JAPAN THROUGH AMERICAN EYES

FRANCIS HALL

JAPAN THROUGH AMERICAN EYES

THE JOURNAL OF FRANCIS HALL
KANAGAWA AND YOKOHAMA
1859–1866

EDITED AND ANNOTATED BY F. G. NOTEHELFER

FROM THE CLEVELAND PUBLIC LIBRARY · JOHN G. WHITE COLLECTION OF ORIENTALIA

PRINCETON UNIVERSITY PRESS · PRINCETON · NEW JERSEY

Efforts were made to locate the literary heirs of this work but without success.

Library of Congress Cataloging-in-Publication Data

Hall, Francis.
Japan through American eyes : the journal of Francis Hall, Kanagawa and
Yokohama, 1859–1866 : from the Cleveland Public Library, John G. White
collection of orientalia / edited and annotated by F. G. Notehelfer.
p.   cm.
Includes bibliographical references and index.
ISBN 0-691-03181-9 (CL : acid-free paper)
1. Japan—Description and travel—1801–1900. I. Notehelfer, F. G.
II. Cleveland Public Library. John G. White Dept. III. Title.
DS809.H18   1992
952'.025—dc20   91-36385

The costs of publishing this book have been defrayed in part by an award
from the Books on Japan Fund in respect of *Crisis and Compensation: Public
Policy and Political Stability in Japan, 1949–1986* and *The Artistry of Aeschylus
and Zeami: A Comparative Study of Greek Tragedy and Nō*, both published by
Princeton University Press. The Fund is financed by The Japan Foundation
from donations contributed generously by Japanese companies.

For
Daniel T. Dale
Missionary and Friend
a truly joyous human being
who reminds me of Francis Hall
and about whom it can also be said
"Everything he has touched he has brightened!"

ILLUSTRATIONS

PREFACE

The journal presented in this volume represents a rather extraordinary discovery. It is not often that a major historical work comes to light after a hundred years of quiescence. Nor is it generally the case that the author of such a work is a completely unknown and forgotten man. And yet, if you had asked me five years ago whether I had ever heard of Francis Hall or his Japan journal, I would have answered decidedly in the negative. I doubt, moreover, that any of my colleagues in the field of nineteenth-century Japanese studies—here or in Japan—had heard of him either. And yet, Francis Hall, as the biographical essay that accompanies this study indicates, was far from unknown. America's leading business pioneer in Japan, correspondent for Horace Greeley's *New York Tribune*, world traveler, opinion maker, "Japanese Frank Hall," as he was later hailed in his home town, was hardly a nobody. Nor were his talents unrecognized in their day. In 1866 J. C. Hepburn, the leading missionary-scholar of his generation, paid him the ultimate compliment when he wrote home that Hall was not only a "very intelligent" and "agreeable" person, but "as well versed in Japanese matters as any man living."[1]

It is my hope that with this publication, Hall's journal will take its place alongside the writings of Townsend Harris, Henry Heusken, Joseph Heco, Ernest Satow, and others active in late Tokugawa Japan, as a major source of information on the treaty port, and on life in Japan on the eve of the Meiji Restoration.

Hall's work was first brought to my attention in the spring of 1985 by Margaret Case, my editor at Princeton University Press, and by Alice N. Loranth, the head of the Fine Arts and Special Collections Department of the Cleveland Public Library. The Hall manuscript had come into the Cleveland Public Library's John G. White Collection of Orientalia through the efforts of Mrs. Loranth, who encouraged its purchase in 1983. Mrs. Loranth was convinced that the manuscript merited publication and sent it to Princeton University Press. The press in turn solicited my help to evaluate and possibly edit the work.

As sections of the manuscript reached me in Los Angeles, I became increasingly enthusiastic about the journal and its content. At the outset it was hard for me to believe that a work of this size and quality could have remained unpublished for so long. Wishing to learn more

[1] Letter from J. C. Hepburn to J. C. Lowrie, D.D., dated Yokohama, July 2, 1866, original in the Presbyterian Historical Society, Philadelphia; copy in the Yokohama Archives of History.

about the provenance of the manuscript, I contacted Karl Zamboni of Zamboni and Huntington, the Palo Alto bookdealer who had handled the manuscript's sale. Zamboni informed me that he had purchased the journal with other materials "from a member of the Hall family in Southern California at about the time of World War II," and that it had remained in his possession until its sale to the Cleveland Public Library.

The manuscript consists of some 885 ledger-sized pages. The first section is written in two bound ledger books, while the remainder consists of loose-leaf pages. From the nature of the material it is possible that Hall initially intended to spend only a year or two in Japan as correspondent for the *New York Tribune* and traveler. And that he hoped in the process to compose a book that he could later publish for which he brought his ledger volumes. Successful business ventures in Yokohama extended his stay, and in the end the loose-leaf pages mounted. Still, it is remarkable that all these pages have been preserved intact without a single omission.

It is clear that Hall initially used his journal to record materials that he subsequently incorporated into his articles for the *New York Tribune*, the *Elmira Weekly Advertiser*, and the *Home Journal*. By the end of his stay in Japan he had written close to seventy articles for the *Tribune* alone. But while there is a substantial overlap between his journal entries and the articles he published in American papers and magazines from 1859 to 1863, by 1864 his growing involvement in the Yokohama trade demanded much of his time. This meant that the entries in his journal from 1864 to 1866 became thinner and sparser. Rather than duplicating his observations, he now often recorded his impressions directly into his articles. In order to balance out the final years of the journal, I have consequently taken the liberty of incorporating a number of these articles into the text, being careful to indicate their separate origins. This helps to provide a clearer picture of his later years in Yokohama, while at the same time providing the reader with a better sense of his public writings.

To deal with the journal directly some general observations about the manuscript may be

in order. Hall's handwriting is by no means easy to decipher. His fondness for multiple styles of initial letters, his habit of stringing words together, and his extensive vocabulary, which includes several foreign languages and many Latin botanical terms, are constant challenges to the reader and transcriber. It took me nearly eighteen months to complete the entire text. Annotating the transcribed text posed additional problems. Many of the individuals who appear in the journal are recorded only by their initials, and in the case of numerous Japanese even these are missing. As may be imagined this does not facilitate accurate identification, and while I have worked hard to identify as many individuals as possible, some have remained anonymous, while in other cases there is always the possibility of error. I am pleased to note, however, that Hall's entries, which I have checked against the historical record with care, are remarkably accurate.

In editing the work, there is the further problem that at the time that Hall arrived in Japan, there was as yet no standard orthography for romanizing Japanese. J. C. Hepburn, with whom Hall lived in Kanagawa, had not yet invented the Hepburn System. This meant that there was little agreement on terms as simple as the name of the country. Hall speaks of Japan as Nipon, Nippon, Niphon, if not something else. Yokuhama, when he arrives, becomes Yokohama not long thereafter; the tocaido becomes the Tokaido; Edo can be Yeddo or Yedo, and even Jeddo. Osaka remains Oasaca throughout. And these are only the place names. As editor I have attempted to create some order out of this chaos by adopting the standard use of place names as much as possible. On some occasions I have paired the readings used at the time with current equivalents. It is still not clear to me why Hall continuously referred to Hodoyaga, one of the stations on the Tōkaidō, as Hodoriya. For terms such as saki, which Hall was known to enjoy, I have used the more standard sake, a spelling that Hall also adopted in his final years in Yokohama. In all instances where the Yokohama dialect was involved, or where Hall gives sentences (or parts of sentences) in the vernacular I have transcribed them exactly as I found them in the original.

In editing the journal I have left its content largely intact. Indeed, one of the strengths of Hall's journal is that it ranges extensively over a wide variety of topics. Hall can be ethnographer, demographer, sports writer, social observer, economist, student of children, diplomat, and savvy trader in turn. Students of history who are drawn to new forms of evidence will find the range of material presented here attractive. To cut this text to my own preferences and prejudices would be to do both Hall and his modern reader a disservice. There are, however, one or two areas in which I have exercised my editorial privileges. Hall faithfully records the weather and temperature for virtually every day that he resided in Japan. In fact, he felt that he was performing something of a public service in this regard, and the first issue of the *Japan Herald*, which was published in Yokohama on November 1, 1860, carried his "Table of Meteorological Observations at Kanagawa from November 1st 1859 to November 1st 1860." But as these observations can be extensive, and in later years often constitute the only entry for a particular day or date, I have taken the liberty of removing them from the published version of the journal after 1861. The first year's entries give a good sample of their content, and should the reader be interested in such materials, the original text may be consulted.

My efforts to trace the background of Francis Hall took me to a number of locations and archives where I was graciously helped by many individuals. Alice Loranth, and her very able assistant, Motoko Reece, in the Fine Arts and Special Collections Department of the Cleveland Public Library were of great assistance in searching out and locating related materials, and in steering me toward individuals and sources. A trip to the Hall Memorial Library in Ellington, Connecticut, Hall's birthplace, was kindly assisted by Laurel S. Best, the director of that library. While there I was shown a variety of materials on the Hall family, the Ellington School, and the Hall Family School for Boys. Although the Hall Memorial Library was surprisingly lacking in Hall's personal writings, it did include two 1873 oil paintings by Charles Wirgman, Hall's friend, and a number of Japanese ceramics and fans that Hall brought back from Japan. The library also displays a photographic portrait of Iwasaki Yanosuke and his wife to commemorate the gift made to the library by the Baron Iwasaki on behalf of the time he spent studying with Hall's brother Edward in the early 1870s.

From Ellington, Connecticut, I made my way to Elmira, New York, Hall's hometown of later years. It was there that he established his bookstore before going to Japan, and it was there that he spent his final years. In Elmira many helping hands provided assistance. Alfred G. Hilbert, the staff historian of the Chemung County Historical Society, and Thomas E. Byrnes provided information on the Francis Hall Papers in the Society's collection. Donna Wertheimer and Herbert Wisbey of the Elmira College Library assisted me with their collection. Carolyn Bossard of the Steele Memorial Library helped me to locate a number of local newspapers. Michael Aung-Thwin of Elmira College provided gracious hospitality.

A year as visiting professor in the Institute for Humanistic Studies at Kyoto University in 1986 allowed me to follow up the Japanese side of Hall's experiences. In this I was helped by a number of friends at the Institute, including Masamichi Asukai and Toshio Yokoyama. Site visits to Yokohama and "Kanagawa" were greatly facilitated by Takashi Utsumi and Saito Takio of the Yokohama Archives of History and by the director of those archives, Shigeki Toyama.

A special thanks goes to my research assistant, Christopher Friday, who spent many hours in pulling out Hall's articles from the *New York Tribune*; to Yoshiaki Katada, who followed up a number of Japanese leads; and to Lesley Ann Beneke, who provided invaluable assistance in copyediting the manuscript.

Financial support for this project came from the Academic Senate of the University of California at Los Angeles, and UCLA's Sasakawa Fund. Support from the University of Kyoto for my year at the Institute of Humanistic Studies is also gratefully acknowledged.

Finally, I wish to thank the Chemung County Historical Society, the Cleveland Public Library, the Steele Memorial Library, the Hall Memorial Library, the Yokohama Archives of

History, and Harvard University's Baker Library for permission to cite materials in their collections.

I also wish to express my appreciation to the Yokohama Archives of History for the photographic illustrations that they generously provided from their excellent collection. The woodblock prints by Sadahide and Hiroshige II reproduced in this volume have been made available through the courtesy of the DAVAL Foundation from the collection of Ambassador and Mrs. William Leonhart of Washington, D.C.

In place of a bibliography, I have relied on the notes that accompany the text to cite all books, articles, and archival materials used.

JAPAN THROUGH AMERICAN EYES

A SKETCH OF THE LIFE OF FRANCIS HALL

Connecticut and New York

The author of the Japan journal presented in this volume, Francis Hall, was born in Ellington, Connecticut, on October 27, 1822.[1] The sixth son in a family of sixteen children, he spent his early years on the family farm. But the Halls were no ordinary farmers. The family, which had come to America from Devon, England, in 1636, was not only prolific but well established. Hall's grandfather, "Deacon Hall" as he was generally known for his church activities, was a prominent merchant who owned substantial property, an iron forge, and a slaughtering and meat-packing establishment. It was noted of the Deacon that when he went to Boston on horseback to make his purchases, the weight of the cash in his saddlebags was often greater than his own.[2]

Francis Hall's father, John Hall (1783–1847), also was a man of considerable education and local influence. A Yale graduate in the class of 1802, he briefly taught at his alma mater before ill health forced him to abandon his hopes for a professional career. He returned to Ellington and joined his brother-in-law, Levi Wells, in business. But preferring the life of a gentleman-farmer to that of trade, he purchased an extensive farm near town, on which he built a large and beautiful house, and practiced what was described as "agriculture on scientific principles."[3]

Scientific farming, at which he appears to have been quite successful, was not, however, the only interest of the elder Hall. Politics seems to have had its place as well. In addition to serving as justice of the peace and judge of the county court, he ran successfully for the

---

[1] For biographical details I have relied on Ausburn Towner, "Francis Hall," in *Our County and Its People. A History of the Valley and County of Chemung; From the Closing Years of the Eighteenth Century* (Syracuse, N.Y.: D. Mason & Co., 1892), pp. 628–39 (hereafter cited as Towner, *Our County*). There is also a family genealogy in the Hall Family Papers at the Chemung County Historical Society, Elmira, N.Y., as well as at the Hall Memorial Library, Ellington, Conn.

[2] "Hall Family Genealogy," typescript transcribed from handwritten document, Hall Memorial Library, Ellington, Conn. As this genealogy shows, the Halls of Ellington were descendants of the Halls of Taunton, Massachusetts. The family had a long history as iron masters in the Taunton area.

[3] "John Hall" in David Field, comp., *Yale University. Class of 1802* (New Haven, Conn.: Privately Printed, 1863), p. 67.

Connecticut legislature in 1815 and 1819, and unsuccessfully for Congress in 1817.[4] Yet, despite his varied ambitions, the elder Hall's principal achievements came neither in farming nor in politics, but in education.

In 1825 John Hall founded a coeducational academy that emphasized classical studies. And in 1829 the original school, which had largely served to educate his growing family, gave way to a new educational institution. The Ellington School, as it came to be known, soon established itself, as the *New York Tribune* later observed, "as one of the most famous schools in the country."[5] Designed to prepare young men "for various departments of business, or for admission to college," the school offered a classical education in Latin and Greek, as well as more contemporary studies that included classes in penmanship and English grammar; rhetoric and elocution; modern foreign languages, such as French; and traditional disciplines, such as mathematics, the sciences, geography, history, and philosophy. From 1829 to 1839 the school experienced its most famous decade. Under the direct supervision of Judge Hall, and staffed largely by Yale graduates—including Alphonso Taft, the father of the American president, William Howard Taft—it attracted students from throughout the United States as well as from the Caribbean, South America, and even Bombay, India.[6]

Although ill health caused the elder Hall to close the Ellington School in 1839, the family's role in education was carried forward by Hall's elder brother, Edward, who founded the Hall Family School for Boys in 1844, a school at which he taught for thirty years.[7] It was to this school, which annually took no more than twelve pupils, that Francis Hall in 1872 sent Iwasaki Yanosuke, the young man who later became head of Japan's leading industrial concern, the Mitsubishi Company.[8] Moreover, it was to commemorate the educational achievements of his father and elder brother that Hall, in 1902, presented the citizens of Ellington with the Hall Memorial Library, a splendid $40,000 structure, which a New York paper called "one of the finest gifts ever made to a Connecticut town," and to which the Baron Iwasaki made his own contribution of $2,000.[9]

If the Hall schools made Ellington into a

---

[4] Ibid., p. 68.

[5] *New York Tribune*, December 6, 1903, pt. 2, p. 14.

[6] For a description of the Ellington School see "Early Ellington Village, From the Middle 1700's—Through 1915," Assembled and printed by the Calendar Staff, the Congregational Church, Ellington, Conn., December 1952. Unp. Also "Ellington Goes to School," typescript, pp. 1–4, and "Notes of Interest About the Hall Schools," typescript, pp. 1–2. All these pamphlets can be found in the Hall Memorial Library, Ellington, Conn.

[7] Edward Hall's Family School for Boys is briefly described in "Notes of Interest About the Hall Schools," Hall Memorial Library, Ellington, Conn.

[8] Iwasaki Yanosuke was sent to the United States to study by his brother Iwasaki Yatarō in 1872. The *Iwasaki Yanosuke den* (Biography of Iwasaki Yanosuke) says that he went to the United States through the good offices of Walsh, Hall, & Co., but his biographers note that virtually nothing is known about his school years in the United States other than the fact that he made unusually rapid progress with the English language. As the Hall Family School under Edward took no more than twelve students, who lived with the family of its headmaster, this appears to have been the perfect opportunity for a Japanese student to learn English. The death of Yanosuke's father and family business needs

seem to have cut short his stay in the United States after only seventeen months. Edward Hall died in 1875. For a discussion of Iwasaki's trip to the United States see Iwasaki-ke denki kankokai hen, *Iwasaki Yanosuke den (jo)* (Tokyo: Tokyo Daigaku Shuppan Kai, 1971), pp. 54ff.

[9] The Hall Memorial Library was dedicated on November 11, 1903, nearly a year after Hall's death. Work on the library was started under his supervision in 1902 and completed by his three brothers, Frederic Hall, Charles C. Hall, and Robert Hall, who served as executors of his will. According to the *New York Tribune* Baron Yanosuke Iwasaki gave $2,000 to the library to "establish a Japanese exhibition and for the purchase of books." Had this money been used to buy books on Japan, Ellington might have established one of America's first "Japanese Collections," but unfortunately the executors of Hall's estate seem to have had other plans. Iwasaki's gift was used to pay for a set of stained glass windows portraying John, Edward, and Francis Hall. Indeed, other than a few trinkets, and two Charles Wirgman portraits (one of a Japanese official and the other of a Japanese woman with umbrella—dated 1873) the library contains few Japanese materials. It is regrettable that the library never became the repository for Hall's papers. That it did not, and that Hall chose to be buried in Elmira, not in the family plot in Ellington,

center of "culture and learning," as local history notes, they also provided the environment in which Francis Hall matured.[10]

We do not know exactly when Hall first entered the Ellington School, but it is clear that his father had distinct ideas on the upbringing and education of children—a subject on which he wrote extensively. A strict disciplinarian, he firmly believed that education was a family responsibility and that it related not merely to the intellect but to the formation of character. "It is a truth incontrovertible and of momentous bearing," he wrote in his book, *The Education of Children*, "that all children, without exception, possess tempers that are irascible; dispositions which are selfish; propensities, of various kinds which tend to evil; that they are impatient of restraint; that they dislike obedience to parental authority any further than it comports with their own inclinations; that they are averse to regular industry; and that they prefer the pleasures of sense to all other gratifications."[11] The elder Hall was convinced, moreover, that education in the home was the responsibility of the father, not the mother. "There is something in a father's sternness, and firm dignity which admits of no substitute."[12] Indeed the parent-child relationship was to be firmly controlled. "The kind of intercourse which is maintained between parents and children forms no considerable item in the process of education and has its attendant errors." He wrote, "There are two short words which, under proper management, have a wonderful effect in teaching children deference to their superiors. These are *Sir* and *Ma'am*."[13]

Sir and Ma'am were certainly elements of the manners Hall learned at home, but they also indicate the distance at which parents were placed. Hall writes little about his mother, Sophia, who died when he was only six, or his stepmother, Harriet, who died a few months before his departure for Japan in 1859. Cabled that his father was dying in September 1847, Hall, who later came to be universally remembered as a kind, gentle, and extraordinarily generous human being, and about whom one writer observed "whatever he has touched he has brightened," replied that going to his father's bedside would "require a sacrifice greater perhaps than my duty would require." He insisted that his affairs were "in the worst possible situation for leaving." In an effort to explain, he added: "How much I have thought in my lifetime, even from very early years, what an event it would be to have father die, and in my youngest days it seemed as if that would be the bitterest grief of life. I used to think I could not live without him much less be happy." But "immersion in the cares of life, and the working with my own hands for my daily bread," he continued, has "removed the feeling of entire dependence on him." In losing his father, he now felt, they were all losing their "best friend." Finally, he asked his brother Edward to express to his father once again "the deep and manifold obligation I feel towards him, that to him I owe all the good that may be in me either in regards to this world or to that to come."[14]

While the foregoing suggests a sense of duty and obligation toward his father, there was apparently little warmth and affection in the father-son relationship. Given the size of the family, as well as the Judge's involvements in the school, business affairs, and scholarship, family relationships were by necessity stretched somewhat thin. Hall is too polite in his letters to record that many of his bench mates at the Ellington School saw his father's two chief characteristics as being his "green glasses" (necessitated by his poor eyesight) and his "harsh temper."[15] Indeed, parental responsibilities

suggests something of the combined sense of veneration and distance with which he viewed his family and hometown. For the Iwasaki reference see *New York Tribune*, December 6, 1903, pt. 2, p. 14.

[10] "Early Ellington Village," Hall Memorial Library, Ellington, Conn.

[11] John Hall, *On The Education of Children, While Under the Care of Parents or Guardians* (New York: J. P. Haven,

1835), pp. 13–14.

[12] Ibid., p. 45.

[13] Ibid., p. 97.

[14] Letter from Francis Hall to Edward Hall dated Elmira, New York, September 30, 1847, Hall Family Papers, Chemung County Historical Society, Elmira, N.Y.

[15] "Ellington Goes to School," Hall Memorial Library, Ellington, Conn.

seem to have been delegated to Francis's oldest brother, Edward, at a early age, and at age eighteen, more in keeping with Japanese than American practices, Edward became his legal guardian.

Hall does not tell us when he entered the Ellington School, but as the school's program was designed for boys from the age of eight to sixteen, we may presume that he started his education there in 1830 and completed it in 1838. This would have placed him at the school during its most illustrious decade, and brought him into contact with other young men from throughout the country and abroad. We do, in fact, have a letter of his, penned in 1834, in which he writes that he is "receiving lessons" in "Historical Greece, Latin Grammar, and Greek" from Alphonso Taft and Samuel G. Brown.[16] "I like living at the school very much," he added, and, in response to his older brother's question of how his grades stood, he reported that he had received forty-three "Perfect" marks, fifty-three "Goods," five "Mediums," and no "Poors" or "Failures." While noting that his results were considerably better than those of his brothers, Maxwell and Wells, he added apologetically, "I expect that you would think that my marks would be better."[17]

In keeping with the elder Hall's ideas on education, life at the Ellington School was highly austere. As one writer has noted, the Judge ruled over the school with "inflexible Puritanism."[18] Hard work and discipline were two of the school's basic themes. Moreover, to many of his students it appeared that Judge Hall was particularly given to the pursuit and performance of what struck them as a dreary and monotonous form of outward religious life. Even Hall, who later got on well with missionaries and preachers, seems to have found little to attract him to his father's brand of Christianity. And yet, it must be said on the Judge's

behalf that he could be as hard on himself as on his students. Those under him recognized his essential fairness. And some even remembered small kindnesses. Donald G. Mitchell, the "Ik Marvel" of nineteenth-century American literature, who was Hall's classmate, remembered the Judge as a "kindly, dignified gentleman."[19]

Of life in the school Mitchell wrote:

When I hear boys of near kith today complaining of the hardships they endure, I love to set before them a picture of the cold chambers opening upon the corridors in that huge building. We dressed there by the dim light coming through ventilators over the doors, from lamps swinging in the hall. After this it was needful to take a swift rush out of doors, in all weathers, for a plunge into the washroom door, where we made our ablutions. Another outside rush followed for the doors opening upon the dining-hall, where morning prayers were said. Then an hour of study in a room reeking with the fumes of whale oil lamps went before the summons to breakfast. There were two schoolrooms. The larger was always presided over by a teacher who was nothing if not watchful. The smaller was allotted to the higher range of boys, and here the superintendent appeared at intervals to hear recitations.[20]

It appears that Hall completed his course of study at the Ellington School in 1838. This was a year after the great financial panic of 1837, which boded ill for the family finances and may have contributed to the closing of the school in 1839. In later years Hall frequently wrote to Edward seeking to know his father's "pecuniary circumstances," while enclosing small contributions to the family's budget.[21]

---

[16] Samuel Gilman Brown later became president of Hamilton College. See *Dictionary of American Biography* (New York: Charles Scribner's Sons, 1964), vol. 3, p. 153.

[17] Letter from Francis Hall to Edward Hall dated Ellington, Conn., February 2, 1834, Hall Family Papers, Chemung County Historical Society, Elmira, N.Y.

[18] Waldo H. Dunn, *The Life of Donald G. Mitchell: Ik Marvel* (New York: Charles Scribner's Sons, 1922), p.

28. Dunn wrote: "Ellington was a typical New England boarding-school of that day, with many resemblances to contemporary English institutions of the same kind. Its founder and principal was Judge John Hall, a Yale graduate of 1802, who, without being brutal, ruled with inflexible Puritanism."

[19] Ibid., p. 39.

[20] Ibid., pp. 39–40.

Clearly the pursuit of a college education at Yale was now financially out of the question. Hall decided to take up teaching instead. For the next two years, at the ages of seventeen and eighteen, he taught district school in the winters, "boarding 'round" from house to house as was the custom. For his first winter's effort he received $36. This was barely enough to pay for the "slender outfit" of clothes he had bought on credit and the watch he had rented for the winter at $1.00.[22]

In the summers Francis, or Frank, as he now preferred to be called, clerked at the bookstore of his elder brother, Levi Wells, in Springfield, Massachusetts. In October 1840 he wrote to Edward that he did not mind the idea of teaching another winter, if he could get "a *good school*," by which he meant a school that would pay him $60. "As far as the utility of the thing is concerned," he added, "it might be better for me to serve my clerkship out at once, and not put it off any longer, for I am now most eighteen."[23]

Any misgivings that the family may have harbored about their eighteen-year-old's ability to survive on his own were quickly laid to rest. "I like my business quite well," he wrote, "and have not been homesick yet." "If I wander away from here," he informed the family with a new sense of confidence, "I shall not probably go home before I leave for good."[24]

Here we have early signs of the independence that was to lead Frank Hall to Japan two decades later. Determined to make his own fortune, like so many a New England lad, he seems to have been ready to move on to new opportunities. Ellington, despite the home and family ties, would have to be jettisoned for the broader world. But as any reader of his Japan journal will sense, Ellington and the family also left their imprints on Hall. Not least of these were the aesthetic sensibilities and love of nature that so clearly expressed themselves in later years. Hall's father, despite his Puritanism, was not only a highly cultured man but one sensitive to his natural environment. As one student recalled, the Judge lived among "gardens and orchards," and his splendid house was surrounded by walks that were lined with lovely shrubs and trees.[25] Moreover, the Judge's example seems to have been emulated by the other citizens of Ellington with the effect that, "now there is scarcely a country town in Connecticut," one observer wrote, "which strikes the eye of the traveler with so much delight; where the houses and buildings, the courtyards, gardens and farms, exhibit so much neatness and taste, and indicate so much thrift and happiness; or where shade-trees are so common along the roads."[26]

Complementing his love of nature and the budding aesthetic tastes that were linked to his home and early education, Hall also developed a fondness for music and books. Teaching school in South Coventry, Connecticut, in the winter of 1840, he wrote home that in addition to the flute, which he had learned to play earlier, he was "learning to sing" at a singing school, and proudly noted that he had recently "purchased a book that cost me 77 cents."[27]

[21] The full financial details are not clear, but Hall's father seems to have "given up" the family farm in 1838 and the school in 1839. The school may have been for sale in 1840, for we have a letter from Hall to his brother Edward in which he writes: "Whatever the prospects of the school, if the people of Ellington wont pay 30 cents on a dollar for the stock they ought to remain as ignorant as Arabs." Letter from Francis Hall to Edward Hall dated South Coventry, December 31, 1840, Hall Family Papers, Chemung County Historical Society, Elmira, N.Y. In 1845 Hall wrote to his brother: "How or what is father's pecuniary condition? I sent him a few dollars at Thanksgiving time and will try to send more before long. I think I can say that 'I wished I was rich' and commit no sin in so doing, the disposal of a few loose hundreds would do me and others so much good." Letter from Francis Hall to Edward Hall dated

Elmira, N.Y., December 15, 1845, Hall Family Papers, Chemung County Historical Society, Elmira, N.Y.

[22] Towner, *Our County*, pp. 629–30.

[23] Letter from Francis Hall to Edward Hall dated Springfield, Mass., October 3, 1840, Hall Family Papers, Chemung County Historical Society, Elmira, N.Y.

[24] Ibid.

[25] The student was Donald G. Mitchell. See Dunn, *The Life of Donald G. Mitchell*, p. 39.

[26] "John Hall" in David Field, ed., *Yale Class Histories*, vol. 1, 1804–1825 (Hartford: Connecticut State Library, 1912), p. 67.

[27] Letter from Francis Hall to Edward Hall dated South Coventry, Conn., December 31, 1840, Hall Family Papers, Chemung County Historical Society, Elmira, N.Y.

The latter was clearly an extravagance, when, as he added in his letter home, "my pantaloons are worn pretty thin" and "my overcoat is pretty well worn so that I burst it on the shoulder."[28]

Hall's sense of humor, his ability to get along with others and make friends quickly, his realistic assessment of situations, and his willingness to laugh at himself, traits which were to serve him well in Japan, were clearly apparent even during these early years. Hall usually found himself marching the middle path between extremes. No dreary Puritanism for him. Exposed to austerity at his father's school he saw no reason to make a virtue out of deprivation. "This sleeping in cold beds isn't what it's cracked up to be," he wrote home from South Coventry.[29] Temperance, which he appears to have supported in principle—there is even a pledge he signed for a year—also got only limited support. Pleasantly recalling fireside discussions of politics and theology at the home of friends that always included a "pitcher of hard cider," he wrote to his brother, "it will hardly do, I suppose, to talk much about cider in these temperance days, though I don't think I should refuse a good glass of such as I used to find in Coventry."[30] Nor was he prepared to refuse a good cup or two of similar conviviality in Japan a few years later. Even Hall's eye for the ladies, of which we can find ample evidence in his Japan journal, appears to have been the source of considerable merriment and family banter. Taken to task for his flirtations by the more dour Edward, Hall wrote back, "As I remarked in my last [letter] I agree with you perfectly in your views of one's conduct toward the other sex; that no one ought by any conduct of his to allow them to cherish feelings of regard for himself."[31] And yet, two paragraphs later he wrote, "Has Harriet C. forgotten about 'setting her cap for me'. I think she is the one that threat-

ened it, at any rate the Watrous girls acknowledge *who* it was."[32] Later he added, "Those blackeyed roguish girls at Christian Corners I know I shall not forget very soon. I don't see how the young men of Coventry can hold out against four such pairs of piercing eyes."[33]

In 1841 Hall began to clerk in a bookstore in Syracuse, a business into which his brother Levi Wells bought not long thereafter. Hall liked Syracuse, and he quickly made friends there. Describing an active social life, he wrote home, "You see I do not feel quite like a stranger in a strange land. The more I see of Syracuse the more I like it. My acquaintance among the men of the place is pretty extensive, but with the ladies I am little known."[34] Although the town was growing rapidly and business was good, Hall's stay in Syracuse was cut short by the reorganization of the bookstore. Moreover, having completed his clerkship, he was ready to step out into the business world.

Having apprenticed in the book trade Hall set his sights on owning a bookstore of his own in Elmira, New York. What attracted him to Elmira was the westward expansion that was spearheaded by the boom in railroad construction. Elmira was about to be "opened up" by the Erie Railroad. This made it particularly attractive to a young businessman who hoped to get in on the ground floor of a new urban center. In March 1842 Hall went to Elmira to explore his prospects. At the time the railroad was still a good distance away, and Elmira was little more than a frontier village with less than 2,500 inhabitants. A recent fire had burned down a good part of the business district and Hall had difficulty in finding a building to rent. But here, as later in Japan, Hall's agreeable personality and pleasant manners seem to have turned the tide in his favor. Impressed with the young man's enthusiasm and lively interest in their community, several of the leading citizens of Elmira warmly encouraged him

[28] Ibid.

[29] Ibid.

[30] Letter from Francis Hall to Edward Hall dated Elmira, N.Y., September 23, 1842, Hall Family Papers, Chemung County Historical Society, Elmira, N.Y.

[31] Letter from Francis Hall to Edward Hall dated Syracuse, N.Y., February 16, 1842, Hall Family Papers, Chemung County Historical Society, Elmira, N.Y.

[32] Ibid.

[33] Letter from Francis Hall to Edward Hall dated Elmira, N.Y., July 12, 1842, Hall Family Papers, Chemung County Historical Society, Elmira, N.Y.

[34] Letter from Francis Hall to Edward Hall dated Syracuse, February 16, 1842, Hall Family Papers, Chemung County Historical Society, Elmira, N.Y.

to proceed with his plans for a bookstore, and one of them offered to build him a modest, two-story, frame building on Water Street beside the Chemung River. Two months later, in May 1842, Hall arrived in Elmira with a wagon-load of books. He had purchased his inventory with a $500 loan from his brother Levi Wells, and with the few additional dollars he had saved from his teaching and clerking years, he optimistically "opened for business" in his still unfinished store. Hall was nineteen, full of hope, and brimming with ambition to succeed.

But he soon learned that success, in the form of profits, could be elusive. Elmira was almost entirely dependent for its economic well-being on the lumber trade. The year he arrived lumber prices were plummeting, and all businesses suffered. "Business," he wrote, "is dull," and "nobody pretends to lay out a sixpence for the most common necessities of life without grumbling about 'Hard Times.' "[35] Indeed, Hall's first year in the book trade was a difficult one. Even with cheap board at $2 a week and lodgings in the store, it was hard to turn a profit.

Prospects for his second year, 1843, did not improve. With few customers to keep him busy Hall had time to gaze out of the windows of his store. He wrote home:

I have been interested for a few days back in watching the rafts that float down the Chemung by the hundreds. I have before written you that my store is on the river brink, consequently I have a fine view of them as they pass. A bridge crosses the river a few rods from the store, and a number of the rafts have been broken to pieces on the piers to the great danger of the raftsmen. From forty to fifty thousand is the usual number of feet [of lumber] in each raft. The lumbermen are usually a

hard set of fellows. It is calculated that over a thousand rafts go down this season. This you know is our staple commodity, and lumber answers to us what wheat does to the Genesee Valley.[36]

But conditions on the river did not inspire confidence. "As the market for lumber is not likely to be very brisk," he warned, "trade in Elmira will probably be dull all summer."[37]

While he liked Elmira in these early years, writing, "I am very much pleased with the place and people, have formed many agreeable acquaintances, and receive many attentions," he seems to have felt quite isolated in his new location. "We are rather out of the way here," he added, a little "among the bushes." "We need the completion of the New York and Erie Rail Road. Then we shall be within a few hours ride of the city."[38] As to his remaining in Elmira, he seriously questioned the prospect. "It is doubtful," he wrote, "whether I remain here long, provided a purchaser for the stock of books can be found. We pay our way, but the capital would be more productive at Syracuse."[39] Later in the same year he wrote that his business had improved a little and a note of optimism can be found in his letters for the first time. "I hope it will eventually increase enough to make my location permanent," he wrote to Edward, "I think I have done better remaining here than I should have done at Syracuse."[40]

By 1844, his third year in Elmira, his bookstore showed some profits. "Wells made the suggestion," he wrote to Edward, "that in the spring I take the store entirely on my own shoulders. If I remain in Elmira, I think I had better do so, and as prospects are now I shall probably stay another year at least."[41] By 1845 all references to "leaving" were dropped, business was moving steadily ahead, and Hall was becoming used to the town. While he contin-

[35] Letter from Francis Hall to Edward Hall dated Elmira, N.Y., September 23, 1842, Hall Family Papers, Chemung County Historical Society, Elmira, N.Y.

[36] Letter from Francis Hall to Edward Hall dated April 21, 1843, Hall Family Papers, Chemung County Historical Society, Elmira, N.Y.

[37] Ibid.

[38] Ibid.

[39] Ibid.

[40] Letter from Francis Hall to Edward Hall dated Elmira, N.Y., June 28, 1843, Hall Family Papers, Chemung County Historical Society, Elmira, N.Y.

[41] Letter from Francis Hall to Edward Hall dated Elmira, N.Y., January 3, 1844, Hall Family Papers, Chemung County Historical Society, Elmira, N.Y.

ued to express his sense of isolation, writing home, "I know of nothing in our place that would interest you," he had, in fact, already determined to assist in the cultural and intellectual transformation of the town.[42]

As Ausburn Towner later noted in his history of the Chemung valley, "Mr. Hall's influence on the business, social, and literary life of Elmira was marked from the first."[43] To start with there was the Hall Book Store which served as a rendezvous for kindred spirits throughout the region. The store itself was rather unusual in that it was the first store in the community in which there were no counters. In the center of the store there was a glass showcase, so that the customer was never "outside," and the proprietor or attendant was never "behind the counter." Hall's aesthetic sense was manifest in the arrangements. Already a great walker, as his Japan journal confirms, and an enthusiast of plants and flowers, Hall's early morning rambles into the surrounding hills never failed to provide a wide variety of wildflowers that were tastefully arranged on the central showcase in spring and summer.

While aesthetics had its place, so did modernity. The first telegraph instrument "that ever ticked in the village of Elmira," we are told, was set up in his store in 1847.[44] When the railroad finally reached the town in 1851, Hall served as express agent, as well as importer of the New York papers, the *Herald* and the *Tribune*.[45] By the 1850s his bookstore had become the gathering place for the region's intellectual community. These included local literary figures as well as members of the abolitionist movement, such as Thomas K. Beecher, Henry Ward Beecher's brother, who served as minister in Elmira's Congregational church. Hall tried to keep in stock the best literary works. It was during these years that *Uncle Tom's Cabin*

and *David Copperfield* were first published in semimonthly installments, which Hall had rushed to his store by express.

To what degree Hall subsequently became familiar with Elmira's most famous writer, Mark Twain, is difficult to determine, but he maintained wide contacts with other American writers and poets. In fact, Hall seems to have become something of a promoter of literary men in the town, instigating at his own risk a series of lectures that brought to Elmira such figures as Ralph Waldo Emerson, Edwin Percy Whipple, Bayard Taylor, Horace Mann, J. G. Saxe, Oliver Wendell Holmes, and E. H. Parker.[46]

Although he never shared his father's interest in active politics, Hall was deeply committed to public affairs. At the same time, gradually improving financial circumstances also permitted new personal considerations. Hall's letters home from Elmira tell us little about the number of "piercing black eyes" he encountered in the village. But in the summer of 1846 he wrote the family that he would be coming East in October, adding, as if by afterthought, "Before I leave I expect to be *married*."[47]

Hall's bride, Sarah Covell, was the daughter of Miles Covell, one of Elmira's most prominent citizens.[48] At the time of their marriage in October 1846 Hall had just turned twenty-four. Sarah was still nineteen. A particularly "sweet and attractive woman," we are told that the marriage was "looked on with exceeding favor by the whole community."[49] Sarah was a warm and sensitive individual, and, Hall wrote home, he hoped they would find her as "pretty" as he did. But the domestic tranquillity that married life provided was not to last long. In the spring of 1848 Hall reported that while his own health had improved, the same was not true for Sarah. "Sarah's health is not

---

[42] Letter from Francis Hall to Edward Hall dated Elmira, N.Y., December 15, 1845, Hall Family Papers, Chemung County Historical Society, Elmira, N.Y.

[43] Towner, *Our County*, p. 632.

[44] Ibid., p. 633.

[45] Ibid., p. 632.

[46] Ibid. The Charles C. Hart Autograph Collection in the Manuscript Division of the Library of Congress contains a letter from J. G. Saxe to Hall dated December

13, 1852, in which he agrees to speak in Elmira. The same collection also includes a letter from Horace Mann to Francis Hall dated January 3, 1856, which discusses the terms for a forthcoming lecture by Mann.

[47] Letter from Francis Hall to Edward Hall dated Elmira, N.Y., August 17, 1846, Hall Family Papers, Chemung County Historical Society, Elmira, N.Y.

[48] Towner, *Our County*, p. 631.

[49] Ibid.

good," he wrote. "Her physician says however that her lungs are not affected and that a general debility is her greatest difficulty. A residence of a month next summer on the seashore would do her good."[50] But there was little cause for optimism. A few weeks later he wrote the family that Sarah was "very much emaciated and just able to go upstairs at night and down again in the morning. She lies on the sofa most of the time. . . . I do not think you will see her at Ellington this summer."[51] Hall's worst fears were quickly realized. On August 4, 1848, Sarah died.[52]

Sarah's death had a profound impact on Hall. Despite his eligible widower's status, and the wealth that his Japan years produced, Hall never remarried. While his Japan journal amply illustrates that he continued to be attracted to women and enjoyed socializing with the opposite sex, no one was ever allowed to take Sarah's place. Indeed, Sarah's death seems to have plunged Hall into a deep depression. Nor was her death the only cause of this crisis. Hall had suddenly become surrounded by death and illness. In 1846 his sister Harriet Reed died. This was followed in August 1847 by the death of his favorite brother, Maxwell, who had been clerking for him in Elmira. Two months later his father passed away on October 2, 1847. Then it was dear Sarah's turn. And two months later, his sister Maria died.

Confronted by death on all sides Hall thought of giving up his work in Elmira. If he could find a purchaser for his stock he would make a "change," as his family advised, and join Wells in Syracuse. "Since Sarah's death I feel little attachment to this place," he wrote home, and "Wells is anxious to have me go to Syracuse."[53] "Were I to sell out this fall," he noted in his next letter to Edward, "I should take quite a vacation before I made a fresh start."[54]

But a favorable selling opportunity never arose. On December 1, 1848, Hall wrote home that "the blight which Sarah's death . . . has cast over the household is painfully apparent." He was more and more sadly aware of the difference of his "present condition and that of a year ago."[55] Hall's solution was to bury himself in his work. To do this he moved back into his store. "While I am here," he wrote the family, "my mind is constantly occupied with something, and I find it better thus to be."[56]

Hall's ambivalence about staying on in Elmira in the wake of Sarah's death seems to have been partially overcome in the early 1850s by his renewed commitment to his work. The bookstore prospered, and Hall took on new responsibilities. Keeping himself occupied meant increased public involvement. A few years earlier Hall had written his brother Edward: "Our Academy is a miserable affair. I wish we had you at the head of the male department and some good female teacher with you."[57] Now he seems to have become increasingly interested in the educational opportunities Elmira afforded. A part of this interest focused on the Lyceum movement, for which, as we noted earlier, Hall became a sponsor, but a second seems to have centered more directly on education, particularly on the establishment of Elmira College.

Plans for what became Elmira College were first made in 1851 at the Second Dutch Reformed Church at Albany, which was then pastored by the Reverend Isaac N. Wycoff.[58] The

[50] Letter from Francis Hall to Edward Hall dated Elmira, N.Y., April 18, 1848, Hall Family Papers, Chemung County Historical Society, Elmira, N.Y.

[51] Letter from Francis Hall to Edward Hall dated Elmira, N.Y., May 29, 1848, Hall Family Papers, Chemung County Historical Society, Elmira, N.Y.

[52] *Elmira Weekly Advertiser*, August 10, 1848.

[53] Letter from Francis Hall to Edward Hall dated Elmira, N.Y., September 9, 1848, Hall Family Papers, Chemung County Historical Society, Elmira, N.Y.

[54] Letter from Francis Hall to Edward Hall dated Elmira, N.Y., October 2, 1848, Hall Family Papers, Chemung County Historical Society, Elmira, N.Y.

[55] Letter from Francis Hall to Edward Hall dated Elmira, N.Y., December 1, 1848, Hall Family Papers, Chemung County Historical Society, Elmira, N.Y.

[56] Ibid.

[57] Letter from Francis Hall to Edward Hall dated Elmira, N.Y., August 6, 1846, Hall Family Papers, Chemung County Historical Society, Elmira, N.Y.

[58] Gilbert Meltzer, *The Beginnings of Elmira College* (Elmira, N.Y.: The Commercial Press, 1941), p. 11. The goal, Meltzer tells us, was "to establish an Institution which should hold the same rank in Female Education as that which Colleges and Universities have long held in the Higher Education of Young Men" (p. 23).

goal was to establish a high quality institution of higher education for women. The result became one of America's first women's colleges, which although initially proposed for Auburn, New York, eventually settled on Elmira as its permanent site. One of the central figures in planning Elmira College was the former China missionary Samuel Robbins Brown, who headed the school's founding board of directors, and with whom Hall was to travel to Japan in 1859.[59] A generous gift of land and money made to the school by one of Elmira's founding fathers, Simeon Benjamin, in 1854, assured the school's successful opening under a revised charter in 1855. While Hall's original contacts with the college are not precisely indicated, he subsequently spent twenty-five years on the school's board of trustees, and one of the college's leading prizes, the Hall Prize, bore his name.

As the establishment of Elmira College indicates, the mid-1850s were years of considerable growth and expansion in the town. That Hall remained an active member of the community can be seen in the fact that he regularly served as one of the village's trustees, and, in 1856, despite his formal declination to run for office, was elected to the presidency of the board of trustees.[60] This was equivalent to being elected mayor of Elmira. Hall's term in office was noted for several important accomplishments. One of these was the establishment of a free school system. The second was the development and dedication of Elmira's Woodlawn Cemetery. Having in mind a new kind of cemetery, Hall hired the re-

nowned New York landscape architect, Howard Daniels, to design and lay out one of America's first mortuary parks.[61] Years later, while visiting the graves of the Tokugawa shoguns, he was pleased to observe that the Japanese had developed the same idea centuries earlier.

The third incident of note during his tenure as "mayor" involved what Ausburn Towner has described as "one of the most exciting events" of which "the annals of Elmira can boast."[62] With the arrival in Elmira of Thomas K. Beecher in 1854, and with the support of locally zealous "free" Presbyterians, abolitionist sentiments mounted. Elmira was an active station on the Underground Railroad that sent blacks north and on to Canada. Indeed, the local community included a considerable number of black families. And, as we have already observed, the Hall bookstore often served as the place where Beecher and others of this persuasion met and discussed the "vexed and intricate questions of the day."[63]

In the summer of 1858 Hall was confronted with a highly explosive situation. Rumors spread rapidly one day that there was a Southern slave driver at the Brainard House, the local hotel, and that he had with him a slave he had captured in the northern part of the state and was attempting to return to servitude in the South. An angry crowd, including many of the town's blacks, assembled, first in the street, and then in the lobby of the hotel, calling for the release of the black man. The crowd was on the verge of violence when Hall arrived at the hotel. Climbing up to a balcony,

---

[59] Samuel Robbins Brown (1810–1880) was born in East Windsor, Connecticut, but in 1813 the family moved to Ellington where they lived until 1818. His mother was a hymn writer and active supporter of foreign missions. Brown graduated from Yale in 1832 and in 1838 went to China as a teacher with the Morrison Education Society. He returned to the United States in 1847 due to the failing health of his wife and brought with him some of the first Chinese students sent abroad, including Yung Wing. From 1848 to 1851 Brown taught at the Rome (New York) Academy, and in 1851 he became the pastor of a Dutch Reformed Church at Owasco Outlet near Auburn, New York. It was at this time that Brown became active in the establishment of Elmira College, serving as chairman of the first Executive Committee, searching for a site, and es-

tablishing the school's curriculum. With the selection of Elmira in 1854 Brown spent a good deal of time there in working out the school's plans. It was during these years that he came into contact with Hall, although the families appear to have known one another from Ellington days. On December 11, 1858, Brown applied to the Dutch Reformed Board for missionary service in either "China or Japan." For details regarding S. R. Brown's life see William Elliot Griffis, *A Maker of the New Orient: Samuel Robbins Brown* (New York: Fleming H. Revell Co., 1902).

[60] Towner, *Our County*, p. 633.

[61] Ibid.

[62] Ibid., p. 634.

[63] *New York Tribune*, December 6, 1903, pt. 2, p. 14.

he calmly assured them that the laws must be observed and peace preserved. "If this fugitive wishes to return home with his master," he told the crowd, "he shall go. If he don't want to go back there is no power on earth that shall force him from this place for that purpose."

A deputation of three local blacks was quickly organized to interview the runaway slave. The man in question, it turned out, was elderly, had indeed run away, but had grown homesick and felt uncomfortable with his newly acquired freedom. He had sent word to his master requesting to be taken back, and his master had come North to fetch him. "It's no use," the black delegation reported to the crowd, "he wants to go back with his master." But given the strong local feelings, there were those who proposed rescuing the fugitive, whether he wanted to be rescued or not. The crowd was slow to disperse, and Hall sensed there would be trouble the following day.

Hall's premonition proved correct. The next day an unruly mob gathered at the railroad station to interdict the pair's departure. Hall and the local sheriff had anticipated possible outbreak of violence and had taken the precaution of quietly sending their Southern guests on to the next railroad station by carriage. By the time the crowd realized what had happened, it was too late, and a potentially explosive situation had been effectively defused. Hall was widely complimented for his skill in handling this situation. As later in Yokohama, his quiet good sense in the face of potential violence served him well.

To China and Japan

Hall's reasons for going to Japan in 1859 were never openly stated. However, a number of circumstances were pushing him in new directions. In September 1858, three months before S. R. Brown wrote to the Dutch Reformed Board offering to go to Japan as a missionary, Hall sold his bookstore in Elmira to his brothers Frederic and Charles, who formed the new firm of Hall Brothers.[64] As noted previously, Hall had toyed with the idea of leaving Elmira earlier, but had never been able to come to a successful financial arrangement that would allow him to get away. In the meantime, frugality and sound business instincts had made the store increasingly profitable, so that Hall had accumulated a fair sum of capital that could be put to other uses. With the store transferred to his brothers, he was free to make new plans.

By the autumn of 1858 and the early months of 1859 Japan was suddenly in the news. Word of Townsend Harris's newly negotiated Treaty of Amity and Commerce with Japan, a treaty that promised to open a number of Japanese ports, including Kanagawa, to American residence the following July, aroused a great deal of interest. This was particularly true of the church, which saw in the "opening" of Japan a renewed opportunity to Christianize this long-closed and tragically anti-Christian country.[65] Upstate New York, where the Dutch Reformed denomination was strong, was particularly agitated over these prospects. It was therefore no accident that S. R. Brown,

---

[64] *Elmira Weekly Advertiser*, November 14, 1879, clipping in the Chemung County Historical Society, Elmira, N.Y. The firm of Hall Brothers, which was originally founded by his brothers Frederic and Charles C., was expanded in 1863 to include a third brother, Robert A. Hall. Hall Brothers ceased operation in 1879 when the firm was sold to Preswick, Morse, & Co.

[65] There was a further direct connection between Elmira, or more specifically Elmira College, and the emerging interest in Japan. In 1845, some years before the Perry expedition "opened" Japan, Dr. B. J. Bettelheim had been sent to Loochoo (Okinawa) by the Loochoo Naval Mission, a Protestant missionary society formed by officers of the British Navy. The goal of the organization was to penetrate Japan's closed doors by starting a Christian work in Naha. Bettelheim was a medical doctor and a man of considerable intellectual

talents. A British subject of Hungarian birth he went to Naha with his wife and two children and worked there until 1855 in the face of considerable local, and Japanese (Satsuma), opposition. In 1855 Bettelheim came to the United States in an effort to secure funds that would enable him to undertake work on the main islands of Japan. Bettelheim enrolled his daughter, Victoria R. Bettelheim, in the first class of Elmira College. Victoria had lived in Naha for ten years and was one of a mere handful of Westerners who had firsthand experience with the Japanese of the Ryūkyū Islands. For a discussion of Bettelheim's life see Otis Cary, *A History of Christianity in Japan* (Tokyo: Charles E. Tuttle & Co., 1982), vol. 2, pp. 18–27, 35. For reference to Bettelheim's daughter see Meltzer, *The Beginnings of Elmira College*, p. 106. Elmira's local interest in Japan seems to have been aroused further by the 1858 request trans-

Guido Verbeck, and Duane B. Simmons, the three pioneer Dutch Reformed missionaries to Japan, all had strong ties to this area.[66] Having been selected for the Japan field, they spent the early months of 1859 solidifying their support by deputizing the parishes in this region.

Given the fact that Hall was an active layman in the church and had worked closely with S. R. Brown in the establishment of Elmira College it seems only reasonable to conclude that he was kept abreast of their plans. At the same time, there was a second component in Hall's attraction to Japan. As he later admitted, travel and travel literature had come to fascinate him more and more in the 1850s.[67] Such interests were further underscored by his friendship with Bayard Taylor. Taylor was widely known as America's leading nineteenth-century traveler and travel writer. An interesting speaker on the Lyceum circuit, he had visited Elmira on several occasions at Hall's invitation, and the two men seem to have developed a fondness for one another.[68]

At the time of their acquaintance, Taylor had just published his first account of Japan. This had been the product of his trip to Edo Bay with Commodore Perry in 1853. Taylor's book, *A Visit to India, China and Japan*, which appeared in 1855, predated Perry's official description of his expedition to Japan by more than a year and presented the American public with its first extensive portrait of the Japanese.[69] Written almost entirely from memory, because Perry confiscated his notes and journal, the book gave an intriguing picture of America's efforts to open what had been a forbidden and mysterious land. Combined with the letters he sent to the *New York Tribune* at the time of the expedition, Taylor's writings stirred a wide interest in things Japanese.[70]

Given the briefness of his stay, Taylor was convinced that his account was little more than the first step in America's introduction to Japan. He was of the opinion that Japan presented a golden opportunity for an important book, and for a time he toyed with the possibility of writing that book himself. On a visit to Washington, D.C., in the summer of 1855 Commodore Perry suggested to him that he "apply for the appointment of United States Commissioner to Japan."[71] The post, Perry hinted, should be particularly appealing, in

---

mitted from Nagasaki to the major American missionary boards (Episcopal, Presbyterian, and Dutch Reformed) by S. Wells Williams, E. W. Syle, two visiting China missionaries, and Chaplain Henry Wood, of the *Powhatan*, that each board select and send missionaries to Japan in the near future.

[66] The Dutch Reformed Board took up the challenge to send missionaries to Japan early in 1859 selecting S. R. Brown from his Owasco-Elmira location, and seeking out a "Dutchman," Guido Verbeck, who then resided in Auburn, and whose bride, Maria Manion, belonged to Brown's church. The third member of the board's Japan team was Duane B. Simmons, a medical doctor. Because of Japan's long associations with Holland, competency in the Dutch language was considered an important asset for anyone working in Japan, and the Dutch Reformed churches were seen as excellent recruiting centers.

[67] Towner, *Our County*, p. 636.

[68] Towner writes: "A happy acquaintance with Bayard Taylor no doubt intensified this desire [to travel]. The long winter evenings in the old book store had been largely given to books of travel" (ibid.).

[69] Hearing of the Perry expedition, Taylor had rushed to China and used his political connections to have himself included in the trip to Japan. Perry, who

was not very favorably disposed to having him along, finally agreed to take him on the condition that he become a member of the crew as "Master's Mate." This placed him directly under the Commodore's immediate command. Not a line for publication would be allowed, and at the end of the journey his journal would have to be turned over to the Navy Department. See Marie Hansen-Taylor, ed., *Life and Letters of Bayard Taylor* (Boston: Houghton, Mifflin and Co., 1884), vol. 1, pp. 250–51. Taylor never received permission to use his journal, so his book *A Visit to India, China, and Japan, in the Year 1853* (New York: G. P. Putnam & Co., 1855) was written largely from memory. The official account of the expedition, M. C. Perry's *Narrative of the Expedition of an American Squadron to the China Seas and Japan*, appeared in three volumes. Volume 1 was published in 1856, and 2 and 3 in 1857 and 1858.

[70] Although his journals were confiscated, Perry did allow Taylor to send "letters" to the *New York Tribune*, which he personally reviewed before releasing them for publication (Hansen-Taylor, *Life and Letters of Bayard Taylor*), vol. 1, p. 251.

[71] See letter of Bayard Taylor to his mother dated New York, July 9, 1855, in Hansen-Taylor, *Life and Letters of Bayard Taylor*, vol. 1, p. 300. Taylor writes: "I went to Washington on Thursday evening and returned

had hoped to take in Macao on the way back, to see the city of the "pious father, Francis Xavier, the first apostle to Japan, whither my own steps were tending." But this was not to be. Taking the steamer *Feima*, or Flying Horse, he headed back for Hong Kong. Twelve miles from Whampoa a storm blew up and the captain refused to go out into the open river. The storm turned into a "three day typhoon." Hall finally managed to make his way safely back to Hong Kong to his "old familiar quarters" on the *Surprise*, but the ship, despite his hastened return, was not ready to leave for several days. "Finally on the morning of the 29th of September," he wrote, "we weighed anchor, dropped out of the fleet, and catching a light flaw of wind and favorable tide, rounded Green Island, and stood out through the Leema passage."

The start out of Hong Kong was not particularly auspicious. On the second day the *Surprise* ran down a Chinese junk that foolishly tried to cross its bow. The vessel was completely destroyed and a child was killed in the collision. The following day one of the American crew members fell overboard.

"For a week we beat against head winds and seas," Hall wrote home, "breaking ropes, splitting sails and rolling and tossing about most uncomfortably. Our course was shaped towards the south end of Formosa Island for the outside passage up the coast." The ship managed to reach Formosa on October 3. Now "the wind blew fresh from the eastward, dead ahead," Hall wrote, and they "were three days rounding the south end of Formosa, and then stood out into the Pacific."

Here storms gave way to fine weather. "The days," Hall wrote, were now "cloudless and serene, and the nights, under a full moon and over a sparkling sea, faultlessly beautiful. We sat on the moonlit deck amusing ourselves with a round of household games till the middle watch. Never were nights more lustrous." But for a sailing ship, fine weather meant slow going as the "winds were light and calms fre-

quent." At last, on October 16, they were near the mouth of the Yangtze. "The wind and tide being with us," Hall noted, "we soon sighted the light ship at the entrance of the Yangtsi Kiang and passed out of the green sea water into the turbid flood of this great river." "The Yangtsi," Hall told his American readers, "belongs to the trio of great rivers, disputing with the Mississippi the claim to the second place in the world for length and volume of water. It is thirty miles wide at its mouth, and its waters are as muddy as the Missouri's. Islands, the deposit of its mud, are continually rising in its broad estuary. No other river rolls through more cultivated fields, or among such numerous and populous cities and villages. Its Southern shore was low, but picturesque, with trees, villages and herds of cattle and sheep."

Due to unfavorable head winds, the *Surprise* could not cross the bar of the Woosung and therefore had to anchor outside for the night. But the arrival of the missionaries had been anticipated by their friends upriver. "A light boat had come down from Shanghai to meet the Missionaries who were with us," Hall wrote, "and we were not long in availing ourselves of the opportunity to get up to the city." "We had to tack the whole distance, twelve or fifteen miles, but the thoughtfulness of the ladies who came down to welcome the missionaries, had provided an appetizing pic nic dinner. So we sailed cheerily up the Woosung, between its rich alluvial shores, vivid with the freshest vegetation and dotted with trees, till we dropped anchor near the American consulate." Having arrived in Shanghai, Hall wrote, "the hospitality of the East again awaited me, and I was soon domiciled amid home surroundings."

As it turned out, Hall had little time to see Shanghai and its environs. He wrote home, "I saw nothing of Shanghai beyond the foreign settlements." The city, itself, he noted, is "situated on the Woosung, twelve miles above its junction with the Yangtsi Kiang." It is located in "flat, but highly cultivated country. The houses of the foreign residents are plain but spacious, each one standing in an ample breadth of well-shaded and improved grounds. Before the city are anchored a hundred foreign vessels, and above there is a wilderness of junk masts." He regretted that he was "unable

---

rival in Japan, are taken from "Wanderings in the Orient," Number Eight, "China to Japan," *Elmira Weekly Advertiser*, February 18, 1860.

to see the native city," and consoled himself with the thought that "in all probability I should be there again."

The reason for Hall's abbreviated stay in Shanghai was that shortly after arriving in that city, the missionaries received word that a bark, the *Mary and Louisa*, was about to sail for Japan.[86] As there was still no regular shipping service from Shanghai to Kanagawa, this represented a golden opportunity. The problem was that the vessel was scheduled to leave in three days. According to Towner, the *Mary and Louisa* was quite willing to offer passage to the missionaries, but was not willing to transport to Japan a possible merchant competitor.[87] Hall's initial request for passage was consequently denied. But even this obstacle was overcome. When the *Mary and Louisa* sailed for Kanagawa on October 21, she carried not only Simmons and Brown (Verbeck had decided to go to Nagasaki) but also Frank Hall. As he wrote home, he was happy to commence the last stage of his six-month journey, as he had begun to be "weary of the monotony of sea life" and was anxious to try something new.

And yet, at Shanghai, too, departure was not without incident. As Hall describes the scene, by noon of October 21 the steam tug *Meteor* had commenced towing the *Mary and Louisa* down the river toward the bar at its mouth. "We steamed down the Woosung in a brief time," he wrote, but "just inside the bar, and obstructing the channel was a large fleet of junks." "There was no possibility of a passage through them without collision," Hall recorded, "so the pilot ordered full steam and crash, crash, we went among the junks, cutting one down to the water, staving in the stern of a second, and dismasting a third, fortunately with no injury to ourselves." With what injury to the hapless Chinese boatmen and their families we are not told. Hall, whose quiet good sense and disdain for arrogance allowed him

to survive in the dangerous world of Yokohama for the next seven years, was obviously concerned by what he saw. "I was sorry for the poor fellows," he wrote, adding in his typically balanced fashion, "Notwithstanding, they will, despite many similar accidents, continue to anchor in the way of the shipping passing up and down."

Proceeding without further incident, the *Mary and Louisa* entered Van Diemen Strait just south of Kyushu on the morning of November 17. Here Hall hoped to get his first glimpse of Japan. "Nor was I disappointed," he wrote home, "for through the gray light of the early morn I could make out the bold coast and bare rugged hills of the southern extremity of Kiusiu."

"Japan, so long looked for was at last visible," he wrote, and "I doubt if Marco Polo was better pleased with his first glimpse than I with mine.[88] How distant did these shores look to me in that remote corner of the world's map when I first contemplated sailing thither! Inagosima, a volcanic peak 2500 feet high on an island opposite, was sending forth a light smoky vapor. We continued in sight of the shore of Kiusiu all day, whose appearance gradually improved. Numerous villages were seen with their square houses and thatched roofs. Many of the hills were terraced and cultivated to their summits."

But if daylight introduced Hall to what appeared to be an enticing and tranquil coastline, by nightfall he was in the midst of the kind of storm that had wrecked many a vessel on Japan's treacherous shores. "On the evening of the 29th," he wrote, "we encountered the severest gale of our passage from New York, lying to several hours under the close-reefed top-sails—after splitting fore-top-gallant sail and main-top sail into ribbons. The U.S. steamer *Powhatan*, which was near us, but less protected by the land, lay to for 12 hours, los-

---

[86] See Towner, *Our County*, p. 637. Also Griffis, *Verbeck of Japan*, p. 67.

[87] Towner, *Our County*, p. 637. Since Towner got his account from Hall it seems likely that this interpretation is correct, but in his "Wanderings in the Orient," Number Eight, Hall simply wrote: "On our arrival at Shanghai, I learned that there was immediate opportunity of being forwarded to my destination in Japan by the

barque Mary and Louisa, to sail for Kanagawa in three days" (*Elmira Weekly Advertiser*, February 18, 1860). The *Mary and Louisa* was under the control of Captain Benjamin Jones of Brookhaven, New York.

[88] Hall is mistaken here. Marco Polo never visited Japan and his accounts of Zipangu (Japan) were based on information supplied by the Mongol invaders of Japan in the thirteenth century.

ing sails and suffering some damage to her spars. It was the severest blow she had experienced during her present cruise."

As if the storm was not enough to unsettle Hall and his missionary companions within sight of their goal, at nine o'clock, just as the gale reached its height, the cry "Fire!" "Fire!" was added to the confusion. As Hall wrote, "Thick smoke was pouring out of the carpenter's room, and there was a light flame blazing up." Hall had read about fires at sea, but as he noted, "A ship on fire on such a night as this—in such a howling tempest—who could live to tell its tale!" Fortunately quick action averted disaster and the fire was brought under control. With time the storm also abated, and it was as if the final obstacles to their reaching Japan had been overcome.

"Early on the morning of the 30th, we made Cape Idsu, fifteen miles distant," Hall wrote, and "we had a clear view of the promontory and its broken ranges of hills running diagonally to the coast line. To the north-east towering high above the volcanic ridges, Fusi-Yama, snow-crowned was seen rising aloft in silent majesty. The rising sun glittered on its frosty crest and on the snowy ridges of a long mountain range. Thirty miles distant the island volcano of Oho-sima emitted clouds of smoke that hung suspended in midair." Soon they entered Edo Bay, "but calms and baffling winds," Hall noted, "made our progress slow." They now "encountered fishing boats by the hundreds, with crews of robust, poorly clad men," and "off Uraga two boat loads of officials came off to us and wished to know our nationality." "The answer of 'American,' and the sign of the stars and stripes," Hall added, "gave satisfaction to the two-sworded gentlemen and they rowed back again."

Hall was delighted by what he saw.

All that has been said about the beauty of Yeddo Bay and its shores has been deservedly said. As we sailed on, the villages grew more numerous, the hills less difficult and the ground better cultivated. We were so near that we could see the white and brown houses, hear the shouts of children, the barking of dogs, and the ringing of bells. I was never weary of watching the peerless beauty of Fusi-Yama, which at every advance appeared to lift-itself higher and higher among the clouds. Unlike the peaks of the Alps and the Andes, it has no rival summits to detract from its apparent height, but stands in clear unbroken outline, monarch of all, in cold, solitary grandeur.

With the *Mary and Louisa* safely anchored near the Kanagawa strand, Hall wrote, "We arrived in Yokuhama bay, fifteen miles south of Yeddo, on the evening of November 1st. I had completed my long voyage of 20,000 miles in safety. And though I had gone so many miles away, it was pleasant to think, that with fair winds, I was only thirty days distant from the western boundary of my native land. In the morning I should see the shores which were to be my abiding place for an uncertain future."

"The morning dawned," Hall wrote, and "before me lay a land pleasant to behold of hill and meadow, of field and forest. There was another sight that fastened my gaze. High above the clouds, dazzling white with the freshly fallen snow of yesterday's storm, rose a mountain's summit. The cloud-shadows were chasing each other across its snowy fields, the morning sun flushed its crest with a rosy hue"; here he stood at last facing "matchless Fusi-Yama!"

Hall's Japan

Neither Hall, nor many of his Western contemporaries who entered Japan in the latter half of 1859 knew much about the internal affairs of the country in which they were about to reside.

The tranquillity and splendor of Mount Fuji, which impressed Hall as he stepped off the *Mary and Louisa* onto Japanese soil, belied the turmoil in which the nation found itself. The Perry expedition of 1853–1854 served to highlight the gradual disintegration of the old regime. By the fifth decade of the nineteenth century the once all-powerful Tokugawa shogunate was little more than a shadow of its former self. Its economic and political power had been vitiated by the very forces of change it had set in motion two and a half centuries earlier.

Peace and stability, the shogunate's highest priorities, had resulted not only in a well-established order but also in economic transformation. Urbanization, the commercialization of agriculture, the growing wealth of city and rural merchants engaged in the protoindustrial production, flourishing domestic trade, increasing access to education—all these indicated the degree to which Japan was moving away from an agrarian-based feudal society.

Even among the elite, the samurai, there was dramatic change. Once battle-hardened, sword-wielding, and largely illiterate men of action, the warriors Hall encountered were, for the most part, ledger-toting, brush-wielding bureaucrats, or "officials," as he viewed them. If there was a problem with all this, it was that the Tokugawa shogunate was ideologically and economically incapable of integrating itself effectively into the new order that was confronting it on all sides.

The Pax Tokugawa, it must be added, was achieved only by closing Japan to outside influences. But the effort to keep the world at bay by locking out all Westerners—except a handful of Dutch—in the late 1630s was also costly. Cut off from Europe during the scientific and industrial revolutions, Japan, which had boasted technological equality with the West when firearms were first introduced in the sixteenth century, was now seriously behind. This was particularly true of the fields of military technology and hardware. The Tokugawa regime was pressured, therefore, not simply by domestic change, but by the growing force of Western nations whose search for markets was backed by unprecedented military power.

The arrival of Perry in 1853 merely confirmed an expanding problem. Russian pressures for better relations with Japan, which dated to the late eighteenth century, were followed in rapid succession by those of Great Britain, the United States, and France in the first half of the nineteenth century. Faced with a mounting cry to "open" the country, even the servile Dutch advised the Japanese that isolation was no longer a feasible policy. And yet, within Japan there was no clear consensus on what was to be done. On one side stood the realists, including many within the shogunate, who argued that Japan had few choices in the face of superior Western military and technological force. As they saw it, the nation could seek an accommodation with the West by opening the country to trade and foreign intercourse—hoping that with time the incorporation of Western technology would allow for new choices. On the other side there stood the self-appointed protectors of the realm whose strident voices swelled in the ever-mounting cry "revere the Emperor, expel the barbarians." For such men there was little hope for an accommodation with the West. As they viewed it, the idea of opening the country to trade and a period of self-strengthening would simply lead to loss of will. For men of this disposition it was better to confront one's enemies directly. To lose one's life in striking down the enemies of the throne, whether foreign or domestic, was preferable to the slow disintegration of accommodation that, they insisted, robbed men of their will as well as their virtue. It was the very existence of such men, as Hall quickly discovered, that made life in treaty-port Japan precarious.

Hall's experiences in Japan were to be shaped by the events of the 1850s of which he initially knew little and only gradually grew conscious. At the surface level the Perry Treaty of 1854 resulted in only minor concessions on the part of the Japanese. The Kanagawa Treaty of Friendship, as it was known, simply called for the opening of two ports, Shimoda and Hakodate, to American ships, a limited trade, and the exchange of consular representatives. This was a far cry from the full commercial treaties the United States and European powers wanted. The shogunate, which quickly signed similar treaties with the Europeans, therefore had some reason to feel satisfied, having blunted the chief Western thrust to open Japan to trade and commerce. But not without cost. Confronted, as it was, by an unprecedented foreign threat, the shogunate tried to bolster its position by seeking the advice and support of the daimyo throughout the land. This was a clear break with tradition, and the results were unanticipated. Instead of supporting the limited opening of the country that shogunal officials regarded as inevitable, many of the daimyo (feudal barons) insisted that the shogun should live up to his title of "barbarian-quelling general" and throw the Westerners out. The Tokugawa effort to gain broad daimyo support for the opening of the country therefore backfired. In place of unity the shogunate was confronted by an increasing national debate. This debate focused on how the West should be dealt with and what reforms should be carried out at home to meet the Western threat.

This debate was further complicated by the arrival in Shimoda of the American consul, Townsend Harris, in 1856.[89] Harris was determined to convince the shogunate that trade with the West was inevitable and that it would be far wiser to conclude an amicable settlement with the United States than to await the more forceful demands of Great Britain and France. To this end, as we have noted earlier, he was able to effectively use the Arrow War in China to argue that the joint British and French expedition that was in the process of subduing the Chinese would thereafter be sent to Japan to achieve the same ends.

With time the American consul's arguments and stubborn persistence paid off. On July 29, 1858, the shogunate signed a full commercial treaty with the United States. This treaty, which was popularly known as the Harris Treaty, served as a model for similar treaties signed in a matter of weeks with Great Britain, France, Holland, and Russia. The commercial treaties basically set the conditions for treaty-port life. As the Harris Treaty stipulated, in addition to Shimoda and Hakodate, several new ports were to be opened to trade and foreign residence. The first two, which were scheduled to be opened on July 1, 1859, were Kanagawa (Yokohama) and Nagasaki. Starting in 1860 and running through 1863 several other locations, which included Niigata and Hyogo (Kobe), as well as Edo and Osaka, were

to be made available for trade and residence. In addition to opening these sites the treaty set tariff rates and import duties at low levels, and established the system of extraterritoriality under which foreign residents in the treaty ports were subject to their own consular courts and not to Japanese law. While no Japanese territory was ceded to the treaty powers, as was the case in China, treaty rights extended to an area approximately twenty-five miles inland from the ports. Hall's many excursions from Yokohama and Kanagawa were restricted to this area, and while he occasionally went a few miles beyond treaty limits, travel to the interior required official government permission. As his journal indicates, even trips to Edo were not permitted without an official invitation from one of the Western legations.

Despite such restrictions, the concessions made in the commercial treaties clearly placed Japan in an "unequal," or semicolonial position. Well intentioned and "realistic" as the shogunate may have been, the signing of these treaties unleashed a new furor of national debate about Japan's future, its relationship to the outside world, and the overlordship of the Tokugawa house.

In an effort to stem the decline of Tokugawa authority Hotta Masayoshi, the minister responsible for drafting the Harris Treaty, once again turned to the daimyo for advice, and furthermore sought to gain court approval for the proposed treaties with the West. This was tantamount to openly admitting weakness and allowed a growing number of radical samurai, as well as some of Japan's leading daimyo, to rally to the side of the emperor and further challenge Tokugawa legitimacy. When the emperor refused to endorse the treaties, Hotta was forced to resign.

The demise of Hotta brought to power Ii Naosuke, one of the leading men of his age. As lord of Hikone, Ii had established himself as

---

[89] Townsend Harris has provided us with one of the other important journals for the late Tokugawa years. Harris's journal covers the years from 1855 to 1858. See Mario E. Cosenza, ed., *The Complete Journal of Townsend Harris: First American Consul and Minister to Japan* (Rutland, Vt.: Charles E. Tuttle Co., 1959). A second major journal was that of his secretary, Henry Heus-

ken, which covers the years from 1855 to 1861. See Robert A. Wilson and Jeanette C. van der Corput, eds., *Henry Heusken: Japan Journal, 1855–1861* (New Brunswick, N.J.: Rutgers University Press, 1964). Oliver Statler has utilized these journals and placed them within the context of Japanese domestic politics in his *Shimoda Story* (New York: Random House, 1969).

an able administrator and headed a group of Tokugawa vassals who were bent on restoring the shogunate's prestige and authority. In keeping with the troubled times, Ii was granted the position of "great elder," which was equivalent to the shogunal premiership, a position that was filled only during times of crisis, and he immediately took strong steps to restore shogunal control. One of his first acts was to sign the Harris Treaty. When summoned to explain this decision to the imperial court in Kyoto, he refused to go. Instead he placed under house arrest several of Japan's leading lords who had been active in the growing proemperor movement. Among these was Nariaki, the lord of Mito, whose son Keiki was rejected as shogunal heir, and in whose territory Ii carried out a widespread purge of proimperial intellectuals.

Ii's efforts to breathe new life into the declining fortunes of the Tokugawa regime, while temporarily successful, came to an abrupt end when, as Hall records in his journal, extremist samurai from Mito assassinated him on his way back from Edo castle at the Sakurada Gate on the snowy holiday afternoon of March 24, 1860. Hall's opinion that "this affray may prove the forerunner of important events involving the empire in political difficulties, and threatening the situation of foreigners" was soon confirmed.[90]

Those who followed Ii as leaders of the shogunate possessed little of his forcefulness or political acumen. And while further reforms were attempted, as Hall's journal shows us the shogunate was now adrift, caught between a tide of mounting anti-Tokugawa sentiment and antiforeign xenophobia. Unable to control the currents that buffeted it, the shogunate desperately sought allies. When the lords of Chōshū and Satsuma suggested a "union of the court and shogunate," the Tokugawa accepted the proposal, hoping to use the prestige of the court to shore up its own declining

status. Under the elders Ando Nobumasa and Kuze Hirochika, who succeeded Ii, the marriage of princess Kazu-no-miya, the sister of the Emperor Kōmei, and the Shogun Iemochi was consummated in 1862.[91]

But to bring about such an alliance the Tokugawa were forced to make a number of important concessions. These included the appointment of officials friendly to the court, the revision of the hostage system, and the relaxation of the requirement of "alternate attendance" whereby feudal lords had been forced to spend a good deal of their time in the city of Edo. Most indicative of the changing relationship between court and shogunate was the agreement that the shogun would travel to Kyoto to consult with the emperor and his court regarding matters of national policy. When Shogun Iemochi set out for Kyoto in the spring of 1863 it was the first such journey on the part of the Tokugawa since the seventeenth century. Hall notes in his journal that on this occasion not even the "usual repairs" were to be made to the roads and bridges, that the inns were "not to be refitted as usual with new mats," nor was any "new furniture to be provided." Hall concluded that this lack of "decent respect, is an indignity put upon the reigning Tycoon by the hostile faction who have in a measure usurped control" (JJ, November 18, 1862).

With Tokugawa prestige in decline, power, as Hall observed in the early 1860s, was shifting to new forces. Satsuma and Chōshū, two of the largest and strongest "outer" domains with long-standing anti-Tokugawa feelings, now came to the forefront in national politics. Both sought to ally themselves with the imperial cause through close ties with the court.

Satsuma took the lead in this effort in 1862 by taking up the theme of the proposed court and *bakufu* (shogunal government) alliance. At the same time it was authorized by the court to bring order to Kyoto, which had been dis-

---

[90] Francis Hall, Japan Journal, March 25, 1860 (hereinafter cited as JJ).

[91] It is worth noting that the marriage of Princess Kazu-no-miya was not the first such marriage alliance between the court and shogunal house. On February 29, 1860, Hall witnessed the procession of Michi-no-

miya, the niece of the Emperor Kōmei, who was on her way to Edo to marry Tokugawa Mochitsugu, the Lord of Kii and brother of the Shogun Iemochi. This marriage was part of Ii Naosuke's efforts to bring about a union of court and shogunate.

rupted by growing numbers of masterless samurai, or *rōnin*, who called for the overthrowal of the shogunate and the expulsion of Westerners while proclaiming themselves supporters of the imperial house. It was under Satsuma's influence that Keiki was made guardian of the young shogun in Edo, and that the shogunate was forced to accept the lord of Fukui, Matsudaira Shungaku, as a reformist elder. It was Matsudaira who brought to an end the hostage system and allowed the entourages of daimyo wives, which Hall describes, to leave Edo for their provinces. It was also under his influence that "alternate attendance," the linchpin of the Tokugawa system, was reduced to a meaningless one hundred days every three years, and the city of Edo, as Hall records, suddenly lost a large part of its population as well as its role as national political center.

From Hall's perspective in Yokohama, these were years in which Japan seemed to be slipping into anarchy. Life in Yokohama had always been precarious. In February 1860 Hall recorded in his journal, "there are seven foreign graves on the bluff of Treaty Point, six of the occupants died violent deaths, five out of the six having been assassinated in the streets" (JJ, February 29, 1860). In 1861 he recorded the death of Harris's secretary Henry Heusken. The British legation in Edo was attacked the same year and subsequently both the British and American legations were burned down. On September 14, 1862, four Britishers riding on the Tokaido near the village of Namamugi were set upon by samurai in the procession of the lord of Satsuma. C. L. Richardson, one of the men of the party, was killed, and two of the others were seriously wounded. The British government angrily protested and demanded the arrest of the murderers as well as the payment of a large indemnity.

Satsuma was not alone in its antiforeign stand. Mito *rōnin* were a constant threat to Yokohama, and the most radical group of all were the Chōshū activists, who increasingly defied not only the shogunate but also the more conservative elements of their domain. In Kyoto radical activists, or *rōnin* from Chōshū and other territories, became increasingly violent in their support of the emperor. Assassinations became common, and these were directed not only at their more moderate rivals, but at all who were alleged to have cooperated with Westerners, or who were in any way connected with the foreign trade.

Even the court seems to have been impressed, if not intimidated, by the radicalism of its Chōshū supporters. It was into this hotbed that Iemochi stepped on his journey to Kyoto in the spring of 1863. Virtually a prisoner, he was forced to accommodate the court and its supporters by establishing June 25, 1863, as the date for the expulsion of all "barbarians" from Japan. On June 21 Hall noted in his journal, "The Japanese Governors visited General Pruyn [the American minister] this evening. . . . they admit that the Tycoon is compulsorily detained at Kioto and that he has given the orders for the expulsion of the foreigners. They said that these orders were received ten days since and required compliance within thirty days. They had not attempted to execute them, and would not because they knew they were impossible" (JJ, June 21, 1863).[92] As Hall's observation shows, the shogunate now found itself in the awkward and embarrassing position of issuing expulsion orders that it knew it could not enforce.

Indeed, the situation was even more complex. While the shogun blithely called for the expulsion of Westerners in Kyoto, the men left behind to manage shogunal affairs in Edo and Yokohama were desperately trying to deal with the British ultimatum, presented on April 6, which called upon the shogunate to pay an indemnity of £100,000 for the two lives lost in the attack on the British legation, the assault on the Richardson party, and the subsequent burning of the legation buildings. The English demands, which also called for the arrest and presentation of Richardson's murderers, were backed by an expanding force of ships and guns that arrived in Yokohama under Admiral

[92] The journey of the shogun to Kyoto and the difficulties the shogunate confronted in the spring of 1863 are extensively discussed in Conrad Totman, *The Col-* *lapse of the Tokugawa Bakufu, 1862–1868* (Honolulu: University Press of Hawaii, 1980), pp. 67ff.

Kuper. The British position was unequivocal. The Japanese were given twenty days to reach a political settlement and pay the indemnity, or face Kuper's guns. As Hall notes, for the next two months Yokohama constantly found itself on the edge of war as deadlines approached, were violated, and replaced by new deadlines. Occasionally there was pure panic. At one point native merchants fled the city en masse; on another occasion it was the foreigners who desperately sought shelter for themselves and their goods on the foreign shipping in the harbor.[93] Even during calmer intervals there were constant rumors that bands of proimperial *rōnin* were planning to attack the settlement.

On June 21, 1863, after another agreement to pay the indemnity had been aborted, Hall wrote in his journal, "A communication is received from the Admiral today in which he says that peaceful negotiations having failed to bring the Japanese to terms, he shall employ measures of coercion, which he will not institute for eight days inclusive of today, unless the Japanese take the initiative before. Thus matters will soon be brought to a final issue. He recommends the removal of the women and children on shipboard." "Our hopes of peace," Hall added on June 23, "are alternately raised and depressed."

Hall records that the indemnity was suddenly paid in full on June 24, 1863, the day before the proposed "expulsion of foreigners," announced earlier in Kyoto, was to go into effect.[94] What he did not know on that day was that he, or more specifically Walsh Hall & Co., his firm, was already directly involved in the next stage of the antiforeign drama.

On June 21 Hall had dispatched for Shanghai the American steamer *Pembroke*. This

steamer made its way into the Straits of Shimonoseki on the afternoon of June 24. While at anchor there shortly after midnight, in fact at one o'clock on the morning of June 25, the *Pembroke* was attacked by an armed bark and a brig belonging to Chōshū. The steamer managed to get up steam and escaped to Shanghai with little damage. Hall was at dinner with the American minister, Robert H. Pruyn, on July 10 when one of the governors of foreign affairs from Edo arrived with the foregoing "urgent news," which was confirmed by a report from Shanghai the following day. On July 15 word reached Yokohama that the French dispatch steamer *Kien Chang* had also been fired on by Chōshū shore batteries.

Chōshū's decision to take matters into its own hands and to initiate the expulsion of "barbarians" by firing on Western ships in the Straits of Shimonoseki set the stage for an escalated confrontation not just with the West but also with the shogunate. On July 11, the day after word of the *Pembroke* attack reached Yokohama, the American warship, the *Wyoming*, under Captain McDougal, was sent to the straits. The Americans reached Shimonoseki on July 16 and after being fired on by Chōshū batteries, McDougal retaliated by sinking the Chōshū brig and another recently acquired steamer, as well as silencing several of the domain's shore batteries.[95] Four days later the French retaliated for the attack on their steamer and sent ashore landing parties that destroyed several additional forts and their ammunition.

While the Americans and French were dealing with Chōshū, the British were determined to finish their negotiations with Satsuma over the Richardson murder. Despite the shogun-

---

[93] On May 6, 1863, Hall wrote in his journal: "Today a regular panic has seized the town; the native population are fleeing in the utmost haste. Everyone believes war is inevitable and is hastening to escape from the vicinity of the sea. Scarcely a native merchant has the nerve to remain, but all offer their wares at any price they can get. The excitement among the foreigners is hardly less." On June 22, 1863, Hall noted, "the foreign merchants are generally busy removing their merchandise and valuables on shipboard."

[94] The decision to pay the British indemnity seems to have been made with some haste, perhaps with the

knowledge that Chōshū was determined to begin the expulsion of foreigners the following day. Hall notes in his entry that the payment was delivered at 4 A.M. The delivery of the twenty chests of coin was unusual at this hour and awakened Hall. See also Totman, *The Collapse of the Tokugawa Bakufu*, p. 72.

[95] On July 24 and 25, 1863, Hall dispatched a long account of this battle at Shimonoseki to the *New York Tribune*, which covered almost the entire front page of the paper on October 2, 1863, under the heading "The Naval Fight With the Japanese."

ate's payment of the main indemnity, the murderers had not been produced, and there was still the matter of a £25,000 demand on Satsuma. As Hall records, the British fleet sailed from Yokohama on August 6. On August 15, after several days of negotiations, Satsuma batteries suddenly opened fire on the British. The fleet responded by sinking three of Satsuma's steamers and burning down a good part of the city of Kagoshima. But while the destruction ashore was extensive, Hall noted that the British did not escape unscathed, "having lost sixty killed and wounded, including among the former the Captain and Lieutenant Commander of the *Euryalus* flagship of Rear Admiral Kuper" (JJ, August 21, 1863). To Hall it seemed that "the strife between Japanese exclusiveness and Western liberalism is fairly grim" (Ibid.).

In the wake of the Kagoshima confrontation, Satsuma quickly admitted the failure of its antiforeign policy, paid the £25,000 indemnity, and developed a great respect for the British navy. New vessels were soon bought with British aid, and some of Satsuma's young men were secretly sent abroad to learn more about the West. If the dire lessons of August 1863 encouraged Satsuma samurai to abandon a self-destructive xenophobia in favor of a willingness to learn from the West, the same was not yet true of Chōshū.

Chōshū's power within the court had expanded with its aggressive antiforeign stance. It had attempted to ally itself in Kyoto with the more radical men around the throne to pursue its expulsionist plans, and it had even tried to get the emperor to take personal command of an expedition against foreigners. Indeed, when the shogunate sent a special emissary to Chōshū demanding that it call off its attacks on Western ships, the extremist samurai killed him as he was attempting to leave the domain. But Chōshū was not alone in seeking court influence. Satsuma remained an active rival, and on September 30, 1863, Satsuma and Aizu forces carried out a coup d'état in Kyoto driving out the Chōshū forces and thereby greatly reducing that domain's influence at court. Moderate nobles now replaced the more radically inclined Chōshū allies, some of whom fled the city with the retreating Chōshū forces.

Meanwhile Chōshū's xenophobia was hardly diminished. The forts destroyed by the Americans and French in 1863 were quickly rebuilt and the Straits of Shimonoseki were again effectively closed to foreign shipping. Occasionally even Satsuma vessels were attacked. In the summer of 1864 Chōshū tried to restore its position in Kyoto by marching troops on that city, but on August 20 these troops were defeated by the samurai of Aizu and Satsuma. At the same time Chōshū's continued belligerence against the West resulted in another naval confrontation with the foreign powers. This time the expedition sent against Chōshū included not only the Americans and French, but also the British and Dutch. The combined fleet left Yokohama on August 28 and 29. On September 5 the fleet attacked the Chōshū fortifications, and on September 18 Hall recorded in his journal, "Late last evening the *Perseus* returned from Shimonoseki bringing the first news of the Allied Fleet's success against Chosiu. The forts were easily silenced, and a subsequent landing party completed the work. The casualties were few, 12 killed and 54 wounded." Chōshū, like Satsuma, had at last come to realize the futility of armed confrontations with the Western powers.

Chōshū's effort to attack Kyoto and her confrontation with the West finally convinced the shogunate to take stronger action against this recalcitrant domain. An expedition of 150,000 troops loyal to the Tokugawa house was assembled in Hiroshima to confront the rebellious "Prince of Nagato," as Hall referred to the lord of Chōshū. The threat of invasion quickly led to a reorganization of the domain in the closing months of 1864. The radical samurai leaders who had attacked Kyoto with mixed battalion of samurai and commoner troops, and who had tried to push their proemperor policy at court, were replaced by conservatives who opposed the domain's role in national politics. As Hall recorded in his journal on January 22, 1865, "The rumor is current that Chosiu has made terms with the Government by ordering three of his ministers, who have been most active in prosecuting the rebellion, to commit harakiri." On January 24, 1865, the Chōshū conservatives accepted the Tokugawa peace terms, which included the forced suicides, an official apology, the return of a number of radical nobles who had left Kyoto with the retreating Chōshū troops, and the disbanding of the mixed rifle units of samurai and commoners.[96]

The "victory" of the Tokugawa and their allies in the Chōshū expedition was more apparent than real. While the Tokugawa shogunate was determined to use this opportunity to rebuild its declining power and authority, this was not easily accomplished. Although it was able to tighten its military control over the Kyoto court and even managed to gain French support and technical assistance for a military buildup, these efforts were largely inadequate. Attempts to regain its national position by restoring the alternate attendance system ended in complete failure. Moreover, Chōshū's attacks on Western shipping further saddled the regime with an indemnity of $3 million, which seriously undermined its financial position. In short, most of its reform efforts were too little and too late.

Indeed, the situation in Chōshū was also far from settled. While the conservative faction that took over the domain in the fall of 1864 had been able to carry through most of the conditions outlined in the "peace settlement" with the shogunate, it was unable to disband the mixed rifle units and to control the radical samurai who had founded them. By the spring of 1865 Chōshū found itself immersed in a civil war. The outcome of this struggle was a victory for the reformist group whose mixed units won victory after victory against the regular domain forces and finally seized control of the castle town, setting up a new administration.

With the victory of the reform faction, Chōshū was once again clearly in rebellion. And the shogunate was once again faced with the task of mounting an expedition against it. But by this time the shogunate possessed neither the military superiority nor the widespread support it had enjoyed earlier. Organizing a new expedition proved to be a slow and difficult task. Almost a year went by in an effort to gain sufficient support, and when the expedi-

tion was finally organized and sent in the fall of 1866, several of Japan's leading lords, including the daimyo of Satsuma, refused to participate. Chōshū, for its part, had used the interim to further modernize its military units. In doing so the domain was supported by the British, who in distinction to the French, cast their lot with the reformist-minded young samurai of Chōshū and Satsuma rather than the Edo government. In the struggle that ensued, Chōshū's more determined and better prepared and equipped troops outfought their numerically superior shogunal opponents.

By the end of 1866, the year in which Hall left Japan, the shogunate was in its death throes. Soundly defeated by the Chōshū army, it had been forced to sue for peace. In the latter stages of the campaign it had been deserted by many of its allies, and its authority as a national government was gone. While some of its friends continued to maneuver and search for ways in which it might be preserved through compromise and power sharing, the end of the Tokugawa regime was clearly in sight. Perhaps nothing foretold this more clearly than the secret alliance of Chōshū and Satsuma concluded in March 1866. Both of these domains had transformed their previous xenophobia into a willingness to learn from the West, and both envisioned a new Japan in which the country would have to be modernized and taken beyond its feudal past.

As Hall left Yokohama in the summer of 1866, the Meiji Restoration was virtually complete. A year later the drama that saw the last shogun, Keiki, return his authority to the emperor was proceeding toward its final act. With the announcement of an "imperial restoration" by the samurai of Chōshū, Satsuma, and their allies on January 3, 1868, that drama was complete, and Japan, as Hall had envisioned, entered its modern age.

---

[96] For details regarding the peace negotiations with Chōshū see Albert Craig, *Chōshū in the Meiji Restoration* (Cambridge, Mass.: Harvard University Press, 1961), pp. 246ff.

Kanagawa and Yokohama

"My feet at last stand on Japanese soil," Hall wrote home early in December 1859.[97] After seven months he had finally arrived in "this land so long forbidden to strangers." A country "from which its own citizens once departed could never return except to meet a certain death. Whose shores were so inhospitable that the shipwrecked mariner escaped the sea only to find a more cruel fate on shore . . . a land which sat by itself far away on the sea, absorbed in its own intolerant selfishness till America, which had flung its own doors open to the born of every clime, came knocking at its gates and demanded admittance for herself and the wide world."[98]

Here we have much of the mid-nineteenth-century American view of Japan. In fact, Hall wrote quite honestly, "When I left home the interest felt in Japan was, I might say, a romantic one. Much had been written and printed of the beauty of Japanese scenery, the fertility of Japanese soil, the loveliness of its climate, the honesty and simplicity of its people, and their anxiety to see and learn more of the American people."[99] "Everything written or said," Hall noted, "was rose tinted." As he made his way to the Far East, "other reports began to come in." The "Japanese reputation," he observed, "did not stand so high in China. There were stories of governmental hostility and popular dislike, so that at the last it was uncertain whether so much as a shelter for one's head could be had." But, as he added, "I still kept on my way more anxious than ever to know something positive of this hidden nation." Having settled in Kanagawa with "all necessary creature comforts," he clarified his position, "I anticipate no little pleasure in my study of this land and its people."[100]

If, as the foregoing indicates, Hall's intentions were to study and to report on Japan for the *New York Tribune* and *Elmira Advertiser*, he did not announce these plans to the Japanese authorities who questioned him about his reasons for coming to their country. To the normal inquiry of one officer regarding his profession Hall replied that he was a "traveller." "That was a new profession to him," Hall wrote in his journal. "He repeated the name several times and wrote it down in his book, 'travellyerr,' for future research, buckled on his two swords and departed" (JJ, December 24, 1859).

As his journal indicates Hall settled in Kanagawa, initially taking up residence with J. C. Hepburn and his wife at the Hepburn's temple, the Jōbutsuji, and subsequently moving with Duane B. Simmons and his wife into another temple building. As he wrote home, "I have been fortunate in finding a temporary home with an American family, the comforts of which almost cause me to forget that I am so far removed from that great bill of particulars which you call *necessities* of life in the States."[101] At the time, he noted, the foreign population of Kanagawa consisted of the American, British, French, and Dutch consuls, the American missionary families, and "perhaps half a dozen individuals besides."[102]

Hall described his new setting to his Elmira readers as follows: "Kanagawa lies on the northwest shore of Yokohama bay, and opposite to it on the south-east coast is the new town of Yokohama which, in spite of treaty stipulation, is the entre pot of foreign commerce. Kanagawa is a long straggling city of two or three streets in breadth lying on the Tokaido or great highway from Yedo to Oasaca. It might properly be called a suburb of Yedo, for on each side of the Tokaido is a continuous row of dwellings and shops to that city, broken by two short intervals only."[103]

Hall was taken with life on the Tōkaidō. "From early morn till night this national high-

---

[97] "Wanderings in the Orient," Number Nine, "Kanagawa and Yokohama," *Elmira Weekly Advertiser*, March 24, 1860.

[98] The foregoing quotations are from ibid.

[99] Ibid.

[100] Ibid.

[101] "Wanderings in the Orient," Number Ten, "Life in a Temple," *Elmira Weekly Advertiser*, April 28, 1860.

[102] Ibid.

[103] "Wanderings in the Orient," Number Nine, "Kanagawa and Yokohama," *Elmira Weekly Advertiser*, March 24, 1860.

way is a scene of busy life," he wrote. "Crowds of people are passing through it, from the haughty grandee of the empire with his suite and numerous train of attendants, to the naked coolie with his burden pole of bamboo. At every step, one is met by pack horses carrying their heavy burdens of produce and merchandise in bales of straw slung on either side. From men and women in the houses, from swarms of children in the street, from the passing laborer and traveller on the road, the stranger is saluted at every foot of advance with 'Anata Ohio,' or the national 'How do you do?' "[104]

About Kanagawa itself, he noted, there is "nothing specially attractive." Its houses and shops were "humble and unpretending," and its many temples could "boast no greatness of extent, no beauty or grandeur of structure, not even the gaudiness of Oriental architecture." Indeed, Hall concluded that "from their weather-worn and crumbling aspect one might suppose that even Buddhism was a religion going to seed or at least in the over ripeness of decay." As Hall summed up the town, "Everything within and around Kanagawa wears the immutability of generations."[105]

If Kanagawa struck Hall as drab, this was hardly the case of the natural setting in which the town was located. "The country round about is picturesquely beautiful," Hall wrote home. "It is broken into innumerable gently undulating eminences. Between them and around them spread rich fields bristling with the ripened rice, or emerald with the young growing crops. The low hills are fringed with sparse woods, or laid out in ridge divided fields and cultivated with horticultural nicety."[106] As Hall's journal indicates, he was soon out on excursions into the countryside, and by the end of his stay he had visited a large number of the villages in the Kanagawa-Yokohama region.

Studying Japan, which seems to have been Hall's initial goal, meant studying the customs and language of the Japanese people. In his efforts to wrestle with Japanese, Hall was for-

James Curtis Hepburn. Physician and missionary scholar who created the system of romanizing Japanese that still bears his name.

tunate in several respects. His shipboard lessons had already introduced him to the elementary forms of the language, and living with J. C. Hepburn and S. R. Brown in Kanagawa allowed him to work with two of the leading missionary-scholars who were then engaged in similar language studies. The three men seem to have shared both the difficulties and accomplishments of their efforts. Hall later spoke of two years of "hard study."[107] And while it seems questionable that he reached the level of Japanese competence indicated in his obituary, which claimed that he "mastered the language, so that he could speak, read, and write" Japanese "with as much fluency as a native," he did make considerable progress.[108]

---

[104] Ibid.
[105] Ibid.
[106] Ibid.

[107] Obituary of Francis Hall, *Elmira Weekly Advertiser*, August 29, 1902.
[108] Ibid.

Kanagawa on the Tōkaidō. Photograph by Felice Beato.

By the time he moved across the bay to Yokohama in the fall of 1860 he had developed an elementary conversational level sufficient to communicate with most Japanese regarding day-to-day matters. Still there were a number of amusing episodes. Four months after his arrival his servants returned one night after an evening on the town "redolent of sake." "I put them outdoors," he wrote, "and scolded them to the best of my abilities in Japanese." "I did my scolding, book in hand, first looking up some ugly word and then firing it off at their heads at a venture." By this method he succeeded in telling them that they were "*drunkards* and *smelt bad*." But he was not convinced of the moral force of his admonition, even though one of them returned the next day with "red eyes and woebegone expression, and promised to practice all the virtues for an uncertain time to come" (JJ, February 3, 1860).

Three months later he felt better when "a Japanese girl hearing us talk imperfectly in her own tongue would believe nothing other than that I was a Japanese 'like Heco [Joseph Heco].' She would not be convinced to the contrary" (JJ, May 18, 1860). By the second and third year of his stay in Japan his Japanese had become sufficiently good to allow extensive communication with the natives. Raphael Pumpelly, the mineralogist who accompanied Hall into the Oyama district in 1862, recalled that Hall's language skills got him out of several scrapes, including one where they were refused lodgings. "Mr. Hall, who spoke the language well," Pumpelly wrote, "besieged the hostess. By persuasive politeness he carried the point, where force would probably have failed and been followed by serious results."[109]

As Pumpelly notes, Hall's skills at dealing with the Japanese were aided by his personality. Hall's friendly, open, and generous traits served him well in Japan. He made friends quickly, often among the common people he

[109] Raphael Pumpelly, *My Reminiscences* (New York: Henry Holt & Co., 1918), pp. 294–95.

met on his almost daily hikes from Kanagawa and Yokohama into the surrounding country-side. His sense of humor, love of plants and flowers, and fondness for children seem to have cut through cultural barriers. His delight in joining Japanese on their festival occasions, his willingness to enter into their revelries, to partake of their generosity, while at the same time offering his own, all these seem to have convinced the Japanese that here was a foreigner who was genuinely interested in them and their culture.

While Hall had come to Japan to study, observe, and write, his business instincts soon involved him in the Yokohama trade. On November 24, 1859, less than a month after his arrival, he recorded in his journal, "Concluded to write home for my funds" And on August 10, 1860, his "treasure" from home arrived, "having been nearly five months on the way" (JJ, August 30, 1860). Meanwhile, like other foreign merchants, he seems to have been active in the export of gold specie. Since the gold to silver ratio in Japan stood at five to one, whereas the same ratio outside of Japan was closer to fifteen to one, exporting Japanese gold and bringing in foreign silver was highly profitable. On December 22, 1859, after totalling up his first month's expenditures in Japan at "a little less than $17," he added that he had "sent to Olyphant today by the *Excelsior* in Lowrie's hands 120 kobangs," that is, 120 of the standard Japanese gold coins (JJ, December 22, 1859). Hall subsequently traded in a variety of goods that included art objects and antiques, particularly lacquer, as well as silk and tea.[110]

If everything around Kanagawa wore the "immutability of generations," Yokohama, to which his business interests drew his attention, was entirely different. "Yokohama is new, a growth of today," he wrote home. "No western city springing up of a night on the furthest prairie's edge ever grew more rapidly."

Our treaty with Japan provided that on the 4th day of July, 1859, Kanagawa should be opened as a port of trade, and place of residence to foreigners. So hither on the 4th of July came vessels whose trading flags had dropped in every sea, merchants who had made gains in every clime and were zealous to be the first to trade in these seas. They came into the bay and on the low Yokohama shore where three months ago nothing was to be seen but a shingle beach backed by low rice fields and swamps, behold! a city had sprung up. Surely it was a dream or a visional phantasy. They rubbed their eyes and looked again, but still there were the long rows of streets, the Custom House compound and its tiled roof buildings, public offices and warehouses, all real and substantial. They landed and found wide streets, cleanly kept, flanked with rows of stores whose shelves were filled with attractive wares and on whose new mats sat the smiling, obsequious merchants. Another quarter of this town, risen so miraculously, was appropriated to dwell-

---

[110] On January 17, 1862, the *Elmira Daily Avertiser* ran the following announcement: "Our citizens have now the opportunity of examining and purchasing the first installment of Japanese curiosities, composed of articles of luxury and use, recently sent to Hall Brothers from Frank Hall now in Japan. . . . The large consignment now exposed for sale, embraces most of the articles of Japanese household use and luxury. There are dressing cases from the size of a bureau to the diminutive jewel-safe; shawl, handkerchief and glove cases; stacks of boxes piled up one on top of the other, or shutting together into one large nest, designed as the receptacles of those nameless little powders, puffs and perfumes of a lady's toilet; cases with magical concealed drawers; platters and waiters of all shapes; punch and rice bowls, fruit dishes, peculiarly constructed tops and toys, wooden eggs containing seven diminishing sizes within each other, childish play things and Japanese charms to be worn about the person, tea and coffee sets of porcelain and shell and lacquer ware, the porcelain set being of the two dimensions used by Americans and Japanese respectively; smoking apparatus containing drawers for tobacco and metallic cisterns for the ashes and fire and hooks for placing away the pipe." Hall seems to have gone beyond merely sending objects for sale, however, "much knowledge," the article continued, "is also gained by examination of the series of Japanese architecture, scenery, modes of planting a[nd] rearing fruit trees and shrubbery, in which they with the Chinese are such adepts, of birds native and peculiarly sacred, of social customs of dignities and ranks in society, and especially of that cunning workmanship in which they are unsurpassed."

ing houses for the use of the foreign population that might here gather.[111]

As Hall noted, all these preparations were part of a "game" being played by the Japanese government to locate the foreign businesses and merchants at Yokohama instead of Kanagawa. The reasons for this "game" were quite obvious. Kanagawa lay "on the great national highway from Yedo to the south-west, on which were constantly passing high officials, royal corteges, and the trains of the Daimios or hereditary princes. As they passed along the humble citizens prostrated themselves to the earth in abject humility." Foreigners, he noted, were not prepared to show such respect. "It would be a bad example to set . . . this walking along erect and covered before so much royalty," he wrote. "And it was without doubt to prevent the effect such conduct might have on the minds of the people, more than anything else, that led to this attempt to substitute the Yokohama side of the Bay for Kanagawa." Hemmed in by the sea on one side, and by salt marshes on the other, Yokohama, Hall wrote, served as a kind of "mitigated Desima."[112]

But there were also advantages. "The anchorage on the Yokohama side of the bay chanced to be much nearer shore than the opposite or Kanagawa side." And, as he noted, "The shipping had come for cargoes, the merchants had come for trade, they could not wait in the haste to be rich, on questions of national policy. True this was not the place named by the treaty, it was a genteel confinement," he added, "and national self-respect demanded the stipulated place," as Townsend Harris, the American minister insisted. "But here were houses," Hall wrote, "here were stores, here were spacious go-downs and native produce

ready to fill them. The custom house was here, the piers were essential, so it was not strange that commerce carried the day against national honor, and quietly accepted what the representatives of the foreign powers steadily and properly refused to accept, Yokohama in place of Kanagawa."[113]

By the time his capital reached Japan, Hall concurred with the general opinion regarding Yokohama's advantages. Although he wrote in his journal that his reason for moving across the bay in October of 1860 was largely to relieve Mrs. Hepburn of the burden of taking care of him as well as Dr. Simmons and his wife, the advantages of Yokohama for his growing business interests were obvious (see JJ, September 13, 1860). While both Hall and Simmons purchased separate lots in Yokohama's "New Concession" in December 1860, they continued to live together in a house they had taken over from F. E. Boyd that stood near the customs house not far from the Japanese part of the city.[114]

Hall's botanical interest took him to Nagasaki as early as June 1860 to meet Philipp Franz Von Siebold, the German doctor and botanist who had originally come to Japan (under the Dutch) in 1823. Hall's acquaintance with Von Siebold served to create new contacts that influenced his later years in Yokohama. While in Nagasaki he met John Greer Walsh, the American consul in that port. Walsh, and his brother, Thomas Walsh had already founded Walsh & Co., the first American trading house to operate in Japan, and their representative in Yokohama, Dr. George R. Hall, was another amateur botanist with whom Hall soon became friendly.

Dr. Hall, like his namesake Francis, was one of the pioneer traders in Japan who has been

[111] The description of Yokohama is from "Wanderings in the Orient," Number Nine, "Kanagawa and Yokohama," *Elmira Weekly Advertiser*, March 24, 1860.

[112] Ibid.

[113] Ibid.

[114] "List of Americans holding land in the New Concession, December 24, 1860," Despatches from U.S. Consuls in Japan, National Archives Record Group 59: M135, Kanagawa (also Yedo), 1861–1897. The site of Hall's and Simmons's residence is clearly marked on Simmons's 1860 woodblock print map of Yokohama

now in the possession of the Yokohama Archives. What this map shows is that Hall and Simmons lived in a house that fronted the wharf and constituted one corner of the Custom House compound. See Maruya Tokuzo, *Gokaikō Yokohama dai ezu* (Edo: Hōzendō, 1860) in Yokohama Archives of History (cover bears the initials D.B.S.). Simmons marked this map to show not only his Yokohama residence, but the land he bought, his previous temple residence in Kanagawa, S. R. Brown's temple, and a number of other sites.

Detail of Sadahide's 1860 Print: *Complete Detailed View of Yokohama Honcho and the Miyozaki Quarter*, showing the Customs House complex. The white dot marks the building in which Hall and Simmons lived.

largely forgotten.[115] Indeed, the two Halls, though unrelated, have often been confused with one another. Two years older than Francis Hall, George R. Hall had graduated from the Harvard medical school in 1842. By the time Francis Hall encountered him in Yokohama the doctor was already well known in the Far East. Dr. Hall arrived in Shanghai in 1846 when that city boasted only seventeen American residents. His decision to go to China seems to have been influenced by the King and

Olyphant families of Newport, Rhode Island, who were longstanding merchants in the China trade, and by his friend Edward Cunningham, who became vice-consul at Shanghai from 1852 to 1854, and who was closely connected to Robert Bennett Forbes, a partner in Russell & Co., one of America's leading trading houses in China. In 1850, after establishing the Seamen's Hospital, which later became the Shanghai Hospital, Hall sailed home to be married. Later in the same year he returned to Shang-

[115] Given the fact that we know very little about the residents in the treaty ports of Japan it is hardly surprising that two men with the same name should be confused with one another. What makes this even more confusing is that both Dr. Hall and Francis Hall worked for the same firm. A few Japanese scholars have described them as "brothers," but to my knowledge the two were unrelated, although Dr. Hall's connections in Newport and Massachusetts seem to have included the Delano family, and Francis Hall's sister, Sophia, married William A. Delano. Both Edward and Warren

Delano, Jr., had been members of Russell & Co in China in the 1840s. The only account of Dr. Hall's life and career in China and Japan can be found in Richardson Wright, *A Gardener's Tribute* (New York: J. P. Lippincott Co., 1949), pp. 119–42. Wright was a former editor of *House and Garden* who stumbled across Hall in relationship to the many plants the Doctor brought to the United States from Japan in 1862. The following biographical details on Dr. Hall are from Wright's biographical sketch.

hai with his bride, Mary Beal, to live in the substantial house he had built on five acres of land.

Growing instability in China that spread in the wake of the Taiping conquest of Nanking in 1853 convinced Dr. Hall that Shanghai was no place for women and children. In 1854 he sent home his wife and three small boys. At the same time he decided to abandon his medical practice in favor of the more lucrative field of trade, joining Edward Cunningham in a variety of trading ventures. In May 1856, three months before Harris arrived in Shimoda and two years before the commercial treaties were signed, Cunningham and Hall sailed for Shimoda and Nagasaki to explore trading conditions in Japan.[116] With the completion of the commercial treaties Hall decided to set up business in Japan.

George Hall's arrival in Kanagawa corresponded with the opening of the port in July 1859. As Joseph Heco, the Japanese castaway who became an American citizen, and who accompanied Harris to Kanagawa in July, noted, it was Dr. Hall who took the side of the merchants in the dispute over Yokohama as the location for the new port. Heco wrote that Hall "on his own responsibility procured a plot of land on the Yokohama side, and proceeded to establish himself there. This was quite in defiance of the Consul's view, but Dr. Hall was a practical man and saw the immense advantages over Kanagawa possessed by Yokohama in facilities for shipping."[117] The lot Dr. Hall selected was No. 2 on the Yokohama Bund, and it was only later that Jardine Matheson & Co. selected No. 1, and Dent & Co. numbers 4 and 5. By December 1859, George M. Brooke recorded in his journal that the doctor was "building a fine house"[118] on his new site, a house that recalled his splendid Shanghai mansion, and which eventually became the site of Walsh, Hall & Co.

In the garden of his house George R. Hall continued to amass a great variety of plants. When the well-known botanist, and plant hunter, Robert Fortune, arrived in Japan in 1860, he entrusted most of his collection of Japanese plants to the "safety of Dr. Hall's garden" until they could be packed in Wardian cases and sent to Europe.[119] The doctor himself is largely remembered for the great variety of Japanese plants he shipped back to the United States at the time of his return in 1862. Indeed it was Dr. Hall, more than any other American, who introduced America to Japanese plants, particularly to the great variety of trees and shrubs of variegated foliage.[120]

[116] Edward Cunningham wrote a description of this trip that was published in the *North China Herald*, June 21, 1856. See also Cozenza, *The Complete Journal of Townsend Harris*, pp. 173–74. See also Eldon Griffin, *Clippers and Consuls: American Consular and Commercial Relations with Eastern Asia, 1845–1860* (Ann Arbor, Mich.: Edwards Brothers, Inc., 1938), p. 332.

[117] Joseph Heco, *Narrative of a Japanese* (San Francisco: American-Japanese Publishing Association, n.d.), vol. 1, pp. 216–17.

[118] George M. Brooke, Jr., ed., *John M. Brooke's Pacific Cruise and Japanese Adventure, 1858–1860* (Honolulu: University of Hawaii Press, 1986), p. 183.

[119] Robert Fortune, *Yedo and Peking: A Narrative of a Journey to the Capitals of Japan and China* (London: John Murray, 1863), p. 144. Fortune also made another great find in Dr. Hall's garden in Yokohama—the male plant of the *Aucuba japonica*. The female plant of this species had been introduced to Europe much earlier, but without the male plant it could produce no red berries, so Fortune was very pleased with his find. "Let my readers picture to themselves all the aucubas which decorate our windows and gardens, covered during the winter and spring months, with a profusion of crimson berries.

Such a result, and it is not an improbable one, would of itself be worth a journey all the way from England to Japan" (ibid., p. 61).

[120] See Wright, *Gardener's Tribute*, chapter 6, "Pills and Plants, The Tale of Dr. George R. Hall, who eventually chose between them," pp. 119–42. Hall's collection of Japanese plants went to three locations in the United States: his own Rhode Island garden, the Parsons Nursery at Flushing, Long Island, and the garden of Francis Parkman in Boston. Hall gave his name to several important species, which included Hall's Honeysuckle, Hall's Amaryllis, Hall's Magnolia, and Hall's Flowering Apple. Wright quotes Mr. Parsons, who headed the Flushing nursery as writing: "Dr. Hall speaks of the great variety of trees in Japan with variegated leaves, and which are among these. They will give a new beauty to our lawns, and be more permanent than flowers. It gives us much pleasure to speak at this early period of the arrival of these plants and seeds in this country, both because we wish the horticultural world to know how much it is indebted to the enterprise and plant love of Dr. Hall, and because a collection so rich and so varied has never been obtained from any country, even by the best English collectors, while the simi-

While Hall's journal does not indicate specifically how the two Halls became acquainted, it may well have been their common love of plants that became the source of a growing friendship. On December 25, 1860, Hall notes in his journal that he had Christmas dinner with "Dr. Hall," and in 1861 he mentions numerous horseback rides with the doctor into the countryside surrounding Yokohama. By the end of that year, the journal shows that George Hall arranged a meeting with the Walsh brothers and apparently made preparations for Francis to take his place at the firm. On January 2, 1862, Hall recorded in his journal, "Dr. H. and Mr. Walsh spend the evening with me." And the following day, Hall noted the departure of his "friend," Dr. Hall, on the *What Cheer* bound for San Francisco. On January 15 he wrote, "went to Walsh and Co.'s this morning to mess and keep house for them till some more permanent arrangement can be made."

The "more permanent arrangement" mentioned here was a limited partnership with the Walsh brothers that officially began on May 1, 1862, and was initially to run for three years. As part of this partnership Walsh & Co. was renamed Walsh, Hall & Co. in the spring of 1862, and with time the original partnership was extended until March 30, 1866.[121]

There is a strong possibility that the above arrangement was designed to allow Dr. Hall to return to his Yokohama house and position after being reunited with his wife and family in the United States. Indeed, Dr. Hall and his family did start on a trip to Japan in 1865, but the sudden death of his wife enroute intervened, and the doctor abandoned his plans to return to Yokohama. This caused Francis Hall to extend his partnership in Japan until the spring of 1866, when Mr. Cunningham took his place. In 1874, Dr. Hall's son, Chandler Prince, went to Japan and joined Walsh, Hall & Co. in Kobe where he continued to be active until his death in 1897.[122]

The firm Hall helped to found in 1862 quickly established its reputation as the leading American trading house in Japan, a reputation it maintained well into the Meiji period.[123] It is a tribute to Hall's integrity and sound trading practices that even after his departure from Japan in 1866 the firm continued to use his name. Walsh, Hall & Co., like Jardine Matheson & Co., its British counterpart, went through a princely era in the late Tokugawa and early Meiji years. Chiefly a commission house, Walsh, Hall & Co. became a major force in the tea and silk trade. Hall, it is reported, shipped the first cargo of Japan tea to New York.[124] And he is also known to have pioneered in the shipment of tea to the West Coast. The firm, as his obituary points out, "made much money," and Hall regularly dispatched vessels in the middle 1860s that carried million-dollar cargoes of silk to the United States and Europe.[125] By 1866 he had made a comfortable fortune.

In the meantime his firm had also begun to develop close ties to Iwasaki Yatarō, the founder of Mitsubishi, and to the House of

---

larity of the Japanese climate to our own renders this collection of peculiar value" (p. 137).

[121] *The Japan Herald* of May 17, 1862, carried the following notice: "Mr. FRANCIS HALL is this day admitted a partner in our business at this port, which will hereafter be conducted under the name WALSH, HALL & CO. The business of this firm will be strictly that of Agency and Commission. WALSH, HALL & CO., Kanagawa, 19th April, 1862."

[122] Wright, *Gardener's Tribute*, p. 138. It seems that Dr. Hall accompanied his son to Japan in 1874, for the *Japan Weekly Mail* lists G. R. Hall arriving in Yokohama from San Francisco on February 7, 1874.

[123] Ernest Satow remembered Walsh, Hall & Co as the "leading American firm" in Yokohama when he arrived there in the fall of 1862 (*A Diplomat in Japan*, p. 27). See also M. Paske-Smith, *Western Barbarians in Japan and Formosa in Tokugawa Days, 1603–1868* (Kobe: J. L. Thompson & Co., 1930), p. 266. Harold S. Williams writes, "Walsh, Hall & Co, was doing an enormous business; the partners were looked upon as merchant princes, and everyone recognised it as ranking among the No. 1 American firms." See *Foreigners in Mikadoland* (Rutland, Vt.: Charles E. Tuttle & Co., 1963), p. 204.

[124] "Francis Hall Obituary," *Elmira Weekly Advertiser*, August 29, 1902.

[125] Ibid. On November 1, 1864, Hall reported in his journal: "The *Nepaul* which left this morning with 1850 bales of silk, value $1,000,000, struck a rock in Uraga channel and returned leaking badly. A good deal of silk injured."

Mitsui.[126] It is regrettable that the records of Walsh, Hall & Co. have not been preserved, but it is clear that the firm's relationship to Iwasaki Yatarō remained close. Iwasaki first met the Walsh brothers in Nagasaki in 1859–1860 when Thomas Walsh was establishing his company there, while his brother, John Greer Walsh, served as U.S. consul. In 1867 Yatarō returned to Nagasaki to head the Kaiseikan, the commercial bureau of his domain, Tosa, which was then in financial straits. A substantial loan by Walsh, Hall & Co., in exchange for monopoly rights to Tosa's camphor, allowed him to consolidate the domain's debts on the eve of the Restoration.[127]

The relationship between the two houses was further cemented by Iwasaki Yanosuke's experiences in the United States, both at the home of the Walsh family in New York, as well as with Hall's brother Edward at the Hall Family School for Boys in Ellington. Yanosuke, who took over the leadership of Mitsubishi in 1885, later stated that his "success" was "largely due to the training he received under the instruction of his teacher, Edward Hall."[128]

While the records of Walsh, Hall & Co. remain sketchy, we do know that by the early 1870s the firm was shifting its focus from becoming a trading and commission house to becoming a firm active in the industrialization of Japan. This was in keeping with early Meiji policy. In 1872 the firm, in partnership with several other foreign investors, founded Japan's first modern paper mill, the Japan Paper Making Company, in Kobe. In 1877 Walsh, Hall & Co. bought out its partners and founded the Kobe Paper Mills. Two years later Iwasaki Yanosuke bought a half interest in these mills.[129] When John Greer Walsh died in Kobe in 1897 his brother Thomas decided to return to the United States. In the process he sold the remaining Walsh, Hall & Co. interests to Yanosuke and the Mitsubishi Co. Therefore, it may be fair to conclude that Walsh, Hall & Co. ceased to exist in 1897.[130] Meanwhile the once splendid quarters of "Ameichi" ("The Number one American Company") in Yokohama and Kobe were sold to the Hongkong and Shanghai Banking Corporation.[131] But by this time Hall had long disassociated himself from the firm and devoted his time to his American business interests and his lifelong passion for travel.

[126] The contacts with Iwasaki Yatarō and Mitsubishi were close, as I have indicated earlier. In 1873 Frederick Krebs, who served with Walsh, Hall & Co. since his arrival in Japan in 1868, joined Mitsubishi as one of its first foreign employees. See the *Iwasaki Yanosuke den* (Tokyo: 1986), vol. 2, p. 52. Also *Iwasaki Yatarō den* (Tokyo, 1986), vol. 1, pp. 37–71. William D. Wray in his *Mitsubishi and the N.Y.K., 1870–1914* (Cambridge, Mass.: Harvard University Press, 1984), p. 555, n. 84, tells us that before Masuda Takashi set up Mitsui Bussan he acquired his knowlege of foreign trade during a one-year apprenticeship as an employee of Walsh, Hall & Co.

[127] Under Gotō Shōjirō the Kaiseikan had accumulated very extensive debts due to its purchases of ships and guns from foreign firms such as Kniffler and Co. and Alt & Co. In 1867 Iwasaki Yatarō obtained a loan of 300,000 ryo from Walsh, Hall & Co. to pay off these debts. By 1871 the total debt owed by Tosa to Walsh, Hall & Co. was $195,000. This debt was partially taken over by the new Meiji government which paid Walsh, Hall & Co. ¥219,501 in November 1871. See *Iwasaki Yatarō den* (Tokyo, 1986), vol. 1, p. 593. Also Tanaka Sogoro, *Iwasaki Yatarō den* (Tokyo, 1955), p. 94.

[128] "Dedication of the Hall Memorial Library; at Ellington, Conn., Nov. 11, 1903," pamphlet in the Collection of the Hall Memorial Library, Ellington, Conn., p. 23.

[129] For details regarding the Kobe Paper Mills and the relationship between the Iwasaki family and Walsh, Hall & Co., see *Iwasaki Yatarō den* (Tokyo, 1986), vol. 2, pp. 471ff.

[130] The *Iwasaki Yatarō den* (Tokyo, 1986), vol. 2, pp. 480–81, states that not only had John Greer Walsh died in 1897, but this was the same year in which the unequal treaties granting special privileges to foreign trading houses in Japan ended. Thomas Walsh, now seventy, therefore decided to "turn over his trading company to others," and to sell his interests in the Kobe Paper Mills to the Iwasaki family. It appears that this was the formal end of Walsh, Hall & Co.

[131] Williams, *Foreigners in Mikadoland*, p. 205. The fact that Walsh, Hall & Co. was in some financial difficulties in the late 1870s can be seen in the fact that it needed to borrow £130,000 from Mitsubishi in 1878, a loan for which it gave as collateral the assets of the Kobe Paper Mills. The loan was entirely repaid by its due date in 1889 indicating that the firm's financial conditions subsequently improved.

Hall as Observer and Recorder

Hall, as we noted, went to Japan to study and to write. His initial goal was to be an observer and recorder. As correspondent for Horace Greeley's *Tribune* he was also committed to the policy of that paper: "To print the information daily required by those who aim to keep posted on every important occurrence, so that the lawyer, the merchant, the banker, the economist, the author, and the politician may find whatever he needs to see."[132] Hall's goal was to provide such information for his American readers. His journal therefore ranges widely over a great variety of subjects. Matters of everyday life, living conditions, health, education, business practices, local prices, Japanese customs, theatrical performances, sporting events, festival days, the flora and fauna of the land, and a large number of other topics run through his daily observations.

Politics is given its fair due as Hall attempted to come to grips with and inform his readers about the complexities of the Japanese political system. Living in the treaty port, as he did, he was naturally concerned with diplomatic issues. And these occasionally involved him directly, as he sometimes served as acting American consul in E. M. Dorr's absence. Indeed, when Dorr's health gave way in the spring of 1861, Harris offered Hall the Kanagawa consular post, a lucrative position, which he did not accept (JJ, April 18, 1861).[133] Hall's obituary states that, with the announced departure of Harris from Japan later in the same year, the "citizens of Kanagawa petitioned the government to make him minister."[134] If such a petition was proposed, and we have no further evidence that it was, it seems unlikely that Hall, who left Elmira because of mounting official duties, would have allowed it to go forth. He did, however, serve as a founding member of the Yokohama Chamber of Commerce in Feb-

ruary 1864, and as the journal indicates, was active in various community affairs.[135]

While Hall was taken with the natural beauty of Japan and the Yokohama environment, he was predominantly people-oriented. His early observations quickly confirmed what had become clear to the members of the Perry expedition, namely, that the common people were basically friendly to foreigners, while officials and other members of the samurai class remained cool, aloof, and occasionally hostile. Dealing with the Tokugawa bureaucracy, he concluded, required particular patience and forbearance. "To do business promptly is no part of Japanese usage," he wrote the day he tried to land his goods. "The whole business transaction of the Custom House for these four hours could have been performed by any American of ordinary capacity in a half hour." But in Japan, he explained, "everything is so tied up by routine, and hampered by forms that the greatest stretch of patience is necessary to do any business with officials." He was convinced that the Japanese "played" at business, and venting his frustration wrote: "The perfection of how not to do it belongs to this empire" (JJ, November 4, 1859).

At the same time Hall was conscious of the power of Japanese officialdom over the Japanese people. From interference with the work of Hepburn and Brown's carpenter, who had begun to build a stable for their compound only to be officially informed that these men were "only physicians" and therefore had "no need for horses," to the Yokohama merchants who were arrested for "making too much money," the influence of the authorities was only too obvious. As Hall noted, "the fear of the Governor is the ghost that haunts every Japanese home" (JJ, December 15, 1859).

Official coolness and intransigence contrasted to the general friendliness and curiosity of the treaty-port merchants and the people of the farming villages around Yokohama. Hall

---

[132] Richmond Croom Beatty, *Bayard Taylor* (Norman: University of Oklahoma Press, 1936), p. 56.

[133] Hall wrote, "went to Kanagawa to meet Mr. Harris per invitation. He thought it probable, owing to Mr. Dorr's precarious situation, that he should be obliged to appoint a new Consul and offered me the place if the

contingency should arrive. I declined to accept the post."

[134] "Francis Hall Obituary," *Elmira Weekly Advertiser*, August 29, 1902.

[135] M. Paske-Smith, *Western Barbarians in Japan and Formosa*, p. 219. Also Towner, *Our County*, p. 638.

liked the farmers he regularly visited. As the journal shows, in many villages he was well known, and the boys would shout "Here comes Mr. Hall," certain that his arrival would mean a shower of brass buttons and copper cash.

Hall was particularly observant of the world of children.

During more than a half a year's residence in Japan, I have never seen a quarrel among young or old. I have never seen a blow struck, scarcely an angry face. I have seen the children at their sports, flying their kites on the hills, and no amount of their intertangled strings or kites lodged in the trees provoked angry words of impatience. I have seen them intent on their games of jackstone and marbles under the shaded gateways of the temples; but have never seen the approach to a quarrel among them. They are taught implicit obedience to their parents, but I have never seen one of them chastised. Respect and reverence to the aged is universal. A crying child is a rarity seldom heard or seen. We have nothing to teach them in this respect out of our abundant civilization. I speak what I know of the little folks of Japan, for more than any other foreigner I have been among them.[136]

One can gain a sense of Hall's charm in his description of his contacts with Japanese children.

Of all that Japan holds, there is nothing I like half so well as the happy children. I shall always remember their coal-black eyes and ruddy brown faces with pleasure. I have played battledore with the little maidens in the street, and flown kites in the fields with as happy a set of boys as one could wish to see. They have been my guides in my rambles, shown me where all the streams and the ponds were, where the flowers lay hid in the thicket, where the berries were ripening on the hills; they brought me shells from the ocean and blos-

soms from the field, presenting them with all the modesty and a less bashful grace than a young American boy would do. We have hunted the fox-holes together, and we looked for the green and golden ducks among the sedge. They have laughed at my broken Japanese and have taught me better; and for a happy, good-natured set of children, I will turn out my little Japanese friends against the world. God bless the boys and girls of Nippon.[137]

On many occasions Hall records warm receptions from local citizens, particularly in the years from 1859 to 1862, before political tensions mounted to the point where such friendliness became dangerous and invited *rōnin* reprisals. From time to time his journal captures the spontaneity of these first encounters that were filled with cheerful naivete. Hall recorded a delightful scene in the spring of 1860. On a hike to Treaty Point he met "a young girl who had just finished weeding her patch of beans." The young lady "asked if she might walk with me," he wrote, and "certainly she could, and therefore she took me by the hand and we went down the hill swinging our arms as I have so often seen country lads and lassies do." "Her bonhomie and artless confidence," he recorded, "was charming" (JJ, April 12, 1860). A few days earlier on another walk he had encountered two young lasses gathering cresses. They, too, asked him to join them as they made their way along a stream. Hall recorded that they "admired his boots" and "said very complimentary things" about them, while he "admired theirs." They were barefooted! They also knew where he lived, and as he parted from them to take a path that struck off into the hills, they tried to dissuade him by calling after him: "The mountain path is hard come with us" (JJ, April 1, 1860).

While Hall's contacts with the merchants of Yokohama convinced him that the Japanese knew the tricks of trade as well as anyone, he admired the common people for their curiosity, interest in the outside world, and desire to learn. He noted that the Commercial Treaties

---

[136] Francis Hall, "Japanese Little Folks," *Elmira Weekly Advertiser*, January 26, 1861.

[137] Ibid.

were quickly translated into Japanese and had such a large sale among the native merchants and farmers that the price dropped to an insignificant half an ichibu for all five volumes. "The treaties," he lamented, are "not half so well known at home" (JJ, May 2, 1860).[138]

Hall also admired the common classes for their willingness to work hard, and often for their skills as craftsmen. He was particularly taken with what he saw as the contrast between the energy and dynamism of the commercial classes, including a portion of the agricultural sector, and the fixed, stolid, and even reactionary qualities of the feudal elite. Of the samurai he wrote home, "The soldier is the idlest, most worthless man Nippon produces, but he has the privilege of caste, and uses it to make all sorts of exactions upon those more humble than himself."[139] "I remember the thoughtful expression of a merchant's face to whom I had narrated the honorable position of the American merchant," he wrote. " 'That is right,' said he, then lowering his voice, as if fearful of being overheard, 'but we are the most despised people in Nippon.' "[140]

Hall's response to these class divisions, as he wrote to the paper in Elmira, was, that "the time must come when all this shall be changed, when idleness and the sword shall no longer be badges of virtue, when the farmer and trader shall know his value in the realm, and knowing it, shall assert those rights which generations of feudal oppression have taken from him. This lesson will be learned through unrestricted foreign intercourse. There may be war and bloodshed," he added, "as when the feudal system of the Western world was extinguished, but the end is sure."[141]

In Hall's journal we get a good picture of the process through which the arrival of Westerners helped to destabilize the old order. Hall was aware that Westerners could not help but exacerbate domestic tensions between the feudal elite and the lower orders, particularly between the samurai and the commercial classes. "I do not wonder," he wrote, "that the hereditary nobles should feel jealous of the foreigner who stands erect, uncovered, and regardless before them and teaches daily lessons of practical equality" (JJ, May 9, 1860). Echoing the very reasons for the Tokugawa government's efforts to keep Westerners as removed as possible from the native population, Hall added, "With equality and prosperity of the people, the rule of feudalism must fall to the ground." But, as he also realized, "It will not be given up without a bloody contest, and I believe the day is not far distant when this land will experience all the horrors of war." As Hall saw it the forces for change were already in place. "Commerce with its leveling tendencies will meet the aristocracy of caste and birth and one must go to the wall" (Ibid.).

Hall was conscious of the mounting contradictions in the society around him. "I hear it said again," he wrote, "that many of the Daimios maintain a state beyond their resources, and they resort to forced loans from the prosperous merchants of their principalities to sustain their living expenses" (Ibid.). He noted that merchants tried to keep their wealth circulating as much as possible in order to avoid such levies. He furthermore observed that there was a list of Japan's most "impoverished" lords. "One of these bankrupt Daimios passed along a few weeks ago," he wrote, "with no end of baggage, soldiers, servants, and retinue. The Tokaido was full from morning till night with his train. The Japanese were in front of their houses kneeling to the earth as the great man passed by." And yet, he added, "There is not a boy in the Tokaido who does not know that this grandee cannot pay the debts he incurs in keeping up all this pomp." Moreover, the very people who kneeled abjectly before the lord in public, spoke of him behind his back with some disdain as *Nippon ichiban bimbo daimyo* [The Poorest Daimyo in all Japan].[142]

---

[138] The widespread circulation of the commercial treaties in Japan has also been commented on by Irokawa Daikichi, who located copies of the commercial treaties (as well as the Perry Treaty) that were preserved by villagers in out of the way and often isolated villages. See Irokawa Daikichi, *Meiji no bunka* (Tokyo: Iwanami Shoten, 1970), p. 47.

[139] "Wanderings in the Orient," Number Seventeen, "The Japanese Merchant," *Elmira Weekly Advertiser*, August 25, 1860.

[140] Ibid.

[141] Ibid.

[142] Ibid. See also JJ, March 23, 1860.

"For all his social disadvantages, the merchant in Japan manages to thrive, nevertheless," Hall wrote, "in Yedo, Miako, Oasaca, and other large cities, he accumulates great wealth."[143] Hall recorded various rumors that indicated the growing concern of the elite with capital accumulation among the merchants and farming classes. "Money the world over is power," he noted, "and even the despised Japanese merchant sometimes gets along too fast to please his superiors." This could lead to the imposition of "squeeze," or a "public job" at "ruinous prices," Hall observed.[144] "It is said of late that the erection of water mills for making mochi and hulling rice has been prohibited by the Emperor [shogun], for the supposed reason that thereby wealth might be accumulated" (JJ, May 9, 1860).

Hall's economic observations and insights could be quite penetrating. Long before other Western writers, Hall wrote of the potent possibility of a wealthy peasant (*gōnō*) and urban merchant alliance, and the threat that such an alliance posed for the Tokugawa regime. Escorting the mineralogists William Blake and Raphael Pumpelly into the Oyama district in 1862, Hall compared the Yokohama region, which largely produced rice, with the upland regions through which they passed. This was a silk-producing district. And as Hall noted, "The change in production from the shores of the bay is not more marked than the appearance of the hamlets and houses. While in the mulberry districts more land was under cultivation, the hamlets were sparser and less thrifty in appearance than the hamlets of the rice districts."[145] "On the other hand," he noted, "the spacious proprietaries of the large farmers were much in advance of anything seen in the bay. They were the seats of evident wealth comparing favorably with many residences of that rural metropolis Yedo. Lines of

hedges or walls of stone, wood, or turf, or all combined, enclosed these country houses entered by wide and solid gateways built of enduring wood." Within were "spacious one-story mansions" that were flanked by "white storehouses" that sat amidst splendid gardens. "It was easy to see," Hall wrote, "that the owners of such places were the great factors of the silk crop." "In two days," Hall wrote, "we have passed many of these extensive farm houses and have seen the same striking contrast of rich and poor which are found in all districts of extra hazardous and valuable crops, whether it be cotton, silk, tobacco, or lumber—contrasts less apparent in districts producing crops that have a more even valuation from year to year as the great food staples of life, as one may by example compare the manufacturing and grain districts of England, or the cotton, tobacco, and grain districts of the United States." Not only did such "Japanese planters" have large incomes, often from "sublettings," but they "wear, when abroad, two swords and are sometimes attended by a train of sword bearing servants." "They belong to the most independent body of the state," Hall continued, "holding lands by an inalienable tenure, possessing revenues and servants and demanding and receiving universal respect. A formidable commonality could at any time be found in this empire," he wrote perceptively, "by the union of the hereditary farmers and the wealthy merchants of the great trading centers. A fact which the great chiefs and the imperial [shogunal] government show their knowledge of by the respect paid these classes of men." "To these men," Hall wrote in conclusion, and one cannot help but wonder how he came upon this insight, "the Mikado alone is a sovereign power" (JJ, April 3, 1862).[146]

While Hall was a good observer of the economic transformation that Japan was undergo-

---

[143] "Wanderings in the Orient," Number Seventeen, "The Japanese Merchant," *Elmira Weekly Advertiser*, August 25, 1860.

[144] Ibid.

[145] William Phipps Blake (1825–1910) and Raphael Pumpelly (1837–1923) were American mineralogists hired by the Tokugawa government to carry out a survey of Japan's mineral resources. Pumpelly made an extensive study of Hokkaido. For a discussion of their

years in Japan see Yoshida Mitsukuni, *Oyatoi gaikokujin (2) sangyō* (Tokyo: Kashima Kenkyū Shuppan Kai, 1968), p. 128. Pumpelly later wrote his own reminiscences of this trip in his book, *My Reminiscences*. The quoted portions that follow are from JJ, April 3, 1862.

[146] Like other Westerners in the mid-nineteenth century Hall usually refers to the Tokugawa shogun as "Emperor." When he speaks of the head of the Imperial House in Kyoto he usually uses the term "Mikado."

ing, he was also interested in social conditions and social change. Here, too, Hall could be highly perceptive. Writing in February 1862, he repeated an earlier observation that Buddhism appeared to be seriously in decline in Japan, particularly in the last quarter of a century. "In my own mind," he wrote, "there can be but little doubt that Western civilization has insidiously helped to effect this, for the Japanese have not been ignorant of what was going on in the world about them, and their own improving civilization has led them—slowly to be sure and almost imperceptibly yet gradually—to follow after and strive to imitate it." "Buddhism, when it has yielded," he added, "has yielded to nationalism and disbelief. As this is seen mostly at Yedo, the courtly city where foreign affairs have been best understood, it is additional reason to believe that light from the West streaming in a feeble ray through the pin point at old Desima had its influence." Hall was convinced that "in its own isolation Japan was very slowly improving" and he based this on the fact that he heard "so commonly of improved popular customs and opinions differing from those they have had in their earlier history." Through their contacts with the outside world the Japanese were "slowly drawing in to themselves a knowledge of a better life and civilization existing beyond their shores." "They had books," he wrote, "of sterling value that they could read, they had a hundred imported articles, in instruments and results of art, mechanical skill, improved ways of the healing art, tangible evidences of the value of Western civilization." And now Hall raised the fundamental question that has intrigued students of nineteenth-century Japan both in the West and in Japan. "Thus I am often led to think," he wrote, "that had Perry never opened Japan to the West and the Dutch remained a century longer at Desima that Japan would have improved in civilization steadily if not rapidly." Indeed, he was convinced, that the "gain to this people" would have been "far greater and more permanent" had they been left to "*ask in*" Western civilization "in their own way, without compulsion or restraint" rather than have it "*forced* upon them as now" (preceding quotations from JJ, February 16, 1862). Not many Westerners of his generation were able to see Japan this clearly in 1862.

While Hall may have had his doubts about the process of forced Westernization that he felt was ushered in with the coming of Perry and the commercial treaties, like most Westerners he stubbornly resisted changing his own social values to accommodate those of the Japanese. On occasion he was not above sewing the seeds of discontent—unconscious as this process may have been. The following scene had clear implications for a society in which only the samurai and daimyo were privileged to ride on horseback, and in which women were seen as "beasts of burden," more in the category of the horse than rider.

After dinner I escorted Miss B[rown] on a horseback ride on the Tokaido. We took a brisk trot of nearly two miles on this thoroughfare. A lady on horseback was a novel sight to the Nipponese. Everybody rushed out of doors, the near ones shouted in advance that a "foreign woman was coming on horseback," and so we rode down a long file of men, women, and children. Pedestrians scrambled out of the way, women picked up their children, pack horses and their drivers were so bewildered by the novel apparition that instead of clearing the road they stood stock still. The *betto* [groom] shouted "clear the way," dogs barked, for we came down the road at a spanking pace. When we turned our horses' heads for the return, far as the eye can see the street was full of people watching us and waiting our return. The houses must have emptied their contents in the streets. We came back at a hard trot, the girls from the tea and other houses gazed with a look of admiration to see one of their own sex so elevated, the old ladies shouted *yoka* [Great!], and the general look of the natives was one of gratification. Some of the men shouted after us, but happily we could not understand their derisive epithets, we finished our ride without accident. (JJ, February 15, 1860)

"Accident" was, of course, always a realistic possibility in the turbulent Yokohama environment in which Hall lived. As stated previously, his journal includes a long string of assassinations. While he was aware of the danger and often went about armed, he did not allow the environment to inhibit his adventuresome spirit and curiosity. "It seemed odd," he wrote of one of his forays into the countryside, "to start out for a walk by putting a revolver in one pocket and a copy of Tennyson in the other!" (JJ, April 15, 1860). Hall realized that popularity alone could not protect him from the assassin's sword. That lesson had been taught all too clearly by the assassination of Harris's extremely popular secretary, Henry Heusken, in January 1861. By the end of his stay in Japan Hall was well aware that, careful as he may have been, he had been extremely lucky.

But the journal also indicates that Hall was occasionally willing to "push his luck," particularly during the early years of his residence in Kanagawa and Yokohama. One of these occurrences took place when the lord of Owari passed through Kanagawa on the Tōkaidō early in 1860. Hall wanted to see this lord's procession, which was often said to have included some five thousand persons. He also knew the risk. "To stand up before such royalty, to stare at him even," he wrote, "was not only a breach of etiquette but a crime." It was suggested that he watch the whole affair from a friendly merchant's house, peeping through the cracks in a wall. Or he might kneel down and look up from under his cap. But he concluded that this would be "compromising the independence of an American citizen" (JJ, March 2, 1860).

Instead, he, Dr. and Mrs. Simmons, and Dr. Hepburn decided to climb a cliff that overlooked the Tōkaidō in Kanagawa in order to view the procession from an open space at the top. Hall knew that "looking down on" a feudal lord was itself a breach of etiquette, and although ordered away from the site once by the advance guard, he and the missionaries returned after the Japanese had been ordered to their knees below. From his perch on the cliff Hall was able to use his binoculars to see and describe the procession in great detail. But everyone knew that a confrontation was in the making. And as the lord of Owari's palanquin approached, no one knew what the outcome would be.

Hall described the scene that followed: "no sooner had his norimon [palanquin] reached the open spot in front of the hill, than there were the eyes of all the attendants and all the people crouched on their knees along the roadside turned up towards us. What was going to happen once the occupant of the norimon, Owari no Kami himself, was in communication with his attendants, who came crouching to the side of the norimon," he wrote. "Was he going to send orders to have these foreigners, who were gazing at him with profane eyes, hurled headlong from the hill? He had but to move his hand and it would have been done."

Fortunately for Hall and the missionaries, this was not to be the case. "No, more sensible fellow," that he was, "he had his norimon stopped in the spot, slid back the closed grating like window, and with an opera glass, a veritable opera glass, took a good long look at us," Hall wrote, "directing, gallant fellow that he was, the most of his glances at Mrs. S[immons], who is comely and fair to look upon. When it came my turn to be stared upon, I lifted my hat and bowed with as much grace as a man could muster sitting down dangling his legs over the edge of a cliff." Surrounded by his courtiers, the lord of Owari stared at the group for several minutes before moving on. Hall concluded that Mrs. Simmons must have been "the first foreign lady he had ever seen" (JJ, March 2, 1860).

Hall's Japanese friend, Sadajirō, later warned him that he had been exceedingly foolhardy and unusually lucky on this occasion. A different lord might well have been far less accommodating. And a few years later after the deaths of Heusken, C. L. Richardson, and a number of others, Hall readily concurred in this view. At the same time, what this incident reveals is the obdurate adherence to a different set of social and political values that Hall and his fellow Westerners asserted in the treaty port, which rubbed away at the fabric of Japan's traditional order. Hall recalled that when he was up on the cliff he was accompanied by several Japanese who went down "like a shot" when the heralds ordered everyone to their knees. He remembered, too, that one of the men said to him, "it may do for you to look that way, but it would not for me." And yet there were, no doubt, many among the Japanese on their knees, who like the women seeing Miss Brown on horseback, were prepared to mutter to themselves a quiet *yoka*, and even in the foregoing response to Hall there is the admission of other possibilities and a different social order.

Hall's journal is particularly interesting in that it manages to catch many of the social tensions of the late Tokogawa years. As an avid observer of festivals, he noticed some curious patterns to the way in which they were organized and celebrated. Present at the first Yokohama *matsuri* (festival) (July 18–19, 1860), he preserved a detailed account of what he saw. "It is the gayest scene of popular festivity that it had ever been my lot to witness," he wrote. Hall compared it to a "Boeuf Gras Festival" in Paris, or "Carnival" in Rome. "These shows are not attended without considerable expense," he wrote, "but there is not another nation I believe in the world where so large a portion of the popular earnings are expended for pleasures." He was convinced that this was due to the fact that "status in life is so unalterably fixed in Japan, or rather so difficult to change, that the lower classes have little reason, as they certainly have little disposition, to hoard up useless money, but more wisely employ it to purchase pleasures and indulgences which, if profiting little, produce no other harm than spending some time and substance, making them with all these drawbacks one of the most, if not the most, contented people in the world" (JJ, July 18, 1860).

What Hall observed but did not analyze sufficiently, is the fact that *matsuri*, had increasingly become escape valves that allowed feudal tensions to be dissipated between the classes. He recorded that in Yokohama the festival was purely for the common people. "Nowhere did I see an official take any hand in it except as spectators," he wrote. One of the main performances mimicked authority by presenting a farcical daimyo's train passing through the streets of Edo in which the feudal lord riding in his palanquin was a fox and the retainers flanking the "lord" were "men clad in female attire, their faces painted and colored like so many harlequins." The palanquin was "preceded by pike and standard bearers, armor bearers, weapons bearers who wound along with a peculiar slow and mock dignified step, for this scene was evidently a half-caricature." In addition to poking fun at the feudal elite, the townspeople participating in the festival used every opportunity to appropriate the dress and behavior of the samurai and upper classes. "At first glance," he wrote, "one would suppose officials were largely in the procession for most of the processors wore two swords and the peculiar code of dress proper to a man of rank." But he soon realized that these were the townsmen playing samurai. Nor was Yokohama peculiar in this regard. As Sadajirō told him, "These days are holidays of the people par excellence, where they wear not only the swords and dresses of superiors in rank, but have every license permitted them of speech and behavior." "At Yedo," he noted, "the samurai and yakunin [officials], particularly the former, remain within their own enclosures" during these festivals. This was because in the past "serious riots" had broken out between the samurai and the people engaged in such festivities. "For two days," Sadajirō told Hall, "the people are supreme."

The quest for freedom from social restrictions that runs through Hall's descriptions of festivals are paired with other social observations. Hall already mentions the "dancing mania" that was sweeping parts of Japan long before the Meiji Restoration; he was intrigued by the number of "pilgrims" who were engaged in all kinds of travel—including trips to observe the "barbarians" in Yokohama (JJ, May 12, 1860).[147]

---

[147] Hall wrote: "Sadajirō told Dr. H[epburn] that a few years ago near Oasaca a dancing mania possessed the people, it began with one person and continually extended to a multitude. It was undoubtedly one of those phenomenas which we have witnessed from time to time in America of which the 'jumpers' of Kentucky are an example." What Hall mentions here sounds a good deal like the "eejanaika," (literally, "Why not, it's okay!") dancing hysteria that broke out in the Kyoto-Osaka area in 1867. Hall often mentions pilgrims. On August 6, 1861, he wrote in his journal, "Yesterday and today great numbers of pilgrims have been in the streets who are returning from visits to sacred places, *O-yama, Fusi-yama*, etc. The greater number of them are clad in white cotton, white cotton sack, tight cotton trousers, umbrella hats, sandals of straw, a long staff, and a bundle of necessaries hung about the neck completes the equipment. . . . The officials about the foreign settlements are especially vigilant lest in this guise men intent on harm may enter among the foreigners."

As we have seen earlier, Hall was interested in assessing the economic circumstances under which the Japanese lived. Here his journal gives us a mixed picture. On one side we see generally well-off townsmen and rural families who are prosperously engaged in trade and agriculture, who live in clean, well-kept houses, send their children to school (particularly the boys), and appear to have some surplus to spend on entertainment and travel. Very observant about children, Hall noted that much of the street peddling and entertainment was directed toward them. He records numerous instances of top spinners, gymnasts, and various other street entertainers, as well as hawkers of toys, candies, and other goods attractive to the young.

What Hall's journal shows is that the use of money, as well as the consumerism that he discussed earlier in reference to the entertainment spending of adults reached down into the world of children. The reality was that children had money in Japan; this was rarely the case in nineteenth-century America. And this would indicate that in the Kanagawa and Yokohama portions of the Kanto Plain, families had been able to accumulate a sufficient economic surplus not only to free them from the dire necessities of child labor (thereby providing the leisure for education), but at the same time reaching a sufficient proportion to allow some sharing of this surplus with their children, and thereby supporting a surprising degree of conspicuous consumption on the part of the young.

Hall furthermore records elements that we now know were related to the growing economic prosperity of the agricultural sector of late Tokugawa Japan, but which were not clearly understood until quite recently. We know, for example, that rational family planning resulted in a very stable population in eighteenth- and early-nineteenth-century Japan. This was, in fact, central to the accumulation of an economic surplus. But it was not until very recently that we have learned that in the sex selection of family planning during this period the preferable first child was a daughter, and not a son as previously supposed.[148] The reason was quite basic and simple. The labor of the mother was more valuable in the fields, and if the first child was a daughter, she could be quickly pressed into service as a babysitter, allowing the mother to return to her work. Hall, who knew nothing of these demographics, was nevertheless repeatedly struck by the number of little girls, some only six years of age, who were carrying another child (usually a baby brother) on their backs. If the fact that Japanese children had money was one contrast with life in America, this was certainly another.

While Hall recorded a fair amount of prosperity in the Yokohama region, he also commented on the large number of beggars that seemed to be everywhere. Shortly after his arrival he wrote, "the beggars were numerous and troublesome with importunity." A few, he noted, seemed to be beggars from disease, but the majority appeared to be "professional beggars." "They had a sinister expression of countenance." He added, "Their hair was cut short to about a half inch in length, their clothing and whole appearance filthy beyond measure. Many boys were among them" (JJ, November 15, 1859). There were also a large number of religious beggars, some of whom asked for alms for reasons other than dire necessity. Hall concluded that begging was itself a kind of business. He was taken with a nun he encountered asking for alms, whose well-rounded face he described as "by no means shriveled with spare diet and late vigils" (JJ, December 24, 1859). On another occasion he encountered a group of priests who had perfected the arts of intimidation. Hall found these in the middle of

---

[148] G. William Skinner's studies of villages on the Nōbi Plain have shown that there was not only rational family planning but clear sex selection with a preference for a female first child. Skinner's work further updates Thomas C. Smith's findings in *Nakahara: Family Farming and Population in a Japanese Village, 1717–1830* (Stanford, Calif.: Stanford University Press, 1977), which first indicated that family planning (through infanticide) was a central part of the rational peasant's strategy to maximize economic gains in an increasingly competitive agrarian economy. See G. William Skinner, "Conjugal Power in Tokugawa Japanese Families: A Matter of Life and Death," in *Sex and Gender Hierarchies*, ed. Barbara D. Miller (University of Chicago Press, forthcoming).

the night "chanting an inharmonious song" and "keeping time with a rattling staff of rings" in front of a local house. "Such serenading," he wrote, "is not to be coveted at the dead of night. The fellows were doubtless sure that anyone would give a few cents rather than be disturbed long after the midnight hour" (JJ, June 11, 1860).

Hall was somewhat suspicious about the actual economic conditions of most beggars because he had already familiarized himself with the economic conditions of the outcasts, or *eta*, who he presumed would be the most economically deprived members of the community. But Hall's visit indicated otherwise.

> I went to the quarter of the leather dressers. The houses were in a thick cluster with no apparent regularity of streets. A few hides were stretched and drying in the sun. There was nothing about this quarter to indicate any special poverty except a number of houses that were underground. A cellar was dug and over it a straw roof placed with a paper window in the floor. In the quarter generally the people were as well clad and looked as prosperous as other parts of Kanagawa. Some of these leather dressers are said to grow rich in their proscribed traffic. Persecuted they truly are, being forbidden to marry without their own guild, or to enter the houses of others. They are said to be particularly affected with ophthalmia, though this was not apparent in my walk. (JJ, April 21, 1860)

While the outcasts lived better than he expected, and some beggars were asking for alms for reasons other than pure economic want, Hall was no Pollyanna about genuine poverty when he encountered it. Passing near the English consulate on his way to church one rainy Sunday morning he encountered the type of individual who had not shared in the economic blessings of the age. The poor fellow was sitting under the dripping trees by the wayside eating his meager dinner of rice and a few slices of sweet potatoes. Hall wrote, "His matted hair hung over his face and he was protecting his shivering limbs with a mat of straw. He looked healthy and strong enough to labor, but

as he sat cowering under the dripping trees, with wet and cold and ate his not over nourishing meal, my heart smote me with pity. He asked for nothing, but I could not refrain from dropping some coppers in his hand, though I knew the probability was, that too, would go for sake. So let it go, thought I, and may you forget your poverty and cold, though it be but for a brief hour" (JJ, May 6, 1860).

It is therefore clear that while Hall observed a good deal of prosperity in the Yokohama region, he also found some poverty of the type just described. Hall had a good eye for social problems and in his journal he covers a variety of social issues. These include suicide, crime, violence, the treatment of women, abortion and abortionists, the life of the outcasts, and a variety of other issues that run the gamut from sanitation to prostitution and drinking.

Despite his close contacts with the missionaries, Hall was no prude. His journal gives us one of the best descriptions of the Yokohama Gankiro, the well-known Yokohama "tea house," or brothel. Hall found the establishment sumptuous, neat, clean, and well-organized. Among the "ladies" he noted, there was "some exposure of person," but "not made with the brazen effrontery of London, Paris, or New York." In the end, he concluded that a "short inspection was long enough." "The place is yet incomplete," he wrote, but given its proposed size and scale when finished, it "will certainly be an extraordinary fact in the history of a people" (JJ, December 13, 1859).

Visiting Hokkaido in October 1860 he commented on the "Oshiwara" of Hakodate, writing, "it is a quarter of the town by itself."

> The lower front of each house is a large apartment open to the street except so far as the vertical bars separate it. These apartments are handsomely matted and papered, and at evening time when they are brilliantly lighted, seated in a row across the room are the showily dressed bedizened courtesans. Their garments, long trailing robes of silk or of bright unusually gaudy colors and oftentimes expensive. Their faces and necks are whitened with powder, and their cheeks and lips glow with artificial dies. Their headdress is the

result of great painstaking on the part of the most skillful of hair dressers and is fairly burdened with the weight of hair pins and ornaments of metal, shell, and precious stones. They are kneeling on the mats with their brazier of charcoal before them and pipes, tobacco, and tea for an occasional solace. They are of all ages from the little miss in her first teens to the hardened outcast of double her years. And there they sit while the crowd without wander up and down gazing at their uncovered beauty. Occasionally one comes forward to the lattice in obedience to the call of some acquaintance from without. Many faces were beautiful and have not yet lost the look of innocence. Indeed so little shame attaches to this life in Japan that those hard, horrible visages one may meet in the street at home are wanting here. (JJ, October 5, 1860)

Hall further noted that in Hakodate one could "hire a mistress" for $15 a month, which was "less than half the cost of the other ports" (Ibid.). His journal contains a number of descriptions of courtesan life that show he pursued his interests in this subject throughout his stay. But Hall's continued good relations with the missionaries would indicate that "indulgences," if they occurred, were handled in a highly discreet manner. Hall was above all an observer, and this was one of the many aspects of Japanese life he thought worthy of recording.

This is not to say that he was not capable of his own flirtations and amusements. On his trip to Hokkaido in 1860 he had encountered a young lady, the "belle" of her village, who was a relative of a very ill child. Hall tried to assist the child, for which the child's grandfather brought him a several quarts of beans—a gift Hall rejected because he did not know who the old man was. Later, as he became aware of

his mistake, he was ashamed and tried to find the old man to make amends. Going back to the house of the ill child, Hall wrote, "I had the luck of a romancer in meeting at this house the village belle, who was daughter of the old man and proffered to escort me to his house. Soon we went together through the street to the no little amazement, I have no doubt, of the gossips of Toni-no-shta [the village], what pretty Okoma was doing with that hilarious bewhiskered *tojin*" (JJ, October 3, 1860).[149] Hall described what followed.

The old man was alone and had fallen asleep over his simple dinner and his potations of sake, a sleep so sound that it required a good deal of shaking, which Okoma laughingly bestowed upon him to arouse him. He was at length awakened and made to comprehend the purport of my visit. He clasped my hand warmly in his, thanking me over and over again, laughing with that peculiar chuckle that belongs to old age. But when I came to say good bye to him and Okoma, and placing my arm around the waist of the village belle gave her a kiss, which she received with mingled blushes and smiles, the old man's chuckle broke out into a peal of laughter. He evidently thought it, as did I, the best joke of the season. (Ibid.)

Here we have a brief portrait of Hall's deep feelings and concern for others, as well as his whimsical charm. To Westerners there was nothing unusual about such conviviality, but it was rather extraordinary in Japan where, as Hall observed on another occasion, kissing was definitely "one of the lost arts" (JJ, July 19, 1860). If kissing was out, flirtations of other kinds could be readily engaged in. Hall recalls another charming scene that took place in the graveyard behind his temple at Kanagawa. It shows us that he had not entirely given up on

---

[149] The term *tojin*, which literally meant "Chinaman," was used as a general word for "foreigner" in late Tokugawa Japan. *Tojin baka*, or "Foreign Fool" was an epithet that Hall notes was regularly used toward foreigners in Yokohama leading to various confrontations. The term was later proscribed by the authorities

but as Hall notes clever Japanese who wanted to get around the proscription now simply saluted foreigners with "*tojin baka-ri*," or "*Anata baka-ri*." By trailing off on the *ri* they turned "foreign fool" into "only a foreigner." See JJ, August 11, 1860.

"blackeyed roguish girls." Indeed, this scene is delightful in that it combines the Japanese curiosity about Westerners, which resulted in the popularity of the "Yokohama prints," which directed the skill of Japan's woodblock artists to foreigners and foreign life, with the equal fascination Westerners like Hall felt about the Japanese.

Hall tells us that for several days a group of middle-aged women had been visiting the cemetery behind his temple to burn incense at a new grave. They were accompanied by a young lady of seventeen or eighteen, who was dressed in considerable style. Hall was sitting in his room observing this scene one Sunday afternoon. "I think the young lady is coquettish," he wrote. "She paid little attention to any pious offices for the dead, but strolled leisurely about adjusting with coquettish air her handsome garments, casting furtive glimpses at this house as if to say, I wonder if the foreigners see this handsome young lady of Nippon" (JJ, April 8, 1860). One of the older ladies caught sight of Hall looking out the window. She "smiled, jolted the young lady, who looked up and smiled, then I smiled, then another old lady smiled, and finally we all smiled together. The young lady walked airily as though she was treading on so many invisible eggs. She no doubt thought to herself, that young man is gone up, he could not resist, I knew he couldn't, and then she looked again out of her almond shaped eyes, which opened so little that they seemed like slits in white birch bark, for her skin was powdered to that hue."

As in Hokkaido, Hall seems to have enjoyed himself immensely. "Now I flatter myself," he stated, "that I am not the worst looking fellow in the world seen through a window at a distance of several paces, and a flirtation in a graveyard was an original sensation, as I repaid look for look. The battery of my glances was loosed as rapidly as hers, and I thought the kindly way in which the old ladies smiled and showed their blackened teeth told that my shots told. The young lady smoothed down the folds of her crape scarf, took out one of her long metal hair pins, and scratched her head. She no doubt felt something."

And now Hall shows us that he can give us his own verbal equivalent of a "Yokohama print." "But I haven't told you how the young lady was dressed," he wrote.

Her hair was a miracle of brushing, camellias and iris, and formations. It is not describable, the way it was on her head like a fan expanded at the sides, like wings "loosed over the ears [and] fell away from the forehead in puffs," was skewered up by tuning fork pins of shell and white copper, silver washed, adorned by spangles, tied up with silk cords—a ballroom belle's is as nothing in comparison, and the time spent on that head must have been only possible in a land where time, like everything else, is very cheap. She was whitened with powder, and reddened with rouge, and her thin lips were brilliant with vermilion. One long loose robe covered her figure. It was gathered about her waist by a broad girdle and tied in a miraculous tie in the rear. The girdle was 1/2 of a yard wide at least, and was tied in a square knot behind like a gentleman's cravat. The robe was a light blue silk elaborately wrought in front in flowers of red and green. At the bottom it was bordered with a roll of red stuff as large as my wrist. The sleeves were deeply hanging sleeves edged with red and sewed together so as to give just room for the play of the arm, which was left bare to the elbow. Underneath the outer robe were several under robes of thin crape silk folded over the bosom so as to display their clean, gaudy folds. Her feet were covered with white cotton socks, and the thong of her straw slippers passed between her toes and across her ankle. She looked as fresh, neat, and clean as a snow drop. I had seldom seen one so richly dressed. The old ladies were evidently very fond of her. They finished their devotions at the grave and again disappeared out of the gate, still casting Parthian glances in their retreat. They knew their young companion was irresistible in her charms and, I have no doubt, wondered that I didn't fly through the window and over the old gravestones to testify my submission. (JJ, April 8, 1860)

One wonders how his brother Edward would

have responded to this scene, and on a Sunday too!

Like other Westerners in the treaty port, Hall commented on the production and consumption of alcohol in late Tokugawa Japan. This remains one of the largely unstudied topics of this period, but drinking, too, seems to have provided some release from the rigidity of the Japanese social system. Shortly after arriving Hall wrote, "The frequency of sake shops is noticeable. They are fully as common as grog shops at home. The liquor, which tastes like a cheap whiskey, though less harsh, is said to be very intoxicating. It does not appear to be drunk where sold, but the common laborer, boatmen, etc., have their earthen jug, which a single tempo replenishes. Drunkenness is common, and any day towards night there is no lack of red eyes and faces, rising tongues, and staggering gait." "Intemperance in drink, and intemperance in lust," Hall concluded, "are the national sins of Japan" (JJ, November 5, 1859).

The alcohol referred to here seems to have been some form of *shōchū*, rather than sake, but it is worth noting the price. To fill up one's "jug" cost a mere tempo, or "penny," as Hall described the coin most frequently requested by beggars. No wonder Hall found a ready supply almost everywhere. Moreover, lest the sentiments expressed in the final sentence of the foregoing passage be taken too literally, it should be pointed out that Hall, unlike the missionaries, was quite fond of a "stiff one" now and then. In fact Hall enjoyed drinking with the Japanese. On December 30, 1859, he recorded in his journal, "I amused myself while waiting with warming my fingers over the ferry master's brazier, talking Japanese, and drinking hot sake with him" (JJ, December 30, 1859). Early the following year he wrote, "A native traveller invited me to his room and offered me a share of his dinner, which consisted of fish fried and steamed in oil, eggs broken and boiled with vegetables, hot sake, and tea. I tried the fish and tea which was good. I tasted the hot sake; it has a not unpleasant taste and contains a small proportion of alcohol, less than ale. The people drink a great deal of it before showing intoxication. This traveller was emptying his second jug—

small, brown, earthen jugs hold a pint, reminding me of Dutch beer jugs—and his flushed face and reddened eyes showed that the hot beverage was beginning to take effect" (JJ, January 20, 1860). Hall also enjoyed sharing an occasional bottle with his fellow treaty porters, and the "chowder parties" he describes would hardly have been as lively without the potations that accompanied them.[150]

But while Hall was no teetotaler and had given up his "pledge" years before, he did not approve of the excessive drinking that seems to have been common in Japan. "The intemperance . . . of this people is immeasurable," he wrote on another occasion (JJ, November 25, 1859). Shortly thereafter he made an estimate of the scope of the problem. "An intelligent Japanese," he wrote, "informs me that one half of the Japanese are addicted to sake drinking and one tenth are sake drunkards—one-tenth of those who drink that is" (JJ, December 24, 1859).

Hall's problem with drunken servants has already been noted, but he was not alone in facing such difficulties. Mrs. Hepburn was equally unhappy with one of her servants, Kami, "whose love of sake made him so worthless that he had to be dismissed" (JJ, June 6, 1860). She now wanted Hall's friend, Sadajirō, to find her a servant "that did not drink." Hall noted that Sadajirō, "brought one that he said did not drink, but he said it was difficult to get a servant in Nippon that was good for anything that did not drink. 'All that are active and intelligent drink, and all that do not drink are fools,' he said" (Ibid.). He also recalled that S. R. Brown had been told the same thing when he tried to find a nondrinking teacher. Hall concluded that this illustrated the "universal prevalence of drinking" in Japan.

The use of alcohol, as Hall described it, was very much a part of the lower orders of Japan. Needing coolies to transport some baggage, he commented that "they came, bare legged fellows with ragged wrappers around their shoulders, a dirty set of vagabonds as one could hope to see. There is a colony of three hundred or so of them living together. They are

---

[150] For a typical description of a "Chowder Party" see JJ, September 5, 1860.

poor men who have no house, no clothes, no family, who live by coolie jobs, drink sake, and gamble. The government furnishes them shelter and if two or three hundred laborers are wanted, you apply to the government and the government knows where to get them" (JJ, April 2, 1860).

To indicate how these men worked, Hall described a *kago*, or sedan chair, ride from Edo to Yokohama in 1860, which cost two *ichibus* and a few gratuities. "The day was rainy and the street muddy. The bearers flagged, went slowly, and wanted something to drink, they drank and moved on more lively, then flagged again, besides it was raining and they ought to have more sake. So there was more sake and something to eat." He then paid about another *ichibu* in gratuities, which it was the custom to ask for. "If the day is pleasant, the bearers are very hot, if cool, they are suffering with cold, or their passenger is too heavy, or sits unevenly; they always have some excuse for extorting extra pay and are quite as clever at it as our hack drivers." The sedan chair bearers are "young single men, or improvident fellows," he noted, "who spend all their money in gambling and sake drinking" (JJ, May 2, 1860).

Finally, Hall recorded that the coming of the West had merely provided new possibilities for Japanese who desired to imbibe. On a trip to Nagasaki in June 1860, he observed that "foreign wares" had become very common, "particularly glassware such as decanters" and "drinking glasses." Moreover, foreign forms of alcohol were also being rapidly imported. "I was more than once stopped in the street," he wrote, "and asked if I would not buy 'gin for one dollar a bottle' " (JJ, June 30, 1860). By 1860 it was therefore quite obvious that the average Japanese, if not his government, was ready to reach out to the broader world, and was already well on his way to the highball and martini.

Hall as Correspondent and Interpreter of Japan

Hall lived through one of the most turbulent and confusing decades of Japanese history, as the Tokugawa order gave way to the forces for change that led to the Meiji Restoration. Following in the wake of Bayard Taylor's book and the official reports of the Perry expedition, Hall's writings soon became the major source of American information on Japan. In the six-and-a-half-year period spanning his arrival in Japan in 1859 and his departure in 1866, Hall submitted more than seventy articles to the *New York Tribune*. Given the importance of the *Tribune* to American public life, it is possible to argue that Hall served as America's leading "opinion maker" on Japan during this crucial age. Moreover, despite the fact that a number of these years overlapped with the news demands of the American Civil War, Hall's monthly correspondence received both extensive space and prominent placement. Occasionally, as on October 2, 1863, when he reported the naval skirmish between the USS *Wyoming* and Chōshū ships and forces at Shimonoseki, he dominated the entire front page of the paper.

In keeping with the *Tribune*'s policy, Hall's goal was to inform the American reader as widely as possible about things Japanese. His articles, like his journal, cover a wide variety of topics, which range from an extended series on Japanese agriculture to elaborate descriptions of the city of Edo. Needless to say, the political situation in Japan was one of his dominant concerns, and he wrote extensively on every twist in the tortuous unfolding of the *bakumatsu* drama. Hall's obituary noted that "he loved Japan" and that "no American was ever more thoroughly Japan-ized."[151] Indeed, from the start, Hall appears to have projected a positive image of Japan. As we have seen, he was highly impressed with the Japanese people, who, except for the feudal elite, are pictured as intelligent, hard-working, neat, and orderly. If there was an initial villain, it was the "Government," which constantly interfered with trade and with Japanese-foreign contacts. "There is no doubt," he wrote in one of his first "letters" from Japan, "that the present Government is opposed to foreign intercourse, and seeks to obstruct trade all that the treaty will allow." "The Government is a grand mo-

[151] "Francis Hall Obituary," *Elmira Weekly Advertiser*, August 29, 1902.

nopoly," he wrote, "from the hire of a temple to that of the servant who cooks your rice and the coolie who carries your parcel in the streets."[152] Everything required government permission.

Hall was convinced that one reason for the government's lack of enthusiasm for trade stemmed from the shogunate's ignorance of the true conditions of the West. He therefore strongly supported the departure of Japan's first mission to the United States, which left in 1860. As he wrote in the *Tribune*, "Their visit cannot fail to have a salutary effect upon our relations with this people." For, as he added, "Words do not, and cannot, convey to them any true impression of the resources and power of the Western nations." Indeed, he observed with some amusement, "They think there must be some humbug about a map that gives Niphon so small a place as it actually occupies among the nations of the earth."[153] In addition he recorded that the commissioners wanted to take their own rice and charcoal to the United States, and were particularly concerned about "their saki remaining good for so long a period." But if these were amusing anecdotes surrounding their preparations, Hall thought that there were also more profound consequences. "The departure of this embassy," he wrote, "breaks down forever the barbarous edict that consigned to death every man who left this land and sought to return." "May we not hope, too," he added, "that the little Japanese steamer, the first vessel for centuries that has dared to sail away from these coasts, is but the van of a fleet; that the ancient maritime skill of this people is again to be restored, and that the rising sun flag shall again appear in Asiatic ports in the peaceful pursuits of commerce."[154]

Japanese ignorance about America and Europe, Hall was quick to add, was matched by the average "news from Japan" that was "published in many of the journals of England and the United States." A British member of parliament, he lamented, went about informing his countrymen that "Japan produces coffee abundantly, and that the finest in the world!" An American paper announced the emperor had "ordered that the cities of Yeddo, Nagasaki, Simoda, and Hakodade should be united by telegraph, and that the line was being built from Yeddo to his summer residence." This was "astounding news to us," Hall wrote. The same article added that the whole "Imperial fleet" was being "turned into steam propeller," and that one vessel, the *Niphon*, had "already left on a voyage of discovery." As Hall insisted, in all this so-called "news" there was not "one word of truth," yet it is a "fair sample of the 'latest news from Japan' brought back to us by every mail."[155]

At the same time Hall admitted that both gathering and interpreting "news" in Japan was no easy assignment. Although he surrounded himself with intelligent and informed Japanese such as Honda Sadajirō,[156] and had excellent contacts with the major diplomatic figures of his age, which included Townsend Harris (later Robert Pruyn), Harry Parkes, Rutherford Alcock, Leon Roches, Duchesne de Bellecourt, Graeff van Polsbroek, and several others, deciphering Japanese events could be a baffling effort. Not only was it difficult, but one often had to make abrupt changes in one's perceived notions. Originally, he had given the Japanese the benefit of doubt in several of the early Yokohama assassinations by noting that Westerners often provided cause by openly insulting the Japanese. But after two inoffensive, elderly Dutch captains were wantonly cut to pieces on Yokohama's main street in March 1860, he wrote, "We look in vain for any provocation to the deed."[157]

[152] Francis Hall "Letter" datelined Kanagawa, Japan, November 24, 1859, *New York Tribune*, February 22, 1860, p. 6.

[153] Francis Hall "Letter" datelined Kanagawa, Japan, January 12, 1860, *New York Tribune*, April 23, 1860, p. 6.

[154] Francis Hall "Letter" datelined Kanagawa, Japan, February 15, 1860, *New York Tribune*, May 1, 1860, p. 6.

[155] Francis Hall "Letter" datelined Kanagawa, Japan,

February 25, 1860, *New York Tribune*, May 16, 1860, p. 6.

[156] For a brief biographical sketch of Honda Sadajirō's life see the journal entry under February 20, 1860. Honda was a highly educated and well connected physician and scholar.

[157] Francis Hall "Letter" datelined Kanagawa, Japan, March 4, 1860, *New York Tribune*, June 22, 1860, p. 5.

Hall was not above his own mounting frustrations, and these could not help but color his writings on occasion. "The longer foreign merchants reside here," he complained, "the more, of course they become acquainted with the people, their language, and customs, and the keener they become in detecting the throwing of obstacles in the way of their trade by the authorities." "Nothing is more evident," he continued, "than the reluctance of the Japanese to treat the foreigners with liberality. They either do not know how to grapple with the large transactions of commerce, or they will not."[158] Hall was particularly annoyed with the all-pervasive influence and meddling of Japanese officials. In the fall of 1860 he wrote,

The Japanese grow daily more and more close in their espionage of foreigners. "Their impertinence is at times intolerable." You can have no dealings with any merchant, or with your own servants, without their knowledge and possible interference. They have gone so far as to take servants out of foreigners' houses for no shadow of offense, and forbid any man to be in foreign employ without permission of the authorities. Every house-servant must pay a share of his wages to the Governor. The fisherman may not sell us a herring, the market-woman a fowl or an egg, or the grocer a handful of potatoes without repeating it to the proper official. If we cross the ferry between Kanagawa and Yokohama an official is stationed there to count noses and record them in a book, and also the number and description of all boxes, parcels, or bundles into which he will pry with cunning fingers, if possible." "The Japanese authorities," he concluded, "persistently go on their own way, and no effort

is made seemingly to resist their petty aggression."[159]

One of Hall's major complaints against Townsend Harris, the American minister, was that he made no effort to counter such Japanese behavior.[160] Hall noted that foreigners were better understood in Nagasaki. "It was pleasant at Nagasaki," he wrote when visiting this port, "to be out of the way of insolent officials, and not to encounter a party of sword-bearers at every step."[161]

Hall's early hope that the shogunal mission to the West would serve to break down the rigid prison of feudalism in Japan was not immediately confirmed. As he noted when the commissioners returned, "the greatest indifference was manifested," by the government and "not a boat put off to welcome the returned Envoys."[162] But noting the mounting split between daimyo factions and the shogunate, he added, "the Daimios are inviting the members of that embassy of high and low degree to their houses for the purpose of inquiring into American affairs. We hear but one report of the tale they have brought back of the wealth and greatness of the Americans, the splendid houses, the great ships, and the wonderful railroads." "These stories," he observed, "have come to the ears of the common people with no diminution of their repetition."[163]

By 1861 Hall sensed the growing tension between the Tokugawa and what he called the "Princes," or daimyo of Japan. His interpretation of the assassinations of Westerners, including the death of Heusken, now led to a new argument. As the *Tribune* reported, "In the opinion of our correspondent, the recent murders at Yedo have been committed not so much from hostility to foreigners as from a desire on the part of a turbulent faction of the

---

[158] Francis Hall "Letter" datelined Kanagawa, Japan, May 10, 1860, *New York Tribune*, August 20, 1860, p. 6.

[159] Francis Hall "Letter" datelined Kanagawa, Japan, October 29, 1860, *New York Tribune*, December 29, 1860, p. 8.

[160] "Oh for an hour of the bold sagacious spirit of Perry," Hall wrote in obvious criticism of Harris, "who knew so well where to stop their petty intermeddling, is the feeling of every annoyed foreigner" (ibid.).

[161] Francis Hall "Letter" datelined Kanagawa, Japan, July 10, 1860, *New York Tribune*, October 11, 1860, p. 6.

[162] Francis Hall "Letter" datelined Kanagawa, Japan, November 15, 1860, *New York Tribune*, January 30, 1861, p. 6.

[163] Francis Hall "Letter" datelined Kanagawa, Japan, December 29, 1860, *New York Tribune*, February 28, 1861, p. 8.

feudatory princes to involve the Imperial [shogunal] Government in a foreign war, with the expectation that during the trouble and confusion which would be sure to ensue they could bring about a revolution and drive the reigning dynasty from the throne, to which some of these princes have themselves hereditary pretensions." As the *Tribune* continued, "The Government of the Tycoon, though perfectly aware of these designs, is too weak to venture to offend its powerful vassals, and therefore reluctantly connives at their outrages, which it dare not repress, though fully conscious of the danger it incurs from submitting to them."[164] Again Hall put the alternatives most perceptively. The shogunate "has before it the alternative of a foreign war or a domestic rebellion, and perhaps both of these evils at the same time, and is deficient either in power or in decision sufficient to put an end to its embarrassment."[165] This analysis, which Hall developed by the opening months of 1861, was to be confirmed by the events that followed.

By late 1861 and early 1862 Hall was increasingly concerned about the possibilities of civil war in Japan. "I can well imagine that in a comparison with the stirring events which are taking place nearer home," he wrote alluding to the American Civil War then in progress, "what may be going on in so remote a corner of the earth as Japan may seem matters of small moment, yet these too are a part of the world's record and progress, and even here the fate of twenty-five millions of people hangs trembling in the balance." "Today," he added, "the whole Japanese mind is troubled by the fear of imminent revolution in the State." "A break-up of this Government, if it comes," he warned, "would, amid the claims of contending rivals, carry Japan back to the times of three centuries ago, when every powerful prince was in the field seeking such alliances as the interest of each dictated. Thus we may hope that if the threatened wreck comes, a liberal foreign

policy may yet prove the strong point on which a wise Government may rally as against the divided aims of selfish chiefs."[166]

The situation was even more confusing by late 1862. "Nothing is so difficult to understand in Japan," Hall wrote, "as the peculiar complex character of its political institutions. The knowledge of today seems contradicted by the events of tomorrow. To foretell what will be is impossible; to be sure of what has happened is not always attainable." "That an extraordinary ferment is now at work in the country among its ruling classes," he wrote, "we all know by what is occasionally thrown to the surface. A revolution, if not a reform of ideas, is going on, thus far peaceably, but at times threatening more serious results."[167] Hall believed that the daimyo, "ever full of intrigue, were never more full of it than at the present moment." As he saw it, Japan was divided in several "parties" or factions. The first he identified as the "progressive party" who "either coveting foreign intercourse or viewing it as an inevitable necessity wisely seek to make the best of it." This group he saw as headed by the shogun and included a "class of men, by no means small, who, truly patriotic, are sincerely desirous to profit their country by whatsoever is to be gained by intercourse with more enlightened people." This group was further backed, he wrote, by many small daimyo who had thrown in their lot with the Tokugawa. In opposition to the "present reigning family," Hall identified several distinct groups. First of all there were the "aspirants to the throne," he wrote, of whom "Mito's family is most conspicuous." And secondly there were "those Daimios who, through selfish interest or fear, are hostile to foreign intercourse." "There is a third class," he wrote, who are "adherents of the Mikado or Spiritual Emperor, who are jealous of the growing centralizing power of the Tycoon's Court at Yedo." The chief representative of this camp, he felt, was the daimyo of

---

[164] "The Condition of Japan," an article composed by the editor of the *Tribune* "from the letters of our correspondent." *New York Tribune*, April 11, 1861, p. 4.
[165] Ibid.
[166] The quotations in this paragraph are from Francis

Hall "Letter" datelined Kanagawa, Japan, September 1, 1861, *New York Tribune*, November 11, 1861, p. 6.
[167] Francis Hall "Letter" datelined Kanagawa, Japan, November 20, 1862, *New York Tribune*, February 6, 1863, p. 3.

Satsuma. "Thus the country," he wrote, "has been full of reports of the machinations of one or the other of these parties. One day Mito is dead and the next is heard of as an active plotter against the throne and foreigners. Today the Emperor is poisoned and tomorrow the Mikado repudiates the treaties and demands that his faithful leaguers shall 'wipe out as with a sponge every foreigner from the land.' "[168]

Hall's articles reported on the mounting chaos that followed in the wake of the abrogation of the alternate attendance system and the shogunate's inability to pursue a clear-cut foreign policy. While his articles reflect the apprehension that many Yokohama dwellers felt about their safety, he rarely lost his balanced perspective. "We have had so often such a 'Wolf!' 'Wolf!' cry," he wrote when the city was threatened once again in 1863, "that many are wholly incredulous of any danger, while others are sufficiently alarmed to remove their treasure on board the shipping. Your correspondent," he assured his readers, "is inclined to the belief that although the Japanese authorities are sincere in their apprehensions, this is but a repetition of the menaces which have so often been made, to produce disquiet when no real intention exists of carrying them into execution."[169] Confronted by the further escalation of tensions that accompanied the arrival of the British fleet in the spring of 1863, Hall retained his stoic composure. Conscious that British demands for a large indemnity to pay for the loss of life suffered in the attack on the British legation in 1861 and the wanton killing of Richardson on the Tōkaidō in 1862 might well lead to war, Hall wrote with a sense of resignation, "We calmly await the issue of the twenty days, and their event of peace or desolating war to a people who for three centuries have known the blessings of unbroken peace. Not less anxiously do we wait for the results to ourselves and our property, for on us and our

property would fall such blows as the Japanese may have to give."[170]

By summer Hall reported that the Japanese government had come to an agreement with the English. "At present war seems to be averted," he wrote, "but it is of no use to disguise the fact that it is a temporizing, unwilling settlement on the part of the Japanese, and that since the party in Japan who are hostile to foreigners are largely in the ascendant, and of late have gathered force, the evil day is only averted." "We live," he cautioned, "over a smoldering volcano, which any day may burst out, involving more or less of us in destruction." "The irrepressible conflict between an old but powerful feudalism and modern social progress," he warned, "has yet at no distant day to come off on these shores, and I am mistaken if the Miaco party do not soon bring on the trial."[171] And yet, gloomy as prospects appeared, he was not willing to accept the worst, writing: "Let us still hope for peace to thrice unhappy Japan, who in an evil hour, not of her own seeking, opened her long-closed doors to such troublesome guests."[172] Finally, Hall provided his own analysis, finding "amid all these belligerent prospects" some "rays of hope." "The government of the unhappy Tycoon," he reasoned, "is likely to be crushed between two forces—the hostile Daimios, or the English. To remain neutral will be annihilation and so it is to be hoped that he will choose the wise course of meeting the demands of the English, and if need be accept foreign aid against his powerful enemies at Miaco, who are the enemies of foreign intercourse and progress also."[173]

While Hall reported faithfully on the complex political issues that dominated 1863, he was also struck by the irony of certain contradictions. As life in Yokohama became more precarious, and the cry to close the port and expel all "barbarians" mounted, the number of

[168] The foregoing quotations are from ibid.

[169] Francis Hall "Letter" datelined Kanagawa, Japan, January 3, 1863, *New York Tribune*, March 20, 1863, p. 3.

[170] Francis Hall "Letter" datelined Kanagawa, Japan, April 14, 1863, *New York Tribune*, June 26, 1863, p. 4.

[171] Francis Hall "Letter" datelined Kanagawa, Japan, June 15, 1863, *New York Tribune*, August 28, 1863, p. 5.

[172] Francis Hall "Letter" datelined Kanagawa, Japan, June 24, 1863, *New York Tribune*, August 28, 1863, p. 5.

[173] Francis Hall "Letter" datelined Kanagawa, Japan, June 23, 1863, *New York Tribune*, August 28, 1863, p. 5.

foreigners increased steadily. Yokohama, he wrote in November 1863, "is crowded with foreign houses and foreign industry." "We are," he wrote, "all told English, Americans, Dutch, French, Prussians, Swiss, Portuguese, and nondescript, four hundred souls, already stifling for room." More were arriving monthly, and the demand was reflected in land prices. A standard lot, he observed, which two years earlier had sold for $265 now cost between eight and ten thousand dollars. (Two years later, in 1865, he recorded that a two-acre waterfront compound sold for $200,000.) "Commerce," he recorded, "reaps ten millions annually of silver dollars." While this was the "gross," he estimated that "the net profit is also a sum of fat cyphers marshalled by a not overlean digit." Silk and tea, he noted, had become the "great staples of the Japan trade," followed by cotton, copper, camphor, coal, new tobacco, and various edibles sent to China. Japan, once "*terra terribillis*, if not *terra incognita*" had thus become a "foster child of commerce." He wrote,

And commerce comes here full panoplied, as when, centuries ago she conquered the *Mare Mediterraneum*, and so passed by to Britain, who now returns to the East. She comes with her sword and cannon, and her resonant fife and drum fill the quiet air of these isles; for today, as I write, twelve hundred British soldiers and marines are parading our streets, to give the Japanese an impress of their strength. She comes with her virtues and vices, and it will take the Eternal Accountant at last to decide whether "the opening of Japan" brings civilization to a fearful debit or a glorious credit in the books of the Ages."[174]

While Hall was willing to submit his own interpretation and analysis of the Japanese scene, he was increasingly conscious of the difficulty of predicting events in Japan. Early in 1864 he wrote: "Of all the countries in which to win the reputation of a prophet I would pronounce Japan the most difficult. Better a 'rain maker' in South Africa than a seer in Nippon. So it is that if my letters at one time speak encouragingly of remaining peace and prosperity for Japan and the foreigners on her shores, and at another of wars and rumors of wars, it is because my correspondence must be a reflex of the prevailing feeling at the time, now tending in one direction, and now in another."[175] By 1864 Hall was growing increasingly impatient and felt that "it is high time some conclusion that shall be felt as binding by all the Daimios and their followers is reached. Even a determination to undertake the expulsion of the foreign element," he added, "would be better than this incertitude which is leading more and more to petty anarchy."[176] But shortly thereafter he once more accepted the Japanese reality, writing, "Affairs in Japan continue with the same halting steps toward progress—as often recalcitrant to the old desire for seclusion—groping, stumbling, with the indecision of a blind man, inimical and dangerous to the foreign element in the Empire, puzzling to the diplomats, and wholly inexplicable, I trow, to the *Tribune*'s fireside readers."[177]

In the summer of 1864 Hall captured something of the difficulty that any firsthand observer faces in deciphering day-to-day events. The past year, he felt, had revealed little more than "hopeless contradictions and weary surmises." "At the Court of Yedo," he wrote, "the Tycoon has been the puppet of his ministers; flying between Yedo and Miaco the shuttlecock of adverse parties. Deposed ministries have followed deposed ministries in rapid succession. Tycoons, Mikados, supreme councilors, regents, governors, no-kamis, daimios friendly, and daimios hostile, have flitted before our eyes with all the changefulness of the magic lantern's phantasmagorfs. The same ir-

---

[174] The foregoing quotations are from Francis Hall "Letter" datelined Kanagawa, Japan, November 30, 1863, *New York Tribune*, February 13, 1864, p. 4.
[175] Francis Hall "Letter" datelined Kanagawa, Japan, January 4, 1864, *New York Tribune*, March 18, 1864,

p. 1.
[176] Ibid.
[177] Francis Hall "Letter" datelined Kanagawa, Japan, January 14, 1864, *New York Tribune*, March 22, 1864, p. 1.

resolution, born of hopeless doubt and ignorance, still hangs like lead on the conduct of
ministers and admirals, which weighted them
down when first the fleet came into our waters."[178] Hall noted the difficult situation in
which not only he as a reporter, but diplomats
such as Rutherford Alcock, who were "skilled
in Oriental diplomacy," found themselves. "For
where everyone, even the most experienced,
are ignorant," he wrote, "where each government official is more skillful than his fellow in
the art of lying so as to simulate the truth, who
shall tell whether it were better to strike or forbear. So we are drifting on the surface of the
flowing time, steering neither to this side or
that, hoping only that some propitious wind,
tide, or current will float us into our haven of
ease."[179]

What Hall's articles and journal entries capture so distinctly is the fluid state of Japanese
affairs in the 1860s. Here are all the actors
who eventually make the Restoration. Indeed,
here we can even see the outlines of policies to
be pursued, such as those of the shogunate.
But nowhere is there the slightest sense of certainty about the outcome. What history has
neatly packaged for us as the "Meiji Restoration" with the clarity of hindsight, was in reality a kaleidoscope of rapidly shifting images
and forces. To predict the outcome of this turmoil was, as Hall realized, beyond normal human capacities. And yet, surrounded by
confusion and uncertainty, as he was, Hall
maintained a sense of optimism about Japan's
future. "It must be admitted," he had written
in 1863, "that the Japanese have betrayed a
wonderful progress in the art of war, and that
they have shown themselves to be far ahead, in
this respect, of every other nation in Asia."
"Their present difficulty with the great powers,
whether it may be peaceably settled or by war,"
he added, "will probably give a new impulse to
the mental faculties of the people, and help to
elevate them to a higher level of civilization."[180]

Occasionally Hall used his *Tribune* articles to
try to bring reform to the treaty port. He
noted, for example, in reference to the "inac-
tion" of the fleet, that "the irksomeness of delay is magnanimously borne by the fleet, whose
profit, arising out of their ichibu exchange,
now reaches the enormous sum of $50,000 per
month!" Earlier, Rutherford Alcock had casti-
gated Yokohama merchants as the "scum of
the earth" for their avariciousness in convert-
ing dollars to *ichibus*. "Let it be known then,"
he wrote, "that by the grace of this same Minister, so sensitive to mercantile honor, a system
of ichibu jobbing is going on here by officers
wearing her Majesty's livery to which the offenses of the so-much abused merchants were
harmless peccadilloes. The story of this business—so discreditable to her Majesty's high officials, and not to hers only—must some day be
made known, then home governments and
home people will be equally astonished and
ashamed for such weaknesses—to use no
rougher term—in high quarters."[181] Hall regarded such payments as an "enormous subsidy from the Japanese Government," which
he felt was "dangerous to public morals and
official integrity" and should be "swept away,"
he wrote, "before it accomplishes its legitimate,
I had almost said inevitable, work."[182] But as
he also pointed out, this "subsidy" was not limited to the fleet. Hall noted that all ministers
and consuls, including the American representatives, also received special exchange privileges. "The amounts thus exchanged by
foreign officials doubles and trebles their salaries," Hall noted. "Do the astute Japanese suppose they get no return for this favor? Is it
wholesome for the purity of official inter-

[178] Francis Hall "Letter" datelined Kanagawa, Japan,
August 11, 1864, *New York Tribune*, November 10, 1864,
p. 7.

[179] Ibid.

[180] "Japan," editorial comments based on the "account
of our correspondent," *New York Tribune*, October 2,
1863, p. 4.

[181] Francis Hall "Letter" datelined Kanagawa, Japan,
August 11, 1864, *New York Tribune*, November 10, 1864,
p. 7. Hall noted that the English were not alone in re-

ceiving "subsidies" from the Japanese government. In
his journal he writes: "The American Minister [Robert
Pruyn] is down for $70,000 worth of exchange for a
single year, some of which is put down by the Japanese
'as compensation for leaving Yedo!!' The American
Consul figures for large sums given also as compensation." See JJ, August 2, 1864.

[182] Francis Hall "Letter" datelined Kanagawa, Japan,
August 11, 1864, *New York Tribune*, November 10, 1864,
p. 7.

course," he questioned, "that a diplomatic representative should receive from the sovereign to whom he is accredited *twice the salary* that he gets from the country that sent him thither? Yet these are the stern facts."[183]

Hall's efforts to change such practices were not limited to published articles. In 1865 Consul George S. Fisher asked him to comment on the state of the Yokohama trade. Hall observed that there was some dissatisfaction with the duties imposed, with government interference, and with the role of Japanese monopoly organizations. But by far the greatest problem involved the currency and currency exchange rates. Hall reminded Fisher that the treaty Harris signed called for a "weight for weight" exchange between the dollar and Japanese coinage. "Yet what are the existing facts?" he wrote.

> The merchant who arrives in Japan in the pursuit of his legitimate calling is met at the threshold by an extraordinary state of affairs; two currencies for two divisions of foreigners. He sees the foreign merchant buying the produce of the country with a Dollar, which instead of passing weight for weight, passes for barely two-thirds its weight and value in the local coinage, while at the same time the foreign ministers, consuls, or other delegated representatives of foreign powers, the admiral and officers and sailors of the fleet, [and] the general and subalterns and men of the military force on the station receive for the same dollars, as a privilege and perquisite of their class from the Tycoon, the dollar's full value in exchange at the government treasury.

Hall felt that this contributed not only to the evil of "class distinctions," which a Republican government should be slow to condone, but to a decline in "sound public morals." Hall reminded Fisher that "in the year 1864, according to records in the Custom House at Kanagawa, there was exchanged by said Custom House for the resident foreign officials,

the naval and military force stationed here, a sum not far from three millions of Dollars at the net profit to the recipients of this favor of one millions of Dollars." Hall added that the problem had become so great in the summer of 1864 that "a larger sum was actually employed month by month by the official, military, and naval representatives at this port in a coin exchange than was employed in the whole commerce of the port!"

It struck Hall as ironic that it was the foreign merchants who eventually had to pay the price for all this by buying the coin necessary to carry out their trade from the very officials who had been sent to protect and preserve the treaties. The result, he felt, was currency instability that interfered with a healthy trade. Hall estimated that at least 10 percent of the entire Japan trade went to supporting such special arrangements with foreign officials, and he was convinced that both Japanese and Western traders paid the price of these exactions. But what upset him even more was the ever increasing demand for "indemnities" by the foreign powers. "The demands made upon the Japanese Government for political offenses whether as condonation for blood or as indemnity for offenses at Kagosima or Shimonoseki or elsewhere in money have been grave mistakes," he wrote. For while they have been "aimed as a punishment upon the Government and the principal classes in Japan," he pointed out, "the blow has really fallen upon the productive and mercantile interests of the land, which have had to pay for crimes in which they had no share." As Hall saw it, this made no sense. "We have indirectly punished our friends for the faults of our enemies," he wrote. "In each fresh money demand on this government there is a fresh exaction on the producers and traders. We in effect place a mortgage on the productive industry of Japan ultimately to be discharged by ourselves." Hall summed up his position to Fisher as follows: "Let us then have an end to money demands as indemnity for crimes, an end to official speculation in the coinage of the realm, and asking of our protectors only security for life

[183] Francis Hall "Letter" datelined Kanagawa, Japan, November 15, 1864, *New York Tribune*, February 15, 1865, p. 1.

and labor, free intercourse on both sides, the simple guarantees of the treaties and commerce will work its own silent irresistible ways."[184]

Hall's efforts to reform such abuses seem to have resulted in a number of positive changes. The British abandoned their "exchange privileges" late in 1864, and the Americans followed suit not long thereafter.

As the foregoing indicates, Hall had no tolerance for the cupidity of public officials. He criticized E. M. Dorr, the Kanagawa consul, for his lack of "honor, honesty, or gratitude, save as they may serve some selfish end he desires to promote" (JJ, November 13, 1861). At the same time, while Hall in the end refused even to serve temporarily in Dorr's place, it is worth noting that he regularly nursed him in his increasingly debilitating illnesses. For an individual who was proverbially kind to others and whose generosity and kindnesses were widely commented upon, it therefore seems curious that Hall was so adamant in his criticism of Townsend Harris, the American minister.

Shortly after his arrival in Japan in November 1859, Hall commented on Harris's advice to the Yokohama merchants, writing, "We shall take all his advice at its proper valuation, for we are not without reason for believing that he is not always competent to give advice" (JJ, November 28, 1859). A few weeks later Hall noted,

Our American merchants resident at Kanagawa, or rather Yokohama, throw much blame on Minister Harris for lack of a proper care of American interests. It is difficult to arrive at the truth when self interest rules a man's opinions, hence I should be unwilling to say how far the charges of want of energy and ability can be sustained. I am however inclined to believe that Mr. H. is not the vigorous actor and sound thinker he may have been before age and infirmities sapped his vigor, and therefore I can imagine that in dealing with a government like this it would want the healthy look at affairs and the decided tone that an

enfeebled body cannot yield in full to the mind. (JJ, December 14, 1859)

When Harris asked the American merchants to meet with him early in 1860 to try to get them to move from Yokohama to Kanagawa, Hall recorded, "there were but few present" (JJ, January 16, 1860), and those who came decided that they would not move from Yokohama unless forced to do so.

Although he met Harris socially on a number of occasions in Kanagawa, and once accompanied him to Kawasaki on the edge of Edo with the missionary S. R. Brown, Harris never invited him to see the city, even though he knew he was the correspondent for America's leading newspaper. When he was finally invited to visit Edo by the officers of the *Hartford* on October 31, 1860, a year after his arrival in Japan, Hall noted in his diary that the invitation was doubly welcome "as I was not indebted for it to Consul Dorr or Minister Harris" (JJ, October 31, 1860).

Hall's portrait of Harris in Edo is one of the few "snapshot" images we have of him. "Mr. Harris is a man of middle size, full figure, blue eyes, gray hair, in his manner inclined to an excessive show of politeness," Hall wrote.

He does not look as if he had suffered much from the cares of his office, or his long seclusion in Japan, having rather the appearance of a bon vivant, a little blase more than that of a soul and body suffering *en verite*. One need not hear him speak for five minutes before making the discovery that there is at least no man in the world who knows but the American Minister at the Court of Yedo is a great man. Nor should the guest trouble himself to frame fitting speeches, for sorry chance will he have to fire them in among the thick, rolling volley of words that tell the experiences of the speaker, with all the unreserve of a man who thinks what he has seen, done, and supposed, be fitting themes for every hour and all ears. (JJ, November 1, 1860)

[184] The foregoing quotations dealing with the exchange problem are from a letter from Francis Hall to Consul Fisher dated Kanagawa, November 1, 1865,

Despatches from U.S. Consuls in Japan, National Archives Record Group 59: Vol. 2, M135.

When Hall and Joseph Heco stayed over in Edo for an extra night at the invitation of the French representative, Abbé Girard, Harris tried to have them expelled from the city. "Mr. H.'s opposition to American's visiting Yedo amounts almost to a mania," he wrote in his journal. "Like a Grecian Cerebus he sits at the gate yelping at every approach." "One might suppose from his anxiety," Hall wrote, "that the integrity of the Japanese Emperor [shogun] depended on his keeping at bay every American; they would hardly dream it was his own integrity, or reputation for integrity, he was claiming to sustain" (JJ, November 5, 1860). Little wonder that when Harris came to Yokohama on Christmas Day, 1860, to "spend the day with his countrymen," Hall wrote, "Alas! his countrymen are not willing to spend this day with him. Mr. Dorr invited a number of us to dine with him, but we all found convenient excuses not to go. The only Americans present at the dinner were the Captain of a vessel in harbor and his wife. Mr. Harris has alienated himself from the goodwill of his countrymen by his official and personal neglect of them hitherto and the refusal to meet him at dinner was a marked token of their disesteem for the man" (JJ, December 25, 1860).

But Hall's severest criticism of Harris was reserved for the days following Heusken's death. Noting that Alcock had rallied the foreign community behind his decision to leave Edo and had explained his stand in a circular on Japanese affairs, Hall contrasted Harris's actions with those of his British counterpart. "It is pretty certain," Hall mused, "that our Minister has forwarded no dispatches home. He is [in] no condition either to write them or to attend to American interests. He 'was so shocked by the murder of Heusken that it has rendered him extremely nervous and incapable of sleep and utterly prostrated him.' We know what this means. What a disgrace it is," Hall continued, "how unsafe it is to be represented at such a juncture by a man who has no control over his appetites. Is it all false that we hear from Yedo that he has 'walked up and down his rooms like a mad man with a pistol in each hand,' or the still more shameful thing, that he requested the officials to bring him a woman 'to sew buttons on' and when they brought a

woman for that purpose he exclaimed 'what did you bring that old hag for, I don't want her to sew buttons on, I want to + + + +.'" "And this is the man," Hall concluded, "who is thought at home to be such a fit representative of our country to this semicivilized people, who is supposed to be the zealous promoter of civilization and even Christianity" (JJ, January 31, 1861).

Given the fact that Hall was extremely circumspect and never wrote about anyone else using such language, these are quite extraordinary entries. Needless to say, these were private observations, not intended for publication. In fact, they show the relationship between his journal and his published articles. On the day Harris left Japan Hall simply recorded, "Mr. Harris leaves Japan" (JJ, May 11, 1862). On May 28, 1862, Hall wrote to the *Tribune*:

> Ex-Minister Harris left on the 12th for the States, via Suez. Consul Dorr has been gone some weeks. Whatever may have been the cause, the implacable feud existing between the American residents and their retiring officials was both unpleasant and detrimental to public interests. The story is too long for your columns, and too uninteresting to your general readers. At home, Mr. Harris is widely known as the negotiator, single-handed, of our present treaty, and for it he will have honor to the end of our common history. Whether his policy with the Japanese of later years has been best calculated for the good of all concerned, we leave to time to determine. Your readers will care little for the details.[185]

Hall appears to have gotten on a great deal better with Robert H. Pruyn, the new minister, and with Pruyn's son, as well as with Consul Fisher, whom he regarded as more genuinely interested in both the American citizens residing in the treaty port as well as in America's national interests in Japan.

And yet, while Hall was often highly critical of Harris, and occasionally of Dorr, as the

[185] Francis Hall "Letter" datelined Kanagawa, Japan, May 28, 1862, *New York Tribune*, July 30, 1862, p. 3.

foregoing indicates, he was also frequently sympathetic to their positions. Even Harris's decision to stay in Edo, which he saw as risky, made sound diplomatic sense to Hall in that it prevented the American minister from becoming obligated to British and French "guns" in the bay, and allowed him to play the complicated game of placing a "non-belligerent" America between Japan and its "rapacious" European foes.[186] The fact that Harris hoped to have Hall serve as American consul in Kanagawa as late as the spring of 1862 furthermore confirms that on the formal, interpersonal level the two men retained a certain respect for each other.

Hall's relations with the Yokohama community and with the Japanese remained excellent. Indeed, at the time of his departure from Japan in the summer of 1866, the American community in Yokohama threw a massive party for him at the French Hotel and there were similar celebrations at Walsh, Hall, & Co. He sailed for home on July 5, 1866. As he wrote in his journal, "It was a delightful summer day, such a day as I would have had to say adieu to dear old Nippon, which I was leaving with so much regret. Those were after all, I saw, golden years of my life that I had passed on these shores" (JJ, July 5, 1866). And as his later life confirmed, these had, indeed, been "golden years" in more than one respect.

Hall's Post-Japan Career

Hall returned to the United States a wealthy man. As he noted in his journal his "settlements" with Walsh, Hall & Co. had been made on a "liberal" and "satisfactory" basis and he could not help but be pleased with the results of his "years of travel" (JJ, July 5, 1866). Returning to Elmira in November 1866, Hall re-

ceived a warm welcome. The *Elmira Advertiser* noted that he had "not grown old or changed much" but had "simply mellowed" with the passing years. "A little more greyness frosts his hair," the editor wrote, "but the old genial heart, kind as that of a woman, is still there, and the old vigor and elastic spirit still keenly flashes forth." The paper reported that he would "for the present" make his "residence" in New York City, "where the details of his business can be more readily supervised," but it also went on to assure him that the people of the town "could not easily forget one of Elmira's earliest benefactors and a truly faithful friend."[187]

We are told that shortly after his return to Elmira an American publisher "offered him a considerable sum to write a history of Japan," but that he preferred to pursue his business and travel interests.[188] Indeed, Hall used some of his Japan capital to build the Hall block on East Water street in Elmira, in which the Hall Brothers Book Store was prominently located. He also invested substantially in the creation of the Syracuse Chilled Plow Co., of which he was a founder, first vice-president, and a large stockholder.[189] In addition there were investments in real estate that reached as far as Puget Sound on the West Coast. To what degree Hall maintained his relationship with Walsh, Hall & Co. is not entirely clear. One of his obituaries states that he returned to Japan in 1869 and "sold out his interests"[190] at that time, but if this happened, and we have no further evidence that it did, there are also signs that he continued to be on good terms with the Walsh brothers and that, as in the case of Iwasaki Yanosuke, he pursued his Japanese contacts well into the Meiji period. Unfortunately the records for these years are not currently available.

What information we have on Hall's post-Japan years indicates that he continued to pur-

---

[186] Hall wrote in his journal: "Mr. Harris has no support from any American force in these waters, where he is, he places himself in the protection and honor of the Japanese Government, if he retires to Yokohama, he places himself under the protection of British and French guns, a position which I presume any American Minister would be glad to avoid if possible. Furthermore, the policy of the American Government in the East is a settled one of no armed interference, the af-

fairs of China have sufficiently shown this, why then should Mr. Harris take a definite stand with no prospect of his government's backing him" (JJ, January 21, 1861).

[187] *Elmira Daily Advertiser*, November 12, 1866.

[188] "Francis Hall Obituary," *Elmira Semi-Weekly Advertiser*, August 29, 1902.

[189] Ibid.

[190] Towner, *Our County*, p. 639.

sue his interests in book and art collection;[191] and he devoted the remainder of his time to his two chief passions—travel and philanthropy. Hall's wealth provided him with ample leisure for travel, and he seems to have extended the curiosity that took him into the countryside surrounding Elmira and Yokohama to the world at large. It was later said of Hall that he visited more lands than any other nineteenth-century American except Bayard Taylor.[192] In 1892 Ausburn Towner wrote of Hall's travels: "Since 1867 he has traversed well-nigh most of the globe, certainly the most interesting part of it, taking up his journeying year after year in both hemispheres, on every continent, and amidst the isles of the sea."[193] But if he indulge himself in travel, he matched that self-indulgence with charity to others. Hall's philanthropic commitments included the founding of the Steele Memorial Library and the Arnot-Ogden Hospital in Elmira. For twenty-five years he served as a trustee of Elmira College, worked for the board of education, and was active in several of Elmira's churches.[194] One of his final charitable efforts was the construction of the Hall Memorial Library, his gift to the people of Ellington, Connecticut, to commemorate the educational work of his father and brother.[195] It was shortly before the library's completion that Hall died in Elmira on August 26, 1902, at the age of seventy-nine.

In considering Hall's life, one cannot help but wonder how such an individual, and the journal he composed, can have remained unknown for so long. Is it not a sad comment

upon us as American historians of Japan that while we know many of the obscure Restoration heroes on the Japanese side, we know so little about the Americans who were active in nineteenth-century Japan? It seems odd that there is not a single reference to Hall in an American historical study of Japan. Walsh, Hall & Co., America's leading trading house in the treaty port, is equally unknown. This would matter little, if the men and institutions in question were nonentities. But as Hall's writings reveal, this was hardly the case. As America's leading opinion maker on Japan in the 1860s Hall was a man of considerable influence. That his journal has not been published previously, is truly regrettable.

On the other hand, like many other nineteenth-century Americans active in Japan, Hall also allowed his Japan experiences to slip into obscurity. Freed from the financial needs to make Japan part of his professional career, which drove men such as William Elliot Griffis and Lafcadio Hearn, who followed him, Hall returned to his private life. While Japanese observed that Hall and his company set the standard for integrity in the treaty port and consequently earned much respect for the United States and American businessmen, Hall displayed little of Townsend Harris's preoccupation with his image in Japan. Hall simply went on with his life. If there is anything that shines through his Japan years as well as his life in America it is Hall's remarkably even and likable personality. As Thomas K. Beecher noted, "Francis Hall was the best balanced man I ever saw. No one ever saw him angry."[196] Or

---

[191] "Francis Hall Obituary," *Elmira Semi-Weekly Advertiser*, August 29, 1902.

[192] We do not know precisely what happened to Francis Hall's collection of books. While his will indicates a bequest to both the Steele Memorial Library, as well as to the Elmira College Library, there is no evidence in the collections of these libraries that Hall's books became part of their holdings. Hall's will authorized his executors to distribute his "furniture, books, pictures, bronzes, porcelains, art objects and collections and articles of personal use" among his relatives and friends to the sum of $2000 per individual. The records of his estate show that his collection of paintings was sold in New York. In this regard it is worth noting that the two Wirgman paintings now in the Hall Memorial Library

in Ellington, Connecticut, were regarded as being of no particular value and were consequently removed from the New York sale and sent to the library by the executors of his will. See "The Will of Francis Hall" and the "Hall Estate Papers" in the Hall Family Papers, Chemung County Historical Society, Elmira, N.Y.

[193] "Next to Bayard Taylor," the Elmira papers stated, "he was the greatest American traveller, Greenland and Iceland being the only two countries he had not visited" (*Elmira Semi-Weekly Advertiser*, August 29, 1902).

[194] Towner, *Our County*, p. 639.

[195] For a discussion of this library see the *New York Tribune*, June 12, 1903, pt. 2, p. 14.

[196] "Francis Hall Obituary," *Elmira Semi-Weekly Advertiser*, August 29, 1902, p. 5.

as the head of the Syracuse Chilled Plow company put it, "He was a man possessed of uncommonly clear foresight and sound judgement and his intercourse with his associates was at all times cordial and friendly. I know of no instance in the 26 years when a difference of opinion or judgement marred the warm friendship constantly existing between himself and the other members of the company."[197] "Francis Hall," a friend of his summed up at the time of his death, "was a refined, educated, hightoned gentleman, quiet and unobtrusive to a degree, whose desire was to know the whole world, exceedingly fond of literature, art and music—a level headed businessman, generous to his friends and the public alike, of decided opinions but never obtrusive going about doing good in every way."[198] "Through all the years of his residence in Elmira," the writer added, "it may be said of him that he never spoke ill of any man, nor has any man been heard to speak ill of him. When one stops to think of how few men this may be truthfully said, it hardly seems necessary to add further words of praise."[199] Indeed, about how many men can it be said with equanimity, "Everything he has touched he has brightened."

[197] "Francis Hall Obituary," *Elmira Daily Advertiser,* August 29, 1902, p. 5.

[198] "Francis Hall Obituary," *Elmira Semi-Weekly Advertiser,* August 29, 1902, p. 5.

[199] Ibid.

THE JAPAN JOURNAL OF FRANCIS HALL

1859

Tuesday, November 1, 1859

After a passage of eleven days from the lighthouse at the mouth of the Yang-tsi-kiang I arrived in Yokohama bay on the evening of Nov. 1st 1859. It was just past sunset of a misty, rainy evening. The sea and shore was covered with an impenetrable veil of vapor. I left the deck where I had been watching for land and went again below to the cabin to finish letters to send back.

Wednesday, November 2, 1859

A clear and autumnal morning. During yesterday's storm Fusi Yama [Mount Fuji] has received an accession of snow, for it shines white, more lustrous and beautiful than ever in the morning's sheen. Its dazzling cap of white is relieved by a soft-rosy flush of the early sun.

There is a wonderful charm about the superb mountain, quite indescribable. It rises so peerlessly above all surrounding objects, the clouds float so gracefully about its hoary crown, it is so symmetrical of form that I am never weary of beholding it. The look of the country, or as the farmers would say at home, the "lay of the land," as I view it from shipboard is inviting. The shores have a graceful sweep around the waters of the bay. They are gently undulating, the higher grounds alternating with trees and cultivated fields laid out like so many gardens. Kanagawa lies on the north east shore of the bay and Yokohama on the south west. They are apparently about three miles apart; the houses seem to straggle along connecting one with the other. On the Yokohama side, on a prominent and picturesque elevation, are the buildings of the Governor's residence, surrounded with many trees and cultivated fields of regular oblong shape. On the same side, the long row of Custom House buildings and the new stores of the natives and go-downs of the foreign merchants are to be seen. The flags of the American, English, and Dutch Consulates float on the Kanagawa side. Fishermen's huts dot the bay here and there. Clustering like bees amidst their hive we see the workmen engaged in constructing a new fort at Kanagawa.

Soon after breakfast we went ashore at Kanagawa and called upon the American Consul, General Dorr.[1] We found him not far from the landing, living in a temple on the hillside.[2] The building was of a single story in height with the four sided peaked and curved roof such as I had seen in China. It was wholly built of wood and had a thatched roof of two feet thickness. It was perfectly plain in its exterior and by no wise to be compared with the Buddhist temples of Canton. Its situation was fitly chosen on a hilly ridge skirting the main street of Kanagawa. The approach is from the street over a stone walk flanked on either side by houses occupied by the priests. A walk of a few rods leads to a flight of stone steps up the steep hill-

---

[1] The American consul in Yokohama was Eben M. Dorr, a Californian, who was agent for Augustine Heard & Co. of Shanghai. In the nineteenth century, on-site commercial agents were often appointed to consular positions. Dorr was consul in Yokohama from 1859 to 1862. As we shall see, Hall sometimes served as acting consul in Dorr's absence.

[2] The American Consulate was located at the Honga-kuji, a lovely temple that was located on an elevated site in the cleft of hills overlooking the Bay of Yokohama.

side over which hang the branches of the enclosing wood, giving a close shade and a dark atmosphere. On the level ground at the top of the steps is a gate, or propylaeum, consisting of a cross timber resting on two pillars. We found the General at home, and received from him a very cordial welcome to Japan. His apartments were arranged a la Japanese, except that he had placed glass windows in lieu of some of the paper screens. Charcoal fires burning in braziers of brass and copper gave a pleasant warmth. The charcoal is not brought into the rooms until thoroughly ignited so that there is no unpleasant effect from the fumes of carbonic acid gas. The charcoal is used either in its natural state, or it is pounded up and made into balls with rice water. These last can be bought of the size of a large apple at the rate 3000 per $4.

We learned from the Consul that Dr. Hepburn[3] and wife had arrived two weeks since and were also living in a temple where they had ample quarters for us all. This was welcome news when we had looked upon the probability of none, or very poor, quarters. Following the path through the fields among garden-like patches of rice, turnips, and vegetables, we came to Dr. H[epburn]'s temple,[4] passing the British Consulate on our way thither, located in another temple.[5] We received a cordial welcome from Dr. H[epburn] and his lady who had been expecting the entire company of the missionaries ever since their own arrival a fortnight since. We found them in a roomy temple far enough back from the main street to be quiet and retired. The buildings were old and out of repair except such as Dr. H[epburn] had already made.

They were enclosed on three sides by a vigorous growth of trees, evergreens largely, clipped and trained after the favorite manner of the Japanese. Outside of this protecting wall of trees and shrubs were the cultivated fields and gardens of the people.

Dr. and Mrs. H[epburn] were already beginning to feel at home. They had experienced great civility from the people. Mrs. H[epburn] had amusing accounts to give of the curiosity of the Japanese, she being the first female resident of Kanagawa. The temple was besieged by crowds of gazers for the first day or two till their presence was so obtrusive that it became necessary to shut them out of the premises. They were in every room of the house, invading even the sanctity of the bedroom. She could not dress or undress without someone opening the shutters to see the new wonder. In the street she was followed by crowds eager to examine her clothes and without hesitation of turning up the bottom of her dress to explore the underdresses beneath made by hoops and crinoline. Their own mode of dressing being quite the reverse. Their clothing being filled at the top and tapering to a silken under garment at the nether extremities.

It was speedily arranged that we should come ashore at once and rough it as we best might. The Consul had also proffered the hospitality of his house. We returned to the ship to dine and then took a boat to Yokohama and walked through the streets and among the shops. We encountered numerous parties of sailors on leave from the *Powhatan* in pursuit of sake and more questionable gratifications. Two or three were lying dead drunk on the platforms of stores. Officers and men from the

---

[3] Dr. James Curtis Hepburn (1815–1911) arrived in Kanagawa on October 17, 1859, as a missionary for the Board of Foreign Missions of the Presbyterian Church. Hepburn had been a missionary in China from 1841 to 1845. In Japan he became best known for his medical work and for his studies of the Japanese language. He published the first Japanese-English dictionary in 1867, and his system of romanizing Japanese is still widely used today. Hepburn's unusual linguistic gifts gave him a central role in translating the Bible into Japanese. For a biography of Hepburn see William Elliot Griffis, *Hepburn of Japan* (Philadelphia: Westminster Press, 1913).

[4] Hepburn's temple was the Jōbutsuji. Hall photo-

graphed this temple and many years later sent a copy to William Elliot Griffis, who published it in his *Hepburn of Japan*, p. 90. There is a detailed large woodblock print map in the collection of the Yokohama Archives of History that belonged to Duane B. Simmons that pictures the temple among the other buildings of Kanagawa. See Maruya Tokuzo, *Gokaikō Yokohama dai ezu* (Edo: Hōzendō, 1860) in Yokohama Archives of History (cover bears the initials D.B.S.). Simmons marked the Jobutsuji as "My Temple in Kanagawa," and he marked the Jōryūji next door as "Mr. Brown's Temple."

[5] The British consulate was located in the Jōsōji.

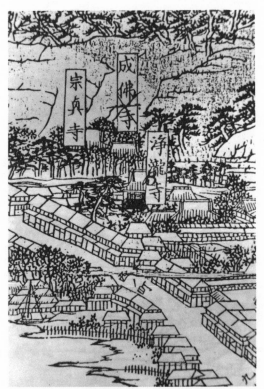

Detail from Sadahide's 1860 map: *Gokaikō Yokohama dai ezu* [Great Map of the Opening of the Port of Yokohama]. Simmons marked the Jōbutsuji, Hepburn's temple, with an (*), writing "My Temple" on his map, and marked the temple next door, the Jōryūji, with a (B) indicating that this was the temple at which the Browns resided.

Powhatan and *Highflyer* were making purchases of the things curious to foreign eyes in which the shore abounded. Prices, we were told, were enhanced by the sudden access of purchasers.

Yokohama had all the newness of a western town or a New England factory village. It has been recently built by the Japanese government to draw thither the foreign population from Kanagawa. Kanagawa is the port mentioned in the treaty. It lies near to Yedo [Edo] and might in truth be called a suburb of Yedo as the houses extend almost uninterruptedly to the Capital. It is [on] the great thoroughfare of travel over which there is a frequent procession of the travelling trains of princes and grandees of the empire, before whom all the common people bow, or rather squat, to the earth as they pass. As foreigners could never pay such obeisance and would be exhibiting a marked contrast to the custom of the people, it is supposed to be the prompting motive of the desire to remove the foreign trade and population to Yokohama, two-miles-and-a-half across the bay to one side [of] the "tokaido," or national highway. Accordingly the government laid out a new town on the Yokohama side. The streets were laid out wide, the stores were new, and merchants brought thither from ruined Shimoda, and other towns, who filled the stores with wares attractive to strangers. The Custom House was built here also. Another portion was allotted for residences, where houses and godowns were built expressly for the traders. That nothing might be wanting to make all this attractive to the representatives of Christendom, directly adjoining the foreign quarter was a street laid out and built up for "tea houses." Hither were assembled scores of girls who led a life to which no shame is attached in this country. There was another advantage over its neighbor possessed by Yokohama viz., a better anchorage. The shipping could lie conveniently near Yokohama, but not within two miles of Kanagawa. These combined inducements had prevailed. At the time of my arrival the only foreign residents of Kanagawa were the American, English, and Dutch consuls. The merchants were all on the Yokohama side, numbering thirty or forty. The Consuls refused to recognize Yokohama as a port. They had recently selected a seaside strip of ground on the Kanagawa side, and thither they were endeavoring to bring over the traders, with what success remains to be seen.

Everywhere we went we heard the salutation "Ohio." The Japanese struck me as a pleasant, affable, good natured people. They were sociable among themselves, laughing and chatting heartily. The dress of the common people was quite as free as their manners. The coolie class were either naked, with the exception of a loin cloth, or wore a long loose cotton robe open all the length in front and which revealed quite as much as it concealed. To this dress others added cotton trousers. The next grade wore petticoat, trousers, and a full loose robe with wide hanging sleeves of cotton or silk material.

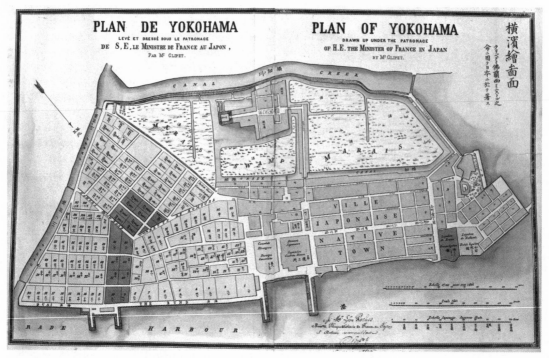

Plan of Yokohama, 1865, showing the lots assigned to the foreign community. Walsh, Hall, & Co. was located at No. 2 on the Bund facing the harbor.

The sleeves served as pockets also, having a few stitches in the looser opening. Some wore one and some two swords according to rank. Their heads were bare, the crown being shaved on the top of the head, the side hair short and combed smartly down, the back hair brought forward, gathered into a little roll of a finger's thickness, stiffened, tied, and curved outwardly. The females wore a loose dress and petticoat. The dress being full in the shoulders and diminishing to their naked feet. The married women were distinguishable by their blackened teeth and plucked eyebrows. The girls had good looking faces, rosy with health and rouge, and whitened with powder.

The stores were under buildings of one and two stories, the fronts being open to the street. The goods were arranged on shelves or stood in boxes on a single platform or series of ascending platforms. The platform that constituted the main floor was spread with mats, fresh and clean. On the mats were squatted the sellers around a brazier of charcoal fire, smoking, talking, or drinking tea. Wherever I stopped, goods were freely shown and I was often invited to a cup of tea, or proffered some eatable like sweetmeats, cakes, or nuts. No Japanese treads on their mats till he has left on the ground his sandals. We Americans were less particular, leaving our footprints wherever we stepped for it was inconvenient to draw off our boots. Each store had, as with us, its own class of merchandise. Silks and spices, goods, lacquered ware, porcelain, provisions, had each their own place.

A shop for the sale of the beautiful little Japanese dogs interested me especially. It was a menagerie on a small scale. In the front sales room were the vivacious little fellows in cages, in a back room a whole pack of them was let loose upon the floor. A long yard in the rear was appropriated to various animals. There were monkeys from the Straits, a black bear, cranes several feet high, and even goats and sheep were caged up as curiosities. There were a variety of birds, the most beautiful of which were the golden and silver pheasants, the latter, with its white plumage bedecked with scallops of silver and the curving plumage of its tail, the most distinguished prisoner of all. The owner of the grounds beckoned me into a small apartment in the yard where was a spread covering some great treasure in natural history, I inferred, from the sly looks and cautious procedure of the showman. The cloth was removed and a box produced looking as if it might be an infant's coffin. The lid was carefully removed, then several thicknesses of cotton wadding and lo here was a mermaid—mummified to be sure, but none the less a mermaid. Fancy the corpse of a beautiful maiden with curling locks of dark hair terminating in a scaly body and bony fin—imagine it for such was not this mermaid.[6] It was the grinning skull of an hideous ape, fleshless and eyeless, an ape's shoulders and breast, clearly joined to a fish body. Here and there were little bits of fur remaining. Antiquity was well counterfeited. The whole thing was a well devised imposture. No seam of the joining of an animal head to a furry body was to be seen. For aught that was apparent to the eye the

nondescript was a veritable production of dame nature. Yokohama although new could boast some stenches of an ancient odor.

Thursday, November 3, 1859

Heavy rain all day, did not leave the ship.

Friday, November 4, 1859

After breakfast went to the Custom House with Mr. B[rown][7] and Dr. S[immons][8] to get a permit to land our effects. The Custom House swarmed with officials. It is a long building of one story, tiled roof, and side wall of papered screens with intervals of plaster. Around it were numerous godowns and storehouses. It faces the sea from which it is separated by a wide street; the grounds are enclosed with a high fence, the court is strewn with coarse gravel and small stones. Stonewalks lead to the main building. At its outside door, on their knees, are menial attendants, who, when accosted by a superior, knock their heads against

[6] Commenting on the prevalence of such "tricks" in Japan, Edward Barrington de Fonblanque writes in *Niphon and Pe-che-li; or Two Years in Japan and Northern China* (London: Saunders, Otley, and Co., 1863), p. 141, "That most candid of charlatans, Mr. Barnum, tells us in his memoirs, that the real genuine mermaid, which he exhibited in his museum at New York to admiring thousands, was obtained from a Yankee ship-captain, who reported having procured it in Japan.

In the course of a shopping tour in Yokuhama, I came across several specimens of the same kind, and I had puzzled over them for a long time, utterly at a loss to reconcile their strange incongruities, partaking, as they did, of man, beast, fowl, and fish, before I discovered, or rather suspected—for discovery required a dissecting process—that this *lusus naturae* was ingeniously manufactured, by the hand of man, out of a composition of paper, pulp, leather, and glue.

The shopkeeper, who dealt principally in livestock, dogs, chickens, singing-birds, etc., did not attempt to deny the ingenious fraud when taxed with it, but assured me that he sold a great many to the Funi-Yaconins (ship-captains), who never doubted his word when he assured them that the nondescripts had been caught in the interior of Japan."

[7] Samuel Robbins Brown (1810–1880) had been one of Hall's fellow passengers on the *Surprise* from New

York. He and Duane B. Simmons had also accompanied Hall to Kanagawa on the *Mary and Louisa*. Brown had served as a missionary to China from 1839 to 1847. After returning to the United States he was sent to Japan in 1859 by the [Dutch] Reformed Board. In Japan he became renowned as a teacher, translator, and missionary. He was a founding member of the Asiatic Society of Japan. He published one of the first guides to the study of Japanese, *Colloquial Japanese* (1863), and played an important role in the translation of the New Testament into Japanese. For a biography see William Elliot Griffis, *A Maker of the New Orient: Samuel Robbins Brown* (New York: Fleming H. Revell Co., 1902).

[8] Duane B. Simmons was sent to Japan as a missionary doctor by the [Dutch] Reformed Board. After a year as a missionary he went into private practice in Yokohama. Simmons was subsequently to make a name for himself as a physician, founder of a major hospital, and legal scholar. In later years he was closely associated with Fukuzawa Yukichi, lived in the Mita compound of Keio University, and devoted himself to research on Japanese feudal villages. Simmons died in Japan in 1889. See *The Japan Weekly Mail*, February 23, 1989, p. 179. Also Ozawa Saburō, "Meiji bunka to dokutoru semenzu," in Osatake Takeshi, ed., *Meiji bunka no shin kenkyū* (Tokyo: Ajia Shobō, 1944), pp. 311–44.

Sadahide's 1860 Print: *Complete Detailed View of Yokohama Honcho and the Mi-yozaki Quarter*. Walsh & Co. (later Walsh, Hall & Co.) was located just below the American flag in the lower right. The lower left shows the Miyozaki Quarter including the Gankiro.

the ground and scarcely dare to lift their eyes while spoken to. Each Japanese that enters knocks off his sandals of straw before touching the scrupulously clean mats that cover the floors of the piazza, the hall in the official rooms. On the right side of the hall was a suite of offices occupied by the officials. On the left was the long room where money is changed, and the general reception room. Crossing the entrance hall beyond these rooms was another hall where the Governor had his rooms. Interpreters in English and Dutch were present. The English interpreters had a very limited knowledge of that language. They could understand our request, which was a very simple one backed up by a note from our Consul. As there was no press of business we expected a speedy reply. To do business promptly is no part of Japanese usage. We waited for an answer and got none. We caught our interpreter and another, and were told it would come immediately. We went out into the street, walked till we were weary, went back and there was the same answer, "very sorry you wait, but the permit will be ready in a few minutes." We did wait from nine o'clock A.M. till one P.M., time enough for every official in the building to

have examined our papers. When it came, the interpreter had the assurance to say that it "had been ready long time but he could not find us." The whole business transaction of the Custom House for these four hours could have been performed by any American of ordinary capacity in a half hour. But in Japan everything is so tied up by routine, and hampered by forms, that the greatest stretch of patience is necessary to do any business with officials. The whole thing was a play at business just such as one should expect of a group of boys "playing store," or girls playing tea parties. The perfection of how not to do it belongs to this empire.

The tedium of our story was relieved by watching the operation of changing Mexican Dollars for Ichibus. As I have said, the money changing department is on the right of the entrance hall. It is a long room one half of which is occupied by a platform raised a couple of feet from the dirt floor of the remaining half. This like all Japanese floors is covered with mats. A half dozen officials are squatted on the mats. Beside them is a block for counting money upon, a pair of scales for weighing, ink box and pens, and a few boxes of coin. There is no other furniture. Standing in a group on the earth floor and confronting them are the merchants and merchant clerks, princes and officers on leave from the men of war, sea-captains and adventurers like myself waiting their turn for receiving ichibus for dollars weight for weight. By treaty it was agreed that the Japanese government should exchange their silver coinage for ours weight for weight. Under the excuse that they were unable to coin silver fast enough, this portion of the treaty has been tardily complied with. At times during the summer it has been impossible to get a single ichibu, at others, only the smallest sums. Until recently, so many dollars per capita were doled out one, two, three, or more as the case might be. Now they have adopted the rule that a prorata distribution should be made on the amount applied for. This would have been very well had not the applicants put in claims for larger amounts than they really needed. So for the last two or three days applications have been made by millions and tens of millions in amount. Day before yesterday they received ten dollars on each million, yesterday an applicant for $15,000,000 received $38. Preposterous as all this was, the Custom House treasurers steadily ciphered away at the percentage to be distributed, an act more creditable to their patience than their business knowledge. They must have believed the foreigners made of money. There was a general strife among the applicants to see who should claim the greatest amount. Millions, quatrillions, sextillions were small figures today. Pages of paper were covered with figures. One enterprising sea-captain, procuring a roll of Japanese paper at least 50 feet long, inscribed it with a row of figures from one end to the other. This day's work ended the matter. Japanese arithmetic was incompetent to this enumeration of the sums wanted, much less to calculate how much each could have of the $2000 to be divided among the whole. I may as well state here that the rule was then adopted that no person should apply for more than $5000 on one day. Under this rule the highest sum paid out for several days was $50 to one person.

Our permit to land was received so late in the day that it was impossible to procure light-ers for the day, and so our landing must be again put off. In the afternoon went to Kanagawa. In walking through the fields met old acquaintances, to wit, the daisy, violet, dandelion, and thistle. Their familiar faces were pleasant to behold in this land so far from where I had been accustomed to meet them.

Saturday, November 5, 1859

A wet day again and cold. Too wet to move our effects. Overcoat and overshoes were decidedly comfortable. Despite the wet, went ashore to Yokohama and took a walk among the shops. Found the active tradesmen affable as ever, took tea and cake with them and made some small purchases. Yokohama has a breadth of three streets only. The one furthest removed from the water is occupied by Shimoda merchants entirely. Wares are sold in this street cheaper than in the front street being less frequented. Beautiful silks were to be had here of eight and ten cents a yard, such as retail at home for 75 cents and $1.00 per yard. Capt. J[ones][9] bought a handsome fat bullock for $10. The merchants live in the rear of their stores. I passed one establishment where three or four females were sitting, and among them a young and well looking girl. The latter smiled most graciously and beckoned me to a seat at her side, the mother seconding the invitation. At another store three children were playing with one of those exquisite little Japanese dogs. To my desire to buy him they replied by expressive gestures that they could not part with him. In the rear of Yokohama are extensive rice fields and swamps, in the midst of which I saw an extensive range of buildings going up, and learned, on inquiring, that they were for the accommodation of the Cyprians who were to be moved thither. It was a perfect place amid the marsh miasmas to plant these greater mansions of society. A solitary sportsman was tramping through the tall reeds and grass of the swamps in pursuit of his game.

The frequency of sake shops is noticeable.

---

[9] Captain Jones was the captain of the *Mary and Louisa*.

They are fully as common as grog shops at home. The liquor which tastes like a cheap whiskey, though less harsh, is said to be very intoxicating. It does not appear to be drunk where sold, but the common laborer, boatmen, etc., have their earthen jug which a single tempo [penny] replenishes. Drunkenness is common, and any day towards night there is no lack of red eyes and faces, rising tongues, and staggering gait. Intemperance in drink, and intemperance in lust, are the national sins of Japan.

The fruits in market are grapes of excellent quality and of delicate flavor, which are sold usually at one ichibu the basket of six or seven pounds, depending upon the quantity of straw in the bottom. Persimmons are abundant, large, and cheap, and of better flavor than the Chinese. The pears, which are apple shaped with a speckled rusty coat, resemble the Chinese but are larger, more juicy, and of better flavor. I see also chestnuts, both large and small, and have bought butternuts, smaller and of milder taste than those of the States. There are other nuts in market new to me. The vegetables I have seen are long turnips of mild flavor, radishes less crisp and tender than our own, onions with a long instead of a bulbous root, Irish potatoes small but good, sweet potatoes hardly equal to New Jersey ones, carrots altogether like our own, and others. No rice can be better than the Japanese. It costs here about one cent per pound, but its exportation is strictly prohibited. Good brown sugar is to be had for 4 cents per pound, and white for twice that sum.

At short intervals along the streets are wooden fire engines. Two tubs like half-barrels stand on the ground full of water, on these stands a third, and on top of that is the engine, a square box which has two pumps worked by a lever, like an engine break. What the pumps are I cannot say, but I suspect that they are made like their hand pumps on the squirt gun principal [sic]. Frequently when I stop in the streets I am surrounded by curious people to whom my clothing is a curiosity, the woolen cloths were particularly. Today I had india rubbers on. These were much noticed and approved by "Yoka," "Yoka" [Great!]. One man determined to know the whole mystery exam-

ined closely my overshoes, then my laced garters minutely, then my pantaloons, and turning up the bottom of them was passing his scientific investigations on my ankles and shin bones when I moved on, not knowing where his thirst for knowledge might lead him. I had with me a folding umbrella. I showed them its operation, which seemed to gratify them very much. Suddenly I saw every man of them dropping on his knees—the Governor was coming. As far as his excellency was visible, his subjects bowed themselves down. He was mounted on a spirited horse and accompanied by a long train of umbrella bearers, sandal bearers, trunk bearers, etc. The train was preceded by an official bearing a rod with metal rings whose jingling gave warning of the coming greatness.

The Japanese are up to the tricks of trade. Today while in a shop with Dr. S[immons] the merchant beckoned him into a backroom and produced a gold idol, an inch high, which he was ready to sell subrosa for quarter its American value in exchange for ichibus. The Dr. paid the price, five ichibus, and afterwards had the satisfaction of learning that his idol was a bronzen divinity. Capt. G.,[10] a few weeks since, purchased a vest pattern, which any man not expert as a silk inspector would have believed an honest fabric. In this instance the material was half paper, most ingeniously counterfeiting the silk worms threads. Capt. G. also says that at Nagasaki stealing had become so common that a Japanese wife refused supper to her husband who had worked all day for foreigners unless he brought home some stolen gains!

Sunday, November 6, 1859

Morning stormy and cold, remained on shipboard ti!l afternoon, then went ashore with Mr. B[rown] and Dr. S[immons] to walk around from Yokohama to Kanagawa. We followed the shore. One of the first sights was a mother conducting her young daughter to town for purposes which her signs made mani-

---

[10] It is not clear who Captain G. was, but it is possible that this was Captain Gaby of the *Azoff*.

fest. The girl looked simple and artless. She was quite young, well dressed and painted and reddened after the custom of the country. It was a pitiful sight to see this young creature going to be sold at the shambles of sin. Not far behind was another girl older and not so handsomely attired. She too was accompanied by her mother who pointed to her daughter as we passed with unmistakable intent. And yet all this is done as a matter of course. Little of shame, or wrong, is attached thereto. Several times during this walk, nods, beckonings, and even words reminded us continually of the natural vice.

The road to Kanagawa is of recent construction. It is a broad causeway, or dike, separating the sea from the low lands beyond, wide enough for carriages to meet and pass. It is raised several feet from the surrounding level and macadamized most of its extent. There are several hundred feet of substantial sea wall and several bridges thoroughly and strongly made. There is a workmanlike finish about them not to have been looked for in this country. They are built across arms of the sea and canals filled by the salt water tides. The face of the country is remarkably uneven. There is a succession of dry hilly ridges of irregular course between which are low marsh lands. Both the valleys and ridges were under systematic cultivation. The land was divided into garden-like plots by rows of grassy turf or embankments. Buckwheat and rice was ripening for the harvest. Some cotton fields were yet unpicked. There was a large growth of turnips, which send long roots down into the light rich soil free from stone or gravel.

After a walk of three miles we came into the main street of Kanagawa. It is the great highway to or from Yedo and the provinces. There is always a throng of business and pleasure travel flowing through. Wherever we passed, the people never ceased staring at us till we were beyond their vision. We passed a blacksmiths shop, before it was a trough of water in which pincers just like our own were cooling. It was an accustomed sight. There were bakeries where were made a thin round cake in shape like ginger snaps. They were cooked in a coal fire in irons like waffles. They are a great article of consumption, and have a pleasant

taste. Numerous tea houses are by the wayside where travellers stop for refreshments and lodgings, they are the hotels of the country. Many of them were large houses looking very cleanly. Sitting on mats within, one could see, as we passed, the girls belonging to the establishments. Some houses had stalls for horses also, and there were other houses of a less inviting aspect, probably of a cheap grade. Occasionally, too, there are sheds by the wayside with seats and tables underneath, where the humblest traveller can rest without charge and be fed at little cost. Shops where rice was pounded were very numerous. The operation is exceedingly simple. The rice is placed in large wooden bowls—trunks of trees hollowed out. A beater, to one end of which a large wooden pestle is attached, is worked at the other end by a man treading upon it, a slow and laborious process. At every tenth shop, I should say, might be seen from one to four naked fellows, save the loin cloth, rising and falling at their work. Passing along the Kanagawa road were numerous travellers on foot and on horseback, often with a train of attendants and baggage carriers.

Called on Dr. and Mrs. Hepburn and returned to the ship. Met on my walk the daisy, dandelion, violet, and thistle.

Monday, November 7, 1859

The day was fine and water smooth. After breakfast a large lighter was alongside to receive our baggage and boxes. A little before noon we had all on board and crossed over to Kanagawa. As all labor and service is a government monopoly, so far as concerns foreigners, we applied for 50 coolies to take our baggage up to the temple. They came after a considerable delay. Most of them were naked except the loin cloth worn as a suspensory bandage. Like all other orientals, they knew but one way of moving such burdens, viz., strength and stupidity. The lighter pieces were carried on their shoulders and the heavier were slung to bamboo poles carried also on the shoulders. They went to their work good naturedly, evidently wondering what all this meant. The ploughs and brooms attracted a great deal of notice. A keg of Epsom salts belonging to Dr. H[epburn] had its head broken in. I took a quantity out on a board and treated the crowd, some like Oliver wanted more, but I preferred not to run the risk of physicking half Kanagawa and being hung for a poisoner. The majority however had the good sense to be satisfied with the first dose. At the landing is a boat house and near it is a tea house. Around them were gathered a band of curious people. They were all eager to learn the American name of everything. People travelling turned aside to see what was going on. Men brought their families. We put all our effects unreservedly into the hands of the carriers, placing no scratch on them. It was a government job, and nothing was missing. By five o'clock all things were stored in our new home and we sat down to our first dinner and meal in Japan. There are four servants Tomy,[11] Kami,[12] Kooni [Kuni], and Kimpatchi, awkward louts as ever served. When Mrs. H[epburn] came she gave them, and ordered them to serve, dinner. The fish came on to the table dripping with oil in which it had been cooked unscaled and uneviscerated. In the evening the 3rd Governor called with interpreter and suite. They spent some time in looking at maps and illustrated books, which appeared to please them most of all. They were exceedingly courteous, profuse in tones and expressions of pleasure. We hear that last evening a Chinaman was killed by a Japanese for some supposed insult. We made up a couple of beds on the floor and took our first night of sleep in the empire of Japan.

Tuesday, November 8, 1859

Went to the ship and thence to Yokohama. Found the Custom House giving out $50 on each $5000 today. Mr. B[rown] bought a vat of handsome light brown sugar for four cents per pound. Went into some iron and copper shops, and find a great variety of household and mechanical utensils. Some well, others poorly, made. Copper is largely used, comparatively as freely as iron with us. Bought some Japanese bread and sponge cake and returned home to a late dinner, where I ate for the first [time] a prawn curry, which is a most palatable dish. The night was noisy with ringing of bells at the temple and the sound of human voices in crowds. Tomorrow is a holyday among the Buddhists.

Wednesday, November 9, 1859

Morning fine, went to Yokohama. On the way across the bay noticed to the north a peculiar smoky haze like a drifting smoke. Found this notice posted up at the Custom House. "Today is Holy day. No change and work." So we took a boat to the *Powhatan* steamer. The cause of the haze was revealed, a rising wind out of the north was drifting down the smoke from Yedo, the sea was getting rough and while we were aboard the *Powhatan* our boatmen became so alarmed that they left us and started for the shore. Fortunately a boat was just going ashore from the *Powhatan*. We had a

---

[11] In his series of articles, "Wanderings in the Orient," that he wrote for the *Elmira Weekly Advertiser* Hall wrote about Tomy [also Tomi], "To-my, Saki loving To-my, is our man of all work. He is poor. To him belongs that common blessing of poverty—a houseful of children; to provide for whom and to keep his own and his wife's saki bottle full also, is difficult. . . . To-my is a very devout man in his way, for he divides his spare coppers with impartial hand between Amida and his appetite for saki" ("Wanderings in the Orient," Number Twelve, *Elmira Weekly Advertiser*, May 5, 1860). Robert Fortune, the botanist who visted Japan in 1860, also remembered Tomi. Noting that he needed a native to assist him in gathering botanical specimens he recalled that Tomi was recommended. Fortune writes, "Tomi had been a kind of pedler, and had wandered up and down the

country for many years. Everybody knew Tomi, and Tomi knew everybody. Latterly he had been in the service of some foreigners at Kanagawa, who gave him a high character for intelligence and activity. But it was rumored that Tomi had, in common, I am sorry to say with many of his countrymen, one serious fault, and that was, he was particularly fond of saki—the wine, or rather whisky, of Japan. It was added, however, that he rarely indulged until the evening and that he was generally to be depended upon during the day. . . . Tomi was now my daily guide all over the country, and I must do him the justice to say he performed his work to my entire satisfaction" (Robert Fortune, *Yedo and Peking* [London: John Murray, 1863], pp. 51–52).

[12] Kami seems to have shared the same weakness for sake and was later dismissed by Mrs. Hepburn.

hard pull back over a rough sea the spray of which gave me a good drenching.

In the afternoon the priest of the temple called. He was a smooth shaven, fat, pleasant faced man hardly fifty years old. He wore a stiff dress of brocade silk with wide flowing sleeves and an undescribable hat, neither mitre, cap, or helmet, but a compound of the three. He was accompanied by a lad who had a suspicious resemblance to him. Perry's expedition and the beautiful plates gave him manifest delight. He was able to recognize the portraits of several there given. After dinner took a walk to a high peak nearby which overlooks all the country and out to sea for many miles. It is used as a lookout station for which purpose a house is built on its summit. The prospect was a beautiful one, especially that of the bay with its picturesque shores, hazy waters, and numerous fishing boats. Found pinks and blue gentians.

Thursday, November 10, 1859

Went to Yokohama. Morning pleasant and warm. Had hardly arrived when there was a cold change. Wind was threatening, so went back to Kanagawa and spent the remainder of the day studying Japanese with our neighbor.

Friday, November 11, 1859

Thermometer 7 A.M. 35°. Hard frost. The day later Indian Summer. Walked to Yokohama. At two iron shops observed cast iron caldrons capable of holding two barrels of water. Between Kanagawa and Yokohama are numerous tea houses. They look clean and inviting. As I passed along the road I saw several girls come out from one of them and take the bridle of two travellers' horses and strive with the force of smiles and other charms to induce them to tarry and rest. So had the old Japanese story tellers said was the custom. At another time I saw two of them take an old shorn monk by either arm and lead him, not unwill-

ing to be led, to a seat on the clean mats. The licentious character of the people was much manifest by unseemly signs and beckonings. As I stopped a moment to look at some novelty I was slapped on the back by a woman whose blackened teeth proclaimed her a wife, at the same time that she said "Yokohama moo-some."[13] This was done as if the most innocent thing in the world was meant.

After dinner took a walk up the Yedo road. There are numerous temples scattered along a little way back from the main street, but they are generally exceedingly humble structures. It was about five o'clock and the bathing houses were active. The doors were open showing inside men and women bathing and drying themselves, or actually scrubbing each other. Although naked, the women were not careless of exposing their whole person. As before, I was struck with the numbers of travellers, some of whom were persons of distinction judging by their retainers. I met one retinue of not less than fifty persons, first came two men with long poles bearing what appeared to be plumes of fine flax, then followed baggage bearers, norimon [palanquin] bearers, a saddled horse and all requisites for the road by day or night. The whole train were neatly clad in blue cotton clothes.

Saturday, November 12, 1859

Thermometer 35° 7 A.M. A warm beautiful day. Passed it in examining contents of trunks, boxes, and my cases of clothing, etc.

Sunday, November 13, 1859

Thermometer 34° 7 A.M. Our coldest morning, passed quietly within our own limits, which are very retired and quiet. The trees that surround our grounds were vocal with the music of birds, of one in particular bearing in size and color some resemblance to our king bird with a note like the robin. Services appropriate to the day were held in our sitting room.

---

[13] *Yokohama musume*, or Yokohama girl, was a term that came to be associated with many of the "ladies" of the houses of pleasure that were part of the Gankiro which Hall describes at a later point in the journal.

While we sat around our fire at evening the tolling of the temple bells deep and sonorous in tone called to mind the evening church bell at home, and I sat looking into the coals lost in home reveries.

Monday, November 14, 1859

Thermometer 38° 7 A.M. Fine day, warm and hazy. Went to the *Canvass Back* after breakfast, thence to Yokohama. Quite out of patience with a Japanese iron worker at the long time wanted to make a chisel and oyster knife. Oysters prove to be excellent and cheap. An ichibu's worth has made a dish at our table for three meals. The oyster is more nearly round than the American oyster, fatter, has a larger heart, requires no salt in cooking and is scarcely inferior to the finest Baltimore oysters. In my walk today I saw a fanning mill like the old pattern in New England. I was informed that the figures on the back and front of Japanese clothing indicate the name of the man's house. I am doubtful of this.

Tuesday, November 15, 1859

Thermometer 64° 7 A.M. Passed the morning in pressing leaves and flowers. Then took a long walk towards Yedo. Kanagawa certainly abounds in a wolfish species of dog and queer looking bobtailed cats. The dogs run and howl at my approach, puss is less timid than cats are wont to be, which shows she is less abused. A species of orange hedge is very common. Stopped on my way at a school. The boys and girls were in separate rooms, the former having a male, the latter a female, teacher. I went into the boys room, there was a general rush to the door when I passed, and when I fairly stopped at the threshold the school was in an uproar. The master, an old gentleman in spectacles (wisdom assumes a sage look in Nippon too), look[ed] hopeless of his power to keep order. The boys were sitting on benches behind desks, but now they were on top of benches and desks, wondering at the stranger. They had been writing, and like all young copy book urchins they were smeared with ink. Hands

were black and faces were besmirched. There was no use in school keeping as long as I remained, and I left. The old school master took the whole with a pleased face, but Madame, who had come in to look after some of her girls that had their share of curiosity, frowningly sent them back and soon inclined to frown at me, but as I fear no school marm sans spectacles I smiled, the school marm smiled, then we both smiled, till her stained teeth gave her mouth the look of an ebony knot hole.

The roadside inns were frequent. An ordinary traveller can get a supper of fish and rice, lodging, and breakfast like his supper for four tempos or eight cents. On a summer's day, I imagine, the airy rooms and clean mats truly show an inviting look. The beggars were numerous and troublesome with importunity. They are a most degraded looking lot of outcasts. A few seemed beggars from disease, but the most appeared to be professional beggars. They had a sinister expression of countenance, their hair was cut short to about a half inch in length, their clothing and whole appearance filthy beyond measure. Many boys were among them. One dreadful diseased old man had a little kennel by the way side, his needs were too visible to be fictitious. A man and two boys dressed in finery like our Indians wearing a headdress with plumes were wandering from house to house. The nature of their occupation I did not learn, for I was so much more of a curiosity than they that their occupation, whatever it was, [was] gone. A cluster of boys arrived, an itinerant attracted my attention. The man carried a small assortment of candies and cakes. He had also a wheel, a foot or so in diameter, with lines radiating from the center to the circumference, dividing it into sections. A sort of teetotum was spun around this wheel and wherever it stopped some article was indicated of his wares. A boy put down his single cash, round went the teetotum and he was the winner of a stick of dirty looking candy. Another urchin, who did not appear to have confidence in his luck, purchased outright, and got for the same money four times as much. So it was evident the first boy was a loser. I noticed many young men among the travellers. Sometimes a mother and her neat looking daughter. Then some old soul of a fellow would come along in a chair. I met many such men having a most remarkably worn out, dissipated look. Women were frequently to be seen travelling alone by chair.

There is a ferry from Kanagawa to Yokohama under government care. A tea house stands at the ferry. The price of ferriage to Kanagawa, two miles, is 50 cents. Each ferry boat carries a flag furnished at the toll house. I saw that most appeared to pay by tickets. Labor is very cheap, a house carpenter gets 300 cash a day. Dr. S[immons] went to Yedo today.

Wednesday, November 16, 1859

Morning warm and pleasant. Went to Yokohama in the afternoon. Visited the theater. It is a rough building thrown hastily together. The people were assembling for the evening play and I stepped in. It was a veritable theater. There was the stage and its curtain, the gallery, and all the seat arrangements of a metropolitan theater. The part corresponding to the pit was divided off by bamboo poles into squares capable of holding a half dozen persons. Behind this were two or three rows of raised seats with high backs, answering for the boxes. A large audience were in waiting. Refreshments were handed round, and families had brought their teapot and eatables with them and were making their evening meal. Others were smoking. The galleries were filling up, and like theater galleries at home, were frequented by the fair and frail. I did not stop to see the play as I wished, for it was growing dusk and I had yet the bay to cross to reach home. This evening the carpenter at work on the repairs to our temple brought a shinjo, a present, as is customary with the Japanese. It consisted of crisp cakes made of rice, pleasant to the taste. They were contained in a neat box. To the outside was fastened a bit of dried fish in paper which always accompanies every

gift. While at Yokohama I met a priest, or doctor, who has been at work preparing Dr. H[epburn]'s house. He had been paid off this morning and had evidently come to Yokohama for a good time, for he was very merry with sake and familiar. Dr. H[epburn] moved into his new quarters today.

Thursday, November 17, 1859

Morning warm and cloudy. Towards night rainy. Called at the *Mary and Louisa* for Mrs. J[ones][14] and went to Yokohama shopping. The Japanese are annoying by doing many things in public which are better done in private. Purchased scarfs and porcelain ware. Took tea in the upper room of a silk house and saw many cheap and beautiful fabrics. At one crockery store Mrs. J[ones] was taken into a backroom and treated to tea, cake, and sweetmeats, the portion not eaten was put in a box and presented to her as usual. She attracted great attention from the natives wherever she went. When she first reached Japan she was a great object of curiosity. To the natives it was a wonder how she could wear so many clothes in hot weather and when she stopped in the store they would fan her. They did not comprehend the mysteries of crinoline. Crossing the bay in the morning my boat was surrounded by a large black duck, the fishermen were also very busy with their nets. The government forbids any further exportation of copper under the pretense that the emperor needs it to rebuild his palace which was burned last Saturday evening.

In my absence learned that the Mayor of Kanagawa[15] had called upon Dr. H[epburn] and had demanded his Chinese books. Dr. H[epburn] refused and said he would consult the Consul. Mrs. H[epburn] had in the forenoon unpacked some pictures among which was a crucifixion. They were in her bedroom,

[14] This was apparently the wife of Captain Jones of the *Mary and Louisa*.

[15] This was the governor not mayor. Joseph Heco reports that the two governors, Sakai Oki-no-Kami and Mizuno Chikugo-no-Kami were removed from Yokohama at the end of August 1859 in response to Russian

demands following the death of two Russian sailors. The governor at this time was Shimmi Buzen-no-Kami Masaoki who served in this capacity until his departure for the United States on February 13, 1860, as head of the Tokugawa shogunate's mission sent to exchange ratifications of the 1858 treaty.

and this one was placed behind the rest face to the wall. The officials walked into the bedroom, without waiting for an invitation, and began examining the pictures. One of them spied this and turned the face around, and lo, there was the cross hated of the Japanese, trampled by them under foot, and the religion it had symbolized by them overwhelmed in blood. Their curiosity was greatly excited. "Who is it?" said the Governor. "Jesus Christ" was the reply. Ques. "Who killed him?" Ans. "The Jewish Rulers." Ques. "Why did they put him to death." Ans. "Because he rebuked them for their sins." Ques. "Who are these on either side." Ans. "They are two thieves." Ques. "Why were they put to death at the same time." Ans. "To humble and dishonor Jesus the more." There were other questions and answers of similar import. When Dr. H[epburn] handed the Mayor one of the Gospels printed in Chinese and said "that would tell him all about Jesus," the Governor said they only wished to take his Chinese books to the Custom House to examine them and would return them. Dr. H[epburn] was steady in his refusal. The Governor and suite left. He was polite and courteous throughout. Dr. H[epburn] at once informed the Consul, who upheld him in his refusal.[16] About noon a slight shock of an earthquake was experienced.

Friday, November 18, 1859

Went to Yokohama to make purchases for Gerny and Ranlett.[17] Day cloudy but without rain. Spent all the day trafficking.

Saturday, November 19, 1859

Went off to the *Canvass Back* to breakfast with Capt. Clark.[18] Found him a very agreeable acquaintance. He is from Baltimore. Went again to Yokohama to complete yesterdays transactions. Loaned $200 to Capt. Jones to be used to our mutual advantage. Many Dutch trinkets are sold as Japanese. Yangaro, who has been indefatigable in his attentions to us, and is, I think, a government spy, is charged by the carpenter who did Dr. H[epburn]'s work as having levied blackmail on him for se-

[16] J. C. Hepburn wrote to Walter Lowrie on November 22, 1859, "There was another incident [that] occurred at this inst. which quite startled me and which I felt at first disposed to regret exceedingly. Some friends in New York had presented us with a set of pictures of Bible scenes, of large size, color and put in gilt frames—my wife had that morning, had them unpacked, and they were standing in our chamber, just by the door of the room where we were entertaining the Japanese officers. Whilst I was busy showing some of them the wonders of the microscope, others had got into the chamber, and were admiring the pictures. They turned to one that greatly attracted their attention and soon they all gathered round it. It was the picture of Christ crucified between the two thieves. I was for the moment much taken aback knowing their prejudices & hatred of the cross. I however endeavoured to make the best of it and answered as well as I could, through the interpreter, all their questions as who Jesus was?—who killed him? why they did so? who those were that were crucified with him? I had thus an opportunity of telling them some things about Jesus and of the reasons of His coming into the world and dying to save men. They said little to each other and seemed rather bewildered. As I said above. I was disposed greatly to regret this event fearing they might take us for Romanists & Jesuits (Perhaps they may think so of us. Time alone can disabuse them of this notion and teach them to distinguish between true and false Christianity) but when I reflect on all the circumstances of this incident I see so plainly the hand of Providence in it, that I must believe that God has some wise and good intention in it. The picture, however, we have laid aside, as well because I think it offensive to good taste as from motives of policy." Quoted in M. Takaya, ed., *The Letters of Dr. J. C. Hepburn* (Tokyo: Toshin Shobo, 1955), pp. 25–26.

[17] Gerny's identity is not known; Ranlett was Captain Ranlett of the American Clipper ship, *Surprise*, which had taken Hall to China. See Ausburn Towner, *Our County and its People. A History of the Valley and County of Chemung* (Syracuse: D. Mason & Co., 1892), p. 636; also Carl C. Cutler, *The Story of the American Clipper Ship: Greyhounds of the Sea* (New York: Halcyon Press, 1930), pp. 158, 337–40, 414. George Henry Preble refers to him as the "renowned Captain Charles A. Ranlett," in *The Opening of Japan: A Diary of Discovery in the Far East, 1853–1856*, ed. Boleslaw Szczesniak (Norman: University of Oklahoma Press, 1962), p. 375.

[18] John M. Brooke in his diary referred to a Capt. Clarke of the *Canvasback*. See George M. Brooke, Jr., ed., *John M. Brooke's Pacific Cruise and Japanese Adventure, 1858–1860* (Honolulu: University of Hawaii Press, 1986), p. 178.

curing the job. The Dutch Consul was aroused last night by someone attempting to enter his room by sliding one of the screens. He had no weapon, but went to a hand organ standing in the room and began to grind out the music. The burglar very properly refused to listen to such music and left. Why should Italy be any longer oppressed since she is so fully armed with this formidable weapon, which her sons know so well how to use.

Sunday, November 20, 1859

A delightful morning of bright sunshine and soft air. Birds singing on the branches, the fearless crows cawing in the tall trees, the doves sunning their quakery dress on the temple eaves, roses and camellias in bloom. A pleasant day throughout. Service was held at Dr. H[epburn]'s by Rev. Mr. Brown being the first service of the protestant mission. Twelve persons were present, including 2 ladies. Yangaro planted himself on the steps watching what was going on.

Monday, November 21, 1859

Cloudy and cold. Went to the *Mary and Louisa*, loaned Capt. Jones $50 more. Returned and breakfasted at Dorr's, where I gathered some ten flowers for pressing. Rainy afternoon and evening.

Tuesday, November 22, 1859

Morning at home, at noon went to the *Mary and Louisa*, then went over to the *Banson Brek*[19] which was discharging coal vats, a large vessel belonging to the emperor, a gift of the Prince of Satsuma. She was a great unwieldy tub of an affair built after some antiquated Dutch model

and could carry, I should think, two thousand tons. Called on the British Consul in the afternoon. While there the Governor of Yokohama came to dine accompanied by his suite and a large train of attendants. Took a walk back into the field at evening. The people were busy harvesting rice, which was growing in great abundance. The winnowing was done in this way, by a fanning mill like the old fashioned ones still in use in many parts of the United States,[20] and by a pair of fans made of bamboo covered with paper, a split bamboo forming the handle and giving a back spring like a pair of sheep shears.

Wednesday, November 23, 1859

Looking out from the dining room windows this morning at Dr. H[epburn]'s I saw what I had often seen before, a woman putting fresh flowers before the graves in the adjoining cemetery and burning incense sticks. All the temples so far as I have seen have grave yards attached, the graves being thickly together and having monuments of thick flat or square stones standing on a pedestal. Some of the stones are covered with inscriptions, all have something on them. A place is hollowed out in the pedestal into which fresh water is frequently poured. Often a separate stone is placed for this. Fresh flowers are continually brought and green twigs. Chrysanthemums and camellias seem to be more commonly used. The poor of the Japanese are buried. The richer are burned and their ashes deposited in the ground. In burials the body, after being washed and the head being wholly shaved, is placed in a sitting position in a coffin. Into this coffin are placed a few cash for expenses, perhaps a pipe and tobacco, and little rice and the favorite trinket of the deceased, gifts from friends, which are to give him a good setting out for his long journey.

---

[19] This may have been the *Yakkan-maru*, the "old hulk," that Joseph Heco says was sent by the Japanese government to store the coal for the U.S. steamer *Powhatan*, that was to take the Bakufu's 1860 mission to the United States. See Joseph Heco, *Narrative of a Japanese* (San Francisco: American-Japanese Publishing Association, n.d.), vol. 1, p. 236.

[20] For a contemporary photograph depicting this procedure see Yokohama Kaikō Shiryō Kan, eds., *F. Beato bakumatsu nihon shashin shū* (Yokohama: Yokohama Kaikō Shiryō Kan, 1987), p. 148.

Winnowing rice with a pair of fans made of bamboo covered with paper. Photograph by Felice Beato.

These customs remind one strongly of the burial customs of the North American Indians.

Dr. H[epburn] had today an application from a man who wished to learn English but who was so afraid of the government's unwillingness that he proposed to come as a servant. We bought a quarter of beef of the *Mary and Louisa*. Tomy shouldered it at the landing, and after he got it to the house cut off a slice secretly. The Japanese are fond enough of animal food when they can get it, I suspect. Workmen have commenced repairs today on our temple. Went to Yokohama and had a rough passage back in a little boat. We were in the trough of the sea and danced about most fearfully. I was drenched to the skin. It was a dangerous sail. A boatload of twelve Japanese are said to have lost their lives by being swamped.

Thursday, November 24, 1859

Breakfasted at Dorr's after a farewell trip to the *Mary and Louisa*. At Yokohama in one of the stores I found a group of new merchants anxious to learn English words, especially the salutations and simple words that they could use in their trading. So I squatted on the mat with them and gave them an hour's tuition. Our double consonants trouble them very much, a sound like "th" and even the sound of "h" alone it was difficult for them to get hold of—l and s are almost identical with them. The second syllable of their alphabet (ro) they pronounce with a peculiar combination of the letters d.l.r.; it is neither one of them alone, nor is it all combined together. It is almost impossible, or perhaps quite, for our organs rightly to understand the sound. Sat up late tonight preparing letters for the *Carthage*. Concluded to write home for my funds. Thanksgiving day at home and have had many thoughts of friends far away.

Friday, November 25, 1859

Busy all morning with letters again. Took a row over to Yokohama to exchange ichibus. We met there a German Jew[21] who will furnish one with kobangs [gold coins]. I went to his

---

[21] Hall later refers to him as the Jew K. This may have been L. Kniffler, whose firm Kniffler and Co. is listed in *The China Directory for 1863* (Hong Kong: Shortrede & Co., 1863), p. 55.

house. He had rented a house among the Japanese, had two servants whom he paid $4 a month for service and furnishing the table. He had sent to Yedo and hired a mistress for $33 per month. I accidentally saw her and he told me when it was no longer of any use to make concealment. She was like most of the Japanese women, of small stature, was about nineteen years old, rather plain looking. She was amusing herself with books, colors, and music. Gave my merchant scholars another lesson. In the evening went off to the *Carthage* with Mr. and Mrs. H[epburn]. Our boatmen were full of salt and sake and made indecent gestures. The intemperance and licentiousness of this people is immeasurable.

Saturday, November 26, 1859

To Yokohama for ichibus and kobangs. $45 changed yesterday and today. Obtained fifty kobangs of the Jew. Shopping in the streets, I stopped at a store where was a man, wife, and wife's sister in attendance. Stores and houses are all together. Very commonly in some of the front shops there is another room in which are kept articles of a choicer description, especially such as Europeans and Americans would be apt to buy. I was invited into the back room to look at some browns and cornelians. Then the old gentleman cautiously opened a drawer and brought out some kobangs. These I did not buy as he asked too much. The wife was present, a laughing, talking lady telling me how cheap her husband was offering his wares to me. She handed me a silk Japanese coat to put on, which I did. She declared I would make a good Japanese. So I have been told before and do not feel at all flattered thereby.

I was about to go when the old gentleman reached to the top of a case of drawers and took down ten boxes carefully wrapped up. He undid them and out of each box took three books full of vile pictures executed in the best style of Japanese art, accompanied with letter press. We were alone in the room, the man, wife, and myself. He opened the books at the

pictures, and the wife sat down with us and began to "tell me" what beautiful books they were. This was done apparently without a thought of anything low or degrading commensurate with the transaction. I presume I was the only one whose modesty could have been possibly shocked. This is a fair sample of the blunted sense and degraded position of the Japanese as to the ordinary decencies of life. These books abound and are shamelessly exhibited. The official that comes into your house will pull perhaps an indecent print from his pocket. I have known this to be done.

I walked back from Yokohama as the sea was again very rough. Two Japanese were tried today by the authorities in presence of the English Consul for entering a foreigner's house and stealing 1500 ichibus ($500). They were found guilty and condemned to death. The Consul endeavored to have a milder punishment inflicted, but no, such was the penalty under their laws and it must be paid.

Sunday, November 27, 1859

Thermometer 34° 7 A.M. Morning cloudy, day cold and commenced raining early in the afternoon. Rev. Mr. B[rown] held service in Dr. H[epburn]'s rooms at 12 N. The only strangers present were our Consul, Capt. Clark, and Judge Cleary of California, now naval store keeper at Shanghai.[22] At 11 A.M. there was a slight shock of an earthquake lasting a moment. The *Hellespont* steamer came in and brought letters from Shanghai but none from home. Rain very heavy in the evening.

Monday, November 28, 1859

Morning cold and cloudy. After breakfast went to Yokohama to exchange coin. The storm of yesterday has covered with snow nearly all the visible portions of Fusi, and crested with white the peaks of the neighboring ranges. The merchants of Yokohama report that they are obliged by their government

[22] John M. Brooke simply refers to him as "Mr. Cleary, Naval Storekeeper at Shanghae." See Brooke,

John M. Brooke's Pacific Cruise and Japanese Adventure, 1858–1860, p. 177.

to report all things bought of or sold to foreigners. In the afternoon went with Mr.
B[rown] to Yangaro's home. His wife was there
with plucked eyebrows and blackened teeth as
becomes wives in Nippon. Her house keeping
was a credit to her. Every room was remarkably neat. Holland itself could not show a
neater cottage. The ground around the house
was equally neat. Saw the fleur de lis blooming.
Saw also a pile of stones which once belonged
to an edifice that had been overthrown by an
earthquake. We saw in the house a beautiful
finished musical instrument like one we saw
among the Chinese made of two similar sets of
bamboo reeds fitted into a bowl shaped piece
of ebony, silver mounted. It was a handsome
piece of workmanship, valued by its owner at
$67. He had also several bamboo flutes, a hol-
low section of bamboo nearly two feet long
with 4 finger holes on each side and one on
the opposite side. Instead of an embouchure
the player blows into the open end. It was difficult for me to understand how the tone could
be produced when using so large an orifice. Its
sounds were soft and flutelike. He then went
to a drawer and brought something which he
said was very valuable, and suiting the action
to the end, placed in my hands three or four
of very obscene pictures. His wife stood close
by and it was apparent from the demeanor of
both that there was not a shadow of suspicion
in their minds of the immodesty of the act or
of the pictures themselves. They had shown
them as something really very choice and
worth looking at and preserved them with
great care. They brought us some refreshments consisting of cold roasted sweet potatoes, a lime and persimmons, with hot water in
teacups for drinking.

We are told today that Fusi Yama is worshipped, and that all the mountains have their
appropriate gods. Received a line from Dr.
S[immons] in the evening. Minister Harris ob-

jects to persons applying for ichibus in quantities of $5000 as is customary. He also advises
that we should not go out after dark. We shall
take all his advice at its proper valuation, for
we are not without reason for believing that he
is not always competent to give advice.

Tuesday, November 29, 1859

Morning cool. Day warm and clear. After
breakfast took a walk to the Yedo road and as
usual were annoyed by beggars. See fine turnips in the market, also carrots, some of the
latter measured 30 inches in length. Yesterday
I saw a lot of turnips which averaged two feet
in length and some measured 26 inches. At
frequent intervals, intervals so frequent as to
be astonishing, casks are sunk along the side of
the great highway, which are used as urinals.
They are emptied of their contents so often
that little or no effluvium from their contents
is experienced by passers by. The highway is
kept very neat, swept regularly at least once a
day, and from the porous nature of the soil
water does not stand long. I saw at Loureiro's[23]
some beautiful Japanese clocks. A spring was
the motion pauser. I hear that at Yedo watches
can be neatly repaired. Also that saddles are
made after the American pattern, and a great
variety of glass made. Despite the very common neatness of houses and frequent bathing,
the Japanese are said to be inflicted with a certain insect about the head which grows to an
enormous size, large as mosquito! At all events
K., the Jew,[24] complains that his mistress has
brought them abundantly to his house.
Blekman[25] reports another earthquake last
night.

[23] Jose Loureiro, Portuguese and French consul and
member of Dent & Co. See Fortune, *Yedo and Peking*, p.
40. Fortune refers to him as "an old friend of mine, Mr.
Jose Loureira [*sic*], the manager of Messrs. Dent and
Co., of China, who was also consul for Portugal and
France." Fortune met him in Yokohama in 1860.

[24] See footnote 21.

[25] Blekman [sometimes spelled Bleckman] was secretary and interpreter of the French legation. See *The
China Directory* (Hong Kong: Shortrede & Co., 1863), p.
55. See also, Meron Medzini, *French Policy in Japan During the Closing Years of the Tokugawa Regime* (Cambridge,
Mass.: Harvard University Press, 1971), p. 31.

Wednesday, November 30, 1859

To Yokohama, cloudy day and cool. Two or three shops have been closed by the authorities for selling more goods than the government wished to restrict them to, and for dealing in kobangs. These are plain violations of both letter and spirit of the treaty, which permitted free trade unmolested by official interference. Oranges are abundant in market today. I could buy a box of them holding a half bushel for an ichibu. Persimmons are also very abundant. The supply of grapes is unabated at an ichibu the basket of six or seven pounds.

Thursday, December 1, 1859

Heavy rain all the morning ending about noon with a thunder shower. Afterward clear and warm. Went to Yokohama. Find two more stores closed in Shimoda street, among them my acquaintance of book notoriety. Our Consul and Minister protest against these treaty obstructions of trade. The carpenter at work on the temple has today spent a good deal of time in our room talking over Japanese affairs. He says that near Miaco are hills whose sands are so strewn with gold that the sandals of the people are shining with the adhering metal. If any dares to dig, or carry away, the gold, which belongs to the Spiritual Emperor,[26] his hand would be paralyzed. He states that the Japanese believe that all mankind sprang from one pair. He was very curious to learn about the world. He thought Japan was a country exactly square. My musical box astonished him greatly, and when I made him put his fingers in his ears and then rested one end of a cane on the lid and the other against his teeth, his wonder was very great that he could hear better with his teeth than with his ears!

Friday, December 2, 1859

Morning cloudy and cold. Went off to the *Canvass Back* to breakfast and then to Yokohama. Morning still, wind began to rise early, and when I returned at 10 A.M. a fresh breeze was blowing and the bay was rough, wind increased till sunset and then subsided. Contracted with the carpenter for furniture. When out early I always meet many fish sellers. They carry suspended on a bamboo pole shallow baskets or tubs, three, four, or more resting one on the other. Later in the day I see these baskets washed and drying in the sun. Travellers hurry along the road, their faces tied up, a servant follows carrying baggage. My india rubber heads astonish Tomy.

Saturday, December 3, 1859

Fine clear warm day till 3 P.M., then cloudy and colder. Went to Yokohama. I learn that the Shimoda family man, wife, girl, even servant are in jail. I have seen lately wild boars in the market. Gen. D[orr] furnished some for our table. It is stronger in taste than our fed pork and I think decidedly inferior.

Sunday, December 4, 1859

Morning warm followed by a cold change. Sabbath service as usual. Only two strangers present, Gen. D[orr] and friend. In the afternoon had a pleasant walk back into the country. The rice is now mostly harvested and all the other fields are covered with crops of vegetables. Peas are four to six inches high, wheat is very thrifty and a few inches above ground, turnips are of all sizes from the first out of the ground to the full grown root. Walked toward cottages pleasantly situated in a copse on the hill side. The shears used to trim the thatched roofs in shape of blade and handles are identical with our own shears. Last night fired on

[26] In speaking of the "Spiritual Emperor" Hall is referring here to the Imperial House in Kyoto. Hall also uses the term Mikado to refer to the Emperor in Kyoto. Like other Westerners in nineteenth-century Japan Hall often refers to the Tokugawa shogun as the "Emperor," and to his government as the "imperial government." On occasion he also refers to the the shogun as the Tycoon.

the dogs that prowl around the house, wounding one.

Monday, December 5, 1859

Thermometer at sunrise stood at 29°. Water and ground frozen. At one P.M. it had risen to 49°. A strong S.W. wind blew all day, chilly and cold. Notwithstanding the temperature, many of the Japanese had no covering over the lower parts of their bodies except the insufficient one of their long surtout like robe. A norimon bearer might occasionally be seen with no clothing at all beyond his "T" bandage. Went to Yokohama to do some trading. Merchants more than usually cautious, took tea and cake with them. Dr. S[immons] returned from Yedo today. He speaks of Yedo, a city full of trees as though built in a forest, temples are very numerous and with their spacious grounds occupy a large portion of the city. The grounds of the Daimios, or Princes of the Empire, are also very spacious and cleanly kept. [They] themselves are very hostile in their feelings towards all foreigners, not unfrequently, half unsheathing their swords, while the lower people throw stones and use the opprobrious epithet of *tojin baka*, a foreign fool. The general account I get of Yedo is that it is an immense city of wide streets, humble houses, spacious temple grounds and ordinary temple structures, extensive grounds of the resident princes and much ornament of trees and shades. It is magnificent only in sin. The grounds of the Emperor's Palace, lately burned, are six miles in diameter. I saw at Yokohama today another evidence of the depraved taste of this people, being some beautiful porcelain saucers ornamented with the vilest pictures. In further illustration of this Dr. S[immons] mentions the masks and children's toys which he saw at Yedo.

Tuesday, December 6, 1859

Cold S.W. wind prevailing all day. To *Canvass Back* to put Ranlett's goods aboard. Catechized Tomi all the evening in the language. The faithful old fellow gaped and yawned and drank water, enjoying the importance it gave

him evidently, while at the same time the place of a schoolmaster was hard for him to sustain. He told me that the place at Yokohama, which I supposed was the property of the Governor, was the residence of one of the Daimios. And also that the grounds between us and the American Consulate belonged to Oki no Kami and told us how he lived at Yedo and kept his servants here and wore two swords. I told him I was *Barrytown no Kami*, "Prince Barrytown," and wore a pistol showing him my revolvers.

Wednesday, December 7, 1859

Fair, wind blowing so violently that it was difficult to cross the bay and did not attempt it. We have today another evidence of the unfriendliness of the government by the Governor's refusal to let S[immons] have the temple which he had engaged before going to Yedo. Mistakes of beginners in a new language are always amusing. For instance at breakfast this morning S[immons] wishing the servant to bring him a tumbler of water requested him to bring him a house, while B[rown] wishing to know if all of certain fields belonged to the Prince of Oki inquired if *all heaven* belonged to him! Mrs. H[epburn] was sick and was unable to superintend our breakfast, so Dr. H[epburn] and myself undertook to look after the cooking. We tried to cook a steak by frying. There was a lack of fat to fry it in, and we concluded to put a little water with the dish. Kooni tried to make some hot rolls, such flat heavy affairs were never before seen. Kooni looked at them, and only said "mooshi kashi" [muzukashii], "difficult." However, with the aid of our Japanese boys, we managed to get a passable steak and some eggs made, breakfast enough for anybody.

In the afternoon I had the honor of a visit from Tomy, Tomy's mother, Tomy's wife, Tomy's daughter, and one or two more beside. I showed them all my curiosities, played for them on the flute, but the little music box was the greatest wonder of all. I treated them to persimmon figs, and never were simple people more delighted. And while sitting around our fire at night, grateful Tomy came in with a pot of Nippon tea. I sent for hot water and gave the faithful old fellow a hot sling as an "American *tea* good for the backbone." He ran for his teacup poured out a cup full from the tumbler, which he did not know how to use, took two or three swallows. His very eyes snapped as he uttered the ejaculation "mai," which is expressive of pleasant taste. Such a beverage had never crossed his lips before, I dared say.

Thursday, December 8, 1859

Morning cold and water frozen. Read papers from home. Spent a part of the day at Yokohama assisting Mrs. H[epburn] to make purchases. Hired a body servant for eight ichibus or $2.07 per month.

Friday, December 9, 1859

Spent all the day at Yokohama assisting Mrs. H[epburn] to make purchases. Much annoyed by the crowds that perpetually followed us. While trading at one store Mrs. H[epburn] standing with her back to the crowd, one of them turned up her dress a foot or so. I turned around just in time to boot the man, who looked up as much as to say "what did you do that for." At a crockery store the merchant, wishing to entertain us, stopped a strolling company of gymnasts in the street. The performers were three young boys. They were dressed in loose trousers and coat all in one garment as our boys are dressed at home. On their heads they wore a false head with more a general shape of a dogs head. This was surmounted by a plume and a veil fell down before their faces. Their feats were the usual tumbling exploits of the circus, somersaults, etc., in which they displayed a great deal of skill and agility. The boys were from six to eight years old and were accompanied by a man who, during the performances, beat a tambourine with a stick. I had a hurried glimpse of the Fire Department of Yokohama in procession. It was evidently a procession of the officers only. They were dressed in fancy robes of large black and white plaids. Their engines were borne in procession. They consist of a square box capable of holding a half barrel of water in which a lifting pump is worked by a brake sufficient for one man on a side. Its

power and efficiency is very small. The usual position of the engine is resting in a tub of water of half barrel capacity which in turn rests on two others. These are placed at short intervals along the street ready for use.

Saturday, December 10, 1859

Yokohama is gay today with lanterns. They are hung before every store and each corner is surmounted with an umbrella, covered with gay figures, to each rib of which a long slip of bamboo is fastened covered with gaily colored papers. The streets are full of people. It is a great sacrificial day among the Buddhists. On my return home I purchased a brazier and ordered it sent to the house. Instead of the brazier, in the evening the merchant came to say that he dare not send the brazier lest the Governor should cut his head off. This is the common story since the burning of the emperor's [shogun's] palace. Anything made of brass or copper the merchants fear to sell. The brazier in question was bronze, and I directed my servant to go back with the merchant and bring the brazier, which he did. The fuel for the braziers is either charcoal, or charcoal pounded and made into a round ball with an admixture of clay and rice water.

While writing tonight my attention was attracted by the chanting of a prayer in the adjoining graveyard. I went to the window and saw a burial by moonlight and the light of lanterns. The old woman died yesterday while saying her prayers. She was 82 years old. Tonight they were interring the body. Her companion, the old priest, was muttering prayers over the grave which the workmen were now filling up, and several nuns robed in white silk with white hoods on their heads were standing by. N.B. See next day.

Sunday, December 11, 1859

Another beautiful Sabbath day after a frosty night. The birds are still singing merrily in the trees, the rosebush in the hedge is red with buds, the camellia buds, too, on the tree near the house are bursting out with beauty. The chrysanthemums are gone in our garden, though in my neighbor's they are still plenty. Service at 12 M. by Mr. B[rown]. None but ourselves present, except Henderson the invalid sailor from Dorr's. I was mistaken last evening in supposing the burial I saw to be that of the old nun. It was Kimpatchi's (our former servant's) father. The white robed nuns were the family mourners, white, as with the Chinese, being the mourning color. The old nun was buried today. Tomy had told us while at dinner that we should see the procession pass through the old grave yard. The old fellow has been very officious all day long in his attention to the priestly family that are bereaved. I have heard his loud voice as he bustled in and out of their little cottage. When we rose from the table we went to the door and heard the monotonous tones of the praying priest and the incessant ding dong of the little bell. But above the sound of prayer and the tinkling bell was old Tomy's voice as he marched first out of the house to drive the boys out of the compound, or the sheep into their pen, and then back in again to superintend the last offices of the departed. The house of mourning was inside the compound. Again bareheaded Tomy passed his head out of the priest's gate shouting *achira, achira, miroo watakusidomo yukeri*, "there yonder look are we going." We returned into the house and went to the windows overlooking the old grave yard, and there we saw the procession emerging from a wicket gate that opened through an evergreen bordered path into the grave yard. Tomy was at the head marching along with conscious pride of place and looking up to the window to see if we were observant of this ceremonial of which *magna pars fui.*[27]

First came the bier of plain fir wood borne on the shoulders of four men. On this was the box containing the body which after the custom was cinched into a box two feet square in a sitting posture. This was covered with a white fall of neatly embroidered silk, surmounted by an ornamental cover of gilded wood such as is seen in the main room of their temples descending from the ceiling. Behind the bier followed the three attendant priests bearing incense, the little bell beaten in prayer, and a plate of rice cakes and confectionery. A few of the friends and neighbors followed then. They wound through the grave yard and out into a bye street whither I followed them, anxious to witness for the first time the cremation of a dead body. The procession proceeded along the banks of the stream just outside of the town where was a place set apart for similar ceremonies. The coffin, or box, was taken from the bier and placed on a bed of charcoal, which extended below the surface of the ground. More coal was heaped around and above the coffin, and over this were placed bundles of rice straw till a little mound of straw was made like a hay rick in our summer meadows, this was bound tightly down by cords of straw, and above this evergreen branches were placed. One of the attendant priests next lighted the pyre, and then all of them commenced muttering in low tones their prayers, striking the little bell rapidly at the same time. They held in their hands rosaries of beads and sticks of burning incense. After brief prayers, one who seemed to be a family friend went around among the spectators bowing to the earth and thanking them for their attendance. Those who have attended New England funerals have heard the same public thanks for attendance. Then more prayers were muttered in a sing song tone, then in a pause in which the priests laughingly chatted with those about, asked for a pipe which was filled and lighted at the now blazing pyre. A few whiffs, some more prayers, another smoke, and I left the worthy brothers of the shaven head and long robe alternately smoking and praying. The straw burns down and makes a thick ash over the ignited coal under which the body is allowed to slowly consume away for nearly twenty four hours when bones and flesh are alike calcined ready for inurning. There was little solemnity about the scene, the persons present laughing and talking unreservedly. The place for cremation was under some old evergreen trees around whose trunks were trailing vines.

[27] "He was the important one."

Monday, December 12, 1859

We have today further rumors of the unfriendly disposition of the general government. Among them it is said the French Consul at this place has secured word from the Consul General at Yedo that he need not be surprised at any day to be compelled to leave Japan in common with all foreigners at very little notice. Genl. D[orr] quite alarmed Dr. H[epburn], who was making a professional visit upon him, by saying that the Japanese rulers were so inimical that it would not be strange if the foreigners were expelled any day by force, if indeed our lives were safe at all. He afterwards moderated this language in conversation with B[rown]. It is understood that the representatives of the foreign governments at Yedo have come to a dead lock with the Japanese on their demands. On the other hand, Consul Alcock has filed a long document making complaint of the foreigners for their manner of demanding ichibus at the customs. Although the foreign merchants may have violated good taste and even decency in the list of sums handed in, I think little fault should be found with them for the effective way they took of breaking up an evil principal of distribution which the Japanese themselves had inaugurated. It is stated from reliable sources, i.e., Japanese authority, that all natives crossing the bridges to Yokohama are searched for kobangs. Dr. H[epburn] offered Yangaro today ten ichibus a month for one hour per diem of instruction. Y[angaro] replied that he dared not do it for fear of imprisonment. Mr. Lowrie[28] came today from Nagasaki. He reports that thieving was so extensively practiced at N[agasaki], that Liggins and Williams,[29] the missionaries, are compelled to keep a night patrol.

I made some inquiries today respecting prostitution in Yokohama. I learned that the girls living in the public quarters are chiefly daughters of Yedo shopkeepers and are hired out for that business in payment of thirty ichibus. That this was the common employment of such girls from such families. I cannot satisfy myself as yet whether the tea house girls are all common. Though the same informant declares that they are of the common lot kind, selling their favors for a few tempos, Mr. Harris thinks that they are like the restaurant girls of our own country liable to be loose, though not so classed professionally. Thermometer today 37°, 7 A.M.

Tuesday, December 13, 1859

Started with Henderson this morning for a walk to the old town of Yokohama. Ferried over the bay. The old town of Yokohama lies to the westward and southward of the new town. As I passed along I noticed new houses going up by the bay literally. The old town is quite different from either the new or Kanagawa. It is a large village of brown cottages among which wind paths three to five feet broad, for streets laid out with the regularity of the new town it has none. These streets and walks are very serpentine and bordered with evergreen hedges and bamboo polings all through the town, giving a not unpleasant effect. Indeed nothing could be more rural. We found the inhabitants at their usual rural and domestic occupations. They were very civil, invited us into their houses, and set before us tea and hot sake. After leaving the village we ascended the hills beyond from whence we had a large view of the bay and surrounding country. The latter was beautiful, rolling from far as we could see, and cultivated, every foot of it, most carefully. Every hill slope was terraced into every variety of irregular patches. Wheat was the most common crop. Still going on we

---

[28] This appears to have been Reuben Post Lowrie, the son of Walter Lowrie, the Secretary of Missions for the Presbyterian Church, who served as a missionary to China and who died in Shanghai the following year (1860). Nineteenth-century China missionaries were often sent to Japan to recover their health in the comparatively more temperate climate of Japan.

[29] Channing Moore Williams and John Liggins were the first Protestant missionaries to come to Japan after the opening of the treaty ports. Both were dispatched to Nagasaki from China by the Mission Board of the American Episcopal Church. See Otis Cary, *A History of Christianity in Japan* (Tokyo: Charles E. Tuttle & Co., 1982), vol. 2, p. 45.

came to a small village of thirty houses or so picturesquely situated in a little vale.

From the heights south of Yokohama new town we had a clear view of the bay and its shipping, and the town, and its new clean looking shops. It looked like a baby's playhouse. Between us and the town were extensive flats devoted to rice culture. The water from the hills was gathered and led into one patch after another. Beside these were reservoirs scooped in the earth, probably for purposes of irrigation in dry weather. In these flats a broad canal wound around like an ox bow, wide and deep enough for burden boats. There were long dikes faced with stone, and there was one in particular, running parallel with the new city, showing that these flats are sometimes connected into a sea of water leaving the city on a long tongue of land, a mitigated sort of Deshima.

We crossed these flats where the water was frozen in the ditches and came upon the new Sodom building for the reception of the public women. It is a small town of itself, and its buildings cover many acres in extent, I should judge eight or ten. We went to the main building and were astonished at the size and completeness of the preparations being made. This building was a hundred and twenty five feet long by sixty broad, two stories in height. The lower story was divided into offices, reception rooms, and some bedrooms. Occupying a large quadrangle in the center was an artificial lake crossed by an elaborately furnished bridge. This design was certainly pleasing. A wing connected with this lower story was set apart for Chinamen especially. A man and boy showed us freely about the premises. On the lower floor we went into one large apartment or sort of common living room, where twelve or fifteen girls were seated about on the mats, talking, smoking, painting their cheeks, whitening their necks, dressing their hair, and similar toilet devotions. One threw her dress off her shoulders, baring her figure to the waist, and commenced pounding her neck and shoulders with the utmost sang froid. I have omitted to state that at the entrance of the building a placard was put up notifying that "all noisy persons would be ejected." There was a second placard in English and Dutch announcing

terms of the privilege of the house. We ascended to the second story, which was a broad gallery around an open space looking upon the lake below. This gallery was divided into bedrooms of good size, fitted up with clean mats and handsome silk covered mattresses and comfortables. Everything was new and is yet unused seemingly. One large room was for a refreshment room and was fitted up with table, chairs, and lounges. The walls, and particularly the ceiling, were handsomely, though rather gorgeously, papered. There were seats in the same room for musicians. I was informed that this building is not a dwelling place except temporarily for the girls who live in houses adjoining. The whole was a successful attempt to render vices alluring and attractive. I must not omit to mention that ample washrooms, etc., were provided. A broad causeway leads to this Sodom from the town and the entrance is through a massive gate just within which is a police station and ample police.

Leaving this building we saw long rows of other buildings divided into small cell like apartments, each having its inmate whose deportment was in nowise unlike those in similar situations at home. One building was a bath house very complete in all its arrangements. In another, which was open to public view, a dozen girls were asleep under thick comfortables, and in the same apartment were a score at least of little girls. I could not understand this room at all. There was some exposure of person, but not made with the brazen effrontery of London, Paris, or New York, but in the general national absence of the virtue of modesty and decency. A short inspection was long enough. The place is yet incomplete and when finished will certainly be an extraordinary fact in the history of a people.

On our return to the street we stopped at a merchant's house to hear his little girl play on an instrument, name unknown. It was several by 4 1/2 feet long, [and] had thirteen strings. The playing fingers were protected by lozenges of ivory secured by rings. Yangaro states that an edict has been issued from Yedo prohibiting the Japanese to use the salutation "Ohio," except towards persons with whom they have business. At old Yokohama I heard repeatedly the salutation of *"tojin,"* and once *"tojin baka,"* "foreign or China fool."

Wednesday, December 14, 1859

Our American merchants resident at Kanagawa, or rather Yokohama, throw much blame on Minister Harris for lack of a proper care of American interests. It is difficult to arrive at the truth when self interest rules a man's opinions, hence I should be unwilling to say how far the charges of want of energy and ability can be sustained. I am however inclined to believe that Mr. H[arris] is not the vigorous actor and sound thinker he may have been before age and infirmities sapped his vigor, and therefore I can imagine that in dealing with a government like this it would want the healthy look at affairs and the decided tone that an enfeebled body cannot yield in full to the mind.

Our fall or winter weather continues delightful, we have had now a long succession of frosty nights and clear sunny days, with a dry hazy atmosphere. It is nearly the perfection of fine weather.

Thursday, December 15, 1859

I had today a long talk with some Yokohama merchants. Nowhere are ranks more rigidly observed than in Japan. The common man takes his tea from a flat tray, the Officer from a higher cup stand, and the Daimio from a still higher one. I was shown the washbowl of a Daimio's wife, which was a large lacquered bowl with four handles and a lacquered kettle like an old fashioned tea kettle for a ewer. Emperor and Daimio have a plurality of wives, so do some of the officers, the common people have one. There is an official name for the wife of each class, and a special name for the children of each. The Daimio will not speak to a merchant, who is of the lowest order of commoners. Marriages take place as early as eighteen years with males and fifteen with females. I notice daily in the streets a family group walking about to see the sights, a father, mother, and one or more children. Our carpenter, who comes in almost every evening to talk with us, confirms us tonight that the seat of the memory is in the liver! That a man has a good memory according as his liver is large or small! He has been trying to persuade S[immons] not to go to his temple near the hill, and hastened telling us what adders, boa constrictors, fleas, hornets, mosquitos, cockroaches, and even lice will invade his repose if he undertakes to dwell there! The secret is that he is afraid of the government, which has opposed S[immons] in having the temple. The fear of the Governor is the ghost that haunts every Japanese home.

Friday, December 16, 1859

I saw at Yokohama today a large cornelian stone of several pounds weight and was informed that they were abundant of a smaller size. I have seen a round ball of polished quartz crystal the size of a large orange. A day or two since, the mayor of Kanagawa brought some copper pyrites to the house for identification.

Saturday, December 17, 1859

Our delightful winter weather continues. Each day is clear and sunny and air is still. The Japanese impress the fine weather and splendid waters of the bay for fishing. Fish grow daily more abundant and cheap. A fish that in windy or rainy weather would bring an ichibu now sells for 1/2 that sum. A great variety of shell fish are consumed, bivalves such as clams and oysters and univalves like the mother of pearl oyster and several varieties of spiral shell fish. Pheasants are occasionally to be had in the market. Eggs are sold 80 for one ichibu.

Sunday, December 18, 1859

Sabbath day. Service at 12 M. Rev. Mr. Lowrie of Shanghai officiating. Several strangers were present today.

Monday, December 19, 1859

Went to Yokohama early in the morning returning in time for a horseback ride with Mr.
B[rown]. We had the Genl's. [Dorr's] horses
and took a trot of five or six miles on the Tokaido towards Miaco. The grooms attended us
walking and running all the way near the
horses' heads. They carried a coil of ropes in
their hands which it is the custom of the country to fasten to the bits, the groom still retaining the other end, we felt capable of managing
our own animals. Our horses had broken under the Genl.'s care to American saddles and
bridles, and had been indifferently shod by the
grooms. The horses are kept up in stable, fed
on grass, rice, beans, peas, etc. Their stables
are always neat, every bit of ordure as fast as
dropped being swept up and removed. The
horses of the country generally are a poor,
meager looking set, like a poor man's horse
past work at home. There are a few good and
shapely animals owned by the wealthy and officials. They all possess one common peculiarity
viz., a great meagerness of hairs and steep
pitch from the hips to the tail. The horse is the
only beast of burden, and a constant string of
them is daily passing on the Tokaido and
bringing in burdens from the fields. Another
office of our grooms was to shout "Hai," "Hai,"
to every living obstacle in our way so that we
might have a clear road. So on we darted
through the street, men and women rushing to
the door at the unusual clatter, and children
following after shouting "*anata Ohio,*" "*Nippon
Ohio,*" "*tojin,*" and even "*tojin baka.*" If we had
been a grand cavalry corps of a regimental parade there could not have been more excitement. Of course I sat very upright and looked
as martial as possible.

We passed a school and there was a general
rush, as with a district school in Conn. when
the elephant and brass band of the menagerie
goes by, the boys with books in hand rushed
pell mell to the school door, their instructor
looking after them hopeless of order so long as
we were in sight. Several of the boys had paper
and pens in their hands. I hoped we afforded
them a fruitful theme for composition, if that
delectable exercise is introduced in Japan. And
I don't know why it should not be, for they

have well sweeps, old fashioned winnowing
mills, and today I heard a cooper at work with
a regular rub-a-dub-dub. How the people flew
from right to left and left to right to keep out
of our way. There was a decrepit old man in
the middle of the street, him the foremost
groom caught around the body and had lifted
him quite out of the street before he knew
what had happened. The tea house women
caught with the last drained cup in their
hands, while the girl from the balcony windows of the second story smiled and nodded
approvingly—of our splendid horsemanship I
suppose. After a brisk trot of a mile and a half,
or two miles, we came to a sharp angle in the
streets and then passed some very large
houses, in the general but of a single story in
height. The sliding screens were thrown back
and we could see the clean mats and airy
rooms running far to the rear, frequently terminated by a little bit of a garden or a fancy
piece of rock work in a small yard. In these
houses a group might occasionally be seen
seated around a brazier drinking tea, or sake,
or partaking more substantial refreshments.
Following this, the great highway, for a mile
more at least, we at length came into the open
country.

Thus far the road had been bordered by a
constant succession of cultivated fields, the low
ground covered with rice stubble, and the rolling lands back with green crops of vetches, turnips, onions, cabbage, etc. The ground became
more broken as we proceeded and the road
wound up a moderate hill between rows of
aged firs. They were fine old trees. I dismounted to measure one of them and found
its girth to be twenty feet. The rolling lands on
either side for the next mile were only partially
cultivated, on the left particularly were large
tracts of arable land covered with low beech-
wood. Not even a scattering house was to be
seen. So after we thought every foot of Japan
is either populated or tilled there is room for
more. Possibly, too, the population has been
exaggerated. Along the road side under the
firs were occasionally booths for the resting
and refreshment of travellers. Some of these
halting places were simply a bank of earth covered with matting making a raised seat of a
few inches. To even this there was an atten-

dant girl who had a tea pot over a little earthen furnace of coals and a few cups as her stock in trade. There is a halting place for even the poorest. Beggars with short coarse hair, tattered clothes, and staff were more than numerous with their peculiar incantation of "*tempo anata stots tempo*," "a penny Sir one penny." Travelling priests, shaven and shorn, followed the road for alms. In penance sake the rich and the princes also of the realm travel as beggars incognito. I know not how many times I may have turned a deaf ear to alms seeking royalty.

A gang of laborers were scattered along the road cutting the dry grass around side bushes which they burned. They were repairing the road, making water courses at the sides of the road, bringing on earth where it was needed, planting young firs at short intervals on either side. Another gang were busy sweeping the road, gathering the refuse and dry leaves to be burned. The whole breadth of the road was varying from two to three rods, the roadway itself broad enough for carriages to meet and pass without difficulty. A great deal of coarse gravel and small stones has been drawn on the road from time to time, so that its surface is often uneven and rough. Growing by the roadside was a small berry bearing plant resembling our wintergreen and belonging to the same family. After riding out six miles we turned about and came home. The school had been let out and the youngsters we found as bold and noisy as any district school let loose. Our footmen were pretty well blown by the time we reached home.

Tuesday, December 20, 1859

Today we have news from Yedo. The government stipulates that there shall be no further interference with trade, and that coin except copper may be an article of sale and purchase. Rice, wheat, and copper coin are the only articles forbidden exportation.

Japan seems to be not more prolific in soil than in children. The streets are full of them. They seem always to be merry and good natured. I have not seen a quarrel yet and rarely see a child crying. The secretion of the noses, however, seems to be as abundant as among civilized youngsters. Every day they gather round our gate, which is an open sunny spot, to play their little games. Spinning tops and bounding ball are the chief amusements. In the latter sport they keep the count in a musical singing way. Girls of ten or twelve, say one third of them, have a babe strapped to their backs. Kite flying is another popular amusement. The children are great patrons of the itinerant peddlers of fancy goods, confectionery, etc. I saw a group of them today very much interested in the goods of a peddler who carried dolls, figures of dogs, rabbits, cats, and other animals. These itinerant hawkers are very numerous. I often see the teahouse girls chaffering with them. A priest with a shaven pate was passing a neighboring tea house today when two of their Abigails besought him so casually to tarry that he nearly paid Swift's price for his escape. Dined with Dorr in the evening and had a pleasant game of whist with Henderson, Mr. Shoyer, [30] and Mr. Law.[31]

---

[30] Raphael Schoyer is listed as a Yokohama "auctioneer" in the *China Directory* (1865), p. 235. John M. Rosenfield in his article, "Western-Style Painting in the Early Meiji Period and its Critics," states that Schoyer was a "journalist," a claim based on the publication of the *Japan Express*, which Schoyer used to advertise the goods in his auction rooms. Hall speaks of him only as an "auctioneer" in later sections of the journal. But M. Paske-Smith tells us that Schoyer was a native of Baltimore and served as "leader of the community in civic matters" having been elected as the first chairman of the Yokohama Municipal Council in 1865. Unfortunately he was "overcome by excitement" at one of the first council meetings and collapsed of apoplexy. Hall

had been suggested for this position, but had declined due to his planned departure from Japan. Schoyer's wife was an excellent hostess and amateur painter who taught a number of Japanese artists, including Takahashi Yuichi, the essentials of oil painting. For the Rosenfield reference see Donald H. Shively, ed., *Tradition and Modernization in Japanese Culture* (Princeton, N.J.: Princeton University Press, 1971), p. 195. For Paske-Smith see *Western Barbarians in Japan and Formosa in Tokugawa Days 1603–1868* (Kobe: J. L. Thomson & Co., 1930), p. 269.

[31] I have not been able to trace Mr. Law, but he was later Hall's cabin-mate on the *Azof* when he went to Nagasaki in June of 1860.

Wednesday, December 21, 1859

Mr. Lowrie left us today, went to the boat to see him off. Passed on the way two itinerant nuns soliciting alms, which they received in a wooden bowl. They wore long black dresses and dark hoods with capes falling over the shoulders. They get a cash or more at every house. I saw too an officer visiting from house to house and collecting cash, evidently for some religious purpose as he carried in his hand a slip of paper with the print of an idol thereupon. Today is one of three monthly *yasumibi*, or "days of rest." The carpenter told us this evening that he often has to pay blackmail on his building contracts to the Governor. If the Governor knows of his building he will during the progress of it "squeeze" him to the amount of one tenth. If he can get his job finished first he is not troubled. The poor people in Japan must be the victims of all sorts of exactions.

Settled up monthly bills today and found living expenses for the month to be a little less than $17. Sent to Olyphant[32] today by the *Excelsior* in Lowrie's hands 120 kobangs and 75 quarters ditto.

Thursday, December 22, 1859

A raw cold day, more like one of our bleak November days than anything we have experienced as yet, wind blowing from the north. Took a long walk through the fields. Everywhere I saw the same evidence of patient cultivation that I have so often seen. I walked out to where there was a pond made by damming up a small mountain stream and used for irrigating the rice fields. Large birds of the crane or stork kind were in the paddy field, and ducks were in the rushes of the pond. The crops are now all gathered, though still the greater portion of the fields seem to be occupied by next year's wheat, and vegetables for early crops next spring such as turnips, rad-

ishes, peas, broad beans. The forests are as brown as our own in December, the deciduous trees having shed all their leaves.

Friday, December 23, 1859

Passed the day within doors writing letters. Tried the experiment of copying letters by dampening Japanese paper and pressing it on the written sheet with my feet. It executed very well. Genl. D[orr] informed us today that the chief minister of state at Yedo, who has been so hostile to foreign interests, has just been removed on account of *ill health*, the usual Japanese method of removal. Four ships only remain in the harbor, the smallest number since my arrival.

Saturday, December 24, 1859

Going to the ferry today I met another nun begging from house to house. She carried in one hand a lacquered bowl for the receipt of alms and in the other a small bell. Over one hand hung a rosary. On her head was a black hood with a large cape falling on the shoulders. Her robes were of the same color, they were a gown with large loose hanging sleeves. She had a good natured fat face, by no means shriveled with spare diet and late vigils. A little girl accompanied her. The morning was cold and most of the travellers in the road were well clad with two or three thicknesses of thick cotton stuffs, one of which was generally wadded. A light blue handkerchief was drawn over the head and lower part of the face, which was sometimes concealed, all but the eyes. They wore on their feet the blue cotton socks so generally worn with a straw sandal underneath, the thongs of which passed between the great toe and other toes, the great toe being separate from the rest like the thumb of a mitten.

In the Yokohama market today I saw wild boar meat, hares of large size, pheasants at an

---

[32] D.W.C Olyphant was the founder of Olyphant & Co., the American trading house in Canton. Olyphant was well-known as the "one American who always refused to handle opium" in the China trade. He was also a strong supporter of the missionaries and often offered them free passage to China. See Jack Beeching, *The Chinese Opium Wars* (New York: Harcourt Brace Jovanovich, 1975), p. 56.

ichibu a pair with plumage so splendid that it seemed a pity they should be killed to gratify one's appetites [in] lieu of an ordinary farm yard fowl. The Carpenter made us a shinjo of a half basket of oranges, excellent ones worth in the market an ichibu a basket.

The Mayor's interpreter called again today. He pretends to be taking lessons in English from Dr. S[immons], but I more than half suspect he is only a spy. He gave us some instances of such opinions as even literally well informed Japanese have of foreigners. He thought that our American ladies generally wore beards, and was quite surprised when told the contrary. He wanted to know why foreigners wore such heavy beards, as it gave them encyfilas to wear so much hair! He had noticed that foreigners had very red faces!— which he called encyfilas, and so thought it better they should shave the front and top of their heads like the Japanese. He wished to see our clothes and hair brushes. S[immons] handed him his hair and clothes brush. After examining them, he said the clothes brush did not smell quite so bad as the hair brush, for that smelt very bad. He then told S[immons] that his hair (which happened to be much disarranged) did not look well, and he had better fix it like mine, which had happened to be brushed only a few minutes before he came in. He varied his conversation with frequent smoking. He was inquisitive to know our professions, where we were going to live when our houses were done, etc. I told him that I was a traveller, that was a new profession to him, he repeated the name several times and wrote it down in his book, "travellyerr," for future research, buckled on his two swords and departed. An intelligent Japanese informs me that one half of the Japanese are addicted to sake drinking and one tenth are sake drunkards, one tenth of those who drink that is.

Sunday, December 25, 1859

Christmas Day in Japan! And a beautiful day it is. A crisp frosty morning, thermometer 23°, followed by a bright beautiful day. Picked a couple of rosebuds just ready to flower and camellias from trees in full bloom. Friends at home were often thought of and spoken of by us all. Service at 12 M. as usual. News comes today of the shipwreck of an American vessel on the rocks near Sumatra and loss of four lives, no names given yet. When I awoke this morning the temple bells made me fancy I heard the Christmas bells of home.

Monday, December 26, 1859

Another day like the preceding. Called on Mrs. Capt. Baily at Yokohama who treated me to Christmas cake and wine. Green ornaments of the camellia leaves and sacred bamboo were good substitutes for the holly and pines at home. A high official from Yedo, fourth in rank, is here today on the annual tour of inspection into the public offices. Barges with cabins built on deck draped with striped blue and white cotton convey him and suite. The Japanese steamer is down from Yedo to carry him back. The streets are neater and more carefully swept than usual today. Dr. S[immons] states on authority of Mr. Harris that a prisoner of state is never put to death until he has been made to confess his crime by torture. Today we, the gentlemen, commenced housekeeping in Mr. B[rown]'s apartments. Henderson the sick sailor is our cook. We had a great time getting our dishes together and getting the table in readiness. The quantity was ample as well as the variety. We had fish that had been fried an hour too long, baked venison that Mrs. H[epburn] sent us, pickled ministers face from the General's, rice that stood till it was cold, and eggs hard as a rich man's charity. Mrs. H[epburn] and the Dr. came in to laugh at us, but we made good dinner of it despite all the drawbacks of bachelor housekeeping. While at Y[okohama] today exchanging ichibus with a crockery merchant he invited me into his back room and brought me tea and sponge cake. The tea was hot, so he very kindly poured it into a large saucer and blew on it vigorously to cool it!

Tuesday, December 27, 1859

Genl. D[orr] went to Yedo today. The Japanese mode of travelling among the higher ranks is either by horseback or in a norimon. The latter is a house in miniature. It is an oblong box, long enough for a man to recline in, wider at the bottom than the top with a sliding screen window on either side and a roof slightly projecting and with a double slope on the top for wet weather, it is provided with a tent of rain proof coverings of either paper or cloth. A stout bar runs over the top longitudinally, projecting four feet beyond either end. The norimon is supported by this on men's shoulders. Two or four carriers, with a relay of as many more, are employed. It is no joke to carry one of these. With its burden inside, one end of the norimon taxed my strength to raise it from the ground. These carriers however make off with it at a rapid walk, accelerated frequently to running. Inside are cushions to recline upon and any other comforts the road may require. The noble traveller takes in addition a saddle horse which [he] uses a part of the time. He is preceded by servants who bear long staves and clear the way and followed by a numerous retinue of sandal bearers, bed bearers, clothes bearers, cooking utensil bearers, etc. These articles are carried in packages, or in lacquered trunks, fastened to a pole carried on the shoulder. The size of the train and its outfit is in proportion to the status of the traveller. The retinue of a governor of a province, of the daimios, or hereditary princes, of whom there are 264, are large and attired in befitting garments.

Wednesday, December 28, 1859

At Yokohama today inquiries were made by the merchants for woolen cloths and spotted shirtings and friction matches. Woolen cloths I learned on inquiry they like, but they are un-

willing to pay the prices for them. They appreciate the comfort, but do not like to purchase it. I do not wonder at it, for their wadded and quilted gowns, which they wear in winter, are very comfortable, the material is cheap, and they have become so accustomed to its clumsiness, that they no longer regard that which would be its greatest objection to us accustomed to the ease of bifurcated trousers and close yet easy fitting coats. I made some very good exchanges today with buttons. I bought a box of paper for walls, being a series of pictures of Japanese females, the *jooroya* [courtesan] class. The seller informed me that at both Yedo and Miaco, especially the latter place, they occupied very extensive quarters. One building contains as much room as all the stores of Yokohama together. I can well believe even this story judging by the extent of the same buildings at Yokohama. The one building I suspect is a series of dwellings. At Yedo temples are adorned with portraits of the most celebrated courtesans of that city.

Thursday, December 29, 1859

The *Contest* arrived today with the missionary families. Mrs. B[rown] and children, and Miss A[drian],[33] and Mrs. S[immons]. The ship was coming up the bay as I was crossing. I went off to her more in hopes of letters than of seeing any friends, but then I found them. Luckily I had a large boat and after finishing my business at Yokohama I took the party ashore and surprised the husbands at dinner.

Today we have had our first snow. It snowed rapidly between 8 and 9 A.M. and whitened the ground. The scenery as I crossed the bay was beautiful, the hills were whitened where the fields were tilled, and the contrast between them and the evergreen trees was strikingly picturesque and beautiful. In the distance was the snowy pearly head of Fusi.

[33] Caroline Adrian was a member of S. R. Brown's church at Owasco Outlet, New York, who decided to accompany Brown and his wife to Japan in 1859. Going to Japan at her own expense, she hoped to start a Christian work among Japanese women, but Kanagawa and Yokohama proved inauspicious for these efforts

and she subsequently left Japan disappointed. Following her stay in Japan she joined the [Dutch] Reformed Church mission at Amoy, China, where she died in 1863. See Griffis, *A Maker of the New Orient: Samuel Robbins Brown*, pp. 119–20.

Friday, December 30, 1859

I saw today for the first time a specimen of Japanese top spinning. I was returning from Yokohama when on the Tokaido my attention was attracted by a crowd of boys gathered around a top spinner. He was a grizzle headed tall man with a merry twinkle about his eyes and a constant smile on his face. He stood on one side of the public road with a travelling nest of boxes before him in which were tops great and small. In front, and on either side of him, was a group of happy urchins with smoky black eyes, semi-shaved heads, reddened upper lips and tattered nether habiliments. There were young girls with great fat babies strapped to their backs, all intent upon the merry top spinner till I, too, stopped to look, when their attention was directed and divided between the *tojin* and the showman. The later had all the peculiar shrewdness and readiness of his craft, alternately talking to his tops and to the spectators with an occasional clue that a few cash would be acceptable. The novelty of a stranger looking on increased the crowd by the addition of more boys and all the idlers of the neighborhood. The passing travelers, too, stopped till the highway to Yedo threatened to sustain a temporary blockade. I flattered myself that the itinerant spinner of tops was flattered by my distinguished presence, for he addressed himself to his work with increased zeal.

Taking a large top in his hand he twirled it between his palms till he had communicated to it a rapid motion when he tossed it high in the air catching it first on one finger then the other, the top losing none of its steadiness or motion, spinning now vertically and now horizontally. Again he held it on a little stick six inches long and with the index finger of his right hand he described the plane of its horizon, the top leaning over as his finger descended and rising erect as he poised his fingers directly above it. Then he tossed it again in the air and caught it on the sticks of his fan on which it spun rapidly, and away it went into the air again and fell horizontally on its axis, but still hummed away. The top conjurer talking to it all the while as if it had been a thing of life with the occasional diversion of a smile to his auditors. At every new feat of dexterity a score of brown little faces were turned upon me and I was asked "is not that good." Good, said I, the little fellows clapped their hands in glee at my approval of their national pastime. Now he tied the end of a cotton cord, or thread, to his box cover and reeling off twenty feet or so, he started a fresh top which he dexterously placed on the cord and it went spinning along while he held one end of the cord till it reached the box, and then it hopped off and spun till exhausted. There was great applause then in which I heartily joined.

A small shower of copper cash having passed over, he inverted a tea cup and sent another top spinning around its bottom rim. As before it followed the swaying motion of his index finger. And now he looked wise, and we all, boys and *tojin* alike, knew something grand was coming, and we stood on the tip toe of expectation. Deliberately did the cunning spinner build up a little tower of carved wood to the height of 18 inches, its top was a round apex of an inch diameter. On this he poised an egg on end, on the top of this egg he balanced another horizontally and on top of that pair a third. Again he twirled fiercely in his hands the longwise handle of the top, and catching it up on a thin narrow slip of brass from that he delicately slid it off onto the apex of the uppermost egg, where it spun away quite as much at home as if on the robust earth. Ah! didn't we bareheaded and barefooted boys, baby burdened girls, and travelling stranger, make the welkin ring with approving shouts. Whereat dignified Nippon gentlemen with two swords buckled to their sides looked very grave. The stranger had evidently demeaned himself in their eyes. This last trick would have been better if the wax that held the eggs together had not been of a different color from the shells. The eggs were real for he broke one to convince us. With a smiling bow he signified that the play was over, and so we separated boys, babies, top spinner, and stranger each to their homes.

Mr. B[rown]'s family landed their effects today. I went down to the ferry and stood with Mr. B[rown] superintending the unloading of the boxes and their removal to their destination from 6 P.M. till 10, for this work was all done slowly. The great piano box consumed half that time in its removal. The only mechanical process known to the Japanese are "strength and stupidity." The box was fairly enveloped in straw ropes and was finally carried off by fourteen men. Six Irishmen would have done much quicker, better, and easier. I amused myself while waiting with warming my fingers over the ferry master's brazier, talking Japanese, and drinking hot sake with him. The conversation developed some of the usual immodest tendencies of Japanese thinking.

Saturday, December 31, 1859

The morning opened clear and bid fair for a warm pleasant day, but the sky began to thicken with clouds and about one a violent snow storm set in with a strong wind from the north. I was at Yokohama exchanging money and was fairly caught. The sea had become very boisterous, but to go around by the highway was to meet a violent snow storm from the north full in the face, and contrary to advice of Capt. King[34] and others I concluded to cross the bay. My servant was with me. Just as we were pushing off from the shore I saw Dr. S[immons], wife, and Mrs. Capt. Steele[35] putting off in another boat for the *Contest*. They proceeded but little ways before they turned about and came ashore again. Schoyer made no attempt to cross, but hired kangos [palanquin] to carry him and servants around by the road. I found the sea rough and the water came over the bows a little. Our boat had a narrow escape from being dashed against the piles that protect the sea wall, and had just safely passed them when, in spite of the boatmen's exertions, a collision with a junk at anchor appeared for the moment inevitable. I think we should have been thrown against it if I had not ordered the boatmen to turn around and pass it astern. We then kept along the shore to where a point made out into the bay. From this point, I judged, that a few minutes

of vigorously pulling would fetch us over the roughest of the way to where the water was somewhat sheltered from the wind by the hills on the Kanagawa shore. So we struck out across the bay. The waves tossed our light boat about and my boy was fain to lie on his face in the bottom of the boat through fright, sea sickness, and the freezing cold storm which chilled the very marrow of my bones. He did not move his head till we had reached, as I had supposed, smoother water and were about to land. The storm continued in its violence for an hour and a half, when it subsided, the heavens cleared off, and the thermometer fell in the still cold to 20° fahrenheit by the following morning.

---

[34] Captain King was the captain of the schooner *Wanderer*. King replaced E. M. Dorr as the representative of Augustine Heard & Co.

[35] Mrs. Captain Steele was the wife of Captain Steele of the *Contest*, the ship that brought the wives of Brown and Simmons from China. "Steele is one of those practical old fellows, down upon everything that other people admire," John M. Brooke wrote in his journal. "This is however in part affectation." See Brooke, *John M. Brooke's Pacific Cruise and Japanese Adventure*, p. 203.

our unwilling "Minister Resident." The latter gave him however a terribly severe blowing-up for coming, a proffer of some dinner, an unwilling bed, and an escort of four soldiers and an officer on the way back the next morning!!

Monday, January 2, 1860

It is reported that there are three wrecks near the entrance of Shimoda harbor. Capt. Price of the *Nymph* has reached Yokohama. In his disaster he lost his mate, one passenger, and four sailors in an attempt to go ashore. Cargo all saved. Dr. H[epburn] returned from Yedo on Saturday evening much pleased with his visit. Minister H[arris] was a few days ago insulted in his own yard by a retainer of one of the Daimios who ran against him and used offensive epithets. Mr. H[arris] struck him with his riding whip. The affair goes to the government, showing the hostile feeling against all foreigners and their friends. Minister H[arris] says that an interpreter once prominent at court when he was negotiating his treaty is now degraded and so poor that he was unable to appear respectably. Another interpreter at Nagasaki, who had made great progress not only in the language, but in general science, and was a hard student, he borrowed some foreign fashions, allowing his hair to grow on the top of his head, sitting in chairs, and eating at a table. He suddenly disappeared, and his fate remains unknown to this day.

Tuesday, January 3, 1860

There was a great fire at Yokohama today. Several foreign houses and godowns were consumed. I had an opportunity of seeing the Japanese fire department in action. The alarm

1860

Sunday, January 1, 1860

The opening day and first Sabbath of the New Year. It was a clear frosty morning with an exhilarating atmosphere, the "glad New Year." My thoughts were often with the friends beyond the seas, with whom it was then the eve before New Year's morn. I know how busy my brothers were in the old store where I had toiled so many Christmas' and New Year's eves so, that when the ten o'clock of their eve came around I was rejoiced for their sakes. Service as usual, and a millennial rather than a New Year's sermon from Mr. B[rown]. Only one stranger present. The active merchants of Yokohama care little for gospel ordinances.

Van R. [Eugene Van Reed][1] has been to Yedo with a Japanese pass, without aid from

[1] Eugene Van Reed (1835–1873) was a native of Reading, Pennsylvania, who arrived in Yokohama aboard the *Wanderer* on June 30, 1859. Van Reed worked for a time as clerk in the American consulate in Kanagawa, as well as a representative for Augustine Heard and Co. He was also in business for himself as a trader of rice and arms, and subsequently as a broker for contract labor. In later years he served as consul general for the Kingdom of Hawaii. Van Reed had

learned Japanese from Joseph Heco in San Francisco and established close ties with representatives of Satsuma while in Yokohama. At one point he was on the verge of signing a "private" treaty with Satsuma to handle all of Satsuma's foreign trade, a plan that came to naught when the bakufu arrested his Satsuma negotiator. On the occasion mentioned here Van Reed managed to get Japanese papers to go to Edo, which brought him into conflict with Townsend Harris. Van

Eugene Van Reed from a woodblock print portrait by Sadahide, 1861.

ter. Each engine was furnished with a reservoir that would hold five or six pail fulls of water. This was continually replenished from tubs filled at the sea side, which was not far off. Each tub was fastened to a stout wooden pole and like the engines was carried on the shoulders of two men. There were a score of them throwing a feeble stream as large as my little finger upon this great fire. I thought of Samuel Gulliver.

The fire was serious and the excitement was great. One entire block was in flames when I got onto the ground. Ladders of bamboo were placed against the street now, and up these clambered men bearing in their hands what appeared to be large square paper lanterns inscribed with Japanese characters. One of them had an addition of paper streamers. The bearers ran along the ridges with the alacrity of apes. Whether they were intent on some fire business, or were only guides to the gang of men that followed and who began to strip off the tiles, I cannot say, but wheresoever the fire made new headway these lantern men frantically were mounted to the ridgepoles and raised their paper banners aloft. The Japanese deserve credit for their willingness and zeal. There were at least two thousand men on the ground and all hard at work bringing water, carrying off goods from the godowns or demolishing the buildings. The latter appears to be the only effectual method they have of stopping the ravages of fire. Their engines are farcical against a large fire, but they are provided with ladders, hooks, etc., and with the breaking out of a fire they swarm in and around the exposed contiguous buildings and go to work to tear them down. Japanese houses are light and this is rapidly effected. The foreigners assisted in this in a more effectual manner. Under the superintendence of some former ship captain, ropes were secured to the corner posts

bells tolled and there was a rapid gathering from all parts of the town, the neighboring village of old Yokohama, and a great many from across the bay from Kanagawa. The fire department was out in force. Every available fire engine was brought to the ground, each one borne on the shoulders of two men. These engines are nothing more than large squirt guns worked by a lever of two man power. There were also simple pumps, three feet long with a piston working precisely like a squirt gun, one end of the pump being placed in a pail of wa-

Reed's career needs further historical evaluation. Clearly one of the most colorful and independent men in the treaty port, he has often been maligned for his business dealings—particularly his role in sending immigrants to Hawaii in the late 1860s. The best account of Van Reed's life can be found in Albert Altman, "Eugene Van Reed: A Reading Man in Japan, 1859–1872," *Historical Review of Berks County* 30, no. 1 (Winter 1964–

1965). For a recent Japanese account see Fukunaga Ikuo, "Vuan Riido hyōron," *Eigakushi kenkyū*, no. 18 (November 1, 1985), pp. 59–74. See also Joseph Heco, *Narrative of a Japanese* (San Francisco: American-Japanese Publishing Association, n.d.). A number of Van Reed's letters dealing with this period can be found in the Augustine Heard Papers, Baker Library, Harvard Business School.

of the buildings and were easily thrown down. There are regular fire stations in the town where ladders, hooks, and other apparatus similar to that of our hook and ladder companies is kept. Here also are bells and a regular watch to give alarms. There was one exceedingly frantic individual rushing about making wild gestures towards the advancing flames as if he had power to exorcise the demons of fire, but I could not see that the elements paid much respect to his gesticulations.

The officers of the fire department were on the ground in large force giving directions. They were distinguished by their handsome robes of silk and colored brocade and handsome fire hats, altogether a very *distingue* dress. Each wore in addition two swords and bore in his hand a short baton of finished iron, or steel, which he used to attract attention while giving orders. There were others who wore on their heads a close fitting skull cap from which a [flap] hung down so as to enclose the head and face and protect the shoulders. This was met by a stout dress covering the whole person. It was doubtless designed for protection against water, fire, and smoke, for I saw them in the thickest of the fray. In front of one of the godowns, towards which the fire was spreading, was a high pile of seaweed in straw matting. Thin little wooden pumps sufficed to wet this down, and then, by pulling down the adjacent buildings to the level of this barricade of wet straw, the flames were arrested at length.

I must give the Japanese credit for unwearied exertion and fearless exposure to danger. I saw one of them carried off who had been made senseless by a fall. I assisted to carry away a ship captain who was knocked senseless by a falling timber, and I heard of a Chinaman who was badly hurt. No fatal accidents however. As soon as it was evident that the fire was under control, the Japanese inscribed a large number of boards with characters, using mud for ink, and these they put up on end on the remains of the charred but unfallen timbers, some fixed purpose again I suppose. Both Governors and the Vice Governor were in attendance mounted on horseback. After the fire was subdued the people were busy in removing the goods to a safe place and it was really pleasing to witness the cheerfulness of their labor.

Wednesday, January 4, 1860

The reported loss by the fire is $100,000 of which $60,000 was in silk. A deputation visited on the Governor last evening to solicit the employment of coolies to remove the ruins of the goods. He replied with exceeding *naivete*, "when the Japanese take hold of a fire they do not leave it till subdued and everything is safe." Considering their facilities for such subjugation the remark was rather pleasing to the Committee. One of the first sights that met my eye when hastening to the fire was somebody's pretty mistress fleeing for life. The fire and the ruins revealed also to the wandering eyes of the officials some contraband goods such as Kobangs, a particular kind of fish, etc.

The crew of the *Lady Inglis*, an English barque, shipwrecked at the entrance of Shimoda light some ten days ago arrived last night. They had sailed in open boats from the scene of the disaster seven days to Y[okohama]. They struck a rocky reef at 10 P.M., the wind blowing fresh and under double reefed topsails at the time. They remained on board till the following forenoon, when she settled down by the stern and they took to the boats. They landed first at Shimoda where they were furnished with fuel, water, and such provisions as the country afforded. They were restricted to the beach. From thence they sailed along the coast, stopping when necessary for food, which was always kindly furnished. A Dutch vessel and an American barque, names unknown, are also reported as wrecked. The foreign residents have had a meeting today to devise protection against loss by fire, and the English further to protest against the attempt to remove the foreign population to Kanagawa. Witnessed the delivery of nine boxes of specie to Henderson and the delivery by him to the Japanese authorities.

Thursday, January 5, 1860

The loss by the fire was exaggerated in the first accounts. The total loss is probably $25,000. The morning was delightfully clear and warm, but the north wind in the afternoon blew a cold ugly blast, the sky was clouded in. I was awakened at 12 A.M. by the violent throes of an earthquake that shook the temple to its foundation. For a moment I had fear for my safety, for every joint of timber creaked, the casements rattled, and the sliding screens were shaken as by a fierce blast. The shock was double, and while each lasted, seemed to come in waves of increase and diminution. The whole could not have lasted over a minute, or a minute-and-a-half. It reminded me of the jar sometimes produced by the heavy wave like rolling of a thunder burst. I was relieved when the thudding heaving earth was restored to rest. There was something both grand and awful in the idea of the solid earth being so moved from her foundations. It was not surprising then, when in the morning I heard, that many of the Japanese moved out of their houses in fear last night.

Friday, January 6, 1860

Azof arrived, no letters or papers from home. Why don't they write? Went off to the *Contest* with apparel from the ladies for the wrecked Captain's wife of the *Lady Inglis*. News received of the great conflagration at Nagasaki.

Saturday, January 7, 1860

Passed the day at home putting my new room to rights. Made the acquaintance of Dr. Lindo [Rudolph Lindau], an envoy from the Swedish [sc. Swiss] government.[2] There is a bakery near our temple from whence we have once got some very nice rolls and where they make also those thin light rice cakes. I stopped

in as I passed yesterday and saw two men each standing in a barrel. Their legs were naked, and their garments tucked up around their middle. They were kneading and mixing the dough. One of them was up to his knees in an uninviting looking mixture of such consistency that he had some difficulty to keep his feet in motion. It is lucky, thought I, that we don't always see how what we eat is sometimes prepared. I should not have relished their light rolls so well the other day, if [I] had seen these barelegged fellows treading out the dough. Yet, at the time, I detected no flavor of the heels.

Sunday, January 8, 1860

Service as usual at 12 M. About 2 P.M. there was a very slight and transitory shock of an earthquake. The late earthquake is represented to have been more severe at Yedo and of several minutes (four) duration. People there left their houses, not only natives, but members of the diplomatic corps.

Monday, January 9, 1860

The news today is that the Yokohama merchants are to be allowed quick possession of their several places and great is the rejoicing thereat. The news needs confirmation.

Tuesday, January 10, 1860

Auction today of the *Nymph*'s effects. Daily auctions after the manner of our own are held at Yedo, so the Japanese tell me. Shimamori of the Custom House was curious at the sale, looking at this thing and that. The medicine chest attracted his attention particularly. I gave him to taste tincture of rhubarb and a solution of camphor. He made no wry faces, smacked his lips said it was good. Personally he inquired if I did not want my money changed. Certainly

[2] Rudolph Lindau subsequently became a literary figure of some reputation in Europe. He published several volumes dealing with his Japan experiences which include: *Aus China und Japan* (Berlin: F. Fontane & Co., 1896), and *Un Voyage Autour du Japon* (Paris: Librairie de L. Hachette et Cie, 1864).

I said. Well said he "go in and I will change it." I went into the Custom House where he appeared laughing behind the counter and said I might wait a little. He was greatly delighted at this Rowland for my Oliver.

Wednesday, January 11, 1860

Coming up the street today I passed the stand of a travelling peddler, whose wares, toys for children, were spread out on a board. There were dolls, picture books, tops, and play things of various sort, and among them toys of a description too indecent to describe. Every day convinces me more and more of what an utter want of modest[y] in some things pervades this people. *Powhatan* arrived today from Hong Kong.

Thursday, January 12, 1860

Minister Harris arrived from Yedo today. It appears to be fully settled that the Japanese Commissioners will go to the United States.

Friday, January 13, 1860

As a specimen of the treatment received by the Japanese females from the men, the following is a fair example. Bohē [Buhee][3] is a Japanese merchant of good standing. He is a partner in several stores at Yokohama and Kanagawa and is well to do in the world. I met him at our landing today with his wife and two daughters, good looking girls of 15 and 17 years old I should say. I offered him a seat in

my boat which he declined. I met him afterwards at his store in Yokohama with his family. He asked me into the family room back of the store, introduced me to his partners, and called for tea, hot water, and hot sake. These were brought and I tasted them all, but the salt turnip which was with the sake was horrible. So some sponge cake was brought, and then he sent out and bought a cigar for me while the rest smoked their Nippon pipes of tobacco. When I came in they seemed to be just ready for dinner, there were the salted turnips, boiled rice, and some indescribable stew on the coals of the brazier. Bohe deliberately ate a hearty meal. All the time the wife and daughters stood without in the cold patiently waiting for him. There was no unkindness in it, it was the Nippon way, and wife and children seemed just as happy as though they had waited in the warm room within. They could not be treated as equals of the husband and father, they had kindness but not respect. Yet I often see at stores the husband consulting his wife over a sale, and not unfrequently she appears to be the dictatress of terms, and the man second in business transactions. So I often see a woman seated around a brazier with two or three men talking familiarly.

Saturday, January 14, 1860

Lysoon[4] today bought some lumber for shipment to Shanghai. For three quarters inch and inch stuff he paid about the rate of $5 per cwt. It must prove a profitable speculation for him. Met in the evening Commodore Tattnall at Gen. Dorr's. Allusion was made to his conduct at the Peiho affair.[5] The old Commodore felt

[3] This merchant appears to have been Saigaya Buhee, who is listed as one of the Kanagawa merchants who opened a store in Yokohama shortly after the treaties went into effect. Saigaya is listed in an 1861 directory of Yokohama merchants of Kanagawa origins. See Kanagawa Kushi Hensan Kankō Jikko I-inkai, eds., *Kanagawa kushi* (Tokyo: Dainihon Insatsu, 1977), p. 241. Hall sometimes writes his name Bohee or Boohee, the latter would clearly be Buhee by Hall's transliteration scheme. Joseph Heco refers to him as Saikaya. Heco writes, "a man called Saikaya, a silk-dealer well known in the town, brought the samples [of silk] to the Consu-

late. He had heard of my history, and shewed a great wish to talk with me about what I had seen, and he and I became firm friends" (*Narrative of a Japanese*, vol. 1, p. 230).

[4] The name would indicate that this was a Chinese merchant, but I have not been able to trace him further. Many foreign firms, including Walsh & Co. used Chinese compradores in Yokohama.

[5] Commodore Josiah Tattnall was in charge of the United States East India Squadron. The "Peiho affair" stemmed from the effort by British and French forces to enforce the treaties of 1858 between England,

confident of the approval of his government tacitly at least. The only apology he had to make was that any one must be placed, as he was, amidst the slaughter of kindred blood before they could determine what a man should do in a like emergency.

Sunday, January 15, 1860

Service as usual by Mr. Brown. 22 persons present. In the evening the first Christian Communion was held in Mr. Brown's house.

Monday, January 16, 1860

The resident Americans at this port were invited to meet Mr. Harris this morning at 12 at the Consulate. There were but few present. Mr. H[arris] addressed them respecting their location in Yokohama. The reasons assigned for insisting that Kanagawa alone should be occupied by foreigners were these. When the treaty was in process of negotiation it was his wish to have the foreign settlement at Yokohama, requesting to include it, the Japanese objected, and he officially asserted that Kanagawa alone should be the port. After the treaty was negotiated, then the Japanese wished him to take Yokohama. He refused now. So his main reason was that as a question of faith with the Japanese, and of honor, our government could not consistently accept Yokohama. He gave as other reasons that the Japanese

could isolate foreigners at Yokohama as completely as at Deshima. He furthermore thought that trade would be promoted in the end by a removal to Kanagawa as the merchants would be brought in more direct contact with the people and would buy more of our imports. He further contended that the Kanagawa shore was better protected from the elements, and read finally a clause in the treaty which he regarded as giving the Consul necessary powers to make a forced removal.

The merchants, on the other hand, opposed any change, because ships could not lie so near the Kanagawa shore, and even lighters could not approach at low water within several hundred yards. Hence a greatly increased expense of receiving and delivering freights. Because there were no provisions on the Kanagawa side for business, viz., the Custom House and wharves, and they ought to have some assurance that they could have them before leaving Yokohama, where they had them both. That they were already established at Yokohama and the removal would be attended with great expense and loss, and that if the Japanese chose to grant more than the treaty asked for it was no compromise of national honor to accept *more*. Some desultory conversation occurred when Mr. H[arris] announced that he had nothing more to add. The merchants conferred among themselves a short time without coming to any definite conclusion as to what course they should take, but the feeling was manifestly against a removal from Yokohama unless forced so to do.[6]

France, and China that called for the residence in Peking of English and French ministers. The Americans had signed their own treaty with China in the wake of these treaties, but in 1859 the Chinese suddenly refused to allow Western ministers entry to Peking. The British and French were determined to fight their way up the Peiho to Peking, but at the Taku forts they met with serious resistance and four of their gunboats were sunk with considerable loss of life. Although the Americans had adopted a position of neutrality in the confrontation, Commodore Tattnall independently engaged in this battle on the British and French side, justifying his action with the famous line that "blood is thicker than water." See John K. Fairbank, Edwin O. Reischauer, and Albert M. Craig, *East Asia: The Modern Transformation* (Boston: Houghton Mifflin Co., 1965), p. 170. See

also George M. Brooke, Jr., ed., *John M. Brooke's Pacific Cruise and Japanese Adventure, 1858–1860* (Honolulu: University of Hawaii Press, 1986), p. 243n.

[6] The issue of Yokohama rather than Kanagawa as a center of merchant activity dated to the opening of the port on July 4, 1859. Joseph Heco recorded that when he, Harris, and Dorr arrived in the port on June 30, "We observed building everywhere in progress on the Yokohama side." " 'I observe, Harris,' " he quotes Dorr saying, " 'that they are erecting houses on the flat opposite to Kanagawa. I suppose the Japanese Government intend this for a second Deshima, but of course we cannot accept that sort of thing.' " " 'Certainly not,' replied the Minister. 'But that will be a battle you will have to fight since you are the Consul of the port.' " Despite Dorr's efforts, Heco notes, "At length, however Dr. Hall

While I sit writing this evening I hear on every side the barking of dogs. Kanagawa abounds in a breed of wolfish curs that growl and bark furiously at the white stranger. They hang around the house, but we have given over shooting at them for they are legion. The cats are large and would be quite handsome but for a great abbreviation of their caudal appendages. Rats are numerous, nightly they scamper over the ceilings in droves.

A fire was discovered in Elmstone's[7] compound at 3 A.M., supposed to be the work of an incendiary. Extinguished without much damage.

Tuesday, January 17, 1860

Took a long walk with Henderson on the Tokaido. Nothing of interest occurred till we passed the turning off place to Yokohama. We then came into a part of the road much less frequented by foreigners and were, of course, objects of curiosity. Scores of children dogged our footsteps, following now on one side and now on the other, and oft times running ahead of us reminding of boy days and trainings and following the soldiers. They kept up an interminable string of *"Anata Ohio," "Nippon Ohio," "dochiye, dochiye"* [Where are you going?], *"tempo stots"* [a penny please], etc. After two miles walking we came to a break in the houses and were rid for a while of our boy escort. We entered another village again and encountered a fresh swarm of bareheaded urchins whose outcries heralded our approach. Our route was the same as that pursued some days since on horseback in company with Mr. B[rown]. We continued our walk till we passed the village also and emerged into the open country beyond. A pretty stream with a deep and sometimes a lovely bed flowed near the road side. At one point when it turned the corner of a cliff it had found a subterranean passage, disappearing in the hill on one side and emerging on the other fifteen yards distant. Our walk had extended now five or six miles, and the country beyond, presenting few attractions to foot weary pedestrians, we turned about.

In the last village we passed through were numerous Japanese tea houses or inns. As we reached them on our return their clean look and quiet attracted us to seek a little rest. We approached one, but no sooner did we show signs of entering than all the attendant girls fled as if old Nick himself were at their heels. Away they scampered out of doors and windows, laughing, looking over their shoulders and casting Parthian glances in their retreat as if after all their flight was needless. We entered hoping to reassure the timid ones by our good behavior. Two married women remained behind and civilly escorted us through the house, but were so evidently ill at ease that we took pity on them and left them, though a little rest would have been acceptable. There was quite a crowd in the street by this time watching us

of Walsh & Co. was found bold enough to back the merchants' view of the case. On his own responsibility he procurred a plot of land on the Yokohama side, and proceeded to establish himself here. This was quite in defiance of the Consul's view, but Dr. Hall was a practical man and saw the immense advantages over Kanagawa possessed by Yokohama in facilities for shipping. The land he occupied is now known as No. 2 Bund [this was first the home of Walsh & Co. and after 1861 of Walsh Hall & Co.]. After that a guest of Walsh & Co. secured the lot next to No. 2, now known as No. 3, while Jardine and Matheson soon after selected No. 1, and Dent & Co. Nos. 4 and 5." The Dr. Hall referred to here was Dr. George Hall, no relation to Francis Hall, but subsequently a friend, who convinced Francis to join Walsh & Co. at the time of the doctor's departure from Japan in 1861. See Joseph Heco, *Narrative of a*

Japanese, vol. 1, pp. 200–201; 216–17. There is an interesting map of Yokohama published in July 1860, which confirms the fact that Dr. Hall established the American presence on the Yokohama Bund even before William Keswick established the English presence there. This map shows the waterfront lots in sequence of their occupancy and clearly indicates the first lot to be "American" and the second to be "English." See Kanagawa kenminbu kenshi henshūshitsu, eds., *Kanagawa kenshi, shiryōhen* (10) *kinsei* (7) (Tokyo: Dainihon insatsu kabushiki kaisha, 1978), n.p.

7 C. T. Elmstone is listed as the Yokohama representative of Sasoon, Sons & Co. in *The China Directory* (1862) (Kong Kong: Shortrede & Co., 1862), p. 51; he is also mentioned as Capt. Elmstone in Brooke, *John M. Brooke's Pacific Cruise and Japanese Adventure*, p. 173.

with great curiosity. There was a still larger house adjoining which seemed to have no occupants save a man and his wife. This we entered, but no sooner were we inside than there was a grand scamper of women and girls who were inside and whom we had not observed. Away they flew out of the back doors and wherever there was egress. The woman of the house, with a gesture of the hands, beckoned us not to come any further. I told her and her husband in the best Japanese I could muster for the occasion that we wished merely to see the house. She appeared a little reassured and we took a look at the rooms. This house had but one story but was very large, on the ground it was divided by the sliding screens into numerous small rooms about ten feet by ten each. There were thirty rooms, possibly more. They had no furniture except the mats on the floors. The traveller brings his own bedding, either on his back, or by the hands of a servant. Refreshments are obtained at the adjoining refectories. Girls can always be seen passing in and out of these tea houses, or inns, with a tray of refreshments from some cook shop nearby. The only man in the house followed me about evidently not quite sure of my intentions. Seeing the poor people were annoyed evidently by our presence we turned to face them. The people belonging to the house were clustered together near the door. There were two or three married women, and peeping over their shoulders were the frightened girls. Approaching the mistress of the house I offered her a trifling present, for I have provided myself for such emergencies. She refused, I insisted, but she only refused the more. I reached above her shoulder and offered it to one of the girls; she turned and ran away. I then was about to lay it on the mat, but the mistress seemed so afraid of us, *timeo Danaos et dona ferentis* [sc. I fear Greeks bearing gifts] that I was ready to put my *shinjo* back in my pocket and say *Sionara*, or good bye.

"Well," said I to my companion "we are likely to be compelled to make our long walk without rest or so much as a cup of tea, but we will not give it up yet." All this neighborhood seemed to be houses of entertainment, and we passed on, whenever we made any signs of halting, all fleeing, till we came to a house where a good natured looking fellow was standing in front of his house, or just within it. "We will try this" we said. The house was small compared with the others. Two women were over the fire and a buxom lass was with them. At first they all seemed a little shy but gathering courage, the women poured out some tea and told the girl to bring it to us. She started with the two cups on a tray and timidly approached us. When near enough so to do she reached out the tray at arms length, but no sooner did H[enderson] put out his hand to take a cup than quite overcome she dropped tray, cups, and tea, on the floor and ran as if for life. The scene was so ludicrous that we burst into a roar of laughter. The old ladies laughed too and once more filled the cups and brought them to us. While we were drinking, the fat cheeked girl came back cautiously. So when we had finished the tea, I motioned to the girl that she must come and take the cups. Somewhat restored in her mind she did so and as I placed mine on the tray I laid with it a present. She was no longer afraid but went herself to get our cups refilled and brought them to us. The people were now quite friendly and took us all through the house, and as for the girl, the revulsion of feelings was so great that she looked as if every drop of her blood was rushing to her face, which was deep scarlet and her cheeks were glowing like coals of fire. She covered her face with her hands and said *atsi atsi*, hot! hot! No doubt it was.

By this time the neighbors seemed to have recovered their confidence, for when we entered another house nearby we were civilly received and shown through the house and then asked to walk upstairs where tea and sweetened hot water was brought us. The little upstairs room was crowded by the street idlers who followed us in. We sat down and drank their moderate drink and talked with them. As usual they were curious to examine our clothes and everything we had about us. Two girls waited upon us. H[enderson] gave his cigar to one of them, which she smoked and declared very good, but when I took some shiny beads out of my pocket the cigar was soon forgotten. The damsel at once left H[enderson] and came and sat by me. The beads had won her away and it cost H[enderson] his kid gloves to win her back.

The common arrangement of all these tea houses so far as I have seen is usually this. The front part of the house is occupied by the family. The houses are long, and in the rear is a second house perhaps. If so, there will be a little court between the two where there is a pond of water, some evergreen trees, and perhaps artificial rock work with flowers. There are piazzas around this little court, and here is a favorite place for the family or traveller to sit. This little summer house in the rear is intended for a more retired place. When I go into these houses I am usually asked to go up stairs, there is a view to be seen either of the bay or the handsome fields around. There is generally one flight of stairs to the front chambers and another flight in the rear. We had not gone far from this last house when we came to another where were a number of girls. There was no backwardness here, we were invited in, shown through the house, and offered refreshments, which we declined. There were half a dozen girls here evidently of a very low class. We passed one or two other houses like this. These I suspect were not tea houses but licensed houses of prostitution. As to the character of the teahouse inmates generally I am at a loss to determine from what I have seen. That they are all open houses of prostitution I doubt. I saw in one of them in their sacred recess images of things that it would not do to name to ears polite.

We made another halt at a house managed by three married women, who earnestly beckoned us in. Weary, as well as hungry, we concluded to make a halt here. We were most kindly treated. We were taken into a room by ourselves, a brazier of charcoal was placed before us. The three women were joined by yet another, an old lady of a prepossessing face. They were anxious to serve us. First they brought hot tea. Then they roasted over our brazier coals on a nice gridiron a thick cake of rice batter. This they gave us to eat hot with sugar. It was delicate and palatable. Then they brought *mekans*, a sweet orange that grows on the island of Sikok [Shikoku]. They pressed us to eat and wished us to carry away some of the rice cakes and seemed sorry to have us refuse.

But I explained to them that our pockets were not big enough and they appeared content. They were very chatty and talked me up to the full extent of my acquaintance with the language. They called in two little girls, one thirteen [and] one sixteen years of age, sisters. They appeared modest girls and were delighted with my gifts of beads, combs, etc. And when we paid them an ichibu for our entertainment they were greatly delighted and were urgent in their invitations that we should come again. We did not make another stop till we were nearly at home. Here we were served with hot water in which was steeped a stew of blossoms like the strawberry flowers. The taste was not particularly pleasant. Here were also three married women and four girls who were very quiet. One of them looked very ill. I was astonished here by one of the married ladies asking one to play "bean porridge hot." Whether the game is a Japanese one, or one they have learned, I do not know. Without further adventure we reached home.

Wednesday, January 18, 1860

A quiet day, spent mostly at home. Did a little shopping in Yokohama for Mrs. H[epburn].

Thursday, January 19, 1860

The street, stores and houses are beginning to put on their holiday garb as the New Year approaches. A carpenter who has been making chairs for Dr. H[epburn] brought his work home this morning and received his pay—twenty ichibus. A couple of hours after, his wife's mother came to inquire for him, when it appeared that he had taken the money and run away with it, leaving a wife and family behind. There was great trouble among the poor people, workmen had lost their wages and family its head. As I passed the shop they stopped me to tell me all about it and were in a state of great terrible excitement. I could only recommend them to inform the officers and hope the deserter may be speedily caught.

Two boys rowed me across the bay today. They worked with a will, and though the day was cold and drizzly with a Scotch Mist one of them bared the upper half of his body to the skin.

Friday, January 20, 1860

Went over to Yokohama by boat and returned walking around the bay. Stopped to rest at a *chaiya*, or tea house. A native traveller invited me to his room and offered me a share of his dinner, which consisted of fish, fried and steamed in oil, eggs broken and boiled with vegetables, hot sake and tea. I tried the fish and tea which was good. I tasted the hot sake, it has a not unpleasant taste and contains a small proportion of alcohol, less than ale. The people drink a great deal of it before showing intoxication. This traveller was emptying his second jug, small brown earthen jugs hold a pint reminding me of Dutch beer jugs, and his flushed face and reddened eyes showed that the hot beverage was beginning to take effect. He grew, moreover, less reserved in his conversation, which finally took action towards the all prevailing theme in Nippon. Our attending servants were two chipper women with blackened teeth. They were as usual especially polite and attentive and seemed really solicitous about my hands, which were chilled with the long walk. They repeatedly asked me to hold them over the fire, and finally one of them, first warming her own hands, commenced rubbing mine. I asked them what the people would do on the New Year's day. "They would rest from work, eat, drink sake, walk leisurely about, visit the country, make excursions on the water, play battledore, dance, sing, and play an instrument, make visits, give and receive presents," doing in short very much as fashionable New York might do on the same day. I made them some trifling presents and departed with urgent invitations to come again.

Saturday, January 21, 1860

Took a long horseback ride on the Tokaido. Mr. Harris was to return to Yedo and Mr. Brown and myself escorted him as far as Kawasaki, and the river Logo,[8] which is the boundary line laid down by the treaty to the limit foreigners are permitted to go in the direction of Yedo. The day was fine. We were in the saddle a few minutes before eleven and started off at a brisk trot. We hardly slackened rein till we reached Kawasaki. Mr. Harris was further escorted by two officials who were deputed to the duty by the government and who were also mounted. Our horses were good stuff for Japanese horses and we made the seven or eight miles by quarter past twelve. We had horn saddles and stirrups, but our two officials used the Japanese saddle and the heavy curved stirrup much like the Mexican. A little more than half way one of our attendant cavaliers was rolled in the dirt by a slip, stumble, and fall of his horse. They rolled over together and we were gratified to see our companion get up again little hurt except in his feelings. With short intervals of open space the road was hemmed in by houses on either sides.

The streets were looking handsomely today under their New Year preparation. All along the street in front of the houses were planted for the occasion young pines and firs and the tall slim bamboo canes. This long vista of evergreens had an exceedingly beautiful effect so that the village seemed planted in a summer grove of pines where branches were waving in a summer holiday. From the eaves of the roofs hung fringes of rice straw two feet in length. Over the doorways this was interrupted by a rosette of green leaves, mostly a species of fern. In the center of the rosette of green was a large orange, over which were laid horizontally a string of dried persimmon figs, a strip of fish, or a roll of charcoal wrapped around with paper. The inns and tea houses had in addition a large crawfish boiled to bring out its bright red color, which grasped the orange

[8] The River Logo was in fact the Rokugo, or the name given to the lower stream of the River Tama along which Kawasaki is located. It constituted the treaty limits beyond which foreign residents of Yokohama were not allowed to travel without special permission to visit Edo.

with its claws. And some added bits of bright colored paper and other ornaments. The straw fringes were also frequently ornamented with bits of paper tied in at frequent intervals.

Through two green lanes we rode, our attendants shouting to the people to clear the way. The country, as at Kanagawa, was broken with low ridges and flat intervals till we were within two miles and a half of the river Logo, when a break in the continuous walls of the houses gave us the first glimpse of the immense flat champagne country which surrounds the capital city of Yedo, and which for fifty miles from the bay is one unrelieved level of lands, not swampy but moist and intersticed with streams from the little riverlet to the more majestic rushings of the river Logo, a river about the breadth of the Chemung above Elmira.

The flat lands, which are divided into numerous fields and patches were covered with wheat and rice stubble. Tall cranes, blue and white, were stalking about, and numerous wild geese were as contentedly feeding as domesticated ones in their own poultry yard. The Tokaido follows the trend of the coast hills, near Kawasaki the lowlands wet by the tides turn it a little more inland. Over this road Mr. H[arris] passed on his first journey to Yedo from Shimoda. He pointed out to us an inn where he halted and stated that all along the road the inhabitants of the houses and shops prostrated themselves on mats by the road side as he passed. We could not accompany Mr. H[arris] beyond the river Logo, and on its banks we all halted at the inn of "Ten Thousand Felicities." Is not this a suitable title for a hotel, always provided its felicities are great as set forth? How much more suggestive than the "Smith Hotel," or the "Hotel de Brown." Our *betto*, or groom, had according to the custom of the country run on foot with the horses, keeping pace with them. He ran ahead to the hotel of the felicities to inform them of the distinguished arrival. The hotel is situated where the highway makes a sharp turn down to the ferry. It was in a corner of the angle thus made and on the other corners were similar inns. They were the usual low buildings open to the streets with mat floors and sliding partitions. A narrow street turned off from the highway and led into the court of the myriad felicities.

Groups of men and women were seated on the mats within partaking of their meals. One group consisted of man, wife, and daughter, the latter looking very neat and clean in their fresh looking garments and clean light kerchiefs tied over their heads. On our return in the afternoon I saw the same group trudging along the road three miles from the inn. We reined up our horses in the courtyard and dismounted, and while we went into the inn our smoking animals were provided with stabling, for this was a house of entertainment for both man and beast. The landlord met us at the door, bowing low to the mats, and conducted us upstairs into a room that had a spacious view across the open country. There was no furniture in the room except a pair of pictures, scenery in outline, in which I saw, as I have seen before, that the Japanese have knowledge of the art of perspective drawing. Over the sliding screens was a fine lattice work of unpainted wood in squares and hexagonals. There was a piazza off the south side, and thither we had brought a low bench and covered it with a cotton rug and had us be seated. We were exposed to view from the court in the rear and whither gathered a crowd of boys and girls to stare at the strangers. There was a group of smiling, bright eyed girls standing together twelve to fourteen years of age who were made very happy by the present of an ichibu to be divided among them. Meantime our attentive Abigail was ready with tea which was handed to us, each cup on a lacquered tray of the proper size as becomes dignitaries, for in Japan, one soon learns, there are aristocratic degrees among teacups and trays. A group of girls stood in the stairway watching our movements with eager interest. If we ventured near them, away they scampered down the steps, as though greatly frightened yet laughing the while and showing their unfailing white teeth. Mr. H[arris] conciliated them to a nearer approach by cutting off some of his gilded buttons and presenting them. While we were taking our tea and rest above stairs our attendant officers were taking their rice and sake down stairs.

We parted with Mr. H[arris] at this place who kept on his way to Yedo while we returned. We went down to the ferry with Mr. H[arris]. Ferry boats do not differ much the world over. The river Logo is crossed by flat bottomed boats let across with poles. I noticed in the river a large number of timber crafts. After bidding adieu to the Minister we mounted our horses again and struck off by a horse road into the country to visit a large temple.[9] Our way wound among the stubble fields and through extensive orchards of the pears. These orchards were systematically planted in rows. At the height of five feet from the ground the trees had apparently been grafted with four sets of grafts, as these grew up they were cut back and trained horizontally till the whole orchard presented an even flat surface like a house floor with young twigs standing up above, which too were symmetrically as well as systematically cut back. I have never seen in any home orchard of peach, apple, or pear such thorough cutting back as these pear orchards presented. The stumpy arms and branches were curious to behold, yet the upper surface of the orchards presented an even level. It is to the thorough system of cutting back, the fine large fruit is indebted for its handsome appearance. I hope when spring returns to visit something of the Japanese mode of culture.

We passed some temple grounds noticeable for their beautiful hedges of orange and the cryptomeria Japonica. A ride of a mile brought us to the temple we were in quest of. The temple grounds were surrounded by a moat a yard across and full of water. On the opposite side of the moat was a solid stone wall six feet high also enclosing the grounds. Above the wall stood thick rows of evergreen trees, pines and firs and evergreen oak. But above all rose the black massive tiled roofs of the temple itself. The wall was about two hundred feet in width by three hundred in length. We followed down one side of the wall, turned a corner into a narrow street paved in the center with stone and flanked by tea houses which led us to the temple entrance. We passed through a gateway in the wall into the open court. A broad stone walk led up to the temple. On the right was a massive oblong tank hewn out of a solid stone and filled with running water. On the rim of its basin were a few copper cash left by devotees. A little further to the right were the priests' apartments in a large spacious building. On the left was the bell tower, a square structure built on a massive stone foundation ten or twelve feet above ground and fifteen feet square.[10] On either side of the walk, just at the foot of the temple steps, there were bronze lanterns not less than ten feet high fashioned in the shape of a Chinese pagoda. Before us stood the temple. It was seventy five feet in front by fifty deep, I should judge, and was a sight to behold with its immense timbers of polished and carved Kiaki[11] wood. A wood whose grain resembles our chestnut in color, but which has the hardness and beauty of our black walnut. The tiled roof was elaborately wrought and adorned with shiny ornaments of brass, colorful heads of dragons grimaced at us from the facade. The pillars in front were shod at their bases with heavy castings of copper. Ascending a flight of several stone steps, on which a man was prostrating himself in worship, we stood within the vestibule. It was a narrow hall several feet in width extending across the front. At either end were shrines with grim idols seated therein. Sunk in the floor was the treasury box, which was eight feet long, four wide, and as many deep, it was covered with a grating of wood secured by a lock. In front of the box and facing the altar kneeled a worshipper who, before he rose, wrapped a few cash in paper and tossed them into the treasury. I looked in, there was a small and low mound filling the box and I suspect the jolly fat priest I saw within does not wait

---

[9] From subsequent visits it is clear that this was the Kawasaki-Daishi, or Heigenji, a Shingon temple dedicated to Kōbō Daishi, which dated to 1128. This temple was a popular tourist attraction during the bakumatsu period.

[10] For a photograph of this bell tower taken by Felix Beato, a contemporary photographer who was active in Yokohama during Hall's period of residence there, see Yokohama Kaikō Shiryō Kan, eds., *F. Beato bakumatsu nihon shashin shū* (Yokohama: Yokohama Kaikō Shiryō Kan, 1987), p. 59.

[11] Keyaki, or zelkova.

for the box to run over before he empties it.

The vestibule was separated from the main room by a wide screen of large dimension in the middle and sliding doors on either side of the screen. At the entrance was something like a long counter covered with paper and books behind which were several men who had altogether a business air about them. We entered the main room than which there could be nothing more scrupulously neat and clean. A large portion of this room was occupied by the altar and its belongings. It would be impossible to convey anything like an adequate impression of what I saw here. It was one grand glitter of brass and gilding rising gradually from the floor to the ceiling. The articles were so numerous and nondescript in character that I can compare them to nothing seen outside of a Buddhist temple. Amidst a profusion of brass cups and wares, brass flowers, tripods, pedestals, urns, etc., were many lighted lanterns standing on elegantly wrought bronze pedestals, braziers were burning with endless flame, but conspicuous above all were the candelabras of brass fashioned after the similitude of the lotus flower. They were ten feet high, and the broad leaves, the closed and half opened buds, the full opened flower, and the heavy lead receptacles were beautifully fashioned. Behind them brocade hangings of gold and silver tissue formed a little recess in which were more elaborate ornaments on which was flickering the light from some concealed blaze. But amidst all these ornaments I saw no idols. On the ceilings there were panels executed in colors with rare taste and beauty. There were flying Amidas as gracefully drawn as many temple angels in continental cathedrals. We were politely received by the attending priest, who escorted us about, showing us all that was to be seen. We were particularly grateful with a work in brass which stood on the vestibule and was covered up. This he ordered to be uncovered. On a pedestal of massive brass were three figures in bronze of grotesque appearance supporting on their shoulders a round tablet with twelve faces. Each face was a little panel six inches long and four high, and in each panel were figures in bronze of various animals executed with a skill and fidelity that I think cannot be surpassed anywhere. The dog,

wolf, bear, ape, rat, dragon, deer, wild boar, etc., were represented in natural postures and habit. I must confess that I strongly coveted those bronzes and should they have been detached should not have hesitated to have chaffered with the priest over a bargain for them. There was a massive basin in brass which the father seemed very proud of and which he desired us to lift. I did so, but it taxed my strength to the utmost. During our visit we were followed and attentively regarded by a crowd of idlers. Inviting the priest to return our visit, which he seemed inclined to do, we parted. As we passed by a tea house at the entrance, attention was drawn to a colossal statue of another Japanese divinity of a less celestial type.

Sunday, January 22, 1860

Service by Mr. Brown. Attendance increasing.

Monday, January 23, 1860

Today is Japanese New Year's, the same in China. Our servants and the people we have come in contact with have been looking forward to this day and often talking to us about it. At midnight the temple bells began to toll and were heard at intervals till morning. The Japanese do not make so much parade over their New Year, at least in Kanagawa, as the Chinese do. Last evening the streets were brilliant with huge lanterns hung before every door. The manner of decorating the houses I have already mentioned. Today, our servants tell us, will be devoted to leisure walks in the country and amusements generally. Making calls is an important feature of the day. We had hardly arisen from the breakfast table before we had a call from the head priest of this temple. He was out in full dress, silk brocade gown, brocade mitre on his head, and silk scarf across his shoulders. As usual he was very affable and brought a New Year's gift of some cake (Azuheimake) in a neat little box tied with a band of red and white cords made of some vegetable fibre. On the top of the box was the customary bit of fish wrapped in a variegated paper. The old man hardly stopped to pay us the compliments of the season and smilingly bid us goodbye bowing low to the ground. I walked out to see what the people were doing.

The streets were full of men, women, and children all in their holiday garb. I crossed the fields to the Consulate. On my way I heard a loud buzzing noise. I fancied a big blue bottle fly about my ears or the sound of many bees in the clover. But the sound was too loud for that. Then I saw groups of well dressed children kite flying. They gave the kites string and others rapidly drew them in again, and I saw it was the kite that made the noise. There were a half dozen of them over my head, and looking across the fields I could see many more high in the air, "buzz," "buzz" they went. The kites were square, oblong, bird shape, butterfly shape, all shapes, and painted. The large square ones were most common with pictures of the emperor, a stern looking man got up in elaborate costume having all the colors of the rainbow. The butterflies were next the favorites and there were many nondescript ministers. Not only boys, but men were happy in flying their humming kites. The noise was made by a thin shred of bamboo stretched taughtly across the top of the kite and played upon by the wind. The boys were in fine feather and wanted one to try their kites, which I did, and were much pleased when I told them that American boys also flew kites.

The priest attached to the temple occupied by the Consulate made his New Year's call soon after I did. His present was some packages of white paper neatly tied up, enclosed in a wrapper with the donor's name thereon and laid upon a tray. At the consulate [I] got H[enderson] to accompany me on a walk to Yokohama and the country. At Yokohama we found the shops closed. Here or there was one that had a shutter off just as on a holyday at home there will always be some craftsmen and traders who even on holydays lie in secret wait for any chance trade that may drift along in the accustomed channels. The greed of gain is as unblushing under a brown skin as a white. In the compound occupied by the officials extensive calling was in progress. The officials singly or in pairs or companies were going from home to home to make their calls accompanied by a servant. At the gateway of the house, the caller exchanged his street shoes for another pair carried by the servant, on this second pair he walked to the entrance of the house and left them off as he stepped on the mats with his stocking feet. And then such obeisances as were made at the doorway between the caller and the called upon can be seen nowhere out of Japan. Facing each other they fell upon their knees on the mats and again and again bowed their heads to the mat, lifting their faces towards each other, smiling and drawing in their breath with a sibilant growl and then knocking their heads on the floor again. Generally the callers did not enter the houses, but contented themselves with ceremoniously leaving their cards. These were their names written on strips of paper of a fingers length and breadth. At the doors of the house, and just outside, was a lacquered stand on which was placed a box to receive the cards. At other houses a wooden bracket was fastened by the side of the door and the cards were slipped on a spindle. Sometimes this spindle for receiving the names was placed at the outside gate. No doubt this custom of a ceremonious giving of cards is centuries old, and who knows that ours was not borrowed therefrom. The officials were all handsomely dressed. Light blue robes were most commonly worn made of silk with family or official coat of arms thereon. My own servant came out with a new silk robe and a family coat of arms.

From Yokohama we started out into the country making our way through the swamp. The causeway was full of people passing and repassing from the houses in the swamp. For it was a holiday there too, and the poor girls were tricked out in all their finery, with lips painted vermilion and face and neck thickly coated with white. It was a sad sight to see the troops of little girls of years too tender to know any crime wandering about in childish simplicity and delight. One, a pretty creature not more than ten years old, was handsomely dressed in black silk trimmed with red. Her headdress was elaborately made. Resting on the top of her head and among her shiny black hair was a butterfly with outspread wings formed of crapes of various colors patterned with bands of gold and silver braid. It was ingeniously fashioned. This little queen of the opening year, playing unconsciously about the serpents dew, was attended by a group of girls, a dozen or more of the same tender age. There was no envy of their little leader in their looks, but instead they seemed proud of her. I made her very happy by the present of a string of beads to add to her holiday finery, and hoped that she at least might be spared the fate of those around her.

We followed the causeway leading toward Kanagawa till we were just outside of the village, and there turned to the left passing through a small village, and here too the children were happy in their holiday. There were three little girls playing battledore, as beautiful and happy looking children as one could wish to see. Everywhere today I am delighted with the pretty looks of the children. Long as I live I shall carry their memory with me, and when in other lands I shall see children at play I shall wish again that I might see the black eyed crown and glowing cheeks of the little girls of Nippon. This village was in a little vale among the hills, completely embowered in the shade of the holly and evergreen oaks. There was one superb hedge of green not less than fifteen feet high trimmed to an exact evenness of surface. We struck out for the country following a broad path that wound around the foot of the hills and past thatched cottages buried in hedge and shade. My companion, who had spent some years on the continent, said they reminded him of the chalets of Switzerland. There was a temple on the top of a round low hill with tall and straight fir trees growing all around it, one of the sort of picturesque spots I know of. We climbed up and found many men there, officers with swords, but to what use the temple was now converted was a mystery. It had the air of some official place. We passed other wayside shrines, which are always numerous wherever we go. Many of them are charmingly situated on eminences surrounded by groves of pine and oak. Cleanly kept paths lead to them across the fields, often hedged in and shaded, and well cut steps of stone lead up

the mountain side to the shrine. Today all these places were in holyday attire. There were offerings of flowers, of garments, of salt, placed before them.

A walk of four miles brought us into the Tokaido again in the village of Hodoriya [Hodogaya]. Our coming had been spied by the children across the fields. When we entered the Tokaido the wide street was fairly blockaded by them. There must have been a hundred following us at once, all talking and shouting together saying it was New Year's day, and were we English, American, French, or Dutch. And when I said we were Hottentots they repeated the word Hottentot wondering what new nationality this was. The boys told us where we could find tea and sweet cake, but the pretty girls playing battledore pleased one more than the rowdy kite flying boys. One woman offered us hot water to drink, standing in the door of her house, which she was afraid to have us enter, but we passed such hospitalities by till we came to our former resting place near a little bank. Here we were kindly received as before by the household, and hot tea and hot sake and raw eggs and oranges were brought us. The old ladies seemed delighted to have us once more for guests and I made the coy serving girl forever happy by the gift of a few buttons to wear on her robe where it folded across the bosom.

But the day was passing, the sun was low and we hastened on passing through such swarms of children, that it was a wonder where they all came from. So happy too they all were with the annual holiday, I played battledore with one little girl and another much to their joy, and among a group of boys I scattered handfuls of cash. On the top of the last hill we met a group of former acquaintances, and we had to stop once more to play battledore with a pair of timid young damsels and their less timid black toothed chaperons. Soon the sun had set and we stopped no more. Tired and gratified with our New Year among the gay Nipponese we were not sorry to return. Prominent among the offerings at the various temples were large cakes or loaves of unbaked rice flour. In some places there was a prodigal display of them, but nowhere did I see such large loaves as at the houses in the swamp, the largest of which were two feet in diameter, and there was one of a peculiar shape appropriate to the place.

Tuesday, January 24, 1860

Took another walk today with Dr. H[epburn]. We went back into the country, the beautiful appearance of which greatly gratified us. I was specially pleased to see some isolated farm houses with granaries, sheds for animals, manures, etc. We came, too, upon a small pond whose sides and ends were lost in a nearby marsh. Numerous waterfowl were sporting on the surface. To the great regret of the children, who today as usual officiated as guides, we had no firearms with us. In these walks we frequently encounter little wayside niches with objects of worship in them. The humblest of them had not been respected in the general New Year's decoration.

Many of the neighboring Japanese females called in the afternoon at the temple. They had all the curiosity of children about everything that was new and nearly all they saw was both new and wonderful to them. They wandered from one object to another asking some questions that we could answer and many more that we could not. In one set of visitors were three females, two married and a young girl. The latter from the respect paid to her by her companions, and from her superior dress, belonged evidently to a better class. Her garments were of silk, the under garments of white figured silk. Broad belts of fine material girded her waist. Her head dress was very elaborate. The hair being gathered in one heavy fold on the forehead tied with silver cord and ornamented with long hair pins of shell, in shape like a tuning fork. I sat in my room and they were [in] the adjoining apartment, the screens were closed. I put my music box in motion and immediately, without asking leave, they were in my bedroom. They were delighted with the music box, but true to the woman instinct the large mirror attracted still more. They stood before it and adjusted their great shiny masses of hair. Then my bed was a wonder to people who sleep on the floor. It was evident they appreciated its comfort, for first one half reclined on it and then the little damsel was lifted on it by her chaperon that she might see how soft it was. Then she must put my cap on, but the little miss said no it would disarrange her hair. A few buttons increased her delight more. Just before sunset the streets were again gay with children and young girls who were flying kites and playing battledore. The street was handsome with their bright faces and picturesque costumes. I only wished that New Year's might come oftener, it was so delightful to witness their enjoyment of their simple pleasures. Their clean toilettes set off their handsome dark hair in which a sash of red crape was twisted, and their ruddy olive complexions, their dresses gay with trimmings of crimson, scarlet, and purple, and their clean white stockings, quite thrilled my heart. And too there were numbers of girls in their holiday attire carrying a babe on their back, and baby was got up sumptuously in brown silk and scarlet crape. May their happy faces never know what clouds of sorrow sometimes cover the sky.

Near my residence are grounds and extensive buildings belonging to [Sakai] Oki-no-Kami. On Friday last one of his retainers here in charge, for the Prince himself lives at Yedo, was disgraced for drunkenness and committed suicide by Hara Kiri.

Wednesday, January 25, 1860

Made a visit to the *Powhatan* in company with our people of the Mission. Hospitably entertained by the Commodore, partook of a cold collation and were treated to music by the band. Saw the preparations made for carrying over the Japanese embassy. The Embassy consists of twenty men of rank and fifty-one servants. Their own steamer is to accompany them, Nagasaki built by the Dutch.[12] They were desirous to bring on board two hundred

---

[12] This was the *Kanrin Maru*, which sailed as the escort to the official Embassy. The vessel was a 300-ton corvette built in Holland. It was manned by a Japanese crew selected from the shogunate's Nagasaki Naval

boxes of presents, but the *Powhatan* had no storage room for so great a number. They also wished to carry their norimons and ample supplies of sake, rice, charcoal, etc., just as if they were going to a desolate land. They are mere children in their ideas of what is before them.

Thursday, January 26, 1860

High wind all day, no boats crossing the bay. Passed the day in reading, writing and walking.

Friday, January 27, 1860

The exchange of money which has been interrupted for several days by the advent of the New Year's holidays was resumed today. On my return from the Custom House I saw a boatman sitting in his boat having taken off his upper garments which he seemed to be intensely examining unmindful of weather at the freezing point and the whipping north wind. Coming nearer to him I saw he was industriously engaged in killing certain "small deer" with which the preserves of Japanese garments abound.

Saturday, January 28, 1860

Took a ramble in the country again today in company with the Dr. and Mrs. H[epburn] and Miss B[rown].[13] We visited a beautiful valley about a mile and a half distant where are numerous temples and *Gakoomong* [gakumon] or school houses. The name of the collection of Buddhist temples is *Buikenjhi* [Bukenji].[14] I have seen nothing so picturesque in the vicinity of Kanagawa as the locality of these temples. There are five of them besides numerous school buildings, whither shortly will gather young priests from all the adjacent country for instruction. Our party were all in raptures of delight over the retirement, neatness, and beauty of this place. Clean walks, evergreen hedgerows, and trees both graceful and majestic, shed an air of such quiet beauty that each exclaimed "who would not live here." We entered one of the temples, which we found much superior to those on the Tokaido. In summer this must be a charming spot indeed. I shall say more of it after other visits.

Leaving the little valley and its numerous temples we climbed the adjacent hills and found ourselves on an elevation commanding a view of the surrounding country, the bay of Yedo up and down for many miles, and the distant ranges of mountains. There was a fleet of fishing junks far out in the bay looking in the distance with their white sails like a brood of gulls on the water. A ship under full sail was just coming in to her anchorage. We could in the extreme transparency of the air see the break of the waves around her cutwake, and better than that we could see with our glass the stars and stripes floating at her masthead. The hills across the bay were very clear in their outline, we seldom see them so distinct, while to the southwest the blue outline of lofty ranges

---

Academy, and sailed to the United States nominally under the command of Kimura Setsu-no-Kami, but Kimura was heavily assisted by Lieutenant John M. Brooke. For an interesting discussion of the first Japanese embassy to the United States (1860) see Masao Miyoshi, *As We Saw Them* (Berkeley: University of California Press, 1979). For Brooke's role see Brooke, *John M. Brooke's Pacific Cruise and Japanese Adventure*, pp. 213ff.

[13] Julia Maria Brown was the oldest daughter of S. R. Brown. Born on February 18, 1840, she had just turned twenty. She later married John Frederic Lowder, whose mother, Mrs. Lowder, married Russell Alcock in 1862. Lowder served as junior assistant in the British consu-

late at Hakodate in 1862 and 1863.

[14] The Bukenji was a Nichiren sect temple known for its scholars and students. The temple was greatly expanded in 1719 to include five school buildings, twenty-five dormitories, and more than three hundred students. The temple complex was thoroughly refurbished in 1858 and so was once again in its prime at the time that Hall saw it. In 1871 and 1885 fires destroyed a number of the temple's buildings, and those that survived were subsequently destroyed in the 1923 Kanto earthquake. The site remains famous for its many lovely cherry trees. See Yokohama shi yakusho, eds., *Yokohama shishiko—Butsuji hen* (Tokyo: Meichō Shuppan, 1973), pp. 864–66.

broke the horizon's edge, but still further was Mt. Fusi and its eternal snows. We were on an extensive plateau broken into low ridges covered with fields under cultivation, old woods, and many plantations of young firs. Of the latter there was one thrifty nursery near a Sintoo temple. On my way homeward we found the boys on the cliffs overlooking the Tokaido flying their kites. A couple of them clambered up the camellia trees and gathered for us some of the freshly opened blossoms. The cold weather of the past month checked their blooming, but the week past we have had milder weather and I see the buds not only of the camellia waking into life but also of the plum and cherry and other trees whose names I do not know. These are the first throbs of returning animation in the pulsations of the coming spring. In my room a dwarf cherry full of blossoms diffuses a fragrance like that of the hyacinth. These blooming dwarfs are a substitute for our winter blossoming bulbs at home.

Sunday, January 29, 1860

A Sunday morning walk. Last night was frosty and cold. This morning the sun has risen clean and warm. The air is delicious to breath. In our front yard the sparrows are flitting about shaking their wings in the warm sunbeams which fall into our enclosure so pleasantly. A crow has just flown into the old pine near the bell. His glossy black coat throwing back the sunlight as from a mirror. There he sits now singing his morning hymn in his deep bass voice, harsh and rough as if he had bronchitis. I go out into the streets, the sun fills them too with its morning radiance, but the streets seem unusually quiet. Sent on by the charming freshness of the new day I followed along this little back street till I came to a temple where men are busy gathering the new year decorations, which last night were taken down throughout the streets, into bundles for the fire. Only the store houses keep them up, and they will keep them up four days longer when streets and houses will subside into their everyday dress and the people, too, till another New Year brings new holidays.

I leave the streets and the temple and strike across the paddy fields toward the hills. The air sweeps strong and chill down the valley, the wind is north. The wet rice fields are frozen and the little narrow paths of turf that divide are frozen so that they bear me up. The tall blue cranes are picking their morning meal out of the frozen mud. There far away to the southwest I see the snowy peak of Fusi. It looks dazzling white and cold this morning. I take an out of the way path across the fields and over the hill. An old pine, stout with resistance to centuries of storms, is on the summit of the hill on a mound. From the pine I overlook the bay, all its waters are lost in the misty distance. The fishing fleet are sailing out to their daily labor, the foreign merchant ships lie idly at their anchors. I leave the hill top and wander on by the secluded path til I am lost among low ridges and groves of cryptomerias, young pines, chestnut, and oak. I meet no one in the path, and the quiet seems indeed that of the Sabbath. But Japan has no Sabbath, so I know that the quiet still air of the country is its every day garb. It is a country of quiet.

The air is so exhilarating and I still wander on and on into new paths, over more hills, then I dip down into a little valley where there is a small hamlet of a few thatched cottages. The simple people are not used to the stranger, perhaps have never seen a white man before, for the woman with dirty face and disheveled hair who suddenly meets me at the corner of the hedge screams as Laura Matilda screams when she sees a caterpillar and runs as fast as her clumsy clog shoes will permit. Then all the village turn out and stare at the stranger. Only one has the courage to speak, and he asks, "where am I going." When I tell him I am walking for pleasure he stares still more, for it is evidently an idea that he cannot comprehend, how there is pleasure in so doing.

I leave the little hamlet behind me and strike into the woods and fields again. I am surprised to see so much wild uncultivated land. I could almost fancy that I am in some rural portion of New England where the old woods have been cut off and new forests and underbrush is springing up, but the richness of the soil, the easy slope of the hills, the little narrow valleys and especially the absence of rocks and stones forbid any such fancy. But I look again, it may be New England yet, for here hard by the path are heaps of opened chestnut burrs. I see too the young white and black oaks and there is even, if eyesight did not deceive, the tag alder forming a border to this grove of pines and the pines, too, look like New England. No, the pines are planted in rows like an orchard, and now I see the young oaks are so planted also. There are evergreen oaks and glossy camellias, and yonder comes a horse laden with straw panniers and shoed with straw shoes, and his driver wears a handkerchief on his head, and a quilted fabric around his body, and a man follows behind with buckets of manure dangling from either end of a pole which is borne on his shoulders, and he wears straw shoes and loose cotton robes—no this cannot be New England.

I wind around among the crooked paths till I get a glimpse down a long valley of the sea, and there floating from its high staff on the hill is the flag of the American Consulate. I am approaching home again. The sun has risen higher and now numerous people are crossing the fields. There are men in twos or threes, who like myself appear to be walking without apparent purpose. Here are three women going to the fields to rake up the rushes and long grass with curious bamboo rakes. I hear on the hill the sound of a woodchopper's axe and I see his faggots of wood tied up with strong ropes, making small bundles which will be swung over the horse's back and so borne to market. Horses are going and coming with loads and men are passing with their buckets of manure and children are flying kites and shout across the fields, "*Ohio Anata Ohio.*" An old bareheaded man bent with his age passes me and salutes me as he goes by. I think how

friendly the common people of Nippon seem when met out of the streets, and so thinking I came again to the old temple that is my home.

Monday, January 30, 1860

Today comes the news from Yedo that "Dan"[15] the confidential servant of Mr. Alcock was killed last evening at 5 o'clock. Dan was himself a porter of Messrs Fargo and Co., San Francisco, being one of the Japanese sailors shipwrecked on that coast. His knowledge of both English and Japanese rendered him invaluable to the British Consulate. But his manners gave much offense to the Japanese. He was puffed up with the pride of place and became insolent and abrasive to the people. He had also an unfortunate intrigue with a tea house damsel which resulted in her imprisonment, and that of her family, and his being shunned in every tea house he entered. Last evening he was playing with some children in front of the Consulate when he was approached from behind and struck through the back with a short sword, expiring almost instantly. The murderer escaped. The Japanese find themselves to be a vindictive people, and the common practice of wearing side arms supplies a ready means of practicing their revenge. There is wisdom in those civilized laws that forbid the wearing of concealed weapons.

Tuesday, January 31, 1860

Another mail from the States today and still nothing for me. We hear of another disastrous fire at Yedo on the 29th. Major Boyle[16] of the English Army is here and has made a contract

[15] Dan, or "Dan Ketch," whose original name was Iwakichi (later changed to Denkichi) was one of the castaways of the *Eiriki-maru* along with Joseph Heco. Perry permitted him to join the *Mississippi* on her return to the United States from China in 1854 and the sailors gave him the name "Dan Ketch." In 1859 Dan returned to China and was hired by Rutherford Alcock to serve as interpreter for the British legation in Yedo. In the process he became a British subject. Back in Japan he flaunted Western ways and dress and antagonized many of the natives. Even Alcock saw him as

"obnoxious" and was warned to send him out of the country for his own safety. See Katherine Plummer, *The Shogun's Reluctant Ambassadors* (Tokyo: Lotus Press, 1985), pp. 244ff; Sir Rutherford Alcock, *The Capital of the Tycoon* (London: Longman, Green, Roberts, 1863), vol. 1, p. 331; see also W. G. Beasley, "Japanese Castaways and British Interpreters," *Monumenta Nipponica*, vol. 46, no. 1 (Spring 1991), pp. 96–97.

[16] It is not clear who Major Boyle was, but the Japanese records list one H. L. Boyle, an Englishman, as residing in Yokohama during this period. See *Yokohama*

with the Japanese Government to furnish 3000 horses for the coming campaigns in China.

Wednesday, February 1, 1860

I hear today respecting Dan, the murdered servant, that he has received warning more than once that his life was in danger. The Consulate at Yedo was so informed. Not only that, they were threatened with fire and were even requested to make choice of another temple to flee to when it should happen. Dan was in the regular employ of the British government as interpreter, was registered as a British subject, and the offense is political as well as personal. The brother of the girl before spoken of is said to be conspiring and consequently becomes suspected. The murderer wore a basket over his face, such as I saw two soldiers of the deceased King wearing when begging on the Tokaido, a long basket covering the head with a bamboo grating before the eyes that may see and not be seen. The beggars were clad in robes of pure white and wore swords in black velvet coverings.

In the evening I went to a temple on the hill near the Consulate, a Sintoo temple frequented by boatmen.[17] Tonight the temple was illuminated by rows of lanterns suspended in front and large lanterns at the gate. A broad way paved in the center with stone led from the Tokaido up to the temple. A flight of stone steps led up to the temple, which was situated on a little flat rock half way up the hill. The temple itself was small and plain. Like other Sintoo temples it had no idols but a polished metal mirror stood in the niche usually allotted to the idols. There were significant gilded carvings and the customary brazier, temple service of cups, lamps, candelabra, lotus flowers, etc. At the left of the temple was a little porch occupied by a colossal mask representing an ogre-like face with a monstrosity of nose and a long grey mustache. The particular significance of it I could not learn. As this was a boatman's temple it might have been one of the old sea kings for ought I know. At any rate its devotees were numerous and the crowd of people repeatedly called my attention to the big nose, as if on it hung all the hopes of the poor fishermen for the year. There were numerous votive offerings hung up around this masque, a half bushel of the top scalp locks of the boatmen were tied by a string and hanging there, beating about in the wind, dust, and rain, till they were furry with dirt and age. There were rude pictures of pinks on little square boards also hung up. Pictures of birds, beast and dragon. I recognized one naval picture, that of the great clumsy craft built by the Prince of Satsuma at Nagasaki. This was a fair representation of that ship. There was a futile effort at a war steamer, another tablet hung up, and the American flag was flying from the masthead. Who of our gallant Commodores and Captains has been praying for luck at this nautical temple and hung up this votive tablet? Or was it a thank offering of the bold Japanese who punched Commodore Biddle[18] down, or

---

shishikō, sangyō hen, p. 31. Boyle may well have accompanied Edward Barrington de Fonblanque, who wrote *Niphon and Pe-che-li; or Two Years in Japan and Northern China* (London: Saunders, Otley, and Co., 1863), who arrived in Japan in January of 1860, and who writes: "A few days after my arrival at Hong Kong, General Straubenzee determined upon despatching me to Japan, for the purpose of reporting upon the resources of that country, with reference to its capability of furnishing supplies for the expeditionary army in China;— and, if practicable, procuring several thousand horses for the purpose of military transport" (pp. 6–7). Fonblanque worked out a deal for horses with the Edo government on January 13, 1860 (p. 35). Alcock confirms the arrival of a "Commissariat Officer" who wanted to buy three thousand horses. See his *Capital of the Tycoon*, vol. 1, p. 329. Unfortunately he does not give the officer's name. Fonblanque later made it possible for Hall to go to Nagasaki on one of the British Army's chartered vessels.

[17] This would have been the Susaki Myōjin, which stood next to the Hongakuji where the American Consulate was located.

[18] Commodore James Biddle arrived in Japan in 1846. Like Perry who followed him he hoped to "open" Japan diplomatically and to secure the better treatment of American sailors stranded on Japanese shores. In the process of negotiating with Japanese authorities, Biddle was often subject to unruly Japanese conduct, and on one occasion when he went to receive the shogun's reply on a Japanese boat he was physically assaulted and pushed back into his own vessel by one of the samurai.

only that of some poor boatman escaped from being run down by one of our great seamonsters. I both recognized and was recognized by the boatmen, many of whom I had employed. The kind old ferrymaster came up while I stood there to make his offering. The worship was short, the worshipper stood a moment before the shrine, bowed his head, lifted up his supplicating hands palm to palm, muttered a few words, then wrapped a few cash in a piece of white paper and threw them on the temple mats and departed. Some paid their prayer to the big mask also, but little cash only. Whereas the temple mats were literally covered with their cheap offerings. It takes fifty cash to make a cent and less than half that number was the usual offering. The priests in attendance, four or five, seemed pleased to see us and gave us oranges.

A few steps below the level of the temple was a large statue sunk in water. Here the women came and touched their hands and faces with the sacred water and wiped them on a row of figured cotton cloths suspended near. The avenue to the temple was thronged all evening. For some distance either side on the Tokaido were the stands of fruit and toy sellers and hucksters. Their wares were spread out on stands and lighted by paper lanterns suspended from bamboo poles. Children's toys, prints, and eatables were the principal wares offered for sale. There were oranges and dried persimmons, and sticky looking confectioneries, rice cakes, fish dipped in rice batter and fried in oil, crabs and prawns served up hot or cold, and tea and sake. There were miniature swords and boats for the children, dolls without clothes that could and could not cry, jumping jacks, sugar cats and wooden dogs and tiny houses and pictures of the great emperors among others, as pleasing to the Nipponese as similar toys to similar little folks at home.

Thursday, February 2, 1860

The rumor today is that two persons have been arrested for the murder of Dan. The girl's brother is still missing. Yangaro, the merchant, spent the evening at my room. I taught him English and he taught me in turn Japanese. Speaking of the families of Daimios, he told me that their children were betrothed at a very early age. If the betrothed husband died before, or after, consummation of the marriage the bereaved maiden was thenceforth doomed to a life of single blessedness. He naively remarked that he thought that was very bad. I agreed with him. Earthquake about 6 P.M., slight.

Friday, February 3, 1860

Servants were out last night frolicking and came home late in the evening redolent of sake. I put them outdoors and scolded them to the best of my abilities in Japanese. I think the moral force of my remarks was somewhat blunted by the want of words. I did my scolding, book in hand, first looking up some ugly word and then firing it off at their heads at a venture. I succeeded in telling them they were *drunkards* and *smelt bad*. The lecture was received with heads on the mats in counterfeit humility. Kami's father came, a severe looking old man the intensity of whose looks was heightened by the loss of an eye and the smallpox footprints. He took his erring son aside, promising to whip him. I think he confined the whipping to his tongue, but Kami however came back with red eyes and woebegone expression, and promised the practice of all the virtues for an uncertain time to come, and so ended our household event.

A pleasant old lady called this morning accompanied by a pretty lass of eighteen her niece, as modest as pretty, and by an intelligent

---

The official Japanese reply to Biddle's request was also lacking in respect, and to many Americans this incident displayed the results of a "weak" policy toward Japan. The Perry expedition was consequently designed to demonstrate appropriate American force, and Perry refused to submit himself to any of the conditions that had led to Biddle's demise. For a discussion of the Biddle expediton see Harry Emerson Wildes, *Aliens in the East* (Philadelphia: University of Pennsylvania Press, 1937), pp. 227–32.

looking man, a native physician who she said was her son. The mother looked too young to have so old a son. Yet she assured me she was sixty years old. While talking with her, to my utter amazement, she removed from her mouth her upper teeth! I saw that her grand looking teeth, which I had no suspicion of being other than natural, were artificial. They were fastened to a plate which was fitted to the mouth on the same principle as dentists employ—the principle of suction, but yet were made of wood throughout. She allowed the ladies to examine them, but she was unwilling that I should see them, except as she held them in her hand. Tonight the streets are noisy with drums and shouts, it being some religious fete night.

Saturday, February 4, 1860

Returning from the Consulate this evening I was passed in the streets by two boys, one behind the other running. They were naked except a white cloth around their heads and another around their loins. The foremost one bore a lantern and following close upon him was the second, tinkling a small hand bell. They were forerunners announcing the coming of some propitious deity as near as I could understand. As the thermometer was barely above the freezing point I hoped the bare little fellows might not have far to run. But I daily meet naked men and conclude I live among a race susceptible of bearing cold.

Sunday, February 5, 1860

This morning there are bonfires in the fields and the open courts about the temples. It is another religious festival, and so during the first thirty days of the new year these sacred days, or rather days devoted to some special object, will frequently occur. The straw fringes and other house decorations of the New Year, which were taken down a few days since and put by for this day, are now made into bonfires. Each little street or neighborhood had its own bonfires. I went into the fields back of our temple where "our folks" bonfire was blazing

famously under the superintendence of Yangaro. Men, women, boys, and girls, surrounded the fire, and some were roasting amidst its embers cakes of rice flour. Others inserted their cakes in split bamboo poles and so heated the cakes more cleanlily. These cakes were to be taken to their houses and there eaten by the family, they were supposed to have virtue in driving away disease throughout the year. The boys, full of glee like all boys, were scattered over the fields setting fire to the dried grass.

Monday, February 6, 1860

I took a long walk today along the hills that overlook the Tokaido. I was on more elevated ground than I have been before and could see far up and down the bay and over a great breadth of country. Everywhere the characteristics of the country are the same. The whole surface is broken up into little hills of every possible shape and size with narrow and long valleys intervening. The valleys are almost wholly cultivated, but a good proportion of the hill slopes are left to a growth of scrubby underbrush, tall bamboo grass, or forest patches of pine and fir from the young trees just set out with the regularity of orchards and every intermediate age to old forest monarchs. The lowlands are both wet and dry. There are numerous small streams whose water is carefully husbanded for the irrigation of the rice fields. I see few stones except in the beds of the brooks and then not numerous. In the hills are great beds of clay and sandstone from which numerous springs and wells are fed. Along the Tokaido are some abrupt clay and sandstone cliffs, the sandstone soft and friable. The people have scraped out little basins along the road side, where the sweet waters from the hills gather, and supply the neighborhood. I have only once seen any fish in any of the streams and those were very small.

I visited today a temple which had a picturesque situation a few rods back from the highway at the foot of one of the hills. The temple was clean looking, and its grounds were in the best order. Nothing unsightly, no rubbish of stick, straw, or stone detracted from the inviting look. A boy priest met me at the gate and invited me to walk in. We passed into the grounds in the rear, which had been laid out against the hillside with more than a rude taste. A small grotto had been scooped out of the soft rock which on one side of the ground had a perpendicular face. In the grotto were plants standing in pots waiting for the breath of returning spring to revive their beauty and bloom. Others hung in short baskets from the ceiling. At the entrance was a spring of clear water which, as the day was warm, I found refreshing. From the grotto a path led to a bamboo bridge that spanned an artificial pond fed also by the mountain spring. There were still other basins of water scooped out of the rock. The entire slope for half the distance up the hill is covered with smooth turf among which wind the respective paths. The turf plots are adorned with a variety of trees quaintly trained and the walks bordered with flowering shrubs. Rustic gates of bamboo interrupted the walks where they opened unto broad platforms or shelves in the hill side designed for resting places, and having a grand look out upon the bay and shore of Yokohama. I fancy this place will be charming in the summer time, and I shall hope then to revisit it and say more about it.

I visited another temple, a Mia,[19] situated on the top of a high narrow hill and reached by a long flight of stone steps from the Tokaido. There was worshipping there. It seemed to be resorted to by parents with their children. I passed many fathers and mothers taking their little ones up the steep stone stairs and I found the little temple at the top full of bright eyed children crowding around the priest, who seemed to be performing service for their special benefit. I stood in the doorway and looked on, but the kneeling priest paid no attention to my approach although the noise of the multitude should have told him a stranger was nearby. Before him was a brazier of fire, several brass cups half full of water, and twigs of evergreen oak. His clasped hands were ever and anon raised to his face, a few words muttered then some faggots were laid across the

---

[19] A *miya*, or Shinto shrine. Hall did not always distinguish between Shinto shrines and Buddhist temples.

fire like a child's cob house, and as the flame devoured them he touched the brass cups with a metal rod, picked off leaves of the oak, and threw them down near the fire, muttered more prayers, evidently reading from a book of prayers that lay open before him. But so long as the children stood in the door they paid scance regard to the priest, but were continually shouting to the vociferous welcomers. The priest seemed in nowise disturbed by the noise of his young flock, but continued his prayers and offerings. I bid them there goodbye, and the little fellows with one accord said come again tomorrow. As I returned down the steps I thought of the Sunday Schools at home in contrast with these little pagan worshippers.

A mile or so from this temple was another. To this one also a broad stone walk led from the Tokaido. The temple was small and mean. On either side of it were several little out buildings like cupboards with a roof. In one were a number of lamps, in another a great heap of used up pens, while others were empty. There was a school here and the pens, smashed, blunted and broken, were the children's pens. I was surrounded at this place by a crowd of children and young men. They were kind, though rather pressing and noisy in their zeal to do me service. There was nothing attractive about this place except the pleasant retired situation and some fine old trees that formed a background of living green. There was a flat leafed cedar they called the "Tree of the Sun" (Hinoki), a name to which its great height and symmetry entitled it.

It is perhaps within bounds to say that in every group of children like this, one half the girls capable of sustaining the weight of an infant, had one on their backs. Little toddlers just able to clearly walk themselves carried another little bundle of humanity wrapped in blue cotton and crimson crape. As I turned to go away and was half way down the stone walk back to the street, a half clad girl perhaps twelve years old with rounded pretty face followed me and asked if she might go with me. How can you, said I, you have a child to carry. I can leave the child she said. But I told her she must not go. What the poor child's thoughts, or wishes, could have been, I could not know, but she was in truthful earnest. Before this I asked another little miss if she would shinjo on me one of a pair of white copper rings that she wore. She asked the older ones about her if it would be right to do so, and when they said yes she pulled it off and handed it to me. I made her more than happy by the gift of a few matches in return. I was much amused yesterday after giving some to a couple of priests who called upon us. I lighted one to show them how to do it. Then they began to talk between themselves, looked puzzled, and laughed heartily. They were saying that if they lighted them to show them to their friends, the fun was all over, and at last asked me if it were not so. I told them yes, then they laughed again as much to say what good does a present do a man that he can't show to his friends. Yet they are very glad to get hold of matches and will pay high prices for them.

I followed the hill top till I came out into the Tokaido in the village of Hodoriya [Hodogaya]. The women of a tea house where I had stopped before once saw me coming down the road and beckoned me earnestly to stop. I did so. Before when I had been here, I had found the house very quiet and free from visitors. Now several parties were dining on fish and rice. A man was asleep in the retired room where I preferred to take my tea, so the old ladies took me to an upper room in front. At the landing at the top of the stairs I stumbled upon another pair of sleepers, and in the only room there was, behind a screen, a girl lay asleep or awake, but I was hardly in the room before she was up and dressed, which in Japan is about one and the same thing. A hibatchi was brought, I asked for tea and it came as soon as prepared with a plate of oranges. The little serving girl recognized me, and, I believe, was really glad to see me again. Why not? I gave her buttons before. Then came the old lady of old, a nice old lady, bringing me a shinjo of a book. They had many inquiries to make, asked after H[enderson], who was the one with me before, and wished me to take

him some oranges. And next time I came, they said when I left, I must bring him again, only the little serving girl who enjoys my small gifts said "no, *anata stori*"—come alone. I left and the children who are great visitors' guides led me to a cock fight a little way off, but it was not amusement to my taste and I struck across the fields for home.

Tuesday, February 7, 1860

My long walk of yesterday in the warm sun has over fatigued me, so I am little sorry that today proves a wet one and confines me for the most part to the house. Busy myself preparing letters by the *Powhatan*. The carpenter was in this evening. He had much to tell me about Udano mountain, which was the special case of a very good kami. No bad man could ascend this mountain, no matter how strong he was when he got to a certain height he could get no further but would fall on fours and paw the earth like a horse. But there is a temple, *Zenkoiji tera* [Zenkōji],[20] situated on a hill to which no bad man can attain. At a certain height he would be turned into a dog, or swine, or cow. He could return to his proper shape, and this experience always made a good man of him. Then there is another mountain in which, if a base man should strike at a tree with an axe with intent to fell the tree, the axe would fall against his own leg and chop it off! So too, if one should draw a bow at the sun the arrow would pierce the sinning marksman. Or if he should defile a temple with impurity, sickness would seize the sacrilegious wretch.

The first created man came to the province of Ishya [Ise?]. He had no wife but begat children of a serpent that came out of the waters. He and his immediate descendants after death became Kamis and now watch over Nippon. The greatest priest in the empire lives in this province. It is a seat of learning. From thence are distributed annually almanacs with tables

[20] Zenkōji is a temple located in the city of Nagano in Nagano Prefecture. It is affiliated with the Tendai and Jōdo sects and is said to have been built in 642 to house the first Buddhist image sent to Japan in 552 by the King of the Korean kingdom of Paekche. While its ac- tual origins remain clouded, historical records of the early ninth century clearly make reference to it. By the Tokugawa period it was best known for its Amida fig- ure that was thought to have miraculous powers.

of eclipses and rising and setting of the sun, etc. On the first of each year every house receives from the temple at Iseya [Ise?] a list of sacred days, lucky and unlucky days. These are presented but a small gift of corn is expected in return.

Wednesday, February 8, 1860

Busy all day with letters. In the evening went to Yokohama with Henderson to send some papers. Did not return till midnight.

Thursday, February 9, 1860

Today the embassadors to America embarked on the *Powhatan*. They were received with a salute of seventeen guns and the national flag of the Empire was raised at the fore. The *Powhatan* steamed down to Yokohama in the evening. Inquiring in the evening what certain lights on the hill were I received the popular Japanese account of will of the wisp. These lights are foxes out taking a pleasure walk on the hills lighting their lanterns while they do so. The lanterns are their own illuminated breaths. So they walk backwards and forwards, and should a simple man or a drunkard come along they would lead him astray into water and swamps. Of good men they were afraid, but were a terror to all bad men. I would like these strange creatures, I said, and I was promised the sight. I want I could catch one. If I approached one it would turn into a girl. Well, said I, I will catch the girl then. But the people thought I could not do that.

Friday, February 10, 1860

The *Powhatan* is at anchor today busy with a court of inquiry. Formal complaint was made by the British Minister at Yedo that the officers of the ship had used undue influence to get ichibus. Hence the court of inquiry, which only

showed that no improper course of this kind had been taken. Large amounts of ichibus had in some cases been granted, but as favors and not through fear.

The Commissioners, we hear, are very happy aboard the ship.[21] An amusing anecdote is told of one. The interpreter presented himself to the officers of the deck and stated that "a high official" had a very singular but common want which it would hardly do to spread in full upon these pages.

Saturday, February 11, 1860

Took a short walk in the country in the afternoon. Came upon a little hamlet at the foot of a hill on the top of which hill was a small temple. People very glad to see me and particularly desirous of having my pistol.

Sunday, February 12, 1860

Sabbath service as usual. First snow storm of the season. Storm began at 2 1/2 P.M. with wind N.N.W. Snowed fast till sunset making three inches on the even ground. The evergreens are beautiful in their snowy mantles.

Monday, February 13, 1860

A clear sunrise and brilliant landscape. The contrasted white of the sun and the dark green of the foliage are charming to see. But the sun comes out warm and soon gathers to itself the white drapery of yesterday's storm. The disappeared birds gather again in the old pines in front of the temple and hail the returning warmth with grateful songs. Rode to Yokohama in the afternoon and found the low portions of the road very muddy. By night the snow in exposed situations has disappeared. It yet lingers in shady spots, and the tops of the distant hills are white.

[21] This was the day on which the *Kanrin Maru* sailed for the United States carrying a portion of the official mission. The *Powhatan*, which carried the Japanese ambassadors, did not depart until the 13th.

Tuesday, February 14, 1860

The carpenter came to Brown today with a doleful face and said that he had been forbidden by the officials to continue his work on a stable which he had begun for B[rown] without delay. B[rown] repaired to the Consul's and stated the interference. Dorr immediately dispatched a messenger to the Honjin, or Mayor's office, requesting him to call. He did call making his appearance at the Consulate with his suite of attendants. Upon being informed why he was sent for, viz., to know why any official had dared so far to overlook treaty rights as to interfere with an American citizen in that manner, the Mayor disavowed the act. He said he had not only given no orders to the carpenter, but did not know who could have done so. He promised to call at Mr. B[rown]'s house and rectify the matter and discover who had made this officious interference. Accordingly he came to B[rown]'s house and sent a servant to summon the carpenter. The latter came, his usually dark olive color changed to an ashen gray, and went through the customary prostration. The Mayor told him to go on with the work after inquiring how large accommodations he was about to build. Tarakagi[22] (the carpenter) departed with a lightened heart. He returned in the evening and said that this very Mayor, who had so solemnly protested his ignorance of the whole transaction, was the man who had personally given orders to him not to go on with the work, saying that the residents in this compound were "only physicians and had no need for horses." This is a fair sample of Japanese diplomacy and honesty.

Tarakagi gives me the following legends. Seven hundred years ago about seventy five miles from Yedo lived the prince Kiomori [Taira Kiyomori]. He was ordered to build an island in one day between sunrise and sunset. So he gathered his materials and a great number of laborers and when all was prepared one morning at break of day the great work was commenced. The island was rapidly cut of the deep under the labor of so many busy workmen but the night approached, the sun was near its setting, and there was a good hour's

work yet to be done. One hour more and the island was finished. And what was worse, if the work was not completed in one day this land would all settle back into the sea again. Kiomori was a wise man also, and a magician, and when he saw the sun about to set he went out by himself and with his fan he beckoned to the sun and commanded that for one hour it should stand still. The sun stood still, the island was finished, and remains to this day a monument of Kiomori's great power and wisdom, in resemblance to the biblical tale of Joshua commanding the sun "stand thou still upon Gibeon; and thou, Moon, in the valley of Ajalon."

There is another legend similar to that of the "Wandering Jew." There are old men who wander up and down this empire who have been bidden to remain on earth. They are old men with white hair and long white beards. No one has power to harm them; fire will not consume or water drown them. They are met in the street but are unknown, and so will they wander on for ages to come. The popular belief places them in the rank of kami rather than ordinary men.

Wednesday, February 15, 1860

After dinner I escorted Miss B[rown] on a horseback ride on the Tokaido. We took a brisk trot of nearly two miles on this thoroughfare. A lady on horseback was a novel sight to the Nipponese. Everybody rushed out of doors, the near ones shouted in advance that a "foreign woman was coming on horseback," and so we rode down a long file of men, women, and children. Pedestrians scrambled out of the way, women picked up their children, pack horses and their drivers were so bewildered by the novel apparition that instead of clearing the road they stood stock still. The *betto* shouted "clear the way," dogs barked, for we came down the road at a spanking pace. When we turned our horses heads for the return, far as the eye can see the street was full of people watching us and waiting our return. The houses must have emptied their contents in the streets. We came back at a hard trot, the girls from the tea and other houses gazed with

---

[22] Or Terakagi.

a look of admiration to see one of their own sex so elevated, the old ladies shouted *yoka*, and the general look of the natives was one of gratification. Some of the men shouted after us, but happily we could not understand their derisive epithets, we finished our ride without accident.

Thursday, February 16, 1860

Spent most of the day at the Consulate taking testimony in the *Salvage* case. After adjournment took a walk with Gen. D[orr] and Mr. H[enderson] to the hill, and called at some of the teahouses and chatted with the inmates and travellers. One pockmarked traveller who was frolicking with his wife was specially polite and hospitable.

Friday, February 17, 1860

A heavy rain all day from the north, 3 inches water fell. At 2 P.M. I went to Yokohama and found the streets nearly impassable with water. A little after three I started to return, but on reaching the ferry on the Yokohama side I found my boatmen had deserted me. A heavy swell was rolling in from the South, the rain was increasing and they left to return to Kanagawa. I had difficulty in getting another boat but an ichibu tempted a couple of boatmen to take me across. Just as we reached the Kanagawa shore the wind chopped around to the south and the rain fell in torrents. This southwind was very warm, the thermometer rose fifteen degrees in less than an hour from 40° to 55°. In an hour the rain poured in torrents, the wind blew a gale, and then it cleared up as suddenly as the squall had come in.

Saturday, February 18, 1860

At the Consul's taking testimony. Returned home quite exhausted. My boy seeing me resting on my bed wished to know if I was ill. When I replied no, only tired, he offered to give me a shampooing in the Japanese way. I lay down on the mats and he commenced kneading my limbs and joints, pressing the flesh and rubbing it. This process was extended to the back and was finished by a vigorous tatoo beaten on my shoulders. I have not been so thoroughly tickled for years, but I will allow the process seemed to relieve me of fatigue.

The *Medina*, which left a day or two ago, was driven back by yesterday's gale with the loss of bowsprit.

Sunday, February 19, 1860

Sabbath services as usual. Mail arrived at dinner. No letters from home.

Monday, February 20, 1860

Sadagaro [Sadajirō], Hepburn's teacher,[23] brought me today a shinjo of scented envelopes. He sat down and we had a long talk to-

---

[23] Hepburn's teacher was a man named Honda Sadajirō. Honda entered Hepburn's service as the "son" of Suguru Kenri (possibly the "Old Inkyo" of the diary). The elderly Suguru was an acquaintance of the Ise merchant, Takeguchi Kizaemon Nobuyoshi, a supporter and patron of Katsu Kaishū and Saigo Takamori, who had a store in the Fukagawa district of Edo and wanted to set up business contacts in Yokohama. According to Kizaemon's diary, *Yokohama no ki*, "Honda was a physician from Echizen, thirty three years of age, whose occupation was medicine, and who came to Edo. He was deeply interested in studying Dutch [or Western] medicine. Consequently he entered the service of the great Doctor Hepburn in order to learn this field, doing so as the son of the old man (Suguru Kenri). Dr. Hepburn wanted to learn Japanese, so they both taught each other." See Kanagawa Kushi Hensan Kankō Jikkō I-inkai, eds., *Kanagawa kushi*, p. 233. Hall describes him as a "native doctor" which seems to correspond to the Takeguchi account. While Hall continues to refer to him as Sadagaro, I have taken the liberty of using his proper name, Sadajirō, in the remainder of the journal. Honda Sadajirō was more than a physician, however; a disciple of the Kyoto Confucian scholar, calligrapher, and nanga painter Nukina Kaioku (1778–1863), he had wide-ranging interests and was well informed on a broad range of topics. See *Takegawa Chikusai nikki* in Yokohama Archives of History. Chikusai

gether. He first premised what he had to say
with the remark that the people in general
were not permitted to say much about the empire and its officers, and he charged me over
and over again not to repeat what he said. The
subject of dissection came up (Sadajirō is a native doctor), and he said that dissection was
practiced in Japan. This is in contradiction to
previous testimony. He himself had witnessed
dissections and they were common at Oasaca.
Yet, I am told that at Yokohama, when Dr.
Duggan applied to the Governor for the ca-
davers of the criminals, the Governor refused,
and was much horrified at the request. Fatsijo
[Hachijōjima] is not the only penal island of Japan. Various other islands are so used by governments, among others Oki, and the large
island of Sado. Ordinary criminals, as well as
state criminals, are exiled to these islands. The
most powerful prince of the empire is in the
province of Kaga to the north of Yedo. At the
present time there is said to be a large emigration to the island of Yeso. The emigration is
from the populous central provinces about Oasaca and Miaco. The reason assigned is that
the wood in these provinces has been cut off,
all the land is under cultivation, and the mineral wealth is mostly exhausted. Yeso is yet rich
in wood, minerals, and uncultivated fields and
the poor classes emigrate thither. The mountainous provinces of Mutsu and Dewa in the
northern part of Nippon are also rich in mines
of iron, copper, and gold. The extreme northern part of these provinces is famous for its
fine breed of horses.

Tuesday, February 21, 1860

It has been duly announced for some days
past that wrestlers would exhibit their skill at
Yokohama for "fire thing days." I had heard so
much of the fame of the wrestlers of Japan
that I did not omit so good an opportunity to
see them. It is a favorite amusement of the
people.

The wrestlers are picked men. They are
gathered from the lesser walks of life. Wherever among these a man is noted for his size,
strength, or agility, he becomes a wrestler by
profession. He is attached to the retinue of
some prince, wears his coat of arms, and becomes one of his body of servants. He does not
shave the crown of his head, as other Japanese,
but permits his hair to grow long, gathering it
in the usual knot on the top.

They assemble in the arena where they exhibit each morning at eight o'clock for practice. The practice, of which I was not an
acquaintance, is a rough and tumble practice.
They are naked with the exception of the loin
cloth. In the morning practice in the arena, if
wrestling in pairs as in the exhibition, a number enter the arena and try their strength in
seeing how many each can master in wrestling
or throwing. They also made sudden rushes at
their adversaries, lowering their heads to a
level with their shoulders, and striking their
opponents on the heart over the pectorales
majores, the great muscles of the chest. Or
their opposing heads clash. Blood flows freely
from the nose and mouth and the large puffy
discolored tumors rise on the chest from the
force of the blows. To protect their heads in
some measure in the arena their hair is permitted to grow on the crown unlike most of their
countrymen's. After this exercise, which occupies two or three hours, the combatants bathe,
take refreshments, and rest till afternoon,
when the regular spectacle commences.

The place of exhibition in Yokohama is a
rude enclosure formed by the walls of adjacent
buildings and rough boards nailed to high
posts. It is sufficiently high for a gallery, which
is supported by upright or transverse timbers
lashed together with twisted straw ropes. The
building, if so it may be called, has no roof. Its
audience holding capacity is just about equal to
one of our large circus tents at home.

I entered from one of the side streets of Yokohama, through a boarded lane on either side
of which were hucksters' stalls. The whole ar-

---

visited Hepburn and Hall on a number of occasions. He
was a friend of Takeguchi Nobuyoshi. For a published
portion of Takegawa Chikusai's diary see Yamazaki Uji-

hiko, ed., *Izawa bunka shi* (Tsu: Tōa Insatsu Yūgen
Kaisha, 1956).

rangement was strongly suggestive of a rural show in the States. Walking through the lane, I first came to the ticket sellers, who were seated on a raised platform protected from the weather. The tickets were oblong bits of wood, between a quarter and a half inch thick and inch and a half wide and five inches long, inscribed with Japanese characters. The price of a ticket was two tempos, but they were not intended for foreigners, and I was waived in by a gesture of the ticket seller's hand till I came to the entrance. One ichibu was the price of a foreigner's admission. I mildly suggested to the three or four men who guarded the door, and who from their size and appearance might have been retired sporting gentlemen, that this was making a good deal of distinction. No, they said, it was Nippon Hoshiki, Nippon custom, and I might come or stay out as I pleased. It would not do to stand upon ichibus before such sporting characters, so I paid the money and walked in.

The arena was a sand platform raised a foot or two from the ground. The sand being kept in its place by a quilting of straw ropes and matting. It was a rod square. A circle was enscribed within by a further demarcation of straw ropes. A roof covered the whole resting on four tall posts. In a convenient position to the arena was a wide raised seat of boards set apart especially for foreigners. The ground immediately around the arena was divided by poles into small squares, each square having board seats capable of accommodating a half dozen people or so. There were Japanese figures on the backside of each square exactly as opera chairs are numbered at home and distinctly served the same function. These squares were occupied by a large audience of common people, the two tempos spectators. Back of these seats under the gallery were raised seats, the boxes of the establishment, and the gallery also was similarly divided. There were privileged seats for which the occupants paid extra prices (I think from one to two ichibus.) In one of the gallery divisions, fitted up with some extra care with screens and cotton tapestry, sat an official whose duty it was to see that everything was done in order. A suitable police force was in attendance.

The performance had begun when I en-

tered. The wrestlers were medium built men. They were naked, except a stout cloth put around their persons in the shape of a T bandage. This was drawn closely and held very tightly.

The contestants sat on the ground on cushions on either of two sides of the arena and were called in by a herald who stood in the sanded arena to see that there was fair play. His shrill voice was constantly heard while the wrestling was going on. His wand of office was a handsomely lacquered, fan shaped baton and his black tassels and crest.

Another pair from either side of the arena was called up. Their undergarments were thrown off as they raised themselves up revealing their naked figures. They stepped easily and confidently into the arena, each one as he stepped up picking up from the ground a bit of straw, breaking it, and throwing it aside incidentally to put on an air of indifference.

At the feet of the posts supporting the roof of the arena were pails of water, and on the posts hung baskets of salt and paper for rinsing mouth and nose when necessary. The next step was to take a swallow of water and after that each took a little salt between his fingers touched it to his tongue. Then each standing on his own side of the arena back to back raised first one and then the other foot high in the air and stamped with force the sand, swaying himself also as if to render each joint supple for the impending combat. There then was another drink of water, another bit of salt was taken, and the combatants faced and approached each other, sprinkling the salt on the ground between them.

Salt in Japan is the great emblem of purity. Perhaps it was to purify themselves and the ground wherein they might fall that it was used. Coming together in the circle of the arena they bent down facing each other with their hands resting on their bent knees or squatted close to the earth. Having taken a good look at each other they would rise, perhaps go back to the posts, take another swallow of water, another taste of salt, and again face each other.

This was often repeated several times with great deliberation. Perhaps one would make a sudden spring and push at the other when his officer would cry out *Mada*—not yet! or *Mate*—stop! The herald sometimes interfered after two, three, and sometimes half a dozen feints of this kind, and as many water drinking and salt tastings, they appeared to get a fair start slowly rising and extending themselves and closing in upon each other.

It was necessary for the victor to either throw or push his antagonist out of the circle, or to throw him fairly to the ground. The first attempt generally was to force [him] out of the circle. This was done by thrusting with the open palms, striking and hitting with the head, or grappling around the body by main strength of lifting and pushing combined to force each other beyond the circle. While doing this, if a good opportunity occurred of making a throw, they availed themselves of it. There was less real skill of throwing and gripping than I expected to see. Their more common hold was a grasp and lock around each others arms, and if a clutch could be had of the waistcloth, this gave advantage. The wary wrestler was aware of this and avoided such a grip by thrusting out his body.

It was seldom the contest lasted long, a fall to the ground, or a push out of the ring, soon happened to one or the other. The wrestlers often issued a loud cry as they closed in and continued uttering ejaculatory sounds, but quite as often they were very quiet.

Some of the wrestlers rubbed sand between the palms of their hands so that they might have a more secure hold, and rubbed their arm pits with the same, perhaps that in a close embrace their brawny smooth bodies might not slip. I was often surprised when one had a strong grip of the other's waistcloth to see how often, and apparently easily, the wrestler would clear himself from this hold. Little tripping was done, though a few times it was very handsomely done.

One heavy, fat man of immense brawn was pitted against a small active man who carefully watched his chances and with a dexterous twist of his hands, and a lift at the same time, sent his heavy opponent spinning heels over head clear off the platform. Very often one was hurled from the arena down among the spectators, and often both in a close clutch rolled together out of the arena.

Several pairs of the wrestlers had performed, when from side rooms on the right and left emerged a score of new wrestlers who walked into the arena and circling around it went gravely through a pantomime motion of their hands raising and extending them and then they retired—these were the next set who were to exhibit. This was several times repeated as the afternoon wore away. They came in to exhibit their bone and sinew to the admiring spectators.

Each set that came in was larger and larger, till finally with much ostentation came in a score of giants. They were indeed giant men of tremendous limb and muscle. They appeared fat, but their training, while it gave them this appearance, gave them in fact solid muscles as any one could see by close examination. Each of them who were old and renowned wrestlers wore an apron in front extending from his waist to his feet. Their aprons were made of silk and satin nobly embroidered. They bore their names and the coat of arms of their prince. Except this and the loin cloth they were bare.

These huge fellows were known favorites, for they had often been similarly engaged. These had their own herald, who was handsomely draped. They were called into the arena by pairs also. The selection of the pairs is made by the judges, so that often there were seemingly disproportionate matches, a tall one was matched against a short, a slender against a heavy man. But the result showed that the race was not always to the swift, or the battle to the strong.

The efforts put forth by these men were tremendous exhibitions of strength. The largest of all the wrestlers, and I think I saw sixty different ones perform, was a man six and a half feet high on his bare feet. His opponent was six inches less in height but of heavy compact frame. The former was a man of splendid proportions, arms neck chest legs all belonged fittingly together. After the usual preliminaries and feints these giants closed in. Each in a moment had the other in an unyielding grasp. There seemed to be no attempt to throw, it was an exhibition of sheer strength to see which could put the other out of the ring. The latter of the two succeeded in heaving his antagonist to the circumference of the ring, a step more and the victory was his, but that victory hung doubtful.

These animals, for such they were, put forth their utmost strength, one to keep his position in the ring, the other to crowd him one step more back. There they stood apparently immovable, every muscle rising and quivering with the tremendous strain till they stood out in bold relief. Then the larger one seemed to gather himself for one great effort—his limbs stood stiff and rigid, his fingers were corpse-like and bloodless from the tenacity of their grasp, his face was livid with the mounting blood, his eyes were bloodshot, but as if all the fire and energy of his being was concentrated in one rigorous effort he strongly and steadily raised his antagonist from the earth and was able to lever him outside of the magic circle, that and nothing more, not a foot not an inch. There was an evident sensation of relief to both when the contest was decided. And now rose a shout of applause, the tall wrestler was evidently a favorite, indeed he and his antagonist were said to be the 3rd best pair in the empire.

Full a dozen or more of the wrestlers were over six feet in height. Their's was the perfection of animal nature. They looked animal, not brutal. There was neither ferocity in their looks or manners. During the whole exhibition there was nothing of the glaring looks and malignant expressions mentioned in Perry's book.[24]

On the contrary they all had the usual Japanese kind nature. The vanquished bore his defeat with the *utmost* good humor, the victor seldom showed any exultant feeling. There was sometimes a gesture of satisfaction, and once or twice the conqueror laughingly sat down on his prostrate foe. One, only, showed signs of anger, but he was so thoroughly vanquished that he was discreetly quiet. The

larger and older wrestlers often used their open hands to strike their opponents' heads, faces, and shoulders with force during the contest. In no instance was blood drawn.

At intervals the herald appeared and announced that a man, giving his name affiliation and residence, had presented a certain wrestler with so many ichibus, or any other gift. Their gifts were made and announced in the ring irrespective of his becoming victor or vanquished. When some wrestler had made a skillful throw an admiring spectator would take off his upper garments and throw [them] to him. These garments were borne away and afterward returned to their owner, who is expected to redeem them with any present he deems proper.

So fond are the Japanese of this amusement that they not infrequently spend ten, twelve, or fifteen ichibus on their favorites, a great sum for them to pay. The audience were decorous, not boisterously offensive. As usual refreshments were largely consumed during the exhibition. Programmes, pictures, and biographies were passed around and sold.

Several officials honored the spectacle by their attendance. A few women only were present. In Yedo it is improper for them to attend such shows—not so in the country. There was a pretty girl in the gallery with her friends. She seemed to pay little attention to the play, being chiefly occupied with her refreshments and pipe. It was hardly like an opera hunting lady at home to see her, when she wished to move about a little, climb over the gallery rail and go down a ladder, unconscious that the gallery rail had caught her garments and exposed her unprotected limbs in all their proportions. She would not have cared if she had known it, for in Nippon it was nothing more than the exposure of one's face.

In their training the wrestlers consume animal food freely. I was frequently struck with

---

[24] In reference to Japanese wrestlers the Perry volume stated: "As the spectator looked on these over-fed monsters, whose animal natures had been so carefully and successfully developed, and as he watched them, glaring with brutal ferocity at each other, ready to exhibit the cruel instincts of a savage nature, it was easy for him to lose all sense of their being human creatures, and to persuade himself that he was beholding a couple

of brute beasts thirsting for one another's blood. They were, in fact, like a pair of fierce bulls, whose nature they had not only acquired, but even their look and movements." See Francis L. Hawks, comp., *Narrative of the Expedition of an American Squadron to the China Seas and Japan performed in the Years 1852, 1853, 1854, Under the Command of Commodore M. C. Perry* (New York: D. Appleton and Co., 1857), p. 432.

the smallness of their hands and the tapering proportions of their arms. During the performance some individuals came around to collect pay for the cushions we and the others sat on, which, it seems, was an extra. This was true Yankee enterprise.

Wednesday, February 22, 1860

We are honored today by the entry of a Daimio with his train. It is Matsudaira Etsizen-no-Kami,[25] he is the owner of the land about Yokohama as [Sakai] Oki-no-Kami is lord of the Kanagawa soil. I was surprised to see his train, which consisted of 1000 soldiers and 200 servants. His soldiers were well equipped, and were supplied in part with percussion lock muskets. Bleckman, the English interpreter, was passing the Yokohama causeway at the same time and was rudely treated. One seized his horse by the bridle and another raised his fist as if to pull him off, but he struck them back and being well mounted was soon out of the way. Sadajirō tells me that there are only some ten or twelve Daimios to whom the people are obliged to kneel when passing the Tokaido. In Yedo, where the Emperor lives, they must kneel to still less, something like half the number. The Daimio and his servants do not all wear the same coat of arms. The Daimio wears his own, his soldiers another, and his servants another. Thus each Daimio may have two, three, or more coats of arms. When one of these large trains halts for the night they are quartered in inns, temples, and private houses, who receive large recompense. I have heard the Matsudaira's revenues in rice alone to be 1,000,000 sacks per annum. It is an incredible amount.

Thursday, February 23, 1860

I visited today the hill near the American Consulate on which is an edifice that had often excited my curiosity. The grounds are prettily laid out outside of the enclosure. The main gate was closed, but I entered a side gate and was hardly inside before a servant came out of the house and beckoned me away. I continued to walk, saying that I only wished to pass through on to the top of the hill. So I persisted in coming further in. An old man came out of the house and asked me to leave. I told him I would go, slowly halting till I had a survey of the grounds. They were tastefully laid out and decorated with turf, trees, and flowers. The only house was quite plain. But I was interested in the appearance of the man. He was tall and slender with a fine beard and prepossessing intelligent face which bore a troubled sad look. His head was unshaven, and he said that this was not a temple. This strange old man interested me very much, but he spoke so rapidly that I could understand little that he said except that he appeared anxious that I should leave. His face looked so sad that I am sure if my presence was unpleasant to him I did not wish to remain. I made inquiry respecting him and learned that there are many similar places. Their occupants are disgraced soldiers of the emperor. A soldier of high rank has committed some offense, its dire penalty is Hara Kiri, but instead he is banished to these solitary places where he must evermore reside. He is not permitted to go among the haunts of men. On certain occasions he robes himself in white, wears over his face the basket veil that I have before spoken of that his face may not be seen and goes from home to home begging alms. It was men of this set that I had seen about New Year's time. My imperfect knowledge of the language prevents my understanding as fully [as] I wish the condition and fate of these exiles from society.

Friday, February 24, 1860

A fine open spring like day. Went off to the shipping and after my return took a walk with Lars on the cliffs, where we have a charming view of the bay. Stopped to rest at a chaya there, entertained with refreshments, music, etc. One of the damsels gave us an amusing il-

---

[25] At this time Matsudaira Echizen-no-Kami was Matsudaira Mochiaki who succeeded Matsudaira Yoshi-naga (Shungaku) as lord of Echizen in 1858 after the latter was forced from office in the Ansei Purge.

lustration of the way Americans dressed by arraying, as well as she could, her own garments in similar style.

Saturday, February 25, 1860

I find my information respecting the occupant of the house on the hill near Dorr's to be substantially correct. These, or similar places, are occupied by men who having committed some offense for which Hara Kiri would be the proper atonement, instead of thus expetiating, occupy for life these secluded places. The treatment of adultery I find to be this. The injured husband is permitted to slay his wife and paramour, if he slays the paramour alone and allows his wife to escape, he will himself be imprisoned. He may slay the wife and permit the man to escape. Notwithstanding this severity the offense is said to be very common and is often compensated with the injured husband by the payment of money. So, too, if a man buys a girl of her parents for a mistress, and any other man interferes, he is allowed to slay the offender as before.

If two parties become angry and quarrel and one slays the other, the survivor commits Hara Kiri both from fear of punishment and that his children may not be disgraced. For such is the law of Hara Kiri that whoever becomes obnoxious to it and fails to perform it is not only disgraced himself, but his family are forever tainted.

Sunday, February 26, 1860

I sat in the long twilight of this Sunday evening watching the sun go down in the West. I thought of it as departing far towards the land where lie all the memories of other days. My heart followed the sun to those far distant lands. And while the twilight paled out and the shadows gathered round the head of Fusi

Yama, I passed in spirit over the seas and stood with the rising sun over the sweet valley I had left. And I went into that upper room where a group of brethren stood in a sorrowful parting. I felt once again the affectionate grasp of the hand, the tender embrace. I heard the last sweet, sad sounds of adieu and saw again the moistened cheeks and my heart was sad, for what delights had the world to compare with the friendship and love of the dear ones at home. And I gave an hour to pleasant memories of the friends I love and then gathered my spirit again to come back to the real of my life in this far away country.

We sat around our evening fires tonight, the Consul was with us, it was past ten o'clock, when B[row]n came in from accompanying a friend to the ferry and told us there was another murder at Yokohama. Who, it was not known; we supposed some of the drunken Russian sailors we had heard of as being on shore today. To satisfy ourselves, with the Consul at our head, we went to the Honjin, the official residence on the Tokaido to inquire. We found a strong police force watching the streets. At the intersection of other streets with the Tokaido at the leading out of all the paths to the county grounds were posted numerous lamps lighted and the crossings barricaded by ladders and ropes. There was a police officer in nearly every house. Messengers had been dispatched to all the surrounding country and villages where the same policies would be carried out. We found a large number of officers at the Honjin but no interpreter, as we turned into the street again we met Dr. Lindo[26] and Snell[27] mounted on horseback hastening to Yedo preceded by an officer. From them we heard that this evening, about or between half past seven and eight, Capts. Decker and Vos[28] of two Dutch vessels in the harbor had been slain in the main street of Yokohama. One of them was an older man of fifty-eight years, two days in port only, he was a quiet and peaceful old man. They left their friends at the hotel at

[26] Rudolph Lindau describes his discovery of the murdered Dutch captains as well as his ride to Edo with Schnell in his book, *Aus China und Japan*, pp. 300ff.

[27] Edward [or Eduard] Schnell was a partner in Schnell & Perregaux, a Yokohama firm which is listed

in *The China Directory* (1865) (Hong Kong: Daily Press, 1865), p. 239.

[28] Decker was Captain of the Dutch ship *Christian Louis* and De Vos was Captain of the *Helena Louise*.

seven twenty P.M., and soon after eight the tidings came that they were killed. They were found cruelly cut, one had his nose cut off, his mouth cut away and his head laid open, the other was cut down from the shoulder and his head was nearly dissevered. The hand of one was found grasping his cane a hundred feet distant from his body, as though he had attempted to fight. For previous murders there had been perhaps provocation, for this it does not appear that there was the slightest.

Monday, February 27, 1860

Yokohama is overcast with gloom. I have never before seen it wear so still a look. The stores are closed and the foreigners in consequence can do but little business. The street gates are closed and guarded. Among the foreign merchants there is a general feeling of distrust and uneasiness. For where will the blow fall next, who will be the next victim to this unseen but terribly felt presence of hate or revenge. No one believes that the unfortunate victims of last night's tragedy could have given the slightest cause or provocation. Were they the mistaken victims of some man's animosity, or were they acting in compliance with the wishes—possibly orders—of some one of the implacable Daimios? Behind the Yokohama hotel in an outbuilding lay the two bodies. A native surgeon and assistant was busy sewing up the gaping wounds. The men were literally cut to pieces. One blow had cut down through the shoulder of one cleaving its way half through the ribs and laying open the cavity of the chest. It was a fearful testimony of the force of the blow from the ponderous swords of the Japanese. Another blow had severed the head nearly from the shoulders, and there were other deep cuts about the body. The old man had one hand clean cut off at the wrist in

a slanting direction as if the hand had been held up for protection. The other hand was partially severed, the forehead and nose cut away, the left eye cut down and a deep cut across the mouth and cheek and other blows about the head and neck. There were fourteen wounds on one and nine on the other. It would seem that there had been a slight attempt at flight. The spots in the streets had been covered with sand and sprinkled with salt, the emblem of purification. A Chinaman who was nearby saw the attack and fled into a shop close at hand whose proprietor fled with him into an inner room. He saw the hand severed while it was grasped by one of the assassins, and today he has disappeared, probably hidden through fear of being compelled to testify of what he knows. Last evening the same futile attempts were made at Yokohama as at Kanagawa for the arrest of the murderers. A guard of marines was promptly sent on shore from the Russian gunboat [*Japonitch*] and when they made their appearance in the Custom House grounds the Governor was evidently disturbed. They stood sentinel during the night over the dead bodies and guarded the foreign settlement.

Tuesday, February 28, 1860

No discoveries are made today respecting the unhappy tragedy of Sunday. The funeral is postponed on account of the heavy storm of snow and sleet. The ferries are still suspended.

Wednesday, February 29, 1860

This morning at an early hour the Tokaido was honored by the presence of a distinguished female.[29] She was a niece of the present Mikado and was passing from her home in

[29] The lady in question was Michi-no-Miya, the niece of the Emperor Kōmei, who was on her way to Edo to be betrothed to Tokugawa Mochitsugu, the Lord of Kii and brother of the Shogun Iemochi. This was part of a Court Bakufu alliance begun by Ii Naosuke and continued after his death by Andō Nobumasa and Kuze Hirochika. The same policy led in 1862 to the marriage of Kazu-no-Miya to Iemochi. The *Ishin shiryō kōyō* (To-

kyo, 1941), vol. III, p. 266, shows that Michi-no-Miya entered the Wakayama mansion in Edo on March 1, 1860.

Edward Barrington de Fonblanque encountered the same procession. He writes: "M. de Bellecourt had arranged that he would accompany me to Kanagawa today . . . to attend the funeral of the murdered Dutchmen . . . [official objections were made and finally reathe southern provinces—from Miaco, with a large retinue to Yedo. She is there to be betrothed to a younger brother of the reigning taisio [shogun]. The marriage will not be consummated for two or three years to come. She is thirteen years old. I should have been gratified with a sight of so distinguished a princess, but the ladies were borne in closed norimons not to be seen of vulgar eyes. Furthermore the authorities of Kanagawa had stationed interpreters at all the streets leading down from the foreign residences. This was a precautionary act lest foreigners meeting the royal courtage might be subjected to severe insult as Bleckman was a few days since.

There is an inn a little ways up the Tokaido devoted especially to the use of Daimios and distinguished persons. I visited it a few days ago and found it a very spacious building with a large number of rooms. There was a large kitchen with a well, inside large boilers, and ranges suitable for extensive culinary operations. The entire premises were in the most perfect order. Today the arms of the Minister of Foreign Affairs are over the door and at a neighboring teahouse are the arms of another distinguished official. The Minister and other officials are down from Yedo, report says, on account of the murders. Respecting the murders no progress is made towards the discovery of the assassins. Two Jews from California state that on the evening of the 25th they were stopped in the same street by the armed men who held a lantern to their faces and asked if they were Americans, being assured yes, "all right," was the reply in English, and they passed on. No importance was attached to the circumstances at the time, it being so common

---

sons given]. There was, it appears, a large procession on its way to Yedo, comprising no less a person than the daughter of the Mikado coming to be wedded to a great prince. . . . We had proceeded about five miles on our way, when the advanced guard of the procession came in sight . . . verily the *trousseau* of a Japanese princess is a splendid affair, since the nuptial *impedimenta* formed an unbroken column of nearly four miles. . . . By the time we arrived at the river [Rokugo], the *cortége* assumed a more distinguished appearance. . . . Our Yaconins now showed symptoms of nervousness. . . . M. de Bellecourt, however, said that a lesson inculcating the sanctity attaching to the representative of the Emperor of the French was indispensably necessary, and that there could not be a better opportunity of asserting the right of an European to proceed, without let or hindrance, along the high road, no matter who might pass. We accordingly rode on, single file, and on the side of the road, so as to avoid possibly interfering with the order of the procession. The Yaconins were now fairly at their wits' end; at first they dismounted and led their horses; then, as some savage-looking members of the procession shouted at them, they made a last desperate attempt to turn us back, and finding us inexorable, they fairly turned tail and vanished, man and horse, leaving us to our fate. . . . M. de Bellecourt's two grooms, with monstrous deformed eagles emblazoned on their coats, could not resist the example of their superiors, and disappeared suddenly, but my betto proved faithful, and walked by my side. . . . As we progressed, we were repeatedly motioned to stop or turn back, and at length a two-sworded man approached, and laid his hand upon my bridle. A gentle tap over his knuckles from my whip induced him to relinquish his hold, but our position was becoming unpleasant. As far as we could look before us, on the straight road, we saw nothing but armed men, to every one of whom our presence was an affront; but retreat was as dangerous as advance, and to have got off our horses and stood in the road would it appears, have been derogatory to our characters as European gentlemen. Several officials now placed themselves in our path, as if to check our progress. M. Bellecourt, in the most polite manner, assured them, in purest Parisian accent, that "*Comme Chargé d'Affaires de l'Empereur Napoleon il s'arrêterait pas soit même pour Sa Majesté le Mikado.*" . . . Again we proceeded—again were we stopped; and this time, a consultation was held around the norimon of a man of high rank, at the end of which a gentleman dressed marvellously like the Knave of Clubs, and bearing the largest fan I ever saw, even at a pantomime, rushed up, and, walking by our side made way for us, and enabled us to pass the whole cortége without further molestation.

And now *the* norimon approaches. The principal men preceding it are mounted, and around them are footsoldiers, carrying matchlocks and crossbows. The Knave of Clubs prostrates himself before the chair; we pull up and salute the invisible princess; then come more cavaliers, and more armed men; by degrees, the norimons become smaller. . . . The Knave of Clubs, having played his game out, makes a parting bow. We say "Allegato," and "Sionada," at which he laughs; and, with a wave of the big fan, he shuffles off. . . . We bragged a good deal at Vyse's dinner-table in the evening about having so pluckily maintained the dignity of our respective countries, but I suspect we both wished ourselves well out of it at the time" (*Niphon and Pe-che-li*, pp. 93–99).

for such questions to be asked in the day time. Among the many foolish and unfortunate rumors is this that all foreigners will be cleared out in twenty days. The people we come in contact with most, the humble classes, speak of the deed as base and express regret whether they feel it or not. They fear the punishment of war, and upon them would the cuts of war fall heaviest. They reap benefits from foreign intercourse. Most of them possess great ignorance of the reason of such a deed, though all concur in saying it was done by the soldiers, a two sworded class. S.'s servant says he thinks it was the work of soldiers of the disaffected daimio, all the more powerful of which are hostile to foreign intercourse. He further says that it is generally believed that the daimios are preparing weapons of all kinds large and small in anticipation of an outbreak someday (His fable of the strong men from the mountains and the want of faith in flesh eating fiends).

The funeral of the deceased shipmasters took place from the Yokohama Hotel this afternoon. There was a general concourse of the foreigners from the shipping and the resident establishments. There was a detachment of armed marines from the Russian steamer *Japanese* [*Japonitch*] and the British gun brig *Camilla*. The Governor was present. There were stories in circulation about the Russians forcing the Governor to attend, but they were without foundation. The bodies were placed in fir coffins painted black and draped in their national colors. The coffins were borne by other shipmasters and brother masons. The procession went out to the foreign burial ground on the bluffs beyond old Yokohama, and Japanese by thousands lined the way looking on with eager puzzled curiosity. Arriving at the bluff the Governor took a respectful leave and Mr. B[rown] read the funeral service of the Episcopal Church. The Masons went through with their ceremonials, the bodies were lowered to the graves and as earth fell to earth, ashes to ashes, and dust to dust, the Russian marines fired a volley as the last ceremony of respect to the unfortunate Hollanders. There are seven foreign graves on the bluff of Treaty Point, six of the occupants died violent deaths, five out of the six having been assassinated in the streets. The surrounding hills were full of Japanese looking on. The Governor and his suite awaited the return of the procession in the village of the old town and took a final leave of the foreign representatives present. The following circular has been issued to American residents from the Consulate:

United States Consulate
Kanagawa Feb. 28, 1860

In view of the inhuman murder of two Dutch shipmasters in the streets of Yokohama on evening of the 26th inst. by the hands of Japanese and of the evident insecurity of life there, the undersigned desires that all Americans should be extremely cautious in leaving their houses after dark. Especially not so to do without lanterns before and behind them. That such lanterns should have the name of its owner distinctly inscribed thereon in Japanese characters and that Americans should go prepared for self defence in case of unprovoked attack.

The Japanese Officials are authorized to arrest and bring before the undersigned all unruly persons, and masters of vessels are desired to warn their crews against any misconduct on shore.

Police regulations as suggested by the foreign representatives will be adopted by the Japanese government for the further security of life and property.

(signed) E. M. Dorr
U.S. Consul Kanagawa

Thursday, March 1, 1860

Passed the day in taking testimony at the American Consulate in the case of the wrecked barque *Nymph*.

Friday, March 2, 1860

The servants were particular to inform us this morning that the Prince of Owari and his train would pass through the Tokaido on his way to Yedo. In rank this man is the 2nd in the empire—the emperor himself only taking precedence. I was desirous to see what I might of the cortege of a man whose travelling train is said frequently to contain five thousand persons. But how should I see him? To stand up before such royalty to stare at him even was not only a breach of etiquette but a crime. I might go into a friendly merchant's house and peep through some cracks in safety. I might kneel down by the roadside with the Japanese and cast furtive glances from under the frontispiece of my cap, but either of these courses would be compromising the independence of an American citizen besides being an insult to the supposed omnipotent protection of the celebrated American bird which figures very conspicuously on 4th of July occasions, the Mosquito coast, and the waters of the Paraguay, but of about as much value in other waters, to use a vulgar but forcible expression, as the last year's domicile of his young eagles would be. There was one place where I thought even the Lord of Owari might be stared at with impunity. There is a high cliff by the Tokaido side, which the earthquakes have split and rent asunder leaving a perpendicular face of clay and soft sandstone abutting on the road with room for a few houses between. This cliff commands a view of the Tokaido for an extent of two miles or more and the passing cortege would move along its base. Fortified with an excellent Munich Glass I took my station on this hill in the forenoon. I found S[immons] and his wife there also. As far as we could see up and down the Tokaido the people were in front of their houses and stores awaiting the train.

Our elevated position was soon espied from below and a hundred voices cried "there are foreigners on the hill," and a thousand eyes looked up to see the foreigners who had the presumption to take so conspicuous a position to observe his noble lordship. Then strong legs began to propel certain curious and sturdy bodies up the hill which I should have said is ascended by a flight of a 150 stone steps and on the top of which is a house, a government lookout on all that passes in the bay in front. We waited and looked and waited and looked again till weary alike of the tardiness of his lordship's coming and of the curiosity of the crowd that was gathering thicker and thicker about us. We left the hill and the crowd followed.

It was a clever maneuver to get out of the crowd for when we came back after half an hour we had the hill to ourselves and the balked Japanese were already pinned down on their knees below by the cry of the herald in advance of the cortege, "*sta iri*," "get down." Dr. H[epburn], Dr. S[immons] and wife, and myself were on the hill top and half a dozen Japanese. We were espied also and the herald with gesture and shout commanded us also to fall down. The Japanese went down as if shot and Dr. S[immons] followed suit, Mrs. S[immons], Dr. H[epburn] and myself continued standing, though presently Mrs. S[immons] sat down beside the Dr. All the moving line of warriors and pack horses had been moving in advance with the baggage of the Prince and his servants and attendants. The train now coming was his personal guard of honor. First came in single file the heralds with their long staffs of office, and these were followed by a file on each side of the street of soldiers bearing two swords and insignia of the princely household. They were neatly dressed in dark Japanese suits, with close fitting leggings. On their heads they wore white flat hats having a slightly raised apex to the crown. These were woven of bamboo. The train was scattered along at irregular intervals and the white hats could be seen for two miles in length moving like a great snake with white scales along the winding Tokaido. Arranged in their proper order in the procession were the pike bearers, sword bearers, umbrella bearers, sandal bearers, and others carried small trunks on shoulder poles, the trunks made of wood or paper and lacquered a plain brown or black color. Then came the royal falcons perched on the arms of their bearers as in the old days of the falcon hunters of England, by their side were the bearers of the falcon poles. Others followed bearing baskets on poles, neat round baskets, and then more soldiers on foot. The procession had been filing along slowly in this manner for nearly an hour when the train began to move in a more compact mass, for the Lord of Owari himself was approaching.

I was standing conspicuously at the edge of the cliff. Dr. H[epburn] had left me, and Dr. S[immons] and wife were sitting down. We had attracted from the first the attention of all the train but now a group of two or three richly dressed officials stopped and looked, went forward and spoke to others who returned to the

Aerial view of the Tō-kaidō in Kanagawa show-ing cliffs from which Hall and his companions ob-served the Lord of Owa-ri's train. Detail from Sadahide's 1860 map: *Go-kaikō Yokohama dai ezu.* Simmons marked the Tō-kaidō on his map with a K.

opening of a street that led from the foot of the hill whereon I stood until a dozen or so of the sworded gentry gathered in the opening. I was looking at them through my glass when one of the officials stepped forward and beck-oned to us, to myself particularly, to leave. As we seemed in no hurry to go, they concluded best not to stop the procession on our account and moved on. The passing train now nearly filled the street, a body of bowmen passed with bows on their shoulders and were followed by the quiver bearers with quivers full of arrows. Then came a dozen lead horses having a groom on each side and beautifully capari-soned, they were fine looking animals. A group of fifty or sixty musketeers followed, their arms covered with water proof piece casings of leather or paper. Then there was a large cluster of two sworded men preceded by a tall plume of cocks feathers surrounding a norimon.

No sooner had this norimon reached the open spot in front of the hill, than there were the eyes of all the attendants and all the people crouched on their knees along the roadside turned up towards us. What was going to happen once the occupant of the norimon, Owari no Kami himself, was in communication with his attendants, who came crouching to the side of the norimon, was he going to send orders to have these foreigners, who were gazing at him with profane eyes, hurled headlong from the hill? He had but to move his hand and it would have been done. No, more sensible fellow, he had his norimon stopped in the spot, slid back the closed grating like window, and with an opera glass, a veritable opera glass, took a good long look at us. Directing, gallant fellow that he was, the most of his glances at Mrs. S[immons], who is comely and fair to look upon. When it came my turn to be stared upon, I lifted my hat and bowed with as much grace as a man could muster sitting down dangling his legs over the edge of a cliff. It was impossible to see more of his majesty than a brown hand and wrist coming out from the folds of white crepe, said hand and wrist being attached to an undistinguishable mass of body within. Surrounded thus by his courtiers he gazed at us for several minutes. I presume Mrs. S[immons] was the first foreign lady he had ever seen. The train moved on and was brought up in the rear by a motley group of infirmed servants and baggage bearers. This body guard, people of the prince, contained seven hundred men; of the attendants behind it is impossible to reckon the number. I think it not all improbable that several thousand persons passed preceding and following this immediate body guard.

Sadajirō came in the evening to talk over the events of the day. He said our being on the hill to observe was a matter for much comment among the Japanese. It was a great breach of Japanese etiquette according to his account that we should thus openly gaze at so distinguished a personage. We ought to have gone within some home and looked out unseen ourselves. Moreover, it was dangerous for us to do so, another prince less friendly might take such displeasure as to order his soldiers to shoot at us. A Japanese who was crouching down on the hill near me, not daring to be seen, said to me as the prince's norimon moved on, "It may do for you to look that way, but it would not for me." The old saw has no force in Nippon, "Even a cat may look at the King." Here the great mark of politeness would be to "turn your back towards the royal cortege."

Sadajirō says that in case of the death of the present emperor without issue, there would be a great strife among the Daimios for the succession, that forces would be freely used to get each other out of the way, and that it would devolve upon the Mikado to settle the disputed succession.

Saturday, March 3, 1860

The wayside chapels are adorned today with colored flags. It is the beginning of the rice planting season and the deities, under whose special protection the rice crop is, are propitiated today. The flags are inscribed with the name of the kami under whose care the rice crop is supposed to fall. The fields are rapidly assuming a vivid green. The wheat looks very luxuriant, the peas and turnips are also starting. It is only in favored spots that the grass has seemed to change. Cherry and plum trees are daily blossoming. The camellia trees are putting on a brilliant show of crimson blossoms, the birds are beginning to nest, "for the winter (we hope) is over and the spring has come."

Sunday, March 4, 1860

Took a walk in the old burial ground today with Sadajirō. The oldest monuments he thinks are four hundred years old. He read from some that were over a hundred years old. The early and the later rains have impinged against the stone surfaces for so many generations and the mosses have eaten at them with their unfelt teeth so that inscriptions have become illegible and the once smooth surfaces are rough with corrosion, some that had corners broken off have been thrown over by earthquakes. The stones are square pillars standing on pedestals with the name of the deceased, when he died, and a few have the family coat of arms carved and gilded on the stone. Yonder round monuments with a smooth rounded or oval top are the monuments of priests, and the rounded tops are the similitude of their once shaven crowns. Each family has its own burial spot bought of the temple. Usually it is only large enough to deposit the coffin, each successive member of the family dying being placed in the same spot one above the other. If there is more wealth, a family will have room for several burials side by side. There were few such however. One monument stood over the remains of the whole family for generations and I frequently counted a single monument with between twenty and thirty names upon it while some had fifty or sixty. Many simply told that here a husband and wife lay side by side. In the families of the great each body has its own undisturbed resting place, as with us the graves ranging side by side. The poor, unable to raise a simple monument of stone, had long sticks of wood placed at their graves. The largest monuments all stood over the spot; where the poor were indiscriminately buried, their names unpreserved even. A payment of a few zeni [copper or iron cash] gave them burial there. The bodies of the priests are similarly buried, but more pleasing than the family monuments, since the evidence of family remembrance is religious observance evidenced by the continually fresh supply of green branches and clean water before the graves. There were some monuments so old that there was no lineage left to continue their pious offices, the green mosses took the place of the green branches and the rain and dews supplied the purest of waters. I have often wondered at seeing heaps of little stones about the shrines of some of the many shinto kami. I learn they are placed there by children who having no zeni to sacrifice, bring in lieu of them, these smooth pebbles.

Monday, March 5, 1860

There are no tidings yet of the late murderers. There is small reason to hope they will ever be given up. I shall not be surprised if the government substitutes fictitious criminals however. The Russian corvette has been desired to remain as a protection to foreigners. The conviction gains ground that these murders may be the result of a political maneuvering on the part of those out of power who in case of a war would be the gainers thereby. The unusual friend Mr. Harris found among the Daimios at the time his treaty was negotiated has disappeared. He can gain no tidings of him. He has written him and sent him presents but he is doubtless in disgrace.

Bathing. In Yedo, Miaco, and Oasaca public bath houses open to all passing eyes are not permitted. Baths in these places are strictly private. Nor do the better classes bathe in public elsewhere. If there are no private bath houses, the better class have their baths at home. The Honjin, for instance, has its private baths. The young ladies I saw bathing there the night of the murders were the property of underlings only. One of them was in the bath tub, an earthen tub round in shape capable of holding two barrels of water. A fire was under and the young lady was enveloped in a cloud of steam as she lay cooking inside. I was curious to know how much boiling a musume needed before she was done. Her companion, entering inside, was partly hid behind the bath tub. Ruth half hid in the corner and was polishing off her shoulders with a towel. At the public bath houses the water is changed only once a day. The price for a bath is all the same, in the morning clean water as in the evening mud. The price is eight zeni to a common man, a doctor or a soldier pays half as much more because he has some clothes or two swords to be taken care of and is allowed more abundant water. If he has an assistant to rub him down he must add as much more as twenty-four zeni in all. The bather after using the hot bath finishes off with a douche of cold water and then perhaps, as I have often seen, walks naked through the street to his house.

Tuesday, March 6, 1860

Dorr went to Yedo last night at a little past midnight accompanied by Mr. Brown and Henderson. I was empowered with his functions during his absence. There was a great alarm at Yokohama last evening. It was reported that a man had been slain in Kanagawa, then that the American Consul's cook was the victim and lastly that the Consul himself was killed. This of course produced great consternation. A messenger was dispatched to the Russian Corvette which sent a guard of fifty men ashore, the crew beat to quarters and guns were fired to let the Japanese know that they were on the alert. A large portion of the foreign residents at Yokohama mounted such arms as they have prepared for desperate deeds. The Japanese on their part were quite as much alarmed at the firing of the Corvette and swarmed on the house tops to see what was to pay. The street gates were closed that no passage could be had. The officials gathered at the Custom House. The truth at last came out. A native night patrol in Kanagawa saw a sailor lying dead drunk in the street, taking it for granted that he was murdered, a notice was dispatched to Yokohama accordingly and all this hubbub occurred before the truth could overtake the error. Passed the day at the Consulate taking testimony.

Wednesday, March 7, 1860

A quiet day at the Consulate. Yesterday's rain is succeeded by a blowing March day. French Minister and Consul called in the afternoon. No discovery is yet made of the cause or perpetrators of the late murders. There is an unpleasant feeling of insecurity among the foreign residents. The streets after nightfall are shunned as much as possible. The following is the circular issued from the U.S. Legation at Yedo and addressed to the Consul at Kanagawa:

Sir,

The barbarous murder of two quiet and unoffending Foreigners in the main street of Yokohama on the night of the 26th inst. is a matter of grave importance and gives me deep concern for the safety of the American citizens residing within your consular district.

In the purpose of promoting their safety, I have to recommend to all American Citizens the observance of the following precautionary measures.

1st. That no one should leave his residence between the hours of sunset and sunrise except in case of absolute necessity.

2nd. When such necessity exists, they should be attended by persons bearing lights, and if possible by two or more Japanese as a guard. They are also recommended to arm themselves (at night) with defensive weapons, but such weapons are only to be for self defence, and in cases of absolute necessity.

I am of the opinion that the strict observance of the foregoing recommendations will secure the personal safety of the Americans in your district. Japanese of respectability do not leave their houses at night except in extraordinary cases, and in the exceptional cases they are always attended by guards with lights. The reason given for these precautions, is, the admitted insecurity of the streets at night.

While we have an undoubted right to claim from the Japanese Government the same protection that it gives to its own subjects, we are not relieved from the duty of taking the same precautionary measures for our own protection that the Japanese themselves adopt for that purpose.

I would also recommend to all American Citizens and shipmasters that they should watch the conduct of sailors when on shore, and that, when they discover any evidence of civil disturbance among the sailors that they should cause them to be arrested and taken before you.

I am credibly informed that during the afternoon of the 26th inst. a number of intoxicated foreign sailors were conducting themselves in a very riotous and disorderly manner in the streets of Yokohama and it is quite possible that some persons outraged by them have sought their revenge which has unhappily fallen on quiet and orderly persons.

I have requested you to communicate the foregoing to all American citizens now residing within your consular jurisdiction and also to those who may hereafter arrive therein.

(signed) Townsend Harris

Thursday, March 8, 1860

At the Consulate.

Friday, March 9, 1860

Do Do.

Saturday, March 10, 1860

Do Do. *Page* arrived from San Francisco with President's message and late papers. Commenced snowing in the middle of the forenoon and snowed all day melting as it fell.

Sunday, March 11, 1860

At the Consulate. Sunday services by Dr. H[epburn]. B[leckman], the English interpreter, was in to sit and dine. He had a deal of talk to get off as usual. A large share of his conversation was upon the late murders, and he is evidently ill at ease in his own mind. He inclines to the belief that the murders may be instigated by Mito, a disgraced Daimio, who hopes to bring about trouble between the present dynasty and the foreigners whereby he may gain advantages.

Monday, March 12, 1860

The fall planted crops are growing rapidly under the influence of the great amount of moisture combined with a moderate degree of temperature. The slopes of the hill laid out in garden like patches are vividly green with the advancing crops of wheat, beans, and peas, radishes, turnips, etc.

Tuesday, March 13, 1860

At the Consulate.

Wednesday, March 14, 1860

Mr. Dorr returned from Yedo today.

Thursday, March 15, 1860

Went to Yokohama today, the first time for several days. I find new preparations to render the streets more secure. Gateways are erected at all the intersections of streets and at convenient distances across the streets. Today it is said the authorities are on the lookout for five men who have arrived from Yedo without any ostensible business and without reporting themselves to the authorities. They are supposed to be assassins in disguise. The Kuubo[30] has an army of 80,000 horse ready for the field and under his immediate control at Yedo.

Minister Harris came down today. The Prime Minister has expressed to him in the strongest manner the desire of the government to find the murderers of the Dutch shipmasters and their unsatisfaction at their inability to do so. I learn from Mr. H[eco] that others than the Samurai, or soldiers, are entitled to wear two swords. Men who have rendered some service to the state are privileged to wear two swords and to give their children a military education. These latter by this education and position belong to a higher caste and are candidates for promotion in the state. As their profession is honorable they are supported by their relatives without resort to menial labor. Yet having neither offices given to them and no occupation they become gamblers and destitute till perhaps they are cast off by their friends. The highwaymen [and] hired assassins are largely recruited from this class, and it is altogether likely that the Yokohama

30 Kubo, or Shogun.

murders have been perpetrated by men of this character. If a murder has been committed by a retainer of a Daimio knowing that such an act, although not commanded by his master would still give him pleasure, it is by no means an easy matter for the government to obtain possession of the person of the offender. Like the follower of a Highland Chieftain, as the retainer of a feudal baron he would fly to his lord for protection, and any attempt to snatch him thence would array the lords of the empire into two parties at once. This might be the beginning of a civil war that once lighted would set the whole empire in flames, for like the feudal chieftains of old there are always those who expect to profit by internal dissension and the throne itself might fall to parties, who, now out of power, would hail any such convulsions.

Friday, March 16, 1860

Yesterday the patron gods of the rice crop were again propitiated. The Honjin was adorned with brilliant lanterns in honor of the day. I have put in press today a specimen in bud of a flower used by the natives, the poorer class, to blacken their teeth. It is infused in oxide of iron water.

Dr. H[epburn] exhibited his magic lantern last evening to our servants and a few Japanese. They were much pleased. Among the diagrams were two astronomical ones representing the motion of the star system, the tidal influence of the moon, the procession of the seasons, eclipses, relative motion of the star system. Sadajirō and Yangaro, particularly the former, seemed to appreciate them and understand them as well as average men at home would; if they did not, they put on the appearance of so doing and looked as wise as any of us. This reminds me too, that during the day I was introduced to a Yedo man who had with him a magnetic battery in a portable case. It was beautifully made and I could hardly believe him that it was indeed Nippon made. The weather for a week past has been wet and cold, even a little snow fell. Notwithstanding the fall planted crops continue to grow vigorously.

Saturday, March 17, 1860

I have now heard from so many various sources this account of the troubles that possibly bring about the repeated assassinations that I deem it worthy of mention. The father of the present emperor died year before last suddenly and, as is generally believed, by poison. This poison is said to have been administered by Prince Mito who is the third man in the succession if the present emperor should decease. The Prince of Owari is first in the succession, the Prince of Kiusiu 2nd and the Prince Mito 3rd. On the death of the late emperor so satisfied were the supporters of the throne of the manner of his death that several princes of the realm lost their lives and Mito himself only saved his own because he was of the blood royal. He was degraded and imprisoned in his own house, where he still remains. His followers are said to be the cause or perpetuation of the murders hoping to involve the present government in a foreign war which will lead to its downfall. I should have said also that the poison is supposed to have been administered by the physicians of the emperor under influence of a bribe, at all counts this physician was beheaded.[31]

By this close confinement of Mito many of his soldiers are left without support and are ready for any deed of desperation. Ingkio, the head priest of Jobootsugi [Jobutsuji], who returned yesterday from Yedo, says that there are frequent quarrels among Mito's homeless followers and those who are better off, that there have been repeated assassinations among them. Norimons on route have been pierced through with spears and swords and their occupants slain or severely wounded. Such is the current story among the Japanese.

[31] The Shogun Iesada died on August 14, 1858, of a severe illness. Joseph Heco gives a similar account of Iesada's death in his *Narrative of a Japanese*, vol. 1, p. 246, saying that Iesada was poisoned by the court physician at the instigation of Mito Nariaki, that Ii Naosuke discovered the crime and removed Nariaki from his position as "vice shogun" and forced him to retire to his domain.

Just at evening the Mayor and suite called upon Mr. Brown and stated that, owing to the insecure position of foreigners, they desired to keep a regular guard of two soldiers at our gate night and day. Mr. B[rown] gave his consent. H[enderson] and myself are hardly satisfied that this is the real object of this guard, they may act as spies as well. However, under B[rown]'s consent between eight and nine of the evening a two sworded official called and left his card stating that he was the guard detailed for duty tonight. He was armed with two swords and a lantern.

I inquired of Sadajirō this evening whether the houses were partitioned off into fives and placed under the watch of one man. He says it is so, that the oldest man among the five families is the head man. It is his duty to report all offenses to the government, this he does not always do, however, for he is liable to be fined heavily together with his whole neighborhood without cause, a practice equal to that of confining a witness in jail. The result is that if an offense has been committed within the circuits of the five families they are very apt to absent themselves in the country and be very ignorant of any occurrences.

Sunday, March 18, 1860

Service by Rev. Mr. B[rown]. Illustration of the poverty of the common people, it is said by the people here that the expense of erecting the street gates which was assessed on the residents of Kanagawa and could not have been large yet disrupted them so much that many left and went into the country rather than pay so small a tax. The weather continues rainy and cold mist and rain has fallen all day but the crops are growing vigorously nevertheless.

Monday, March 19, 1860

We hear this morning of the shooting of a Japanese at Yokohama last night by the Russians from the Corvette. It is said to have been accidental.

The succession to the Japanese throne is not of necessity from father to son. There are three princes called the brothers of the emperor. The prince of Mito, the prince of Owari, the prince of Kiusiu. The title of the "brothers of the emperor" in their families descend from father to eldest son. The families of these four persons, if numerous, are drafted away by a sort of adoption so as to keep about a certain number of male children who are educated and prepared from their youth for the possibility of attaining the throne. On the death of the emperor, the Daimios of the realm select from these families the imperial successor, the most eligible one. It is understood that this successor should be taken in the direct line of the deceased king where there is a suitable person. A failure to the succession among so many families it is hardly possible to occur. On the death of the late king two years ago the present incumbent was selected. Prince Mito was dissatisfied with the selection and, under cover of hostility to the policy [of] admitting foreigners to the country, was suspected of designs tending to the overthrow of the present dynasty. Consequently he was restricted some months since to a genteel confinement within his own premises, his title was taken away and given to his son. The power of the Mikado is merely minimal, he is a cypher. He has the creation and disposition of titular honors, but he acts under advice from the Kuubo at Yedo and dares not contravene the instructions from thence. New statutes altering the organic or fundamental law of the empire must have his approval, but he never negatives what the temporal princes approve. If there is a division of opinion among the Daimios he merely waits till they agree among themselves before giving assent or dissent.

Levies of troops are made on the princes or Daimios in case of need according to his revenue rated in so many bales of rice—so many soldiers to each specified number of bales.

Tuesday, March 20, 1860

Shinjo's. Boxes or packages containing presents, beside a bit of fish wrapped in paper are also cunningly tied with strings. These strings are five neat little cords made of paper. Etiquette prescribes that there must be exactly five except in case of marriage gifts between the betrothed or their friends when a sixfold cord must be used, or a double cord of five making ten. The five cords are kept flat by a ferule of paper. If the person making the present is in mourning the cords must be white, if not, half white and half red should be used, the white half being on the left of the tie. This tie, if the gift is from an inferior to a superior, should be a bow knot, if equal to equal or superior to inferior, a plain square knot is appropriate. Presents are constantly made, the bakery [and] the confectionery always have a supply of boxes ready for use, gifts of little delicacies of food are very common and the value of the gift has less to do than its appropriateness. So the gift may be a quart of beans, a half dozen eggs, a few sheets of common paper, as well as a box of cakes, confectionery, or some little curio.

I noticed the children today playing a game like the "jack stones" of school boy days—instead of stones little bags of sand were used. The children always appear happy and contented at their plays. I do not remember a single instance of quarreling among them.

Wednesday, March 21, 1860

At the emperor's audience the only persons admitted to the presence chamber are the king's titular brothers on one side of the room and the king's councilors on the other. The king, or emperor, is seated in a chair standing on a raised platform or dais. The retinue, servants, and soldiers of the emperor are not appanages of the crown, they are the retainers of his family. The present emperor is not a son of the late emperor. The body servants of the emperor have shaved heads like the priests, while those of the Mikado in addition blacken their teeth. The Mikado never eats twice from the same dishes and never wears the same dress a second time. Plain dishes and coarse dresses are his ordinary daily fare. His supply money is meagerly doled out to him from his

imperial brother at Yedo and while he is nominally the greater sovereign he is in fact a minor cypher in that government of the realm (on authority of Harris).

Thursday, March 22, 1860

The long continued rains have made the streets of Yokohama almost impassable by reason of mud and puddles of water. Kanagawa is a little better only. The rains are not violent, and the fall of water is inconsiderable for the duration of the falling weather. Vegetation advances day by day, field flowers are beginning to spring forth, and trees and shrubs put on their blossoming daily.

Friday, March 23, 1860

To[day] Yetzizen no Kami[32] passed through the Tokaido on his return from Yedo to his own province. This is the season of the year when the changes are made. I encountered his train at a halt while walking in the Tokaido. His servants were scattered about in groups in the stores and tea houses, resting from their burdens of baskets, panniers, boxes, etc. These were the immediate personal attendants of the Daimio. The bulk of the baggage and norimon bearers had passed on ahead. Some of the norimons were gaily decked with plumes of colored papers and the naked bearers wore a bright yellow loin cloth and a fillet around their heads of the same color, shouting a rude chorus as they hurried by. Several of his attendants wore yellow insignia. This is the color adopted by the priesthood, and why used by him I did not learn. I passed among the train of baggage bearers and through groups of sworded men without molestation, though it was the same Daimio's attendants that insulted the English interpreter lately.

When opposite the Honjin an official whose pleasant face I had often seen came out and joined me. He inquired if I was going to the

---

[32] Although he is identified only as Echizen no Kami, the context suggests that this was Matsudaira Mochiaki, the lord of Fukui, and not Abe Echizen no Kami Ma- satō, who served as Kanagawa bugyō from 1861 to 1862 and as Senior Councilor from 1864 to 1865.

house. I told him yes, we walked together till we came to the street leading to our house where he halted and asked me if I would look at the Daimio and his body guard, who were just then appearing from the other Honjin. We accordingly stopped and a confused mass of soldiers came across the bridge preceded by pike bearers, then came three lead horses well caparisoned, and finally the norimon of the Daimio himself surrounded with a crowd of attendants. His lordship was housed within, out of mortal sight, but for all that down on their knees went every man in the street. One poor fellow who was not quite quick enough had his wide straw hat knocked over his eyes and was hustled very much as men in a crowd are sometimes hustled in a home mob. The train passed by, and my attendant left me, wishing me good bye. This looked like a simple act of politeness on his part, but it was more than that. He had seen me passing along the street, and knowing that I was likely to meet the Daimio and his followers, joined me to prevent any insult happening to me. It was very cleverly and handsomely done. This Daimio or Lord of Yetzizen does not enjoy a very enviable reputation at home. He is a Daimio of impoverished estate, said to be the 2nd poorest Daimio in the realm. A Daimio near Hakodadi takes precedence of him in impoverished finances and is known as the *itsi bimbo Daimio* [first among the poorest daimyo], and the famous Prince of Owari is 3rd on the list of bankrupt princes. The maintenance of a great army of retainers and the arming of them has impoverished both the lords of Owari and Yetzizen. They have borrowed money in their own provinces, forced loans, which they will not repay, and though their estates are some of the finest in the empire they are known as my informant says "by every child in Japan as the bankrupt Daimios." Men of substance are leaving their princes through fear of these forced loans, thus still further impoverishing the princely estates.

Saturday, March 24, 1860

Today is a holiday in the calendar of Japan. It is a holy day especially for women and children, who dressed out in all their finery are expected to pay visits to each other and take a friendly cup of tea and discuss, no doubt, the last bit of Kanagawa street scandal. But alas the day is miserably cold and snowy, and the *oldest inhabitant*, for this individual I have already heard of in Nippon, says he never knew it [to] snow on this day in his lifetime before, nor at this season. The snow ceased about noon leaving the streets so dirty that I should miss seeing all the pretty damsels of our village out in clean white socks and lacquered pattens. As I was walking leisurely through the first street outside of the compound I heard someone calling me, "Hall Sama." Looking around I saw Kami's smiling face. "Would I turn back and make a call on his father," who was celebrating the day. I went back and received a hilarious welcome from a group of men sitting on the seats of a large thatched cottage. This was Kami's paternal roof and the old gentleman, who has but one eye and leers diabolically out of the remaining orb, invited me to sit down on the mats and join his home circle. I asked him how many he had in his household. Sixteen he said, he was the head, that man, pointing to another, was the 2nd head and that one, pointing to a stout fellow of twenty and upwards, was the "boy." What relationship all this group of men stood to him, I did not understand. At the side of the door a little pavilion had been formed. A strip of white cloth stamped with the family crest in large gold figures was arched over a little recess. This recess had a series of narrow ascending steps on which were placed a great variety of knick knakery—principally handsome children's toys, dolls of boys and girls, richly dressed in spangled robes, playing on instruments of music and variously represented as amusing theatricals. There were plates of refreshments which were brought to me to taste, and a peculiar kind of white sake, sweet and very pleasant. Then followed hot sake of another kind. Before offering me these, I heard them talking among themselves whether I would be likely to accept. But I did, and the principle people were very much delighted.

From my first landing in the country till now I have been impressed with the belief that the Japanese have no reverence for their religion. Sadajirō today led off on this topic of his own accord and I spoke to that effect. The present Buddhist priesthood are very ignorant, they profess a creed that they know nothing about, they learned to mumble over the prayers when they were children, and that is the extent of their knowledge of their own faith. But a few of them were never able to read their sacred books and of their tenets and doctrines they for the most part knew nothing. The very children mocked them in their recitations of their prayers. The common people secretly despise them, and their offerings were so small that for the last twenty five or thirty years the priesthood had become poor and Buddhism had rapidly declined in its force and influence. Nor, so far as I can see, does Shintooism, the ancient faith, rally and take its place. Where ancient systems of belief or unbelief are growing effete among the learned and the better classes the system of Confucius professedly obtains, as it does in China among the Mandarins and scholars, but in reality there is a disbelief in all these forms. I do not believe that Germany is today more imbued with rationalism than Japan is with practical atheism. Naturalism, or a belief that Nature in herself by her own laws is capable of working out the daily procession of events, that she is herself cause and effect, seems to be a wide spread belief among this people. Whether this may be construed unto an opening prepared for the spread of a vital Christianity I hope may now be solved. It was no doubt owing to the impoverishment of Buddhism that temples have been so freely leased to strangers.

Towards night, the wind having partially died, I took a walk on the Tokaido to see what the people were doing on this holiday. I found them gathered at their houses in groups around their hibachis, bathing, eating and drinking, and from among houses came the shouts of laughter and revelry. Since the streets were too foul for out door rambling the people were making the best of it within doors. I also visited a very pretty temple this afternoon built five years since, one of the cleanest and best kept that I have yet seen.

Sunday, March 25, 1860

Once more I have to chronicle a bloody record, but this time the quarrel is confined to the Japanese. Yesterday at 2 P.M. as the Prince Regent, the Gotairo,[33] was returning from the palace accompanied as usual by a large train of attendants, his norimon was attacked by a band of fifteen or twenty armed men. The assailants met the cortege within the second wall of the imperial grounds. They were there disguised as menial servants bearing baggage of some Daimio. Rain cloaks, Kappas, completely disguised their real character. At the proper moment these disguises were thrown off, and the pretended menials were men in complete armor, armed with swords and pikes. Two pistol shots were fired into the norimon, but after a severe struggle the assailants were beaten back. Heusken's letter to Harris reports that ten of the Regent's men were slain, two of the assailants captured, who immediately committed hara kiri. The Japanese version is that four of the assailants were slain and six of the Regent's party. That a part of the assailants fled, and a part went into the premises of two of the Daimios. Some of them say the Regent was wounded or slain and others not, but that since the Regent was assaulted a year ago in a like manner he has always gone to the palace disguised as one of his own train and some other person has occupied the norimon. The assailants are recognized as servants of Mito.

---

[33] This was the Tairō Ii Naosuke, the Daimyo of Hikone, who served as the leading political force in Japan from 1858 to 1860. It was Ii who signed the Harris Treaty in 1858 without imperial approval and who carried out the Ansei Purge in 1858 and 1859 and thereby earned the hatred of pro-Imperial and anti-Western loyalists. Ii's removal of Mito's lord, Nariaki, from office earned him the hatred of Mito samurai who were largely responsible for his assassination outside the Sakurada Gate of the shogunal palace.

There is great excitement among the Japanese. This affray may prove the forerunner of important events involving the empire in political difficulties, and threatening the situation of foreigners. The guards at the Legations were again increased. Our own night patrol is strengthened to three men. The servants have just been in to say that they are directed to bar the gates at bedtime and then to hunt the yard with lanterns to see that no bad men are concealed. The Honjin officials here requested Ministers Harris and Bellecourt not to attempt to return to Yedo tomorrow on horse back but to go in an official boat.

Monday, March 26, 1860

The day is stormy and the ministers have not departed for Yedo. The Regent is reported dead today. By some reports he is said to have been poisoned in his tea after escaping from the affray of the day. It is also said that his previous attack happened on this same holiday just a year since. Seventy soldiers or officials have been added to the force at Kanagawa today. It is amusing on the whole to see our three guards solemnly marching into the yard eight or ten times today with their paper umbrellas over their heads, marching for the kitchen direct, inquiring each time if any bad fellows have been about, and enjoining watchfulness on the part of the servants, and they solemnly march out again.

Today the guard house is finished at our gate and I presume our reliant watch may now rest undisturbed. The guard at Simmons's last night arrested a one sworded fellow who appeared to be prowling about without any business and sent him over to Yokohama to the Governor's lockup.

Mito was suspended from his rights of office as Daimio and from his family heirship to the throne by his attack of a year ago on the same Regent. Daimios sometimes voluntarily resign their honors in favor of their oldest son. The sons when numerous not infrequently join the ranks of priesthood from which they may again be recalled to political life by the death of the brother who was expected to inherit the family honors and titles.

Tuesday, March 27, 1860

The news of the Regent's death is confirmed today. He died of the wounds received in the attack on Saturday last. At Yokohama there is a great deal of excitement among the foreigners respecting their personal security. Arms have been distributed among them, and they have some sort of organization for concerted action in case of an attack. The various compounds are connected by gates. In case of surprise the rallying point is fixed at the Yokohama Hotel and the mode and order of resistance and escape is arranged. There is a night patrol of ten persons. Today the guard house is placed in our compound.

Wednesday, March 28, 1860

The assassins of the Regent are said to have been arrested and another source says that a body of one thousand of Mito's followers have gone to another Prince to stir up insurrection.

Thursday, March 29, 1860

The foreigners at Yokohama have been exercised by all sorts of alarms and rumors respecting their intended assassination by the followers of Prince Mito. Yesterday a fleet of boats were coming down the bay to surprise the fleet and the foreign settlement, and there were other rumors of the approach of a band of three hundred sworded men. Everyone is fully armed, in fact, some of the gentlemen are walking arsenals. Yesterday they ate their dinners with their revolvers by the side of their plates. On our side of the Bay we have felt no such apprehensions. We do not fear, that is, a general massacre of the foreigners. There may be isolated cases of assassination as before, but even these are well provided against. The Japanese have furnished all our places with a constant guard, and even this we hardly feel to be necessary.

Friday, March 30, 1860

According to terms of dispatches received at the British Consulate, Mito has fled to his estates and thirty-six of his followers have been executed, a part of whom had been under torture of the rack to extort confession. Two of the condemned were roasted to death, the others decapitated. Mito is now placed in a position of open hostility to the government, and if he has men or means to take his revenge we shall hear more from him. At the time of the attack on the Gotairo the train of the Prince of Kiusiu and Owari were in company. Owari and his followers sought refuge by hastening away and Kiusiu's gathered around their master's norimon to act simply on the defensive. Mito has doubtless been the cause of the assassinations at Yokohama hoping to bring trouble upon the present dynasty. Failing in this, he has aimed a blow at the government itself. What will be his next move we cannot say, it may be a more decided and formidable attack upon foreigners in the empire.

The *Azof* arrived yesterday, reports that fourteen days before her departure from Nagasaki a Dutch steamer had sailed with Superintendent Curtius on board bound for Yedo Bay. The non arrival of this vessel excites some apprehension as to her safety.

I met this evening just at sunset a train of fifteen females returning from a funeral. They were all clad in white, white long robes and white girdles about their waists. There was something particularly strange in their appearance, particularly in the contrast of the clear white color of their mourning robes with the somber hued evening dresses of the other passers by in the street.

Saturday, March 31, 1860

Heusken is down from Yedo today and reports a state of quiet. He affirms the statement that a number of arrests have been made, but thinks the report of their execution premature.

I had the sight today of an interesting document, being the Journal or Diary of an old gentleman seventy years old. When a man in Nippon has so prospered that in his old age he can lay down the toils of life and live in the repose and quiet becoming to old age he has the title of Inkio. This was the daily journal of an Inkio kept with remarkable neatness. Its uncouth Japanese characters were of course perfectly unintelligible. Sadajirō read some portions aloud to us explaining its meaning as he went along. The most interesting part of it was the daily account of impressions put down previous to the time of Perry's landing. There were the first exaggerated reports, that America was to send a fleet of 300 ships with hostile intent, the gradual narrowing down of that immense armament to the real size and purpose. A copy of the King of Holland's letter in which the pacific intentions of the fleet were announced in advance. There was an account of the extraordinary preparations made to receive this fleet if it should assume a hostile character. The provision of arms and gunpowder, the repairs of the forts, the general practicing of the people in the use of arms. Then the feelings of the people, the general wish of the Daimios to resist, by force of arms if necessary, the newcomers. The pacific desires of the emperor in opposition which prevailed. Then there were the details of the approach and arrival of the fleet in the Bay of Yedo, all the sayings and doings in accordance with our own published accounts. There was one statement particularly noticeable, which was that when one of the steamers got aground, the hostile party were exceedingly clamorous to embrace the opportunity to make an attack, and that if the vessel had not been promptly got off this purpose would have prevailed. So says the Inkio's journal, speaking also of the throwing overboard of heavy articles to lighten the ship. I think Perry's Journal speaks only of the grounding of one ship, the *Macedonia*, in his account of which he speaks of the ready assistance provided him by the Japanese officials to get her off. The two accounts may not conflict, the Inkio's Journal gives possibly an inside view of the matter which the Commander could not have seen and in a few moments he might have found his seeming friends so many enemies. The Journal alludes to the fact that heavy guns were moved towards the scene and this initiative step was taken. The names and armaments of the various ships were correctly given in the Journal. In its proper place the Journal gave some particulars of the Mexican War, names of Taylor and Scott, the conquest of California, the discovery of the gold mines and the great rush of people thither. A better knowledge of the language would doubtless bring many interesting things out of this Journal.[34]

Sunday, April 1, 1860

A misty, cloudy morning has given way to [a] clear, warm day. The sun shines out with such force that languor is born of the warm damp air. Thermometer in the shade 73°. After church I took a walk into the fields. I passed Yangaro's house. He was sitting on his clean mats looking over his account book and gave me a hospitable invitation to join him. His young and pretty wife behind her screen reminded me of a little mirror that I had given her a few days ago. His old mother would have [me] walk in and "asobi," or pass a little leisure time. And when I said no, then I must stop when I returned. A half dozen youngsters were paddling in the brook stripped of their clothing and hunting for little fish. An old lady squatted down by the brookside was bathing in the muddy stream. I followed the brook out into the fields and wandered by its side. Its swollen stream was running over a ledge of rocks, and we have christened the Falls St. Mary's after the first young American woman that has come to reside near its banks. The alders just bursting out into leaf hung over the stream, the wild rose bushes fringed the banks, the camellias threw their circular chalices into the rushing stream. The cryptomeria is in blossom on the hill, the rapeseed plant in the plains. Far up the valley stretch the green fields of wheat, the fragrant wind steals through the belt of pines. The peasantry are weeding their fast growing crops or leading their laden horses to market. Directly they will

come back to return to the fields loads of muck and manure to make good the loss to the ground. I see men, their brassbound saddles flashing in the sun, as they wind along the narrow path on yonder hill. Two little girls were gathering cresses from the wet fields and brookside. Their long garments were tucked up within the waist girdle and with bare feet and legs these little lasses of ten or twelve went laughingly on their errand. They pointed to my stout boots and their naked feet, and when I told them these boots were easily removed they laughed right heartily. And now they said if I would walk a little faster I might keep in their company, so I and the bare little damsels walked along by the brook together, one chatted as we went, "Where was I going?" Only to walk. "Was I all alone?" All alone. Then they showed me their cresses and said they were good to eat. They knew too where I lived, and then they would stop to admire and say very complimentary things of my boots, and I in turn admired theirs! Then they waded into the stream and their slender limbs glistened in the water like white lily stems. So we walked and chatted till I turned off into a path that led up the hill. They tried to dissuade; the hill path was hard. I had better keep with them and go to the Bookenji [Bukenji] temple. And as I disappeared in the wood path I heard the voices of the little cress gatherers calling to me to come back, and so wherever I go I shall whenever I think of the 1st of April, 1860, think of the happy bare legged cress gatherers shouting to me "the mountain path is hard come with us."

There is a memorable old pine on the hill top. It stands all by itself its circumference is some number of feet and inches, I don't know how many. It is a favorite walk to go to the old pine standing all alone on a mound that appears artificial, for there I have a grand lookout to the distant blue hills and over acres and acres of rice fields, wheat fields, and forest. In front is the deep blue water of the bay and the many hill tops beyond. I can count the white sails and see when they disappear around the point as they sail up to Yedo. And when I turn around I see the snowy cone of matchless Fusi Yama.

[34] Unfortunately Hall does not tell us who the seventy-year-old retired author of this remarkable journal was.

Monday, April 2, 1860

The blossoms in the trees, the song of the returning birds, the vernal scene of wood and fields are not the only indications in Nippon of returning spring. The attire of the inhabitants is as much so. While the trees are leaving out, they are leaving off, and gentlemen in Paradise shirts and Eden pantaloons are seen again in the streets. Twenty coolies were wanted this morning to carry baggage to the boat and they came, bare legged fellows with ragged wrappers around their shoulders, a dirty set of vagabonds as one could hope to see. There is a colony of three hundred or so of them living together. They are poor men who have no house, no clothes, no family, who live by coolie jobs, drink sake, and gamble. The government furnishes them shelter, and if two or three hundred laborers are wanted, you apply to the government and the government knows where to get them.

Tuesday, April 3, 1860

Nothing parallels a fashionable lady in crinoline so well as a Japanese merchant astride of his horse on a rainy day. The horse is loaded both sides with bales and parcels till he occupies half the street in passing. On top and among the ware sits the rider. He wears a rain coat or cloak of oiled paper buttoned around his neck and made so large that it spreads out and protects not only himself but all the burden with its ample folds. Taking his head for the "primp taper waist," the figure swells out to the largest periphery as the stiff crinoline-like oiled paper covers alike the rider, the beast, and his burden.

An official announcement is posted on the doors of the Custom House today saying that the Regent is out of danger. Japanese officials were passing around Yokohama today inquiring at each foreign residence. What weapons of self defence they had, and whether all the inmates could use a pistol, women as well as men. The answers were noted down.

A shop custom of Nippon is this. If today I step into a store and make a purchase and on the morrow, or a day or two after, pass the same store, the shopkeeper, or his wife, daughter, clerk, or whosoever I made the purchase of, says "I thank you for your purchase yesterday," or the day before as it may happen to be.

Wednesday, April 4, 1860

Sadajirō denies emphatically that the Regent is yet living. He says the government so reports for thus is their custom. The people are apprehensive of a war of factions between the partisans of the slain Regent and the followers of the Daimio of Mito. To use Sadajirō's expressive phrase: "The xxxxxxxxx of everyman in Nippon were xxxx or xx with fear." I bought of him today several dwarfed specimens of flowering trees, camellias, cherry, orange, and two unknown varieties.

Thursday, April 5, 1860

Still we have contradictory reports about the Regent. Our officials at Yedo say "he still lives," our Japanese friends that he is dead. Bulletins are put up at the Custom House emanating from the British Embassy which speak quiet and express confidence in the good intentions of the Government.

Friday, April 6, 1860

Many centuries ago, say the Japanese chronicles, Fusi Yama was born in a night rising at once to its majestic height. Their books have cuts of this event representing the people looking on in astonishment. The precise date of this event is given in their annals, *quien sabe?*

Busy with home letters. We are all settling down into quiet. Walked out to the Guard House towards Yokohama. In addition to two sworded officials there was a stack of percussion lock muskets, Hollander make. An official was present to inspect them. He told me that he knew Perry, Adams, and Brown of the Japan Expedition.

Saturday, April 7, 1860

A fine clear day after many rainy ones. Improved it by a long walk under Sadajirō's guidance to visit a celebrated temple and get a fine prospect. The day was charming, we shunned the Tokaido and went through the fields green with the young wheat, peas, and beans, or yellow with the rape flower blossoms. We wandered among all sorts of pleasant little valleys and sequestered brooks gradually rising to higher ground and finally came to a hill that commanded altogether the finest prospect one has seen in Nippon. At our feet lay the bay of Yedo, across which white sails were flitting. The tide was low and on the long reach of bare sandy shore the Kanagawagians were out by the hundreds gathering mussels and clams. They turned over the soft mud with their fingers, or a narrow hoe, and gathered their crop of shellfish in wicker baskets, washing them occasionally to clean them.

At our left was the village of Kawasaki, and we could see the large pines near the temple of Daisi. Beyond, the bay stretched up to Yedo, and had the city any elevation, or if we had good glasses, we might have seen the city itself. On our right was the Bay and village of Yokohama and the foreign fleet. All around us lay low hills cultivated with garden-like exactness to their summits or covered with groves of pines. I saw many fine old trees. Behind us was the [most] imposing sight of all, the white peak Fusi Yama. The atmosphere was uncommonly clear. I was on higher ground than ever before and I never had so grand a view of Fusi and the neighboring mountains. The summit of Fusi was so pure, so white, looked so calm, so soothing, we could see below the snow line. There's something quieting to one's feelings in looking at such a mountain. It is itself such an image of repose, stands so majestically still, you think a convulsion of nature even might not disturb its serenity. Nothing else soothes my feelings as such a sight unless it be the vast still ocean, or the hushed wood of a mighty forest. Yet the mountain has the advantage, for while it soothes it elevates the soul to its own heights in the blue heaven. The elevated ground of today revealed to me new snow clad peaks and many beside that were wood crowned without snow. The other sunny peaks were very distant, the uncovered range was much nearer perhaps not more than 25 miles distant. I had not seen so fine a panorama of hill and mountain since I passed Iaru [possibly Java]. The whole sweep of the country between the point on which I stood and this chain evidently partook of the character of the surface about Kanagawa. Rolling land broken up into low hills covered with much wood. Each new walk reveals to me how much uncultivated land there is even so near the great capital. The woods are planted timber. Both sides of the Tokaido are lined with old trees wherever the houses are interrupted. From this distance the summit of Fusi looks very smooth, save a mighty excression on the south east side (see above [April 6]). We perceived several small temples situated on the summit of hills, or in picturesque woods. Their builders had a good eye for location. We did not see the temple we came to look for after all. The day was warm, we walked many miles up hills and across valleys, and the temple evidently receded as we advanced till at last, wearied by the distance and heat, we turned back. Wood violets were abundant along the way. Many other flowers were peeping out. The peach is now coming into blossom.

Sadajirō pointed out to us a row of houses occupied exclusively by leather dressers. Their calling is a degraded one and they are outcasts. They are compelled to live by themselves debarred from all intercourse with others. The hides of all animals are theirs by right without cost. They are universally afflicted with sore eyes.

The officials are at last satisfied of the Regent's death. Two revolvers that had been fired and thrown down were found near the scene of the attack. The Regent is said to have received two balls in his person. Our future quiet will now largely depend on the character of the new Regent.

Sunday, April 8, 1860

There was a burial in the graveyard a few days ago, since then I have seen several women middle aged and old coming to the new grave

Scene on the Tōkaidō near Kanagawa. Photograph by Felice Beato.

to burn incense tapers and perform other pious offices. They are normally accompanied by a girl seventeen or eighteen years old dressed in considerable style who walks about apparently merely to air her fine habiliments. They were out today. I was sitting in my room after service. I think the young lady is coquettish. She paid little attention to any pious offices for the dead, but strolled leisurely about adjusting with coquettish air her handsome garments, casting furtive glimpses at this house as if to say, I wonder if the foreigners see this handsome young lady of Nippon. One of the old ladies at last caught me staring out of the window, smiled, jolted the young lady, who looked up and smiled, then I smiled, then another old lady smiled and finally we all smiled together. The young lady walked airily as though she was treading on so many invisible eggs. She no doubt thought to herself, that young man is gone up, he could not resist, I knew he couldn't, and then she looked again out of her almond shaped eyes, which opened

so little that they seemed like slits in white birch bark, for her skin was powdered to that hue. Now I flatter myself that I am not the worst looking fellow in the world seen through a window at a distance of several paces, and a flirtation in a graveyard was an original sensation, as I repaid look for look. The battery of my glances was loosed as rapidly as hers, and I thought the kindly way in which the old ladies smiled and showed their blackened teeth showed that my shots told. The young lady smoothed down the folds of her crape scarf, took out one of her long metal hair pins, and scratched her head. She no doubt felt something.

But I haven't told you how the young lady was dressed. Her hair was a miracle of brushing, camellias and iris, and formations. It is not describable, the way it was on her head like a fan expanded at the sides, like wings "loosed over the ears [and] fell away from the forehead in puffs," was skewered up by tuning fork pins of shell and white copper, silver washed, adorned with spangles, tied up with silk cords—a ballroom belle's is as nothing in comparison, and the time spent on that head must have been only possible in a land where time, like everything else, is very cheap. She was whitened with powder, and reddened with rouge, and her thin lips were brilliant with vermilion. One long loose robe covered her figure. It was gathered about her waist by a broad girdle and tied in a miraculous tie in the rear. The girdle was 1/2 of a yard wide at least, and was tied in a square knot behind like a gentleman's cravat. The robe was a light blue silk elaborately wrought in front in flowers of red and green. At the bottom it was bordered with a roll of red stuff as large as my wrist. The sleeves were deeply hanging sleeves edged with red and sewed together so as to give just room for the play of the arm, which was left bare to the elbow. Underneath the outer robe were several under robes of thin crape silk folded over the bosom so as to display their clean gaudy folds. Her feet were covered with white cotton socks, and the thong of her straw slippers passed between her toes and across her ankle. She looked as fresh, neat, and clean as a snow drop. I had seldom seen one so richly dressed. The old ladies were evidently very fond of her. They finished their devotions at the grave and again disappeared out of the gate, still casting Parthian glances in their retreat. They knew their young companion was irresistible in her charms and, I have no doubt, wondered that I didn't fly through the window and over the old gravestones to testify my submission.

Monday, April 9, 1860

A rare case of an attempt to reduce a dislocation came to my knowledge today. Drs. B[ates] and H[epburn] were called on shipboard to a man whose shoulder was out of joint. After ineffectual attempts to reduce it, a watch tackle was hitched to the arm and an attempt made in that way to reduce it!

Tuesday, April 10, 1860

A fair sunny day. A pleasant sail across the bay to Yokohama. Made the tour of the shops and returned at sunset.

Wednesday, April 11, 1860

The rainy season has had a two day interruption of fair weather. The farmers are just beginning to break ground for the rice crop. The wheat comes on rapidly, choice pieces are nearly a foot in height. The colewort is generally in blossom, its yellow flowers intermingled with the green wheat fields give a pleasant look to the fields and cultivated hillsides. I observe the farmers are particular to stir the ground often with their clumsy hoes and to keep the crops free from weeds. The deciduous trees are budding and leaving out, a few like the chestnut and oak, and some varieties that I do not know, still hold back their summer promise. The grass is hardly started, it looks as brown and sere as a month since, as a general thing. Take it altogether, the weather is like a month later in our latitude, the fall sown crops having more the growth of the last of May or the 1st of June while the grass and deciduous trees are no more advanced than with us in early May. I have not yet seen so hot summer-like days as some I experienced the week of my leaving home, the 1st week in May 1859. The winds hang perseveringly north. Since March 1st we have not had all told more than a week of clear sunshine. It has rained two days out of three.

Thursday, April 12, 1860

There are rumors of fighting near Oasaca between the rival factions in the empire. There have been collisions already to the north in the province of Hitachi, Mito's own principality. The Governor has asked the Consuls to go to Yokohama temporarily, till the troubles are over, saying if the disaffected dare slay the Regent they will not hesitate to slay any foreign officials they may desire.

The customary rate of interest in Japan is 12

percent, but small sums are frequently loaned at usurious rates. A man borrows a few ichibus for a day for which he agrees to return a half ichibu for interest. He must pay this by "crow caw" next morning, as that is the word instead of cock's crow. If he delays an hour over that time he must pay one ichibu as interest and so on increasingly for each hour's (Nippon hour) delay.

Took a walk to Treaty Point. The upland fields in that direction were looking very thrifty. Wheat being the principal crop. Found a few flowers in bloom, a little blue bell that was particularly pretty. A young girl who had just finished weeding her patch of beans asked if she might walk with me. Certainly she could, and therefore she took me by the hand and we went down the hill swinging our arms as I have so often seen country lads and lassies do. Her bonhomie and artless confidence was charming.

The farmers are very careful to keep their crops well weeded out. Everything is sown or planted in drills and they often pass their long narrow hoes between the rows cutting up the weeds, stirring the earth, and throwing it slightly up in ridges around the plant, whatever it may be. Some of the valleys are one cloth of field with the sweet scented colewort blossoms. The broad bean is pretty generally in blossom. In my walks I find the dandelion, burdock, plantain, rhubarb, all familiar plants.

Friday, April 13, 1860

Another day of rain. Busy arranging botanical specimens.

Saturday, April 14, 1860

The number of soldiers in Yokohama is very much increased and we hear confirmation of the reports that parties are arming in the interior for a struggle. With us, all appears on the surface quiet, and yet, the storm may burst over us at any moment. After dinner took a walk with Yangaro. We went to a neighboring hill, here there was a fox hole and a little chapel near it. The people believe that galleries run under the hill and these galleries are peopled by white foxes which are good geniuses and they propitiate them with prayers and offerings. We then visited an old farm house situated in a picturesque niche in the hill. There was a good deal of Nippon taste about the place. There was a chain of little fish ponds in which I saw goldfish fifteen inches long. The sweep of the hills enclosed this work on three sides and the chord of the arc was bordered with a thicket of ornamental and shade trees. There were several varieties of single and double camellias, and flowering peach and cherry trees. The peach blossoms were double like laces and were much the size and appearance of the Burgundy kind. A broad walk led by a circuitous path up the mountain and this was bordered by fine specimens of the azaleas not yet in blossom. The ponds were said to be full of the lotus plant. Scattered among the forest trees on the hillside were flowering peach, cherry, and camellia trees. The spot must be a delightful one in the summer season. It belonged to a family in decay. Through an opened screen I had a glimpse of a room in which were four swords and two old muskets, remnants of a better day when the family had renown. The care bestowed upon the grounds was further testimony to the truth of what my guide told me. The proprietor made at first as if he would have expected a fee for the privilege of seeing his grounds but I laughed it off as a joke and told him when I came again I would bring him a gift. So he bid his girl bring us some tea on the back piazza that overlooked the lake, and a cool delightful retreat it will be from the summer sun. The tea was very peculiar, it had some blossoms in it which had first been salted. The flavor imparted thereby was not particularly agreeable.

Sunday, April 15, 1860

Just after service we had a visit from an official attended by a suite of about twenty persons. He was an officer of considerable rank and had come down from Yedo to inspect the situation of the foreign residences. With what intent does not yet appear. After dinner I took a walk over to the old pine tree on the hill where I sat and read. It seemed odd to start out for a walk by putting a revolver in one pocket and a copy of Tennyson in the other! The day was delightful and the aspect of the country with the fresh crops pleasant to the eyes. I descended into a little secluded valley, that I had somehow heretofore overlooked. I found a picturesque spot; there was a pond green with slime into which a little stream fell. There was a temple enclosure at whose entrance was an old magnolia tree. The trunk was larger than my body but the top was decayed, and instead was a numerous growth of shoots a few feet long tipped with the pure white blossoms. Some that I gathered measured seven inches across. It was evident from the curiosity of the people and the shyness of the children that I was probably the first stranger that had found his way into this valley. A girl of seventeen or eighteen who was bathing came nude as she was to the door, where she finished drying herself with a towel looking at the stranger at the same time.

Monday, April 16, 1860

Picnic today at Treaty Point. Richards[35] came over from Yokohama with a large boat and invited us all to a day's recreation. So we packed up our hampers of cold meats and sandwiches, our pail of coffee, our jars of pickles and preserves, and somewhat to keep the chill off, and started. We were a great curiosity to the frequenters of the Tokaido as our train passed through to the boat landing preceded and followed by baskets and hampers. We could hear the people inquiring of our servants what was going on among the foreigners. They told them we were out for a day's recreation. This was something they understood very well, for the Japanese in like manner spend a day of leisure with family and friends on the water or in the fields. The day was fine, the bay smooth, and a little more than an hour's

pull brought us to the Treaty Point, where we disembarked. The shores were bold, but a little path in the face of the cliff led us up to the groves of pine and cryptomeria on the top of the hill. We spread our cloth on the grass under the trees where there was a grand lookout upon the bay and its fleet of fishing boats and soon had a bottle opened amply. The natives gathered around with large curiosity. Seeing that we picked up flowers, the children gathered and brought them to us. With many a pleasant sally and pit, the lunch made the pines of Nippon sound off. When we were through we offered the coffee and beer to the natives. It was pleasing to observe the cunning look of one fellow in particular as he sipped, smacked his lips, turned up one eye, and said *mai*, that is "it tastes good." We offered them the cold meat, telling them it was the flesh of animals. Some refused it, but most took it. Yet they did not all eat it, but wrapped it up in a bit of paper for further discussion. We strolled along the cliffs after dinner to the flagstaff, zenith battery, cross the guns on the conical isolation hill that forms the extreme top of Treaty Point. The Natives followed us in crowds wherever we moved. We gathered quantities of the "Forget me not" by the path side. Then three or four of us scampered down the steep hill to the shore. Through the camellia trees we darted, falling or sliding where the ground was red with the fallen petals among the thick bamboo grass down to the rocky shore. This hillside was covered with a grove of camellias more superb than anything I have yet seen. And the fallen petals were to [be] scraped up by handfuls. I measured the girth of three of these trees standing near each other. Their circumferences, from two to three feet above the ground, were respectively 40, 45, and 48 inches. Their height did not exceed forty-five to fifty feet.

On the other side of the hill was a neat Buddhist temple. There were a hundred people around it including several officials. I threw a handful of buttons among the crowd who were

[35] C. H. Richards is listed in the 1862 and 1863 *China Directory* as an American merchant residing in Yokohama. Richards was a well-to-do consignment merchant who was active in the Yokohama trade. See M. Paske-

Smith, *Western Barbarians in Japan and Formosa in Tokugawa Days, 1603–1868* (Kobe: J. L. Thompson & Co., 1930), pp. 342ff.

soon on all fours after the glittering toys. The lookout upon the bay at this point was very beautiful. We were at the zenith where the bay turned far as the eye could see to the southward and to the north. The white junk sails were going up to Yedo. Across the bay in smoking distance was the outline of the high lands of the Principality of Kadsusa [Kazusa], at our feet swept the waters of the gulf on a bold pebbly shore. We enjoyed the leisure of the day and the scene to the full of our bent, and reentered our boat. A fair wind was blowing fresh from the South. Up went our square sail and we swept rapidly by the bluffs of Treaty Point, the thatched roofs of old Yokohama, and the young city of the new town, and again landed at Kanagawa.

The following case has been related to me by an eye witness of the conclusion of one act in the life of a young girl. A certain foreigner, doing as most foreigners in this part of the world will do, had bargained with a Japanese merchant for his young daughter for a mistress. This is a common event to the young girls, daughters of the inferior classes. But all these tender maidens are not indifferent to the shame and degradation of such a life. By night the father brought his daughter to the man's house. She was young and pretty, not more than thirteen years old. But when her father was about to leave her, she burst into tears and besought him to take her along again. So evident was the grief of the young girl that the heart of the libertine was touched even to compassion and he made her go in peace.

Tuesday, April 17, 1860

A warm day, writing by an open window most of the day. Peach and cherry trees are now in full blossom and rape plant ditto. There is a splendid show of cherry trees in bloom at the fisherman's favorite temple on the Tokaido. In my evening walk, I came upon a little lake made by a dam thrown across a ravine to collect water from the rice fields. On it two mandarin ducks were swimming. The little flowering thorn of which I have seen so much I am now satisfied is the Pyrus Japonica.

Wednesday, April 18, 1860

A strong south wind has been blowing most of the day. It is the season for change of the monsoons. Late in the afternoon I crossed the bay but did [not] much enjoy sailing in a Japanese boat at the mercy of a huffy wind. The evening was pleasant and I walked back. A gang of laborers were digging a trench near the seaside. The water that leaked in was thrown out by treadle water wheels each worked by one man. It was lifted by the buckets of one about four feet into the reservoir and then the bucket of the 2nd took the water and lifted it four feet more to where it could be carried off. The water lines discharged continuously with a large flow. The causeway had its usual string of passing people, laborers, soldiers, travelers, market men and women, laden horses coming in, unloaded horses going out. On the Tokaido the teashops and inns were full of business. The second story windows and balconies of the latter were full of heads who were looking at the immense volume of Mrs. Capt. McD's voluminous skirts, lost in wonder at such an apparition. The summer is certainly coming, the ladies are growing more free and easy of costume, and the common men ignore any costume. The ballooned skirts are quite eclipsed by some of the crape silk clothes of the females with prints of fans, pine trees, and occasionally one carries even Mount Fusi or a waterfall concealed under her garments.

This morning I saw a party of three starting out for a holiday to wit, mother and two daughters. The oldest girl was head adorned and face painted most elaborately and her long trailing dress of pea green silk brocade with leaves and flowers gave her a dashy appearance on the promenade. As the weather grows warmer the bathing house doors are again thrown open and there is no end to the Venuses and Appolos in *costume* one may see about sunset who having come out of the bath sit complacently drying themselves with a towel. As an evidence of Japanese regard for their Sunday, both Simmons and my servant made the long journey to Yokohama today on business, each forgetting that it was their Sunday when the Custom House was closed.

Thursday, April 19, 1860

The wind of yesterday has increased to a gale, the water of the harbor is lashed into white, there is no crossing for boats. In the evening it blew a hurricane and rain fell during the afternoon and evening. Henderson tells me that our Consul recently handled the officials stationed at his gate roughly. The officials at the Honjin desired Heco to inform Genl. D[orr] that if, in future, he had any trouble with the guard to inform them, but if he took the law into his own hands they would not be answerable for the consequences. Heco is afraid to tell the Genl.[36]

I tasted today some wine made from the native grape; it had very much the flavor of one of our home made grape wines.

Friday, April 20, 1860

Yesterday's gale suddenly subsided during the night and the morning is clear and delightful, altogether like a summer morning at home after showers in the night. Employed the fine morning for a walk to the hills in search of wild flowers and pleasure. Joe [Joseph Heco] was with me and we had a grand ramble of it along the south side up the hill and among the fringe woods. The fields were golden with colewort, whose blossoms filled the air with their scent. We found many varieties of wild flowers, forget-me-nots, lupine, violets. We could not help enjoying the delicious atmosphere. Joe was in fine spirits, is a capital companion and under the "greenwood tree" we made one of our most delightful mornings in Nippon. We halted under the "Pine" to rest and look at the fleet of ships coming down from Yedo, where they had been detained by

the gale of the last two days. There were not less than three hundred under sail coming down as if one fleet. Something bit Joe while under the Pine, luckily no poison adder or centipede.

The laborers are long preparing the rice fields. In the streets and in the fields the laborers are again nude, except the waist cloth, but I have seen several children today completely nude. Who shall say our Tokaido innkeepers do not understand their calling. What could have been more grateful to the two travellers I saw stopping at one after their warm day's tramp than to have a serving woman bring tubs of water for their feet and assist to untie their sandals. In the evening we had our first thunder shower for the season.

Saturday, April 21, 1860

In the lower part of Kanagawa along the shore of the bay the boatmen and fishermen are collected together. I walked among their houses this morning. Owing to the high winds of the last two days there was little fish for sale, but I did not fail to notice how clean they kept their fish nets and the barrels in which they exposed them for sale. From the fishermen's quarter I went to the quarter occupied by the leather dressers. The houses were in a thick cluster with no apparent regularity of streets. A few hides were stretched and drying in the sun. There was nothing about this quarter to indicate any special poverty except a number of houses that were underground. A cellar was dug and over it a straw roof placed with a paper window in the floor. In the quarter generally the people were as well clad and looked as prosperous as other parts of Kanagawa. Some of these leather dressers are said to grow rich

---

[36] Heco had good reason to fear Dorr's volatility. Invited to dinner at the consul's with Captain Brooke of the *Fennimore Cooper* in late July 1859, Dorr asked him how he had gotten on with a certain Captain H. of a revenue cutter in California. Heco, who had suffered under the captain, called him an "unprincipled man," to which Dorr took offense saying "He is my friend, and if you dare to repeat such words at my table again I'll kick you out through that door!" Heco's right to express himself became a point of debate between Dorr

and Captain Brooke. Dorr announced to Brooke, "If any man dares to interfere with my business at my table, I should just like to shoot him right across this pig's head!" [which he was carving]. Brooke responded "General D., I accept that challenge. Choose your weapon and step outside!" It was only Eugene Van Reed's diplomatic skill that managed to avert a catastrophe. Finally, a calming "drink" seems to have soothed hurt feelings all around. See Joseph Heco, *Narrative of a Japanese*, vol. 1, pp. 218–20.

in their proscribed traffic. Persecuted they truly are, being forbidden to marry without their own guild, or to enter the houses of others. They are said to be particularly affected with ophthalmia, though this was not apparent in my walk. In the fields saw barley headed.

We hear on authority of the Dutch Consul that an envoy sent by the Government to Mito was beheaded by his orders and that there have been other violent deaths. The Government will send another envoy, but they find some reluctance on the part of all to go on so dangerous an embassy.

Sunday, April 22, 1860

Clear and warm. Strong south-west wind again in the afternoon and rain in the evening.

Mr. Goble[37] has been trying in vain to get a house. He first looked about for himself among the neighbors and found a tenement which its owner was willing to rent. The government approved and the price agreed was forty ichibus a month, an enormous rent, but there seemed to be no help for it. Then the officials told Mr. G[oble] that as the house was in among the native dwellings and it would be difficult for them to protect it, if he would let the house go he might hire a temple wherever he could find one. Mr. G[oble] was of course pleased with this plan and gave up the house and commenced search for a suitable temple. Temples were plenty and at first his prospects were fair for renting one, when suddenly no temple could be had at any price. As the case now stands it would seem as if the government having first got him away from the house, then privately discountenanced the renting of any temple. This opinion is sustained by the report from our neighbors that the Japanese who first

offered to rent his house without consulting the officials has been punished by confinement to his house. Although this is a direct violation of the treaty, it is difficult to bring it home. The man who is punished would deny it through fear of a worse fate should he inform against the officials.

Heco gave me a few days since an interesting account of his meeting his brother after he arrived in Japan.[38] When he arrived here in July he sent word to his brother who lived near Oasaca to come to Kanagawa to see him. He was standing at the entrance of the American Consulate a short time after this just at evening. A Japanese came to the gate whom he knew at once to be his brother. The recognition was not mutual for Heco had gone away a little boy and now returned a man in American clothes. He addressed his brother as such then took him into a native house and by his inquiries soon convinced him that he was in reality his brother who many years ago was driven from the coasts of Nippon by a storm and was supposed to be lost. Then the tears began to rain down the brothers' cheeks, and said Heco, "when I saw the tears come from his eyes, it made my tears come, of course I couldn't help it." When his brother came to part with him to return to his friends, Heco gave him some presents he had brought from America for the family, but he was afraid to accept them lest they might bring him into trouble with the officials. Among other things were some pictures which he desired, but if he took them he could have no good of them as he would have to keep them secret. There was a Daguerreotype of his restored brother, however, which he wished to take to his living relatives and he returned to carry that away with him. On arriving at Oasaca he was stopped for having this foreign picture and was kept in restraint at Oa-

---

[37] Jonathan Goble had been a marine on the Perry expedition. A deeply religious man, he had befriended a Japanese castaway, Sam Patch, who accompanied that mission from China to Japan and subsequently was influential in his conversion to Christianity. Goble and his wife, Eliza Weeks, came to Japan as missionaries of the American Baptist Free Mission Society, arriving in Kanagawa on April 1, 1860. For a brief time he, his wife, and two children resided at the Jobutsuji with the Hepburns and Browns. Cut off by the American Civil War

from funding from home, the Gobles lived in considerable poverty. At one point Goble supported himself as a cobbler while his wife took up tailoring. Goble is better known for his invention of the *jinrikisha*, which he used to help his disabled wife get around Yokohama, than for his missionary accomplishment. See Otis Cary, *A History of Christianity in Japan* (Tokyo: Charles E. Tuttle & Co., 1982), vol. 2, p. 52.

[38] For Heco's own account of this meeting see, Joseph Heco, *The Narrative of a Japanese*, vol. 1, pp. 209ff.

saca for thirty days until a message could be sent to Yedo to know the royal wish. After this delay permission came down from Yedo that he might return the picture and go home to his friends. Such is Japanese surveillance. We hear too that Yangaro has had to give up a book presented to him by Dr. H[epburn].

Monday, April 23, 1860

In the evening we heard a bell rapidly tolled and supposed it to be a fire alarm, but our servants came in to tell us that some *loning* [*rōnin*] had entered a temple below us to rob, and the alarm was given to collect the officials.

Tuesday, April 24, 1860

The only additional particulars we have today of last evenings disturbance, are that two robbers entered a temple next to the Holland Consulate and with drawn swords demanded of the priest his money. He was frightened out of his wits and fainted at the apparition. The alarm was speedily given and the booty-less robbers decamped. Many of the people think the intention was to attack the Dutch Consul, but the circumstances hardly warrant this conclusion. When the alarm was given the officials were apprehensive that such might be the case and the gates were at once secured.

At Kawasaki collisions between Mito's men and the Regent's friends are reported, and several deaths have resulted.

Walking in the Tokaido this morning I saw a man catching birds. He carried in his hand a long bamboo pole, one end of which was smeared with a viscous substance and strongly adhesive. He had a peculiar whistle in his mouth which imitated the chirping of a bird. They hovered about the adjacent roofs attracted by the sound. When opportunity offered, the bird catcher with a dextrous snap or push of his pole struck the birds with it. Which entrapped by the bird lime were easily secured and put in a basket the bird catcher carried on his back like a trout basket. At Yedo these bird catchers are seen daily plying their trade. The falcons, or hunting hawks, of the Emperor and his princes are thus supplied. In Nippon the ancient custom of falconry is still maintained. Large and small hawks are trained for this purpose. In the trains of the Daimios, as they pass through the Tokaido, these birds are often seen perched on the wrists of their keepers.

I visited again this afternoon the homestead under the hill where I lately found so many camellias. There were many people gathered there and it was evident that my appearance was looked upon as an intrusion. While I was debating whether I had not better go and leave these people to themselves, my former acquaintance made his appearance and received me civilly. I brought him a little present of soap, a mirror, and some lucifer matches. He was much pleased with these trifling gifts and a change came over the faces of the whole assembly. I was invited to walk into the back piazza that overlooked the fish pond and was surrounded by a crowd of curious people. The owner of the place gave me to understand that some religious ceremony was going on in the next room and invited me to look in. I did so and saw at a glance the cause of the odd looks with which my first entrance was met. A corpse deposited in the usual square coffin was awaiting burial and I had intruded upon the friends and neighbors which gathered there. The coffin draped in plain white cotton or silk stood upon a simple bier of unpainted pine. Before it two candles were burning and branches of the evergreen oak were laid and joss sticks were smoking. Two men, relatives of the deceased, were kneeling and evidently rehearsing prayers. A fat funny looking priest and his attendant stood in the back part of the room taking no part in what was going on. I sat in the open door and the master of the house by me surrounded by the people as before. Without any regard to the praying friends they talked on loudly. He told me that the deceased was his wife, that she was a very good wife and he felt bad and then laughed as if it was a very good joke. Then he put his hands to his eyes, said she was a true woman, and he had cried a great deal, and all went into a roar of laughter in which the bereaved husband took the lead. All the noise did not appear to disturb the prayers within who finished their devotions and then came and joined us. The chief mourner was a Samurai from Yedo who had come down to attend the funeral. He came and sat by me also and was very affable. I took my leave with little delay for I knew their custom was to bury the dead when the sun was low. So I left them after taking a drink of water and a pipe with them and was warmly invited to return. Some years back the head of this house was a soldier of rank, but the family property had gradually dwindled away and the present master was a farmer and a poor man. The family weapons were retained as heirlooms.

Wednesday, April 25, 1860

We had a visit from the head Governor today. He was accompanied as usual by his interpreter and a suite of twenty persons or so. He wore on his head a white flat hat rolled up a little at the sides. His trousers were large and loose of embroidered silk. He was very affable and pleasant, was much interested with Dr. H[epburn]'s superior stereoscopes. He remained about ten minutes and left. At his approach all our servants fled to the furthest room. The fear of these officials is great among the people. Nothing can exceed their abject humility. They are so entirely under the surveillance of officials that nothing they do appears to escape notice. A merchant endeavored to enter our compound today but our guards positively refused him admittance, why not, we cannot say. Any of the common people that chance to be in our houses at the time of a visit from officials are always frightened and make their escape unseen if possible.

Thursday, April 26, 1860

After breakfast to the Bookenji [Bukenji]. Found a new species of arum, height 2 feet with remarkably elongated spadix, the spadix terminating in a filament two feet long! Found the cypripedium. Saw the purple magnolia in blossom. Also a shrub having a blossom with the odor of the azalea and same shape but small and white. There were a number young priests at the temple under tuition. The grounds were in perfect order, neat as possible. One or two of the houses were the neatest

of anything I have yet seen in Japan. The handsomest fir I have seen stands within the temple enclosure. It is a symmetrical cone of even slopes to its summit. There were cherry trees in handsome blossoming. The temple was not open today.

From Sadajirō I learned today that the Dosia powder which is said to have the virtue of rendering flexible limbs that have stiffened in death is well known in Japan. Its sale is a monopoly enjoyed by the Buddhist priests, who bring it from India. Its efficacy is believed in by the common people. S[adajirō] himself did not believe in it, though he thought the same affect could be produced by rubbing the soles of the feet or the arms or face with earth, but particularly with clay.

I have heard it stated that whenever a Japanese fells any forest trees he was obliged by law to plant a tree for each tree felled. This a not law but a common custom. Each man does as he pleases. I saw yesterday a clearing where near each tree felled another had been set out. I observed that the trees set out were cut down to about a foot above the ground although their diameter was an inch and a half to two inches.

The tree which produces the vegetable wax furnishes also the lacquer varnish which is obtained by incisions in the bark. The berries of the tree yield tallow from which the candles in ordinary use are made.

The season in Nippon admits of but one rice crop annually except in one province, Awa I think, where two are produced.

In pursuit of business and wealth Oasaca stands at the head of all places in Nippon. Yedo is an imperial city, a city for the residences of government officials and the princes of the Empire. Oasaca is the commercial imperium. It is said to be handsomely laid out with wide and spacious streets. Brick and stone are there used in building. Its merchants are men of large capital and wealth to whom the whole kingdom is tributary. Thither come the products of the various provinces, to be distributed again as they are wanted. The products of the estates of the Daimios are sold to the Oasaca capitalists, who frequently advance funds on the incoming crop of this year or next. These merchant princes are posted as to the capabilities of the empire in production in any one year and when the state of the crop and market warrants they buy up by secret agents the article in which they wish to operate for rise and not unfrequently are said to hold for a year or two or more till they can secure the profit they wish. Even the Yedo merchants are second to these and are purchasers at Oasaca. Credits of a year are given, though it is customary often times to credit in this way: the seller will not trust the buyer with goods but he will lend him money for which he takes a note wherewith to pay the funds. There is some distinction made in collecting which renders this mode preferable that I do not quite understand.

Not long since there was a considerable amount of ivory imported by the Dutch from India. There was so much that no Yedo merchant dared buy it but it should fall in value. An Oasaca merchant stepped into the market, bought all the ivory there was, and reaped a large profit by his control of it. Auctions are a common way of disposing of merchandise in Oasaca. Samples are shown and the bidding and sale is conducted as near as I could ascertain, much as with us. The auctioneer cries the price exactly as with us. Each trade too has its own street. There is a rice exchange. At very early day all rice dealers gather in the street where the rice merchants transact business. Perhaps 2000 may assemble. The buyers are indicated by wearing a napkin thrown over the shoulder, the sellers have the same thrust under their waist girdle. There is a head man who superintends all the transactions. The buyer says he wishes to purchase so much rice and makes a deposit to bind his bargain. His offer is put down in writing and some seller agrees to fill his order. At noon the offers and acceptances are closed and the delivery of the contracts commences. If the seller finds that rice is up and he cannot fill without loss, he pays the difference, if rice has fallen the buyer makes good the difference. The business seems to be done very much as at our stock boards. Paper money entirely corresponding to our bills are also used at Oasaca. There are banks too, of deposit, individual banks, on which checks are drawn. There are brokers large and small. In the large trade transactions of Oasaca specie is not used generally but paper money in some shape, possibly bills of exchange, checks, or current notes.

Friday, April 27, 1860

An unknown Japanese committed suicide today by hanging himself to a camellia tree on the hill near the American Consulate. Suicide by hanging is not uncommon and its causes are as various as with other people. This man was not recognized by any of the people living in Kanagawa.

Had a pleasant walk with Joe [Joseph Heco] into Inaguchi valley and so on beyond into one of the most picturesque hamlets I have seen. It was on one side of a large valley surrounded by trees and hedges. The farm fields and houses were better than usual. The yards better kept and had some beautiful flowering shrubs. On the opposite side of the valley was another long straggling hamlet picturesquely situated among trees and hedges. The walks today, skirting the woods and forest knolls, often reminded me of wood paths at home. We came back over the highlands near the Bookenji [Bukenji], finding on our way a new variety of blue flowers remarkably pretty. We should not have seen them perhaps if we had not sat down to rest ourselves on the green bank, gathering rest and enjoyment from the delights within our reach. The walk along the ridge home just before set of sun was one of the rural pleasures that never satiate.

Saturday, April 28, 1860

Among other accounts from Fusi Yama that I hear of the people is this. That near the summit one old crater in the summit crater is full of water in which are fish. They say also that there is a crater in action about two thirds of the distance up. I have frequently seen what appeared to be smoke spewing from one side of the mountain. The fact that Fusi is covered with perpetual snow would indicate the improbability of a lake in its extinct crater.

Sunday, April 29, 1860

On my morning walk at a farmhouse not far distant I found some remarkably beautiful azaleas. The flowers were four inches across, were of a very white color with carmine dots on the inner side of two of the petals of each flower. The bush on which they grew was low (calyx 5 cleft petals and perfume strong). There is a flowering tree which scents the air for a great distance with the honey suckle's perfume. The flower is quite small, white, and its leaf similar to the honey suckle. It is borne on a small tree, not a shrub like the azaleas.

Monday, April 30, 1860

Took a horseback ride in the afternoon with Miss B[rown] into the country. We took some new paths and found a landscape which in the appearance of its woods and make of the ground resembled parts of New England. The bridle paths through the woods are very pleasant.

It is said that the Japanese custom of shaving the face and head is comparatively modern. Two hundred years ago the hair was grown and beards were worn. The Mikado and the males of his court and household do not shave the head. The hair is gathered and tied in a knot behind. Prince Mito who is famous nowadays wears both his hair and beard.

Today ends my first year's absence from home. It has been a year of varied experiences and a great contrast to my previous life. With the year's end, I close this volume.

Kanagawa Jobootsoogi [Jobutsuji] temple, May 1st, 1860.

Tuesday, May 1, 1860

Today commences my second year's absence from home. A year ago tonight I left Elmira for New York to take shipping for this distant land. Since then I have travelled many thousands of miles, and many a league of water lies between me and my country. The sincerest wish of my heart is that before this year's close I may be reunited to the friends from whom I then separated. The day has been one of slow, drizzling rain, but it was mail day, for the *California* must leave, and I have had ample occupation within doors. Sadajirō left us last evening to go to Yedo to bring back the Chinese geographies which he took up there some time since. Inquiries have been made respecting them from the Honjin, Custom House duties demanded of Dr. H[epburn], and S[adajirō] is very uneasy lest he get into trouble.

Wednesday, May 2, 1860

Sadajirō has returned today and feels that he is now secure. He has got the geographies back without being discovered and breathes freely. I learn from him some of the customs of the road. He paid today two ichibus and brought down a kango [palanquin]. In addition to this he had to pay some gratuities. The day was rainy and the street muddy, the bearers flagged, went slowly, and wanted something to drink, they drank and moved on more lively, then flagged again, besides it was raining and they ought to have more sake. So there was more sake and something to eat. He then paid about another ichibu in gratuities and such is the custom. If the day is pleasant the bearers are very hot, if cool, they are suffering with cold, or their passenger is too heavy, or sits unevenly, they always have some excuse for extorting extra pay and are quite as clever at it as our hack drivers. The business of furnishing coolies for the road on any route is farmed out to some one or more persons who receive all the fees and pay the Kangoyas and bearers. A bargain must be made before hand with them, for they begin with asking large prices. The Kangoyas are young single men, or improvident fellows, who spend all their money in gambling and sake drinking. They report themselves to the Kashira, or the contract man, that they are ready for hire. He pays them small wages when he wants them, and if they can get their eating and drinking besides out of their passengers they will have their wages for further dissipation. The privileged class, officials, and samurai always travel cheaper than merchants, mechanics, or farmers. They squeeze the Kashira so much because they know he has a lucrative business and makes it up out of others.

The ferriage from Kanagawa to Yokohama is farmed out the same way, and here the classes above mentioned all go scot-free from Governor to samurai. It is the custom of the land. The ordinary price of ferriage is half a tempo (one cent) and the revenue of this ferry for 6 months has been 4800 ichibus or $1000. With the increased growth of Yokohama and the advantage of summer months I should think that revenue the next six months would be more than doubled. This is a large revenue. The business is managed by several assistants who keep a list of all the boats and boatmen employed, what is paid them for food, the number of persons crossing, and the monies received. I infer that no rent is paid to the government for the ferry beyond the free carriage of the officials, which is cost sufficient. This same class of samurai and the followers of the Daimios compel all the inns to furnish them food and lodging at low prices, compel the merchants to sell them their foods cheaper than to others. It is said that if a merchant is known to have purchased any article at a low rate, a yakunin, if he chooses, may step in and compel the merchant to resell the article to him at the price paid. And he is lucky to get that. I suspect these are some of the illustrations of the way the poorer classes are squeezed. When the Daimios in person travel the road, they are said to be extremely liberal.

Sadajirō brought me today copies in Japanese of the Treaties with the Americans, English, French, Russians, and Dutch. They are in 5 books, were originally sold for one ichibu for the whole five, but the sale of them has been so large that the lot are sold for the insignificant price of half an ichibu. They are scattered all over the kingdom and generally used. The same treaties it is safe to say are not half so well known at home. Heusken sends word that Mrs. H[epburn]'s saddle cannot be fixed at once because all the men who understand the business are busy with work for the Daimios who desire to adopt our style of saddle.

Thursday, May 3, 1860

The foreign community were the subjects of a fresh excitement last evening, particularly at Yokohama. In the course of the afternoon and evening bodies of soldiers arrived at both places. At Yokohama two pieces of artillery were also brought into the place. These were arrivals of fresh contingents of soldiers to protect the foreigners and the government officials, owing to rumors of an attack from Prince Mito's followers. These rumors are various, but it seems that there was special alarm yesterday arising from the report that a party of Mito men variously stated from three to sixty had entered Yokohama and were to be followed by more. According to reliable Japanese accounts "inflammatory handbills" have been posted and circulated for some days past announcing that the followers of Mito to the number of 30,000 would attack Yokohama with swords, muskets, and artillery. The attack was first set down for the 10th of the current month and then for the 13th, which is today. These notices were distributed in the Japanese manner by writing on a board and placing it in a conspicuous place, or by printed handbills posted and circulated. It would seem a very questionable policy in an attacking party to thus announce their intentions, and thus the Japanese must have regarded it, for on the 10th one heard of no undue alarm and excitement, and the people looked upon it as a move to frighten the officials and foreigners. But on top of this came the story of a small party having effected an entrance into Yokohama and a further report that the attack was to be made by water, the assailants coming from Mito's dominions in junks. All this together produced some anxiety and fear on the part of the officials at Yokohama. [Sakai] Oki no Kami, under whose military superintendence Kanagawa is situated and who is responsible for its defense, sent in last evening a contingent of soldiers from one to three hundred according to different accounts. Echizen no Kami, under whose jurisdiction Yokohama lies, sent in his contingent then also of like number and the 2 field pieces. A large force was placed on guard duty at both places during the night. Only the officials at Kanagawa knew of this fresh alarm, at Yokohama the preparations made and the presence of an increased force at once aroused the foreigners to a high pitch of excitement. Some of the more timid counseled a flight to the ships. All held themselves in readiness for an attack, weapons of every description were put in order, plans of action debated, and boats made ready in case an escape by flight became necessary. The shipping in the harbor were all apprised of the situation of affairs on shore and were to have boats in readiness with all the men and weapons that could be made available. The Vice Governor was active in furthering all necessary preparations. A night of some anxiety wore away without any hostile demonstrations. Today we see parties of the soldiery strutting about the streets in their neat uniforms. At Yokohama a large force is quartered in the Custom House whither the two field pieces have been brought. We learn nothing new today. I am inclined to believe, and do firmly believe, the whole affair is but a game either on Mito's part to frighten the authorities, or, what is quite as likely, the authorities may be magnifying a small matter to frighten the foreigners.

No new Regent has been appointed in place of the one slain. It would seem that this office and its title may not be placed upon a new party. If the Regent dies, his son may succeed him, but no new one is created. The superintending of the government is however entrusted to one selected for the purpose. Such a man has now been selected and it is Matsudaira Oki no Kami[39] who not long since was deposed as Prime Minister. He has ever shown

an implacable disposition towards foreigners and was particularly obnoxious to the foreign representatives. It is he who is said to have insulted Minister Harris at his receptions. His appointment to this high place is ominous of more ill to foreigners than all the rumors respecting Prince Mito.

Dr. Hall [George R. Hall] two nights since was accosted by a man and found a thief in his bedroom. He secured him and handed him over to the authorities.

I frequently encounter the Japanese postmen. They travel fast, making the distance from Yokohama to Yedo, twenty miles, in three hours. They are nearly naked and carry their dispatch in a parcel tied on the end of a rod and borne over the shoulder, or in a wallet fastened by a cord around their necks. I have never seen them running in pairs, as said by the Dutch. They wear cotton socks on their feet, the Tokaido is free from loose stones and offers no inconvenience to such light shoeing.

The farmers are busy with rice planting and have commenced sowing the seed. The ground which has been flooded with water is dug up with a bent fork of four prongs. The water is again let in, when with a wide harrow or the same fork the whole is sliced and worked over till it is an even surface of mud and water. On this the rice is sown. Then the mud is whipped with a bamboo pole on the end of which a few leaves and twigs remain till the paddy is worked below the surface and the rice planting is completed.

Spent the forenoon at Simmons's photography;[40] got good pictures of a priest and a boy

---

[39] This appears to have been Kuze Hirochika who with Andō Nobumasa came to head the shogunate in the wake of Ii's death. Kuze had served as a senior councillor of the shogunate from 1852 to 1858 when he was removed from office for openly criticizing Ii's Ansei Purge. Hall appears somewhat confused here in reference to Matsudaira Oki-no-Kami. He seems to have mixed up Matsudaira Echizen-no-Kami (or Matsudaira Iwami-no-Kami Mantarō, Kanagawa bugyō [magistrate] from 1859 to 1863) with Sakai Oki-no-Kami. Neither were, of course, synonymous with Kuze Yamato-no-Kami.

[40] This is one of the first references we have to photography in the Kanagawa-Yokohama area. From the reference here, and later in the journal, it appears that Dr. Simmons at this time established a photographic

studio, or room, which Hall regularly used. Simmons had brought with him a camera as part of his missionary "outfit" purchased by the [Dutch] Reformed Board. When he subsequently resigned from the Mission he was asked to return the camera to S. R. Brown, whose daughter appears to have become something of an amateur photographer using it. Some forty years later, when William Elliot Griffis was in the process of writing the biography of S. R. Brown, he contacted Hall about photographs of Brown for the book. Hall noted that what photographs he had of the early days were "in book," but that he would be able to provide Griffis with a photograph of the temple they lived in. Hall's photograph can be found reproduced in Griffis's *A Maker of the New Orient: Samuel Robbins Brown* (New York: Fleming H. Revell Co., 1902), p. 148, as well as on page 90

Picture of the Jōbutsuji in Kanagawa. This is the only extant photograph taken by Francis Hall, who seems to have taken some of the earliest photographs in Kanagawa-Yokohama. Hall sent this photograph to William Elliot Griffis for his biography of S. R. Brown.

priest. They were much delighted therewith. An old nun who was with them refused to have her picture taken. She evidently had some conservative scruples about such work! I was sorry not to get an impression of her stupid sleepy face as she stood with a rosary hanging from her wrist. I tried unsuccessfully to get a picture of the Dr.'s roguish eyed little Japanese girl. The Dr. has taken her for a servant, but the authorities are disposed to interfere and threaten to take her away.

Sadajirō's affair seems to have passed by. The officials came again today to inquire about the books. S[adajirō] had got them all back from Yedo the evening before except a few that he had sold, and the Dr. showed them to the officials. The ostensible ground of complaint was that no duties had been paid, that a Yatoi, a hired man, had no business to sell books, nor had Dr. H[epburn]. It was the business of a merchant to buy and sell and did not belong to the professional men such as Dr.

H[epburn] was. This of course was none of their business, but it afforded a pretext for meddling, which they are all ready to do. A few days since a merchant, who was entering our gate to show some silks which B[rown] had requested to be brought, was denied admittance by the yakunins at the gate and B[rown] had to remonstrate sharply with them before they assented to his entering. They said a merchant should sell his wares at his store. A threatened appeal to the Governor brought them to terms.

The streets this morning are lively with squads of Oki No Kami's soldiers. Their uniforms of a dark green with star crests look handsome. A large number of them are clad in mail. You do not see the armor, but you hear its rattling noise as they move. We learn nothing new of the picture of affairs today. I see the baggage and lanterns of the fresh recruits passing into the Daiba[41] between the English and American Consulates. The Yokohama

of Griffis's *Hepburn of Japan* (Philadelphia: Westminster Press, 1913). In his letter to Griffis, Hall also notes that "Mr. Brown's daughter, Mrs. Lowder, was an amateur photographer" who might also be able to assist him in finding photographs to illustrate his book. We have no record of what happened to Hall's photographs. For

Hall's letter to Griffis see Francis Hall Letter to the Rev. Wm. Elliot Griffis, Elmira, N.Y., May 3, 1901, in the manuscript collection of Elmira College Library, Elmira, New York.

[41] The *daiba* was a fortification where samurai were quartered. There were two *daiba*, or "forts," in Kana-

people are in fine spirits, and, though prepared for an emergency, feel little alarm.

Friday, May 4, 1860

The excitement over the threatened invasion subsided as rapidly as it rose. The government, acting on the safe side, keep up a large show of force. Soldiers are regularly quartered in the Custom House compound. At Kanagawa most of Oki no Kami's contingent have disappeared. The garrison force at the Daiba is augmented, but they do not appear much in the streets. The servants report that the government are pressing men into service from the ranks of the farmers who are first chosen in preference to other callings, paying six tempos a day for their wages. Our guard at the gate appears to be made up in part of these recruits. There is a lad of eighteen among them, who, like other youths in trainer's clothes, is fond of showing off. He struts about with an important [air], brandishes the bamboo pole, and plays cut and thrust at the six inoffensive stone gods under the little chapel roof, and stabs all the trees and posts in a savage heartless way. Even poor puss came in for a share of his demonstrations and frightened fled behind the stone images for safety. The altar was no protection for this young aspirant for military service, who continued to bait poor puss till she had to beat a vigorous retreat into the top of a pine tree, safe from all juvenile warriors.

Today comes a report that [the] young Emperor [shogun] has been slain. It is not at all unlikely, but we may wait days before we shall know its truth or falsity in this land of duplicity. A meeting of the foreign residents is called at Yokohama this evening to consider means for self defense.

The change from moderately warm weather to a heated time has been rapid. The thermometer this morning at sunrise stood at 63°, rising to 80° at noon. In going out to walk I found this temperature at first quite oppressive, but the south wind blew up fresh and strong and after the first half hour the heat was bearable. I followed up one of the alluvial expanses that stretch inland between low hilly ridges. The country people were coming into Kanagawa, bearing burdens of produce or home manufactures for sale. Led pack horses with straw bales of various country products were frequently met. Many of the horses were laden with bundles of faggots and rushes, little mountains of bulk but light in weight, monopolizing all the breadth of the country ways. These horses look shy at the strange apparition of foreigners, stand, snort, stand obstinately still, or make a clean break into the fields. I met a family group, as I often meet them, trudging along on foot with a happy contented look. A girl of thirteen or fourteen with pleasant face, and skinny, was clad in blue robes with a red crape undergarment beneath showing at the roll of the neck, in the slashed opening of the sleeves, and where it hung a little below her outer garments around her otherwise naked ankles, naked from ankle to knee. At a little distance the dress looks picturesque with its bright colors. In winter the primary colors are dark. Now I see lighter shades begin to come into the streets.

My walk led me on under the shade of trees that arched the path with their grateful shade, where in the moisture and coolness ferns and violets rested in luxuriescence of growth. I came into a little hamlet scattered among a growth of bamboos and firs, surrounded with living fences of trees and flowering shrubs, that I visited a few days ago. A brisk little woman who keeps a wayside teahouse recognized me and invited me to sit down on her cool mats in the shade of the thatched roof. I was glad to do so after a warm walk. She brought some hot tea and showed me her crop of beans of which she appeared to be proud for their really luxuriant growth. The boys as usual made their appearance and conducted me from one cottage to another, hid among the trees, and everywhere I met a hospitable

---

gawa, which are clearly shown on the 1860 map of Yokohama and Kanagawa that Simmons marked. See Maruya Tokuzo, *Gokaikō Yokohama dai ezu* (Edo: Hō-zendō, 1860) in Yokohama Archives of History (cover bears the initials D.B.S.).

reception, and wherever I found flowers they were willing to pluck them more freely than I wished to have them. There were very many persimmon trees in the hamlet. They resemble our butternut trees in appearance, size, and formation. I found many beautiful varieties of azaleas, white, red, and purple.

My last stop in the hamlet was at a farm house and out buildings so hid in a bamboo thicket that it was invisible till I entered the enclosure through a shady path. A woman sat at her loom in one part of the house and in another room was a cluster of school children squatted on their mats and cushions before their little low writing desks. They at once jumped up when they recognized a stranger and asked me to come in saying it was "play spell." I accepted their hearty invitation and went into the school room. There were not more than a half dozen or so scholars there. Each had his little table on which was his copy book and writing materials. The copy book was made of some sheets of Japanese paper sewed together, the writing material were the reed pens of the country, india ink, and a tablet to grind the ink upon. The desks were black with ink and hacked, not with Yankee prick knives, but with the paper cutting knives of the school boys. Their copy books were smeared with ink into one general blot, for it seemed that as each page was finished the whole was blacked over. By the side of each copy book was the master's copies in a little book shaped like books of copies at home, long and narrow, only they opened on the long edge unlike ours. One sheet of paper which lay on one of the tables was the delineation of a foreign head and face with long beard and hat, which I at once saw was the work of the little fellow that lingered at his desk to make the hasty sketch of the *tojin* when my entrance interrupted him. Now came in the women from the nearby houses to look in. I kneeled on the cushion before one of the tables and taking the pen, while one of the boys rubbed some fresh ink on the tablet, I commenced writing the arabic numerals and our alphabet to their great delight. I was surrounded by an attentive group. I filled one page, and then a fresh paper was brought for me to fill. The people have always a desire to possess any written or printed characters of a foreign language.

Then the women went and one came back with a pot of tea and another brought some round rice cakes filled with persimmon—much like dried apple sauce. Another brought in a bowl of preserves, but such preserves they were, small peaches preserved in salt and their own acid. A little went a great way. By this time the schoolmaster made his appearance. He was a man of fifty years, taller than most men among this low statured people, had a pleasant face and quite the air of a pedagogue. He brought in some better paper, his own box of pens, and I must write some characters for him, and all were pleased that I was going to do something for the schoolmaster. I did my best and filled a page with my very choicest chinographs ending off with Mr. Buchanan's name, who I told them was the American emperor. And I hereby respectfully inform his Excellency the President of the United States that the bare mention of his august name made a decided sensation among the boys assembled.

The school master brought in a beautiful jug of sake and having drunk a cup full himself offered it to me. He was much pleased with what I had done for him. Of course I was elated with my success and must now display a flight into the region of the arts. The "big girl" of the school took her place on the opposite side of the low writing desk and saw that I was supplied with ink and paper. I made a bold attempt with a free spirit at the American Flag. Notwithstanding my stars were of all shapes and sizes, and the stripes of black, and the staff inked and wobbly, I was glad to see that the sketch was recognized. This excited so much applause that I determined upon a house. Three or four of the boys were behind me examining my boots, rolling up my trousers to make such brief explanations as they might while the rest commenced a running commentary on what I was making. The old school master was attentive to the sake jug. I had got the foundation timbers laid, the uprights set up, and was putting on the roof, when the lookers on concluded I was drawing a horse, but when I had finished the roof put the chimneys on and window in they all said with one voice it was a junk. A sensitive artist might have felt disparaged by such criticisms but nothing daunted I persevered till the big girl pronounced it a house and all assented thereto, the master drinking to the discovery. A tree which they were divided as to its being a fish or a dog came out right [at] last, and the master filled and emptied his cup again.

The school master, whose eyes began to twinkle as his head grew full and his jug grew empty, pronounced me a clever fellow with the pen, and my chinographic exploits were all folded up with many thanks. The master took a parting drink all to himself, asked me to come again, while a few of the lads volunteered to escort me to all the places where the flowers grew and out into the stout young pine woods whose perfumed breath filled the air. In this morning walk I came to the first enclosure I had seen where there was anything like a garden. Here I saw paths bordered with plants and shrubs among which were azaleas, columbines, and a species of primulaceae or polyanthus. These are common in a variety of colors with ovate and serrate edged petals. My walk home led me through a wooded dell so cool and shaded that last night's dew lay in drops on the white violet's caps.

The long withheld permission to leave the country has at last been granted under restrictions. The party leaving must bind himself to return. If taken away as a servant the party so taking him must promise to return and leave with the Consul of his flag a money pledge that he shall come back within a specified time.

The American Consul went to Yedo this noon and I have assumed his place till he returns. Having occasion to go to Jobootsoogi [Jobutsuji] and return after dark my escort shows in what an unsettled state this empire is. A man bearing two lanterns with the insignia of the consulate preceded me and another in like manner followed me. On either side of me was a yakunin with a lantern and two swords, when the path was wide enough to admit this order of procession. In the path through the fields, first went the lantern bearer, then a yakunin, then myself, then behind me the same order, a yakunin, a servant with two lanterns bringing up the rear. I carried a stout cane in one hand and my pistol was placed where it could be handled without a second's delay. This precaution, we are assured by the government, is absolutely essential against secret attacks.

Saturday, May 5, 1860

At the Consulate. A dismal rainy day. Walking through the Tokaido I was presented with some extraordinary clusters of azaleas, light straw color and red bordering on orange. They were more like lilies than any azaleas I had ever before seen. I picked some of the flowers and laying them on a table resting the open throat on their petals I found the largest measured a foot in circumference! From tip to tip in full diameter the measurement was four inches. I had some white ones of the same size. Yangaro brought me a monster, heavy and hotly scented, that measured two feet in circumference! The azaleas are grown in the yards of the farmers and merchants having no special cultivation beyond being half protected under the friendly branches of a belt of trees.

The Japanese tell the following pleasant fable. The cardinal numbers from one to nine inclusive have the terminal syllable "soo," except five which is itsoosoo, doubling the same, ten is "to," and the fable runs that ten complained to the other numbers that he had no "soo," to his name and he believed five was a thief and had stolen the "soo" that belonged to him for he had two "soos."

In the emperor's service is an official whose duty it is to try all the sword blades wanted for the imperial service. His seal of approval is sought for on sword blades throughout the empire. They need only his stamp to make them at once valued and salable.

Until within eight years houses of catamites were quite common, patronized mainly by the priests. They have fallen into disrepute of late years under the royal favor. There are said to be still at Yedo these houses for the nefarious prostitution. The boys are dressed like girls and faces are powdered in like manner.

The reported meeting at Yokohama last evening was a fizzle. All that was done was by Schoyer, who impressed the opportunity to sell a table at auction.

The expenses attendant upon the interment of the suicide who hung himself on a tree near the Consulate were assayed upon the people. His funeral expenses, according to the official who took charge and the posting of public notices amounted to about thirty ichibus, or ten dollars. This was assessed on owners and occupiers of landed property. All these burdens fall heavily on a poor people. So when the other day a priest fell in a fit before the Honjin, the principal consternation was lest there were more funeral expenses to be met. On examining the priest it appeared that he was from Yedo and was returning home from a travelling expedition with a box of respectable dimensions full of ichibus. In cases like the suicide the person being unknown, a description of the person is posted in public places for recognition. The same manner of advertising by posting is common from advertising wares for sale, to rewards for thief, in short as we would do at home.

Sunday, May 6, 1860

A rainy Sunday at the Consulate. On my way to church in passing through the lane near the English Consulate I saw a poor fellow sitting under the dripping trees by the wayside eating from a straw plate his meager dinner of rice and a few slices of sweet potatoes. His matted hair hung over his face and he was protecting his shivering limbs with a mat of straw. He looked healthy and strong enough to labor, but as he sat cowering under the dripping trees, with wet and cold and ate his not over nourishing meal, my heart smote me with pity. He asked for nothing, but I could not refrain from dropping some coppers in his hand, though I knew the probability was, that too, would go for sake. So let it go, thought I, and may you forget your poverty and cold, though it be but for a brief hour.

Monday, May 7, 1860

At the Consulate. Rainy. The authorities came to inquire if the Japanese hulk on board which the United States has had coal stored could be used by them to place a police force aboard. One of the Japanese steamers is anchored in the harbor, which with the force on the hulk are designed as protection to the settlement from the landward [seaward?] sides.

Tuesday, May 8, 1860

A fine day after a storm of three days continuance. Thermometer at Sunrise at 44°. Dorr returned today with Heusken from Yedo. Heusken tells me that the Japanese still pretend that the Regent is not dead, but that as the son is old enough to take the reins of government he has assumed them. No new regent is appointed but the young emperor is new at the head of affairs. Mito, when he fled to his province, took possession of a suite of buildings occupied by an imperial officer having driven him out. It was to this place an ambassador was sent by the government to remonstrate and negotiate with Mito, and he replied by cutting off the ambassador's head. A daimio of high rank has been lately assassinated in Yedo, but who is yet unknown. Probably from this arose the report that the young emperor was slain.

Apricots are growing in size and are now as large as ordinary peach stones, raspberries have more than half their growth. Mr. Harris sent Mr. Hepburn a day or two since a collection of plants from Yedo. Among them were little camellias four or five inches high covered with a bud ready for blossoming. The Dielytra Spectabilis [Bleeding Heart] was also among them. In the street I saw a Hydrangea today and little dwarf pines three or four inches high. Flowers, flowering plants, and shrubs are daily brought for sale and appear to find a ready market.

Wednesday, May 9, 1860

Two or three weeks back Mrs. H[epburn] had a scholar desirous of learning our language. He was a very pleasant amiable fellow of delicate organization, small hands and feet, and wrists like a musician's. He has not attended upon his lesson for several days until today. He apologized for his absence saying that he had been sick. He afterwards confessed that he was the official whom our American Consul in a fit of half anger and half drunk severely chastised at his gate because he said he caught him asleep. It was for this that the authorities requested Heco to inform Dorr that for a repetition of the offense they would report him to his superior at Yedo, and if he took the law into his own hands he must run the risk of the consequences.

For three days the train of one of the princes of the empire has been passing through the Tokaido. His effects and baggage bearing his crest have been passing for three days, last night the main body and the immediate escort of the Daimio himself went by. The night was chosen to avoid collision with foreigners. It was the wish of this daimio to visit Yokohama, but at the request of the authorities he abstained from so doing through the same fear. Today the rear of the train passed by. I was standing at the foot of the Consulate steps when a body of about fifty men went by escorting an official of the prince's household. He was above the average size, dark complexion, prominent nose and sharp eye. His dress was of rich brocade silk marked with figures in gold. His attendants wore dark suits, the usual wide hats and were armed with muskets and swords. Some of them were fierce looking fellows. Most of them looked pleasant, and there were others who had a bold defiant gaze, for all turned their eyes on me as I passed. I do not wonder that the hereditary nobles should feel jealous of the foreigner who stand[s] erect, uncovered, and regardless before them and teaches daily lessons of practical equality. With equality and prosperity of the people the rule of feudalism must fall to the ground. It will not be given up without a bloody contest, and I believe the day is not far distant when this land will experience all the horrors of war. Yedo is an imperial city in the strictest sense, a court residence when the dignitaries of the realm are gathered there. Commerce, with its leveling tendencies, will meet the aristocracy of caste and birth and one must go to the wall. I am inclined to think it would have been better even to have opened the port of Yedo to the traders. I hear it said again that many of the Daimios maintain a state beyond their resources, and they resort to forced loans from the prosperous merchants of their principalities to sustain their living expenses. Prosperous merchants, manufacturers, and farmers generally keep their wealth circulated as much as possible through fear of

forced levies. Removal from one principality to another cannot be effected without permission. This is only in the largest principalities. It is said that of late years that the erection of water mills for making mochi and hulling rice has been prohibited by the Emperor, for the supposed reason that thereby wealth might be accumulated.

Thursday, May 10, 1860

I have been pleased with hearing today that the memory of honest old Will Adams, or Ange as he is called, is perpetuated by having a street named after him in one of the pleasantest portions of Yedo. I cannot learn that any of his descendants are living. I inquired diligently of my informant if there were any traces of the Catholics descended from the old Spanish and Portuguese stock. He knew of none. I asked if there might not be some who secretly maintained the faith handed down from father to son. He did not think it possible. At the time of the extirpation of the Catholics the names of all the Christian families who remained of the natives unexecuted were marked in a book. Their houses were often visited by officials to discover if there was any trace of the uprooted faith lingering in symbols, books, or practice. So rigid was the surveillance that he regarded it as effectual.

The same man relates of the great Hide Yoshi, the first Taiko Sama, that he was originally a farmer of low extraction, that he was small of stature and an unprepossessing countenance, but possessed a great shrewdness and ability. From the peculiar expression and confirmation of his countenance he was always called "monkey faced." After wandering about and having the reputation of a highwayman he became the betto of the Prince of Owari in whose service he acquired the distinction which finally led to the command of armies and the occupancy of the throne. At his death he left a son by one of his concubines. She seems to have been a dissolute woman abandoning herself to incontinent conduct like Queen Catherine, and wholly neglected the education of the child, who grew up an ignorant youth. Disgusted by her vices and the training of the child, Iyeyas [Ieyasu], supported by a party, and who is represented as a man of large abilities, headed a revolution. But the adherents of the throne were powerful. Armies were raised and after various encounters a decisive battle was fought in which the forces of the young emperor were ten to one of his opponent. The battle commenced early in the morning and by noon Iyeyas saw every division of his army swept away but one. Leading these, his reserves, in person he restored the fight and after a desperate struggle prolonged till nearly night remained master of the field. This success gave him the imperial throne and from him are descended the present line of emperors.

The law of succession to estates in Japan is by primogeniture. These may be children by the wife or by the concubines, the eldest of all succeeds for the children of the *mekake* or mistress never know her as mother which title is applied to the wife alone. Polygamy is only limited by the wealth or tastes of the male. One woman only is called wife, all the rest are concubines. If the husband chooses he may put away his wife at pleasure.

Schools are generally private at Yedo. S[adajirō] says there are public schools. Mr. Harris says there is one such designed for children of the princes, but it has no pupils.

The gifts brought by Perry are all stored in the emperor's houses at Yedo and are seldom seen. All the people have ever seen of them was in their first exhibition at Yokohama.

The publishing and sale of obscene prints and books is contrary to law. Once in a year or two the imperial officers make a descent on the publishers and vendors confiscating not only the books and wooden stereotype plates, but the entire contents of the shop where found. On a repetition of the offense one to two hundred lashes are administered. I am more inclined to think from the frequency and openness with which such books are sold that if there be any such law it is mainly a dead letter.

Green peas were offered today by the vegetable sellers. They were too young to be

shelled without trouble. Pieplant is also in market, but it has none of the tartness that makes it desirable for cooking.

Friday, May 11, 1860

Nippon can boast of a great variety of beggars. This morning a woman and child were begging in the Tokaido. The woman's dark skin was completely coated with white paint, she was a funny looking fish but the curious thing was that she carried on her back a large doll after the manner of carrying infants. She attracted attention by beating a piece of bell metal. A great variety of beautiful pinks and carnations were for sale in the streets. Also a fine root of the Kalla and one of the Diety tree.

Went to Yokohama to see what I could do towards getting a building lot. Found that the Americans, weary of vexative delay and the inability or unwillingness of the foreign representatives to render aid, had resolved to help themselves. Some Californians led the way by "staking out claims" in true California style. Talbot[42] and I followed suit, carrying our "locations" to and on the first bluff near Treaty Point.

Japanese traders again report that the sale of oil and silk has been suspended for one month. They are forbidden any more to bring "musters" to the foreign houses, probably because sales made in this way would be less under the espionage of the government officials.

It has been said that the Japanese generally are not fond of flowers for the reason that they are not so universally and skillfully cultivated as among the Chinese. My own experience is to the contrary. The flora of Japan is not so large and varied as that of China, but whatever Japan has is diligently cultivated. The traffic that I see daily at this season in the Tokaido is a sure evidence that the people are fond of plants. Every store has its little back area of shrubs, dwarf trees, or plants, or else in the front are one, two, three, or more pots of plants in flower. Then whenever I go in the

---

[42] This may well have been W. H. Talbot who is listed as a British resident of Yokohama in Paske-Smith, *West-* *ern Barbarians in Japan and Formosa in Tokugawa Days*, p. 357.

country all the better class of farm houses have more or less flowering shrubbery and plants. I have gathered my best specimens and varieties of flowers at these farm houses. Whenever I return from my walks with my hands laden with flowers, they are always noticed by the people in the streets and houses by which I pass. "Here comes a stranger with flowers," "beautiful flowers," "the prettiest flowers," "truly beautiful," such are the exclamations I hear as I walk by not from one or two but at every step. If I happen to gather a flower new and beautiful I hear these comments. One will say "Beautiful flower, what is it?" And the answer is perhaps "I never saw it before, it is very handsome." The old women who come in to sell rushes and faggots for fuel have a handful or two of gathered wild flowers on the top of their burdens.

Japan abounds especially in flowering trees and shrubs; evergreens and flowering trees and shrubs are the two features remarkable in the Japanese flora above all others that have so far come under my notice. Of ferns and creepers there are too a large variety, but of low herbaceous plants the variety, in this part of the empire at least, is small. But if other proof were wanting of the characteristic fondness of the Japanese for flowers and flower culture, this is convincing that in no other part of the world have such floral manners been exhibited. It is to be noted in this how this people left to cultivate the arts of peace lap on to our civilization born of tumult with theirs vegetating in quiet. As with us, some florist produces a new variety and it at once becomes the rage. Princes, officials, soldiers, merchants, farmers all participate in the frenzy. The plant, or flower, is bought and sold at fabulous prices, even children gamble on the new production and fortunes are lost and won in a season's passage. Twelve years ago there was such a furor respecting a very insignificant flowerless plant without any bearing of crop either. It became the fashion of the day, and valueless though it was for any ornamental use, enormous sums were paid for single specimens. Two, three, five hundred and a thousand ichibus were paid for a single plant. At length the emperor interfered forbidding its sale and purchase, and it was not till imprisonment and

strifes were frequent that this florimania was suppressed. So when the narcissus was introduced many years ago from Holland, three and four hundred ichibu were paid for a single bulb. The rage for the pink seems to have equalled anything else. Florist pinks, carnations, furcatus [Dianthus furcatus or alpestris] were produced by the cultivators and as the variety was great the gambling in pinks pervaded all classes and ranks. The children staked all their spare cash on the speculation. Extra varieties were sold for 2000 ichibus. To this day I am told that a pair of the handsomest carnations are often sold for ten ichibus. They are described as large and showy as our finest ones. I have seen great numbers of carnations offered for sale within a day or two, as yet none equal to our best varieties at home.

Nor is this fashionable sporting confined to flowers alone. At the time Perry visited Japan a spotted rat supposed to have come from his ships made its appearance. It was known as the "American rat," and was at once bred for sale. This wonderful rat was in brisk demand. Princes and men of substance indulged themselves in the luxury at the cost of fifty ichibus for each. The pet rat, after the manner of his kind, made himself at home, reared a numerous progeny, till the "American rat" would have had as much paid to get rid of him as was paid in the first place to have him.

Saturday, May 12, 1860

Today the street was all astir with the news. Several state prisoners were to be escorted through the Tokaido who had been arrested at Miaco (as Kioto is generally called here) for being participators in the attack upon the Regent. It now appears that seventeen men were engaged in that attack. Three were slain on the spot and seven others were so wounded that fearful of discovery they committed hara kiri. The other seven went to Kioto but their whereabouts was for a long time unknown. According to the popular version they went to Kioto to make an attempt to seize the Mikado believing that if they could get hold of the sacred person recruits would flock to their standard and a successful revolt would be initiated.

At all events they got into conflict with the Mikado's servants, were worsted, and to prevent being taken prisoners five disemboweled themselves. The remaining two were brought up today on their way to Yedo. They were in closed norimons and escorted by a guard of eighty men armed with muskets and swords. The event was magnified by rumors of a great battle near Fusi Yama in which the rebels were defeated and 250 of them taken prisoners and were escorted to Yedo under a guard of 1000 men! Such I found the prevailing impressions at Y[okohama] this morning.

The Japanese have sent another ship into the harbor, and it is said that every boat or junk approaching Yokohama is searched for the vagabond soldiers of Mito. The Governor of Yokohama when inquired of what this means, replied "Oh I know nothing about it, the Government send them here and I am bound to receive them, and take care of them, that is all I know about it."

I made a botanical excursion in the forenoon and gathered specimens of three varieties of sagittaria [arrowhead], four of ferns, ten flowering trees. In the way in another walk I added the flowering blackberry and a creeper with a deep blue flower. In my morning walk I found near a farm house at the foot of a hill a grand specimen of the purple flowering wisteria. There was a little chapel in a grove of cryptomeria, hidden in leaves above and ferns below also, and the wisteria where it sprang from the earth and for two feet above had the enormous measurement of five feet in circumference! Its gnarled and twisted trunk, which was deeply encircled by its growth, gave something more than this measurement of solid wood, a few inches difference perhaps. About ten feet from the ground the trunk separated into many branches, wreathing and turning like so many serpents of anaconda size. A large keaki tree had been cut partially in two and thrown down to give support to the vine. Over this and a grove of palms stunted by its weight the wisteria had spread itself to where, forming a twisted mass of growth, it was a picture of the wild profusion of vegetable growth. The palms like so many columns spreading their leafy capitals to support the festooned roof

above had the appearance of an old colonnade in ruins and overgrown with creeping vines.

There were two farm houses that had the same hill for a background and in front were belted in by a fringe of trees and hedgerows. They were large and with their ample yards were in better condition than the average of country places. Two women were keeping the house, one an old woman seventy years old (I have not yet heard of one over seventy), while the men were working in the paddy fields nearby assisted by women. I do not often see women doing field work. They are often met bringing in faggots and rushes for firewood, perhaps that much belongs to their household duty of keeping their pot a boiling. Here there were several up to their knees in the soft [mud], smoothing and raking the paddy fields for the season's crop which is nearly ready to be transplanted. The women of the house were weaving or preparing charcoal balls from burnt refuse wood, rushes, straw etc., agglutinated with rice water. There were several outhouses. One was a granary, another was an repository of tools where I saw our New England fan mill. In a corner of the same house was a tub of some fermenting vegetables that had a smell as stout as sauerkraut in a Dutch cellar. There was a stall for a horse, and under a shed was the rice huller. In another place was a rude contrivance for weaving a coarse straw rope matting. In all the larger farm houses, there is the manure shed for storing dry manures, with great tubs for preparing liquid manures. Into these are thrown all sorts of refuse vegetable and animal matter to undergo decomposition producing like the manure pits in the field the most intolerable stenches. There were handsome azaleas in bloom and some bushes with buds nearly ready to expand.

The inside of the houses are dingy with smoke and dark with smoke discolored paper windows. The kitchen is a confused collection of pots, kettles, tubs, dried herbs, and the simple domestic utensils. Over a fire hole left in the floor edged with stone swings from an iron crane the tea kettle or perhaps a large kettle. Then there is the cooking range which is a small furnace with two or three places to set a

Farm houses along the Tōkaidō. Photograph by Felice Beato.

pot or kindle a fire underneath, the smoke making such vent as it may. The bake oven is an iron cauldron set in earth. The fire is kindled underneath and the oven is covered with a dish shaped iron cover on which coals are placed. These are the common living apartments. There is another room cleaner and with fresher mats where the family altar is set up and the household sleeps, and, if quite well to do in the world, there will be an altogether genteel room as clean sweet and fresh as new mats, papered or plastered walls, and a little day's care can make it. There are no house shoes at the farm house door but there are strips of paper with printed characters, picture of some small animal like the white fox or the image of a protecting kannon [Buddhist diety of mercy], which has been bought of the priest for a few cash. They may come from a calendar of lucky and unlucky days or an almanac. I am generally received kindly at all such houses. After tea is offered, and if there are

any flowers, I am free to pick as many as I choose. A few buttons to the youngsters are an ample return if I choose to make any return.

I picked May strawberries in this walk growing along the wayside. They are small and utterly insipid. One, which had a fair strawberry size, was juicy but flavorless. In Japan they are only used as medicine, tasteless as they are. I cannot conceive of what virtue they may be possessed.

I secured this forenoon excellent photographic negatives of Yangaro and his wife. They were much delighted.

Sadajirō told Dr. H[epburn] that a few years ago near Oasaca a dancing mania possessed the people, it began with one person and continually extended to a multitude. It was undoubtedly one of those phenomenas which we have witnessed from time to time in America of which the "jumpers" of Kentucky are an example.

Sunday, May 13, 1860

Sabbath service as usual. Passed the day quietly at home.

Monday, May 14, 1860

Sadajirō came down from Yedo this morning and says the city is unusually quiet through fear of danger growing out of the disturbed state of affairs. He says that one of the Regent's assassins disguised himself as a servant and remained in Yedo. His master, suspecting him on account of a nasal tongue said to be peculiar to the people of Mito's province, examined his effects and found his bloody garments.

Brown, with the aid of his teacher, has been reading from the Nippon blue book the revenues of the Daimios. It states that 25 Daimios have an aggregate revenue of $28,000,000 in rice. The largest revenue of one person is $3,000,000 (Q.E.D.)

Tuesday, May 15, 1860

I went to Yokohama today and made an unsuccessful attempt to get my claim fenced in. But both the land and houseowners and the carpenter could not stir a foot in the matter without permission of the official. Their consent was hopeless and so the matter fell through after a three hour's toil in the hot sun. In my pursuit of this business we were conducted by the carpenter to the headman of old Yokohama. We found him in a farm house that had been converted into an office place. He said he was the head of all the carpenters, and if we wanted any work, all we had to do was to go to the Custom House and get a writing to him from their Somebody no Kami! Then he would set the laborers at work. Of course we could not expect any government assistance in squatting.

The Japanese are likely to oust Goble out of

his house after all. The clamor is that the ground belongs to the old priest of this place and he is unwilling to rent.

Japanese merchants say they are now required not to sell any oil or silk again for a limited time. They are forbidden to bring musters to the houses of the merchants. And again they are notified that all their buying for the foreign supply must be of a trading monopoly at Yedo. I think I see in this last an attempt to crush the treaty, which says trade with foreigners shall not be obstructed, this being trade among themselves, a plan to control the prices.

Wednesday, May 16, 1860

Consul Dorr gave a breakfast to us Kanagawagians. It was a handsome entertainment and was only marred just at its close by an accident to Miss B[rown].

Thursday, May 17, 1860

Writing letters for the San Francisco mail. Mr. Harris came down from Yedo today. Mr. H[arris], Genl. D[orr], Dr. H[epburn] and lady, and myself took a horseback excursion in the country. Dined at Dorr's.

Friday, May 18, 1860

Went to Yokohama. Hear that Gen. D[orr] has penned a circular to Americans requesting all who have staked any claims to lots to remove their mistakes. Tiffin at B. and T.'s.[43] A Japanese girl hearing me talk imperfectly in her own tongue would believe nothing other than that, I was a Japanese "like Heco." She could not be convinced to the contrary. Made some purchases to send home by the first opportunity.

I find I have been mistaken as to the privilege granted of leaving the country. Japanese will be permitted to leave on condition that

---

[43] B. and T. are not identified. B. may have been N. D. Boyd of W. Kemptner & Co. from whom Hall later purchased a lot in Yokohama; T. may have been

Talbot, with whom he sometimes dined thereafter, and with whom he had "staked his claim" on the bluff.

they soon will return and that provision will be made by themselves or the person taking them away for the support of any family they may leave behind.

Saturday, May 19, 1860

Spent the morning writing letters. Slight shock of an earthquake about 12 1/2 P.M. After dinner called on Mr. Harris and took a walk with Dr. H[epburn] who piloted me through a new and very picturesque wood more like home woods and scenery than anything I have yet seen. Our path debouched into the extensive valley which I had visited before. Two low hills crowned with a variety of trees were planted as the residences of two princes many years ago. In the civil wars of the empire they became appanages to the crown. Their mines are said to be still viable. A large stream was flowing to the southwestward—where can it empty? Saw three new flowering shrubs growing in its grounds. Stopped at a farm house and asked for a drink of water, as usual it was readily and cheerfully brought. At a sort of road corners we came upon a posting place of imperial edicts. They were on boards or tablets hung beneath a roof. They were very old in their promulgation, the tablets being renewed as they became illegible with time. One edict forbade the firing of any gun or other firearm. But another was far more interesting. It offered a reward of $300 for any information that could lead to the detention of any follower of the "Kiristaru," "Romane," or the "Bruddesan" faith. Here was the old edict of the days of Taiko Sama renewed from time to time. It is a dead letter now, for alas! the persons against whom it was raised have long since been extirpated. After the days of the persecution a register was kept of any family who had given adhesion to the new faith and they were watched, their houses frequently searched, so that there was no hope of escape. What will become of these edicts if any modern converts shall be made?

On the opposite side of the valley from the tablets and under the hill was a house and store of a farmer merchant. Its white fire proof walls and black tiled roof were very neat. It rested amid shrubbery and looked as charmingly picturesque as any woodbine cottage at home. At a neighboring house I got some fine specimens of the white flowering brambles, like double white roses, 2 and 2 1/2 inches in diameter.

Dr. H[epburn] had two patients today enfeebled by excessive venery. They had no disease, this was all their trouble. It illustrates the character of the people. The princes leading idle lives and enjoying the several delights of their harems are said by Mr. Harris to be frequent subjects of paralysis and epilepsy and are commonly a feeble debauched looking lot of men.

Sadajirō asserts positively today that the priests of all the temples have been forbidden by the government to lease their temples to foreigners.

Sunday, May 20, 1860

A rainy Sabbath day. Services as usual.

Monday, May 21, 1860

Read letters from home from Alfred and Edward.[44] Mr. Harris said today in conversation that when the Russian frigate *Diana* lay at Shimoda a Japanese came secretly aboard one night, and satisfying himself that no Japanese were about, cautiously withdrew from his breast a cross. Its full import he did not understand, it belonged to his family and all he knew was that its possessor must not worship idols. He knew the names of Jesus and Mary. There was an indistinct glimmer in his mind of some other religion, but what it was he knew not. This was stated on the authority of Count Mouravieff who stated also that the Japanese was secretly conveyed out of the kingdom. Mr. Harris expressed the belief that there were

[44] Edward was Francis Hall's oldest brother, who carried on the family's educational enterprise in Ellington, Connecticut, at the Hall Family School for Boys. Alfred was one of Francis's younger brothers by his father's second wife.

remnants of the old faith existing about Sekai which would some day come out again.

The respect shown in Japan to the aged is universal. When I tried sometime since to hire a temple the priests refused on account of their old mother whom they did not wish to turn out of her accustomed home. I have never seen a quarrel among old or young but once. That was between Tome's wife and a man and was only a war of words. I have never seen any fighting among men or children. Nor have I ever seen a child punished. The case is widely different in China, where persons will become so infuriated as to tear their own clothes off and throw themselves into a well or other water.

Cucumber came into market today four or five inches long of good flavor. They were brought in little shallow straw baskets containing two each. The multiflora iris are in bloom, small and insignificant to what I expected. I saw green blackberries today.

Tuesday, May 22, 1860

Among the edicts posted together with the one against Christians was one requiring the return of the emperor's hawks, and another respecting harboring fugitives from justice.

Today has been signalized by the baptism of the first English child born in Japan, Miss Emma Japan Elmstone, daughter of Capt. Elmstone. The Capt. came over from Yokohama in a tilbury, a vehicle that has greatly astonished the simple Japanese.

The tide was extremely low today and it was amusing to see the Japanese women coming off from the ferry boats carried on the backs of the boatmen. I rode off that same way myself cracking a joke with my sure footed carrier about two legged horses.

Wednesday, May 23, 1860

At the flower store on the Tokaido I bought a few days ago a handsome flowering shrub. It had a ball of earth held mainly with straw about its roots and when I got it home I directed my servant to set it out. He came into the house laughing a few minutes after and showed me that I had been tricked. It was a branch of a shoot set in earth and made to look like a rooted tree. I told the keeper of the flower shop, he averred his innocence of the cheat and sent up a Chrysanthemum to the house to take its place. Receiving two or three days after another specimen of the first shrub, he also sent me that without charge, showing his wish to deal honestly by me.

A horse drawing a tilbury ran away in the causeway to Yokohama spilling the load of Capt. E[lmstone], wife, and child, who were returning from the christening. They escaped without injury. Such a vehicle produces so much consternation among the Japanese horses endangering the safety of horse, driver, and luggage, that the farmers and burden carriers have petitioned to the Governor to have the nuisance abated. I hope the Governor will assent to this request.

Thursday, May 24, 1860

I procured at Yokohama a book of plates from copper plate engravings executed by Japanese artists. It is now fifty years since the art of engraving on copper was introduced by the Dutch. The work was very creditable comparing equally with English engravings on copper fifty years ago. In this book were pictures of the Joroya houses at Yedo and at Oasaca. It appears that the customs of the empire respecting them vary at different places. In Yedo the Joroyas are confined in their recreations to their own street or quarter, while at Oasaca and Miaco they walk about at their pleasure. Their quarters at Oasaca are said to be the most extensive in the kingdom, occupying many houses. There are nine of the first-class Joroyas and five hundred of inferior ones at Oasaca. At Oasaca one who purchases the favors of a Joroya is allowed uninterrupted intercourse, while at Yedo if a second person or a third calls for the same person one must share her favors with all. The price of the first grade is 6 ichibus but there are other expenses such as shinjos and refreshments, which are at the option of the visitor.

We hear today that the *Excelsior*, which left

here on the 22nd, is on the rocks near Perry's Island.

A Japanese Custom House official was caught stealing a bottle on board of a ship, being barred admittance to the cabin on that account he brought back the bottle although nothing had been said to him about the theft. He understood what was the matter.

The use of Chinese characters and words was introduced by the Buddhist priests, though many of them now are far too ignorant to understand them.

A singular custom prevails at Yedo which reminds me of the Lion's Head at Venice or the Mayor's Complaint Book at New York. A large box like our ballot box is placed in an acceptable situation where persons having any complaint against [an] official, no matter how high his station, deposits his written accusation. This is done anonymously and the box is so placed that any passer by may readily deposit his ballot without attracting attention. This is done in a given day at least once a year and sometimes more, twice, or thrice. The ballot is open from sunrise till late in the afternoon when the papers are taken out at a large building used for such assemblages and the charges are publicly read. If they are afterwards discovered to be true, the offender is deposed from his place or otherwise punished. So too, if any one wishes to deposit a word of commendation of any official he may do so. Since these ballots are examined by officials themselves I imagine they manage it quite cleverly enough to protect themselves as a general thing. If not electing by ballot, it has a chance of unelecting by ballot.

instance of Japanese official shrewdness at a recent interview with the Governor. The Governor inquired of the mint stamp on our coins, is it not the guarantee of their correctness. Certainly it was. Is not the standard one given for all the coins? Certainly. Is the Mexican dollar the American dollar? No, the mint does not issue dollars for general circulation. Yes, says the Governor, here is one, and here are two half dollars, at the same time producing them, and, one dollar, in the half dollars, does not weigh the same as one of the dollars. The dollars the governor had was one of the California mint made for the China trade. It is of extra weight to compete with the Mexican dollar in the China market. The secret was that American merchants tendered payment of their export duties in American half dollars between which and the Mexican dollar these is a difference of 8 percent in weight. The Japanese were therefore unwilling to receive the half dollars particularly as they had got hold of an American dollar which was heavy up to the Mexican standard. They looked upon the half dollars as debased coin. The Consul did his best to explain the fear of extra weight dollars, but I think the result will be that the half dollar will eventually be depreciated and thrown out of the Japan trade.

Inquired of S[adajirō] today about the two Japanese who came up to Perry's Squadron at Shimoda and asked to leave the country. He says the facts are well known, that the two men are still living, one of them was a distinguished teacher of military tactics. The common report is that these two were representatives of a party of ten that wished to get away and sent these two to pioneer.[45]

Friday, May 25, 1860

Raspberries in market resembling Yellow Antwerps, may not the Dutch have received them from Japan?

Call from the Consul today who relates an

Saturday, May 26, 1860

Earthquake this morning at 3 A.M. which wakened us all out of sleep. It was the severest but one that we have experienced.

---

[45] This entry shows that Sadajirō's information was not always accurate. The two men in question were Yoshida Shōin and Kaneko Jūsuke. Yoshida Shōin was the important late Tokugawa ideologue who favored the pro-Imperial and anti-Western position that was

projected under the slogan "Revere the Emperor and Expell the Barbarians" (*sonnō jōi*). Under the influence of another important teacher, Sakuma Shōzan, Yoshida decided to go to the West in order to study conditions there so that Japan might strengthen herself. He and

Spent the early morning at the photograph room and got an indifferent likeness of the Honjin interpreter. In the afternoon took a long walk with Dr. Hepburn. Found the multiflora iris abundantly in bloom and wild raspberries ripe. Our return brought us past Bookenji [Bukenji] where we saw the priests sweeping the broad avenues. I admired more than ever the beauty of this spot—the clean streets, the neat houses, the well trimmed hedgerows, the beautiful shrubs and trees, and the air of quiet that pervaded the place.

Some young priests were returning from a walk with flowers in their hands as they advanced up the hilly path they met one of their superiors, when all in a line together bowed to the earth retaining their bent position a half moment, then all rose with a word of welcome from the white robed priest to whom they presented their flowers. The farmers were busy with their fields, transplanting rice, cutting grass and weeds, which they threw into the submerged fields for manure. We stopped at one snug farm house where, in its hidden seclusion, no voices of the world reach. The man was repairing a saddle out of doors, within an old woman was sewing with spectacles on her nose and a buxom girl was plying the bang shuttle of a cotton loom. It was an apparent picture of happiness. I cannot help believing that the peasantry of Nippon live more quiet contented lives than most any people of earth, savage or civilized.

It seems that the mound on which stands my favorite pine is artificial, being the burial place of a Daimio in bygone days. This reminds me of the old custom of the Norridgewock Indians in interring their chiefs under a young maple. In my country walks I frequently see a straw rope extending across the road from the top of high poles. To the ropes are attached strips of paper with charms written thereon by priests to ward off sickness from the vicinity—to keep disease from stalking by.

S[adajirō] mentions a fact, if it be one, that I have never before heard. He says the Emperor has 20 female personal attendants. They are neither wives nor mistresses. He calls them his guards. They never appear publicly, are chosen for their fine appearance, suitors for gain are said to reach the Emperors ear more directly through them than by any other source.

An orchid which I bought a few days ago for half an ichibu, or rather pair of them, is now in bloom. The flowers are white and rose tinted and of exceedingly delicate and pervading odor. The handsomest single and double fringed poppies I ever saw are now in bloom. They are truly superb.

Sunday, May 27, 1860

Sunday services by Mr. Blodget.[46] Saw the first gathering of the new crop of rape seed.

Monday, May 28, 1860

Rain from the north and northwest. Thermometer down to 58°.

I have two specimens of Japanese miniature gardening. One is a box of earth 4 1/2 by 9 1/2 inches. It contains two cedar trees growing out of a bank of moss, a maple tree, wisteria vine, two box trees, a clump of ferns, one of cilas, and one of grass and weeds. Under the maple is a miniature rockwork and under the vine is a miniature arbor. A fence of bamboo partially

---

Kaneko tried to get Perry to take them to the United States in 1854, but were rejected and later imprisoned for their efforts. Kaneko died in jail in 1855. Yoshida's sentence was commuted to house arrest in 1856, and in 1857 he organized a school, the Shōka Sonjuku, where he taught a number of samurai such as Takasugi Shinsaku, Ito Hirobumi, and Yamagata Aritomo, who became important leaders in the Meiji Restoration. Yoshida was subsequently implicated in an unsuccessful assassination plot against the high shogunal official, Manabe Akikatsu, and executed in Edo on November 21, 1859.

[46] The Reverend H. Blodget was sent to Shanghai in 1854 by the American Baptist Board of Foreign Missions. See William Dean, *The China Mission: Embracing a History of the Various Missions of All Denominations Among the Chinese, with Biographical Sketches of Deceased Missionaries* (New York: Sheldon and Co., 1859), p. 163. Blodget and his wife had come to Japan for the sake of her health and were staying with the Hepburns.

encloses it. The design is to represent the pleasure grounds attached to temples, tea houses, or the better private dwellings. The little dwarf trees are all healthy, well rooted and growing. Then I have another box 8 x 15 inches very similar except on a little more enlarged plan. It contains two fir trees, two cedars, two climbing vines, a maple, and two varieties of plants unknown. One of the pines is growing out of a rocken mossy bank and has been trained and treated with a great deal of pains. It is probably two or three years old and is just now putting out its young shoots of the present year's growth. The Japanese offer a great variety of these for sale. Some are smaller even than the smaller one I have described, while others not more than two feet long by one wide will have the whole arrangement of a Japanese *niwa*, or yard. There will be the house itself and all the outhouses and sheds belonging to it, a garden with a great variety of trees and plants, a miniature lake with tiny goldfish, artificial rock work, and hedgerows with all the variety of dwarf trees and plants in a healthy state of growth. The cost of such a toy which must have required a large outlay of time and patience may cost a dollar.

Tuesday, May 29, 1860

Another day of rain. A horse dealer brought me his sorry crop to look at today. I could not buy.

Wednesday, May 30, 1860

At Yokohama today among the flowers offered for sale by a flower merchant were some ferns. The long fern roots had been taken up and were braided in wreaths or trained on cross bars, whether this had been done before the growth of the leaves I could not say positively but there was every appearance of their having been so cultivated. It has been trained against an upright piece of bark their roots resting in a little pocket at the bottom.

In the Tokaido in the afternoon I passed a traveling peddler. His goods were carried under a canopy gay with colors, ornamented with pictures and jingling pendants of brass. Wreaths of these same ferns were also suspended around the canopy. I met also the servants of a Daimio who was going to make a halt for the night in Kanagawa. This intention was announced by painted boards affixed to long poles of bamboo placed at short intervals in the street. The black square boxes which I have so often seen S[adajirō] tells me contained the armor of the soldiers. Several warriors passed but we did not meet the main body. We halted at the Inkio's house, a sorry little place off the Tokaido. The little front yard was full of flowering plants and shrubs among which was the Yacae plant. I was treated to some tea made from the first young leaves of this season, the flavor was pleasant. S[adajirō]'s wife was here. She had colored her teeth and plucked out her eyebrows so that I did not at first recognize her. S[adajirō] says she did this in obedience to custom but felt very bad and wept while she did it. He said he could not bring her to our place with her eyebrows and white teeth for the officials thought, if she came that way, she "was B[rown]'s, or H[epburn]'s, or my mistress." This reminds me that the common people believe that Miss A[drian] who lives in B[rown]'s family is his wife No. 2. We returned home through the fields. The first of the rape seed is gathering and the barley is being cut.

The fields about Kanagawa belong to the crown. The land holders paid originally for the lease and now an annual rent of one half the rice grown. The other crops belong to the farmer. I have heard that they are entirely his own. H[eco?] understands that a money impost is levied on all crops but rice, in lieu of the half share paid on the rice. All the land in the empire is held by the crown and daimios, the latter receiving the same tribute and in turn paying to the crown a small tribute, about one fiftieth. The owner of the land is obliged to keep all the paths and roads in order and see that the streams are free from obstruction and ready for irrigation. If these are deficient the farmer reports to the officials who look after the owners interest and he makes all needed repairs.

The evening primrose is called the "Evening Beauty or Belle," the same word being applied to it which is applied to a Joroya when she is dressed for the evening's allurements.

The Embassy to the United States has been heard from. A whaler touching at Hakodadi [Hakodate] brought letters from them to their friends dated at the Sandwich Islands. They had a passage of 22 days to the Islands, had lovely fine weather, and enjoyed themselves.

The farmers and other residents on the lands proposed to be opened to foreigners at Yokohama are very unwilling to leave them. They have remonstrated to the Imperial Court.

Thursday, May 31, 1860

The last day of May with a half clouded sun and clear refreshing atmosphere. A walk with Dr. H[epburn] at noon. The banks were covered with the scarlet snake-berries, how much we wished they could be converted into delicious strawberries which they are in form and colors. The boys met us with their happy shouts and were ready as usual to guide us to a pretty prospect, to flowering trees, and where the wild raspberries were growing. Two of them were returning from their school at Kanagawa, their copybooks were tied up in a satchel on their backs hanging from their necks. There was the usual supply of babes, for children in Nippon are early taught to carry double, one little girl had a bouncing year older strapped on her back and a young infant in her arms while she herself could not have been more than nine years old, or not so many. We tried to tell the boys that this was an awful burden for the little girl, and to shame their gallantry into her relief, but the youngsters only laughed. They saw their mothers as beasts of burden, and why not their little sisters. New flowering shrubs as usual. Returning across the hill a blackeyed boy hailed me as an old acquaintance, said I had given him buttons, and he thanked me and wished to show me where I could find the raspberries. I told him not then. I must come day after tomorrow, he said, then there would be some flowers in bloom, and he pointed to a low small leafed variety of azalea just then coming into blossom.

Friday, June 1, 1860

Yesterday a horse dealer was to bring me some horses to look at. They did not come, and [when I asked] why, there was the usual complaint of official interference at the gate. So today I have been and selected four horses to be brought to our compound tomorrow by my official request. These interferences are provoking enough to us, but I fancy still more to the poor people who would like to come and sell a few vegetables. An old woman came this morning to sell some raspberries, we had abundance in the house and did not want them. The woman appeared to be really distressed that we did not take them and the secret of her trouble was that she expected to be upbraided by the officers for coming to sell what we had not ordered to be brought. Today Goble's teacher, a friend of his from Yedo who expected to be employed as teacher by Richards, and Brown's stable boy have all been arrested, for what we do not know. The Honjin officials say they know nothing about it (lying of course) and that some under officials have done this. But all these instances only illustrate how this people are at the mercy of all the two sworded class whether yakunin or samurai.

Saturday, June 2, 1860

I have waited at home all the morning for the horses to be brought to me but they do not come. Now the dealer comes and tells me that two of the horses are sold. I believe it to be a ruse to cover the poor fellow's fear of the yakunins, at all events the horses are not at the stable nor will the man produce other than two sorry looking steeds that I will not have. One feels a desire to be revenged of such treatment, but how can I hit the yakunins without the blow recoiling on the head of the horse dealer. The Consul was a long time at the Honjin last evening in the affair of our missing servants. The officers denied knowing anything about the affair, said it was the work of an under officer, etc. General D[orr] was resolute, he knew the men had been seen bound at a Hatangoya [hatagoya], or inn, and demanded a search. Two or three inns were searched and no one found. The Consul still persisted, and finally in face of all their previous objections they produced the boy Kako and said the other two were undergoing an examination and could not be produced. Such is the unblushing affrontry of a Japanese official. The Consul then today made a demand of the Governor not only that these two servants shall be produced, but that the officials shall be dismissed from the gates of the Consulate and residences.

Such is the surveillance in Kanagawa that a native is fearful to step in any house but his own except by permission. At Yokohama natives passing the gates into the foreign quarter must have leave of the gate keepers.

So, too, a tax is levied on silk entering Yokohama that has been purchased outside of ten percent. Such are some of the infractions of the spirit and very letter of the treaties.

My attention was attracted this morning by the sound of several voices singing in chorus. I went into the streets and saw that it was a procession of begging priests. There were 25 of them going in single file through all the streets with a half chanting, half sing-song drawl receiving such alms as they could collect in small lacquered wooden cups. They were dressed alike in long dark robes covering an under robe of white and long, and which was close fitting to the skin, white socks and sandals of straw. Their heads were covered with the large bowl shaped traveler hats like the lower half of a corn basket which serves to keep off the rain and sun alike. A loop of straw falls over each ear, and a string passing under the chin from one loop to the other keeps the hat on the

head. This is the favorite hat of the common people and the soldiers. Lacquered hats made of paper with a slight convexity only are worn by the gentry. These last ranging in their ornamentation with the rank of the wearer.

Capt. Thompson of the *Sportsman*, who arrived a day or two since, brought five shipwrecked Japanese that he picked up off the coast. He saw a strange object in the water, altered the course of his ship, and found three persons on a raft. By signs they made known to him that ten others were to the leeward when with commendable humanity he put about and succeeded in saving all the survivors of the crew of the junk lost in a recent gale. One junk had twelve and the other sixteen souls on board. The Japanese authorities seemed much pleased with his kindness to their unfortunate countrymen.

Sunday, June 3, 1860

Bishop Smith of Hong Kong[47] held a service at Yokohama today. Mr. Goble conducted the services at Kanagawa.

Monday, June 4, 1860

My servant Iwasaki[48] came into my room this morning full of smiles. I knew something had happened to bring such joy into his grave face. He had come in to display his new clothes cut after the Chinese fashion with close sleeves. It was very much better he said. I asked him if the Japanese did not laugh at him, no he said

[47] George Smith, the bishop of Victoria (Hong Kong), later published *Ten Weeks in Japan* (London: Longman Green, 1861) based on this visit.

[48] It is unclear who this Iwasaki was, but he may have been a member of Iwasaki Yatarō's family. It is well known that Iwasaki maintained close ties to Walsh Hall & Co., and that his younger brother, Yanosuke, was sent to the United States to study in 1872 under the auspices of this firm. What is not known is that Yanosuke went to the Hall Family School for Boys in Ellington, Connecticut, where he lived and studied with Hall's brother Edward. Yanosuke subsequently became the Baron Iwasaki and ran the Mitsubishi Company after Yatarō's death in 1885. Yokohama records indicate that

Hall's servant's name was Yasaburō (using the same characters common to Yatarō and Yonosuke's name). Yasaburō was also the name used by Yatarō's grandfather, and Yanosuke was the third son, so it is conceivable that he might have used this name in Yokohama. Unfortunately I have not been able to find corroborating evidence that Yanosuke was in Yokohama at this time. If Hall's boy servant Iwasaki Yasaburō was indeed Iwasaki Yanosuke then Hall's decision to send Yanosuke to his brother's home and school makes a good deal of sense. For the name of Hall's servant see Fujimoto Jitsuya, *Kaikō to kiito bōeki* (Tokyo: Tōkō shoin, 1939), vol. 2, p. 286.

they all admired the style. Some men from the
Emperor's steamer whom he had met at an inn
had pronounced favorably on the imitation. I
suspect if the people were left to themselves
they would readily imitate foreigners in many
customs. Sadajirō, who has been wearing a
shirt for several days, is an object of great curiosity whenever he appears in the Tokaido. He
says he is envied more than laughed at.

Tuesday, June 5, 1860

Spent the day in making purchases of articles to send home and in getting them ready.

Wednesday, June 6, 1860

Took my box to Yokohama and made arrangements with White to have it go to California care of Wells Fargo and Co. and to be
shipped from there to N.Y. via Cape Horn.[49]

Mrs. H[epburn] wished Sadajirō to get a servant for her in place of Kami, whose love for
sake made him so worthless that he had to be
dismissed. S[adajirō] brought one that he said
did not drink but he said it was difficult to get
a servant in Nippon that was good for anything that did not drink. "All that are active
and intelligent drink and all that do not drink
are fools," he said. It was so when Brown
wished to hire his teacher. He was told the
same thing. It illustrates the universal prevalence of drinking and Maj. Olyphant and oth-

ers who speak of the Japanese as a remarkably
temperate people are wide of the truth. How
he could ever have been out after midday and
not encountered scores of sake drinkers it is
impossible to conceive.

The almanacs promise rainy weather almost
daily for a month and a half to come. Like our
own, the Japanese almanacs foretell the
weather, give lucky and unlucky days, etc.

Thursday, June 7, 1860

Rainy day. Earthquake at 10 1/2 A.M. making
the third successive morning that we have experienced them.

S[adajirō] brought in a journal tonight copied by the old Inkio from a manuscript of
Manjiro who had gone as interpreter to the
Embassy to America.[50] Manjiro was shipwrecked, picked up by a whaler and taken into
Howland.[51] He spent several years in the Sandwich Islands and America and returned to Japan about nine years ago. The book gives an
account of his adventures and his observations.
There are several well executed pictures in it
of a railroad and cogs, telegraphy, drawings of
wearing apparel, very good pictures of coat,
vest, shirts, trunks of different styles. There is
a map of the world in good drawing representing the two hemispheres. It is difficult to make
out the names after they have been rendered
by one Japanese into Japanese and then translated back by another into English. I could
make out the names of Dr. Judd and Mr.

---

[49] This seems to have been the first of numerous
shipments that Hall sent off to his brothers' store in Elmira. On January 17, 1862, the *Elmira Daily Advertiser*
announced: "Our citizens have now the opportunity of
examining and purchasing the first installment of Japanese curiosities, composed of articles of luxury and use
recently sent to Hall Brothers from FRANK HALL
now in Japan." Hall Brothers held an exhibition to
which they invited "all of his friends, as well as the public generally, to examine the choisest specimens of Japanese art and skill ever imported to this country." Hall
had excellent taste, especially when it came to lacquer
ware, and Elmira may well have been the first American
community to receive a large volume of such works in
the early 1860s.

[50] The manuscript mentioned here appears to have
been the four-volume edition of Manjiro's life that was

produced by Kawada Shoryū and Manjiro at the request of the Tosa Daimyo, Yamanouchi Yōdō, after
Manjiro return to Japan in 1851. In 1918 Stewart Cu-
lin, the Curator of the Brooklyn Museum, found the
original manuscript at a second-hand book sale in Tokyo and bought it for the Brooklyn Museum. As no
known copy of the work existed in Japanese libraries,
Manjiro's son, Nakahama Tōichirō, was delighted to
find that his father's work was still extant, and using it
produced the standard biography of Manjiro: *Nakahama Manjirō den* (Tokyo, 1936). For a biography of
Manjiro in English see Emily V. Warinner, *Voyager to
Destiny* (Indianapolis, Ind.: Bobbs-Merrill Co., 1956).

[51] This is not a place-name. The *John Howland* was the
whaler that picked Manjiro up and took him to Honolulu.

Cook[e][52] of the Sandwich Islands and President Taylor's. The book was an account of his every day life and a recital of American customs, such as marriage customs, funeral ceremonies, dress, business and employments, religion, observance of a day of rest once in seven days, etc. In New York he remarks that drinking is very common and drunkards frequently seen, though he says it is contrary to law.

Manjiro returned to Loo Choo [Ryūkyū Islands] in a whaler and hence to Nagasaki where he was well received by the Prince of Satsuma who made his case known to the Emperor. The Emperor at once sent for him, gave him a place among the officials, and he now is an important man in the Empire. His return led our conversation to the custom or law of the empire respecting the return of shipwrecked Japanese. S[adajirō] sternly denies that it was ever the custom to put such to death. He says the Dutch "lie" about it. If a man left by design it was otherwise, but shipwrecked mariners were always joyfully welcomed back. I alluded to the case of the Morrison.[53] He said that if the Morrison had gone to Nagasaki she would have met a kind reception. Her appearance off Uraga alarmed the Governor of that province and he felt bound to repel the supposed intruder. He indignantly denied the imputation, but I am not sure the Dutch sailors were wrong.

Friday June 8, 1860

A long ride into the country and came out on to an elevated rolling plateau that commanded an extensive view of the circumferent country. The fields were covered with grain, with here and there a forest wood. The whole aspect of the country was much like the farming lands of New York, more than I had ever seen before. The woods were heavy with the frequent rains, so much so that I was compelled to lead my horse down some of the steep declivities. I observed in several places that between the wheat rows another crop of beans was just coming up.

Mr. Heusken states that at Yedo there are a hundred families, descendants of recanting Catholics in the days of persecution. They are supported at the expense of the government and employed as spies to ferret out any traces of other Christians. The story may well be doubted for more than one obvious reason.

Here is another apocryphal story related on the authority of Sadajirō. He says that about twelve miles from Yedo is a large extent of wild land covered with a low growth of underwood which is used for the raising of imperial horses. They are suffered to herd and grow wild. The tract is so extensive that a wayfarer would readily lose his way unless guided by marks which are placed there for the purpose. I am not sure but there might be such a tract of marshland, but I doubt to its being put to such a purpose.

The same authority declares that the daimios owning uncultivated estates freely offer house and land to farmers who are willing to cultivate the soil.

Simmons has the 3rd Governor under treatment for the itch. He has recently cured a Custom House official of the same disorder.

The jolly priest who owns the temple has friends to visit him today. They are enjoying the evening in the open verandah, which is brilliantly lighted. They are drinking tea and smoking, and I should judge from the peals of laughter that the sake bottle is going round. I hear the jolly priest clapping his hands to call the shave headed boys to replenish the cups. I called on him today and found him enjoying the cool shade of his rooms and affable as usual. He gave me some very good confectionery.

---

[52] Dr. G. P. Judd and Amos Starr Cooke were American missionaries to Hawaii who were kind to Manjirō and his fellow castaways.

[53] The *Morrison* was an American brig that sailed into Edo Bay in 1837 ostensibly to return several Japanese castaways. Aboard the ship were both missionaries and merchants who hoped to "open" Japan for religious activity and trade. The unarmed vessel was fired upon by shore batteries and quickly withdrew and returned to China. See Harry Emerson Wildes, *Aliens in the East*, pp. 197–210.

Saturday, June 9, 1860

Spent most of the day in photographing. A vessel arrived today from Shanghai reports the disturbance of the Anglo-French Alliance in China. The loss of the steamer *Renni* is reported in the bay of Uraga in the blow of three weeks since.

Sunday, June 10, 1860

Mr. Heusken is down from Yedo. He places entire confidence in the story of the hundred families mentioned yesterday. He says they live in a body very near the American Minister's.

Monday, June 11, 1860

The penal islands of Japan are Hachijo [Hachijōjima], Oho Shima [Ōshima], Miaka [Miyakejima], on the south coast, and Sado Shima in the north. Sado contains valuable silver mines and convicts sent thither are employed in the extraction of the precious metals. Hachijo is famous for its fine silks worked by criminals. Formerly degraded princes were employed in these works, but of late years the custom has been to confine the offender to his own quarters at Yedo and place him under constant guard. Servants of the daimios, inferior officials, and all classes of common men are still sent to the penal islands to engage in the employment indicated.

Brown's teacher[54] confirms Sadajirō's remark that shipwrecked Japanese are not executed. He says they were allowed to return but were assigned a house at Yedo in which they were confined and fed at the Emperor's expenses. If any of them had become valuable by their knowledge of foreign affairs they were promoted to the service of the Emperor or some one of the princes.

Beside the port of Irato, or more properly

Hirado, the Portuguese established themselves largely on the island of Amakusa.

After dinner with the American Consul yesterday I returned home through the Tokaido accompanied by my servant and an official. The streets were quiet, the houses dark, the lights being extinguished and the shutters drawn to. A train of night travelers was coming down the road preceded by a lantern on a high pole, each man moreover bearing another lantern in his hand. A large train moving at night with these brilliantly colored lanterns is a sheer spectacle. Under the roofs of one of the shops a travelling restaurateur was fanning the coals of the movable kitchen. Before another house a half dozen begging priests were chanting an inharmonious song keeping time with a rattling staff of rings. Such serenading is not to be coveted at the dead of night. The fellows were doubtless sure that anyone would give a few cents rather than be disturbed long after the midnight hour. A few roadsters with burden pack horses were improving the cool night for travelling.

The government compels each one of our servants to pay a monthly tax of half an ichibu out of their wages.

The belief in the transmigration of souls is universal among the common people. Sadajirō when taking his new house a few days ago was, at the urgent solicitation of his friends, compelled to call in a charmer to protect the house from all evil spirits. S[adajirō] himself is too intelligent to believe such nonsense, but he was obliged to conciliate his friends. By laws of the realm every Japanese must be personally attached nominally to some Buddhist temple. Twice a year he pays a tax called a contribution for the support of this gospel. S[adajirō]'s tax is an ichibu each time. Trampling on the cross has been common until within a year or two. Now it is only required when a man is suspected of Christianity.

Births are required to be registered in books kept for that purpose and the priests are re-

---

54 Brown's teacher was Yano Riuzan, who is described by James Ballah as "a shaven-headed Buddhist, a *yabuisha* or quack doctor . . . who was selected by the Shogun's Council of State for a language teacher for Dr. S. R. Brown. On my arrival November 11th, 1861, he

became my teacher." Yano is recorded as the first Japanese to receive baptism as a Protestant Christian in 1864. See Cary, *A History of Christianity in Japan*, vol. 2, pp. 55–56.

quired to keep a list of all deaths in their respective temple parishes.

I hear frequently a whistle in the streets, it comes from wandering shop performers who give this notice of their approach on a bamboo whistle.

The farmers are all busy today cutting their barley. It rains so nearly every day that this would seem difficult to get it in a dry state. The Japanese manage it very cleverly however. They take the cut stalks in their hand and ignite them near the head, the flame lasts long enough to burn the stalk off close to the head, singes the long beard, and this process dries the straw of the ear so that it is ready for the flail without scorching the grain. The country was full of smoke today from the burning straw. One group would burn off the ears, another thresh out the grain, and yet another were winnowing it with two large bamboo fans united by a bent piece of bamboo in the shape of an oxbow. Many women were in the fields employed at the light work.

Tuesday, June 12, 1860

A day of incessant rain, no going out of doors. Busy with letters for the *Onward*.

We hear of the destruction of the *Norway* by fire off Angier. She was the noble ship which I had visited in Hong Kong harbor. She started for Havana with 1200 coolies. I hear that a few days out the coolies rose on the ship but were overawed by the guns from the barricade at the break of the poop. The ship was afterwards fired several times and finally burned off Angier. Capt. Major's family escaped.

Wednesday, June 13, 1860

Fair day. Morning writing letters, in the evening went to Yokohama with Mrs. H[epburn] and Miss B[rown], returned to dine with Am. Consul. Heard a good anecdote of Japanese

skill. Minister Alcock had a Chubb lock that needed repair. He entrusted it to a Japanese locksmith who brought him back not the original Chubb, but one so exactly in imitation of it that the fraud was not at once discovered.

Thursday, June 14, 1860

Rainy, spent the day writing home letters.

Friday, June 15, 1860

Mrs. S.[55] of Yokohama who spent the day here relates a good anecdote of a Japanese merchant who, desirous to evade the prohibition of taking supplies to the foreign houses, wrapped four pieces of silks around his body by passing two pieces into one big sleeve, around his back, into the other sleeve and the other two in like manner around his chest. Also two men brought a couple of suits of armor to sell hidden in a box which appeared to have eggs packed in chaff. So there were several dozens of eggs on top. Their deceptive boxes passed all the guard houses from Yedo without detection. If they had been detected the punishment would have been severe, possibly death. The risk was taken for a few ichibus profit.

The servants at Yokohama are required to pay one-and-a-half ichibus per month to the officials and are desired to give information of all that is transacted in the house.

Had a long and pleasant ride in the afternoon on which I passed some beautiful scenes. We, Dr. H[epburn] and Miss B[rown], rode over the tops of the hills that gave us a panoramic view of the bay, with the shipping at anchor, the rolling ridges of the country, the fields where men, women, and children were busy gathering the barley and wheat harvest. The land from which the rape seed has been taken is now being covered with young cotton plants and beans, sweet potatoes, taro, etc. The

---

[55] Mrs. S. is not clearly identified. This may have been Mrs. Raphael Schoyer, who resided in Yokohama at this time and was something of an amateur artist. See John M. Rosenfield, "Western-Style Painting in the Early Meiji Period and its Critics," in Donald H. Shively, ed., *Tradition and Modernization in Japanese Culture* (Princeton, N.J.: Princeton University Press, 1971), p. 195. Mrs. Schoyer was also known for her lavish parties.

soil being thus made to produce two annual crops. But little of the rice appears to be transplanted as yet. We skirted along the hills and passed one curve where an artificial bank of earth had been raised several feet. Its sloped side was covered with green turf and the top with a row of young cryptomeria. A valley lay along in front. A little further we came to a broad embankment that served to draw back the waters of a large pond, a reservoir of water for a large plain covered with paddy fields. A noisy brook was running over the small rocks under a hill where trees overhung its waters, it was like a mountain stream of home. The large valley was fringed about with forest trees, with here and there a house opening among them. I was reminded again of Java.

S[adajirō] tells me relative to the rent of land that the rice rental is paid according to the productiveness of the soil. Good rice lands pay 1/2 to the proprietor of the soil. Some extra lands may pay even more. Poor lands pay a smaller percentage and very poor pay nothing. This is in discretion of the imperial officer. Of course here is a good opportunity for bribery and the revenue collector is persuaded by a liberal *douceur* to report land as worthy of a very small tax.

Saturday, June 16, 1860

Mrs. S[immons] left on the *Onward* today for California and home.[56] We were all down to see her off. The wind was ahead so that it was impossible for the *Onward* to sail from her anchorage. After a couple of hours aboard ship we returned. Mail from England in the afternoon brought me Fred's[57] letter of 27th of March. Towards evening took a sail on the bay at invitation of Mr. Richards.

Sunday, June 17, 1860

A rainy Sunday. Mr. B[rown] held service to a small audience. Mrs. S[immons] did not leave till early this morning.

Monday, June 18, 1860

Removed my effects to Dr. Simmons' temple, half of whose temple I have hired and with whom I am to dwell.[58] Left my pleasant home at Mrs. Hepburn's with many regrets, for my stay there has been exceedingly pleasant. Mrs. L., who called today, relates the following anecdote of Japanese officers. An American rented a house of a Japanese paying him therefore fifty ichibus per month. He reported to the Government to whom it seems he was to pay one third of the rent received that he received twenty ichibus only. The government have recently discovered that they have been cheated and came a few nights ago at midnight and carried off the lessor and his son to prison.

B[rown]'s teacher returned yesterday from Yedo. He did not find his son there, but found him here on his return, still confined within a house. He was permitted to converse with him through the closed screens of his apartment without seeing him. He does not know where the other two are but supposes they are confined in some other house.

Tuesday, June 19, 1860

The rapeseed harvest is gathered and the seed cleaned. The straw is gathered and burned and seeming waste of fuel and manure when every such thing is usually so clearly economized. The barley is cut and mostly threshed. The wheat is being gathered. Be-

---

[56] Mrs. Simmons returned to the United States ostensibly to take care of an ailing parent, but as we will see subsequently there were also other reasons for her return.

[57] This was Francis Hall's brother Frederick who had taken over his bookstore in Elmira at the time of his departure for Japan in 1859.

[58] M. Takaya, in his *The Letters of Dr. J. C. Hepburn* (Tokyo: Toshin Shobo, 1955), p. 33, states that the temple in which Dr. Simmons resided was the Sōkōji. This temple stood beside the Jōbutsuji where the Hepburns lived. Simmons's woodblock print pictorial map, now in the Yokohama Archives of History, shows both temples.

tween the rows of rapeseed and barley and wheat another crop of beans is coming up and the young cotton plants. This appears to be the universal method of rotating the soil and crops.

Engaged a passage on the *Azof* for Nagasaki. In the afternoon a walk with Miss B[rown]. Mr. B[rown]'s boy servant is restored to him today.

Wednesday, June 20, 1860

Busy with preparations for voyage to Nagasaki.

Thursday, June 21, 1860

Ditto. Earthquake at 4 1/2 P.M. A company of Shilling Mountebanks were passing the street this afternoon, I called them into the yard to see them perform. The performance was principally with caps and balls and balancing sticks. One was the performer and four others kept time with music on a samisen, flageolet, fife, drum, and cymbal. The performer had a ball made of red yarn three or four inches in diameter, also two sticks length of an ordinary drumstick with a flat head also covered with red yarn or cotton cloth. The company were dressed in long blue robes stamped with blue figures of wreaths of leaves. The performer commenced by throwing the ball and his sticks into the air, keeping them all going and catching the ball on one stick gave it a rebound and caught it on the other. Then he did many skillful feats of balancing the ball on the sticks, or throwing the ball up, catching it on his forehead, eyes, or mouth, or the fold of his dress at the base of the neck, or holding one of the drum sticks in his mouth horizontally the ball was balanced on it and rolled back and forward by a curve of the head, then by a jerk of the head tossed up, caught on the eye or back of the neck again. He then took a stick a foot long and an inch in diameter with one concave end and which he balanced on his head or mouth, threw up the ball and caught it in the socket. It was a clever thing to do when he rested the ball on the stick gave a little toss

of his head threw the ball off and caught it on his forehead without losing the stick's balance. Another trick was this. He balanced one of his sticks on his chin, then another horizontally on this and another vertically on that, on the top of this last was the same red ball, after a moments balancing he caught the horizontally [placed] stick quickly, and with it eased back the one on which the ball rested over his head into the hands of an attendant and caught the ball on the tip of the stick that rested on his chin! He did this repeatedly and continuously, the attendant passing the sticks propelled over his head back into his hand. He then balanced two of these sticks on his tongue and placing the ball on one he, with a muscular effort of the tongue, sent the ball from the top of one stick to the other backwards and forwards repeatedly without a failure. Besides there were many less skillful slights of hand such as balancing the stick and ball on his fingerends, etc. The fife performer was as clever in his way, making up wondrous faces of astonishment and putting himself into contortions of amazement at the sights greatly to the delights of the crowd, for all the men, women, and children of the neighborhood had gathered in our compound to see the show, to say nothing of the crowd outside of the bamboo polings. The children applauded Mr. Merryman with shouts of laughter and cries of "Jodsoo," by nature the same the world over, and when the clown sang a song no doubt very comical for those who could understand it he brought down the crowd. The performer then said that was part one, price one ichibu. There were three more parts at the same rate of demand for them. But I dismissed the motleys to another day.

Earthquake at 4 1/2 P.M.

Friday, June 22, 1860

Packed my trunks and went aboard the *Azof* in the afternoon expecting to sail at 3 P.M. Found the steamer would not leave till early the following morning and returned ashore and took tea with Mrs. H[epburn]. Went aboard again at 8 P.M. and passed the night. No pilots to guide us through the inner passage having been provided by the Japanese there was no hope that the *Azof* would take that route. But my passage being secured and baggage all aboard I concluded to keep on however disappointed I might be in the change.

Saturday, June 23, 1860

We wakened at daylight this morning by the various noises incident to a steamer getting under way. It was early dawn and I only took one look out of my port to see that the sea was smooth and sky fair and relapsed into slumber again. Around about 8 A.M. we had left Treaty Point disappearing behind us and were moving down the bay. With the progress of the morning hours and of our steamer we had a change of weather. The coast was shrouded in a hazy veil of midsummer vapors. A south wind came up dead ahead and beat up an ugly head sea. Our progress was slow. The *Azof*, though a handsome well built good sea boat, had an insufficient auxiliary engine of but 80 horse power. The haze thickened as we proceeded so that, after leaving the inner bay and major channel, we had only occasionally glimpses of coast headlands and points—or the islands and rocks that beset and make dangerous the way. Before breakfast the rough sea had already affected me so much that I went to my berth rather than the nine o'clock breakfast table. In the afternoon as I lay sea-sick in my berth I missed the motion of the screw, our engine had stopped. My roommate, Mr. Law, came below to tell me what a narrow escape we had. In the obscurity of the weather we had come so near upon a rocky reef that rather than attempt to pass by its outer side as usual, the engine was stopped, the spanker and jib shaken out to catch the wind and thus the current, here very strong, let us safely around the inner side between the reef and shore, but so close that L[aw] distinctly saw the black ugly shapes of the rocks below water waiting for their prey.

Sunday, June 24, 1860

A rainy day, the shore completely veiled in the wet misty clouds. We had run slowly all night, partly of choice for safety sake, by compulsion of head winds, waves, and a strong current of four knots. At 9 A.M., as I stood on the deck, suddenly the steep cliff of a rocky islet shouldered itself out of the fog, almost athwart our way. Thank God it was daylight as two minutes more of our course would have sent us hopelessly to destruction. Well does the coast maintain its ancient reputation for storms and mists and dangerous navigation. How much are surveys needed and how much a lighthouse or two and an occasional buoy would tend to the preservation of life and property. Capt. G[aby] of the *Azof* says he uniformly encounters more or less bad weather. Last winter and spring nearly every ship reported a gale, or more or less heavy weather on this passage, and during the summer the weather has been thick and palling. Passed Cape Idsu about noon having made barely 80 miles since leaving our anchorage. Compelled by sea-sickness to cling to my berth most of the day.

Monday, June 25, 1860

Still wet, thick, and lowering by throws. The running being fair I was enabled to come out on deck and to take my breakfast with the rest. We have still headwinds and seas. We can scarcely accomplish a 100 mile figure per day. We have the considerations of a roomy cabin, social rooms and clean beds, good fare, attentive stewards and pleasant company. Our crew is most Malay, a few Hindostanee and African firemen. Their natural characteristics are strongly marked. The Malay are most short and lithe with broad low noses, broad faces inclined to stupidity or half senseless expression. The Hindostanees are tall and spare with a grave expression of countenance, Caucasian in movement as well as kind in feature. There are one or two Goa Portuguese looking like Hindoo half breeds whom centuries of oriental life and habit have reduced to nearly the oriental breed. It was pleasanter to look at the Africans whether because of their known associations or because they carry with them everywhere their peculiar African characteristics it were difficult to say. But there sit a pair of them who have their respite from work down in the hot depth of the furnace room and sit down on the deck close by the smoke stack as if they could not leave it even in their play hours, stretch out their great ugly feet and talk, laugh, and gesture with African vivaciousness and content with the joy of the present hour knowing no trouble for the future. Who tells a story with such a rhetorical form of expression as Coffin-Lid, his thick lips wrinkling with laughter or curling with venom, how his great eyes roll about and his gesturing hand is never idle. His companion listens intently. Your African is a bundle of attention till it comes his turn to tell a story of other days and adventures.

Among our passengers are Mr. Morrison,[59] Consul at Nagasaki, who has been up to visit Mr. Alcock and Yedo and report says made himself unpleasingly notorious at our Kawasaki tea house. Like myself he is sea-sick, only much more so. We have, too, Lord Richard Grosvenor, who with Mr. Cavendish, was hunting in the Red River when I was at St. Anthony's in the fall of '58.[60] Our first officer, Mr. Bird, parts his hair in the middle of his forehead, has a half feminine voice, and strives to be jocular.

Tuesday, June 26, 1860

A showery day. Wind, sea, and current still adverse. The landmarks of the coast are invisible in the vapory haze.

Wednesday, June 27, 1860

A fine day of fair wind. Yet our slow craft does nothing better than six or six and a half knots per hour. Thoroughly convalescent I have enjoyed the day on deck. Showers as usual towards night. Our course today has been directly across what is put down on the Charts as Cape Josa [Ashizuri Saki], its extreme point being 25 miles inland from its position as laid down. Cape Daibosaki makes out

some twelve miles seaward from its place on the chart reads. And the whole coast line of the northwest coast of Nippon is by recent surveys of the *Active* found to be 30 miles out of its position on our maps and charts. The island is that much narrower. This is from 37° to 39° 30' North. Rocks and islands exist where none are laid down, while others occupying conspicuous positions on the charts exist nowhere but on the charts. About 5 P.M. made Cape D'Auville [Toi Misaki] and hope to be in Van Diemen Straight [Ōsumi-kaikyō] before morning.

Thursday, June 28, 1860

A beautiful summer morning at sea. A soft breeze is blowing from the north, the blue waters are dancing and sparkling in the sunlight. Sunny days in other seas were widely recalled. Cape Chichakoff [Sata Misaki] is visible on our starboard a few miles distant. Calm and beautiful lie the green wooded shores under the slumberous veil of the summer haze. So still and quiet is it that it looks like an enchanted land. Not a sail flecks the deep blue of sky or sea, for these shores are ever so silent and dreamlike. We see distant mountains and inward threading vallies, the classic vistas of the Japanese coasts. Now on our bow the beautiful solitary cone of Mt. Horner [Kirishimayama], its wondrous symmetry seems chiseled out by art, a Fusi Yama in miniature. I leaned over the hull resting my head in my hands for an hour, watched the change of shores, and felt the soft morning air breathing health into my nostrils. Oh but these were days of watching beauty at sea when the haze fell on fresh and the blue waters are crested with foam, and the ever ranging coastline is seen in hazy distance, for what leagues of traveled spaces and longing days of home shores do they not compensate us. In the middle of the afternoon we passed the Simplegards Rocks, reefs dangerous to the mariners, and the scattered islands of

---

[59] G. C. Morrison, the British consul in Nagasaki, was subsequently seriously wounded in the attack by *rōnin* on the British legation in Edo in 1861. See Sir Rutherford Alcock, *The Capital of the Tycoon*, vol. 2, p. 166.

[60] Hall wrote elsewhere "among the half dozen passengers on board was a traveling Englishman whom I

had met twenty months before in the wilds of the North-West, on the head waters of the Mississippi" (*New York Tribune* October 6, 1860). Lord Richard Grosvenor was the Second Marquis of Westminster (1795–1869). Mr. Cavendish is not readily identifiable.

Koshiki. Lying in the uncertain distance was Amakusa, the favorite retreat of the fathers of the Romish Church in Japan. The wind freshened as night came on and threatened unpleasant weather. It proved a threat only (there was a heavy gale in Yedo Bay this day).

Friday, June 29, 1860

In the early morning we were entering the Bay of Nagasaki. Rising in the cold morning light was a semi-circular trend of hills more abrupt and less wooded than that about Yokohama Bay. We followed the serpent like trail of the channel between islands and the main land. On either hand these beautiful islands rose out of the water green from sea to summit, terraced and cultivated with the prevailing Japanese exactness and industry. Batteries placed in directions that commanded all the approaches to the inner bay frowned down upon us. They were heavy pieces of ordnance housed under sheds, a few guards only were visible. Soon we pass bloody Pappenberg and memory recalls the bloody days when the funeral pyre of martyrs lit up her rough island shores and their dying agonies invaded the unpitying air. Today Pappenberg frowns down from its grim cannon mouths planted on every slope upon Christian ships entering the Bay. There is no terror in their aspect. On our left is a steep inaccessible island wooded to the summit half hid amid whose foliage are yet other batteries. A stone stairway protected by a guard house leads from the water up to the top. On either side on the shores are Daibas and Official stations of the Emperor or of the Princes of Satsuma and Oomura. Soon we pass a file of brick buildings with a tall smoke stack. It is a steam foundry wholly managed by the Japanese. One more turn in the narrow inlet and before us lies Nagasaki. A few more turns

of the screw and we swing round to our anchor.

A heavy wind sweeps down the river gorge that forms the head of the bay and it is difficult to get a boat to go ashore. A brig near us is dragging its anchor. While we wait we have a view of Nagasaki from the sea. In the front ground is Descima crowded with buildings new and old, for under the new regime many new structures are put by the old ones. I looked with an undeprivable interest at its long rows of two storied white houses built with much control and precision and Dutch taste, at the green doors and window blinds, at the summer verandahs where doubtless many a summer day like this the Dutchmen long expectant of the Batavia Ships sat in listless idleness waiting for the annual tidings from home. Or in the twilight and evening enjoyed the cooling breeze from the bay still sweet though it blew over tainted Pappenberg, enjoyed their pipe and schnapps and the solace of Nippon's brown daughters.

Bold hills green with vegetation, though sparsely covered with trees, rising to varying heights of a thousand to 2000 feet bend round the bay. Against them and between them lies the city of Nagasaki, for the most part on the waterfront of the bay and between two hills. Clinging to the sides of the hills everywhere are Buddhist and Shinto temples, the long flights of stone steps leading thereto are plainly seen and standing about them are the tombs and other assorted monuments writing a *memento mori*[61] across the entire brow of the city. The flags of the Consulates are flying in the breeze, grey clouds sweep across the lovely summits of the highest peaks, and faintly borne across the water are the compound sounds of the restless life of a great city.

After some delay procured a boat and went ashore. After paying my respects to Consul Walsh[62] I called on Mr. Verbeck,[63] my former

[61] Reminder of death.

[62] This was John G. Walsh, the American Consul in Nagasaki, who with his brother Thomas Walsh founded Walsh & Co., one of the first American trading houses in Japan. It was this firm that Hall joined in 1862. With Hall as a partner, the company changed its name to Walsh Hall & Co. and under his management it soon established itself as the leading U.S. trading house in

Yokohama.

[63] Guido Fridolin Verbeck was one of the pioneer [Dutch] Reformed Board missionaries who sailed to Japan with Hall on the *Surprise*. Verbeck later became renowned not only as a missionary, but as an advisor and educator under the new Meiji administration. For a biography see William Elliot Griffis, *Verbeck of Japan* (New York: Fleming H. Revell, 1900).

shipmate on the *Surprise* on the voyage out from America. I found him living on the hill a mile or so from the harbor. On my way thither I was pleased to meet in Nagasaki the wide clean streets of the standard Japanese pattern. They were generally paved in the center with three or four stones laid edge to edge making a substantial stone pavement of four or five feet width. This is the Japanese side walk. At the side of the streets were paved stone gutters. Now, as afterwards, I remarked the entire cleanliness of the streets. The situation of Nagasaki contributes to this. Three considerable streams flow down the hills and disembarque themselves into the bay. Innumerable small rills are led down the hill sides and flowing through the gutters keep the city clean of impurities. Wherever I went I heard the tinkling of these streams and occasionally their fall over a terrace on to the next level below. There are other streets destitute of the center walk of stone but with hardbeaten earthways swept frequently during the day and clean as a floor. The houses were generally clean. Many of them in Nagasaki are of two stories, for Kiushu [Kyushu] is not so earthquake shaken as are our houses on Yedo Bay. As you ascend the hill the houses are built on terraced plateaus supported by walls of stone and sitting so that the floor of one house is on a level with the roof of its next-house neighbor. Running up the hill along the sides of the streets are smaller walls. These walls are covered with a variety of mosses and creeping vegetation among which I saw ferns and ivy. Leading away from the streets were broad stone stairways with flights of 50 or 100 and even two hundred stone steps conducting to temple or shrine half hid amidst pines and cypresses at its top. Many of the temples were very old and in incipient decay. There are said to be 72 in the city, a few more only than Kaempfer speaks of two centuries ago. The temples differed in nothing from others I had seen, though I may except one, evidently very old and thoroughly Chinese in its architecture and arrangement.

Everywhere I walked I encountered the familiar salutation of "Ohio" and the less familiar one of "Button cashay" or "give me a button." The children seemed to me less ruddy

and healthy looking than those I had daily met for six months past. Perhaps it was a fancy opinion. The larger of the three rivers mentioned is crossed by numerous stone bridges spanning the stream with a high arch destitute of key-stone. Some, one at least, had a middle pier and double arch. The earthquakes of eastern Japan would I think soon overthrow these. Many of them are so overgrown with clinging vines that they resembled holiday arches of twined evergreens. There were several flouring mills on one of the rivers. A few locks, timbered without sides into the river bed, diverted enough water to draw a breastslot wheel and a small case of stones by the simplest arrangement of cogs. The bolting was done by sieves propelled by water and hand. The miller carried the grist as it fell from the stones to the sievry in wooden baskets. It was now the rainy season and the rivers, swelled to an unusual degree, were breaking lively over their rocky beds. In the dry season these locks give too small diversion and the wheels of the mills stand idle. This was the first mechanical application of water I had seen in Japan.

Just at evening I walked out with Mr. V[erbeck]. As we passed through Tera Matz [machi], a temple street, we heard the noise issuing from a theater and had the curiosity to see what a theater in Nagasaki might be. The half clad barbarian who attended the door confronted us at the entrance and demanded the admission price, as the play was nearly over we compromised with him for an ichibu to admit the party of three to the gallery, which in a Japanese theater is the humble part of the house. Through dust and dirt we clambered up a stairway so steep and with steps so narrow that it needed a little practice to do it adroitly and safely. At the top we found ourselves in a room a hundred feet square spanned by a roof unsustained except by the side walls without columns or pillars. Our usher speedily ejected a half a dozen natives from their seats and gave us a little enclosure to ourselves. He then bustled about to find a board for us to sit upon in foreign style, asked us, if he should bring us tea, sake, or other refreshment which we declined, assured us the play was very excellent and left us to enjoy it.

The coup-d'oeil was certainly a remarkable

one. The house was full of steaming humanity, sultry in a hot day the last day of June. The general floor was covered with seats divided off into small enclosures by posts and bamboo rails and answered to the pit. The galleries, which were on the sides of the house, were similarly divided off. A few of their apartments or "boxes" were fitted with seats covered with mat cushions and adorned with screens for the use of officials and dignitaries of whom few were present. There were two boxes on the side of the stage whose occupants were screened from public attention by curtains of bamboo slats. They could see but we could only see them by the occasional flutter of a fan or the movement of a body. As I have said the play was going on and nearly finished. The pit was crowded with men and women and children dressed and undressed, some were fanning themselves, some were watching the actors, some were asleep, others were catching certain nameless insects and others were imbibing tea or sake or finishing their rice, for Japanese theater goers take their refreshments with them. There was quite a disturbance just after we entered whether a certain paper window should be opened for ventilation or not. Paying no regard to the play the audience turned around to that attendant who was trying to do something with a screen that would not be done with, shouted to him their various wants whereby the poor fellow was so bewildered that he beat a retreat and the commotion subsided. But I have seen just such a noisy audience in their temple worship and at a funeral. They evidently desire to "free their minds" on all occasions when it is proper for common people to speak. The good intentioned people crowded about us and assured us over and over that it was *very good*, *highly agreeable*, and the actors experts in their way. Several seats were occupied by frail Nagasakian beauties who delight in public shows. Their demeanor was altogether quiet and modest.

Judging from the play by its last scene or two it might perhaps have been called "The Enchanted Blacksmith." An anvil and forge was brought on to the stage, there was a deal of hammering, and one of the actors resplendent in red silk and gold thread was grievously wounded by an unlucky blow which threatening to be mortal, his lady love appeared and a sentimental gentleman in blue silk, and who seemed to talk poetry, so measured were his accents, and was a rival of the red gentleman. The lady fell at the red gentleman's feet and shed tears and talked sweet and romantically and he shed tears and groaned with death pangs and evidently went on to make some horrible complaint to the young lady and her father all of which ended by the gentleman in blue receiving the disconsolate young lady who was so plastered and painted that whether she grew pale or red by turns was impossible to tell. Then the gentleman in red had a great deal to say and died very hard, in fact the curtain fell on his struggles and abbreviated his moaning, the actors all drawn up in one imposing group precisely as in a theater at home.

During the play, boys from the audience ran across the stage whenever they wished regardless of the actors or the acting. An orchestra at the side of the stage sang choruses from a set of books to the accompaniment of drums, sambie, and cymbal. Then scene shifting was used. The actors stood on a turn table and behind there was a screen and whenever the scene was to be shifted the turn table was set in motion and they were whisked out of sight like so many solar planets and their star arrived into sight from the other side of the screen.

A Japanese theater is conducted on a plan altogether different from ours. It is an affair of a day to attend the play. In the morning two or three different plays are begun and as many scenes acted from each. In the afternoon the morning's work is resumed and finished. Thus one may hear in the morning the first acts of a theater play, leave then, and return in the afternoon and hear it completed without being obliged to attend the whole. The stage manager announced the close of the play by striking his bits of wood together and the audience arose to depart with as little tumult as would be seen in a more civilized audience. It was a common sight to see a man going home with his teapot in one hand and the mat he had squatted upon in the other. When we left four men and a shaven headed doctor who sat near us gathered themselves around a tub of sake to make a final carousal over it, hospitably inviting us to share.

Saturday, June 30, 1860

Instead of the horse as a beast of burden the use of the bullock or uncastrated bull is universal in Kiusiu [Kyushu]. His load is packed on his back [and] he is guided by a rope halter fastened to his nose. Foreign wares were common in native shops, particularly glass ware such as decanters, drinking glasses of all sorts, and jars with ground glass stoppers, of these last the Japanese are very fond, using them to put therein confectionery, tea, sugar, tobacco, etc. So too there was a great deal of French porcelain and perfumes, Holland earthenware and medicines, spices from Java, some broad cloth and calicoes. I was more than once stopped in the street and asked if I would not buy "gin for one dollar a bottle."

With the virtue of foreign medicine, many of which are known in Japan only by the name of the pharmacopeia, the people are becoming rapidly acquainted. Quinine is nearly as well known in Asia as in Europe. Dr. Meerdervoort,[64] the resident physician at Desima, has a class of 20 pupils whom he regularly instructs in a building provided by the Government. Learning the art to kill is no less popular than learning to heal. Japanese soldiers for some time past have been under the discipline of Dutch Captains and drill Sergeants. Books on mathematics and astronomy are eagerly sought for. So too geographical works, of all of which Rev. Mr. V[erbeck] has distributed many copies printed in the Chinese characters. With the Chinese character every one in Japan with any pretension to education is familiar.

In the afternoon in company of Mr. V[erbeck] I ascended Mount Higo, the loftiest of the elevations that form the background to Nagasaki. The ascent was gradual but the way was everywhere strewn with stone, and the mountains covered with fragments of calcareous rocks. Streams were running down the hillside and were made to water successive terraces of rice fields. Thus, for many hundred feet above the level of the sea the ground was irrigated sufficient for the moisture loving paddy and the hills were adorned by the wild green of the young blades. The farmers were still busy with transplanting the crops. Scattered too all over the face of the hills was the waxtree, a tree of middle size, its bark bearing a strong resemblance to the ash, and its leaf to the locust. They were now full of the green berry from which the wax is extracted. The tree fruits similar to the wild cherry, except there are several stems of the berries in clusters. Our path up the hill was a stony way frequently ascending a short flight of stone steps. The stone walls that banked the terraces of the new fields were covered with a profusion of vines among which was the low blackberry, the color of the ripe fruit was a deep red. There was a profusion and variety of ferns laced and creeping. I gathered many varieties. Wading through the long grass and climbing over the rocks that crowned the hill we reached its summit short of breath and with a giving out sensation about the knees. A beautiful panorama of ocean, bay, city, mountains, forests, and hill rewarded our toil. For many leagues we could see all the indentations of the coast lines of the southern promontory on which Nagasaki is built, winding inlet, deep bay, and shallow cove, alternated with bold headlands and low points aiming seawards. At our feet lay Nagasaki, fan shaped, the "Yedo road" forming the handle. The ominous islands and rocks that bejut the approach dotted the ocean surface. The atmosphere was remarkably clear and we had on one hand in view the primary inlet of Hizen and on the other the Bay of Kiusiu [Kyushu], the deep gulf of Simabara and yet further in the distance beautiful Amakusa. Lifting its truncated [peak] to an elevation of several thousand feet was the volcano, Benten Yama. Its inactive crater was distinctly visible at a distance of eighteen miles. There are two clouds of vapor on its side, but whether mistbanks from above or the rising steam of the

[64] Pompe van Meerdervoort, Johannes Lydius Catherinus (1829–1908) was a Dutch naval medical officer who was invited by the Tokugawa shogunate to teach medicine at the naval training school in Nagasaki. He returned to Holland in 1862 and subsequently wrote

Vijf jaren in Japan, 1857–1863 (Leiden: Firma van den Heuvell en van Santen, 1867–8), 2 vols. Portions of this work have been published in Elizabeth P. Wittermans and John Z. Bowers, trans. and annot., *Doctor on Deshima* (Tokyo: Sophia University Press, 1970).

hot springs that there abound we could not say. Wunzen Yama was notorious in its days of Christian persecution. At its foot, in the Gulf of Simabara, was the city of the same name where the native Christians made their last rally and heroic defense for their lives and faith. After a siege of several months Simabara only yielded when Dutch guns trained upon them by Dutch artillerymen made any longer contest hopeless. Then the sea was reddened with the blood of the massacred defenders, the fiery mouth of Wunzen Yama's crater received others, and still others were plunged in the boiling springs of sulphur water. So died out for three centuries Christianity in Japan.

I asked Mr. V[erbeck] and W[illiams],[65] intelligent missionaries at Nagasaki, if they had met any traces, however slight, of the old Romish faith. They had not of themselves and the most modern trace was a tale of twenty years since related by Mr. W[illiams]. A Nagasakian who with others was compelled to perform the annual trampling on the cross was a descendant of the former Christians. Of all the rites he had retained as handed down to him he only knew that after each trampling ceremony he had to wash his feet in sake and drink the liquor after. He only knew it was a custom but it was doubtless one which had been handed from generation to generation and was the form of purification prescribed by his ancestors for the act of trampling the sacred emblem.

On the summit of the mountain embowered in trees was an old half decayed shrine. Mosses and ferns were invading its sanctity and creepers hiding its incipient decay. We descended the hill by a long circuitive path to the Yedo Road passing in our way a little grot before whose entrance was another shrine. There was a pool of clean water within the grot overhung by ferns and a dripping spring from above supplied the pool. We returned to the city by the Yedo Road, a simple pathway covered with loose stone above, scarcely two and twelve broad, and quite unlike the thronged thoroughfare of the same road when it terminates in the ocean-like city of Yedo. The number of foreigners in Yedo[66] is estimated between forty and fifty.

Sunday, July 1, 1860

Rainy day, quite ill today and remained at home. There is a young American[67] here who is making somewhat of a sensation as a preacher; he is less than twenty years old and came out from the states on his own cost and charges.

Monday, July 2, 1860

Still rainy, spent a good deal of time among the lacquer shops. The shops are not so pretentious and showy as the gayer bazaars of Yokohama, indeed it was difficult to find where the best shops were, so little display was made of goods and wares, the best of which are kept out of sight in a back room or upstairs. I found much the same wares in Nagasaki as at Yokohama. The particular work known as Nagasaki works, inlaid mother of pearl, was here more abundant, so too were the straw work, and there were many highly ornamented tables of Miaco work which I had not before seen. The porcelain which was from Hizen was less showy than the Yedo ware but of more useful patterns and structure. There was not so much discrepancy between the price asked and taken as I had been accustomed to. Made several purchases.

The fruits in the market were plums of good quality, peaches as yet unripe, *Yama mo*, a berry with a kernel like a cherry and flavor something strawberry like, loquats with a pleasant scent and taste. The vegetable sellers

---

[65] Channing Moore Williams mentioned earlier.

[66] Given the context it seems more likely that this is an estimate for Nagasaki, not Edo.

[67] The American was Paul Bagley who Hall later refers to as the "charismatic boy preacher." Bagley remains a largely unknown figure in the history of nineteenth-century Christianity in Japan. Bagley appears in the 1862 *China Directory* as residing in Yokohama, and he is mentioned on several further occasions in Hall's journal, particularly at the time of Hall's trip to Hokkaido in September and October 1860.

offered cucumbers of distorted lengths, small onions, string beans, a fecund summer squash of remarkably good flavor that cooks dry like a winter squash, egg plants and a muskmelon in shape like a short thick cucumber or summer squash.

Mr. V[erbeck] was at the house when I returned. He told me that not many months since a Greek priest came to Nagasaki in a Russian ship and did not scruple to make the sign of the cross in public or private as he chose. The young Buddhist priests would mockingly make the same sign and seemed to think it a very good joke.

The Buddhist priesthood at Nagasaki struck me both from observation and inquiry as having more influence and respect than at Kanagawa. V[erbeck] told me there were many intelligent men among them who were capable and willing to defend the faith.

In a stage representation of Hara Kiri the victim appeared on the stage clad in white surrounded by his friends one of whom read a paper reciting his intentions and making suitable comments on the occasion. Then with a short sword the self immolator made two cuts across his belly, one horizontal, one oblique, and a third across his throat. The man who can persevere never to make the third is regarded as a hero of constancy and courage.

Tuesday, July 3, 1860

Went to Desima. This famous island can be no better described than in Kaempfer's language, "In shape it nearly resembles a fan without a handle being of an oblong square figure the two larger sides segments of a circle. By my own measuring I found the breadth to be eighty two common paces and the length of the longest side two hundred and thirty six." No doubt he had paced it often enough to know. The buildings on Desima are a row of residences facing the sea, long two story build-

ings built with a painful exactness like Dutch houses in the old country. There were verandahs whose pleasant look out on the bay must have rendered them attractive spots to the Dutchman, where at evening toil they watched the shipping in the Bay and solaced themselves with schnapps, tobacco, and the society of the brown girls of Nippon. In the rear of the dwelling were godowns, or fire proof storehouses. In the upper loft of one of them I found the Bazaar where the Nagasaki merchants have gathered their wares in variety to supply the foreign shippers. There was nothing essentially different in the wares offered here from those sold in the shops except that all were brought together. If the prices were a little higher here than in the street shops, the goods were also a little better. The island occupied by the Chinese formerly is within a stone cast of Desima. The Chinese use it now for storehouses alone, they live on the mainland in their own *yashiki*, a compound of buildings enclosed by a high wall and to which admittance is sedulously denied except to their own people.

On my way back to V[erbeck]'s I passed the Joroya quarter, the principal portion of them occupied the entire block of two story buildings, and several levies in adjoining streets were also occupied by them. Everything was quiet and orderly, though several hundreds are said to live the infamous life. I did not enter the building, its interior arrangements were not so inspiring by report as those at Yokohama. Through the latticed windows I saw the half nude girls making their toilets.

Wednesday, July 4, 1860

The anniversary of the "ever glorious 4th." Little demonstration was made by the few Americans resident at Nagasaki. The *Fennimore Cooper*[68] fired a salute and was finally run aground by a pleasure party on board.

---

[68] The *Fennimore Cooper* was the surveying vessel that Captain John M. Brooke brought to Japan in 1859. The vessel was driven ashore at Yokohama on August 21, 1859, and subsequently condemned and sold at auction. The buyer, Dr. George Hall of Walsh & Co., had her rebuilt in Yokohama. See Brooke, *John M. Brooke's Pacific Cruise and Japanese Adventure*, pp. 149ff. Captain Brooke returned to the United States in company with the Japanese mission that sailed on the *Kanrin Maru* in February of 1860.

In company with V[erbeck] I made a call on Dr. Von Siebold[69] according to a previous arrangement made yesterday with his son, a noble lad of twelve years with fair hair and sunny blue eyes. He lives in a temple on a hill among the Japanese population far away from other foreigners. Our way thither led us through some remarkably tidy and well built streets both paved and unpaved. A flight of stone steps led us up to the temple grounds, a terraced plateau with foundation walls of stone and ornamented as usual with a variety of evergreen trees. The Japanese veteran received us at the door and gave us a cordial welcome. There was a warmth in his greeting that preimpressions derived from others, particularly from the historians of Perry's exhibition, had not led me to expect.

The Prof[essor] is a man 62 yrs old, of middle height and size, florid complexion, the eyes and hair strongly inclined to gray. I had in my hand as I entered a few leaves and specimens of trees which I wished to identify. Catching sight of them he hardly waited for the customary salutations before he said "I am a Botanist" with great enthusiasm of manner. Thirty seven years ago he came to Japan at the age of 25, and his long residence, interrupted by an interval of home residence, had endeared the Japanese people to him of whom he spoke in expressive terms of attachment. He feelingly deplored the rough usage they sometimes encountered nowadays at the hands of thoughtless foreigners. He spoke particularly of horseback excursionists dashing at full speed through the streets taking the center paved way belonging to foot passengers and riding reckless of whomever was in the way. "It is only people who never were on horseback before that do this," he added with playful sarcasm.

His botanical researches have been very thorough. Of the flora of Japan he has 2000 specimens to which he still makes additions. Beside these he has a very extensive collection from the flora of northern Asia. Eight hundred volumes contain this collection. Of the trees and plants in Japan he has identified 300 varieties as coming from China. The palm which we see so much was brought from China. Of pines he enumerates 37 species. Of the beautiful maple 60 species and 120 varieties. One of the trees which I wanted to identify having a leaf similar to the Lombardy poplar known as "the peacock tree" in China he called "Salisburia Adianthifolia." One hundred and fifty years ago four of them were taken to Europe, and having been sold for "forty pieces of silver" each, were known as the "forty silver piece tree." They were scattered and as the male and female flower exist on separate trees they were never fruited until an industrious botanist assisted nature by bringing the fructilizing pollen from one to the other. (Qua. Is not this the story I have read before modified?) After his return from Japan to Europe while walking one day in Carlsruh [Karlsruhe] unexpectedly he encountered one of the trees. "I removed my hat and bowed as to an old and respected friend," said he. He proposes to remain in Japan two or three years longer and will then return finally to Europe where at Leyden he has his house and a garden of 600 Japanese plants.

[69] Philipp Franz von Siebold (1796–1866). Von Siebold arrived in Japan in 1823 as part of the Dutch settlement on Deshima. A pioneer of Japanese studies, he taught the Japanese Western medicine in Nagasaki and was closely associated with the leading Japanese students of Dutch studies. During his stay, Von Siebold gathered a considerable body of information on Japan that he subsequently published in his *Nippon, Archiv zur Beschreibung von Japan* and numerous other works on the flora and fauna of Japan. In 1829 his acquisition of materials deemed "secret" by the Tokugawa authorities—including several Japanese maps—led to his expulsion from the country and the arrest and imprisonment of several of his associates. Siebold returned to Japan with his son Alexander in 1859 and worked for two years for the Netherlands Trading Company. He wanted to be appointed Dutch representative to Japan in 1863, but was refused because his policies were regarded as running counter to Dutch interests. Hall, who shared Von Siebold's love for botany, made a point of keeping in touch with him. For a reevaluation of Von Siebold's second stay in Japan see Prof. Herman J. Moeshart (University of Leiden) "Von Siebold's Second Visit to Japan, 1859–62" (Paper presented at the Meeting of the European Association for Japanese Studies, Durham, UK, September 1988), abstract published in *Bulletin of the European Association for Japanese Studies*, no. 29 (June 1988), p. 25.

Nagasaki streets are varied as in other cities. There is a "Broadway," "Temple Street" (Tera Matz) [Tera machi], "Whiskey Street" (Sake Matz) [Sake machi], "Low Street" (Squi Matz) [Hikui machi?] etc. Passing through one of the most frequented thoroughfares we stopped to examine the odds and ends of a street dealer who had a low table on the sidewalk covered with old laid aside articles, second hand goods, just such ones as one meets in any American or Continental city. Among the curios I noticed a copy of "Dr. Danskin's anus vase" and feigning ignorance asked the dealer if it were a cooking utensil. "Yes" it was. Then seeing by my smile that I had chaffed him, he by significant gestures gave me to know that he understood the true use of the article.

We stepped into a temple enclosure where we found a boys school. It was "play time" and a bevy of urchins rushed to the door to see the strangers. Like any schoolboys they had faces and fingers grimy with ink and looked a deal of roguery out of their black eyes. A few girls were among them. "How many scholars have you," we asked. Roguish glances passed from one lad to another and one says low, "tell him five hundred," "tell him a thousand" says another. The boy addressed hesitated, "five thousand" wickedly suggests another. "Fifty," honestly answered the truth loving fellow.

Wrestlers were performing in Nagasaki, and everywhere we went in streets and shops handbills were posted announcing the fact. The print shops sold their pictured representations, the book shops their biography. Handbills gave a history of their previous matches, and what they would essay to do now. The people were talking about it. The boys were playing wrestler in all the streets. We stopped half an hour in a crowd to see one naked man and his little boy of five or six years going through in mimic show the wrestlers feats. It was circus week in a country village repeated *mutatis mutandis* [with the appropriate changes necessary].

In the afternoon a Japanese official called in honor of the day and left his card after Japanese custom.

Towards evening Mr. and Mrs. V[erbeck] and myself walked to "Ippon Ki," "The Solitary Tree." We started, expecting to find it after a ten minute walk or so. But we walked on and on out of the city into the country, on rough stony paths up hill and down and at sunset we were five miles out of town at the desired spot. Some thirty years ago the Gov. of Nagasaki had given permission to the resident physician of Desima to have a botanical garden at this spot for the propagation of foreign plants. Its winding paths, shady walks, and natural and artificial terraces were overgrown in the long neglect of past years. There was only a trace of its former beauty. There was a house on the spot from wherein the present keeper brought forth chairs of ancient Dutch model and a table, and placing them on the green ground brought us refreshments of tea, pickles, and confectionery. We made merry as we could considering we were five miles from home in the dark in a strange land and already well tired. At 8 P.M. we started back, picking our way as best we might over the rough road and were glad to reach our house safely, refresh ourselves with a cup of tea, and go to bed.

Thursday, July 5, 1860

In the morning took my luggage aboard the *Azof* preparatory to my return to Kanagawa, but finding she would not leave till 3 P.M. returned to the city. V[erbeck] was receiving a call from three priests and a young boy priest. The priests were intelligent old men, and, as usual, delighted with the sight of everything foreign. Mrs. V[erbeck]'s appearance in crinoline was a subject of considerable comment among them. A glass headdress of hers was a miracle of a wonder. How could glass be spun thus into threads. Refreshments were given them, most of which they wrapped in paper to take away with them.

As I put off from the shore again in the afternoon to take the steamer I passed a boat sailing across the bay to have a picnic on the opposite shore. It was a boatload of both sexes with their refreshments, rice, tea, sake, etc. Some girls were getting their shami's ready for music. They were happy and doubtless bound to be "jolly."

We were under weigh a little before 4 P.M.,

and soon left behind us the beautiful Bay of Nagasaki. Its hill crowned shores shone pleasantly in the afternoon sun. The coast batteries grinned their last defiance, the mounded land of Pappenberg receded behind a bend in the inlet and out among the green islands and bare half sunken rocks we steered out to sea.

Friday, July 6, 1860

Smooth sea and slight head wind but we have the current that sets eastward through Van Diemen Straight in our faces. This current was full of drift and seaweed, and once a root that lifted up two prongs deceived us to a momentary belief that we saw a boat with men in it. This deception is not uncommon and when sometimes, as here happened, a bird lights on the stump and flaps his wings like a signal of distress it is not strange that boats have put off to rescue the supposed distressed mariners. In the afternoon we had on one side the beautiful cone of Horners Peak and opposite in a farther distance with its head wrapped in clouds and smoke was the volcano island of Iwoga Sima [Iō-shima]. At nightfall we passed Cape Chichakoff and the triangular arch at its extreme point.

Saturday, July 7, 1860

Headwinds and rough head sea. The Sea moving counter to the current was very tumultuous. Passed a Portuguese Man of War. Seasick afternoon and evening.

Sunday, July 8, 1860

Fair day. Sea P.M. rough. Engine stopped three hours for repairs.

Monday, July 9, 1860

Fair day and fair wind. We made rapid progress. Sea covered with dancing crests of white foam; a misty haze around the horizon. Passed between Cape Idzu and Vries Volcano [Ōshima] at 5 P.M. Entered Yedo Bay early in the evening and moving under a clear starlight made an anchorage at Kanagawa a little past midnight.

Tuesday, July 10, 1860

Consumed nearly all day in getting my effects off the steamer, part of them having been delivered to the wrong person. Found friends all well. Mr. Blodget, who has occupied my rooms in my absence, is just leaving for Chefoo. Mr. and Mrs. Nevius[70] have arrived at Dr. Hepburn's, and Mrs. Hewell, an invalid from Shanghai, has my old room there.

Wednesday, July 11, 1860

Quite ill today with a summer disorder that has hung about since I left Kanagawa. Earthquake at 2 P.M. John Corky (?) of N.Y., a fellow passenger by the *Azof*, died today. He left N.Y. for China on a voyage to seek his health. From China he crossed to Nagasaki. Finding his health still failing he came to Kanagawa hoping to catch a vessel to California. One would leave in a few days, but he, poor fellow, was summoned for another journey.

Thursday, July 12, 1860

More ill and unfit for any effort. Keep the house closely.

---

[70] John Livingston Nevius (1829–93). Nevius was a Princeton graduate who went to China with his wife, Helen Coan, in September 1854. They were active in Ningpo, Hangchow, and Chefoo. In 1860 Nevius and his wife came to Japan to consider working in the Japan field under the Presbyterian Board but soon gave up the idea and returned to China. See Boleslaw Szczesniak, ed., *The Opening of Japan: A Diary of Discovery in the Far East, 1853–1856, by Rear Admiral George Henry Preble* (Norman: University of Oklahoma Press, 1962), p. 343.

Friday, July 13, 1860

Mail from home. Letters from Fred and A.C.A. The remains of Corky were interred at 7 A.M.

Saturday, July 14, 1860

A very hot day. Sharp earthquake at 7 P.M.

Sunday, July 15, 1860

Very hot. Too ill to go even to Yokohama to Church where services are now held. In the afternoon there was a funeral in the burying ground near to us. The hearse was preceded by men bearing parti-colored staffs surmounted with dragon heads and others with glass lanterns. Mourners clad in white followed. It was the funeral of some one of more rank and station than usual. There was the same indifference to the funeral ceremonies, loud talking and even laughing mingling with the priest's drawled monotonous prayers.

Monday, July 16, 1860

Since I left Kanagawa the new regulations forbidding subjects of other than the Five Treaty Powers has gone into effect. The foreign Consuls and Ministers having given the edict their official sanctions. Vessels of either of the Five Treaty Powers bringing such persons will be required to take them away again.

The Portuguese Man of War which we passed on our return brought over from Macao the Governor of that colony to negotiate a treaty with Japan in accordance with the stipulation made in the Holland Treaty.

The wheat crop had universally been gathered in my absence which had hardly begun

when I left. The crop is said to be light this year and not well harvested owing to the unusual amount of falling weather.

The Japanese steamer *Kandin Marrah* [*Kanrin Maru*] has also returned from San Francisco. On her return she was wholly navigated by the Japanese though she had one or two white men as passengers. The Japanese are greatly delighted with their visit and brought back many souvenirs of their American made acquaintance. Manjiro, the interpreter and 2nd in command, brought back a sewing machine.[71] He informed Mrs. B[rown], at whose house he called to get some instruction how to use his sewing machine, that he had translated Bowditch's *Navigation* into Japanese.[72]

Wednesday, July 18, 1860

Today and tomorrow are two great holidays at Yokohama, matsuri days as the people call them. Although Benten, the deity of the sea, is particularly honored, the day is a holiday fete rather than a religious festival. It has, moreover, the special sanction of the Governor for it is of course the first festival of the kind since the settlement of Yokohama. Similar matsuri days are observed at this season throughout the empire. Its character will be best known by a narration of what I saw.

Landing at Yokohama in the middle of the forenoon the city was brilliant with ornament and spectacles. The streets were full of people. In front of all the shops scores of gay colored lanterns were hung, and the shop fronts were adorned with rosettes and streamers of various colored papers. Platforms had been built so as to extend the shop floors out to a line with the projecting roofs which usually overhang Japanese houses a few feet. These were covered with new mats. The wares had been wholly removed from the front shops or compactly piled up so as to leave the mat floors open for

[71] It appears that Manjirō's mother was less enthusiastic about her much prized sewing machine. After trying it out she discarded it because in the garments sewed with it the threads could not be pulled out for laundry purposes as they could with traditional stitching. See Warinner, *Voyager to Destiny*, p. 187.

[72] Manjirō had indeed translated Nathaniel Bowditch's, *New American Practical Navigator* into Japanese in the mid 1850s. The task required eighteen months, and, as he remarked, "aged him three years." See Warinner, *Voyager to Destiny*, pp. 173–74.

visitors and guests. Of these there were many who had come from Yedo and other places to see the spectacles and were sitting quietly on the mats talking socially and partaking of tea, pipes, and more social refreshments.

The wider and rear parts of the shops were wholly concealed by reversible screens stretched across the rooms. The screens themselves were curiosities. They were many of them elaborately ornamented with colored drawings of animals, birds, fruits and flowers, or representing historic scenes. They were much handsomer than any I had before seen and were doubtless heirlooms in families and brought out only for special occasions. There was one with elaborately carved woodwork made from a native wood that resembles rosewood. Many of them were very ancient. Others are plain and not a few made wholly of plain gilt paper. A rail ran in front of the shops from post to post over which were hung ornamented mats of gay cotton carpeting. Everybody wore countenances full of smiles. Railings were temporarily constructed so as to set apart the center of each street for the processions and spectacles.

Every foreigner was welcomed with *Konichi Nippon Suntaki,* "Today is Japanese Sunday," a recreation day being always their idea of Sundays, and they were made welcome to the hospitalities they had to offer. The whole population were in holiday dresses and the tout ensemble of the street was as if a thousand rainbows had been shattered into four or five foot fragments and gone stalking about in curious pose, the robes of every imaginable hue. It was a carnival with play and "general training" combined. Already groups of people were parading the streets accompanying some grand spectacle got up for the occasion. These spectacles were usually a triumphal car surmounted by a tower of several stories on top of which was some allegorical or historical person or scene. I sat on the mats of a friendly Japanese trader and among the groups that passed were these: the first was a car which showed borne aloft an artificial grotto, a mimic cascade, a pine grove in which a tiger was crouching, and a gigantic dragon. These scenic representations were fabricated mostly of paper, for these people do everything with paper, and the tower was twenty five or thirty feet high.

Second was a tower on the first story of which was a group of musicians playing on drums of different sizes and shapes and the shami [shamisen], above them was a canopy of handsome silks and paper flowers, and standing on the summit was a colorful female figure with long hair flowing down her neck and a gorgeous dress of brocade silks and gold silken tissues. She represented an ancient heroine of Nippon celebrated in the annals of their wars and deified after her death. A pine tree twelve or fifteen feet high stood in a tub of earth behind her. This car was drawn by two bulls, as were all the larger and heavier ones. The lighter ones were borne on the shoulders of men. Standing among the musicians was a man dressed to represent a fox with a grotesque fox head adorned with a long beard. He was constantly tossing his head and arms about and played the animal well.

Third was a similar tower with musicians and fox headed performer surmounted by a colorful statue of a Nippon demi-god bearing aloft over his head an immense bell.

Fourth was a less imposing tower and canopy hung with variegated lanterns.

Fifth was an artificial bridge forming the foreground of a stage representation. Actors appeared on this bridge and rehearsed a brief pantomime.

Sixth was a beautiful cupola of artificial trees and flowers.

Seventh was a bullock drawn canopy with musicians, as before, surmounted by a colossal flute player. A masked character diverted the spectators by his grotesque gestures.

Eighth was a representation of the train of a daimio passing through the streets of Yedo. The norimon was preceded by pike and standard bearers, armor bearers, weapon bearers who wound along with a peculiar slow and mock dignified step, for this scene was evidently a half caricature. The norimon instead of a Prince had another fox riding within who sat in dignified state. On each side of the norimon walked three men clad in female attire, their faces painted and colored like so many harlequins.

Ninth, tenth, eleventh, and twelfth were cars

supporting miniature houses representing one or more apartments. These were occupied by female players from the houses of prostitution attended by their duennas. These enacted a variety of plays, pantomimes, and dances. They were the accomplished girls of the institutions to which they belonged. Their dresses, though too showy for a refined taste, were not more overdone than the stage habiliments of our tragedy queens and kings. They were made of the most expensive silks and brocades printed in colors and wrought with satin, gold, and silk threads. A few of the faces were deserving of the epithet of handsome.

On the first day of the spectacle there was no order to the procession. The different parts of it wandered through the streets as they pleased, stopping here and there to exhibit their play or pantomime. It was the gayest scene of popular festivity that it had ever been my lot to witness. A Beouf Gros festival in Paris or a Carnival in Rome are its nearest counterparts. Persons familiar with similar displays in China had never seen like brilliant effects of costume produced, for however barbarically gorgeous this was, there was not a tawdry or mean thing in the whole. All was as fresh and bright as new dresses and new spectacles could make it. These shows are not attended without considerable expense. But there is not another nation I believe in the world where so large a portion of the popular earnings are expended for pleasures. I believe this to arrive in part from the fact that status in life is so unalterably fixed in Japan or rather so difficult to change that the lower classes have little reason as they certainly have little disposition to hoard up useless money but more wisely employ it to purchase pleasures and indulgences which if profiting little produce no other harm than spending some time and substance and making them with all these drawbacks one of the most, if not the most, contented people in the world.

The festival of the matsuri is purely one of the common people. Nowhere did I see an official take any hand in it except as spectators, or in front of the Governor's stand during the procession of the second day, where two or three were charged with the duty of keeping order. The people were unrestricted in the manner and mode of the enjoyments. The expense of this festival was said to be 3000 rios equal to $4000, half of which was raised by subscription, mostly from the merchants and master mechanics, the other half was donated by the government, and to this sum must be added $1500 more as individual expense of the merchants and others in fitting up their shops and carrying out the programme. The whole direct expense thus could not have been less than $5500. The city is divided into street divisions or *tomes* [*chōme*], something like our wards, except that they are on a much smaller scale. Each tome receives its proportion of the fund raised and gets up its own share of the exhibition in its own way. This leads to a rivalry for excellence and no doubt the fund is often increased by the zealous ward partisans. The dresses of each ward worn in the procession are also distinctive. The spectacles exhibited one year, and the dresses worn, are never employed a second time. The towers, canopies, and towers are taken apart, the dresses are given to the poor and the next matsuri must differ as much as possible from the preceding one. Members of different trades and professions combine to represent themselves, which is sometimes done by scenes of labor and occupations taken from their own calling. Thus among the spectacles exhibited was one of the merchants, another of the house builders, and a third of rice cleaners.

Elbowing my way through a crowd that stood bareheaded in the hot sun before the official station in rear of the Custom House and around one of the stage cars, I had an opportunity of seeing a pantomime performed. A group of officials were sitting within the open house squatted in grave dignity on mats watching the players. There were three of them, girls from the joroya houses, one of whom was dressed to enact the part of a man. The stage was, as I have described before, the representation of an apartment. There were the lattice windows, the papered walls, the ceiling papered in figures of gold and flowers, it was a bijou of a place, just such an one as had I Aladin's ring I would have spirited away for a garden summer house.

Two female attendants accompanied the actresses to render assistance in changing dress, shifting scenes, and looking after their elaborate underrobes. They were young girls from seventeen to nineteen years old, though it was difficult to judge, for not the smallest portion of the natural hue of their face or necks could be seen through the white paint and vermillion which was thickly overlaid. Their dress, which the change of dress required in the play and which was made in sight of the spectators, was a richly wrought outer robe that fell in a train at their feet, a scarf of crape about the neck, and one or more sashes about the waist usually of velvet or satin with silk and gold and silver embroidery. These sashes were a foot or more wide and tied and gathered in front or behind in an enormous tie. Under this were several robes of white and colored crapes and silks, the more worn the more honorable the dress. Such a dress must have been exceptionally burdensome in the heat of the summer. It is said, on authority that I am inclined to believe, that not a year passes that life is not lost among poor girls who sink with the heat and exhaustion on the rounds of their play. The feet are either bare or covered with a white sock and further protected by a light straw sandal or wooden clog. The head dress with its towering mass of hair and forest of hair pins is utterly indescribable. In addition to their own masses of dark hair they used wigs so that their heads are a mass of folds and plaits. The pictures of Japanese girls which seem to us so impossible, and which really are unnatural representations of Japanese females in their everyday costume, are all borrowed from one of these full dressed girls. The joroya girl is the pet of the empire, it is her picture that adorns alike the palace, the temple, the house, and the inn, that is seen on their cooking ware, multiplied on their furniture, adorn their books and improbable as they seem, nay even grotesque as they are, they are not misrepresentations of a girl dressed for the stage or attired to render her shameless calling attractive. The vermillion colored lips, the high arched brows, the oblique position of the eyes are there by the skillful laying on of colors. (At Nagasaki I fell in with a native artist who had learned to paint in water colors after the European style and who executed some very desirable things.)

The heat was intense but patiently stood the crowd watching the players, the hot sun falling on their shaven crowns in a manner that would have been a speedy death to an European. The omnipresent fan when not doing duty to cool their faces was held as a shield over their heads.

With some difficulty I succeeded getting a good standing place on a bench under the shelter of a projecting roof and was a looker on at the theatricals. Coming forward from behind the temporary screen of a bamboo curtain the actresses advanced to the front of their short stage and kowtowed to the dignitaries on the mats. Then to the music of drums and shami commenced their dance, if so it might be called, for it was a series of movements with feet, body, hands, and arms, more or less graceful, but with none of the characteristics of the saltatory motion we are accustomed to call a dance. Beating time with an occasional and regular stamp of the foot they would advance to the front, bend their bodies gracefully forward, saluting each other with the tips of their extended fingers, whirl about retire to the back of the stage and again advancing would join hands, or laying hold of the swinging sleeve of each other's dresses sway from side to side with a seesaw motion and raise their arms aloft or extend them horizontally, each finger moving, for they were never at rest but the whole body was in a slow measured motion that kept time to the uncouth music. Again they would face each other throwing an arm across the opposite one's shoulder, whirl about, stand back to back, throwing their arms aloft till their finger tips met or eyed each other with furtive glances over the shoulder. After the strangeness of the scene wears away, however unmeaning or graceless these motions at first may, or usually do, seem, they grow gradually more pleasing. It is seen that the whole is the result of necessary training, and that long and severe. These motions are not made at random but come in their proper place to the time of the music which had no melody in it but served only as a time marker. The more closely I watched the more was this apparent.

Then commenced a play in pantomime. A chorus of performers sang the recitative from books, and acting, instrumental and vocal music all harmonized in time. The music was written in ugly blots of Japanese characters and there was something indescribably ludicrous in seeing a half dozen middle aged grave looking men singing, with an earnestness that reminded me at once of Hogarth's picture, page after page of their books. Especially when the character of the play began to develop itself. There was occasional applause at some well executed maneuver on the part of the performers. On one side of the stage was the chorus; on the other the instrumental performers. As the play progressed the wardrobes were frequently changed and the more cumbrous garments left off. The scope of the play was indistinct until near the close when a family scene was enacted in expressive gestures that could not be mistaken. It was the birth of a child, nothing was omitted [from] the drawing water from an imaginary well to the bathing of the imaginary infant. All this was looked at without the faintest idea of indelicacy on the part of the spectators. The people were quiet, the officials wore their grave smiles of approbation, and the chorus bawled in stentorian words all that was necessary to fill up the sufficiently expressive pantomime. Bowing their heads low to the floor the curtain dropped and the car moved away. The attendant women frequently renewed the paint on the performers' faces, which the perspiration threatened to obliterate. Poor girls, they were the idols of the hour, yet why pity them, it was their great joy to win such triumphs.

Throughout the day similar scenes were enacted and groups of gaily dressed people wandered up and down the streets. Refreshment sellers, hucksters, and crock shops did a thriving business. The first watermelons of the season were produced today and large luscious plums had been brought from distant markets to honor the occasion. For in all these features the world's shows like these are alike. When evening fell there was no intermission of the sport. The street lanterns were ablaze and shed colored lights through their tinted papers. The patient bullocks and still more patient men dragged about the dragons and heroines and gods. The plays were reenacted and the gaudy dresses and painted faces were more attractive in the less intensive light of lanterns. It was an unreal scene. The foreign spectator was bewildered with the glare of light, the glittering of colors, the miming cars, the showy females in the house show, many graceful dances; it was a scene conjured up by a wizard's spell. All night long the revel lasted, there was no sleep. Strangest of all, there were no fights, no scenes of brutality, and in a land where intoxicating beverage is only less free than water hardly a person drunken with rice wine. No, such scenes on frolic days belong to lands of a more boasted civilization.

Thursday, July 19, 1860

With the morning dawn the fete was renewed if that may be called a renewal which had not been discontinued. Today all the different spectacles, and plays, and the people interested in setting them up were to pass before the Governor in grand procession. A stage had been fitted up in front of the Custom House on which was seated the Governor, his friends, and the chief dignitaries of Yokohama. The stage was draped with cotton cloth bearing the official colors of black and white stripes alternating. When I reached the ground the procession had already commenced to move. The street was blocked with a dense mass of spectators as yesterday standing bareheaded in the sun. Making my way through the crowd I found a place under the Governor's stand out of the sun which I shared in common with sworded gentlemen, gentlemen's servants who were there to fan their masters, and a few foreigners. The Daimio's retinue was passing when I arrived and it was evident from the smiling faces of the officials that they appreciated and relished the joke.

A slight of hand performer was trying his tricks. I recognized in him the same performer with cups and balls whom I had seen once before at Kanagawa. His tricks too were much the same. He had one clever additional one. Placing on his forehead a rod a yard long he rested on top of it a fan horizontally. Then on the butt end of the fan he balanced vertically a short rod of the form and length of an ordinary toddy stick [that was] cup shaped at its broad extremity. On the top of this was placed a cup full of water. He balanced this for a moment dexterously and then by a slight motion of his head gave the cup and stick on which it rested a rapid whirling motion. This he continued for some time without spilling a drop of the water. Then he dexterously withdrew the fan from between the upper and lower rod leaving the shorter resting on the longer one, and again whirled the cup so as to throw out its contents. After the cup was emptied, holding the short decanter shapen stick in his hand, he poised the cup upon it and tossed it high in the air, caught it again in the little socket, and repeated this several times amid the applause of his spectators.

The juggler passed by, then the horsemen bearing the same fox headed rider and his male attendants in female attire stopped in front of the Governor. The pretended females executed a dance in a burlesque way, and while they were yet performing, suddenly appeared among them a monstrous green dragon. The dragon was made by two men standing several feet apart who had thrown over themselves a green and painted cloth terminating in a dragon head. There were too many red Nipponese legs visible below the cloth to make the cheat very perfect but they imitated very well the quick motion of the ugly head and the undulating progress of the body which a respectable dragon might be supposed to have. The dragon appeared in the middle of the performers who fled shrieking with fright, and the monster followed with an appetite apparently as voracious as his famous counter part of Wautley. The cries of the distressed damsels amused the fox resting in his lair in the norimon. The fox slides back the door and appears as the champion of the ladies who have gathered behind him. The fox is a human dressed in white tights with a brief tail projecting astern and on his head is a mask with the face, head, mouth, and eyes of a fox. He has a long white beard which foxes generally do not have. In his hand he bears a paper broom secured to a bamboo rod a yard or so long. The white fox is a guardian genius in Japanese allegory as such he has ceremonious tokens paid to him something very like sacrifices. The white fox turns to the damsels, beckons them assuringly, and leads them on to face the green dragon that is again approaching.

Dragon and fox come face to face, fox takes one satisfactory look, whisks his broom in the dragon's face and beats a retreat. The dragon pursues more intent on the damsels than on the fox who fly around the fox for further protection. So again they all cautiously approach the monster, there is considerable dodging between dragon and fox. The monster's jaws are opened and the fox's broom is flourished and a variety of wonderful antics gone through with; the fox again wheels, falls into the dirt, and goes through altogether some comical scenes till the farce is ended by his retreating to his norimon, the damsels disappearing in the crowd, and the dragon goes off with unappeased hopes for a maiden's flesh.

This passed by, then came a car bearing a miniature house like those already spoken of and three stage girls. These girls as they rode through the streets were encircled by a curtain. The car stopped, its superstructure revolving on a pin was turned about so as to bring the actresses face to face to the Governor to whom they made a low bow with their heads firm to the floor. The girls were young, pleasant faced, and one of them was simply so handsome that she "carried off the hearts" of more than one looker on. Her figure was slight and graceful. A familiar pose with these girls is to stand with knees bent forwards and the body thrown backwards as far as possible, the head inclined to one shoulder and an upward look of the eyes, the arms and hands being raised so as to bring the hands about the line of the head. This position is retained while the young danseuse moves slowly backward and again advances, inching her head first to one shoulder and then the other, marking the time with a tap of her foot and the rhythm of her swinging hands and arms. As before the play was entirely in pantomime accompanied by a band of musicians, drums, and cymbals who stood under a canopy on one side and a group of singers who sang the story of the scene from books to the accompaniment of the shami on the other. The music occasionally in its preludes and interludes had a show of an air but the singing was like Windham Bray [?] in direful discord at a camp funeral. For the Japanese do not, like the Chinese, consider the perfection of music to consist in the highest screams, its value being in ratio to its force, but they indulge rather in low dolorous notes. As the play progressed in nearly every car the gorgeous dresses were laid aside and the girls at last stood forth in plain, and several times, scanty attire. The number of dresses some of them wore was burdensome. The folds of the different dresses were made to show in their dress sleeves that fell to the ground and in the plaited trails or rolls of each different one that folded across their bosoms.

Another group of actresses who passed by at first enacted a scene of high life. One of them in male attire seemed to personate a man of rank. Then there was a delicate young girl to whom he appeared to devote every attention. She had her female servant and there was a very pretty rehearsal of a love scene [:] the playful fondness of two lovers, a quarrel, the girl in a fit, the man sulky, then a reconciliation. Then came a shifting of the scene, the noble personages dwindled to fishermen and standing in a stage boat they went through the motions of rowing, keeping time still to the music that accompanied. They had lifted their fine dresses and stood now with bare arms and short dresses that fell half way to the knee. Thus they presented the boat scene and were still happy lovers and ended with a dance somewhat after the style of their sisters, or their maids, the ballet girls.

Then came a couple supposed to represent the Imperial pair. The lady was a wonderment of dress. Her wrappings must have exceeded in number, as they certainly did in bulk, those of an Egyptian mummy. Her face was less pleasing than others we had seen. She rose with great dignity, made a grave bow to the Governor, as if he was honored in seeing, as much as she in being seen, and after a few stage poses subsided to a seat and the cooling of two attendants who constantly fanned her. She had too many dresses of brocade, satin, silk, and crape to be lively.

Thus went by each spectacle of the day before. Preceding the spectacle furnished by each *tome* [*chōme*] came two, four, or more girls dressed as policemen and bearing in their hands the iron staff and rings of that office. They preceded each division, then came the chief presenters of the scenes in handsome holiday dresses. Then the exhibition furnished by each section followed by a band of musicians under a canopy and next a movable kitchen with furnaces and fire to furnish tea, rice, and hot sake as occasion wanted. This refreshment apparatus was indispensable, some of the divisions having two. The rear was brought up by the people of each section, every one attired in new and holiday clothing, the dress of each section differing from any other. These dresses were usually cotton stuffs printed in gay rawtone tints as one half of one color and one half of the other. Thus the upper half of the robe would be white and the lower blue, or red, or multicolored. [in the margin: In the procession were two men each bearing on his back a ———— of colossal proportions.] The lacquer merchants who appeared by themselves wore purple short silk dresses. On their heads they wore broad hats of split bamboo trimmed with rosettes and streamers. At first glance one would suppose officials were largely in the procession for most of the processors wore two swords and the peculiar code of dress proper to a man of rank. This was a holiday and the people were playing soldiers, wearing two swords, wooden ones though they were. So each man was followed by a servant who bore on his shoulders a chair or camp stool and a long handled fan with which he kept his master cool, fanning him from the rear as he walked along. Some sections made up by shouting, their lack of any other show.

After the procession had thus passed for several hours came the rear divisions being the part of the programme assigned to the joroya quarters. First came four little girls as miniature policemen with miniature staff and rings followed by a body of a dozen girls dressed in male cotton loose over robe of red and white, tight trousers, sandals and bamboo hat, others with loose trousers gathered ala turc below the knee. These little girls were attended by ten male servants, each of whom took care of them and fanned them. The other girls had each a male attendant with fan. Then followed a beautiful little house on a car with lattice work, verandah, and bamboo screens all around to hide what was passing within. This, like the others, halted before the Governor, the curtain was raised and exhibited three girls of sixteen or seventeen years of age in the act of prostration before a superior. These were richly dressed like the others that preceded them and accompanied by music and singing. They enacted a brief play wholly in pantomime and presently sat down on a low seat which at once revolved backwards and was certainly the most remarkable piece of scene shifting I ever saw, far ahead of the Nagasaki turn table. As the three girls disappeared, up were to view two little girls ten and eleven years old apparently. They were a pair of pretty creatures and how sad it was to think of the life before them. I can never forget their clear sweet childish tones in which after saluting the officials with fairest grace they began their little play. One had the part of a boy. He came onto the stage with an umbrella in his hand, a box slung over his neck, and a bamboo reed. They were children at play in the fields. He dipped his reed in the box and blew imaginary soap bubbles in the air while they marched about as if planting flowers and they chatted of the landscape before them, rehearsing in charming elocution a little dialogue. There was a little bye play of love between them and a bit of childish quarrel, the pouting lips and defiant look of the girl, the teasing indifferent air of the boy could not be surpassed. Then the quite impulsive reconciliation, one moment all frowns, now all smiles, was unimitable. There was no kissing for kissing is one of the lost arts, I have never seen it in Nippon where it is not the thing. It is no exaggeration to say that the acting of these children would have drawn the same applause anywhere that they did here. They could be a fortune to some enterprising businessman. Although the acting I have seen in Japan is neither to be compared with anything one may see in Drurie Lane or Broadway, yet I have been often struck by the many resemblances in stage tones and stage airs between the actors of Nippon and those of England or America.

The children presented their play, the three

damsels of the 1st scene advanced to the front, and the five in front paid their kowtow, and the curtain fell on one of the prettiest scenes of my Nippon life. The car was a favorite and continued, after the procession was ended, to perform here and there in the city, and so much had the sweet little children pleased me that I saw them twice again go through the repeated play.

Thus ended the festivities of matsuri. The towers and costumed canopies paraded the streets a while longer, but one by one they withdrew to the temporary houses built for them in their respective wards, the night came on, the crowd grew less, the returning boats were full of country people going home, the little child actors gave their last rehearsal in a shower of rain, the lanterns were dimmed, and Yokohama settled down to a two nights repose in one.

Friday, July 20, 1860

Quietly at home exhausted by over exertion in the hot for two days previous.

Saturday, July 21, 1860

Today the lots in the new reservation at Yokohama were sold at public auction. I should say private auction, for our worthy American Consul permitted none to be present except intended purchasers. The lots had been appraised of an equal valuation of $255 which sum was necessary to clear them of present occupants. The purchasers rather than pay anything beyond this in the competition of an auction sale had the day before quietly got together and drawn the lots by lot, so that today as each lot was put up the one who had drawn the lot the day before made his bid of the assessed value and no one offered more.[73] *Somebody* was outwitted by their mercantile shrewdness!

---

[73] Hall purchased Lot 23 in what came to be known as the "new concession." Simmons purchased Lot 31 (later renumbered as lot 82). See letter of E. S. Benson dated Yokohama January 11, 1862, in Despatches from

U.S. Consuls in Japan, National Archives Record Group 59: M135, Kanagawa, 1861–1897 (Washington D.C.: National Archives and Record Services, 1985).

Sunday, July 22, 1860

During my absence to Nagasaki the Sabbath services have been changed from Kanagawa to a hired room at Yokohama. Mr. Nevius who recently arrived from China alternates with Mr. Brown in conducting the service. Mr. Goble preaches on shipboard to the crews.

Monday, July 23, 1860

Making improvements in our front yard. Under Dr. S[immons]'s regime it had become unsightly with grass, weeds, and neglected shrubbery. These I am having cleaned up, the trees trimmed, the fish pond cleared up, etc.

Tuesday, July 24, 1860

Call from Heco today. Among the news he brings me is that three princes have committed hara kiri at Yedo very lately, one of whom was the Prince of Kaga, the most powerful prince of the empire in revenues. The story is that these three were appointed to bring Mito to terms on some ground of settlement of the old feud. They made a proposition of settlement, but Mito, who is said to be a man of extraordinary parts, defeated their proposition by showing that it would be contrary to Japanese law, usage, and propriety. According to old custom the three princes being defeated in a proposition on state affairs committed hara kiri.

Mito is said to be gaining in popularity. His policy is declared to be to admit foreigners for trading purposes, but to insist upon them conforming to Japanese law and usage as the Japanese would be compelled to do in foreign countries, and to grant to foreigners nothing through compulsion. Like heroes in other civilized lands, Mito has a reputation for some extraordinary preter-natural achievements. For instance, it is said of Mito that in early youth, being possessed of uncommon shrewdness and discernment, at the age of seven he feigned a loss of the power to hear or speak. This cheat he practiced many years. It enabled him to hear all that was said among the inmates of his father's court, the declarations and policies of public men who paid no regard to a deaf and dumb boy except to treat him with the respect and deference to which his rank entitled him. Thus his mind not distracted by the many idle ceremonies and amusements of the indolent life of a prince's court was educated by a study of books and particularly of such as gave information of foreign affairs and the political economy of an empire like Japan. I have before heard it stated that there was no man in the empire so conversant with foreign matters, how foreign rule is administered, foreign laws and customs, as Prince Mito. At the age of nineteen he paid a ceremonious visit to the court of the Mikado, and returning from thence to his family with the faculty of speaking and hearing, declared that to the spiritual offices of the Mikado was he indebted for their restoration.

Large shipments of forage are going forward to the English army in China—hay, beans, and peas.

Wednesday, July 25, 1860

B[rown] has been making inquiries respecting the system of taxation and has found it much as I have already recounted. The lands are hired of the crown or the great princes for which the people pay in kind from 2/10 to 4/10 of the produce (my information 1/10 to 5/10) or a money compensation instead. Nonland holding classes such as merchants, mechanics, etc., pay an annual money tax.

Thursday, July 26, 1860

At the ferryboat landing the officials who sit there require every man to take off his hat that passes there in going to and from the boats. This applies to Japanese only of course.

The tides are low now and we are frequently obliged to be carried off to our boats on the shoulders of the Japanese. It is sometimes a little difficult to manage with cane, umbrella, etc. The Japanese women are used to it, they throw their arms around the bearers' necks, who throw their arms back under the fleshiest part of the riders' body behind, and thus with her bare red legs hanging straight down (not a-straddle) the Japanese girl goes laughing to the ferry boat.

The dollar is gradually falling in price, a hundred at the present time being worth 235 Bus. The Govt. on Monday, at least, have posted an official notification that the dollar was worth 2 Bus and 5 tempos.

The guard houses were all removed from the foreign houses in Kanagawa a few days since. But the Japanese, with true Japanese pertinacity, have put up new guard houses in the streets contiguous to the same residences, and which, for all purposes of espionage, answer to them as good a purpose. Belcour [Bellecourt][74] and Vyse[75] both declare their belief that among our very servants we have government spies in men who have temporarily assumed menial employment. B[rown]'s teacher says there are spies, but who, or where they are, no one knows. He thinks there are forty such men in Kanagawa wholly unsuspected in their avocations.

My attention has been drawn in the streets to little miniature cages, and on examining them I find they have not birds but singing crickets for sale. The cricket's note is made with their wings and gives a pleasant sound. The young girls wear the little cages and their insect songsters as head ornaments. Musical hair pins.

Friday, July 27, 1860

In the morning a walk in the fields to gather wild flowers. The tiger lily, yellow and spotted, has been in bloom for two months and now there is a more superb variety in blossom, large white blossoms with a streak of lemon yellow running longitudinally the center of the petals and purple spots sprinkling each petal. It is a showy yet delicate flower. Japan abounds in lilies. After a succession of hot days rain began to fall in the afternoon accompanied with a little distant thunder and lightning. The storm increased till at 5 P.M. we had a heavy

gale and the rain falling in torrents. The farmers say this rain is "like old gold" for it has fallen just in time to benefit the paddy fields.

Saturday, July 28, 1860

A fine bright day succeeds yesterday's storm. The gale was heavy on the bay. The junks tossed up and down at their anchorage as if they would part company with their cables. Loureiro's new house, yet uncompleted, was blown down. The tea houses on the cliff by the roadside that overlooks the bay are pleasant retreats on hot mornings like this. The cooling breezes that come over the bay, the airy rooms and clean mats invite to rest and indolence. In an hour that I passed a large white cat lay quietly on the mat and in the sun above mistress was busily engaged in picking the fleas out of pussy's fur. Puss' half closed eyes and outstretched jaws showed she enjoyed the old lady's attentions. A little further on a man was reclined full length on a mat floor while a boy was performing a similar kind office on his head.

I took a walk to Bookenji [Bukenji] in the afternoon to gather a twig of the handsome maki[76] that grows there.

The old man who has been trimming the dooryard has taken a week to do what a sturdy Irishman would have finished in a day. He has done everything neatly and well. An orange tree that he brought me today has sixty-five oranges on it and the tree is less than three feet high. These oranges are small, the long diameter 1 1/2 to 2 inches, the short diameter 3/4 to an inch. Their flavor is between an orange and lemon, less sweet than the former, less sour than the latter.

Sunday, July 29, 1860

Mr. N[evius] preached at Yokohama. Two or three Japanese came in as lookers on and quite a crowd was attracted outside by the singing. A

---

[74] M. du Chesne de Bellecourt was French Minister to Japan from 1859 to 1863.

[75] F. Howard Vyse was British Consul in Kanagawa.

[76] This was the Koya maki or umbrella pine that is pictured in Robert Fortune, *Yedo and Peking* (London: John Murray, 1863), plate following p. 46.

heavy shower came up in the afternoon and the rain again fell copiously. No thunder or lightning and little wind.

Monday, July 30, 1860

Sadajirō returned from Miaco two or three days since from where he has brought his mother. He is full of life and spirit as ever, improved in general looks, and if we may believe his story has had "a good time." Among the other marvels he relates that at Miaco they are raising horses on the grandest scale. A large place has been set apart and prepared for them and he saw gathered there a multitude of horses reputed to be 27,000. England and France are badly served in the slow way horses are dealt to them if there is such an equine reservoir as this.

The pilgrimages to Fusi are numerous this year. This is a year set apart for females to visit Fusi and occurs once in sixty years. Japanese women must be long lived or many must die without seeing Fusi.

On his way he met five travellers on the road wearing foreign shoes and seven wearing Chinese shoes.

The rains have been very heavy there as here. He and his travelling companions had occasion to cross a river which the rains had swelled to a torrent. They reached the bridge at night and crossed it by light of lanterns. When they reached the opposite shore they found the country inundated and essayed to wade. They soon got beyond their depth, a priest was swept away in the darkness and they managed to return leaving the poor fellow to his watery fate. By daylight the remainder again crossed over and found the priest safe in a tree where submerged branches had proved his salvation. "We all wept tears of joy to-gether," says S[adajirō]. The crops have generally been good, better than usual. The silk crop has not been so good for 20 years, the rape seed is poorer than usual owing to untimely rains in early summer. He reports the merchants as impatient to open trade with foreigners.

Recent quarries of colored marbles have been opened near Miaco, near ancient gold mines which had been mined as far as Japanese miners could go. The new currency of the Emperor is illy received in central Nippon as it is thought to be much debased. The ichibu is debased with white copper alloy.

Mount Fusi is not in eruption nor has it been for very many years amounting to centuries.

There was a good deal of sickness there, so we hear the same of Yedo. It is a kind of cholera or cholera morbus induced no doubt by excess of vegetable diet. S[adajirō] says he upbraided the people for their faith in wooden and stone gods and their belief in mountain gods and gods of stone. His missionary work is to be doubted.

The *Forest Eagle* which left this port twenty days since with a load of horses for China returned last evening having lost one hundred and twenty of them.[77] She reports heavy weather; her cargo owing to imperfect storage broke loose and stove her water casks; the peas soaked in the water, fermented, and the stench is so horrible that it is impossible to go down in the hold.

The Portuguese envoy has negotiated his treaty with the Japanese Government. The material ratification obtained is the reduction of the duty on wines to 5 percent.

[77] Edward Barrington de Fonblanque, whose cargo of horses were aboard wrote: "I shall never forget the scene presented by one of my transports, the *Forest Eagle* which sailed for China with above two hundred horses. . . . The horses had all been stowed between decks, and a line of stalls, which had been constructed with as much strength as a Japanese carpenter could bestow upon them, having given way during a hurricane, the poor beasts, half maddened with fear and tortured by their hurts as they rolled among the fragments of their boxes commenced an onslaught upon one another, which death or sheer exhaustion only terminated. . . . Only seventy horses survived and of these several had had their eyes kicked out, or were otherwise so mutilated as to render their destruction necessary" (*Niphon and Pe-che-li*, p. 128).

Tuesday, July 31, 1860

Today commences the matsuri at Yedo. Many people have gone thither and we have found it difficult today to get fish because Yedo has demanded it all. Sadajirō confirms the statement that these days are holidays of the people par excellence, where they wear not only the swords and dresses of superiors in rank, but have every license permitted them of speech and behavior. At Yedo the samurai and yakunin, particularly the former remain within their own enclosures. In former times serious riots have occurred between the samurai and the people engaged in their festivities so that of late years the former keep within doors. The people are supreme for two days.

I have noticed in the bay crates sunk in the shallow waters a little larger than ordinary crockery crates with small interstices. These I learn contain live fish for the imperial table at Yedo. A particular fish called tai, esteemed the best, is caught and kept in large numbers so that in bad weather the royal table may not lack.

In the afternoon Dr. S[immons], Dr. H[epburn] and myself took a boat to go and examine the bluffs along the coast near Treaty Point. We found the same soft clay rock that we have on the Kanagawa side. The formation was this. Surface earth say eight feet thick, then a large mosaic deposit of shells almost wholly bivalves, then another stratum of earth in which these marine deposits were bedded of nearly equal thickness to the upper stratum, then a clay rock say ten feet thick, then a bed of beach gravel almost the same thickness, and lowest a deep bed of the same clay rock twenty feet thick or twenty-five above the sea level and how much below I could not say. The different strata were horizontal without any apparent slip or upheaval.

Wednesday, August 1, 1860

Horseback excursion into the country. The rice crops look promising. The upland rice which was seen between the wheat drills before the latter was gathered is also coming on finely. Remarked the numerous small streams which everywhere abound.

Thursday, August 2, 1860

A Court of Inquiry is being held in the matter of the *Forest Eagle* that lost 127 horses out of 200. Went to see Major F[onblanque] about the chances of a trip to China and Tai Lin Bay, report unsatisfactory.

Friday and Saturday, August 3 and 4, 1860

Busy with letters for the home mail. Simmons is about day and night at Yokohama and I have quiet times. The four servants have little to do. I was amused to see the whole force out trying to catch one poor chicken for my dinner. I found it difficult to cater for me, so I live on few courses and simple. A stewed or roast pigeon makes a good dinner, eggs and rice or a fried fish my breakfast.

Sunday, August 5, 1860

Spent the day at home. Dr. S[immons] returned today and brought Talbot back with him. I had dinner nearly ready when they came. It made a good dinner for three and see how cheaply one may live in Japan. Our first course was boiled fish, *akatai* (grouper), the Emperor's favorite dish as my servant took care to remind me. This cost 10¢, then a roast chicken cost 7¢ flanked by boiled rice, squash, egg plants, value of the vegetables 2¢. 3rd course an egg curry, value hardly appreciable but the whole cost was within a quarter of a dollar including bread, butter, and a desert of baked fruit and other accompaniments. We could not have done so well at a Chatham St. restaurant. We had Dr. H[epburn] and his wife to dine the other day when we had five courses from soup to desert—soup, fish, beef, curry, and fruit, vegetables, etc., for less than a half a dollar. We have amusing times with our marketing especially in trying to get tender chickens from the sharp little woman that keeps the poultry and pig yard. Made a capital discovery yesterday in baked apples and pears. I may yet become famous as Soyer [Schoyer?].

Monday, August 6, 1860

To the *Pruth* this forenoon. My betto came today,[78] a likely looking man. He had hardly arrived when a betto from an adjoining stable who had hoped to get the same place came into the yard and made a disturbance. I had to eject the disturber summarily several times before he would stay disturbed. A curious specimen of Japanese modesty today. I stepped into a store to buy a trifle. The proprietor was as nearly naked as he could well be and would not wait upon me till he had got his garments. He called to a girl or young woman in the adjoining apartment to bring them. So she came bare to her loins bringing a robe to hide the man's nakedness.

Tuesday, August 7, 1860

Tried my new horse and saddle by a ride into the country. Find the weather full warm for such exercise. On my return I passed a farm house where an old couple entirely nude were taking their evening bath from a tub in the door yard. A rural scene truly. We exchanged salutations and they were no more disturbed to be seen bathing out of a tub in common than I was to be riding horseback. I saw a more comical sight in the street. A fat man with only his loin cloth on stood in the center of the street fanning himself. It was not so much this that made the scene comical as it was to see that he was specially endeavoring to cool that portion of his physique which schoolmasters are so fond of warming up in the persons of ill behaved urchins. Fleas fairly rousted me out of bed tonight.

Wednesday, August 8, 1860

Drying and arranging botanical specimens. A Yokohama merchant who was in said he thought that men who drank sake and ———— did not interest themselves in such things. He said there were men in Miaco who followed such pursuits and they were temperate in all

pleasures and added they wore beards too like myself! I have heard it said before that it were generally believed in Japan that men engaged in intellectual pursuits must abstain from bodily and sensual delights.

Thursday, August 9, 1860

By the arrival of the *Princess Charlotte* yesterday I received my treasure from home it having been nearly five months on the way. Shower at evening with a single flash of lightning. We have very little of either thunder or lightning.

Friday, August 10, 1860

Took a long ride in the afternoon which led us into a beautiful valley covered with rice. A fine stream of water ran along the margin of the valley, overhung by bamboos and trees of various kinds. Cottages were scattered here and there in the shade on either side of the valley. The scene was a parklike ornamental landscape.

Saturday, August 11, 1860

Belcour [Bellecourt] when riding down from Yedo yesterday was saluted with *tojin baka* from a house on the way side. He at once pursued the man to his house and threatened summary vengeance. Identifying the place he came on to Yokohama and complained to the officials, informing them if he was thus insulted again he should use his pistol. The authorities have issued a proclamation to the people forbidding them to salute foreigners at all and what might be the consequences if they did. As a commentary on this text I was saluted in the afternoon with "*Anata Baka-ri*." If the speaker had stopped at the hyphen he would have said "You fool," but pausing a second he added the final syllable which makes another and very harmless Japanese word signifying "only."

Went with Dr. S[immons] to visit the work

---

[78] Hall's *betto*, or groom, was a man named Hikozō who, like his servant Yasaburō, was listed in the official

records. See Fujimoto Jitsuya, *Kaikō to kiito bōeki* (Tokyo: Tōkō shoin, 1939), vol. 2, p. 286.

on the great canal at Yokohama which is to separate the foreigners from the native people. It is a great work in which hundreds of men were clustered busy as bees carrying off the excavated earth in baskets of ropes swung to poles. It seemed as expeditious as paddy's wheelbarrow. The canal in progress is 120 feet wide and at its mouth emptying in the ocean is 30 feet deep. Land was being prepared for the new native settlement above. The water was removed from the canal by a series of water wheels that lifted it rapidly from one level to another. Crossing the bay we encountered a boat load of Fusi Yama pilgrims dressed in white clothing with a bell suspended at their sides. In Yokohama met several more. What must be the power of superstition that at this season of the year starts thousands on a long foot pilgrimage to distant shrines.

The change to a slightly cooler temperature seems to justify what the Japanese say of their season, that after the 6th of August the weather daily grows a little cooler, the wind varying again to the north.

Sunday, August 12, 1860

Ill this morning and did not go to church at Yokohama. At sunset took a short walk in the fields by myself finding several varieties of plants in bloom.

I hear today that the Governor of Yokohama has protested to the American Legation against the conduct of Van Reed [Eugene Van Reed] in visiting Yedo a few days since without permission. The Consul has protested against the action of the Japanese authorities in throwing up a large embankment at the canal outlet in Yokohama.

Monday, August 13, 1860

At noon I walked up to Jobootsoogi [Jobutsuji]. The air was hot and still. In every house the inmates were lying stretched on their mats courting or enjoying slumber. In one, two men, naked all save their loin cloths, were asleep, at the door of another sat a woman nursing a child with her clothes thrown off her body to her hips; another woman in equal dishabille sat in a doorway opposite; at the next house a woman and her child lay at full length on the mats, the child naked, the woman with a printed cotton cloth lying across her loins; at another men and women lay together on the mats asleep three quarters nude. Mrs. Tomy's boys and girls were wholly nude. So it was wherever I passed.

The air is full of the sounds of insect life. The insects supply the place of birds. We hear scarcely a note save that of the hoarse callings [of] crows, the sparrows so noisy in winter are now quiet. But there is a locust that sings loud as a bird, a real trumpeter, his note shrill, vibrating, is fairly deafening. There is the swelling and diminuendo note of the grass hopper, the chief of crickets, and the song of a small insect like a beetle half bird cry half insect utterance as the male and female sing responsive to each other. There is the singing cricket with long legs who raises his wings perpendicularly till they cross like a pair of shears and give from them a sweet vibratory note. Separate the wings ever so little and his song dies away. Everywhere there is an incessant hum of insect life. Sounds strange coming from strange insects.

Towards evening took a long ride into the country; reached high land whereon I had a far reaching and grand landscape view of rolling hills, woods, and distant mountains.

Tuesday, August 14, 1860

The pilgrims to Fusi Yama are daily more numerous. I meet them in the street and on the bay clad in their white robes. The inns are nightly well filled with the passing travellers. The only value attached to the pilgrim's excursion, beyond the pleasure which I imagine is the more considerable part, is that by so doing they propitiate the local deity of the mountain who will secure to them a happy abode after death.

Wednesday, August 15, 1860

Sadajirō called on us this evening. He has just presented me with a couple of books of his own made to be used for herbariums. He is as communicative and inquisitive as ever. I mixed for him a little claret sangaree which he enjoyed very much and afterwards having tripped on the steps to the hall declared he was "small drunk." He has the greatest desire to ape foreign manners. I had given him a shirt with a stand up collar; Dr. H[epburn] a pair of white pants, then I added a cravat, with all this toggery he looked like a civilized demoralized half-breed savage. He was anxious to learn an American song. So Dr. S[immons] and myself taught him Yankee Doodle. It was a comic scene to see him in foreign gear singing our patriotic song; he was especially careful to imitate the tones of our voices.

The story we had a few days ago of the hara kiri of three princes is probably untrue. The three great princes of the Empire are 1st the Prince of Kanga [Kaga], 2nd the Prince of Satsuma, 3rd the Prince of Mootsu [Mutsu]. They are of the oldest family, most powerful in revenues and retainers. The eighteen principal daimios who outrank all others are those whose ancient lineage is longest and most honorable. After these follow an innumerable host of smaller daimios.

Thursday, August 16, 1860

Received from the *Wanderer* today my safe and four boxes from home, also June home letters. I had no difficulty in getting my effects ashore. The vigilant official was lulled to sleep by a shinjo of a perfumery bottle. These are the bright days in our calendar when the mail brings us letters from the friends beyond the sea. We devour them eagerly and impatiently not knowing what news pleasant or unpleasant each line may reveal to us. We are supplied abundantly with papers. The Japanese look upon the newspaper as a great curiosity.

Friday, August 17, 1860

Mr. and Mrs. S[choyer] gave a breakfast today. A company of twenty four persons assembled at their house in Yokohama at one P.M. and of that number eleven were ladies! A goodly gathering of our fair sisters in a distant land. All were married ladies and most of them residents of Yokohama and Kanagawa. The house built after Japanese style was profusely decorated with evergreens and flowers, the doorways converted into living arches and the posts wreathed with camellia and spruce. In the back yard adorned with trees a fountain was playing. It was a summer fete in a park. Breakfast! was served at 2 P.M. This dejeuner as our invitation said, was in the godown which was so hidden under green branches and flowers that it seemed a rustic booth erected for the occasion. The table was similarly ornamented with a pretty display of fruits added— melons, pears, plums, grapes, confectionery etc. There was a variety of courses by Chinese cooks, wine flowed liberally and after a pleasant time of two hours and a half we finished our breakfast at 4:30 P.M.

An hour or so was passed promenading, chatting, etc., when we again assembled in the dining room to see some Japanese slight of hand tricks. The performer was a very intelligent looking man clad in silk garments both outer and inner. A band of Japanese music played a lengthy and inharmonious overture, the conductor addressed a speech to his auditors who were none the wiser for what he said, bowed his [head] several times, the juggler did the same and commenced with trick no. 1. This was the well known ribbon trick in which the ribbon which was of fancy colored paper was produced from a bowl which had been shown to be empty. No. 2 was much cleverer. An empty bowl was placed on a low stand, shown freely to the audience and then from a tea kettle a pint or so of water was poured in. A good deal of byplay followed with a lacquered box, then a platter was brought the bowl emptied upon it and lo! the water was alive with eels three, four, and five inches long, a score or a score and a half of them, but how he had managed to get them there was the puzzle. In trick no. 3 he showed us ten sheets of clean transparent paper which were separately placed one by one on the same low stand, another ten were counted off and similarly disposed of. A cup was filled with water and inverted on the stand so as not to spill a drop. One or two sheets of the paper were withdrawn to show that it was thoroughly wetted and the conjurer then drew from beneath the cup a score of pictures printed on small sheets of paper clean and dry which he distributed among the audience.

No. 4 was the famous butterfly trick. Twisting a piece of light paper and holding it so as to get the wings and body of a butterfly he placed it on the end of his finger and fanned into the air. The insect hovered about the performer's head face and shoulders simulating the peculiar movements of the real little creature. He held another half open fan with the other hand and the butterfly over and above the fan now on this side and now on that retreating, returning, alighting and darting off again till growing less fearless it alighted on one end and still fluttering his wings half flew and half walked to the other as the insect does and seemed to search for the flowing nectar. Another butterfly was added, the two disported together now up now down and away coquetting famously. The performer held a bowl, they hovered daintily around its rim, peered inside, and fluttered without, one inside and one out at the same time and finally settled down within, from where they again flew out and alighting on the performer's hand he crushed them between his thumb and finger, fanned again, and lo! the dead butterflies were created into a shower of tiny bits of paper. The secret of this trick was apparent, invisible threads prevented the mock insects from flying only so far and by skillful practice direction was given to their movements thus restrained.

No. 5 was a lantern in which a bit of candle was placed, then withdrawn, its wick bored out, again replaced, and the lantern closed. By a few strokes of the fan the candleless lantern glowed with an interior flame.

No. 6 was a more elaborate ribbon performance. A little water was put in a bowl, 2 bits of paper thrown in thoroughly wetted as was plainly manifest. Holding one of the wetted pieces in his thumb and finger he fanned it into a thousand pieces of clean, dry, paper. Holding the other wet paper in his hand plainly before us all he gave it a toss when out from it flew several narrow strips of paper ribbon many feet long; two eggs were in the tangled end of the four ribbons, then there was a mass of wide gay colored ribbons which he stuffed away, and behold in his hand was an umbrella which he opened and retired amid a shower of applause! The beauty of the trick was no means adequate to the care seen to be employed.

No. 7. An empty box of lacquered ware is mysteriously filled with water and the performer catches a small fish with hook and line.

No. 8. A long box is shown with three bits of board within inscribed with characters. These are taken out and distributed among the audience. The performer then undertakes various schemes for withdrawing the attention of the audience and at the end asks for the three bits of board to be brought back, two only can be found. He is astonished, insists upon the audience giving it up, and as a last resort opens his box again and there sure enough it is spirited back somehow. The trick is a prior arranged collusion with the host.

So finished the juggling. Now the numerous lanterns among the trees in the yard were lighted and the scene was wholly oriental in its caste—trees, fountains, and gay lanterns with promenaders and a band of music from the shipping. I came away as the tables were being set for a grand dinner, after which dancing was to follow. But it is impossible to get boats at a late hour and I preferred leaving to an all night stay. Fireworks were going off as we bade adieu to the evening gayety.

Saturday, August 18, 1860

Heco breakfasted with me this morning. We were talking of the superstitions of the common people. H[eco] gave some instances. Not long since a native girl in service was so cruelly treated that she drowned herself. Her master's boy bathing a few days ago at the same spot was drowned, the people believing that the girl's spirit in revenge dragged him down into the depths. If a man is deranged it is commonly said that a fox has taken possession of him, entering by his armpit, and the man becomes demented. So too if a fox has been stoned by a boy, he may come at evening time in the guise of another boy or companion rap at the door and entice the offender away and put him to death. A native tells me that all white and yellow cats are males, and white, yellow, and black females. So scarce is a male of the latter kind and so sagacious, that junk masters will give one hundred ichibus for one as it will foretell bad weather and other dangers by clawing and shrieking.

Sunday, August 19, 1860

Attended service at Yokohama.

Monday, August 20, 1860

Had a call from the old Inkio this morning who came to see my iron safe. Showed him also views of Washington with which the old man was much pleased and told me how many years ago Washington was born and the date of the Revolution correctly. He brought me a shinjo of a watermelon.

Tuesday, August 21, 1860

A Yokohama merchant called this morning to express his gratitude to Dr. S[immons] for curing him of the itch. He brought a shinjo of some fine pears. Consul D[orr] returned from Yedo last evening. Minister Harris' audience with the Emperor [shogun] resulted very satisfactorily. A personal guard of 100 men was with him in addition to the retinue of the Kami who accompanied him. He and his suite (Consul D[orr] and Mr. Heusken) rode in norimons, their led horses following. The distance to the palace was three miles, which was thronged by a dense crowd of people all the way. Reaching the 2nd palace enclosure the norimons of the suite rested, they proceeding on foot. The delegation were received in an outer room where Representatives D[orr] and

H[eusken] remained while Minister Harris proceeded between files of attendants to the 3rd audience room. The Emperor was seated in a chair on a dais raised a foot in height. Mr. H[arris] approached within a half dozen mats of him, read his address to which the Emperor made reply and Minister H[arris] retired. The whole ceremony occupying not more than twelve or fifteen minutes. The audience chamber was plain, devoid of furniture, with the customary mats bound with white. A handsome gilt landscape paper covered the walls. More [than] three hours after Mr. H[arris]'s departure from the palace a high functionary came to his residence to inquire if all had been satisfactory to the Minister. On receiving an affirmative answer he expressed delight, and gave Mr. H[arris] a present from the Emperor and concluded by inviting him and Mr. D[orr] to a dinner on Wednesday with the particular request "that they would come with empty stomachs." So ended this long talked of audience which in Minister H[arris]'s mind has supplanted nearly every other idea, less solicitous how his countrymen's interests were faring than how he should be received by the Emperor. D[orr] says he tried on his new clothes, court costume, several times to see how they looked, pleased as a boy.

Sadajirō called in the evening to take another lesson in "Yankee Doodle." He now sings two stanzas with a considerable unction.

Kissing he says is something never done except by Joroyas. I have never seen a kiss given or received in Japan. It is one of the lost arts in Nippon.

Ordinary wages seem to be four tempos a day and some mechanics may receive a tempo more. It is said the Emperor pays high wages for this reason. The ancient custom was that imperial laborers would work an hour in the morning, break off, take breakfast and a long rest, work another hour, stop again till after they had dined, do another work perhaps in the afternoon and cease altogether for the day. This was the established custom of the Empire. The consequence was that imperial work was never likely to be completed and now if the emperor has work that he wishes done in reasonable time he pays two to four ichibus per-diem to get [a] good days work! Large jobs of work are let by contract, not to the lowest bidder, nor the highest, but the medium bidder. The port lately built is said to have made the contractor rich, whereas the canal is likely to impoverish the jobbers. In the latter case after the contractor has been compelled to do his utmost the government renders assistance. Labor for the Mikado is done for no wages beyond food.

At Mr. H[arris]'s late audience although he alluded to the Embassy in America the Emperor deigned no allusion to it. The subject was treated coldly by the Prime Minister, who only expressed the desire that it would speedily return. Instead of receiving honors from their prince and countrymen the four ambassadors are quite as likely on their return to be degraded because they have been the recipients of foreign favors.

The servant of Mr. H. a Yokohama merchant with his intended committed suicide a few days since. He was a dissolute fellow in debt to his master for borrowed money. A girl living in "The Swamp" was his intended wife, but seeing poverty and disgrace staring them in the face, [and] no means of repaying the money, they concluded to put an end to their lives. He went to her house and first stabbing her in the throat afterwards dispatched himself. The Japanese believe that the couple who go out of life in this manner will be happily reunited in the world of spirits.

The Japanese have a saying that if you have sweetmeats never show them to one with long teeth for persons with long teeth are supposed to have a particular fondness for choice eatables. So too a long or large nosed man is supposed to be a wise as well as an amorous man.

Wednesday, August 22, 1860

Genl. D[orr] invited a number of ladies and gentlemen to the Consulate to see the present of confectionery sent by the Emperor to Mr. Harris and which Mr. H[arris] had sent down for the purpose. The present was enclosed in a plain unpainted pine box two feet long and high by a foot and a half wide. The box was in two parts, one lapping like a cover over the other. Removing the cover four trays of the

same unpainted wood were exposed to view each filled with a great variety of confectionery arranged in the most tasteful manner. The eyesight was the sense principally gratified, for the candies and cakes were far less agreeable to the taste. The whole were rice flour, bean flour, and sugar variously compounded, and though we admired the taste displayed in the arrangement and the pretty harmonizing of colors we should, any of us, have preferred a pound of sweets best to the whole box full. On the outside of the box in a white paper tied with the usual cords of white and red paper were ten strips of dried fish (the limpet) each stripe a foot and a half long and half of an inch wide. This is the imperial style and no one else would dare to use *ten* stripes, or stripes of such size. We had a fine frolic over the Emperor's candies assisted by the General's wines.

I saw today a pleasing instance of respect for the unfortunate. A blind priest came down the mountain side alone. When near the bottom he appeared puzzled to find his way, groping here and there with his long staff. He then raised a cry repeated two or three times. A little girl ten years old in a compound a little way off answered his call and running thither met the blind man with a merry laugh, and talking in kind tones took him by the hand and led him on his way. How many American children would have done so for a blind wayside beggar.

Thursday, August 23, 1860

Today is set apart to propitiate the deity who presides over the wells. The streets are ornamented with tall bamboos from which are suspended streamers of colored papers and on the streamers songs are inscribed. Over the road where are numerous springs gushing from the side of the hill are hung strips of colored paper and arches festooned with strips of inscribed cloth two feet long by half a foot in width. All the wells are to be cleaned out today. The servants have called upon me to contribute one ichibu towards cleansing the great well that supplies this neighborhood, so that the water Kami may be propitious and keep us supplied with the indispensable fluid. The

Milky Way, the "Celestial River" of this as other unlettered people, is venerated today. On either side of the Milky Way is a cluster of three stars, if these unite on the same side the augury is for abundant supplies of water. There is another superstition connected with the day. The women thread their needles by moonlight and sew on children's garments believing that they will thereby become expert in the use of the needle.

At 5 P.M. took a horseback ride with Dr. S[immons] and Rev. Mr. N[evius] up the Tokaido to the plain beyond the Yokohama crossing and then off among the hills, through shady paths, bending around towards home, striking the familiar path across the high plateau.

Friday, August 24, 1860

Writing at home till evening and then a sail over to Yokohama and return by moonlight. Received a shinjo of some handsome pears and views of Yokohama.

The name of yesterday's holiday is "Tanabata," the popular idea is that the Milky Way is a celestial river which supplies the terrestrial founts of whatever description. The stars alluded to are popularly said to unite in marriage. Hence too the young men and maidens observe the day writing songs on slips of paper which they offer to the Milky Way to secure success in their love suits. The children do the same thing that they may become wise. The garments sewed upon by the women are offered to the stars also. The strips of paper fluttering from the bamboo poles are those inscribed by the children and the young folks.

Saturday, August 25, 1860

Today was held at the Consulate the examination of Mr. [Van] Reed on the charge of having gone to Yedo! The Governor sometime since addressed the American Consul stating that Mr. Van Reed had on a certain day hired a boat at Kanagawa to sail on the bay; that after leaving the shore he compelled the boatmen in spite of their remonstrances to take

him to Yedo where he visited several places, purchased some articles and all, as the Governor alleges, in contravention of the treaty which says Yedo shall be opened in 1862, and begs that Mr. Van Reed may be punished for the offence. A day was appointed for the trial at the Consulate. Van Reed appeared, the Governor's charges were read to which Van Reed pleaded not guilty, and demanded a trial according to American law as stipulated by the treaty. Under this sanction he required the presence of his accusers and the proof of the charges made. The Governor not being present the court adjourned to another day when the accusers again failing to appear adjournment was again had to this day. Today the 3rd Governor appeared accompanied by an interpreter and ometsuke, and the six boatmen who had been held in durance. The charge was reiterated and the six boatmen were ready to say that Mr. Van Reed had been in Yedo, this the officials thought quite enough to convict any man, they said he was guilty and that was quite enough, but they proposed to question Mr. Van Reed and when informed that the criminal in America could not be questioned without his consent, but himself could question, they thought it a very strange custom. It was so in conflict with their ideas of justice as administered in Japan, where a yakunin's word would be sufficient to condemn. Said they, why question the boatmen, they were tools "hands and feet, Mr. Van Reed was the head," "ask the head not the hands and feet." No accusation being sustained the court again adjourned to give the Governor once more an opportunity to proceed in due form.

The principal deity of Fusi Yama who is adored by the pilgrims is a female called "Sengen" or the "Thousand Eyed." She is said to be an ancient Japanese deity. Buddhists and Shintos alike make the pilgrimage to Fusi.

Japan has had its female authors, two of whom are especially renowned for their great wisdom. According to Japanese story an ancient Mikado desired to present to his subjects books which should teach them all rules by which a good life should be regulated, and two females of his court produced a number of volumes containing many nice sayings, apothegms, and moral lessons. Their names were

"She" [Sei Shonagon] and "Moorasaki" [Murasaki Shikibu]. There are many reflections contained in them, so says Sadajirō, like those of the Bible and he quoted one which said that life forever was fleeting like the smoke or the dew on the grass. Horseback ride P.M.

Sunday, August 26, 1860

Attended service at Yokohama.

Monday, August 27, 1860

The heats of summer are now sensibly mitigated by the prevailing northerly winds, thus proving correct the declaration made by the natives early in August of such a change in the season.

The Embassy to the United States have stated that Yedo has hospitals for the sick. I have inquired of an intelligent Japanese physician who tells me there are two institutions of that kind without patients. Patients who enter them receive so little care and attention that it is looked upon as sure death to enter one of them. The physicians appointed to attend them are unskillful men. They receive the Emperor's pay, make annual reports of the successful condition of the hospitals, but no one uses them. At Oasaca, he says, there is a large hospital founded by the wealthy merchants which is much better conducted.

Tuesday, August 28, 1860

Cloudy with a strong wind from the S.E. At home all day, towards evening ordered my horse for a ride. Betto was so drunk that he could not mount after getting into the fields. I got away from houses. Crossing a paddy field came to a ditch without a bridge and in dismounting to lead my horse across jumped into the soft mud. Betto got back a half hour after I did. I took away the clothes I had given him

and told him that I could not permit a drunken man to wear my crest! in the street. His wife and all the servants are anxious lest I should discharge him. Drunkenness is the national vice and it is in vain to expect complete sobriety of all, and useless to dismiss a servant for drunkenness unless his habit becomes troublesome. A new one might be just as bad.

Wednesday, August 29, 1860

Writing till dinner, after dinner made an excursion for plants and found several new varieties. My walk led me to the little lake beyond the American Consul's. Dined at the Consul's in the evening with Dr. S[immons]. After dining we enjoyed the delicious moonlight till a late hour. Troy[79] was under the trees near the flag staff playing the clarionet. The night was radiant with beauty. When the moonbeams fell on the long rushes that lay on the steep hill side there seemed a cascade of waters falling down the hill. The trees on the top of the hill stood out boldly against the sky. A soft wind stirred the leaves and we could hear the lap of the light surf on the beach not far off and see the glimmer of the beams on the bay. So sitting and enjoying ourselves till midnight we started out to give the Jobootsogi [Jobutsuji] ladies [Mrs. Hepburn, Mrs. Brown, Miss Brown, and Caroline Adrian] a serenade. We stopped on our way at the Honjin to send some officials after the General's runaway servants and then made our way through the streets and closed gate into the rear of the Jobootsogi temple. Following the narrow paths among the grain and pulse we came to the low hedge of the garden enclosure and walking softly found the gate through the short evergreen hedge near the house open. This gave us access to the friendly [cover?] of a pomegranate tree where we should be unobserved. Troy then woke the night with his sweet music. The noise of sliding shutters told us the house was aroused. Creeping out unobserved we followed round to the old Bell House in the compound yard and ser-

[79] Joseph Heco wrote in his diary on March 1, 1861: "My old friend, Thomas Troy, turned up in Yokohama, and I was delighted to employ him as my clerk." See Joseph Heco, *Narrative of a Japanese*, vol. 1, p. 277. Troy later served as a member of Dent and Company. See *China Directory* (1863), p. 55.

enaded the H[epburn]s. We were leaving when Miss B[rown] came out and asked us in to take some refreshments in the piazza. We were only too happy to comply and spent a pleasant half hour in the moonlit piazza or the hedge surrounded enclosure. It was a night to be remembered.

Thursday, August 30, 1860

Today commences a three day holiday time. Next to the New Year holidays these are the most important. As at New Years, accounts are settled up among all classes of business men. During the three days the people abstain from fish. They are Buddhist holidays. On the three days all abstain from work who have living parents, those who have one parent alive abstain on the 2nd and 3rd day and those who have no parents living rest on the last day of the three. The graveyards have all been cleaned and put in order. Last night paper was burnt before the house doors in the belief that thus the spirits of deceased friends would visit them. Today likewise for the same reason paper and joss sticks are burned in the graveyard.

Friday, August 31, 1860

Groups of well dressed women and children are in the street today paying visits to the tombs of their ancestors, adorning the graves with green branches and flowers. As Dr. and Mrs. H[epburn] were returning from the landing just at dark they were followed by a man evidently drunk who persisted in taking hold of Mrs. H[epburn]'s oildress. He was rebuked and struck by the officer attending, but did not desist for after they had turned into the street leading to the house he came up unperceived from behind and dealt Mrs. H[epburn] a heavy blow with a stick or pole that he carried in his hand and escaped.

Mr. L. of Yokohama has a little boy six years old. He was discovered to be missing last evening and after several hours search was found at the Gankiro in care of the girls who had petted him, fed him, and adorned his person with bonbons and gifts. It was touching to see the little fellow among the depraved girls who were, in their care of him, acting the true instincts of their nature. But the Japanese always show a fondness for foreign children. The young of all animals are pets.

Saturday, September 1, 1860

Today is famous in the annals of western civilization on the shores of Japan as inaugurating the first horse race. The foreign citizens according to programme held the Yokohama races 1st season on a spot of ground prepared near the Bluffs. It was a half mile course on a firm sandy bottom. Its situation was picturesque. Bordering the home stretch were the undulating hills of the bluff covered with profuse vegetation. On the other sides were the green vegetation of the plain and the town of Yokohama. The course was marked off by posts and ropes. A judge's stand, and stand for the spectators was erected, which was filled with foreign population. Numerous entries were made. The contest was amusing at the least. There was running and trotting. Some horses would not go at all, others went where their riders did not wish them to go, and riders went where they did not wish to go. The animal showed his native stubbornness to the full. Several gentlemen were unhorsed but fortunately nobody hurt. A Hurdle race was the most exciting in which interpreter Bleckman's horse shied the track and pitched his master into the field.

Sunday, September 2, 1860

Services at Yokohama. Sitting in my room at home before sunset a package of home letters just arrived was put into my hand. They could not have come at a more welcome time. Letters always acceptable are doubly so in the quiet of a Sabbath day.

Monday, September 3, 1860

We have a little news of Allied successes on the Peiho and other news of English and French atrocities at Shanghai. Capt. McC.[80] of the *Moneka* saw a body of French soldiers attack the Chinese quarter without provocation. He saw them enter a room where a man lay asleep and shot him in cold blood; he saw them enter another room where a man was cooking rice and they disemboweled him with their sword bayonettes as he stooped before the fire. Such are the refinements of *civilized warfare* at which barbarianism might blush. The English in their turn committed a gross and wanton attack on some rebel shipping near Ningpo with whom they had no quarrel.

Tuesday, September 4, 1860

Our last news from the States is that the Embassy are either so frightened and disgusted that they refuse to visit any further places or desire to return home as speedily as possible. We do not sympathize much with the Japanese when we remember the insults and injuries that have been inflicted upon foreigners in Japan and allowed to pass unpunished. The civilities bestowed so superabundantly upon them are in marked contrast to the cold politeness and civility extended through fear of us, shown by the Japanese at home. We know just what heartless souls are concealed under the smooth exteriors of this people.

Took the longest ride of any I have hither to had into the country. An elevated hill gave me a perfect command of a landscape at once grand and beautiful. Great vallies that hid away among hills, woods crowned the heights and mountain ranges closed in the background. Our ride was so extended that Mr. N[evius] and myself were overtaken by night before we reached home. Before the farm cottages we frequently saw the women performing their ablutions close by the roadside. Knowing no shame because they were unclothed. One, as if not sufficiently conspicuous,

was taking her bath on a spot elevated several feet where she stood as nude but less graceful than the Venus in her charms.

Wednesday, September 5, 1860

Made one of a chowder party today. Five of us took a large boat from Yokohama manned with six sculls. We were provisioned with all the materials necessary for a Chowder, cold meats besides, and as we were putting off S——s with his usual propensity for melons darted ashore but soon reappeared again with a huge melon under each arm, which he added to our basket full of muskmelons already aboard. Looking over our stores and making the roll call of chicken, bread, salt, pepper, butter, pork, potatoes etc., a steady aye aye from some one of the party was answered. There were several suspicious bottles with slender necks and one pretentious jug that had somehow got aboard and no one stood sponsor for them. And when a demijohn was produced we each and all thought that the jolly god Bacchus himself must have stowed in the hold if tall B——n had not asservated [it] was only a supply of water against some unforeseen emergency. An assertion that he immediately proved by making a lemon colored mixture from the contents of the jug and demijohn united.

The wind in skipper's phrase was dead ahead so we sculled out of the harbor and skirted the shore toward the Treaty Point. Time was beguiled with books, pictures, and songs. Not over confident in our fish hooks we pulled for the fishing boats in the bay. Out of a fish reservoir, a huge basket anchored by the fishermen in which to keep their fishing spoils for market, we caught with an ichibu's silver hook the finest fish I have seen—a noble *akai tai* (red tye). So all our elements for a chowder were now safe and we abandoned ourselves to the carelessness of quiet winds. Few hours sculling brought us to Mississippi Bay which we crossed in another hour and made a landing in the shady cove which we at once christened "Chowder Bight." There was a broad sand beach littered with shells. A small stream of fresh water ran out of a narrow valley that ex-

---

[80] This was Capt. McCaslin, whose full name is mentioned in the entry of September 12, 1860.

tended inland. On one bank of the stream was a bold bluff, on the other a sloping hill crowned with pines.

It was a choice spot and we unloaded our stores and the boatmen's rice kettle and furnace. The boatmen speedily confined themselves to sleep on the sands. B——s and B——n tried their fishing lines in the streams. I left S——s chatting with A———n on the grassy bank while I, having first gathered my hat full of shells, started up the carina to search for plants. I followed the little stream to where a long slope led to form the neighboring hill at right angles. I crossed the stream [and] ascended the slope through fields and thickets of bamboo grass and bushes to the summit. There I had a panorama of the Bay of Yedo before me, its smooth lake-like surface and winding shores were more picturesque than usual in the uncommon transparency of the atmosphere. A transparency in which the distant mountains came near and which in this East is said to betoken a gale. There were windy paths on the summit of the hill to which I had clambered. One of them led to a grove where at the foot of an aged and immense pine tree a stone idol was set up cut in alt relief in the surface of a flat stone, its base was surrounded by pebbles brought thither by those too poor to offer anything else.

I spent a pleasant half hour on this hill, alone, in the heart of Nippon enjoying the freshness and beauty of nature about me. I filled my hands with new ferns and plants and returned to my comrades whom I found sheltered in the grass by the shore enjoying their repose. So I again started and followed the shore along vaulting cliffs of soft sandstone overhung with vines to where a number of Japanese men [were] engaged in getting timber aboard some boats. They were very curious to see my pistol, which they handled with great fear lest it should go off and kill them unaware. The respect for the foreign revolvers is only second to the respect for the *Ty sho* [shogun]. I plucked from the cliffs some ferns more beautiful than any I had hitherto gathered in Japan among which were some creeping ferns. The tide was rising over the beach and the shelving sandstone and I returned to "Chowder Bight."

Pistol practice amused us for awhile, empty bottles were shot and trees were riddled and finally an exchange of shots at each other's hats was agreed upon when some chaps and felt hats were so perforated that the owners might congratulate themselves that their heads were not inside of them. On our landing we had buried our bottles of potables in the wet sand of the rivulet's bottom and corralled our melons in a dam of sand and rushes to keep them cool. A round water melon became the next target and was riven and splat in all directions. When the sport grew wearisome, adventurous jumps across the stream where it had collected in a broad pool were attempted. Jumps were short and jumpers landed in the water. There was then a show of soaking shoes and stockings splashed and dripping trousers, and muddied unexpressibles before this was done with.

Now a fire was kindled under the boatmen's kettle and the chowder put in preparation. Onion so mild as to bring hardly a tear was sliced with new potatoes, bits of salt pork and fresh fish, the royal tye, were side by side. These were placed in the fishermen's kettle in concentric layers with bread, seasoned with pepper, flavored with wine and a dish steaming hot and savory was soon ready. The kettle was laid on the grass and with cups, plates, and clamshells for spoons we began our repast. B——s was bathing when the meal began but so savory was its aroma that he rushed from the salt waves, made a hasty toilet with his shirt, and sat in the grass sans culotte to share the enjoyment. Natives gathered from the country to witness the scene. We assigned the farther side of the stream as the bounds to their approach, where, squatted on the grass, they for the first time saw *tojins* dine.

What a banquet we had on this spread of the grass with the whispering pine leaves for our tent hangings and the boom of the surf for our orchestra. Rapidly disappeared the chowder. The group was a scene for an artist. B——n lay on his elbow as if at a Roman banquet under a pine by himself. B——s in his cool dress and bare limbs, squatted among the tall grass on the brink of the bank, A——n had a trunk to himself, H. sat on a stone propped against a tree, S——s sat in the grass with legs outstretched and wide apart the open space covered with fragments of a watermelon he was intent upon devouring. With his plethoric firm round face and broad brimmed hat he was the model for a bon vivant. A priest who had come out of a temple not far away came in his flowing black robe and beads on his wrist to see who were in his domain. We offered him a glass of claret which he tasted and declared delightful, we urged him to drink it up, it is not Japanese etiquette to decline and he gulched it down with wry faces at its acidity. The fragments of our feast, which were many, were given to the boatmen. The day which had been cloudless and serene drew to a close. Sport ended with the feast, we gathered our poles and lines, our revolvers, our spoils from the fields and shore of shells and flowers, cleaned our utensils in the brook, got aboard, weighed our pronged anchor, and just at sunset with a fresh following breeze shot out of the bay towards home. The evening was starry and cloudless, we gave our huge sail to the wind and sped rapidly over the waters. Fishing boats returning from a days labor crossed our tracks. On we sped by the starlight, till we made the lights of Yokohama. Here we landed most of our party and by the light of the new rising moon we crossed Yokohama Bay to Kanagawa and the day was done. I, a New Englander born, had eaten my first chowder in Japan.[81]

Thursday, September 6, 1860

Owing to long absence of rain the Japanese have begun to draw off the waters of their lakes or ponds to supply the moisture so necessary to the paddy fields. It is five years since they have done this.

Friday, September 7, 1860

The long needed rain falls today in copious showers. It will secure the rice crop and all Japan will rejoice.

---

[81] Unfortunately the context does not help us to identify those who accompanied Hall on this pleasant outing.

Saturday, September 8, 1860

Among the begging pilgrims of Japan is one class called *Rokoo Joo Rokoo* (66) because they take it upon themselves to visit each of the sixty six different provinces of this Empire. They consume about six years in this pilgrimage. Another class which are called *Ichi sen* (1000) pilgrims take the vow of visiting 1000 different temples, the principal ones of the Empire.

The Japanese have a saying "Whether is it better to have a new roof to one's house, new mats to the floor, new clothes for the body, or a new wife." The choice of wisdom is said to be that of a new wife.

Sunday, September 9, 1860

I was awakened before light this morning by the roar of a tempest without. It was the beginning of one of those typhoon storms that belong to these latitudes. The rain fell in a deluge of water and the vehemence of the gale was such as to endanger the safety of crops and dwellings. The storm increased in violence as the morning advanced, the barometer rapidly falling. Wind from the N.E. From daylight till noon without was a scene of wild uproar. The blasts came in gusts with the suddenness, force, and roar of artillery. Shingles were flying from roofs, trees were going down and even houses all but fell before the fury of the blast. Our kitchen was partly unroofed and wholly deluged with water. About noon S[immons] and myself putting on some old clothes went out to see the wreck of the tempest. The rain beat our faces stinging like hail so that we were obliged to protect them. The creek that flows through Kanagawa had over flowed its banks and submerged the floors of many houses. We waded through our street where the water was flowing along nearly leg deep. In the middle of the flood we met a girl, a woman grown, wading like ourselves, with her dress gathered about her hips. She gave us merry greetings and kept on her way. Our cottage was a complete wreck. In B[rown]'s temple, several of the inmates were driven out of their beds by the rain that seemed to penetrate everywhere without resistance. We anticipated hearing of much destruction in Yokohama. The injury to the rice crop in this vicinity must be very great. The storm lulled at noon and at evening a dead calm reigned.

Of marriage customs I hear, that when a husband loses his wife it is considered the most proper thing not to marry again and men of the best stamp ever after lead a single life. If a daimio loses his wife he may take another if he chooses, but if he dies his wife may never more marry. She shaves her head like a priest and lives on as unwedded wife. His concubines go back to their families or take husbands if they like.

Burial customs differ with different religious sects. The Buddhists wash the dead body and dress it [in] white clothes. Before burial prayers are recited before it, fires are lighted and rice is placed on a tray. If the family is able to bear the expense the body is first placed in a box of Paulownia wood handsomely finished and this box is again placed in another of unpainted pine. The body is dressed in white and with the lower classes the head is shaved, with the upper it is not. The body is seated with legs crossed and hands lifted and joined together as if in the act of supplication. A rosary hangs from the wrist. Prayers are written on paper and deposited with the dead and 6 (six) copper *moong* [*mon*] to pay the admission fee to the regions of *Amida's* blest. For they believe in a good and bad place hereafter. A dignitary has his swords placed with him in the coffin. Here the dead are born to the place of sepulture, I have before described. The priest preceding the coffin with beads and muttered prayers, the family friends bearing lanterns and dragonheaded wands with paper streamers, an offering of rice cake borne sometimes by a girl clad in white, and mourners following clad also in white garments.

Capital punishment is inflicted for many offences. The murderer is bound to a crucifix and after that a spear is thrust entering at either armpit and coming out either side of the neck. Each armpit having been pierced another is thrust through the neck from shoulder to shoulder. The thief may be bound or have his head cut off. The man who commits arson is bound to a crucifix and is burned to death by lighted faggots placed around him.

If a husband detects his wife in criminal intercourse he may slay her and her paramour as I have before mentioned. Unless he witnesses the offence he may threaten death but not commit it. A third party is called in who imposes a penalty in way of a fine or administers a harsh reprimand and the wife may be put away. If a man's daughter is seduced away the parent may banish her from his house or if the man is unmarried demand him to marry her, or seek a small pecuniary compensation or rebuke him in words, but there seems to be no grave punishment for the offence. The banished daughter may become a *Joroya*, a house servant, or be received by her seducer.

Monday, September 10, 1860

The havoc of yesterday's storm is visible at Yokohama, where roofs were blown off, houses wrecked, boats driven ashore or sunk and a general destruction of property. The Schooner *Nankin* was driven ashore but got off again today without damage. One large junk was driven ashore and sunk and many cargo, passenger, and fishing boats were stove on the beach whither they were driven and sunk. In the foreign quarter a dozen godowns were blown over and many more injured. Several of these were new fire proof warehouses, supposed to be proof not only against fire but the other elements. Large amounts of valuable foreign and Japanese goods were stored in these such as Manchester goods, drills, muslins, and native raw silks and tea. The loss to the foreign population is estimated at $100,000. The rain falling with such force and abundance penetrated the hard finish chunam covering of the warehouses and the mud walls, so that many of them not wrecked have had their walls partially dissolved as it were. The foreign residences were in like manner inundated, the frail mud walls offering little resistance to the penetrating storm, so that the families were driven out of the windward side of their dwellings. Amid all this wreck the only loss of life of which I hear is on our side of the bay where a man was killed by the crumbling of a cliff under which he was washing his rice at some spring. Among the native population of Yokohama the loss also has been great.

Tuesday, September 11, 1860

A conversation with Sadajirō modifies what I have written about burial customs. Shaving the head is a matter of choice, there is no fixed rule. One coffin is used by common and poor people, wealthy people two or more. A Daimio has five, one within the other, the Emperor's fixed number is seven. The higher classes are placed at full length as I have elsewhere stated. A man of rank is dressed in his *Kamissimo*, or the flowing trousers belonging to his station. Two swords are placed within made of wood. His real swords are sometimes placed on the outside. Formerly these trappings were perquisites of the priests and are so understood now, but money is received universally instead. So among the lower classes money is paid that the grave clothes may be retained. Formerly it was the custom when a girl was buried to inter her with many garments laid in the coffin, but they were so universally stolen by the priests, who would dig the graves for them, that the custom has fallen into disuse. Nor is it now the custom, as anciently, to place money itself in the coffin but so many bits of paper representing the money. This money is to pay ferriage across the River of Death that divides this world from the next—the Styx of the Ancients.

The common people say the late gale was owing to the attempt of foreigners to ascend Fusi, last year's gale was because of the admission of foreigners to Japan, and why said a questioner were gales of previous years, "Oh because the Kami knew foreigners would come."

Wednesday, September 12, 1860

The completeness and minuteness of the espionage in Japan is something astonishing. Every article of food that we buy for our daily consumption is reported at the *Honjin* by the purveyor, so of every other purchase. I doubt not we are thoroughly observed in all our ways from morning till night. If we cross the ferry to Yokohama one of the boathouse men reports us on bended knee to his superior after forcing his head against the broken stone that forms the pave in front.

For the first time a vessel is preparing to leave the Bay in ballast unable to obtain cargo. The *Moneka* Capt. McCaslin, the consignee, applied to the Custom House authorities for stone ballast which they at first refused, they could not allow the soil of Japan to be carried away, at any rate without leave from higher authorities!

Sad disasters from the late gales are reported involving the loss of several vessels and many lives. What of the reports are true and what are false it is impossible to say. The Prussian steamer that arrived here nearly two weeks since, when about half way from Shanghai encountered a heavy gale. She was towing a yacht designed as a present for the Tycoon. In the gale the hawser parted and that is the last that has been seen or heard of the yacht and her burden of thirty souls. In the gale of last Sunday a Japanese bark was driven ashore at Shimoda and out of the fifty five souls only five or six were saved. Third, the wreck of a ship is seen on Cape Idsu and another vessel still is reported missing. The passage from China to this port bids fair to become the grave of many a mariner.

Thursday, September 13, 1860

After many decisions and changes Mr. S[immons] and wife have concluded to accept my proposal to leave my present temple and go to Yokohama. I contemplate the change with no satisfaction. I shall leave my delightful house which I was enjoying so much with exceeding regret. My desire to compensate Mrs. H[epburn] for her kindness to me by relieving her of the care of S[immons] and wife is my only motive for the change.[82]

[82] It appears that there was some friction between Mrs. Hepburn and Dr. and Mrs. Simmons. Mrs. Simmons had been brought up as a Unitarian and consequently did not share the strict Calvinist attitudes of the Hepburns. She led an active social life, which included dancing and playing cards with other members of the

Friday, September 14, 1860

Busy endeavoring to get ready to leave Kanagawa, I find it difficult getting a place to my liking at Yokohama but I shall persevere if success is attainable.

Is the Mikado worshipped? The Mikado is regarded by the people of Japan as above all kami's, he is the brother of the sun, moon, and stars, and their superior. His prayers to the heavens will bring rain or drought, heat or cold, fruitful seasons and health. They are inclined to worship him, but the officials of the Empire forbid it. Yearly at Miaco some sort of homage is paid to the symbols of his power, viz., the mirror, the sword, his seal. The former is an emblem of purity, and of the clearness with which all faults are beheld, the S[word] is emblematic of justice, and the third is the royal approbation and the seal of his unbroken descent of family. Yearly he is drawn through the streets of his capital in his magnificent ox cart. At such times the men crouch to the earth and the women kneel on their mats within doors, and the people, if permitted, would recite the changeless trisyllabic prayer of the Priests *Namida Namida* [*namu amida*] but that an officer precedes the cortege to forbid it. The Mikado worships Heaven. The old story of his motionless position on the throne for hours lest the affairs of the world go amiss is now, as it has always been, a fable.

Today tall bamboo poles erected in the streets proclaim that the Princely Kami whose name they bear on a tablet affixed will sleep tonight at Kanagawa. Tomorrow is the annual gathering of all the Daimios to pay their respects to the Emperor on the anniversary of his ascent to the throne. Gifts will be presented by all, gifts of the obang (the great coins of gold), articles of gold, down to the humble tempo of the Daimio's servants, for all must share in the royal present making.

Saturday, September 15, 1860

Morning at Yokohama looking up new quarters. Look around also among the shops but find it difficult to make purchases so long as a dollar is worth but two ichibus. In the afternoon on the hill above the temple collecting grasses and seeds. My occupation attracts some attention from the people and children, who seem to wonder what I want of such trash. Six little girls eight to ten years old followed me, four of them carrying double.

Sunday, September 16, 1860

The *Berenice* returned last night bringing back the Fusi Yama party. Mr. Alcock and two of his suite remained at the Springs of Atami. I hear generally the trip was both successful and delightful but no particulars as yet.

---

treaty port community. These activities were regarded as "worldly" by the older missionaries. When she returned to the United States on June 16, 1860, to look after an ill parent, Hepburn wrote home, "Her heart is not in the missionary work." Dr. Simmons was also criticized by Dr. Hepburn, especially for accepting pay for his medical services from the residents of Yokohama (Takaya, *The Letters of Dr. J. C. Hepburn*, p 32). Simmons left the [Dutch] Reformed Board in 1860 and became a private physician in Yokohama. In 1862 he sold his house, auctioned his household effects, and returned to the board the entire sum it had spent to send him to Japan. Brown noted that Mrs. Simmons disliked Japan and urged her husband to return. Simmons left Japan for the United States on September 3, 1864, but he later returned to Japan and spent much of the remainder of his life in Tokyo until his death in 1889. See letter from S. R. Brown to Philip Peltz dated November 8, 1862, in Michio Takaya, *S. R. Brown shokan shū* (Tokyo:

Nihon kirisutō kyōdan shuppan kyoku, 1980), p. 110. For an obituary of Dr. Simmons see *The Japan Weekly Mail*, February 23, 1898, p. 179. Earlier Hepburn had written that, despite the servants, "my wife has still a pretty heavy burden of household care on her, more than she is well able to bear. We have Mr. Brown, Dr. Simmons & Mr. Hall of the Dutch Society eating with us" (Takaya, *The Letters of Dr. J. C. Hepburn*, pp. 22–23). It seems strange that Dr. and Mrs. Simmons, who lived with Hall at the Sōkōji, should remain under the "care" of Mrs. Hepburn. Hall, for his part, was extremely grateful to Dr. and Mrs. Hepburn, and many years later left her a bequest of $1,000 "in grateful recognition of their friendship and kindness while I was resident in Japan." See "The Will of Francis Hall," File # 3006, in Chemung County (N.Y.) Surrogate Court, Elmira, New York. At the time of this entry Mrs. Simmons had already left for the United States.

Monday, September 17, 1860

Agreed with Boyd[83] today to take the premises at Yokohama—paying him $50 for privilege and improvements.

The care assigned for blacking the teeth and plucking the eyebrows of married women is that [it] is a mark and seal of their loyalty and devotion to their husbands. The male servants of the Mikado are likewise said to blacken their teeth to signify their loyalty to him.

Tuesday, September 18, 1860

Among the polite accomplishments of the ladies of Nippon are painting, flower and screen painting, fan painting, needle work and embroidery—a young lady is not accomplished that cannot make up her own garments—and the art of arranging and preserving flowers. I took some tomatoes around to Yangaro's today as they are a novelty in Japan and in return his mother and pretty wife must bring me some handsome flowers. The old lady took occasion to tell me that she had been carefully taught how to cultivate flowers, how to arrange them tastefully in vases, and how to doctor the water they were placed in so as to prevent the leaves from falling away or the petals withering. There were treatises she told me on the proper medicine for every kind of plant. The old lady had an evident pride in her knowledge on this issue. Her back parlor is a model of good housekeeping. I always have to apologize for intruding upon them with my shoes, but she waives all apologies. A common ornamentation of Japanese houses was here, a scroll hanging on the wall in a little recess sunk a foot or more from the plain surface of one side of the room. It represented a female deity of pleasant face attired in flowing robes of silk attended by two young girls bearing salvers in their hands of fruit and flowers. The livening of the features, the drapery of the garments, and particularly the coloring was highly creditable to the artist. On a stand in front of the picture was an antique vase of bronze in which were branches of the Japanese larch. In good houses of merchants or farmers this arrangement is often seen and before the picture homage is paid. In contrast with so much refinement was the reply made by mother and wife when I called and inquired for the husband who was temporarily absent. The reply so illustrative of Nippon manners I cannot repeat here in English. (*Yangaro Chōdsu surimas*).[84] Y[angaro]'s wife before she plucked her eyebrows or blackened teeth was a Nipponese beauty. She is of a gay lively turn, is always becomingly dressed, though I suspect she is fully conscious that her full bust is both fairer and handsomer than the generality of her sisterhood's, or she would not be so prodigal in its display.

Wednesday, September 19, 1860

The returned party from Fusi Yama reported the best of treatment everywhere on the road. The ascent required ten hours and was somewhat toilsome the path laying over the scoriae and cinders of former irruptions. From base to summit were fourteen houses of rest. There was but little snow on the summit and that had just fallen. The thermometer stood 58° in the sun. The circumference of the crater was two miles, its long diameter being 1500 yards and its short diameter 600—depth 800 yards. There was a spring of water near the summit. The height of this extinct volcano is 13,900 feet, another peak has an altitude of a little over 14,000. The scenery on the route is spoken of as exceedingly beautiful in its varied expression, while the view from the summit is not surpassed by any mountain view in the world if equalled.

---

[83] This may have been F. E. Boyd. The location of Simmons's and Hall's new Yokohama residence is clearly indicated on Simmons's map now in the possession of the Yokohama Archives of History. This map shows that Hall and Simmons lived in one corner of the Customs House complex that faced the wharf. This corner location backed on the Custom House compound, but did not have direct access to it. See Maruya Tokuzo, *Gokaikō Yokohama dai ezu* (Edo: Hōzendō, 1860) in Yokohama Archives of History (cover bears the initials D.B.S.).

[84] "Yangaro is on the toilet."

Thursday, September 20, 1860

Storm, stayed at home and busy with letters. We are in for a long equinoctial.

Friday, September 21, 1860

Still the rain comes incessantly. No walking, no riding. No crossing the bay, but a dull staying at home shut in by leaden clouds that impart their hue to everything around them. What an equinox is this! Dined at the Consul's where I met Mr. Gower,[85] one of the Fusi Yama party. He expresses great delight with his trip and showed me some fair pencil sketches. The party were all mounted but Eusden who went in a *norimon*. They met nothing but kindness from the people on the route. Forty or fifty miles from Kanagawa they passed over Mount Hiacone (?) where near its summit they found a lake fifteen miles (?) in extent, 6,ooo (?) feet above the level of the sea (?).[86] The stream of ——— [Saki gawa] they crossed on men's shoulders as usual with travellers. Intelligence of their coming had preceded them and everywhere the tea houses, the customary halting places of the Daimios, were ready for their sole use. The [party] reached Mount Fusi after six days travel. They describe it as a solitary cone, densely wooded at its base, with an ascent made difficult by the scoriae and cinders of the extinct volcano. A spur, a mountain of itself, shoots up from one side. The recent heavy rains had cut up the path but in anticipation of this visit they had again been repaired. The crater has a long diameter of 11oo yds, short diameter of 6oo, a depression of about the same. Its height above the sea level was 13,99o feet. One cone on the crater's edge was nearly a hundred feet higher. A spring and small pond of fresh water was found near the summit. From the summit was a magnificent prospect. Seaward Oho Shima, or Volcano Island, the Broken Isles, Rock Island, and other islands of the coast were in view, while landward drift away to sides and rear a magnificent country of hill and vale. Apparently nearly across the island of Nippon other peaks were seen rising in altitude with matchless Fusi. Ten hours accomplished the ascent, which was rendered toilsome by the loose cinders and lava.

Saturday, September 22, 1860

I learn today that I can have a passage to Hakodade [Hakodate] on the *Berenice* if I provide my own bedding. This is soon provided for. I have a Japanese mat made for my berth, and a sheet comfortable and my shawl with carpet bag for a pillow suffice for the rest.

There is a village school in the compound just across the street whose noisy hum of children reading, and louder strains of children singing I have often heard the summer past. Today I paid the school a visit. The school was in a one story brown house with shingle roof. The teacher, a shaven headed doctor, was outside varnishing or oiling some paper umbrellas set out to dry in the sun. He was completely nude save the loin cloth. He seemed to my eyes hardly a model for a school master of one of our High Schools. Just at the door was a stand for the deposit of umbrellas and sun shades, and at the door numberless wooden clogs betokened that school was in.

I entered the door without ceremony and found myself at once in the school room, a large open room with smoke begrimed walls and paper windows and mat floors. In an instant a hundred black eyes from under as many darky foreheads overshadowed with black hair were fixed upon me. The glances were from the fifty scholars seated at their low

---

[85] The first ascent of Mount Fuji by a party of Westerners was made by Sir Rutherford Alcock on September 11–12, 186o, and the journey up the mountain is described in his *Capital of the Tycoon*, vol. 1, pp. 395ff. S. J. Gower accompanied the party and made a number of sketches, some of which were reproduced in Alcock's volume. Edward Barrington de Fonblanque was also one of the climbers and the trek up Fuji is discussed in his *Niphon and Pe-che-li*, pp. 147–63. Gower later worked for Jardine Matheson & Co. in Yokohama. Like others living in Yokohama, Hall also dreamed of climbing Mount Fuji, but treaty limits on travel in the interior prevented him from doing so.

[86] Question marks are in the original text.

desks on the mats astonished at the stranger's intrusion. Study was arrested, copy books shoved aside, and at least 1/2 of the school were immediately on their feet. Aroused by the stir, the school mistress, for most Japanese schools have their male and female teachers, came out from an inner room to see what occasioned the unusual disturbance. She was a sedate looking woman of forty years or so, the saturnine expression of her countenance heightened by the somber color of her garments and her blackened teeth. I thought of Shenstone's schoolmistress,[87] perhaps because the contrast was so great. The naked master came in also from his out doors occupation to bid the boys again to their tasks and restore order. I told him as well as I could in my imperfect Japanese that I had to "visit" the school. The boys and girls were not easily restrained. Though at the master's reproof they took their places again, yet first one and then another would rise on tiptoe and with mischievous smiles and glances were not to be balked of their curiosity.

The boys and girls were together, but there was a little room apart where the mistress had her select class of girls by themselves. These came out into the main room to see what was astir. I had my music box with me and asked permission to play it for the children's benefit. The permission was readily given, for the teachers were just as curious about this as the scholars. When I wound it up and started it order was immediately at end. The school was fairly disorganized. The children crowded around piling over each others shoulders to get nearer. Their efforts to see and hear quite prevented for a while the latter. The nude preceptor called them to order, the urchins would subside for a moment only to break into a fresh uproar. One or two little youngsters were crying lustily because they could not see for the "big boys." It was not till the master became angry and menaced with imperious tone and gestures that anything like order was restored. The children were delighted with the curious toy and it played for them to their full satisfaction.

Closing my musical entertainment I entered the "ladies department." The mistress, who was a stoutish dame of forty years or so, received me graciously. I looked about the room to see how it compared with a young ladies seminary at home. There were no globes, maps, or blackboard, for school appliances were few. Several *Samisen* hung against the wall, in one corner there was a cupboard where the girls could put their little bundles, copy books, the dinners they brought etc. A shining copper boiler filled with water was bubbling over the fire of charcoal to supply the indispensable tea or simple hot water for drinks. There was a little piazza just without the room where the girls had their umbrella stand and several pots of plants stood by an open window. I squatted down on the mats by the old lady's side and begged the favor of hearing some music from her pupils. Quite after the honor, she responded by calling out the name of one of her girls. In answer to the call a little girl came in from the outer room, a young child of unkempt hair, disordered dress, and dirty fingers. Her feet were bare and soiled to blackness with the dirt of the streets. A drop of nature's jewelry trembled at the tip of her nose. She was modest with us and came timidly into the room and seated herself on the mat opposite the mistress. I asked her age and she gave it as nine years. No doubt the young musical prodigy of the school had been selected to astonish and entertain me. There was the usual delay of getting ready common with young female debutantes, and while the mistress was tuning her *Samisen* the little girl was uneasily fidgeting, several of the other girls came into the room and kneeling down asked some favor of the mistress. It was too evidently only an excuse to come in to see what was going on. After giving what appeared to be words of direction to her little pupil the mistress began a tune which the little girl accompanied with her voice. It was a long song about the winds and the flowers and the blossoming cherry trees and had little of music in it to my ear. To the Japanese the young singer might have been an incipient Mali-

---

[87] William Shenstone (1714–1763) wrote in *The Schoolmistress*, 1737, stanza 6. "Her cap, far whiter than the driven snow,/Emblems right meet of decency does yield."

bran,[88] to me she was a fabricator of harsh sounds. The first one of other young singers.

I thanked the lady for her music, bows were exchanged and I left the female department for the main room. Here school was nearly out. The children were passing in their copy books to the oldest of the girls who seemed to be a sort of mistress for she examined the exercises as she laid them one by one in a drawer. A large firm looking lad was assisting her and they exchanged many smiles and glances, a school girl flirtation no doubt as they leaned across the low desks to speak to each other. Now the young mistress takes her stand by the side of the nude preceptor, a queer juxtaposition of the girl, and the children come up one by one to take leave. It is clear that the girl has the thread of their fate in her hands for she appears to report to the master as each one comes up, the boy makes a low bow to his preceptor and goes out with his bundle wrapped up in cloth for home. So one by one they take a bowing leave as I have a hundred times seen in our own district schools. There pupils frequently came long distances to the schools, which are dismissed always early in the afternoon. I found myself among a group of the youngsters going home. They recognized me with smiles of good nature. A boy not more than eleven years old wearing his two swords passed by. There was no recognition of his humble companions, who eyed him askant, as he walked through them with gravity becoming the son of some man of rank.

Sunday, September 23, 1860

Went aboard the *Berenice* this evening with Dr. H[epburn] taking our beds and bedding for the voyage to Hakodade.[89] The captain was not aboard and the officer of the deck had no instructions in regard to passengers and we were obliged to wait until the Capt. came off from the shore about midnight. We got under the deck awnings until a shower drove us below, and eked out the miserable hours of waiting as best we could. The Capt.'s coming relieved us and his frank cordial manner at once assured us that we had fallen into good hands. We had had some Japanese mats made on shore to fit our berths and covering these with comfortables and blankets we were made comfortable ourselves. Dr. H[epburn] and myself had a large room to ourselves and anticipated a pleasant voyage before us.

Monday, September 24, 1860

We were under weigh at 8 A.M. The morning was fair on the bay, but to the southward dark sullen masses of clouds overhung the waters and it was not without anxiety that we headed towards them. It was the typhoon season, and we knew by experience what that meant and what dangers of storm and wreck were hid in its inner regions. Late disasters on the coast did not serve to dispel one's dread of encountering one of these tempests. The clouds lifted however as we approached them, and a rainy morning gave way to a clear day and an unusual transparency of the atmosphere in which the shores of the gulf were distinctly visible. Hodowara and its batteries that guard the narrowing channel of Uraga were in plain sight as we turned a pivot and there appeared the deep-set bay of Uraga, where a large fleet of junks were lying at anchor. The shores were bristling with cannon for in this pass are the outer defenses of the bay of Yedo, and it is here that Perry made his first halt in his progress towards the capital. The cultivated fields, the terraced hills and the dark cypress groves looked charmingly in the bright sunshine for the day had turned out to be one of "the perfect days."

The *Berenice* is an old steamer of the East India Co. navy. She has been in commission twenty five years, is still a staunch tight old ship using her original engines with one renewal of boilers made a couple of years since.

---

[88] Maria Felicita Malibran (1808–1836) was a contralto renowned for her opera performances in Europe and the United States. Her father was the well-known Spanish tenor Manuel Del Popolo Vincente.

[89] For J. C. Hepburn's description of the trip to Hokkaidō see his letter to Walter Lowrie dated "Steamer 'Berenice' Pacific Ocean, October 8, 1860," in Takaya, *The Letters of Dr. J. C. Hepburn*, pp. 35–40.

She is not fast, but what was better she inspired us with confidence in her seaworthiness, better than mere speed. Capt. R. had seen twenty years service in the Indian navy, and to good qualifications as a seaman added those of a gentleman and man of extended general intelligence. He had two native pilots on board who had experience on the coast. The gun brig *Camilla*[90] had been due a long time at Kanagawa and there were fears that she might be wrecked on the coast, so our pilots were particularly valuable, knowing as they did each headland and bay so that we could keep as close to the shore as possible.

Although the day had turned out so fair and to my inexperienced [eyes] and to most experienced ones as well there were not the slightest indications of foul weather, yet our pilots said we must run only till noon but lie by in a sheltered bay over night and not go outside till morning. Accordingly when we approached Cape Sagami about noon, instead of passing out into the Pacific, the *Berenice* was turned about into the bay to Tate Yama and dropped her anchor a little after twelve. If anything could make amends for this unpleasant detention it was that we were in such a beautiful spot. We had anchored inside of two rounded button like islands in deep water not far from the shores of the bay that swept around with a circumference of several miles. At the foot of low hills was a large village, and in whichever direction we looked were hamlets half hid in the luxuriant tree growth of these islands. The low cottages are for the most part detached, each nestling amid its own particular shrubbery. In the distance we could see the heavy roof of a temple lifting itself above the surrounding foliage. Great numbers of fishing boats on the shore indicated the occupation of the inhabitants. It was an era in the history of this pretty bay to have a steamer anchor in its waters and we were surrounded by boats from the shore bringing off the curious people. At least a thousand people were soon collected about us and were eager to come aboard. As they were crowding about us under bow and stern another boat came off bearing men in

authority dressed in robes laid off in red and white squares. They were the police of the village and at a word from [them] the crowd of boats fell back to a more respectful distance. These again were followed by officials from the shore who came off to inquire why we anchored here and if we wanted anything. They were civil and respectful throughout, but when they left us did not return to the shore but anchored themselves at a little distance as if to watch us. They were busy making notes all the time they were aboard of what they saw and heard. The boats of the villagers were forbid any further communication with the ship except to bring us some fresh fish. We whiled away the afternoon in watching the different groups in the boats making sketches of the beautiful scenery of the shores and the bay. As night came in the boats of the villagers left us, but two guard boats remained, one on each side of the ship, ostensibly as they said to keep the other boats from annoying us, but in reality to watch our movements.

It was a clear moonlight night, and if the bay, its islands of green, and the picturesque shores had been beautiful by day they had a strange beauty under the softer light of the night. Our crew partook of the influence of the scene and danced by moonlight on the open decks to the sound of the violin. Our crew was of mixed nationalities. Besides our white crew made up of all sea faring peoples we had Malays, Bengalese, Hindoos, half caste Portuguese, Mozambiques and Zanzibar negroes, and our Japanese pilots. I used to be interested in seeing them at their meals. The Musselmen have their own cookery separate from the rest. Each mess brought out is great pans of curried rice and meats and sitting on the decks dipped it out with their gathered fingers and conveyed it to their mouths. I learned there was a nack how to eat with ones fingers as well as with chop sticks or knives and forks. After the meal came a smoke. A water pipe made of burnt earthenware or bamboo was the favorite instrument for enjoying the after dinner smoke.

---

[90] The *Camilla* left Hakodate on September 2, 1860, and was never heard from again. She appears to have foundered in the typhoon of September 9. Some 130 men went down with her. See Rutherford Alcock, *The Capital of the Tycoon*, vol. 1, p. 421.

Tuesday, September 25, 1860

We weighed again and were under way at 6 A.M. and were soon outside of the heads of Capes Sagami and Susaki [Cape Sunosaki] and turned our bow to the eastward, coasting close to the shores till we had rounded Cape King [Cape Nojima] also and with bow turned to the north east were outside of Dai Nippon [Honshū] fairly on our way to Yeso [Hokkaidō]. But we met a heavy swell rolling in from the Pacific, which speedily sent me below with my old foe sea sickness at my heels. In the early part of the day the shore line was low mountains of exceedingly wrinkled and broken surface and sparsely covered with trees. The narrow breadth of soil between them and the water was thickly occupied by villages, where brown roofs made an almost uninterrupted line along the coast. Hundreds of fishing boats were dancing over the rough waters.

After passing Cape Tori-Yama [Katsuura] the aspect of the shore changed, the wrinkled hills were replaced by low lands scarcely discernible from the ship's deck. Later in the afternoon we passed the mouth of a large bay and made Cape Boi [Cape Inubo] at 6 P.M. near the mouth of a large river.

In the afternoon the ship's fire drill took place and some of us were startled, believing that it was real.

Wednesday, September 26, 1860

Thermometer 69°–71°.

In the morning passed *Koojee-Yama*, at noon were opposite *Utsu* [Ōtsu] in Lat. 37° by ship's observation. At 5 P.M. were abreast Arihama. Cape Kinko san [Cape Kinka-zan] the most easterly extremity of Nippon in sight thirty five miles distant.

The day [was] one of the loveliest of sea days. Land in the distance and again bold. Our pilots say it is one of the best rice districts of Japan. At 10 P.M. abreast Cape Kinko san.

Thursday, September 27, 1860

66°.

Last night was so brilliant with the light of the full moon that as I lay in my berth I could watch the changing shores in its beams through the window by my head. Was this not the romance of sea voyaging and was it strange that my eyes forbade slumber. The morning was as cool and delicious as the night had been bewitching. The mountains that guard the coast rise higher as we proceed northward. We are now on ground familiar to whalers and the quick eyes of the deck officers catch now and then the white spray of a blow. At 8 A.M. we have made Cape Tooni [Todo saki] and at 10 1/2 A.M. are off the coast of Nambu, a rich productive region with a large coastwise trade. It is the seat of Sendai, Mutsu-no-kami one of the very first of the Daimio in resources and revenues. There are not more than two or three his equals. Noon observation gave us Long. 142° 10' Lat. 39° 45'. Shores still mountainous and heavily wooded and weather delightful. At 5 P.M. we were opposite Hachinohe. By noon observation we were distant from Hakodade 180 miles. In the afternoon it clouded up and threatened rain. The wind, which had been blowing freshly all day from the S.W., shifted to the N.W. About noon we passed some very picturesque scenery. Bold banks rose perpendicularly from the water and from their summits spread inland a breadth of table land covered with groves interspersed with cultivated fields. Back of the table land were successively three ridges each towering above the other as they receded inland. Again this changed to a shore of bold rocky cliffs and again towards night subsided into low sloping banks like the alluvial shores of a river. Few villages visible today but much timber land. As very many pits were visible on shore which, as the country is so heavily wooded, I suspect were charcoal pits.

Friday, September 28, 1860

Last evening there was every indication of a storm, the clouds were gloomy and lowering, the barometer fell rapidly, and there was an ominous stillness in the air. A little before midnight we hove to and waited for daylight as the shores were too low and indistinct for our pilots to make out the essential headlands. All night there was a murky stillness in the atmosphere which caused us to fear an outbreak of the tempest. We were under weigh at 5 A.M. the wind then blowing fresh from the S.W. again, barometer low and sky threatening. Made the entrance to the Straits of Sangar [Tsugaru] in the middle of the forenoon with Cape Jerimo [Esan misaki] on the isle of Yeso in sight bearing East of North. As we entered the Straits the wind blew very fresh out of the N.W. and a strong tide and current running out our progress was very slow. A little after noon we passed the volcanic mountain of *Yake yama* ("Burning Mountain") [Mt. Esan?] from which occasional puffs of steam floated off into the clear atmosphere. The rim of the crater towards the sea was broken away and its reddened sides were plainly visible. The course of former lava streams flowing into the sea, and the paths cut by the devouring element through the forest sides were distinct through the pure atmosphere. We were now fairly within the straits, our staunch steamer battling nobly against wind, tide, and current. This current is that part of the gulf stream of this coast which flowing northeasterly is divided by the Islands of Japan and the western branch passing along the coast of Corea again reflects to the east through the Straits of Sangar. The dark blue waters turned their white caps in the face of the breeze, and the falling sunlight was shattered into ten thousands of jewels. Few passages can be more beautiful than this between the opposite shores of Yeso and Nippon with their bluff shores of living green. Slowly we approach the hilly promontory behind which lies the bay and city of Hakodade. There are few trees on the steep declivities, but here and there are paths through the green turf connecting the little fishing hamlets that everywhere skirt its base. Now we catch a glimpse of the conspicuous white buildings of the Russian Consulate, the masts of native shipping, and again they disappear. We sail every point of the compass before we reach the harbor's anchorage, the winding channel curling round precisely like the tail of the letter S. On a projecting point is a solitary battery of a few guns; we take a long sweep around it and

before us is the land locked harbor of Hakodade. As we entered the sun was sinking behind a black mass of clouds where a thunder shower was trailing along the hills out of which the lightning glowed and the rain fell into the mountain gorges. To add to the beauty of the sunset hour a full moon was rising on the opposite side of the heaven's sphere. The harbor was full of junks, but not a foreign flag was visible. "How like Gibraltar" exclaimed everyone that had seen that renowned fortress. "Here is the city on the promontory, the tongue of land that unites it with the main land, and yonder shores of Nippon beyond the straits are not these Africa." Narrowly escaping shoaling we came to anchor at 6 P.M. abreast of the town.

Saturday, September 29, 1860

Thermometer A.M. 62°.

A clear sunrise and beautiful morning with a cool breeze from the north. A Russian corvette has come in during the night and dropped anchor near us. It is like a crisp October morning in the Middle State. From the ship's deck we have the best view of the position of Hakodade. It is built at the foot and on the side of a bold promontory which consists of three peaks, the central one rising about 1500 feet above the level of the sea. It is connected with the main land by [a] long narrow low neck of sandy land interrupted by occasionally sandy knolls that have been heaped up by the wind and tide. The bay in front of the town is an oblong oval shape. The opposite shores are two miles distant, covered by a wide strip of low land mixing with an easy slope into an enclosing ridge of wooded hills. The hill on which the town lies is mostly bare of trees but covered with green grass and strewn with rocks. At an angle of the bay a fort is in the process of construction. Few harbors in the world, I imagine, are more secure than this, and still fewer could be made so suitable as a safe resting place for a nation's navies as this might be under impregnable batteries on the bold promontory and the commanding positions of all the approaches. Conspicuous objects on the shore are a cluster of white buildings, two stories, of foreign style. While we wonder what they are, a puff of smoke rolls out from the sides of the corvette, it is the eight o'clock gun and simultaneously from the ship and the white buildings on shore rolls out the flag of the Greek Cross—it is the Russian in these northern waters, whose influence creeps like a mysterious shadow down from his home in the frozen north. I cannot blame him if he looks with covetous eye on the more fertile soil of Yeso lying under a warmer sun, and the goodly harbor of Hakodade, icebound as he is in his own coasts for more than half the year.

After breakfast we went ashore, boating through a wilderness of junks and a spider's web of cables and anchor floats, landing at the Custom House steps of stone. We paid our respects firstly to our Consul Mr. Rice,[91] whose picturesque proportions and beard like an ancient sea-king, I have no doubt, makes a suitable impression on the dwarfed Japanese. He received us with great cordiality, for Americans are not yet become so common but that it is pleasant to exchange greetings among each other in a far away land. In his company we took a walk about the town. When he first came to Hakodade, now some three years since, there was a population of about seven or eight thousand since when it has grown rapidly, having increased to seventeen thousand. Wherever we went this growth was confirmed by the great number of new buildings and still the process was going on. This is owing mostly to the stimulus given to the place under increased foreign intercourse, but in part also to a natural growth of Yeso stimulated by the efforts of its princely land owners. At least such is the account given by the Japanese themselves, that emigration has been large to Yeso owing to inducements so held out by landowners, which has brought hither settlers from the densely populated parts of Nippon. Many whale ships touch here and traders going backwards and forwards to the Amur river (see tables).

We walked out to the new fort which is building after an improved manner with faces and angles so as to wholly command the harbor. For some cause the work is at present suspended. Near the fort is an old battery which hitherto has constituted the chief defence of the harbor where several large brass guns were mounted on barbette. Near these also was a shell foundry where a half dozen men were employed in casting shells. This is the first I have known of shell casting in Japan, it having been commonly affirmed that the process was unknown in this land.

The streets up the hill were occupied by residences of officials and private dwellings, the lower part of the town is occupied by business. On the hill, too, is the foreign population, with their houses scattered among the native population. The streets were generally of good width of from one or two rods, usually the latter, and as elsewhere in Japan were scrupulously clean. The situation of the city gives the best of draining. Shade trees, shrubbery, and hedge rows were also common. The stones taken out in constructing the houses and streets had been usefully employed in building stone walls at the side of the streets as at Nagasaki, but they were not so picturesquely overgrown with vines and creepers as at the latter place, the hot moist air is wanting to produce them. "Water Street," the main business street and thoroughfare of the city located as its name indicates near the water's edge, has much the general appearance of the Tokaido at Kanagawa. The buildings of one and two stories were occupied as stores in front while the family lived in the rear or up stairs, but the houses were generally poorer than about Yedo Bay though Kanagawa itself, like Hakodade, is a fishing town. Bark is much used for the siding of houses placed vertically and secured by transverse strips of wood a short distance apart. Tile roofs also were more generally replaced by shingle roofs which were kept in their places not by nails, as with us, or by wooden pegs, as at places to the southward, but by stones from a baby's to a man's hand in

---

[91] Elisha E. Rice was initially (1857) commercial agent, later (1858) American consul at Hakodate. He was a tall and heavy-set man, who like Hall, found himself in various differences of opinion with Townsend Harris. Rice enjoyed the company of merchants while Harris generally disdained them. Harris regarded Rice as illiterate.

See Mario E. Cosenza, ed., *The Complete Journal of Townsend Harris* (Rutland, Vt.: Charles E. Tuttle Co., 1959), p. 376. An interesting description of Rice can be found in Oliver Statler, *Shimoda Story* (New York: Random House, 1969), p. 412.

bigness, so that the field of brown roofs looked down upon from above looked like our hill pasture land of New England in this same autumn time. The roofs were further adorned with one or two tubs of water each standing on the ridge for convenience in case of fires. The shops were filled with the simple wares of the country to supply the great wants of food and clothing and, having few articles of a fancy character, presented small attraction to a novelty seeker.

In the midst of the shops and houses of Water Street is the "Star Hotel," a small inn kept by Mr. Bradford, an American. We went to it to seek quarters ashore and found Mr. B[radford] superintending the process of clapboarding the house in Yankee style. He will need no other sign, for its novelty will distinguish it from its humbler neighbors. The inn was small and being in part unfit for occupancy through the present repairing we should have found no quarters therein if the landlord had not kindly consented to give up his own room for Dr. H[epburn]'s and my accommodation. Our quarters secured we went to the Custom House for boats and were charged the extortionate prices of two *Bu's* each for boats to go off to the *Berenice* for our baggage. But it was the customary price and there was no use in grumbling, though we could not help thinking the foreign Consuls should resist such an excessive tax on the visitors. We tried to put off ourselves in a small boat, but the bay was so rough from a freshly blowing norther, that after we had moved out a little ways and got a good wetting and ran some risk of swamping we turned back. Thus we were furnished a boat so large and buoyant that the waves knocked that about so that we were compelled to go ashore again. Finally in a third boat and after a third attempt we were properly quit and got along side the *Berenice*. Putting our effects aboard we got ashore at dark in time to dine with our friendly Consul and his assistant Mr. Pitts. The latter gave us an interesting account of his shipwreck last year on a rocky ledge off one of the Kurile Islands. The crew were saved, and much of the cargo, as the weather was favorable. While lying here they were hailed by the Russian Steamer which had Mr. Rice on board as a passenger returning

from the Amur. They were so secure in their position that it was decided best for them to remain with the saved cargo. After the steamer had left a storm arose so severe as to wash all the cargo away, all their food, and broke over the reef with such violence that they were often submerged and only saved themselves by hard clinging to the craggy ledges. Then followed a starving process which would have been complete but for shell fish which they fortunately found abundantly and rain water from the crevices of the rock. Among the drift of the wreck swept on the reef during the subsidence of the storm were a great many boxes of matches. These they opened hoping forlornly that at least one match might be found that would ignite and after trying box upon box one fortunately did strike fire so [they] had the three great requisites of fire, food and water. In this way they lived for many days (three weeks I think), and were finally rescued by the Japanese schooner which had been sent after them.

After dinner we called upon Mrs. Fletcher, the wife of an American resident. She was content with her lot amid many privations in hope that her husband would be pecuniarily rewarded in properties and that a few years at most would send them home with ample worldly goods and gear.

It was some feast day among the people, and as we returned home late in the evening the streets were illuminated with transparencies hung across the streets at frequent intervals with pictured historical, legendary, and religious scenes.

We took possession of the room so kindly given up to us and returned to our beds but not to sleep. No sooner were lights extinguished than rats walked in through unguarded crevices and holes and ran over the ceilings across the floors and on to our beds. By the moonlight we could see them in their nocturnal gambles peering with cunning eyes out of their holes or with whisking tails curvetting on the walls and about the floor till sleep was impossible. Mosquitoes, too, added their bill of exactions and when good Dr. H[epburn] after relighting his lamp discovered additional foes clambering about his bedposts and bedding and even caught a Japanese body guard on his own person I laughed outright and amused myself for an hour or two lying in wait on my bed with my cane in my hand, and trying to avenge myself on the disturbers of my nightly rest. The welcome morning light came after a sleepless night coming through the little latticed window which opened out over a sea of stony brown roofs and revealing to us the aspect of our apartment by daylight, trunks, boxes and clothes indiscriminately scattered about, tawdry paper on the walls, and Japanese distorted pictures put there adorning them, a bedstead in two corners of the room, one of which had been hastily constructed the evening before of pine planks, a pot for a wash bowl and a great glass pitcher like a planet wandered out of its sphere. It was half Japanese, half prairie cabin.

Sunday, September 30, 1860

Thermometer 56°–72°.

A perfect October day, clear, warm and no wind. Took a walk before breakfast on to high ground commanding a view of the adjacent country. The walk led me near the Russian Consulate consisting of several houses built in European style and occupied by the Consul General, a Russian doctor and his lady, and a hospital for seamen and soldiers. Near this also is a Japanese *odaiba*, a troop barracks in parallelogram. After breakfast climbed the heights above Hakodade in company with Dr. H[epburn]. We passed the line of the houses and entered a large cypress grove where [a] dark mass of foliage had attracted my attention when viewing the city the first morning from the ship's deck. A small *mia*, or wayside chapel, stood at the entrance of the grove, and well worn paths threaded it in every direction. It was a magnificent grove. The trees were tall and shapely, rising with unbending columns fifty to seventy feet before the tufted heads of the grove knit together to form an impenetrable shade. As I walked into its silent depths there was an impressiveness that I never felt in the forest before. Under this green roof of ten thousand columns were no sounds of bird or insect life, its repose was absolute. The only plants that seemed to flourish in its shade were the knotted ferns growing in clumps here and there. The ground was moist, slippery, and crumbling, making our progress slow. Again we emerged out of the grove into the clear sunlight above. The ground was thickly strewn with rough trachyte rocks and the interstices between the sharp edges of the stones was hidden by luxuriant grass and low shrubbery so that we took many treacherous steps. We were out of the beaten way for on turning a short distance to the right we struck onto a well worn path leading up from the town below. Near the summit on a rocky platform was another *mia* of a solitary, deserted air. Its paper windows were fluttering in rags and its weather boarding was growing grey and weak with age and neglect.

Another hundred feet and we stood on the summit of the hill 1135 feet above the sea level. The prospect before us rewarded well our toil. At our feet were the brown roofs of the town, and coming around in a long ellipse of several miles was the entrance channel to the bay which shone clear and calm at the foot of the hill on which we stood. In front of us were the moor-like lands across the bay and the swelling background of hills. There too were the wooded mountains of Yeso, and two volcanos were emitting light wreaths of smoke and vapors. Back of us were the Straits of Sangar and the shores of Nippon, where we could look one way into the sea of Japan and the other into the broad Pacific. So too, far away to the left in an indistinctness of the coast we could see where Matsumae, the seat of the feudal chief of that name, the lord of Yeso was situated. The harbor bustled with junks, and shipping out with the morning wind were several departing to Nambu, Oasaca, and Nagasaki with their cargoes of sea weed, fish oil, potatoes, and coal. Like children we could see the friends of the departing traders following along the bay waving and shouting farewells and wishing "good voyages" to the outward bound. At the present time there were about 200 junks in the harbor, though frequently there are three and four times that number. They come up with the southerly winds of Spring and Summer bringing silk, cotton, rape seed oil, sweet potatoes, and the products of the more genial southern islands, and going back in the fall with the N.E. winds laden with returns. An American schooner arrived that morning, two Japanese, and the two steamers were all the craft of foreign size. The summit of the hill was adorned with several idols roughly hewn out of the circumjacent stone and set up on pedestals of trachyte. Honey bees were swarming about their heads in enjoyment of the sunshine. I thought of Fremont's rocky mountain bee and wondered if these also might not be pioneers of the civilization to come to the city below. At any rate there were suggestions of home and house comforts in the faces of the broad daisies that looked smilingly out of the grass and the purple asters such as adorn our own October hills.

In the afternoon, it being Sunday, young Bagley, the boy preacher from California who had been a shipmate on the *Berenice*, preached the first Protestant sermon in Hakodade at Mrs. Fletcher's to a small audience. In the evening we dined with Mr. Hodgson, H.R.M.'s Consul, and were agreeably entertained by his hospitality and that of his charming wife.[92] They are about leaving Hakodade and will go away with us in the steamer. They occupy the priest's home of a Buddhist temple and will leave with some regret the beautiful landscape garden attached. Even in charming England they will recall the spreading heads of the dwarf yews, the lawn, the grass, the little lakes, the fragrant hedges with regrets.

H[epburn] and I had a great time renovating our room before nightfall. We overhauled the bedding and dispensed with some whose stained and dirty appearance would have added a thorn to our slumbers, slaughtered the mosquitoes with our napkins, stopped up the rat holes, and had as a reward a refreshing night of slumber.

Monday, October 1, 1860

Thermometer 58°–74°.
Another pleasant fall day, after breakfast walked through the town out to the sandy neck which separates the bay from the straits and across it to the straits. We wandered for an hour on the sandy [beach] searching for shells, but found little to reward us for our trouble. A heavy swell was rolling in landward and pulsating on the beach. There were traces of other waves driven by fierce winds that had heaped up the shifting sands in banks and hills or gullied deep water channels. There was a small fishing village, and some of the houses nearest to shore were half buried in the sea sands which had piled up to the very eaves, as I have seen snow drift in a winter's storm. These half buried huts were deserted by their former inmates. The poor people in the village were exceedingly shy, and some fishermen we found on the beach stretching their sea weed to dry were reluctant to answer our few inquiries till their reserve or dread had worn off. When we went about Hakodade both houses and streets indicated the humble condition of the inhabitants.

We had in contemplation a trip twenty five or thirty miles inland to the volcano of Sawara and busied ourselves this afternoon in making preparations for the jaunt which was to be a horse back one and promised some new experiences.

Tuesday, October 2, 1860

64°.
This morning our little inn was an unusually busy aspect with the preparations of our trip to Sawara-Yama. There were four of us to make the party Dr. H[epburn], Rev. W. P. B[agley], the surgeon of the *Berenice*, and myself. Horses had been supplied by our Hakodade friends, small stout ponies, and we had beside three mounted servants, one acting as guide, one as hostler, and the other a coolie hired out of the streets had charge of the sumpter mule, which was a one eyed horse of shaggy coat and cadaverous aspect driven by a rope tied around his nose. My pony was hired of our landlord, a little quick footed black fellow who was half

[92] For a description of the Hodgson's life in Japan see Christopher Pemberton Hodgson (1821–1865), *A Residence at Nagasaki and Hakodate in 1859–1860. With an Account of Japan generally. By C. Pemberton Hodgson . . . With a Series of Letters on Japan by his Wife* (London: R. Bentley, 1861).

covered up by the Mexican saddle which I rode. The bridle was a Japanese one with clumsy iron bit and long reins of purple crape that gave it decidedly a stylish appearance. We were to be about three days and provided amply of stores. We had a half dozen or more basted fowls, boiled ham, twenty pounds of crackers in tins, and several bottles of ale, besides tea, sugar, and condiments, knives and forks, and other small necessaries of a campaign where provision might not readily be obtained. These we calculated would be an ample supply with possible eggs and fish and certain rice and potatoes from the natives. We were much indebted to our indefatigable landlord for his attentions to our comfort. Having seen that all was ready, every saddle girth tightened properly, and the sumpter horse's burden secure, we filed out through the streets in pleasant anticipation of the adventure.

For my own part I was not a little vain of my personal appearance on the most stylish horse and with the most brilliant outfit of the party. I had no doubt the amount of leather in my saddle made a suitable impression on a people among whom leather is luxury, and there was no doubting the effect of my bridle reins of purple crape or the white and purple rosettes and tassels of the head and tail.

My well founded pride as all worldly pride is apt to receive a sudden check. Just outside of the city's limits there was a brook to ford or rather a small river and I was riding in advance as became one so properly caparisoned. So clear and inviting did the stream look flowing over its pebbly sands, that moved thereby my horse showed signs of a desire to drink. I pulled up the bridle rein when my gallant charger conveniently availed himself of the halt to lie down in the tempting water for a bath. His country breeding was evident but too late came its knowledge; a smart blow rescued me from an entire submersion and we rose, I instead of a gallant chief on a noble charger nothing but a disconsolate workman on horseback. But such mishaps were only trifles and seeking a bit of green turf secure from curious eyes I relieved my toilet in the most obvious and hasty way and mounting again finished the drying by a sharp trot in the sun and wind.

Beyond the sandy neck we found the plains opposite Hakodade of much larger extent than they had seemed viewed from the bay. They were smooth and level like a western prairie, it being several miles in a sight line from the water's edge to the foot of the hills. Through this plain ran several parallel roads just as the humor of the passers by had cut them out, in this way giving another point of prairie resemblance. The greater part of the plain was uncultivated, but was covered with a scrubby growth of low trees and bushes, brakes, weeds, and briars. Along the road side the asters, golden rod, with their blooms disported the soil with thistles, brakes, and the abundant artemisia. The spots under cultivation were enclosed by fences of turf. As we got farther away from the city and bay, the country began to put on its true rural life. Instead of the plains with their fuzzy bushes and turf fences we came upon neat farm houses and well cultivated fields. Many of the homes were quite new, showing that Yeso was growing in the country as well as city, and we came to small villages composed entirely of recently erected houses where the manufacture of silk was the universal occupation.

The different physical aspect of Yeso was at once apparent, for the low knoll-like hills of Nippon we had wooded mountains with long slopes of green fields that seemed just the fields where cattle would thrive. The resemblance of the conformation of the surface to the temperate climes of the States was not greater than that of its tree growths. There were maples, their leaves now turning with autumnal frosts, chestnuts, oaks, persimmon pear trees, and new to us in Japan were apple trees, wild cherries, and weeping willows. A large heap of potatoes in a farm yard was a familiar sight, so was a row of thirty apple trees which appeared to need only the ingrafting of choice varieties to yield fine fruit in place of their present gnarly little fruit. Fences of posts and small timber along the roadside were common, though the turf fences were used as well. To add to the resemblance of home scenes were the flowers blooming about the houses, asters, cock's combs, balsams, amaranths, coreopsis, chrysanthemums, and even the stately sunflowers. Horses were feeding in the stables near the houses, cordwood in many instances was stored up for winter's use, and about the houses were patches of vegetables such as beans, onions, carrots, squashes, corn, a small kind of celery, turnips, a small kind of pumpkin, and at one place I saw a fine bed of beets, a vegetable scarcely known in Japan, [as well as] tobacco. The country was well watered with small streams flowing over beds of small stone and gravel.

Such was the character of the country throughout our afternoon's ride to the village of *Toni-no-shta* ("foot of Mount Toni")[93] where we were to pass the night, 15 miles from Hakodade. The road was a wide smooth road throughout, in no wise inferior to our best country roads at home. Our horses had proved not only tractable, but sufficiently fleet and serviceable. At 2 P.M. we arrived at the "half way house" of Toni-no-shta. The remaining half of the road would be more mountainous, and the latter part of it through blind paths, and though it was possible to push through to the mountain, we thought it better to remain, especially as the clouds betokened rain. The landlord of the little inn, a peasant with a broad homely face expressive of good nature and hair growing almost into his eyes, received us at the door and held our bridle reins and stirrup as we dismounted before the inn.

The inn was built on the roadside where three ways meet, a plain house of one storey with thatched roof, one half of which was kitchen, the other half was divided into small apartments for guests. All was neat and attractive. We were conducted into the rear room of the house, which is the "front room" in Japan, and opened onto a verandah which in turn opened into the garden of fruit and vegetables and flowers. We sat down in the verandah opening into the shady garden while our host brought us refreshments, tea and sweetmeats first, and after a little interval boiled potatoes and eggs.

We rested ourselves on the clean mats and the verandahs a while and then took a walk into the village. This consisted of thirty or forty houses on the main road at straggling

distances apart built close upon the street. They were comfortable looking cottages and their inmates were disposed to every civility. The children brought us chestnuts and some wild berries from the mountains. In one home where I entered a little child lay sick before the fire, she looked very delicate and seemed to lift her head with difficulty. I gave her some little trinket from my pocket and her eyes brightened with joy. Her mother, a comely woman, and her grandmother were taking care of her. Another inmate of the house was a girl of seventeen with a fair fresh countenance of modest grace and we thought her fairly entitled to be called the "belle of the village." We found now for the first [time] the wild hop growing luxuriantly. To the natives it was simply a useless vine for which they knew no value. We told them its properties and uses and advised them to gather them to sell to the foreign merchants at Hakodade (on our return two days afterwards we found they had been gathering them according to our suggestion). At one home there was a gathering of the neighbors to rethatch a roof illustrative of their appreciation of the value of mutual assistance.

Returning from our walk through the village we found our sumpter horse arrived with our provisions, and while our dinner was being prepared we took a walk in the old lady's garden. The flowers in bloom were chrysanthemums, bachelor's buttons, balsams, asters, cock's combs, hollyhocks, pinks, all old fashioned favorites at home, and among those passed out of bloom I saw azaleas, peonies, columbines, and the flowering almonds. It's vegetables were as various, viz., eggplants, radishes, squashes, corn, beans, onions, and tobacco. Among its trees were the peach, pear, and cherry, the pear trees were large and lofty trees more like fruit monarchs than the bearers of such small insignificant fruit as we saw.

We returned to the house. The landlord brought in our hot potatoes and eggs, we unpacked our hampers of cold meats, and seated upon the mats a la Japanese with the paper shutters thrown open so that we could look out

---

[93] This was most likely the village of *Toge no shita*, "at the foot of the pass" leading to the lakes of Ōnuma and Konuma, which lie below the two volcanic peaks, Komagatake and Sawaradake.

onto the pleasant garden, commenced our meal. Our long ride and the novelty of situation gave zest to our appetites. The people of the village peeped slyly through the open doors to watch our novel proceedings, and a group of youngsters with treasures of chestnuts and baskets of a small pulpy fruit of sweet taste of the size and appearance of a potato ball waited for us to become purchasers without.

After supper came a smoke upon the verandah and we congratulated ourselves that we had halted at the foot of Mount Toni for the night as the rain clouds had gradually thickened over head and now the large drops were beating up the dust in the flower borders and washing the growing leaves. Night closed in, our landlord closed the shutters and brought in his parlor astral lamp what was a saucer of oil with a lighted pith wick enclosed in a paper box with translucent sides. We unrolled our packs, spread our blankets and shawls on the mats, the landlord supplied us with wooden head rests softened by a few thicknesses of paper that had a greasy suspicious look as if used by many a head moistened with camellia oil.

We put on pillow cases of clean paper, and with our four heads in the four corners of the room and our feet coming together where the lamp stood in the center, like the radiating points of the compass, we disposed ourselves to rest till our monotonous chat and the pattering of the rain without lulled us to deeper repose. Repose do I say! There was a smothered exclamation from the corner where our surgeon had pillowed his head in a carpet bag, not profanity, but still short and ejaculatory, which was reechoed by the young dominie who was done up in two Japanese quilts to my right, "fleas," said the physician with a boom of vexation from another corner, "fleas," I took up the refrain accompanying the word with brisk manual practice. "I shall never sleep," said the surgeon. "Let's take the road," said the physician. "There are no such fleas at Nagasaki," said the dominie, and all was quiet once more. Then silence was broken by objurgatory exclamations and pithy remarks like occasional shots after the fray, but the music of the rain drops mastered the bites of the insects and it

was broad daylight under a leaden covering of clouds when our shock-headed host opened the shutters and let in the sweet breath of the morning air. The sun was struggling with great fleecy volcanos of vapor out of which came the sullen roar of the distant thunder like the dying rage of the baffled spirit of the storm.

Wednesday, October 3, 1860

We had intended to have been on the road betimes, but we had overslept ourselves in the dark room and under the cloudy morning. It was already past seven o'clock, and we hurried up our horses, and prepared our alfresco meal again on the verandah, but the breakfast call was poorly responded to. One was knocked by yesterday's ride, such an innovation was it upon his usual mode of life; another was a little invalided, and another had no appetite. I think the quantity of last night's hard boiled eggs and bacon had something to do with our satietary condition.

The sun was high when we mounted, the landlord brought his bill of twelve bus for the accommodation of our party and saw us in the stirrup, a few stragglers of *Toni-no-shta* gathered about the inn door, and more small boys with fresh relays of chestnuts hoped for a farewell trade. We had hoped to have visited the volcano, and by an early start, and a hard day's ride, to have returned to our present quarters, for we heard dismal stories of our possible accommodations for the night at the volcano and danger to our horses from prowling bears since we must picket them out. It was clear now that we should fail to make *Toni-no-shta* again today. We filed off through the street of straggling houses and were soon climbing Mount Toni.[94]

At first the road was rough with large blocks of stones thrown onto the road by the mountain torrents, and gullies produced by the same cause, and slippery with the recent rain, but this was soon replaced by a broad country road where two carriages might drive abreast in the

---

[94] They were, in fact, going up the pass to the Ōnuma lakes.

best conditions of travel. We wound slowly up the hill amid the trees and foliage dripping with last night's shower and came out upon the summit on a point of ledge where suddenly a magnificent landscape view burst into sight.

We were on a hill that overlooked the whole valley through which we had rode yesterday afternoon taking it at one sweep, wood, hill, hamlet, the flowing plains about the winding channel of Hakodade harbor, and, last of all, the city itself, clear and distinct against the background of the promontory on which it glittered in the sunlight like a gem in a coronet. We gazed in mute silence, for, familiar as five of us had been with scenery in all parts of the world, that landscape sight came upon us with the force and bearing of an inspiration.

We rode on over the mountain, and as if nature would be lavish of delights, as we descended the broad country road on the opposite side of the hill high up in the hilly fortresses nestled a lake, the gleam of whose waters shone through the foliage that arched our pathway. We descended to the very level of the lake bed, and then our way wound around the mountain's side, the grand old forest trees waving benediction above us and the lake coiling like a python among the hills below. Everything was glistening after last night's storm with a new face, the air was full of pleasant fragrances, a soft wind moved among the pines and beeches, little cascades created out of last night's floods leaped in merry playfulness across our way or with a wondrous artfulness threatened to cut us off. The road bed was sometimes usurped by the mountain rills which our horses seemed to splash through with visible sensations of delight. Across the lake the smoking truncated cone of Sawara was puffing out its vapory clouds, but a short distance as the bird flies, though we had a detour of several miles to make around the foot of the lake to reach it.

The vegetation of the temperate zone was about us, birches white and black, beech, several varieties of maples, the chestnut oak, the black, white, and evergreen oak, two varieties of ash, the Spanish and common chestnut, tall hydrangeas, and climbing over these white cypress contrasting agreeably with the scarlet berries of the ash and other trees and the glistening green of the evergreen oaks.

Here again our young dominie who is liable to sudden fits of inspiration conceived the idea of putting all this beautiful panorama of sky, wood, hill, and water onto his sketch book. Less confident of his artistic prowess than he was, we represented the inconveniences of stopping the whole party to humor him and the risk of his separating from the guide, but he was obstinate, and when was there a young dominie that was not.

We left him and rode on through the woods without him, but we had not proceeded far before we heard him coming splash through the water courses and plunging through the deep mud holes, for our road had now changed for the worse at the foot of the hill. He showed us the results of his hasty labors and we felt a relief in knowing that if through our temporary desertion the bears had come out on this mocker of the beautiful, as they did upon the mockers of old, a Turner or a Copley would not have been lost to this generation.

For a few miles more our road was through woods and the marshy margin of the lake occasionally alternated with open fields and ample lands. Since leaving Toni-no-shta we had encountered few homes and not a solitary hamlet. There were large wastes of land uncultivated and extensive tracts of timber. Here and there only a scattered farm house with its inmates had any sign of life. We were now not more than five or six miles distant from the foot of the volcano, but between us and it was a low swampy bit of ground covered with small trees, ferns, and rushes.

We turned off from the main road we had been pursuing. Our guide appeared a little uncertain of his way for the paths were various and obscure. But striking onto one we directed our course toward the steaming cone of the volcano. The narrow paths were miry and heavy with the recent rains and the black ooze of the swamp splashed over us at every step. A couple of miles of alternate wet and dry road among the scrubby trees brought us to the margin of a clear and flowing stream on the banks of which was a house inhabited by a solitary old man. From him our guide gathered new directions and we crossed the stream.

Our path for a mile or two was comparatively good, but at the end of this the trail became less distinct and involved with paths made by the peasants who had small patches of corn among the trees and rushes, and who came out to gather their winter's fuel and rushes for thatching their roofs. There were occasional hummocks of land, low knolls rising out of the surface of the plain, patches of spruce timber and tall grasses, so that we could see but a little way in any direction. The volcano was smoking mockingly near, but how to reach it was the question. There was another small river between us and it and we must keep the path that led to the ford, too much detour to the left would bring us into impassable swamps on the edge of the lake which we had been skirting for the past hour or more, to the right we should come upon the sea.

There was but one house near the mountain, and to that we wished to go, for it was evident there was no chance for a return to Toni-no-shta. But the guide who was to show us the way was perplexed, lost his reckoning, and finally led us into a labyrinth of swamp, jungle, and water. We floundered on through mud and mire, now on dry land, and now up to our sodden girths in water, dark pools lay across our path of uncertain depths, all full with last night's heavy showers, but our good animals patiently encountered it all as if they were accustomed to such things. The more our guide strove to recover his position the more helplessly we became entangled, and as if to mock us, the head of Sawara rose clear in the sunlight close at hand. We urged our horses up the hummocks, through the bushes and wild briars, but no paths were visible, only the mountain so mockingly near. We were fairly lost in sight of our journey's end and retreat seemed about as impossible as advance, for the whole swamp was laced with various paths by which the peasantry entered in the dry season to gather rushes and fuel.

We told our guide he must go back and beat the bushes for some native who had more woodcraft than he, and the Doctor and myself taking the lead made a push to regain a dry part of the plain which we had crossed some-

time before. We reached this, and while our guide had gone back for assistance we let our horses crop among the tall grasses while we undid our hampers again and made a picnic meal on the turf. Here our young dominie who had all along shown a disposition to have his own way, regardless of the wishes of the rest, became impatient of the delay and prepared to go on by himself confident in his ability to find the way. We urged him to keep company with us as the safer plan, for although he might reach his destination, he might miss the little inn and a night among the hills in a country infested with bears was a risk too serious to be taken. Out of sheer obstinacy he was determined to go; it was the wilfulness of a boy and not the cool courage and determination of the man. It was clear that the more we remonstrated with him the more he was bent upon carrying out his own purposes so we let him go his own way, and bidding us adieu he struck off onto a leading path and was soon out of sight.

He had hardly disappeared before our guide returned bringing with him the old man we had left by the house at the river side to act as our guide. Our horses were called in from their foraging, packs and saddles were again adjusted, and we were soon following in the wake of the gray headed old man among the high rushes. We pushed forward with all haste to make up for the lost time, crushing the deep cups of the fringed gentians under our hoofs, hoping we would overtake our clerical brother. We came to another small river, the outlet of the lake. It was from this point our guide had turned back three hours ago, believing he had mistaken his path. We crossed the stream and soon after struck out of the main path where a finger board in unintelligible Japanese nailed to a tree had fallen into the mud. The true road was so much the most unlikely one to be the right one that we felt confident our comrade must have gone astray at this point.

In a moment more we were riding through a sea of rushes high as our heads mounted as we were. We congratulated ourselves that we had not left Toni-no-shta yesterday afternoon and been caught in its storm amid these intricacies with our ignorant guide. A couple of miles through the tall rushes and we came out onto the forest that fringed the lake and in a few moments more were at the little cottage by the lakeside.

It was the same lake we had seen early in the forenoon and we were soon at its foot. Behind the cottage flowed the outlet of the lake off into the woods beyond. Across the lake were the scarred sides of Sawara, and on its margin were heaped up the scoriae of former eruptions where the lava stream had flowed into the lake. We inquired for our comrade, but he had not been seen and he could have come to the house by no other road and our forebodings that he had mistaken his way were fulfilled.

The little house was not an inn but the residence of a factor in sulphur who gathered the crude masses from the volcano and extracted the valuable mineral by a rude smeltery under a shed near the house. He was hospitable, giving up his little house to our use. We left our horses in the good care of our bettos and took a guide for the immediate ascent of the mountain, for the day was already far spent. Our guide was one of the workmen employed in collecting the cinder sulphur from the volcano. No superfluous clothing encumbered his small person; any garments he had were like a puritan bed quilt in the last stage of rag and tatter. His feet and ankles were clad in stout coarse leggings against the rough chafing of the loose pumice stone.

It was about 3 P.M. that we went down to the lake and embarked in a small dugout canoe to cross over to the mountain's foot. A rude bridge of logs spanning the lake's outlet led to a path through the woods on the opposite shore, but the canoe would land us more directly. A light breeze crinkled the surface of the lake which was beautifully set in the hills, with its shores fringes of evergreen woods. We were soon over and were landed on a pile of scoriae that heaped up against the resisting water when the lava streams had passed years ago. The last eruption of the mountain was variously dated back ten, twelve, and fourteen years. The sulphur factor, who should have known, said the first (ten) date.

Though our path was over the rough pum-

ice stone or ankle deep in scoriae we had the satisfaction to see that it was a long lazy slope of not more that three miles from the foot of the lake. The whole mountain presented a wide scene of desolation, bleak and bare of vegetable life, and white with the fire leached stone and ashes. Here and there a line of charred timber, overthrown, uprooted, and lying heaped up in dire confusion, trees of huge growth, showed what forests the burning tide had desolated. There were sharp ridges of heaped up lava showing the flow of the streams, and one broader than the rest was the line of ascent to the crater. Patches of new vegetation were fighting for existence in barren soil. Less than half way to the summit were two deep gulfs side by side from which apparently a stream of lava had sometime flowed towards the lake, as this river had broken out in that direction and the course of the flow remained as distinctly as if in a dried up river bed of sand.

The sharp pumice stone and the cinder ashes told rapidly on our boots and sole leather, and we began to think of the possibility of a barefoot descent. The atmosphere was of great purity and transparency, and as we rose the north wind blew upon us with increasing force and coolness. We could now see the abrupt broken peak of Komanga standing over the crater with its shattered sides.

The ascent grew steeper and yet steeper, the air so cold that we buttoned up our coats tightly about us. One hour and a half of rapid climbing brought us to the rim of the crater where the wind was so cutting that we were glad to dip below the shelter of its rim to shield ourselves from it. Still above us and forming the wall of the crater on the side of the mountain opposite to that by which we had ascended was the peak of Komanga, a sheer mass of rock 300 feet above the crater level and circling it on the north and east sides. On the western side the circular rim was less than thirty feet deep, and towards the south it was broken away by its last eruption and fell in one long slope towards the sea whose blue waters were sparkling and whose Volcano Bay lies three or four miles distant. The crater proper had a long diameter from north to south 3/4 of a mile, east to west 1/2 a mile, and this space was covered with jets of steam sending up the wreaths of vapor which the wind floated off to the seaward.

We had paused for a moment on the crater's rim for the surgeon, but he had lagged so much behind in the ascent that the Dr. and myself went down into the crater without him accompanied by our guide. The floor of the crater was smooth and looked moist and hard as the beach left by the returning tide. So it was hard for the most part, but occasionally the crust, moved by some primordial head of steam, quaked and quelled under our feet. It seemed a little hazardous to walk in among the spouting masses of sulphurous vapors that bespoke the cavernous earth below, and when we had gone in a little way and the ground gave back a hollow reverberation to our tread and the steam arose in pits before, behind, and on every side of us Dr. H[epburn] would turn back. So I said the sulphur workmen come here almost daily and we can go with safety wherever they can.

The steam pits ran in lines across the crater in every direction. There would be a slight elevation of the earth, or little ridge covered with a hard shiny crust, and along this ridge every few feet, often at closer intervals, were the steam fissures. There were here and there slight chasms and earth depressions and gullies made by the rains which swept down from the peaks above or were gathered in the crater. Most of the jets were noiseless, others escaped with a sharp hissing sound, and we were attracted to one which was roaring loudly and was escaping with the noise and pace of a blowing off from a monster engine. We went up to the slightly marked elevation and saw an opening down into the bowels of the earth of the size of a barrel from which the colorless gas was escaping with such force and violence that it did not take on its white vapory robe till two or three feet above the surface. Absolute contact with such a fiery vapor would [have] hoisted us like a rocket, still I could peer in closely enough to see that the opening instead of descending vertically at once was connected with a horizontal gallery about three feet below along which the fierce flow of imprisoned gases was rushing to enter life and liberty. Still further on, nearly across the crater, was a bank

of earth from which the steam was escaping with less violence but in greater volume. Indeed it seemed to be oozing gently out of the earth's pores over the whole bank. Here it was our guide said they extracted the sulphur.

Following him I plunged into the thick cloud of vapors, steamy and hot. It was a sulphur vapor bath on a grand scale. Several times I thought I must retreat when clouds thicker and more strongly charged enclosed me till my breath stifled for an instant and I gulped for a fresher dryer air. But the guide was clearing away the crystalline masses to get me a good specimen. I could see the bank crusted and brilliant with the deposits of alum and sulphur like a winter's snow bank. Stooping down so as to bring my thermometer in the escaping steam near its orifice it soon went up to its range which unfortunately was only 152 F. I do not think it would have risen much higher. And now our guide chipped out a mass and placed it yet hot and glistening in my hands and we retreated out of this pit of Avernus.

We recrossed the crater amid its steaming vapors and clambered up its crumbling side where the north wind again smote us with an intensity increased by the contrast of the vapory warmth we had left behind. The mercury that a few minutes before had leaped up exultingly in its tube, as if in secret sympathy with the gases escaping from an imprisonment which it had never escaped only to be prisoned again in this constricted glass house, now retreated again and marked only 58° cold by its contrast. We had just climbed out of the crater when our surgeon, half exhausted, came up, so we descended again to its warmer level while he went in amid its wonders.

The wind whistled sharper and colder, the sun hung low in the west near to its setting, when we started together for the descent without having seen the missing dominie. Night was coming on rapidly and our fears were greatly excited at the prospect of his passing a night out in the cold in the bleak mountains, or below, exposed to prowling wolves and bears. But we knew not whither to look for him, and our own safety demanded our return without further delay. We had descended half way and had come again to the broad sloping descent, when by mere chance, turning to look back once more on the peak of Komanga and the rising vapors of Sawara, I saw on the crater's rim our missing dominie leading his horse. How had he got there? It was not the time to speculate how he got there, or to exercise our just indignation at his obstinacy and folly, but there he was, with the red light of the departed sun fading out in the sky, and sure without help to be benighted on the mountain, for none but the astutest path craft could take a man over this undistinguishable lava flow.

The dark was coming on rapidly and we were in danger of losing our own way but the dominie's trouble and danger was greater, and we rushed to send back the guide to him hoping that we could make our own way to the ferry. The guide turned back and we made our way very well by the way marks of stones that had been placed at short intervals to guide the sulphur miners.

But now our surgeon knocked up with fatigue fell behind. We urged him forward and remonstrated with him against the danger of being left behind on the mountain. Our footsteps were retarded. Dr. H[epburn] and I could easily have made the ferry by running before the night fell, but the surgeon could hardly move forward. The darkness came in rapidly and we lost all traces of our path. The cairns were no longer visible with new lava ridges distinguishable from deep gulches. With feet already sore by walking over the mounded pumice we stumbled on in the dark, directing our course towards the trees on the margin of the lake.

Deeper still grew the darkness, we had wandered off the broad ridge and were as completely lost without our guide as we feared the young dominie would be. I am afraid we thought hard things of his obstinacy that had led to his being belated on the mountain and our losing our guide. The surgeon could scarcely drag one foot after another. Coming suddenly upon a deep furrow we knew by the approach to it at right angles that we were moving around the mountain directly opposite to the way we should go. So we faced about and knowing by the slight ascent of the land that we were near the foot and properly concluded that if we followed the other way we

should have a chance of coming within the hail of the guide and dominie, who, if they had kept the path, must be nearly as low down as we.

The star light sent but a faint glimmer over the field of burnt out scoriae, the lake timber was lost in the gloom, and we made our uncertain way over ridges through hollows and entangled among the charred timber as we best might. Dr. H[epburn] went on ahead hoping to get a hail from our guide. I remained with the surgeon, who begged to lie down and threatened each moment to give out, but I promised to stay by him if for all night. We hollered to keep up communication, and just when the Dr.'s voice grew fainter and fainter with the distance and threatened to be lost altogether, I could perceive by its tone and reflection that he was probably answering the hail of our guide. So it proved, he had encountered him just as we calculated and his long experience soon led us down to the front of the lake.

The people at the sulphur merchant's on the other shore and our servants had lighted great bonfires to guide us, but the screen of the woods prevented our seeing their glow till we were quite at the lake's margin. We heard the shouts of our servants coming towards us by the wood path around the foot of the lake, and directly they issued out of the forest with glowing torch lights of straw. They were relieved of anxiety by our return, and we at once filed off into the old wood to go around the lake. It was a picturesque night sight. The broad wood path followed close to the water and the fitful glare of the straw torches shone on woods and water and over winding file of men. We thought of old days in America's wilds as the trunks of trees and thick clumps of bushes came into light and passed into shadow while the torch glare shone on the faces of our Japanese red as our own Indians. We heard the rush of the lake outlet over its bed of stones and were soon crossing its bridge of two logs thrown across the rapid, but the dominie's horse had to swim across where it was broader and staler which he was reluctant to do and yielded only to much persuasion and many blows.

A fire was blazing in the middle of the wide

room of the rude cottage, and we were glad to throw ourselves down on the floor. The dominie and surgeon were completely knocked up by the day's fatigues. The former gave us an account of his adventures after leaving us. He missed the right path at the place we supposed he would, where there was a fallen guide board, taking a path to the right instead of the left. This after an hour's riding or two brought him to the foot of the long slope which I have already spoken of as leading from the broken down side of the crater to the sea. Finding the ascent with his horse practicable he rode up the mountain unto the crater where he expected to find us, or at least hoped so. But we had made our descent into the crater and had then started on our homeward way.

Then for the first time he felt the probability of a night out on the barren ashes and debris left of an eruption. He determined to scale the crater's rim from a point opposite to that where he had entered, and then, if he saw nothing of us or any shelter, to descend the mountain as far as possible, and when the darkness prevented any further progress to light with his matches a fire among the charred timbers for warmth and protection against prowling bears. But thanks to a good Providence he was spared the unpleasant alternative by recognizing us on our homeward way and being in turn recognized.

We made our preparations for the night. Wood was heaped on the glowing coals in the middle of the room and a teapot swung over them; our hampers were unpacked and our stores assorted from the chaotic confusion into which the long ride had thrown them when salt was lovingly blended with sugar and cold ham had fraternized with moist fowls. The bee's butter, which was the surgeon's chief solicitude, had escaped all the dangers of a rough jolting on the pack pony's back. Our beasts were already provided for by the *bettos* whom we had left at the hut as we went up the mountain. They were tethered to young trees in front of the house near to each other and enclosed by a series of circle bonfires to keep off the bears that might prowl in the adjoining wood.

The rising and falling light of the blazing fires threw strange lights into the dim night, and the dark forest, casting fantastic shadows onto the bosom of the still lake, as if weird shapes of gigantic form were walking or hovering over its surface. Within we sat around the cheerful fire on which the kettle was bubbling with sounds of good cheer and ate our evening meal. In this lovely spot by the lake we seemed more like a band of outlaws snatching rest and repose amid dangers, with fires to light up the picket of horses as if in sudden emergency to mount and away again. My comrades had lost their appetites in their over fatigues. I alone was able to eat like a famished lion and keep time and accord to the chomping teeth of our feeding animals without. We passed over the unfinished feast to our servants who made up for all our lack.

Our repast finished, we sat around the expiring embers smoking and chatting over the day's adventures, our languid flow of talk taking time from our wearied bodies. The dominie had already laid himself down in a corner. The surgeon was bolstering his heavy head on his knees and our servants were dropping off into sleep, when there were snorts and heavy plunges from our horses without. Our servants sprang to their feet shouting *kooma* [*kuma*], *kooma*, a bear, a bear. We rushed out just in time to see our horses, with glaring eyes, tugging at their halters, and one of them break loose and rush into the forest. Our semicircle of fires having almost died out while our bettos were inattentive, a bear had prowled so near as to alarm the horses. The servants hastily twisted torches of straw, and I started with them into the woods, as I had the only pistol in the party.

The torches gleamed among the trees, and soon one of the men shouted to me to discharge my pistol to frighten the bears. We soon had the satisfaction of seeing him return with the missing animal who was standing shivering with fear in the thick woods. He saw the glare of the animal's eyes, who sulkily retreated as the lights came into sight. We saw that our horses were again secured, heaped up the fires with fresh wood, and bade the servants keep alternate watches during the night to guard the animals and replenish the fire while we unpacked our blankets and prepared for repose.

There was a little room off the main room of the house where two could sleep. Thither the physician and I repaired, leaving the dominie and surgeon in their chosen corners without, with their feet to the fire. We spread our shawls and blankets on the floor, pulled off our boots, and wrapped ourselves up for sleep. The fatigue of the day brought to most of us a deep slumber, for myself, somewhat less fatigued than the others, my rest was divided between sleeping and wakefulness. About two in the morning I was aroused from the semi-unconsciousness of this slumber by a great noise and hubbub without.

I heard shouts, saw the mats of the sleeping Japanese whisked in the air and the fire now sunk to a bed of coals scattered by some sudden movement, as instinctively I raised my pistol and rushed to the open doorway. I could only distinguish the word *kooma, kooma*, again, and was sure that a bruin must have found the corral of horses belit with fire and made his way into our midst. A half moment's glance at the horses feeding quietly without in the light of the blazing fires told me that their instincts could not have been deceived in allowing a bear to pass them undisturbed.

There was a door leading out into the forest from the side of the house opposite to the horses whose existence I had not perceived the evening before and this was now wide open. "What is it," said I to the terrified *bettos* who stood with eyes grown suddenly immense in their surprise. "We do not know," they replied, but "where is the master," they added, pointing to the empty corner that had been occupied by the dominie when we retired. They did not tell me so, but it was clear they had not a bit of doubt but a bear had entered the door, and noiselessly slipping over the surgeon who lay sleeping before the open door, had carried off the dominie into the forest as a punishment, or rather a revenge, for yesterday, and his escape from the mountain when he had well nigh become their legitimate pray.

It was a puzzle to me how the man had got over the surgeon's body without arousing him, for he was only just now sitting bolt upright rubbing the remnants of slumber out of his eyes and wondering what all the fuss was about. With pistol on cock I stepped out of the open doorway in time to encounter, not the bear, but the dominie coming in. I slapped him a vigorous blow over the shoulder as he walked into the fire without saying a word, and said, "you have been dreaming dominie, your day's adventures have come back again in your sleep." "So they have," he said, "and I have not been fully awake till your blow brought me back to life and reality. I have been dreaming." Then he relapsed into a solemn silence looking down into the fire while we all laughed heartily.

To the Japanese, who were gazing wonderingly at what all this meant, I pointed to the still half stupefied man, and then tapping my head with my forefinger, they smiled in comprehensive recognition of my meaning. Our night camp had been wholly aroused, and as we gathered around the fire the somnambulist after some persuasion said, "I was dreaming; I thought I was still on the summit of the volcano's rim hanging as it were on the mountain peak and resolving in my mind how I should get out of the scrape in which I seem involved. My horse's bridle was in my hand, and I was pondering over the mischances of the day, when it seemed to me that some one shouted 'The Bears, run for your life.' It seems I did run, but how I could have got over the body of the surgeon which lay lengthwise sleeping in my way and escaped through a door that I had never seen before, I cannot tell more than you. My first consciousness of my situation was when you," turning to me, "slapped me so familiarly on my back." "Well," said we, "your dream has been more frank than your waking hours in telling us that you are not quite so fearless of bears as you would have us believe yesterday."

So after a merry laugh over this new alarm we turned into our beds again and slept soundly till morning.

Thursday, October 4, 1860

We did not make the early start this morning we intended, our slumber had carried us a little beyond the sunrise. The morning by the still lake side was one of captivating beauty. Not a wrinkle flecked the crystal water surface, the deep forests that enclosed its pebbly margin were glistening with dew on every leaf; floating around the peak of Komanga was a thin wreath of steamy vapor; our campfires were smoldering in ashes.

Kneeling on a couple of stones at the lake's clear rim I performed my morning ablutions in the grandest of washbowls, but alas no maid's lips came up to salute mine as they might have done to the original of the Faun of Praxiteles. While the remnants of our last night's supper were being spread anew for the morning's breakfast, I wandered off into the woods fragrant with pines and sassafras to gather leaves and blossoms. The half wild dogs bounded out of the coverts and fled away with a yelp and howl at my approach, but my pleasant work was not half done among the ivy wreathed trunks and the vine festooned elms before my companions called me back. We ate our breakfast, seasoning it with the mementoes of last night's alarms. The hospitable merchant who had given up his little house for our care and gone to sleep amid the fumes of his sulphur manufactory presented us with a bill for only what grass and firewood he had brought for us, the recompense for the use of his house he left to our own liberality which we exercised to his satisfaction.

We mounted, took a farewell look at our night's quarters by the side of the Sulphur Lake, and rode off into the woods and out through the tall rushes into the swamps which yesterday had been to us such a labyrinth of hillocks, bushes, fathomless mud holes, and intersecting trails. My horse appreciated the idea of going home and was impatient of my gathering the woodside seeds of flowers, and hardly gave me time to give a morning hail to the hermit of the brookside who had come to our relief yesterday, but bounded with a snort of welcome into the open roadway that led towards his familiar crib.

I had more leisure from preoccupying thoughts on my return to notice the beauty of the autumnal woods. That morning's ride winding about the lake is an ineffaceable recollection. How like a segment of heaven's own clear arch lay the lake amid the mountains, reflecting in its bosom nothing more human or sinful than the environing forest, the wings of

the birds sailing on the boundless lake above, or the stars of midnight. The rays of the autumnal sun sparkled on the little streams that ran across the road or flowed in our very pathway and bombarded the dense line of the forest, making breaches only here and there in the ramparts of living green. A multitude of scarlet berried ash and holly and sacred bamboo and of trees unknown stood like torches among the leaves and the seed vessels of a peculiar species of maple hung with all the grace and more than half the beauty of a crimson fuchsia. Ducks and wild geese were swimming among the reedy margins of the water; trains of horses and bullocks wound along the road and among the hills. Sometimes a train of a dozen bullocks with a single driver at the lead or thirty or forty horses trained to a brisk walk wound through the defiles of the hills.

We clambered up again the hill which commands such a view of Hakodade bay and harbor and descended its other side into the village of Toni-no-shta, whose villagers gave us welcoming recognizances, and dismounted at the little inn where shockheaded landlord awaited our approach. Here we made our noon halt, and our host brought in a basket of tempting fish which he had secured in anticipation of our wants. The children, too, were ready with their baskets of acorn like chestnuts and fruits. One man showed us with pride a half bushel of hops he had gathered at our suggestion to try the market.

As we sat once more on the piazza opening out [upon] the flower garden, an old man came to us with a few quarts of beans and muttered over some unintelligible Japanese which I interpreted into a desire to sell them. I declined the purchase, he insisted, and I finally left him and his beans and took a walk through the single street of the village. Halfway up the hill I met the pretty village maiden I had seen on my way out. She was going Rebecca-like to the well with two buckets suspended from a pole across her shoulder. Her head was enclosed in a neat muslin wrapper and as she smiled her welcome I thought her prettier than ever.

I went on to the house where the little child lay sick and alas the poor thing could no longer lift its head. I had brought a pocket full of crackers for the little invalid as the most acceptable gift out of our small stores which were gratefully received. Returning to the inn I found that the old man had persisted in disposing of his beans, and during my absence had poured them out before one of my comrades and departed. Then it occurred to me what I had been too dull to perceive before, that the old man was, after all, desirous to make a present rather than to trade. So, hastily snatching up some trifles, I started after him, but he had disappeared from the street.

As my only resource I went back to the house where the sick child lay and inquiring for him discovered that he was this little child's grandfather and had been vainly trying to make me a present in return for the little attention I had bestowed on the child the day before. More than ever was I eager to find him and make amends. I had the luck of a romancer in meeting at this house the village belle who was a daughter of the old man and proffered to escort me to his house. Soon we went together through the street to the no little amazement, I have no doubt, of the gossips of Toni-no-shta, what pretty Okoma was doing with that hilarious bewhiskered *tojin*, to her father's house.

The old man was alone and had fallen asleep over his simple dinner and his potations of sake, a sleep so sound that it required a good deal of shaking, which Okoma laughingly bestowed upon him to arouse him. He was at length awakened and made to comprehend the purport of my visit. He clasped my hand warmly in his, thanking me over and over again, laughing with that peculiar chuckle that belongs to old age. But when I came to say good bye to him and Okoma, and placing my arm around the waist of the village belle gave her a kiss which she received with mingled blushes and smiles, the old man's chuckle broke out into a peal of laughter. He evidently thought it, as did I, the best joke of the season.

I had occasion to note the hospitality of this people removed from foreign contact. Into whatsoever home I intruded my face with curiosity I was welcomed, invited in, and tea or sake or both placed before me with sometimes fruits or eatables.

My comrades were half through the dinner when I returned to the little inn, but I bore their jokes at my prolonged absence well since the belle of Toni-no-shta and I knew a flavoring sauce more than they. After dinner we at once mounted and took a new road towards the city, which again afforded us many a pretty bit of rustic scenery, whether of brawling brooks, farms, houses, gardens, cultivated fields, or several of them combined. As a whole the farm houses were inferior to those I had been familiar with in Nippon, but there were also more new ones. This homeward road had many houses upon it, and one or two large villages. The populace were generally industrious, and we had no lack of salutations from children playing by the road side, women in the doorways, or laborers in the yards and fields. Certainly the outward look of it all, if not one of great worldly prosperity, was one of happiness and content.

A rain shower overtook us as we passed around a mountain spur and came into the streets of a fine village which, from it proximity to Hakodade, bore more signs of thrift. Spacious houses under the shade of grand old trees, or half hidden among hedge rows, replaced the wooden cottages of the open country. Small streams were again universal, a better watered country there is nowhere, and this end of Yeso at least might be made into something little short of a paradise.

Now we debouched again onto the great plains that begird the head of Hakodade Bay where our path lay alongside of numerous sand hillocks that the winds blowing in from seaward had heaped in irregular line of sea wall. Seeing native pack horses coming down on the sea beach we rode through the sand and found a little road bed on the scarce beaten sands of the shore. It was a pleasant ride along the ocean's rim where a gentle swell was pulsating on the beach and the air that crossed the water came to us laden with so much freshness. The water rolled in to our horses' hoofs with the incoming tide and coming to a little inlet that intercepted our way we breasted our reluctant horses over it.

Soon the rising tide drove us from the beach back to the highway and we were among the scattered fishermen's hovels that formed the first outlying suburb of the city. Our horses were so knocked up with the to them unaccustomed jaunt, that not even the familiar location any longer infused any life into them. We were swallowed up in the crowds that were passing out of the city after the completion of their day's business.

Train after train of pack horses were coming and going, and laden bullocks were blocking the road. The loads of wood, charcoal, and vegetables with which they had been burdened going in were coming out with rice, seaweed, oil, clothing stuffs, and other household necessaries of life to be scattered broadcast up and down among the vales of Yeso. I counted one train of fifty horses. By the roadside was a drove of 300 horses that had been purchased by the English Commissariat office for the China campaign, but with the news of the late successes came orders to resell the animals and they had this day been disposed of at $1 per head, a loss of $15 to $20 on each.

There were a few officials going in and out of the city, not moving as in the Tokaido on foot or riding in a norimon, but mounted on horseback with their followers like small bodies of very irregular cavalry. As they came along the dusty thoroughfare it was sufficiently amazing to see the *chonin*, or common people, popping off their horses and popping on again as the trains swept by, for plebeian blood must not remain mounted before official dignity, and sometimes their motions were accelerated by a tap from an attendant's spear or in their own haste to do the little great more reverence they tumbled into the dust. As we entered the city proper we were at times brought to a dead stand still by the blockade of animals. While I was in Hakodade I should estimate the daily passing of horses over the neck of land that unites the promontory with the main shore at not less than 3000.

We rode up to our inn door and were welcomed back by its hospitable landlord; our horses more rejoiced than we at our journey's termination. The animal which I rode, being tender footed, was not able to leave his stable again while I was in Hakodade. Thus ended our day's jaunt, which had been one of the pleasantest episodes of my wanderings. Everywhere we had received uniform and marked hospitality without drawback of a single rudeness or churlishness. We had been free from both the espionage and interference of officials, so different from what it would have been on the shores of Yedo where we may not stir without being jealously watched. Bears we had been threatened with, boors none.

Friday, October 5, 1860

I witnessed a burial procession this morning differing little from those I was familiar with passing our own temple yard at Kanagawa. But the custom of burning the dead is much more prevalent at Hakodade than in the vicinity of Yedo, in fact, it is almost universal. Dr. H[epburn] and myself had started this morning to cross over the hill to a settlement on the other side particularly to a porcelain manufactory and some pleasure gardens near thereto. As we descended the opposite face of the hill we came upon one of the places for cremation. It was a fit place, a wild spot among the rocks, great mounds of trachyte, low bushes, and vines, enclosed by a wall of rough stone. There was a Buddhist chapel also surrounded by monuments of stone near to the enclosure.

We clambered over the rough trachyte and made our way into the enclosure where the fires were even now alight. A grinning sexton in rough clothes was watching a burning pile and adding fresh faggots thereto amid whose flames we saw a half consumed body. The Sexton of Isnay, so call him, was of a cheerful countenance and looked as though he might have been as pithy and sententious of speech as his fellows of Denmark. But there was a wall within the walls, a wall half turf half stone, where in a less open spot and under a roof the cremation was more extensively accomplished. One was certainly a place for outsiders, and the other for the gentle folks.

We could have entered at once but the smoke bearing its rank effluvia was drawing through the gateway. A breach in the wall to the windward favored us, and clambering over it we were within a small enclosure where under a shed roof four bodies were in various stages of consumption by fire. One fire with its ashes was quite cold and among the cinders a relative of the consumed one was searching for any calcined reminiscences of the departed. The second fire was being quenched with water, and the other two were yet blazing fiercely. There were several attendants here but the chief of them was a grim cross-eyed fellow in gray robe and leggings of straw who smoked his pipe and stirred up the embers with equal nonchalance.

Despite his avocation, the sinister look of his face, and unsavory order of his garments, he was communicative so far as our imperfect knowledge would allow him to be. All were burned, he said, who could afford, and it was only the very poorest who denied the purification of fire to their departed relatives. The teeth were extracted before burning and then with the tobacco pouch and pipe, and ashes, were enclosed in a box and buried in the temple cemeteries. The little enclosure was neatly kept and everything was decorous unless it were the idle boys of the neighborhood who gathered around despite the smoke that flew in their faces and were having their own laugh and talk. I have never seen any seriousness in the face of death among the Japanese and the cross-eyed sexton smoking his pipe was no more solemnized by his occupation than are the mourners in white who follow the coffin of kindred flesh to its last and long home. We bade the sexton adieu holding our breaths till we were sure we were beyond a whiff whose flavor would be sure to linger in our memories longer than most memories of deceased virtues and so happily vices too.

The porcelain manufactory was carried on in a little cluster of houses and sheds at the front of the hill. The men were enjoying a long dinner hour's rest when we entered within the fence that enclosed the buildings. We waited for them to resume their work, and then we were free to inspect all the processes and ask any questions which were answered civilly. "No admittance" did not turn us back from the doors, as it would at home, nor did the questioned workmen instead of civil answers bid us go to fires warmer than their iron bake ovens. Seated on their legs on a platform before paper windows four or five men were painting cups and saucers after patterns, behind them as many more with simple hand lathes were moulding and shaping various vessels, others were preparing the plastic clay. Without in the yard were ranges of baking ovens made of what had been unburnt bricks; a stream of water led by bamboo pipes from the neighboring hills furnished a constant supply; the clay was brought by boats from another province 60 miles to Hakodade. Most of the work was the common porcelain of the country, though on one shelf we saw specimens of a few elaborate patterns.

We rested ourselves in the tea garden another mile beyond which was the counterpart of many similar places with its miniature lake, rustic bridge, rock work and flowers, dwarf trees and hedge rows. Rhododendrons were growing luxuriantly among the scattered artificial rock works. But the season for such places had passed by and besides ourselves there was but one party of guests.

There are fewer Buddhist temples at Hakodade than at Kanagawa but the respect paid to them and their services was something very different. At the latter I had been accustomed to see temples day after day with only occasionally a worshipper, and all the religious services were confined to festival days or the ringing of bells and muttering of prayers by an ignorant priesthood. At Hakodade, on the contrary, the temples were seldom without worshippers and twice in the day, at daylight or sunrise and in the middle of the day, there were regular services numerously attended. I went at two o'clock this afternoon to the temple near the American Consulate. I should think there were 200 people assembled within the temple and kneeling on the mats before the shrine.

The steps before the temple were covered with Japanese sandals and clogs, and squatted on a mat by the door a beggar boy was seeking to earn a few copper or iron cash by cleaning and brushing the same; a few coins were tokens that his efforts met a partial success. The temple was of capacity to hold 800 persons; it was devoid of ornament except the carvings of the friezes which were capital similitudes of the 12 signs of the Japanese zodiac, and the ceiling panelled in squares and ornamented with rich woods and colors. The three personifications of Buddha's images of wood life size with the alter service stood within a recess behind a veil.

Lighted lamps were burning before them on branch candlesticks, each socket being a lotus in blossom.

The people were reverently kneeling in silence with clasped hands and by far the greater number were men. As they came in each one after kneeling drew out from the folds of his dress a surplice or double sash which was suspended from the neck and fell over the shoulders rather than across the chest, these prayer aprons were usually of fine silk and bore the family crest of the wearer. After the audience had remained for some moments kneeling a priest in flowing yellow robes kneeling before the audience with the side of his face towards them took a book out from its handsome wrapping of silk brocade heavy with gilt and spreading it open on a low reading desk, read from it a few moments and then began a rapid exhortation. His manner was that of an actor uttering a soliloquy in measured cadences and monotonous tone. What with the kneeling audience, the burning lamps, and the peculiar manner of the priest to say naught of his robes I might have imagined myself in a Catholic as well as a Buddhist temple. The address or sermon lasted half an hour or more and thus twice in a day at four temples in the city are held like services oftentimes to crowded houses. To the right of the altar numerous offerings of rice were heaped up in paper bags whose contents would have made several bushels and the floor and mats were thickly covered with iron and copper cash.

Not far from the temple is a street running back and up the hill built up on either side with the best houses of the city. The very character of the buildings in so excelling others would alone have indicated the locality of the "Oshiwara" (Places of prostitutes). Not only the street up the hill, but others at right angles with it were similarly occupied. It was a quarter of the town by itself. By day all is quiet and decorous about them, but at evening the scenes are of gayety and dissipation.

The lower front of each house is a large apartment open to the street except so far as the vertical bars separate it. These apartments are handsomely matted and papered, and at evening time when they are brilliantly lighted, seated in a row across the room are the showily dressed bedizened courtesans. Their garments long trailing robes of silk or of bright unusually gaudy colors and oftentimes expensive. Their faces and necks are whitened with powder, and their cheeks and lips glow with artificial dyes. Their headdress is the result of great painstaking on the part of the most skillful of hair dressers and is fairly burdened with the weight of hair pins and ornaments of metal, shell, and precious stones. They are kneeling on the mats with their brazier of charcoal before them and pipes, tobacco, and tea for an occasional solace. They are of all ages from the little miss in her first teens to the hardened outcast of double her years. And there they sit while the crowd without wander up and down gazing at their uncovered beauty. Occasionally one comes forward to the lattice in obedience to the call of some acquaintance from without. Many of the faces were beautiful and have not yet lost their look of innocence, indeed so little shame attaches to this life in Japan that those hard horrible visages one may meet in the street at home are wanting here.

Each night when the streets are lighted the crowd marches up and down the streets and the youth of Japan take their lessons in vice which has become familiar to its sight and is daily set before them by the rulers of the land. Many of the girls are placed here by their parents without regard to their wishes, and what is worse this young girl seldom turns with loathing from this life till it is too late to retrace her steps. A life of ease, fine clothes, and abundance to eat and drink are but too fatally alluring to the daughters [of the] poor in this land as well as others.

On one corner of the main street is an immense building of two stories erected for the foreign community, but its numerous apartments find few occupants. Many of the girls within their cages cover their faces whenever a foreigner gazes in with their fans; whether it is done from a dislike to foreigners or to heighten their charms by an affectation of modesty they do not possess I cannot say. I know they were not always the youngest or fairest who do so. From these houses mistresses are hired out to the foreign population at $15 per month, less than half of the cost at other ports. The singing girls attached to these houses are a class by themselves.

Saturday, October 6, 1860

The further removed the foreign settlements are from Yedo and its court influences, the less difficulty there appears to have been with the native authorities. This is so with Nagasaki, compared to Yokohama, and yet more so at Hakodade. This is owing in part to the fact that the settlement at Hakodade is smaller, there is less trade, and of course less conflicting conditions, but also to the fact that officials on both sides take more responsibility in adjusting difficulties without reference to a higher power. There is less espionage at Hakodade, the entire number of officials was said not to exceed 300, though I suspect this does not include the garrison of the princes in whose military jurisdiction Hakodade is. The foreign population is not in a community together but is scattered about the city where inclination leads them, Bradford's inn being in the very thickest of the city in its principal street. He never has been particularly molested, though I think he has two or three times had stones thrown at his house probably for provocation given by some of his transient guests. The foreigners go about the streets at night freely with or without lanterns. I saw plenty of sailors enjoying their shore leave after Jack's own heart in unlimited possession of grog, and noisy and troublesome as they must have been, the inhabitants get along with them very quietly.

There was one class of population that I regretted I missed seeing, these were the "Ainos," or "Hairy Kuriles," supposed to be the autochthons of this island and the Kurile group to the north. There is a large settlement of them at Volcano Bay thirty miles from Hakodade, and when I returned from the trip to the volcano I regretted to find that I had been very near to them without knowing it. They are people of small stature and are noted, as their name denotes, for their hairy bodies. The men universally wear long beards hanging down over their broad chests. They are described as a poor, inoffensive people subsisting by fishing and some simple manufactures much like our N.A. Indians. Once each year in the fall they pay a visit to the Governor of Hakodade from whom they receive gifts of food and clothing to assist them through the winter, which is long and cold to a people living in frail houses and with neither skins or woolens to protect them. The procession last year was 2000 in number and such a show of long beards must have presented a striking appearance.

Stretching to the northward from Yeso is a series of islands reaching up to the peninsula of Kamchatka belonging nominally to the Japanese Empire and inhabited by this singular hardy race. These islands are little known to the rest of the world having nothing to tempt either the avarice or cupidity of other people. Not so with the long island of Saghalin [Sakhalin] lying between the Gulf of Tartary and the Sea of Okhotsk. It lies in the path of Russian vessels sailing out from Amour and is valuable for its coal mines to the Asiatic navy of this colossal empire. There has already sprung up a conflict of jurisdiction for this island between the Russians and Japanese, the former being in actual occupancy of one end of the island mining coals extensively and the latter on the northern end whither this summer they have sent over many soldiers embarking from the fort of Hakodade. Already I felt within the sphere of this great power's influence, that silent crisis, the influence from whence it comes you know not, you only feel that it is.

In the streets of Hakodade Russian accents were commoner than our own, the handsome buildings of her consular residency are the most conspicuous objects of the city, and in men's rooms, and at the tables, it was not the great Mississippi, or the vast breadth of western prairies, that was talked of, nor yet what the Thames was rolling seaward, or what was done under the shadow of St. Paul's, but the grimy commerce of Amour, the fertile plains prairie-like in richness and extent that Russia had acquired of her weaker southern neighbor, the mineral wealth of Siberia, and the boundless material resources of this young empire and how the slightest touch of the wire at St. Petersburgh was promptly and faithfully answered six thousand miles away, six thousand miles in unbroken extent, what is the spasmodic drum beat of England to the measured tramp of progress of such an Empire as this.

Russia feels sadly the want of a harbor on this side of the world. Since the Crimean War, Petropavlovsky has been deserted as a naval or military station, Okhotsk is falling into decay, and the resources that sustained these places are now centered in Nikolaevsky, which is the headquarters both winter and summer of the Russian forces in the East. Poor winter quarters they are indeed, blocked up with ice half the year and the troops dying of scurvy in their barracks. Emperor Harbor will bring only a mitigation of difficulties. But there is a harbor which the Russian bear looks at with covetous eye from his poorer winter home, a harbor spacious, safe, and that can be made as impregnable as Gibraltar, a harbor where the summer lingers long and the winter brings just a necessary allowance of cold for the northern constitution, a harbor to which timber, iron, coal are all cheaply accessible. More important even than Constantinople to Russia in the West is Hakodade to Russia in the East.

Business was dull at Hakodade, there was not a foreign ship in the harbor loading for any port. The available exports are few and come under the head of chow chow as the china traders call it. Fewer whalers than usual had touched at this port during the past year, Nagasaki dividing the trade in outfits with Hakodade; indeed whalers had been in a measure discouraged from attempting outfits here, finding it difficult to get what they needed (See table furnished by Consul Hodgson to me of the trade of the port and the number of vessels touching there).[95]

Among the imitative manufactures I saw here were silver forks and spoons fabricated after foreign models, excellent hinges and screws, the latter laboriously filed out by hand. Bradford's inn was furnished with well made sash and clapboarded after the Yankee style; though clapboarding was quite common among the natives. A very common weather boarding of the houses was made of bark placed vertically. Of their own manufactures the best thing I saw was a smooth bore rifle with match lock handsomely finished and mounted.

Man is here much less a beast of burden, the abundance and cheapness of horses and oxen

answering a better purpose. There was very little use of the norimon, the horse supplanted that also. Until I came to Yeso I had never seen a mare in Japan and seldom a cow, here they were abundant, sustaining the usual proportionate relations of the sexes. On Nippon and Kiusiu the mare is kept for breeding purposes and are neither for sale at the open ports nor to be seen at all.

There were very few beggars in the streets though the humble houses with roofs of straw or shingles and stones and sides of bark bespoke a condition of life not many ounces from poverty. But Dr. H[epburn] and myself thought we observed a ruddier look of health in the population as a whole. Instead of doing up their hair in such elaborate headdressings as is universal in Nippon, at least half of the women wore their hair combed smoothly back and gathered in a simple knot held by a back comb. Nor were the boys' heads so commonly shaved, but their hair was also combed back smoothly from the forehead. This may have been that scalp diseases were not so fearfully common as among the young children about Yedo bay. Nor did the people show such eager curiosity. I went about the streets unobserved

[95] This table is not included with the manuscript, but it was published with his letter from Hakodate dated October 26, 1860, which was published in the *New York Tribune*, December 29, 1860. The table follows:

	Imports	Exports
July 1 to Dec. 31, 1859	$12,760.43	$ 86,309.24
Jan. 1 to June 30, 1860	$ 7,203.14	$ 40,377.00
July 1 to Sept. 30, 1860	$ 3,605.14	$ 8,226.35
Total for Sixteen months	$23,685.30	$135,123.63

Foreign Ships Entered into the Port of Hakodadi

	1859	1860
Russian men-of-war	26	5
American whalers	36	17
American merchant ships	12	10
English merchant ships	10	9
English men-of-war	5	4
Dutch men-of-war	1	1
South American merchant ships	1	—
Dutch merchant ships	—	1
Russian merchant ships	—	1
Total	91	48

The above table is for the whole of the year 1859, and nine months of 1860.

and not boisterously saluted with "Ohio" at every step, or surrounded with a curious crowd wherever I stopped.

But I cannot speak so well of the dogs, the best fed and conditioned race of street monarchs I ever saw. They ranged the streets in bands seeming to have their particular patrols and were fed from door to door. They look formidable with their large size, wolfish head and eyes, and bristling necks and tails, but at the first sight of a *tojin* down drops the tail and away the animal goes to the nearest alleyway where he stands barking and howling as you pass and all his comrades take up the refrain and pass you on from dog to dog, band to band, street to street, and you find yourself heralded in advance wherever you go as effectually as if by a yakunin's *sta iro* (the order given to kneel by a herald preceding a dignitary). Their very yelp seems to say "*tojin, tojin,*" and a housewife's drying turnips are safe from any foreign thieves thus preached about.

Sunday, October 7, 1860

Remembered as the anniversary of a brother's birthday whose days on earth were finished sad years ago.[96]

The *Berenice* was to return tomorrow and I took a farewell look at the beautiful bay from the hill. The distant hills were covered with a thin haze which gives a landscape such a strange inexplicable charm. The volcanos were puffing up their steam clouds from what unseen engine deep in the bowels of the earth? What were the buried titans so industriously forging? Junks were outward bound on the fair morning wind and friends of the departing were following along the shore waving hands and shouting farewell words.

My week's stay had been the height of pleasurable enjoyment, the cloudless autumn day and the subtle joy in the atmosphere would alone have produced this, and I shook my head incredulously at the foreigners who talked of cold winter storms and summer's cloudy days of rain, and would name the cli-

[96] This was his brother William Maxwell, who died in 1847.

mate only with objurgations. I had seen none of it, and why should I believe in aught but the delicious autumn time I had felt. Dined with our Consul, to whom I was indebted for kind attentions, early in the evening, and left my inn and its attentive landlord, whose only fault was his too modest charges, at 8 P.M. to embark.

Monday, October 8, 1860

Thermometer 54°–Latitude 41° 29′ M.

We were up anchor and away at six of the morning. With steam, tide, and the current we passed rapidly out of the Straits of Sangar, but abreast of Yakeyama, or Burning Mountain, our engine was stopped for repairs. We made sail on the foremast, but progressed slowly the remainder of the day. Our engine was again serviceable at 8 P.M. in good time to steady us in a heavy seaway, for the wind was blowing freshly and our open ports took in water. There was a great tumbling of unsecured baggage in the night.

Tuesday, October 9, 1860

Thermometer 54°. Latitude 39° 50′, Longitude 142° 38′.

Wind blowing fresh and a heavy sea, and of course my sensitive stomach rendered serviceless. At 10 A.M. we were opposite Cape Tooni, at 6 P.M. opposite Kinko San. Sea fell to quiet towards night and we had a magnificent view of the sun setting behind the hills of Nippon. A junk had a narrow escape of being run down by us.

Wednesday, October 10, 1860

Latitude 36° 30′, Longitude 141° 36′.

A lovely morning at sea, the water smooth as a lake, our spirits were full of exhilaration as we walked about the decks or lounged on the bridge. At 7 A.M. we were opposite Kadji Yama. We have run farther out coming down barely keeping the headlands in distant sight, and what surprised us, we had a strong current bearing us southward at an average distance from the land of 20 miles. Coming up and keeping in shore we had failed to find the northerly flow of the Kuro Siwo. At 6 P.M. we were opposite Cape Boi. A bright starlight night. At 2 A.M. the officer of the deck saw a burning village.

Thursday, October 11, 1860

At 7 A.M. we were abreast Cape King, and rounding Susaki had a fine view up the bay, beautiful in the sunny sheen and under the sporting wind, beautiful with its great fleet of fishing boats with their white sails like gulls over the water. A brig and barque were ahead of us pressing at the bay under full canvass and it was not till we reached Mississippi Bay that we passed them. At 12 M. we anchored before Yokohama completing our voyage in 78 hours of which there was at least eight hours delay by our being under slow sail while the engine was out of repair. As our ship's best rate was only 7 knots, the aid of a homeward current had been plainly marked.

Returned from Hakodade today arriving at 12 M. Found all friends well. Few changes have occurred since I left. The poor *Camilla* has not been heard from and we fear she has gone down with every soul on board. So I hear of other disasters by storm. The *Mary and Louisa* has arrived from Shanghai after a passage of 25 days. For seven days she lay battling with the tempest on a lee shore and barely saved herself. The *Henriette Louise* has had a passage of 65 days hence to Shanghai! What a stormy coast. Let none who are not compelled by urgent necessity tempt the dangers of the Japanese coast in August and September.

The Prussian envoy has not succeeded as yet in making a treaty. The Japanese so far refuse

to make one. Attached to the expedition is Mr. Heine[97] formerly of the Perry expedition.

Prince Mito is within a few days reported dead.[98] He is supposed to have died by foul means. The Japanese are used to the poison cup. Some say poisoned by his enemies, others by some of his followers recently dismissed from his employ. At all events it seems pretty certain that the great bugbear of the foreigners and the Japanese government is gone to his account.

Then I hear that the Japanese are determined to open no more ports even under the treaty and again that they will open Oasaca instead of Yedo in 1862.

Some excursionists availing themselves of the treaty privilege of going ten ri have recently been into the country, but they were dogged wherever they went by Custom House officials dispatched after them and the inn keepers were instructed to charge them prices so exorbitant as to deter others from following in their footsteps.

Friday, October 12, 1860

The work on my new residence at Yokohama was wholly stopped in my absence by the Japanese who said my lease from the former proprietors was good for nothing. I think they were quite right, but I thought it best to leave the house and talk to them afterwards. They seemed inclined not to give possession at all, but Dr. S[immons] after many interviews won their consent. Today I have been to look at it and find the work progressing favorably. Made a purchase of several pieces of handsome lacquered crockery.

Just before dinner our house was invaded by all the old married ladies of the neighborhood with their children. It was a holiday belonging

---

[97] Peter Bernhard Wilhelm Heine was a German artist who accompanied the Perry expedition. He provided many of the graphic works used to illustrate the official account of Perry's visit to Japan. Heine subsequently published his own books: *Reise um die Erde nach Japan an Bord der Expeditions-Escadre unter Commodore M. C. Perry.* 2 vols. (Leipzig: Hermann Costenoble, 1856); *Japan: Beiträge zur Kentniss Des Landes und Seine Bewohner.*

2 vols in one. (Dresden: Woldemar Urban, 1880). A portion of the first volume has been published as *With Perry to Japan: A Memoir by William Heine*, trans. Frederick Trautmann (Honolulu: University of Hawaii Press, 1990).

[98] Hall's information is fairly accurate on this occasion. Tokugawa Nariaki, the Lord of Mito, died on September 29, 1860.

to this temple and they, with freshly blackened teeth and clean clothes, were making pastimes of the day. They requested the privilege of looking through our rooms which was readily accorded to them. Every article new and strange to them excited expressions of approval and curiosity, from the clothes on our persons to the lamp on the table and the clock in the corner. The music box yielded them a fresh delight. Handling my clothes and inspecting my shirt the old ladies begged me for my shirt buttons. As this would be inconvenient, I proffered a compromise in some brass buttons I had. In an instant twenty hands were thrust out to receive the coveted gift of a gilt button. I gave the buttons out to women and children and some hands came back twice with Japanese craftiness and even old ladies strongly plead for one more. When they found no more were to come every hand with its button was raised to the forehead and the head bowed in token of thankfulness, the children bowing to the floor. The ceremony finished I was immediately told by the invited women to accompany them to the priest's house where ceremonies were being performed in honor of the day. By signs and words they intimated I should have a measure of sake. In vain I plead business decisions urgent of time, the black teethed women were inexorable as fate and I had to promise to come after dinner.

So after dinner I went. At the priest's house where the idols formerly belonging to the temple are kept I found a crowd of people of both sexes. In the room that held the service of Buddha's worship eight priests were kneeling before an image of Buddha chanting prayers in unison. On the altar were lighted candles, burning incense sticks, offerings of fruits, flowers, and vegetables. The priests were kneeling in a row on either side of the room facing each other, the senior priest kneeling between the rows facing the altar. As they chanted in not inharmonious tones their prayers they accom-

panied them with an occasional rhythmic beat on a wooden drum or on one of two bells. There was none of the attention or apparent devotion on the part of the people who looked on such as I had just seen in the temple worship at Hakodade. The men were smoking and talking, the women chatting merrily, and the children playing with a mirth sacrilegiously merry for worship. Satisfied with what I had seen I did not wait for the promised sake.

Saturday, October 13, 1860

Night before last Yedo was visited by one of those destructive fires which so often ravage the city. One temple, a theater, and many houses were consumed. The illumination of the fire was distinctly seen here. Many lives were lost in the theater.

Rode into the country this afternoon. The rice has ripened during my absence, the beans and millet have been gathered, the cotton picked, buckwheat is in bloom and the fields are being prepared for fall sowing. Radishes are already in the ground and coming up. Concert of music by the Prussian band at Dorr's in the afternoon. Among the many rumors of what the Japanese propose to do, we hear that they now propose to abandon Kanagawa and Yokohama to the foreigners and remove the Tokaido further back from the sea and thus be out of our way.

Sunday, October 14, 1860

There has been no lack of services suitable to the day even though we live in a heathen land. The Prussians had service on their frigate, English prayers were read on the *Berenice*, Mr. Goble preached in the hulk *Sapan*, Abbé Girard[99] held high mass at Yokohama, and Mr. Nevius preached to a congregation of some

---

[99] The Abbé Girard, or Prudence Seraphin Barthelemy Girard (1821–1867) was one of three French Catholic missionaries dispatched to the Ryūkyū Islands in 1855. Father Girard arrived in Yedo on September 6, 1859, just in time for the formal ratification of the French treaty with Japan. He temporarily served as in-

terpreter there for the French consul general. Later he was active in Yokohama. For a brief biographical sketch see Paul C. Blum, trans., "Father Mounicou's Bakumatsu Diary, 1856–64," *Transactions of the Asiatic Society of Japan* (third series), vol. 13 (Tokyo, 1976), p. 54.

forty souls. And this is in Japan where so much as to name the Christian religion threatened death to the offender.

Monday, October 15, 1860

The marriage customs of the Japanese so far as I have learned them are very simple. The parents of the young man ask of the girl's parents their daughter in marriage. Or vice versa, for it is quite proper for parents to ask for their daughter the husband they wish her to have. If the parents are consenting the young folks are brought together to see each other. If judging by a face interview alone they are not mutually pleased, or do not coincide with their parent's wishes, they separate, and other connubial companions are sought by their parents. If pleased, a day is fixed for the marriage, the hour appointed, the friends gather, the young couple arrayed in finery in presence of their friends without further ceremony become man and wife and feasting and drinking follows. The bridegroom then takes his newly wedded spouse to his house or that of his father's. On the following day the young man's mother goes in company with the bride to visit all their friends seeking like friendship for the young couple. If a boy and girl without the first introduction of parents conceive a liking for each other they consult their parents or nearest relatives or friends to make the customary proposals and arrangements. A courtship seems to be as unknown as kissing.

Tuesday, October 16, 1860

General Dorr gave today a grand fete to the Prussian Commodore. A long table is spread in his dining room which is ornamented with evergreens, camellias, and flowers. The Prussian Band is stationed under the trees in the yard, the rooms of his spacious temple are thrown open to a large company of ladies and gentlemen who wander about them, or prefer the open air of this bright October day. The collation was ample, wine abundant, company in high spirits, and our Consul, who does these things always well, had his usual success.

The *Overland Mail* brings me news of the broken alliance between France and England and of serious difficulty growing out of the Synai persecutions that may lead to war. Such news has the intensest interest in a little community like this made up of all nationalities far from home. So too there is news of more fighting in China, a battle at Tang Chan 12 miles from Pekin and of the capture by the Chinese of a flag of truce borne by Henry Parkes, the correspondent of the *London Times*, and officers of the staff. Elgin threatens all sort of disasters if a hair of their heads is touched.

Wednesday, October 17, 1860

A rainy day, busy in doors all day with letters for the home mail. Received yesterday and today one letter from L.W.[100] and papers from home. The singular mistakes made by letter writers to our home papers always amuse me. Think of Mito as lord of 31 provinces, as having fought several battles and been driven to the mountains 20 miles from Kanagawa! Nothing could be more absurd or untrue. How shall I believe foreign letter writers or travellers when I again tarry at home unless I know the writer or traveller?

Thursday, October 18, 1860

Making preparations to move to Yokohama. Ride on the Tokaido in the afternoon.

Friday, October 19, 1860

Busy as yesterday. Crossing the bay today, I saw the most curious fishing party I ever have seen. A yakunin accompanied by his servant were fishing in the shallow waters near the boat house. They had tucked their garments up and waded into the water up to their thighs and there they stood, the servant respectfully a little behind his master with a large pail to take the fish in and also to adjust tackle and bait. I

[100] Levi Wells Hall was one of Francis's older brothers.

recommend the example to some of our pleasure fishing parties at home.

Saturday, October 20, 1860

Moved a few of our things today.

Sunday, October 21, 1860

Rainy day writing letters.

Monday, October 22, 1860

Took boatloads of household effects to Yokohama favored by a fine day and smooth sea. Took up our quarters in our new house. Dined in the evening with Talbot not having yet our kitchen in readiness.

Tuesday, October 23, 1860

Fairly started housekeeping in our new home and finished bringing over the last load of our effects.

Wednesday, October 24, 1860

Putting things to right, to Kanagawa in the afternoon, returning saw a prisoner tied by ropes and led by an officer. He was eating a potato given to him by his conductor.

Thursday, October 25, 1860

Hartford arrived. Took an evening walk with Knight, Heco, and Duus.[101]

Friday, October 26, 1860

Went to Yokohama and arranged daguerreotype rooms. Fusi Yama clothed with snow.

Saturday, October 27, 1860

My birthday. Dined at Brown's and spent the day photographing.

Sunday, October 28, 1860

Rainy day. Closing day for the *Onward's* mails. Busy writing letters to friends at home.

Monday, October 29, 1860

To Kanagawa; called at Consul's, Hepburn's, and Brown's. S[adajirō] reports that Manjiro, the interpreter, has been confined to his home since his return from America. He has been taking daguerreotypes at Yedo with considerable success. Heco relates that he saw a galvanic battery recently of Japanese construction and that its maker had borrowed a barometer to make one after. Called on Lieut. Beaumont of the *Hartford*.

Tuesday, October 30, 1860

Called on Flag Officer Stribling of the *Hartford*, but did not find him aboard. Visited the different parts of the ship under the guidance of Lieut. B[eaumont]. She is a noble ship and everything on board seems to be managed worthily of her. The good order and neatness that everywhere prevailed was admirable. These features make our little navy noticeable wherever it goes.

---

[101] Mr. Knight and two other gentlemen, Est and Smith, had come to Japan from San Francisco to procure a cargo of lacquer ware. Knight later talked Joseph Heco into leaving the American consulate and joining him in a trade partnership. See Joseph Heco, *Narrative of a Japanese*, vol. 1, p. 235; see also Brooke, *John M.*

Brooke's Pacific Cruise and Japanese Adventure, p. 171. This appears to have been J. H. Duus, later of Lindsay & Co., who is listed in *The Chronicle and Directory for China, Japan, and the Philippines for 1865* (Hong Kong: Daily Press, 1865), p. 243.

Wednesday, October 31, 1860

Consul Dorr gave a dejeuner today to the officers of the *Hartford*. It was a breakfast of cold meats handsomely set forth as our Consul knows how to do it. Most of the Americans resident at Kanagawa and Yokohama were present as also many English, French, and Dutch residents. The band of the *Hartford* played under the cover of the great cherry tree. The day passed pleasantly to all concerned. The pleasantest incident to us was an invitation from the ward room officers of the *Hartford* to be their guest on their intended trip to Yedo tomorrow. I joyfully accepted the invitation, which was doubly welcome as I was not indebted for it to Consul Dorr or Minister Harris.

Thursday, November 1, 1860

Went on board the *Hartford* this morning at eight o'clock accompanied by Heco.[102] Met a warm welcome from the officers and sat down to breakfast with them. The wardroom mess I found a genial lot of men. The names I remember are 1st Lieut. Walbach. 2nd. O. Blanning. 3rd Myers. 4th Law. 5th Du Bries. Surgeons Troipler, Carson, and Hay. Chaplain Barton. Purser ———. Master Lee, Capt of Marines Garland, Lieut. of Do'. Dawson. At nine A.M. we made steam and were under weigh for Yedo. The twelve miles of our steaming presented no incidents, nothing of note.

We reached our anchorage at Yedo in an hour and a half, passing the Prussian frigates *Thetis* and *Arcona*[103] and exchanging salutes with them. The waters of the head of Yedo Bay are very shallow. The *Hartford* drawing sixteen or seventeen feet was anchored five miles from the shore. The shores of the bay are low, while far inland we could see the blue peaks of a high mountain range. Abreast of the city are fire forts—earth parapets with stone facing—and guns mounted on barbette. These forts have been constructed since Perry's visit. They have no formidable look, and to an attacking boat party approaching from the south the first put would cover the guns of all the rest. There was a considerable earthwork and battery on shore. The forts are built out in the shallow water a mile and a half from the mainland.

From our anchorage ground there were few indications of our nearness to one of the greatest cities of the world. The bay was still and almost lifeless, not busy with native craft as we would have expected. Here and there on shore were visible a few mast-junks, and a small number of fishing boats were scattered about the bay. The Prince of Satsuma's unwieldy, useless hulk was anchored near the forts. Along the shore we could see scattered among trees yet unscathed by autumnal frosts the tiled roofs and white walls of more conspicuous buildings.

A party of us went ashore in the ship's cutter. We passed between the silent forts and their grassy slopes of green. The brass guns, mostly of small calibre, were bright, but not a soul was to be seen about the ramparts. As we neared the shore we could discern the thick houses of a great city. Low hills of irregular form were covered with temples whose peaked roofs were embraced in the shade of overhanging trees and whose walls were hidden by living walls of hedge. Picturesque spots along the bay were occupied by the tea houses and places of pleasure resort. The white walls of the Princes' enclosures shone out from among the shrubbery and rising above the humble roofs were the mosque-like *shiroi*, or cupolas, denoting princely residences.

Our boat landed us at the Custom House wharf, a solid work of stone with steps leading up from the water's edge. Japanese officials received us and politely inquired whither we would be conducted. We told them we wished to look at the city, and without the least delay

---

[102] For Joseph Heco's account of this visit to Edo with Hall see his *The Narrative of a Japanese*, vol. 1, pp. 257ff; see also Haruna Akira, *Hōryū—Josefu Hiko to Nakamatachi* (Tokyo: Kadokawa, 1982).

[103] The *Thetis* and *Arcona* were the ships that had brought Count Friedrich Albert Eulenberg, the Prussian representative, to Japan. Eulenberg was in the process of negotiating a commercial treaty with Japan at this time. For details see Hermann Maron, *Japan und China* (Berlin: Otto Janke, 1863).

three or four two sworded men were detailed to accompany us whithersoever we would go. The Custom House grounds were secluded from the city by a high fence, its buildings are simple wooden offices where a few officials are stationed to look after the wants of the national representatives that visit Yedo, for none others are yet permitted within these waters.

We first paid our respects to Minister Harris, who received us courteously. Mr. Harris is a man of middle size, full figure, blue eyes, gray hair, in his manner inclined to an excessive show of politeness. He does not look as if he had suffered much from the cares of his office or his long seclusion in Japan, having rather the appearance of a bon vivant a little blase more than that of a soul and a body suffering *en verite*. One need not hear him speak five minutes before making the discovery that there is at least no man in the world who knows but the American Minister at the Court of Yedo is a great man. Nor should the guest trouble himself to frame fitting speeches, for sorry chance will he have to fire them in among the thick rolling volley of words that tell the experiences of the speaker, with all the unreserve of a man who thinks what he has seen, done, and supposed, be fitting themes for every hour and all ears.

The residence of the American Minister is in the western suburbs of Yedo, [a] mile and a half from the Custom House landing. The walk thither was through streets of shops crowded with buyers and sellers, hucksters, venders of small wares, then by the walled enclosures of some daimios, and again through a quiet street of humble houses, clean chalets where little yards were separated by green hedges and adorned with shrubbery. Again we descended into a little valley through which flowed a small stream and no building had been permitted to stand on its banks for a large breadth either side so that the city stream retained its country life and meandered gracefully between green banks skirted with clumps of trees.

Mr. Harris occupies the dwelling apartments of the priesthood attached to the large tem-

ple.[104] His interpreter (Mr. Heusken) occupies a small house within the same compound. A large number of officials are posted within the same grounds as a guard. The Minister's residence is pleasant, the backcourt is shut in by a high hill covered with fine old trees. Here is a fish pond with some remarkably large gold fish or carp.

After paying our respects to Mr. Harris, under the escort of some officers we took a walk into the city. Everywhere we found wide and clean streets. No filth, no noisome stench offended any sense. The contrast between this and Chinese cities could not have been greater. There was every variety in our walk. Now we were passing through the compact buildings and spacious streets and dense population of a city, now we had a bit of a country road bordered by fresh turf and shade trees, again a brick walled lane, a rural path, a babbling brook and rustic bridge hard by the spacious residences of a feudal daimio prince. So mingled is Yedo of city and country.

In one street a party of police were endeavoring to arrest a couple of offenders, there was a mob, a rush, a great struggle and pulling of hair as we passed by the excited multitude. Our official guides conducted us to Atago-Yama, or Belleview, as the Yedo foreign residents politely call it. This is an elevation from whose summit the whole of Yedo may be seen and it is the only accessible eminence where a like view may be had. A flight of 84 stone steps fifteen feet wide conduct to the summit. On the summit and occupying the face of the entire brim of the hill were tea booths where we were welcomed by the low bows and polite salutations of the attendant girls. The booths were divided into separate compartments each one with its Hebe of the celestial beverage. Each one strove by meaning smiles, persuasive beckonings of the hand, and polite favors of Japanese speech to induce us to patronize their booth. I do not know how it happened, but it did so happen that when we had made our selection and seated ourselves on the low benches covered with mats that we found ourselves in the tea booth presided over by a

---

[104] This was the Zempukuji. For a contemporary photograph of this temple taken by Felix Beato, the Yokohama photographer, see Yokohama Kaikō Shiryō Kan, eds., *F. Beato bakumatsu nihon shashin shū*, p. 109.

Zempukuji, site of the American Legation in Edo. Photograph by Felice Beato.

bright eyed nymph of sixteen, for she told me in a confidential way, showing all her many white teeth at the time, that she was not a day more, and the prettiest out of the dozen or more who are the hill goddesses of this spot. To be sure her face was powdered and there were broad bands of white extending down her neck and disappearing under her garments in rueful contrast with the dingy skin left untouched, for this is Japanese style, and her sore fingers were symptomatic of a common cutaneous disorder. But one forgets the little drawback to female beauty after a short residence in Japan, so when the belle of Belleview brought us our hot unsugared tea in little blue porcelain cups we drank it thinking only of her sloe black eyes, glossy hair, and shining teeth.

The view from the hill was a superb one. There under a sleepy autumnal curtain lay the great city of Yedo—Yedo so long the marvel of the world, Yedo with its streets unbetrodden by white men till [now] save by the few abased Dutchmen that wandered occasionally therein bringing tribute from Desima, or some especial favorite like Spanish Rodriguez[105] or honest Will Adams[106] of centuries ago. Yedo with its mysterious tales of princely feuds, its spectacles of princely retinues, its court-gayeties and popular festivities, where population aforetime has been counted by as many millions as London, Paris, Rome, and St. Petersburg combined. It was one great sea of black and white roofs broken here and there by some temple's lofty head or the *shiroi* of the princely courts. Far as the eye could see to the northward and eastward stretched the great city till lost in the obscure distance; its extreme length cannot be less than sixteen miles or its greatest breadth less than six.

All over the city you see interspersed the green crests of trees, for there is not such another city in the world for parks and ornamental grounds. The density of the city is so broken by the innumerable recurring structures of the daimios that it has not the look of compactness seen in most of our home cities. There was something in the landscape before us that reminded more than one of our party of the view of Philadelphia from the top of Gi-

---

[105] João Rodrigues (1561?–1633) was a Portuguese Jesuit who served as interpreter and commercial agent for Toyotomi Hideyoshi and Tokugawa Ieyasu. See Michael Cooper, *Rodrigues the Interpreter: An Early Jesuit in Japan and China* (Tokyo: Weatherhill, 1974).

[106] William Adams (Miura Anjin) (1564–1620) was a commercial agent, informant, pilot, shipbuilder, and interpreter for Tokugawa Ieyasu. See P. G. Rogers, *The First Englishman in Japan* (London: The Harvill Press, 1956).

rard College, but what greater possible contrast could there be than between the Quaker city and its multiplied interests of manufacturers and commerce and this city of court residences. From the extreme left of the hill we could see the moat and massive wall that surrounds the Emperor's palace.

We descended the hill and were conducted into one of the business streets with a view to making some purchases. This street was narrow; the shops crowded with wares were open to the street, but so great was the throng of people attracted by the stranger's presence that it was impossible to do any shopping in the din and confusion and we retreated out of the crowd. But everywhere we went the following crowd was so great as to take away the pleasure of our walk, and night coming on we returned to the landing place to meet the boats from the ship.

The wind had turned and was contrary, and after a couple of hours spent in beating the bay of Yedo by moonlight we furled our sails and took to our oars arriving on board at eight P.M. Dinner was passed but the wardroom with their ready hospitality brought forth their good things and made us at home. The rooms were full, and more than full at night, and several swinging cots were hung up to accommodate us. I had a good night's rest in Lieut. Law's room left vacant by his absence on shore.

Friday, November 2, 1860

Went ashore today at noon. Went to Iempoogi [Zempukuji] (the residence of Mr. Harris) and found my horses had arrived from Kanagawa. We had today a party of six or eight from the ship. Horses for all were readily obtained from Japanese stables. A scrawny lot of nags which had Japanese saddles with stirrups weighing five or six pounds apiece were not very worthy. Our mount in the temple yard was amusing, what with the ignorance of riders and obstinate temper of the horses. But finally we were all mounted and escorted by four mounted officials and preceded by as many bettos as we had horses we dashed out into the street briskly.

There was some awkward riding to begin with, some hard talk about horses hides and eyes, some lagging behind, some getting on too fast, the officials meantime begging us to keep in a body and not separate. Our first pull up was at Belleview again. The damsels received us with many low bows and thanks for yesterday's patronage and each invited us to her particular booth. We stood by our yesterday's acquaintance and received cups of hot tea again from her disordered hand. There was a great crowd of people on the hill intent upon watching us, among them some girl faces that surpassed our tea house belle.

From Atago (Belleview) we started for the temple of Asaksa or Kanon [Asakusa Kannon, or Sensoji]. This temple is the most famous in Yedo. Thither flock pilgrims from all parts of the empire to make their offerings and pay their vows. The street leading to it was so blocked up by the coming and going crowd that with difficulty we approached its outer, or first, gateway. From the first to the second gateway, a distance of several hundred feet, the walk was one impacted mass of people. We dismounted, and with our officials and policemen with iron staffs and rings to precede us we slowly made our way through the throng. A broad stone walk led up to the second gateway and on either side of the walk were continuous rows of booths for the sale of small wares such as the distant pilgrim might purchase as mementoes of his visit. Children's toys occupied by far the greater part of the space, and many a child in distant parts of the island prizes his tiny pair of swords, his miniature horse brought from distant Yedo and famed Kanon. But this I noticed everywhere in Yedo, the numerous shops for the sale of children's toys. I have every where observed that childhood in Japan is cared for relatively as well as anywhere in more favored lands of civilization.

We endeavored to make some trifling purchases ourselves but the curious throng so pressed upon us that we gave it up after securing a trifle or two. The second gateway is a massive structure of wood. Heavy columns support a roof weighty with carvings and ornaments of half barbaric taste. We passed through its deep portals and stood within the temple grounds. Before us was the temple, a building of a single high story. A singular network of timbers projecting over the side walls were intended both as supports and ornaments to the superincumbent mass of the tiled roof. There were a few gilded entablatures shining conspicuously on the vermillion ground of the body of the work. The grounds about the temple were ample, venerable trees of many decades of growth screened the uncovered pilgrims from the midday sun. The majestic salisburia [gingko] was monarch of them all. Flowering cherry and peach trees, camellias, the tall Japanese elm, and evergreen holly and oaks blended together their boughs. In the blossoming time of spring these temple grounds must be a sight of breathtaking beauty.

In a grove put at the left of the temple stands a pagoda of several low stories, of quaint arabesque or moorish architecture. A crowd of pilgrim worshippers were ascending and descending the steps. Preceded by our officers we also ascended the half score of steps and were swallowed up in the crowd of worshippers within. The temple within was neither more spacious or remarkable for its ornamentation than others I have seen. There were the same massive pillars of the Japanese elm with wreathed carvings, the same paneled ceiling of gilt and colors that I had seen often before, but never before such a crowd of worshippers. The multitude with difficulty made way for us till we stood before the immense wooden chest that receives the offerings of the faithful Buddhists. Imagine a contribution box fifteen feet long by five broad and three deep. Its cover was made of stout bars of wood with wide interstices and a large padlock barred sacrilegious plunderers, as we walked around the box a shower of iron cash was constantly flying over our heads into the charity box. The eager worshippers absorbed in their devotions mechanically made room for us but paid no more heed to us than if we had been so many pillars of wood. The earnest face of one supplicating old man was especially to be noticed as he stood praying with lifted eyes and clasped hands from which hung his rosary of wooden beads.

Behind the cash box was the inner recess where knelt the chanting priests before their given idols. A light transparent screen alone separated them from the people without. There was a large number of women and young girls within this veil, who womanlike ceased their prayers to stare upon the strangers. The girls were clad in holiday attire and looked handsomely in their fresh garments, bright faces, and well dressed heads. Our attendant officials proposed to conduct us within this higher spot, but the forbidding priests closed the door in our faces and we could only gaze at the celestial deities and the earth born beauties through the light lattice bars. And, I add, the latter got by far the greater part of the gazing.

Contiguous to the temple are pleasure gardens and tea houses, and from a side door of the temple we crossed a narrow street into the tea gardens. We followed stony, winding paths between trim hedgerows and dwarfed pines and spruces and under vines of wisteria, passing one little cottage after another with their pleasant verandahs looking out into the neatest of yards where graveled walks led among trees, flower beds, and fish ponds. Within the cottages groups of people were taking their tea or more substantial repasts. After passing several of these embowered tea cottages we were brought to one more retired than the rest, where we also might refresh ourselves. The curious crowd were shut out by the barred gates and satisfied themselves by staring at us over the hedge tops. We took our cups of tea and looked out of the windows in the room upon open fields of rice in the very heart of Yedo, all belonging to one temple enclosure.

We again left this tea house and followed paths again bordered by shrubbery and the showiest chrysanthemums were in bloom, till we came to another little group of cottages entirely hid among the trees from outside observations. Into one of these we entered while our ready host set before us a dinner of eggs, prawns cooked in batter, rice, hot sake, and fruit. We made out a good dinner for our appetites were sharpened by a long ride and tempted by the cleanly look of everything about us. A tray of sweetmeats concluded the repast and I noticed among them candies wrapped in mottoes. Some of the mottoes translated by our interpreter at hand had the lovingness of those we pass to our sweethearts at home.

Scattered about the temple were numerous shows and spectacles which were well patronized by the pilgrims. A gallery of wax figures and a wrestling match were the more enticing amusements. The afternoon was growing late and we had time to visit but one place. So we omitted the wax figures which are said to be equal to Madame Tussaud's famous models and entered the mat enclosure where the wrestlers were providing exhibitions of their strength and skill. This exhibition was much inferior to the one I saw at Yokohama last winter, but it had a feature of attraction in the boy wrestlers who displayed their young muscles. From behind a screen of mats a dozen nude boys entered the arena. They wore a girdle around their waist and embroidered silk aprons in imitation of their elders. It was amusing to see their self satisfied strut as they slowly marched in, and all the little aping of the ways of the adult heroes of the ring. They formed a circle around the bed of sand on which the matches are wrestled out, made some revolutions with their bodies and hands and again withdrew. A boy herald then called two of them back and they were pitted against each other for a trial of muscle. They went at it with all the readiness and good nature of boys. The strife was a brief one, being ended by the throw of one into the soft sand.

After this two adult wrestlers came into the ring and went through the same process of feints that I had seen at Yokohama before engaging in interest. One wrestler of middle size but of well knit frame was the victor in three successive matches. His last opponent was nearly his equal and there was a great show of strength and tact before the victory was decided. There was a side scene among the spectators which had nearly ended in a more serious fight growing out of the attempt to eject a couple of men from the gallery who appeared to have taken a higher seat than their rank in life entitled them to. Hot words and angry glances were exchanged freely and men-

acing shakes of the hand, but the police interfered and restored order.

The sun was getting low and we passed out of the temple grounds pressed by the eager crowd. The river Ooka [Ōkawa],[107] or Great River, flows through the heart of Yedo and runs near the temple of Asaksa. We could return by the river in boats and so concluded to do. A short walk brought us to the river bank close under the bridge of ——— [Azuma Bashi], the upper of four bridges which cross this river. The river Ooka is about the breadth of the Chemung at Elmira, flows with a slow current and has a varying depth of a fathom to a fathom and a half. It is the great artery of the city. Boats of various sizes are plying up and down distributing to the warehouses merchandise brought from the junks in the harbor or carrying out exports to other points. More numerous were the passenger and pleasure boats, flat bottomed boats of firwood with sharp bows, broad amidship, low gunnales, made of unpainted wood, but kept as well scrubbed and clean as the most notable housewife's white fine table. A cabin is built over the boat amidship with roof of wood and side windows of sliding screens and fitted with seats. In these boats pleasure parties were numerously seen on the river enjoying their pipes, their meals, or perhaps it would be a devoted Japanese Walton pursuing his favorites for eating amusement.

The bridge above us was filled with people watching as we embarked in three separate boats and pushed off into the stream. A single scull propelled by two men shot us rapidly down the stream. The banks were lined with dwelling houses and stores interrupted here and there by a tea house from whose balconies overhanging the river came the sounds of noisy mirth. Open as the balconies were to the river we could see the groups of singing girls making merry for their lords who sat around the dishes that contained their feast. All stopped to stare at us and the girls waved their hands and shouted Japanese welcomes. We passed by the Imperial grain houses on one

[107] This is the lower section of the Sumidagawa, which is known as the Ōkawa.

bank and on the opposite great rice ware-houses of the daimios. Now we floated under a bridge over which a mixed multitude was passing and now by the gardens attached to some prince's residence, or by his palace walls. Canals led away from the river into the city and everywhere boats were dropping out of these canals into the river, or out of the river into the canals, for a numerous system of canals gives boat access to every part of Yedo. Now we passed again by the mouth of an inlet and had picturesque glimpses of bridges and green banks of country streams.

But night overtook us before we had reached our landing place near the river's mouth. The boatmen lighted their paper lanterns and suspended them in the cabin, we stretched ourselves on the bare benches, listened to the "hay-hah" of the pulling oarsmen, the shouts of the revellers in passing boats, watching the lights on the shore from palace, cottage, and tea gardens and the red streak of the sky in the distance where a fire was burning among the close tenements of the city.

We turned out of the main stream into a broad canal and after proceeding a little ways landed in a dark deserted looking portion of the great city. Here our horses met us and a troop of yakunins and servants were shouting in the dark and running hither and thither in the darkness. Yedo is not a safe place for benighted travellers when drunken samurai are strutting about and we mounted in haste. We plunged into the broad open streets lighted with lanterns of gay colored paper representing landscapes, temple views, flowers, and the like, bettos and yakunins alike shouting to the crowd to clear the way.

Where the population was dense we moved slowly along but at each open space we pushed our horses into a brisk trot. Thus we rode for a half or three quarters of an hour through streets of shops, streets of residences, and those hemmed in by barracks of daimios, till we reached the boat landing. The evening was far spent and we proposed to the Custom House officials to give us a sleeping place on their clean mats, they were nothing loth themselves, but were afraid Mr. Harris would think it a violation of the treaty. The six o'clock boat

had gone back to the ship and we took a government boat and went off to the *Hartford*.

Saturday, November 3, 1860

We were ashore again this morning and were in the saddle by noon. We rode first to Atago and took another cup of tea with the Belle of Belleview. From thence we rode to the Emperor's Palace. The imperial residence at Yedo is situated in the very heart and center of the city. Three walls and fosses, each widely separated from the other, surround the royal abode and adjacent building and grounds. We passed the center moat unconscious that we had penetrated within one of the three winding lines. And so might we pass it daily without its attracting our attention. We were now riding among the princely residences of the great chieftains of the empire. Large areas of space were inclosed by walls of solid masonry, and within were the houses of the Kamis usually denoted by a *shiroi*, or mosque-like cupola, the numerous houses of their servants and retainers, and many of them had ample room for lawns, gardens, and groves of evergreen trees. More commonly these enclosures were formed by ranges of wooden buildings following the entire outer circuit of the ground and occupied by the soldiers and other followers of the house. Wide and massive gateways surmounted with the coat of arms or insignia of the family reminded us of the feudal days of old when mail clad warriors issued forth from the heavy gateways for feast or fray. Here was the warder looking out by his loophole by the gate as of yore, there were mail clad warriors within and almost any day servants may be seen in the passing trains of nobility bearing their masters' hawks on their hands. So too are the bowmen, and the spearmen, and the swordsmen seen in each daily retinue.

But the fair damsels of court and hall are no longer visible to vulgar eyes. The Japanese lady of quality lives in the never broken seclusion of her own home. She has her garden and ample room for all pastimes within the sacredness of the family enclosure and only on some special holiday or religious occasion does she

Compound of the Lord of Arima in Edo. Photograph by Felice Beato.

ever go forth, and then borne in the jealously guarded and closed norimon.

Riding past such places as these through many a street we came to the broad moat and high wall of the second enclosure. We passed at a rapid pace the bridge over the moat and through the heavy gateway already open and unguarded. The space between the second and third, or inner wall is almost wholly occupied by the residences of the greater daimios. Their ample grounds adorned with shrubtrees and hedgerows were like so many country seats. We took the broad road that follows the moat outside of the third wall. It was like a country road in rural New England, this road daily traversed by haughty princes who could summon their armed thousands to the fields. There was a sword grass turf on either side of the road and at large spaced intervals on one hand were the palaces of those nearest the throne. There were the houses of Owari, and Kiusiu and Mito, titular brothers of the King, the domains of the great Prince of Kaga, first in the empire

in power, the solid walls of the late Regent's residence, and here abutting on the road and the moat, where the road leads around the grounds of Kiusiu, is the very spot where the Regent was assassinated last winter, a still, quiet spot it is by the moat side.

On the right of the road is the moat that encloses the royal grounds. It lies deep between two banks of sloping green turf which workmen are now clipping. It has a varying width of two to three hundred feet, trees overhang its dark waters, lotus plants cover its surface with patches of their dark green leaves, wild geese and ducks swim in and out fearless of any marauder who dare touch the emperor's birds. Crowning the steep bank that rises full fifty feet from the opposite side of the moat is the last or inner wall. A low battlement of stone crowns the high wall of earth. Hither we catch here and there glimpses of tiled roofs. The Palace itself was burned down last winter and is now slowly rebuilding. Groves of pine and cedar skirt the walls, each trained so that the green represents a broad flat surface, a floor of living green. Hedges of all kinds, orange, evergreen oak, camellias, etc., overtop the battlements. Massive bridges of stone ending in double gateways of superior strength and archways of stone cross the moat at long intervals.

I only wanted to hear the warden's challenge, the blast of the trumpet from the walls, and see with knightly concern and pleasure a score of horsemen dart out of the gate to believe that baronial times had returned upon earth. In and out of the palace enclosure norimons were carrying and going with trains of attending servants. We halted our horses opposite one of the gates just at the break of the hill where we had a fine view of the city below. It was a gathering point of streets, and while we stood there several Japanese gentlemen passed by on horseback clad in fine silk robes with bare heads. They rode easily despite their clumsy Japanese saddles and heavy stirrups. Their horses were richly caparisoned and numerous servants on foot in neat attire followed them. Many of them were youths, some were boys whose light complexions and their delicate faces bespoke a different mode of living from the common people about them.

Opposite the gateway is a teahouse under the cover of imposing Salisburia [gingko] trees. We alighted from our horses and walked behind the screening hedge of camellia, sat down on the clean mats of the tea house and took our tea. One learns to drink a deal of tea in this way. But what surprised me most was that behind this tea house, in the very focus of the great life of Yedo, was a large area of open uncultivated ground. A part of it was used by the Japanese gentlemen as a race course. Unfortunately we saw none of the sport.

We left the tea house and the Imperial grounds to ride to Ogee [Ōgi-ya],[108] a noted tea house and place of recreation in the country. After leaving the imperial grounds and passing out of the second wall we ascended rising ground. It was both in its streets and buildings what the upper part of N.Y. is to the lower. Gradually as we galloped on the houses grew sparser and at the end of a brisk two hour's ride we were riding in pleasant suburban roads bordered with gardens of fruits and flowers or vegetables, and groves of cypress and fir. At the foot of a hill where there was a small cluster of cottages we found Ogee.

We dismounted before the open piazzas of the hostelry before the dozen girls of the establishment, who with their masters at their head, were bowing low and bidding us welcome. The villagers from the neighboring [village] had gathered round to mark the newcomers. How bright and clean the polished floors of the piazza looked, and what lessons of neatness were the snug rooms with their fresh paper and clean mats. We turned into the slight paling that fenced the yard and its stunted pines, artificial rockwork, and fish ponds, from the street. The kitchen of the establishment was in front of the building and cook with pouting face and bare arms and scullion with taut hair left the charcoal fire of the stone range and the great shiny copper caldron of tea water to stare and say their welcome too.

Ogee is a series of tea cottages built in a summer dell on a brookside. A swift stream tumbles over a fall at the head of a little gorge and bounds on its serpentine course amidst trees and rocks. On one side, overhanging the stream with their long tasseled arms were the native spruces, on the other, a cluster of tea cottages scattered here and there under cool shade and surrounded by gardens of flowers, one and two stories in height, and with spacious verandahs opening towards the bounding brook and the thick grove beyond. Groups of Japanese were enjoying themselves in the open rooms. There were young girls with the sambie, the Japanese guitar, making their harsh music to please the ears of a little family

[108] The Ōgi-ya was a celebrated teahouse located in Ōji Village. Ōji was a favorite Edo excursion spot during the spring and autumn, widely acclaimed for its cherry blossoms and maples. The tea houses Ōgi-ya and Ebi-ya were located along the banks of the Takinogawa. Not far distant stood the Temple of Inari. Felix Beato photographed this tea house during the bakumatsu years, see Yokohama Kaikō Shiryō Kan, eds., *F. Beato bakumatsu nihon shashin shū*, p. 115. Also *Once Upon A Time: Visions of Old Japan. Photographs by Felice Beato and Baron Raimund Von Stillfried* (New York: Friendly Press, 1986), p. 61.

Tea houses at Ōji. Photograph by Felice Beato.

party who were laughing loudly and chatting boisterously over their dinner of fish, vegetables, rice, tea, and sake. There was a gay party in one room, a man was seated on the mats with three females around the remains of such a meal. One female with blackened teeth, who he said was his wife, was very jovial, a young girl in the corner was shy and timid, the third was the singing and playing girl whose company is not shunned by the Japanese wife, outcast though she would be at home, here she is the favored companion of the holiday excursion.

The man called to me as I passed and told me in broken Dutch that he was gedrunken, a truth confirmed by his flushed face and empty sake jug. In mingled Dutch and Japanese he said he was having a good time, that the hilarious woman with black teeth was his wife, and a good woman, and that the timid little girl in the corner, who looked up at me out of her frightened eyes, he would give to me. I contented myself with tossing some brilliant buttons to her which reassured her and she bowed forward and touched her forehead to the mats in expression of thankfulness.

A summer house, octagonal in form, on the brink of the swift water was assigned to us. We had ridden far and divesting ourselves of our accoutrements were glad to throw ourselves down on the soft mats where we could see the glittering cascades, the sun falling through in flecks of light, the great oaks, conifer, and salisburias, and the gay parties dancing, playing, and feasting in the neighboring cottages. The always grateful tea, luscious purple grapes, and sweet cakes were set before us by the active housemaids preparatory to our fuller meal which we had ordered.

While this was preparing we walked out to a hill planted with various kinds of Japanese flowering and shade trees. There was a short smooth turf under the trees. The hill which contained several acres was a bit of park scenery or like the pleasure grounds of other lands. From the further brim of the hill we had a wide view of a great flat country of rice fields extending for miles and bordered by woods, this too so near the great city. It was a magnificent stretch of landscape.

While we were on the top a party came out from the city to enjoy, like us, a day's recreation at Ogee. The head of this party were two children, who by their numerous attendants were scions of some family of rank and station. They were young and by their delicate faces showed that they had been house plants; in immediate attention upon them was one who offered to act in capacity of tutor and guide, behind them was a stout placid looking old man who by his shaven head and dress could be none other than the family physician, behind them were a numerous retinue of servants. All were kneeling on the ground behind their young masters, who were looking at the prospect before them with childish curiosity. The mentor of the party had a telescope with him of foreign construction which he adjusted to their eyes, but the youngsters' vision wandered more to the strangers from other lands who stood near them and the holiday at Ogee will be associated in their minds not with the grand landscape or the pretty teahouses but the curious strangers whom they for the first time had seen.

Our dinner was ready for us when we returned. There was rice and eggs and a large grouper, a fish of delicate flavor fried in tasteless vegetable oil and dished with bean soy. There were fore-relishes, salted radishes and a tender knot of greens and other dishes of indescribable Japanese composition. All were scraped clean and for the most part palatable, the only drawback was our clumsy use of chopsticks in which none of us had yet become proficient. Did you ever try to eat soup with two knitting needles, if so you can imagine the depth of our embarrassment. There was cold sake and hot sake, and cured sake, and tea in abundance, and our good appetites gave a hearty relish to our Japanese dinner.

Nobody could be more attentive than the smiling damsels who waited upon us, one of whom lured me into a wild chase after her through the intricacies of the neighboring houses and grounds and was merry as a witch to think what a fruitless chase she led me. I

saw her afterwards telling it with infinite zest to her companions. Our horses were again brought out, for horses and bettos had been enjoying their meals also, our moderate bills were paid, and the assembled household gathered on the edge of the piazza to bid us adieu, bowing low, profuse of thanks, and bidding us come again soon. The little miss that led me such a chase bore her roguish smile to the last.

Our guides led us back through other streets, remarkably fine and open streets. The great establishments of the Princes of Kaga and Yetsizen were on our homeward route. We came into ———— [blank in original] street the great commercial street of Yedo. It is a wide street like Broadway, and like Broadway a swollen stream of human life of all ranks and conditions was pouring through it, occupying not the sidewalks as in the case of Broadway, but the center of the street. The shops were two stories in height of unequal size or architectural finish for while some were handsome fireproof structures with polished block walls others were the plainest of wooden buildings and mean shops. At one large silk warehouse, in extent equal to our largest Broadway shops, a mixed multitude of shoppers were sitting on the mats chaffering with the attendants over their intended purchases.

We dismounted from our horses to undertake a little purchasing for ourselves. In vain our yakunins tried to keep back the passing crowd, in vain the policemen of the street shouted to clear the way and rattled their iron staves and rings, the curious crowd still gathered around us rendering shopping and even locomotion itself almost impossible. After visiting a few stores among which was a lacquer store where beautiful wares of lacquered works inlaid with silver and gold were ravishing alike to eye and purse, we abandoned any idea of shopping amid such disadvantages particularly as the Japanese shopkeepers doubled and trebled their prices hoping that in our uncomfortable haste we would give all they asked.

We were glad to mount again and urge our horses through the crowded streets. We again passed Nippon Bas, the famous bridge of Yedo from which all distances throughout the empire are rated. It differed from other Yedo bridges only in its side railing which was supported by high ornamental posts tipped and ornamented with copper. At set of sun we were in the street that housed one of the emperor's temples and burial place of his ancestry, wide streets enclosed it, but a paling fence and lofty hedge rows screened the interior from observation of barbarian eyes. We could only see the leafy heads of venerable shade trees, the flowering rows of althea and camellias as we dashed past where the streets were wide.

It was again dark before we reached Iempugee [Zempukuji] and turned our horses out to the bettos' hands. There was a mile and a half walk to the landing, my companions with two officials and the lanterns had hurried on ahead of us, leaving Heco and myself to follow. Two yakunins were with us with lanterns and the gatemen of each street as we passed. We walked on unmolested till we came into the street which is bordered on either hand by the barracks of Satsuma's followers making a blank wall on either side of a narrow street. We had gone halfway through when we overtook three young men each two sworded and who from their swaying gait had evidently been carousing. We were walking briskly as we overtook them and just as we passed, the middle man of the three accosted us in Japanese, endeavored to draw his sword and break away from the other two men trying to restrain him. The officials immediately fell in behind us and putting their hands on Heco begged him to hurry. We quickened our pace, for however successful our revolvers might have been against three, the first pistol shot would have brought down on us a host of Satsuma's men. Discretion was here certainly the better part of valor, and we went on our way as rapidly as convenient without running. We took a Japanese boat again and returned to our vessel.

While returning from Ogee we had a specimen of native archery. In an open field a party of men were shooting at a target at sixty or seventy yards. Their arrows were sent with more force than skill. I saw the target which was two feet in diameter hit only once out of a multitude of shots.

Sunday, November 4, 1860

Our party were divided on shore today. Heco and myself rode alone accompanied by two yakunins. We took the road again to the imperial grounds, passed through the massive gateway of the middle wall and followed the countrylike road that follows the back of the moat that encloses the imperial residency. It is the pleasantest ride within the city. There were few persons in the streets and these were of the privileged class, it is altogether like a ride in the rural suburbs of Boston. We stopped for a moment at the tea house opposite the gate and then took a street that lead down the hill alongside of the imperial moat and inner wall.

Contrary to my expectation I was surprised by seeing a quarter occupied by dingy shops and low mean houses in close proximity to the impressive residences, in fact, occupying one side of the street as the moat did the other. From this quarter we emerged into a populous quarter and our way was through a fine street of large mercantile shops. There were many foreign goods in these shops, the most common being glass ware and bright colored calicoes and handkerchiefs. Each business was distinct, having its own sale shop exclusively. There were bookstores gaudy with high colored pictures arranged to attract notice, toy shops crowded with an infinite variety of small wares, comb stores, spice stores, inkstand stores, tobacco and pipe pouch stores, pipe stores, sake shops redolent of spiritous fumes. On one corner we saw the largest shop in Yedo for the sale of cotton fabrics, the Stewarts (?) of Yedo. It was a large building of two stories with the lower one open to the street on two sides, built fire proof. At least two hundred persons were seated on the mats of the great bazaar, a 100 feet square busy with buying and selling. There was the seller displaying his fabrics or sipping his tea with his customers or reckoning his accounts on his calculating board. Well dressed men and women were intent on their purchases and a troop of thirty or forty boys were bringing the goods to the salesmen from shelf or drawer or handing about tea in tiny porcelain cups on newly lacquered trays. The tea making apparatus occupied a conspicuous place in front of this bazaar.

There was a large furnace of stone and a bright copper boiler high as a man's head and large as his body. A Japanese woman presided over this mammoth tea urn and continually replenished the cups of the serving boys. It was a busy scene of life where business, pleasure, and comfort were happily blended.

This portion of the city was very dense and much of it recently rebuilt after a devastating fire. The streets were scrupulously clean. We were subjects of curiosity to great crowds of gazing people as we approached the river Oka once more. The street leading to the Riogokoo [Ryogoku] bridge, or "bridge of two provinces", so called from its being a connecting link between the two provinces on either side of the river, is the great thoroughfare between the portions of the city lying on either sides of the river, was more crowded with people than any other hitherto seen. It is a wide street and its center was occupied by stands for the sale of all sorts of refreshments reminding one of old Market St. in Philadelphia. Salutations of *tojin*, *tojin baka* were numerous from the rabble here collected. Over the bridge a steady full stream was constantly passing.

Our yakunins and the policemen of the neighborhood preceded us to clear the way. As we passed over a fine view of the river was afforded, crowded with burden boats. It is the great artery of Yedo; from it numerous canals penetrate into all parts of the city to facilitate the transmission of heavy merchandise. Having crossed the bridge we were within the southern suburbs, so called. A close compact quarter occupied by dwelling houses and merchants. Here are the foremost merchants of the city, dealers in rice, grain, and all raw produce. Their fire proof warehouses are built on the canals and large boats load and unload cargoes at their doors. But we must not forget the milling crowd gathered about the southern end of the bridge. It was like a country fair where are all sorts of devices to gather the idle pennies of passers by. There were refreshment booths in front of one of which was a tempting display of game, a wild deer lay on a board and near him were braces of pheasants and other small game and a large wing bat, large as a barn door fowl! There were sing song booths, singing girls, gambling sheds, show boxes, slight of hand performers, tumblers, harlequins, and importunate beggars pertinaciously plied their calling.

From the bridge we followed down the bank of the river. We passed a temple[109] famous as the burial place of the bones of 108,000 souls perished long years ago by an earthquake which tumbled the houses in ruins and fires followed, consuming thousands unable to extricate themselves. Another temple was notable for the numerous handsome stone monuments chiseled and cut with no little care. Then we rode by fifteen relatively large buildings like warehouses, near the water's edge. These contained the imperial barges. We had glimpses through a few crevices of the high poops resplendent with vermillion and gold as we passed.

We drew up at last at the temple of Hatchiman or "80,000," but 80,000 what I cannot tell.[110] It is an unpretending temple in a quiet quarter of the city. There was nothing remarkable or curious about, save a colorful idol in bronze on a high stone pedestal in a sitting posture with a great rain hat on his head. There was one of the quietest of little tea rooms nearby where we were received kindly and sat down on our mats to await the preparation of dinner. This soon came most cleanly served. There were boiled eggs, fish cut into small pieces and well fried, an omelet of egg, rice, boiled and afterwards rolled in thin cakes of batter, also in sea weed, there were sweet cakes of rice, wheat, or bean flour, hot tea and hot sake.

This quarter had been visited by foreigners only once before and consequently all the neighborhood were in the qui vive. They climbed the fences and gates which had been

---

[109] This is the Ekō-in, which was built to commemorate the more than 100,000 dwellers of Edo who lost their lives in the great Meireki Fire of 1657. See *Murray's Handbook to Japan* (London: John Murray, 1913), p. 134.

[110] The "temple" Hall visited here was the Fukagawa Hachiman Shrine. Hall appears to have understood Hachiman to mean 80,000 rather than the Shinto God of War.

shut against them, mounted the trees, and a swarm of youngsters had climbed up the given god of brass and were clustering like so many bees around his head, astride of his arm, standing on his shoulder, embracing his neck. We had a good dinner nevertheless at a moderate charge, for these simple souls had not yet learned to charge *tojins* several prices more than their own people for the same things. So for this very comfortable dinner for four and a dinner also for our bettos we paid fifty cents aggregate.

On our return we recrossed the river by the bridge Etai [Eitai], the longest bridge over the river and nearest the sea. On our homeward ride we passed the street occupied by the large sake dealers. The whiskey scent was in the air. We rejoined the rest of the ship's party at the landing and took leave of them as Heco and myself were to remain a day ashore by invitation of L'abbé Girard, interpreter to the French Legation. So at the landing we bade adieu to our good friends of the *Hartford* and rode back into the city to the Abbé's where we found good cheer and a warm welcome awaiting us. A conversation on Japanese affairs in which we all felt interested beguiled our time till midnight.

Monday, November 5, 1860

This was my last day in Yedo. We were to devote it to a ride into the suburbs. We had camped so agreeably on the Abbé's sitting room floor that we rose late, breakfasted late, and the forenoon was far spent before we were mounted to go to Jooniso[111] [Jūnisō], or "The Twelve Spirits." The ride today was different altogether from those of the preceding days. The streets and houses were like those of more rural places. Bamboo palings, unpretending hedge rows, scant yards enclosed the neat houses which were uniformly humble in character. One hour's ride brought us quite out of

the city proper into the pleasant rural precincts of Yedo.

Smooth well kept roads, wide enough for two to ride abreast, separated cultivated fields and open meadows. It was much like the rural scenery about Kanagawa. I noticed the changed tints of the maples along the roadside. Jooniso is a summer resort of the Yedo people. Its attractions are a little lake lying between two sloping ridges of well kept turf dotted with flowering and shade trees. Benches are scattered about under the trees, and built on sites across one end of the little lake are the tea houses. There is a fine grove of tall cryptomeria by one of the tea houses and in a deep ravine nearby a noisy waterfall. It is sufficiently quiet and picturesque for a few hours rest and is much resorted to by the Yedoites.

Groups of visitors were scattered about the grounds where guests were drinking the ever ready cups of hot tea. Those who wanted more substantial repasts occupied the open houses which connectedly formed a covered bridge across the lake. A crow perched on a tree was watching a dining party with sinister intent. They are impudent fellows, these great Japanese crows, because nobody molests them. This gentleman in black, after eying the tempting repast till appetite overcame his caution, flapped his broad wings and swooped under the roof and astonished the little dinner party by picking up a roll of rice wrapped in sea weed and flying off with it in his beak. The crows of Jooniso are doubtless accustomed to laying their tribute on transient guests. I had seen many fine gold fish in Japan but the native fellows in this pond were monarchs before all. I stood in one of the tea houses where a servant clapped his hands and the great golden carp 15, 18, 20 inches long or more came swimming up from the deep water for the meal that awaited them. These were accompanied by another kind of large fish some of which were over two feet in length. There was no indecent scrambling for the falling

---

[111] Jūnisō was a popular Edo picnic site. The main attraction was a pond famous for its carp, which was located near the Jūnisō Gongen temple which was dedicated to the gods of Kumano. See *Murray's Hand-* *book to Japan*, p. 139. For photographs of the temple and cascade see, Yokohama Kaikō Shiryō Kan, eds., *F. Beato bakumatsu nihon shashin shū*, pp. 116–17.

crumbs, they swam leisurely for the floating morsels and devoured them with the dignified air of fish who know their position in society and that there were crumbs enough for all. One of our yakunins distinguished himself here by falling over the old large tea pot and crushing it, for which he seemed greatly mortified.

On our return we passed through a wide street resembling the Tokaido and there were large inns and houses of prostitution; from this again through a crowded quarter of the city, where we were hailed with *tojin baka*, to the imperial walls. Our yakunins were acting as guides today and now took us through a portion of the city near the imperial palace entirely occupied by daimio palaces. More than once this ride reminded me of the suburbs of Boston, the wide streets overhung with shades, the warren ones threading between beautiful hedge rows, the spacious grounds tastefully adorned with trees and hanging gardens had more a suburban rural air than the heart of the greatest city of the world as it really was. The grounds belonging to Kiusiu were extremely picturesque. So too was the residence of the royal astronomer on the summit of an intramural hill to which walks winding among trees and shrubbery conducted by an easy ascent.

After half an hour's ride among these city palaces we passed the grounds of Sendai Mutsu no Kami, in wealth and revenues the third in the kingdom. His grounds were a wide square. The houses within the enclosure were completely shut from view by a fine old grove of flat cedars which itself was worth a long journey to see.

We were back to the Abbé's hospitable quarters by set of sun. We had taken our dinner and were enjoying the social evening together when we were interrupted by a call from a Japanese official. He had come on an errand from Minister Harris, who forgetting the civility due to a gentleman's roof, had sent to make the following inquiries. "Why these gentlemen had not returned on the *Saginaw*?" "Why they were not at the American Minister's?" "By whose permission they had ridden to Jooniso?"

I would not recognize the right of Mr.

H[arris] to put such inquiries, and was for sending back a curt answer. I did request Heco to interpret the following. That "I came up on the *Hartford* and was stopping with the Abbé by his request. I was in the territory of the Emperor, if he was wronged by my being here I was ready to answer civilly any questions on the part of his officials, that it was his territory not Mr. H[arris]'s; if I was recognizing anyone it was the Emperor and would answer to his officers." The official had previously stated that Mr. H[arris], and not the Government, prompted the inquiries. The official declined giving the message because "it would make Mr. H[arris] very angry."

I rested here and left the matter with Heco and the Abbé who were desirous of sending a message less likely to be provocative. Mr. Heco therefore returned the following message: "I came up here by special invitation of the Commodore. I called the first day on shore on Mr. H[arris], and as he did not ask me to stay at his house, of course I did not. The Abbé invited me to remain a day with him, and I have done so. The ride to Jooniso was in company with Japanese yakunins."

The official left us to finish a quiet evening together and we saw and heard no more of our Minister. Mr. H[arris]'s opposition to Americans visiting Yedo amounts almost to a mania. Like a grecian Cerberus[112] he sits at the gate yelping at every approach. One might suppose from his anxiety that the integrity of the Japanese Emperor depended on his keeping at bay every American; they would hardly dream it was his own integrity, or reputation for integrity, he was claiming to sustain.

Tuesday, November 6, 1860

We were up early in the morning ready for our departure from Yedo. The owner of the stable was on hand with his account current ready made out as all such things are done in Japan. The price for the stabling of our horses and sheltering and feeding our bettos had

---

[112] Cerberus was the three-headed dog that according to classical mythology guarded the entrance to Hades.

been half an ichibu per diem for each man and horse. The yakunins and their grooms were waiting for us in the court. The Abbé was to accompany us. We took a cup of coffee and a biscuit, to sustain us till we reached the hospitality of Kawasaki, committed our luggage to the care of a coolie, and went out for the mount.

It was a cool November morning, sharp and blowery with a northwind. The sky was clear and the sun already rising aslant over the tile roofs of Yedo as we sallied out of the gate with our attendant yakunins and bettos and bade adieu to Yedo. We pushed through the narrow street of the suburbs and emerged into the Tokaido, or the great eastern sea way, that following the trend of the coast, is indeed the great highway by the sea for all who travel from Yedo to Miaco.

Early as it was in the morning, travelling Nippon was earlier than we. Already the Tokaido was full of travellers to and from Yedo. The crisp autumn air gave a ruddier look to their faces than their wonted good color. There were men and women on foot trudging merrily along alone or in groups. The women were attired for travelling, a figured cotton headdress covered their heads and sometimes half the face also, their garments were shortened and only a thin covering of red or white crape covered their limbs below the knees, or left them entirely bare from knee to ankle. When not attended by a servant to carry their baggage, they bore an umbrella in their hand and a little pack on their backs. The men were bare headed and bare limbed or they also wrapped their heads in cotton cloths and encased their limbs in tight fitting leggings. Soldiers with their two swords came swaggering along, norimons hurried by with their inmates well preserved from outside light or air, and their tattooed bearers in relief parties trotting along at their side. Now there would be a mounted party moving easily and at leisure, or it would be some dignitary approaching on foot to the imperial city with his insignia of office borne aloft before him, his led saddle horse following, his norimon and numerous armed attendants following that, and baggage bearers bringing up the rear. Pack horses laden with bags of straw, boxes, or basket panniers moved both ways in unbroken steadiness. Coolies supporting heavy burdens between them from poles of bamboo were as universal as the pack animals. Threading their way through the crowd with nimble dexterity came the flying feet of the dispatch bearers on their way to the great city. Their letters were enclosed in small oblong boxes fastened to a stout bamboo pole and suspended over their shoulders as they ran.

Again we passed a little travelling party of females. In the lead was an elderly woman clad in sober garments trudging along with staff in hand, following her was the prettiest girl I know of in Nippon. Her cheeks fair as many European's were aglow with moving exercise. She had a blue figured scarf prettily enswathed around her head, her well developed calves peeped out from the bright crimson chemise that fell below her over garments of wadded cotton. Her rosy lips parted in a smile of recognition displaying her fine handsome teeth as I came up with her and I knew her face as the *mekake* [mistress] of a merchant friend and by all odds the prettiest woman, as I have said, in Nippon. Following her were other females and the rear of the party was brought up by a well dressed man accoutred with his single sword as is customary with the servant thus employed to travel with a party of females, but I had no eyes save for the rosy cheeked lass in the chemise of crimson crape, as fair a sight as one would care to see of a November morning.

Sinagawa [Shinagawa] is the first village below Yedo but it is in fact only a continuation of Yedo. Indeed from Yedo to Kanagawa, a distance of seventeen miles, the succession of houses on both sides of the street is scarcely interrupted. At Sinagawa are extensive shops and numerous tea houses and inns of the larger scale. We were for some time between the spacious views on either side, buildings of two stories running far back from the street. Their floors were highly polished and their mats clean as usual. These inns have a large business from their contiguity to Yedo, being the halting places of travellers just before entering the city and the pleasure resorts of large parties from Yedo. The samurai class who lead an indolent, vicious life frequent the Sinagawa inns to an extent that renders them unsafe for foreigners. They come for a carouse and bring their mistresses with them or find them in the large joroyas of Sinagawa and would at such times be reckless of what they did.

We passed through the suburbs at so early an hour that we saw only the travellers who had tarried overnight getting up early for the road again. Several contiguous inns had been occupied the night before by a travelling grandee and the street was nearly blocked up by the crowd of servants and baggage preparing for the morning's start. Handsome horses, fair limbed black animals with long flowing tails, stood before the inns. The saddles were gay with colored leather embossed in fanciful figures and stirrups painted with green and gold. A net work of green silk cord protected the animals from insects. Their long tails were covered with bags like ladies back hair nowadays and spotted leopard skins covered the saddle seats. Elaborately finished norimons were awaiting their inmates at the doors, servants were busy putting the baggage in packs and securing it to the horses' backs. The armed attendants were lounging about the open doors smoking their morning pipe waiting for the train to move on.

I met another class of travellers, young lads belonging to these high bred families as we could know by their fine silk dresses, their light figures, pale complexions, and their numerous attendants. The roadway of the Tokaido has been made for the most part with course gravel from the sea beach and is smooth and hard as a macadamized road, other portions of it are smooth shell roads over which it was a pleasure to ride at a fast speed. The open spaces, which were few were always bordered with trees, pines, and the beautiful cryptomeria.

Under these trees the beggars station themselves sitting on mats at the road side and begging for tempos. "I am a poor man only one tempo I beg you for," "I am in distress only one tempo." Other beggars in helpless infirmity or disease were daily brought here by their companions, some were very importunate throwing themselves across our way and following after us. The beggars are never teased in Japan and are seldom refused a mong, or the 50th part of a cent, the smallest of coins.

As we rode along, Mount Fusi, whose head was now white with winter's snow, was a conspicuous feature in the distant landscape. The Japanese have a book of "The forty four views of Fusi from the Tokaido." As they also have a book of views of different places in Yedo from which Fusi may be seen.[113]

A few miles this side of Yedo toward Kanagawa we passed an execution ground. Standing on a board with features ghastly in death we saw the head of a recently decapitated criminal. Another board inscribed with Japanese characters related the crime for which he was punished. There is another execution ground on the great road leading north from Yedo towards Hakodade and two others seldom used on roads leading westward into the country. The reason for the selection of such public places is obvious.

We left the execution ground and its ghastly victim behind us glad to gallop out of its sight. A more pleasant scene was an attractive tea house in the midst of a garden whose attendants came out begging us to stop for "one cup of tea." We were loth to refuse the bowing maidens but hurried by to the banks of the Logo [Rokugo], that noted stream of which our Yedo Minister is the grim Charon who turns an importunate ear to all entreaties to happiness. The Logo is a small river of no great depth navigable for some miles by the flat bottomed boats. Its headwaters are in the mountains whose blue peaks we can see thirty-five or forty miles distant. Two flat boats ferried ourselves and horses across. Unlike Avernus, the exit from Yedo is easier than its entrance, no guards question you why you came back, however they may hound you going in.

We reached Kawasaki in the middle of the forenoon and drew up at one of its several

---

[113] As a book collector and book dealer Hall was interested in such works. But while these references are no doubt to works such as Hokusai's "Thirty Six Views of Mt. Fuji," (*Fugaku sanjū-rokkei*) and Hiroshige's "One Hundred Views of Famous Places in Edo" (*Meisho Edo hyakkei*), Hall does not seem to be aware of the artists who created them.

inns where a bevy of slip shod damsels awaited us. We were ushered upstairs into the honorable room and a half dozen girls set about at once to make us comfortable. Seats and cushions were brought, braziers of charcoal, cups of hot tea, bottles of warm sake, trays of sponge cake and fruit with the least delay. And the handmaids squatting upon the floor began to upbraid the Abbé that he had neglected their hostelry of late and gone to other places.

The good Abbé tried to defend himself but the voluble tongues of the girls were more than a match for him. He was compelled to promise better for the future. Then they took him to task because he did not properly return their salutation when he passed and they bowed and said "Ohio." "You never say Ohio and nod your head just a little," said they, "but Mr. B[ellecourt], the Minister he bows low and smiles." The Abbé was again discomfited and made to promise better things.

We separated from the Abbé who was in haste to return to Kanagawa while we were desirous of visiting the temple of Daishi a mile off the road. We ordered our dinner to be prepared while we walked to Daishi (This temple I have elsewhere described).

On our return from Daishi we found our room comfortable with all the luxuries a Japanese inn knows and all the available damsels of the household ready to keep us company and amuse us. So we squatted in a circle around the glowing brazier of coal, Heco, myself, and six or seven girls. Full of chat they were and wished to know all the doings at Yedo and Yokohama, telling us the latest gossip in return. One item was that at another inn some police were with a poor unfortunate who had vainly endeavored to escape from the Joroya of Yokohama. She had been overtaken here and was being taken back to her life of infamy.

Dinner was served. We had a prawn and vegetable soup, fried fish, boiled eggs and rice, green relishes of pickled relishes and a preparation of beans, sweetmeats, cakes, grapes, persimmons, and pears. The nearest girl assisted me to manage the clumsy chop sticks or I might never have got the dinner to my mouth. We shared our repast with them, and they enjoyed the tea, sake, and cakes more than we did. The plates were removed and after dinner we had a merry time. The girls sang and played for us on their sambie, showed us some Japanese plays. In return I taught them the mysteries of "bean porridge hot" and tea plantation dances. A half dozen girls were down on the mats at one time trying this difficult step and as their garments are open in front with only a girdle around their waist there was of course an astonishing display of legs. They thought the dance a famous one, however, and were never weary of repeating it. While not chary of their personal charms in some respects the tea house girl is modest in others. Her class is entirely distinct from the Joro. She is forbidden to sell herself under penalty, and I have not yet seen the foreigner who has known one to transgress.

After enjoying the naivete and playfulness of the girls till it began to dull, we prepared for the remount. Our hats, riding sticks, etc., were brought us, we paid our bill, eight ichibus, rather an extravagant one, and escorted by our fair attendants descended to the open court of the inn where our horses and bettos awaited us. Master, mistress, and all the girls stood on the piazza as we started, bowing us a low adieu and bidding us "come again."

We rode on in the pleasant autumn sunlight now among the hamlets and now through the pine shaded wood. On either side were extensive plots from which the laborers were gathering the fall rice. Flocks of wild geese and ducks were here and there seen in the fields. Tea house damsels rushed out of their houses to decoy us first seizing our bridle reins, and cups of hot tea were spilled in their eager haste. One woman partly succeeded in stopping my horse, and before I knew it a man was at my horse's head with a bucket of water for him, and the old lady was spilling hot tea on my leg in her desire to get it up to my mouth. We ended the day at Kanagawa by 2 P.M. and so finished a memorable trip.

Wednesday, November 7, 1860

Paid visits to Kanagawa friends. Met Capt. Schenck of the *Saginaw* at Dorr's. A more humorous character it has not been my lot to meet for years. His fund of mirth and anecdote was inexhaustible. At Dr. H[epburn]'s I found a "Sewing Society in Session," a sewing society in Japan. We had before the church, the hotel, the billiard room, the race course, and now this new civilizer is added. Truly the dawn of the Japanese day advances. The ladies sewed in the afternoon, the gentlemen dropped in in the evening after the approved way and for "auld lang syne" we had a game of "Blind Man's Bluff" in the evening.

Thursday, November 8, 1860

At home writing up my Journal.

Friday, November 9, 1860

The long expected *Niagara* arrived today at noon.[114] Her advent was received with the greatest quietness by the Japanese. All the enthusiasm was on the part of the foreigners. A few coolies gathered on the beach to stare at the "big ship," but paid no attention to a boat load of the under officials who had come off to report to the authorities and to send dispatches to Yedo. These came on shore and paid their salutations to those they met as apathetically as if they had just come in a Nagasaki junk.

I went off to the *Niagara* which was only lying to to communicate with the shore and had the gratification of meeting Lieut. M[ay] who had come direct from kindred and friends at home. Chance meetings of old friends are everywhere agreeable but nowhere so much as when they meet on the outer rim of the world, as it were, reviewing a thousand associations buried under years of absence. In the evening I had a holiday time opening the boxes which the *Niagara* had brought me. Each article provided by the care and attention of friends was

thrice welcome. Indeed I was both pleased and a little sad for I was reminded how far separate I am from all I hold dear, but pleased to see with what judicious care my wants had been provided for.

Saturday, November 10, 1860

Surprised today by a visit from Consul Rice of Hakodade. He is here in his full proportions of six feet five and official insignia. Gave up the day to showing him our young lions and lionesses and to negotiating a sale of ichibus which ended in my securing the purchase myself of 7600.

Sunday, November 11, 1860

A headache and cold kept me from church today. Mr. R[ice] spent the day with me.

Monday, November 12, 1860

The *Saginaw* is down from Yedo today. The Embassy have been received as quietly at Yedo as at Yokohama.[115] The Japanese are endeavoring to return some of the civilities shown their embassy by attentions to the *Niagara*'s officers. A temple has been set apart for their use which the officers can occupy while on shore, provisions are to be supplied, and horses placed at their disposal. The *Niagara* is to be victualed for the return voyage with such victualling as the country has.

Tuesday, November 13, 1860

Alert left for Honolulu this morning, a blowy norther blowing all the day.

[114] The *Niagara* returned the ambassadors who had gone to the United States on the *Powhatan* in February 1860 to exchange ratification of the Commercial Treaty with the United States.

[115] The following day, November 13, 1860, Father Mounicou recorded in his diary: "The Japanese Embassy returned from New York in a large American steamer. The officials were disturbed at what they found upon arriving at Edo. The Japanese have resumed their overbearing manners. A great many guns and cannon were unloaded. An American officer has entered the Japanese service as instructor in artillery fire and firearms. While the Consuls of the other nations look askance at this, the Americans seem proud of it." See Blum, "Father Mounicous' Bakumatsu Diary, 1856–64," pp. 64–65.

Wednesday, November 14, 1860

A rough day on the Bay which is made impassable for small boats. Preparing letters for the *Saginaw*.

Thursday, November 15, 1860

Saginaw left us today. A large party were on board to see her off. We hear that the man fired at by the Frenchman recently attacked in Yedo was wounded and that his friends vow vengeance.[116]

Friday, November 16, 1860

Manjiro,[117] who recently returned from America, for some offence has been confined to his house for a few days. Bohee [Buhee], a Kanagawa merchant, has been similarly punished as he alleges for no offence but because the government have been led to believe that he was making money too fast.

We have another story from Yedo to this effect. Thirty of young Mito's men came to the Prince of Satsuma's residence and demanded

to see the Prince. He refused to see them. What their object was is not known. Now these men propose to fight Satsuma men, but the latter refuse. Satsuma is the second most powerful prince in the empire.

Saturday, November 17, 1860

A call today from some Yedo men, one a samurai, one a lacquer merchant, one a book seller. They are all learning our language by themselves with such printed aids as they can find. The samurai, who has a knowledge of the Dutch, has learned the most rapidly by the aid of his Dutch English dictionary and speaks quite well.[118] The others are young men of a great deal of vivacity and their attempts to talk in English are sufficiently amusing. They are good examples of the desire on the part of the Japanese to learn foreign languages and with their earnestness and the rude aid of their imperfect books reminded me of self teaching scholars at home. They will all master our hard tongue after a while. At Hakodade I met a ship carpenter who had in two years picked up a fair conversational knowledge of our tongue. We exchanged presents as usual.

---

[116] The Frenchman in question was M. Natal, the color guard in the service of M. de Bellecourt. Natal was an Italian by birth who was also M. de Bellecourt's valet (Blum, "Father Mounicous' Bakumatsu Diary, 1856–64," p. 74). As Hall's diary indicates an attempt to assassinate him was made on March 7, 1861.

[117] Nakahama Manjirō had accompanied the 1860 Tokugawa embassy to the United States sailing to San Francisco with Captain Brooke. Upon his return to Japan, as Hall notes, he regularly associated with Westerners in Yokohama. But Manjirō's Western contacts, particularly his visits to Western ships, were regarded with suspicion by some in the shogunate, and for a time he was placed under house arrest for allegedly disclosing secrets to the Americans (Warinner, *Voyager to Destiny*, p. 197).

[118] There is no clear indication of who this "samurai" was, but there is a possibility that this was Fukuzawa Yukichi who had visited Yokohama in the autumn of 1859 and had made the troubling discovery that English, not Dutch, was the prevalent language of the treaty port. Fukuzawa writes in his autobiography that on his visit to Yokohama he stopped at "a shop kept by one Kniffer. He was a German and did not understand much of what I said to him, but he could somehow un-

derstand my Dutch when I put it in writing." The merchant "Kniffer" was quite likely L. Kniffler who had established Kniffler & Co. in Yokohama and whose firm is listed among the first treaty port houses in *The China Directory for 1863*. Kniffler may also have been the "German Jew K." who Hall met shortly after his arrival in Kanagawa. Fukuzawa tells us that he "bought two volumes of a small English conversation book at Kniffer's store in Yokohama," and that with access to a Dutch-English Dictionary he obtained at the Bansho Shirabesho he commenced his studies of English late in 1859. On February 10, 1860, Fukuzawa left Japan on the *Kanrin Maru* as personal steward to Admiral Kimura, bound for the United States as part of the 1860 embassy. He did not return until high summer of 1860, when with the aid of a Webster's Dictionary he obtained in San Francisco he started his studies of English in earnest. "After my return," Fukuzawa wrote, "I tried to read English books as much as I could and for the benefit of the students, I taught them all English instead of Dutch. But as yet my knowledge was not sufficient; I still had to have much recourse to my English-Dutch dictionary." See Fukuzawa Yukichi, *The Autobiography of Yukichi Fukuzawa* (New York: Columbia University Press, 1966), pp. 97; 99; 122.

Sunday, November 18, 1860

One in the succession of clear autumnal days which we are now enjoying. It is like our Indian summer of the northern states. After church I took a walk into the country. It was all new to me for my rambles hitherto have been on the Kanagawa side. I walked out into a long beautiful valley laying between low hills where the farmers were busy gathering rice. The foliage of the trees on the hill sides were nearly as varied as our own autumnal foliage, the tints less vivid however. Some of the maples were as deeply reddened by the frosts as our own, so too the sumachs were clothed in deep crimson. A thin haze covered all this varied beauty as with a veil. Asters, daisies, and golden rods were thick by the path side and along the margin of the wood paths the blue gentian opened its azure cup.

I passed by the *odaiba*[119] of Matsudaira Yetsizen no kami situated under a hill ridge. Within its earth embankments several hundred men are said to be stationed. But I was more interested in the beautiful grounds that lay without. Enclosed by a narrow moat were a succession of cottages, or rather of houses, for they were large and ample, occupying a large space at the point where the hill bordered the valley. Grounds handsomely laid out in gardens, lawns, and shade, and enclosed by hedges of rhododendrons, live oak, and maki[120] surrounded the houses. Avenues between dense hedge walls led from the verdant to the houses.

Into one of these I entered which brought me to a large residence of evidently some official on the Daimio's estate. I never saw more beautiful hedges. These were made of maki. I walked between the rows which were fully ten feet high and three or four feet thick, a great wall of green relieved by the white tips of the maki. At the corner two trees had been trained with horizontal branches and these clipped circularly so that they are two corner posts of green foliage. A woman and a couple of girls came to the door as I entered the yard. I asked permission to look about which was

readily conceded and a gate at the side of the house was thrown open.

Entering through this I found myself in as lovely a little spot as one could desire to see. A spacious yard was enclosed by [a] hedge and the ground was laid out in a landscape garden. In the center was a miniature lake with rocky margin overhung by trees. Various walks conducted under the shade of trees into a close thicket beyond. There was a mound of close shorn turf, groups of dwarfed trees, and clumps of flowery plants disposed with a good eye to effect. Into this fairy spot the principle room of the house opened by a broad piazza. We sat down on the hard polished floor of the piazza and talked with the half dozen women of the household who were very civil and brought us fire for our tobacco. I have seen no place in Japan which I would more covet as a residence. From this place I took a path up among the hills and valleys everywhere picturesque in contrived wildness and cultivation.

Monday, November 19, 1860

During the past summer a monument has been erected to the memory of the Russian officers murdered in the streets of Yokohama little more than a year ago. Four square columns rising from a heavy base of stone support a square crenated roof on the top of which is a gilded copper dome surmounted by a cross. Between the pillars at the back of the monument another large gilt cross stands. The bodies of the murdered were disinterred today and removed to their resting place in the vault of this monument with great ceremony. The marines of the two Prussian frigates paraded on shore, and a large body of sailors in blue jackets and white collars armed with cutlasses. A procession was formed of the marines, sailors, diplomatic functionaries, and citizens preceded by a band and the standards of the various treaty powers. It was intended by such an effective display to show the Japanese that all the nations were one in an affair like this. The procession was followed by large and

---

[119] Fort, or fortification, as well as barracks for samurai.

[120] Chinese black pine.

larger crowds. At the grave the Prussian chaplain said prayers and made an address. During his exercises two photographic cameras were busy taking views of the scene.

The *Niagara* arrived from Yedo today. The Japanese conclude to dispense with Lieut. Vries' services for which we are all heartily glad.

Tuesday, November 20, 1860

The streets are lively with officers and crew of the *Niagara* enjoying their shore leave. The Japanese bazaars are crowded from morning till night. Jack is drunk and noisy in the streets.

Wednesday, November 21, 1860

A wet day, employed it in quietly writing within doors all day.

Thursday, November 22, 1860

May came off from the *Niagara* this morning. We have had a long talk over past times and many inquiries have been made after absent friends. The attention to the *Niagara*'s people absorb a great share of our time. I have spent most of the day assisting May in his shopping. Drunken sailors are plenty.

A betto was leading a yakunin's horse down the street today and a sailor seeing the empty saddle without waiting for an invitation proceeded to mount. The betto was in trouble, but finally succeeded in getting Jack off. Another, half sans cover, was mounted on a horse which a Japanese was guiding. He had an umbrella over his head and pipe in his mouth evidently enjoying his day ashore.

Friday, November 23, 1860

Mrs. S[immons]'s birthday, in honor of which the Dr. invited a few friends to dinner. We had a pleasant gathering. After dinner Chaplain Stewart called. He was at one time the intimate friend of Louis Napoleon during his exile in America. Their friendship still continues. He related many interesting anecdotes of the Emperor.

Saturday, November 24, 1860

A wet disagreeable day spent mostly in shopping with May. Picked up several more articles to send home by the *Niagara*.

Sunday, November 25, 1860

Chaplain Stewart preached today to a small audience. Our friends who came over from Kanagawa were caught by a blow in the bay which necessitated their return by norimons. We had a peculiar time storing the ladies away in these inconvenient vehicles. The wind increased to a gale and cut off all communication with the opposite shore and the shipping in the harbor. Many of the *Niagara's* men and officers were on shore unable to join the ship which was to sail at daylight. The Japanese boatmen refused to face the heavy wind and sea. A few were taken off in the ship's boats and the rest dispersed to find shelter till morning.

Monday, November 26, 1860

The *Niagara* instead of leaving today as expected is detained by an investigation into an affair in which some of her crew were concerned yesterday. Some of the men on shore leave, a party of ten, attacked the newly arrived Secretary of the French Legation and robbed him of his watch and revolver, severely bruising him and tearing his clothes partly off from him. He fired two or three shots from his revolver before it was taken, without effect. He identified the principal sailors on board today who were put in irons. After a conference with the French Minister it was decided to leave the men in the hands of the Captain for such punishment as he deemed necessary. The *Niagara's* men had had no leave since they left home and were very drunk, noisy, and troublesome in the streets. It is a pity that we must thus air our infirmities before the Japanese or any other people, but Jack must and ought to have permission to go ashore, and, so long as he has it, will be drunk and quarrelsome. From my own observation since I have been here I think the crews of American men of war have been the worst of all. The contrast between their conduct and that of the crews of the two Prussian frigates is indeed very marked and altogether in favor of the Prussian.

Tuesday, November 27, 1860

During the Fall the foreigners have been in the habit of going out on hunting excursions being absent sometimes one night. This practice was disliked by the Japanese, and officials were always dispatched from the Customs House to follow and take note of their proceedings. A request was made last year of the Consuls that foreigners should abstain from hunting, but the neglect of this request has been openly winked at. The Japanese appear now determined to stop hunting by their own power. A party were out yesterday fifteen miles from Yokohama. One of them Telge, a Prussian, had strayed away from the rest and had bagged some game when he was accosted by three or four Japanese who came up apparently to admire his weapons and skill. They praised his gun which they said was a "fine gun," and called him a "skillful hunter" slapping him familiarly on the back. The hands thus familiarly laid on were not taken off and in a trice the Prussian found himself securely held in their grasp and was immediately bound, thrust into a Kango covered with the Kango's rain suit and was started off as a prisoner. It chanced however that the prisoner, and his captors, who did not know that any other foreigners were near, were met in the road by the Prussian companions, who seeing a man's leg dangling out of the chair thought their companion must have got tired out and

was taking a ride back. The Prussian hearing their voices told them he was a prisoner and was speedily liberated by his comrades who were in too strong force to be resisted.

Today a more serious occurrence has happened.[121] In the afternoon the English Consul at Kanagawa was appraised by one of his servants that a foreigner had fired upon and severely wounded a yakunin. He at once repaired to the Honjin but was met by a deaf ear to all his inquiries, and a pretence that there was nothing known about a wounded yakunin or any such affair. But he persisted in entering the house and found indeed an officer with his arm between the elbow and shoulder shot to fragments.

The Consul called in Drs. H[epburn] and S[immons] and proffered to render assistance. The Drs. examined the wound and decided nothing short of amputation would answer and that was necessary to save the man's life. This they refused to have done, saying it would be necessary to apply to the Governor for permission to amputate. The Consul then told them that if the yakunin died he would hold himself to no responsibility for the death. They refused moreover to give him any satisfaction as to who the prisoner was or where he was.

S., Dr. H[epburn]'s servant, saw the affray. He said the foreigner was passing along the street, and when opposite the Honjin several men, yakunins with swords, came out after him. As they approached him he faced them and waved them back with a fowling piece which he carried. He continued to move his gun horizontally in a semicircle waving them to come no nearer. As they pressed close upon him he fired, one of the yakunins fell, the remainder closed in, secured him, placed him in a kango and started off towards Yokohama.

At Yokohama the foreigners were ready on hearing the news to march anywhere to the rescue if the place of confinement could be found and the Consul would give them leave. It was not till evening that the missing man could be known. Then Mr. Moss was found ab-

---

[121] The Moss Case, as it came to be known, which Hall records here is also discussed in John R. Black,

Young Japan: Yokohama and Yedo, 1858–79 (Tokyo: Oxford University Press, 1968), vol. 1, pp. 53–55.

sent and it was known that he had started yesterday on a hunting excursion, and had invited friends to meet him at dinner this evening.

Wednesday, November 28, 1860

The issue of yesterday's affair has been this. Consul Vyse finding no clue to the whereabouts of the missing man determined to demand him of the Governor in person and to enforce the demand. He obtained the cooperation of the Prussian Commodore, who agreed to sustain him with an armed force. Late in the evening a large force of marines left the Prussian frigate in boats fully armed and taking with them two boat howitzers. They rowed quietly into the mouth of a small creek that flows into Yokohama bay at the foot of the hill on which stands the Governor's house.

The Governor's residence is a half mile from the main town of Yokohama. At the same time Consul V[yse], accompanied by an armed body of English residents to the number of twenty five fully equipped with guns, bayonets, pistols, and swords proceeded to the Governor's by the high road. The men were stationed inside the Governor's yards while Mr. V[yse] went in and demanded of the Governor the person of the missing Englishman. The Governor denied all knowledge of the man, his whereabouts, or the transaction and persisted in this statement in answer to Mr. V[yse]'s repeated demands. The Consul then told him that unless the man was at once produced he should make the Governor a prisoner himself. The Governor affected not to believe this, but the Consul assured him he was in earnest and had the means at hand to carry out his intention.

It had been prearranged that the Prussian force in the creek below should land at the signal of a blue rocket sent up from the party on shore. The rocket was ready in the Governor's yard, the match lighted, when the Governor concluded to yield and surrender the prisoner. He accompanied Capt. V[yse] to the jail which is near the Governor's house and they entered. Mr. V[yse] proceeded through several apartments shouting "Moss are you here," when he received an answer from the confined man. At 2 A.M. Moss was released from his incarcera-

tion and taken to the Consulate to await the action of the English authorities.

From Mr. Moss we get the following narration. He had been in the country hunting and had remained out over night at a farm house. He was coming home through the Tokaido with his servant following behind carrying a wild goose which he had shot. When near the boat landing he heard a noise behind him, turned round and saw his servant in the hand of several officials who were securing him.

He turned back and told them the man was his servant when they called upon him to stop and began to approach him. He drew his gun, cocked it, and waved it before them to keep them off. Finding they hesitated he let his gun still cocked stand on the ground holding it with his left hand. Almost immediately he felt a blow on his head from behind which disabled him and rendered him partly unconscious. He remembered after falling hearing the gun go off, but it was not by his aid. The hammer had fallen probably in the scuffle and had discharged the gun. He was at once pounced upon while down, turned over on his face, and his hands tied behind him. While down he was stamped upon, struck over the head with the iron batons carried by officials, and was afterwards struck several times.

He was removed into a house near by where he was kept till some time after dark and was near by Mr. Vyse at the very time the officials were denying all knowledge of his whereabouts. He was then thrust into a Kango securely tied and put into a boat. In what direction he was taken he could not tell. From the boat he was landed and taken to the place where he was found. It was the inner one of several apartments with an entrance so low that he had to creep in. His cell was a cage of stout bars without mats or any protection from the cold and no food was given him. He knew not where he was, for what he was arrested, or what would be his fate. Cognizant of their cruelty he was prepared to expect any fate, even death. Speaking of his release he said "no sound ever fell so pleasantly on his ear as Mr. Vyse's calling him by name."

It had been fully determined between Consul Vyse and the Prussian Commodore if Mr. Moss was not surrendered to take the Governor prisoner on board of the ships and to seize the two Japanese steamers in the harbor.

Another tragedy occurred yesterday. A Chinaman riding through Kanagawa ran over and killed a child.

Thursday, November 29, 1860

The Anniversary of Thanksgiving in the States. Minister Harris recommended the observance of the day by the Americans in Japan, but his recommendation was unheeded save for the very few who would have kept the day in memory without any suggestion from him. Mr. H[arris] is so unpopular with his countrymen abroad, and has the reputation of doing so much for effect, that they were not at all willing to please him in this matter. The missionary families observed the day with a few others. There were religious services at the American Consulate in Kanagawa very thinly attended. Minister H[arris] was present. After services I went to Rev. Mr. Brown's and dined with several others. Mr. B[rown]'s family being of New England extraction we had a good deal of the spirit of the day with us. Old associations connected with this festival were brought up and talked over, and absent friends were duly remembered.

Friday, November 30, 1860

Passed a rainy day arranging botanical specimens. Mail arrived, no letters.

Saturday, December 1, 1860

The examination of Moss commenced today at the English Consulate. The Japanese objected to Moss's presence during the examination of a yakunin as witness saying that a prisoner could be present only when an inferior was under examination. This being re-

fused, after a long struggle on their part, they desired that "he might be placed behind a screen." The Japanese deny that they intended to arrest Moss until after the gun was fired, and declare that he fired the gun. Moss claims $30,000 damages of the Japanese for injuries.

Sunday, December 2, 1860

Visited Kanagawa after service. While at Dr. H[epburn]'s the 3rd Governor came to pay a call bringing with him the head of the Yedo police, a mild looking man who had little the look of a thief taker. A large retinue accompanied them.

Monday, December 3, 1860

Dropped in a few moments at the English Consul's in Kanagawa to hear the examination of Moss. One of the yakunins who made the arrest was giving evidence. The testimony went through a double interpretation from Japanese to Dutch and then into English. The witness was very cool and quiet giving every answer carefully so as to commit himself the least possible. The three officials who attended to the examination on the part of the Japanese were strict, deliberate looking men. The officers all swear that Moss fired the gun whereas the people who witnessed the transaction say he did not, but they dare not testify to this effect against their officials. The Japanese in lieu of our oath of affirmation affix their seal to a written declaration of their truthfulness and if afterwards the subscribing witness is found to have perjured himself honor drives him to *hara kiri*. The wounded man openly declared that if he recovers he will revenge himself on Moss, and if he dies, his friends will revenge him.

The day being fine I induced Knight and Robinson[122] to join me in a ride into the country. We went out into the long valley that I

---

[122] It is difficult to identify Mr. Robinson, as none of the directories for the period list an American by this name in Yokohama at this time. On April 2, 1862, Hall accompanied a Mr. Robinson and the two geologists,

Blake and Pumpelly, into the Hachioji region. Although Hall clearly wrote Robinson in his account of the trip, Pumpelly wrote that a Mr. Robertson accompanied them. The *China Directory* for 1862 does list one

have so often desired to follow up. I found it to continue on for many miles gradually lessening in breadth. A large stream flows through it. At two different points the different roads in the valley were made to converge so that all the travel must pass two bridges across the stream. Each bridge had a gate and attending officials. At the second one, several miles distant from Kanagawa where there were a few houses, we halted at a tea house for rest and refreshments. We obtained tea, boiled eggs, and some candies that were unusually good. While we were resting, it was curious to notice the older of the two gatekeepers watching and inspecting us as if he wished to be sure of knowing us when he saw us again. The innkeeper wished to know what countrymen we were. No sooner had I replied American, than the old gentleman in the blue robes hastened to jot it down. The inn keeper spied a pistol peering out from K[night]'s pocket and hastened off to report that also. So long as they were civil and unobtrusive we did not mind their watching.

The valley we passed through had been covered with rice now just gathered and appears to be exceedingly fertile. The northern side of it was bordered by one continuous village of well to do houses. We had passed many fine farm houses on the south side, whose neat buildings and out buildings, fire proof structures and granaries, handsome yards bordered with hedges of holly or spruce denoted unusual thrift. I frequently saw splendid specimens of chrysanthemums, some of them having thatches of straw over them to keep off the frosts. A pet canary in a cage swung before the door of a cottage bordered with hedge and flowers had an enticing look of home about it. I made a note in my memory to ride around the valley on the opposite side at my earliest leisure.

We struck across the hills on our return and were rewarded by finding a pleasant path through the woods and glimpses of magnifi-

cent scenery. In the distance were successive ranges of mountains perhaps thirty miles away and between us and them one grand sweep of plains dotted with forests, cultivated fields, and rural hamlets. It was a sight that would reward us for a long day's journey. Having been four hours in the saddle we reached home a little after dusk.

Tuesday, December 4, 1860

Passed the day at home writing.

Wednesday, December 5, 1860

A present of tea is annually sent from the Mikado to the Tycoon. It is carried in state in a richly lackered box accompanied by a numerous retinue. Wherever it passes the people must kneel to the earth as to royalty itself.

Thursday, December 6, 1860

Went over to Kanagawa for a ride. In company with Dr. H[epburn] and Mr. Brown rode out to the great valley again. We crossed it where it had a breadth of five or six miles and found it a succession of rice, wheat, and barley fields all under fine cultivation. I note everywhere the utter absence of need. Everything is sown in drills and the rows are always perfectly straight. The ground is laid off in patches about 100 feet square and a line of turf that one may walk upon is the dividing line. When the crops are sewn the drills in one patch will not correspond with those in the other, but be diagonal to them. Thus the lines are continually varied which breaks up the monotony of appearance and gives the whole country a look of a garden. The women are beginning to gather rushes for the winter's fuel. We met today two girls under heavy loads of rushes and

S. Robertson as an American resident in Yokohama. It would seem odd that Hall could mistake the name of someone with whom (as his account of the Hachioji trip indicates) he was well acquainted and who had spent some time in Japan.

the poor things crouched against the bank as if mortally afraid of us. It was nearly dark when we returned.

The result of Mr. Moss's examination has been that he is bound over for trial. After three days' examination the Japanese officials refused to attend any longer saying they had wasted time enough. The yakunins who made the arrest have been rewarded, some of them receiving as much as 150 ichibus.

Friday, December 7, 1860

The English Minister has issued a circular forbidding English residents from hunting any kinds of game or wearing pistols between sunrise and sunset and cautioning them not to resist any Japanese officials making arrests. The circular excites general indignation among the English.

Saturday, December 8, 1860

The Japanese arrested a Chinaman today for riding horseback contrary to a new regulation of theirs. The English citizens assembled today and made a protest to Mr. Alcock and the Home Government against Mr. A[lcock]'s new regulations as to firearms. A series of resolutions were passed, among which was one expressive of their determination to wear pistols openly so long as Japanese—not officials—wore swords.

There seems to be little doubt of the man wounded by Moss expressing a determination to have blood for blood, and that if Moss leaves the country alive somebody else's head must pay the penalty.

A Japanese merchant has runaway owing several thousand dollars to the foreign merchants; to one $8000 to another $3000. Such rascalities thus far have been on the side of the Japanese, for not a single instance have I heard of any defrauding of the Japanese in like manner.

Sunday, December 9, 1860

After church service took a walk in the country a short distance. Found camellias in bloom, also the blue gentian, asters, golden rod, and a few others. Some members of the returned Embassy from America visited Yokohama today attended by a large retinue.

Monday, December 10, 1860

After writing busily till afternoon went to the Japanese theater. The building with its arrangements of seats, galleries, and stage was much like those I have before described. The people were divided off by cross timbers into small squares where families were sitting taking their meals and listening to the play at the same time. The stage scenery, dress, curtains, etc., were an improvement on what I had hitherto seen. The same turntable arrangement was used for shifting the scenes that I saw at Nagasaki. In nearly two hours we watched the progress of the play, getting the thread of the incident by the pantomime and Heco's explanation. The play had begun in the morning and lasted all day, but unlike our plays the different acts are quite complete in themselves. In instance we came in at five P.M., but saw a complete stage play the plot of which was something like this:

A servant of an officer goes into a teahouse where another officer is recreating himself and gives offence, which results in his being deprived of his master's spear that he carries. He is sent back to his master thus disgraced.

2nd Scene. The two officers are seen in angry colloquy respecting the incident in which the owner of the spear is told that he can have it back in exchange only for his servant's head. This scene is enlivened by a by-play of the servant who is half stupid apparently, but who comprehends the term of the exchange and draws his thick quilted garment around his neck as if to shield it from a blow. He finally rises to go when his master asks him what he is about and he says he wishes to go to Yokohama.

3rd scene. The master tells the servant he

must take his head off and exchange it for the spear or else humiliate himself before his brother yakunin. He expatiates on his sorrow at being compelled so to do as his servant has always been faithful. The servant says he is willing to die but he has an old blind mother whom he must support. The master moved by his servant's supplication says he will take the mother as his own and to dignify the death of his servant says he will make a yakunin of him and he shall commit hara kiri. The servant is delighted with the idea of being made a yakunin or samurai, tosses aside his old short sword with expressive contempt and receives the long swords of a samurai. His satisfaction is less evident when his master succeeds to instruct him how to commit *hara kiri*. This scene is well enacted, the evident disgust of the servant at the operation, his feints at performing it, his shrinking from the first scratch, etc., is admirable. Finally he does the deed, the master cuts his head off, and the dead body is covered with a cloth, and then *walks* off the stage instead of being borne off. A wooden head is produced which the master now wraps up in a cloth.

Scene 4th. Yakunin no 2 is seen in a room waiting impatiently for the head of the offending servant. Yakunin the first comes upon the stage with the head still wrapped up and so informs the other he is ready for the exchange. The exchange is made and yakunin the second dashes the head he has received on the ground. The master now tells him that he promised his servant that he would avenge his death on his head. A combat ensues between the first yakunin with the spear and the second with his sword. The second is slain, his head is cut off and the victor places the head face to face to that of the servant's and talks to his servant's head saying that he has avenged his death. This seemed to close this part of it, and the subsequent acts were distinct.

The next representing a scene between a merchant who for ten Kobangs had bought a girl of a princess and the woman has sent the girl away. The disappointed merchant demands the girl or the money, the woman replies that the girl was worth more, that the foreigners at Yokohama would give more for her. A quarrel ensues and a fight in which the

woman uses brows and nails after the feminine mode.

Another scene follows in which a prisoner is brought to an inn in a Kango. His bearers sleep and the prisoner is released by a servant in the guise of a blind shampooer. There follows the astonishment of his guard, then attempts to retake him in which there is some good tumbling and somersaulting, indeed the whole of this scene is quite like a performance of the Ravels. There followed another scene representing the same prisoner crucified and his wife comes to mourn, but Ravel-like he escapes from the crucifix and there follows some more pantomime and tumbling. I could not pick up the thread of these last scenes or see any connection to what had gone before.

We went into the green room between two of the acts and saw the actors preparing themselves for the stage. There were two series of apartments one above the other, and the actors were busy with paints, false wigs, and wardrobes. They received us very civilly, and like their class at home were unusually polite in their address. One was painting and dressing to represent a girl, another entirely nude was squatted on the floor busy with paints and powders which he had around him in saucers. Each actor seemed to have his own dressing room. I saw a foreign mirror in one of them.

About the whole arrangement and performance of the theater there were many points of resemblance with those at home.

Returning home late from a ride a few evenings since just at dark I heard the sound of a conch shell in the vallies. I learned that it is the call of the bath house keepers to signify that the bath was ready.

Tuesday, December 11, 1860

Writing and shopping.

Wednesday, December 12, 1860

A severe northeast rain storm. Musical soiree in the evening K[nigh]t and M[ors]e assisting. K[nigh]t is going to China tomorrow. We have a sociable evening and make a late lunch on a cold duck left over from dinner and separate about one A.M.

Thursday, December 13, 1860

Among items of news gleaned from Japanese sources is one that the late Prince of Mito and the Prince of Satsuma were discovered in a correspondence respecting a union against the present dynasty. Again I hear that the great princes are mutually jealous and distrustful and feel much less concerned about their foreign, than their internal, relations. They are said to be very active in building forts within their own provinces and arming their men with weapons, muskets, pistols, etc., of Japanese manufacture.

In Japanese affairs the eighteen greater daimios take no part except in great emergencies. The Emperor's immediate and constant advisers are the Gosanki [*Sanke*], his titular brothers, but as they are often absent the Gosankio [*Sankyō*] are his advisers who always remain in the city, having no country estates. The Goroju [*Rōjū*], or council of five self elective, are the originators of public measures, and really the governing power, as the Emperor would seldom interfere with their acts. The Goroju is made up of smaller princes supposed not to have such great state interests as would bias their opinions as would naturally be the case if taken from the members of the more powerful princes. The eighteen daimios are an upper council of state whose will would be supreme when united on any policy. They are the last appeal, it is they who choose the Emperor. They hold their councils in the "hall of a 1000 mats" and are presided over by the Emperor in person. The selection of the Goroju is confined to a certain number of princely families. In like manner the Gotairo [*tairō*] is chosen from one of three families.

Friday, December 14, 1860

Spent an hour or two today among the wrestlers. The exhibition on the whole was better than last year's. The pavilion or canopy over the wrestling ring was tastefully arranged.

Four poles supported a roof of latticed bamboo, directly under which a purple and crimson curtain five or six feet in breadth was hung. The poles themselves were wrapped with strips of ribbon one white and blue combined, a second white and purple, a third white and green, the fourth white and red. The wrestlers are divided in classes according to their skill. Each class has his own umpire. The umpire of the first class was handsomely attired in silk with the imperial arms impressed thereon. In this class were the best wrestlers of the empire, one of whom was the acknowledged wrestling champion of Japan. I saw him afterwards engaged in a match with the 2nd best of Japan. It was a great display of mingled skill and strength devoid of anything brutal. When the victor had partly lifted his antagonist out of the ring and placed him against one of the pillars they stood for a moment looking laughingly into each others' faces. Some Japanese were about the foreigners stands very eager to engage in bets. A numerous public had seats in the galleries by themselves.

After the exhibition was concluded I went into the dressing, or rather undressing, apartment which was on one side of the enclosure. The stalwart wrestlers received us very kindly. The umpire of the first class took off his outer jacket and showed it to me. It was lined within with a white silk on which were painted pictures of heroes and notorious women, some of which were of a character highly indicative of the corrupt taste of this people. I have no doubt this exhibition is as free from any depraving tendency as the Olympic games of old.

Saturday, December 15, 1860

Went over to Kanagawa at 8½ this morning to have a long country ride. Our party was Mr. B[rown] and Miss B[rown], Mr. Nevius, Mr. Insley, Mr. Goble, and Duus. We rode out into the great valley where a broken bridge prevented our crossing the river of Suruma[123] at the usual place and turned us off into the

---

[123] This seems to have been the Katabira-gawa which may have been called the Tsuruma-gawa by local residents as it flowed from the direction of Tsuruma.

country to the right. The character of the country differed little from that near the bay. The hills were smaller, lower, and more abrupt, inclined to the conical form. We must have entered a silk district as the mulberry trees were very abundant, forming the division rows of the fields and crops. The tree is headed back so as to secure a yearly abundance of young suckers which produce larger leaves. We went out twelve or fifteen miles and fortunately carried our lunch with us as we were unable to procure anything to eat except sweetmeats and cakes. We reached home at 5 P.M., having been in the saddle six hours.

Sunday, December 16, 1860

A gale of wind from the north has beaten up such an ugly sea that there is no crossing the bay, so our Kanagawa friends were absent from church. A mail arrived yesterday and brought me no letters. Dr. S[immons] is disconsolate at not hearing from his spouse.

Monday, December 17, 1860

Today closed Moss's trial before the English Consul and three assessors, terminated in a disagreement as to a verdict. It was a prejudged case so far that the verdict was to be left with the British Minister to whom the case now goes. Two mails from home arrived this evening. I had a three hours enjoyment of reading my letters which only those far away from home can understand.

Heco says that the daimios at Yedo are very much interested in making inquiries of the returned Ambassadors as to American affairs and that the talk is that when the Embassy goes to England a daimio of high rank will go.

Tuesday, December 18, 1860

Spent an hour or so this morning seeing the wrestlers practice. They are divided into classes according to their experience and skill and the head man of the class exercises his subordinates. The practice is more interesting than the wrestling matches because there is more freedom of action and a greater display of muscular effort, a little more rough and tumble in fact. The head wrestler will exercise with four, six, eight, or more successively as his class may happen to be.

In the practice there is some of the rough work described by Perry. Butting with the head, or rather forcibly striking the forehead against the master's breast and shoulders is universally done, bringing bloody noses in consequence. Nor does the man struck always escape bruises as old scars sufficiently testified. It was really interesting to see some of the older professional ones humble their younger brethren so easily. One fellow of splendid frame stood like a rock against the shocks of the forceful head blows, though when he willed he could easily hold his adversary at arm's length. Then he would let his hands fall at his side and butt his adversary out of the ring with his shoulders, and finally stood on one foot, and using no hands, fairly drove by butting a stout competitor out of the arena.

The neophytes were put through till exhausted, they were thrown down, pushed down, struck down with the flat of the hand, batted down, thrown over the wrestler's head till the poor fellows could hardly stand. There was no danger of injury, and the whole was done with a smiling good nature. There were various set-tos in other parts of the enclosure among the younger wrestlers. The attention bestowed upon the favorite and skilled men was noticeable. If they fell in the dirt a half dozen hands were ready to wipe off their nude skins, indeed someone was wiping them, all [of] them, as a horse would be groomed. Water was brought to them obsequiously, and they bowed to the earth before them when beginning their morning lesson. It was amusing to see at every pause in the exercise a half dozen gather around the master and hang on him beseechingly that he would give his next attention to them.

Wherever the head wrestlers go they are followed up by the younger ones doing servants' service. They do not allow them to help themselves in anything, at the bath they wash them and wipe them dry, masters were never so attended by their pupils elsewhere. One of the wrestlers came to H[eco] and myself and wanted to know what he should do for sore eyes. He showed us a moxa on the tip of his great toe and another between two toes and several on his back that he had burned to relieve his eyesight.

Wednesday, December 19, 1860

Morning shopping and writing. Had also a long visit from an astronomer from Miaco, an almanac maker. He is a priest, a young man, and had a nervous organization. His face was thin and pale, and his hands delicate as a woman's. He told me there were a few others at Miaco like himself who studied this science. He could calculate eclipses but not the orbit of a comet. There are none in Japan who can do so. At Yedo there are two observatories, or rather houses occupied by astronomers, who give their attention wholly to this science. This man corrected me once or twice when I made mistakes. He was desirous to learn how to calculate a comet's orbit, but it was beyond my knowledge to tell him.

In the evening attended Sewing Society at Mrs. Nevius' and had a pleasant time.

Thursday, December 20, 1860

Mr. Moss received his judgement today which was, that he pay the wounded man $1000, be confined three months in the Hong Kong jail, and be banished [from] the country. The entire community without regard to nationality are indignant and outraged. It is a judgement contrary to justice and humanity, and one which could not have been obtained in any court.

Friday, December 21, 1860

Two French men of war have arrived in the harbor having Admiral Charnier[124] on board.

[124] Vice Admiral Charner.

Saturday, December 22, 1860

The straightforward diplomacy of French Minister Belcour [Bellecourt] commends itself to all foreigners. While passing through the streets of Yokohama he met the Governor and his train, to whom he bowed politely, but in return received the epithet of *baka* from one of the attendants. Without more ado he seized the offender at once, and after first compelling him to apologize before all present, he had him sent off to the Custom House under arrest with promise of punishment. A French merchant was robbed a few nights since of $2000 worth of goods, the Minister demanded the offender and that he should be punished in his presence to the extent of the Japanese laws. The Japanese replied that they could not find the offender, "very well says the Minister, you must pay over the $2000 then, a government that can watch the foreigner to knowing every step he takes day or night is capable of knowing its offenders, and if the man is not punished it is because some official screens him." So, too, he has demanded unequivocal settlement of private claims of French merchants who have been defrauded by the Japanese.

The chief office of the *ninsoku* [coolies] is near our residence and there are more or less of these latterdemalions in the vicinity. This afternoon one of them started a fire in the street with some old straw bales, bits of board, etc., and soon a large number of these half clad fellows were enjoying themselves by the general warmth.

Sunday, December 23, 1860

Our coldest morning so far, ice formed last night an inch thick, followed by a pleasant day. Walked with T[albo]t out to Treaty Point.

Monday, December 24, 1860

To Kanagawa by boat and a ride back in company with the Am. Consul. Evening at Talbot's.

Tuesday, December 25, 1860

Christmas Day. Sent the servants to the fields and woods for flowers and green branches and rode over to Kanagawa to pay my respects to the American families there. Dinner at Gobles, and after dinner rode out with Mr. N[evius] towards Yedo. Had a distinct view of Yedo Bay and the shipping from the hills. Returned to Yokohama and dined with Dr. Hall[125] in the evening. Minister Harris is down from Yedo, having come down "to spend the day with his countrymen," but alas! his countrymen are not willing to spend this day with him. Mr. Dorr invited a number of us to dine with him, but we all found convenient excuses not to go. The only Americans present at the dinner were the Captain of a vessel in harbor and his wife. Mr. Harris has alienated himself from the good will of his countrymen by his official and personal neglect of them hitherto and the refusal to meet him at dinner was a marked token of their disesteem for the man.

Wednesday, December 26, 1860

A stormy day, rain alternating towards evening to snow. Housebound all day.

Thursday, December 27, 1860

A bright day after yesterday's storm. The ground was white in many places with snow, but the purity and freshness of the atmosphere enticed me into a long walk in the country. The paths were often heavy with mud, but there were many remaining spots under the hedgerows where the frost buried turf was dry and the air was sweet with the odor of fragrant leaves. There was a long path across the paddy fields bordered by some grand old live oaks, and I stopped at a cottage and got a handful of roses blooming in the open air.

Friday, December 28, 1860

Mail day for the *Daniel Webster* and so busy all day long preparing letters for home. We hear today that a late Governor of Yokohama has committed suicide at Yedo by *hara kiri*.[126] It grew out of disagreement upon some question in regard to foreign trade with the Goroju. After his death Simme [Shimmi] Buzen no Kami, the chief of the Embassy to America advocated the same ground and said if not sustained in opinion he should commit the same act. But the Goroju yielded either to his threat or arguments though too late to save his friend the late Governor with whom he had formerly been associated.

Saturday, December 29, 1860

Lanrick arrived today with a home mail. Boat to Kanagawa and a horseback ride with Dr. H[epburn]. The roads very muddy and sticky from thawing frost and recent rains. Thus far our winter has been more cloudy and wet than last winter.

Sunday, December 30, 1860

The American bark *Coquimbo* put in here last evening in distress leaking badly, making three feet of water per hour. She left Hong Kong sixty five days since with 300 Chinese (60,

---

[125] Dr. George R. Hall, who was no relation to Francis Hall, was the Yokohama representative of Walsh & Co. For further details regarding Dr. Hall see the biographical sketch of Francis Hall that accompanies this volume.

[126] Joseph Heco records that this was Hori Oribe-no-sho, the former governor of Kanagawa and then governor of foreign affairs. The reason for Hori's suicide was that he stood by the conditions of the Harris Treaty regarding the export of flour against the wishes of Andō Tsushima no Kami, who sought to prohibit the export of this commodity due to rising flour and wheat prices in Edo. Convinced that he had offended Andō at the meeting of the Rōju, Hori committed suicide in his palanquin on his way home. The shogun, fearing that Hori might do so, sent a messenger pardoning him for disputing with the senior council, but the messenger arrived too late to prevent the act. Hori's son was immediately appointed governor of Kanagawa. See Joseph Heco, *Narrative of a Japanese*, vol. 1, pp. 265–66.

women) on board for San Francisco. She experienced heavy weather and has for forty days worked hard at the pumps to keep afloat. An attempt will be made to repair her.

In the last twenty four hours we have had many rumors respecting the French. Now they are about to bombard Yedo, and now they have landed several hundred men, and again a steamer has been dispatched for reinforcements from the Chinese squadron. The Japanese themselves have taken alarm and on Friday evening put a garrison in the new fort at Kanagawa. Doubtless the French Minister has been firm in his demands for redress of all grievances and hence the flying rumors and alarm of the Japanese.

The $2000 demanded as restitution for the robbery of a French merchant has been repaid.

Monday, December 31, 1860

The last day of the year and one that has quickly flown so full has it been to me of new interests. Long before this I had expected to have been absent from Japan, but I am still a lingerer on these shores and perhaps another New Year may still find me in these ends of the earth. Tonight my heart goes across the Pacific and the width of the continent beyond to the friends from whom I have been so long separated. When shall I again be in their midst to say the greetings of a "Happy New Year," and my heart weary of absence only answers when? I know it must be long, and I shudder when I think of the changes that may be.

1861

Tuesday, January 1, 1861

New Year's Day, made calls on Kanagawa friends, returned to Yokohama to dine with Richards,[1] back to Kanagawa in the evening at a "Candy Pull at Mr. B[rown]'s," and back to Yokohama at midnight. So much for New Year's festivities in Japan. The day was sunny and warm, how our callers at home would enjoy such a first of January temperature.

Eighteen hundred of Mito's men have been discharged from their master's employ say the Japanese and have turned vagabonds, robbing and plundering where they can. The people of Kanagawa and Hodogaya are in fear lest their houses are fired and the yakunins are, in truth, here to catch them, lest the foreign settlement should be disturbed. These men say they will seek to enter Yokohama disguised as servants, or day laborers, and commit their crimes of pillage, arson, or murder. These discharged

[1] C. H. Richards was one of the leading American commission agents in Yokohama at this time and founder of C. H. Richards & Co. See Yokohama Shiyakusho, ed., *Yokohama shishi kō—Sangyō hen* (Kyoto: Rinsen Shoten, 1986), p. 50.

soldiers seem to consider it less disgraceful to rob and plunder than to earn a living by hard labor. A murder was committed near Kawasaki two or three nights ago by these vagabond soldiery.

Wednesday, January 2, 1861

Today the town is full of rumors. Each one has his own story. This much is reliable, that a high official came down from Yedo to see Mr. Harris on the 1st. The object of his visit was to inform him that a band of 600 lordless men were intent in attacking the foreigners both at Yedo and Yokohama and desiring that Mr. Harris with the other officials at Yedo would go within the citadel for safety as it was difficult to protect them where they were. Also to request that the Consuls would remove from Kanagawa to Yokohama. Rumor says that Mr. Alcock will accept the proposition and move within the imperial citadel.

The English fleet came down from Yedo last night and Rear Admiral Jones and the English Consul have had a long interview with the governor of Yokohama. The admiral says to the Governor, if you cannot seize this band of marauders, show me where they are, and I will take them for you. The Governor declined the proffered aid. The Dutch brig of war was ready for any emergency last evening, her guns were loaded and shotted. The French have a guard on shore at the Consulate in Kanagawa and the French settlement in Yokohama. This band of six hundred are said to be encamped on an island in Yedo Gulf, but this is a rumor of doubtful complexion. They are not Mito's men altogether, but are said to come from three different daimios. The Japanese authorities have thrown several hundred soldiers into Kanagawa and Yokohama for defence. These are supplied by Oki-no-Kami at his fort, or barracks, in Kanagawa and by Yetsizen-[Echizen]-no-Kami at Yokohama. Three daimios have received orders to provide each a contingent more for the protection of the settlements. Muskets have been distributed to the various guard houses on the public roads and a close watch is kept by the government on all who enter Yokohama.

It is a little remarkable that this new disturbance arises like the others at a time when there is a fleet of men of war in the harbor. All these stories of truth, fact, or fable, make little impression on the foreign community. We have become accustomed to alarms, and we are incredulous as to there being the amount of danger the Japanese represent. Some ulterior design is covered up under all this stir, and the whole hubbub is quite likely to arise from the difficulties within themselves than any virulent hatred towards the foreigners.

Dr. S[immon]'s teacher confirms the story related to me by Heco a little time since of 36 of Mito's men after their master's decease coming to the Prince of Satsuma and saying that they were pledged to their dead master, to implacable hatred towards the foreigner, and desiring him to further their designs. This the Prince of Satsuma did not do, but took them into his employ till the Government should make some provision for them instead of letting them loose as a band of assassins.

Mr. B[rown] of Kanagawa has had in his employ for some months a Japanese teacher and the teacher's son, a lad of sixteen or so, as house and stable boy. Soon after his employ the boy robbed Mr. B[rown] of some trifles and was arrested by the authorities in the manner I have related in a previous part of my journal. Of late he has been pilfering more extensively, taking not only many small articles about the house, but [he] opened Mr. B[rown]'s safe and took out a hundred ichibus. He was exposed by some of his companions, and many of the things, and most of the money, were restored.

Mr. B[rown] was desirous to discharge both father and son from his employ but the old man pleaded so hard saying they were without any means of support that Mr. B[rown] was inclined to be merciful and strove to reform the boy. Then the other servants rebelled and said they would not remain if Mr. B[rown] kept Kakoe, for they would be regarded in an unfavorable light by the yakunins. It is Kakoe's third offence and Mr. Brown, who has gone to Yedo, has taken the boy with him hoping to get him a place of security. He could not go to Yedo by himself, for wherever he went he must report himself to the nanooshi [nanushi], or headman, of the street and tell who he was or where he came from. Today Dr. S[immon]'s teacher and our servants both say that the Japanese have knowledge of his offence and are watching for him, for if they take him he will probably be executed. But they state a singular fact, that Jobootsugi [Jobutsuji] temple and its grounds is a crown gift to the priests and that by Japanese law no one can be arrested in the temple grounds. If this be true it accounts for the mode in which Kakoe was arrested before with two others. They were called as if on some errand without the gate and there arrested.

Thursday, January 3, 1861

We hear nothing new of the state of affairs and all surface wise seems sufficiently quiet.

I had a visit today from two yakunins and two doctors. One of the yakunins has been here twice before, when I have been out, to purchase if possible Goupil's Head of Washington[2] that hangs over my desk. Today he found me in and was importunate that I should sell it. I told him no, it was a man all Americans loved, our great chief, and I could not part with it. He urged me saying that I could replace it, he had come from Neegata on the opposite side of the island and could not come again. He knew all about Washington, he said, he was the greatest general, and in all the world there was none like him. He knew about our Revolution, its continuance, the length of Washington's career, and his desire to get the portrait was so earnest that it was really hard to refuse him.

I never saw a child take the refusal of any coveted article so much to heart. The tears almost stood in his eyes. He took out his memorandum wallet such as all Japanese carry and taking out a sheaf of paper folded it into an oblong strip and then placing in it a gold coin of a little over a dollar in value laid it on the mats and getting down on his knees lowered his head to the floor and pushed it towards

me. I told him nay, I would send to America for another and in a few months he should have it. But he could not wait he said and he lived so far away.

I had some cheap colored prints of the Presidents on one sheet of paper which I showed him and offered one to him. He smiled and then turning his face up to Washington's portrait rubbed his hands together and for another half hour implored me to gratify him. Then he sat down in my chair and looked steadily at the noble looking head in rapt admiration. He again approached me and placing another gold piece in the paper again prostrated himself to the floor in earnest entreaty for the picture. It was really hard to refuse him, but if I parted with it I should lose the privilege of showing to the Japanese the portrait of a man whom many know and all esteem.

He at last with great reluctance consented to wait till I should send to America and get a copy for him. The two physicians, his companions, were very intelligent looking men, one of them had a face of southern Europe, really a Spanish looking fellow. He was anxious to buy a photographing apparatus and to study medicine. I have never seen a group of Japanese with whom I have been more pleased.

Friday, January 4, 1861

Again do reports thicken about our ears of coming harm to all foreigners. The Embassies at Yedo are to be sacked, the foreign settlement on the bay to be extirpated! The government urge, with all apparent seriousness, the Ministers to come within the citadel walls at Yedo, the Consuls to leave Kanagawa and go to Yokohama where they may be more easily protected. But as the foreign representatives will not accede to their demands, they have doubled the guards about the embassies at Yedo and the patrol at Kanagawa. At the latter place there is a nightly patrol of a guard armed with muskets and bayonets. As in the

---

[2] This was a mezzotint of Gilbert Stuart's portrait of George Washington engraved by Edward Girardet and published by Goupil and Co. See Charles Henry Hart, *Catalogue of the Engraved Portraits of Washington* (New York: The Grolier Club, 1904), no. 379, p. 174.

disturbances of a year ago, so now, contingents of soldiers have been sent into Kanagawa and Yokohama by Oki-no-Kami and Yetsizen-no-Kami respectively. Guard boats patrol the bay and every Japanese entering Yokohama is closely scrutinized. Yet, for all these indications, we believe in no danger personal to ourselves. The trouble, if there is one, is between the government and a band of outlaws, discharged soldiers of the late Prince Mito.

Saturday, January 5, 1861

The Dutch brig of war was ready for action last night with shotted guns and every preparation for emergencies that might occur. Today towards evening a hundred and fifty of Yetsizen-no-Kami's soldiers marched through Yokohama with two field pieces and were posted in the Custom House compound for the night. Yet nobody takes alarm except a few worthy Dutchmen.

Thursday, January 10, 1861

I was taken violently ill on the evening of the 5th with what proved to be varioloid.[3] Saturday I had severe pain in the head, chills, etc., in the evening a high fever followed the chills and I had a sleepless night. Sunday, high fever all day and another restless night. Monday morning the eruption appeared but we were not aware of its nature till Tuesday. The attack was a mild one and the eruption light. Confined to the house all three days and for the most part to a couch chair being weak, feverish, and suffering a good deal of headache. Able to read, but not to write.

Friday, January 11, 1861

Convalescent. The eruption has mostly dried up, my tongue is clearing off and appetite slowly returning. Severe headache in the morning is my chief annoyance.

Saturday, January 12, 1861

Much better today, left my easy chair and have written a little. Headaches mitigated. Snowed most of the day, melting as it fell.

Sunday, January 13, 1861

Still convalescent. The pleasant skies overhead tempt me to go out, but the ground is everywhere wet and the streets muddy, so I must fain wait till another day.

Monday, January 14, 1861

I had risen this morning and was dressing when there was an alarm of fire. Looking out of my window I saw the smoke pouring out of one of the godowns in the Custom House compound. I hastily finished dressing, by which time our little household was in great alarm, for we were closely connected with the C[ustom] H[ouse] buildings. S[immons] was for removing everything at once, for the flames were bursting out fiercely and dense curtains of smoke issued forth. I begged him to wait till I went to the spot and saw first what our danger was. I hastened into the Custom House yard and saw that two long godowns, or warehouses, separated from the Custom House buildings by a narrow street, were all in flames. A great crowd of people were gathered striving to arrest the conflagration by their feeble means of squirt engines and tearing the adjacent buildings down.

If the large Custom House buildings ignited our chances of escape were very small. Seeing the danger of this so imminent I returned to the house to take some measures towards moving out when lo! I found the house already stripped. S[immons] yielding to his own fears, and the persuasions of friends, had consented to the removal of our effects. We continued the work and had nearly emptied the house when word came that the fire was under control and the Custom House, and thereby ourselves, safe. So we stopped and contemplated

---

[3] A mild form of smallpox that is sometimes incurred by individuals who have been vaccinated against small-pox, or who have had the disease previously.

Japanese fire brigade with pump. Photograph by Felice Beato.

the wreck we were in, our furniture, bedding, books, and personal effects were scattered, and our neat floors were a mass of filth from the mud trodden in. My recent illness was forgotten in the necessity of action. Our friends came to proffer assistance, among them were many Japanese who had assisted in removing, and were now ready to help us replace. Our old Kanagawa friends who had come across the bay found us and were very kind. Two merchant's clerks from a crockery store rendered us much assistance. Indeed the Japanese were very obliging and faithful. Our English and American friends offered house, room, and anything we wanted, but we only accepted a breakfast from Allmands[4] as our household was in great disorder. With the aid of so many willing hands we soon had our goods and chattels back in the house and by noon order was restored.

Nothing had been broken, stolen, or lost, which was truly remarkable. We must replace our soiled mats with new ones which is our chief, indeed our only, loss. The Japanese did well with their means in stopping the fire at the point they did. Fire is an enemy they dread and one they are taught to combat. They have large fire companies distinguished by showy parti-colored dresses and their fire implements are small force engines that two men can carry and work, firehooks, ladders, and axes for tearing down buildings. The chiefs of the fire brigade came out with leather helmets and capes, oftentimes iron and copper helmets, carry a baton with which they enforce orders, silk trousers are a part of their attire. Others wore thick quilted hoods and dresses covered with great blotches of red and white. I have never seen the Japanese so showily dressed as on occasion of these fires. Mounting the roofs in advance of the flames are men bearing aloft paper flags, streamers, and talismans to keep off the evil genius of the fire and when the flames are subdued a crowd of people clamber up the roofs that have been saved and with their paper flags, inscribed with characters appropriate, exult over the extinguished elements.

We have been the recipients of gifts from our Japanese friends in token of their joy at our escape. One sent us half a bushel of oranges, another a sponge cake, another some small cakes. Heco, our neighbor, has been showered with boxes and baskets of oranges,

[4] John Allmand was the head of Allmand & Co. See *The Chronicle and Directory for China, Japan, and the Phil-* *ippines for 1866* (Hong Kong: Daily Press, 1866), p. 233.

cakes, sake, etc. So, many other foreigners, have received gifts even such as were in no wise exposed. These tokens of good feeling were very pleasant to behold. The warehouses burned were filled with foreign goods incurring a loss to different parties of fifteen or twenty thousand dollars.

Tuesday, January 15, 1861

I am now quite restored to health again. Went to Kanagawa in the afternoon to call upon my friends there.

Wednesday, January 16, 1861

We are all shocked this morning by the news of Heusken's assassination at Yedo last evening. The poor fellow was returning from the Prussian legation at half past nine P.M., when he was attacked by a party of seven men and so severely wounded that he survived but three hours. I wait to get the particulars more fully before writing them down. Only last Sabbath evening Dr. S[immons] and myself were speaking of Heusken and his habit of being out in the evening so much at Yedo, and wondered how it was he escaped if Yedo was so dangerous as we were told. We attributed his immunity from danger to the fact that he was widely known and universally popular at Yedo, but alas! even these have failed to protect him, and it would even seem that he was laid in wait for to be cut down in cold blood. A great gloom is cast over the foreign community and no one can feel himself perfectly secure any longer.

Our household is turned upside down today repairing our floor mats which were ruined at the time of the fire.

Thursday, January 17, 1861

Mail arrived today bringing me a letter from Charles and Fred[5] and a supply of papers.

[5] Charles and Fred were two of Francis Hall's brothers.

Friday, January 18, 1861

At Kanagawa today and called on the American Consul who is yet sick in bed. From him I gathered some particulars of the murder of poor Heusken. He read to me Mr. Harris' letter. Heusken had been taking dinner and spending the evening at Akabane, the Prussian headquarters, as was his wont. He was engaged moreover in assisting them to engross the newly made treaty. About half past eight he started to return home, a mile distant. He was mounted and attended by three mounted yakunins and four bettos running in advance with lanterns after the usual custom. When about halfway home, as they were riding along, one of the yakunins in advance, and just as they had turned a corner, his party were attacked by men springing upon them from either side. The lanterns were struck out of the bettos' hands, simultaneously one of the yakunins' horses was cut, another struck over the head, and Heusken received a thrust in his right side. He urged his horse into a gallop, rode two hundred yards and exclaimed, "I am wounded and dying," and fell from his horse. Thus the whole affair was begun and ended in an instant, no second blows were given, and all escaped unharmed except Heusken. The attacking party, he thought, was seven men, but in all probability there were more considering what was so rapidly and successfully done.

About twenty minutes to ten Heusken was brought to the American legation, the first knowledge any foreigner had of the event. He was conveyed from the ground on poles, and a Japanese who was present said his shrieks of pain would sing in his ears to his dying day. Prompt medical assistance was administered by Minister Alcock, who was formerly a surgeon in the English Peninsular Army, and by the surgeon of the Prussian embassy. Heusken had received a thrust in the right side laying open the abdomen, wounding the intestines and spleen. He lingered till half past 12 and died in the arms of L'Abbé Girard, who administered to him the last consolation of the Catholic religion to which the dying man was attached.

Mr. Heusken had often been warned against the habit of going out evenings, but for two years he had gone and come in the evening at all hours and laughed at any idea of danger. Yet, Yedo is unsafe at night to her own people and particularly so to foreigners. He trusted somewhat perhaps in the high estimation in which the Japanese people always seemed to hold him. He was a favorite among them, for his universal kindness and patience with them. Wherever he rode in Yedo he was hailed with shouts of his name, indeed his name had almost become a synonym for foreigner as it would be shouted to any foreigner who passed the streets. The duties of his official station were always discharged with great fidelity. No one man had so much to do with the making of the foreign treaties. Each and all of the treaty Powers are indebted to him for valuable services, English, French, Russians, Dutch (?) [question mark in original], and lastly the Prussians. The Queen of England in acknowledgement of his valuable services presented him with a costly gold snuff box, but he received a more distinguished acknowledgement of his services when Lord Elgin removed his valuable watch from his own person and transferred it to Mr. Heusken. His untimely end has cast a gloom over his associates that time will not soon expel, nay more, they have reason for personal solicitude when the least obnoxious person of their number has been so wantonly slain.

Who committed the deed? No one knows, at least no one who will divulge. Whether they were the outlaw soldiery of Mito, of whom we have heard so much and against whom the Japanese ministry especially cautioned Mr. Harris, or whether they were soldiers of some daimio hostile to foreigners, or to the government, it is impossible to tell. To one of these two classes they doubtless belonged. It was not a drunken raid but a deliberately planned act. The skill and celerity with which the deed was accomplished, the lying in wait, the manner of attack, all prove this. The most noticeable feature of the transaction is that so large a party of men could lie in wait for their victim at that place without suspicion. Between the Prussian and American legations the government had erected guard houses at each sixty mats, or 360 feet, and how so large a party of men had repaired to this spot and remained unseen of anybody that would report them is a little

strange. It is vain to hope that the offenders will ever be brought to justice. The government is powerless to seize them out of the hands of their master, whoever he is, hence the anxiety of the government to prevent a crime they cannot punish. Today the remains of Heusken are to be interred at Yedo and we are not entirely free from suspicion that the Japanese may show disrespect, or ill will, to the funeral cortege.

Dined today with Mr. Nevius, and while going thither with Dr. and Mrs. H[epburn] we were followed and insulted by a young man drunk with sake. We paid no attention to him but he insisted upon obtruding himself upon us in an insulting way. H[epburn] and myself bid him go away, and when I turned around and met him face to face he threw his garment off from the handle of a short sword that he carried. The first impulse was to knock him down, but Mrs. H[epburn] begged we should do nothing to him but he should revenge himself afterwards upon them. I stood ready at the least movement towards his sword to take the initiative myself but a companion came up and persuaded him away. We called an officer who promised to have him arrested and bound. He afterwards reported that he had done so, but he may, or may have not.

Saturday, January 19, 1861

We have rumors today of fresh troubles at Yedo. The story goes that just before the hour of Heusken's funeral yesterday the Foreign Minister came to Mr. Harris and begged that he and his associates would not go to the funeral, that there was danger of an attack upon them. To this the Minister paid no heed but attended poor Heusken to his burial. A company of 50 marines were furnished by the Prussian frigates. Open demonstrations of ill will were shown to the funeral escort. Mr. Harris, distrustful of his personal security, went on board the Prussian steamer last evening and all the legations were to strike their flags today and go aboard the ships. The Prussians have refused to receive their treaty saying, "They would not accept a treaty signed with blood." Such are the rumors that have been current this afternoon and have excited a great commotion in Yokohama. The probability of extreme measures and their consequences have been the general talk, and no small anxiety has been felt.

On my own part I cannot help believing that most of all this is idle rumor that has grown as it passed from mouth to mouth. Though the events are far from impossible, and it would not be strange if they should occur, I shall be slow to believe in advance in any such alarming condition of affairs that would be fraught with so much danger to us all. We hope to know the truth of matters tomorrow.

Snowing all day, at sunset four inches deep.

Sunday, January 20, 1861

Consul Vyse returned from Yedo this morning and hired the Yokohama Hotel for the use of [the] English Legation, who are expected to remove from Yedo on Wednesday. In view of the insecurity of life at Yedo all the legations have determined to remove to Yokohama where they may be protected under the guns of the foreign shipping, except Mr. Harris. He does not feel that there is any insecurity of life that demands this step which his colleagues are about to take. I agree with Mr. Harris that there is no danger that warrants the foreign ministers in leaving their posts. Their lives cannot be greatly exposed so long as they remain within doors at night and go out with proper precautions by day. The removal from Yedo is a grave step that may lead to fresh complications.

From the Japanese we hear that the large daimios declare their intention to go to their own provinces if the ministers withdraw and pay no further court to the present government which has shown itself so weak.

Heusken was buried on Friday with all honors. It is repeated on authority of the French Consul that the Japanese Ministers cautioned Mr. Harris of danger of an attack upon the funeral cortege, nevertheless no arrangement was intermitted. The body was borne in a coffin with the American Flag as a pall, supported by sixteen bearers in American uniform, and escorted by a guard of marines from the Dutch brig. Preceding the body was the Prussian band, a body of Prussian marines, the flags of the five treaty powers, and in advance of this the five Japanese Governors of foreign affairs and the chief of the late Embassy to America, each with his customary retinue of retainers. Following the body were Mr. Harris and Mr. De Witt[6] as mourners in chief, the members of the foreign legations, and naval officers from the men of war in the harbor. All went off quietly with no symptom of disturbance and so closed the last act in the drama of Heusken's life and death. Mr. Portman[7] has been called to Yedo to act in Heusken's place.

Monday, January 21, 1861

The recent events at Yedo are the all engrossing topics of conversation among us. No new facts of importance are known. It appears that Heusken was carried home on that fatal night by his bettos and there was indifference enough to his fate that the pool of blood where he fell remained painfully visible to the procession that carried his remains to the grave. Usually the Japanese are quick and careful to obliterate all such tokens of violence.

The refusal of Mr. Harris to leave Yedo places the other legations in a dilemma. If they sought any moral effect by leaving Yedo in a body that effect is greatly nullified by the refusal of the representative of the country most injured to unite with them. If they look to measures of a more decided character the position of the American Minister single handed and alone will be an argument against them at their courts at home. We can suppose that the retiring embassies have reasons for leaving of the gravest character which are unknown outside, reasons to which perhaps the American Minister should lend ear for the common good. Or they may take the stand that the Government is not wholly clear from being a *particeps criminis*, that her disavowals now are no stronger than they have been in proved falsehoods before, that at least the Govern-

---

[6] J. K. de Witt was Dutch Consul General in Nagasaki.

[7] A.L.C. Portman served as interpreter and later secretary of the American legation in Edo.

ment, out of eight murderous assaults—seven of which have proved fatal—must in some cases have known where followers of the offenders were, and through more fear of offending a powerful person at home, than a foreign power abroad, have maintained a close silence. At any rate, to justify the abandonment of their posts in the eyes of the world, they must show that Mr. Harris is playing the part of a bravado or notoriety hunter, or that he is refusing to take the best steps for the common weal of the Treaty Powers.

Another point, Mr. Harris has no support from any American force in these waters, where he is, he places himself in the protection and honor of the Japanese Government, if he retires to Yokohama, he places himself under the protection of British and French guns, a position which I presume any American Minister would be glad to avoid if possible. Furthermore, the policy of the American Government in the East is a settled one of no armed interference, the affairs of China have sufficiently shown this, why then should Mr. Harris take a definite stand with no prospect of his government's backing him.

Tuesday, January 22, 1861

There is no change in the aspect of affairs today. The prevailing impression is that the Japanese government are playing a treacherous part, an opinion in which I cannot yet coincide. Among the Japanese the belief appears to be general that the murderers of Heusken were not *ronin*, but followers of some disaffected daimio. This gives a still more serious aspect to the affair. I glean a few additional particulars respecting the death and burial of Heusken. The men who attacked him sprang upon him with loud outcries, his horse sprang forward, but was hindered an instant by the horse of one of the yakunins which, having been struck, faltered. H[eusken] rode on unconscious that he was wounded till he fell from his horse exhausted by the loss of blood. He was picked up and carried home by the bettos. His mistress had warned him some days before that his life was in danger, whether it was a general fear or derived from some special circumstances is unknown. Returning from the

funeral the procession passed the body of a man who had just been murdered in the streets. We now hear that the Emperor's guard has refused to do duty any longer at the Embassies and that their place is supplied by changes of men furnished in turn by the daimios (?) [question mark in original]. The princes of Sendai, Kaga, and Satsuma are said to be at the head of the movement to leave Yedo and retire to their own provinces.

Wednesday, January 23, 1861

At Kanagawa I learned a few additional particulars of Heusken's murder. The wound he received was found to be more severe when he was laid out than at first supposed. It had entered his right side and passed through his body, the wound appearing on the left side. His intestines protruded through the wound. The yakunins who were with him as soon as the melee was over hastened to Mr. Harris's [and] gave the alarm to the guard. A party of them returned to the place, and placing Mr. Heusken on a door carried him home.

Thursday, January 24, 1861

Nothing further transpires of importance in relation to recent events. Rumors of displays of hostile feelings by the Japanese arise one moment to be contradicted the next. Very few have any real fear as to results, the general impression being that the cloud of difficulty will blow over as others have done before.

Friday, January 25, 1861

Nothing transpires of interest.

Saturday, January 26, 1861

The *Encounter* is down from Yedo today having Mr. Alcock on board. The French Minister has also come down and is at Kanagawa. The Prussian Treaty is signed and they are preparing for a speedy departure. The *Elbe* leaves tomorrow with dispatches. Nothing new from

Yedo except that we hear that Mr. Harris is sick.

Sunday, January 27, 1861

Minister Alcock came ashore today at Yokohama and occupied his new quarters. He and Mr. Belcour [Bellecourt] took a formal leave of Mr. Harris at Yedo yesterday. Mr. Alcock communicated his departure on the eve of leaving to the Governors of Foreign Affairs with the reasons for so doing. We now hear on good authority that the Japanese themselves requested the detention of the English men of war. It is given out that the English and French will now demand a full and satisfactory settlement of all difficulties before they return to Yedo. Among other causes of offense the sentence of imprisonment of Mr. Moss is one.

Mr. Harris takes an extreme Japanese view of the position of a foreigner at Yedo. He is willing to admit for himself that he should not go out evenings as Yedo is notoriously unsafe to her own citizens, but when he adds that a Foreign Minister should only go out as a Japanese dignitary would, i.e., accompanied with a large escort of yakunins in the daytime also, it is granting too much to the customs of a foreign people. Even this would be tolerable were the danger from irresponsible men, the common thieves, or the murderers of society. But since it is now well established that the assassinators must be followers of some one or more daimios acting with the knowledge and consent of their chief perhaps, the case is at once changed. To be asked to protect yourself against such emissaries is an insult to the Minister and people who sent him. The Government knows who the offending daimios are, and if they will not reveal them, let the Government take the *onus*. Either let the civilized world punish the prince who turns assassin, or the government that hides him. If the arm of the assassin is sustained by a power in the state, if the murderer is shielded by a feudal chief, honor, national as well as humanity, demands condign punishment to the offenders. Living in semi-durance through fear of a ruling chief is another thing from protection from private assassination.

And now we hear directly from Yedo that the guards about Mr. Harris's house are under the personal superintendence daily of one of the Governors of Foreign Affairs. At Yokohama Mr. Alcock permits no Japanese official about his place except on direct business. Four guards from the English shipping patrol constantly in front of his house.

Called on Dorr today and found the poor man quite ill. I feel some anxiety about him. Bleckman is sick with varioloid. He was deserted of all his associates through fear and left sick and alone in his house without anything to eat. Dr. Hepburn takes care of him.

Monday, January 28, 1861

The *Elbe* left today bearing the newly made treaty with the Prussian Government. The treaty was signed on the 24th. No additional privileges are granted by it. From Yedo we hear that Mr. Harris is ill and Consul Dorr is not so well. Mr. Alcock has issued a circular today setting forth the reasons for his removal from Yedo.

Tuesday, January 29, 1861

At Kanagawa removing boxes, etc., from Sokogee [Sokoji],[8] as Mr. Nevius and lady are about returning to China. Each day brings

---

[8] The Sokoji had been the home of John Livingston Nevius and his wife during their stay in Kanagawa. Nevius and his wife had been missionaries of the Presbyterian Board in China and had originally been selected to go to Japan with J. C. Hepburn. Hepburn convinced them to come to Japan in the summer of 1860 to see how they felt about working in Japan, and for a time they lived with the Hepburns at the Jobutsuji. In her biography of her husband Mrs. Nevius writes: "When we had decided to remain some time in Japan, my husband and I removed to a little temple called So-ko-gee. It stood at the foot of a very steep hill, upon the top of which was a 'lookout,' with an extended view far over the bay and the surrounding town and country." After studying Japanese for six months Rev. Nevius and his wife decided to return to China. See Helen S. Coan Nevius, *The Life of John Livingston Nevius* (New York: Fleming H. Revell Co., 1895), p. 201.

with it some absurd rumor. Today we have it that four of Mr. Harris's servants were killed last evening and he is compelled to cook his own meals as no servants will any longer stay with him. Such fabrications need no refutation.

The tea-trade has received an increased activity owing to the good sales made of the cargoes of the *Georgianna* and *Troas* in England, the first direct shipments. They are said to have paid a 100 percent profit. Silk and chow chow trade is dull, so of lacker ware and fancy goods.

Wednesday, January 30, 1861

A storm day mostly passed within doors writing letters for the *Cadiz*.

Thursday, January 31, 1861

Still occupied the same as the *Cadiz* does not leave till tomorrow. Minister Alcock furnished us very kindly with a copy of his circular late issued on Japanese affairs. He is pleased with the interest manifested by the Americans in what is going on and that his position will be known in America, since he and Mr. Harris disagree. While not one Englishman made a copy of his dispatch at least half a dozen copies were made by Americans to forward home.

It is pretty certain that our minister has forwarded no dispatches home. He is [in] no condition either to write them or to attend to American interests. He "was so shocked by the murder of Heusken that it has rendered him extremely nervous and incapable of sleep and utterly prostrated him." We know what this means. What a disgrace it is; how unsafe it is to be represented at such a juncture by a man who has no control over his appetites. Is it all false that we hear from Yedo that he has "walked up and down his rooms like a mad man with a pistol in each hand," or the still more shameful thing, that he requested the officials to bring him a woman "to sew buttons on" and when they brought a woman for that purpose he exclaimed "What did you bring that old hag for, I don't want her to sew button on, I want to + + + +." And this is the man

who is thought at home to be such a fit representative of our country to this semicivilized people who is supposed to be the zealous promoter of civilization and even Christianity.

Friday, February 1, 1861

At Kanagawa assisting Dr. S[immons] to remove his medicines, etc. Tide was out and we waited till sunset before we could embark and had a disagreeable time of it.

Saturday, February 2, 1861

The five Governors of Foreign Affairs were down yesterday and sought an interview with Mr. Alcock, but he refused to give them one. No change in public affairs, everything quiet.

Sunday, February 3, 1861

A beautiful sunny winter day. After service walked over to Kanagawa and paid a visit to our sick Consul and rode back by the Tokaido and through the fields.

Monday, February 4, 1861

Morning writing, in the afternoon rode over to the Consul's with Dr. H[epburn]; remained with the Consul to look after and take care of him all night. He received letters from Harris saying that he was recovered from his "bilious attack!" and was busy preparing dispatches for the government.

Mr. Alcock issued a circular today requesting the British subjects to notify him of all grievances and infractions of the Treaty that have occurred in their trade intercourse with the government, which they can substantiate with dates and verifications.

The Japanese, to keep the peace of Yokohama more secure, have now forbidden any samurai except such as are in government employ to enter Yokohama for any purpose whatsoever. At Yedo every man who receives a guest at his house must report the same to the proper official and is allowed to entertain none whom he does not know. The inns report the number and quality of their guests, but this last is said to have been always the custom.

Tuesday, February 5, 1861

A French steamer arrived this evening and reports a vessel outside bottom-upwards, supposed to be the *Neva*.

Wednesday, February 6, 1861

The Japanese are busy with their preparations for New Year's. They are planting pines and bamboos in front of their houses and hanging fringes of straw to the eaves of their houses, over the doors are rosettes of green leaves, paper, oranges, and to crown all a large prawn. Merchants are closing up their accounts and everyone who is not able to square up at New Year's is a broken merchant. Hence we find some of them very anxious to sell goods in hand.

A painter called on me today with samples of his work. He had an artist look about him but his work, however pleasing to Japanese eyes, had small favor in mine. I bought two or three pieces of him. He was on his way to Yedo "to spend the Holiday."

Thursday, February 7, 1861

A wet day with a northerly wind. About 2 P.M. the wind suddenly veered to the southward and in half an hour there was a surprising change in the temperature. From a few degrees above freezing the thermometer suddenly rose to 67°, and so instantaneous was the change that on an alarm of fire being given at that time more than one examined their own premises supposing from the extraordinary warmth that the fire might be very near. Continued so warm all the day and evening that fires were dispensed with. Not only this, but there are other indications of approaching spring. The wild plums are blossoming and the Japanese are selling dwarf cherry trees in bloom and crocuses.

Friday, February 8, 1861

The English have held a meeting today to consider the circular of Mr. Alcock calling upon them to state their grievances. A memorial was drawn up and presented to the meeting with resolutions. There was harmony except upon one point which was whether the present condition of the currency question was one that called for official interference. The merchants engaged in selling imports advocated more interference believing that if the dollar was raised to its proper standard their trade would suffer. On the other hand the large tea and silk buyers were sufferers by the dollar's depreciation and were in favor of bringing the dollar up to the standard of weight for weight as provided by treaty. Beside there was a general agreement that there could [be] no reasoning in favor of depreciating the relative value of a trading currency that was not fallacious. The general interests of commerce must be best subserved by a dollar passing for its true legitimate value. The sellers of imports carried the day however!

Saturday, February 9, 1861

Another day of storm. In the house all day writing. We hear nothing new in political affairs beyond flying rumors having no definiteness.

Sunday, February 10, 1861

Japanese New Year's. So begins the New Year Holidays. Festivities are kept up for three days, though the holiday season is supposed to have a week's longer duration. On these three days nothing is cooked in the house, and the food needed has been prepared for the occasion the night before New Year's. Giving and receiving visits and abstinence from labor are the prevailing notions of the way to spend a Japanese New Year's. Through every open door is seen the "Short Bread," round cakes of rice, in size and quantity proportional to the means of the householder, from the size of an egg to that of a half bushel measure. This is afterwards carefully preserved and eaten throughout the year for certain supposed specific value in insuring health and prosperity. The cakes are adorned with green sprigs, bits of colored paper, or garnished with fruits. All are dressed in their best clothes, new ones being generally provided for at this season, and even the poor girls of the *joroya* receive today new robes from their master growing rich with illicit gains. The streets are made lively and picturesque with their adornments of evergreen trees and straw wreaths, but still more by the bright colored dresses of the girls and children.

It is a holiday that young Japan especially looks forward to with pleasant anticipation. To him the incoming year is vaguely foreshadowed in such delights as young America anticipates when he dreams of St. Nick and his tiny team on the merry roofs. Today he will have a new kite and new clothes and in the streets or the open fields will send his paper birds aloft till the air is full of whizzing monsters, ugly ogres, great winged birds, curvetting children, for our Japanese boy sees no beauty in a plain bowed kite or a parallelogram of paper and sticks, he must have them of every similitude of man, bird, beast, and monster and with a thin reed secured to the top so that it will hum in the air. As I passed a toy shop today there was a crowd of little fellows with smooth hair, shining faces, and clean garments edged with bright colored silks chaffering noisily for new kites, and troubled whether to choose the hideous face of an ancient hero, or fabulous monster, or the pictured representative of just such a boy as themselves. But young Japan is not always noisy, he is seldom so except when excited over a game of jackstones or a game which, if it is not "I Spy," might just as well be. It is not the little boys either who are alone fond of kite flying, but the big boys too and sober parents who review their youth in their children's pastimes.

In the officers' quarters stately visits are going on with a great deal of ceremony, there are long genuflexions, much knocking of the head on the mats, prim fellows in their highly stiffened gala dresses followed by servants bearing umbrella and shoes go about from house to house leaving their cards at the door or thrusting them on a spindle at the gate, or they go within and are received by the mistress of the house with so many salutations that you think they will never have done with it, and hot tea is poured into porcelain cups, and ancient saucers of choice old lacker and gold are filled with the beverage especially made for new years, *toso* they call it, and a nest of trays is opened displaying the choicest results of the housewife's culinary skill in preserved shrimps, sliced cuttle fish, household triumphs in preserved beans and salted radishes and choice confectionery from the shops. Pipes are smoked, and, possibly as a final *bonne bouche*, the good housewife with great show of ancient porcelain and tiny boxes of choice lacker proceeds to prepare the famous ground tea, whipping it to a creamy froth, more salaams and sucking of breath through the closed lips and then the visit is over.

The children of the officials, very pretty in their figured silks and sashes of crimson and scarlet and purple crape, and the little girls with faces artificially whitened till not a vestige of the original color is left, with vermillion lips, hair in great shining coils of midnight, broad girdles gathered in buns behind half as large as themselves, and socks of spotless purity, are playing in the open streets or in the house areas in charge of blooming abigails who smile sweetly as abigails always do when they have pretty children to take care of. If a pretty child in clean clothes and amiable temper doesn't make young ladies smiling and good natured I would like to know what will. There goes a brave little fellow not more than four years old, he is strutting proudly in his new silk trousers and a gala robe such as his father wears and two swords tied to his side, the child is father of the man the world over. The girls are playing with bats and birds.

Heco and myself made a few calls after the Japanese custom. One of them was upon a large silk merchant who happened to be out visiting himself, but the hospitalities of his house were maintained by his head clerk, himself an old man, and his wife. We passed through the front shop into the rear where were the living apartments of the family. The wife received us with great cordiality. She was a good looking tidy woman less than forty years apparently. There were several girls also sitting around a brazier of coal and all in their holiday dresses. We were received with an easy courtesy, and a graceful modesty on the part of the young folks. The look and air of the house betokened a man of substance in its owner. The few comforts and luxuries of a Japanese house were all here and truly there was something of an air of home about the spacious tidy apartments and the circle of inmates. Nothing could be more scrupulously clean than the walls, ceilings, and floor mats. The kitchen, which was open to view, was no less tidy. Every article of household use was clean and in its place and the well scrubbed coppers of the high cooking range from which the bubbling steam was escaping were emblems of good housewifery.

Seats were brought us and at a single word from the mistress one of the girls with unembarrassed but modest manners came forward to serve us. I have always noticed this, that the young females of a household need but a word from their elders to serve with cheerfulness and alacrity. This one brought the always ready tea, tea cups, tray, sake cups, and a sake kettle of white metal. Kneeling before us she first filled the tea cups and handed them to us. Then at a word from the mistress she filled the sake cups with *toso*, a sweet sake made very palatable by some ingredients added to the rice liquor and handed them to us. We found the flavor very agreeable without any heady quality. Then opening a nest of trays she filled from them little plates with a small fish dried and preserved in oil, cuttle fish similarly prepared and cut in shreds, leaves made into an agreeable sweet confection, and salted radishes. These articles were not only clean but palatable.

We sat and chatted over the viands and drinks for an hour, and all this time there was nothing to mar the air of well bred gentility which prevailed. I was astonished myself at finding such a family picture. About the room were articles hanging up such as books of account and memorandum, household utensils, and all in their places. We rose from our seats at the mistress' request and walked out upon a verandah which formed one side of a little paved enclosed area. The verandah led to a *sitsui* [ōsetsuma] as usual but no one would imagine it unacquainted with Japanese customs. He would have wondered perhaps at the stone basin with its clean wooden ladle but never

grasped its uses. This little opening among the buildings, a well let into the sky, was perhaps twelve feet long by five wide enclosed on all sides. On two sides was a tapestry of braided shavings, a rustic ornament of the Japanese worthy of imitation. A small pine tree and a few shrubs were growing here and on the verandah were some pots of dwarf cherries now in bloom.

The best room of the house opened upon the verandah and we were asked to seat ourselves here, where the sun fell pleasantly on the mats. In this room was the "show bread" and branches of flowering plums were placed in the corners. Then we were invited to partake of a cup of powdered tea, the choice drink of a Japanese social hour. Going to a little cupboard the hostess brought out a small box rich in lacker and gold tied up in a silk wrapping. Out of it she took a porcelain cup which she said was a family heirloom many years old, a box of the powdered tea, and the utensils for making it. One of the girls brought hot water and two old and crackled porcelain bowls. With a wooden spoon she dipped out a little of the green powder into one of the ancient bowls and pouring hot water upon it she then whipped it or beat it with an apparatus of bamboo splits that came also out of the box, beat it till it was all of a creamy foam, the sign and test of its quality, and so preparing a bowl for each gave us to drink. There is nothing pleasing in the taste of this tea, indeed it is too strong for most palates, but its exhilarating effects are at once apparent. It is made of tenderest and youngest of the freshly sprouting leaves. She assured us it was excellent to take after too much sake drinking. Then she talked with us on the uppermost topic in the Japanese minds at present, the prospect of trouble between Japan and the foreign powers. She said the upper classes of Japan were too effeminate to cope with the foreigners. "They lived too much in the house, were waited upon by servants, could endure no hardships, fed poorly, were slow in thought and action," whereas the "foreigners were rapid in all they did, lived well, on beef that made them robust, were capable of fatigue and strong with active life." All of which was very sensible, and true as sensible. So we passed a pleasant hour, and leaving with oft repeated invitations to come again went away impressed with the family scene we had witnessed.

We next called upon our friend the Doctor. His wife and handmaidens had gone out for a holiday, but still he gave us a hospitable welcome, prepared the tea with his own hands and served out the *toso* and the refreshments. From the Dr.'s we went to call upon the head of a famous establishment. Nowhere were we received with more ceremony, nor was it possible to imagine from the behavior of the family inmates that we were in other than a private family. The master of the house, a fine looking man, sat before us and at our side was his delicate looking wife. In came two female attendants bearing boxes and trays. First we were served with tea as before, after this the large tray box of refreshments was opened, then three sake saucers were brought in on a lackered stand, each handsomely ornamented with gold. Each saucer was larger than the other, taking off the uppermost and smallest one he extended it to the waiting girl who made a point of pouring in some of the liquid, then he touched the saucer to his lips as if to drink, then carefully turning the rim he had touched towards himself and away from his guests that they might not touch their lips to the same place he handed it again to the girl who filled it and he passed it to Heco. After he had emptied it he went through the same process and handed it to me, and so every time he offered us to drink. The wife and the waiting girl picked up the morsels of food in the chop sticks in whose use we were awkward and conveyed them to our mouths. While we were thus eating and drinking the New Year's Cheer, twelve or fifteen girls in their bright holiday dresses came in and knelt behind us and began to eat the confectionery they had just been out in the street to buy. Two of them were seventeen or eighteen years old perhaps, but the others were little girls ten to twelve years old, they were singing girls and actresses. It was a touching sight, their faces were as sweet and innocent as children's could possibly be, in heart and conscience they were spotless as their years, but Good God where were they and what was their future. It makes me sick and sad to my heart's core when I think of that New Year's group. It is no made feeling, no mere sentimentality when I say I could weep

for them. I love childhood, if there is anything left on earth good and lovable it is that, especially that of the little girls of such tender years, and no childish faces could be more innocent or artless in outward seeming, it makes my heart ache when I think and write of them. If civilization and Christianity may save such as these, God speed the day when their light shines on these islands. It was enough, I turned my footsteps away, but never shall I forget that New Year's group so long as life lasts.

Monday, February 11, 1861

A curious phase in diplomacy came to light today. Beyond the canal that invests Yokohama are the bluffs of Treaty Point. These are highlands commanding a view of Yedo Bay in every direction, both salubrious and picturesque in position and have long been coveted by the foreigners for residences. The Japanese would never give them up to any entreaty of the foreign representatives but with quite a contrary purpose went to great expense to dig a canal thirty feet deep and a hundred wide as an impassable line of demarcation. It was well understood that the bluffs could not be had and all thought of it was banished. But since the withdrawal of the Ministers from Yedo it appears that the bluffs were again thought of as desirable for official residences. The English Consul Vyse in a conversation with Dorr, the American Consul, gave a plain intimation that when the English fleet expected here should arrive the bluffs would be seized. Consul Dorr at once communicated this to Minister Harris at Yedo and the result was at a single interview of Mr. Harris with the Minister of Foreign Affairs he obtained a concession of the bluffs in question as a grant to all the Treaty Powers for occupation for building purposes. We can well imagine the line of argument Mr. Harris used to obtain so easily what had been so persistently refused. The Japanese preferred to anticipate a forced concession on the part of England and France by a voluntary gift to all through the American Minister.

We have this much as benefit arising directly from the attitude the English and French have taken. Had the withdrawal from Yedo never taken place, we should not have had the grant of the bluffs of Treaty Point. This movement on the part of the Representatives of these powers has given great uneasiness and real alarm to the Japanese government.

Tuesday, February 12, 1861

A disagreeable day of rain and snow. We have plenty of visitors come in to look over the files of our papers received by yesterday's mail bringing full returns of Lincoln's election. We heard the news a fortnight since via England and the Red Sea telegraph.

Wednesday, February 13, 1861

A cloudy day spent at home in writing, etc.

Thursday, February 14, 1861

Visit to Kanagawa and found our Consul slowly convalescing. I have an interesting pupil today, it is Ōtsuru,[9] a Japanese girl of seventeen years old. She is a yakunin's daughter at Yedo, but spends much of her time with an old lady here, a friend. She is a teacher. Heco introduced me a few days since and calling again today, I found her seated at her low writing desk busily at work. She showed me her work and I found her truly a master of the difficult Japanese characters. Her childish innocent ways pleased me greatly and when in obedience to her wishes I wrote our arabic numerals for her and essayed to teach them, I was yet more pleased with her avidity to learn and her aptitude. In a half hour's time she thoroughly mastered the nine digits and their combinations up to 100. Her face glowed with childish delight at her success and she exclaimed laughingly that if I would but teach her she would

become an interpreter. The old lady declares that she has a great fondness for writing and I must come and give her another lesson. The old lady dispensed her rice cakes and tea and I departed.

Friday, February 15, 1861

While taking a walk this morning with Heco we dropped in upon his friend the merchant on whom we had made a New Year's call. We were hospitably received as before. I was witness to the most singular minor surgical operation I ever saw. There was a scrawny looking cat in the room which they said had the diarrhea and they were going to apply moxas. One of the girls got the moxas ready, puss was caught and firmly held by the old lady by the head and an old man grasping the four feet. This was one of the stump tail breed of cats, and his candal appendage was not more than two inches long. But the young lady operators in feline surgery applied the moxas to the tip of poor puss's stump and burnt several upon it. Puss struggled fiercely but she was in tight grasp and had to submit to this extraordinary operation.

The wind which blew too fresh in the morning to permit any landing of cargo so abated that I went off to the ship and got my boxes. I landed them without being compelled to pay any customs and then had a joyous time in opening *boxes from home*. A pleasure that no one can appreciate so well as those who like myself are so distant.

Saturday, February 16, 1861

Dr. S[immons] was sent for this evening to dress the wounds of a Japanese who was shot while committing depredations in De Konigh & Co.'s[10] yard. The firm had missed many arti-

---

[9] While it is clear that Ōtsuru was the daughter of a samurai in Edo it is difficult to establish her identity or to determine what she was doing in Yokohama. Although she was introduced to Hall by Joseph Heco, the latter makes no mention of her in his *Narrative of a Japanese* (San Francisco: American-Japanese Publishing Association, n.d.). Hall later sees her appearances and disappearances as somewhat mysterious. It is also clear

that he was quite smitten with Ōtsuru. But unfortunately he does not tell us anything further about her life after her return to Edo, which appears to have been necessitated by illness and a desire to enter religious orders.

[10] De Conigh, Carst & Lels. See *The China Directory for 1862* (Hong Kong: Shortrede & Co., 1863), p. 55.

cles and had set a watch when the thief was caught in the act and in attempting to escape was wounded, though not severely. Being taken he made confession that he was one of a gang of twelve thieves whose names he gave up to the police. Immediately the gates were all closed and before morning nine of the twelve were arrested.

Sunday, February 17, 1861

The *Mary and Louisa* left us this morning for Shanghai with a mail. Mrs. Jones, who has been among us for a long time as an invalid, goes with the bark hoping to reach home where she may die among her kindred. How forcible to an invalid so remote from home must seem the Oriental benediction "may you die among your kindred."

Monday, February 18, 1861

Went down to the bluffs and ascended them to see their feasibility as a place for residences. The bluffs near to business are bare of trees and so exposed to the high winds of this latitude as to prove a large set off to the pleasure of living on high ground overlooking the Bay. On the other hand, the more desirable spots, where trees and shelter are to be had, are too remote for businessmen. I feel content for the present with my choice of a lot on the lowland.

Tuesday, February 19, 1861

A beautiful warm spring forenoon tempted me across the bay. Consul D[orr] is improving. We have through him Mr. Harris's reply to the position taken by Minister Alcock in his letter to the Minister of Foreign Affairs dated Jan. 21 or 20th. It is a fair diplomatic paper but fails to meet the real issue proferred by Mr. Alcock, which is, that if the assassinations are committed by daimio followers, they are committed under the cognizance of those who are the government *de facto* if not *de jure*, and as such demand the gravest considerations. Mr. H[arris] arguing, on the assumption that the murders are the work of private individuals

implicating no one but themselves, the Government cannot be held responsible. The argument is therefore conducted on totally different premises. I am fully satisfied by the concurrent testimony of all Japanese that Mr. A[lcock]'s premises are the true ones. Nor does Mr. H[arris] take the true view of the retirement of the Ministers to Yokohama as to its effect on the Japanese, for we have every reason to believe that it has had a serious effect on the Japanese and is a movement which they deplore, not rejoice over. Also I must totally dissent with Mr. Harris when he says the murderers of the Regent have only been arrested in part and none of them punished beyond imprisonment. Mr. H[arris] must take his information, coming as it does from those who have a motive to deceive, with allowances. The best informed Japanese that I have met all agree in declaring that not one of these assassins now lives. Those who survived the attack promptly committed hara kiri after making themselves known to the Prince of Kaga and exhibiting to him the severed head of the Regent. We shall have doubtless Mr. Alcock's rejoinder.

In the evening ―――― and ―――― [blanks in original] called and we made an opening of the case of liquors received a few days ago from home. We had a festive evening.

Wednesday, February 20, 1861

Ōtsuru the yakunin's daughter is sick, I found her lying on the mats wrapped in thick quilts with her head on a wooden pillow. A blind doctor and shampooer was performing acupuncture, working with his hands underneath the quilts. I was surprised to learn that this operation was commonly performed by these blind men. He was puncturing the abdomen and side to the little pain of the patient seemingly. But I observed that he was very silent and worked with the greatest apparent care.

Thursday, February 21, 1861

Mr. Alcock has issued a rejoinder to Mr. Harris' note of the 12th inst.,[11] said to be a brief! document of *sixty* pages or more. These documents will be interesting as matters of history, differing as they do in regard to questions of vital interest.

Called on Ōtsuru today and found her much better, her eyes sparkled with delight at the prospect of being taught our alphabet. As usual I found her reading, for she seems to have a real fondness for books.

Friday, February 22, 1861

Took a long ride with Dr. H[all] today to Kanagawa. The succession of clear days has dried the roads to some extent. There are some signs of advancing spring in the tasseled birches (or alders?), the wild plums and apricots, the dandelions, crocuses, and narcissus. The field crops as yet are stationary, the buds of a few only of the trees are swelling. Located a lot on the bluffs.

Saturday, February 23, 1861

In the morning went again to the bluffs to obtain a more accurate bearing of the lot located yesterday. Made application to the Consul yesterday and to the Custom House today for a spot above the temples near the canal. Dr. and Mrs. H[epburn], Miss B[rown] and Howard[12] came over to take a ride out to the bluffs. The day was warm and uncommonly fine and we had a charming ride to Mississippi bay. On our route we passed many superb camellia trees in full bloom. They appear, to my accustomed eye, as beautiful as ever they did when they were more novel. Some of those we saw today were fine large trees making a splendid show with their crimson petals and shiny green leaves.

Took a walk with Heco in the evening, a superb moonlight night. H[eco] receives warning how he exposes himself to the fate of Heusken from a friend.[13]

Sunday, February 24, 1861

After church service had a pleasant stroll in the country with Dr. S[immons] and M.[14] The day being warm and exceedingly spring-like, the contrast with our own home winters were discussed as we felt the soft air and walked among the green hedgerows and saw the camellias burdened with blossoms. Swarms of children were at play, today and tomorrow being children's holidays. There was kite flying in every direction. Tomorrow is the prisoners holiday when they are provided with good food and some freedoms are allowed.

Monday, February 25, 1861

Storm has succeeded our late fine weather. Busy within doors writing.

Tuesday, February 26, 1861

Received the loan for perusal of Mr. Alcock's rejoinder to Mr. Harris. The controversy is a fruitless one as regards any good likely to come out of [it] either to the foreigners or the Japanese. There are disputed facts and controverted inferences, hints at misconstructions, accident or wilful, which so long as they are kept within official dispatches will do no harm if they do no good.

---

[11] For Harris's letter to Alcock see Joseph Heco, *Narrative of a Japanese*, vol. 1, pp. 274–77.

[12] It is not clear who Howard was. F. Howard Vyse was the British Consul in Kanagawa, but Hall rarely refers to individuals by their Christian names, although this could be an exception.

[13] For the next six months Heco was repeatedly warned to be careful of his life. On September 16, 1861, he wrote in his diary: "These warnings had of late waxed far too frequent for my comfort." As a result he decided that discretion was the better part of valor and left Japan on a trip to the United States. See Joseph Heco, *Narrative of a Japanese*, vol. 1, p. 278.

[14] It is not clear who M. is, but it is possible that this is W. H. Morse who later worked under Hall in Walsh, Hall & Co.

Wednesday, February 27, 1861

Dined today at K.'s[15] where I met the French Consul, Col. D.[16] of the French Army in the East, and several others. There I learned that the conferences between the retired Ministers and the Japanese have been brought to a successful termination. The Ministers are to return to Yedo on Saturday 2nd March. They call it a "glorious victory," but really we learn of no new advantage gained except that the returning Ministers are to be honored with a national salute from the Yedo batteries. It looks more like the famous march of the King of France immortalized in nursery song, than a conquest worthy the great fuss that has been made about coming down to Yokohama. Mr. Harris has replied to Mr. Alcock's rejoinder and there are open questions of veracity between them. Mr. Alcock refuses to hold any further correspondence with Mr. Harris, charging the latter with descending to the use of language which it would be unworthy [of] his notice! The "War of the Ministers" forms a toothsome subject for an after dinner chit chat or an idle hour of talk, but I opine its ripples will have little disturbing force beyond these shores.

Ōtsuru, the Japanese maiden, would be a little heroine anywhere else. Her winning ways make friends of all who see her. I called there today and had an hour's talk with her. The brave little girl is as resolute in her determination to become a Buddhist nun as any disappointed maiden at home might be of entering a convent. But Ōtsuru is not a disappointed maiden; she cares not for the joys of wedded life, she says, she only hopes by a good life to view the joys of a Buddhist paradise. Already her name is enrolled in the Paradise of Amida and she longs for the day when she will go back to Yedo to the old temple and put on the robes of the nuns, which she has already made with her own hands, to take her new name which has been already selected for her; for it seems that the Japanese maidens when they join the sisterhood like their Catholic sisters assume a new title. She says with sorrowful look that she will go back to the temple only to die, and I am ready to believe her, for she looks so frail and delicate. Today she complained of suffering bodily pains and so it is almost every day. But she was cheerful and after all did not seem to shrink from that saddest of all fates, an early death while youth's sweet blossoms were crowning her. I do not wonder that she is delicate. In the morning the little boys and girls of the neighborhood come to her house to be instructed by her and the remainder of the day she occupies in household duties or more generally in writing of which she has a passionate fondness and then she tells me that she sits up till nearly midnight sewing. She does not go abroad in the daytime for lately she told me that when she went to a temple to worship she was rudely treated by some foreigners.

Ōtsuru has had other trials; her gentle demeanor and winning ways have attracted attention from those who have weighed gold against the poor girl's virtue, but though tempted by sums exciting to Japanese cupidity and which must have been to the young girl very large contrasted with her own slender resources, she turns them all aside with her sweet smile and says firmly no, her only wish is to become a priestess of Amida. But there is a reason stronger than her simple love of purity which shields her. She has two brothers who are officials in government employ and such a degradation of their sister would be to affix an indelible stain upon them. The younger brother was here today, and told Heco that he had heard his sister had been sought for not only by foreigners but Japanese, but sooner than see her thus go astray he would "take her life." So I hope that thus closely guarded she may escape the too common lot of her country women.

[15] Hall does not indicate whether this is his old acquaintance, the Jew K., or someone else.
[16] The French Consul D. was apparently M. le Vicomte de la Tour Dupin who was the provisional Vice-Consul for France in Yokohama and Kanagawa.

Thursday, February 28, 1861

The life of a prince, or noble, in Japan is no enviable one. The stories of the olden time are realized again in the present. I think it is Mr. Olyphant who says that *hara kiri* is nearly an extinct custom in Nippon, but it is no more so than secret assassination and family feuds among the great chiefs which the longer I remain here, the more common I perceive they are. I have in the stories of today abundant confirmation of what I have recently stated in this journal, viz., that the whole land is in a disturbed condition and full of mutual jealousies and feuds among the princes. But these same reports also show how carefully every attempt is made to conceal untoward events. It is now currently reported among the well informed common people, and I have no reason to doubt the truth of the report, that the late Prince of Satsuma committed *hara kiri* two months or so ago on account of his implication with Mito. His successor is a youth not yet out of his teens. Osakawa [Hosokawa], Prince of Higo, was quite recently slain in his own house while washing by an assassin who had concealed himself on the premises; yet difficult as it would seem, the murderer escaped. He was slain at the instigation of Mito.

Mito had nine sons, one of whom succeeded to his titles and honors and the remainder became daimios of inferior rank. Of these latter the most conspicuous one openly disavowed the policy of his father. For this he was slain in his own bed, but the assassin did not escape, the bitter hate engendered among these princes sparing not even a son. But strangest of all we are now told that Mito, the old prince who compassed the death of the late Regent, is himself yet alive, that his reputed death was a cunning sham to keep himself out of harm's way while he plotted further his diabolical schemes. In all this narration there is nothing that transcends the limits of Japanese possibility or even probability, they would be as natural events here as a quiet death in bed in a Christian land.

Friday, March 1, 1861

Sadajirō, who was in to see me today, discredits what I have written about the violent deaths of the men named yesterday. He admits the suicide of Satsuma and the reputed existence of Mito, the rest was news to him, but does not therefore wholly discredit it. This but illustrates the difficulty of getting correct and precise information from this people of which there has been no more striking instance than the utterly various belief of the American and English Ministers respecting the facts of the murderers of the late Gotairo, the former asserting that only a part have been arrested and none executed, and the latter that every one who survived the attacks had been seized, condemned, and executed! Yet both of these ministers derive their information from government officials!

Saturday, March 2, 1861

The English and French Ministers have departed for Yedo today under heavy salutes and in the midst of a drenching storm. As yet nothing of magnitude transpires as the favors or concessions granted by the Japanese to bring about this retracing of their steps. I cannot but believe they were quite too glad to get back on any terms.

Sunday, March 3, 1861

Enjoyed a pleasant walk in the country after morning service and brought handsome clusters of the camellia. Called upon Ōtsuru again today and found her again ailing, nothing more than a dyspepsia brought about by the extremely secluded life which she, like many Japanese girls, leads. She had a new trouble to tell me today, only a few days ago she had been insulted in the streets and yesterday some foreigner had entered her house and rudely seized hold of her, frightening her as she said very much and making her heart beat fast. The color mounted on her face and her black eyes sparkled, her lips quivered as she told me of it. The poor child seemed grievously wronged. When questioned "why he should do so," I told her he was a bad man to annoy a defenseless girl like her, and it was only because so many of her sisterhood were frail as well as fair that foreigners took such licenses. She said she would go back to Yedo to her good old temple and never come to Yokohama more. I had given her a woolen tippet a few days previously which she now brought back and said she must not receive while her foster mother was away, when she came back she said with all artlessness I might bring it again.

Monday, March 4, 1861

Inauguration Day at home. We are full of conjecture as to its important events. Our last mail brought us tidings of the days succeeding election and their great turbulence, the threats of disunion and the crisis in financial affairs. We seem to be standing aloof at some great immeasurable distance looking on at events in which we have no share like disembodied spirits watching mundane affairs. Yet there is not one of us but feels that the union is safe despite the alarmists. In honor of the day I inaugurated the "genius of republicanism." Roberts "little nigger" is suspended against the wall with his feet standing in a bouquet of camellia blossoms, nig's favorite red color. The bouquet is in a hanging vase and the inevitable darkey is up to his knees in flowers. A narcissus which in the morning was in bud has towards evening blossomed in the imp's face, we remember the ancient fable and call it a good omen. Suspended to a lead pencil which is thrust under the folds of his solitary garment of pink calico is the "flag of our union." The darkey's face grinning benignantly over the scene gives a wonderfully curious aspect to the floral ornaments. May the days go well with the new administration and our beloved union settle down in quiet.

Tuesday, March 5, 1861

A rainy day mainly occupied in writing up my journal.

Wednesday, March 6, 1861

Calling on the old priestess today I learned that she had not yet returned from Yedo but that Ōtsuru had started off in all of yesterday's storm to go up there.

Thursday, March 7, 1861

Natal, the Frenchman who was wounded at Yedo last summer, was fired at in his house as he was going to bed last night.[17] As he has had a quarrel with a countryman and has been fired at by him before, we attribute this to him now rather than to the Japanese.

The *Scotland* brought up the mails from China today; letters from home once more.

The old priestess is back from Yedo bringing Ōtsuru with her. I stopped at the house a moment today and found the poor girl tired out with two consecutive days' rides and really quite ill; and yet her foster mother says she must go back tomorrow. There is a mystery about the old lady and this girl I cannot fathom and its inscrutableness gives a zest to the charm of unravelling it. I remonstrated with her against sending her back tomorrow and begged for a day's rest for her, I hope effectually.

Friday, March 8, 1861

Not so; the little priestess and school mistress went back to Yedo this morning and we shall not see her again. I shall miss her pretty childlike ways and her smiling face and almost the only Nippon girl who has had virtue and intelligence enough to render her an object of interest for more than a few moments acquain-

---

[17] Natal, an Italian by birth, was the color guard in M. de Bellecourt's service. He was also Bellecourt's valet. See Paul C. Blum, trans., "Father Mounicou's Baku-matsu Diary, 1856–64," *Transactions of the Asiatic Society of Japan* (third series), vol. 13 (Tokyo, 1976), p. 74.

tanceship. A long walk in Kanagawa. New flowers on the hills over the sea.

Saturday, March 9, 1861

Among the Japanese rumors are prevalent that the death of Heusken was an act of vengeance. The story goes that he struck a two-sworded follower of some daimio who offered to resent it on the spot but was restrained by a comrade, the one who interfered was rebuked by his master for it and to make amends assisted in the subsequent assassination of Heusken. Another version differing a little is that it was after the act of vengeance the avenger was rebuked not for killing Heusken but for not having done it at the time which would have been braver than to have waited and laid in wait for him in the night. From H[eusken]'s known peaceable disposition the whole story is likely to be a fabrication.

Sunday, March 10, 1861

The warm clear weather of the last few days has left its mark upon the vegetation. March 1860 was wet and cold quite in contrast with this. I believe this is the usual weather for the season such as we have it now. Wheat and barley have made a perceptible growth. A walk in the country today was rendered delightful by the beauty of the camellia blossoms, the apricot, and wild plums. Dr. Hall and myself had a charming walk over to Mississippi Bay. The south wind lightly ruffled the lake-like waters of the bay and a thousand sails were coming up before the south wind. The gate of Uraga Channel in the distance seemed blocked by the white wings of the junks. Farmers were busy carrying out manures and stirring the earth among the wheat rows, and here and there a woman assisted in the weeding. Others were gathering twigs and rushes on the hillside for fuel and others were probing for the baculio, a singular vegetable growth looking like the root of a tree. The wheat, barley, and broad beans have established two or three inches of growth already, so also with the vetch. Self-sown straggling rape plants were blossoming in sunny spots under the banks, where also I found today the first pyrus japonica in bloom. Dandelions have been in bloom a fortnight or more and now the temple enclosures are adorned with the blossoms of the apricot and plum, some of which are double and sweet scented. The alders have been in blossom for ten days past. In an old grave yard attached to a temple I found in blossom what I take to be a species of evergreen saxifragas from its highly scented leaves and aromatic taste.

This temple was one of the many charming spots of this land. It was situated half way up the side of a low hill and was hidden from the road by a thick grove of grand old cypresses and an underwood of low trees, shrubs, and a table of ferns, lilies, and irises. Half the trees were adorned with the evergreen ivy. The temple, a very old one and half decayed, was closed and there were no signs of life. One bell swung over the doors and another ponderous was suspended under a bell house. We climbed up some steps to a mia on ground elevated above the temple and were in a grove of young pines that covered the surface of the rounded hill; a planted grove of fifteen years growth perhaps, sweet scented and beautiful as heart could desire. It is not altogether that the priests have chosen the most picturesque spots, though this is usually the case, but long years of taste and assiduity have added to and embellished nature itself. These temple grounds, not more than five acres in extent, had such a variety of beauty in old and young pines, embowered paths, staircases of stone, green hedgerows, flowering trees, open terraces, as would make them a luxury of costly acquisition in our countries where land is only deemed fit to be spanned by railroads, cut into ditches, or devoted to townships.

When I see these Japanese villages clustered in a shady, sheltered, valley or dell, the copses of pines and firs so beautifully dotting here and there the innumerable hillocks, the belts of trees along the field edges conspicuous among which are the brilliant and glistening camellia japonica, the very picturesqueness with which these fields are cut out in the hills or spread open among the vallies with their intersecting divisions of turf walks, no marring fences to offend the eye, with the pleasing regularity and yet undeviating directness of the drill sown crops so that the lines of two fields strike each the other at just the proper and harmonious angle and then those wonderful country roads bordered by hedges, overarched by trees, winding round the hills, threading up the vallies, in always just the right spot where a landscape gardener would have put them had he taken all Nippon under contract, the cultivated terraces with their paced and trimmed banks rising bank above bank against the high hill tops, when I see all these and add thereto some of the farmhouses with their neatness of house and grounds, hedges of box, yew, and the whole wood of evergreen trees, and borders of flowers, I ask if this is the accident of savage nature and half savage man or is there an instinctive taste to those to whom Providence has given so fair an heritage, in keeping therewith, or is the cultivated taste of long experience united to an eye for all that is beautiful in nature. Or shall we accept this as a better lesson than all those that nature yields up her best beauty when she is the most assiduously cultivated for our common necessities, that she bountifully gives the most of her charms where the most is exacted of her homelier qualities.

On our return home we visited another temple to which was attached a Kompira where the retroverted queues of seamen and the long tresses of women hung as votive offerings before the door. This temple had also its rear yard of arborous and floral adornments and dug out of the hillside was a cave in which a well had been sunk for the purpose of obtaining cool water in summer. Indeed our whole walk today, which had extended to several hours and a good many miles, had been beguiled of all its tediousness by the beauty through which we moved.

Monday, March 11, 1861

We were aroused from our slumbers at half past one this morning by a fire alarm. In the thick Japanese quarters of the town occupied by merchants and small shopkeepers a conflagration had started which threatened to be very serious. The fire bells were rung and drums beaten at all the police and fire stations and as usual the Japanese were gathered by thousands to assist in extinguishing the flames. All are compelled to do service and for this purpose there are large fire brigades with showy conspicuous uniforms. Every householder too keeps more or less fire hooks which he must carry with him to the fire, their use being to pull down buildings. The policemen or yakunins act as foremen and give all the directions and compel every man to work, so that fires of formidable aspect are often extinguished by mere force of numbers each bringing his little resources to bear. The head men, generally the town officials, are conspicuous objects with their shiny metal helmets, long capes of leather falling over their backs, breasts, and shoulders, to their waists, urging on the men to work with their steel batons. In our country, you see no such industrious crowd endeavoring to extinguish a fire. The only exempt persons here are we foreigners and native yakunins. Even at a fire a yakunin comes with his usual retinue and the Governor's train is never so showy as when he comes to tour during a conflagration. He came down last night and was a shining splendid figure mounted on his richly caparisoned horse. He wore his fireman's suit. A helmet of white copper to which was attached the cape of embossed and gilt white leather falling down to the saddle seat and meeting the saddle cloth heavy with gilt emblazoning. This cape was buttoned over the face leaving barely room to see. He was preceded and followed by his retinue, several of whom were similarly dressed as to style of cut, but not in ornamentation. As his train passed along the streets with the fire glistening on their helmets and pikes and with paper lanterns borne aloft on high poles, the scene was truly imposing. Indeed, the presence of so many hundreds not to say thousands of lanterns of every imaginable device as are borne out at a fire is alone a sight worth going a far ways to see. Last night several small engines belonging to foreigners did essential service and between them, the native squirt guns, the tearing down of buildings, but especially the barriers of fire proof godowns, the conflagration was stayed after raging nearly three hours and burning down many houses and warehouses. Some fireproof godowns were destroyed that were exposed to an intense heat of ignited wood charcoal, a heat that would have burned down our fire proof buildings in America. One coal merchant lost seven warehouses out of eleven. Today the Governor sent to the Consuls 50 pigs and 300 fowls to be given to the foreigners who assisted to extinguish the fires.

I heard a rather good bon mot of a Californian today at R. and Co.'s[18] auction rooms where some clothing of the murdered Dan was to be sold making the third case within a short time of the sale of murdered men's effects, "hell," said he, "if things keep on, clothing will be plenty, for we shall have a sale of murdered men's clothes every day!"

Tuesday, March 12, 1861

Rode to Kanagawa and returned to write letters for the [Henry] Ellis's mail.

Wednesday, March 13, 1861

Went out to ride again today in company with Dr. Hall. We started without any definite ideas of where we would go and ended by going to Kanasawa, a town on the lower shore of Mississippi Bay. We had a good ride through an interesting country, riding some ten or twelve miles to the point of destination. The road everywhere abounded in picturesque scenery, rounded, conical hills like the bluffs of our western rivers and intervals of valleys where the brown chalets were nestling amid living green. The country in the vicinity of Kanasawa is rough and the soil—except in the vallies—not remarkably fertile, so one would judge from the scanty wheat fields. From the summits of some of the hills we had superb views out unto the distant mountains and down into long deep valleys, or far away on the gulf made white with hundreds of sails.[19]

Descending one of these mountains, or rather hills, by a circuitous roadway cut out of the soft sedimentary rock we saw spread before us the town of Kanasawa. We rode through its streets wide and clean, receiving a hundred salutations from the cottages as we passed from old men and women and little children and mothers standing in the doorways with children in their arms, passed by the ancient temples and mias with their customary surroundings of trees and the still more ancient burial places, rode down to the beach where men and women were engaged in large numbers in manufacturing salt from sea water and then on to an inn where we left our horses and ordered dinner while we continued our wanderings on foot.[20]

We had the entire village escort of boys at our heels shouting "Ohaio," "Anata Ohaio," and begging for tempos and attended in this way visited every spot whither this juvenile mob directed us, for I have found by experience the boys are the best guides to all novelties, seeming to know instinctively what would please us. They could not well go amiss for the very spots that would attract us are the resorts of their own travelling and pleasure seeking countrymen. The advent of a menagerie of strange beasts in a quiet New England town raises not half the excitement that the advent of a foreigner in a Japanese hamlet does. So with their shouts of *Cochi* and *Coco* they took us by an old temple buried out of sight amid its splendid old pines and firs, having moreover a stout wall of stone old and mossy, in and out among the houses, past the country seat of a small daimio with its clean outer yard, its wall of stone, and stockade of young trees. We could see that the ground within was broken and diversified and heads of trees peered over the walls and fences, all pretty and parklike and patriarchal. Patriarchal for here living among his tenantry in dignified seclusion he is both chief and patriarch. Everything was silent about his domains, not a warden or sentinel

---

[18] R. and Co. was probably C. H. Richards & Co.
[19] Photographs of this scenery can be found in Yokohama Kaikō Shiryō Kan, eds., *F. Beato bakumatsu nihon shashin shū* (Yokohama: Yokohama Kaikō Shiryō Kan,

1987), pp. 42–43.
[20] A picture of the inn at which the two Halls stopped can be found in ibid., p. 44.

was stirring, and we walked on where the street went between piles of rock in which niches were cut and images placed for wayside worshippers.

Now on an elevation that jutted out among the salt marshes covered with water, like a promontory, we saw stone steps winding up a hill, and here it was it seemed that the boys wished to guide us. We turned off the main street and took a lane that led us under a gateway and into the thickly shaded court of a temple. Here a young priest joined us and guided us up the flight of steps we had seen to the summit of the hill where we found seats and a neat building, half temple, half tea house. Here we roused two more priests up from their noontide repose and they all made us welcome. The young priest had brought along his tea pot, but before he could kindle his charcoal an industrious housewife came bustling out of breath up the hill with two cups of tea on a salver. We sat down on the mat covered benches and addressed ourselves to the prospect before us. There were the splendid waters of Mississippi Bay covered with fishing boats and its pretty green islands of American nomenclature Perry and Webster. Below us lay the village and on the sea sands were the salt gatherers. The priests brought out a telescope of Japanese manufacture some three feet long, but of feeble power compared to my little pocket Munich Glass. Then they offered us more tea and sweetmeats and cakes and brought out their little wares for sale, such as views of the place, fans with the same view, and other fans neatly put up in ornamented paper wrappers designed as mementos of the place and one of which I bought for the stout comely waiting girl at the inn to which we now turned back for our dinner.

Our boy escort did not leave us till we had returned to the inn, nor even then, but gathered outside of the bamboo paling to see what further the tojins would do and to indulge in boy comments on our horses that stood within munching their beans. Dinner awaited us. We ascended to an upper room that looked out upon the sea and found our low table and seats ready for us. The master of the house kneeled down by our side while the ruddy faced, fair armed servant girl brought in the platters of fish so beautifully fried, the snowy rice, and the eggs, and the little tea pot. We had our option to eat our dinner with chopsticks, lead forks, or fingers and conspired by a judicious use of them all. The fish was delicious and the whole cleanlily served.

We were honored during our meal with the presence of a young gentleman freshly shaved and clean, to whom so much deference was paid by the rest that we knew he was the indispensable spy come to watch us. What cared we for the one spy when one by one boys, girls, and men and women began to come in from the streets to see how a tojin would eat. We gave a welcome to them all, for their curiosity is harmless, and as for the official he was welcome to note what he would.

Kanasawa is a place of some notoriety in Japanese history, if we may believe the popular legend. Here it was some six hundred years ago that China ships came to trade and hither was first brought the religion of Buddha from India and on the hill where we had just been in a temple was for a long time preserved the first sacred books of that faith which now covered the whole empire.

But there was a more interesting legend about the name of our inn, *Adzumaya*, or the "Eastern Hotel," as the words may signify and are now generally accepted, but a Japanese doctor fond of ancient lore said such was not the original derivation of the name. Then he told me how many years ago in the flourishing days of the Mikado when Tycoons were not thought of, one of the Mikados was at war in this region. He had brought with him his beautiful bride as the companion of his campaign, but alas while he was sailing up the Bay of Yedo from Uraga to Yedo, a great and fearful storm arose and his fleet was so tossed about and its passengers put to difficulties that his wife was lost, swept into the remorseless sea. When some days after he passed by the place where his wife was lost, the sea was covered with great waves that came up his ship's sides as if they would enter and the bereaved Mikado said the waves were the spirit of his lost bride, and so the place was named after his "sea bride," but, said the doctor, the old legend has been forgotten and as the words may signify "Eastern Hotel," so it is now called. I have faith in the doctor and his legend, I love all such legends and shall ever assert that I dined this day at the Sea-bride's Hotel.

We finished our repast, paid our bills, and remounted for the return amid the vivas of the urchin crowd who had gathered in increased force. "Good bye," and "come again," made the welkins ring, while standing on the inn piazza the inmates of the house, as is custom bound, stood to give us farewells of good cheer, and standing by a post with their arms around each other shouting good bye till they were red in the face was the stout girl who bore off my fan and her companion in service who was in no wise jealous of the gift, for I have never seen any such little envies among these simple peasants.

We rode back by another road nearer the sea which took us through a large fishing village Soongita [Sugita] on the bay. Here we saw orchards of plum and apricot trees in full bloom reminding us of the apple orchards in blossom at home. We trotted on the sea beach for some miles and then striking off among the hills made a short return to Yokohama, which we reached at sunset having made in all over twenty miles since eleven A.M.

Thursday, March 14, 1861

Made a friendly call on the old priestess who gave me a kindly welcome and many thanks for looking after her welfare the night of the fire which threatened ruin to her. She told me with many tears that her adopted daughter Ōtsuru had grown worse since she went to Yedo; that she had the best of physicians, none of whom gave her any relief. She could no longer hold up her head or eat anything. The old lady was much distressed and received with every show of gratitude my proffer to send something that might tempt the sick girl's appetite by her sister who was going up to Yedo

tomorrow. So I went back to the house and got some little delicacies for her which the old lady was quite overcome by the receipts of and promised they should be forwarded early in the morning. I was gratified to witness the evidences of the old lady's strong affection for her adopted daughter, for it is seldom we see any exhibition of such feeling, not that they do not possess it, but that whatever indications they give to each other of it, is kept in the seclusion of private life.

Call from Minister Harris.

Friday, March 15, 1861

Snowing all day. Packing boxes to send home and studying the Japanese characters.

Saturday, March 16, 1861

Called on Minister Harris at Dorr's. He informs me that every man attached to the late Embassy to America, high and low, had received some mark of approbation from the Imperial Government, the Ambassadors themselves having been promoted and receiving additional revenues. Simme [Shimmi Buzen-no-Kami Masaoki] has now the title of Awa-no-Kami. Mr. H[arris] seems entirely satisfied with his relations to the Government. He stated among other things that the Tycoon had been recently married to the only daughter of the Mikado, a miss of fifteen, but I think he must be mistaken in this as the Japanese still speak of the marriage as a prospective one, and that the intended bride has not left Miaco as yet, but the officials have received orders throughout the whole line of the Tokaido to have the highway repaired and put in order for her progress through it.[21]

The quay is heaped up with sacks of rice today being the pay of the Governor and Custom House officials.

---

[21] It seems that Townsend Harris confused the marriage of Michi-no-Miya, the niece of the Emperor Kōmei, who married Tokugawa Mochitsugu, the Lord of Kii and brother of the Shogun Iemochi, with the pro- posed marriage of Kazu-no-Miya, the sister of the Emperor Kōmei, who eventually married Iemochi in March 1862. Hall had witnessed the procession of Michi-no-Miya to Edo on February 29, 1860.

Sunday, March 17, 1861

Rode with Dr. Hall into the country and followed the country paths till we debouched into the highway leading to Kamakura. We passed through a great deal of wild uncultivated country, more than one half being covered with timber and low trees or lying fallow. As we approached Kamakura cultivation was more general and we passed many hamlets picturesquely situated as usual in the hollows between the hills. There were some farm houses also surpassing in extent of outbuildings and exterior indications of thrift any I had hitherto seen in Japan. One of these from its numerous buildings, its slopes of turf and walls of stone, its park-like enclosure, we mistook at first for an official residence and that of a small daimio, but coming to a second one where extensive repairs were going on, and a large, and for this country elegant, house had been constructed, I made inquiries and found they were indeed farmers' houses. Such indications of worldly prosperity among the tillers of the soil were gratifying. The latter house had three fireproof warehouses.

In the vicinity of Kamakura we rode through a long street lined on either side with houses and passed many temples whose old edifices and venerable trees indicated an ancient foundation. These temples were very numerous. We rode around the stone walled enclosure of one of these, a superb inclosed park of venerable cedars (C. Japonica), the temple buildings themselves being hidden behind the foliage. Within were broad flag walks, ponds of lotus flowers spanned by bridges of cut stone, breadths of turf, stretching back to the hills in the rear up which we saw a flight of stone steps and then our vision was lost among the cedars. As we rode past we could see a range of buildings on the hill to which doubtless these steps lead, dwellings of the priests undoubtedly. We passed one little mia in front of which, out of a spot of ground not four rods square, was a complete epitome of Japanese landscape garden. Every thing was there in dwarfed proportions, trees, lines of hedges, ponds, rockwork, old walls of mossy stone, flowering plants, and bits of green turf. Could I have set this down in the Central Park it

would have been its greatest wonder and completest triumph of the gardener's skill.

We ascended a hill on whose summit was an inn where several yakunin's horses were feeding. As we dipped over the other side Kamakura lay before us and [the] most conspicuous object of all a park of fifteen or twenty acres above whose cedar tops we could see the peaked roofs and red gables of the various buildings that constitute the temple of Hachiman founded by Yoritomo six hundred years ago. Kamakura was the seat of Yoritomo's court and the street of old temples through which we had passed coming hither were the relics of the ancient court. Hachiman yet remains in all its glory. We rode through the street to an inn on a corner facing this temple and heard our names shouted from the balcony of the 2nd story. Looking up we saw the familiar faces of some Yokohama officials who like ourselves had ridden out into the country and to whom the horses belonged we had passed on the hill.

We dismounted giving our horses to hostlers and were shown up stairs into an upper room adjoining our official acquaintances. One was the land officer of the Custom House and two others were well known interpreters. They were just finishing their dinner. Taking out the screens that separated our room from theirs they gave us a hospitable welcome offering us tea, sake, and fish. The village by this time was apprised of the advent of *tojin stori*,[22] "two foreigners," and there was a crowd of two or three hundred persons before the house, men, women, and children.

We ordered dinner and our black toothed landlady gave us a guide to the grounds of Hachiman temple while our dinner was preparing. I was the more inclined to hurry off when I saw one of our friends dig out the eye of a large fish and placing the unsightly globe on a platter and dishing it with soy, looked ominous of offering it to one of us.

We entered the grounds of Hachiman followed by a rabble of a hundred people who were content with watching our movements in no wise annoying us by their orderly curiosity.

[22] Tojin "stori" means one, not two, foreigners. Hall, no doubt, meant to write "tojin futari."

Kamakura lies on the sea and from the entrance gate of Hachiman a long colonnade of venerable cedars extends to the water a mile distant. This colonnade occupies the center of a street and had a most striking effect. The grounds of Hachiman are laid out with great taste and are seen today in no doubt the same arrangement they had six hundred years ago. Yet, there was nothing to impress the great age of this place on one unless it were the trunks of some old trees which were propped up and preserved with religious care, so long as there was a twig or leaf of vitality remaining on the huge girth of the tallest and largest cedars I have ever seen in Japan. I saw nothing in Yedo to compare with this. There were serpentine walks among the groves and avenues laid out at right angles from the main avenues which passed through from north to south and east to west. Groves of cedars alternated with lotus ponds and glades of turf. The main avenue led us through a gateway to an open court where several temple buildings were arrayed within the quadrangle. The roofs were covered with copper and from one of them there arose a spiral spire of the same material. The buildings were all painted with vermilion and on the facade were paintings and sculptures, the former preserving all their tints with remarkable freshness. The subjects were generally fruits, flowers, animals, and birds.

Above this court was a walled terrace to which we ascended by a flight of thirty or forty steps, a broad stone staircase of 30 feet width. On the level of this terrace we stood again among another series of temple buildings similar to those below. To the left was an artificial mound surmounted by a small chapel from which we had a view of the adjacent country and the bordering gulf. My Munich pocket glass which I was using became an object of great curiosity, and the few who were permitted to look through it out of the whole crowd who wished so to do were astonished to see the

waters of the bay and the sailing junks brought within arm's reach as it were.

The simple curiosity and respectful behavior of this crowd of people was indicative of the fact that they had seen few if any foreigners before. From our lookout we could see the coppered roofs and red gables of other temples among the grand old cryptomerias taller than they. Except the noise we and our impromptu escort made, everything else was silent amid these groves and temples. The doors of every building were closed and forbade us access and we saw only one or two priests in their long yellow robes leaning over a parapet wall. How difficult it is to connect the present with the dim past I proved when I strove to regard all this as the work of Yoritomo, the conqueror of the Japanese nobles and the pacificator of the realm six hundred years ago—the betto, who ran with his master of Owari's horse six centuries ago even as our bettos ran with us today, and afterwards the Emperor, who dividing with the Mikado the temporal and spiritual rule of the empire, left him in his own court of many centuries foundation at Miako and built his own capital at Kamakura. We would gladly have paid our respects to the stable boy's shrine, and been satisfied with a touch of the armor he wore in those bloody wars for his sepulcher is here and here his armor is kept till now in this old city, but it was forbidden us so to do.[23] So we gave one more look at the cedars of ancient girth and contented ourselves with believing that Yoritomo saw them planted long before America was thought of, save by her own wild aborigines.

We found dinner awaiting us at the inn, and the ladies of the house, for this establishment seemed to be presided over by three ladies of black teeth and shaved brows, ready to wait upon us. Fish cooked in oil and bean soy, boiled eggs and rice made our meal as usual. In chop sticks we were beginning to be expert

[23] It is worth noting that Hall makes no mention of the Kamakura Daibutsu on this visit. Indeed, it seems that Hall and his fellow Westerners living in Yokohama and Kanagawa were kept quite ignorant of the Great Buddha's existence at this time. It is possible that the Buddha, like Yoritomo's tomb, was still off limits to for-

eign eyes. As Hall notes, foreigners were not yet a common sight in Kamakura. Contemporary photographs of the Hachiman Temple complex can be found in Yokohama Kaikō Shiryō Kan, eds. *F. Beato bakumatsu nihon shashin shū*, pp. 46–49.

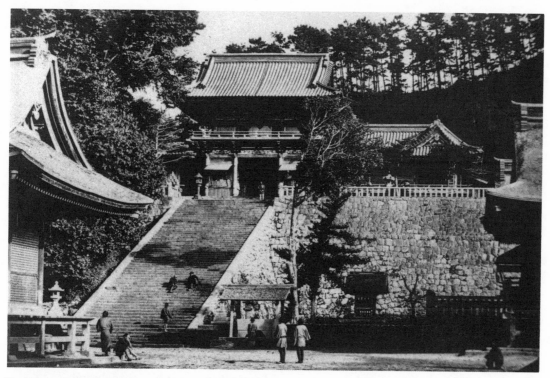

Hachiman shrine in Kamakura. Photograph by Felice Beato.

already. Our social officials in the next room cracked jokes with our landladies while the crowd without watched the low windows to catch any glimpses they could of what was going on within. Our hostesses had many questions to ask us, begged us to stay all night, and were disposed to all civil and polite attentions. We appeared occasionally at the windows to gratify the crowd with the sight of the strange hairy faced men and threw handfuls of iron cash for the children to scramble for. Our horses came round to the door, we paid our moderate bill and mounted amid rousing saionaras (good byes) of the household and the people gathered about. Desirous of testing the shyness of the rural population, before mounting I held up a button in my fingers and picking out a bright eyed little girl in the crowd approached her saying I had a present for her. But no sooner did [I] advance towards the crowd than they broke and fled and the little miss catching her toes in the ridge of a little knoll disappeared suddenly behind it, there

was a tumble of white socks and red crape in the air as she disappeared.

Among the popular accounts of the temple is this that if a woman has committed some fault punishable with death she may save her life by fleeing thither and remaining from three to five years.

On our way back we met a party of females on their way to the temple. On the part of many of the people, particularly the females, there is great timidity respecting foreigners. We saw this today when coming out through the country bridle paths. If we encountered, as we often did, females travelling alone or two or three together they would frequently hurry out of the way as if some wild beast was in pursuit, and we had only to call out to urge them into the fastest flight they were capable of.

Instead of returning by the country roads we struck off towards the Tokaido entering it at the village of Totska [Totsuka]. This village like others on the Tokaido is only an enlargement of the stream of houses that follows this road throughout its whole distance. There were many good shops, a great number of inns, numerous joroyas whose painted and bedecked inmates flocked to the doors and windows to see us pass not waiting always to complete their toilette. We joined the Tokaido's incipient stream of life and our horses understood they were now fairly turned homewards. Travelling on this road must be a pastime to the people. I have often wished to don Japanese garments and become one of them. There is always plenty of company on the road, attractive inns that at every few miles invite to repose, and tea houses and wayside refreshment places filling up the spaces between the villages. And these accommodations are graduated to every man's ability to pay. Most of the wayside halting places are in charge of women of middle life, but we found one today where a bright eyed girl presided over her teakettle under a little shed. She sat on a bench as we passed and looked so smilingly and happy with her companion, a pup, that she held by her side, that her travelling countrymen, if they have any appreciation of youth and good humor, should be sure of patronage. Between Totska and Hodoriya [Hodogaya] we rode through a long avenue of very old and large pines, one of which measured 20 feet in circumference and was hardly an exceptional one for size. Hodoriya was, like Totska, largely devoted to inns, tea houses, and kindred establishments. It being near night and after the labors of the day were over we had the greater part of the population in review as we passed along its street. It was seven o'clock when we reached home and had finished our day's jaunt of over thirty miles.

Monday, March 18, 1861

Writing of Yoritomo yesterday I have erred in confounding him with Hideyoshi as to his having been originally an hostler. Yoritomo on the contrary was of royal descent or rather noble descent. The date of his reign as Kubo Sama is fixed at 1185 A.D.

Tuesday, March 19, 1861

Busy at home packing boxes.

Wednesday, March 20, 1861

Rode to Kawasaki with H.P.K.[24] The rides at this season are delightful, vegetation is starting, flowers are blooming, and the weather is soft and warm without being too hot for the road. On the Tokaido we saw preparations making for the approach of the imperial bride in the repairing of the roadway and trimming of trees. What a preparation for a young bride to make smooth a roadway of 400 miles! We were welcomed at the old inn by the landlady and her numerous attendants and everything done to please us of which they were capable. We had our dinner and while partaking it had the company of the old landlady and seven or eight of her female attendants all kneeling about us to serve us and keep up a lively chat. The old lady is an invalid and I mixed for her from my pocket flask a weak brandy sting which she drank with many exclamations of delight. When she had finished it she politely asked for "just a little more," and I mixed a stout tumbler full of which they all partook thinking it a most delicious beverage. It warmed the cockles of the old lady's heart, gave new life to her circulation, and brought back sparkles to her eyes and a better color to her face than its former ashy hue. She rubbed her hands in gratified astonishment at the unwonted flow of the vital fluid through her chilly fingers, rubbed her cheeks, laughed at the girls whose ruddy brown cheeks were all aglow with the subtle essence of the grape, declared they were all a "little drunken," but that it was "very pleasant." She had not felt so well for many a day and persisted in calling the drink a medicine and would I "spare her a little" of the raw material so that "tomorrow she might have another draught." I told the old lady that if she would let her salted and pickled vegetable alone and eat more meat and

---

[24] It is not clear who H.P.K. was. Rather than one individual the letters may have stood for three friends, as the context suggests.

take a little of this daily she would be better, for she was not old in years but in looks. The secluded indoor life of these Japanese women who have not active household cares combined with their vegetable diet relieved only by a little fish is conducive to many disorders, particularly dyspepsia.

A shower gathering on the hills warned us to be mounted and away again. A brisk trot kept us for a while amid the scattering drops from the edge of the cloud and finally carried us out of it altogether. Before us was a clear sunshine falling upon the hill of Kanagawa and behind the horizon was black as night with a broad belt of the storm cloud from which we had escaped.

The Japanese have been impressed by the good service of the foreign fire engines at the late fire and are making inquiries as to their cost. Our engines would be a great service to them, they have such a well organized fire department and its officers can command the services of those who are not willing to work. But they are all compelled to be present and do service at conflagrations.

Inquiring today whether the Japanese who are so undemonstrative of affection exhibit in private life those strong feelings and attachments we are accustomed to see in enlightened countries, the answer was a decided affirmative. In this land where there is so strong a regard for the distinctions of class, marriages of love from one class to a lower one are not infrequent. A daughter of a samurai, or yakunin, or a hatamoto, will elope "all for love" with some low born peasant. Suicides growing out of similar unequal attachments occur. In these cases the lovers die together; the girl attires herself in her robes of silk, the young man dons his best garments, they bind themselves together with cords and take the fatal plunge into some stream or lake.

Thursday, March 21, 1861

The progress of vegetation has been rapid for several days. The wheat and barley fields on the top of the bluffs present a beautiful sight. They are like one great spread of gardens with their exactness of culture. Not a weed or unsightly shrub visible, but rows of grain lacing the fields in every direction divided by turf paths into small garden like patches.

Friday, March 22, 1861

In conversation with our Minister a few days ago he stated that he "had recently learned a fact of much interest" which was that "our American potato was introduced by Com. Perry into Japan at Hakodade and had become an article of so general culture that last year 1,500,000 piculs were raised on the island of Yeso." I have heard this statement before when at Hakodade last summer, but repeated inquiries serve to convince me that its introduction was anterior to Perry's arrival, though I do not doubt that he may in some way have stimulated its use. I suspect however from the well known slowness of all orientals to introduce novelties in their diet, and from the general culture of the potatoes on Yeso, that its first introduction was before Perry's time and such is the weight of testimony. No Japanese of intelligence with whom I am conversant places its introduction at so modern a date. A Japanese doctor assured me today that it had been well known for more than fifty years, others ascribe its introduction to the former Portuguese or Dutch settlers, and at Hakodade I heard it credited to visits of whalers at a more modern date. So that the whole goes to show that the potato has been known for some indefinite period and has gradually come into use being now raised abundantly on Yeso as my journal in former pages attests, though on what data Mr. H[arris] states the amount I am at a loss to know for the Japanese have no agricultural statistics; one must take the average of guesses!

Our conversation again turned upon the present high price of rice, which Mr. Harris attributed solely to a failure in the crop. This the Japanese deny. On the contrary, they say, last year's crop was a fair crop, but that the rise is owing to the purchase of other articles offered so largely by the foreigners, partly to the fact that the daimios are storing up large quantities of rice in their warehouses which they first kiln dry, and that the rise is partly prospective and speculative in this way: the farmers are this season putting their fields largely to those crops which they are permitted to sell and not to rice which they are forbidden to sell and on which they pay a larger rental to their lord or master. The large merchants have bought and hold it on speculation. The price this year is five Bus in place of two Bus the ordinary price. Twenty-seven years ago a failure in the crop carried the price up to seven Bus.

Saturday, March 23, 1861

Notwithstanding the Japanese promised the occupancy of the Bluffs to both the American and English Ministers, they now turn about and deny that they ever conceded more than their occupancy by the foreign government representatives! It is a specimen of the un-blushing prevarication of Japanese diplomacy.

Mr. Alcock has issued a circular to his countrymen stating that it now (!) appears that Mr. Moss was very wrongly treated by the Japanese and intimating that his punishment was too severe! It would seem that the storm of indignation raised against the British Minister both here and in China must have opened his eyes to the fact that he is not quite the autocrat he appears by his official acts to have considered himself. At the time of his unrighteous judgement rendered in that case I think the American Minister was the only one who professedly upheld him. In his circular Mr. Alcock now says that hereafter Japanese officials who undertake to arrest foreigners shall wear a distinct governmental badge, and that every prisoner arrested shall be brought at once before the Consul. These are precisely the points on which the foreign community quarreled with Mr. A[lcock] at the time of the Moss affair in which they claimed this at the hands of the Japanese and Mr. A[lcock] resisted them, and now he brings forward their propositions as original ones of his own! Thus far in Japanese treaty history the merchants in their collective capacity have shown more sagacity and practical intelligence than the rulers sent to rule over them of which this is but one instance.

Sunday, March 24, 1861

The spring weather this season is peerless. It is almost impossible to remain in the house a moment, the beauty of earth, air, and skies so calls and demands one to go abroad. Just now too, soft moonlit nights add their charm to the pleasure of this Japanese spring. The spring does not burst out with the suddenness and over warmth of intertropical regions, neither does it linger with the heavy tardiness of our northern climes. But it comes gently tripping along like a bride to her long expected lover's arms, neither too formal nor yet too easy, still with a shy confidence, wreathing herself that she may be welcome in her beauty with wreaths of orange and camellia blossoms and the double sweet scented blossoms of peach, plum, and apricot. It is one long beautiful glorious May morning and so abundant are the evergreen leaves that we have already forgotten there has been any winter.

Fresh rumors of Mito and his men are again rife. The old man is said to be indeed alive and to have been living during all the time of his reported death with shaven head and disguised as a priest. His followers are reported as making forced loans at Yedo with the view of a descent on Yokohama. We have had so much of this wolf cry that we pay little heed to it any longer.

Monday, March 25, 1861

Another incendiary fire last night destroying little property. Many fires have been kindled within the past week, which has led to a suppression of the old system of a noisy police. Hereafter the night police are to make their rounds quietly, the most sensible innovation upon old custom the Japanese have made for a long time.

Saturday night there was a fight in the Oshiwara between a party of Chinamen and Japanese resulting in the death of one of the former and wounding of several more. Love and liquor were at the bottom of the quarrel. A foreigner who interfered to rescue his servant was badly beaten. I had a call today from my old acquaintance of Neegata, the admirer of Washington and covetor of the fine portrait I have of him. He came to say good bye to me. Observing that he was without swords and in the garb of a merchant I asked him why it was, "to pass the gates without difficulty" he said.

Tuesday, March 26, 1861

We learn that the Japanese have granted permission to their merchants to trade in their own ships to China and Siam. Really Japan is shaking off her old exclusiveness.

Wednesday, March 27, 1861

A day of storm and rain spent in writing letters for the *Kingfisher*'s mail. Capt. dined with us in the evening.

Thursday, March 28, 1861

The *Kingfisher* bearing our home mails is ashore this morning in the mud of Kanagawa flats. Among Americans the constant theme is *our country*; have we any longer our union? Anxiously we wait for the next mail; [I] was at Dr. H[epburn]'s today, he tells me [he] has now a constant influx of Japanese patients. The fields of rape begin to bloom.

Friday, March 29, 1861

Dr. H[all] and myself had another long ride in the country today. We started with the intention of visiting Fujisawa and Ino Sima [Enoshima] but after riding three hours through the country paths found we had made little direct progress and so concluded to abandon the attempt to reach Ino Sima but struck off towards the sea. This brought us into a wild country among a range of high hills near the coast and not far from Uraga. Our path was a solitary horse path over the summit of the hills which we traversed for an hour and a half. It was indeed a wild country, the hills were rugged, bold, and precipitous with here and there patches of pine or Japanese cedars and uncul-

tivated except an occasional field of grain in the valleys which showed by their stunted look how uncongenial the soil was. Infacerus rocks were thickly scattered about, half hid in the tall grass and furze, and our path was sometimes hewn through an opposing ridge of the same. The scenery was a picture of grand, sublime solitude and desolation. On every side were these rugged hills standing up like needle points between which were the deep chasm-like valleys.

Our narrow path wound past sheer precipices or overhung deep gulfs where far below were the green tops of the Japan cedars dwarfed by the distance. The only persons we met during the solitary mountainous ride were a couple of peasants who had been gathering small firewood among the hills. The prospect from the higher peaks was the most magnificent I have ever seen in these islands. In the rear of us rolled the billowing train of hills till they subsided into low hilly ridges and plains and uprose again against the range of snow capped Hiacone many leagues distant. Fusi still farther beyond was half hid in a veil of clouds that stretched a dark curtain over the southern horizon. To the westward the inland country stretched away, one magnificent plain dotted with hamlets, severed with rivers, belted with forests till eyesight was bounded by distance only and the pall-like rain clouds. Eastward was the broad shiny belt of Uraga Channel bounded by a blue range of the hills of Awa, while to the southeastward we gazed straight through the gateway of the heads into the broad open gulf where a shaft of sunlight bursting through the clouds lay like slumber upon the quiet sea.

From the hills we descended into a broad road that connects Kamakura with Kanasawa and turned our horses' heads to the latter place, that we might get rest for ourselves and food for our horses that had unflaggingly carried us over the mountains and plains for seven hours. We rode into the long straggling town and passed the Hotel of Adzumaya where we had dined before. Though its landlords heartily beckoned us with their hands from the verandah, I always had a fancy for trying new hotels, and my companion agreeing therewith, we rode through the town to a new one that we had observed when here before. We drew reins before its open piazza and were at once received by the inmates and what portion of the village could conveniently assemble on so short a notice.

The house was not so well calculated to provide for strangers as its aristocratic rival, the Hotel of the Sea Bride, but we observed that its rooms were more spacious and newer, and its attendant handmaids not only more numerous but in freshness and beauty wholly eclipsing Adzumaya by the sea. So we overlooked the fact that one went out to buy a frying pan for our fish and that it took half the neighborhood to arrange for our horses, but preliminaries being settled we went upstairs to the room of honor where our dinner was served and made more palatable by the unusually comely and tidy damsels who waited on us. For thus it is the custom that the young ladies of the house who are comely and well favored should do their best to entertain the guest. They sit near you endeavoring to anticipate your wants, they must pour out the tea into your cup with their own hands, fill up your libations of sake, and the utmost honor you can do them is to offer them a taste from your own cup, or hand with your own hand some portion of the viands. They presume not on your familiarity, for the inmates of these houses are respectful and wholly decent and are not to be confounded with their frailer sisters of the joroyas. These were so unusually diverting with their pleasant ways that we regretted when the hour came of remounting.

As we rode out of the village we met several peasants bringing wood to market; their horses were not only laden but themselves, each one having strapped to his own back one third as much as was put upon his horse. This is all economic division of labor to which I call the attention of civilized teamsters. We rode once more into the village of Sugita and along the sea beach the salt water splashing against our horses' hoofs, struck off again into the hills that girt the bay, and riding among the cultivated fields were in two hours again at home.

Noticed today several flowering shrubs, particularly the holly, a low species with beautiful blossoms.

Saturday, March 30, 1861

A couple of highwaymen, *ronin* or disgraced soldiers, as the Japanese call them were arrested near Kamakura a few days ago. They entered a small village and going to a merchant's house demanded his money. He feigned great fear and a ready compliance inviting them into his upper room and setting tea before them. Then he went below again to get his treasure but managed instead to send information of what was going on to the headman of the village. Alarm was at once and quietly given and the robbers were beleaguered. They left the house and took refuge on a pile of firewood, but the populace, who had turned out in a body, belabored them so with missiles of wood that they were at length compelled to surrender despite their long swords. It is rather surprising that in a country so populous as this, containing so many soldiers by profession, the highwaymen should exist in such numbers and with so great apparent impunity. A samurai, or soldier, is disgraced or discharged and at once turns footpad. He robs and slays his victims not only in less frequented roads but in the Tokaido about the populous villages and even in the streets of Yedo itself. The footpad and the highwayman was a notorious, almost a chivalric, character in the feudal days of Europe and in the feudal days of Japan he is seemingly a necessary part of the institutions of the society. I never hear of any determined attempt to put these pests and outlaws of society down. What is called the hill or country road,[25] in distinction from the Tokaido or sea way, which leads from Yedo through the island, is said to be so infested by these men that travelling there is at all times insecure and the sight of a dead body kicked to one side of the road is not an uncommon one.

Whenever I have pressed the Japanese to tell me why the Emperor and his vassal princes do not, with their numerous soldiery, put this system of ruffianism down, I get invariably the reply, "the Emperor's soldiers are old family soldiers, old, infirm, or, if young, yet effemi-

[25] The Kiso Kaidō or Nakasendō, the other main road that connected Kyoto with Edo.

nate, and are both afraid and unable to cope with these men who often are found connected with large parties. Many of the daimios' soldiers are no better and if the daimio of a country so infested cannot put them down the more distant or powerful daimios care nothing about it." Their own personal safety is secured by the large trains with which they travel. The murdering and plundering falls upon the merchant usually and he belongs to the lowest orders of Japanese social life. In the Province of Fitatsi [Hitachi], belonging to the notorious Mito, in one corner thereof, a hilly district, is a famous rendezvous of vagabonds, ronins, and discontented spirits from all parts of the kingdom. There are said to be at this time five or six thousand of them. The nucleus of the band are three hundred or so of Mito's own followers who have been discharged from service, and who have gathered to themselves outlaws from all parts of the kingdom, ronins, disgraced soldiers, even many from the lower classes of the people who are not entitled by rank to wear two swords, but having committed crimes against the state, or stimulated by the mere love of the wild lawless life, have attached themselves to the fortunes of these desperate men, till several thousand have congregated together bidding defiance to the government.

These outlaws have a complete organization; each new comer is required to pay a small sum (5 rios) to the leaders, to arm himself with two swords, and to adopt their uniform which is a plain black. Mito, instead of giving encouragement to these men, is said now to be so sorely perplexed by them that he has appealed to the government for aid to crush them. The feeble government officials are insufficient to do this and we hear now that the Tycoon has ordered the neighboring daimios to form into levies sufficient to surround and cut these men completely off. The outlaws, on the other hand, are reported to have set down the 3rd day of the 3rd month as the time for making a descent on Yokohama. It is only a repetition of last year's false and foolish alarms.

To illustrate how frightened the people of Yedo are and how little protection they seem to have from their own rulers we hear that having at last succeeded in making arrests of some of the parties who have been levying forced contributions on the Yedo merchants they turned out to be only *ninsokus*, or common burden carriers, who had disguised themselves in good clothes and wearing two swords, or one, and using the name of Mito's men had repeatedly succeeded in their daylight robberies in the heart of the city. In another instance a fierce looking fellow wearing a long sword presented himself at a Ban Sho, or street guard house, and demanded sake and food. The frightened officials complied and inviting him in conceived the happy idea of carrying their hospitalities so far as to render the man drunk and in their power. They succeeded as the man's inebriated sleep breathing testified. Carefully they secured his long and dangerous sword, it was unusually light for so terrible a weapon, they unsheathed it, when lo they had been taken in their own castle by a poor vagabond who had only a bamboo splint in his sword sheath!

It is only of the soldiers of Satsuma and Hosokawa Prince of Hizen [scil. Higo] that the Japanese speak with respect.

Sunday, March 31, 1861

After service took a walk to the temple of Miokagee[26] hoping to have a quiet rest in the silent surroundings, but in vain for my hopes. Young Nippon caught sight of my coattails through the foliage and I was at once beset. I firmly rid myself of them by a little ruse and as I sat down under the balsamy pines, I heard the urchins whooping and shouting as they endeavored to find me again. It was a game of hide and seek and the little fellows had half surrounded the hill, but I managed to elude them, but came out of the woods near a cottage when a little girl spied me and as usual came to bring some flowers in hopes of a gratuity of coin. I enjoyed the game, gave her some zeni and darted off again into another

---

[26] The Myōkaji was a major Nichiren sect temple in the Yokohama area. See the Yokohama Shiyakusho (eds.), *Yokohama shishikō—Butsuji hen* (Kyoto: Rinsen Shoten, 1986), pp. 779ff.

path while she ran to bring up the boys. I gained the cover of some live oaks and camellias on a little mound where there was a chapel, and secure from sight listened to the shouts and chatter of the boys as they strove to regain the track I had taken. I have no doubt they talked till bedtime of how I eluded their friendly pursuit.

Ino, my old body servant, while waiting on the table this evening entertained me with gossip of the court.[27] His uncle, he says, is a servant of the Emperor, of rank entitling him to forty followers in the street. He has been himself to court in his uncle's suite as servant wearing two swords and thus has seen not only the present Emperor but the two previous ones. The late Emperor's widow according to his account is one of the strong minded women, strong bodied as well. She was a sister of the late prince of Satsuma and is a large muscular woman. She is skilled in horseback riding, handles the long spear like a soldier, and can lift from the ground a sack of rice weighing five piculs! A few years ago during an earthquake she picked up the emperor in her arms and carried him out of the house! "Very strong" she is, he says. The bridal cortege of the present Emperor's wife will not pass through the Tokaido till September. She will be attended not only by her escort of armed men but by a train of 1000 women in norimons. This will be a rare sight if it is so.

That the government officials misuse their places we have had a late instance. At Hodoriya [Hodogaya] the officials endeavored to collect an unjust tax and unauthorized. The people rose in a body and resisted so firmly that the officials were obliged to give way.

Monday, April 1, 1861

Preparing mail for *Kingfisher*.

Tuesday, April 2, 1861

Preparing mail for *Kingfisher*. The little dancing girls; passed an hour among these interesting children whose tidy appearance, pleasant faces, and polite and winning manners cannot fail to attract and engage regard. I was much amused with their respectful obeisance to Mr. E.[28] who sat a silent looker on.

Wednesday, April 3, 1861

Went out to the *Kingfisher* in K.'s[29] yacht; sailing was delightful. The *Kingfisher*, having lightened herself 300 tons, floated off the mud bank whereon she has been resting so long. Alarm of fire in the evening from our neighbor's where the last day or two a sailor grog shop and boarding house has been opened. It was fortunately extinguished with little damage.

Thursday, April 4, 1861

A charming day following the late rains. Closed up my mails for the *Kingfisher* and went over to Kanagawa. Impressed the opportunity to lodge a complaint at the Consul's against our neighbor's grog shop. Vegetation on the Kanagawa side is more forward. The rape fields are in bloom, filling the air with pleasant fragrances. The rich fields between the English

[27] One wishes that Hall would have been more specific about his "old body servant" Ino. From the description that follows, Ino appears to have been from a samurai family. If his uncle had the right to forty retainers and served the shogun personally, he was obviously a samurai of high rank.

[28] This was probably Richard Eusden, the secretary of the British legation. Hall tended to use the term Mr. for members of the diplomatic corp.

[29] Here again it is not clear who K. is, but the fact that K. owned a yacht, could indicate that this was W. Keswick who headed Jardine, Matheson, & Co. Jar-

dine, Matheson & Co. was located at Number 1 on the Bund, and Dr. Hall of Walsh & Co. was located at Number 2. As the journal indicates, Francis Hall had become a good friend of Dr. Hall's, and later headed Walsh, Hall & Co.'s operations at Number 2. What is clear is that Hall was already making the kind of contacts that would allow him to become one of the leading figures in Yokohama trade in the years that followed. Keswick had arrived in Yokohama with the opening of the ports and by 1861 was a well-established Yokohama trader, who like Dr. Hall had already made considerable money in the Yokohama trade.

and American Consuls are a picture of beauty, one broad carpet of green and gold. Handsomer fields I never saw in our rich country. As I was walking along the path bordered on either side by these green fields, a funeral train crossed the valley with its train of attendants. The mourning women in their white robes, the neighbors of the deceased bearing the crape clad pall, it was a picturesque sight to see it winding through the valley with its streamers of white papers just before the sunset hour. A half hour afterwards I saw them all assembled at the temple, the body laid before the altar between two young priests in long robes, one of whom was conducting the funeral service reading from a book and the other making occasional responses. Once again was I reminded of the points where the church of Buddha and that of Rome touch each other.

Friday, April 5, 1861

Intended to have started for Ino Sima [Enoshima] this morning but the threatening look of the clouds prevented. Magnolia are all in bloom, dwarf glycines, a plant or shrub resembling a deutzia, holly and some unknown wild flowers. In Dr. H[all]'s garden saw fine lettuce beds from which he has been picking for a fortnight, the Japanese are also bringing fine lettuce to market, horseradish, and other vegetables.

Saturday, April 6, 1861

Mail from the States today. Its secession news exciting the liveliest interest. Raw silk immediately fell one fourth in price, much to the astonishment of the Japanese who were unable to understand so sudden a depression.

Sunday, April 7, 1861

A muggy oppressive summer like atmosphere.

Monday, April 8, 1861

A temperature similar to yesterday. The strides of vegetation in the warm moist atmosphere are rapid. Nothing can be more beautiful than the fields of rape in bloom and the waving grain which I saw on a walk today. I observed another good point in Japanese husbandry which I have had occasion to notice before, the planting of young trees by the farmers. They feel the full force of the Scotsman's remark to his son, "plant trees Jack for they will grow while you are sleeping." The nursery patch of young trees is common among the farms and the planted forests are to be seen uplands in every stage of growth, many of them beautiful with their straight regularly planted trunks and the open vista under the branches unchoked of brushwood. A common way of planting is to set out the young trees in an old forest to come on as the larger ones are felled.

Tuesday, April 9, 1861

Packing boxes to send home.

Wednesday, April 10, 1861

Mr. Alcock left today for Shanghai and Hong Kong on the *Encounter*. Divers rumors are afloat as to the cause of his absence, but all point to the Moss affair as the most probable.

Conversing today with an old flower merchant, he told me that thirty years ago when the daffodil was first introduced one hundred and fifty rios were paid for a single bulb, now a penny each will buy all one wishes. In the early pages of my journal I have noticed other instances of a flower mania in Japan.

Thursday, April 11, 1861

Packing boxes for home.

Friday, April 12, 1861

This is the great holiday for females, "The Doll Feast," of which I have an illustration by the Nagasaki painter. It is the anniversary also of the Regent's murder a year ago at Yedo, and the day set down for the attack of Yokohama by "Mito Men." The thick dropping shafts of the rain, those long flexible spears, are the only weapons we are called upon to encounter.

Saturday, April 13, 1861

To Kanagawa and called upon Dorr whom I found very ill.

Sunday, April 14, 1861

After service had a walk in the country and stopped at one of the temples so often to be found on some picturesque eminence overlooking a valley. This one was girt with cherry trees in full bloom. The priests, a young man and an elder, received me very cordially. I cannot imagine a life more retired and quiet than that of these monkish priests. They drawl out a few prayers daily, and squatted on their haunches eat and smoke, read or sleep by turns. At parting they gave me an orchid which was growing in the recess of a paper window.

Monday, April 15, 1861

Passed two or three hours interestingly at the Japanese theater witnessing the performance of a troupe of boy actors from Yedo. Their acting is an imitation of their elders and the poetical and dramatical parts of Japanese life was remarkably excellent. That of one little fellow, six and a half years old, was so extraor-

dinary that he would at home have occupied the head of a bill poster in red letters as the "infantile prodigy" and taken rank at once with the little Batemans.[30] It was amusing to see him strut about the stage hardly able to bear the two swords of the official character he represented, or to move by the clumsiness of his rich brocade dress. All his parts were enacted with so much mock gravity and seriousness that its satire on older children's life absorbing affairs was broad and ludicrous.

The foreigners after the curtain fell called for the stage hero and he appeared at one of the side scenes entirely nude. He was the recipient of plentiful gratuities. The female characters on the Japanese stage are always represented by males dressed for their assumed characters, in this instance the personation of young ladies and girls, was so perfect that though knowing it the fact I could not disabuse myself of the belief that they were just what they seemed to be. The wardrobes were all new and glittering and, if valuable, interesting as illustrating the customs of the higher classes. The female wardrobes were superb as well as showy, one in particular of crimson and gold which being thrown off displayed a yet richer underdress of blue and gold elaborately worked with the needle. I saw for the first time the long loose trousers which trailing behind the wearer give him the appearance of kneeling. These are still worn by the daimio on great court occasions.

The theater is a favorite Japanese amusement in which a whole family will share taking with them their refreshments, their meals, or buying them at the cook shops attached. Some of the groups of well dressed females were very pretty. On entering the theater the spectators slip off their outside sandals and come in in their stockings or on the clean inner sandal and the usher follows with the sandals or clogs for street walking. Friendly visits are paid from box to box and a liberal amount of tea drinking and gossiping is conducted.

---

[30] This reference is to the children of Sidney Bateman, the actress and playwright, whose three daughters Kate, Ellen, and Isabella became well-known child actresses. The Batemans made their first appearance in New York City in 1849 when Kate and Ellen played Richard III and Richmond at the ages of four and six years. See Allen Johnson, ed., *Dictionary of American Biography* (New York: Charles Scribner's Sons, 1929), vol. 2, p. 45.

Tuesday, April 16, 1861

Dr. H[all] and myself started on another excursion to occupy a couple of days. We left Kanagawa at 8½ A.M. and took the Tokaido to Fugeesawa [Fujisawa]. The morning was clear and warm but we met less road travellers than we expected. From Kanagawa to Totska [Totsuka] was familiar ground. Beyond Totska the road became more picturesque and interesting. It was bordered on either side by ancient pines and cedars, which spreading their gnarly branches over the road gave grateful shade to the passing travellers. For long distances the interlocked branches formed a lofty colonnade, an arch of green, and the roadside was thickly set with blossoming shrubs and hedges. The country on either side was rolling, but much of it was uncultivated.

We reached Fugeesawa [Fujisawa] at noon and as very few foreigners had been there before us we were beset by the usual crowds of young men and boys, while the inhabitants of the houses all came out to stare at the strangers. We rode on through the village answering back the *Ohaio*'s that greeted us on every hand. An elderly man from the official station preceded our horses and kept the street clear for our passage, driving back the crowds of children that pressed close upon our horses' heels. The buildings of Fugeesawa looked older and blacker than usual, its shops and inns were smaller and less attractive than those of Totska. Having satisfied our curiosity in looking at the village we turned back to an inn where we were well received with every mark of courtesy. We rested at the inn an hour to suit our horses and rest ourselves. The villagers crowded about us so that it was difficult to move about, yet they were wholly respectful. We were conducted to a back room away from the noise and crowd of the street where we ordered refreshments. Lucky were the villagers who were the landlord's friends and having the entree of the house could make the usual inspection of our garments, but above all to see how the tojins ate. At this place we were the special objects of interest to a group of good natured fat middle aged women who gratified their curiosity in handling us all we could permit. These interrogatives and investigations

are sometimes more inquisitive than modest. We were urged to tarry over night with the proffer of favors which were supposed to be a great inducement. These favors are lip service only, not from any indisposition on their part to pay them but from official prohibition.

Our destination was to Ino Sima [Enoshima], the "Island of Temples," which lies off the Tokaido, three miles distant in the outer Gulf of Yedo. We mounted our horses amid many "good byes" and invitations to "come again," and turning off the great highway by the side of a stream of considerable magnitude which flowed seaward resumed our journey.[31] The country was in a high state of cultivation near to Fugeesawa, and the soil having an admixture of sand the crops were in a great state of forwardness. The broad beans were in full blossom and the pease beginning to blossom. We crossed the stream already mentioned by a ferry boat. As we approached the sea the country became more and more sandy. Flourishing in the light warm soil were many peach orchards now in full bloom. Yet nearer the sea the sand was heaped up in hillocks by the winds blowing in from seaward on which a coarse long grass found scanty existence. From among these hillocks we debouched on to the broad sand beach and before us was spread a magnificent prospect of land and water.

Though the faintest breath of a wind scarcely crossed the waters of the bay the surf was rolling in and tumbling on the beach in one long line of emerald white. Newport beach is not finer or more grand. To the left trended the coast of Nippon bending in a long arc about the waters of the Gulf and ending at Cape Sagami. To the right was the rocky and hilly coastline towards Cape Idzu, which was indistinctly visible in a murky atmosphere. Seaward, veiled in the darkness of overhanging clouds, was the undulating outline of Oho Sima [Ōshima], or Volcano Island, while just before us a half mile distant rose the abrupt island to which we were bound.

The shore here bends sharply round and a long reach of smooth sand beach extends to the island and connects by a low tongue to the mainland. The tides do not rise high enough

[31] This was the Sakaigawa.

to cut it off, but its smooth worn sands gave evidence that the storm waves often and again ride over it. Scattered over the sands were great numbers of fishermen drying their nets. They left their occupation to stare and shout at us, and the boys saluted us with uncomplimentary epithets. But we have always found the fishing villages more rude than the inland towns. A man who had run by our side a mile or more back announced himself as a landlord and solicited our patronage and as his inn was the first house we came to we resigned ourselves to his hands.

Ino Sima [Enoshima] is an island of two miles in circumference rising boldly out of the water and surrounded with rocks and reefs where a storm driven ship could have little hope of any rescue. It is rocky though well covered with trees and foliage and has a striking appearance as approached from the land. It is called the "island of temples" and is one of the most noted resorts of pilgrims in the empire.

A single narrow street leads up by a steep path from the low beach and steps have been cut in the solid rock to facilitate the access. The lower part of the street was occupied by inns which were crowded with people making a visit to the temple shrines. Numerous priests were going and coming among whom was one old man of venerable appearance whose thin long beard was bleached to snowy whiteness. Two young priests and another pilgrim were ascending the hill at the same time and invited us to go with them. We were glad to be under such guidance and joined their party on its pilgrimage to the different shrines.

There are three Buddhist and three Shinto temples on the island according to their account to which paths winding among the rocks, trees, and shrubbery conducted. The roofs of the temples were seen embowered amid the foliage as we approached the island from the beach. The temples were situated on level plateaus to which were flights of stone steps. They were all of them old and unpretending structures. The pilgrims paused before each to mutter a prayer over their clasped hands and to make an offering of a few cash. In this way we rambled over the island by the picturesque paths which led not only to the temples and shrines but to each spot which commands a fine view of the sea and adjacent lands.

One of these places [was] where there was a look down a sheer precipice falling abruptly to the water's edge into which the waves were chasing each other and boiling and surging among the rocks. It was a fearful chasm to look down into. A winding staircase of stone nearby led down to the water, and just as we were preparing to descend we were greeted by a beautiful vision. A group of twelve or fifteen girls coming up the staircase caught sight of us on the temple shelf above and started away among the shrubbery like a drove of startled deer. A pleasant word and the offer of gifts arrested their flight and while one of them timidly, yet with a smile, came up to receive what I offered, I had a moment's inspection of the beautiful group. They were all young apparently from ten to fourteen years and, in charge of female attendants, were visiting the wonders of the island. They were uniformly clad in red petticoats figured with white that fell to the knees and over the upper part of the body was the customary loose sack with flowing sleeves. On their heads were little hoods barely covering the top of the head, blue slashed with white. Their faces were painted and some of them had the exposed parts of their limbs covered with white powder. The bright colors contrasting prettily with their shining hair and dark eyes made the group not only one of beauty, but their shy graceful manners at once warm one's heart. For myself nothing I have ever seen in Nippon of animate or inanimate nature ever pleased me half so well. We descended the stone steps and a rough tortuous path that overhung the sea till we came down among the rocks which just here formed a large platform of stone. The surf just rising to the level of the rocks sent little streams running hither and thither over their surface.

Under the cliffs rising above us fifty to seventy feet we walked till we came to a large cave into whose open mouth the waves flowed and ebbed. The cave which heads under the island is at the entrance thirty feet high by twenty wide, and is evidently the work of the waves in some long ago years. Near it two wrinkly old crones had started the tea business among the rocks scarcely out of the water's reach and were dispensing the beverage to the pilgrims who were constantly going [in] and out of the cave.

Picking our way over the rocks and followed by a score of boys we with our guides entered the cave as far as daylight could lighten us, or a hundred feet or more. Here was a shrine on which lamps were lighted and near it a stream of pure cold water was gushing out of the rocks. A single attendant of the shrine was selling indulgences to explore the cave in the hither darkness and we too applied for the same, backing up our request with persuasive bribes.

The attendant, grimy with smoke, denied us and our gifts, "we were the first strangers who had ever come thither," he said, "and it might not do." Finding all persuasion pointless we watched the entrance of others. The females entered by the right of the shrine, and the males by the left, each and all bearing either torches or lamps. The popular superstition is that there are two cavernous paths leading under the island from behind the shrine which at some considerable distance is united in one and so in the bowels of the earth this subterranean path goes till it finds an outlet in a cavern of Mt. Fusi seventy miles distant! Two men in olden days, says the legend, went through to the mountain, an adventure which no one nowadays is bold enough to attempt. There is little doubt however that this is simply a cavernous opening under the abrupt island rocks for the low portion of all the adjacent country indicates that it goes no further. We imitated the pilgrims in bathing our hands and drinking at the gushing spring and withdrew.

Outside were a group of divers for the awabi, or pearl oysters, who for the consideration of an ichibu desired to gratify us with an exhibition of their skill in diving among the rocks amid the boiling water for the fish. Two of them stripped and creeping down to the water's edge stood or squatted with inflated lungs watching the wave for the right moment, a plunge and they were lost amid the foam, but after a half minute's absence reappeared on the surface, one of them with the awabi which he had plucked from the rocks and the other with a large prawn or lobster.

We left the pearl divers and clambered up the rocks again, strolled for a while longer among the picturesque island paths till it was time to mount and away. Frequent along these paths were little shops kept by women for the sale of mementos to the pilgrims. These consisted of a variety of shells, curious dried fish, sea weeds, corals, and various shell ornaments. We regretted that we were unable to carry these away. We descended again the narrow street amid a crowd of spectators to the beach where our landlord had well looked after our horses. As we rode away the crowd of young men and boys which was now very numerous followed us with loud shouts and even threw after us shells and bits of coral, being as rude as they dared to be.

Our direct road to Kamakura, where we proposed to spend the night, was for three or four miles on the sea beach. It was delightful riding thus by the sea under a sun not too warm and with soft air coming from off the water and the roar of the ocean swell as it fell exhausted on the sands. Leaving the beach we rode for a while inland, then again upon the beach, till we came to the long colonnade of trees which comes down to the water's edge from the temple of Hachiman a mile distant in Kamakura.

By the one side was a belt of pines also which had a uniform lean to the land of 20° so imposed by the force of the summer southeast gale. We struck across a broad plain which was covered with wheat and barley the latter of which was just coming into head, a sea of green flowing between the hills. Thus far today we seemed to have been without espionage but since leaving the last village two miles from Kamakura we had been followed by a well dressed respectable man whom at first we took for a fellow traveller, but as he kept an even pace with us and when once we turned back and rode through the avenue of trees to the water followed us even there, we concluded that as the otona [headman] of the little country village he had felt it his duty to escort us to the next town that he might, if hereafter called upon, be able to give account. However we lost sight of him as we rode into Kamakura.

As we drew up before the inn door near the temple of Hachiman, the same inn we had stopped at before on a previous visit, a crowd of villagers had collected to await our approach. Among them we recognized the face of a fat jolly official who had made himself so friendly and sociable on a previous visit, the face of our landlord, and the women of the inn who gave us welcome and bade us dismount. We asked if ourselves and horses could have shelter for the night as both we and they were tired with a long day on the road. A ready acquiescence was given and our horses were at once led into the back yard and we were ushered with every attention to our old quarters upstairs. We were more solicitous for our beasts than ourselves and went down again to see that they were provided for. This was not a stabling inn, but a shed used to shelter the rice harvesters was cleared out and with a few boards and straw ropes two stalls were well and securely put up in a short time. A carpenter with hammer, saw, and nails would not have done so well or so quickly. The Japanese are adepts at tying up a building from a temporary house shed to a theater, and there is the advantage not a board is marred by saw or nail. Our horses were well furnished for and we turned back to our room to rest ourselves on the clean mats and to be the center of a knot of the more important villagers who had a thousand questions to ask.

The celerity with which we travel on horseback compared to their easy ways on the road never fails to astonish them, and exclamations of surprise went from mouth [to mouth] when I told them we had left Kanagawa in the morning, halted at Fugeesawa, visited Ino Sima, and were now at Kamakura an hour before sunset. A distance of not more than thirty miles but a rapid movement in their eyes.

Supper was served, a fine fresh carp fried and dressed with soy, boiled rice, eggs and tea. The evening passed away pleasantly among the inquisitive people who examined our clothes, our persons, tested the fineness of our hair, the smoothness of our skins beneath, for there is nothing for which the Japanese have more admiration than the white skins of the foreigners. We were cautious who handled us or our clothing, for the children of our host had hands nearly raw with cutaneous eruptions and a young girl of fifteen years who honored

us with her presence for an hour was no better off. A burner of charcoal warmed our apartments and a candle of vegetable tallow diffused an equal amount of smoke and light. This was afterward removed and the night lamp brought in which is a saucer of oil with a pith wick at the edge placed in a tall paper covered frame. A pot of tea was ready at any moment and we sat and chatted till weary when one of the female servants and the eldest little girl amused us for an hour with a Japanese game of forfeits. Our fatigue brought an early drowsiness to which the dull pattering of the now falling rain on the tiled roof assisted and we indicated our wish to sleep.

Thick quilts were brought in and spread upon the mats, quilts which we could not inspect too narrowly, our male guests withdrew and the landlady and one of her servants waited to see us in bed and to cover us up before she could leave us. We had experience enough of Japan to make no other night toilet than to withdraw our boots. With my head on a wooden pillow made soft by a thin cushion I lay down, the buxom servant girl covered me up, closed the screen between us and another apartment where some of our late companions for the evening were sleeping, adjusted our lights, bade us good night and withdrew. Each one of our evening companions had done the same before leaving us wishing us "good rest," the little children bowing their heads to the mats as they said it. An official from the neighboring Honjin slept in the house below. Our fatigue brought us speedy repose.

Wednesday, April 17, 1861

At early daylight the outside shutters were withdrawn and a servant girl opening the screen thrust her head in to say "good morning" and again withdrew. She looked in again and finding us awake brought in a cup of tea and some pickled plums which she assured me were excellent to take in the morning. The landlady made her appearance next and proceeded to make some strange inquiries with a grave desire to be enlightened in a way that I could not gratify her curiosity. I called for water and was taken below stairs to a wash stand

under the verandah and supplied plentifully
with warm water in a copper basin but no tow-
els. The Japanese traveller of any pretension
carries all such requisites with him.

The morning was heavy with rain and wind
and it seemed as if we were to be weather
bound for the day. Other travellers who had
halted at the inn the evening before, provided
with their rain cloaks and hats, started out in
defiance of the storm leaving us to while away
the day as we best could. Fortunately about
nine o'clock the clouds broke away, the wind
and rain lulled, and we prepared again for the
road.

Bidding adieu to our hospitable hosts, we
started out of the village attended to the gate
by the dignitaries of the village who then took
leave of us. Our enthusiastic man followed us
without to his house and there in his eager desire to exhibit us to his wife seized our bridle
reins and fairly stopped our horses. We had
been lionized sufficiently and broke away from
his friendly detention.

The morning was fresh and beautiful after
the rain and the young green of the leaves had
that lovely brilliancy of hue which follows the
washing of the rain. Just outside of the town
among the hills we passed the tomb of Yoritomo so that I had been mistaken in supposing
that I had seen it before at the temple of
Hachiman. On one side of it was the tomb of
an ancient Prince of Satsuma and on the other
that of the lord of Mori. Long flights of stone
steps led to these tombs which were little chapels like the Shinto mias. The road from Kamakura to Kanasawa is the beau ideal of a
country road with its farm houses nestling
among the evergreens and cherry blossoms, itself winding through a beautiful valley bordered by woody ridges through some of which
the path had been cut like railroad cuttings.
These cut cliffs were overhung with trees and
ferns and shrubs, and creepers innumerable
clothed the rugged sides with living green. Numerous streams crossed our path or ran along
the road side tumbling in rapids over their
rocky beds or running smoothly amid the
grasses. The late rain had gemmed every leaf
with glistening pendants, the larches that overhung our road dripped their liquid crystals in
our path and tiny cascades innumerable ran

over the faces of the rocks and leaped to the
rivulets below. Pleasant odors were wafted in
our faces from the fields of colewort and the
blossoming cherry and peach trees.

A little before noon we halted at the tea
house of Kanasawa where groups of smiling
damsels bid us rest and take a cup of tea. We
remained till the clouds now thicker again
warned us to be off. We had not ridden far before a Scotch mist enveloped us, the road, too,
instead of the hard bed we had had in the
morning became more and more muddy and
we rode on towards Yokohama wet with the
rain and splashed with the dirt. We reached
the shelter of our own houses just in time to
escape a heavy shower and found that our bettos had started that morning in pursuit of us
with rain cloaks. I may add that they returned
at 2 A.M. the following morning, having in that
time gone to Ino Sima and back or as far as we
did, illustrating their trained powers of endurance for the road.

Thursday, April 18, 1861

Went to Kanagawa to meet Mr. Harris per
invitation. He thought it probable, owing to
Mr. Dorr's precarious situation, that he should
be obliged to appoint a new Consul and offered me the place if the contingency should
arrive. I declined to accept the post.

Friday, April 19, 1861

A charming day improved by a pleasant
walk on the bluffs. Feeling a little wearied by
my late ride.

Saturday, April 20, 1861

We hear that the Japanese are bent on keeping Oasaka closed in spite of the treaty. Sadajirō, who has just returned from Yedo, reports
that the disaffected men of Mito have been disposed of. They were summoned to meet their
lord and after a discussion of affairs, they confessed that they had been doing wrongfully,
the leader of them committed *Hara Kiri*, the

better portion of them were taken back into Mito's service and the others dispersed or imprisoned. Doubt seems to hang over the fate of old Mito, lately it was asserted that his death was feigned and now we hear again that he is really dead.

Sunday, April 21, 1861

After service a walk on the bluffs.

Monday, April 22, 1861

Had an interview with Von Siebold who arrived on the steamer *Scotland* two days since. He remembered my visit to him last summer in Nagasaki and gave me, as then, a cordial greeting. I found him in excellent health today and in his usual flow of spirits. Age has not subdued his activity or ardor. His table was covered with plants and roots which he had already been gathering from the hills and vallies about Kanagawa. His visit to our section of Japan has been at the request of the Government, for what purpose has not yet transpired. At all events he said he should remain here a few months and we propose to have some walks together among the fields and woods to which I look forward with great pleasure.

He entered freely into discussion of Japanese affairs and I was sustained in some opinions I had formed of the political condition of this country by his maturer and better trained judgement. He regards the present government as very weak and unable to check or control the powerful daimios. Since the year 1600 the house has been four times usurped, legitimacy is lost, or is little represented by daimios whose families were anciently of the imperial family. Mito, Owari, and Kaga [scil. Kii] are of those who claim a right to the throne of the Tycoon. Hence spring difficulties with the foreigners who are used by those opposed to the present dynasty to bring upon it trouble and foreign complications. The murders of foreigners may have had their rise out of this spirit or they may have been committed by bravados who wished to try their new swords on some more distinguished mark than an ordinary Japanese.

Dr. Von Siebold does not regard the policy of Russia as aggressive towards this country. On the other hand he takes the ground that Russia prefers rather to preserve Japan in her integrity to act the part of a friend to her than to seize upon and occupy the country herself. The government of Japan is an absolutism and as such demands the sympathy of Russia.

Tuesday, April 23, 1861

Spent the day photographing.

Wednesday, April 24, 1861

To Kanagawa, Dorr's and Mrs. H[epburn]'s.

Thursday, April 25, 1861

Took a long ride on the Kanagawa side of the bay. Deciduous trees are rapidly leafing out, barley coming into head, rape blossoms falling. By the roadside a cat had killed one of the large fangless snakes which abound in this country. Returning home I saw a good illustration of the Japanese care for old things in a board fence in front of a man's house the panels of which were made of old worm eaten wood. I have often seen such wood used for ornaments, and flowers trained upon old stumps are favorite designs for yard and garden ornaments.

Friday, April 26, 1861

Short walk with Dr. Von Siebold whose enthusiasm for his favorite studies is unlimited by his years.

Saturday, April 27, 1861

Photographing unsuccessfully.

Sunday, April 28, 1861

In the afternoon took a walk on the bluffs and nothing in the face of nature could be more beautiful than the lovely aspect of fields and valleys and hills all clad in their new summer robes of vivid green. The wheat and barley fields now in their full growth were waving in the wind, through openings in the leafy woods were glimpses of green hills beyond down in the vallies among the pines and cedar the thatched roofs of the cottages were more than half hid, the bay was flecked with foam and on its surface flares of mist-like cloud shadows were chasing each other. K.[32] and I lay on the green cliff over the water watching the junks come and go, thus breathing of the winds in the deep till we were lulled into sleep and the afternoon was nearly spent. How much I wished Fred or Dr. W., or the two Johns, or the brothers out of the old store, or any of my old companions for a Sunday afternoon could have lain on the grassy slope with me.

Monday, April 29, 1861

S[adajirō], the Japanese, speaking today of robberies says the erotic propensity of the Japanese leaves them to commit robbery more than any other crime. So well known is this that at every Oshiwara minute registers are kept of every person entering, his name, residence, personal appearance, the hour of arriving and departure, the money expended for courtesans, for food, wine, dancing girls, etc., which register is provided daily to the authorities for the better detection of all criminals. This has passed into such a custom that foreigners are so registered as well as natives. A native man of rank, wealth, or position desirous to keep his visits to such places secret readily compounds the matter with a small sum of money.

[32] This may have also been William Keswick.

Tuesday, April 30, 1861

Went to Kanagawa. General Dorr, our Consul, too ill to be seen. Muragaki, late Ambassador to America, is Governor of Hakodade; before leaving for the post he purchased of Consul D[orr] his horses and carriage to take with him, paying $300 therefore.

Wednesday, May 1, 1861

A low barometer all day indicating storm and wind which did not come.

Thursday, May 2, 1861

Today was the appointed time for the execution of a Japanese accused of having fired various buildings in Yokohama, the penalty of which is death by stake and faggots. At nine A.M. the criminal was paraded through the streets as a public spectacle. He was mounted on horseback, clothed in a loose white cotton robe with his hands and feet secured by ropes of straw. He was held on the horse by attendants on either side, the animal being led by two more. He was preceded by a squad of police and yakunins on foot and another squad followed in the rear attended by a mounted official. Directly in front of the criminal was a large paper banner, setting forth the crime for which the prisoner was to suffer, his name, age, and the province to which he belonged, and behind him a board was borne similarly inscribed. Following him also was a man carrying the pole and sling of a ninsoku emblematical of the rank to which the victim belonged.

A great concourse of people lined the streets and followed the procession and I must do them the justice to say they behaved orderly, exhibited no brutality of feeling and even less levity than would be witnessed at a public execution at home. The criminal was a most forlorn and pitiable looking object. He had been in confinement for a hundred days, was exceedingly emaciated, his lips were swelled, his eyes tumid, and he looked as if he had little capability of suffering remaining.

After being led through the principal streets he was led out of town past the Governor's residence to his place of execution, a knoll of elevated land in the midst of beautiful groves and cultivated fields, as if in mocking contrast to his fate. Shortly before reaching the fatal ground the procession was halted in a shaded lane and refreshments were given the man who had but a long quarter or at best a half an hour to live. He ate heartily of the rice and other food and his attendants gave him bountifully draughts of sake which must have further helped to stupefy the little sense he had remaining.

On the summit of the knoll in front of a grove of cedars an acre of ground had been set off by stakes and ropes in the center of which a pillar was erected. To this pillar the criminal was bound by lashings around his feet, body, hands, and neck, of straw ropes. But so feeble was he that he did not hold his head up till another rope had been tied to the top knot of his hair and passed around the post. I suspect, as it is asserted by the Japanese common people, the prisoner either voluntarily, or with the aid of his executioners, is thus strangled into insensibility before the faggots are fired. From where I stood I could see his breathing became labored and his respiration reduced to twenty four in a minute. The tying completed, the ropes of straw were next plastered with clay to prevent their burning off and bundles of a long coarse dry rush were heaped about and over him, till he was buried out of sight.

Three of the higher officials sat at a little distance overlooking the affair while the others acted as police. A half dozen men were employed in carrying out the details of the execution. At a signal from one torches were lighted and the pyre ignited at every point simultaneously. The flames leaped over the dry rushes as if they had been powder, and quick as a headman's axe, quicker than the hangman's rope, the victim within must have been stifled. In two or three moments the rushes were burned away exposing the blackened scorched body still fast to its pillar, yet faster in death. Torches of lighted straw were placed to the mouth and nostrils to make assurance doubly sure, other parts of the body were searched

but there was no longer [of] life a sign. The head attendant, then most of the supervising officials on bended knee, made report that the deed was accomplished, water was thrown on the smoking embers, and the body was left to stand for three days a public spectacle before being wholly consumed.

The Japanese claim that their rulers deprecate passing a capital sentence and say that the Governor of Yokohama in this instance would not have punished the man capitally had he persisted in his innocence instead of confessing his crime. This hardly coincides with the well known use of the rack to compel confessions.

A story of romantic interest is related, the parties to which resided in Yedo many years ago. A merchant having been burned out in a sweeping conflagration had a temporary abode among the priests of a temple. While living thus a strong attachment sprang up between his only daughter of fifteen years and a young priest. It was impossible that her hopeless passion could have fruition in marriage for this was contrary to the tenets of Buddhism as well as in opposition to her father's wishes. But she nurtured her illicit attachment till it became an all devouring passion. Afterwards when her father had rebuilded his home and taken her thereto, shut up in its seclusion she could no longer see her enamoring priest. Despairing of meeting him again she resolved to burn her father's house, hoping that they would thus be driven to the compound of the monastery again. She lighted the flames and then tolled herself the alarm bell. The flames devoured other houses than her own home and the fact of her first giving the alarm having aroused suspicion she was arrested and confessed her guilt.

By Japanese law acts committed by a female fifteen years old or upwards are regarded as the acts of adults, less than that age they may plead the favor of infancy. The Governor of Yedo moved by the great beauty and constancy of the young girl, and willing to save her had arranged a mode of escape. Her father was told to instruct her to reply yes to all the Governor's queries. When the examination began the tender hearted Governor [asked], "You are fourteen years old?" The girl instructed to shun falsehood disobeyed her father's instructions and replied that she was not fourteen but fifteen. Japanese law had its course and the brave girl was burnt at the stake but became not only the heroine of the hour, but her memory is perpetuated on the Japanese stage where the story of the girl who refused to lie to save her life is a favorite representation.

There has been one other instance of a female executed for the same crime according to the native story tellers. This too was a tale of love. A girl, "beautiful and lovely," is to be wedded, but being poor she asks of her lover ten kobangs to purchase her bridal outfit. The ungallant lover refuses, and the maiden's love turned to anger has all the fierceness the poet gives it. In revenge she fires her betrothed's house, but unfortunately involves many others in his ruin. She is at once suspected, and on her examination before the Governor confesses her crime and gives the reasons therefor. "I condemn you to the stake," says the just Governor, "but since it was for the want of a poor ten kobangs that you did the crime, I will loan you that sum which you are to repay me one half ichibu per year and when the sum is repaid your sentence shall be executed." Ten kobangs being the equivalent of forty ichibus, the erring damsel had a lease of life as well as money for eighty years, and though justice was balked of its victim the way in which it was done was so captivating to the eastern fancy from the day of Harun al-Rashid till now, that the Governor's praises were in every mouth.

Friday, May 3, 1861

At home writing, walking in the fields, and paid a visit to Consul Dorr, who is better.

Saturday, May 4, 1861

A long walk with Mr. Fortune[33] who is again in Japan making collections of plants, trees, in-

sects, etc. His intimate knowledge of the flora of northern Asia, his wide experience as a traveller, and his social qualities make him an interesting as well instructive companion.

Sunday, May 5, 1861

The head of the secret police whose daughter, a little girl of sixteen years, is under S[immons]'s medical treatment for syphilis spent an hour with us this evening. He is a man having a police force under him of thirty men, five of whom are at Kanagawa, and seems to have more knowledge of Japanese execution of justice than anyone I have hitherto met. Speaking of the recent execution he says the prisoner was so reduced by want of food that he could have lived but a few days longer if he had not been executed. "Why a want of food," we asked. He said he was too ill to eat, which meant his confinement in the rigors of a Japanese prison had made him too ill to eat. I asked him if the prisoner about to be burned was not permitted to strangle himself or was strangled by the officers, that, he replied, depended on the will of the man who was the executioner who permitted it or not as he chose, though generally he said the victim was strangled into insensibility before the flames were lighted. This man's crime was an attempt to fire Kemptner's[34] godowns and other smaller offences. Revenge for blood he says is only permitted in the heat of an encounter; a cold blooded pursuit and revenge afterwards is not allowed, differing on this point from information I have otherwise had. Punishment by the husband for adultery is also allowed only when the parties are taken in the act. If a kinsman has been slain and the murderer is afterwards arrested his fate depends on the will of the relatives of the murdered; that is, they have influence to procure the murderer's death or imprisonment, or even his entire escape, as they choose. The murder of parents, brothers,

[33] Robert Fortune was a well-known botanist who visited both China and Japan in the early 1860s. He subsequently published *Yedo and Peking* (London: John Murray, 1863) in which he described his travels and findings. Chapter 13 of his book deals with his return

visit to Kanagawa and Yokohama in 1861. As an amateur botanist Hall enjoyed his outings with Fortune.

[34] W. Kemptner & Co. was an English trading house. See *The China Directory* (Hong Kong: Shortrede & Co. 1862), p. 52.

sisters, near relatives, counterfeiting, and arson are crimes invariably demanding capital punishment. Women are liable to the same penalties as males. When a criminal is to be executed capitally his fate is not made known to him til the day of his execution, nor is the particular day known to even the officers of justice till on the very one of the execution of the sentence.

Monday, May 6, 1861

Chusan arrived bringing no letters for me. The secession news fills us all with unpleasant sensations. That the country and great sisterhood of states we left united should be rent into fragments is not only most deplorable to us, but an unhappy page in the world's history.

Tuesday, May 7, 1861

House cleaning.

Wednesday, May 8, 1861

Dr. Von Siebold called in the afternoon and was as usual full of life and in a conversational flow. He examined my mineral specimens with much interest. In course of a conversation carried on to some disadvantage through our imperfect understanding of each other, he advanced the to me novel idea that Ghengis Khan and ——— [Yoshitsune] the brother of Yoritomo were one and the same persons. He is said to have fled to Yeso after his defeat by his brother, from thence to Saghalin and the Amour, where we first hear of the great Tartar conqueror. The dates of the lives of Genghis Khan and the Japanese coincide. The idea is a novel one and, if true, one of the most interesting facts of history.

Thursday, May 9, 1861

House repairing.

Friday, May 10, 1861

A sudden change in the temperature, thermometer falling to 56°. Caught cold. Dined in the evening at Walsh's, met Loureiro, Hooper, Clarke, and others. Some amusing anecdotes of early life in Japan were narrated. S. goes on Sunday to Nagasaki to reside.[35]

Sadajirō, who comes to my house almost daily, now tells me that anciently the interment of a mirror with one deceased was universal and that the custom still obtains among the princely families. It is obviously derived from Shintoism. Another bit of information which I doubt is that the art of making porcelain was introduced from China not more than 250 years ago, nothing but earthen having been previously employed. The written character for porcelain is still the name of its first introducer.

Saturday, May 11, 1861

Very ill in the evening from my cold which threatened local inflammation. Hot foot baths and diaphoretics gave me some relief, no sleep.

Monday, May 13, 1861

Confined to the house by the effects of the cold and much prostrated. Goble comes in and tells me he has hope of being employed by the Prince of Higo to erect a lumber mill on the island of Amakusa! As all his encouragement is derived from a physician of Higo it cannot be called very reliable.

[35] This is the first reference to any direct contact with the Walsh brothers in Yokohama. Hall had already become friends with Dr. Hall, the agent for Walsh & Co. But as reference on this occasion is to Walsh, we may presume that this invitation came from Thomas Walsh and not Dr. Hall. It would also appear that he was introduced at this dinner to some of the leading traders in Yokohama. Edward Clarke was the head of Dent & Co., H. J. Hooper headed Heard & Co., and Eduardo Loureiro was in charge of his own trading firm.

S. would appear to have been Von Siebold, who was on his way back to Nagasaki.

Tuesday, May 14, 1861

B[lekman] the French interpreter says that the Japanese have formally notified the foreign representatives that they will not open Yedo and Hiogo (which must include Oasaca) according to treaty stipulation and if the Foreign Powers make it a case of quarrel they must meet the consequences. Dr. H[epburn] confirms the statement.

Wednesday, May 15, 1861

Distinguished strangers from Yedo have paid Yokohama a visit today including one of the Ministers of Foreign Affairs and several other dignitaries of less note. They have visited the foreign location and been out upon the bluffs inspecting the proposed sites of the consular and other residences. The respect paid to these upper people by officials below them, and the servility of the common people, marks strongly the class divisions of Japanese society. Able to walk out today.

Thursday, May 16, 1861

Preparing letters for the *Onward*.

Friday, May 17, 1861

Today is Buddha's birthday and a great day among his followers. At Kanagawa it was a great holiday at the beautiful temples of Bookenji [Bukenji]. I went over to Kanagawa by boat and then, taking my horse, rode out through the fields by the pleasant rural paths that lead to Bookenji. Truly all Kanagawa was making a holyday of it. Last year this anniversary was a day of heavy rain, but no day could be finer than this. The aspect of the country covered everywhere with new leaves and growing crops, animated with groups of well dressed people and children threading the little lanes up the valley of Bookenji, was a charming picture of the happiness of peasant life in Japan.

Unwilling to disturb the numerous parties who were either going or returning by the same path, I walked my horse slowly along enjoying the sight. I overtook one group after another, all of whom greeted me with smiling faces. First was a group of children of all ages merrily trotting along looking so ruddy, bright, and clean in their gay clothes and with their well trimmed hair that now as ever I can hardly believe they grew up into the rougher looking peasantry that fill the farm houses. The little girls with their glittery hair ornaments, their fillets of crape, their bright crimson undergarments rolling away about the throat and falling about the knees, their well washed faces and hands, not to say the powder and paint to which I have become so accustomed that I no longer regard it a blemish, their wide cinctures of silk and satin gathered in their great ties behind, their clean sandals, and above all bright happy faces were my companions by the way.

There were groups of old women walking slowly together and merry housewives showing their black teeth as they trudged laughingly along with their little charges. And there were men, singly or in groups, bare headed, or with a handkerchief twisted around the head or a great bowl shaped hat covering them from the sun. There were fathers with one, two, or three children going to keep this holy day, one in particular I noticed whose little daughter was most gaily dressed and painted and riding on his shoulders balancing over her head her tiny paper parasol of pictures. So all over the plain these sun shades were floating along as it were over the tops of the grain. Other parties were coming away. Some with mementoes in their hands. Children with toys, little vases of gold fish, tops, and some sensible boys had pots of young trees which they should plant and in after years still retain a remembrance of the visit to Bookenji. There were parties of young men flushed with health and sake, and young soldiers respectful and quiet.

As I got nearer the temples I dismounted, and giving my horse to my betto proceeded on foot to the avenue that leads up the long slope on which the temples are, terminating in a flight of steps and a little mia at the top of the hill under the shade of a venerable pine of more than 20 feet girth. Entering this avenue lined on either side with hedgerows of shade trees I found it full of people, mostly children. On either side of the principal temple gate were rows of refreshment tables, stands of confectionery, fancy articles of dress such as hair pins, tobacco pouches, combs, and children's toys innumerable. Each table was besieged by a crowd of little traffickers. Further up the hill on a broad green mound near another temple and under the shade of trees were parties picnicking in the open air. It was a charming open spot begirt with the trim cottages of the priests and overlooking the avenues through which were wandering the gaily dressed throngs. With their mats spread upon the grass for seats and tables alike these people gave themselves up to the enjoyment of the day with as much apparent zest as any party of picnickers on the banks of the Connecticut or Hudson. In one spot would be a party of genial men, at another a group of boys and girls taken care of by some tidy matron, or again the more pleasing family group where parents, children and friends forget together that they were the sons of toil. At the temple nearby a young priest was vociferously praying to an audience mostly of women and young girls. He needed to exert his lungs as he did for the mostly shifting throng of comers in and goers out would have drowned a meeker gospeller. Offerings of cash tied up in white paper were deposited in or on the offering chest.

At the main temple in front of the door a metal image of Buddha a finger's length was elevated in a shallow dish of water on a high pedestal. The more frequent worshippers here were father and mother and children who came together and performed a sort of vicarious baptism. Instead of sprinkling their own children they poured libations of water over the metal Buddha and as the liquid flowed back into the receptacle they dipped their fingers in it touching their eyes with it and their children's and sometimes drinking thereof. Plentiful offerings of cash were here too.

Wherever I moved about I was treated kindly and amid many hundreds met not a single frown. Several recognized me and one trio in particular who were taking their fish, rice, and sake under the shade of a neighboring campanile insisted upon my sharing their meal. So I sat down under the throat of the bell and partook of their food while a crowd gathered around to observe me.

Pleased with my kind reception everywhere I went back to the boy vendors and loading myself down with tops, mirrors, hair pins, globes of glass filled with water and abundance of cakes by the outlay of what seemed a small fortune to the boys, but a trifle in itself, I went back again to the belfry where the merry children were scattered about among the trees. I soon had a crowd of bright faces around me and first giving the tops to the boys, throwing them hither and thither among the grass, I called for the little girls and made many a one happy with the simple gift of a hair pin, comb, or mirror. If they enjoyed it so did I. Then with my paper bag of cakes I tried to console those who had not been fortunate to get anything more valuable. Of course this put me in the best footing and I was beset from all sides to join the little parties at their meals and one stout wife had my legs out from under me before I could resist her husband's proffered sake. So passing among the groups and exchanging salutations, I bid them goodbye hoping they would not regret that a foreigner had intruded on their religious festival. I am sure they did not. Happy saionaras followed me as I went to remount.

On my way back among the returning parties I passed two little girls of ten, one of whom was bewailing her finery soiled by an unlucky fall in the mud. It was a sad ending for her day of pleasure, but I lifted her up into smiles again with giving her the last of my small pocket change. These days among the people when they have thrown off their toils are among my pleasantest days in Japan.

Saturday, May 18, 1861

The Tycoon has addressed a letter to the President of the United States desiring that the opening of the remaining ports stipulated for under the Harris Treaty, to wit, Yedo, Oasaca and Hiogo, and Neegata, or other port on the West Coast, be postponed. Accompanying the letter was a memorial from the Goroju, or Imperial Council of Five, setting forth the difficulties of opening so many ports within so short a time, the embarrassments of the Government to properly regulate commercial intercourse, and claiming a certain amount of discontent on the part of the people which they feared would increase to a point difficult to control. Therefore they pray that the time of opening these ports be extended seven years.

No doubt the Japanese labor more or less under the embarrassments of a novel position, but they are notoriously such prevaricators to carry their own ends that all they claim must be taken with large allowances. There are no inherent difficulties in the way of opening these ports at the appointed time that would not exist seven years later. The opening of Yedo so far as trade goes might be well omitted altogether, it would only be the question of conceding so much to an Asiatic despotism that does not know how to appreciate high motives. The Japanese have encouragement to make the demand from their success hitherto in carrying out their own views, and the language of the late correspondence between the American and English Ministers growing out of Heusken's murder was of a character to give license to an attempt yet further [to] impinge not only on the spirit but the very letter of the Treaty.

Who are the "people" who are restive? The lower classes are not formidable to the powers that be, unless aided by a faction among the daimios, and the only people the Government fears are the daimios and their dependents who for selfish ends would seize any pretext to overthrow the present dynasty. It is possible that the central government is too weak to maintain its proper discipline against its opposers at so many points, and it is precisely this, I opine, that urges the request. The same letter and memorial is also issued to the Treaty Powers in Europe.

Sunday, May 19, 1861

Trying the benefit of daily horseback rides on my cold and weak chest. Today rode among the beautiful vales of Kanagawa accompanied only by my betto.

Monday, May 20, 1861

Rode to Kanagawa on horseback and returned by boat before breakfast. The country begins to show the effect of a long absence of sufficient rain. The boat ride reminded of old tropical mornings, the bay was smooth as glass, the waters were rippling against the beach, and the dark morning clouds overhanging the rich foliage of the shores gave it a darker hue and slumberous calm. I could almost believe myself rowing ashore at Java with my Malay boatmen. On the shores the showy white flowers of the viburnum look like rifts of snow among the green leaves.

Tuesday, May 21, 1861

The chief of the police being in in the evening we questioned him upon many things, among others why our servants were obliged to pay a squeeze of eight tempos per month to the yakunins. He replied that the compensation went to a man who kept a register of all foreigners' servants, their names, ages, where they came from, and other particulars of personal identity. It was but one example of the absolute knowledge this government endeavors to obtain of all its subjects, particularly those in foreign service. Wages were spoken of, six ichibus per month was a high rate of wages for a Japanese to pay, the majority received but three or four. A woman servant would receive her living, clothing, and one or two ichibus per month. Carpenters get six to eight tempos per day. Stone masons eight, but these I think are better wages than were formerly paid before foreigners came.

Merchants are allowed to wear silk, so he says in contradiction to others, servants not, even servants of a prince.

Salutation depends on the rank of the person saluted, the head only may be inclined, or the head and body, or the head and body and the hands brought forward and placed on the knees, then slid down half way to the ankles, quite to the feet, then kneeling down and inclining the head at various angles till the most humble salutation brings the forehead to the floor.

Prisoners at Yokohama are variously treated, but as the jail is seldom full they have usually room enough to move about and lie down. At Yedo, where the jails are oftentimes crowded, twelve men are put into a room a mat square or six feet square, thus huddled together they can take no rest by any change of position from kneeling closely impacted together. Their food is only rice, unless their friends pay for better fare, and who may also pay for more spacious lodgings. They are often whipped and a long confinement ends in release by death. The merry paper hanger, half doctor half priest, whom we knew at Kanagawa and who was put in jail a year ago for selling coins, particularly copper cash, died in jail quite recently.

The whole system of courtesanship is a regular one. A man of rank who takes a concubine out of a family is expected to maintain a large circle of his mistress's relatives giving not only food and clothing but also fulfilling frequent demands for money, for the man of rank makes no stipulated price. A merchant, or man of low class, on the other hand, bargains with the parents for their daughter buying her for one, two, or more years and paying for her from one to three hundred ichibus according to her marketable value, which depends not only on her comeliness of person but on her manners, disposition, her accomplishments, such as singing and dancing. Hired from the houses of prostitution all prices are paid from three ichibus monthly to fifty or more. The girl who is purchased for a term of years is for that time the absolute property of her lord and may be sold by him again even to the public shambles. For the regular courtesans various prices are paid. A girl of poor parents and no accomplishments may be bought for 20 or 30 ichibus per annum, or for a term of twelve years for 200, while one more accomplished will demand from one to two hundred per annum, but she must be of an exceptional class to bring so high a price. The former girl sells her favors for two tempos, or eight if her visitor tarries all night, the latter receives for her master 6 ichibus. The prices paid for these poor creatures, as stated above, I believe are rather above than below the mark.

Wednesday, May 22, 1861

Indoors all day writing for the *Onward*.

Thursday, May 23, 1861

Finished letters for the *Onward* and went to Kanagawa to Consul Dorr's. Unexpectedly met there Mr. Fortune who has just come down from Yedo, whither he went on invitation of Mr. Harris, but it appears . . .[36]

Friday, May 24, 1861

The native theater is again opened having as an attractive novelty a mixed company of males and females, the latter personating the male characters but not so successfully as the boy troupe lately presented female characters. The leading actor was the female who had charge of the troupe and was the teacher of the others. She was a woman of thirty years or

---

[36] This sentence is not completed in the journal, but Fortune in his book *Yedo and Peking* elucidates the missing portion. As is indicated above, Fortune had gone to Edo at the invitation of Harris because Minister Alcock was absent and Mr. Myburgh, his temporary replacement, refused to grant Fortune permission. Fortune published the angry exchange of letters between himself and Myburgh, in which Myburgh wrote: "I care not to be informed now for what object you have come to Japan, or that Her Majesty's Minister would have granted you permission to visit Yedo had he been here—I only know that you are a private individual in a private capacity in this country, and that you have not asked for nor received the requisite sanction from the British authority here to come up to Yedo. It is of no consequence to me now what you were given to understand at Kanagawa; but you must have been well aware that the American Minister has not the power to grant you, or any other British subject, permission to visit Yedo" (Fortune, *Yedo and Peking*, p. 195). Hall had had a similar run in with his minister, Harris, earlier and thus could sympathize with Fortune. He objected, however, to Harris's willingness to invite others—including citizens of other nations such as Fortune—to visit Edo, when he was exceedingly reluctant to extend such invitations to the citizens of his own country.

so and her pupils were girls from twelve to eighteen. The playing was Japanese, good, and a scene where a mother endeavors to have a last interview with her child who is to be put to death by being immersed in a caldron of boiling water for assisting to a murder broke down even Japanese insensibility. Visible and audible weeping prevailed throughout the audience, among men as well as women, one old man looking on with streaming eyes.

As the audience dispersed some women who passed H[eco] all said "we have been crying a great deal." So who shall say that the Japanese stage, rude as it is, does not hold the mirror up to nature. In this execution scene the boy was brought on the stage strung in a rope basket over a coolie's shoulders, and his father, who was to suffer with him, came on to the stage [on] horseback bound in the usual manner of criminals and preceded by officers with staves and a tablet inscribed with his offence borne aloft. The horse was represented by a framework made to represent that animal and covered with a shaggy cloth of bay color, while two men did the legs and locomotion part; the head was moveable and there was some by play between the animal disposed to be refractory and his attendant who lead him by the bridle.

We went behind the scenes and were as usual courteously received; admitted to the dressing room of the young ladies who suspended no toilet operations on our account. One with her garments off her shoulders and hanging from her girdle was rubbing her neck with white paint, she rose up to welcome us and in this demi toilette escorted us around. Another girl in similar dishabille sat in front of the manager, both squatted on the mats, while the latter was painting her eyebrows. In another room was another group dressed and half dressed and some were eating. This scene was accompanied by characteristic comment from the group of Japanese about, in which some of the girls did not scruple to take part. My seat was during the play where I could see behind the dress curtain and between acts I was surprised by an apparition of a half nude female leaning over the balustrade of stairs that led up from the rear of the stage. A few moments satisfied our curiosity and giving the young ladies some trifling presents I left them

and resumed my seat. These gifts were afterwards acknowledged from the stage by repeated bows from behind the scenes.

Saturday, May 25, 1861

Closing letters for the *Onward*.

Sunday, May 26, 1861

At church. Afterwards reading in my room in the afternoon.

Monday, May 27, 1861

Rain preceding night and all day. At home.

Tuesday, May 28, 1861

Horseback ride on the Kanagawa side, found the people commencing the rape harvest. Rice had begun to be transplanted, the wild honey suckles were in bloom and I gathered raspberries in the woods. Coming back on the Tokaido I met a group of little misses who were having a holiday. They were from ten to twelve years old and were attired alike in dark maroon dresses embroidered at the bottom, with crimson crape petticoats, sashes of dark red silk and satin, and fillets of red crape in their hair. From the cincture of the waist a charm hung pendant in front. I gave them a merry salutation and they ran before and with me to a tea house which was their headquarters and where three or four well dressed comely matrons looked after them.

In one room was a dais covered with cushions on which three of the girls were sitting and before them knelt all the others; they were enacting some simple game or play of kings and queens. Seeing me dismount before their tea house they scattered in every direction laughing and shouting, but a friendly word soon brought them back about me, and sending the landlady after some cakes and confectionery, we were soon on the best of terms. After I had given the cakes, then I must take a little of each one's cakes as a token of friendship. At my request they all rose in a flock and mounted the dais as happy as possible. I rose to go, but they all came around me again bowing low and thanking me, wishing me many a goodbye and that I would come again.

Wednesday, May 29, 1861

A proposed ride to Kanasawa and Mississippi Bay prevented by the rain.

Thursday, May 30, 1861

To Kanagawa early and found the Kanasawa excursionists had passed me on their way. They returned at evening after a pleasant day and spanking ride.

Friday, May 31, 1861

A Japanese physician to whom I have been giving instructions how to make mirrors was in today quite delighted with his success.[37] He thinks he is on the highway to a fortune. The making of mirrors, lucifer matches, and soap, has especially attracted attention of the people for the supply of common everyday wants.

Saturday, June 1, 1861

Walk in the country. Wild roses, honeysuckles, deutzia in blossom, barley fields ready for the harvest.

Sunday, June 2, 1861

Fiery Cross arrived from Shanghai bringing news from America to the 11th of March including Lincoln's inauguration. The prospect of a permanent division of our beloved country saddens the hearts of all her sons abroad. The *Fiery Cross* made great dispatch it being but 15 days since she left our port for Shanghai. Our home mails are unfortunately on the *Ringdove* which is acting escort to Minister Alcock.

Monday, June 3, 1861

Called on the Japanese doctor today who is quite delighted with his success in manufacturing mirrors which I have taught him. He is the first manufacturer of them in Japan.

Tuesday, June 4–Wednesday, June 5, 1861

Busy packing boxes to send home per *Fiery Cross*.

Thursday, June 6, 1861

It appears that his August Majesty the Tycoon is not wholly unapproachable. On certain occasions his domains are thrown open to the gentry of Yedo and the common people who are cared for and fed in good old baronial style. These occasions are the accession of a new Emperor, a royal marriage, the birth of a son, the building of a new palace, or any other great time of rejoicing in the imperial household. There has been lately such a convention, the occasion being the finishing and occupancy of the new palace. All property holders were invited to the Emperor's castle and made honorable guests for a whole day. They were freely supplied with eatables and drink and entertained with spectacles of a theatrical character. Better than this, they had free audience of the Emperor and were permitted to talk with him freely on all public or private interests. The unbending of monarchy on these occasions is a striking feature in this government.

---

[37] While we do not know the name of this doctor-entreprneur, Walsh, Hall & Co. did end up the major importer of mercury (used to make mirrors) into Japan in the mid-1860s. See letter from C. D. Mugford to Albert F. Heard dated July 26, 1864, Heard Collection, Baker Library, Harvard Business School (Heard I, V. HM-57, Folder II, Letters of C. D. Mugford).

On such an occasion the princes and nobles of the realm are less honored than these guests from ordinary life. They have the direct ear of the Emperor with whom they may talk without the intervention of intermediates. A free subject of converse at this time was the high price of food and the happy result was that at the solicitation of the Emperor an immediate reduction in price was arranged of which I have lately written, viz., on rice of 15 percent, peas and beans and oil of 25 to 30 percent! Having heard this interesting statement from various sources I give it full credit.

Friday, June 7, 1861

Shipped 8 boxes of assorted Japanese wares per *Fiery Cross* for New York and quite rejoiced to get them off.

Saturday, June 8, 1861

To Kanagawa and called upon Mr. Fortune to look at his collection of plants, among them some singular maples, a row of beautiful ferns, a colored deutzia and some other novelties. He has been much annoyed by the theft of some of his rarities. Dined with Dr. and Mrs. H[epburn].

Sunday, June 9, 1861

A delightful day after the rains. Walking down the street with K.[38] he was accosted by a native merchant with whom he had some misunderstanding as to affairs. K. declined to have any conversation then and there, the merchant as usual was pertinacious and obtrusive and insisted upon following. K. after repeated warnings to him to leave lost patience,

perhaps not unreasonably, and struck the man with his open hand, even this did not serve, nor did a second slap, till K. irritated beyond control knocked the man down, then one of the merchant's partners came to his aid and shared the fate of his fallen comrade. I then interfered and urged K. away, but as we were leaving the spot one of them threw his wooden shoe after us hitting me in the back of the neck, whereupon K. turned around and gave the first one he met a severe blow in the face and knocked them both down again. I once more interfered and drawing K.'s arm through mine persuaded him away. The Japs[39] were sufficiently punished to keep quiet. Indeed they were but children in K.'s brawny strength. I was very regretful of the occurrence, but should have cared much less had it been some other day. K. immediately turned home and reported the affair to the Custom House, where of course it will be buried in oblivion.

Monday, June 10, 1861

Busy closing letters and invoices for the *Fiery Cross*, which leaves tomorrow noon. Towards evening took a walk on the hills and found the farmers busy securing their barley. The whole population seemed to be in the fields, men, women, and such children as were old enough to do labor. In gathering the harvest of wheat and barley, which is done at a "catching" season for rain, females are seen at work in the fields, so also they are employed in transplanting and again in gathering the rice. Today some were cutting the grain, some were whipping the heads over coarse wooden sieves or bars of wood, others were burning off the heads, others were thrashing, and all over the face of the country was to be seen the smoke rising from the burning refuse straw which is generally burned on the fields where it grows.

[38] K. is not clearly identified, but he may have been William Keswick who headed Jardine, Matheson & Co. Hall identifies K. as "brawny" in strength and this would fit other descriptions of Keswick who was also "foreman" of the local volunteer fire brigade, a position which Harold S. Williams tells us "was generally held by a Keswick or some such similar stalwart of one of the

princely hongs, provided he had brawn and waist line, and enough wind to run a mile." See Harold S. Williams, *Shades of the Past* (Tokyo: Charles E. Tuttle & Co., 1959), p. 18.

[39] It should be noted that this is the first use of this term in the journal.

The crop of wheat and barley about us is good. And now farmers are sowing on the same lands a crop of beans.

Punishment of criminals. S[adajirō] says when a man has been imprisoned for stealing he is marked on the arm with a transverse line of india ink. In a second offence he receives a second line, and if he is found already twice marked, for the third offence he is executed.

Tuesday, June 11, 1861

A heavy rain today shutting all within doors. The *Fiery Cross* left at 12 M. and must have encountered a gale going out. 4½ inches of rain fell according to Dr. H.'s[40] observations.

A *merchant's residence*. In Yokohama lives a merchant Nakai [Nakaiya],[41] whose residence is one of the curiosities of the place. It is situated on the principal business street and consists of one large main fireproof building used as a shop and residence and several outbuildings, fire proof warehouses, etc. The building is conspicuous to one passing in the street by its dark heavy tiles, roof timbers, and its massive perpendicular sign over the main entrance. Curtains of dark blue cotton emblazoned with the merchant's name and marks depend from the eaves in front till they sweep the earth and enclose the narrow sidewalk. Occupying two thirds of the front is a fish pond of masonry four or five feet wide and full of gold fish. This is fenced by pickets from the street. The entrance is into a large room open to the street covered with mats, where a few clerks and boys in waiting remain. A quiet still spot is this unindicative of traffic, and just now Nakai, whose fortunes are on the wane, has little traffic.

My visit was with Dr. S[immons], who had the master of the house as a patient. One of the attendant boys ran into an inner room to announce us and then returned to usher us in. A sliding screen door let us first into the kitchen, a large room in the most tidy condition, from which we turned aside into a narrow hall or open passageway which led us around two sides of an enclosed court not more than fifteen feet square and occupied by an outbuilding, a miniature pond of water and a large aviary whose birds were hopping merrily about on the branches of a natural tree ten or twelve feet high. Passing around two sides of this we turned again into another hall which brought us to the door of the living apartment. Entering this we found the master of the house lying on thick quilted mattresses under silk coverlets spread on the mats in the center of the room. Three attendants were with him, a man, his own concubine, a woman of pleasant exterior, and a little servant girl. The room was an elegant one, for Japan a luxurious one, and for any country a comfortable, pleasant, and remarkably tidy one. Some foreign comforts had been engrafted upon the Japanese simplicity of house adornment. Glass windows occupying one side of the room opened into a little court of trees and flowers, birds hung in handsome cages within the recessed windows, curtains of gay shiffs festooned them and on the broad bench of the window were ornamental articles both native and imported. The mats were of a remarkably fine texture and bound with white after the style of the imperial palace at Yedo. This visit was made in the spring and at the time pots of flowering cherry trees adorned the room among them some artificial trees so accurate that it needed the touch to detect their fabrication of paper. The projecting timbers and uprights always visible in a Japanese house were handsomely lackered in black and the plastered walls were covered with a neat hanging of paper representing the blossoming cherry trees. In one recess were some articles of antique design and a Japanese landscape painting. Three sides of the room were hung with french colored engravings of scenes in the Crimea campaigns[42] and allegorical pictures of the old mythology whose half

---

[40] This was most likely Dr. Hall not Dr. Hepburn, as Hall would not have had a chance to see Hepburn in Kanagawa on this day.

[41] Nakaiya Jūbee was one of the leading Yokohama merchants active in the silk trade. In addition he traded in a great variety of items that ranged from paper to tobacco. See Yokohama Shi, eds., *Yokohama shishi* (Tokyo: Tosho Insatsu Kabushiki Kaisha, 1970), vol. 2, p. 16.

[42] These were quite likely the works of Felice Beato and James Robertson. Beato and Robertson had cov-

nude gods and goddesses were attractive to Japanese taste in art. A nude Pandora opening the fatal box was conspicuous.

By the side of the invalid's couch was a tray covered with foreign articles in glass, a decanter, an ornamented bottle, vases, glass sugar bowl, etc. While we had been inspecting these things the little handmaid had prepared some fragrant tea which she offered to us kneeling on the mats and the concubine served us with little lumps of rock sugar from the glass sugar bowl. At our desire to see more of his house the little maid threw back the screens that separated an adjoining apartment which was the chief room of the house. It was bare of furniture but was covered with mats of a size I had never seen before. The walls were covered with hangings of silk exactly fitted on which were painted the birds of Japan. The gold and silver pheasants, the snowy herons, etc., in proportional drawings and colored to life. The ceiling was covered with fan shaped devices— on a white ground—of flowers, landscapes, historical characters, divinities in a not unpleasing though strange mixture. These too were beautifully colored. This room opened upon the aviary before mentioned and its tapestries were in harmony therewith.

Going back through the first room then out of it and crossing a narrow passage to an room directly opposite we were in the merchant's private room. It was a fireproof structure of walls of enormous thickness where were contained his books, papers, and valuables. Light was admitted through a grated window of small dimensions. This room was well appointed in all its furniture from the handsomely wrought low desk at which the merchant wrote to a large iron safe of English manufacture in one corner. Various papers were neatly folded and arranged on shelves and the bare spaces of the walls adorned with French engravings among which was the familiar "Dream of Happiness." Few merchants live

in so royal a style and I am told men of rank and wealth seldom surround themselves with such luxuries as did this merchant. He said he would not be allowed to do it in Yedo. A parting cup of tea and some more bits of sugar and we left the merchant sick on his mats wretched amid all his elegant surroundings.

Wednesday, June 12, 1861

Stepped into the theatre with H[eco] a little while, where a mixed company of men and women were playing. The scene was [one] where an outcast child after long years absence returns home with a daughter and stands outside of the paternal gate in the midst of a snow storm (of cotton wool and paper) vainly beseeching admittance of her stern father. The mother stands at the gate and would gladly admit her but for the father's command. She finally lies down in cold benumbed and her little daughter disrobes herself to cover her more warmly. This is an affecting scene after the Japanese way as the wet eyes in the audience bear witness. A comic scene follows in which the half drunk master of a house holds a revel with his friends and becomes the victim of love for one of the young ladies present. The mother of the said young lady (a man dressed as a woman), a tall gaunt character, favors the suit and is a highly amusing character. The brother of the girl however has sold his sister for money which gambling has put him in need of. The daughter and sister is to be compelled to lodge with the purchaser, a fate she avoids by putting him into a sleep of intoxication when she withdraws from the apartment and a friend of her more favored suitor steals in and steals out with the sleeper's valuable sword and the curtain drops upon the horrified sleeper now awakened as he discovers his great loss.

Today the current talk is that Mr. Alcock re-

ered the Crimean War. Beato was a close friend of Charles Wirgman, the artist and correspondent for the *Illustrated London News,* who may well have brought to Japan some of Beato's photographs, or to be more exact the engravings made from them by the engraver

James Robertson (who was Beato's brother-in-law). Beato arrived in Japan in 1863 and soon became the leading Western photographer in Yokohama. For a brief biographical sketch of Beato see *Once Upon A Time* (New York: Friendly Press, 1986), pp. 12ff.

fuses to accept as an envoy to England a titular Kami only. He claims that a prince of rank only should be the chief ambassador.

There is a hitch also in the Emperor's love affair and the proposed marriage with the Mikado's daughter is likely to be broken off.

Today is one of the great holidays of the year, "the Flag Feast." Temples are adorned with long paper flags, processions move in the streets with poles covered with variegated paper streamers, priests blowing conch shells. The Shinto priesthood in scarlet robes and something on the forehead looking like a butter pail and held on by a string passing behind the ears and coming forward to the chin or nose propitiate the divinity of health in procession through the village. Their rites are needed for there is considerable sickness among the natives, some kind of a congestion, a fever that terminates both rapidly and fatally.

Toward evening the streets towards the Gankiro are alive with visitors to that place, H[eco] and I watch them, here come two norimons with servants, in the first is a fine looking elderly man whose soft white features betray his gentler life if not blood, in the second is his pretty daughter of fifteen or sixteen and they are going to visit this place as all Japanese do with their families as an everyday proper thing. We visit by invitation the little group of dancing girls and find the children preparing for the evening stage for there are guests from Yedo to be entertained; we are pressed with hospitalities but the sight of two young ladies gorgeous in fairest colors, embroideries and scarlet crapes, sashes, and with tortoise shell hairpins and ornaments after the pictured style, consumed our appetites and we leave them to their own enjoyments. At another place the girls in holiday dresses and happy amid their poor life are boating on the murky ·water, young fresh and fair faces among them enough to sadden anyone.

Thursday, June 13, 1861

Yesterday's holiday, 5th of the 5th month, is called Osekoo[43] and is one of the principal holidays of the year the others being the 1st of the year, the 3rd of the 3rd month, seventh of the 7th moon, 8th of the 8th moon, 9th of the ninth moon. Yesterday's was in commemoration of the return of the Mikado thirteen or fourteen hundred years ago from the conquest of Corea and China and is especially observed by the princes and officials. At Yedo it is a day on which the daimios pay ceremonious visits to the Tycoon.

Friday, June 14, 1861

Weather very warm, mosquitoes and fleas troublesome.

Saturday, June 15, 1861

S[adajirō], who comes in now nearly every day for instruction in English, tells a good story as thus. The Japanese are very fond of eels and men too poor to buy the coveted luxury sometimes hang about the cookshops to inhale the savory odor of a food their purses will not buy. To such an one the master of a cook shop once presented a bill for a year's smells in front of his kitchen, one hundred ichibus. Very well says the gourmand of smells write your receipt and I will go and get the money. Presently he returns and spreads the money on the table and picks up the receipt while the inn keeper prepares to pick up the money; not so says the epicure of eels recessing the money back into his own pockets, I have *smelt* your eels and you have *seen* my money and I think we are quits.

Building of secret rooms and underground vaults is prohibited without license growing out of the common practice of using such places in

---

[43] What Hall is referring to here is the Go-sekku, or the five traditional, popular festivals of Japan. *Jinjitsu* (the first day of the first month), *jōmi* (the third day of the third month), *tango* (fifth day of the fifth month—the festival mentioned here), *Tanabata* (seventh day of

the seventh month), and *chōyō* (ninth day of the ninth month). These festivals have been celebrated in Japan since the ninth century. See E. Papinot, *Historical and Geographical Dictionary of Japan* (Ann Arbor, Mich.: Overbeck, 1948), pp. 127–28.

former times for secret crimes, the manufacture of counterfeit money and the like. A building of any size is therefore frequently inspected during its erection. Underground passages were once as common in Japan as ever in old feudal warlike times in Europe.

Lately there have been arrests in Yedo of girls practicing prostitution without the licensed houses. Followers of daimios are forbidden to resort to the licensed houses and as infringements of this rule would be known by the inevitable spy system of Japan, they resort to other means. Go-betweens are employed to find peasants willing to prostitute a daughter. The young lady is ostensibly a music or writing teacher and she may have several lovers from whom the family derives a good income although one third of it must go to the pimp and one third to the lower yakunins in whose supervision the family are. Once in a few years the government makes a sweep of all such girls, as this year for instance, and the offenders are punished by a 1000 day's service in a regular joroya. One hundred and thirty or forty were so arrested this year and many more fled the city.

A thousand days service to the Emperor is not an infrequent punishment of small offences. An inveterate gambler for instance may be condemned to 1000 days labor in the Emperor's oil mills.

The girls named above will not be received by the best houses who prefer to buy children and educate them to their infamous life.

H + + +[Heco?] tells me of two girls living on the main street of Yokohama, one of whom is the object of the French Minister's attentions. He says she is called coquettish by the Japanese and I asked how she manifested her coquettery, "Oh she goes to the bath twice a day and that kind of thing!"

Sunday, June 16–Friday, June 21, 1861

Weather clear and hot, thermometer ranging from 75° A.M. to 90° P.M. until the afternoon of the 20th when we had a heavy thunder shower, the only one worthy of the name since I have been in Japan. Wind veered to the north and grew cold. On the 20th A.M. H.B.M.'s gun boat *Ringdove* arrived with mail, bringing news of the 1st week of March in the states. 21st A.M. a British bark brought a mail of a fortnight later date.

During this week we have had most beautiful moonlight nights. The throngs of Japanese in some parts of the town enjoying the evening were very great. H[eco] and I sat on a bench in front of Takara Daia's[44] home one evening enjoying the fair evening, his wife playing the hostess bringing us cold water, sake, rock sugar and tobacco, and fans to disperse the mosquitoes. Afterwards a stroll with H[eco] in the suburbs.

Tuesday, June 25, 1861

Breakfasted with the Hepburns. High wind P.M. increasing to almost a gale.

Friday, June 28, 1861

The Tokaido in the vicinity of the Honjin at Kanagawa is nightly haunted by a ghost according to Japanese account. It puts on the mortal shape of a Joro in full costume of that class and at the witching hour of night walks up and down the silent street. Nobody confesses to having seen it and although I find the Japanese generally say that this is a false ghost yet from their manner it is evident they have faith in true ones being allowed to revisit their earthly haunts at times.

Sunday, June 30, 1861

Closing the month of June which has been a month of fine clear hot weather very different from the June of 1860 which was wet and comparatively cool. The June crops, rape, peas, barley, and wheat have been well secured and are good. Following the removal of these

---

44 This would appear to have been Takaradaya Tarōuemon who dealt in lumber, coal, and raw silk. See

Yokohama Shi, eds., *Yokohama shishi*, vol. 2, p. 15.

crops is the putting in of the 2nd series of crops beginning early in July, and the transplanting of rice, sweet potatoes, and taro. Beans, cotton, goma, upland rice, millet, and buckwheat follow the before raised crops. Notwithstanding the season for gathering crops has been dry I observe the Japanese still consume the bulk of the straw mixing the ashes with night soil and other manures and making a compost for these fields. This season with its absence of rain is better for the rice than last year's abundance, for the country is so well watered by numerous small streams that all the lowlands are easily irrigated in a succession of terraces without resorting to raising water as is common in China. Observe the cleanliness of the culture, the freedom from weeds.

Monday, July 1, 1860

Went to Kanagawa by agreement to take a walk with Mr. Fortune to observe particularly the habitat of a beautiful lily whose bulb is largely consumed as an edible.[45] The day was overcast and we had an agreeable ramble of three hours through the country paths till we came to the object of our walk, a bank under a grove of Japan cedar where a year ago I had seen this lily starring the emerald slopes with its brilliant blossoms. On our way I found a few new both to Mr. Fortune and myself. There were perhaps forty stalks within the space of a square yard and no more to be seen in their neighborhood. The farmers were busy in the fields still transplanting a little rice, sowing millet, buckwheat, and goma, or thinning out the cotton plants. We saw clumps of gardenia in bloom in the farm house enclosure as also the sacred bamboo. We returned to the temple where Mr. F[ortune] is domiciliated and I had the pleasure of examining his fine collection of insects.

Tuesday, July 2, 1861

Busy preparing mail for the *Fiery Cross*. Towards evening taking a walk through the main street I was witness to one of the Japanese customs. I was standing in front of a crockery shop talking with its inmates when a man halted at the entrance who had come there to stop or transact business. He had a bundle on a pole over his shoulder and his dress and feet were soiled with the dust of the road for he had just come from Yedo. Signs of recognition were exchanged, but the usual ceremonious salutations of the Japanese were not gone through with until water had been brought for the new comer to wash his feet and legs and a napkin to wipe them. He sat on the sill of the house to do this, performing his pedablutions with feet in the street. This accomplished, and a clean pair of sandals from his pack put on, he then entered upon the clean mats and gave and received the usual formal salutations with head touching the clean mats. It was a novel custom and wholesome that required a man to wash his dirty feet before he could salute the household into which he was about to enter.

Wednesday, July 3, 1861

Note of conversation with S[adajirō]. Nippon was anciently divided only by its seven great highways having no political divisions whatever. Subsequently five grand divisions were made and these were again divided into many smaller by the Mikados and placed under the rule of favorites and successful warriors. The present provinces held by Kaga, Satsuma, and Mutsu, are inalienable possessions, their title being derived from ancient Mikados with whom they have family connection. So, too, the possessions held by the Daimios of Owari, Mito, and Kii or Kisiu are inalienable, being originally absolute grants to their ancestors who were blood relations of Gongen Sama

[45] One of Hall's contributions to the flora of Elmira, New York, appears to have been some of the lilies he thought so lovely in Japan. On April 4, 1863, the Elmira *Daily Advertiser* ran an advertisement for Hall Brothers bookstore announcing the sale of a shipment of several dozen bulbs of "The Golden Lily of Japan—The Most Beautiful of all Known Lilies," which had just arrived and were to be sold at from "fifty cents to one dollar" per bulb.

[Tokugawa Ieyasu], founder of the present dynasty.

The distinctions of blood are fully observed in Nippon, it being common to say such a man has a "great deal of blood." Thus, too, there are families without property of great value whose rank is very high. Such are the families of Munasaka [Mimasaka?] and Mikawa, and Yetsigo [Echigo], very ancient and honorable, but not powerful. So, too, the families Kadsusa [Kazusa], Hitachi, Kotsuki [Kōzuke], descended of the old Mikados, but families of small domains and strength. These families Mutsu, Owari, Munasaka [Mimasaka], Mikawa, Yetsigo [Echigo], Kadsusa [Kazusa], Hitatsi [Hitachi], and Kotsuki [Kōzuke] are further honored by the fact that no titular kamis are allowed to have the same title. In point of power the principal Daimios rank as follows:

1. Kaga	} of the	4. Owari	} of the
2. Satsuma	} Mikado's	5. Kii	} Kuubo's
3. Mutsu	} family	6. Mito	} family

Followed by these whose rank and strength are similar:

7. Tsikuzen	10. Hizen	13. Hikoni (Ei-Kamon no kami)
8. Aki	11. Inuba	14. Idsumi (Toda Idsumi no kami)
9. Nangato	12. Yetsizen	

The chief servants of the Mikado in the eyes of the people and by ancient custom rank above the highest princes of the realm. The five highest outranking the Tycoon who he said had not the noble blood in his veins that he had.

According to the old chronicles Japan was first peopled in its southern half by men of marked Mongol features and their kingdom did not extend beyond the mountains that crossing the province of Sinano [Shinano] extend nearly from sea to sea. Beyond the mountains were another race who had come from the north and with whom they had frequent wars on the dividing ridge until at last the southern race overran the island penetrating into Yeso. These northern men are spoken of as of more regular features, larger stature, high noses, small mouths, and this very assertions stamps the whole story with improbability for such is not the character of the nations to the north of this day. If there be any truth it must be this that northern Nippon was peopled by a race of these characteristics for although in the province of Nambu the men are said to be rather fairer and having other resemblances to Caucasian blood, my own experience is that the nation is so thoroughly blended north and south that no argument is to be derived that there has been two decidedly distinct peoples at any time occupying the northern and southern portions of these isles. Men of good stature with regular features, a facial angle with high Roman noses, eyes not oblique are to be frequently seen in all parts of these islands without a preponderance anywhere.

It was a custom of the old Mikados to keep in important positions near to their thrones two Chinese servants, men of learning. Gohookoo [*gofuku*] as the Japanese call the introducers of silk to Japan from China and after whom the goods are called to this day was honored by the Mikado with a post near the throne.

Kaempfer's confidential servant and pupil to whom he was indebted for the valuable information which he has made public was imprisoned, beaten, and some say executed for the offence. Kaempfer's researches were printed in Japanese, probably an abridgement only, but the work was suppressed as far as possible by the government.[46]

In Kanagawa on the Tokaido is a little shop for the sale of small articles tended by a young and pretty girl to whose name a sad history is attached. Her father, in Siebold's Desima days,

[46] Hall's reference is probably to Shizuki Tadao's translation of a portion of the Kaempfer history, particularly the essay that Kaempfer wrote on the seclusion policy. See Donald Keene, *The Japanese Discovery of Europe, 1720–1830* (Stanford, Calif.: Stanford University Press, 1969), p. 76.

was the principal servant or follower of the Governor of Nagasaki. With this man Siebold had a long intimacy. After the discovery of the unfortunate map publisher others of Siebold's friends became objects of suspicion, among others this man then living at Yedo. He was deprived of his rank, banished from Yedo, and went to Corea where he died. His family were reduced to poverty and his wife now keeps house for the attachés of the Honjin while his daughter is the shopkeeper of the Tokaido. Siebold's friend, the interpreter, fared as badly. He was tortured by the pulling out of his fingernails, the breaking of every finger, and was then thrust into jail—others implicated in furnishing him maps were put to death.[47] These are the popular stories revived by Siebold's presence again in these parts.

Last night a comet was visible for the first, situated a few degrees from the "pointers" and below them. The nucleus has a foggy appearance as if a light seen through a fog and the tail (hairs the Japs call it) is broad rather than long. The common people have all the common superstitions of its presaging some great calamity such as cholera, fire, war, famine, or tempest.

Thursday, July 4, 1861

Anniversary of America's Independence and celebrated with some spirit by the Americans. A request having been made to Consul D[orr] by an American for the loan of an American ensign to float that day, he replied by saying that he did not allow anyone to fly the national flag. This moved the spirit of the American cit-

izens to a more thorough notice of the day. Application was made to the English, French, and Dutch ships of war for flags when it appeared the Consul had anticipated the citizens by requesting the commanders to furnish no flags to Americans for the purpose in hand. Whereupon, in the latter part of the 3rd, Japanese tailors were busy fabricating American flags and early this morning they were seen waving from many roofs—Consul D[orr] recognizing his countrymen during the day at the Consulate, and the Americans celebrated the day by mutual calls and festivities incident to the occasion. I joined a party from Kanagawa on a picnic excursion. We took boats to Mississippi Bay, and on its southern shore, in a little cove where there was shade and a stream of cool sweet water, we found a suitable place for our camp fires. The day was cloudy and showering and the grass and trees so wet that rambles inland were precluded; but the natives came to us in numbers watching the way tojins passed a holiday. We amused ourselves on the beach, spread our table cloths on the grass, cooked our chowder in the boatmen's kettle, and with the cold fowls from home fared sumptuously. At 5 P.M. we returned. The sailing today was delightful and for the first time I used the old whaler's flag which Alfred[48] sent me.

Friday, July 5, 1861

Called on Genl. D[orr] and his guests Mr. Hyatt, late consul at Amoy, and his family.

---

[47] The incident referred to here involved Von Siebold's efforts to leave Japan in 1828 after collecting a variety of materials on Japanese life, including some recent maps and drawings. Unfortunately the vessel upon which he was to leave encountered a typhoon and was beached in the harbor. In order to make repairs the cargo was unloaded, and in keeping with Japanese law for imported (though not for exported goods) the cargo was inspected. Von Siebold's cases revealed a variety of contraband articles including maps, drawings, weapons, armor, and a garment bearing the shogunal crest. Von Siebold was formally interrogated, and many of the men who had provided him with information on Japan were arrested. Takahashi Kageyasu, one of those

arrested, who had provided him with a detailed map of Japan—including Yeso—died in prison before sentence was passed, and his brine-preserved corpse was later decapitated. Several of those interrogated committed suicide. In the end, Von Siebold was deported from Japan with orders never to return, and a number of the minor figures in the case were deprived of samurai rank, exiled from Edo, or confined to house arrest. The context does not allow us to state precisely who the servant of the governor of Nagasaki was, but Hall's information that he went to Korea and died there is intriguing. See Itazawa Takeo, *Shiboruto* (Tokyo: Yoshikawa Kobunkan, 1960), pp. 97ff.

[48] Alfred was Francis Hall's brother.

Saturday, July 6, 1861

We are startled this morning by the intelligence that the English Legation at Yedo was attacked last night by a desperate party of Japanese. So many conflicting rumors are abroad that I will not attempt any detailed account of the affair until I can hear with some accuracy. It seems the assailants penetrated to the house, or temple, in which Mr. Alcock resides, and which is situated back from the street in a continuation from the Tokaido a hundred and fifty yard[s] or thereabouts. They were repulsed by the guard regularly stationed at the temple after a sharp conflict in which several of the guard were killed and wounded, and report says the assailants escaped. Mr. Olyphant, Secretary of the Legation, and Mr. Morrison, Late Consul at Nagasaki, who came to the door on hearing the disturbance were wounded, the former severely. The *Ringdove* has gone to Yedo with marines from the French ship *Dordogne* and her own. P.M. the street is full of contradictory rumors but the above is all that can be relied on as yet.

Sunday, July 7, 1861

Mr. Morrison is down from Yedo today. He received but a slight wound though he had a narrow escape. From him we have the following particulars. The household of the English Legation had retired and were about retiring on the night of the 5th between the hours of ten and eleven when Messrs. Morrison and Olyphant, who were still up, heard what at first seemed to be the report of a musket, but which was the noise of some one beating in the door of the main entrance to the house. Mr. Olyphant hastened out of a rear door where he was confronted by a man with a drawn sword who struck at and wounded him. He had a riding whip in his hand with which he parried successive blows when Mr. Morrison closely following and looking out and seeing Olyphant engaged in a deadly conflict fired his pistol at the assailant which momentarily repulsed him and allowed Mr. Olyphant to escape. The ball from this pistol was subsequently found on the ground flattened whence it is supposed the assailant wore armor of suffi-

cient strength to resist a bullet. The flash of a second discharge of Mr. Morrison's pistol blinded his own eyes and revealed his person to the attacking party who now assailed him in turn giving him a slight wound in the arm. Mr. Morrison retreated, and stumbling, half fell into a little recess just within the door and blows aimed at him took effect on the partition posts of this recess cutting one of them in two, Mr. Morrison, however, receiving only a further scratch on one of his fingers. His assailant then retired, doubtless satisfied that he made sure work of his victim. By this time several of the attacking party had gained access to the house and to some of the bedrooms and began to slash at everything within reach. Supposing doubtless that some of the inmates were still in their beds, with their heavy long swords they slashed to pieces mosquito nettings, bedsteads, beds, lamps, and furniture.

While this work of destruction was going on, the household were gathered in the drawing room with the dining room only between them and their fierce assailants. Had these known this, or been less intent on tearing the beds to pieces, it is possible, very possible, that not a soul of the legation might have escaped. At this critical juncture the house guards were aroused, of whom there are some 200 stationed there, and came manfully to the rescue. A short skirmish with swords followed in and around the house which ended in the assailants being beaten back and driven out of the compound leaving three of their number dead and one mortally wounded. Six of the house guards were wounded, one mortally, dying the following day. Though wounded in protecting strangers for whom they had little personal sympathy they were proud of their wounds and the wounded guard died heroically without a murmur at his fate.

Notice of the attack was immediately forwarded to H.B.M.'s Consul at Kanagawa and a file of marines were promptly sent up to Yedo from H.B.M.'s Gunboat *Ringdove* and the French Steamer *Dordogne*. The wounded man of the assailants preserved an obstinate silence as to who and what the attacking party were. According to accounts from the Legation there were seventeen of the attacking party who were dressed as common people each with a white cloth tied around his head after the custom of the lower classes. They presented themselves at the main gate to the compound and were refused admittance by the *Mōng ban*, or gate-keeper, but some of the party effecting an entrance by the side hedges slew the gate keeper for his faithfulness and gave entrance to their comrades. They seem not to have aroused the guard within as they proceeded up the long avenue to the house. Entering the house they encountered the native cook and demanded of him the locality of the apartments. He refused to give the desired information and was severely beaten and wounded therefor. Events then followed as already narrated.

For the first time guards detailed by the Japanese to defend foreigners have shown any efficiency. In this instance they appear to have acted bravely and well, and there seems to be no reason for once to complain that the government officials would not peril their lives to save those of the foreigners.

Monday, July 8, 1861

The Japanese report this morning that five of the assailants have committed *hara kiri* at a tea-house and that three more have been arrested by the government. They further state that a portion of the assailants had been all day previous to the attack eating and drinking at the Sinagawa tea-houses and joined another portion of them from elsewhere and began the attack. Who were the assailants? The reply as usual is *ronins*. Whether they were indeed so, or followers of some chief, will probably be learned from the parties arrested.

For several days past the Japanese have been making preparations for the festival of the *Matsuri* like that of last year of which I have given description in previous pages of my journal. The streets are decorated with lanterns of gay colors and every imaginable device from the owners name simply, to uncouth monsters elaborated in gaudiest tints and landscape views. Above the lanterns were suspended umbrella frames ornamented with rosettes of particolored papers; these were revolving in the wind. In each *cho*, or ward, square mat towers have been erected in which are the two

wheeled carts bearing aloft canopies of flowers, scenic devices, or statues of fabled heroes. The streets had already become gay with the holiday dresses of the people who were to take part in the general processions, white cottons splashed with the most extraordinary colors, waterfalls tumbling down brawny shoulders, Fusi lying with superincumbent weight on the stomach, and great sea crabs sprawling on the backs, over topped with broad hats of umbrella size flaunting with streamers or brocade with paper flowers, when last evening orders came down from Yedo that the *Matsuri* must be suspended so far as any public show was to be made. The holiday could be observed within doors alone. The reason for this was of course the recent unfortunate events at Yedo. Fears were expressed lest advantage might be taken of the festival by "roughs" to commit some harm upon the persons of the foreigners. An unnecessary fear which few of the foreigners shared in.

Towards evening I took a stroll in the streets to see what was going on. The streets were full of people all disappointed with the interference of the authorities, yet all happy and cheerful.

At one large house of public entertainment the proprietor, who had just returned from Yedo, gave a gratuitous entertainment. In the center of his establishment, and surrounded by buildings on every side, was an artificial lake 60 or 70 feet square. Wide verandahs surrounded the lake opening into spacious apartments and outside balconies, artificial rock work on which trees and plants were growing rose out of the midst of the lake, and a bridge of vermilion posts and rails topped with gold spanned its waters. Over the whole was a skylight of paper sashes.

As it grew dark red lanterns were hung around the lake and on the island in its midst and from the second story balconies. A group of fifty singing and dancing girls came in and occupied a raised dais on two sides of the lake while at an angle and between the two was a stage for the players. The open verandahs and the upper balconies began to fill with spectators all attired in holiday garb.

On the dais on one side of the lake a dozen girls were seated, part with lutes in their hands and part with written music, on the other dais as many more with drums of differing shapes and gourds beaten with sticks or the hands. The show-girls were scattered in groups about the lake. All were dressed uniformly, their rich black hair gathered in a knot on top of the head and profusely ornamented with flowers and hair pins and ornaments of shell, metal, and glass. Each wore an under tunic of crimson crape edged with blue satin where it folded over their full bosoms in thick bands. Over this was a net work of white gauze figured with representations of the bamboo, around their waists a cincture of white and blue, and then a particolored skirt of red ornamented with flowers to the knee, from the knee to the feet deep purple. The indispensable fan completed their costume, and with their faces and necks skillfully powdered and lips made ruby with artistic laying on of colors the tout ensemble was pleasing. The whole effect of the scene as it was lighted up by the crimson glare of the red lanterns on waters, bright drapes, and crowded balconies, was decidedly Alhambresque.

At a signal the curtains of the stage were lifted and the little actresses, children of nine to fifteen years, came upon the stage and commenced the rehearsal of an old fragment of ancient legend to the delighted audience. Seats in an eligible portion were assigned us by the proprietor, who seemed anxious we should be pleased, and while I looked on a girl of eighteen fanned me incessantly, modest and polite in her demeanor. Again the curtain fell, the audience and players dispersed in groups, the liberal master of the house distributed refreshments in neat little boxes of unpainted cedar. Ours was given to us on one of the raised platforms lately occupied by the singers who acted as our waitresses and companions, bringing us hot tea and sharing our Japanese lunches of rice, bean cakes, and impossible sauces with more relish than we could.

We visited the little actresses in their retiring room who were anxious to know if we had been pleased with the play. They were funny looking little creatures in their stage dresses begrimed with paint to give their countenances the distorted look proper to a Japanese stage character, for the stage appearance of actors

and actresses are not one whit exaggerated by the uncouth pictures we see. "Am I not a horrid looking creature," said a little girl ten years old with face painted to a deep burnt copper hue, with green eyebrows and blackened corners of the mouth. "Please give me a finger ring," said another with face whitened to a pearly luster and vermilion tinted lips and penciled eyelids, clad in a robe of lustrous purple satin embossed in gold. "Am I not [a] real hero," said the girl of fourteen who personated the male character clad in a gorgeous suit of green and gold with a pair of richly embossed swords hanging from her sash and socks of yellow satin. The classic buskin and the modern flesh colored tights were alike discarded for nature's own unadorned pedestals. Then she took an attitude, shook her head at me with an actor's stance and actor's tone, gave me a tragic line, burst into a laugh, and wheeled away. One male and two female attendants were busy preparing the little actresses for the next play, touching up the shaded colors on face and hands, bringing out showy wardrobes, and consoling the little damsels when listless indifference was at variance with their animated appearance on the stage.

We strolled around the lake under the gay lanterns and among the glittering drapes till the proprietor's call, two pieces of wood struck together, called the attention of the audience to the new act, then we left.

Tuesday, July 9, 1861

Heco and myself devoted some time today calling among the Japanese who seem generally disappointed at the stopping of their holiday. We were received everywhere hospitably. At one place I tasted for the first time the *awabi*, esteemed a great luxury, a univalve shell fish (from which the pearl shell is taken), the dried ones of which are sold to the epicures of China for thirty or forty dollars per pound. It was cooked in oil with dressing of soy and sweet sake and was a palatable, though to my taste a not over luxurious dish. The people were everywhere busy taking down the ornaments prepared for the festival.

At one house [we] saw a group of three

young ladies visiting together and enjoying a feast spread about them in porcelain dishes and lacquered trays. They were attractive, two of them unusually well looking, and all clad both neatly and handsomely, their dresses to their white socks or sandals being scrupulously clean. They were squatted down en mode Japonais, and [a] lute lying at the side of one of them betokened that they filled the pauses of feasting and conversation with music.

"Like linnets in the pauses of the mind."

For a Japanese feast of this kind is a long and leisurely meal, which they know well how to make enjoyable.

Frequent inquiries were made about the recent affairs at Yedo and much concern is expressed by the Japanese lest it lead to general disturbances. Indeed they state that the ill feeling on the part of the hostile Daimios is on the increase, who say that foreigners are altogether too well treated in this land, and that if they remain here they *shall* remain living only under such conditions as they see fit to impose without any regard to the conciliating policy of the Tycoon's government. They apprehend at no distant day an outbreak among themselves at home. The pretext is likely to be the foreign policy of the empire. In connection with this is the report from Yedo today Consul V[yse] gives on authority that Mr. Alcock has received certain information at Yedo that one of the Daimios has sworn to have his blood if he remains in Yedo. Minister [Alcock] has made this the subject of correspondence with the government and demands the name of the Daimio. The government refuses to give it or acknowledge the fact. Minister A[lcock] says this settles the question so far as he is concerned, that he cannot, and will not, leave Yedo under menace. Not placing the fullest confidence in the report, I give it for what it may prove to be worth.

From an account furnished by one of the attaches of the English Legation I have a slightly differing account of the late attack. It is supposed that only fourteen were engaged in the assault who made the entrance at the gate as stated. It was a little past eleven and the household had retired. Mr. Olyphant, who had not

yet fallen asleep, heard a noise which he supposed to be an altercation among the servants and rose up and taking his riding whip went into a hall at a side entrance when he was confronted by a man who had just affected an entrance. He was cut in the arm by a drawn sword, and while parrying further blows with his riding whip called for aid. Mr. Morrison slept in a room adjoining this hall and seizing his pistol rushed out and seeing the combat fired his pistol with deliberate aim at the assailant; at the same moment he received a blow from a second assailant cutting his forehead deeply; he instinctively lifted his hand to the wound which partially stunned him when a second blow slightly cut one of his fingers. The darkness of the place was probably all that saved the men from instant death. For some unknown reason the assailants then desisted and O[lyphant] and M[orrison] escaped into the house. The household had now gathered and according to the account they all escaped into the back yard and stood clustering together on the turf, Minister A[lcock] in the midst, while they heard the crashing blows of the assault within. The guard were now aroused and diverted the attention of the assailants between whom a fierce fight at once began as before said. It appears that after entering the compound they attempted to enter the house at different points. One party fell in with a betto belonging to the house, and on his refusing to point out the way to the bedrooms slew him. A priest at the adjoining temple who came out attracted by the noise was also slain and the cook severely wounded for refusing to impart the desired information. Of the assailants two were slain and one is so desperately wounded that he has been unable the speak since the transaction. Of the defending guard 12 in all were wounded one perhaps mortally. Nine of them were servants of the Daimio under whose guard the British Legation is, and three were the Emperor's men. The day subsequent to the attack three of the assailants were heard of at a tea house in Sinagawa. The house was surrounded by imperial officers and the men seeing all chance of escape cut off attempted to commit *hara kiri*. Two of them succeeded in the attempt, but the third was arrested in time to save his life. The popular belief is that these men were indeed Mito's men, and at the tea house where the three were discovered they were said to have held a counsel for one or more days previous to the attack.[49]

Thursday, July 11, 1861

Sadajirō, who has just returned from Yedo, is in with his budget of news. The late disturbances at Yedo appear to have caused much excitement among the Japanese who are fearful of what may follow in the wake. Swords have risen in price and good ones [have] been in great demand. The *Matchi Bunio* [Machi Bugyō] of Yedo was slain in the streets a few days since while walking in state with the Emperor's train. He was slain by a single handed assailant who escaped, his own immediate attendants being cowed by the boldness of the deed. Of the late attack he gives some additional items. The original intention was that the attack should be made by fifty men who were to rendezvous in front of the gate at the tolling of the midnight bell from the temple at the Imperial burial place. A dog gave a premature alarm and fearing discovery the few who had assembled, 13 according to the account, began their work without further delay. It was their desire to attack the American Legation and for that reason the Americans residing here have been watched since New Years for a suitable opportunity, but the watch there were thought too strong and vigilant and the English Legation was next selected. The casualties of the fray are thus far: the betto and the priest slain, the gatekeeper mortally wounded since dead, a servant killed by an ill directed pistol shot from the house, and seventy-eight of the guard more or less wounded, one of whom, the chief of the Prince of Kahi [Kai]'s men, is since dead, and several more it is thought cannot survive. It is supposed the guard suffered more from wounds given each other than from the ronins in the obscurity of the night.

Dr. Siebold went to Yedo to receive 6000 ichibus per annum from the Japanese government for his information and advice upon foreign affairs but, rumor says the Japanese are disappointed in finding that the Dr. will not meddle with affairs of state and enact the rather doubtful part of informer.

The difficulty at Tsu-Sima [Tsushima] is said to be this.[50] Some Russian soldiers landing there from a war vessel entered a Japanese house where were a mother and daughter and offered violence to them. The daughter fled and alarmed the neighboring farmers, the young men from among whom immediately assaulted and drove back the sailors to their boats killing two of their number. Another party landed the following day and seized two Japanese who were innocent of yesterday's proceedings and carried them off to the ship. The indignation of the inhabitants was aroused and further conflicts occurred when the Daimio of the island appeared and tried to quiet his subjects, but they quickly informed him if he had not spirit enough to take his countrymen's part in such an emergency they would drive him out of the island. Fearing the Russians on one hand and his enraged country-

[49] For Rutherford Alcock's account of this attack see *The Capital of the Tycoon* (London: Longman, Green, Roberts, 1863), vol. 2, chap. 8, pp. 151ff.

[50] The Tsushima problem had begun on March 13, 1861, when the Russian corvet *Posadnik* under Captain Birilev cast anchor in Osaki Bay. Coming in the wake of a British surveying expedition the Russians also surveyed the surrounding waters and claimed that they had come to make repairs to their vessel. Using the excuse of repairs the Russians requested foodstuffs as well as timber, insisted on leasing a site, and appeared to be settling down for an indefinite stay. Russian barracks were constructed. The islanders were suspicious of these efforts and various incidents erupted. Several Japanese were killed and a number of hostages were taken by the Russians. The Japanese dispatched Oguri Tadanori, commissioner of foreign affairs, as well as Mizoguchi Hachijugoro to Tsushima to request Birilev to leave. They also protested officially to the Russians through the Russian consul, Goshkevich, in a formal protest delivered by Muragaki Norimasa at Hakodate. Backed by British naval power and further protests the Japanese finally managed to convince the Russians to leave Tsushima toward the close of 1861. See George Alexander Lensen, *The Russian Push Toward Japan: Russo-Japanese Relations, 1697–1875* (Princeton, N.J.: Princeton University Press, 1959), pp. 448–51.

men on the other he dispatched messages to Nagasaki and Yedo for assistance. Ogoori-Bungo-no-Kami was dispatched thither immediately on the steam yacht presented by Queen Victoria with such troops as the vessel could carry. And the steamer *England* has been sent from Satsuma with further reinforcements to resist any aggressions on the part of the Russians while the question is undergoing an examination. A peaceful settlement of the difficulty is likely to be had.

Friday, July 12, 1861

Another version of the Tsu-Sima affair is that the Russians demanded a joint occupancy of the island and the Governor is resisting with all his power and calling for reinforcements. A third version is that the Russians applied for coal, which, being refused, they proceeded to take it by force and were resisted. The truth will come out before long.

The Japanese are making preparations to throw additional guards and security about the foreign residences, particularly the Consulates at Yokohama. Consul Vyse has received intimations that violence would be offered him and has a file of marines doing duty at his place. From Yedo nothing new except that the English Legation looks like a place of siege with its large forces (stated at 1000) of government guards armed with swords, spears, muskets, and artillery.

Among the current reports of the people is this, that the band of assassins had previous to the night of the 5th been carousing at Sinagawa for two or three days. Their presence there was well known and was reported at Yedo and when towards evening of the 5th they settled their bill (30 Bus) that fact was reported also. No notice was taken of them, and although the government officers at Yedo might not have known their particular intentions they were, in existing circumstances, proper objects of espionage. I stated the above facts to the head of the police at Yokohama, his reply, lowering his voice, was, "You speak

truly, had such things been going on here we should have kept them under our sight."

Saw Mr. Morrison this evening who leaves tomorrow in the *Surprise* for China. His forehead was seamed with the slight wound received in the late affray. From him I had full particulars of it, which he illustrated with a diagram. The main facts are those already given. There were two gate keepers killed, one at the street gate, and one at the inner gate where the house path separates from the other. The betto was killed outside in the subsequent affray. The priest slept in a room adjoining the hall first entered and was doubtless killed by the two men who were first to enter. The house was entered at three or four different points the cook being killed by another party. Mr. Morrison was saved by his servant who slept in the passage way first entered. Rushing out with his pistol handed him by this servant he saw Mr. O[lyphant] engaged as first related. He fired first at the man in armor and again at the second assailant, the latter being wounded mortally the body being found the next day under a tree with the pistol bullet's mark clean through it. This it was that arrested the progress of these two assailants and saved not only their lives but others of the legation, for had these two been successful they would have kept on down the passage way encountering the Legation one by one in a defenseless condition. The native report about the dog alarm is so far true at least that a dog did give alarm and was killed by them, and it is by no means impossible that this may have precipitated the attack as stated.

Saturday, July 13, 1861

Thermometer 94°. The late alarm at the Dutch Consul's was occasioned by some thieving going on among his own servants. From Yedo we hear that the whole Japanese guard is withdrawn from the British Legation and Mr. Alcock relies upon his own guard of British and French Marines. Dined at Dr. Hall's and met Mr. Griswold,[51] American Merchant and

---

[51] J. Alsop Griswold had been American consul in Shanghai earlier and had also been associated with Rus-

sell and Co. See Tyler Dennett, *Americans in Eastern Asia* (New York: Barnes and Noble, 1963), p. 197.

Consul at Manilla, and Dr. Fullerton of the same place. A matter of query was Gironiere's singular story of life in the Philippines.[52] The author appears to have been unveracious only in ascribing as incidents to himself the common experiences of several others.

Sunday, July 14, 1861

Thermometer 94°. "A heated term." Locomotion by day and sleeping by night rendered doubtful.

Monday, July 15, 1861

The long continued heat is producing its desiccating effect upon the light soil of the uplands. Farmers are protecting such crops as are easily affected with covering of weeds, grass, and bushes. The continual roll of thunder from the banks of clouds in the West and Northwest horizon seem to promise rain but the storm divides passing southwardly and northwardly and we only get a sprinkle from the trailing skirts of the passing storm. Both last summer and this I have occasion to notice the frequent gathering of storm clouds to the N.W. of us from whose murky depths flashes of incessant lightning are visible in early evening and sometimes, though rarely, the low muttering of the thunder. These thunder showers, I am told, hang over some mountain ridges about 40 miles inland whose peaks are visible from our bay.

Summer day sights—First: a group of Japanese gossips across the way, married dames having an afternoon bit of scandal. The screens of the house are wide open to the street for the summer fervors are great and a half dozen women, married as their black teeth denote, are lying face downwards and leaning upon their elbows on the mats. Each one has thrown off her upper garments from her shoulders and is bare to the waist balancing this nudity by tucking up her lower garments till her legs are left bare to

her thighs. Their faces are to the center of the room and their feet describe the periphery of a circle. There, lying and occasionally kicking their feet into the air as browsing cattle toss their tails under the shady oaks and fanning themselves at the same time, they are holding a voluble discourse in the smooth flowing liquid accents of the Japanese tongue.

Second—a Sintoo priest sitting under a mat roof where several ways meet addressing himself to the passing crowd for alms blowing a great conch shell rimmed with green ribbons and rattling a staff of iron rings to call the attention of the faithful.

Tuesday, July 16, 1861

Cloudy, slight sprinkle P.M. The intense heat of the past three days somewhat mitigated.

Wednesday, July 17, 1861

Sadajirō tells me today that oil wells are common in the province of Echigo [Echigo] and that application was recently made to the Yedo government to be permitted to sell it to foreigners, but the application was denied. He says also there are places in the same province where gas passes from the ground in such quantities that gathered in bamboo tubes it is inflammable.

Japanese reasoning—Mr. G[oble], the rather truculent Baptist missionary at Kanagawa, loses his serenity of mind at times. Just now the officials are putting up tall post fences about the foreign compounds at Kanagawa with the view of further protecting them, and in so doing about brother G[oble]'s lot trespassed on his *squash* vines. G[oble] became very irate and violent in language to the officials, although, as my informant naively remarks, "not a squash had been ruined, only prospectively." Whereupon the officials gravely consulted "whether it were better to protect brother G[oble]'s household or his squash vines, and at last advices were still in doubt." The neighborhood took the matter up and it was a theme of wonderful gossip why brother G[oble] should be so anxious and distressed about a few

[52] Paul Proust de La Gironiere, *Twenty Years in the Philippines [1819–1839]* (New York: Harper & Brothers, 1854).

squashes which are so cheap in Nippon that the poorest coolie may eat his fill of them. The conclusion of the village oracles was that squash was in America a very rare and costly vegetable, and seeing they had it in such abundance they commiserated [with] the poor missionary who had lost, as they said, what "were to him great treasures." Yet they would say he acted very like a child. This was altogether Japanese. (The story of the travelling fat Dutch Director and his wonderful curiosity.)

Thursday, July 18, 1861

Fiery Cross arrived with mail.

Friday, July 19, 1861

Last night doubled guards were placed at all the gates in Yokohama and there was unusual bustle among the police and yakunins. On inquiry we learned that four men had been arrested at Kanagawa suspected of being *ronins*, but they passed an examination to be peaceful travellers enjoying a feast at one of the Kanagawa inns. If an invading host of the *ronins* had arrived, the excitement at Kanagawa could scarce have been greater.

H. and I had a fine sail this evening in a Japanese boat.[53] We lay off on a long stretch across the bay with a fair wind which both filled our great big sail and brought to us delicious coolness after the midday heat. We were four hours on the water returning at 9 P.M. enjoying greatly the sail by moonlight along the wooded shores whose rough outlines glistened and darkened by turn as the[y] stood out in light or fell back in shade. We slipped noiselessly through the water scarce disturbing the trail of silvery light which the moon left on the waters of the bay. Nearing shore we were challenged by a Japanese sentry boat. I replied "two ronins going to seize Yokohama," they recognized the foreign accents, laughed, said "good, good," and passed by to challenge a lit-

tle fleet of boats whose sails were whitening in our rear.

Saturday, July 20, 1861

S[adajirō] says "the Mikado is considered to own the products of Japan, the grains, the fruits, and the cattle on a thousand hills." This in answer to a question of mine "what territory was the Mikado's, and where did he get his rice?" "All Japan is his," he said, "and he has the right to demand anything that his subjects possess." But how does he actually get his rice?, I said. "Oh," he said, "such is the popular idea, but when he really wants, he makes a demand of the temporal emperor who is only his servant and who must furnish him." The practical of it is that the Mikado receives what the emperor chooses to give, which is said not to be an over liberal stipend.

Sunday, July 21, 1861

The weather which for the past week has been excessively hot was towards evening agreeably mitigated by a strong and cool breeze blowing from the north out of a heavy bank of clouds and in which had been an incessant peal of thunder for an hour or two. The earth is becoming dry and parched with the continued drought. So easily irrigated are the lowlands that the rice does not suffer.

Monday, July 22, 1861

Fair, cool. At the house of W[alsh] and Co. I saw today a happy illustration of the use of the photographic art in representing a bunch of raw silk packed and tied as it was received in London from Japan and which the recipients wishing to duplicate had adopted that mode of description. Dr. H[all], agent of W[alsh] and Co., states that the Japanese factors in seeing the faithful picture at once recognized the product, and by its mode of packing for the market immediately declared the quality of the silk, the province where grown, etc. No verbal description, however accurate, not even a sam-

---

[53] As Hall does not refer to H. as Dr. H. it is possible that H. is Joseph Heco rather than Dr. Hall, especially since they went in a Japanese boat.

ple of the article itself, could have so well indicated the precise staple wanted.

Tuesday, July 23–Thursday, July 25, 1861

Clouds in strata and cumulus lowering about the horizon overspreading the heavens, and a lowering barometer have threatened both rain and storm, but instead we have had daily cool winds from the north and east but no rain. At Kanagawa on the night of the 25th word was sent down from Yedo to the Governor of Kanagawa that an attack was threatened against the place by 400 of Mito's men and enjoining especial vigilance. Consequently the guards were increased at all the foreign residences, a large guard patrolled the streets all night long, and the people were in a great ferment. Additional defenses are being added to the consulates. *Chevaux-de-frise* of pointed bamboo surmount the timber palisades already about the Consulate and a second line of palisade is to be constructed a few feet from that now up within and between which the Japanese guards are to patrol. The government are using all their endeavors to persuade the residents on the Kanagawa side to move across to Yokohama and not a strange thing it would be if the Japanese sought to create more alarm than the circumstances call for with a view to operate on the minds of our Kanagawa friends.

R. of the English Legation corrects some of my opinions relative to the late attack on the Legation.[54] Of the attacking party three were slain on the spot and one wounded taken prisoner; two more committed *hara-kiri* in the manner related at Sinagawa and one was taken before accomplishing his suicide; subsequently three more were made prisoners at Hodoriya who were under medical treatment for wounds received, the native physician having informed against them. On the part of the guard, one only has died, and seven only were wounded according to the legation accounts; but this differs so widely from the common report that I am inclined to believe the government have

suppressed the truth in part. The two gate guards were not killed but wounded severely; neither was the cook or priest killed but wounded; the betto was slain. The government report upon these men is that "they were not *ronin*, but men such as farmers, priests, and doctors, who feeling oppressed by the high price of food consequent upon foreign trade, conceived bitter animosity to all foreigners." A reason having not only a shallow foundation, but, if it existed even, would never have caused such deeds from such men. This question I have already reviewed in this journal and my letters home. A document purporting to have been found on the body of one of the slain has been forwarded to Minister Alcock giving the names of the twelve men who had "pledged themselves in view of the troubles brought upon them by the foreigner 'to do something for the glory of Japan and to give her name renown in foreign countries', which they would seek to do by assassinating all foreigners they could, hoping thereby to drive them from the land."

Friday, July 26, 1861

Towards evening of these warm summer days in the little hamlets about, the passer by will see the steaming family wash tub by the road side and one or two or more members of the family in various stages of the bath having entered the tubs by turns. They seem not ashamed of their nakedness, yet I seldom fail to notice a shrinking look from foreign gaze on the part of the female, for there is a modesty even in the public bath which impels them to hide always those parts of the body which modest women everywhere most desire to conceal. When the sun has gone down I see the lamp lit at the household altar, the smudge is kindled to keep off the swarm of mosquitoes, and the household gathers in the apartments, open on one side to the street, take their evening meal leisurely, and thereafter smoke and chat squatted in a circle men and women together. Then, as evening draws on, the mosquito tent is hung up within doors under which the children go to sleep, or the family gathers to while away the evening hours. But

---

[54] This would appear to have been Reginald Russell, interpreter of the British legation.

in the villages, like this, a common sight is to see them outside of the house sleeping on a wooden settle covered with mats, or more likely lying awake and fanning away the mosquitoes. Their sunburned skins seem callous to the armies of fleas which occupy these islands. Or, if the settle or bench is not there, a mat spread on the verandah floor, or on the ground outside, answers the same purpose, and last night I saw a couple lying on a mat in the middle of one of the most frequented streets of the town, not a bed of roses for only the thinness of an unquilted mat was between them and the coarse cobble stones with which the street is paved.

I often smell in the houses the rank odor of the pickle tub. At *Eshaw's*[55] this evening his fat and laughing servant girl was preparing the evening meal. Taking up the floorboards of the kitchen she brought to view one of these tubs of 15 gallons capacity stewing and fermenting with its sourer than sauerkraut odor. A brine is made of water, salt, and bran which undergoes the fermenting process and in a year is considered unfit to use. Into this brine are thrown indiscriminately, turnips, radishes, cucumbers, mellons, egg plants, fruits, and a general contribution from the garden which there seethe and ferment in the humid brine till they are permeated to the Japanese taste and have acquired an odor and taste alike disagreeable to an untrained palate, and have become so indigestible as to readily account for the national *epidemics* of colic and dyspepsia, since they are the everyday and abundant staples of every one's food.

Saturday, July 27, 1861

S[adajirō] opens his morning budget of news with the report from Yedo that seven or eight men within a few night's interval entered the imperial palace for plunder. "How could they pass all the gates," I said. "Because all the gate keepers are fools, and since even the Emperor's house may be thus entered how can foreigners expect to escape?"

Entering a Japanese house, whether it be a dwelling, a shop, or an inn, I often see among the rafters one or more swallow's nests. Usually but one, and that in a conspicuous place near the entrance. While the dogs roam the streets and appear to belong to the street rather than to individuals, the cat is a domestic institution in every house. There are many fine large specimens of the cat kind to be seen, the Japanese giving the short tailed ones preference to the long tails. Cats of pure white color are common, so are those of the tricolor—reddish yellow, white and black—either blended or more often each color in a distinctive patch. And what is not a little singular, for I have often observed it myself, while the yellow and white cats predominate in males, the tricolor predominates in females. So much so, that a tricolored male is not easily procurable, the Japanese attaching especial value to them. I have frequently tried to get them but have never succeeded.

Most persons resident in Japan have, I think, a mistaken idea as to the ability of persons rising from low ranks to high. I am satisfied that this is indeed quite common. As for instance a man enters the employ of a man of rank from out of the farming, mercantile, or other so called lower classes in Japan, and proving himself to be faithful and competent, receiving the regard of his employer, is gradually promoted to stations of confidence, invested with two swords, and assuming the privilege of a samurai, or, if in government employ, he may receive as high as a *hatamoto* from which rank civil officers of the higher grades are taken such as governors of provinces, etc. I think this is by no means uncom-

---

55 Eshaw, or Eisha [Isha], was a native doctor who was a friend of Dr. Hall's. John M. Brooke described him as a native physician whose practice consisted of applying the moxa and acupuncture. Brooke at one point refers to him as Dr. Ghendio "a good hearted man" whose "house is always open to us." Brooke loaned the doctor $50 for a new house he was building. On his departure from Japan in February 1860 Brooke wrote: "Poor Ei-

sha cannot return the $50.00 he borrowed from me. I tell him that if hereafter he has plenty of money, to pay it to Dr. Hall for me. His new house has probably cost more than he anticipated." See George M. Brooke, Jr., *John M. Brooke's Pacific Cruise and Japanese Adventure, 1858–1860* (Honolulu: University of Hawaii Press, 1986), pp. 168, 170, 202, 208.

mon. I so often hear such men spoken of as having risen from low station. A Japanese acquaintance a day or two since in casual conversation named to me two vice governors who had in early life been farmers. Higher than the *hatamoto* class they may not aspire, the honors above that being hereditary. Though anciently, when Japan was broken up into many petty kingdoms with a doubtful consolidation under the Mikado, men rising from the ranks by military prowess laid the foundation of their family name and were invested with permanent rank by the Mikado. Not a few of the present families of the daimios were thus established at no very ancient date, and the great Tyco Sama was at one time a farmer's boy, or, as others say, a hostler of the Prince of Owari.

Sunday, July 28, 1861

Drought still continues but it is noticeable how well the crops endure it owing partly to the heavy dews but more to the light porous soil.

Wednesday, July 31, 1861

[Entries for 29th through 31st listed together.] Busy at the house making repairs. Taking meals at Dr. S[immons]'s.[56]

Heavy shower 3 A.M., squall during the forenoon. Fine cool breezes all night and today. Murky clouds hovering around, but little rain. Last night was the time set down for a threatened attack by Mito's men upon Yokohama, but the night passes quietly on as usual and we pay no heed to the warnings.

Friday, August 2, 1861

Made a close acquaintance today with an *itach*, or weasel, which Fanny Nangai my little puss had chased within doors and driven up to a refuge behind my writing desk. We made an attempt to capture the intruder, Fanny watch-

ing at one end of the desk while I stood at the other waiting for him to come forth. I cautiously drew out the table when he rushed out gliding nimbly by, avoiding equally well my cane and puss who followed in vain with her cut tail. He left behind the strong fetid overpowering odor peculiar to the *Mustelidae* which is secreted and used for purposes of defense. The Japanese say of it, that if it, the fluid, comes in contact with the skin it causes a yellow tint which not weeks will eradicate. S[adajirō] gravely relates that a friend of his who caught an unusually large one and received the ejected fluid in his face was condemned to a saffron tinted visage for a good eight months!

The singing crickets (?) [question mark in original] are just coming about. I have a present of several today including two varieties, a black and white variety, the former called *suzu mushi* from the resemblance of its tone to a bell's, the "bell insect," while others say the name means an "agreeable wind," or "breath fair." The white is called the *mastu-mushi*, or "pine-insect," mushi being a generic name for all insects. These insects, as well as several other varieties, are praised for their vocal qualities, the "bell insect" above all the rest.

At Yedo are several shops for the exclusive transaction of insect traffic and are called *mushi-ya*, *ya* again being a general terminative to the names of all places of business meaning literally house or shop. At these shops in the summer season are to be found great varieties and large quantities of insects for sale from the soft toned bell insect to the great grasshopper whose shrill piercing notes make the air tremulous with tones of sound that literally deafen the ear and is prolonged for nearly a moment of time. These insects singing in a copse near the sea I have heard a full quarter of a mile out on the bay towards sunset or in the early misty twilight hours after sunset. I have held them in my hand while they uttered their sharp vibrating notes and under the thorax and breast plates of the abdomen have seen a thin white membrane vibrating with the utmost rapidity. I thought I had detected the

---

[56] This would suggest that Hall was no longer living with Dr. Simmons. Simmons built a house for himself at No. 82 Main Street (originally lot 31 of the 1860 "new concession"), which he sold for $4,000 in 1862.

source of the sound, but rudely tearing the filament to pieces with a pin the shrill music from some unseen instrument was as high and loud as ever. (Rats are said to leave the house where these insects are kept. I would if the rats did not. The bugle boarder is naught to one.)

The insects are exposed for sale in various forms of pretty tiny cages made of bamboo or rattan, one very common form being that of two miniature pails or buckets about the size of an ordinary breakfast cup connected with a chain passing through a pulley suspended from the ceiling. The singing hours, those of the *suzu* and *matsu mushi*, are in the evening and [they] must be kept carefully in the shade during the day or they will easily perish. They feed on fruits, and at evening should be sprinkled with a little moisture. Fabulous prices have been paid for some of the *suzu mushi*, for as with canaries, there appears to be a quality of voice recognized by insect amateurs and even 20 or 30 ichibus (seven to ten dollars) have been paid for an extra bell-noted individual. The ordinary price is 1 tempo each and 3 for a tempo is the lowest of the market range.

The proprietors of the *mushi yas* do not limit themselves to the sale of insects, but they raise those they do sell, for as they say, it is not only difficult to catch them from the woods but those so caught, imprisoned of their liberties in the wild wood range or fearful of their captors, refuse to sing as caged insects. The process for raising them is very simple. Towards the close of the summer and singing season they are placed in a box or jar of mixed earth and sand the surface of which is lightly covered with cotton or straw. In the winter season these insects burrow below the surface and emerging again towards spring deposit their eggs. The proprietors carefully expose these to the sun at day, covering them at night, and occasionally sprinkling them with water. Thus is the young insect hatched and cared for till the music season comes round when perfected under the best of masters he takes his place in the market. But by far the largest portion are rejected like applicants for the tuition of the conservatoire for want of good voices and left to make shift again in the world. The family line of good singers alone is perpetuated, and alas, when once the cares of parentage have been assumed voice and life are alike lost in the parent insect.

The belles of Nippon employ the bell insect as an ornament. On the top of a hair pin, or rather dagger, is a little cage of wire gauze large enough to hold one [of] these small crickets, or whatsoever they may be, and with this musical adornment of her shining wealth of hair you may meet her promenading the streets displaying the odor of the camellia nut and the song of the bell insect as she moves along thus realizing the story of the lady famous in our nursery rhyme books, with an antipodal reversal of position only,

Rings on her fingers, bells on her toes
She'll have music wherever she goes.

Sunday, August 4, 1861

The Japanese officials have arrested over thirty girls today living in various parts of the town for misdemeanors with foreigners. They were discharged on reprimand and promises for future good behavior.

Monday, August 5, 1861

H[eco] and I were invited to hear some harp playing a few days ago, but when today we went to the house to hear it, the family were so much frightened by yesterday's occurrences that they were afraid to have a foreigner seen about the house, for however innocent themselves, they know that injustice as well as justice is arbitrary in Nippon.

Tuesday, August 6, 1861

Arrival of the *Houqua* with the mail. I was unlucky enough to draw but blanks. Dates from America to the 1st of June. Yesterday and today great numbers of pilgrims have been in the streets who are returning from visits to sacred places, *Ōyama, Fusi-yama*, etc. The greater number of them are clad in white cotton, white cotton sack, tight cotton trousers, umbrella hats, sandals of straw, a long staff, and a bundle of necessaries hung about the neck completes the equipment. On these garments were various stamped devices in red and white received from the various shrines visited. Some of the garments on the back and breast were covered with these records of the faithful, and they were all stamped with the grime and dust of the road, their garments being filthy beyond endurance of anybody but devotees. Some had little boxes of provisions for the road, a gourd for water, a drinking cup, and carried relics of their visits, pictures, and other easy portable mementos, and one I saw had a bunch of orchids which he had gathered from some sacred mountain. Others cut their staves from the mountain or bring back some sacred water.

There are less pilgrims than usual this year owing to fear of ronins, and it is not unfrequent that bands of plunderers roam the country in this disguise. The officials about the foreign settlements are especially vigilant lest in this guise men intent on harm may enter among the foreigners.

It is customary for large parties to start a pilgrimage, friends and neighbors of the same vicarage, who are both company and protection each to [the] other. Two hundred sometimes start at once. The white pilgrim suits mentioned, I learn on inquiry, are purchased at the mountain (Ōyama, which is open for these visits 20 days) and are afterwards worn in every pilgrimage of subsequent years, receiving each year one stamp, or mark, so that after many pilgrimages the clothes, like some I saw yesterday, are not only soiled, but their surface further hid under the broad seals of the pilgrimages, each as large as the palm of my hand. Doubtless in his native village the veteran whose garments are most hidden under the seals and mold of years is an object of rural envy.

Thursday, August 8, 1861

Went with Dr. H[all] on a boat excursion to Kanasawa. Left Yokohama at 9 A.M. and had a fair wind reaching Webster Island in Mississippi Bay in a little more than two hours.

Dr. George R. Hall. Yokohama agent for Walsh & Co. from 1859 to 1861. Physician and plant hunter.

Sailed in behind Webster Island and entered Goldsborough inlet, the wind still fair. The tide was rushing out of the inlet with great force, but we wound our way into the country past beautiful low wooded hills, picturesque islands and villages, and salt flats, till the wind was contrary and we betook ourselves to sculls.

Long lines of sea wall were built here and there about the inlet to confine its waters in due bounds. Landing at one of these under the roof of a tea house we entered the streets of Kanasawa. The village boys were ready to escort us as usual, a half naked crowd whom we made useful in carrying our baggage to the tea house, our old resort, where we [were] hospitably received. We made a tarry of three hours during which I visited an ancient temple seat in a large park-like ground shaded with tall cedars, scattered about which were the monastic residences and the various temple buildings. The principal temple was a small ancient one built by Yoritomo six hundred years ago. Its worn and venerable look bespoke great age. I gathered some ferns under its shadow and at the foot of the hillock on which it was built a lotus pond stretched with serpentine curve under the cedars. This beautiful flower was now in full blossom and it was a glorious sight to see them rising ashore or resting upon the broad leaves of the lily. A rustic bridge of stone crossed the pond which had a length of nearly 300 feet and a breadth of 50 in the widest parts.

The obliging people who accompanied me sent a boy into the deep ooze of the pond to bring me some of the blossoms and I returned laden with my trophies to the hotel. A music teacher of seventeen years across the street entertained us with a "few select airs" by herself and pupils. The landlord showed us with some pride some tomatoes and turnips growing in his garden, the seeds of which H.[57] had given him last April. All the crops about Kanasawa seemed to be suffering more from the drought than at Yokohama. We partook our dinner of fried fish, eggs, boiled rice with a dessert of melons, and cakes fried in rape oil, took an after dinner nap, chatted with our host and his fair mistress and at 4 or a little after gathered our boatmen for the return.

The tide was flowing in as we pushed away from the tea house wharf and we had to battle against [it]. We stopped at a little village on the left bank of the inlet to visit the salt works. Passing through the village where there is a custom house to receive revenues on the salt and inspect the quality and quantity made, we came to the extensive house and grounds of one of the salt factors which betokened the wealth of its proprietor. Ample houses, fine hedges opening into spacious avenues, a large pond of blooming lotus, and the largest collection of mountain peonies I have seen in Japan added to the general air of the place [and] bespoke the well-to-do-astuteness of the owner.

In a little summer house of one room by the margins of the lotus pond we found an old man living hermit-like by himself. His uncropped beard was white as became a veteran

of 94 years. We were probably the first foreigners the old man had ever seen, and he seemed pleased to discover that we had eyes ears and noses not so very different from his own. Our long beards particularly interested him, and he was inquisitive about our garments and seemed surprised to be addressed in his own tongue. The people about paid him every mark of respect and were evidently gratified that we were also.

In the lotus pond were some pure white blossoms and we engaged with a man who appeared to have power to treat that he should mark the spot where they grew that in the next spring we might obtain the roots. He wanted no pay, he said, and it was agreed that it should be an interchange of presents.

The salt work adjoined this place and thither we repaired under the escort of a dozen guides. Inside of the stone dikes, having gates to let in or shut off the salt water at will, a flat piece of ground is prepared, this one contained several acres, over which the sea water is flooded at high tide. After the water has stood a sufficient period it is again drawn off, the surface earth is scraped into heaps, put into small tubs, and lixiviated, draining into a tub below. The brine thus collected is carried to vats stationed at convenient distances about the salt fields in flat forms a few feet high. From these vats pipes lead to reservoirs under sheds by the margins of the fields where it remains awaiting the boiling process. This is carried on under cover in adjoining sheds. The brine is poured into shallow pans some ten or twelve feet square under which is a furnace. This is fed by fire obtained from the long rushes that grow abundantly about, no other fuel is used, but I observed the boiling was evenly conducted over the whole surface of the pan. By this simple process each batch is made to produce about ten bushels of coarsest salt per day. The business is carried on by the farmers who pay the tax to the government.

We laid in a store of melons and at 6 P.M. started again. The wind blew freshly outside, considerable sea was running, and it was nine P.M. before we reached Yokohama.

[57] As there is no mention of Joseph Heco accompanying Hall on this excursion with Dr. Hall, it seems likely that the H. referred to here is Dr. Hall, who was also known to have an interest in plants and seeds.

Friday, August 9, 1861

After a long protracted drought which had begun to give apprehensions for the incoming crops a bountiful rain is falling and what adds to its welcomeness is that it comes without violent gales as is frequent at this season.

Saturday, August 10, 1861

Frequent and heavy showers during the day with little wind. We have reports from Yedo that six days ago one of the Goroju, or Council of State, while proceeding through the court quarter at Yedo surrounded by his guards and in a street at all times crowded with yakunins and samurai, was assaulted by ten ronin and desperately wounded. Two of the assailants were seized and the rest escaped. They were recognized as Mito's men. Prince Mito declares "they are outlaws over whom he has no control and if the Government can do any better with them they may do so."

The Governors of Yokohama and Kanagawa have been remonstrated with by the daimios to whom the three men lately arrested at Kanagawa belong and who are very indignant that any of their followers should be taken for ordinary footpads. Satsuma is one of the outraged parties.

It is stated on good authority that five vessels have already left the ports of Oasaca and Nagasaki for Chinese ports under the new regulation that native vessels may trade to any foreign ports. These are said to have gone to see what may be done and others are advised (Japanese *must*) wait till they bring back [their] report.

Monday, August 12, 1861

S[adajirō] tells me a curious instance of the singular belief that got ground among ignorant people. It is currently stated in Yedo that the foreign merchants desire to buy human *livers,* supposed for medicines as they have obtained from Chinese medicine the story that for certain diseases human livers dried and powdered are infallible cures. One readily no-

tices the coincidence of this with similar beliefs among ignorant people in civilized lands. This story just now got currency from the report of a boy, who running away from Yedo, was offered food and lodging for his services in Yokohama. Accepting his new master's offer he was taken to a large house where he was fed not on rice but on barley which was the food of several men who were in employ at the same place. Dissatisfied with his place and alarmed by the threat of his master for some misdeed that he would "cut his liver out," he escapes and returns again to Yedo with the doleful tale that he was detained solely for the purpose of having his liver cut out! His friends return with him to Yokohama and the boy is taken up and down all the streets to recognize the place, if possible, of his detention. He finally points out a place, the master of which is dumbfounded at the charge, and on being confronted with the boy, the latter avows his mistake in as much as he had never seen the man before. He is then questioned more minutely and describes the peculiar clothing of those by whom he was surrounded, when it appears that he describes the livery of the Custom House underlings and it is further known that they use barley for food. From these and other coincidences the popular belief is fixed that the lad was in durance among the laborers and porters of the Custom House who either meant to sell him for a slave or to cut out his liver for medicine.

Japanese learning English frequently come to me with an English book they have procured but are puzzled to make out some word or sentence, which frequently proves to be a bit of pedantry on the part of the bookmaker, desirous to show his knowledge and which requires more time to explain to the comprehension of the student than pages of his grammar or geography would. For instance today a man came with an elementary grammar received from the Ambassadors to America and finds something about the "philosopher's stone" in a dissertation on parts of speech. Now it takes a terrible deal of time and hard talking in imperfect Japanese to explain what it means and why it is here and the puzzled student goes away at last wondering, as I do, what the philosopher's stone has to do with verbs and adjectives. Special and technical terms are also difficult to explain, but the Japanese are not slow to take an idea. The same man has a great liking for our newspapers and spells and reads away at their columns with all diligence. Today he was deep in the commercial column but soon brought up against the phrase "no margin for profit." I at once pointed to the margin of his paper and he caught the idea immediately.[58]

A Japanese tailor at work makes good use of his feet. If he has a long seam to run up he squats on the floor as he always does and holds the two edges of his material by his toes leaving his hands free to work; making a sewing bird of his toes.

Saturday, August 17, 1861

Went to Kanagawa. Mr. B[rown] came back with me. He says that some months since the Japanese Government applied to him to furnish him [sic, them] from America two practical and scientific men who should explore the island of Yeso to ascertain its mineral and metallic resources. They wanted men who had not only a scientific knowledge of these subjects but who understood the practical details of mining. They wished also for models to imitate and manufacture, an open barouche carriage, and a one horse cart. Here was something for both ends of the social ladder—a carriage for the gentlemen and an improved labor vehicle for the laborers. Mr. Harris at once ordered these things from San Francisco and they may soon be expected out here. The Japanese are further desirous of purchasing more ships.

Monday, August 19, 1861

It appears from letters received from Yedo that there was an attack, or an alarm of an attack, upon the American Legation at Yedo at 2 A.M. of the 19th. The guards stationed about

Mr. Harris's residence gave the alarm and said that persons were seeking an entrance in the rear. The alarm soon subsided and the probabilities seemed to be that no attack was made, the guards taking unnecessary alarm.

Thursday, August 22, 1861

Sadajirō returned from Yedo last evening. He reports affairs at the capital as in a very unsettled state. Ronins were numerous and troublesome, so numerous that the government was powerless to suppress them. He saw himself one evening a band of more than a hundred together. He denies that any imperial troops have been sent against the ronins in Mito's province, but that Mito's own men have gone thither and everybody knows that is only a farce. The rumor of the death of the Tycoon is still believed by many. The present government from the Tycoon to the Council of State is considered very weak and a formidable conspiracy is reported to be steadily organizing against it at which Mito and the princes of Satsuma and Sendai are at the head.

Yesterday closed a series of three national holidays devoted to paying respect to the memories of the dead. The tombs and cemeteries are visited by all ranks and conditions, the burial grounds carefully cleaned, the tombstones renovated, the basins replenished with water, flowers placed at the family graves and incense burned. The women are foremost in this religious work, wives visiting the burial plots of husbands and children those of parents, all attired in holiday clothes. The sight as they go along the streets intent upon this pious observance is extremely pleasing and the stranger who should for the first time see Yedo during these days would be astonished at the numbers of handsomely dressed females he would meet in the streets. The prince's wife goes thither also on foot with her female companions five or six of whom are all dressed alike so that which is the princess and which her attendants it would be difficult to distin-

---

[58] Once again it is unclear who this Japanese visitor was. If he received a grammar from one of the ambassadors to the United States, he was obviously a person of some importance. His interest in newspapers is also worth noting.

guish. So, too, the daughters of the noble houses go thither with their young companions and may now for once at least be seen in the streets of the great city, since the etiquette of the usage require that they should walk to the tombs, though they may return in their norimons.

One of the Governors of Foreign Affairs is in town today overseeing the location of the foreign Consulates to be built upon the bluffs.

Saturday, August 24, 1861

Confucius arrived with mail.

Monday, August 26, 1861

Neva arrived.

Tuesday, August 27, 1861

Raven, Fruiter, Europa arrived.

Wednesday, August 28, 1861

Thermometer 91° within doors.

Friday, August 30, 1861

The late report of the Tycoon's suicide (by poison) gains credence daily. The event is said to have occurred two months since.

Curiosity prompted me to visit a Japanese circus so advertised. I found it to be only a theater on horseback. There was no display of equestrianism, it was simply doing on horseback what might have been better done on a stage. The display was [more] ludicrous than otherwise.

Saturday, August 31, 1861

The wonderful adventure of the *Illustrated London News* artist[59] and a jealous Englishman!

The courtesans' quarter is not far from my abode. It is surrounded by broad and deep canals into whose muddy waters "one more unfortunate" weary of her life not infrequently drowns her sins and sorrows. This evening floating on these waters were three barges lighted with lanterns and torches and gaily decorated with paper streamers. Under a canopy in the largest barge were seated twelve or fifteen priests in their sacred robes of white, yellow, or black, who, as the barges were slowly propelled along by setting poles, offered incense and "sacrifices of fruit, wine, and coin" and chanted prayers for the repose of the souls of the poor girls who had extinguished life's torch in the waters that now gleamed in the flashes of torchlight and lantern. Mingled with the monotonous tones of the drawling priests were the tinklings of bells and sound of drums. It was a strange spectacle under the starlight of a summer night. The balconies of the pleasure houses which overhung the canals were filled with lookers on at what might be some day done for the repose of their souls as well; nevertheless their careless laughter and songs were heard over the waters in shrill soprano to the chanting bass of the shaven priests.

Sunday, September 1, 1861

Interview with Von Siebold.

Tuesday, September 3, 1861

Visit to Kanagawa and Dorr is sick again. A delightful cool change today.

---

[59] The *Illustrated London News* artist was Charles Wirgman, who was also the editor of the *Yokohama Punch*. There is no indication of what the "adventure" mentioned here was. Hall was a friend of Wirgman's and later purchased two of his oil paintings, which hang today in the Hall Memorial Library in Ellington, Connecticut.

Wednesday, September 4, 1861

Went to the "Circus," or "Horse Theater," as the Japs call it with Heco. A large audience were present in which the fair sex were a large morety. The usual eating was going on among the audience, and between the acts the boys, some naked, some half dressed, put up various antics on the sanded arena to the amusement of their elders, but particularly to a little girl in a scanty red chemise who divided her attention between the boys and munching pears. The riding was nothing, although the horses showed great docility.

We had one act representing a historic tragedy in which three warriors clad in mail appeared, one of whom was a young prince betrothed to a fair damsel who also comes upon the scene resplendent in silk, satin, gold, and her head adorned with a silver diadem of glistening stars and pendants. One of the warriors makes love to the damsel telling her that her young Prince has been slain in battle, but she, remaining true to his memory, is slain by the disappointed chief for her constancy. Again the young Prince appears on the stage where he encounters his mortal enemy in the person of an ancient Nippon hero. The Prince is vanquished, but his conqueror spares his life for he was brought up at the court of the Prince's father and they were anciently friends. He therefore sends the Prince away, but while he is making his escape he is arrested by orders of the chief general and sent back again to his vanquisher who is ordered peremptorily to slay him.

Then follows the tragic scene which moves the audience to tears. The warrior tells the Prince of his former friendship to him, sad is the duty he is compelled to perform; thrice he essays to give the fatal blow and thrice his feelings compel him to recoil, till the young Prince, who in the meantime has been praying with pale face over his saddle, now bids him to delay no longer but strike or he will thrust a dagger into his own bosom. Amidst his tears the grim warrior gives the blow, the Prince falls forward on his horse and at the same time a mock head pale and gory is seen to fall on the sands while the Prince disappears from the stage riding his horse remarkably well for a

dead man. The scene closes with a long soliloquy the executioner holds over the head which he has picked up from the sand.

Then followed a farce. A young man is first married and meets an old friend with whom he takes counsel how he shall manage his household affairs. This gives opportunity for the free use of many jests which are highly received by the audience. Among the young man's troubles are the rats, the play is called "The Rats," one of which of great size has surprised his sleeping bride and eaten off her nose. The countryman, for the older represents a farmer, tells him how he shall set a trap for the mouse, and the young man who is much of a simpleton proposes to watch by the trap. He is directed however to set a trap which proves to be something like our "figure four" trap and go to sleep near by. This is done, when in comes the rat mounted horseback. The rat is of course a man dressed to resemble a rat which is cleverly done with garments of "mouse color" and a capital imitation of a monster rat's head complete to its bright round eyes, whiskers, and sharp teeth. After sniffing about the room, in which the person of the sleeper is ludicrously examined, the rat sniffs the baited trap, examines it, and having taken out the bait, springs the trap and retires. The watcher now awakes and finding the trap sprung expects to seize his prey, but is disappointed and in turn is now assaulted by the rat. There is a long chase around the arena which ends in the seizure of the man by the rat and the bearing of him off to the ceiling. This is actually done by drawing up the two men on one horse to the ceiling and then across the room to a stage prepared to receive them. All the machinery work to do this is plainly visible to the audience which renders the scene still more comical and ludicrous. The farce seemed to be well enjoyed by the audience.

Wednesday, September 11, 1861

From the *Actaeon* surveying vessel now upon the coasts I learn that the island of "Oho-Sima," [Ōshima] or "Volcano Island," is a rugged island sparsely inhabited. There are three villages on the island inhabited by poor fishermen only. No yakunins, samurai, or persons of rank were visible. The island roads, cut through ridges and so overhung with trees as to shut out the sun's rays, were a striking feature. The volcanic cone that gives name to the island is in active eruption emitting not only dense clouds of smoke but flames. The inhabitants deprecated any exploration or ascent of the island for they said it was only to be visited at a particular season of the year, and any attempt to do so would bring upon them typhoons, gales, and disasters. In deference to their fears the volcano was left unexplored.

Thursday, September 12, 1861

Open air theaters in the Oshiwara.

Sunday, September 15, 1861

To Kanagawa to make a farewell call on Mrs. Hepburn who leaves soon for America.

Monday, September 16, 1861

A mail from Nagasaki and the return of the English Admiral from a cruise around the island brings additional information from Tsu-Sima [Tsushima]. The Admiral found the Russians on shore at Tsu-Sima and evidently preparing for a stay. They had erected houses, made a road, and were preparing docks for the repair of ships. They had no difficulty in effecting a foothold there contrary to the Japanese report. Proceeding from thence the Admiral visited the Amour where he found the Russians busy in erecting forts. They have taken possession of the whole of Sakhalin and were living on the most friendly terms with the natives. At Hakodade the Admiral entered a protest to the Governor General of Siberia for the occupation of Tsu-Sima.

The principality of Tsu-Sima appears to be almost independent of the Japanese crown. According to native accounts, in the bloody wars of Yoritomo's time some of the defeated vassal princes fled thither and established themselves and since have had little communi-

cation with the imperial government of Japan. The family of the reigning Prince Soo Tsu-Sima-no-Kami is one of the oldest, if not the oldest, in the empire. For 100 years there has been no visitation of this island by the imperial officers. From Rev. Mr. V[erbeck] of Nagasaki I draw the following items. "On the 1st of April 1858 Capt. Kallendyke, chief of the corps of officers of instruction in Nagasaki, landed at Tsu-Sima with Kimura-Setsu-no-Kami, imperial director of the Navy and Oho-ometski (chief spy) on board a Japanese steamer, and though the Capt. in the same company had been received most politely and shown round in Satsuma, Hirado, and several other principalities and islands, the Prince of Tsu-Sima refused to see either any of the Dutch officers or the imperial high officer himself. They were obliged to leave without accomplishing anything but a hasty survey of the harbor." Capt. Kallendyke writes, "whether there is any proof in this that the Prince has cut the Emperor, I do not know, but it is certain that the imperial and European officers were very unwelcome visitors. In explanation of the conduct of the vassal it must however be remembered that it is more than 100 years ago since the Emperor of Japan has sent any one to this island to enforce his authority. So that the Prince, so far out of shooting distance, may well fancy himself lord and master of his land."

Tuesday, September 17, 1861

Today the *Carrington* left for San Francisco with nineteen passengers, among them Mrs. Hepburn. It was a great number to go from our little community at one time though some of them had been merely temporary residents.

Thursday, September 19, 1861

Dr. Hay and Purser Fulton of the *Saginaw* were my guests today. Met at the table a Mrs. Brooks, the young wife of the Capt. of the *Vikery*, who gave us some interesting accounts of Siberia, Nicolaefski, and the Amour from whence she has just returned.

Monday, September 23, 1861

Visited the *Saginaw* today and afterwards the American Bark *Vikery*, Brooks master. The *Vikery* has recently come from the Amour and Hakodade and from Capt. Brooks I gathered information of the Russians on the Asiatic coasts.

The Russians under the conduct of their late Governor General of Siberia, Mouravieff,[60] and the present one, Guskavitch,[61] have rapidly developed their Asiatic possessions. They have now occupied the whole line of sea-coast from Amour to the northern boundary of Corea and extending inward to the Ussuri River, establishing posts and naval stations at all the important bays and harbors of which there are several fine commodious ones and locating military stations and military roads in the interior. The country between the Ussuri and the coast is rich in minerals, well watered, fertile and highly adapted for agricultural purposes. The Ussuri is navigable for steamers and this past season the Governor ascended it in a small steamer to within 300 miles of Olga Bay in Lat. 43° 45′ to which latter place a post road has been established and a settlement made.

Wherever the Russians have gone they have by every means conciliated the people. In poor districts provisions and clothing have been freely distributed by government officials and the most amicable relations successfully cultivated. Petty chiefs have been compensated for their lost possessions. No nation has ever made such territorial acquisitions so silently and quietly and inexpensively. Her trained men have been "prospecting" these countries for years past with a view to the acquisition of all that is valuable, and it may be safe to infer that the progress of Russia southward will find no check until she has reached the great Chinese wall. Japan no longer has any foothold on Sakhalin, Tsu-Sima has been wrested from her, and it is safe to predict that Yeso will ere many years share a like fate. Capt. B[rooks] declares that in repeated conversations with various Russians and in particular with one high officer, these ideas were expressed without reservations, "Yeso they needed and must have, it was theirs geographically as a defence of their coasts, but for the rest of Japan they cared nothing, having the Straits of Corea, Sangar, and P[erouse] in their possession." The Japanese at Hakodade says Capt. B[rooks] have their eyes thoroughly open to the fate that may await them. The Russians are extending themselves there erecting new buildings, keeping one or more ships constantly in the harbor.

The present Consul General of Japan who resides at Hakodade recently received a domiciliary visit from the Japanese Governor who was one of the recent Embassy to America. It is understood at Hakodade that his position is not a pleasant one as he is jealously watched by his shadow the government spy. On this occasion he managed to inform the Consul General aside as to the object of his visit intimating that he deemed it an unpleasant one, but that he must do it and do it under the espionage of this man. The Government had entertained the idea that the Russians might be covertly arming themselves and their place with a view to making it a stronghold for ulterior operations. It is needless to say that discovered only a mare's nest. However during the past year the Japanese have erected a fort on a sandy neck of land whose guns bear not on the bay, but on the town of Hakodade and particularly on the Russian quarters. This Governor of Hakodade is there temporarily to relieve the late incumbent who has been ordered to make an inspection of the whole coastline of Yeso lest Russians might already have made a quiet occupancy somewhere and also to establish posts of observation to watch any such future contingency. What the Japanese fear and what the Russians seek not to disguise is almost sure to be the fate of Yeso within ten years.

Thursday, September 26, 1861

Confined to the house by illness.

---

[60] Nikolai Nikolaevich Muravev-Amurskii.
[61] Iosif Antonovich Goshkevich was, in fact, Russian consul in Hakodate, not governor of Siberia as Hall states above.

Friday, September 27, 1861

Confined to the house by illness. A Japanese merchant states to me that the usual rate of interest in this country is equal to 8 percent per annum and if more is taken although a writing may be shown to that agreement the authorities will set it aside. Although this statement was made unprompted it requires confirmation.

Tuesday, October 1, 1861

Saginaw left.

Wednesday, October 2, 1861

I have much difficulty in ascertaining the joint neighborhood and family responsibility, the *associated five* of whom the Dutch have made so frequent mention. It still exists, but to what extent, and how binding are the mutual obligations, have never been clear. A casual conversation with a Japanese this evening (S[adajirō]) gave me some light. A Japanese servant in the employ of ——— [blank in original] was found by his master last night with a female companion in his room. I asked S[adajirō] if the woman was not a licensed prostitute would the authorities "interfere in [the] case?" "Most certainly," he replied, "she would be condemned to 1000 days servitude as a public prostitute for punishment." Frequent search, he added, was made by the officials for this class of woman who are called *Jingokoo* [jigoku] (the Japanese word also for Hell!). Moreover [in] the neighborhood where the girl lived the "five associated families" would be liable to punishment in as much as they were supposed cognizant of such notorious acts. So also of gambling, the authorities growing sometimes suddenly virtuous enforce the imperial regulations that already exist against gambling, and while the offender is condemned to 1000 days labor in the Emperor's service the adjoining families are mulcted in some lighter penalty which is heavier on the adjoining houses than the remoter ones. The five houses are part on either side of the street,

and those on the side where the offender lives are punished more severely than the opposite houses. This custom does not obtain among the higher classes, the *sword bearing classes*, but is [in] general prevalence in all cities, villages, and hamlets. The head man of the Five is called *skasadoroo sto* [tsukasadoru hito] and the office passes monthly in rotation. Above him is the *nanooshi* [nanushi], who is head man of the hamlet if small or if as at Kanagawa the place is larger there are two or more. He is more commonly called *tosiori* [toshiyori], "the elder," and is chosen annually, sometimes biannually. In his appointment the villagers appear to have an elective choice, and a system not unlike our ballot system is resorted to.

Tuesday, October 8, 1861

Confined to the house by illness.

Wednesday, October 9–Saturday, October 12, 1861

Confined to the house by illness.

Sunday, October 13, 1861

The "Chestnut Holiday," see next p[age].

Monday, October 14, 1861

Arrival of *Theresa* with mail. S[adajirō] returned from Yedo this morning. He reports the aspect of the city as unusually bustling and gay. The abundance of crops of every description this season, more abundant than have been known for many years, have given joy to all hearts. The farmers are especially rejoicing saying that they have had six years in one, that is a thrice abundant crop and a double price for their products. The Emperor is again reported as preparing for his nuptials with the daughter of the Mikado next month. The Governor of Yedo has made another arrest of street girls in Yedo. Two hundred were arrested and are threatened with banishment to

Yeso for wives to convicts. From S[adajirō]'s account it appears that Yeso is used as a penal colony, that the island is governed by men of hatamoto rank stationed at frequent places, and that to the supervision of these officers convicts are sent. Among the unlicensed courtesans arrested was the mistress of the late Regent.

Friday, October 25, 1861

Ride to the valley.

Saturday, October 26, 1861

After a wet weather spell we have again clear skies and fair autumn weather which have proved of essential service to my health. On Sunday last for the first in a long time I tried a short ride on horseback into the country about Kanagawa and finding that it was of essential service, I started again on Friday with Dr. Hall, took a long excursion on the Kanagawa side to the "Great Valley." The circuitous hilly path we took thither was delightful with its alternatives of hills, valleys, woods, and cultivated fields. We found many more berries in cultivation and everywhere the rice crop awaiting the harvesters. Our halt was at a little roadside tea house where the valley converges between the hills, and where for the first time I had to complain of Japanese inhospitality. We were refused food for ourselves and even water for the horses. We helped ourselves to the latter, and should have done so to the former had our appetites craved the meals we saw preparing for native travelers. As I began to plunder a persimmon tree near by of its large golden fruit the tea house attendants proffered in preference some already gathered, and no doubt had we made any show of violent seizure of their fish, rice, and potatoes, would have yielded those also. The money we proffered them they refused, and I threw it to, or rather at, two officials who were gate keepers, close by, of a bridge that crosses hereabouts an inconsiderable stream, and the copper coin lay in the dirt where it fell for anybody's benefit who might pick it up. The reason assigned for the seeming churlishness was that they were

ordered by the Custom House at Yokohama to report all foreigners whom they fed, what monies were received, etc., and as they lived so far away they could not do it. The excuse was an insufficient one for we are always charged enough to pay a special messenger's charges. The Japanese, while they cannot prevent one rambling within treaty limits, are quite ready to embarrass us, so doing with all manner of hindrance and annoyance. Expressing our disgust at such annoyances in Japanese that fell harmless, because not understood, on the listeners, we turned our horses homewards.

S[adajirō] tells me of mourning customs, that to wear mourning for children is not the custom here. A daimio goes into mourning for fifty days, certainly a period, which some extend to one year. During the season of mourning white garments are worn, the mourner remains in his own house, abstains from all shows and amusements, feasting included. Funeral discourses are also pronounced exhorting to good deeds and a virtuous life after our civilized way of "improving occasions."

Sunday, October 27, 1861

My birthday anniversary, *hew! fugaces annos!* Anxious to improve the fine weather for health's sake. My friend, Dr. Hall and I take his boat for an excursion on the bay. Shall I call it an auspicious day that the sky is cloudless and the bay placid and smooth as a pond. There was a light wind before which we sailed down to Mississippi Bay where the breeze deserted us and we fell back upon our oars and the brawn of our five boatmen. A ship lay at anchor in the bay, just in from Aukland and waiting a favorable breath to take her up to Yokohama. We lunched from our stores of fruit, pie, and cakes on the clean deck of the boat and abandoned ourselves after the repast, H. to a nap, and I to dreaming of friends at home who I knew today held me in memory. At 2 o'clock we landed at Perry Island, small and uninhabited. There was a mia on the island and two tenements which though not old were fast going to ruin. The boatmen were unwilling we should land, it was a bad island they said and brought ill luck to all who had anything to do with it, ever since some years ago a battery had been planted there to the great offence of the presiding kami of the island. It was this offended kami and not the typhoon gales, they said, who had torn the houses to pieces, and as for the battery there was not a trace of it to be seen. A sand beach on the inner side of the island was composed of a clear black sand, specimens of which we were wrapping in paper, when again our boatmen protested for it would bring ill luck and disaster upon our heads. "A boat," said they, "if scoured with this sand would soon thereafter be a wreck." But we told them the ill luck would fall on our heads, not theirs, and persisted in keeping our gathered sand. Like all uncivilized people the Japanese are full of superstitious fears. We stopped at the island but a few moments for there was a long pull before us to reach home again since the breeze had wholly died away. On the shore opposite the island we could see the houses of Prince of Higo's soldiery who guard this part of the coast approaches to Yedo.

We turned our prows homeward, the boatmen stripped to the skin bent to their work with a will, the bay was smooth as a mirror and here and there were fishing boats plying their silent tasks and junks whose long sails hung listlessly from their yards. The glowing autumn day died away and a long ruddy twilight followed the sun's descent behind distant mountains. My birth anniversary had been as perfect a day as heart could wish. Darkness had spread over the water before we rounded Treaty Point; guard boats challenged us as [we] passed on to the pier where a little before seven our wearied boatmen were relieved and we disembarked.

Dinner at Dr. H[all]'s and my health crowned the day outside. At an early evening hour I returned to my rooms and gave my last thought before retiring to friends at home.

Monday, October 28, 1861

S[adajirō] tells me an anecdote, of what he was last evening a witness to, which savors of old knight-errantry days. Since the advent of foreigners here the Emperor has placed gates and guards at frequent intervals across the public highway of the Tokaido for purposes of security to the foreign residents. Last evening a messenger of the Prince of Satsuma was passing through from Nagasaki to Yedo mounted on horseback. At one of the gates where a number of yakunins are always stationed he found them closed as it was then dark. He desired them to be opened for him to pass through. These gates, it should [be added] have always a small gate for foot passengers in addition and at the side of the two larger ones which close the street. The reply was that the large gates would be opened for his horse to pass through but that he himself must dismount and go through the small gate, which in Japanese etiquette would be a token of respect for a submission to imperial authority. No, said Satsuma's messenger, I cannot; in coming hither I have dismounted at the gate (two) where it is customary to do so, but these gates are new, daimios do not recognize them, and now the conversation goes on:

Gate Keeper. "It is my imperial master's orders that no one shall pass through these gates (i.e., the large ones) after they are closed for the night."

Messenger. "And my master does not recognize the authority to do this."

Gate Keeper. "I must obey my master's order and cannot let you pass except in the way prescribed."

Messenger. "And I should disgrace my master to respect these orders and should be punished by him and lose my head; and since were you to disobey your master's orders you ought to share the same fate, let us as brave soldiers fight for the right to admit the disgrace of yielding and let our masters settle this dispute."

At this point the gate keeper finding his courage put to an unexpected test declines such an arbitration but the soldier insists as the only way to save their honors. This chivalry on the part of Satsuma's soldiers is not uncommon. The Prince's followers, who father and son have been feudatories for many generations, deem their lives at their master's service whenever called for, whereas, the imperial soldiers and yakunins are often new men taken from civil life who feel no esprit de corps.

The soldier prefers the arbitration of battle, and now tells the official that he is either a liar, and has not had the orders, or he will fight to maintain them, since the soldier will fight his way through, "which is it?" The official, unwilling to fight, declares now that he has been lying and will open the gate and let him pass. "Nay," says the soldier, "I will not go through. You have lied to me, hindered me on my journey, when my time is fixed that I must not exceed, and your honor requires that you fight with me for the insult, or commit *hara kiri* for having been false to your master."

The yakunin, less sensitive in his honor, refuses to accommodate the soldier who at last goes on his way heaping upon the unfortunate gate keeper, who was really doing his imperial master's bidding, all manner of opprobrious epithets.

The anecdote well illustrates the code of honor that is held binding among the samurai and also the independence of the Emperor's edicts as well as himself by the great chiefs and their followers.

Wednesday, October 30, 1861

Dr. Hall and myself made an early start this morning for a ride into the country. The weather was raw and clouds threatened rain but we ventured a start without any fixed purpose of direction. First to the Tokaido and from thence the large country road leading to Hachinogi, Atsugi, and O'Yama. On the road we pushed out several miles till the thickening clouds and damp air warned us to return. Putting our horses heads about we took up a brisker trot and just reached our houses at Yokohama when a cold rain driven by a northeast gale began to pelt us with its merciless artillery.

Thursday, October 31, 1861

Cloudy and wet. Yesterday's rain lasted all night, a drenching storm, but yielded after breakfast this morning to a cold cloudy autumn day with rain at intervals.

Friday, November 1, 1861

Again a bright sunshine and cloudless sky. O'Yama is whitened with yesterday's storm and Fusi has fairly donned his winter mantle which sweeps far below his glittering crest.

Tuesday, November 5, 1861

At half past 2 P.M. left town with Dr. Hall for an excursion, our bettos accompanying us. It was our intention to pass the night at Kamakura, but finding by the time we reached Kanasawa that to do so would necessitate a ride after dark we halted at the former place. Reining up at the tea house "Foomoto," where we had always received a hearty welcome, we found no one at the doors as usual to greet us, on the contrary, the servants fled into the interior of the house at our approach, and it was only after a little delay that one or two in company with the mistress of the inn came near to ascertain our intentions, which they well enough divined. This change in their hospitalities did not surprise us, on the contrary, we rather looked for something of the sort as a few days previously there had been a difficulty with foreigners at the other and more important inn called Adzumaya.[62]

It occurred in this wise. Two Americans who left Yokohama late in the afternoon arrived at that inn at 7 P.M., or after dark. They found the house outside brilliantly illuminated with lanterns, lights shone through all the windows, and within were heard the sounds of revelry. Regardless of this the two entered the gate within the hostelry yard but no sooner was the clatter of their horses feet heard on the inner yard and the sound of foreign accents than there was at once a great commotion inside. The rattling of swords was heard as of persons putting them on and directly swarmed out of the house fifteen or twenty armed men shouting "tojin pegge, tojin pegge," "foreigners leave, foreigners leave," a cry joined in by the

---

[62] The Kanasawa teahouses are pictured in a Felix Beato photograph of the early 1860s contained in Yokohama Kaikō Shiryō Kan, eds., *F. Beato bakumatsu nihon shashin shū*, p. 44. While Hall lists the inns in Kanasawa as the "Foomoto" (Fumoto), "Ogiya," and "Azumaya," the identification with the Beato photograph lists the inns as the "Chiyomoto," "Ogiya," and "Azumaya."

ordinary inmates of the inn. As these sake flush[ed] soldiers approached the two wayfarers menacingly, they wisely concluded that their greater safety was in flight, but to do this was difficult. The inn is situated on the highway which runs close to the beach of Goldsborough inlet, and a bridge over this highway within a few feet of the house spans an arm of this inlet through which the salt waters flow into the flats to the rear and side of the inn. The soldiers who rushed out of the house blocked up the way out of the gate by which they entered and the bridge over the highway by which they must escape. Fortunately for their escape, however, there was a way left open which one of them had seen on a former visit to the inn. From the limited pleasure grounds common to all such houses a narrow dyke led across the inlet and the salt marshes joining the highway again where it makes a sharp bend around one side of the flats towards Yokohama. Leaving their horses behind them much sooner than I have been describing this, they leaped the slight fence of bamboo that surrounded the pleasure grounds just as one soldier, more audacious than the rest, came to closer quarters with his sword half drawn. They made then hasty retreat over the causeway, sometimes in the darkness plunging into the marshy flats, and made the highway just as a party of their pursuers turned the angle of the road a few rods behind. The inhabitants of the village aroused by the commotion joined in the cry of foreigners run, and run they did, till the darkness covered them and they were safe. They now met their bettos, who in the downward journey lagged behind, and whom they sent back after their horses. These bettos did not rejoin them again till they had gone a long distance homeward saying that on their arrival at the inn they were bound, whipped, and made to confess who their masters were before they could come away with the horses.

The matter was subsequently investigated by the English and French Ministers, when the Japanese stated that though at first the servants of the official who was occupying the inn at that night were excited by the intrusion of the foreigners they intended them no personal violence and they followed them in obedience to the orders of their master to call them back, a story rendered improbable both by the circumstances and the subsequent detention and treatment of the bettos. The official belonged to the class of Hatamoto and as is customary with travellers of rank had secured the inn in advance of his coming. On his arrival his coat of arms and other insignia of rank were placed over the gateway and notice affixed that the inn was taken by him, being according to Japanese usage, so long as he stayed there, his own house. A Japanese traveller seeing these insignia respects them and does not intrude; a foreigner knowing neither their customs, or able to read the customary notice of occupation, by his entrance to the same inn would appear to the guests already there the same as if an intruder upon the seclusion of their private houses.

Such were the circumstances that created no little commotion among the quiet inhabitants of Kanasawa, it was no wonder, therefore, that to our request for a night's lodging for ourselves, servants, and horses, we were met with quiet but persistent refusals, though the excuses were sufficiently amusing. First there was a very sick child in the house, "so sick that she would probably die before morning." That did not signify, we said, we were skillful in the healing art and would do the child good. Then with imperturbable face and a serious look the woman said, "a babe was being born in the house at this very time." This was too ludicrous for our politeness to bear and we laughed so cheerfully that the good woman herself joined us and said no more about the baby. Now it was that "they had no men in the house," the oldest being the landlady's son, a youth of fourteen. This excuse, which afterwards turned out to be true, [we countered] by saying that we had Japanese men servants who would be up with us in a few minutes, and their appearance shortly after seemed to put a new face on affairs, for we at last obtained a reluctant consent to tarry for the night. So committing ourselves to their hands, and our horses to our careful bettos, we entered the house, receiving for the first time during all this long parleying even the common salutation on every peasant's tongue "please come in."

We were shown into the upper room, and now that night had set in and we were certainly quartered upon them for the night, they began to thaw out of their reserve and make amends. Hot tea was brought, our baggage disposed of, cushions placed to sit upon, our horses stabled and fed, and the housemaids one by one came to bid us welcome and then retired to prepare our supper below. Now it was amusing to see the ready Japanese diplomacy of the younger woman who had conducted the previous parleying with us to efface the impressions of their inhospitality. "She was very glad," she said, "that we were going to stay for we had been to the house so often (by daylight only heretofore) that we were friends, and it was only the old lady who was unwilling in the first place, but we were not to tell other foreigners that we had lodgings here for they did not wish to entertain them." It was no doubt a recommendation to us that we did not as most travellers do bring with us our own food and drink, for the absence of the former would not bring into their houses meats of which they have a superstitious repugnance, while the absence of the latter was an indication that we would not get noisy and troublesome.

And now came up the supper of fish, eggs, sweet potatoes, and rice, the head damsel of the house, black toothed and old, serving us instead of the young merrier damsels whom she only permitted to come to the room at long intervals to bring hot tea or some other needed article. Supper removed, she called in two of them to help the social chat that followed. Then she gave me lessons in a game on a chequered board requiring about the same skill as draughts. In turn I showed them some little slights of hand tricks, one of which consisted of loosing a knitted handkerchief made fast around my leg and which the ancient damsel imitated in a ludicrous manner by tying my handkerchief around her leg which she suddenly and unexpectedly bared for the purpose.

We made an early bivouac on the mats using our saddles for pillows and our shawl blankets for covering under which we slept soundly till morning.

Wednesday, November 6, 1861

Kanasawa to Uraga and back. We were up betimes for our long day's ride over the hills, and after breakfast, which was a counterpart of last night's supper with the addition of a cuttle fish, and settling our extravagant bill of six bus, at least three fold of what a native Japanese would have paid, we started on our way. We were compelled to make a long detour around the inlet moving three miles to make one and then struck off through a long narrow valley that lay between the spurs of the projecting ridges which we were to ascend. The valley was thick with the still ungathered rice and the dew lay on its beard in glittering masses. The morning air was cold when we came under the shadow of the hills and the recently risen sun again disappeared. Through a narrow defile cut in the hills we began to ascend the rugged hills that line the coast of this entire promontory below Uraga. Our road was a narrow winding path over the hills and through ravines with but room for one to pass at a time, and throughout the forenoon's ride we scarcely encountered a single passer by.

The usual route to Uraga is by sea, coasting to Ootsu and there taking horse again. Gradually we ascended, sometimes by a hard beaten path of earth and again over a rocky bed cut out and beaten down among the rocks over which our horses slipped and stumbled and slid, reminding one of excursions among the White Mountains of New Hampshire, but still upward among perennial forests of green branching pines and stately cedars and the changing foliage of the deciduous trees, for though the autumn tints imparted by frost are not so vivid as our New England woods, yet the variety of tints was sufficient to fall but just behind our own incomparable autumnal hills. The fall blossoms sprinkled the roadside and hung in masses from the roadside banks. Wild chrysanthemums, the blue cups of the gentian, masses of asters and daisies, and golden clumps of the golden rod and here and everywhere the fall blooming pink and white hydrangeas here thickly growing shrubs. Level patches, here and there sunny ravines, and hill side slopes and terraces were industriously cultivated much to my surprise when there were so many level acres below yet unsubdued. On we clomb till we had ascended out of the forests and mountain gorges and now suddenly burst upon us a magnificent spectacle.

We were on the top of hills that stood directly above the waters of Yedo Bay whose changing outline we could see from the narrows of Uraga Channel till lost in the haze that hung over the broad waters near to Yedo. We had a bird's eye view, as it were, and could see each little inlet and cape, creek and bay, rocks and islands, with great minuteness. Behind us rose the winding waters of Goldsborough inlet that we had left this morning, and there were Mississippi and Susquehanna Bays and their islands of Perry and Webster, and across the channel the shores of Bosiu as plain as though we had been looking down upon a map. In the mirage of the distant haze the white sails of the junks and fishing boats seemed floating in mid air. The scene inland was not less inspiring for our road overhung beautiful ravines filled with pines and cedars whose continuous foliage far below was as a carpet of green.

Again we began to descend till once more we were on the sea level and in the village of Ootsu [Ōtsu], remarkable only as the camping place of a large body of Hosokawa Higo-no-Kami's retainers who man the forts and do coast guard to this entrance of Yedo Bay. Our road was now on the beach sands and we could see only the roofs of the numerous barracks of the soldiery. Foreigners were yet novelties in this village and the cries of the children "tojin kita" [foreigners have come] brought not only the common people to the doors but a number of Hosokawa's soldiers followed us some ways down the road evidently amused as much as the children at the sudden apparition of the mounted strangers in their midst.

Following the beach for a mile we again struck off among lower hills towards Uraga. On our way thither we passed a two sworded individual whose insolent stare at us as we passed said so plainly "only say the word gentlemen and I will spliflicate you at once," that his insolence, as he stood in attitude at the roadside, served much to amuse us. After a ride of a mile and a half a turn in the road disclosed to us Uraga most picturesquely situated where a bight of the bay runs up between two

hills. Not much level ground is left for the population which clusters thickly between the hill and water on either side of the inlet thus giving the name of East and West Uraga to the divided portions of the one town. This inlet, which is three quarters of a mile to a mile long and several hundred yards wide, had at rest, in the secure anchorage, a large fleet of native boats and among [these] a nondescript old hulk painted red, evidently an abortive attempt to do something on the foreign model. Uraga is an important place for the native commerce to halt on its way in and out of the Gulf of Yedo. The great number of large fire-proof warehouses so unusual for a town of its size showed that it was, as it really is, a point for the storage of cargoes that have entered the Bay of Yedo seeking a market. There were many poor and dilapidated buildings, and, on the other hand, there were many fine capacious shops with large stocks whose inmates were busy with customers and spacious dwelling houses. From the appearance of these shops we could see that the place was not only an entrepot for coastwise commerce but the great market town of an outlying country. Uraga is imperial domain, and the residency of a governor appointed by the Emperor.

The crowds of people that surrounded and followed us showed that foreigners were yet an object of wonderment, they were not noisy though, not rude in their exclamations. First having gone some distance down the eastern side of the bight we turned about and crossing the head where a small stream flows in, by a bridge entered West Uraga and proceeded in search of an inn, the crowd increasing at every step. Our search for an inn was for some time fruitless till a man in authority took the lead and guided us to an inn where a street turned up the hillside. Here we were received by the landlord bowing politely to the floor and shown to the upper rear room, the most distinguished apartment, and our orders were taken for refreshments for ourselves, servants, and horses.

A little girl appeared with tea but her heart was so full of mirth that hastily leaving us she broke into an explosive laugh at the head of the stairs. Two yakunins next made their appearance entering the room with a swaggering air which they soon laid aside on being addressed familiarly in their own tongue by persons not all overcome by the greatness of their presence. After a cup, the expected series of questions began, "What countrymen? Where had we come from? Why had we come? How long would we stay and where would we go?" The usual interrogatory for our names was not asked. They could hardly believe my answer that we had come over all those hills merely to look at the place. "Had we no other business? Did we come only to see?" they said. Experience has taught me that so long as I am doing nothing to be ashamed of, but that I have a right to do under treaty privilege, the smoothest way to anticipate and disarm Japanese inquisitoriness and censorship, for it is quite as much the latter, is to lead the conversation and tell them freely my plans and wishes. So I had already told them that I left Yokohama yesterday on a pleasure excursion, passed the night at Kanasawa, come over the hills to Uraga, and all I wanted was rest and food for a little while, a look at their harbor, and I was anxious to be off so as to reach Kamakura before dark, and pulled a map of the country out of my pocket and inquired about the roads.

The two officials were now joined by two others of higher rank to whom they recapitulated all they had thus learned. The landlord was called to know what we had ordered for dinner and directed to prepare it, here too the official being evidently gratified with our choice of their own food. "Did we not want sake?," they asked. "No," I replied, "we did not drink it." I ordered some for them, but they declined and said "they never drank it!" While dinner was preparing we fell into general conversation and my ability to converse with some freedom in their own tongue helped to put us on a favorable footing. Indeed, their treatment was wholly civil and polite throughout. Inquiry was made after our lamented Com. Perry, who first put foot on Japanese soil at this place and here delivered his credentials and letters to the Japanese authorities.[63] Capt. Buchanan[64] was

also inquired after, whose fine physique seems to have made a favorable impression on these people. "Why," said one of them baring his wrist, "his wrist was thrice the size of mine, he was a powerful man." The bearing of Perry, Buchanan, and Adams[65] made a marked impression on these people. "Was Perry sama your highest official," said my boatmen to me one day. When I told them he was dead, "Do you worship him?", was at once the reply.

After dinner we ordered our horses saddled and while they were being made ready we told our yakunin friends that we would walk down to the harbor, and so going into the street they accompanied us following a little in our rear at the same time requesting us "not to walk so fast as was our custom." Thus escorted, and with an additional mob of the people hemming in the streets, we sallied out finding little that was more novel or attractive than usual in Japanese towns. The yakunins forbade any noise on the part of the people and we moved in the center of a silent crowd of admirers. We were chary of our time for we had yet a long ride in prospect and our two sworded friends cautioned us not to be out late so we turned about to our inn for the moment.

Our inn bill for us all men and horses was but thirteen tempos, very moderate compared to the morning's extortion at Kanasawa. Receiving the polite farewells of our sworded gentry we rode off up the hill that led towards Kamakura. One feature of our dinner I have overlooked. When dinner was served the young maiden who could not maintain her gaiety was displaced by a comely girl of sixteen or seventeen who had been got up for the occasion. She was very neatly attired in a gray figured robe secured by the ample obi, or girdle, her hair was not so over elaborate as usual, her face was slightly powdered and her under lip painted a deep vermillion. On one finger she wore a cheap gilt ring of Dutch manufacture. Her manners were exceedingly modest and ladylike, and when she came into the room not only ourselves but our yakunins returned her

---

[63] Commodore Matthew C. Perry, who had "opened" Japan in 1854 with the Kanagawa Treaty. Perry died in 1858.

[64] Commander Franklin Buchanan was in charge of

the *Susquehanna* during the Perry expedition.

[65] Commander Henry A. Adams accompanied Perry on the Japan expedition and was in charge of his flagships the *Mississippi*, *Susquehanna*, and *Powhatan*.

salutation of touching her head to the mats with respectfulness. She then filled our cups and handed them round with a modest grace that incited the remark of one of our friends, "is she not a fine girl"? "Truly," said I, "and of a most pleasing countenance," compliments she acknowledged with a quiet smile and inclination of the head. At the close of our meal I added to her stock of jewelry to her great delight.

Note. Since returning home inquiry confirms my impressions as to the commercial importance of Uraga. It is the entrepot of all the coastwise commerce. Situated near the mouth of Yedo Bay, vessels arriving with cargoes from Nagasaki, Oasaca, Hakodade, etc., are compelled to put in here to undergo examination as to their crews and passengers who are passing in and out, the cargo itself going undisturbed and paying no duty. By an old law of the empire, of which the Dutch have perhaps the reason in speaking of a like prohibition at the pass of Hiakone on the Tokaido, no females are allowed to pass in and out of the bay in any vessel. Thus compelled to put in at Uraga, this place, on that account as well as its commercial situation, reaps great advantages. Cargoes are here disposed of to the large merchants while the ship is released for a new voyage. The report of the markets at Yedo, Hakodade, Mito and other points on the coast is well understood at Uraga, and when a vessel arrives here the owner, frequently finding the Yedo markets dull, sells for reshipment to some one of the other ports, or hiring storeroom unlades his cargo and awaits a turn in affairs. There seems to be no tax on the internal trade of the country, though at Hiogo there is a general supervision of all the native shipping and there is a small tax on each bottom. At this place also the governor seems to hold a sort of admiralty court where all cases arising out of collision or other injury done by one vessel to another are heard for the whole empire. It not unfrequently happens that there is a large arrival of junks at Uraga at the same time and laden similarly when some one or more will pass on to Yedo without waiting for examination in order to get the first of the market trusting to making his peace with the examining officers by a liberal bribe.

At one o'clock we left Uraga for Kamakura. Crossing over a range of hills we descended into a broad valley, the other side [of] which was one immense paddy field where men and women were busy gathering in the crop. This valley extending inland from the sea for some miles then narrows and opens into other valleys so that this whole peninsula of Sagami is intersected by them from the Bay of Yedo to that of Odawara. Our road lay through these valleys and we were everywhere gratified with the beauty and fertility of the country. On the right and left of these valleys, especially the former, were lofty hills whose sides were cultivated in successions of terraces, or covered with the noble growth of cedars. Near Uraga we saw several beautiful groves of Japan cedar which had been planted in ravines and other spots so sheltered from the winds that they had grown straight as a plumb line, these were intended for masts.

Throughout our ride this afternoon we saw these planted belts of timber. We observed again the beauty of the autumnal foliage conspicuous among which were the yellow leaves of the majestic jingo [ginkgo] trees, and the bright tints of the ivy that everywhere abounded. Half-way across the promontory were hills of long even slopes in a high state of cultivation, and, what is rare to see, the farm houses were scattered about their surface instead of being all clustered together in some village. The farmers were everywhere busy gathering their rice and putting in their fall sown crops. Sweet potatoes were largely cultivated and we saw many patches of tobacco. Wherever I go in the country, there I find the temple and mia. The priests form a large morety of the population, and you cannot travel far in any direction without finding their temples occupying the most picturesque positions, which have been tastefully improved by the taste of their leisure living occupants. A broad avenue of trees and a series of well cut stone stairways leading up a hill induced me to dismount in expectation of finding an unusually fine temple and grounds, but both, in reaching them, proved quite ordinary; the handsome avenue was the charm on which the priests had expended all their skill. The favorite flower of priest and peasant, the chrysanthemum, was

now in bloom, and we saw many superb specimens in a temple yard or by a poor cottage
that would have been the pride of a florist in
any civilized land. Again and again we stopped
to see the multiplied varieties, trophies of Japanese horticultural skill. The common people,
particularly the farming portion, I have universally found kind and respectful in all my
rides among them, and this day was no exception to my general experience. Often times,
however, a fear and distrust of the foreigners
is manifested; many a time I have seen the little children set up a howl of fear, and one, or
some shy girl or woman, jumps into the mud
of the rice fields to avoid a meeting on the
highway.

A glimpse of blue water announced that we
had crossed the promontory and soon we were
trotting on the beach of Odawara Bay and the
low pulsation of the placid waters sent a light
wave rippling about our horses' feet. There
too was the island of Yenosima and the smoky
outline of the promontory that ends in Cape
Idzu. Passing through the village of Haiyama
we came to a small river crossed by a ferry.
Here we should have passed over, but we were
directed to keep on and thus missed the road
to Kamakura. Over mountain and hill, and
through almost interminable paddy fields, and
night coming on and yet no halting place,
when suddenly we debouched from a hill into
the plain opposite Kanasawa and recrossed a
stream into that town, the same that we had
crossed to go out in the morning. We were five
miles away from the place we had directed our
bettos to halt at for the night, who were behind us. For their sakes we should have gone
back to Kamakura, but already night was gathering fast and we were fain to rein up at the
inn Adzumaya, the "Sea Bride's Hotel," where
at first we were refused admittance but subsequently succeeded.

Once settled down for the night our host

was very obliging and gave as his reason for
refusing at first that he had difficulty with foreigners before about their bills. We had had a
taste of the good fish cookery of the Adzumaya
last spring and we were not disappointed when
a hot and excellent fish supper flanked by
fried potatoes and boiled rice was placed before us (these fish were kept in a basket in the
sea). To add to our joy our bettos, missing us
at Kamakura, had suspected our position and
had joined [us], though this gratification was
somewhat marred by my betto being taken violently ill after supper in consequence of the
unusual fatigue of the day or something he
had eaten. Our own fatigue sent us to rest
early on the clean mats and brought sound
sleep.

Thursday, November 7, 1861

We rose early and though the weather
looked a little threatening we decided to go to
Kamakura yet. My betto was so much used up
by yesterday's fatigues that I sent him home
and we started off before breakfast for Kamakura. This beautiful ride of five miles through
the mountain passes I have before described
and this morning its autumnal foliage gave a
change of scene to us. A poor breakfast at Kamakura, a renewal of our visit to Hachiman
temple, and the increasing clouds started us
homeward leaving some localities unvisited
which we had come purposely to see. A half
mile out of Kamakura however the park like
enclosures of Kenchogee[66] temple impelled us
to halt and amply were we repaid by an all
to[o] brief view of the most interesting temple
grounds I had yet seen in Japan.

Passing through a wall of green turfed bank
faced with stone we passed up an avenue
which was left in a grove of planted pines and
cedars, trees which had centuries of rains and

---

[66] The Kenchōji was the headquarters of the Kenchōji
branch of the Rinzai sect of Zen Buddhism. It was also
regarded as the foremost of the Five Great Zen temples
of Kamakura. The temple had been founded in 1249
by Hōjō Tokiyori to serve as a major Zen center for a
distinguished Chinese Zen master, and in later years it

received the patronage and support of important historical figures such as Toyotomi Hideyoshi and the Tokugawa shoguns. Kenchōji ships had carried trade to
China in Kamakura times. The four massive juniper
trees in the grounds of the temple were brought to Japan from China.

dews and sunshine that had sent their crowns more than a hundred feet into the sunny blue above, given them ample girth of trunk, and knit with strength their sinewy limbs. Such a walk brought us to the propylaeum of the temple, a massive structure of columns and timbers of the Japanese elm whose facade was covered with carvings of beasts, birds, and flowers, real and fabulous, and in whose side niches were the grim guardian idols of the place. Through this portal were the temples situated in an ample breadth of grounds, temples [more] remarkable for their age than architectural beauty which seemed all to have been lavished on the massive gateway or entrance. Still the same venerable trees overshadowed all. This temple, or rather monastery of Kenchogee, was founded by Yoritomo and the main buildings were declared to be of his times or more than six hundred years old. They looked every month of it. We heard the sounds of worship in the second of the two temples and turned our steps thitherward, but as we approached a group of men and boys commenced hastily [to close] the massive doors to preclude any possibility of our entrance. We contented ourselves with a peep through the windows and saw at least fifty Buddhist monks with shaven heads and white robes performing service. We left the worshippers to the enjoyment of their own privacy, more interested ourselves in the worship of nature outside.

We walked as we thought to the extent of the grounds when a break in the hedge led us into a labyrinth of paths and grounds winding in and out among the trees and to the residences of the monks. These grounds lay at the foot of the hills or extended up their sides and neither pen or pencil can do justice to the wild picturesque and cultivated beauty that met us at every turn. Not less than a hundred monks are attached to this temple, comfort and beauty of whose dwellings must outvie any monastic establishments of Europe in the middle ages—back up in secluded dells, hidden in leafy nooks, buried in shade on a gentle eminence, perched securely among the rocks, were the cottages of the monks, all in excellent repair, each with its neat gateway, or sometimes a lodge, its hedgerows, its flats of flowers,

its groups of trees, grounds ample, so artfully disposed, so cunningly hidden that one was hidden from the other. Surely, thought we, there can be no more, for here are the rocky sides of the hills, when lo! another path sends us off into another ravine and among more cottages. Some of the places were closed by substantial gateways of massive posts and woods as if guarding still costlier treasures from vulgar gaze. To live in such idleness and luxury what exactions from the people are not required by these hundred shaven headed drones. However, this monastery like others was the object of visit from a large region of country and the distant pilgrims were doubtless its chief supporters.

The fresh looking cottages seemed but of yesterday, but the mossy walls of stone and the venerable old trees spoke of long generations ago. How I wished that I could have transported this bodily to young fresh America, it would be a curiosity greater than Niagara, more wonderful than the Mammoth Cave. We were allowed to wander here and there at our own free will and came away reluctantly at last. Once more in the saddle we hurried on to avoid the threatening storm. It caught us, however, four miles out and drenched us thoroughly before we made the shelter of our homes. Thus ended a pleasant journey of 48 hours and seventy miles in the interior of Japan.

Note. In the soft sandstone cliffs about Mississippi Bay are numerous holes, natural and artificial, which are used for manure pits giving the traveller airs more powerful than fragrant. The drips from the rocks often furnishes the water necessary for macerating. Larger openings, mostly natural near Kanasawa, and, which are dug, are used for storage of crops. These openings are in a ledge which shows the traces indisputably of its once having been the sea shore, though now distant half a mile to a mile in places. The natives say that Mississippi Bay has been greatly changed by earthquakes.

Monday, November 11, 1861

Ida Rogers arrived, letter from Alfred and Wells.[67] A few days since the young Prince of Owari was to pass through Kanagawa and word was sent to all the foreign residents of that ilk to keep off the Tokaido while the train passed by. All the morning long the baggage carriers and menials of the train passed on and a little past noon the Prince himself and his guard of several hundred armed men came on. A babe of some four years old lolling his head out of the window of his elegant norimon in infantile undergarment and supported by his nurse represents the sprig of royalty for whom all this parade was essential. Little knew the youngster, pleased with his toys, what it was to be in the royal line to a throne and all the happier he. Not all the pleasures of royalty shall share the charm of the gilded bauble he tosses in his hand.

Tuesday, November 12, 1861

Roused out at 2 A.M. by the fire bells and a bright light shining in my window. A fire had broken out in the midst of the Japanese business quarter and fanned by a strong wind increased to a devastating conflagration involving the loss of a great amount of property. Several blocks in length and five streets in breadth were consumed, at least one half of the business town. I was on the ground early and assisted at saving people all my strength allowed. The scene was a magnificent as well as terrific one, most of the buildings being of light fire wood a large extent was in flames at one time. Here and there fireproof godowns resisted successfully the destructive element. All efforts to extinguish the flames were in vain except the final ones of tearing down the buildings in advance of the fire, and here the foreigners, especially the marines and sailors from the harbor, did yeoman's service. In a few hours thousands were turned out of house and home into a cold northeast storm. They speedily found shelter among their countrymen. The Custom House was imminently threatened at one time, and, by consequence, my own premises, and only the tearing down of a number of houses, residences of officials, prevented the flames reaching the foreign quarter. As a general thing the Japanese labored industriously, both at extinguishing the fire and saving property, and considering their tinder box buildings and feeble fire machines their success is oftentimes praiseworthy. No disturbances occurred and little intoxication. The officials were on hand as usual in force in their gorgeous fire rigs and conspicuous among them was the Governor and his suite. The ridiculous ceremonies of arresting the flames were also gone through with. Refreshments of rice made up into round balls, fish, and sake were freely distributed. The fire lasted five hours before fairly subdued. The flames were spreading with great rapidity across the causeway that leads to the Oshiwara, but were arrested by the timely pulling down of buildings. This place is an island among canals and swamps and is so nearly covered with buildings that loss of life might readily occur. The hundreds of poor girls were sent out of harm's way and put in boats on the canal, and grouped on its bank, while scattered here and there were the groups sitting among their household stuffs saved from the impending conflagration. The scene, houses, buildings, boats, waters, and the huddling females with their heads tied in cotton wrappers was a picturesque one.

This morning I walked among the ruins and examined several of the fire proof warehouses which were now open and saw that in most instances they were effectual in preserving their contents. In every direction were heaps of household furniture and merchandise which coolies were busy moving to places of safety. A cold stormy day followed.

Wednesday, November 13, 1861

Went to Kanagawa [and] called on the recently arrived missionaries Mr. and Mrs. Ballagh.[68] To the Consul's and acknowledged deed of sale of my lot of land to D.C.B. for

---

[67] Both were Francis Hall's brothers.

[68] James H. Ballagh and his wife Margaret arrived in

$1td,200.00 [$1,200.00].[69] Consul D[orr] desired me to occupy his post during a temporary absence at Shanghai; [I] declined, ostensibly because I might go away myself, but really from a firm determination to having nothing to do with a man devoid of honor, honesty, or gratitude, save as they may serve some selfish end he desires to promote.

The industry of the Japanese in rebuilding their work places is most praiseworthy, but not more so than their cheerfulness and entire absence of repining under their losses. Scarcely a lot of ground upon which workmen have not been busy since yesterday morning in cleaning off the rubbish and in many instances erecting temporary accommodations. Yesterday morning (the morning of the fire), when daylight appeared, at once gangs of men were at work designating the site of lost buildings by straw ropes stretched around, officers were erecting fences, all were busy removing the ruins, and merchants so fortunate as to have their wares in fireproof godowns had opened them ready for trade. By night many lots were enclosed, and several respectable shanties had been built and occupied. The energy and activity of the Japanese has been made truly manifest. At other places boards were erected in a heap of rubbish and the lot owner's name inscribed thereon, "staked out claims." I have called on many acquaintances to congratulate some on their escape and condole with the losers, but it was difficult to say which party was the more cheerful. Even my condolences were overpowered by their congratulations at my own escape from a somewhat perilous position during the height of the fire.

Thursday, November 14, 1861

The work of removing the ruins and erecting temporary buildings goes briskly on. Blue flags are fluttering now in the debris to mark individual ownership. In any other country the natural result of such a devastation would be increased prices of rents, lumber, provisions and other destroyed necessaries, but not so in Japan. The government attends to this and visits with penalties any one who takes advantage of a common distress and scarcity to reap increased profits. It is one of the beneficent workings of a despotism.

Sunday, November 17, 1861

Arrival of mail.

Tuesday, November 26, 1861

Rose early this morning and soon after sunrise was in the saddle on my way to Kamakura in company with Dr. G. R. H[all]. The morning was clear, frosty, and cold, with wind from the northward. We took the hill road to Mississippi Bay and had a magnificent view of Fusi Yama deeply covered with snow and the chain of other distant mountains whose higher peaks were also capped with snow. The atmosphere was so pure and brilliant that the rugged faces of those mountains were clearly traceable. A half hour's ride brought us to Mississippi beach screened from the wind by the hills from which we had descended. While the cool norther crisped the bay, the sunshine fell lovingly and warm on the smooth sands, the fisher's huts, and their embosoming trees. From the beach [we rode] into the hills again where

---

Yokohama on November 11, 1861. Ballagh was sent to Japan as a missionary by the [Dutch] Reformed Board and subsequently became an important missionary in Yokohama, who is credited with establishing the "Yokohama Band," one of the major groups of Meiji Christians. His wife's letters written from Japan in the 1860s were later collected and published. See Margaret Tate Kinnear Ballagh, *Glimpses of Old Japan, 1861–1866* (Tokyo: Methodist Publishing House, 1908).

[69] This would appear to have been D. C. Brower of Allmand and Co. Hall owned lot 23 in the "New Concession" of Yokohama, which he purchased at auction on July 21, 1860 for $255. D. C. Brower initally bought lot 24. For a list of American land holders in Yokohama in 1860 see Despatches from United States Consuls in Kanagawa, 1861–1897, National Archives, Microfilm, FM 135–1.

foliage was stained with varied autumnal hues only less brilliantly than our own New England forests. The more pleasing tints were the red brown and purply maroons of the maples and the brilliant yellow of the maiden hair tree and the red stained ivies dyeing the old fortress buttresses with stains of crimson. Down the bluffs again on the beach where the large fishing town of Soongita [Sugita] rested in the lap of the hills and once more up the broad mountain paths towards Kanasawa. How exhilarating the atmosphere, what sublime views of the distant mountains and many a mile of hill and wood between, what picturesque glimpses of the blue waters on the opposite hand, what fragrances from the balsamy pines loaded the morning north wind. Gentians and chrysanthemums still adorned the country roadside and roses and sasanquas bloomed in the hedges and at every temple and almost every farm house the showiest chrysanthemums bent on their stalks beneath their ponderous blossoms. A stranger cannot conceive the frequency of these temples, they abound everywhere in nook and dell, on hill in grove, in town and country, every ten minutes ride will bring you in sight of one till one wonders how the lazy monkhood get their living out of the poor peasantry. Now we descend the last long hill that leads into the valley where lies Kanasawa, and as we descend the winding mountain pass the luxuriant ferns hanging from rocks almost sweep in our faces.

Down in the valley among the hamlets the road nears a winding stream among banks of human life, children shouting to us from the cottage doors, "foreigners, the foreigner is coming, foreigners again, fool, beast, ridiculous," such are the epithets young Nippon greets us with while their elders give us a respectful good morning. The inn of Adzumaya, "The Sea Bride," opens its gates to us and we are not received with the distrust that met us

before. Our horses and tired bettos rest with us here and soon the hot fish and the steaming rice makes up our morning's lack of breakfast. We have to chide the landlord, however, for his fish has not the freshness that becomes an inn by the sea. A long residence on the shores of the bay has made us critical in fish. Our horses are again at the door and we are soon riding up the beautiful valley road and among the picturesque hill defiles that lead to Kamakura. We pass the tombs of the old kings on the hillside on our right which stand at the entrance of Kamakura, Yoritomo's old capital.

The beautiful groves of Hachiman temple at Kamakura delay us not today, but we take its mile long avenue of firs leading to the sea till we come to the Yenosima road. Following out this road for a mile or more we are brought to our journey's end in a hamlet under the hills famous for its old temples. We leave our horses in the hands of our bettos and climb the moss covered stone steps that conduct us to a platform hewn out of the hillside whereon stands a temple hundreds of years old. A polite old man keeps ward over this temple which has no recommendations to the sightseer beyond its antiquity, a colossal image of Buddha sitting apart in its own shrine on the lotus blossom, and some statuettes of the 18 Geni's whose exquisitely cut faces fill me with covetousness, two of them looked as if modelled after some of the fat jolly Spanish or Portuguese monks of three centuries ago.[70] They are all of wood and in lineament and drapery were more skillfully done than I have ever seen in Japan or China. From stone walled platform whereon the temple stands overshadowed with firs, cedars, and maiden hair trees, is a handsome prospect of the Bay of Odawara, its ledges of dangerous rocks, its cumbry reef, and the wooded hills of the promontory of Sagami beyond.

The chief attraction of our day's journey,

[70] The temple mentioned here appears to have been the Hase Kannon, although—as was the case in the Meiji period—the Kannon was not readily visible to visitors. By Meiji times the payment of a special fee was required to reveal the venerated wooden statue, which was usually concealed behind folding doors. It seems that Hall was unaware of its existence and did not make

an effort to bribe the priests to view the Kannon. The statue referred to in the text seems to have been that of Dainichi Nyorai seated on the lotus that was given to the temple by Ashikaga Yoshimasa. See Basil Hall Chamberlain, *A Handbook for Travellers in Japan* (London: John Murray, 1913), p. 103.

and which we had come specifically to see, is a famous bronze statue of Buddha erected by Yoritomo six centuries ago.[71] It stands in a little nook of the hills near the other temple and the image in a sitting position faces the avenue that leads thither. This immense work, whose dimension I give below in detail, is a wonderful monument of half barbaric skill. The image rests on a stone foundation, is handsomely molded, all its line and curves being singularly graceful except the too forward inclination of the head. The falling line of the shoulder and arm and its covering drapery is exquisitely done. The graceful pose of the hands resting on the lap with the forefingers and thumbs brought together as in the attitude of one in thought, and the singularly placid expression of the face give to the whole an air of thoughtful benignity as well as majesty.

A door at the side leads into the interior, whither an old priest with a face full of smiles as became the guardian of such an image, conducted us. We stood within, as it were, a dome which had its apex in the rounded head above, a dome fifty feet high and thirty in its long diameter. Here were shrines and images for the devotions of the faithful and pilgrims flock thither in crowds in spring and the early summer. Light came in through the grated windows set into the back of the image. There was nothing within but the mean looking idols and shrines and the best thing about it was that the sun's rays falling without heated the inside to a pleasant temperature where, no doubt, the lazy monks often enjoy themselves in the clear winter days. On bronze tablets without were imperishably recorded the names of the architect and the pious donors to its erection. Anciently a temple covered the statue but during an earthquake, so says the legend, the God displeased with his occultation came in on the wave of the inundating sea and swept it away. The inundating waves during an earthquake are not isolated occurrences in Japan.

Dimensions of the bronze statue at Kamakura, Daibootsoo [Daibutsu], "The Great God":

Height of Stone Pedestal	4.5	feet
Height of Bronze Statue	50	"
Circumference of the base around the drawn up limbs	98	"
Length of the face	8.5	"
Length of the eyes	4	"
Length of the ears	6.5	"
Length of the nose	3.8	"
Breadth across nostrils	2.13	"
Breadth across mouth	3.2	"
Circumference of thumbs	3	"
Thickness of plate	1.25	inches

The shortness of the days between sun[rise] and sun[set] hurried us away, for we had a homeward ride of sixteen or seventeen miles to make before dark. At Kanasawa we stopped again to rest our horses and take dinner. We chided our host for the fish he gave us for breakfast. We should see him take the one for our dinner alive, he said, and pushing off from the stone quay in front of his house in a boat, he opened a large basket creel and with a hand net took out one whose struggle was sufficient proof that our dinner would be fresh. In twenty minutes thereafter we were enjoying his crispy freshness done in vegetable oil in the upper room of the inn looking out upon the bright waters, the picturesque hills, and the thick hamlets across the inlet. It was past three when we remounted again and leaving our bettos to take their own time home we pressed forward to avoid the chill after sunset air. Just as we ascended the last bluffs that lay between us and Yokohama the sun sank behind the distant hills, but long after its departure when other peaks were shrouded in coming darkness its rays fell on the snowy peak of matchless Fusi and clothed its sides with a firey mist.

[71] It is worth noting that it took Hall nearly two years after his arrival in Japan to make his first trip to the Kamakura Daibutsu. Although the Daibutsu was soon to become one of the major tourist attractions for foreigners visiting Yokohama, and Hall was to escort others to its site in later years, it does not appear to have attracted unusual notice by early settlers in the treaty port. Whether this was due to a lack of curiosity, or due to Japanese efforts to keep foreigners away from it, is difficult to determine.

Kamakura Daibutsu. Photograph by Felice Beato.

Saturday, November 30, 1861

A beautiful November day rode with G. R. H[all] to Kawasaki and visited the temple of Daigi [Daishi]. This is perhaps the finest temple anywhere within miles of Yokohama. Its rich altar service, the huge brass candelabra in shape of the divine lotus, its glittering canopy of bells, its lights ever burning in resplendent lanterns, the spacious area for priests and worshippers, the massive columns, are the attractions within doors. Without are the finest stone monuments I know of in Japan, in two of which lights are burning and a third resembles the obelisk of Cleopatra's needle so remarkably that alike taste must have designed both. The other two are much more elaborate in design, consisting of a series of stories, a tablet supported by caryatides, a candelabrum, and, capping the whole, the four sided peaked and curved roof more graceful and elegant than anything I have ever seen executed in America. My rides in Yedo made me aware last year that in nothing have the Japanese shown better taste or design than in some of their monumental erections.

Noticeable on the road again were the travellers in their norimons. The norimon is so capacious that the traveller carries with him not only his couch for the night but many things for his amusement by the way. A little shelf in front contains sometimes books to read, oftentimes a vase of flowers, or, as in one case today where I saw a cage of birds, three canaries, suspended inside and against one end facing the passenger. On the rear, outside, hung his wooden clogs and his broad brimmed hats. When one has become accustomed to the norimon travelling thereby, if not speedy, is not devoid of considerable luxury. The lighter Kango is borne sometimes very fast, two men today preceded us for a mile or so on a brisk run while our horses were trotting. Flocks of wild geese were feeding within easy gunshot by the roadside.

Examined the famous pear orchards of Kawasaki. The tree at the height of two or two and a half feet from the ground is cut off and grafted; a tree fifteen or twenty years old is thus successfully treated, though it is usually done at a young age. The grafts are permitted to grow erect till at about four and a half feet from the ground they are trained horizontally over bamboo poles placed horizontally cross wise. The limbs of the trees being some twelve feet apart, a continuous flat tree roof is formed under which must be a delightful shade in summer. The upright growing twigs, after sufficient have been trained horizontally to connect with each other, are cut off each year. In the fall the ground beneath is littered with straw to prevent bruises to the falling fruit, which thus grows very large and fair. Grafting is done by insertion of the graft between the wood and bark where it is firmly bound, covered around with mud, sometimes crow manure, and then bound over with straw. Simple as this process is, it is very successful. What is remarkable, however, is the wet nature of the soil where these orchards grow, for nearly all of them at Kawasaki are scarcely above tide water, often surrounded with over flowed paddy fields, a condition we deem wholly averse to the successful raising of the pear. There are many acres of these beautiful orchards at Kawasaki.

Wednesday, December 4, 1861

Earthquake 12½ A.M. The nuptials of the Tycoon with the daughter of the Mikado approach consummation.[72] Within a few days the bride's outfits of furniture and personal effects has been passing through the Tokaido as my informant says, "seven hundred boxes" in all, from one, carried by four men, to the largest carried by fifty men at a time, and this last is by etiquette not allowed to touch the earth. Two hundred coolies are engaged in carrying it resting each other by turn.

A singular custom of the Japanese princes has come to light to me today. The Prince of Dewa, whose province is one hundred ri beyond Oasaca or 236 ri from Yedo has messengers stationed at an average interval of seven ri between his residence in his province and at the capital Yedo. These messengers are bound to give their prince early reports of whatever is of great or small interest. Dispatches are thus forwarded with great celerity, the stationary servants or officials in important matters themselves acting as runners. The importance of a

dispatch is known by certain stamps imprinted on the envelope. Three stamps denoting a matter of great importance that must be pressed forward by horseback. One stamp indicates ordinary importance and may be sent by a hired coolie or runner. These mounted messengers are said to be able to reach Oasaca in 26 hours requiring a speed of 12 miles per hour, indeed this limit of time is said to be fixed and imperative. This custom is a very old one. The Prince of Kiusiu has similar service rendered.

The *Honjins*, or official resting places, which are to be found a few miles apart, or in each principal village of the Tokaido, were established by the great chiefs in common and are so still supported by them. For this reason when travelling in state they have no hotel bills to pay but what amounts to the same thing, they make large presents to the "husband of the Honjin" as he is called. One daimio will perhaps refit the house with mats or other furniture, while another leaves a sum of money for kitchen outlay or the commissariat department. The post of husband of the Honjin is so lucrative that it is much sought for and the present proprietor, if he has no son to fall heir to so valuable a revenue, receives some friend or adopts some young man who is recognized as the "Son of the Honjin," or his heir and successor. Much as we might call Mr. Coleman the husband of the Astor House and his probable successor the Son of the Astor House.

Saturday, December 7, 1861

A south wind is blowing today and I have ridden down to the beach of Mississippi Bay to see the surf tumble in upon the shore and breathe the fresh wind blowing across the water. It was an exhilarating ride to me. In Homoco I saw a characteristic Japanese scene, two

[72] The marriage in question here was that of Princess Kazu (Kazu-no-Miya), the sister of the Emperor Kōmei, to the fourteenth Tokugawa shogun, Iemochi. This marriage had been arranged by the senior councillors Andō Nobumasa and Kuze Hirochika as part of an effort to shore up the prestige of the shogunate by more closely associating it with the imperial court. The mar-

riage was consumated in March 1862. Although some of the princess's baggage made its way over the Tōkaidō, the princess herself travelled by way of the Nakasendō, in part to avoid the unstable conditions along the Tōkaidō. Later Hall reports on Sadajirō's observations of her entry into Edo.

begging boys had stopped in the street and were singing to a small crowd gathered about them from a printed score. In the farmyards men women and girls were busy threshing, cleaning, and winnowing the rice. The young girls do a great deal of labor of this kind and are always very merry over their toil.

Sunday, December 8, 1861

Totska road.

Monday, December 9, 1861

Kanagawa.

Tuesday, December 10, 1861

Almost every day are to be seen travellers on the Tokaido who appear to command more than the usual respect. These are retainers or servants of the Mikado on their way to Yedo to grace the approaching nuptials of the Emperor. In one morning a Japanese friend says he passed seventeen separate companies of them to whom all the people knelt as they passed. These companies were small, for the Mikado's household servants and retainers have rank but few of them any revenues, living at home with but a servant or two to attend them. But by Japanese ancient usage the persons about the body of the Mikado, his court, outrank all other officials. The Emperor seems thus to concede a nominal superiority to the Mikado, but it is but nominal. One of the Hatamoto rank, who heretofore when visiting Kanagawa has occupied the Honjin and displayed every insignia of rank, on a more recent visit was obliged to take the humble quarters of an inn and not permitted to make any ostentatious show simply because it was not etiquette to do so while the Mikado's servants are travelling the same road.

The large pieces of baggage named a page or two back, belonging to the intended, were two chariots such as are used by the imperial household at Miako. To accommodate their passage bridges had to be widened, trees lopped away, and in some instances temporary roadside houses removed. The people along the road are compelled to kneel to the passing baggage and its attendants. And I may here mention that physicians and midwives in Yedo are always exempt from kneeling to passing trains, it being supposed that their business is urgent. The same excuse avails elsewhere on being made known.

The marriage cortege is progressing slowly as they make frequent halts to visit all remarkable places along the road. Though in former times a Mikado's daughter was sometimes married to his Siogoons, or generals, it is said to have been refused to the Tycoons resident at Yedo, and that this is the first instance for many centuries that such a marriage has taken place and is, or rather will be, the occasion of unusual rejoicings. The fate of the Mikado's daughters have been to attach themselves as nuns to the more celebrated temples, particularly that of Ise.

Thursday, December 12, 1861

Rode over the hills to Hodoriya [Hodogaya].

Wednesday, December 18, 1861

Rode to Mississippi Bay.

Saturday, December 21, 1861

St. Louis and governor's visit.

Monday, December 23, 1861

S[adajirō], the Japanese, has just returned from Yedo where he has been to witness the entry of the Emperor's bride. He seems to have been disappointed with the display, which was nothing extraordinary except in its length. The young Empress's female attendants did not form a part, having arrived in advance. There appear to be no festive public occasions, the young Empress is received at the palace of her future lord and four days after (tomorrow) is the first public ceremonial when the Daimios call to pay their respects and are feasted. The Empress is visible to the chief of them only. A few days later the citizens (landholders only) are feasted in the imperial grounds. It is on such occasions as these, also the installment of a new Emperor, the building of a palace, and the birth of an heir, that the people are allowed indulgences of opinion as to the officers over them, and not infrequently on the day subsequent to such a feast some official whose misdeeds have been the free subject of converse the day before finds himself degraded.

Tuesday, December 24, 1861

Merry Christmas Eve at Browns. House decorated with evergreens, lanterns, the wassail bowl and its procession into the Dutch settlement. Neighbor M.[73] finds a strange bedfellow in a strange place.

Wednesday, December 25, 1861

A beautiful day for the Holidays. Camellias, roses, and azaleas in bloom in the country. Dwarf plums in bloom are carried about the streets.

Tuesday, December 31, 1861

A notification is issued to the foreign community that Yedo will not be opened on the 1st prox. as agreed under the treaty. The reasons assigned is that for the present a state of insecurity would attend the residence of foreigners in that city. The notifications intimate that the delay is only temporary.

[73] Unfortunately we do not know who neighbor M. was. This may have been W. H. Morse, who subsequently worked under Hall at Walsh, Hall & Co.

1862

Wednesday, January 1, 1862

The New Year opens with fair skies, though boisterously. All day long the bay is impassable. New Year festivities are inactive. The Americans call on the only two families where American ladies are to be found. Dined in the evening with Dr. Hall.

Thursday, January 2, 1862

Dr. H[all] and Mr. Walsh spend the evening with me.[1]

[1] It would appear that at this meeting with Dr. Hall and Mr. Walsh the details for Francis Hall's joining Walsh and Co. were worked out. The initial arrangements seem to have called for Francis Hall to take Dr. Hall's place as Yokohama agent for the firm. Unlike Dr. Hall, Francis Hall seems to have set his own terms calling for a full partnership, and for the revision of the firm's name to Walsh, Hall & Co. Beginning in the spring of 1862 Walsh & Co. became Walsh, Hall & Co. in Yokohama, although the firm retained its name Walsh & Co. in Nagasaki. The formal partnership with Walsh & Co. began on May 1, 1862, and was to expire on April 30, 1865, but in April 1865 Hall extended it to

Friday, January 3, 1862

The *What Cheer* leaves today for San Francisco, carrying with her Mrs. Owner's broken up household[2] and my friend Dr. Hall. The *Lanrick* brings a home mail.

Monday, January 6, 1862

Cold morning and blustery day. About 5 P.M. a large volume of smoke was seen rising in the direction of Yedo and as darkness came we could see the light of a large fire over the intervening woods and waters which continued till seven o'clock when it gradually subsided. It proved to be a conflagration beginning in the Prince of Satsuma's yashiki and his principal town residence, which was mostly consumed, and extended to the yashiki of a neighboring daimio, which was wholly consumed, and then devoured three blocks of shops and houses, and was finally arrested at the water's edge in which direction the flames were carried by a high wind. The houseless people were at once provided for by Satsuma's servants, himself being absent, with ample accommodations in a large compound which escaped the flames by the seaside, and provisions were distributed as well as shelter given. The following day money and rice were distributed to all who had suffered, and they were assured their houses and shops should all be rebuilt at Satsuma's expense and their stores of rice replaced. One temple was included in this bountiful largess of a chief, who, because a fire had begun in his quarters, felt it a chivalrous duty to repair the loss incurred by the poorer people. The praises of Satsuma were in everyone's mouth,

though this is said to be no isolated act of similar assistance given by the great chiefs of this empire. Two or three years since, a fire originated in Sendai's quarters and consumed the only houses left to a neighboring chief, who had unfortunately had his duplicate town quarters burnt out. The Prince of Sendai at once turned over to his suffering neighbor the use of one of his own spacious town palaces and kept him there with his servants as a guest till his house was rebuilt. The frequency of disastrous conflagrations in Yedo has made it necessary for each Daimio to own two or more town residences, widely separated, to avoid being burned out of house and home. Thus Satsuma has seven, eight, or nine (var. estimated) town establishments.

Friday, January 10, 1862

Today the Empress, who has been ill for several days past, enters for the first [time] the imperial palace, and the Tycoon receives the congratulations of the chiefs of the empire. All official business at Yokohama is suspended.

Tuesday, January 14, 1862

St. Louis left.

Wednesday, January 15, 1862

Went to Walsh and Co.'s this morning to mess and keep house for them till some more permanent arrangement can be made.[3]

---

run to December 31, 1865. In fact, he was not relieved of his duties until March 30, 1866, when John A. Cunningham took his place. Despite his departure from Japan in July 1866, the firm retained the name Walsh, Hall & Co.

[2] This was the family of H. Owner, one of the American merchants who came to Yokohama in 1860. It is not clear why the household was broken up.

[3] Hall moved on this day from his own house to the site of Walsh & Co. (soon to become Walsh, Hall & Co.). Joseph Heco, writing about the location of Walsh &

Co., states in his diary that Towsend Harris was opposed to merchants settling in Yokohama, but "at length . . . Dr. Hall of Walsh & Co. was found bold enough to back the merchant's view of the case. On his own responsibility he procured a plot of land on the Yokohama side, and proceeded to establish himself here. This was quite in defiance of the Consul's view, but Dr. Hall was a practical man and saw the immense advantages over Kanagawa presented by Yokohama in facilities for shipping. The land he occupied is now known as No. 2 Bund. After that a guest of Walsh &

Hiroshige II's *Picture of a Foreign Building in Yokohama*, dated December 1861. The building depicted here is Walsh & Co. just before Dr. George R. Hall's departure for the United States. Hiroshige captured some of the plants that Dr. Hall was shipping to the United States. The company changed its name to Walsh, Hall & Co. after Francis Hall joined it early in 1862.

Friday, January 17, 1862

Last evening at Kanagawa a number of workmen in the employ of a boss carpenter who had, as they thought, ill used them, assembled and tore his house down. The deed was no secret, and it seems such cases of revenge are not rare, the actors openly declaring themselves fearless of consequences, for they may be arrested and lodged in jail and condemned to rebuild the premises. At other times, when a wrong has really been done to them, they are permitted to escape.

Saturday, January 18, 1862

For the past two or three days the servants of the Mikado who came up from Miako with the bridal cortege of their young Empress have been returning through the Tokaido. The missionaries resident at Kanagawa were accordingly requested to abstain from visiting the Tokaido while these dignitaries were en route. On the Yokohama side, the gates on the causeway leading into the Tokaido were closed to prevent foreigners entering on that great thoroughfare parts of three different days. Any hindrance to the free egress and ingress of the foreign residents being a manifest violation of the treaty, energetic remonstrance was at once made by the English and French ministers against this procedure accompanied with a threat to remove the barriers by force, for parties had been actually turned back who desired to pass through. The Government at once disavowed the whole affair and said it was the work of under officials without their sanction, a falsehood so palpable that none but an asiatic would have ventured to have uttered it. This

Co. secured the lot next to No. 2, now known as No. 3, while Jardine and Matheson soon after selected No. 1, and Dent & Co. Nos. 4 and 5" (Joseph Heco, *Narrative of a Japanese* (San Francisco: American-Japanese Publishing Association, n.d.), vol. 1, pp. 216–17). The former Walsh, Hall & Co. property is currently occupied by the Yokohama Sambō Kaikan.

fact is significant of two things: first, that when once all foreigners are removed from Kanagawa, the Japanese will do all they dare to keep us off from the Tokaido and *Desimate* us at Yokohama, and secondly, that the Mikado has a real force in this realm since they dared upon a venturesome treaty breach for the sake of one of his officers that has not been asked for the highest Daimio.

Monday, January 20, 1862

The following tale of love and marriage illustrates some Japanese views and customs. An innkeeper's daughter at Kanagawa so much attracted the notice of travellers by her intelligence and sprightliness, complete with comeliness and a good figure, that at last she was promoted to that great object of a common girl's ambition, a situation in a daimio's family at Yedo as maid to his mistress. Here she served, acquiring at the same time the feminine accomplishments which had hitherto been debarred her in her former humble avocation. While absent from home, her father fell ill with mortal sickness and his daughter was summoned back to Kanagawa. Here she attracted the attention of a young unmarried householder who had also just returned from a temporary absence in pursuit of health. The eyes of the maiden were favorable towards him, and according to custom, the parents met in negotiation of a match, when it appeared the lady's father had other projects for his daughter. He had adopted into his house a young man whom he hoped to unite with his daughter and leave them his business. But death hastened on with rapid strides before paternal authority could accomplish this, and dying the father willed to his daughter his house, his business, his lands, in fact, all his worldly gear, coupled with his injunctions that

she was to wed the adopted son and with him carry on the family business. This latter condition was repulsive to the young maiden who had a soul [that was] above waiting on the chance travellers of a Japanese hostelry, watching at the door to invite the passer by to "turn in and wash his feet," or bathing the dusty feet of weary roadsters. The young invalid now returned to health and his large comfortable house where she might live a quiet matronly life, had more charms for her. Besides, had she not been an inmate of a daimio's household and with her mistress's maidens past the happy hours in the light feminine work of dressing her mistress' hair, embroidering her garments, painting fans and screens, and singing to the accompaniment of a lute? She was ready to abandon all her possessions and cling to her lover, whose parents pressed the match. But her mother said she must be faithful to the dying injunctions of her father and wed the adopted son, and on this point was resolute. Then friends stepped in and urged the widow to take into the house for a husband to the daughter and promoter of the old trade a younger brother of her lover; and give to her faithful swain her older sister as a solace for his disappointment. But the widow says nay; the dying father's injunctions must be fulfilled to the letter, while the maiden vows she will no longer keep tavern and wed the adopted son. And here the matter now rests in dispute and all the Kanagawa gossips are talking how the Gordian knot shall be cut.

Wednesday, January 22, 1862

The *Odin* left at 10 A.M. with the Japanese Envoys to Europe.[4] According to Japanese accounts the inferior places in the Embassy were not sought for. Ota,[5] the interpreter, was quite unhappy at going. Judging by the fate of the

---

[4] The purpose of this mission was to attempt to negotiate an extension on the date for the opening of the ports of Hyogo and Niigata to foreign trade, and the cities of Edo and Osaka to foreign residence, due to the unsettled conditions then prevailing in Japan. The envoys managed to get the British, French, and Russians to agree to a five-year postponement. For a description of this mission see Fukuzawa Yukichi, *The Autobiography*

of Yukichi Fukuzawa (New York: Columbia University Press, 1966), pp. 124ff. Fukuzawa accompanied the mission as an official translator. See also Carmen Blacker, "The First Japanese Mission to England," *History Today* 7, no. 12 (December 1957), pp. 840–47.

[5] This was Ōta Genzaburō who accompanied the mission as interpreter.

American Embassy, neither emolument or promotion was to come out of it, for it is asserted, despite Minister Harris's statements to the contrary, that the principals of that Embassy have received no additional rank or emoluments beyond those they would have been equally eligible to if they had remained at home. So also of the underlings, not one has been promoted, while Katsu Taro, the captain of the Japanese steamer, has been degraded. On the whole they do not stand quite so well as if they had remained at home in the regular line of promotion.

When the present Embassy was mooted an influential daimio volunteered to go at his own cost, but this was not agreeable to the old fogies who hold reins as Council of State. It showed a spirit of enterprise that could not safely be trusted.

S[adajirō] has shown me today a Japanese book printed several years ago giving an account of the opium war in China in which the author holds up the result of that war "as a mirror to the Japanese" if they become involved in foreign difficulties.[6] He upbraids the Japanese for their conceit in their own skill and asks them "what protection have you against foreign vessels of water being a little island with unprotected coasts." "Will you," he adds, "trust to the God of the winds who overthrew the fleet of the Corean hordes to do this again for you." "Only fools act so." For this plain expression of opinion the author was seized and imprisoned, and an unsuccessful attempt made to suppress the work. After seven years imprisonment he was released, but banished to a distant province. When Perry's fleet came to Yedo Bay, the words of the unfortunate author were regarded as prophetic.

At the birth of a child, male or female, it is customary for some relative or friend to present the child with a small dagger, or sword, varying from a few inches to a foot in length and of value according to the ability of the giver. This dagger is supposed to be an amulet against evil, and is deposited by the side of the sleeping child. In after years it becomes not only a charm, but with the girls a weapon of offence, and the young maiden travelling on the road may be seen with it thrust in her girdle, or [tied] to the top of her kango, or even secured to her broad hat that shades her from the sun. When married she carries it with her to her home as part of her dowry. It has on its sheath of paper, or cloth, the name of the owner and the giver thus becoming a means of identification as related in a story as follows.

A traveller stopping at an inn where he lies for several days ill exhausts his money, and to discharge his indebtedness sends his short sword to be sold. The servant of the inn enters a shop to make the sale where it attracts the attention of an officer who desires to look at it. Scrutinizing it closely he inquires whence it came. The servant of the inn relates the story as I have given it. "I must know this sword," says the officer, looking at certain names and marks upon it. "It is the amulet sword of the child of a friend of mine at Yedo. This child, growing up, he came very dissipated, a drunkard and gambler, ran away from home, and doubtless he is the young man reduced to want who desires to sell his birthday sword." So he goes to the inn where he, indeed, recognizes the prodigal son and bears him back to his parents at Yedo.

There is complaint again of a debased silver coinage among the people who say that should the present year be one of scarcity, it, combined with a debased coinage, would render prices so high as to produce a revolution.

Are the common people, particularly the farmers, permitted to keep arms? S[adajirō] says yes, that it is common among good farmers to have both sword and spear in the house, and among the better of them muskets also. That this is particularly so in some provinces, Mito's for instance, and in Kosiu, in the latter

---

[6] This appears to be a reference to Shionoya Tōin's essay *Kakkaron* published in 1859, or to his earlier work dated 1846, in which he warned that in the wake of the Opium War the British would soon shift their attention from China to Japan, would send surveying missions, ask for stores and supplies, and make raids on the coast. Shionoya's writings were based on his translation of Wei Yuan's *Hai-kuo t'u-chih* (1847). Hall's information on Shionoya is quite accurate, and it is interesting that Sadajirō was familiar with this work. The importance of Shionoya's works are discussed in R. H. van Gulick, "*Kakkaron*, A Japanese Echo of the Opium War," *Monumenta Serica* 4 (1939–1940), pp. 478–545.

particularly, where the farmers are so trained to use the sword and spear that they are renowned for their skill and moreover are regarded with consideration by the Government.

Sleeping with the head to the north is regarded desirable for good influences. The Emperor lies with his head to the West, so say the people, because in that direction is the Mikado towards whom it would be highly improper to point the feet.

Female Mikados have been several times known in Japanese history. One ruled for nine years within the last century. A female Tycoon or Daimio is as yet unknown, though the widow of one of the large princes unsuccessfully undertook to establish her right to reign. Should the female Mikado marry, her husband becomes Mikado, in fact, and his descendants are heirs to his throne.

The Mikado is not limited in the number of his wives or concubines. He may select his wife from any families of high rank particularly from the Goseki, five families of highest station about his court. The origin of the custom of female servants about the Mikado is said to have been in the old feudal war times of the empire when the sovereign was jealous of any officials about the throne who might conspire against its security. Nor was this all, a long time of war had left no time for cultivation of diplomatic arts or courtier-like skills, nay, as some ignorant man by prowess in arms might rise to great power in the state, the sovereign for secretaries and councilors relied upon females who still cultivated the politer arts, and by their sex were naturally qualified for the etiquette and forms of a court. We have in the old Spanish and Portuguese chronicles, in the relations of the Jesuit fathers, accounts of women of rare excellence and learning and great court influence, which is hardly to be accounted for from the present position of the sex. But her position at the Mikado's court three centuries since would have been a stimulus to highbrow females to aspire to honor through the cultivation of her talents for public business. In the chivalric day of Europe her position was less enviable. From the Mikado's court this custom of female [seems to end in mid sentence]

Friday, January 24, 1862

Arrival of mail. Great fire in the Oshiwara. A little before 7 P.M., while dining [I] was aroused by an alarm of fire on the western side of the town. Hastened around to my premises from whence I could see a large flame arising from the *Oshiwara*, or courtesans quarter. A strong northwind was blowing at the time and showers of coals were falling in the line of the air current. The almost universal use of tiled roofs prevented the spread of the conflagration to a most disastrous extent, but not buildings with shingled roofs [which] here and there repeatedly caught fire. My own roof was on fire more than once, but the stationing of my servants on my roof with buckets of water and wet brooms was successful in extinguishing the coals that continually fell, not only on my own roof, but those of my neighbors, one of whom was absent, and the other (Brother Bagly) was frightened out of all his common sense, moving his effects and leaving his building, the more valuable of the two, to its fate.

After the danger had subsided, I went down to the Oshiwara and found one half of it a sea of flames, though all the buildings had by this time fallen down and were mostly consumed. Standing on the elevated ground that heads the long street leading to the Oshiwara, the sight was a striking one. That street was from end to end a mass of moving people holding their lanterns above their heads, the lights flowing along in a steady stream towards where a mass of flame was fanning up from the burning buildings as so many burning shapes falling into a central flame to feed it. I plunged into the throng, and found it was not without its difficulties and dangers. There was a tide going and returning at once, rushing violently along with shouts so that one had to keep even pace or be run over. Yakunins with two or three attendants rushed through the mass that had to give place to authority, then a high official with a score of attendants bearing sword and spear and plume, crested and helmeted ploughed through the throng. The police with their staves elbowed their way, members of the fire brigade tramped aside the looker on. Occasionally of these last [there] were stalwart fellows in full shut breeches, loose overcoat of leather, tinselled or gilt metal helmets, and flowing capes of chain or stout white and ornamented leather, [who] marched along with lanterns over their heads and staves of office in their hands. Grouped around the fire were the higher officials in squads here and there in their splendid fire suits, helms glittering with silver, gold, and brass ornaments, and capes of white leather flowing over their shoulders, dresses of embossed leather and tinselled brocades. Their horses picketed nearby in charge of grooms. Everywhere were multitudes of officers, members of the fire brigade, and squads of police, so numerous and disciplined that one cannot help thinking there is no small order system and effectiveness in Japanese rule. The higher officials, who even to the Governor, are always present at a conflagration take little part in any exertion to extinguish [the fire], though doubtless emergencies arise, like the necessity of tearing down buildings, when their word of command is necessary. One too has an idea if the event should become necessary what a host of armed men could spring up in our very midst.

The main building, the Gankiro, was consumed and five or six other large houses of prostitution and one long row of prostitution stalls. A hundred females may have been turned out of their houses. Degraded and reprobate as is the calling of these unfortunate females, one's sympathy was needs be excited to see them grouped out and shivering in the nipping night air. Girls whose sin was not theirs but their parents who had sold them in tender irresponsible years to a life of shame, my feelings were touched for them that they had not only the ordinary calamities of life as this night's to meet, but the loathing and disgust and suffering which many of them must feel, if their word is to be believed, for a life to which they have been hopelessly sold. I saw the mistress of one of the houses whom I had known in other days as a small merchant, and who had, after long and obstinate refusal, at last yielded to the solicitations of her own father to assume the control of his house. She was a young unmarried woman twenty or twenty-one years old of an exterior unusually prepossessing, and in Kanagawa where she had lived bore an irreproachable character.

Even after she had, in obedience to her father's wishes, taken charge of his house, I had been repeatedly assured by those who knew her well that no Japanese could, or did, charge her personally with any act of unchastity. She had been tempted by, to a Japanese, a large sum of foreign gold also, but in the midst of impurity and an impure calling kept her own life chaste. As I was looking upon the ruins of the fire I saw a woman standing by herself gazing abstractly into the flames. No one was with her, she was apart from all the throng. I recognized her features as that of this girl. I called her name several times before she was conscious of my presence. At last she looked up and said, "I have lost all," and pointing to her scanty garments said, "my children (she called them) are safe," and burst into tears. It is rare to see a Japanese show so much emotion, and when I turned my back a moment only she had fled into the thickest of the crowd to escape observation.

Saturday, January 25, 1862

The ruins of yesterday's fire are still smoking, but the lots are being cleared, fences erected, and preparations made for rebuilding.

Monday, January 27, 1862

Today is the 28th of the Japanese month and three days before their New Year's and is regarded as a special day. At Yedo the Daimios pay complimentary visits to the Emperor and to some extent visits of compliment are made among friends that they have passed this year so well with wishes for the same for the incoming year.

For several days the signs of the New Year have been apparent and yesterday and today the trimming of the houses is begun. Bamboos and pines enliven the streets with their green boughs and kites in the hands of the boys and battledores in the hands of the girls are ominous of the good time coming.

I rode out to Hondenga to observe one of the country customs of the season. A sort of fair was going on in the public street which for half a mile was so densely crowded that I was compelled to walk my horse very slowly and carefully. On either side of the street were vendors of all descriptions of household wares, wooden made, cookery, iron ware, mechanics tools, hucksters of fruits and vegetables and provisions generally, conspicuous among whom were the vendors of fish standing behind great piles of salt salmon. All wares entering into the common daily use of the people were abundantly displayed and vociferous sellers were getting red in the face with the loud praising of the cheapness of their commodities. Everywhere it was *makete, makete*. Dry goods merchants and sellers of bulky articles were in the shops adjoining, serving their articles to the chaffering crowds that bent their doors. A large trade was going on and it was evident that the fair was one of general resort from neighboring villages, for I counted familiar faces among both buyers and sellers. A large share was given to the sale of house trimmings for the New Year and toys for children of every description. It was an astonishing and unaccountable share of popular character that some of their toys were of the most indecent description. I saw many a little fellow going away with father or brother or mother or other relative who had made him happy in the possession of a new kite or ball, and many a girl was stepping away fondly with her new shoes or stockings, or head ornaments, or a pair of gaily ornamented battledores. Confections and cake sellers were as busy as though it had been a Christmas at home. Everywhere in the crowd I was well received, generally with exclamations of boisterous delight for *sake* had been here, many called me by name and not once from the thousand people did I hear the word *baka*. As I returned home through the country road it was pleasant to see the farmers going home with their arms laden with new household utensils for New Year's gifts to wives and mothers and toys for children. One group consisted of three yakunins who were quite loaded down with gifts for the little folks which they did not disdain to carry with their own hands. Indeed one of them was quite overshadowed by the large handsome kite he was taking home to the black eyed urchins that would rush to meet him at the gate. They sa-

luted me in a cheerful way as I passed quite unbending from their usual gravity as I exchanged a few words incident to the occasion.

But now a whiff of smoke burdened with not an agreeable scent flies in my face and I turn round and see a few men and a frizzly priest raking up the embers of a spot fire and there is a heap of something covered with coarse sacking. I understand it all, the small fire and the dirty priest. There has been a cremation and the bones have been gathered and will be borne away in that sack to their burial, the dirty priest chanting his monotonous prayers for a requiescat. But clear into the crowds of Yokohama I trace the carriers home from the fair and wish I could follow the gifts home to the happy recipients.

Tuesday, January 28, 1862

This day and tomorrow are busy days with the native merchants closing this year's accounts. The people are still adorning their houses and preparing the great rice cakes.

Wednesday, January 29, 1862

This evening the dry good shops, shoe shops, confectioners, toy sellers etc., are busy as with us the night before Christmas selling gifts for the New Year. Articles of substantial use are much sought for. The girl and boy must have their new clothes on New Year's day, and I find my servants each have their new suits of clothes for tomorrow's holiday. Tonight will be a busy night among traders of all sorts, a year's accounts will be finally closed and large and small sums of money change hands everywhere. Few of the businessmen will sleep till the morning cock crows, many not at all, till another eve comes around.

Thursday, January 30, 1862

Heavy snow, 19 inches. *Japanese New Year.* At 3 A.M. snow began to fall and continued snowing heartily without interruption all day. It was a sudden check to the festivities of the New

Year and the streets were deserted of the customary New Year callers. Despite the storm I went out to see what my Japanese friends were doing and found some at 12 A.M. yet abed, others just aroused, and none overflowing with the festivity of the season. The contrast with last year was striking. Among themselves there was no merry making. The storm was worthy of old New England, all day long it sifted down or drove along furiously with the norther blast, the thermometer scarcely at freezing point, till at night everything was robed with a thick mantle. The snow lay 15 inches deep. Foreigners from snowy climes exhilarated by the familiar presence revelled in the old joy of snowballing and snowrolling, boyhood came back again. We only needed sleighs to enjoy the luxury of a sleigh ride once more.

Friday, January 31, 1862

A warm sun is rapidly melting yesterday's snow. The day is so bright that every one feels an irrepressible desire to be abroad. Snowballs are flitting through the air thicker, but less deadly, than the bullets of Magenta, for English, French, and Americans are pelting each other indiscriminately, and the Japanese collectively, who mostly take it in good heart, though now and then one gets angry and finds it no use to lose his temper as the white balls only come the faster.

The neglected calls of yesterday are resumed today. The yakunins with their servants carrying shoes for the street and shoes for the house, or a package of shinjos, are bearing their cards or calling from house to house. They have all donned the linen kamishimo and wear an air of exceeding gravity and importance. The merchants too are calling, attended by servants bearing a large basket, or box, strung forward from the neck, said box or basket full of complimentary packets of small but significant *tosidamma*, or New Year's gifts. From all I can hear entertainments are not set forth as last year. I saw myself no attempt in that way worthy of mention. I called at Takara Dyah's,[7] the rich carpenter's, and found him and his head clerk in their office devoting the day half to business and half to pleasure. Gifts ready for distribution were lying about the room, of which two plain but very neat fans fell to my lot, though I must confess I rather coveted one of several neat fir boxes like a glove box standing each on its own little stand and no doubt filled with some pleasant confections. My covetousness was for the box, more to show it as a sample of Japanese taste, real taste, than for the contents. The clerk was busily engaged in wrapping up in a neat manner some money presents, putting five bus in each packet. Judging from the appearance of things Takara Dyah's gift bill was no small one. We drank the compliments of the season in first a cup of *toso*, a sweet sake like cordial, and again in rice sake.

Wishing to cross to Kanagawa with my friend, Mr. A[llman]d[8] we had some difficulty in getting a boat, and finding the boatmen indisposed to accommodate us we took a boat which had been got ready for the ferry passengers and pushing it off the beach jumped in to row ourselves over. The astonished Japs looked on in amazement evidently not believing us in earnest and then thinking us incapable of managing the heavy sculls, and this last, I must confess, quite baffled me, though friend A[llmand] took to them like an experienced hand and we gradually made headway. We had now got well off the shore and getting the hang of the long scull we were making rapidly for the Kanagawa shore two miles distant when the Japanese boat officers began to get uneasy on their part as to what might become of their boat and started another boat after us. We at first gave them a race and had got half way across when they begged us to stop, which we did on their promise to provide boatmen and allowed them to come alongside.

At Kanagawa the Tokaido presented an exceedingly picturesque appearance. The straw

[7] This would appear to have been Takaradaya Taroemon who is listed as being in the lumber business in a guide to Yokohama merchants for the period from 1859 to 1867. See Yokohama Shi, eds. *Yokohama shishi* (Tokyo: Tosho Insatsu Kabushiki Kaisha, 1970), vol. 2, p. 15.

[8] John Allmand of Allmand & Co.

fringes of the houses and the rosettes of green leaves over the doors with an orange peeping out, the pines and bamboos thickly planted along either road side contrasted their green leaves with the snowy roofs and the snow of the street which had been gathered in heaps a rod or so apart and made a winding road among the snow hills overshadowed with green foliage. It was a scene such as I have seen in their pictures rudely, but faithfully represented.

Saturday, February 1, 1862

New Year's callers are frequent in the street today which are made the livelier by the presence of women and children in their bright holiday dresses. Kite flying among the boys and men, and battledore with the girls is the amusement of the day.

Sunday, February 2, 1862

A mail from home bringing me a letter from Edward. The New Year's visiting still goes on.

Monday, February 10, 1862

Our streets are daily thronged with travellers. It is to the farming population the least busy season of the year and the good returns from the bountiful crops of the past summer have given them means to indulge in sight seeing. Yedo, and the various places and temples of public resort are thronged in an unusual manner. Many of these travellers, in addition to their usual clothing, wear hanging from their shoulders on their backs a thick cotton quilt some five feet long by three broad. This quilt not only answers the purpose of warmth, when walking, but a cushion when sitting or lying, and a comfortable pad for the hard saddles when mounted. Curiosity to see how we tojins live has brought them in such numbers to Yokohama.

The flashes of heat lightning and the lights of the aurora borealis are regarded by the common people as spirits of the departed still wearing the flaming robes in which they were wrapped when the body was consumed (spirits do not at once go to heaven or hell but wander thus about in an intermediate or purgatorial state).

Sorcerers are common who not only pretend to reveal the fates, to bring good luck, but, as in other lands, they evoke the spirits of the departed who hold converse through them with inquiring mortals. The sorcerer is seized with a convulsion, closes his eyes and goes into a mesmeric trance when his own spirit leaves him and the spirit of the summoned dead man takes possession, for the time, of his body and speaks with the voice and tones of his old life on earth. Thus the barren wife intercedes for children, the poor man seeks a road to wealth, the sick man asks to what doctor he shall trust his life, and the bereaved learn the condition of their departed friends.

Thursday, February 13, 1862

Today at Yedo the public officers of rank pay their respects to the Emperor, and we hear at evening that the time was taken advantage of to commit one of those bloody tragedies with which the course of Japanese events is so frequently marked. About ten o'clock Ando Tsushima-no-kami, Minister of Foreign Affairs, left his residence opposite the entrance to the citadel, or imperial residence, to make a call upon the Emperor. He had scarcely gone outside of his own gate, when his norimon was assailed by ten men attired in ordinary citizen's dress. They were armed under their garments, part with revolvers of foreign make, part with Japanese carbines, and all with long knives and daggers. The disguise of citizen's dress was assumed to enable them to penetrate a quarter where a band of samurai usually armed would be at once suspected unless in attendance upon some noble or dignitary. One or more pistol shots were fired into the norimon, when its occupant, a man of forty-five years of age, succeeded in getting out of it and bravely attacked his assailants, in return assisted by his faithful retainers in large number. The assailants, or assassins, were no match for the long swords and superior numbers of their antagonists, although they fought with the desperation of men whose lives were doomed. Six of them were slain on the spot, another ripped himself open, and the remainder escaped. Prince Ando was wounded by a pistol ball in the cheek and a slight cut in the back, wounds of slight character; one follower was killed, two more are thought to be mortally wounded, and several others have slight wounds. The attack was made, like that upon the Regent, in a spot incessantly crossed over by armed retainers following their masters who are on horseback, or in norimons, and the desperate men who made [the attack] must have counted on the loss of their lives, [in] that they had cast them upon a die which gave them barely a chance in ten of escape. The cause of the assault is readily conjectured to have grown out of the assassination of the Regent. Prince Ando at that time being a public functionary under him and his intimate friend, and afterwards in his capacity of a government officer was active in bringing the assassins of the Regent to a death punishment. He thus brought upon himself the hate of the late Mito's men, and how eager that hate, how insatiable the lust of revenge, was in Japanese breasts may be judged from this undertaking. Indeed, I do not know that we shall be done with the acts of the late Mito's soldiery till they are all killed, or have grown old and died. It has been commonly reputed that this Prince Ando was in danger of such an assault, and now it is said that the next official in rank to him, for similar reasons, stands in a like danger.[9]

It is an old custom that a prince when attacked, if he did not draw his sword in defence, had his estates sequestered to the crown.

Hence first of all he tries to draw, and if death arrests the sword but a single inch drawn from its scabbard it shows the pure intent and suffices.

Today the trimmings are taken down from houses and burned at early morning.

Friday, February 14, 1862

Today is a public holy-day. It is the festival of *M'ma* [Emma], or the prince of devils. According to popular superstition M'ma on this day has a recreation day himself. Ordinarily he is so occupied with the laborious duties of his office, that he is inattentive to the supplications of the still living friends of his victims. Today, however, he has his recreation, and not being so busy, it is thought a favorable time to propitiate him for the souls of the departed who are in his limbo. So, at certain designated temples, images or pictures of M'ma are set up and worship is offered. Children are the chief prompters of this worship, and everywhere in the streets today I have encountered bright groups of handsomely dressed children enjoying their holiday with kites and battledores and little misses in red shirts and scarlet and orange sashes, powdered faces stained lips and showy headdresses, white socks and new shoes, are walking the streets with mothers, aunts, or nurses, happy as the day is sunny. At a little temple under the hill by the roadside inns at Kanagawa is a gorgeous picture of M'ma, and a flock of happy youngsters are rushing up and down the steps shouting to each other and a little fellow has got red in the face beating the big temple drum, and here is a cross eyed boy who rolls one eye under his nose and curls his tongue out of his mouth, as, kite in hand,

9 Andō Nobumasa (1820–1871) was the daimyō of the Iwaki Taira domain and senior councillor (*rōjū*) of the Tokugawa shogunate from 1860 to 1862. When Ii Naosuke, the Great Elder (*tairō*), was assassinated in 1860 Andō and Kuze Hirochika assumed the leadership of the senior council. Andō had attempted to strengthen the shogunate's position politically through a policy that sought to unite the court and bakufu. To this end he arranged the marriage between Princess Kazu and the shogun Tokugawa Iemochi mentioned

above. This act so incensed a group of imperial loyalists headed by Ōhashi Totsuan and several Mito samurai that they plotted the assassination of Andō early in 1862. Despite Ōhashi's arrest his fellow conspirators attacked Andō in the Sakashitamon Incident on February 13, 1862, wounding him as Hall's entry accurately indicates. The attackers were quickly slain. But Andō was not able to continue in office and thus his effort to strengthen the shogunate failed.

he looks up at me so quizzically, another fellow is winding up his kite string with a look of having done some great feat in kite flying achievement, and another shouts "here comes Hall sama," and so I ride by exchanging "Ohaio anata" with the gay urchins.

On this day also the felons in jail are allowed some indulgences. New clothes are given such as need, they are allowed to shave their heads and have a body bath, and a little better food is provided. On the 16th of the 7th month the same privileges are granted—albeit friends may provide the prisoner clothing, food, and other necessities at any time.

Saturday, February 15, 1862

Today is the 17th of the 1st Japanese month and is a festival day in honor of Gongen Sama, who is now commonly called Tosio Shinkio, or "Light of the dawn."[10] This name, which was not given to him until a considerable period after his death, was given because with him there dawned upon these isles the long years of peace which they have since enjoyed. His name, more literally rendered is, "Light from the East," east being put for the point from whence the daily light of the sun begins to shine. His tomb is some distance from the city of Yedo, and is the object of many pilgrimages, but at the Imperial Cemetery in the heart of the city is a wooden statue of this hero, in the temple therein located, the head of which statue is adorned with the venerable hair of the defunct monarch. So today flock thither to this temple Princes, nobles, and men of mean estate, from the wearer of silks and satins to the ragged street porter. Ladies of rank, daughters of noble houses, join the swelling throngs. At the distance of two blocks from the temple, custom compels, in order to preserve the proper honor of the hero, that every norimon rider no matter how exalted his birth or rank, ladies of princely houses as well, must leave their palanquins and approach on foot. So the crowd collects there to see these uncovered ladies of rank joining the common throng

as they can rarely, or never, be seen at other times. At the temple they dip their hands in the pure water basins and lave face and hands, and, if Japanese gossiping may be relied upon, the people standing about may be seen picking up the cast aside paper with which some fair damsel of high birth has just dried her moistened face and hands and bear it away as a memento of its fair owner. Why not, need we go outside of our own republican borders to find a parallel case of flunkeyism?

Sunday, February 16, 1862

If we may believe in Japanese informants, Buddhism in Japan has been on the decline, more particularly within the last quarter of a century. In my own mind there can be but little doubt that Western civilization has insidiously helped to effect this, for the Japanese have not been ignorant of what was going on in the great world about them, and their own improving civilization has led them—slowly to be sure and almost imperceptibly yet gradually—to follow after and strive to imitate it. Buddhism, when it has yielded, has yielded to nationalism and disbelief. As this is seen mostly at Yedo, the courtly city where foreign affairs have been best understood, it is additional reason to believe that light from the West streaming in a feeble ray through the pin point at old Desima had its influence. I believe in its own isolation Japan was very slowly improving because I hear so commonly of improved popular customs and opinions differing from those they have had in their earlier history. The appliances and comforts of civilized life were slowly creeping in, and woman [has] had some chance of an amelioration of her position, yet more and more as compared with other semi-barbarian people. It is by no means impossible that the Catholic fathers of three centuries ago left some grains of good that have borne fruit from hidden, or forgotten, seed and despite all the mercenary character of Desima's traffic, the Japanese therewith were slowly drawing in to themselves a knowledge of a better life and

---

[10] This reference is to Tokugawa Ieyasu, the founder of the Tokugawa shogunate, who was posthumously deified as Tōshō Daigongen (The Great Incarnation Who Illuminates the East) by the Imperial Court.

civilization existing beyond their shores. They had books of sterling value that they could read, they had in a hundred imported articles, in instruments and results of art, mechanical skill, improved ways of the healing art, tangible evidences of the value of Western civilization. Thus I am often led to think that had Perry never opened Japan to the West and the Dutch remained a century longer at Desima that Japan would have improved in civilization steadily if not rapidly; nay more, I sometimes think—considering the character of the people that had been left to *ask in* Western influences through the Dutch as then, and not felt them, as it were, *forced* upon them as now—taken their own way, without compulsion or restraint, the gain to this people would have been greater and more permanent than now. Who should say also, that with enlightenment from abroad, they, wearied of their own effete faith and superstitions, might not have come even to receiving through the same door the faith of the West back again, which they, and the traders of Desima, closed three centuries ago.

In every Japanese house is the "Kami no tana," or "Closet of the Kami," where are the emblems of the old Shinto faith, a sort of household altar. In wealthy families the closet, or shrine, is large and handsomely ornamented with carved woods and ornaments of silver, gold, or their imitations sparingly used. In common families a neat shrine in imitation of a temple, standing on a shelf is very general, and from this down to a simple box with doors contain the simple altar sets of worship. The Shinto shrine must always be of unpainted woods, and though often carved elaborately, shuns bronzed ornaments. There is a lamp for light, the great emblem of this faith, a cup for offerings of sake, a vase for flowers. No incense is burned at the Shinto shrine. In the morning the husband or wife strikes a new light from the flint, for old fire will not do, and lights the lamp at the shrine, and with the same fire kindles a flame upon the hearth, or the hibatchi, to boil water freshly drawn from the well for the morning draught of tea. A libation of sake is poured into the cup, and the supplicant may, or may not, bare the head over his joined and upraised hands as in silent prayer. At evening new fire is again given to the replenished lamp, a few flowers have been added in course of the day to the vase, and the morning and evening sacrifice is complete. But daily prayer, or worship, is no more binding on the heathen than on Christian families, for some light the fire daily or twice a day, others on the 1st day of the month, others on the three holy-days of each month, while my friend S[adajirō] says once a year, on its feast day, suffices him, but S[adajirō] is a Japanese skeptic. In the families who live opposite me last summer, when doors were open, I could see each day at eventide the housewife lighting first the altar flame and then the household lamp. It seemed never to be omitted or forgotten, and I thought it a lesson to us who think we are so much better than the heathen. If we have more reason, have we more faith in our worship?

Not only is there the "kami no tana," but in most houses also the "Butsudan" or Buddha's shrine, always placed below the former, and unlike the former may be highly adorned with colors or other devices. But while the latter may be omitted, the former must be in every house, and this fact is of itself a proof that Shintoism is yet deepest in the heart of the people.

Tuesday, February 18, 1862

We have today a new and probably the true version of the cause of the recent assault on Ando Tsushima-no-kami. Last year Hori Oribe-no-kami, formerly governor at Yokohama, committed hara kiri at Yedo. He left letters addressed to his superiors in office, he being at that time one of the Governors of Foreign Affairs, and to his friends, stating that he had been charged by Ando, one of the Ministers of Foreign Affairs, with having been, while in administration of affairs at Yokohama, unfaithful to his office and country by concurring at the schemes of the foreigners. This opprobrious charge he declared to be false, and to wipe out the disgrace of this stigma he took his life after the Japanese custom. It was stated subsequently that Hori's character was fully justified by his colleagues, and according to

Japanese etiquette Ando should have ripped himself up, and for several weeks it was currently rumored that he had done so. It seems he did not, and now it appears that the assailants of Ando were retainers of Hori who thus sought to avenge their master's fate. The assailants were thirteen, two of them physicians and the third a priest who was armed with a pistol. At the first onset the chief and leader of the Prince's attendants, whose post of honor is always on the left and a little in advance of the norimon, was slain by a ball from the priest's pistol. Then followed the assault on the norimon with long swords for it appears the assailants were after all thus armed. Prince Ando escaped with two or three slight wounds, and some of his men were badly injured. Of the assailants six were slain, one committed suicide by hara kiri, and three, to wit the priest and two doctors escaped.

Wednesday, February 19, 1862

Arrival of *Golden State*, Ranlett, from California.

Thursday, February 20, 1862

Abbé Girard, of the new French and Romish Chapel, some days since commenced daily service therein in the Japanese language. The Abbé having resided in Loo Choo [Ryūkyū] several years, and the last two and a half years in Japan, had become sufficiently proficient in this difficult tongue to enable him to speak understandingly. His mode of instruction was to give explanation of the various pictures hung upon the walls of the chapel depicting scenes and incidents from Holy Writ. Though public proclamation has been made forbidding the people to resort thither, they were attracted to the Chapel in considerable number, not in opposition to this proclamation, but evidently not clearly understanding its import. Thus for several days the Abbé had continued to instruct an audience of fifty or sixty people, when the Governor, instructed from Yedo, interfered by seizing a large number of the auditors, binding them and committing them to jail. They were seized not at the temple, but subsequently to their offence, within their own houses. Some fifty or sixty are said thus to have been lodged in jail. The French Minister, it is presumed, will interfere in behalf of these people. The Abbé's instructions had excited much talk among the people, who, if unrestrained, would have flocked to his little chapel to the extent of its capacity. They were much interested in what was said to them of the Savior's life and teachings, for like the men of Athens the people of Japan are ready to listen to something new. Old women and men wept at the touching story of Christ and the ruler's daughter, showing how easily their sensibilities were affected and were the way open, I doubt not, multitudes would come to hear, if not to believe.

Friday, February 21, 1862

An unfortunate accident occurred yesterday in which a travelling man from the Prince of Owari's domains was run over by a horse which a foreigner was riding and believed to be killed. He was borne away as dead.

Saturday, February 22, 1862

The man who was wounded yesterday is in a fair way to recover.

Sunday, February 23, 1862

Carrington arrived from San Francisco having among her passengers Lady Franklin[11] and

[11] Lady Jane Franklin (1792–1875) was the second wife of Sir John Franklin, the artic explorer who died in 1847 on a polar expedition trying to find the northwest passage. Lady Franklin outfitted a series of missions to find her lost husband. In 1859 she finally learned of his tragic death. In the years that followed she became something of an international traveler and visited many countries, including Japan. See George Smith, ed., *The Dictionary of National Biography* (London: Oxford University Press, 1917), vol. 7, p. 631.

attendants, and Mssrs Blake and Pumpelly,[12] who have come out to make mineral and mining surveys for the Japanese Government, having been sent for at request of the same. The *Carrington's* dates had been anticipated by the arrival of the *Golden State* three days earlier, and which left San Francisco twenty days later than the *C.* The *Golden State* brought as freight a truck cart and a barouche carriage for the Governor of Hakodade also ordered from the United States. The Governor is now desirous of getting a span of foreign horses. He is perhaps more intent on making a display for himself than benefitting his countrymen.

Friday, February 28, 1862

The Governor of Yokohama has today discharged all the parties arrested for visiting the Catholic Chapel. He has done so on the urgent request of the French Minister and Abbé Girard. We all rejoice that this affair has ended so favorably to the unfortunate Japanese. Future transgressors against the country's edict will not be dealt with so leniently. The whole circumstance is indicative of the opposition and difficulty to be encountered in introducing any form of Christian religion.

Sunday, March 2, 1862

Earthquake 2 P.M.

Wednesday, March 5, 1862

Festival of Inari, the Rice God. Today is an important holiday in the Japanese calendar being the festival of Inari, the patron deity of the rice crop. According to Japanese mythology, Inari in some dim and remote age of the past came from heaven to earth and taught the people the use and cultivation of rice. The white fox is his chief servant and minister and shares propitiatory honors with his master. The traveller in Japan beholds wherever he goes by the roadside and in the fields little chapels looking like dog kennels of large size and some of them are no whit larger or better than a dog kennel, which for the most part are dirty and dilapidated and deserted. Now and then a white paper tied to a reed stalk, a straw shoe, a little sprinkled rice or some similar emblem shows that they are not wholly forgotten, while others seem deserted from one year end to another. These chapels are sacred to Inari and his white fox and on this anniversary, the 5th of the 5th moon, there is no chapel or kennel however humble or begrimed with a years dust but is decked with offerings. These are few and simple, flags inscribed with propitiatory words, white paper streamers, green twigs and flowers, offerings of rice, sake, salt, sandals of horses and men, picture lanterns are the chief. Some of these chapels are prettily constructed and picturesquely situated. The Shinto mias are gaily bedizened also with flags and streamers, branches, and flowers natural or artificial, and the avenues tree bordered and stone flagged which lead to these as well as the little chapels of the better sort are lined with pictured lanterns in which the fox comes in for a large share of representation. The

[12] William Phipps Blake and Raphael Pumpelly were hired by the Japanese government to serve as geologists and mineralogists to explore the resources of Hokkaido. Townsend Harris was influential in arranging for their appointments and their contracts were worked out through Japan's commercial agent in San Francisco, Charles Wolcott Brooks. Hazel Jones has pointed out that Blake and Pumpelly, who were expected to work in the interior away from the treaty ports, were provided with contracts that stated that each was to be given the "full protection of life" by "the Government of Japan, while in its service, whether at mines, traveling, or in any of the cities or towns, he acting in conformity to the laws and regulations of said [Japanese] government." Townsend Harris evidently accepted this interpretation, which clearly indicated that Westerners in the interior were under Japanese, not consular, jurisdiction. See Hazel Jones, *Live Machines: Hired Foreigners and Meiji Japan* (Vancouver: University of British Columbia Press, 1980), p. 3. Pumpelly, who became a well-known Harvard professor later, wrote of his Japanese experiences in his book, *My Reminiscences* (New York: Henry Holt and Co., 1918), 2 vols.

children as usual take a moving part in the day's demonstrations being indefatigable in beating the temple drums the tire long day. At the side of the Shinto mias or on the street near them a stage is erected with a mat roof overspread and decked with branches and flowers and hung with lantern[s] whereon amateur mountebanks, volunteers from the populace, perform to the accompaniment of rude music, harlequin tricks, grotesque posturings, and dancings with marked faces of the fox, feigned dragon of six heads, to the edification of their audience of boys, girls, mothers with babes in arms and here and there a paterfamilias with the heir of his house on his shoulders. Or this platform or stage is set on wheels with a canopy overhead gay with colored papers and pictured devices and so drawn about the street to the music of drum, flageolet and shouting crowds of people, halting occasionally to fire its clownlike performances.

In the new village of Yokohama the occasion was taken to inaugurate a new mia which had been just completed. It was built under the hill side and a flag walk arched by the *torii* led thither. In front of the chapel two foxes cut in stone kept watch at its portals, within was the Shinto shrine of a mirror supported on either side by two white foxes carved in wood and in front a cup for sake and a vase for flowers. By the street side the neighbors were erecting a stage for spectacles on which young nippon was rehearsing in preliminary tumblings. In the trees lantern were hung for the evening illumination. Afterwards in the still of the night I heard the cries and shouts of Inari and the white fox's worshipers a half mile away.

Saturday, March 8, 1862

Arrival of *Scotland*.

Thursday, March 20, 1862

The light of a large fire was visible towards Yedo all of last evening and night and today we hear of an extensive conflagration in the heart of the city which raged all night and did an immense amount of mischief.

According to accounts the Japanese Government are taking possession of the "Bonin Islands." Some time since a preliminary expedition went thither and found these islands inhabited by a mixed population of English, Americans, and "their servants" (doubtless Sandwich Islanders) in all 32 souls. And now quite recently an expedition of four ships has sailed thither with colonists who receive a large bounty from the Government and are promised an annual stipend. The Japanese have always claimed these islands but have invariably forbid colonists to go thither. Many years ago, however, colonists were sent thither by the Prince of Owari and another Daimio, who after a short stay returned. More lately, some 30 years since, a secret expedition thither was planned having for its leader an inn keeper who had made a fortune. A vessel or vessels were in readiness, colonists were secretly engaged, and just when on the eve of sailing the carrying aboard of so many utensils of various sorts attracted notice and the expedition was arrested and its promoters thrust in jail. The Japanese name of the islands is Moojinjima [Ogasawara Islands].[13]

Friday, March 21, 1862

The fire at Yedo commenced near the celebrated Nippon bridge and burnt itself out to the water's edge on one side and was arrested by streets on the others, consuming between twenty and thirty chos in the heaviest mercantile portion of the city, covering a space nearly if not quite equal to the whole of Yokohama. "Fires are very frequent," the Secretary of the American Legation writes me, "there being two or three alarms every night."

Thursday, March 27, 1862

Some of the Japanese gossips have a rumor of the detection of a conspiracy at Yedo against the Emperor which one of the faint hearted chiefs divulged and three hundred men have

---

[13] Bonin is a corruption of Bunin, "uninhabited"; Mujinjima, "islands without people," suggest the same.

been arrested in consequence. As the rumor after some days existence gets no confirmation it may be distrusted.

Friday, March 28, 1862

Arrival of mail.

Tuesday, April 1, 1862

The 3rd of the Japanese 3rd month and festival of Hinari. This is a favorite holiday of the women and children—as the 5th of the 5th month is of men and boys—who appear in their houses and in the streets tricked out in all of their fine gear. The little folks, especially the little girls, for it is a holiday in which the males take no part, are looking very pretty in their holiday clothes, and are seen in bright groups about the miyas, temples, and tea shops, or visiting from home to home and walking the streets hand in hand.

I took a long walk of several miles on the Tokaido to witness the observance of the day. At the large inns and tea houses, where many females were employed, the most preparation had been made. In the choice apartment of the house a series of narrow shelves had been erected sloping back from the floor as they ascended to about four feet high. On these shelves were deposited images in full dress of ancient heroes and heroines of the Mikados who are especially propitiated on this day, having the name of "The Festival of the Dolls" as the word *Hinari* indicates. These dolls, which are in number according to the ability of the householder, are showily dressed after the approved Nippon way in full wigs, brocade dresses, abundant underclothes of crape, ample sashes and girdles, swords, and head ornaments, as these heroes and heroines are supposed to have walked in the flesh, and are to this day represented on the stage. Mingled with the dolls are ornaments in miniature patterned after the furniture of the house, the utensils of the kitchen, the fittings of a lady's bedchamber, her implements of domestic and ornamental industry, her writing desk, her musical instruments, her fans, her ornaments

and dishes of viands cooked and uncooked of all kinds are set forth on the shelves till they present a queer conglomeration of dolls, toys, and eatables. In fact all the feminine arts and graces in which the Japanese female desires to excel are symbolized by something on these shelves; here she throws out lures to the departed Mikados to win a good and true husband, or to be helped with the joys of maternity—the image representing an ancient heroine of the Mikados who went to the wars in Corea and was safely delivered of a child being always a conspicuous one. A diamond shaped rice cake is an essential among the offerings of the women, as on the 5th of the 5th month a square one is with the men. Today, too, everyone drinks white sake, a peculiar sweet kind made thick with rice flour, which sellers were hawking about from house to house in large tubs and many a one I saw that had been emptied. This, with tea made of the peach blossom or cherry in which salt has been added, are offered to every guest. Fragrant blossoms of other kinds are also used. Like observances are made in private houses on a smaller or larger scale as wealth and fancy dictates, and doubtless among the wealthy and aristocratic class, most attractive displays are made of gaily dressed dolls, toys, cakes, confectionery and more substantial eatables.

I called at several places where I was made welcome and entertained with peach blossom tea and cakes and white wine from the dolls' plates and goblets. I was pleased to see that the glass ware of Europe had its place on the shelves, ladies' cologne bottles of ground, figured, and gold glass serving to hold the white holiday wine.

Curiosity led me to see how the day was kept among the courtesans, where I found that the headman had taken occasion of this festival as a proper day to inaugurate a new house which had been erected in the burned ruins of the old. Japanese politeness prevents such a visit as this from being what such a visit would necessarily be at home, full of disgusting associations. A stranger from anything he should see or hear could not guess what place he was visiting, so courteous is the demeanor of the master, mistress, and their attendants, and so well behaved and seemingly modest are the courtesans, whose life is not so wholly outcast as it would be in civilized lands. The master of the house had assembled all the girls of the establishment, not less than thirty in number, who were seated on the mats on the four sides of a long room each with a new tray and covered bowl before her of lackered wood. All were in bright new dresses, presents from the master, and their heads were ornamented profusely after the Japanese style as seen in their pictures. Ranged down the center of the room were heaping dishes of food just cooked. Then the master and his wife and several attendants entered, and uncovering the head dishes ordered the distribution of the viands. Could one have looked simply at what was visible, the fresh dress and contented faces of the girls and their holiday feast, and forgotten their sad lives and the vile bondage to which they have been sold by the cupidity or poverty of their parents, the picture could have been to carry away with pleasure on memory's tablets. But knowing that this was only a gilded hour out of their lives, for many a Japanese girl sorrows over and loathes a life she had no choice in entering, even as her fairer sisters would loath it, I turned away unwilling to look at the spectacle any longer. These girls, too, often seem conscious of a foreigner's estimate of them, and they are sensitive enough to feel their degradation and would rather he would turn his eyes away.

Wednesday, April 2, 1862

Made up a party yesterday for an excursion into the country, to consist of Messrs. Blake and Pumpelly,[14] mineralogists and mining engineers sent out to the Japanese Government, Mr. Brower,[15] Mr. Robinson,[16] and myself. Mr. Brower, at whose house we rendezvoused for breakfast this morning, was hindered by business from joining our party. Delay of getting horses and bettos together drew away the forenoon and it was already eleven when we were started. A pack on the saddle of each carried a few necessaries for the road such as toilet articles and blankets for the night, while a broad shouldered coolie was metamorphosed into a sumpter carrying a few packed provisions to eke out the slender larder of country inns. We crossed the Tokaido at Hodoriya [Hodogaya] taking a fine road which leads up the hill to the right of that place and which, on the rolling land above, expands into a broad market road from the interior wide enough for a carriage.

The day was warm, and hazy about the distant mountains, the face of the country brightening daily with the spring growth, wheat, barley, rape, and broad beans, with which the hills were chiefly planted. The golden blossoms of the rape were already spreading their cloth of gold in broad patches over the fields. Our course was west and northwest over rolling lands dotted frequently with copses of planted timber of pine and fir, changing after ten or twelve miles to broad open table lands which stretched apparently to the distant hills many

[14] For Blake and Pumpelly see footnote 12. Pumpelly later wrote about this outing in his *Reminiscences*, vol. 1, pp. 289–301. Pumpelly writes: "Having learned that it would probably be several weeks before we should be sent to Yesso, we determined to see something of the surrounding country, and naturally planned our first excursion so as to include the nearest mountains, the Oyama, on the edge of the treaty limits. Accompanied by Mr. Frank Hall and Mr. Robertson, with our Japanese servants and *bettos* or running footmen, we made an early start from Yokohama."

[15] De Witt Clinton Brower was a friend and neighbor of Hall's who had bought his lot earlier and who was now a member of Allmand & Co. Later Hall mentions Brower's wedding at the legation in Edo on June 9,

1864.

[16] It is curious that Hall writes that they were accompanied by Mr. Robinson, whereas Pumpelly records that it was Mr. Robertson. It seems that this was a mistake on Hall's part. S. Robertson was one of the early residents of Yokohama, who like Hall had purchased one of the lots auctioned in 1860 (lot 8). Hall identifies Robertson as a person with experience in Japan, so we have to presume that he is referring to the same S. Robertson not Robinson. Indeed, the only Robinson I have been able to locate in Yokohama during these years is one J. Robinson who signed the Lincoln condolence book that was presented to the consulate on July 4, 1864.

"Yokohama Musume."
Portrait of a Yokohama
girl by Felice Beato.

miles to the north and west. The winding horse paths over these plains, as well as the thick growth of grass and scrubby brush, reminded us of western scenes of prairie trails. But little farm work was going on in the fields except the stirring of the earth among the drill sown grain and pulse. Three patterns ever recurring in a Japanese landscape of low and brown thatched cottages in the valley hamlets, *miyas* among the green groves of the hills century planted, and temples in the choice picturesque spots whether of hill or valley, were frequently passed.

It was near one of them that, emerging from the thick fir grove which begirt some sacred shrine, we encountered a group of Japanese young ladies clad in holiday attire who had evidently been worshipping at the hidden shrine and now stood under the arching shade clustering about one who appeared a leader to the rest, a girl whose whole look and mien called out a simultaneous word of attention from each of us. She was of stature taller than usual for Japanese females and her dress of rich material, though plain in color, and its many folded thicknesses over her bosom and rich and ample girdle, as well as her conscious air, indicated her superiority to her followers. But the feature most noticeable in her as a Japanese lady was a look of intelligence and refinement which the foreigner rarely, if ever, meets among that class of ladies with whom he is liable to [be] brought in contact. Curiosity prompted me to address some inquiries to the fair group, as I might generally do without fear of giving offence, but the well bred air of this girl repelled [me] from what in this case would seem a discourtesy.

The picture of this group of worshippers by the wayside was the theme of our conversation for a long distance on our road, and what was suggested more particularly to my own mind was the relations given by Xavier and the earlier Romish missionaries of the educated and talented females they had met, stories that by my experience in Japan had seemed extravagantly colored hitherto, but now this picture under the pines and of the fine face at its head breathed a possibility into those saintly tales of old. I had often heard of the females of the wealthy farmers who held their rich lands in hereditary copyhold from ancient kings being noted for their charms, and our heroine of today was doubtless one of these.

Our approach to the silk districts was indicated by the increasing number of mulberry plantations, which, as we approached Tsuruma in the afternoon, had become very numerous. Tsuruma is a cluster of mean houses, poor shops and dirty wayside inns, a halting place for the poorest travellers. Kiso, a little further beyond, is a town of some more pretentions with a numerous population who flocked into the streets to gaze at the unusual spectacle of four passing foreigners. As we advanced into the silk district the villages and hamlets were less numerous, but instead we passed the fine farming buildings of the large proprietors enclosed behind fences of turf, stone, and wood, amid hedgerows and trees, above which the clean tile roofs and white traces of the fire proof store houses were visible indications of

prosperous wealth. We were invited to stop at one of these farms establishments but the day was too far spent to admit of delays. One large establishment with long ranges of fireproof warehouses excelling in extent any similar place we passed was the seat of a large sake factor who bought in all the stocks of small producers, something as Nicholas Longworth[17] does with the lesser vineyard proprietors about Cincinnati. Thus the world over the whiskey trade fattens and thrives.

The country became more broken again, and we ascended a long hill from which the Bay of Yokohama twenty odd miles away is said to be visible in a clearer atmosphere than that through which we vainly looked for the point of our departure. We crossed a large trunk trail leading to Yedo, and soon after the town of Hachinogi [Hachiōji] was visible in a plain before us bordered by low hills. This plain of large extent was dotted with farms, groves, temples, and villages.

It was a little before sunset that we entered the broad single street of Hachinogi compactly built on either side with rows of shops, warehouses, and dwellings, the street itself being about four rods in width. The clatter of our horses hoofs over the half macadamized road brought the inhabitants to the doors as we rode along. It had been a fair day, one of the six monthly such fairs, but buyer and seller had disappeared as night came on. A half a mile trot down this spacious street and we drew up before the open doors of the hostelry of *Yama-Kame*, or "The Mountain Tortoise." Where we were received rather than welcomed. "The Mountain Tortoise" was in repute of being the chief inn of the place, the official "Honjin" (the official halting place of officials and nobles when travelling—every large town on the thoroughfare has its Honjin), but its old look, its worn mats and dilapidated slides, gave it the appearance more of an ancient inn of repute crowded to the rear by

[17] Nicholas Longworth (1782–1863) was one of America's leading horticulturalists, lawyer, millionaire, and patron of the arts. Among the first Americans to succeed in making the growing of grapes a commercial success, he retired from the law and established a reputation as a wine manufacturer. His Catawba and Isabella wines were among the most famous American wines of the nineteenth century. Longworth held extensive vineyards in the Cincinnati area and produced wines both from his own and other regional vineyards. See the *Dictionary of American Biography* (New York: Charles Scribner's Sons, 1933), vol. 11, pp. 393–94.

younger and more pretentious rivals. There [was] no hostelry welcome after the true Japanese hospitality, no obsequious landlord and row of comely servant maids greeted us at the threshold bidding us to dismount, rest, and be at peace. We fell at first into the hands of a half superannuated old domestic and a black toothed female who did not know what to do with themselves or us. Perhaps our formidable cavalcade coming upon them so suddenly had a little dazed them, for we had not come in with the leisurely dignity of Japanese travelling gentlemen, having possibly engaged our inn a day before, or at least by slow approach giving the landlord warning, but we four mounted to-jins at a good sound trot had dashed up to the inn door before the scattered forces and rest of the household could be collected.

The host at length appeared just as we were growing impatient of waiting barely inside the threshold and asked us upstairs in a manner betokening toleration rather than welcome. If our bottle-nosed host was a little glum, he had his reasons; no doubt he liked our ichibus well enough and knew he would get plenty of them for his trouble, but he also knew that travelling about and staying out over night even within treaty bounds was not favored by the Government and who would not perhaps be pleased with any alacrity of welcome or excess of hospitality which should invite more frequent excursions. It was a further token of the estimation in which he held us that instead of giving us the quiet rooms in the rear of the house which are always assigned to honorable guests we were ushered into a front upper room assigned to travellers of a second rank, a room whose dingy walls, torn screens and slides warped by time, or shaken by earthquakes out of joint and place, as well as the brown mats, more indicative of fleas than repose, was by no means especially inviting. But we put a good face on the whole, glad that we got in at all, when we might have expected to have been kept out, stored our baggage about

the room and disposed ourselves around the brazier of coals which the evening chill made welcome.[18]

A dirty scullion from the kitchen brought in our tea, the teapot had on its lid the emblematic tortoise of the house. Groups of curious people gathered in front of the house about the open doorways and intruded themselves into our apartments until we were compelled to invite them out. The landlord came in to take our order for supper out of larder meager enough for foreign tastes, pen, ink, and paper in hand to make note of our bill of fare, that he should be able to report to his superiors exactly what the foreigners ate. We could have rice, eggs, fried potatoes, and salt fish, so these were ordered to be made ready. First came the potatoes cut in slices and baked, a quarter of an hour in advance of the eggs, another quarter of an hour and the boiled rice and fish came, salted *tara*, a species of codfish, poorly cured and whose leathery toughness defied all attempts at mastication so that we were fane to fall back on that Japan *piece de resistance*—eggs boiled to adamantine hardness.

We were filled if not fed. The traveller at a Japanese inn is usually waited upon by some one or more tidy damsels of the house who enlivens his cheer with agreeable manners and conversation, a favor not granted to us. It is their part to pour the oft-drained tiny tea cups, fill or refill the emptied sake saucers, prepare the eggs for eating by taking off the shells, and carving the fish with her skillfully managed chopsticks, so impossible to foreign clumsiness. I asked the landlord where the serving maids were, that I could not think of eating without proper attendance, and laid my chopsticks down. He promised to supply the want, when, after a little delay, in came the former dirty handed Hebe from the cook fires who proffered her assistance so far as we were willing to allow it.

We were favored with abundance of company after our evening meal was finished,

[18] Pumpelly wrote: "Towards evening we reach Hachiogi, and stopped at the best-looking inn, where we were shown to a large room on the second floor. As foreigners generally insisted on wearing their boots on the delicate Japanese mats, it was difficult for them to gain admission to any house where the proprietor had once had his floors disfigured, and when admitted they usually received the poorest rooms" (Pumpelly, *Reminiscences*, vol. 1, p. 291).

chance travellers in the house and villagers, friends of our bottle-nosed host, including two small merchants who occupied the room adjoining to us, one of whom had tarried over his sake potations till his eyes were red and tongue garrulous. Their inquisitiveness at first amusing became at last wearisome and obnoxious.

B[lake] undertook to sketch in his note book, but had no sooner made this display of his talents in that line when his services were at once in requisition to ornament plain fans which the lookers on sent out at once to buy. A folding fan made of pure white paper and polished but unpainted bamboo sticks when inscribed with a gem of poetry, some wise saying of the ancient sages, a picture of a favorite tree or flower, the poetical cherry the most frequent, is the common gift and souvenir between Japanese friends, a token of esteem and an appropriate offering from the lover to his mistress.

While B[lake] was thus diverting the older people, I had succeeded in attracting to my side a group of shy and well dressed little girls who had been timidly watching us from the other side of the room. First the youngest—the youngest are always the most fearless—a dark eyed little miss of nine years came and sat by my side with a child's doubtful look, half fear half pleasure, when a few questions about her age, her going to school, not only wholly reassured, but soon brought four or five more who sat in half circle about me coyly pleased with the novelty of their position as their half repressed smiles and looks at each other indicated. I knew what indelible impressions on childish memories the events of this evening would leave, giving perhaps for the whole of their after lives, and not theirs only, the color to their understanding of the foreigner. So it was that I strove to make an agreeable impression upon them and we were soon on the best of terms.

Their ages were from nine to eleven. Having won their confidence, I amused them for an hour as I best knew how and to their great enjoyment, and then I said to them, "cannot you play some game for me." They caught the spirit of the idea in high glee, one of them running off and returning with a bag of small shells, with which they were soon engaged on the mats in a game something like the Jackstraws of boys at home. In their merry sport they grew quite unconscious that the dingy ceilings and the old screens included the shunned foreigners in the same apartment with them, or how mixed a group the paper astral dimly lighted up. The game went on with that regard for each other and desire to enjoy together which I have noticed so characteristic of the little folks of Nippon, graceful, dignified, and yielding to each other's wishes as so many little misses at home would hardly do.

My frolic with the children attracted the attention of the older people who stood over us looking on with much interest and saying, "Ah, he is fond of children," "he is kind hearted," and similar flattering allusions which showed that the same road lies to the parents heart here as elsewhere. I drew a string of beads from my pocket, and handing it over to one of the women looking on requested her to divide them among the children, and I was again pleased to see that while their eyes sparkled with delight at the sight of the glittering trinkets, they not only awaited in quiet the division, showing no shade of greediness, but were rather pleased that all were to share alike, each assisting the other to string her baubles and making no comparisons. I often ask myself from whence these little heathen gain such commendable ideas of good behavior which the Christian father and mother so often labor in vain to inculcate, or do they act thus only before strangers? Nature is stronger than any made up manners, and not the last reason surely then.

We dismissed our audience by nine o'clock, our neighboring lodger had already gone early to bed, the kitchen maid and our older female brought in our beds for the night, cotton mattresses too short for European proportions for under beds, and the thick quilted pelisses for covering which being made with sleeves the Japanese puts on as he would his day clothes. Our beds were arranged on the mats, our night lamps replenished with oil, freshly drawn tea set down by the brazier and we were left to such repose as we could get. To occupy bedding used in common by haphazard Japanese travellers, suggestive of possible skin diseases and vermin, was not over agreeable. Yet, sleepiness and cold soon wear away an old traveller's scruples, and the heavy quilts which at first lying down are thrown carefully over the extremities creep up with the creeping cold and by morning are found covering the whole body. We came prepared for such emergencies with heavy woolen blankets and first enveloped in these the addition of the Japanese quilt afterwards, if necessary, became tolerable. Our wooden pillows with their little rolls of cotton not thicker than a lady's wrist, could be covered with fresh paper and made clean.

We lay down to our slumbers, some of our number not wholly without misgivings so much had they as new comers heard of former troubles, Japanese treachery, governmental unwillingness that foreigners should sleep away from the settlements, and the positive inhibition laid upon his countrymen to that effect by the British Minister, that they felt not wholly assured of a night of quiet. R. and myself were more familiar and such experiences and thoughts of trouble disturbed our slumbers less than the fleas left behind by our evening companions as souvenirs of their visit.

The streets had become quiet without save the click of the watchman's sticks, the rattle of the policeman's staff of iron rings, or the occasional doleful attempt at song of some belated traveller or late reveler going home. At half hour intervals all night long the policemen prattled before our inn breaking our slumbers with their noisy staves and their sing song utterance, "Take good care of your fires," which one of them in shrill voice sang from house to house.

Thursday, April 3, 1862

We rose up early in the morning and while our breakfast was preparing and our horses feeding for the long day's ride before them we sallied out for a morning stroll. The landlord insisted upon accompanying us, but his benevolent intentions were to some extent thwarted by our dividing in different routes, when his before doubtfully expressive countenance settled down into a look of absolute disgust. It was a delightful spring morning, the streets as yet unobstructed with people, leaving us an uninterrupted view of the town. Hachinogi [Hachioji] lies on the Koshiu Kaido, a fine road from Yedo into the rich district of Koshiu and is made up of a single street a mile and a half in extent, the greater portion of which is well built up with shops, dwellings, and warehouses. At regular intervals down the center of the wide street are public wells where the housemaids were busy drawing water for the day's beginning. This place is a large silk mart for both the raw and manufactured article which is produced in small quantities by hand looms, from house to house, and on fair days, which are regular six times each month, each small producer brings his product to the Hachinogi market for sale. There is no associated manufacture of it as there would be if other than simple handlooms were employed.

The people manifested little curiosity about our visit. No crowds following us in the street or offensive epithets saluting us. The shops were large displaying good stocks very tidily arranged, the division of trades being generally observed. Two shops side by side were devoted exclusively to the sale of pomades for the hair which were displayed in great greasy bowls with wooden spatulas ready for retailing. The rivalry between these two vendors is no doubt as keen as between the original Bearsoil and Macassar vendors beyond the sea. The chief buildings of the place after the temples were the shrines of Venus whose priesthood judging from outward show had better revenues than Buddha's shaven bonzes.

We returned to our inn for breakfast as the morning marketers began to come in and, moving from well to well, opened their baskets of fish and panniers of vegetables, yesterday's fish fresh enough to Hachinogians, but to our tastes, made discriminating by a long residence at the waters edge, not tolerable. We ordered our breakfast perforce a duplicate of last night's supper, substituting a sea weed soup for the unconquerable codfish. While it was preparing, from our upper balcony I noticed the gathering life of the streets, market men, buyers and sellers, horses laden with wood and charcoal, travellers on foot their loins girt for the road, others with broad hats and long staffs and small packs on their backs, all staring at the uncommon spectacle offered by the balcony of "The Mountain Tortoise," gentlemen taking the morning road in their heavy norimons, well-to-do merchants in kangos, girls from the inns and cookhouses drawing water at the wells, children with satchels loitering on their way to the early morning school, shopmen displaying their wares, servants wetting down the dust of the streets or carefully cleaning the highway of sticks, wisps of straw, or the smallest litter. The trim teahouse over the way was hanging out its signs of good cheer and its seductive lanterns while two fat buxom maids who were dusting the opposite balcony on a level with ours telegraphed a good morning with their eyes and followed the impression made by a whole battery of similar glances and little feminine bewitchments of look and motion as much as to say "when you come to Hachinogi again don't forget the inn over the way," and what more would have been said or seen was interrupted by the appearance of the landlady over the way, who chided her girls for tardiness at the balcony work, and by the announcement of breakfast on our side.

Breakfast was soon dispatched, and having distributed some garden seeds, our horses were brought to the door leaving nothing to be done but to discharge our indebtedness to the Tortoise and depart. Thirteen and a half ichibus, or $5, compounded with our host for his civilities and incivilities—quadruple what a Japanese would have paid—but we made no complaint, mentally rating the tortoise a slow fellow, and mounting in the midst of a crowd of spectators, we were prepared to say adieu, first bestowing a handful of copper and iron coin on the heads of the crowd, who, old and young, scrambled lustily to gather it. The household was not drawn up to say "good-bye" and "come again," as good old custom demanded, but instead our solemn bottle-nosed boniface hardly vouchsafed one *saionara*, and certainly never bade us come again as we rode away.

The charm of hills of which Oyama, "The

Great Mountain," is the principal peak were seen half hid in the thick haze towards the south wither we turned our way. The road proved even more excellent than yesterday, and for many miles of this day's ride was wide enough and smooth enough for a carriage track. Three miles out of Hachinogi we ascended by an excellent mountain road to a considerable elevation overlooking the town we had left behind and its circumjacent plain, before us a deep green valley rich with the new crops and uplands swelling in wave-like succession towards the distant mountains. Few mountain roads could be better anywhere, though we passed two gangs of laborers numbering 60 or 70 men who were turnpiking the road preparatory to the wash of the spring and summer rains. A large growth of Japanese cedar overshadowed this road among which were many venerable patriarchs of the forest. Descending into the valley before us we came into the village of Hashimoto pleasantly situated in a valley at the headwaters of the Suruga [Sagami] River[19] one of the principal streams of the empire.

Leaving the valley we came upon broad plains of several miles extent uncultivated and sparsely covered with grass. It was a broad tableland destitute of water and exposed to the summer heats and sweep of the winds and was too unproductive to repay cultivation. We passed through several villages usually situated on the streams which were here very numerous coming out of the hilly range beyond.

Water mills for hulling and grinding rice and other grains were frequently passed. Taking the road through Miso [Mizo], Kami Midsoo [Kami Mizo], we came to Saima [Zama] on the main stream of the Suruga [Sagami] about ten miles from Hashimoto. These villages were all farming towns with their small shops, old houses, temples and miyas looking one very like another. The villagers stood in the open doorways, or at the corners of the houses, staring at the unwonted sight of foreigners, none of whom had ever passed this road before. Now and then one bolder than the rest ven-

[19] Hall refers to the Sagami River as the Suruga. At the time it was usually referred to as the Bannyūgawa. Most treaty-port maps list this as the Sagami River, therefore it is not clear where Hall got his reading, but given the general confusion about place names errors of this type are not unusual for the period.

tured a salutation, but for the most part they were respectfully silent. We made a brief halt at the mill of Kami Midsoo and pushed on to Saima where there was a ferry over the Suruga [Sagami]. The ancient river terraces, full of imported boulders, were distinctively defined as we descended to the present bed of the stream, where we were surprised to see so wide a beach of boulders and river gravel from which during the dry winter months the stream had shrunk to its present swift, but not deep and broad, channel. An island crowned with trees stood in the midst of this river of stone, the present channel being at this time considerably beyond it. The Suruga [Sagami] is evidently a foaming torrent when fed by melting snows or long rains and its entire breadth at such times is between a quarter and half a mile. Picking our way among the loose stones and gravel we came to the stream and a ferry boat which awaited us on its banks. We had anticipated possible difficulty in being allowed to cross this river if not absolute detention, and were ready if necessary to resort to fording and swimming, but no objection was made, and when we passed the swift part of the current we were glad that we had not been compelled to try the ford. The banks of the river were protected from its washing effects by wicker baskets of stones which appeared to answer the purpose effectually. A little beyond the Suruga [Sagami] we came upon the half dry bed of another mountain torrent, the Tsuna-naka [Nakatsu-gawa], which had so shrunken that a temporary bridge had been thrown across. A little further on another stream was crossed by means of a bridge moored by ropes to the shores. All these streams in season of high water must at times wholly cut off any travel.

Having passed through a large village we came upon a pretty temple in a grove of old cedars whose attraction invited us to dismount. The gateway of the temple was comparatively modern and was glaring with a freshly laid coat of red paint. In lodges on either side were the grim guardians of its portals, two hideous, colorful idols of wood. Within were several temple buildings, the principal one of which facing the gateway was a Shinto shrine with its simple emblem of a mirror. Upon its walls were hung a series of pictures remarkable in

their size and some artistic skill, depicting various scenes from the mythical legends of the old heroes and divinities of the land, conspicuous among whom was the dragon tailed princess, whose fair face was in striking contrast to the hideous extremities. The meaning of the allegory is obvious. On the right of the enclosure a more dilapidated structure enshrined a colorful image of Buddha in gilded wood sadly in need of a priestly repairer. Before him stood an antique bronze vase and censor upon which we looked with covetous eyes.

The people of the village clustered about us, pleased with our admiration of their place of worship. To the left of the grounds were spacious dwelling houses where the priests were bestowed in comfortable quarters in which they may lead lives as jolly as any monks of the olden times, with lots of sake in their vaults instead of hogsheads and flagons of wine. Two young acolytes came out whose plump semilong faces bespoke the good cheer within. I have everywhere observed that the priests of all the ordinary temples give the foreigner gracious welcome. They appear not to dream of any defilement of their sacred places by his presence, and it is only when we attempt to enter some renowned holy ground that the least repugnance to our presence is felt. May not this be owing to real prejudices, and not religious scruples—prejudices handed down from Tyco Sama's time which excite fears among the priesthood of good living on temporal, rather than spiritual, grounds, lest innovation shall deprive them of their fat temporalities. If the hate of the foreigner was simply superstitious, would it not be natural to find it chiefly among the lower orders of the priesthood?

It was now past noon and we sought a place to halt and refresh ourselves, but the poor looking teahouses of the small village seemed incapable of supplying our wants, and acting on the suggestions of our bettos we were about to ask accommodations of one of the large farm proprietaries whose inmates, they said, would out of curiosity to see us make us welcome, when just after crossing a mountain stream we came upon a snug little teahouse built where the road crossed a spur of the outlying hills. We were on an unbeaten track where contact with the foreigners had inspired neither dislike nor fear, for it had been the humiliating lesson of our ride that we were best received where the foreigner was least known, and now the master and mistress of the house with all their servants came to the door asking us to "tarry and rest," "to enter and be welcome," giving us such cheerful greetings as the native traveller everywhere receives in Japan. We at once dismounted and, while our bettos led away our horses to their promised provender, we entered the little wayside inn whose cool clean rooms and pleasant atmosphere refreshed our bodies and spirits like a bath.

As in many of the country houses the proprietor was both landlord and merchant, and the place, like others I had seen, was a series of cottages connected by verandahs, in one place interrupted by a rustic bridge over a portion of the narrow garden court. At one end was the store, then the kitchen and house apartments with spare rooms for guests, and connected with them by the little rustic bridge a cottage or summer house of two rooms under the shade of the hill and overhanging trees and in sound of the brook that trickled by the roadside, a picture of seclusion and comfort. We were assigned these rooms and only requested that they were not to be our resting places for the night. The clean firm mats were new, the exposed timbers of the walls and ceiling were unpainted but elaborately smoothed and polished, the ceiling made of narrow strips of stained fir, at one end of the room [was] the chigaidana, or shelves sunken in the wall, and the low platform with its rack for swords. We made ourselves at home and had barely time to divest ourselves of superfluous road gear before one of the tea house maids came in and bowing to the mats said "you are welcome," "may you enjoy your repose," "and be refreshed with food," another bow to the mats and she retired when the mistress of the house came in and gave us like salutations. The girl again reappeared with the tea tray serving the agreeable beverage to us with many complimentary speeches of welcome and inquiries as to our wishes and what would we be pleased to have for our dinner. Expecting only the usual bill of fare we were agreeably surprised to find one could have a clam soup for our dinner,

wondering how this bivalve had got so far into the interior. While our meal was preparing our agreeable waitress served us to confectionery of sugar and rice cake, entertaining us with traveller's chit chat and enquiries as to where we had been and "whether we were on a pilgrimage to the great mountain;" "Ah! that is a noble mountain, will you worship there?" This was hospitality after the true Japanese pattern, particularly pleasing to my companions who were new in the land and were delighted with the hospitality of the inn and the grace and modest demeanor of our maid, experiences no longer obtainable by the foreigner on the shores of Yedo bay.

Our dinner came in cleanlily served in quaint porcelain of true Japanese taste, and handed to us by our landlady and the maid with so much real grace and desire to please that the teahouse of Sandangoora [Sandamura] was one of my own pleasantest experiences. Our rice came in a lackered bowl made to represent the section of a tree trunk. Water was brought in an irregular porcelain dish the shape of a gourd cut in a longitudinal section, a pattern much imitated in the ponds of their pleasure grounds. The sides of the dish represented sections of bamboo the more closely to imitate a garden lake in miniature. Another dish was patterned after a water pail with handle, mortices, and hoops all faithfully copied in porcelain. The morning ride, not more than our pleasant surroundings and well served fare, gave zest to our appetites so that our noon rest was converted into a long halt until the declining sun and yet distant mountains warned us not to linger amid the pleasures of Japanese hospitality. Our bill was five ichibus, or about two dollars, besides which we gave liberal sinjous to the girls of the house which they received with many smiles and thanks.

During our stay the curious country had gathered about the house and often thrust back the sliding paper windows to get a peek at us, and when we closed them again, thrust their fingers through the paper to our kind host's damage. Though I have often seen this done at inns where I have stopped, I have never heard any remonstrances for this marring of windows which seems to be regarded a laudable exercise of curiosity only. When we went out to remount we found all available space about the inn crowded with people who had flocked thither to gaze at the strangers, a crowd wholly respectful and silent as the unprejudiced country folks always are with none but friendly looks. The household came out and stood in front of the inn to bid us adieu and asking us to return again with many repetitions of polite salutation while we on our part had endeavored to leave behind us only agreeable impressions, choosing, as I do always, to put up with any small inconveniences, and what a Japanese traveller would regard slights even, so that I may gain their good will. In this we were all agreed, and I believe in our three days ride of nearly 100 miles on different roads we left no ill impression from any conduct.

We crossed the spur of the hill and came out again upon open plains of large extent planted with wheat and mulberry trees. There was one uninterrupted line of such plantations for four miles in length connected with yet others so that in one body unbroken we saw not less than twelve square miles of mulberry and wheat fields. The ground is marked off in plots 6 mats, or 48 feet, square bordered by a single row of trees. The trunk of the tree is permitted to grow to the height of three or four feet when it is cut off and lateral shoots are thrown off in great abundance from the stumps. These shoots are cut each year to give place to a fresh growth of twigs thereby securing two results: first, an abundant crop of succulent leaves, and second, avoiding too much shade on the ground for the growth of other crops which in all this mulberry district have no room on account of the trees. Why should not this idea be carried out in orcharding at home?

Since noon of the day previous our ride had been through one continuous series of mulberry and wheat and barley fields. In the valleys of the rivers, or where mountain and hill streams could be made to do the work of irrigation in upland terraces, rice was cultivated. On the dry uplands and many broad reaches of tableland there were also rape, broad beans, and peas, and everywhere the indispensable

turnip radish. The intermediate lands, the old river plateaus, were wholly in mulberry and wheat. The change in production from the shores of the bay is not more marked than the appearance of the hamlets and houses. While in the mulberry districts more land was under cultivation the hamlets were sparser and less thrifty in appearance than the hamlets of the rice districts. On the other hand the spacious proprietaries of the large farmers were much in advance of anything seen in the Bay. They were the seats of evident wealth comparing favorably with many residences of that rural metropolis of Yedo. Lines of hedges or walls of stone, wood, or turf, or all combined, enclosed these country houses entered by wide and solid gateways built of enduring wood. Within were gardens, fruit and shade trees, and all the ornamental work of the gardener's hand, the spacious one story mansion flanked by its white storehouses being almost lost amid trees and hedgerows. It was easy to see that the owners of such places were the great factors of the silk crop, the reservoirs into which all the smaller streams were flowing as a reservoir. In two days we had passed many of these extensive farm houses and seen the same striking contrasts of rich and poor which are found in all districts of extra hazardous and valuable crops, whether it be cotton, silk, tobacco, or lumber—contrast less apparent in districts producing crops that have a more even valuation from year to year as the great food staples of life, as one may by example compare the manufacturing and grain districts of England, or the cotton, tobacco, and grain districts of the United States. Others of these opulent Japanese planters held their land patents from ancient Mikados or Emperors in return for services rendered and have large revenues from sublettings. They wear, when abroad, two swords and are sometimes attended by a train of sword bearing servants. They belong to the most independent body in the state, holding lands by an inalienable tenure, possessing revenues and servants and demanding and receiving universal respect. A formidable commonality could at any time be found in this empire by the union of the hereditary farmers and the wealthy merchants of the great trading centers. A fact which the great chiefs and the imperial government show their knowledge of by the respect paid these classes of men. To these men the Mikado alone is a sovereign power.

Here and there along our road were a few hedges often but nothing to indicate its special cultivators. As we neared the mountain, the cultivation of the mulberry gradually disappeared. Here we passed, on our right in a narrow valley between hills, the most imposing farm establishment we had yet seen. Its trained hedgerows, imposing gateway, ample granaries, and beautiful gardens made us long to cross over and ask admittance, but the sun was fast sinking behind the distant mountain ranges where the winter's snow yet lingered. We had been climbing a hill road when our path at its greatest ascent bent suddenly over the lip of a deep winding valley where the sun was pouring a flood of light among the green fields. It was a magnificent landscape, appreciated by native eyes as well as ours, for on the overhanging cliff a platform had been cleared and seats of raised turf made for the leisurely enjoyment of the scene. It was a singular coincidence or adaptation that the very next village we entered in the lowland was called *Hinata*, or "Sunshine," but it deserved its name for after crossing several ridges and spanning many valleys we had entered upon a large plain again where, amid a belt of trees, Hinata came like a burst of sunshine to our enraptured eyes. The mountains were now above us, and we soon entered the winding street of Koyasoo [Koyasu] which begins the ascent. Here we had determined to halt for the night, and riding along its street slowly ascending the pilgrim road to the mount's summit is a broad highway amid houses, we came to *Ebiya* or the "Crayfish House." Its open doors exhibited its ample accommodations and the pleasant apartments in the rear, and we congratulated ourselves on such pleasant quarters as we halted before the gateway to the court within, when the landlady appeared, saying that her husband was absent, and she could not entertain strangers, but we would find a good house a little further on. Not wishing to be intrusive upon the lone female, we reluctantly turned away and rode on to *Kamiya*, another inn yet more attractive than

the last, if possible, where another halt procured another refusal on the score that the house was too busy, but we would find good inns further up the mountain. We had resolved not to force ourselves in anywhere except as a last resort, although it was evident we had received lying answers in both places, but the further up the mountain the better we thought as we rode still on and up the winding mountain road, passing here and there an old temple and many small tea houses and shops, having frequently to ascend flights of steps that became more frequent, longer, and more difficult for our horses as we proceeded.

We had gone this way for a mile, or so, till we had got our horses up as many flights of stone steps as we thought it prudent to take them with any expectation of getting them down again, but yet no further inn, and mistrusting the probability of finding any landlords above more accommodating than those below, we concluded to turn back and become guests voluntary or involuntary of the houses below.

We turned back, but in reaching Kamiya its proprietor had anticipated us by closing the whole house with the outside wooden shutters and completely barring our entrance. Very well, said we to each other, if worse comes to worse we must come back and open them for you, and rode past to the Ebiya. Our hosts of the "Crayfish" had evidently not counted on our return for this house was not closed. Here we dismounted, when the landlady of the house, escorted by some of the hangers on of the establishment, met us at the door and with trembling voice asked us to leave for her husband had gone to Yedo, and someone was very ill in the house (an excuse I had heard falsely made on one occasion last year when seeking a nights lodging at Kanazawa) and evidently showing great perturbation. Being the only one of our party who could converse with them in their own tongue, I became the spokesman for the rest and strove to conciliate the landlady by saying that we were quiet people who wished to give her no trouble, that we had our own servants, had already passed the previous night at a Japanese inn, and it was now growing too late for us to think of going elsewhere. My fear all the time was that the inn keepers might have been forbidden by the government to entertain foreigners, but as no excuse of that kind was urged, I continued my persuasions to overcome her prejudices in which the bettos now joined me. Some of our party were for cutting short the parley and making ourselves at home at once, but I protested against this, confident that with a little patience I should win at last.[20]

The landlady further said she had nothing to offer us for food and did not know how to entertain foreigners in a suitable manner. But, said I, you have nice eggs and potatoes and we have fish with us and will give you no trouble about that. A man now appeared, who if he was not the lady's husband, who had "gone to Yedo," was acting *in loco*, for after a little more persuasion he bade us enter and make ourselves at rest for the night. The private gateway to the best apartments was opened and we were soon most agreeably located in spacious apartments to the rear, such rooms as are assigned to the guests of consideration. The household busied themselves for our accommodation. The front gate and doors were closed to shut out the curious crowd, a brazier of coals was brought in, followed by hot tea and sweet meats, sake, and since we must stay, there was a disposition to make us comfortable. We saw or heard no more of the "sick person." Here, as at every halting place, our names were inquired for, and the number of our Yokohama residences, which were written down by our host for information to any superior who should require the information. We appeared to be the only travellers stopping in the house, for it was yet early for pilgrimages to the mountain and we were quiet and undisturbed in our privacy. The bath fire was lighted, and when the water was heated, we were expected to take it in Japanese style one after another using the same water. Even the first use of a Japanese bath tub for the day is not always inviting, but in this inn which was so neat in all its appointments the bathing room was scrupulously clean and all its furniture likewise from the bright copper wash basins to the well scrubbed and cleaned bathing bench made of strips of fir for convenience of drainage. A Japanese bath tub is not unlike a foreign one in shape, being deeper and not quite admitting the length of a full grown person. In one end of the tub is a small copper charcoal stove in which the fire is lighted, the stove having direct contact with the water, so that fire and water are all in one tub and the bather, once in, may keep up the fire and boil himself to any degree of tenderness. And it is the excess to which this tub bathing is carried that is one cause of the effeminacy and weakness of the indoor classes and the early faded look of the women, though in the latter case, their bad custom of heating themselves over the hibatchi, or brazier, covering the body with heavy quilts is far worse than the hot bath. Another form of bath tub, and the more common one, is the round upright tub which will immerse the low statured Japanese nearly to their shoulders. In both private houses and inns of the better class the bathing room is scrupulously neat and the tubs made of unpainted fir glisten in their well scrubbed purity.

R. availed himself of the bath, and his ablutions received the hospitable aid of one of the maids of the inn, who polished his back and shoulders with wholesome vigor. After him the bettos in turn used the same water, and the infinite series to which bathing by turn in the same water may be extended, and answers the purpose, is an unsolved Japanese problem. After bath came our supper in which our hostess did not belie her promises, for rice and eggs were all that her lean larder afforded, but this eked out with some trotted beef and Tweed Salmon in tins made us a satisfactory meal. Supper over and the table, that is the mats, cleared away, tall brass candlesticks were brought in on which R. placed foreign candles

---

[20] Pumpelly wrote of this experience: "To think of riding back ten or fifteen miles in a rainy night was out of the question, so we determined on returning to the house where we had first been turned away, and obtaining quarters by politeness if possible. . . . Here resolutely dismounting we waited while Mr. Hall, who spoke the language well, besieged the hostess. By persuasive politeness he carried the point, where force would probably have failed and been followed by serious results. Once in we were treated well, not only by the hostess but by the landlord also" (Pumpelly, *Reminiscences*, vol. 1, pp. 294–95).

he had taken the precaution to bring, the Japanese candles being dim and smoky, their large pith wicks requiring frequent snuffing. Our nights quarters were very snug. The room was large, its mats newly fitted for the season's travel, and on its screens were frescoes of the adjacent mountains, and on a pair of ornamental sliding doors which led to the garden in the rear, Mount Fusi and its clouds were represented in outline by an ingenious disposition of the wooden lattice with which the doors were made. The adaptation of such rooms as these, and those where we had halted for dinner, to summer houses at home was remarked by us in common.

Our mattresses for the night were brought in at an early hour and spread upon the floor by the female servants who were solicitous in their quantity and arrangement lest we should not sleep warmly or easily. P[umpelly] and I had the headache after our long jaunt, and with the assistance of the maids, who spread our couches and carefully covered us up, were soon disposed for the night, but in my half sleep I had indistinct visions of a group of Japanese who had come in and squatted upon the mats while being entertained by B[lake] and R. who in broken words of Japanese, that would have puzzled clearer heads than their listener's, were intent upon edifying them. At nine a long continued shock of an earthquake rocked the mountains, and our beds, and as we afterwards found was simultaneous with one at Kanagawa.

Friday, April 4, 1862

We awoke at daylight to hear the falling of the rain upon the tiles and the drops of the eaves and concluding that the mountain spirits had for our intrusion imprisoned us for the day turned over to make a part of it in sleep again. But after an hour or so, in looking out, it was evident the storm was limited and we were only wrapped in a mountain rain which might at any moment give way. The bright copper basins filled with warm water awaited our morning ablutions in a little wash room near our own quarters tastefully fitted up for travellers that they might wash without leaving the matted floors.

One by one the household greeted us with morning salutations and inquiries after our rest and the landlord came in to know our purposes for the day. Without waiting for our order our breakfast, a repetition of the night's supper, was brought in, having been preceded by tea and confectionery. The weather was yet misty and rainy at intervals but by ten the clouds had so far broken away and looked light over the valleys we were to cross on our return that we at once concluded to attempt the ascent of the mountain.

We had no sooner announced our determination, than our landlord and a man in ordinary dress of a policeman who had been hanging about, hurriedly started ahead of us, a movement whose object we well surmised as the sequel showed. The morning was unfavorable for the ascent, the mountains were enveloped in clouds far below the summits which would effectually cut off the fine view we had anticipated over the wide spread lowlands at their base. In fine weather the view hence must be truly magnificent. We had come too far, however, to abandon the attempt, and at once began the ascent of the winding mountain road which is a continuous village as before described. We had made a mile ascent, when, a little in advance, we saw two yakunins awaiting our approach with uncovered heads bowing politely and smiling blandly as if very happy to welcome us and make our acquaintance. Their feet were shod with stout sandals as if for a mountain walk, and on our approach saluted us and joined us without a word of objection to our moving on. At occasioned intervals on the roadside were temples, most of which were in so neglected and decayed a condition that they seemed to have little care, the truth being probably that shrines nearer the summit were those most patronized by the pilgrims who yearly resort hither by thousands and tens of thousands. So far as we advanced the mountain vegetation was unchanged from that of the plains below. Frequent and sparkling mountain streams crossed our path or dashed down the declivities by our side. No rocks, for throughout our journey we had met nothing but river boulders of small size.

A little further on and another bland official joined us, and then another, till by the time we had gained some two miles of ascent we had the attendance of a dozen yakunins and nearly as many policemen with their official staffs, beside an uncounted crowd of common people who joined us where a small teahouse was open at the roadside evidently expecting company.

We were invited by our polite escort to rest and take a cup of tea and friendly smoke, which being a usual mark of Japanese courtesy, though in this instance it might mean more, we did not feel it likely to decline. It was evident that our intention to ascend the mountain, being known or surmised from the night before, preparation had been made to meet us at this spot, and our landlord's advance movement this morning was only to announce our approach. But whether this preparation was to prevent our further ascent, or to escort us, it was impossible from the smooth noncommittal manner to say.

We entered the teahouse and seated ourselves on the mats around a brazier while our new friends disposed themselves in like manner at a brief respectful distance, drew out their pipes, and began to smoke. Then came in tea and trays of sweet cakes and confectionery, the yakunins continuing their smoking, and we talking and laughing over the probable conclusion of this farce of pipes and sweetmeats which was being so gravely enacted.

B[lake] amused himself by sketching the group who laughed heartily as though it were a good joke, but not a word about going up the mountain. We continued sitting thus for some time, when we proposed to break up the assembly by moving on, but as if anticipating our intentions the yakunins consulted a few moments among themselves when a man in plain citizens dress came forward and opened a conversation which was continued at some length by him on one side and myself on the other as to the purposes of our visit, until I declined to hold any further conversations with the yakunins through his intervention but must say what I had to say directly. Whereupon two or three of them came forward. The substance of our conversation was this, they desired to know who we were, why we had come thither, if it was our purpose to ascend the mountains, and if we had a permit to do so from the Governor of Yokohama. To these questions I made answers frankly as to our

persons and purposes, but we had no permit from the Governor since we were within treaty limits and needed no permit. Consultation was then held among themselves, the result of which was that we were in the politest manner informed that we could not go any further without a permit from the Governor, and on my insisting on our rights to go under the treaty they said we were already two *ri* beyond treaty limits. I then took out a map of the country compiled from Japanese authorities to show them that the travelled road was very circuitous, and the only correct way to measure the ten *ri* of the treaty was in a straight line as the bird flew. They fully comprehended this, and it was evident they admitted in their own minds the justice of it, for they said that was a disputed point between the Japanese authorities and our own, and as the former construed it they must be guided, in fact they had special instructions upon this subject after an unsuccessful attempt made last season to ascend this mountain by three foreigners. Finding they were firm though remarkably complaisant, I again told them that I claimed my right to go on, but as circumstances were we need not quarrel. I respected the treaty, and any prejudices they might have as to foreigners visiting sacred places, and I would be content with climbing any of the neighboring peaks which would take us up as far as we had time, or the clouds would permit us to go.

To this they seemed to give a cheerful assent, and we left our cakes and tea for the road again, but soon had our evidence of Japanese duplicity, for we had gone but a few rods higher up when our guides struck off from the well beaten road into an obscure path. I inquired why, and they said this was the path to a high peak on our right as it at first seemed. But the path instead of leading us to that peak led quite away from it and rather down than up the hill. We at once halted and refused to go any further in that direction. They then pointed to the peaks away on the opposite side of the road by which we had come up across the deep gulch and said the two sides of the road were under different officers and we could not go up the peaks this side, but might those on the other. I then told them they knew this before we came to this spot, and asked why had they brought us thither. They were

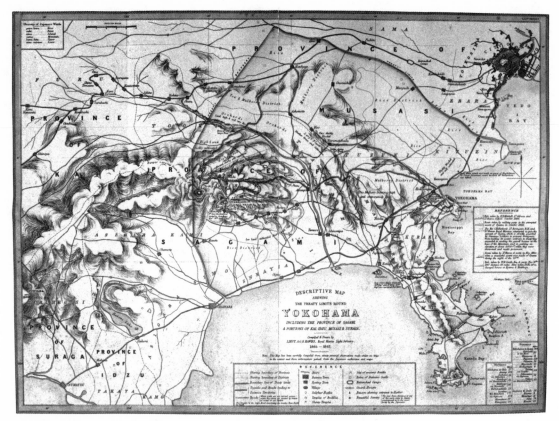

Descriptive map of Yokohama and environs, indicating treaty limits around
Yokohama, 1865–1867.

for once at a loss what to say or do next, but
pointing to the peaks nearby I said we would
go up thither. They assented, and we took another trail which was speedily lost in the rough
ground.

The morning had worn away in delays, the
weather was threatening, and we were anxious
to be back at Yokohama lest a storm and consequent rise of the Suruga [Sagami] and
Tsuna-naka [Nakatsu-gawa] should cut us off
from returning, the cloud limit was not far
above us, and though we felt anxious to thwart
the yakunins' endeavors to choke us off so
cleverly, the victory over them, if attainable,
would be barren of result, and now as we had
got to a place of our own choosing it was
agreed we should make the proposition to return, a proposition accepted with great cheerfulness by our escort who were getting a little

fidgety as to the sequel. Therefore pointing to
the clouds above and the obscured landscape
below I said it was useless to go further and we
were ready to go back. P[umpelly] and I came
down a little in advance and struck into a path
which promised to bring us into the main
more quickly and easily, but had no sooner
made a show of taking this path than our escort interfered saying "that is not the road,
don't go there." The objection in itself seemed
so bald that we determined we would take it
and see what it led to.

We were not long in doubt, for it took us
back into the main road at a bend above where
we had diverged in coming up, a bend that
concealed the final dispositions of our friends
in case we had proved too obstinate at the tea
house conference. At this bend a barricade
had been placed across the road at the side of

a guard house, the barricade being made of a large stick of timber draped with the heavy canvass bearing the armorial bearings of some native chief. If we had not taken this side path coming down, we should have been ignorant alike of guard house or barricade where they had no doubt resolved to make peremptory refusal to our wish to go any further, yet with true Japanese suavity they did not mean we should see their arguments of force. We affected not to notice this, assuming the same indifference they would have shown in our places.

Near the summit of Oyama and approaching its most elevated shrines of the old national religion the road lies through a large torii which has doors that are kept open only during the pilgrimage season of the 5th, 6th, and 7th months, of which time the gates are opened by a priest of high rank who comes from the sacred temples of Miako for that purpose. We had hoped to reach this torii gate, but weather and yakunins alike forbade. Though the females of Japan perform pilgrimages to Oyama they are not admitted to the holiest summit, nor even to this gate, but must halt some ways below.

Our escort attended us on our descent as far as a boundary line in the road marked by stones which they said was their limit, and then, polite and serene to the last moment, bade us good-bye, but certainly did not ask us to come again, that unfailing test of welcome. We passed on our way down a stone image very old and curious from its surroundings of emblems of the reproductive power of life. Our host and hostess when we returned were as affable as ever, and one might have supposed from their interest in our trip they had been eager to promote it instead of spreading information that assisted to thwart us. I again distributed seeds among the people which they were very glad to receive. Our inn bill was fourteen bus, or about $6, which though exorbitant we paid without grumbling. The mountain villagers had assembled to see us off, our landlady bade us a cheerful adieu, and the maids of the inn gave us laughing good-byes, and some even ventured to say "come again" as we turned away from the hospitalities of the "Crayfish."

From the light look of the clouds seaward we anticipated good weather so soon as we left these mist gathering summits behind us, nor were we disappointed, for on the plains below the sun was already shining and yet we had not attained an altitude of fifteen hundred feet.

Our road was through a level country where the mulberry had again disappeared and rice became more common. Our first village was Ishebara [Isehara], a noted halting place for pilgrims bound to the mountains and where [we] saw another fine range of farm buildings whose extent and surroundings denoted the opulence of its owner. The storm clouds still clung to the summits of the mountains, and now our only anxiety was for our horses, two of which already began to show signs of distress. At Tamoora [Tamura] we came again to the river Suruga [Sagami], many miles lower than when we crossed the day before, but still not apparently much wider or deeper, although it had received some affluents. Swift and tortuous as the stream was, boats were gliding over its surface propelled by a fresh wind from the south—literally gliding over, for they did not seem to draw three inches and were steered by a long stern sweep. We now understood how the clams get to the mountains.

The ferry master at Tamoora [Tamura] could not see his way clear to taking foreigners over without an express permission from some village yakunins to whom he wished to open the case. We waited patiently a half hour for this formality and were no nearer the solution than at first, and time was too valuable for more delay, so we astonished the ferry master by taking possession of his poles and boat and proposing to row our own boat. Seeing we were determined he took the responsibility rather than risk chances of his boat and gave us boatmen. We entered the Tokaido one *ri* below Fujisawa where this royal highway was overshadowed on either side by aged firs of centuries' growth, an avenue of shade, till we came to Fujisawa where we halted for dinner between two and three P.M. Objection was at first made to receiving us, but soon recognizing me as an old customer we were kindly received and did ample justice to the freshly boiled carp that were set before us. Leaving

Fujisawa we passed through Tootska [To-tsuka], where every inn was surmounted by the crest of the Prince of Hizen (Nabeshima no kami) one of the most powerful princes of the empire, whose son was returning from Yedo to his province in Kiusiu. The bamboo poles erected in the streets with proclamations of his coming were standing. At Hodoriya [Hodo-gaya] the inns were likewise occupied, and we had only just missed meeting the train on the road. The sun was just setting when we reached Yokohama, having made an excellent day's ride from the mountains.

Saturday, April 12, 1862

In the early pages of my journal I gave account of the merchant Yangaro at Kanagawa and his pretty wife who with their babe and his grandmother constituted a very happy family apparently. But not long since the husband was unfaithful to his marriage vows in the matter of a certain foreigner's mistress, and now she has just run away with an employee of the same foreigner, leaving a good home for no home and poverty.

A change of ministry is reported at Yedo, the late ministry being charged with malversation of office.

Saturday, April 19, 1862

A matsuri, or religious festival, has been in process several days past at the *Benten* temple called *Kaicho*, or "the opening veil." It is a ceremony recurring at stated periods when the sacred images are thrown open more fully to the gaze and admiration of the people, and is held to the great profit of the temple. Crowds of visitors come in daily from all the surrounding country to offer their prayers and make presents of money and rice for the benefit of the temple and its priesthood. The grounds about the temple are occupied with religious emblems, workers of ornament, and spectacles and shows of every description to amuse and allure the visitors. Among the ornamental work are imitations of a Japanese garden, a rustic well, miniature lakes and mountains,

rock work, large and highly decorated lanterns, banners, streamers, and various Japanese devices to which it would be difficult to give name or description. The rustic well is faithfully executed showing its rustic fence of natural wood, the curb of young tree trunks laid up cob-wise, the old bucket resting on a moss covered rock, a shell and gravel walk about it, all in real taste. The rock work, made of tufaceous rock whose particular shapes admirably fit it for the purpose, I have never seen surpassed in naturalness. The rocks are put together as if centuries had passed over them since they were first arranged by some convulsion of nature, a small cave opening is shown, the wear of water is faithfully represented, and the pines on top, the shrubs of althea, minton, the irises, procumbent evergreens and ferns creeping out of every crevice are such exact copies of nature that no trace of man's handiwork is left. I observed with pleasure that this was greatly admired by the native visitors for none but persons possessing some refinement of taste could either execute or admire it.

Besides these the shows of all kinds seemed most attractive. In one place a trained bird picked out numbers from a box in a lottery for cakes and confectionery. Tickets were sold the bystanders and tickets corresponding were placed in a box in a miniature house at the top of a little ladder. At the foot of the ladder was a bird in a cage, which, when its door was opened, hopped up the ladder, thrust its bill into the box, and taking out a number hopped back into its cage. The bird exchanges the ticket with his keeper for a bit of cake, or seed, and the holder of the same number is the winner. At another place is a puppet show where small images of men and women are made to perform many clever things in leaping, dancing, etc. At another place is a performance of dancing girls, at another a tiger is on exhibition, at yet another is the coarse sight of a wrestling match between a girl twelve or fourteen years old and a boy of similar age, both naked except a narrow strip of cloth that barely saves the last outrage in decency. A still more obscene performance was checked because it was thought too indecent to exhibit before foreigners as a specimen of Japanese amusements; and all this for the benefit of a temple! The fair is to be held for thirty days from its commencement.

Friday, April 25, 1862

Arrival of Minister Pruyn, Consuls Fisher and Rice.

Thursday, May 1, 1862

[Start of partnership with Walsh & Co., creating Walsh, Hall & Co.]

Thursday, May 6, 1862

Mr. Harris leaves Yedo.

Thursday, May 8, 1862

Last night Yokohama was again visited by a destructive fire. That portion of the native town which escaped the late conflagration was this time the sufferer and almost wholly consumed. One side of the Ichome street is all that is left of the business town that has not within a short time been consumed. It is estimated that 800 buildings were burned. Valuable merchandise was secured in the fire proof godowns, only two or three of which succumbed. The half of the town burned before was only partially rebuilt when the remainder is laid in waste and Yokohama looks indeed desolate. But with their usual cheerfulness the Japanese take their losses and already this morning ruins are cleared away and temporary structures are going up.

Saturday, May 10, 1862

Letters from home.

Sunday, May 11, 1862

Mr. Harris leaves Japan.[21]

Thursday, May 15, 1862

Great national holiday being Gongen Sama's *Kinichi* ("Soul day") death anniversary. The common people seem to participate little in this anniversary, although the yakunin and samurai class regard it as one of their chiefmost days of observance. The samurai pay visits of respect to the tomb of Gongen Sama thirty six ri from Yedo, where there is a wooden statue life like of this founder of the reigning dynasty, on whose head is said to be preserved the natural hair of this hero whom it represents.

Friday, May 23, 1862

It is reported at Yedo that several of the daimios, among whom are the Princes of Satsuma, Yetzizen, Sendai, Hosokawa, and Arima, have reported to the imperial government that they had severally lost a number of retainers lately, some of them as many as thirty, and they would not hold themselves responsible for any acts they might commit, but gave up all claims of jurisdiction over them to the government. The supposition is that these renegades from service design to lead a life of outlawry like the followers of the late Mito.

---

[21] In his monthly letter to the *New York Tribune* dated May 28, 1862, which was published on June 30, 1862, Hall wrote: "Ex-Minister Harris left on the 12th for the States, via Suez. Consul Dorr has been gone some weeks. Whatever may have been the cause, the implacable feud existing between the American residents and their retiring officials was both unpleasant and detrimental to public interests. The story is too long for your columns, and too uninteresting to your general readers. At home, Mr. Harris is widely known as the negotiator, single-handed, of our present treaty, and for it he will have honor to the end of our common history. Whether his policy with the Japanese of later years has been best calculated for the good of all concerned, we leave to time to determine. Your readers will care little for the details."

Thursday, May 29, 1862

Rain commenced in the night from the N.E. and continued till 9 A.M., when the wind suddenly veered to the southwest and for two hours blew a gale. The French ship *Dordogne* which left this post on the 25th for Shanghai was dismasted off the coast.

Monday, June 2, 1862

Great Japanese holiday (5th of the 5th month) "Nobori" Osekoo [Nobori Osekku], or the "Flag Feast." The origins of this festival, which is a festival for males precisely as that of the 3rd month is for the females, seems a little obscure, though the Japanese common people attribute it to the anniversary of the return from the Corean wars of the wife of an ancient Mikado who conducted a successful campaign after her lord's death. But they talk of so many Corean heroes that one is inclined to believe them all a myth. A favorite article of food today is two kinds of rice flour cakes, or patties, filled with a sweet confection of sugar, bean flour, and other delicacies which are wrapped in the broad leaf of the oak in honor of those old grand war days when the necessities of the times allowed their ancestors no better porcelain. As in the third month many houses make a display of toys for girls arranged on a series of shelves, so in this month there is a similar display of boyish toys but generally partaking of a warlike character. If you are walking the street and look into the open screens of a home of the better class you may chance to see fronting the door a series of narrow shelves, like a lady's flower stand, which is covered with red or figured cloth, and on which, and also on the mats in front, are displayed the toys. There is a horse in the attitude of prancing begirt with rich harnessing and saddlery, there are stands of bows and arrows, swords and spears in rack, flags of quaint device, standards of cock feathers, plumes of horse tails, miniature armor, drums, insignia of royalty, for young Nippon is educated to the belief that warlike prowess may someday make him a chieftain of the first rank even as our democratic boys, "licking their candy and swinging on the gate," may dream of presidencies.

Before many of the houses are two poles erected, one for the husband and one for the wife, and suspended from each is a fixed flag several feet in length, one with the wife's family crest at the top, one with the husband's, and each emblazoned with some painted picture of their own, or the artist's, fancy. Between these poles is suspended a picture of the chief of all the devils who is thus propitiated that he may keep off all the smaller devils of disease and misfortune. But this is particularly a time to use charms against disease, and everywhere along the country roadways and streets men have their heads tied with a green rush, or grass, as a special charm against the headache for a year to come, others bathe today in a hot bath in which a knot of the same herb has been infused to charm away all bodily disease. The children are all clad in their holiday attire and everybody today, if able, has a new dress and is playing in groups about the temples, or the large courts of farm houses, playing "Yoritomo" and "Taiko Sama," and all the heroes and wars of olden days. With the men it was a day of feasting and many a sake reddened face illuminated the streets. At night the tea houses, joroyas, and dance houses were brilliant with lamps and lanterns and noisy with the revel of guests.

Sunday, June 8, 1862

This morning a man was executed at the *Tobe*, or jail, in the Japanese town for theft. His head was to be exposed for seven days to public view and in company with M[aximovitch], the botanist, I rode past the ground. Two upright posts six feet high were driven in the ground on the top of which rested a board, and on this board was the decapitated head of the criminal which had been cut close to its base. Blood had run along the board and stained one of the posts. The face was that of a young man in full health, pale, but not ghostly, and in reply to my inquiries the officer in charge told me that he was twenty-two years old and had been executed for various robberies here and at Kanagawa. It was a repulsive sight of a beautiful sunny day surrounded by all the beauty of nature, for the execution ground is on an eminence amid cultivated fields, overlooking the bay and having a background of young pines. After three days' exposure the head will be removed. A board was posted by the wayside giving an account of the criminal, his crimes, and punishment as a warning to all passers by.

Thursday, June 12, 1862

Mail arrived. I have today learned somewhat of the history of the young man who was executed last Sunday. He was something more than a common thief. He was at one time, not two years ago, an under official, a *staban*, in the Custom House. From the Custom House he went to Kanagawa in an inferior official place, and at Kanagawa became enamored of the pretty daughter of a vegetable seller and sought marriage. The girl disdained his suit, she had a more favored lover. The *staban* then promised to bring the parents a dowry of 200 ichibus for their daughter, a large sum for poor people, and which won their consent, if it did not the daughter's heart. But the maiden was perverse to her parents wishes and slyly held stolen interviews with her lover. A further douceur of 200 ichibus was paid when the house was forbidden the favored lover and the girl was married to the prodigal official. It was a wonder how a man in such a position could secure the means of such liberality, but that was not for them to inquire into.

A few months since, early in the morning, a man was seen lying by the roadside asleep with a large pack by his side. The first passers by were some government officials going to take their morning excursion in archery [and] the use of the sword and spear. In the sleeper's face they recognized the features of the *staban*, and at once examining his pack found, as they suspected, what were evidently stolen goods. They woke the sleeper, who, seeing by whom he was confronted, made no attempt to conceal the facts, acknowledged he was a thief, and was arrested and thrust into jail. While in jail, the torture, or some similar gentle Japanese appliance, wrung from him that he was the author of several daring robberies both at Kanagawa and Yokohama, that he set fire to the Custom House godowns burned more than a year ago for the sake of plunder, and that in

his highway robberies he had twice taken life to effect his purpose. The incentive to all this string of villainies was to obtain money to purchase of her parents the daughter whom he so violently loved and it appears that wedlock had not eradicated the habit. The finale to this tragedy was the scene I saw on the execution ground Sunday morning. By Japanese custom he should have been burned, and why the usual custom was dispensed with I do not know.

Two or three nights since a woman was murdered by another *staban*. She was the wife of a *ninsoku*, a common laborer, for whom he had conceived an unlawful passion and to whom he made clandestine visits, laying the poor woman under obligations with numerous gifts. She, dreading the consequences of exposure if this continued, begged him to forbear and refused to see him at last. His love then turning to jealous hate, he murdered the unfortunate object of his passion. I knew a case last year in its details almost exactly similar.

Monday, June 16, 1862

Left Yokohama at 7 A.M. in company with Mr. Maximovitch, the Russian botanist, for Yedo, whither we had been invited by General Pruyn. We sent our bettos around the bight of the bay to meet us with the horses at Kanagawa, while we crossed in a boat with our luggage and its bearers. At Kanagawa we sent our baggage forward on the shoulders of our coolies and ourselves mounted under a hot June sun. At Kawasaki we were to meet some of our host's family from Yedo, but on riding into the inn yard we found only a yakunin escort who were awaiting us with a letter from the Minister. We halted long enough to breath our horses a moment, take a cup of tea from the ever hospitable hands of our landlady of Kawasaki, and remounted. We had an escort of ten mounted yakunins who bestride little wry Japanese beasts, fuller of life than provender, and, as we found on the road, quite able to keep pace with our own well stalled, well groomed, and conditioned animals. As we rode down to the ferry of the Rokingo Kawa, the Logo of the treaty limits, we passed on its banks two little beggar girls eight or ten years old completely nude asking alms of every passer by.

A ride of two miles beyond the river brought us to the famous inn, or teahouse, of Yamamoto in the village of Omoori,[22] a favorite resting place for passers to and from Yedo. It is not alone the neat cottage inns which are all linked in succession about the edge of the garden and yard which attract the foreign traveller, but the welcoming smiles of the pretty girls who greet one at the entrance. Going to a summer cottage that stood by itself among the trees, we sat down on its clean verandahs which looked out into a garden and orchard of plum trees now full of green fruits, and where an artificial pond lay in irregular outline under the shade of the trees. Rock work, artificial mounds, blossoming trees and shrubs, and garden plants adorned the edge of this rural lake. A wooden bridge spanned its waters, the shiny backs of the golden carp gleamed under its surface, and a pair of mandarin ducks were sunning their marvelous plumage as they swam upon its quiet pool.

We left Omoori and were soon in the Sinagawa suburbs of Yedo, but its spacious inns were quiet; last night's travellers were all now on the road and the inns were taking the midday rest. Our attention was attracted by a group of four Kaga women, who with their peculiar broad hats and guitar in hand, were singing for alms from house to house. The unusual beauty of two of these girls was striking, taller and more slender than most of their Japanese sisters, their faces were also longer and slimmer, and in their movements they showed an uncommon grace and ease, while on their expressive faces was a half sad expression, as if they felt how unjust their fate, to be condemned, with all their charms, to the life of strolling beggars.

We left the Tokaido at Sinagawa in order to pass by the hill of Goten Yama on which the new buildings for the various foreign legations are being erected. The hill overlooks the bay of Yedo and its face has been scraped and a dry ditch dug around it to make easy protection to the foreign embassies. The buildings of the English Legation are already well under way. From Goten Yama we rode by pleasant hedge-shaded lanes into the city and at noon dismounted at the American Legation.

We heard subsequently that the Governor of Yokohama had been very much exercised over our departure for Yedo and had sent a communication to the American Consul at Yokohama that one Hall, an American merchant, had reached Kawasaki on the Yedo road, where he was detained and could go no further. He moreover requested that the Consul should order him back, that he could not stay there overnight, and if the Consul did not send for him, he should be compelled to. It was a strange peak of the Governor, and rather unaccountable, for there was not a moment's detention at Kawasaki or hindrance of any sort, and so far as Kawasaki was concerned, I had a full right to be there. While sitting at dinner that evening at General Pruyn's table a communication was received from the Consul laying the case before him that he might protect me, but I was already enjoying myself under the shadow of his care, unconscious of the Governor's wrath at the insolence of a "merchant" going to Yedo.

We were hospitably received by Mr. Pruyn, who at the time of our arrival was engaged in an interview with the Governors of Foreign Affairs. The American Legation is quartered in the Koori, or priests', house adjoining the temple of Zempookugi, and is situated at the foot of a low abrupt hill which rises from the rear. The house is spacious, but like most such houses, dark and in rainy weather, I should judge, very gloomy. The house and the temple to which it belongs have a front with a common court which is taken up, in great part, by the houses of the guards who are stationed there for the protection of the Legation. In the rear of the house is a miniature lake surrounded with artificial rock work, flowering shrubs of plants, and well stocked with the

[22] The inn that Hall is referring to here as the Yamamoto, appears to have been the same inn that Robert Fortune referred to as the "Mae-Yashiki," *Yedo and Peking* (London: John Murray, 1863), p. 67. A photograph of the garden of this inn, including the bridge that Hall describes, can be found in Yokohama Kaikō Shiryō Kan, eds., *F. Beato bakumatsu nihon shashin shū*, (Yokohama: Yokohama Kaikō Shiryō Kan, 1987), p. 58.

golden carp. The rear verandahs of the house abut the border of this lake and formed a most pleasant sitting room during our stay in the warm summer days. The hill is clothed with a variety of evergreen and deciduous trees which cast their afternoon shadows into the pool below. The carp in the pond are fine specimens, some of them were two feet in length, nor must I forget the noble Salisburia, or Ginko tree, in the front of the house which has a girth of 27 feet. The entire legation grounds are surrounded by a high, close, post and board fence, and still outside of this are double rows of bamboo palisades at short intervals apart. Within these palisades, and for the entire circuit of the grounds from one to three rods apart, are the guard houses of the 300 yakunins who watch over the safety of the inmates below. It does not strike one as altogether pleasant that he is surrounded by these half civilized swordsmen and musketeers. It seems at best but a genteel confinement within your own house, for none of the Minister's household can stir a foot from his gate without being surrounded by half a score, or more, of these supposed to be necessary attendants. But I was particularly struck with it when one afternoon of my stay young Mr. P[ruyn] asked me to take a walk with him through the grounds up the hill overlooking the house, and even then, although guards without number were within easy pistol shot, we could not walk through the brief circuit of the woods without a dozen men following close upon our heels. I would rather stay within doors than to walk at such inconvenience. An American's royalty is not to be hedged in. How we rode out will appear subsequently. The English and French legations, in addition to the native guard, have their own armed patrol, and the former rides out with an attending troop of British Lancers.

After lunch the Minister accompanied us on a ride to the citadel on which occasion we had a mounted escort of twenty yakunins and foot escort of as many bettos running before our horses. We rode into the Princely quarter of the city where the spacious yashikis of the great chiefs flank the broad avenues that cross at right angles, a city well kept and clean, free from noise and filth, with green groves rising above the roofs in every direction till we might doubt if we were in the city at all. So past the spacious barracks and dormitories where the retainers of Aidzu and Mino and Yamato were gazing from grated windows at the passers by, by many a gate with its embossed and copper studded timbers surmounted with royal crests, the old feudal days come again, till our long train swept into the smooth road that skirts the broad moat of the Imperial citadel. The mingled beauty and grandeur of this abode of kings impressed me more strongly than ever. On the left of our road were the stately houses of the Kisiu family, to whom the reigning emperor belongs, on the rising ground where it bends to the right are the castle walls of the late Regent Ee Kamon-no-kami [Ii Naosuke], and here we are treading on the very ground where two years ago he was slain at midday in the streets. On our right the glassy breadth of the moat, seventy yards across where the ducks are hiding among the broad lotus leaves that bridge the water with their flexible piers of green over to the green sloping bank beyond, that, sharp and distinct, rises forty feet to the foot of the citadel walls. There is a smell of new mown hay from where the men are cutting the grass from the moat's banks, keeping them trim and smooth like a cloth of green velvet. The massive walls of the citadel would forever frown above, but the trim hedges within that overlap them, the rare old pines and firs that stretch their pacific arms over them, forbid any grim looks and you think of it as a palace built for beauty not for strength, till this massive double gateway of stone with its ponderous double leaved doors looks another intent. And now here we are on the top of the citadel hill which commands a fine panoramic view of the great city spread everywhere about us. We followed the winding moat which descends from high to low ground by a series of locks, passing other solid gateways and portions of the wall where it rose a mass of solid stone 30 feet from the water's edge. In one place an aged fir planted on the battlements had hung its aged arms down as if to lift up to itself the sparkling freshness of the water below. A large enclosure on our left again, where the click of the workman's hammer was ringing and new roofs were peering over the fences, was pointed out as the foundation of

Edo Castle in the early 1860s. Photograph by Felice Beato.

an Imperial College where the government proposes to have in training more than a thousand youths, chiefly in the study of the modern languages.[23] Turning into one of the gateways and passing through we were within the outer wall of the citadel, a privileged spot except in company of a foreign Minister. It was further than I had penetrated on my previous visit, and I was surprised to find myself riding along another moat of breadth equal to the outer and like it skirting another enclosing wall, while yet within was another wall as I was told.

This part within the citadel was the counterpart of that without. The same wide clean streets with the yashikis of the daimios flanking them on either hand. From the inner position we had a near view of the upper portions of the imperial buildings, and our host pointed out to us the large roof which covers the "Hall of a Thousand Mats." Square turrets of wood

marked the outline of the Imperial Residence, the building itself being hidden by the intervening walls and shrubbery. We were in the shadow of royalty within the most remarkable citadel of the world and longed to open the penetralia within our reach as it were.

We rode in this manner around a part of the inner citadel and emerged again into the more thronged streets of the city. On our way back to the Legation we stopped to visit Atago Yama, from the top of which is the finest view to be had of the city. There it lay, spread before us in the afternoon mist, streets and palaces, gardens and groves, the winding shores of the bay dotted with boats, the city's sea of roofs broken here and there by the loftier roof of a temple, till its boundaries were indistinguishable from the plains beyond. I had a clearer perception than ever of the formation of the ground on which Yedo stands. It is like

[23] This was the former Bansho Shirabesho (Institute for the Investigation of Barbarian Books), which served as Japan's first central institution for the translation, study, and teaching of Western languages and scientific and technical subjects. In 1862 the Bansho Shirabesho was renamed the Yosho Shirabesho (Institute for the Study of Western Books) and moved to new quarters, as Hall notes here. With time this institution became Tokyo University.

that at Kanagawa, a broken series of irregular low hills with intervals between of small and large extent, and covering such a ground is the city built. The hills are still covered with woods, streams still run though the valleys, while a wide margin of turf, copses, and hedgerows still divide the houses and streets asunder, so that the city viewed from an eminence appears an aggregation of villages thicker than in the country, or, if you ride through its streets, it is still the same only there is the citadel, a mound which seems to cluster as a common center, and there are the fine houses of the Princes which are not to be seen in the country.

I was particularly struck with this on a subsequent day when we had been riding in from the suburbs through a long lane shaded by hedges on either side, the boundaries of cultivated fields, no sights or sounds to denote the proximity to a city, when at a pull on our bridle reins, a few seconds' turn in the road, and, like a vision, road and hedges and fields had vanished, and we were in the city streets again. It was like a magical transformation. It is this unseen condition of the city that renders it so difficult to form any estimate of the population, but I cannot place it any higher than on my previous visit.

Tuesday, June 17, 1862

The overcast sky is favorable to the long ride we propose to take today. We have laid out a long jaunt and are to make a field day of it, as General Pruyn observes, whose military experience suggests the comparison so appropriate. We have an earlier breakfast, and between eight and nine we are mounted for the ride. Our wake, as we sweep out into the streets of the city, is noticeable. First go darting down the road our 20 bettos clad in blue upper garments, naked limbs, and white stockinged feet.

My own betto, who is a veteran in the service and looks upon the rest as pupils in the art, clings, despite the warm weather, to his full suit of dark blue cotton shifts with its fantastic crest of the field of our national banner with which I have permitted him to adorn himself.[24] Away he goes springing down the road with light step laughing and talking and shouting to all strangers to clear the way, then follow two, or sometimes four, mounted yakunins, behind them ride our party of five including the Minister, who again accompanies us, and twenty-four more mounted yakunins bring up the rear, so we are quite a troop of horsemen and everybody comes to the windows to see us as we clatter though the streets of the city. We were a sight to be seen, at least so thought the young yakunin who headed our troop and who persisted at one place in taking what the bettos all said was the wrong road. However he had his way, and we soon found wherefore when we passed a sunny little cottage where an old lady and her two daughters stood in their gateway and exchanged salutations with the young yakunin as we trotted by; it was a pardonable vanity that he wished to display his troop as many a field officer on muster day has done before, and I even think he must have sent word in advance that we were coming, or how should the matron and her comely daughters have happened to be in their gateway just exactly at the right moment? We did not begrudge the quarter of a mile extra road it cost 30 more persons, or, if we had, we should have soon lost our jealousy in the sight before us.

We are approaching again the citadel walls which run along a wedge of land parallel with the street up which we are riding. Between the street and the massive walls a wide space has been left free from houses, there is a broad reach of green turf, then the ditch, then another long slope of turf up to the foot of the walls. Bordering the street on the other side are the long ranges of neat substantial build-

---

[24] Hall's *betto* was named Hikozō and the portrait we get of him here is typical of the woodblock prints of grooms we have for this period. See for example the portrait of Eugene Van Reed and his groom produced by Hashimoto Gyokuransai Sadahide about 1861, which is reproduced by Albert Altman in his article "Eugene Van Reed: A Reading Man in Japan, 1859–1872," *Historical Review of Berks County* 30, no. 1 (Winter 1964–1965), p. 9. Hall's *betto* is listed in Fujimoto Jitsuya, *Kaikō to kiito bōeki* (Tokyo: Tōkō shoin, 1939), vol. 2, p. 286.

ings occupied by the followers of a prince. We ride up the road till we are opposite the imposing gateway, we turn, gallop across the bridge of the moat, past the bowing sentinels at the gate and pass through their open doors. This is the famous gateway of (   ) [blank in original] and is with its approaches one of the most interesting sights of the city. We ride within and on every side of us are solid walls, but a sharp turn to the right leads through a secured gate like the first and not more than fifty feet from it. Within were walls of stone and embankments of earth guarding the approaches to the gate in such a way that in the hands of a skillful party its defence could be made formidable. A little further on we come to a stream flowing through the citadel whose banks for some rods on either side have been left in green ground and shade, a curious sight within a citadel's walls. Crossing this stream was the aqueduct which supplies all the imperial grounds with water and is brought several miles from the country.

We ride across the city till we come to the Somee [Sōmei] suburbs noted for their extensive gardens and nurseries and we find these indeed of great extent, for they bordered the road on both sides for at least a mile on one street and half a mile on the other. A very considerable portion of the northernmost suburbs, as we found by this and other excursions, is devoted to growing trees and plants for sale. We dismount and visit several of these gardens. They are quite unlike the Chinese gardens such as the Fati or Pontinqua gardens at Canton, there is an absence of that grotesque gardening which delights in all sorts of fantastic shapes. The Japanese gardener, though he is fond of training his tree to look like a boat or an elephant, is more fond of imitating objects of more grace and more in harmony with plant life. In the gardens of Somee we see very little of the fantastic gardening but a great deal of skillful cultivation and a variety and vigor of growth very interesting. No inconsiderable portion of the trees and plants are of foreign

birth, though the love and proper pride of the Japanese gardener, and worthy of imitation in all lands, appears to be to make the most of the best of what is native to the country, so that by far the most interesting portion of all these gardens were the native growths.

Hybridization and the production of varieties or sports is the Japanese gardener's delight. There is nothing from an oak to a blade of grass that he does not manage to grow, striped, blotched, or mottled in the most curious manner. I saw even the common thistle growing in the largest of the gardens we visited. The general cultivation of these trees and plants in all these gardens was in the same manner as in our nurseries at home, the young trees growing in thick set rows, the choicer ones in pots. All the varieties of the gardener's work was going on, forcing, training, grafting, budding, as we should see it at home. The Japanese have no greenhouses of glass, and even their winter conservatories consist of a straw thatched shed open to the sun, and their heating apparatus is the manure pit or bed of wetted rice straw.[25]

From the gardens we went to the summer houses of Ogee [Oji] and once more reined up before the doors where I had been so hospitably welcomed a year and a half ago. But Ogee was changed. There was no cordiality in the forced words of welcome that the girls gave us at the threshold; none of the ready attention made doubly pleasing by the smiles and grace with which bestowed, that was our former experience. An officer had ridden in advance to announce our coming, and when we came all was as cold, formal, and undemonstrative as he could wish, and as he had doubtless arranged it should be. Nay it has now become almost, if not quite, impossible any more to see the old hospitality of the Japanese inns within the sphere of foreign visitations; if one does not meet right down churlishness he may well be content. Ogee itself was the same, its swift flowing stream, the charming summer retreats upon its banks, the thick copse beyond, but

[25] The gardens of Sōmei are also discussed in Robert Fortune, *Yedo and Peking*, p. 109ff. Fortune wrote: "Park-like scenery, trees and gardens, neatly-clipped hedges, surrounded each other . . . we had arrived at the village of Su-mae-yah. The whole country is covered with nursery gardens. . . . I have never seen, in any part of the world, such a large number of plants cultivated for sale."

prejudice and official interference had blotched out forever all the spirit of the scene. The foreigners themselves were to blame for this, I was told, their own rude behavior having construed a cautious civility on the part of the Japanese, and I well believe this out of my own observation.

We were seated once more in the little octagonal Kiosque by the stream and tea was served by the gracious landlord himself instead of the comely, tidy serving girls whose office it was to wait upon us. I told the landlord he was too old a man to be waiting upon his guest and he should send his waitresses, he bowed and smiled, and only replied it is forbidden. When our dinner was brought I again urged the necessity of more and better serving, but he only bowed the lower, and mouthed the blander saying, "it was impossible." I remembered our pleasant picnic at Ogee with the officers of the *Hartford* and how our meal was enlivened by the gay damsels whose smiles and light humor were more than half the feast as after Japanese fashion they strove to divert the guests, and so I was not sorry to pay even our extravagant bill of seven dollars and bid a long adieu to Ogee.

While our horses were yet resting we took a walk to the "fox temple," a few minutes walk from the tea garden, but found little to repay us for the visit. It is called the "fox temple" because a shrine is built over a fox hole, with a hole left for ingress and egress of the sacred animal about three feet from the ground, and where, from the traces of repeated footsteps, it really appeared as if it was often entered by some animal, not a cunning fox, I am sure, but some marauding puss or amatory tom in nocturnal rambles for plunder or pleasure.

We proposed to visit the famous Quanon temple [Asakusa Kannon] on our way homeward, but instead of going directly thither we took an detour by a pleasant country path through the rice fields and vegetable gardens, and so, skirting the city, we avoided for the most part of the way its annoying crowds. Not that Yedo people were specially troublesome, on the contrary, I had occasion everywhere to remark the extreme civility of the people— there was a change for the better since my previous visit—and I rarely heard even the common epithet *baka* during my stay. Quanon's crowd of devotees were as great as ever, and our yakunin guard were compelled to make a way for us through the throng of pilgrims. The busy traffickers who kept the little stalls that extend from the gateway to the temple steps, a hundred yards, were reaping a hoard of tempos by the sale of souvenirs of a visit to Quanon.

The span of sacred white horses were coming down the steps of the temple as we prepared to go up. These horses are pure white and are daily led up the temple steps as an act of worship before the shrine. Their stalls are close at hand where they live in pampered ease with their glittering harness on, not a whit more lazy, sleek, or useless, than the shaven headed, white robed, monks they so much resembled.

We passed into the temple and among its large crowds of worshipers, not one annoying word or look did we get for our intrusion, nor was there any lull in the shower of iron money that poured over our heads into the treasure box before the altar. We passed out again at a side door and, as in some other lands, it was only a step from the church to the theatre. We entered the latter just as the sumpter was raising up the curtain for a new act. The call bell in Japan is two bits of wood struck together, and this curtain was raised by being lowered out of sight. The performance was after the Ravel style, a series of acrobatic performances hinged on the thin thread of a play. Towards the close of the act a trap door opened in the roof almost immediately over our heads and a man clothed in a long flowing robe with a face made to the last degree hideous was lowered down, suspended over the audience by a hook on the back of his dress. He represented the evil one, and as he swayed back and forwards over the audience grinning hideously as if in pursuit of his victim, I thought from his proximity he might seize and carry off our worthy diplomatic representative, but sinking down, he clutched with his hands a well dressed civilian who was sitting in the next division of seats enjoying the play with his grown up daughter and three or four young children. Clutching him firmly by the back of his [kimono?] he lifted him out of his seat and they were both drawn together up to the ceiling, the victim kicking and flaying and crying out like a lost one. From the unsurprised look of the young lady and the children it was evident they were in the play and had doubtless been seated near us as distinguished guests so quietly that we had looked upon them only as a part of the audience. The curtain closed this act when the manager came forward to the footlights and politely announced that the play was interrupted for the day because the principal performer had the "belly ache," using exactly the words as I give them. I think the audience behaved better under this announcement than a home audience would have done, for they not only did not call upon the manager to refund but retired with quiet sympathetic looks of commiseration for the colic stricken star, saying one to the other "he's got the belly ache, what a pity," and nearly every man I passed nudged me with his elbow and placing his hands over his abdomen said "the play's over, he's got the belly ache." In fact so much was said of this unfortunate occurrence that I began myself to feel premonitions of unripe apples and cucumbers and hurried out, but the doorkeeper, who was the last, pulled me by the coat and said "he's got the belly ache."

This theatrical incident was only surpassed by one I saw in a public performance at Yokohama where in a line with the stage and facing the audience was a cloacine apartment and during the performance two young ladies, altogether the best dressed and most genteel in appearance of all in the audience, entered one by one, each holding the door fast while the other was inside! Nay more, a little boy who had escaped to the front from the care of his mother on being told to come back over and over during the play responded "wait a little mother, I *chozuba stai*" ["I want to use the toilet"].

From the theatre we adjourned to the beautiful and spacious tea gardens which adjoin the temple and would be attractive spots in any land but more so to the weary pilgrims to Asakusa Quanon. These gardens were old and

had many rare and fine specimens of native and exotic trees. Winding walks led to hidden retreats among the shrubbery and parterres of flowers gleamed amidst the foliage. The city with all its noise, and bustle, and heat, was shut out by the leafy barriers that interposed the instinctive forest born stillness.

On our homeward way we passed several ponds, or shallow muddy pools, where gold fish were breeding. In another street the ravages of a recent fire were being effaced by new buildings already nearly complete. The mark of a fire in all old and well established villages is rapidly and thoroughly removed and perhaps nothing can better evidence the parvenu condition of our Yokohama than the contrast in this respect between it and the poor fishing town of Kawasaki on the Yedo road.

Wednesday, June 18, 1862

This was the day that had been agreed upon the Japanese officials for the Minister's visit to the Royal Cemetery[26] and, although the weather was unpromising we concluded not to balk the preparations made for his reception. A larger escort than usual attended us. We were met at the south entrance of the cemetery, which is enclosed by a high bank of fences, by an old gentleman and two younger ones who had been specially detailed for the occasion. We all remarked the frank, open, intelligent countenances of these men. We were received with a grave though pleasant courtesy, and our own guard, which had come with us, were largely reinforced by a number of well clad swordsmen who came a foot. This guard was a token of respect for the place and their visitor, and not a necessary precaution. It is only till quite recently that any foreigners have been admitted within these grounds. We were indeed the second party who had been allowed to visit them. As we passed through the gateway we came into a broad graveled avenue across which, and opposite the entrance, was a small Shinto shrine built on the margin of an

[26] The site referred to here is what later became Shiba Park and which at the time of Hall's visit was the site of the Zōjōji Temple, the Edo headquarters of the Jōdō sect. At the time of Hall's visit the temple, which

was destroyed by fire in 1877, still stood as one of Edo's major temple structures, and its grounds housed the mortuary chapels of several of the Tokugawa shoguns.

extensive lotus pond which was nearly enclosed by the cypress wood that bordered its waters. It was not a little remarkable that the first tokens of worship we saw in this ground were a dozen of the symbols so common in ancient Egyptian temples and the household shrines of the Japanese inns.

We took the broad avenue to the right of the entrance, which on one side was bordered by the monasteries of the numerous priests attached to these grounds who if they were eremites must needs be very jolly ones in their tree enhanced cottages. On the other side of the avenue [was] a narrow moat separated from an elevated ground crowded with a close forest of native trees both evergreen and deciduous. Notices were put up at intervals cautioning visitors not to throw any refuse into the moat, for these grounds are freely open to the common people. As we proceeded, the avenue led away from the edge of the grounds deeper into the interior and was intersected by other avenues, all broad, well graveled, and cleanlily kept. Wherever we went was the same tidiness. The make of the ground is not unlike that of Mount Auburn near Boston, but surpassing even that in the grandness of its forest scenery and the well kept condition of its graveled, hedge bordered avenues. In some places the pines had been trained to lean over the road and had so far lost their perpendicularity and center of gravity as to need the support of large uprights. In one place a simple pine tree had been trained into the shape of a Japanese boat, there was the hull and deck, stern and bow, accurately made by the horizontally trained branches, then the main stem was allowed to ascend branchless a few feet higher and was again spread out to form an awning. Nature is kind to her trees, assisting in Japan to enable them to bear such artificial lines and yet flourish so hearty and strong as does this distorted pine. Give a Japanese man his time and, with a pine or fir tree, a few yards of twine and sticks of bamboo, and his care and patience will work out of the evergreen every shape from a boat to a water fall. He shuns the unenviable animal monsters beloved of the Chinese, though he does not neglect his own sacred tortoise and stork.

Thus we came to the broadest avenue of all those which intersected our path and which

led to the funeral temples of the monarchs of the Empire. Turning into this avenue we saw before us the imposing gateway of the temple and beyond it across a front court the temple itself. Both the gateway and the temple were startling with vermilion though their architecture was only remarkable in the massiveness of its tiled and gilded roof and heavy eave cornices. As we approached the gateway the officials in attendance desired that we should take off our hats on passing through, a request that we were quite ready to comply with, as they did themselves, and as we would do in our own sacred enclosures. Again, as we approached the temple itself the guard drew themselves up in a line on either side for us to pass through, and said we could pass up its steps if we would take our boots off. This we were about declining to do, saying we would stand on the walk below, when word was again passed to us to please pass up the steps boots and all. We did so and looked through the latticed doorways into the interior. Everything within was plain, much more so than many temples I had visited of less note. But there was a good effect in the simple grandeur of the place, there were no detractions from the severe simplicity of the whole by any ornamental works in the grounds. In the entire court, paved with loose stone, where not a weed or a wisp of straw marred its purity, the only buildings were the temple, its gate, and the bell house on one side. This bell is, with one exception possibly, the largest in the empire. It hangs in a bell house also of red painted timbers and its mouth is scarcely six feet from the ground. The bell itself is nine or ten feet high and at its mouth diameter six feet. The thickness of the metal at the flange of the mouth is six inches, but its weight nobody knew. It was rung by a stick of timber suspended without of seven or eight inches in diameter and this swung against its sides. Its deep toned vibrations are heard all over the city. It is only struck at certain hours of the day, and as the hour of our visit was not one of them we could not hear it. The noise works to keep the storks from nesting on the gables of the temple. Recalled the Psalms to exclamation.

In the rear of this temple, or mortuary chapel, are the tombs of the deceased monarchs, but these we were not permitted to see.

We went out of the temple and back into the avenue by which we had entered and following yet further on we passed a gateway leading to the rear of the temple and to the tombs. We could see the black and gilded roofs of these over the intervening walls and that was all the glimpse we had of the mausoleums of royalty, enough to know that they were well cared for in the last offices that man bestows upon man.

We now passed through some striking park scenery, road openings, leafy avenues under the giant cedars, one of which was closed by a canvass with the Tycoon's arms emblazoned thereon, and as there were marks of wheels up that road, we fancied her imperial highness, the young empress, may have this morning taken an airing among the shades of heroes and the cypresses that covered them. We passed out of the cemetery at a gate opposite the one we had entered and were informed our horses were waiting. On our return we rode around the cemetery and estimated its circumference at 3 1/2 English miles! Landscape and garden cemeteries are no modern innovation, it was clear, and with that conclusion we turned our horses heads away from this mausoleum of monarchs.

Thursday, June 19, 1862

Our leisure hours at the legation, before our daily rides and after, were largely occupied with chaffering with the native merchants over the tempting wares they brought thither for sale. There was the lacker-ware merchant, the porcelain seller, the dealer in silks and satins and brocades, the book merchant, the bronze seller, whose wares would have tempted us to a large purchase had not their immoderate prices especially for antiquities been a check. The prices asked for a venerable bit of bronze, an old ivory carving, or rare specimen of lacker were fabulous, yet they seem to have prize hunters enough among themselves to warrant the prices they ask. This article, the cunning dealer assures you as he holds it admiringly in his hands, was once the property of a deceased daimio and by some rare good fortune it has come into his possession and he offers it to you ridiculously cheap. It is enough

to say of any article that it is old, to indicate a highwayman's demand upon your purse. Every morning the merchants came and after breakfast took possession of the dining room and converted [it] into a salesroom of antiques.

This was the last day of our stay in Yedo and we took only a short ride in the afternoon. We visited the temple of (   ) [Korinji] where Heusken was buried. The temple grounds are in the border of the city on the banks of a stream which flows through green and cultivated banks. Its location is picturesque, but itself looked neglected and desolate as we rode up to the gate. Its hedges were broken down or supplied with rushes, the trees that peered above were straggling and untrimmed, nor did its interior look any more cheerful. Wild growing shrubbery, thick weeds, and grasses obstructed the walks, the graves were neglected, not neatly and cleanly kept as usual, and what would be rare in any burial grounds before a single grave was there neither flowers, evergreen branches, or burning incense sticks. We walked among the rank graves till we came to an enclosure of hedge where a fresh looking stone marked the spot where the murdered Heusken sleeps, the slab says "Died in Yedo." The neighboring grave is that of the English linguist "murdered by Japanese assassins" as it recites. The difference of their inscriptions was noticed by the Japanese who felt somewhat aggrieved by the plain truth of the one. A hedge surrounds Heusken's grave, but it, too, showed the general look of neglect, it was uncut and dead grass and leaves strewed the ground, in truth both places look as sad a spot as one might fear at last to lie down in and my heart echoed the remark of one who looked on, "better the grave of the sea." The present Secretary of the Legation told me that this cemetery had been for the most part deserted since these two burials in it, but it looked rather to me as if the Japanese had purposely selected a cemetery out of favor, or neglected, although when vegetation is rank, as in Japan, I know it does not need many months even to cover with the look of neglect any burial place. Mr. Pruyn said he would at once send his gardener to restore this place and put it in order.

We left the city streets and by shady lanes rode out into the open country which was everywhere teeming with abundant crops. The barley and wheat harvest was already nearly complete. We stopped at the temple of "Mengoori" [Meguro] to visit a fountain celebrated for its healing virtues among the devotees.[27] We found the temple close under the foot of a hill and in the rear court two streams of water were pouring out of dragons' mouths from the hill side into a rocky pool below. The water was very pure and cold and the pilgrims who desire to protect their bodies against all disease put their heads under the jets and are supposed to accomplish it. On the facade of the temple under the cover were tablets of bulls eyes that had been targets of successful bowmen and were suspended here as thanks offerings to the deity that gave them the skill.

From Mengoori [Meguro] we rode on into the country through delightful rural roads that recalled the memory of Boston's environs. We passed two pleasure gardens where two artificial hills had been constructed called the great and little Fusi, and so on till we came to a roadside teahouse famous not for its tea, which was of the worst description, or its house, which was small, dingy, and obscure, but a famous wisteria which trellised and spread its shade over the whole yard. And this wisteria deserves fame for it is seven feet in circumference and its thrifty branches had been trained to cover an area of 50 feet by a hundred! It was a roof of green as may not often be seen in a lifetime. The tree, for it seems hardly fair to call it a vine, was said to be 600 years old. Near this was a nursery which had a living rustic gateway, a gateway with a roof and two folding half open doors all from the skillful training of two pines, whose main stems, or trunks, formed the pillars and their arrested branches arched into the roof, then a lateral branch from each trunk was spread and trained to make the leaves of the half opened doors. The resemblance was not far fetched but as close as though a cunning hand had fabricated it of cut leaves, twigs, and branches which he had disposed of at his will, just such a rustic gateway

as we admire when made of dead wood and this was all alive and vigorously growing.

Through the environs of the city, amid continuous planted groves and hedges we rode back till at a sudden turn we found ourselves in the city streets within a mile of the castle walls, the transition was as sudden and bewildering as if we had rubbed Aladdin's lamp and the city had arisen to view and our fraternal access, for such are the surprises we meet every day in Yedo.

Friday, June 20, 1862

Before the Minister's household was stirring this morning my guard of five yakunins were awaiting at the door to escort me back to Yokohama. But owing to delay of getting my own horse in readiness it was past seven o'clock before we rode out of the Legation gates. My guards were pleased with the idea of a ride to Yokohama, and when I offered to discharge them at the River Logo, were more pleased to go on. We rode through the Tokaido to the Sinagawa suburbs encountering not many travellers on the road, as I did once in the month of November. Long before we were stirring the travellers had left their inns which now were quiet and deserted, and had taken the early cool of the morning for the road.

We again left the Tokaido and took a back country road parallel to it in order to visit the temple of *Ikegami* or "High Lake."[28] The change from the monotonous highway to a country road winding among the rich fields and green woods of a low rolling country was most agreeable. The farmers and their wives and children of both sexes were busy securing the barley and wheat harvest, or, wading with bare legs in the overflowed rice fields, were transplanting that young crop. Like most lands in the vicinity of a large consuming city these were in a high state of cultivation and far as the eye could reach were thrifty growing crops of beans, potatoes, yams, eggplants, melons,

[27] This was the Ryūsenji, a Tendai temple known for its image of Fudō, and often referred to as the Meguro Fudō Temple.

[28] The temple at Ikegami was the Hommonji, one of the leading temples of the Edo region, which was venerated as the site of the Priest Nichiren's death in 1282. Much of this massive temple complex was destroyed in World War II.

leeks, arums, while the lower lands, or such as were susceptible of irrigation, were greening with the young rice. Here and there were patches of flowers cultivated in thick masses for market, for every street in Yedo has its one or more shops for the sale of cut flowers. The more common were irises, pinks, and a great variety of chrysanthemums, for there is no season of year except two or three months of the winter when some varieties of this favorite flower are not in bloom.

The temple of the mountain lake is situated on a plateau that overlooks the surrounding country for many miles. We ascended to the temple court by a flight of nearly a hundred broad stone steps making a stairway of a rod or more in width. The landscape view from the top was beautiful, a happy combination of hamlets, rich fields, and the foreground of the bay and its junks and poling boats. There were several temples on the various sides of an open court, only one of which was at all uncommon, and this was the prevailing type of a style more massive than graceful or beautiful, and all architectural effect [was] lost in its one uniform glaring red color. But nature's works compensated in the noble growth of trees that surrounded the temples and then covered a large area on one side which was the cemetery.

A broad avenue leading to a five story vermilioned pagoda was the entrance to the burial grounds which contained tombs of a class I have never met before. They were the tombs of old princes of the empire and priests of ghostly eminence as the care bestowed on these sepulchers showed.[29] Following the winding avenues, which were everywhere darkened and funereal from the overshadowing of the ancient cedars and a stillness only broken by our own foot falls, we passed many a tomb of warrior and priest laid to sleep long centuries ago. The tombs of the Daimios were slight elevations of earth on which a foundation work of heavy stone a rod square was laid. From this foundation rose the stone monuments, four sided pillars with plinth and pedestal and base, the whole elevation being not more than ten

feet. On the sides were cut in deep letters the name of the chieftain and under the cap of the pillar was his armorial bearing or princely crest in gilded bas-relief. The whole was surrounded by a stone railing. The durable look of these monuments, their plain grandeur harmonized with the air of the place. Other tombs were enclosed by a tiled wall surmounted with a roof. The tombs of priests were, many of them, on as large a scale as those of the chiefs, but instead of family escutcheon were large and beautifully chiseled bas-reliefs of the lotus flower and its graceful leaves and stems, the crest of Buddha.

My attendants pointed out some storks which were nesting in one of the tallest pines by the corner of the main temple. A noted bell is to be found at this temple also but I think it is not more than half or two-thirds the weight of the bell at the Imperial Cemetery of Yedo.

From the temple grounds we reached the Tokaido again by crossing the narrowing paths through the submerged paddy fields and halted for a cup of tea at Yamamoto in Omoori [Omori]. The sun bent upon our heads rather too warmly to enjoy the remainder of our road and in pity for ourselves, our horses, and our bettos we made a slow ride back to the bay of Yokohama, where, no little fatigued by several days ride in the hot time of June, I was not sorry to be once more at rest.

Tuesday, June 24, 1862

For several days past our ears have been full of rumors of disturbances in Japan, even so serious as their threatening revolution. The source of these rumors is wholly in the common people and it is difficult to ascertain what, if any, foundation they have. There have been changes in the Goroju, for what causes is not clear. Ando Tsushima-no-kami who was recently assaulted has been removed, and, as is reported, elevated to a high position in [the] treasury offices. His successor Wakasaka [Wakizaka Yasuori] Yamato-no-kami, is said to be a man unfriendly to foreign interests and to have been expelled from the Goroju some two years since for this extreme unfriendliness.

Then we have rumors from Miako that

[29] These graves include not only those of Nichiren and several of his chief disciples but also that of the famous Edo period painter Kanō Tan'yū.

many ronins have concentrated there or in that vicinity, and demand so-called reforms to be instituted in the empire by the Mikado. My Japanese friend S[adajirō] says he has received a letter from a Miako friend which gives the story as follows:

The men who left the service of the Daimio, as mentioned in this journal date of the 23rd ult., and such adherents as they could gather, appeared in the vicinity of Miako. At this time the Prince of Satsuma, or rather the father of the boy who holds the title, and who acts as regent, was on his way to Yedo. Him the ronins stopped on the way and demanded of him that he should represent their grievances at the court of the Mikado. The Prince of Satsuma listens so far favorably that he halts at Miako. The servants of the Mikado, alarmed at this, and fearing that Satsuma is at the head of an insurrectionary movement, with the assistance of friendly daimios threw a strong guard around the inn where Satsuma is and seek an explanation. The Prince states how he was arrested on his way to Yedo by the desires of these men, and that so far from leading a rebellion he had so acted to secure peace; he had already furnished the ronins money and means of subsistence, and sent them on the way to Oasaca. The Mikado's adherents apologized for the course they had taken in surrounding him with guards, and the Prince was satisfied and contented to remain at Miako some days to confer with the Mikado on public affairs.

But some of Satsuma's followers were not so easily pacified for what they deemed an unpardonable affront to their chief. Contrary to his wishes, therefore, a band of twenty-two assaulted this guard who had given them the affront of a surveillance but were speedily overpowered by numbers and all slain. So the matter seems to have rested for a few days, when the ronins reappeared and issued proclamations, as they did before, announcing their purpose to seize the Mikado and the city and inaugurate a revolution.

Great consternation is said to have been produced, multitudes fled into the country, the wealthy took away, or hid, their treasures, trade was suspended, crops were unsold, particularly tea just then coming into market,

while the Mikado confers with his princes as to the state of public affairs. He is now informed for the first time as to the full force of the treaty obligations the country is under, becomes greatly incensed, publicly rebukes his chief adviser, the "Quan bako" [Kampaku] for neglect to keep him informed, and orders him to the close confinement of his house. Complaints are made of the mal-administration of public affairs which has been for many years in the hands of a class who are titled by privilege, and not by rank, that is the titular "kamis," who are the executive power in Japan. Princes complain that the products of their lands which seek a foreign market through the open ports have been subject to an excise for the benefit of the Tycoon, or rather his ministers. The soldiers complain of the indignity of being refused admittance to the ports without being ticketed, or, deprived temporarily of their arms, and various other grievances growing partly out of foreign and partly out of domestic relations.

The Governor of Oasaca committed hara kiri, just why does not appear unless from the menaces of the ronins. The Mikado, acting under the advice of his counselors, at once issued letters to all the great princes of the realm desiring them to meet in council in Miako as early as possible on the affairs of the nation, and the two more important changes suggested are the removal of the smaller kamis from the Imperial Council of State and placing in their stead some of the larger daimios, fully to change the present hostage system whereby a daimio must reside every alternate year at Yedo, and thirdly to require the Tycoon to visit Miako in accordance with ancient usage, but more particularly at this time as etiquette requires having married one of the Mikado's family.

The Japanese authorities deny that any disturbances have taken place; anyone must always be guarded here, as in other lands, from placing too much confidence in popular rumors.

Friday, June 27, 1862

We were all startled today by the report of another attack on the English Legation at Yedo last night. During the day the facts became known circumstantially as follows. Col. Neale, the charge d'affaires sleeps in a room which opens upon a verandah. On the ground in front of the verandah an English sentry paces backwards and forwards keeping guard. I should rather first premise that since the attack upon the legation, almost a year since to a day, the English Legation, in common with the others, has been surrounded by rows of palisades within and between which are posted several hundred Japanese guards. The space more immediately about the house is closely occupied with them, and for the entire circuit of the grounds the guard houses form almost a continuous row. In the vestibule of the house itself are constantly stationed a large number of guards. Beside them the legation is guarded by a considerable force of marines from H.B.M.'s gunboat *Renard*. A police or military train, which is permanently attached to the legation and consists of ten or twelve persons only, acts on guard, and mounted escort duty during the day, the marines patrolling at night. Thus the entrance of any suspicious, or malicious, person would seem impossible.

The sentry on the night in question was pacing before the door and a corporal of marines was doing patrol duty in the grounds. A single Japanese guard was with the sentry before Col. Neale's door. While on duty about midnight they saw some one stealthily approaching in the dark, for the night was cloudy and tempestuous with a high wind. The English sentry challenged and the password was given, for a common pass word is given to English and Japanese. As the man continued to approach the challenge was repeated and again answered, when the Japanese sentry raised his lantern to scan the face of the intruder who was now near, but simultaneously the man sprang forward and with a pike thrust the English sentry with repeated wounds. Col. Neale, who had been awakened by the noise, heard the blows and the exclamations of the wounded man. The sentry drew his sword and seems to have made some resistance although

at nearly the first count one arm was severed at the wrist, the one carrying the musket. The Japanese guard narrates that he drew his sword and attacked the assailant receiving a slight wound but that his light having been lost in the confusion he retreated for fear that when the guard came up as the alarm had been given he would in the dark be confounded with the assassin. The sentry fell before Col. Neale's door covered with wounds. The assassin now appears to have attempted his own escape but in doing so encountered the corporal who was coming up to the scene of action. They immediately engaged each other, the corporal discharging his pistol, or musket, and the ronin fighting with his sword. The corporal was in less space than I can give this narration cut with more than twenty wounds but managed to crawl up to Col. Neale's door also, where he fell and expired at once. The assassin escaped. The tardy Japanese guards now were mustered, bonfires were kindled all about the premises, and they awaited an attack to which they supposed, this, which had already [transpired], was only a prelude. But time wore on and all was quiet.

Meantime three members of the legation who occupied a small house by themselves were much alarmed, being unconscious how much had occurred at headquarters, while those at headquarters were equally ignorant of what might have been their fate. They finally came into headquarters having disguised themselves in Japanese clothing which had been brought them by the guard and were for more than half an hour secreted in one of the guardhouses. The night passed away without further alarms. The sentinel died in the middle of the forenoon, from whose lips and that of the Japanese with him the principal facts were obtained. The spear which had been used with such deadly effect was found on the scene of action showing the marks of the sword cut. This spear was at once seen to be identical with those used by the guard stationed around the premises and at once raised the suspicion of treachery on the part of those sent to protect them. This suspicion was confirmed during the day when on calling the member roll of the guards one was found to be missing, he was searched for and was found wounded at his house and immediately committed *hara kiri*. No clue to his motives for this double deed of treachery and murder has yet been found. Whether it was an act of revenge for the memory of his countrymen who fell in that spot a year ago, or were subsequently executed, the gratification of a personal animosity against the sentry, or an attempt upon the life of the charge d'affaires we can only conjecture. But it certainly is an unpleasant reflection for any Minister resident at Yedo that the guards sent to defend him may prove his most dangerous enemy.

Saturday, June 28, 1862

No further clue is yet obtained to the motive for the deed perpetrated yesterday morning. The various foreign Ministers will make the matter the subject of grave communication to the government.

Wednesday, July 2, 1862

Some further knowledge is obtained concerning the recent transaction at Yedo. The rapidity with which this affair was gone through with, if all performed by one assassin, is not a little remarkable. The sentry on being attacked, and the Japanese with him, raised the alarm and the corporal of the guards, who was not a pistol shot distance, hastened up exclaiming, "what's the matter," and thus confronted the assailant, who, having made sure of the sentry, was evidently about to escape. A conflict between the assailant and the corporal follows, in which the latter is cut up by more than twenty sword wounds. He appears to have discharged his revolver more than once, as four barrels were found empty, to have made use of his sword bayonet, but the skill and dexterity of the Japanese with his two handed sword was too much for him.

The tracks of the assassin in his subsequent escape were followed clearly by the blood, and he appears to have crawled under the verandah of the house and to have reached the temple in the main grounds. Here any further traces of him are lost, and the probabilities are

that he was assisted out of the grounds to his house by the guard, or some of them, who were stationed in that vicinity. This became more probable, for the Japanese themselves relate that he was so severely wounded and weak that he was unable to effect *hara kiri*, and was finally dispatched by his friends in the usual manner by cutting the throat. He had one sword cut, one throat wound, and one or two bullet wounds.

The members of the English Legation, after examining all the circumstances in the case, are inclined to the conclusion that the Japanese sentry, who was with the English sentry at Col. Neale's door, was in fact an accomplice, and although he claims to have inflicted the sword cut found on the man's body, that he only made a feint of assisting the sentry, and that he assisted directly the attack on the corporal. If not he, then some one else of the guard did, for it appears almost incredible that one man in so brief a time could have successfully engaged two well armed men, and cut the second one of them up with so many and fearful wounds. They are not even satisfied that the conspiracy among the guards appointed to defend them was not more extensive but left unexecuted. That portion of the guard, daimios' men to whom the assailant belonged, were at once removed from the grounds and others put in their stead. The Legation grounds have been cleared up of trees, shrubs, and plants so that it may not afford lurking places in the night time and lanterns are so numerously suspended as to make the lightness as of day, a further protection.

Friday, July 4, 1862

This anniversary of our American Independence was celebrated by a gathering of the American citizens, and many other invited guests, at the American Consulate in Kanagawa. Forty or sixty persons were present and at 2 P.M. sat down to a bountiful collation in a dining room draped with flags, ornamented with evergreens and flowers, and inscribed with patriotic sentiments. The portrait of George Washington looked down from the wall over the head of the table where presided

General Pruyn, the American Minister. Good humor and hilarity prevailed. Following the repast were the customary toasts interspersed with fragmentary speeches. The afternoon was wholly spent before the last of the guests had retired.

Two or three days since foreigners were desired to refrain from visiting the Tokaido in the two subsequent days as the cortege of a member of the Mikado's court was to pass through. Yesterday early in the forenoon the cortege passed. The dignitary was an ambassador from the Mikado to the court of the Tycoon, but the remarkable feature in it was that instead of his escort being troops of the imperial household, he was escorted by a guard of a 1000 or so men-of-arms of the Prince of Satsuma.[30] The father of the Prince, who is a boy, was with this train and is described as a stout, good looking man with gray hair and a thin white beard. This departure from the usual routine excited much discussion among the Japanese and is generally held as significant of some important movement. The government had given authority to a report that with Satsuma were some of the ronins who had lately disturbed Miako, and it is certain that unusual precaution was taken to keep foreigners from meeting this train and so out of any possible harm's way. The foreign residents of Kanagawa were not allowed to move out of doors without being followed by a strong guard of Japanese, and at Yedo the members of the Legation were desired not so much as to cross the Tokaido at right angles in order to go there bouts, or to go abroad at all.

The Ambassador is one of the rank *Kange* [*Kuge?*] in the Mikado's court, being among his counsellors, and as such in rank takes precedence of all the daimios and the Tycoon himself. It is reported, whether truly or no I cannot yet state, that the male members of the Mikado's court blacken their teeth like women, and our foreign informant, who saw the train

of some of them on the occasion of the Empress' marriage, bears testimony to the truth of the statement. The news is confirmed of the disgrace of the Quanbako [Kampaku], or Prime Minister, of the Mikado, and of the suicide of the Governor of Miako (not of Oasaca as I had it before).

What is the real occasion of Satsuma's visit to Yedo it is difficult, if not impossible, to state. The Yedo authorities give as the only reason that the old man Satsuma desires to negotiate a marriage for his son, the Prince of Satsuma, now a youth, with some one of the Mikado's family. The people generally regard this visit as the visit of an ambassador from the Mikado to demand of the Tycoon the renewal of the old custom of paying a visit once in three years to the Mikado's court, which now becomes especially imperative since the two reigning families are allied. At the time of the separation of the ecclesiastical and civil power in Yoritomo's time it was formerly agreed that the Siogoon should pass three years alternately at Miako and Yedo. For the three succeeding reigns this agreement was pretended to be carried out. The visits were paid, although the three years were never passed at Miako. At first urgent excuses were found of personal ill health, or something of that sort, for an earlier return, and at last the visits to the Mikados ceased any longer to have any regularity. One thing is certainly established by the recent movements in the empire, that the Mikado's power is something more than nominal and has heretofore been greatly underestimated by us all, as well as the Dutch who preceded us.

The ambassador to Yedo, like all the rank *Kange* has black teeth and an unshaven head. The Mikado's teeth are also blackened like those of the females. The rank of this ambassador is first after that of the Quanbako [Kampaku], and he is called "the keeper of the left hand door" and so in that office leader of all the Mikado's men-at-arms.

[30] This was the imperial delegate Ōhara Shigetomi who was supported by Shimazu Hisamitsu. Conrad Totman tells us that Ōhara's mission was to "bend bakufu foreign policy to fit the *jōi* predilection of the court . . . and to punish those associated with the regimes of Ii and Andō and rehabilitate those injured by them." Tot-

man adds that "formally Ōhara sought unity of court and bakufu, domestic solidarity, expulsion of the foreigners, and consolidation of the peace." See Conrad Totman, *The Collapse of the Tokugawa Bakufu, 1862–1868* (Honolulu: University Press of Hawaii, 1980), p. 8.

Among others Satsuma is charged with laying deeper plots than that of a marriage alliance with the Mikado. He it is who is now charged with having instigated the death of the late Regent, who has caused the removal of Ando Tsushima-no-kami from his seat among the Goroju, and who is now said to be stripped of honors and revenues. All of the Regents' party have been pushed to the wall, and the Mito faction is in the ascendant.

Before the opening of the ports under the Harris treaty the Prince of Satsuma enjoyed an immense monopoly of foreign trade, which he carried on through Loo Choo [Ryūkyū Islands] and China. Through that channel foreign goods were brought into Japan and sold at immense profits. A pound of rhubarb, for instance, sold three years ago for thirteen or fourteen dollars and found its way in by Satsuma's ships, now, thanks to foreign competition, it is not more than a fifteenth of that value. From this source Satsuma derived his revenues, which have led to his present greatness, and now it is said that he is so shorn of these revenues that he is secretly the abettor of that policy in Japan which would drive back all the foreigners to Nagasaki again, or wholly expel them from these shores.

Saturday, July 5, 1862

Bohee [Saigaya Buhee],[31] the merchant, tells me today that it is unsafe to be on the Tokaido after nightfall on account of the bad men who are about. He also gives a different version of Satsuma's and the Mikado's envoy's visit to Yedo. He says that the Mikado, the princes of Satsuma, Hizen, Mori and others are to demand of the Tycoon the positive removal of all foreigners from Yedo.

Wednesday, July 9, 1862

An excursion party complimentary to the American Minister left Yokohama this morning for Kanasawa, Kamakura, and Yenosima.

[31] See footnote 3 for the year 1860 for reference to this merchant.

There were twenty three Americans in the party including five ladies, as many horses, several yakunins for guards and an uncounted number of bettos, chairbearers, porters and servants; between seventy and eighty souls.

The evening previous we sent coolies in advance with baggage and provisions to be left at various points on the road. We followed in boats the next morning. It was a sultry summer morning with but little wind and we were compelled to make a long pull of several hours to Kanasawa where was our first rendezvous. The inn of the "Sea-bride," my old resort, overlooking Goldsborough Inlet was full in its seaward balcony with unusual guests. The landlord and his household were flying hither and thither in a state of bewilderment at such an influx of customers. The street was blocked with horses and norimons, hampers of provisions, bettos rushing wildly about endeavoring to administer a diet of leaves to their charges.

We left our boats at the inlet to await our return while we pushed on to Kamakura for lunch. The sun was shining in all its midday fierceness in the road untempered with any breeze. The rich tints of the foliage relieved the eyes amid this blaze of fire. Never was the shade of the deep gorges on this road before so welcome and glad were [we] to dismount at the Kamakura inn after an hour of such exposure.

While some were visiting the famous temple grounds, others preferred the quiet of the inn. We took the upper rooms of the house and speedily had a crowd of spectators without wondering what so many tojins were about. Benches about a foot and a half high were brought in to serve for tables and our servants were soon busy opening basket and box and spreading out our cold meats. Each one furnished his own tableware but provisions were provided for all in common. We were a hilarious party despite the heat over our cold fowls and meats and the clink of glasses made agreeable music. Below stairs our numerous retinue equal to a daimios' train really took possession of all the house.

After a couple of hours halt our hampers were repacked and our long train again set in motion towards Yenosima. But we stopped on our way to visit the great bronze image of Dai-boots, "the Great Buddha." This colossal image received us all within its ample bosom, and we enjoyed the perfection of Buddhist faith—"absorption in Buddha." The old priest seemed pleased at the unusual number of his pilgrims, and particularly at the tribute money we paid him, and when several of us began to climb into the god's lap and rest within his folded colossal arms he seemed to look upon it [more] as an act of respect than otherwise. This bronze image, as I have before described, is a Buddha sitting upon a lotus lily with his hands brought before him, the thumbs touching, the head bent a little forward as if in silent contemplation. Between the arms and hands thus folded there was room for a double [dozen?] people to stand which conveys some idea of its great size. We poured out our libations, more germane to the merry god of the wine hills of Greece rather than this calm divinity, but I observed the priest was not unwilling to join in partaking them.

Again, through a crowd of wondering people who hemmed the roadside, we took the shady paths that brought us out upon the beach of Odawara Bay. And now the summer heats were tempered by the cool breeze coming from the sea waves, the ocean surf tumbled its waves upon the barren sands with a welcome roar. Out to seaward was the smoking cone of Volcano Island. Yenosima rested like a jewel on the bosom of the sea three miles in front of us, and on its right the mountain ranges of Idzu promontory rolled away in rugged outline seaward. The ride upon the beach sands in the low afternoon sun was charming. Two of our yakunins went in advance to secure us accommodations and came back a mile this side to say that we could not go into Yenosima [Enoshima]; it was very sickly with the measles, there was a public holiday also, and no accommodations to be had. They begged us to turn aside and go to Fujisawa on the Tokaido where we could be better accommodated. We were accustomed to such talk and told the officials we should go only to Yenosima, and to Yenosima we went.

It was a pretty sight at sunset to see our straggling cavalcade crossing the narrow sands which the sea makes on either side, and which forms the communication with the shore. Bet-

tos running and shouting with the horses, coolies staggering under their burdens, and all the population of the island and the adjoining villages clustering like bees in every degree of nudity to witness our advent. The narrow street that by stone steps goes up the hill was blocked with people, and we saw that the inns on either side of it were closed to prevent our ingress. There was one inn which stood at the entrance of the street and commanded a pleasant prospect of the sea beaches where we wished to stop, but this too was closed with wooden shutters and barred. We indicated our preference to stop there. No we could not, the yakunins said, for the proprietor had just died of the measles and his dead body now lay in the house, and the next inn was full of sick people, and the next, and the next.

We were disposed to give the people time to come to the conclusion of entertaining us, and although our ladies were sitting in the street on the stones we forbore a while with all patience, but at last told the yakunins that it was no use to make any further delays we should go no further, and if they did not open the inn doors for us we should open them ourselves, and proceeded at once to take our stand by the doors of the one we had selected.

As usual this show of determination settled the matter and the inn doors were opened and we were in possession of the upper rooms and balconies overlooking the sea. Of course such a sudden interruption gave no time to remove the "dead man," but he had vanished somehow, and we saw neither body or ghost. A footing once obtained, the household were active enough to serve us, and we had no complaints to make on that score. In the upper room we again spread our tables from the hampers which had arrived all safe some hours before we did. But the hot sun had caused some of our cold meats to perish, yet there was enough left. It was a beautiful night with the moon just at her full and after dinner we strolled out upon the beaches to enjoy the coolness of the air, the beauty of the scene, the waters undulating far out to sea in the silvery touch of the moonbeams, the distant mountains on the mainland lifting their solemn peaks into the night sky. The ladies had purchased some Japanese robes and took a sea bath, the gentlemen followed in the same luxury.

When we returned to our inn the debris of the feast had been removed, the mats had been swept, and the full radiance of the moon filled the balconies with light. Travel and fatigue had wearied us all and we prepared to sleep. The ladies had a room by themselves, and from their merry laughter were evidently enjoying the strangeness of their position. The strong cool breeze of the sea cleared away all mosquitoes, and we looked forward to a comfortable sleep. We had come prepared with night garments, mosquito nettings, and some with sleeping blankets and pillows, but the most of us preferred to lie on the clean mats in our pajamas and loose shirts using the wooden pillow of the Japanese, or our own bundles and carpet-bags, for head rests. The scene was like a hotel on convention night for we covered the floor about us as closely as it was possible without contact.

The always pleasant sound of the surf promised to lull us to sleep, but, alas, how vain were our hopes. It was a matsuri day, and if it had been a carnival day of barrel organ even we could not have been more disturbed. The sands in front of our inn was the public square of the place, and here were the people assembled for their sports. Directly under our windows was the tom-tom band, who gave us an operatic entertainment we had not counted upon. Imagine a half-a-dozen wooden drums accompanied by several shrill fifes playing a tune with just three notes—and those discordant ones—from nine o'clock at night till three in the morning, accompanied with shouting and screeching, and all the hideous noises an unmusical people make when they are trying to be jolly, and some idea may be had of our position. A few were happy enough to add their own snoring to the outside harmony, but the most of us lay on our mat couches wondering when the last symphony would come and thinking it would have been a better arrangement of things that a people who are so fond of celebrating holiday occasions with vocal efforts as the Japanese are should have been blessed with some ideas of melody.

Thursday, July 10, 1862

Sleepless, as our night had been, we were out early to enjoy the fine sea bathing and a morning stroll in the pure sea tempered atmosphere. The little rocky isle of Yenosima would be a favorite resort if located on American coasts. It reminds me to some degree of Nahant. An early breakfast was welcomed by ready appetites, some fine fish (the tai) from the baskets anchored out in deep water were added to our own stores.

The island of Yenosima is a rocky islet springing boldly out of the water, not in fact an island, for a narrow strip of sand forms an isthmus to connect it with the main shore. About the sides of the island are masses of fallen rocks among which the waves tumble and leap, and where the hardy fishermen dive down for the awabi that clings to them. The island, covered with trees and grass, is of uneven surface, its greatest height out of [the] water being 150 feet. Its circumference is not more than two miles. Scattered about in picturesque locations are the temples which, though not remarkable for their beauty, are shrines visited by pilgrims from far and near. Though perhaps the chief attraction is a cave in its outward face, an opening into the rocky foundations of the island 30 feet high at is entrance and extending underground some three hundred and fifty feet. Hither come the pilgrims and after laving their hands and lips with the spring water that gushes out of the rock, they are taken into the inner cave carrying lights in their hands. In its lowest part there is room enough to stand upright. In niches in the rocks, or on pedestals at the side of the passages of the cave, about halfway to its terminative branches, are images of various deities to be propitiated. One is a serpent coiling out of a rock representing a real serpent which lives within the cavern and which nobody sees.

We cooled our arms in the bronze basin of the sacred spring and took an underground libation assisted by the guardians of the place. The matsuri had absorbed all the interest of the place and the little shops for the sale of curiosities were closed. We wandered about the island, or boated along its shores till the noon day heats, when some went back to the inn, while others of us, finding a cool spot on the cliffs over the sea where the fresh breeze was invigorating, lay down on the benches of a deserted tea booth in calm enjoyment of the breeze.

There was a temple nearby with a well of very cold water which iced our champagne and here in happy indolence we passed the noontide hours till it was time to return for lunch. This cliff overhung the sea, below the boats were falling and rising with the ocean swell among the rocks. The nude red skinned fisherboys were sporting on the beach. Shouts of children at play came up from below. The musical vibrations of the sonorous temple bells filled the air at intervals mingling with the faint hum of the surf. Crags and rocks were overrun with vines and gave uncertain support to trees of glistening foliage, mimosas and gardenias bloomed among the cliffs, and on the sea were the white sails of hundreds of fishing boats. Low misty clouds were wreathing the picturesque hills of the promontory of Idzu; creeping like ants along the distant beach were new pilgrims coming to visit the sacred shrines. So unlike was it all to the experiences of usual life, were we not dreamers by the sea cliffs?

We spread our last meal at the inn and enjoyed it with hearty good will. Our excursion had been pleasant, no accident or selfishness had marred it, and now we pledged each other in generous bumpers. There was a long time packing up the remnants of our feast. The beggars living in the shade of the great boats hauled up on the beach did not scruple to receive fragments of forbidden meats. A group of jugglers were performing before the inn on the dry sands; below stairs our porters were carting our luggage for the return. People who had rendered any service, great or small, were coming with neatly written bills, our gray headed landlord came with portentious document in hand and knocking his head to the mats presented his "little bill" with great humility, as if he was very sorry to take any pay for his hospitalities. He received his 62 bus and profusely knocked his head several times more thanking me over and over again. The stable keeper swindled us in a bill of 31 bus, and wanted nearly half as many more, and one

sleek faced Aminadab wanted nearly two dollars for ferriage somewhere that nobody knew anything about. But the last bill was paid, the last hamper stashed, the landlord, more gracious as our blessed departure grew imminent, went down on his head again over the gift of our empty bottles and boxes left behind. The people assembled on the sands to see us off, and so we went out of Yenosima.

How delicious the sea wind was as we rode along the beach for several miles, the white foam washing our horses' feet. The air grew drier and hotter as we took the country paths more inland. A short halt at Kamakura and we rode on to Kanasawa where our boats awaited us. Here we found the people all out in holiday clothes enjoying another matsuri. There was a procession of cars ornamented with flowers, flags, and toy figures, others had singers and players, jugglers and mountebanks, and one was a boat on wheels handsomely carved and finished with a house upon it. All the cars were much more ornamental than anything of the kind I had ever seen before. They were heavy with carvings of beasts, birds, and human forms, plants and flowers. A moonlight sail from Kanasawa to Yokohama completed our excursion in a very pleasant manner.

Friday, July 11, 1862

The English Legation leaves Yedo.

Sunday, July 13, 1862

Two days ago the English Legation again formally left Yedo in consequence of the late assault upon the guards. It can only be supposed that they do this from a belief that their life is imperiled by staying. The general feeling in the community is adverse to the wisdom of this step.

Sunday, July 20, 1862

The rains of yesterday have cooled the atmosphere so that walking is again an agreeable pastime and exercise. The two W.'s[32] and myself took a boat to Kanagawa for the purpose of visiting the beautiful temple grounds of Bookengi [Bukenji]. On our way to the ferry we met a travelling aquarium and fern seller. His establishment was a large light frame all about which were hung the fern roots twisted into circles, lattice work, basket work, or various shapes, from which the delicate fern leaves were sprouting. Among the ferns were suspended glass vases in size and form like an ordinary lamp globe in which swam gold fishes. The frame itself was covered with glass ornaments, leaves, bunches of grapes, and a hundred tinkling glass bells. Behind him came a cricket seller for now is the season of the singing gryllae [cricket] and cicadae. He too had a light frame like a long basket. In the bottom, in little cages six or eight inches long by half as many broad, were members of singing insects of various kinds feeding on slices of egg plant or on pears. Then there were quaint little wicker cages of every shape, square, bell shaped, and oval in which to deposit the singing insects as they were sold. And so he went from house to house selling these novel canary birds in cages which the Japanese seem proud of. Even the belle wears the cricket in her hair enclosed in a fine wire, or gauze, cage attached to her hair pins.

We crossed the bay and took the pleasant paths through the fields towards the temple. The landscape was looking particularly fresh and beautiful, the air was cool and delicious and we all felt exalted in feelings as we threaded our way among the shaded paths over the low hill and the outspread valleys between.

The priests' houses at Bookengi were for the most part silent and deserted; it was out of season for the young theologians who here assemble every spring and prepare for the Buddhist

priesthood. In one cottage hanging over the valley below were three young monks taking care of the library by opening the books to give them light and air, and so free them of the mold which attacks everything at this season. Not less than three hundred volumes thus lay open on the mats. They were books of priestly and historical lore, said the good natured lazy monks as they struck fire from flint and steel for their pipes and our cigars, old books and precious. We left the monks amid their lazy surroundings, inert, dull, monotonous lives do these monks lead, left the beautiful temple grounds, and clambering the hills took our homeward way along the cliffs that overlook the waters of Yedo Bay and the beautiful country alternating with plains of rice, fresh and green, wavy hill-like levels, rounded dells, [and] forests of fir which begirt the waters.

The magnificent white and spotted lily had just come into bloom, scenting the woodland paths with its exquisite odor. Gleaming in the mist that overhung the waters were the countless sails of the fishing boats and junks, just filled by the soft south wind that scarcely crisped the smooth surface. Directly below us the snake-like Tokaido crept along between rows of trim houses, or glided into the country between the long time planted cedar rows. Like ants the travellers were creeping by, and under the shade were the clamorous beggars.

Down from the cliffs by a flight of steps and a path made for the convenience of the worshippers of a Shinto shrine we descended to the road below, stopping at a *Kompira*, or sailors temple, cut out of the hill side, the great resort of all the seafaring men hereabouts. On a little platform leveled out of the hill-side stand the buildings. The shinto shrine facing a broad flight of stone steps descending to the street below, on the left, the Kompira shrine, on the right, the largest and best building of all, where the priests live their lazy lives.

But what interested [me] was that among the locks of hairs deposited here by grateful sailors [who] escaped the perils of the sea, votive offering made in an hour of danger, were eleven top locks suspended on an inscribed tablet and affixed to the front shrine apart from the rest.

[32] The two W.'s would appear to have been John G. Walsh and Thomas Walsh, Hall's partners in Walsh, Hall & Co.

I at once conjectured what they might be, and the good natured old priest who came out of his house at my reverences confirmed my conjecture. These were the votive gifts of the eleven shipwrecked Japanese picked up in mid ocean by the ship *Victor* from Hong Kong to San Francisco, and from the latter place sent to Kanagawa, where they had arrived a few days ago. They had sailed away months ago (in Dec. last) from this port in a rice and wheat laden junk for Oasaca, but were driven out to sea in a tempest and for three months drifted like a log on the ocean. Fortunately they had cargo enough of wheat yet undamaged to maintain life all those weary helpless days until they were rescued.

The tablet gave their names, their district (mostly men of Owari), the name of the vessel, and the dates of its departure and their return. Their wives and mothers in Owari do not yet know that husbands and sons are saved and yet daily make offerings to their departed shades. How like the living from the dead will they come back to them.

The old priest brought out some grain and directly a flock of tame pigeons covered the ground, flew about our feet, and even ate out of the strangers hand. We left the priest among his doves and were again in the Tokaido. At a tea house picturesquely situated on a cliff over the sea, where the wind came in through the open screens, we took our cups of tea and rested and Nawo San, shyest and most modest of Nippon's maids with her wealth of dark hair and eyes and magnificent teeth, waited upon us and thought it a pleasure to take all our handkerchiefs to use if they were scented for she said she was "very fond of perfumes." After a half hour's rest on the clean mats we returned to our boat and our home. (At this tea house a priest was taking his meal who was travelling in state with two handsome norimons and many attendants. He was a very brisk, lively old gentleman.)

Wednesday, July 23, 1862

For some weeks past the measles have been prevalent throughout Japan where they have not been known for many years. The spread was so universal as to embarrass all household and business operations; the entire servants of a household were disabled; carpenters had to suspend work; boatmen could not be found; manufacturing ceased, or nearly so. The disease does not appear to have been accompanied with much mortality.

The Japanese at Yedo have found a sovereign remedy for the disorder. At the temple of Fukangawa Hachiman[33] are stalled a span of sacred horses who are fed their daily rations of beans out of a tub. If their tub is put on the head of the worshipper while in the act of devotion, it is found a sure amulet against the measles, as it has long been known a sovereign cure for rheumatism! The virtue of these horse tubs is only excelled by that of the beans themselves fed to the "white steeds" of Asakusa Kanon, a few of which administered to crying children dry up their lachrymal founts. Recommended to impatient young fathers for night use.

Thursday, July 31, 1862

Consul Polsbroek's fete.[34]

Thursday, August 7, 1862

Started at 11 1/2 A.M. in a boat for Kanasawa with the two W's and their friend P.[35] We had a fair wind and pleasant sail across Mississippi Bay and reached Kanasawa about 2 P.M. Here we had, as usual, an excellent dinner of fish. Our horses, which had been sent overland, joined us at this place. After dinner we mounted to ride over to Kamakura and the great bronze image. P.'s horse had not arrived

---

[33] This reference is to the Tomigaoka Hachiman Shrine in Fukagawa Park.

[34] Dirk de Graff van Polsbroek was the Dutch minister to Japan in 1862.

[35] The two W's were the Walsh brothers, but it is not clear who P. was, unless he was the new American minister Robert H. Pruyn.

and he was compelled to hire a kango, but his unwieldy bulk retarded the Kango bearers, and I gave him my horse and took the kango myself. There were three bearers and with my light weight they easily kept along with the horses. At Kamakura we visited the beautiful grounds of Hachiman temple. The lotus ponds were in full bloom and made a magnificent show of red and white blossoms. From Kamakura we went to the bronze image with which my companions were much delighted and astonished. The old priest was as smiling and affable as ever, and as eager for his ichibus.

The ride over the country newly cleansed by showers was delightful. It was 7 1/2 P.M. before we reached Kanasawa on our return, but the night was moonlit and we were not solicitous. We had again a good fish supper, and a little after nine took our boat. As we wound out of the inlet between its green shores by the moonlight, the scene was one of brilliant beauty. But our fatigue overpowered our sentiment, and soon after we had rounded Webster Island and were fairly out on the bay, one by one we dropped asleep on the floor benches, or roof, of our boat. The tide was against us and thus it was one A.M. before we reached Yokohama.

Saturday, August 30, 1862

The measles, which have so generally prevailed in an epidemic form, have of late proved fatal in the secondary effects. Many have died at Yedo and elsewhere. And now the Cholera has followed, not yet in its worst forms, but there are many deaths daily among the natives. In one house four inmates died one after the other. My neighbor Goble buries a little girl today.

Sunday, September 14, 1862

Today there is to be recorded another one of those bloody deeds which have filled already so many pages of this journal. A party of four, three gentlemen and one lady, Mess. Marshall, Richardson, Clark, and Mrs. Borrodaile, left Yokohama to pay a visit to the temple of Daishi-sama about 8 miles above Kanagawa. They took boats to Kanagawa where they were met by their bettos with horses and proceeded on horseback on their ride. About 4 P.M. some of our citizens were startled by the sight of Mrs. B[orrodaile] riding home alone, her horse at full gallop, her dress greatly disordered, her hat gone, and her face marked with blood. She stopped her horse at Mr. Gowers, the first foreign residence, where she gave the information that while riding from Kanagawa to Kawasaki they met a Japanese retinue, were assaulted, and that she had escaped from their murderous hands leaving her male companions wounded, or slain, on the road.

There was a prompt rallying of citizens and officials who mounted their horses to go to the scene of the disaster. The French Minister M. du Bellecourt was particularly zealous, ordering at once a large detachment of sailors and marines with sabers, muskets, and field pieces to be landed at Kanagawa and proceeding thither himself with his mounted and foot guards. Capt. Vyse led also to the same place the mounted guard of the English Legation, their officer being absent. The excitement was intense, mounted citizens in pairs and in groups hastened thither as rapidly as possible. Some of the latter met portions of the retinue still on the road, and when demonstrations of hostility were in one instance shown to a party of five or six, they promptly drew their pistols, and pointing them at the head man in a norimon, brought them thus into a quiet frame of mind. The different parties all brought up at the American Consulate in Kanagawa where they found Mess. Marshal and Clark lying seriously, but not dangerously, wounded.

From their narrative given at this time, and subsequently, it appears that after they left the boats and mounted their horses they rode about three or four miles above Kanagawa without meeting any interruption. True, they met many passers by, menials carrying baggage and groups of armed men wearing the livery of the Prince of Satsuma; such travellers as one may always see in advance of the retinue of some chief or travelling grandee. A notice had been issued from some of the consulates that on the two following days the retinue of the Mikado's envoy would leave Yedo and occupy the Tokaido, but none had been cautioned for this day, and our party of four still kept on.

The bearing of those they passed was wholly civil and respectful. They passed also a well known interpreter of the Yokohama Custom House and exchanged words with him, but he also gave them no intimation that the road was unsafe. About four miles above Kanagawa they met the advanced guards of a moving train and took one side of the road remarking to each other that it was best to avoid any trouble. As they thus halted at the side of the road the guards in advance quietly passed by, although they spread across the road so as to crowd our party quite out of the same.

When the norimon of the chief approached surrounded by his personal guards, one of the latter, a man of large proportions, stepped forward and imperiously waved his hand to our party signifying that they should turn about and retire. Any opposition to their wishes was of course useless, and the party accordingly wheeled their horses about with their heads towards Kanagawa to get out of the way. No sooner had they turned, than the same man who had gestured to them so significantly drew his sword and gave Richardson a severe blow across the loins, a wound which subsequently proved to have been sufficiently fatal without what followed.

They immediately sought their safety in flight, but the guards closed in around them throwing their loose robes off their shoulders and drawing their long swords. Marshall, urging Mrs. Borrodaile into flight, tried also to keep Richardson up with them, who was already giving in from the blow he had received and exclaimed that he was dying. In this struggle to escape Richardson was again and again wounded, Marshall received two shallow cuts across his loins, Mrs. Borrodaile had her riding hat shorn off and Clark's left arm was nearly severed at the shoulder, but riding over and through their immediate assailants they got away from them, and Richardson soon after fell from his horse apparently lifeless. The more advanced guards simply drew their swords but made no further attack on the fugitives who urged their horses past one group

and another till exhausted with wounds and fatigue they reached the American Consulate. Here, while Clark and Marshall halted, unable to go further, Mrs. B[orrodaile]'s horse started again, and unable to hold him, she again fled along the Tokaido. Alone, and fearful of falling into desperate hands, she urged her horse down a narrow path that led to the sea, resolved upon drowning herself in preference. But her horse after taking the water a while again came out upon the road taking the familiar way that led to Yokohama. Once having left the Tokaido and got into the Yokohama road Mrs. B[orrodaile] felt comparatively safe, but did not cease to urge her horse till she reached the foreign residences.

Let us now return to the gathering of officers, citizens, and soldiers at the Consulate. After hearing the story of the wounded men, and Richardson's fate being still uncertain, a mixed company of English, French, and American citizens and soldiery started in search of him dead or alive. Consul Vyse took the lead in the matter. Reaching the scene of the attack the body at first was not to be seen, but a boy proffered to guide them to where it had been disposed in a field or garden by the wayside. It had been decently laid out on a mat, another mat covering it, and a temporary mat roof built over all. His clothes, watch, jewelry and money had been undisturbed, but the body presented a shocking spectacle. The head was nearly severed from the trunk, one shoulder was cleft in twain, there was a deep spear wound over the heart, one hand was severed, and the other partially so, while the bowels protruded from a deep gash in the side and back. From the bloodless character of some of the wounds it would appear that they had been inflicted when life was nearly extinct. One Japanese account stated that after Richardson fell he sat up by the way and asked for water, but at that moment the norimon of the chief again came up with him and the rider bade his followers dispatch him. It is also stated, on the evidence of some of the party who were attacked, that the attack was made by a word of command from the norimon of the chief accompanied with a clapping of hands and with a shout the onset was made.

The body of Richardson was taken back to

Village of Namamugi on the Tōkaidō where Mr. Richardson was murdered. Photograph by Felice Beato.

Yokohama and the wounded were also removed thither from the American Consulate. It now became a question what steps should be taken. The English charge d'affaires received from all hands much censure for his apparent indifference. When urged to send a party in search of Richardson he declined to act. Report charged that he seemed more solicitous for his personal safety than for the welfare of the community. After the dead body of Richardson had been seen by him, after he heard the story of the assault from Mrs. Borrodaile's own lips, he stated to a deputation who waited upon him that he "was not officially informed that any disturbance had happened." It fortunately happened that on this very afternoon an English gun boat and a man-of-war steamer having the flag of Admiral Kuper came into port. With such a force present in the harbor, to wit, eight ships of war of the English, French, and Dutch nationalities, many counselled the seizure of the chief of the train who was known to halt for the night at the village of Hodoriya [Hodogaya], about three miles from Yokohama. To this course the French Minister was strongly inclined, the Admiral hesitated for want of knowledge and jurisdiction, and the English charge opposed it. The Governor of Yokohama, fearing trouble, quickly sent word to Hodoriya and before mid-night the chief moved out of harm's way decamping with all his attendants. This chief is said to be an official high in the service of the Prince of Satsuma.

Monday, September 15, 1862

Today Richardson's body was buried, attended to its last resting place by a large concourse of soldiers and civilians. Last night and today there have been numerous meetings of the citizens and also of the officials. At the former, strong resolutions of censure were passed against Col. Neale and a "statement" of the affair drawn up to be forwarded to the Home Government. The officials seemed to have come to no definite purpose of action and the slow course of diplomacy must take its way. The excitement in the community is very great and Col. Neale is loaded with opprobrium for not taking active measures to secure the offenders.

At Yedo the rumor prevails that the Tokaido is seized by the foreigners and the Mikado's ambassador who had left that city returns.

Tuesday, September 16, 1862

Minister Pruyn is down from Yedo today and there is a meeting of the Foreign Ministers to concur upon measures for the public safety. Some suggest a new Tokaido for the Japanese to travel upon, others suggest the posting of guards at stations along the present one, but no general action is agreed upon.

Wednesday, September 17, 1862

It is now clear that no extraordinary measures of redress will be adopted by the foreign officials. The Japanese government is said to declare its inability to punish the chief offender, as he is a servant of the Prince of Satsuma. But no daimio is more accessible for redress than this prince. His capital city of Kagoshima lies on the bay of the same name, he is the owner of much shipping, among which are the large steamers "England" and "Fiery Cross," recently acquired. For the first time in a long series of assassinations the crime is brought home to its perpetrator, and surely it will be a greater crime if the offender is ultimately allowed to escape. Satsuma, too, holds the fief of Loo Choo [Ryūkyū] islands and has a large and profitable trade therewith.

Sunday, September 21, 1862

The excitement over the recent assault and murder on the Tokaido abates. It has made on the common people less impression than it otherwise would because of the widespread cholera. At Yedo the mortality is very great. The famous Nippon-bas [Nihon Bashi], which is said to be cleansed after every 100 funeral trains have passed over it, is daily purified four times. Numerous as are the priests in Yedo, funerals daily take place without their presence. Sect distinction is disregarded in procuring their services, bodies lie above ground for several days because it is impossible to burn or bury them fast enough. Of the measles which prevailed before the cholera 75,000 are said to have died. Death in many cases rapidly follows the first attack. At Yokohama there are, too,

many deaths. Among the foreigners there has been little sickness except in the fleet where a few deaths have occurred.

Thursday, September 25, 1862

There is a conference of Foreign Ministers today to take into consideration the recent transaction on the Tokaido. The result is not yet shadowed forth.

Friday, September 26, 1862

What transpired at yesterday's conference is not declared except that the conduct of the Goroju was very satisfactory.

The Japanese have their love of humor. I have just seen an amusing caricature called "The Measles War." The picture represents an army of diseases going forth to war on mankind led by the Measles as chief who is depicted with a swollen spotted face. Headache is a warrior with his brow tied up, fever is ruby red, colds and coughs by one in the act of coughing with wide open mouth. Cholera a grim bilious fellow occupies a conspicuous place. This formidable army is attacked by a motley crowd of people among whose banners most conspicuous is the *moong* of the Yedo Oshiwara which is properly supposed to be one of the chief sufferers. They are represented as expelling from their midst the tribe of watermelons, one of which occupies the head of a flagstaff, muskmelons, hard pears, shell fish, and other disturbers of the human system. One warrior is crowned with a hat in shape of a "pleasure boat," for the river boatmen are general sufferers in a community where funerals take the place of feasts. An apothecary among his pills, powders, and ointments is overwhelmed by the emergency and shows sympathy on his face lest the Army of Diseases is defeated. Caricatures are not uncommon among the Japanese.

Wednesday, October 1, 1862

Yokohama races.

Tuesday, October 7, 1862

Commenced loading *Storm Cloud.*

Tuesday, October 14, 1862

It has been stated that a man has been delivered up to the government who was one of the assailants in the recent affray upon the To-kaido, that he is in fact the one who slew Richardson. But who knows that this is the man, or some poor coolie or malefactor, who is made to represent him. Or how shall one man atone for the act of several, or how shall the chief, Shimadzu Saburo, be held guiltless who gave the inhuman order to behead the wounded and dying Richardson? The general government has avowed its inability to punish this man as the soldiers who did the biddings of the Prince of Satsuma will not give him up. Nothing but strong measures on the part of the foreign powers will render our lives secure outside of our settlement. To let such crimes go unpunished endangers the safety of every foreign resident. We can then only wait, asking each other whose turn comes next to be waylaid or openly murdered.

Thursday, October 16, 1862

News received of the stranding of the *Guinea.* The Dutch Consul goes to her assistance.

Thursday, October 23, 1862

From Yedo we have accounts of important changes and reforms in the government.[36] The Tycoon has ordered that hereafter the Kamisimo, or garment of ceremony, is to be laid aside as an official dress and also the long trouser which trailed upon the floor. The custom of these dresses is said to have originated in

Gongen Sama's time and was purposely employed for its hindrance to the free movement of the arms and limbs so that *emuete* would be less likely to occur at royal interviews and state occasions. It illustrates the disturbed condition of society in which it had its origin. So too, which later report is not so well founded, that the system of daimios residing at Yedo for alternate years is also to be done away with as a needless burden and expense upon the chiefs. Wives and families are no more to be kept there as hostages for good behavior. Certain classes of the chiefs are to reside at the court one year in five, others one year in seven, but this is doubtless nominal. Thus Yedo will be left to the imperial court alone. The removal of so large a population from Yedo of the princes and their adherents must wholly change the character and appearance of the city; indeed the complaints of the common people, the merchants, the fishermen, and laborers, are said to be loud and deep against this prospect of ruin staring them in the face. The government consoles them with the idea that the increased foreign trade will make up their losses—an absurd idea that this small trade can sustain a city of more than a million people.

My informants declare this move to be one of the government and a salutary reform inaugurated by it, and yet it is possible that it may have sprung out of quite other motives.

The daimio residency at Yedo was purposely instituted by Hideyoshi, or Gongen Sama [Ieyasu], to cripple the power of the daimios by the exhausting expense of the alternate years of removal, and to prevent them from fomenting disturbance in their own principalities. So, too, the court dress worn, which abridged the full use of their limbs, was a restriction upon them. So that these reforms may have sprung not from a nice paternal government, but from the demands of the hampered nobles. This removal may signify an abandonment of the Tycoon and his court, instead of a change of government policy voluntarily undertaken.

[36] The reforms mentioned here were the Bunkyū Reforms carried out by Matsudaira Yoshinaga with the advice of Yokoi Shōnan. The modification of the *sankin kōtai* had been announced on October 15. Once again

Hall seems to have been quickly and well informed. For details of the Bunkyū Reforms see Conrad Totman, *The Collapse of the Tokugawa Bakufu,* pp. 3ff.

Following so closely upon the announcement of the closing for five years of the port of Oasaca there are those who believe that all this is but a step towards the removing the whole government to Miako; a surmise, which the well declared intentions of the Tycoon to pay a visit to that city, gives some significance to. How are we to account for the removal and disgrace of the late Minister Ando, who was friendly to foreigners and a man of rare intelligence, if reforms were what were really aimed at? Or the later disgrace of Kadso [Katsu], also a friend to foreigners. What mean the frequent embassies to and from Miako, the interference of the large daimios with the reigning dynasty, of which so much has been said of late. Truly Japanese politics are a riddle to those who have not avenues of information. Minister Pruyn was ignorant yesterday of all this movement, except the new dress regulation, until I informed him. And what that dress had its origin in, and what its reform perhaps really symbolized, was to him unknown. So close do the Japanese hold their secrets, and so hard is it for those at the court itself to learn what is being done about them. In this, as in all other matters, we must wait till the record has passed into history before we dare to believe anything.

Monday, October 27, 1862

My birthday's anniversary; another decade of life finished, *hew! fugaces annos.* Invited my friends to dine. General Pruyn, Consul Fisher, Rev. S. R. Brown, Dr. Hepburn, and Mr. Shoyer. Told them that, as I was now venerable and ought to be placed with the elderly gentlemen, I had invited them as fitting companions of sober age to dine with me. General P[ruyn] retorted by proposing the health of the "new Methuselah!" We had a pleasant evening and our table was graced with some American dishes by the thoughtful help of friends at home. A genuine whattleberry pudding and American wines vouched for the remembrance of fatherland. The health of friends at home was drunk with more than usual feeling.

Thursday, October 30, 1862

Earthquake 10 A.M.

Sunday, November 2, 1862

5 earthquake shocks.

Thursday, November 13, 1862

The pressing nature of my business has for many days back caused me to neglect my journal. The business consequent upon the wreck of the *Guinea.* The loading and dispatching of the *Storm Cloud* and *Josephine* to California have left me little leisure. Since my entries of Oct. 23rd the changes going on at Yedo and in the empire have been more clearly understood. The sumptuary regulations as to dress regards not only the upper classes, but a general edict has been issued forbidding the use of silk, foreign camlets, woolen stuffs, and velvets, and restricting high and low to cotton and linen fabrics only. Such sumptuary regulations appear to have been made from time to time in Japan, to have prevailed a few years, and then to have been done away with. What humor prompts the present edict it is difficult to tell. The keeper of some of the large houses of prostitution at Sinagawa was in Yokohama the other day desiring to buy 200 pieces of gray shirting. It is the custom of the proprietors of such houses on New Years Day to present all the inmates with new dresses, and in large houses these dresses are usually of silk and very handsome. This man said he had 140 girls so to clothe, and he wished to buy foreign cottons and dye them, because he could not buy silks or satins.

Hosokawa Hizen-no-kami says he will neither leave Yedo with his followers, or lay aside the wearing of silk. These things are time immemorial customs and he shall adhere to the ancient ways.

A royal edict was indeed issued that the residency system of the daimio at Yedo should be broken up in a great measure. All the large daimio[s] were to retire with their families to their provinces and once in three years were to visit Yedo for 100 days, their families remaining in the country permanently. Certain ones of the smaller daimios were to remain in Yedo with the imperial families as supports to royalty. Connected with this edict was an order to cut off the immense retinue of idle servants attached to the princely families for mere show. It is shrewdly suspected that all these important changes had their origin in a desire of some of the large daimios to emancipate themselves from custom both onerous and expensive. Hosokawa has made himself conspicuous by his determination to remain at Yedo after the old custom.

As might be supposed such important changes produced consternation among the common people of Yedo, a city built and supported by the numerous population which surrounded the court. Not only were the daimios to leave with their many thousands of followers, but, before leaving, they dismissed inferior menials by thousands more, who, without any regular means of livelihood, were likely to become either beggars, ronins, or were to enter into competition in trade and branches of industry which were already greatly curtailed by the removals. The women of the household, servants and mistresses of the princes and their head servant and dame, or conveniences for their numerous soldiery, were dismissed to friends or relatives, some with money saved from wages and bounties, but the greatest part with no accumulated fortunes but their slender wardrobes and diminished chastity. Some of these females had grown old in the service of their Yedo masters, and, originally drawn from the country, had become enamored of the convenience, luxury, and ease of city life, and contemplated a return to the country with aversion. None shared in this feeling more than the wives, concubines, and daughters of

the chiefs who had always lived in the city, where every luxury of dress and food, and every variety of amusement, had stimulated their otherwise inane life. They were to be exiled to the seclusion of their provinces where they would miss the delights of town life, the dissipations of a court residence, the plays, the theaters, the singing girls, the iris gardens, the tea houses, the boat excursions, the matsuris. In Yedo, too, the skillful artisans and handicraftsmen reside; here were all the ornament of person to be found: fabrics of the best manufacture and latest design—for Japan too has its fashions and the city belle looks with disdain upon her country cousins—Kanzashi for the hair, cunningly wrought of tortoise shell and gold and silver, nowhere else such cosmetics for the skin and scented oils and pomation for the hair, such sandals for the feet or rare embroidered robes and girdles. It was worse than banishment to leave all these behind, and one after one the trains began to move out of the city with their melancholy attendants.

But there was a sudden diversion; the populace of Yedo who, and their ancestors, had lived on the court population for centuries were not so easily to be balked. Mutterings grew louder and deeper and broke into open words and threats till one day Yedo presented the unusual spectacle of a mob of the people, who attacked the City Governor's residence with stones till he was compelled to make his escape in female disguise.[37] The temper of the swarming population of Yedo was unmistakable, and suddenly an edict royal appears on the city walls and is distributed through the provinces saying that the former decree is abolished and the old system of daimio residency reestablished. The delight in Yedo is great, a day is given up for feasting and at night the streets

[37] Conrad Totman, in writing about the effects of these reforms notes: "Inevitably reforms of this magnitude hurt some people. The Edo populace was injured by a rapid loss of income stemming from the reduction in bakufu employment and the concurrent exodus of daimyo families. By late 62/int. 8, a reported forty thousand Edo residents had been thrown out of menial attendant jobs, and poorhouses were set up to aid their families. This development came at a time when daily living costs were gradually escalating, with costs of daily

necessities for Edo consumers having nearly doubled from average levels of recent years. In response to the worsening situation discontent grew. Rumors began to circulate that some among those who had lost jobs as servants, merchants, artisans, foot soldiers, and day laborers were planning to assemble in the Marunouchi district adjacent to the castle to protest their hardship" (*The Collapse of the Tokugawa Bakufu*, pp. 22–23). Totman does not mention any actual riots, nor does he mention the temporary issuing of contrary decrees.

are illuminated and processions fill the streets intoxicated with sake and joy in equal proportions. Now again there are some Japanese shrewd enough to believe that since the Government had in the first instance been forced into a measure against its will, it was the secret promoters of disturbances among the people in order to rehabilitate the ancient order of affairs.

It is only a few days ago that an order was issued to construct a new Tokaido several miles distant and parallel to the present one, so that the daimios could avoid meeting foreigners in their goings to and fro between their provinces and Yedo. Of a sudden this order is rescinded because, as is said, and doubtless truly said, the daimios regarded the removal out of the way of the foreigners a disgraceful concession.

It has been settled that the Tycoon goes to Miako to pay his respects to the Mikado in the 2nd month of the Japanese New Year, and a decree has been issued that the usual repairs made to the roads and bridges when royalty goes forth need not be made except where there is positive danger from bad roads and bridges. The inns are not to be refitted as usual with new mats, but on the contrary the Tycoon is to stop only at the Honjins, the imperial resting places or inns in all large towns, or at the temples, and at these places no new furniture is to be provided. It is well surmised that the far departure from ancient custom, and from even a show of decent respect, is an indignity put upon the reigning Tycoon by the hostile faction who have in a measure usurped control. Let us hope, however, that these changes, the new sumptuary regulations, the attempts to break up this horde of idle soldiery at Yedo, this avoidance of charge upon the people while the royal cortege is moving, spring from a sincere desire for reform and to remove all burdens from the people at large.

Wednesday, December 3, 1862

For some days past the daimios and their families have been again moving away from Yedo, for it appears that the suspension of their hegira before was only temporary. We hear, however, little said of the refractory people who apparently acquiesce in this movement which must strip Yedo of so much of its population.

The Tycoon sets an example to his subjects in dress reform by wearing himself only cotton garments. These dress reforms have at various times obtained in this empire. About 30 years ago rigid sumptuary laws were enacted and as rigidly enforced by the then prime minister who made himself famous by an imperial order as to the length of the loin cloth, and shortening it to such an extent that it no longer became of use and gave rise to the use of his name as a practical synonym for stinginess that recoiled on itself.[38]

From Miako we again hear extraordinary rumors. Shimadzu Saburo, the intriguing ambitious chief, father of the Prince of Satsuma, the murderer of Richardson, has been slain by assassins. He had lately received promotion, but his ambition was not satisfied, and those to whom his ambition was becoming obnoxious are said to be his slayers. But strangest of all is the reported disappearance of the Mikado. It is said that since the night of a great conflagration which laid many streets in ruins, he has disappeared and hints are not wanting that he too has been slain. Young Ee [Ii] Kamon-no-kami seems to inherit all the vigor of his murdered father, the late regent, and to be a strong adherent to the fortunes of the Tycoon at Yedo against the powers that rule in Miako. His name is therefore coupled with this event almost, and for modern years, at least since the accession of Tyco [Taiko] Sama, quite unexampled in the annals of the empire. He it was, too, who, hearing that Stotsbashi of Mito's kin was to come in great state to visit Miako, openly declared that he should attack him on

[38] The reference here is to Mizuno Tadakuni in the Tempo Reforms of the early 1840s. A part of Mizuno's reform plan was to push austerities, including a wide variety of sumptuary laws that strictly controlled dress and other forms of consumption.

the road, so that Stotsbashi is fair to go by water. The intrigues of Japanese politics are really quite incomprehensible.

A wreck on the coast and Consul Fisher has gone up to look after it.

Yedo two nights ago was swept by another fire, thirty streets are said to have suffered. The fire was in a quarter which had had, according to Japanese ideas, a long exemption from such a calamity, a fortunate locality having escaped ten or twelve years.

Tuesday, December 9, 1862

Rode with Dr. S[immons] to Kanagawa. Met one of Nippon's tenderly bred daughters walking the road with a stout comely woman who may have been mother, aunt, or governess. The girl's delicate indoor breeding was clearly manifest from her air. She was highly dressed, the long sleeves of her robe nearly scraping the ground. Her under garments were white. Her hair elaborately ornamented and spread out, the face highly rouged and whitened. As we rode by she hid her face, shrinking amid the folds of her attendant's garment. Her age was fourteen to sixteen.

Wednesday, December 10, 1862

A beautiful day. Rode with Dr. S[immons] to Mississippi Bay along the beach, through the gap into the valley, and again through another gap into the Hodoriya road. Paths everywhere in use to dry the recently gathered rice.

Thursday, December 11, 1862

St. Louis arrived.[39]

Friday, December 12, 1862

Today the Tycoon is said to pass down the bay in his newly purchased steamer *Jinkee* to Uraga, a distance of thirty miles or so. While his royalty is passing, no Japanese boats of any kind are allowed to be on the water, every fishing boat is withdrawn, no matter to what hindrance to the daily supply of this staple of food to the dwellers on the bay.

Saturday, December 13, 1862

The Tycoon did not pass down the bay yesterday, as arranged, owing to the foul weather, and today the breeze blows up so freshly that I do not think his majesty will encounter the head sea and its disagreeable train of consequences to his physique, which even royalty doth not hedge in from mortal ills.

Wednesday, December 17, 1862

Yesterday and today we have rumors again of danger threatened to the settlement. Yesterday the Governor of Yokohama communicated to the English and French Ministers that a plot had been discovered to burn the foreign town, in which 150 conspirators were said to be engaged. He, the Governor, could not say how true or false the rumors might be, and it appears that the only foundation for his alarm was that three weeks ago a paper was found one morning pasted to the Custom House gates which threatened destruction to the foreign town at the end of 20 days! Who put this incendiary notice there nobody knows. We have had several such false rumors circulated by the Japanese authorities before, and many, like myself, pay no regard to them; but the authorities wishing to be on the safe side landed men from the English and French men-of-war, the gun boat *Kestrel* was moved [as] close to the shore as possible and filled with marines from the *Centaur*, and a mounted patrol of English

[39] Hall was apparently involved in the sale of the *St. Louis* to the daimyo of Tokushima (Awa). As we will see, the "men of Awa" came to pay for the vessel on December 24.

and French were on duty in the streets during last night. Today the Governor reiterates his cautions to the foreigners—and the *Jinkee* came down from Yedo filled with Japanese soldiers—and some weak nerved foreigners grow timorous. Pistols are belted on again, and we have quite a return to the old days of 1860.

Thursday, December 18, 1862

The visible signs of danger do not increase, but the alarm manufacturers are busier than ever. An armed patrol again tonight; the Japanese land about two hundred soldiers armed and equipped in foreign fashion from the *Jinkee*; one of our English fellow citizens issued a circular "that a detachment of the Yokohama volunteers will be on guard at his house tonight," and invites "all citizens and families who desire protection" to make use of his house. The Americans seem less visibly affected than their fellow citizens of other nations, and indeed the whole affair seems a most ludicrous farce. The utter absurdity of 150 men, whom no man has seen in the flesh, attacking this settlement, which would be defended by more than twice that number of foreigners used to arms, to say nothing of the government forces, is too apparent.

Friday, December 19, 1862

The same vague rumors as yesterday, but no definiteness is yet given to them.

Saturday, December 20, 1862

The excitement about *ronins* has measurably subsided, the grand total result being a few frightened, but nobody hurt.

Sunday, December 21, 1862

We hear today of increased disturbances at Miako; the arming of troops hostile to the government. The envoy from the Mikado who passed up to Yedo a few days since is reported to have made fresh demands of abdication of his power from the Tycoon. The ladies of the Prince's of Satsuma's household today passed up *to* Yedo, when other princes' ladies are coming away. So what again does all the rumor mean? (Error they passed down.)

Tuesday, December 23, 1862

Attended last evening for the first time a Japanese wedding. The bridegroom was our faithful servant Tokoo [Toku], and the bride, the daughter of a well to do merchant.

Wednesday, December 24, 1862

The Prince of Awa's men are at the office today paying for the *St. Louis*. After this vessel was sold to them they hired some of the officers and sailors to remain with the vessel, first having stipulated that they should read no Bibles aboard, intending evidently to forbid any acts of worship.

Thursday, December 25, 1862

Christmas day. My thoughts are homeward. In the evening dined with Consul Fisher at Kanagawa and sat down to a Christmas feast prepared in home-like style.

1863

Thursday, January 1, 1863

A soft mild day. Dispatched the *Emily Banning* for San Francisco and the *Ida* for Hakodade, and in the afternoon made a few New Year's calls. Towards evening the wind blew up cold from the north and [I] had a rough passage across the bay.

Saturday, January 3, 1863

We have had last night the old menace of ronins revived. At midnight last night the French and English Ministers were aroused by a deputation consisting of two of the Governors of Foreign Affairs from Yedo and their train of attendants with the Governor of Yokohama who said they had come to apprise them that they were in danger from the attacks of ronins. That the Government was well informed that the neighborhood of the Tokaido was infested by various small parties of these men who were bent upon the assassination of any foreigners whom they might meet, but particularly foreign officials. They had therefore come to caution them. The American Minister was spending the holiday at the Consul's at Kanagawa, they gave the same information to him, and particularly desired that he would not return to Yedo by way of the Tokaido on account of this danger, but that he would accept the offer of the steamer *Jinkee* which they would place at his disposal. Thus we have again with added particulars the so oft repeated cry of "ronins, ronins." It is fair perhaps to suppose that the Japanese Government themselves believe in the probability of such outlaws being about, although it looks quite as much as a practiced deception to convince the foreigners amid what dangers they live; how they had better remain safely at home; and what good friends the Government is in thus warning them.

The effect on the foreign community is according to nationality. The Dutch are decidedly timorous and full of absurd rumors, the French suspicious but inclined to be defiant, the English disturbed and apprehensive and practicing a caution that smacks of fear, some of their merchants shipping their treasure to the vessels; the American laughing at the alarm and incredulous of any real danger, showing not a little of his native recklessness, it may be time he says, but don't lets worry over it. A mounted patrol is detailed to watch the settlements at night.

[On January 3, 1863, Hall wrote the following letter to the *New York Tribune*, which was published on March 20, 1863.]

Just as the mail is closing for San Francisco by the Timandra we have rumors of one of those threatened dangers with which the young settlement has been so often menaced. There have been, indeed, floating rumors for some days past of bands of *ronins*, or armed outlaws, who were determined upon mischief toward the foreign residents. Once or twice the past month an armed force has been landed from the foreign shipping, and the British gunboat Kestrel has been moored within a cable's length of the shore. A foreign mounted patrol for several nights did guard duty in the streets. But these three rumors were gradually lost sight of until the present moment, when they have been revived with an increased importance given to them by the Japanese authorities.

It seems that late last night or early this morning all the foreign Ministers, who are spending the holidays at Kanagawa and Yokohama, were waited upon by a deputation of two Governors for Foreign Affairs, who had come down from Yedo expressly for the purpose, to apprise them of threatened danger to their persons. The American Minister, who was staying with the Consul at Kanagawa, was disturbed at 4 a.m. by this deputation, who came to apprise him that they had good assurance that bands of lawless men were watching in the vicinity of the *Tokaido* to do mischief upon any foreigners who should pass along that thoroughfare, and that they believed this danger was particularly imminent to foreign officials. They especially desired that he would not attempt to return to Yedo by the Tokaido, as he had contemplated doing two [or] three days hence, but that they would send a steamer down for him. They said they were not able to lay their hands upon the *ronins*, but they had good assurance that they were about.

To these rumors are added many others, which have less foundation, of an attack upon the settlement generally. Some Japanese servants, whose friends reside at Yedo, are said to have been warned to leave foreign employ and to give their masters warning also of the danger.

We have had so often such a "wolf! wolf!" cry that many are wholly incredulous of any danger, while others are sufficiently alarmed to remove their treasure on board the shipping. Your correspondent is inclined to the belief that although the Japanese authorities are sincere in their apprehensions, this is but a repetition of the menaces which have so often been made, to produce disquiet when no real intention exists of carrying them into execution. The *ronin* is half a hero among the Japanese—a sort of Sherwood Forest outlaw, ubiquitous and invincible.

However, these rumors will not be treated with entire neglect, but every precaution of guard and patrol taken to secure against surprise for a day and a night or two, till they pass away.

Sunday, January 4, 1863

The French residents are cautioned, by an official notice, how they go beyond the bounds of the settlement. The English Consul also issues a cautionary circular to the English residents. The extreme beauty of the weather makes me heedless of ronins and Dr. S[immons] and myself take a ride over to Kanagawa and up the "ronin haunted Tokaido," but meet naught but peaceful citizens and quiet travellers.

Monday, January 5, 1863

A few evenings since I had the opportunity for the first time since I have resided in Japan of seeing a Japanese wedding. The groom was Tokoo [Toku], the faithful upper native servant in our counting room. To tell the whole story as it occurred will best illustrate a Japanese courtship and marriage.

A well-to-do merchant in town, whose business is the hiring out of mattresses and sleeping robes to people who have transient guests, has a daughter of 15 years old whom he desires to see well married. The girl has been carefully brought up in seclusion within doors and has now arrived at an age when the prudent parents desire to see her well married. Tokoo's friends hear of this eligible match and think it his fortunate opportunity. Tokoo, who hears of the beauty and fair face of the damsel, and of the wealth and good standing of her father's family, is not averse to entertain the matter. Tokoo has no father living to whom would properly belong any negotiations about the match, so according to custom one Machinoski, a friend, acts in loco parentis and advises him; for it is Machinoski who has recommended the girl to him in the first instance.

Now the next step is that the young people must see each other without both knowing why they are brought together. This is simply managed. The girl's father not only hires out bedding but in the front of his home has a small room which he makes a shop for the sale of various small articles such as pens, pencils, and ink, writing stones, hair and head ornaments, and various small articles of personal use. The females of the house attend the shop. So one day the dear Machinoski arranges it that all the older people shall be away from home and leave the young girl to be shopkeeper; then Tokoo is to visit the shop as if to purchase some trifle, and so the young couple are first to be brought together. Tokoo goes to the shop as arranged, and the young girl, unconscious of the plot laid to show her charms, waits upon him. Tokoo lays down the money for the trifle purchased with unwonted delight and hastens back to tell Machinoski how much he is pleased.

Machinoski now informs the parents, who in turn are first made acquainted with the young man with whom they profess themselves satisfied for a husband to their daughter. And now the damsel is asked whether she remembers the young man who came and bought the trifles at her shop. Well she remembers him, and a fine young fellow he was, and she is willing to marry him. Tokoo's grandfather is now sent for, who lives in the country, and the preliminaries are to be formally settled. A *chooning* [chūnin], or go-between, is chosen by the young man to confer with the parents of the girl respecting marriage portion, dowry, etc., for in all the negotiations those most interested are kept in the background, and the interview that the young couple have had will be all they will see of each other till the wedding day—a luck day in the calendar is chosen for these negotiations.

The parents of the girl are well off and inform the *chooning* that they wish no marriage portion for their daughter, on the contrary, they will bestow favors on the husband. He is to marry in and the daughter is not to marry out; they receive a son and do not lose a daughter. So it is arranged that Tokoo is to bring nothing, but has the promise that before long he shall be installed into the lucrative business of the bride's parents who will retire into the country. The Japanese have these matrimonial distinctions. The parents of the girl, or boy, may seek the alliance. If the girl's parents have the best standing by wealth or position, the young man is married into the bride's family, such was the case in this instance. The custom obtains only with the first daughter married usually; the second daughter should be married off.

This preliminary being arranged that Tokoo was to be received into the bride's family, presents from the bride followed of sake, sea weed, and fish. Had Tokoo received the bride into his family the presents would have been from his parents and himself to the bride. The sake was brought in two new clean fir tubs, and the seaweed and fish which are given emblematically, were wrapped in white papers tied with white and red cords and laid upon little fir tables of unpainted wood. In another paper, and on another table of the same material, is a present of money, ostensibly to buy the bridegroom's wedding garments, but the sum may be large or small in proportion to the wealth of the giver. In such cases if the husband is to receive the bride instead of being given to her, he sends her "money to buy a girdle," which is in fact the dowry he pays the parents for their child. These presents are accompanied with messages of good will. Tokoo's presents, having been received, and this passing of presents constitutes the betrothal, his go-between asks the bride's parents to name the wedding day. A lucky day is chosen when the marriage shall be consummated.

It was at this point that I became personally a witness of what followed. On the wedding day I was asked to witness the ceremony. About 6 in the evening we went to Machinoski's house where we found a small company of men assembled. Tokoo and his *chooning* had just arrived. There were present here mainly the groom's friends and one or two of the bride's.

In one room were placed the betrothal gifts Tokoo had received from his affianced and with them were the presents he was to make in return. The presents were emblematical rather than valuable. There were curious straw ornaments decked with fish roes, emblem of fecundity. There was sea weed and dried cuttle, similarly trussed with straw and adorned with fancy paper and tied with the red and white knots. There was the little fir table with the "girdle money" neatly wrapped in white paper, and there was the chest of drawers, an always indispensable gift to the bride. The male friends assembled in this room around the sides, the bridegroom and his friend Machinoski sitting at the head of the room. Before each was placed a tray, and after the guests had exchanged the most formal salutations with each other, bowing repeatedly to the mats, and the groom had been as formally introduced, and congratulations interchanged, a feast was set before them dish by dish of a great variety of articles both fish and vegetables.

This ceremony occupied some time and it was nine o'clock before the company were ready to go to the bride's house. It was her duty to have come here for a brief visit, before returning to her own house, to finish the ceremony, but the girl being young and very modest about it, this part of the ceremony was waved. A list of all the presents that were to be taken to the bride was made out on a large sheet of paper, the presents themselves carried out into the street before the house and placed in new barrows of clean fir wood.

The procession was formed, servants going before with the gifts, followed by the bridegroom walking in company with his mediator, and they in turn by the remainder of the guests, each bearing lanterns, and brought up in the rear by two servants each bearing on a pole over his shoulder a lackered box in which was the wardrobe of the intended husband.

We wound through the narrow street which were illuminated by our multitude of lanterns and crossed quite over the town to the house of the bride's parents. Here the bridegroom and his friend were met with cordial welcome and ushered into the well lighted house which appeared to be newly matted and fitted up for the occasion. The bridegroom was at once ushered into a side room to meet his bride who awaited him, and this was the second time he had ever seen her face. The room in which he thus meets her surrounded by her friends, her mediator, her single sister and mother, is a little apartment off from the main room of the house which is to be their room in the house after the ceremony.

In the main room the guests assemble and are dispersed about the side of the room, Machinoski taking the head of the room, on the right is the bridegroom's grandfather, next sits the male go-between, opposite to Machinoski is the father of the bride, and on his left are vacant places. Tokoo first comes in and sits down on the left of Machinoski, the bride follows him, coming in modest and blushing, attended by her female friend or go-between and sits beside her future lord. She sits with downcast eyes politely raising them now and then to look at the company and the strange guests with foreign clothes and faces. Her features and expressions are very good and we all inwardly congratulate Tokoo on his apparent good fortune. Her dress is simple and well arranged, the outer robe is ash color, wrought in the skirt with vine and flowers, and gathered about the waist with the heavy folds of her silken girdle which falls in a large square knot behind, this dress is trimmed with red crape and lined with white, and as she sits down its heavy folds are turned carefully outward by her go-between to show the white lining and the borders of other underdresses. The folds of her dress are gathered similarly across her bosom so that the turned over edge of each under garment, the last one of pure white, may be seen, one gradually lapping over the other till her bosom is hidden to her throat. Her rich dark hair is plainly dressed, combed back from the face, and gathered in the usual puff on the top of the back head, where a single gilt comb and hair pin is discernible.

The ceremony begins by Machinoski formally introducing the bridegroom to his future father-in-law who drink together. Then the cup is filled again by the go-between and handed to the bridegroom who hands it to the bride and she touches her lips to it. This sake is brought in a small tea pot of peculiar shape with a silvered spout and to the handle a rosette is tied with the white and red cords, in which rosette is a strip of dried fish. Next the bride's mother is introduced to the young groom, who drink sake together, and afterwards various female relatives are introduced, and at each introduction there is a mutual pledging in the sake cup. Two children, a younger brother and sister, are as formally introduced and this part of the ceremony ends.

The bridegroom now, in presence of the company, slips off his kamisimo, and the bride retires to the adjoining room and changes her dress. She reappears in a plain brown robe, and the gilt comb is exchanged for a black one. She takes her seat by her future husband and the feast is served. This consists again of the simple vegetables and fish food, though some of the dishes are elaborately prepared and made ornamental. One dish in particular attracted our attention. In a large round platter was a miniature pine, and on its green burrs a snow made of grated radish had fallen, a pair of white storks, emblem of longevity, rested in the branches and had their nest there on which the eggs were seen. The stork is typical with the Japanese of longevity and the birds nest in the branches had its readily understood significance. Under the tree were vegetables carved into various similitudes. The dish was helped out to all present and followed by other dishes till every guest's tray was loaded. Bountiful libations of sake were poured out, and everybody drank everybody else's health.

Under the rice wine's stimulus the party grew jolly and the poor bridegroom drank and drank till I feared for his head and heels. The nice little bride barely wetted her lips on each occasion, but by degrees her maidenly reserve thawed out and she smiled happily as brides can smile. It was a pity that we could not understand all the merry jokes that were flying about but some of them were as broad as wedding jokes in rural places are wont to be. After a little while we were invited into the room with the wedding party and the honorable seat on the right of the protempore father, Machinoski, was assigned to me in close proximity to the bride. I might not salute her with a wedding kiss, as her light pouting lips certainly tempted me to, but I could ask her to pledge her happiness in a cup of sake. The go-between filled the flat open cup, which I drained,

and then carefully balancing it on the tip of my fingers, after the custom, bowed my head over it and offered it to the bride. She received it with a modest little "heh"!, the Japanese monosyllable of assent, bowed in turn as the cup was filled for her and wet only her dainty lips, coyly smiling the while. I again drank with the bridegroom, and then addressing myself first to the bride thanked her for receiving my "boy" for her husband and wished them both long life and happiness.

Then I had to drink with the male and female friends further, grandfather, mistress, aunts, and go-betweens, till the fumes of the hot sake made me as exhilarated as the rest of them. The black toothed ladies were especially merry, one of whom I had long known as the landlady of the "Simoda House" in Kanagawa, and who had come in as a helping friend. Another was saluted by all the guests as Tonari o-kamisan, that is "the lady from the next door;" she was a particularly jolly party, and every time she was challenged to drink took full bumpers without flinching. She has evidently a strong head, and was greatly "cheered," but not inebriated. She gave us all urgent invitations to call upon her next day, and impatient of even that delay, lighted a lantern and insisted upon my going to the theater with her just over the way, although it was already near midnight. With some difficulty I evaded her invitations by promising to attend the next night; whereupon she turned upon M.,[1] who had grown more facile with sake, and off they started together but were brought back by some of the rest of the party.

The bride again retired and this time reappeared in a plain rich dark robe which heightened her dark beauty more than before. It was already midnight, and soon, as we were told, the ceremony proper would begin. A screen would be brought into the room and all the company shut off, leaving the bride and bridegroom behind the screen with the female go-between, when would commence the ceremonious sake drinking described as the vital fact of a wedding ceremony in these preceding

---

[1] This would appear to have been W. H. Morse, who was an employee of Walsh, Hall & Co. See *The Chronicle*

and Directory for China, Japan, and the Philippines for 1866 (Hong Kong: Daily Press, 1866), p. 237.

pages. We waited sometime longer, but saw no signs of this ceremony beginning, and fearing lest our presence might prove some restraint, we proposed to go. It was one A.M., when we left the house amid the profuse bowings, gratulations, and hearty adieus of the guests taking especial leave of the blooming bride whose beauty like the night blooming crocus grew with the midnight hours.

We learned the next day that after our departure the formal ceremony of sake drinking was omitted still, but that after a little renewed feasting and drinking the bride again disappeared with the groom to the adjoining apartment where each laid off their wedding garments and put on their night attire and came back into the guest's room. A lady's night robe is a long loose garment flowing to the heels with loose bag sleeves, the garment gathered about the waist with a silken girdle. This night robe among ladies of rank or fortune is made of dark soft silks in crape, sometimes of a mixed fabric of silk and cotton, but more commonly of cotton only. While they were in the guest's room, the female friends spread their couch in the adjoining apartment, mattresses of cotton covered with silk, and thickly wadded silk comfortables. A wooden pillow was placed for each, and between the mattresses, for each has his or her mattress, is placed a roll of soft paper napkins. These dispositions for the night having been effected, the bedroom is cleared and the female go-between now enters the guest room, and giving a hand to each, husband and wife, leads them to their couch herself and spreading the covering over them, when they are left to their marital repose.

We heard of the party next day that she was gay and cheerful as any bride, but Tokoo's wedding dissipation had been too much for him, he sent up to the office begging to be excused from work that day.

After the wedding follow the interchange of visits, making of presents, and other ceremonies already described in these pages.

Wednesday, January 14, 1863

The fine soft air of this winter day tempted me to a horseback ride. Mr. Hogg accompanied me.[2] We took the pleasant country road that lead through the valley and over the hill to Totsooka [Totsuka]. Mr. H[ogg] was delighted with the rural scenery and it was truly pleasant to ride through the sunny valley among the palms, bamboos, and pines which the winter's cold had spared. We came into the Tokaido just as a scattered train was passing along, the Prince of Bizen's family returning to the country from Yedo. Numerous norimons bearing the females of his household passed by, all attended by two sworded retainers. The ladies, some of them, had got out of their norimons and were walking, but few of them were young, and none of them handsome, though we did not see the lady princess herself, or her immediate personal attendants. As we rode into Hodoriya we found the streets quite blocked up with people about the inns and with difficulty made our passage. A portion of the train were halting for rest and refreshment and the norimons, bearers, and attendants filled the street in front.

We made our way slowly through the throng, but just beyond Hodoriya again encountered another portion of the train who were accompanying a large norimon: there were swordsmen, spearmen, and bowmen. We met them at one of the official houses where coolies and horses are furnished, and the street was so blocked that there was no way left for us to turn to one side and pass by the train, the headmen of which began to gesture to us to keep back, and the people crying to us to stop and to leave the road, or go behind the houses, anticipating the probability of some danger to us from the haughty menials who were escorting the lady of the Prince of Bizen. We succeeded, however, at last in finding room to rein our horses up under the projecting roof of a house and waited for the train to come on, and not certain what affront they might put upon us. The soldiers in advance passed slowly by, and then the norimon with

[2] Thomas Hogg was the U.S. marshal in the Kanagawa consulate. See *The China Directory for 1863* (Hong Kong: Shortrede & Co., 1863), p. 55.

its numerous retinue, but no insult of look or gesture was offered us. We breathed freer as they all passed by, the tragedy of Richardson's death being yet fresh in our memories. For three miles we had passed through this straggling train.

Wednesday, January 28, 1863

Today and yesterday daimio trains have been passing along the road and foreigners are warned by the Governor not to be on the Tokaido for fear of harm from stragglers of these trains. The English Consul advises his countrymen in an official circular not to go outside of Yokohama for a week. The process of intimidation, whether well or ill founded, is making slow but certain progress, and we are soon likely to be hemmed in to the little promontory that lies between the Yokohama and Mississippi bays.

Thursday, January 29, 1863

The Japanese ambassadors to Europe return in a French vessel today at noon.

[On February 3, 1863, Hall wrote the following letter to the *New York Tribune*, which was published May 21, 1863.]

Under my last date a month ago I wrote of the many threats against the foreign settlements in Japan, threats to which some importance was attached because of the notice taken of them by the Government itself. But the month has gone by, and though abundantly fruitful of rumors, has brought no real dangers. Still the Government does not cease to warn the Foreign Ministers and Consuls to enjoin upon their subjects great circumspection and care as to going out upon the public highways, particularly since the flight of the Daimios from Yedo, which was temporarily arrested has been resumed. Almost daily the Tokaido is occupied by the long trains of retainers and menials escorting the families and effects of princes, or perhaps the distinguished chiefs themselves, on their way back to their patrimonial estates, which now for two centuries and more have been deserted for life at the Court. The story of the flight of the Princes is worthy the graphic pen which told so well the "Flight of a Tabar Tribe." The breaking up of so many households, the dismantling and desertion of palaces on so extensive a scale, the exodus of nearly a quarter of a million of people from a single city, at whose gates no impatient foe was knocking, is of itself a grand epoch of history. This movement, effected in a time of peace, and done so quietly withal, is one of the remarkable events in the history of nations.

In a ride on the Tokaido, a few days ago, I thus encountered the Prince of Bizen's family on their way to their country estates. The ladies of his household (the Prince himself not being with them) occupied nearly fifty norimons, and were attended by an armed escort and an unarmed train of baggagebearers and attendants who occupied the road, in scattered groups, for more than three miles. Several of the ladies had dismounted, and were walking, who, if they were representative women of the Prince of Bizen's household, vouched for neither its youth nor beauty. Through the open window of one norimon a young lady was visible leaning forward, with her head resting on cushions of silk, fast asleep. In other norimons were little comforts for the road—a shelf of books, a few flowers in a wicker-basket, a canary in a cage, or the young lady's lute, to beguile for the occupant the tedious time of travel.

Among other dignitaries who have thus recently passed by was the Prince of Owari of the blood royal, whose retinue was to be counted by thousands. Also the Mikado's Envoy on his way home from his mission to the court of Yedo, when the Tokaido was strictly closed to all foreigners and sentinels and interpreters posted to insure that the road was kept free for his Excellency to pass. A few days since the Governor of Yokohama issued a circular to all the foreign Consuls, of which the following is a copy:

"As some of the great Daimios are now passing along the Tokadio, which will be the cause of great confusion on the road, and as there are, besides, reports in circulation that some barbarians are walking round, and for all I know, may now be in Yokohama, it is desirable that your countrymen should not go out of Yokohama during one week, from to-day, until you receive another communication from me."

Then follows the request that the Consul will communicate this information to his superior in office and to his countrymen. A deputation of Governors also came down from Yedo to desire the English and French Ministers not to visit that city for the present, as they did not deem it safe. The Government evidently does not feel well assured of its ability to control its own lawless citizens, nor place much confidence in their regard for the lives or property of the foreigners on these shores. No overt acts against the persons of foreigners have followed these intimations or threats of possible violence, but on Sunday morning last the buildings newly erected for the English Legation at Yedo were destroyed, being blown up with powder and consumed. These buildings had first been completed by the Japanese Government, at a cost of $25,000, but were yet unoccupied. The French Legation buildings were partially blown up. These buildings were on the elevated site selected a year ago for the residence of all the foreign Legations, but buildings had as yet been erected for only the two Legations named. The selections of this site for such a purpose, as I took occasion to state in your columns at the time, was greatly impolitic and especially offensive to the feelings and prejudices of the Japanese. The hill of Goten-Yama, as it is called, had been for many generations the pleasure-ground of the people. It is in the Sinagawa suburb, in immediate proximity to the numerous inns, tea-houses, and houses of less reputable character, where all the fast youth and dissolute soldiery of Yedo resort for riot and drunkenness. Its vicinage was the worst possible that could have been chosen in all Yedo. Moreover,

the Tokaido over which so many Daimios and dignitaries must pass in going in or out of the city runs by its foot; an overlooking of them sufficiently repulsive to their ideas of etiquette. All these causes combined rendered this hill most ineligible for the proposed purpose. But obstinate ministerial will had its way, and the offended Japanese made no secret of their vow "that foreigners should never occupy that hill." How well that vow has been kept thus far the incendiarism of Sunday morning tells. A few days before the destruction of these buildings the Japanese gate-keepers to the grounds had been slain for refusing admission to a small party of soldiers who had come up full of wine from the hen-houses below.

A large number of Government officials have recently been disgraced and deprived wholly or in part of their revenues. Their crime was malversation of office, and the greatest offender of all, Ando Tsu Sima-no-kami, the able Prime Minister a year ago, has likewise been disgraced, confined a close prisoner to his house, and mulcted in heavy sums of money. One of his associates in the Imperial Council of Five shares his fate.

The Yedo Government is evidently uneasy at the activity of the Miaco faction, who are thrusting forward their pretensions under the guise of devotion to the Mikado, and the Tycoon is not going to trust his person on a pilgrimage to that spiritual functionary without due precaution. In his precautions he has shown a shrewd cunning. The past fortnight rumor has obtained extensive credence among the Japanese that several French war steamers had visited the port of Oasaca, which is very near to Miaco, and were attempting to land in force. This ruse on the part of the Tycoon's officers, for it is doubtless nothing else, served well to give them excuse for sending a considerable force of Imperial troops in the vicinity of Miaco and Oasaca, where, if they were not wanted to resist any Frenchmen, they would be ready to overawe any attempt at an insurrectionary movement on the part of the discontented

Princes, who are rallying about the shadow of the Mikado's supreme power in the realm. It is rumored that the English Charge d'Affaires has been asked if, in the event of an open rupture between the Mikado and the Tycoon, the latter could have the moral field and Armstrong suasion of his Government.

We have the first tokens of opening Spring in the blooming camellias and apricots, while the dandelions and violets are waking to life under the many banks. My "Spring peas," sown last November daily though slowly grow in green and stature with the aid of a little night blanketing— proof of the mildness of our Winters. With Summers neither too hot nor Winters too cold, surely Japan enjoys the golden mean of climates.

Sunday, February 15, 1863

Today and yesterday the streets are lively with preparations for the New Year holiday which begins on the 18th. The work of trimming the house and shop fronts goes busily on, and already the streets look like long avenues of pine and bamboo. All the shopkeepers are occupied with the New Year's patronage, and every household is busy making ready gifts for distribution. A tailor can no longer be procured, every one is already full of work on the dresses that are to be given on New Year's day. The shoe stores are largely patronized, and at many doorways I see the little folks proud with their new shoes which they are ostentatiously exhibiting. At the book stalls games and amusements are temptingly displayed to the proud parents who cluster there in search of gifts for the children at home. The toy shops are crammed to overflowing with new wares and their shelves are brilliant with the party dressed, big headed dolls that stare at you from the walls. The pastry cooks put on an extra force of hands. The fish sellers reap a silver harvest, and at every turn you meet the stout porters or slip-shod serving girls bearing a tray of fish stuck round with evergreen pine or ferns which they are carrying from one friend to another. In every street are several shops busy making the New Year's mochi, or rice cake, which is indispensable in every household, and is moulded in every fantastic shape. The kite shops are a blaze of bright colors, and hideous faces and shapes of man, beast, bird, and reptile, done in vermillion paper and light bamboo, are ready to be let aloft every fair day for the next two months. Little misses in new dresses and girdles and faces overspread with white and dashed with vermillion are inspecting the quaint battledores decorated with heads and busts done in crape with a view to purchase. New lanterns are suspended from the doorways and eaves, from the silk shops and clothiers parents are hurrying home with the New Year's suit which is indispensable to every man, woman, and child, who can raise money to buy it for New Year. The young maiden hopes for a new girdle and the gay kanzashi from parents, lover, or friends. Everyone is liberal, everyone hospitable on New Year's day, no one need be hungry or naked. The ladies and servants of the households are busy tying up in white paper with red and white silvered twines and rosettes little gifts of fan, a pair of chop sticks, cakes, or articles of more value which will be distributed by the house servant on the New Year's day. That these trifles are not always so graciously received, I had occasion to witness today in the house of a wealthy merchant. A servant had brought in a showy looking parcel, a return gift for some present the lady of the house had made, which she opened and found a little brown sugar, a half pound perhaps, inside. "A thank you would have been as well," she quietly remarked as she laid the parcel down again.

Monday, February 16, 1863

The preparations for New Year's go vigorously on. All day the shops are crowded and the present bearers go about the streets. In the evening as late as eleven o'clock I went up into the Japanese town to witness what was going on. I found the retail shops still open and busy, the shoe shops, drygoods bazaars, confectioners and all. The shop fronts were emblazoned with great paper lanterns and the busy people were still coming and going. Wares were brought out of the godowns and temptingly displayed on the floors and mats. Bookkeepers were up to their eyes behind great account books settling the year's business. About one third of the shops were thus open and the light and noises streaming through the chinks of the shutters of such as were closed, and the clink of money, showed that life was active in all, and the old year's business coming to its final wind up. Households everywhere are up watching the old year out and the new year in, for says the proverb, "He who goes early to bed will come early to years"—a saw for New Year's only.

Tuesday, February 17, 1863

Japanese New Year's. Every shop, office, and place of business is closed today. Those who went late to bed are late risers this morning. But young Japan, each in his or her holiday suit, is out looking fresh and bright as this young year. The boys are kite flying and the girls battledore playing, a few with discreet obasans are going out to make calls. Everyone, child and man, that can afford it are in their new holiday suits. In every house the (———) [blank in original] or new year refreshment trays, are waiting the calls of friends, and libations of sweet toso are prepared for all comers out of the funny little teapots. I made a few calls towards evening and was well received, entertained with refreshments and the cordial like toso. One enterpriser was humorously drunk and protesting that of all the pleasures of life there was none like making money. Others might have their wine and their women, but "give me the dollar," he said with maudlin laughing, burying both hands in his pockets where the dollars were supposed to be. At Kaiya's new mansion his wife received us with great hospitality amid some lady friends she was just entertaining. Sweet beans, chestnuts, and other fruits, boiled and dressed with soy, were offered us. Some nice cuttle fish just received as a New Year's gift from an Yedo friend were broiled over the coals, while cakes, oranges, and toso supplied the dessert. With commendable pride she showed us all through her new house, and she had reason to be proud of it. Nothing could look fresher or neater than her large mansion. In several rooms were found guests, customers of her husband, merchants from the interior who as the custom goes when in town stop with the factor of their wares. The best part of the house was fitted up to entertain official guests. The little courts into which the rooms opened were adorned with trees and shrubs of quaint form trained by the gardener's hand.

Wednesday, February 18, 1863

Today business is still suspended and this is the principal visiting day and day for making little presents among the business people as yesterday was among officials and people of leisure. A strong breeze favors the kite flying and the air is gay with pictures of man, bird, and beast. The air hums as with the noise of twenty clover fields of bumble bees. The streets are picturesque with the pretty maids playing battledore and other simple games by the street side.

Thursday, February 19, 1863

The 3rd of the New Year's holidays and kept much like the preceding. During these three days all business is at rest.

Monday, February 23, 1863

Commenced building. It is not until today that business has been partly resumed. I have signalized it by the commencement of our new godowns and offices.

Saturday, February 28, 1863

We had sometime since rumors that a letter was in existence from the Mikado to the Tycoon in which the former orders the latter as "general of his forces," to abrogate all treaties with the foreigners and to expel them from the country. The veritable existence of such a

A view of the Yokohama Bund showing the Western merchant compounds. This photograph shows the kind of godowns Hall commenced building for Walsh, Hall & Co. Photograph by Felice Beato.

letter has been much doubted but our Minister at Yedo, having procured the document in question, submitted it to the Goroju and demanded if it was authentic. They acknowledged it to be so, but treated it as a *brutum fulmen* [idle threat]. Meantime the preparations for the Tycoon's visit to Miako go on, which looks as if he was not afraid to meet the lion of a Mikado in his den.

Mr. Pruyn is occupied with some important modifications of the treaty with this country, and it is a significant testimony to the strength of the Tycoon's power that at the very time he is ordered "to expel the hated foreigners," that he instead proposes to accord to them new privileges.

Wednesday, March 4, 1863

Today was made glad by the receipt of a great budget of letters from home. Business kept me from reading them all day and till far into the night. It was midnight before I sat down to the feast that had awaited me all the day, and two in the morning before I rose from the repast.

Tuesday, March 10, 1863

Rape in bloom, wheat has grown some inches, sowed pease in the open ground. [written as marginal comment next to 7th, 8th, 9th, and 10th]

Wednesday, March 11, 1863

Yesterday I dropped in to see a tea merchant, a friend of our house. On parting he gave me a present of some tea, "virgin tea," because it was all made by little girls. It was essential to this tea that each leaf should be picked, twisted, and prepared by little girls *dare mada skibbi arimasen!* The tea was affected by gentlemen of quality and none was for sale; it was given only in presents.

Friday, March 13, 1863

Sowed onions, turnip and radish seed in open ground.

Sunday, March 15, 1863

Broad beans begin to bloom. Pyrus japonica also.

Wednesday, March 18, 1863

The Japanese show a good sagacity in letting out contracts for building. Instead of letting to the lowest bidder, it is the custom to let to the next one to the lowest. The advantages of this course are obvious.

Sunday, March 22, 1863

Rape fields in bloom. Several English men-of-war arrived today.

Sunday, March 29, 1863

Arrival of two more English men-of-war and two Dutch men-of-war.

Monday, March 30, 1863

The arrival of so many men-of-war has produced much speculation both among foreigners and natives. On the arrival of the first on the 22nd every Japanese vessel, of which there were two steamers and two sailing vessels in the harbor at the time, quickly left. Admiral Kuper is supposed to have arrived with diplomatic powers, and to have authority to demand reparation for the late outrages, the attack on the sentries at the English Legation, the murder of Richardson, and the burning of the Legation buildings.

Wednesday, April 1, 1863

Garden peas, winter sown, begin to bloom.

Thursday, April 2, 1863

Today it is said on authority of some of the English officers that the demand on the Japanese government is for $200,000, and that Simadzu Saburo, the chief of the train which assailed Richardson, shall be delivered up to the English for punishment.

Sunday, April 5, 1863

A walk in few countries can be more enticing than among our fields. I took a short ramble on the bluffs over the bay. Far as eye could see over the rolling landscape the fields were carpeted with the rich growth of wheat and barley, a bright and vivid green interrupted here and there with patches of rape now in golden blossom. The morning wind was laden with the pleasant perfume of these fields. The rippling banks were pranked with violets, dandelions, the blue gentian, the pyrus japonica. About the farm houses and temples, peach and cherry were in bloom, and in the woods here and there the wild cherry blossomed. My walk extended to Mississippi Bay.

In the afternoon I took Capt. and Mrs. Ames in my boat to Treaty Point and into Mississippi Bay.[3] As we rounded the point into the bay the increased swell made Mrs. A. sea-sick.

Monday, April 6, 1863

Mr. Eusden, Secretary of the English Legation, went to Yedo today bearing the demands of the English Government upon the Japanese for the murder of the English sentries and the attack upon Mr. Richardson and his friends. The nature of these demands has not been made public.

Wednesday, April 8, 1863

A meeting of the English residents was held today to which a letter from the Consul was read, stating the demands the English had

---

[3] I have not been able to identify Capt. Ames and his wife.

made on the Japanese Government, to wit, a sum of money for the families of the two sentries killed at Yedo and for the persons assaulted on the Tokaido last fall, and also that the murderers of Richardson should be given up to justice. The demand was made on the 6th and twenty days allowed for an answer.

The Prussian and Dutch Consuls called upon their subjects for an inventory of their property as a base of reclamation in case of ulterior measures.

Thursday, April 9, 1863

The demand of the English Government is the all absorbing theme. The letters read to the English meeting yesterday are printed. Of the demand, Col. Neale's letter to the Consul says + + + "That reparation comprises the trial and capital execution of the murderers of Mr. Richardson, a heavy pecuniary penalty on Japan for that offence, and a considerable compensation for the sufferers, or their surviving relatives." Of the consequences of a refusal on the part of the Japanese Government the letter further says. After hoping that the Government will comply with the demand, "On the other hand, in the possible contingency which exists of the Japanese Government refusing to accede to these demands, or hoping to evade them by futile arguments or procrastination, it becomes my duty to apprise you of the inevitable adoption in such an event of coercive measures by the Rear Admiral Commanding-in-Chief Her Majesty's naval forces in these seas, now arrived here with a considerable force and furnished with instructions to the above effect analogous to my own."

It is impossible to foresee what the result of this demand will be. Were it confined to a pecuniary demand however large, I think it would be met. I cannot yet believe that the persons of the murderers will be given up. The Government of the Tycoon is powerless to seize them from Satsuma and the ancient custom is that each daimio shall have the sole power to punish his lieges. The proud Satsuma is little likely to yield to this demand. Will he escape it by some subterfuge such as the rendering up of some condemned malefactors in their stead, or the tale that they have already

anticipated justice by the suicidal *harakiri*? At least we shall out of this issue learn something of the temper of the government and the princes.

Friday, April 10, 1863

A meeting of the American citizens assembled at the Consulate today where a letter from Mr. Pruyn, the Minister, was read which, while expressing an individual sympathy with the English, enjoined on all the Americans strict neutrality. The Consul made some remarks *a la the American Eagle*, alluded to the "glorious banner," and expressed his readiness "to die on the last ditch." The meeting resolved to await further developments before taking any action.

In the afternoon a general meeting of all nationalities was held at the English Consulate, which resulted much as the American meeting had. No one was excited, and it was after some desultory talk resolved to appoint a committee to devise plans for the safety of the settlement. When my name was called on the committee, I arose and declined on the ground that the English *charge* and Admiral had taken the matter wholly in their own hands; they knew, and we did not, what overt measures they might take, and that we should leave the matter in their hands till called on by them, or it became necessary to act in self defence. This opinion was at once adopted by acclamation, the resolution recalled, the meeting adjourned, and the *charge* and Admiral left to act on their own responsibility. The Admiral has very indiscreetly advised the ladies to leave Yokohama for a place of greater safety.

Saturday, April 11, 1863

Azaleas begin to bloom.

Sunday, April 12, 1863

The *Encounter* and *Bouncer* arrived.

Monday, April 13, 1863

Barley begins to head, first turning up [of] the rice fields. All remains quiet. The natives are indifferent; do not believe we shall come to blows. Trading goes on quietly as before.

[On April 14, 1863, Hall wrote the following letter to the *New York Tribune*, which was published June 26, 1863.]

The all-engrossing topic for a few days past has been the demand of the English Government on the Tycoon for reparation for the murder of the English sentries at the Legation in Yedo in June last, and for the attack on a party of Englishmen on the Tokaido in September last, when Mr. Richardson was killed and two others severely wounded.

Three weeks since Rear-Admiral Kuper, Commanding-in-Chief all her Majesty's naval forces in the China Seas, arrived at Yokohama in the Euryalus, escorted by three other war steamers. Since that time there have been accessions to the squadron, till now there lie in our harbor eleven men-of-war, several of which are large and powerful steamers. Several others are daily expected as Admiral Kuper has ordered all the available force on the east Asiatic coast to follow him hither.

On the 6th inst. a formal demand was made at Yedo on the Ministers for Foreign Affairs in the Tycoon's Court for full and ample redress for past outrages. All that has been made known to the public of the nature of these demands is contained in a letter addressed by Col. St. John Neale, the English Charge d'Affaires, to the English Consul, requesting him to communicate to the British residents the grave position of affairs. This letter, together with the one addressed by the English Consul to the residents under his charge, I enclose:

YOKOHAMA, April 6, 1863.

SIR: I have already made known to you the purport of a note I have this day presented to the Japanese Government, containing a declaration of grievances and unrequited outrages of which British subjects have been the victims and sufferers, and for which, under instructions from her Majesty's Government, I have demanded a specific reparation within a noted period of time.

The attack upon her Majesty's Legation at Yedo, on the 26th of June last, when two of the guard of H.M.S. Renard were treacherously murdered, and the subsequent barbarous murder of Mr. Richardson, on the 14th of September, and murderous assault committed on the same occasion upon a lady and two other gentlemen British subjects, are special outrages for which reparation is now demanded.

That reparation comprises the trial and capital execution of the murderers of Mr. Richardson, a heavy pecuniary penalty on Japan for that offense and a considerable compensation for the sufferers, or their surviving relatives.

It is sincerely to be hoped that the Government of the Tycoon, influenced by wise and just reflections will yield a ready compliance to the demands thus rendered necessary by these unprovoked and outrageous acts.

On the other hand, in the possible contingency which exists of the Japanese Government refusing to accede in these demands, or hoping to evade them by futile arguments or procrastination, it becomes my duty to apprise you of the inevitable adoption in such an event of coercive measures by the Rear-Admiral Commanding-in-Chief her Majesty's naval forces in these seas, now arrived here with a considerable force and furnished with instructions to the above effect analogous to my own.

Twenty days, dating from the 6th instant is the period allowed as the term which I will await the definite and categorical reply of the Japanese Government, and the nature of which, when received, will decide the adoption or otherwise of coercive measures, the duration and severity of which will be proportioned to the degree of ill-advised obstinacy or resistance which the Japanese Government may assume.

Under such circumstances I have to instruct you to call a meeting of the British residents within your Consular Jurisdiction or of a Committee appointed by them, and make known to them the purport of this dispatch, with a view that her Majesty's subjects may individually adopt such precautionary measures for the safeguard of their commercial interests . . . [illegible line] . . . measures of defense against the contingency of aggression or attack upon the several settlements during the continuance of coercive operations, the Rear Admiral Commanding-in-Chief H.M. Naval Forces, will very shortly propose to concern with the Diplomatic Agents and Naval Commanders of Foreign States on the spot, respecting the adoption of such combined arrangements as may be practicable and expedient. I have to request you to communicate the purport of this dispatch to your colleagues the Consuls of friendly nations residing at Kanagawa—Yokohama with the least possible delay.

E. ST. JOHN NEALE.

Her Majesty's Consul does not deem it necessary to introduce the communication the purport of which he is directed to impart to the community by any lengthened statement.

All her Majesty's subjects in this country are aware of the grave and fatal occurrences which took place on the 26th of June, and 14th September last.

These have naturally engaged the serious attention of the Government, and her Majesty has directed her Charge d'Affaires to demand in her name such reparation and redress as the gravity of the circumstances requires. (Here read the letter of her Majesty's Charge d'Affaires).

I request you will particularly take notice that the object of her Majesty's Charge d'Affaires in directing me to acquaint you with the tenor of his dispatch is to enable British subjects to take such timely measures of prudence and precaution in reference to their commercial and individual interests as they may consider the circumstances require them to adopt.

The Admiral proposes in concert with the Chiefs of the other Foreign Nations such arrangements as may tend best to secure the safety of the settlement.

It is especially my duty in the grave state of our relations with the Government of this country to impress upon you in the plainest terms the expedience and necessity of observing the greatest circumspection and courtesy in your intercourse with the natives of all ranks and classes—to avoid all acts which may lead to complications likely to render still more difficult the position of those entrusted with the control of her Majesty's affairs in this country, and by the exercise of a distinct self-restraint as all occasions of unnecessary exposure to personal risk.

I have only to state that the foregoing contains all the material information which, under present circumstances, it can possible be in the power of her Majesty's Charge d'Affaires to foresee or make them acquainted with. The whole question is in a future, which rapidly approaches, and during which, it is hardly necessary to say, your safety and protection, so far as the same may be practicable, will be an object of anxious solicitude.

CHARLES A. WINCHESTER, H.B.M.'s Consul.

The ultimatum was delivered on the 6th inst. and the terminal day rapidly approaches, when, if the demands be not complied with, our little settlement will be exposed to all the chances of war. There are no indications as yet of what the result will be. The native people about us thus far express only the greatest indifference to the matter; they do not seem to believe that any serious difficulty will occur, let the Tycoon reply as he may. While not so conceited as the Chinese, they have yet ample confidence in the power of their chiefs and princes. Meetings of the foreign merchants and residents have been held to take into consideration our exposed conditions and our means of defense. Not a few are apprehensive that the Japanese, whose ancient cunning and treachery is in mind, may take the initiative before the twenty days are out, and attempt a surprise of the foreign settlement. And Admiral Kuper, who has advised the ladies to seek a place of greater safety—that is, the shipping—or to leave the country altogether, yet does not so much as land a night patrol.

It is unfortunate that at this juncture the Tycoon and the chief officers of his court are absent, they having departed on the long contemplated visit to the Mikado at Miaco, a fortnight since. This visit of the Tycoon to the Spiritual Emperor, where, at the same time, there is to be a great gathering of the most powerful Daimios of the realm, is one of vast importance to the future of Japan. For many years there has been no such assemblings of the country's Chiefs, and we may expect that many conflicting interests will be reconciled or expand into open acts of hostility. The internal and external relations of the country will be more firmly established, or all the land will be ablaze with the fires of civil war. These are the alternatives, and we wait anxiously the result of the Miaco meeting, as well as Admiral Kuper's demands, the latter, no doubt, giving now intensity to the counsels of the former. The volcano on which unhappy Nipon has so long been resting is either to be quenched forever or burst out into magnificent violence. No longer may treachery subdue smoldering.

Should the Admiral fail to get satisfaction at Yedo, it is rumored that he will take his fleet to Oasaca, seventeen miles from Miaco, and demand redress of the assembled powers of the realm, where Tycoon, Mikado and Daimios will be together, and there shall be no shuffling of responsibility from one portion to another of this tripartite power in the rulership of Japan. Or, as say others, he will go to Kagosima, the capital of great Satsuma, whose liege it was that did the foul deeds of the 14th of September, and demand the assassins from under the guns of his hereditary castle, or wreak his vengeance there.

Such are the courses open to him truly, but my own belief is, that before the twenty days have expired, the Japanese Government will give either a complying answer in part, or make such reasons for further delay that the Admiral will be compelled by

"a decent regard for the opinions of mankind," to consider them before taking his "coercive measures." Otherwise, Japanese shrewdness and diplomacy will, for the first time, have failed of carrying its end. They can, too, in honest faith, not diplomatic cunning, give an answer which will demand a hearing and an answer other than at the cannon's mouth. Through Admiral Kuper is said by his countrymen to be ambitious of winning his knightly spurs, he must in this nineteenth century win them in a knightly way, if he would wear them with knightly honor.

We calmly await the issue of the twenty days, and their event of peace or desolating war to a people who, for three centuries have known the blessings of unbroken peace. Not less anxiously do we wait for the results to ourselves and our property, for on us and our property would fall such blows as the Japanese may have to give.

The Wyoming is soon expected, and will be loudly welcomed at this crisis. The French have two war steamers here, and the Dutch two. A part of the Russian Asiatic Squadron is looked for, so that the corps of observation will be full.

Friday, April 17, 1863

A circular has been round today among the English residents emanating from the Consul, the purport of which is that if the Japanese should attack the settlement after the 26th inst., the final day of the grace allowed them to make their answer to the English, the Admiral can give the settlement no protection. This announcement causes great excitement and indignation.

Saturday, April 18, 1863

The English residents, through a committee, address the Minister and Admiral criticizing the course they have pursued in first proposing to defend the settlement, and then abandoning it. The people remain calm and quiet and trade still goes on in its accustomed channels.

Monday, April 20, 1863

The English Minister sent answer to the English citizens through their committee; the nature of which is not yet publicly known.

The American merchants met at the Consul's this forenoon to hear read a dispatch from General Pruyn which exhorts to continued quiet and expresses no alarm at the same time that it rebukes the course of the English officials. The meeting resulted in no action. The unanimous impression was that we could only bide the coming of events. Preparations are making for the removal of the women, children, or others in case of any attack or increased apprehension. These preparations are confined to the French and English. The native merchants are becoming a little uneasy and a few families are said to have left for the country.

Tuesday, April 21, 1863

No new developments today. The native people remain quiet and trade moves on in its accustomed channels. Minister Pruyn is down from Yedo. His visit is to ask an extension of time allowed the Japanese for their answer to the English demand.

Wednesday, April 22, 1863

This morning a rumor prevails that an English surveying vessel has been fired on in the inland sea and sunk. Confirmation is wanted. An informal meeting of the American citizens was held at the house of Walsh Hall and Co. to confer upon the state of affairs. General Pruyn was present and addressed the meeting. He stated his confidence in the good will of the Japanese Government towards the Americans and expressed his belief that in case of hostilities, the neutral powers would be safe under their protection. He returns to Yedo today. An hundred rumors fill the streets now of war and now of peace. Within my own compound everything goes on as usual where more than a hundred natives are employed.

A patrol will guard the settlement tonight.

Thursday, April 23, 1863

The English chaplain and wife take refuge in the shipping. In the evening are rumors quite rife of a granted delay; still all is uncertain. Patrols are stationed at various points tonight.

Friday, April 24, 1863

Rumors are current that an extension of time will be allowed the Japanese. The natives express now some uneasiness lest war may ensue. There have been a few removals.

Saturday, April 25, 1863

It is officially announced that 15 additional days will be granted the Japanese to consider the English demands. Thirty days were asked for, but fifteen were, after some hesitation, allowed.

Sunday, April 26, 1863

The native people are all rejoicing today over the hope of a settlement of the difficulties. This influence was at once felt in the market which stiffened its prices considerably.

Thursday, April 30, 1863

All is silent as to the intentions of the Japanese Government, but feeling the pulse of the native people around us we find there is again a growing anxiety. There is more and more distrust of a peaceful solution. Mr. Portman is down from Yedo and says that in Yedo no less anxiety seems to be felt as to the issue. The guard around the American Legation has had a further increase of a hundred men. The Japanese do not seem so timorous as to the result of a war, that is, they seem to increase in confidence that if war does come they will be able to take care of themselves.

Friday, May 1, 1863

The feeling of distrust among the Japanese increases. The merchants are desirous to realize on their goods. Teas are offered ten to twelve dollars a picul cheaper than before the demands, while silk, which has remained firm up to today, has fallen 30 to 50 dollars a picul. In truth, the Japanese seem to be getting ready for a flight. Families at Kanagawa in vicinity of the port have been removed. Whether this is done by intimations from the government, we do not know, there are rumors that it is so.

Saturday, May 2, 1863

Wheat in head. The feeling is much as yesterday with no new phases of affairs.

Sunday, May 3, 1863

The merchants are, many of them, packing up their valuables and the flight of families to the country has commenced. The fort at Kanagawa has been dismantled and the guns removed. At Yedo the daimios have removed their families, the aged and infirm, women and children, have been enjoined to flee also. The Sinagawa forts are said to be dismantled, the temple near the sea to be occupied by soldiers. Our Minister remains there without any disquiet.

Monday, May 4, 1863

The flight of the Japanese increases. The City Governor of Yedo has advised all the women, children, infirm and aged to retire to the country. The shopkeepers grew daily more anxious to realize for their wares and rumors of threatened attack to the foreign settlement grow more frequent.[4]

Tuesday, May 5, 1863

The excitement greatly increased when it was known this morning that Mr. Stearns had been attacked.[5] Mr. S[tearns] had an unadjusted claim with a native who gathered his laborers and friends and besieged Mr. S[tearn]'s house at an early hour demanding settlement. Mr. S[tearns], thinking to intimidate them went out of the house with his double barrelled gun in hand and ordered them off. His gun was immediately knocked out of his hand, he was surrounded, thrown down, and beaten severely until his native servants interfered for his rescue.

The removal of the natives goes on more rapidly and the Governor of Yokohama confesses that they go by his advice. Foreigners begin to remove their goods to the shipping.

Wednesday, May 6, 1863

Today a regular panic has seized the town; the native population are fleeing in the utmost haste. Everyone believes war is inevitable and is hastening to escape from the vicinity of the

---

[4] To put this in perspective I quote from Conrad Totman who writes: "British belligerence made Inoue [Masanao] sufficiently concerned lest negotiations fail that he alerted daimyo in the Kantō to the prospect, instructing them to prepare for trouble. In orders to the daimyo still in Edo, the senior councillors explained that they were trying to delay any British decisions until the shogun's return [from Kyoto]. If that were impossible, however, they had no choice but to drive the British away even though defense preparations were inadequate. Daimyo and liege vassals were assigned defense tasks in the Edo-Yokohama area, and their women and children were ordered evacuated from the city. As preparations were made, the general populace became panicky. A rash of hoarding abruptly pushed prices up, and some people began selling their possessions even at giveaway prices and fleeing the coastal areas of the bay. Alarmed by the spreading disorder, the bakufu called upon daimyo and officials to take measures to restore tranquillity" (*The Collapse of the Tokugawa Bakufu, 1862–1868* [Honolulu: University Press of Hawaii, 1980], p. 69).

[5] J.O.P. Stearns is listed as an American in *The China Directory of 1863* (Hong Kong: Shortrede & Co., 1863), p. 56. The 1866 directory lists him as running his own firm.

sea. Scarcely a native merchant has the nerve to remain, but all offer their wares at any price they can get. The excitement among the foreigners is hardly less. All day long the wharves are crowded with merchandise to go off to the shipping. Any price is paid for boats or coolies here. The transportation of a package that would usually cost two tempos has gone to three, four, and six times that price. This excitement is intensified by the fact of several assaults having been made in order to collect claims. Mr. Robertson[6] was seized in his bedroom while dressing this morning and was carried off to the rear of the settlement, for what purposes of violence we do not know; he was fortunately rescued. Mr. Schoyer[7] was likewise beset by a large gang of laborers and had to pay them money, which he says was not due, but in all these cases the Japanese had some claims. Servants left their masters robbing them as they went. Macaulay,[8] a landlord, was knocked down by his own servants and robbed. A Portuguese was similarly treated. The confusion grew hourly greater, and when about noon it was heard that Dupontes, a Frenchman, had shot a man for making a similar demand on him, the excitement reached its height.[9] The town was full of coolies whose burden poles would have been dangerous weapons, had they had the courage and determination to use them. They seemed to want only a determined leader to rise against the foreign population en masse. All dreaded the coming of night.

At this time a consultation, or conference, was being had on the *Euryalus*, Admiral Ku-

per's flagship, at which were present the English and French authorities, and on the side of the Japanese the Governor of Yokohama and Takamoto, one of the Governors of Foreign Affairs from Yedo. At this interview the French admiral was present as he had just arrived in the *Semirames* from China. The Japanese asked for more time on the ground that the Tycoon had not yet returned: that he was on the way back and might now be expected in a few days more. The French admiral took the just ground that the reasons assigned for the delay were good, and that when the Japanese recently asked for thirty days extension of time it ought to have been promptly granted for the just cause given, the emperor's absence. It is rumored that he took occasion to speak of the ill timed demand in the first instance when it was openly known that the Tycoon and his court were absent. But the most important affairs of this conference were the revelations of Takamoto, the emperor's envoy, who frankly disclosed that orders had come from the Mikado at Miako not to meet the English demands, but to fight rather for the expulsion of the foreigners. He further said that this antiforeign party was so powerful that it was doubtful if the Tycoon's government could effectually resist it. He was then asked if the Tycoon would accept the assistance of the Allies to put down this hostile faction. His reply was, that was a question he could not decide, he must first submit it to the Goroju.[10]

It was finally concluded at this conference that the Japanese should be allowed fifteen days from that day, the 6th, for their final an-

---

[6] Samuel Robertson. This appears to have been the Mr. Robertson with whom Hall accompanied Raphael Pumpelly and William Blake to the Oyama district in April of the previous year. Robertson's health subsequently failed and Hall saw him off to the United States on August 14, 1864.

[7] Raphael Schoyer.

[8] James B. Macaulay was an Englishman. See *The China Directory for 1862* (Hong Kong: Shortrede & Co., 1862), p. 52. The 1865 directory lists him as owner of a "Livery Stable," and the 1866 one as a "Commission Merchant."

[9] L. C. Dupontes was a member of Remi, Schmidt & Co. See *The China Directory for 1863* (Hong Kong: Shortrede & Co., 1863), p. 55. Father Mounicou's diary

entry for the same date clarifies this affair. Dupontes was having a wall built. The last payment for the work was due upon completion of the work. Despite the uncompleted project the masons, six men, wanted to be paid on a pro rata basis. Dupontes refused to pay them. When he ordered them to leave at gunpoint, one of the men tried to take the revolver from him and in the struggle that followed the man was shot several times. See Paul C. Blum, trans., "Father Mounicou's Bakumatsu Diary, 1856–64," *Transactions of the Asiatic Society of Japan*, vol. 13 (Tokyo, 1976), p. 90.

[10] Takamoto was in fact Takemoto Masaaki, who along with Shibata Masanaka served as Gaikoku Bugyō, or governors of foreign affairs.

swer and that in the meantime the Governor should restore the old order in Yokohama, that the merchants should return to their shops, and the servants to their place. Moreover that the Allies should in the meantime be permitted to take such measures for the protection of the settlement by landing troops, or otherwise as seemed advisable.

Accordingly in the afternoon the Governor issued an *ofoori* [notice] to that intent enjoining upon all the native population to return to their customary avocations. The potent influence of this government was at once seen in the quiet that was suddenly restored, although that very morning the Governor had told the consuls that the lawless coolies were beyond his control. But for this timely notice, nothing but a landing of a large force could have prevented the night following from becoming a scene of horrors.

The Japanese have received a further delay, but there can be little hope any longer of a peaceful solution. The declarations of the Governor at the conference show that the Tycoon seems to have only a choice between a civil and a foreign war, and it hardly seems possible that he would escape the latter by a choice of the former.

Thursday, May 7, 1863

Order continues today but few people return to their old employments. On the contrary there seem to be more removals than returns.

It is a misfortune to the Yedo Government that its emperor is a youth under the care of regents and guardians. The court is consequently full of intrigue on the part of parties ambitious to have the control of the empire. Were he a strong ruler like Taico [Hideyoshi] or Ieyas [Tokugawa Ieyasu] he would before this have put down the hostile chiefs who are attempting to subvert his throne.

Friday, May 8, 1863

Order continues and a few more are returning to their avocations.

Saturday, May 9, 1863

Though the Japanese population appears quiet, the foreign population is full of rumors of hostile intentions on the part of the Japanese. There is a general intention of reshipping such imports as are on hand and all day and every day the *hatoba* is crowded with merchandise for the shipping.

Sunday, May 10, 1863

Very warm. It is wonderful how calm and quiet all appears today after the week's turmoil and excitement. It seems a Sabbath indeed. There is no bustle in the streets no crowd on the piers. I think the Japanese will believe that there is some regard for the Sabbath when they see the turmoil of yesterday hushed to the quiet of today.

General Pruyn is down today and speaks encouraging words. At least he says more time for deliberations is sure to be given the Japanese. He is not sanguine as to the ultimate result, but thinks we have no immediate danger.

Monday, May 11, 1863

The U.S. steamer *Wyoming*, which was reported as ashore below, came in early this morning having grounded last evening in the road. Never were the "stars and stripes" more welcome. Whatever trouble might come now, a place of refuge was open. The hearts of everybody were relieved. The Japanese are slowly crossing back to their deserted houses and shops.

Tuesday, May 12, 1863

A meeting of the American citizens was held at the Consulate today. General Pruyn and Capt. McDougal were present. The state of affairs was discussed, but no definite action taken, which is the general result of all our meetings. After a great deal of desultory talking and passing complimentary resolutions, I put the plain question to the meeting, "What shall we do?" without note or comment. This gave a practical turn to affairs. The Minister said he "should remain at Yedo till within an hour of the opening of the English guns on the city." He gave no advice as to what others should do. Others said what they thought best to do individually, which was perhaps all that could be said.

"All is quiet on the Potomac"—*Curlew* left for San Francisco.

Wednesday, May 13, 1863

Slowly the shops open and business begins again; the Japanese are only sellers not buyers. Silk and tea again rise in price.

Saturday, May 16, 1863

It has been understood since the American meeting that the Japanese were to have yet further time if they wished. They are now allowed till the 27th for compliance. But as it is officially promulgated today that the Tycoon has not yet left Miako on his return, even this delay is likely to prove unavailing. There are popular rumors that Satsuma and Kaga have had a collision at Miako, the latter having espoused the Tycoon's cause. The story needs confirmation to be reliable.

Sunday, May 17, 1863

The country about us is in its full summer glory. All the fields [and] the low mounded hills are teeming with the verdure of the new crops. Wheat and rape seed begin to show the golden tint of their ripening. The woods are luxuriant with rich masses of fresh foliage. No fences mar the view, it is one vast panorama of wood and rolling field and the sparkling waters of the bay fringing all. The only exceptions to the general verdure are the winding valleys left for rice, where the brown soil shows like a muddy stream among the green banks. There, by and by, will be the green spots when others are yellow and bare.

My favorite walk is along the edge of the bluffs that tend inland and overhang the rice valley below through which runs the road to Kanazawa. The ground is high and overlooks wood, field, with here and there a sunny burst between the ridges of the bay water. I mount the little hillocks that the farmer has left when centuries ago these fields were scraped, terraced and levelled, and feast my eyes with the park like landscape that lies between me and the bay, or, on the other hand, I look down into the valley below where lies the town of Yokohama. I see the winding coves of the bay, the broad canals that lead back into the country, the beautiful valley through which they wind overspread with the tender crops now in their richest green. I see the brown cottages clustering along the valley edge, half lost among the foliage and now the irises are blooming on the roof. Strings of men and pack horses are following the winding trail of the valley roads. Beyond this valley lie another range of bluffs, segregated with fields, copses, temple grounds, and, towards the town, by the barracks of the Japanese soldiery. Beyond this bluff I see the break of the rolling land till it abuts against the Oyama range 30 miles off, above whose hazy tops lifts another range of torn and rugged peaks some thousands of feet in height and fifty miles distant, and bringing up the rear of all glorious old Fusi symmetrical and snow crowned, rosy and glittering in its 75 miles of distance. How shall I carry this superb picture with me when I leave Japan. I know it must and will haunt me, and that even amid the delights of a home rejoined I shall at some moments sigh for the walk over the bluffs of Yedo Bay.

Monday, May 18, 1863

Quiet continues. More business and labor is daily resumed, rumors vague and uncertain, news of peace, and now of war, abound.

Wednesday, May 20, 1863

Dispatched the *Alerta* to Shanghai. A few Japanese seem to be moving again today. Some foreigners also place their merchandise on board ship because the limited time is drawing towards its close.

Thursday, May 21, 1863

Dispatched the *Josephine* to Shanghai.

Friday, May 22, 1863

We have news from Nagasaki yesterday and today. The panic and confusion at Nagasaki was even worse than here. The merchants generally removed their property to the shipping and many of themselves went thither also. The English Consul was among those who left the shore. There was the same panic among the towns people who fled as here selling their stocks of goods for what they could get. This fright was much contributed to by the outspoken Governor of that city, who said that if he heard that the Yedo government refused to meet the English demands he should consider war inaugurated and take the offensive. He advised all foreigners without regard to nationality to leave the place, promising them however 24 Japanese hours notice before hostile acts were commenced by him. After that time English men and ships would be seized wherever they could be found. Our latest news left the people of that city in dire confusion and distress, fearing the reenactment of the bloody scenes of the 16th century.

Sunday, May 24, 1863

First strawberries. General Pruyn writes from Yedo that his house was burned down last night, or rather at 2 A.M. this morning, the fire originating in the kitchen, and as he believes from an accidental source.

The 27th rapidly approaches and no announcement of the conclusion of the Yedo Government. The envoy who was to have been here on Saturday sent down word that he could not come, assigning no reasons.

We hear further this afternoon that the inmates of the Legation at Yedo lost everything in the fire, even their personal clothing. Circumstances seem to show that the fire was designed.

Monday, May 25, 1863

An envoy from Yedo is here today holding conferences with the French and English Ministers and Admirals relative to the demands. A settlement without war is confidently hoped for.

Tuesday, May 26, 1863

The result of yesterday's deliberations are not given to the public, but it is well understood that no war is to take place. The *Coquette* goes to Shanghai tomorrow and all that Col. Neale will say, that we may send the news forward, is "that matters look more hopeful, but the foreign merchants had better relax none of their precautions."

Wednesday, May 27, 1863

The *Coquette* left today and after her departure we had hoped for more direct intelligence from the English authorities as to what was agreed upon, but the *charge* yet withholds any definite information.

Thursday, May 28, 1863

It seems to be understood that the present position of affairs is that the Japanese consent to meet the money demand upon them, if time is allowed for its payment, that they say they cannot give up the criminals, or to attempt it would be followed by a civil war. Rumor adds that the English then demand as a substitute the opening of a port, Oasaca, which the Japanese say in reply would be dangerous to give. At all events, the English appear to have receded from the high position they took at the start and to be very glad now to accept compromises. The French Minister expresses himself more pithily than decorously respecting one of the conferences from which he withdrew as he saw "the Japanese were about to —⸺ defile the English flag."

From Yedo we hear that General Pruyn remains there until the Japanese grant him a new residence, which they seem desirous to evade.

The report gains currency and confidence that the Tycoon will not return from Miako unless it be temporarily, but that the court will be removed from Yedo thither.

Friday, May 29, 1863

Very warm. Mr. Walsh of the English Consulate[11] had this P.M. some difficulty on the Tokaido with the retainers of some prince (Mito? So said) at a tea house where they accidentally met. Mr. W[alsh] says that they were intoxicated and questioned him roughly, and then made menacing gestures with their swords, whereupon he drew his pistol, which deterred them till he had time to escape into the street, when they pursued him to the boat landing where the yakunins on duty interfered and protected him from violence.

Saturday, May 30, 1863

Mr. Walsh's affair creates some talk and the assault upon him is believed to have been wholly unprovoked.

Sunday, May 31, 1863

Events thicken upon us. Today the Consuls were called together to meet the native Governor at 1 o'clock. The Governor said he had to apprise them that many ronins were known to be about and desired them to notify their respective citizens that it would be unsafe for them to go on the Tokaido for fifteen or twenty days. That the government would exert its utmost power to put down all these outlaws and within thirty days could promise quiet. Notices were issued accordingly.

Late in the afternoon the Vice Governor who lives at Yokohama came to the U.S. Consul and in the most urgent manner requested that he would at once without delay remove his family from Kanagawa and cause the missionary families to remove also. So urgent and importunate was this request that the Consul removed the females of his household on board the *Wyoming*. The mission families having no place to flee declined to go. The gentlemen of the Consul's house also remained. But during the night again and again urgent requests were made for them to leave at once.[12]

Monday, June 1, 1863

Early this morning I found General Pruyn, his son, and his secretary had arrived from Yedo. It appears also that yesterday afternoon he had been solicited to leave Yedo in so urgent a way that his volition was hardly left to him. The officials of his household guard informed him that a conspiracy of seven hun-

---

[11] P. B. Walsh was junior assistant in the British consulate at Kanagawa in 1863.

[12] Margaret Ballagh, the wife of James Ballagh, who was living in Kanagawa at the same temple where Hall had originally resided, wrote: "This has been an extraordinary and busy day. Last night about midnight, we were awakened by a loud knocking at the gate, and when it was opened, our Minister himself came to the door with quite a guard around him, and bade us arise and get ready at once to leave this place. Early this morning, we were again disturbed by loud knocking at the gate, and a band of officers walked with authority up to our door, with a dispatch from the governor, for us to prepare to leave in all haste, saying that we were

in imminent danger, as the 'Ronin' were not far from the town. But the missionaries proffered in all calmness a request that they should be allowed to remain till after the Sabbath; which was granted at our own risk. After committing ourselves to God, we quietly made such preparations for leaving as the necessity of the case demanded. There are already in the yard, about 100 men, sent by the government to guard us during the night,— certainly very considerate of our wishes and religious convictions. I did not feel the least frightened, but indignant that our Minister and Consul should allow themselves to be thus imposed upon." See Margaret Tate Kinnear Ballagh, *Glimpses of Old Japan, 1861–1866* (Tokyo: Methodist Publishing House, 1908), p. 105.

dred ronins to take his life that night had been discovered and he *must* go. He accordingly went on board the Japanese Steamer *Kandin-maru* [Kanrin maru] and arrived at Yokohama at midnight, remaining on board till morning. Early this morning the mission families began to move, and now Yedo and Kanagawa are at last evacuated. A large body of guards came down from Yedo to protect the Kanagawa families during the night and nobody was allowed to move without an escort.

Today imperial solders armed with muskets, swords, and spears are filing through our streets and taking up guard stations at different points. Small pieces of artillery are stationed at the approaches to the town over the Kanagawa causeway, and in the rear near the bluffs, ammunition has been distributed. The Japanese Government are either in earnest to make such preparations for our defence, or they are trying a system of terrorism upon us on a large scale. We must accept these native guards, while we distrust them, since the fleet in the bay will not land a guard for our defence.

I saw a letter in the hands of General Pruyn today, a translation from a Japanese document to the government officers at Yedo and emanating from the Mikado. The Mikado says that it is understood that all the daimios will retire (from Miako) to their provinces and put everything in order preparatory to the work of exterminating the foreigners which his faithful Siogoon or General in Chief has undertaken to accomplish.

I saw also a second document which stated that if the Siogoon failed in this work he would set upon its execution himself. These documents being shown to the Japanese officials with whom General Pruyn has frequent communication they pronounced the first genuine, the second they knew nothing about.

One cannot help feeling at times that we are surrounded with wily foes and treacherous friends and that the fate of the Portuguese in the 17th century threatens us.

Tuesday, June 2, 1863

From Yedo we have reports that the Government has begun its promised work of putting down the ronins whose depredations on the lives and property of the people of Yedo had become so great as to cause great dissatisfaction with the government. Three, some say five, daimios have been entrusted with the charge of putting down these outlaws. A conflict is reported to have occurred yesterday between these guards and the ronins in which although the former suffered severely, several of the latter were captured. A large body of them, five to seven hundred, are gathered at the yashiki of one of the smaller daimios, but have been invested by the imperial troops. This looks as if the government were sincere in their acts and promises and that the flight from Yedo and Kanagawa was not made without cause.

Wednesday, June 3, 1863

The news is generally confirmed that the ronins are being punished by the authorities. The Governor of Kanagawa and Yokohama a few days since distributed a large sum of money, said [to be] 30,000 ichibus, among the people who had been at the expense of removing during the late panic. This is another instance of the care of the government for the people.

Sunday, June 7, 1863

Walked to Mississippi Bay. The American ship *Viking* was wrecked on Thursday last on Princess, or Mecoura, Island about 60 miles S.E. from Simoda. Her captain arrived here today from Simoda to seek assistance. The *Viking* had no cargo, but 460 Chinese passengers were aboard bound for San Francisco. No lives were lost though the captain was severely injured by a fall. The *Wyoming* goes down tomorrow morning to her assistance.

Saturday, June 13, 1863

The wrecked crew and passengers of the *Viking* were taken on Tuesday to Simoda to await reshipment on their voyage by some other vessel; the *Viking* being a total loss.

We have remained for the week now ended in the same state of suspense as to our future. Almost daily there have been promises of interviews between Col. Neale and the Japanese Ministers in which a conclusion would be arrived, indeed the day has been set two or three times when the ministers would be down from Yedo, but they have not yet come. On Friday evening Col. Neale received a flattering letter from them promising an interview for today and spoke with confidence of his position. But the day has worn away and no minister or Governor of Foreign Affairs makes his appearance. Now we hope for tomorrow.

Meantime we hear of all kinds of proclamations going about Yedo, proclamations that all the ports are to be closed against foreigners, that all persons are to hold themselves in readiness to act for their country, that the daimios have retired to their provinces for military purposes, etc.

The government officers admit the truth of some of these and meantime the Tycoon does not return from Miako. The ronins who were represented as so formidable in Yedo as to render it necessary for General Pruyn to leave, and who were gathered at one daimio's home to the extent of several hundred have been squelched in a very extraordinary and Japanese manner. The government has actually taken them all into its employ, paying them wages and appointing a chief over them! We have heard of such things before in this anomalous country.

The day before General Pruyn left Yedo a man was assassinated near his residence who was said to have been killed by the ronins. From accounts now given General Pruyn by his interpreter Tommy and others, it would appear that this man was a distinguished ronin himself, "the chief of the Yedo ronins," "the very man who killed Heusken, and who had often openly boasted of the deed." He had been slain in a feud with others of his clan. Col. Neale from other sources gets still a more circumstantial version which also represents him as a leader among the ronins, and the avowed murderer of Heusken. An attack was contemplated on the American Legation and was urged for the night of the 30th or 31st May, by the ronins generally. This man opposed this as premature and likely to embarrass their operations against the other foreigners, "if we attack the American Legation we shall slay but three men and alarm all the rest of the foreigners, who will escape the attack we design to make on them on the 24th day of the 4th moon" (June 11th). The others were impatient, and this lead to a dispute and a feud between him and his brothers which ended in his death, some say, by his brothers' denouncing him to the government who put him to death on, or near, the spot where he had murdered Heusken. The other account says this quarrel led to a conflict between rival parties of ronins in which he was slain. It is certainly extraordinary at least that this man should have openly boasted himself to be the slayer of Heusken and been permitted to escape so long unpunished, unless indeed we have to believe, as circumstances indicate, that no *samurai* will be punished by his government for an offence against a foreigner.

From Nagasaki we hear that the city is full of swaggering insolent samurai, and that active preparations are being made for a stout resistance in case of war with the English.

Monday, June 15, 1863

Yesterday and today the English *charge* and the Japanese Governors of Foreign Affairs (two of them) have been in conference. The point reached yesterday was that the Japanese consented to pay the money demanded of them viz. £100,000 paying the first installment on the 19th inst., to wit $150,000, and the balance in weekly payments of $50,000 each. The question respecting the demands on Satsuma for £25,000 and the murderers of Richardson are under discussion today.

[On June 15, 1863, Hall wrote the following letter to the *New York Tribune*, which was published on August 28, 1863.]

Under date of May 9 I gave your readers a brief account of the troubles in Japan, growing out of the English indemnity demand stating, in conclusion that fifteen days more had been granted the Japanese in which to make their reply.

But so ready did the Japanese appear to take up this quarrel, if pressed too far, and so illy prepared after all did the English find themselves to overcome the resistance which now seemed probable, that the fifteen days grew into an indefinite extension, agreeable to both sides.

Repeated conferences were again had between the representatives of the English and Japanese Governments in which the latter exhibited all their native coolness and imperturbable patience, regardless of either threats or persuasions, until they had taken their own time to weigh the chances of peace or war with the outside barbarians.

Meantime we had news from Nagasaki of the repetition there of scenes like those through which we passed at this portion the 4th, 5th, and 6th of May. The Governor of Nagasaki whose patriotic zeal extorts commendation from all, took the English Charge at his word when he said it was submission or coercion. The brave Governor, making no secret of his intention, openly declared that, inasmuch as he did not believe his Government would or could meet the demands, he should regard any official notice that they had not been met as inaugurating a state [of] war: that he should not wait for the threatened coercion, but be prepared himself to take the initiative. He then exhorted all the foreign residents at Nagasaki to be ready to leave the place, promising them forty-eight hours notice of the hostilities, yet, at the same time, cautioning them that he might not be able to protect them against the lawless soldiery of the neighboring independent chiefs. Then, with praiseworthy diligence, he set about the defenses of the harbor in which the Princes of Satsuma, Hizen, and Chikuzen, who have territorial possession adjacent to the bay of Nagasaki, emulated his zeal until all the approaches to the town were bristling with batteries and put in condition for a formidable attack or defense. The foreign residents, such of them as could leave without too much sacrifice, made their escape to Shanghai.

At Hakodade there appears to have been no unusual commotion.

Negotiations dragged on day after day and week after week till the original twenty days of the ultimatum became more than two months of inconclusive diplomacy. On the one hand, the Japanese were reluctant to meet what they regarded onerous and unjust demands; and on the other, the English hesitated to initiate their threatened measures of coercion, while their allies, the French had withdrawn disgusted from the field of diplomacy. In this state of suspense trade was paralyzed, and a condition of open war would have been scarcely less disastrous.

It appeared as if the Japanese intended finally to refuse compliance with the demands, and were only seeking to gain time so as to be prepared for the resistance which they ultimately intended. This view was strengthened by the fact that the Miaco party, with the Mikado at their head, had openly declared themselves in favor of expelling the foreigner at any cost. This Miaco party, so far as could be learned, was rapidly increasing in strength, and for the Government of Foreign Affairs to comply with the demands would be to expose the Yedo party to increased odium among the already discontented chiefs.

The Tycoon did not return from Miaco as promised he would. There were whispers that he had met the too common fate of Oriental royalty—assassinations; at any rate, there was no longer even a pretense of his early return. Whether he was detained as a hostage for the good behavior of the Yedo Government, or whether he voluntary remained, nobody knew. The former opinion seemed most consonant with the known facts, nor was it unlikely that this was but the carrying out of what had so long ago been threatened—the removal of the seat of Government to Miaco, leaving but a shadow of a Court at Yedo.

The anti-foreign party who surrounded the Mikado now pressed their advantages, and the first open act was that Matsudaira Ichizen-no-kami, the Regent, and known to be friendly to foreigners, was removed from office and retired to his principality on the western shores of Nipon. He was succeeded by Prince Mito, who had been the rival and unsuccessful aspirant for the Tycoonship on the death of the late Tycoon, and who now assumed all the powers of actual Sovereign, and maintains them to this hour. Such of the Gorogio, or Supreme Council of State, as were not facile to the views of the Miaco party have been removed.

At Yedo imperial proclamations and orders of council were issued privately to officials, or publicly posted on the walls, pointing to a determination on the part of the Miaco faction to expel all foreigners from Japan. Nations neutral in this quarrel, especially Americans, who flattered themselves that their neutral and friendly position would have respect, discovered that their friendship and neutrality was a rope of ashes. The suspicion daily gained ground that the Yedo Government itself, while professing their dread of the Miaco party, their desire to put them down, and keep the peace with foreign nationality, were playing a deeply treacherous part. Subsequent events afford undeniable proof of this, and no one knows what at last averted the fate that hung over the foreign population in the month of May.

Early in the morning of the 24th of May the residence of Gen. Pruyn, the America Minister at Yedo, who had courageously remained at his post, was burned over his head, involving the loss of his personal property, though the archives were saved in an injured condition. This occurred on a dark, stormy night after a day of pouring rain—the house being surrounded by the usual guard of 500 men, and the fire had originated in an unused and detached apartment—thus the suspicion of incendiarism was too palpable. The American Minister, however, still maintained his ground, and living with his son and Secretary in the small single apartment of an outbuilding, refused to leave Yedo until the immediate preparation of another residence was promised. On the 30th, after many delays and prevarications, the new residence was promised, and Gen. Pruyn prepared to leave Yedo temporarily, or until the promised house was in readiness.

On the afternoon of the day following, he was waited upon by two Governors of Foreign Affairs, who urged his instant departure to Yokohama. A conspiracy, they said had been discovered, in which a body of 500 *ronins* were engaged, that night to attack and overpower his guard and take his life. The Governors were urgent, fairly compelling the Minister from his house, and placing him on board of a Japanese steamer in the harbor, which, the night following, took him to Yokohama. So, Yedo was at last cleared of its last obnoxious foreign inhabitant.

The same day and hour, the American Consul at Kanagawa was similarly threatened and pressed into flight to Yokohama, where now all the foreign residents on the shores of Yedo Bay are for the first time assembled.

These events indicated a crisis at hand, and everyone looked for some more evident demonstration. Yet, after all these indications of resistance, the Japanese suddenly and unexpectedly agreed to the English demands. At a conference on the 13th inst., the Japanese Commissioners promised to meet the firm demands of Col. Neale, the British Charge, by the payment of the sum demanded of the Tycoon, to wit: $440,000—the first installment of which ($140,000) is to be paid on the 18th, and the balance in six equal weekly payments. To secure the fulfillment of this promise, a written bond was given to that effect. The remainder of the demand, viz: that the Prince of Satsuma should also pay $100,000, and arrest and punish the murderers of Mr. Richardson, was held in abeyance for further consultation. The Commissioners gave little hope of the rendition of the men, as they said they had escaped immediately after the murder, and all of Satsuma's attempts to discover them had been unavailing—all of which is probably a mere subterfuge.

Here the matter rests at this moment. A present war seems to be averted, but it is of no use to disguise the fact that it is a temporizing, unwilling settlement on the part of the Japanese, and that since the party in Japan who are hostile to foreigners are largely in the ascendant, and of late have gathered force, the evil day is only averted. We live over a smoldering volcano, which any day may burst out, involving more or less of us in destruction.

It is now but too evident, both from common report, and from known proclamations of the Government—documents some of which are in the hands of the foreign ministers—that, at the very moment the Yedo Government were saying fair words and promising protection, they were secretly plotting the destruction of all foreigners—nay more, the very decree for our expulsion had gone forth, and Mito was placed in power expressly to execute this purpose, which his courage failed him at the last moment to carry out. In the first week of May, the whole foreign population of Japan were on the threshold of destruction; whether they have removed many safe steps away from it is yet to be seen.

A strange affair has come to light amid other revelations. On the 23rd of May, a *ronin* was killed on or near the spot where the late Secretary to the American Legation, Mr. Huesken, was assassinated. It was admitted by Government officers that this man had been slain in a quarrel growing out of the intended attack on the American Legation. He had opposed the attack at this particular time as premature, which led to a breach between him and his comrades, to a street brawl and his death. Or as other accounts say, he was denounced by his own brother to the Government, and afterward assassinated. It now turns out that this man had been an acknowledged chief among the *ronins* of Yedo, and had often boasted of his having been the slayer of Mr. Huesken. Yet the Government, whose officers now confirm that they know the man and the deeds, never had made the attempt to punish him.

Such is the record of this hour. The irrepressible conflict between an old but powerful feudalism and modern social progress has yet at no distant day to come off on these shores, and I am mistaken if the Miaco party do not soon bring on the trial.

The American ship Viking, from Hong Kong to San Francisco with 460 China passengers, was lost on the 4th inst. on Mecoora or, Prince's Island, sixty miles southeast of Simoda. All on board were saved, and subsequently taken to Simoda by the U.S. sloop-of-war Wyoming, Capt. McDougal, which went to their assistance, where they now await fresh means of conveyance to their destination.

Trade, owing to the troubled state of public affairs, as well as the usual dullness of this season of the year, has been for some time past very moderate. Crops of every kind promise a bountiful yield, and only assured quiet is wanting to rapidly advance business relations with these islands.

Tuesday, June 16, 1863

In the discussions of the demands on Satsuma, the Government officers proposed assuming the money demand on themselves. As to the murderers of Mr. Richardson, they said they had escaped after his death and though Satsuma himself had tried to discover them with a view to punishment he had not been able to. No conclusion was arrived at so far as known.

Thursday, June 18, 1863

Today, instead of the 19th, was the time appointed for the payment of the first installment of the Japanese indemnity to wit $140,000 but the payment is postponed for some unknown reason till tomorrow.

General Pruyn read to me today extracts of his home dispatches accompanied with documents showing the perfidy of the Japanese

Government. The more important of these documents are the orders of the Miako Government to Prince Mito to take the reins of the Tycoon's power at Yedo and charging him with the expulsion of *all* foreigners from Japan, the imperial decrees of Mito to the effect that all the open ports were to be closed against the foreigners, the orders of the Supreme Council, or Goroju, for the expulsion of foreigners and exhorting all Japanese to be patriotic. These documents with others incontestably prove:

1st. That the Tycoon's visit to Miako was a compulsory affair. That he is detained there till it is the will of the Mikado and daimios that he should return.

2nd. That there is a large and powerful party in the empire embracing the great majority of the daimios who are bent on the exclusion of all foreigners from Japan.

3rd. That Mito was sent to Yedo and invested with all the powers of Siogoon, or as the word originally implied, "commander in Chief of the Armies," charged with the duty of driving out the foreigners.

4th. That he has failed to do this probably from a just appreciation of its difficulty, possibly, however, in obedience to orders, issuing from a desire to temporize a while longer.

5th. That during the month of May pending the settlement of the demands, the government, which pretended to be par excellence the friend of the foreigner and saying that they would give every protection to neutrals, was at the same time meditating the basest treachery to all.

6th. That there is every reason to believe that if the money demanded is finally met, it is because the small minority who have power in Yedo have shouldered a responsibility, which it is very doubtful if it will be accepted by the Miako faction, who cannot but feel humiliated at what they consider a punishment and degradation, and there is reason to fear will yet seek retribution.

7th. That we are on a volcano which may any moment explode under our feet.

Friday, June 19, 1863

Col. Neale was informed yesterday that there was some delay about the payment of the money, but he refused to extend the time beyond 9 o'clock this morning. The morning came and passed without payment and during the day Col. Neale was officially informed that the obligation to pay given by the Governors of Foreign Affairs on the 14th was given without authority and could not be met. This cool repudiation of a written bond can have but one explanation, namely, that the payment of the English claims on any terms is repugnant to the daimios, who represent the real strength of the country. The Governors representing the Yedo Government signed the bond doubtless intending to pay, but between the time of signing and the hour of payment, finding that payment would be so repugnant to the hostile daimios as to endanger the whole government, they repudiate their written obligation. Our affairs now assume a most grave aspect. Col. Neale refuses to see any of the Japanese Governors until the money is paid.

Saturday, June 20, 1863

Col. Neale having refused to see the Japanese Governors, the consuls of all the nationalities were this morning called to meet the Governor of Kanagawa at the Custom House. On assembling there the Governor informed them of the position of affairs, and stated that the reason the money had not been paid was that a letter had been received from the Tycoon, now at Miako, ordering them not to pay, and again a second letter last evening repeating the order, and saying, that the payment of the demands of the English would put his life in instant peril. The Governor says that this settlement of the claim is hostile to the feelings of the samurai who say, "why do you pay this money to those English fools?" The Governor then avowed the desire of the Tycoon's Government to pay these demands, but they were restrained from so doing by the power of the Miako party. He further promised that unless the English began an attack upon them, all should remain quiet at this port, and merchants and laborers should continue their avocations as usual.

Col. Neale was known to be on the *Euryalus* in conference with Admiral Kuper to a late hour in the forenoon and all awaited with anxiety the result.

In the afternoon Col. Neale gave official notice to the Foreign Ministers, and, through the Consul, to the British merchants, that he had placed the whole matter in the hands of Admiral Kuper, who would take such steps as the exigencies of the case demanded.

Thus, at last, the English claims have left the civil and gone into the military and naval power. War seems inevitable—all hope there yet may be left some road to peace—what Admiral Kuper will do, what measure of compulsion he will employ we can only conjecture.

In due time we shall know his intentions. No alarm fortunately prevails among the Japanese as before, which shows that the Japanese Government have not as before urged them to flight. Every day will now bear its own burden of responsibility.

Sunday, June 21, 1863

A communication is received from the Admiral today in which he says that peaceful negotiations having failed to bring the Japanese to terms, he shall employ measures of coercion which he will not institute for eight days inclusive of today, unless the Japanese [take] the initiative before. Thus matters will soon be brought to a final issue. He recommends the removal of the women and children on shipboard, and assigned the *Coromandel* to receive them so soon as they are ready to go.

The Japanese Governors visited General Pruyn this evening and still held out the olive branch, they admit that the Tycoon is compulsorily detained at Kioto and that he has given the orders for the expulsion of the foreigners. They said that these orders were received ten days since and required compliance within thirty days. They had not attempted to execute them, and would not because they knew they were impossible. They again promised not to disturb the persons, or property, of neutrals, and that their own merchants, mechanics, and laborers, in fact, all the native population of Yokohama, were everyone to remain and continue their business.

Monday, June 22, 1863

The foreign merchants are generally busy removing their merchandise and valuables on shipboard. The natives are still quiet. The Governor of Kanagawa is still busy endeavoring to make some arrangement for the settlement of our complicated affairs.

Tuesday, June 23, 1863

The work of removal goes on as briskly as ever. The *Pearl* and a gun boat have gone out in the bay reconnoitering. Stotsbashi [Hitotsubashi],[13] who has been expected from Miako clothed with full powers, slept at Fujisawa last night. Today he reached Kanagawa and had an interview with the Governor. There are rumors enough as to his mission, but nothing reliable; our hopes of peace are alternately raised and depressed.

The English *charge* and Admiral visit the Custom House this P.M. and some high official is down from Yedo—something in the wind.[14]

[13] Hitotsubashi, was, of course, Tokugawa Yoshinobu, who met with the Kanagawa magistrates, Asano Ujisuke and Yamaguchi Naoki, on this occasion. Yoshinobu had been sent to Edo specifically to take charge of the expulsion of the Westerners. See Conrad Totman, *The Collapse of the Tokugawa Bakufu, 1862–1868* (Honolulu: University Press of Hawaii, 1980), p. 71.

[14] The official mentioned here was Ogasawara Nagamichi, who arrived in Yokohama that morning and who later in the day sent word to the British that he would pay the indemnity. Payment was arranged the next day. See Conrad Totman, *The Collapse of the Tokugawa Bakufu,* p. 72. Hall is quite right in sensing that an important decision had been made. Totman indicates that it is not clear that Yoshinobu and Ogasawara met on this day, but that Yoshinobu's stand indicated "tacit consent" with Ogasawara's decision.

[On June 23, 1863, Hall wrote the following letter to the *New York Tribune*, which was published on August 28, 1863.]

I had scarcely closed my letter of the 15th inst. when a sudden and unexpected somersault in public affairs took place which the delay of the schooner Ford enables me to chronicle, as well as to place before your reader copies of two important documents.

The Japanese Governors on the 13th instant gave their written obligation to pay the first installment of the English demand on the 18th. The 18th came and passed, but brought with it not an ichibu—there was a hitch somewhere, and the Japanese Governors begged for a day's delay. The next day came and passed, but still no money: instead thereof the Governors informed Col. Neale, the British Charge, that they could not pay, and that in giving him a written promise to pay they at once closed the door to any further interview on the subject until the money was paid as promised.

On the morning of the 20th, communication with the British Charge being suspended, the foreign Consuls were called to the Custom House to receive a communication from the Governor. This communication was that orders had been received from the Tycoon at Miaco, forbidding compliance with the English demands in any shape, as compliance would place his life in immediate peril at the hands of the hostile Daimios. The Governor further expressed regret for the false position he had been placed in by his broken promise to pay, but compliance now would cost him his head as well. He still insisted that the Yedo Government desired to arrange this affair, and would commit no acts to provoke hostilities; that all the native populations of Yokohama had been enjoined to remain quiet, and pursue their usual avocations.

On this same day Col. Neale communicated to the British residents the fact that he had ceased all negotiations with the Japanese, and had given the further conduct of the matter into the hands of Rear-Admiral Kuper, commanding the fleet in Yedo Bay—a copy of which notification forms one of the enclosures with this.

On the following day, Rear-Admiral Kuper issued notice (a copy of which forms the second enclosure) to the British residents that, peaceful negotiations having failed to bring the Japanese to do justice, the trial of coercive measures to that end had devolved upon him—promising also that no such coercion should be commenced before the 29th instant, in order to give the foreign community time for the arrangement of their affairs.

The Japanese Governors, cut off from further interviews with the English Charge, now sought the representatives of the other Powers for explanation of their position and purposes. They still claimed for the Tycoon and his Government officers an earnest desire to adjust these difficulties, but unfortunately the young Tycoon himself was at the moment compulsorily detained at Miaco, and had been forced to sign the order of noncompliance with the English demands by the hostile chiefs about him, and whose prisoner his virtually was. They voluntarily stated that ten days ago they had received positive orders form the Tycoon requiring the expulsion of every foreigner from Japan within thirty days—an order they had not attempted to execute, and did not intend to, knowing its impossibility. They avowed their desire for continual peace again, promising that the first blows of war should not come from them; on the contrary, they would do all in their power to preserve Yokohama from attack. The people, they promised, should remain quietly at their business which promises they have so far faithfully kept.

The French Admiral Juarez, who has two steam war vessels in port, and 600 soldiers and sailor-marines at his command, had promised to hold Yokohama "to the last extremity"—and even this small force is, doubtless, sufficient to help us maintain our position here for a considerable time.

Amid all these belligerent prospects there are rays of hope. The government of the unhappy Tycoon is likely to be crushed between two forces—the hostile Daimios,

or the English. To remain neutral will be
annihilation, and so it is to be hoped that
he will choose the wise course of meeting
[the] demand[s] of the English, and, if
need be, accept foreign aid against his powerful enemies at Miaco, who are the enemies of foreign intercourse and progress
also. Thus, though Nagasaki may be abandoned temporarily, being in the infected
portion of the empire, there is good reason
to hope that the whole region to the north
of the Hiacone Mountains will remain tranquil and so secure a continuation of trade
and intercourse at this port, which is the
natural outlet of all the silk, and the most
convenient one of tea.

In obedience to Rear-Admiral Kuper's
suggestions, the foreign residents are generally preparing for the worst, by the removal of their merchandise and effects on
board the shipping of which there is luckily
a fair supply.

Re-enforcements have been ordered
from China and India. The emergency requires rare powers of discretion, patience,
and forbearance in dealing with a Government whose chief is in the hands of his enemies, which sees only destruction whichever way it turns.

Let us still hope for peace to thrice unhappy Japan, who in an evil hour, not of
her own seeking, opened her long-closed
doors to such troublesome guests.

Wednesday, June 24, 1863

We were all agreeably surprised this morning to find that the Japanese Government had
come to terms, and that so early as 4 A.M. a
large installment of money had been paid into
the hands of Col. Neale. We rejoice in the
prospect of continued peace and quiet. Who,
or what, has wrought the change I do not
know. The movements at the Custom House
last night had attracted my attention as well as
broken my rest.

Curious anomaly, all the Ministers receive
this morning dispatches from the Goroju requesting the removal of all foreigners from Japan, that is perhaps a blind for the Miako
government.

The money paid in I learn is the £100,000
demanded of the Tycoons Government =
$440,000 Mexican. The demand on Satsuma
for an additional £50,000 and the murderers
of Richardson is not yet settled.

[On June 24, 1863, Hall added to his
dispatch of the previous day the following
section, which was published in the *New
York Tribune* on August 28, 1863.]

The two accompanying letters were
ready for the Ford's Mail, which closes this
morning, when the Japanese Government
refreshed itself with another somersault.
At 4 P.M. [A.M.] $300,000 of the indemnity
money was paid into the English Legation,
unexpectedly to everybody—the balance of
the claim is to be paid today. Truly, for lying diplomacy Japan must bear the palm of
glory. What act the curtain shall ring up
next who shall dare predict! It promises, at
least, present peace and quiet.

Copy—No. 44   YOKOHAMA,
                               June 20, 1863.

SIR: I have to instruct you to adopt as early
as possible such measures as may be the
most effectual to make known to the British community and to your colleagues, the
Consuls of foreign States, the present situation of affairs in regard to the subject of
the British demands upon the Japanese
Government.

The patience and moderation which I
have exercised in my communications with
the Tycoon's Government, in the earnest
desire of bringing about a peaceful settlement of the avowedly just demands for
reparation preferred by her Majesty's Government, are well known and sufficiently
manifest.

At the most recent date (the 18th instant), those objects which I had in view
were in the very eve of being happily accomplished.

The Japanese Government, through its
Envoys, had, after innumerable difficulties,
solemnly and unreservedly entered into a
written engagement with me to pay the pecuniary demands at short specified inter-

vals, the first payment to have been made on the date above referred to.

That day has been reached and is passed, and the Japanese Ministers have flagrantly, unequivocally and designedly broken their faith.

In the most unjustifiable and audacious manner the Tycoon's Government now seeks to reopen negotiations previous to accomplishing their solemn assent to the settlement of the pecuniary portion of the demands and openly declare their intention to withhold all payments, thus most effectively extinguishing all remaining faith in even their most solemn engagements.

As her Majesty's representative, I have now, therefore, to declare that the utmost limits of my patience (consistently exerted and directed to exact the reparation sought by peaceful means, and which I had good reason to hope had been successfully exercised) is now exhausted.

Her majesty's subjects and your colleagues, the Consuls of foreign States, have, during a period of ten weeks, been at intervals informed that the adoption of coercive measures was an impending contingency, though the probability, or otherwise, of their occurrence, was alternately stronger or feebler to advise, though yourself, British subjects, and the foreign community generally, to be prepared for the worst and most regrettable emergency which could arise, namely, the necessity which might present itself (with a view to the security of their persons and property) of abandoning the open ports, while the Vice Admiral Commanding in Chief has as often and as consistently declared his inability to hold militarily the settlement, if coercive measures were actually resorted to effectually to enforce compliance with the demands.

So long as a chance of honest though tardy action could be anticipated on the part of the Japanese Government, I have scrupulously deferred initiating hostilities by an appeal to force. But I now feel myself urgently called upon to leave the adoption of the only measures which the Rulers of this country would appear to understand or appreciate—namely those of coercion,

to the Admiral in whose hands I will this day consign the solution of affairs.

Thus within a very short period the policy of expediency, invariably adopted by the Japanese Government, may possibly lead them to repair their broken faith by the actual payment of the indemnities, and a more peaceful aspect of affairs may again present itself—or, on the other hand, the Admiral may have deemed it advisable to profit by the circumstances to carry out some of the operations he may decide upon.

Thus also her Majesty's subjects and your colleagues will judge of the measures they may individually deem it practicable and expedient to adopt under all the circumstances here most unreservedly and explicitly set forth.

I need hardly add that I shall not fail immediately to concert with Admiral Kuper and Admiral Juarez (whose frank and cordially proffered cooperation I am assured of) respecting such temporary measures for the safe guard of the community in this emergency as may be practicable.

> EDWD. ST. JOHN NEALE
TO CHARLES A. WINCHESTER, esq.

EURYALUS, at Yokohama, June 21, 1863
SIR: Her Majesty's Charge d'Affaires has placed in my hands the solution of the questions at issue between the Japanese Government and that of Her Majesty, in consequence of all peaceful and diplomatic negotiations having failed to bring the Government of the Tycoon to a due sense of its obligations.

The instructions under which, in this contingency, it will now be my duty to act, will necessarily involve coercive measures to be undertaken by the naval force under my command; and as such measures will probably lead to action on the part of the Japanese, which would endanger the safety not only of British subjects, but also of all foreign residents in Japan; I have to request you will forthwith communicate this circumstance to all British subjects and to the Consuls of Foreign Powers, with a view to their immediately adopting such steps as they may think desirable for the security of their persons and property, the force at my disposal being inadequate for the efficient protection of Yokohama, while carrying out the instructions of Her Majesty's Government in other parts of Japan.

In order that the community may have sufficient time to make arrangement for their personal security, I desire you will inform them that, unless called upon by any initiative act of hostility on the part of the Japanese, to maintain the dignity of the British flag. I shall not take any hostile step until after the expiration of eight days from this date, inclusive.

I have also to acquaint you that all the precautionary measures adopted some weeks since for the speedy relief of the foreign community in the event of any sudden attack or disturbance, will be continued during the interval mentioned, and such additional assistance rendered as will be consistent with the duty of preserving the efficiency of her Majesty's ships.

Under the existing state of affairs, and the great probability of approaching strife and torment, I think it necessary to recommend most strongly that all those who have wives and families at Yokohama should take the earliest opportunity of removing them, at any rate, from the scene of danger, should they themselves determine upon awaiting the issue of events.

AUGUSTUS I. KUPER
TO CHAS. A. WINCHESTER, esq.

Thursday, June 25, 1863

It is agreed that all the daimio men in the place shall evacuate and leave the protection of Yokohama to the Tycoon's soldiers and the foreigners. With this view the French and English are to place a battery on the bluffs S.E. of the town, and it is understood that no two sworded men are to be admitted to Yokohama except such as belong to the Tycoon.

This sudden change in the Japanese movements almost compels me to believe that they have been playing a game of deep deception as regards their inability to pay, their having been ordered not to pay, and their danger from the Mikado's power. So tangled is Japanese policy that no one dare affirm that he understands it.

Tuesday, June 30, 1863

The French hoist their flag on the bluffs over Yokohama.

Saturday, July 4, 1863

Salutes fired by the *Wyoming* and the English and French vessels in harbor. Capt. McD[ougal] of the *Wyoming* had company aboard. Passed a pleasant day there.

Sunday, July 5, 1863

A timely rain after a long dry time and much needed for the crops.

Tuesday, July 7, 1863

The Yedo Government has chartered the English Steamers *Elgin* and *Rajah* to take troops to Oasaca. It is supposed for the relief of the Tycoon who is detained there.

Saturday, July 11, 1863

Last evening while at dinner at Mr. S.'s in company with the American Minister, Consul, and others, a Governor of Foreign Affairs came from Yedo on urgent business as he said.[15] This urgent business proved to be the communication of the fact of an attack made on an American steamer near the straits of Shimonoseki in the Inland Sea. The Governor

---

[15] It is not entirely clear who Mr. S. was, but this may well have been Raphael Schoyer, mentioned earlier. The *Pembroke* was an American steamer under consignment to Walsh, Hall and Co. The *Pembroke* had been sent to China by Robert B. Forbes, who writes: "It was on the 16th of November, 1861, that I dispatched the

said the vessel was fired into by two Japanese vessels belonging to the Prince of Chosiu, and whether it had escaped or not he did not know.

This news is confirmed today by the arrival of a mail from Shanghai. It appears that the steamer *Pembroke*, dispatched by me for Shanghai on the 21st, was the vessel attacked under the following circumstances. When near the straits of Shimonoseki on the afternoon of the 24th she anchored for the night. Soon after a Japanese armed bark flying the imperial colors, which she had passed about 2 P.M., came down and anchored within a quarter of a mile of her. About 1 A.M. in the night, which was very dark, the bark opened fire on the steamer, and soon after was joined by a brig, which coming down under full sail and passing within forty yards of the steamer, raised great shouts and then joining the bark also opened fire on the *Pembroke*. The steamer hastened to get up steam, and, though under fire from both vessels while doing this, succeeded in making its escape with no other injury than the cutting of a topmast back stay.

The Governor called again today on the American Minister in relation to the affair, and for his government wholly disavowed the act and said the perpetrators were no Japanese. This was enough, the opinion of Capt. McDougal of the *Wyoming* was already made up that he should proceed in search of the quasi freebooters at once and impart signal punishment, in which opinion the American Minister coincided. The *Wyoming* began to coal at once and it was arranged she should go to sea on Monday morning. This affair has caused no little excitement and the universal desire is that these marauders may be punished.

Sunday, July 12, 1863

The *Elgin* went to sea today loaded with Japanese troops.

Monday, July 13, 1863

The *Wyoming* went to sea early this morning fully prepared to inflict punishment on Chosiu and ships wherever found. We ardently hope that the proud daimios of Japan will receive a wholesome lesson.

Wednesday, July 15, 1863

The *Hellespont* from Nagasaki arrived today and brings the interesting news that the French dispatch steamer *Kien Chang*, which left there a few days since, while passing through the inland sea was attacked on the 9th inst. at the same place and by the same vessels that attacked the *Pembroke* in which they were aided by the shore batteries throwing both shot and shell. The *Kien Chang* used the two guns she had but pressed on her way and escaped, though not till she had received several shots which did her some injury. The French Admiral takes prompt action in the matter and will dispatch at daylight tomorrow the *Semiramis* (35 guns) and *Tancrede* (42 guns) with a landing force of 400 men. The Admiral hopes to demolish the assailants of the *Kien Chang*. The Dutch Corvette *Medusa* left Nagasaki the day before the *Hellespont* via the straits of Shimonoseki and the inland sea for this port, and the *Hellespont* reports her coming out of the Bungo Channel as she passed. This diversion from a direct route seems significant at this juncture, perhaps she has shared Mowori [Mori] Prince of Nagato's animosity also.

We hope our own gallant *Wyoming* will have the opportunity to deal the first blows.

---

propeller 'Pembroke,' Captain J. A. Cunningham, for Batavia and China, under sail. She was the only vessel during the [Civil] war, furnished with a 'letter of marque' [the right to be armed and seize enemy vessels]; which fact is attested by W. Hunter, assistant Secretary of State, under date of 21st July, 1865." See Robert B.

Forbes, *Personal Reminiscences* (Boston: Privately Printed, 1876), p. 285. As the text indicates, Hall had just dispatched her to Shanghai. The news was therefore of considerable importance to him as well as the minister. John A. Cunningham, the captain of the *Pembroke* took Hall's place at Walsh, Hall & Co. in June 1866.

Thursday, July 16, 1863

Matsuri at Homura today with the usual crowd of gaily decked men, women, and children. The curiously shaded and parti-colored dresses have a very quaint effect. French calicoes were effectively used for cheery dress. The little girls, many of them, wore their gowns off of one shoulder so as to display their crimson and scarlet and fancy colored underclothing.

Friday, July 17, 1863

The *Medusa* arrived this morning and our anticipations respecting her were realized. While slowly steaming through the Straits of Shimonoseki she was opened upon by a well directed fire from several shore batteries and the same bark and brig. These batteries were placed advantageously in a small indentation of the northern shore which enabled them to deliver a converging fire. The firing was rapid and well sustained and the *Medusa* being within point blank range was hit more than twenty times, several shots taking effect within a few inches of the water line. One shell exploding in the engineer's room set fire momentarily to the ship. The action lasted for over an hour, the *Medusa* slowly steaming on. On the *Medusa* four men were killed and four severely wounded. The fire was from guns of six, twelve, and thirty pounders and was well directed. The batteries appeared to be six in number. The *Medusa*'s shells were seen to explode over the attacking brig, the forts and the town of Shimonoseki, but with how much injury there was no means of ascertaining. All things considered the *Medusa* had a fortunate escape. The slightest stoppage of her machinery would have been fatal—or if batteries on the south shore had opened, she would hardly have got away without great loss and injury.

The *Medusa* spoke [with] the *Semiramis* but did not meet the *Wyoming*.

Monday, July 20, 1863

We are all delighted this morning to see the *Wyoming* steaming back into the harbor and hasten to get her news. She too has had a serious brawl with the Shimonoseki batteries and brings back five killed and five wounded. The *Wyoming* reached the scene of action on the morning of the 16th and steamed into the straits, [a] signal gun from the bluffs announced her approach. When she came within range of the first batteries fire was opened on her. The *Wyoming* hoisted her ensign and replied. Under shelter of the batteries lay the bark and brig, already famous, and to them were now added the *Lancefield* steamer purchased by Mowori in this [port] six or eight months since. The *Wyoming*, avoiding the usual course through the center of the channel, steamed in nearer shore so as to pass within pistol shot of the brig and between the *Lancefield* and the batteries, delivering a broadside into each as she passed. She then steamed past the batteries and turned around to return, still delivering her fire as she moved, and receiving the fire of the vessels and batteries. The *Lancefield* now attempted to steam away, but two 11 inch shells not only arrested her progress, but one of them exploded her boilers and a fearful explosion hopelessly shattered the steamer which was now put ashore, everybody jumping overboard to escape. The brig again received further shots and began to settle down. The *Wyoming* having thus been under fire an hour and ten minutes, entering into action at 11 o'clock 15 minutes and [having] effected the work she was mainly sent to do, steamed out from under fire. Her losses were the killed and wounded as named above, and she received 11 shots in her hull none of which were of serious injury. Capt. McDougal praises warmly the action of the officers and crew.

Yedo has suffered another great fire which occurred on Saturday night in the daimio quarter adjoining the emperor's palace, which narrowly escaped and suffered some injury.

Tuesday, July 21, 1863

The fire at Yedo is said to be the most severe known for many years, some say fifty years. The destruction was the greatest in the daimios quarter near the citadel, 30 of their yashikis, or palaces, were consumed, and the flames, impelled by the violent south wind blowing, leaped the citadel walls destroying the Tycoon's palace.

Thursday, July 23, 1863

Japanese rumors declare that the explosion in the *Lancefield* at the late battle of Shimonoseki caused the loss of 40 lives, and that also much destruction and loss of life was occasioned by the *Wyoming's* fire in the town and batteries.

Friday, July 24, 1863

The *Semiramis* returned this morning having left the *Tancrede* behind to repair her trifling damages. These vessels reached the strait on the 20th, but what they did it is difficult to say out of all the conflicting rumors, some of which say they did everything, some that they did nothing. We shall have a semi-official report tomorrow.

[On July 24, 1863, Hall wrote the following letter to the *New York Tribune*, which along with his letter of July 25, 1863, entirely covered the front page of the *Tribune* of October 2, 1863, under the headline "THE NAVAL FIGHT WITH THE JAPANESE."]

The demands of the English Government on the Court at Yedo were met by the payment of £110,000 on the 24th ult., the very day my last letter left, and so the immediate commencement of hostilities against the Japanese was averted. This payment following so much long and fruitless negotiation, promises to pay, and again refusals to pay, was at last made in the most sudden and unexpected manner. The cause

of this final resolve to pay is easily seen. The Tycoon's government were pressed from two sides, the hostile Daimios, who demanded that not a farthing should be paid, and the English fleet, which was ready to let slip the dogs of war in case of any longer refusal. The last pressure was for the moment the strongest; the hostile Daimios might be placated hereafter—the English must be appeased on the moment.

The Tycoon, who, in his forced absence at Miaco, was represented in Yedo by the Gorogio, or Council of State, had already done something to placate the irate Chiefs. The American Minister, the last foreigner residing in Yedo, had literally been smoked out like a troublesome rat in the areas of courts; the burning rafters over his head were unmistakable notices to quit, and he is forbidden to return. At Kanagawa proper, on the north side of Yokohama Bay, the few families there, including the American Consul, were likewise driven out by threats of assassination, until Yokohama alone held all of the hated foreigners. And now, no sooner was this money paid than the Gorogio threw another top to the implacable Daimios *by the issue within three hours after this payment of a formal notice to the ministers' representatives of each treaty power that the foreigners must leave Japan and all the ports be closed!* After humbling themselves to the payment of the English demand, no one of course believed the Gorogio had any hope of carrying the decree into effect, and when called upon for an explanation of this insult to every treaty power they so confessed, and said that it was done in obedience to orders from Miaco, with whose assembled dignitaries they were compelled to temporize.

The Government at Yedo, which was sicker than ever the "sick man of Europe," was in desperate straits. That it would have put the knife to the throat of every foreigner if thereby it could have secured its own position nobody doubted. They, the Gorogio, played a fast and loose game between the foreign chiefs and their own. In their tricky diplomacy they lied themselves into one position only to lie themselves back into another until they had lost the confidence of the most confiding of the foreign representatives. They had paid the hefty demand on their purse, but were still nicely balancing whether they should best subserve their own interests by falling in deadly blows on our little settlement or taking the aid of foreign arms against the Miaco party.

The English fleet still lay in the harbor augmenting in force—their allies the French far more vigorous of purpose had called over troops from China and made a camp on the heights above Yokohama, and prepared the ground for the erection of batteries to command both bay and town, and threatened to take military occupation of the place. The English had still an unsettled demand on the Prince of Satsuma for £50,000 and the murderers of Richardson which they hoped to settle in the bay of Yedo without being compelled to knock at Satsuma's citadel gates in Kagosima on Kiusiu Isle. And the wily Satsuma, it is to be learned, has been mocking the English with delusive hopes only to gain time to render yet more inaccessible to hostile fleets his own mountain-crowned bay of Kagosima, a cul de sac girt with formidable batteries. While Admiral Kuper was contemplating the early movement of his fleet to Satsuma's capital, other events occurred which absorbed the attention of everyone—the commencement of hostilities by the Japanese themselves.

Before proceeding to the narration of those hostilities, it is well to recall the fact stated in a previous letter—that the Daimios in council assembled at Miaco had determined on the expulsion of all foreigners from Japan, speaking through their mouthpiece, the Mikado, to whose long-time unrecognized supremacy in this Empire they had found it convenient to give a new vitality. This proclamation had gone forth that the foreigner was to be driven out and the dispatch addressed to all the foreign Ministers by the Gorogio was only an iteration of that decree. All Daimios had been enjoined to repair to their principalities, put their sea coast in a state of defense and their trainers in fighting order. The

Tycoon still remained in surveillance at Miaco, and to the Gorogio it began to appear doubtful if any concessions to the Mikado would now save his position and power; they accordingly instituted other measures, and having chartered two foreign steamers they loaded them with troops, as well as their own steamers, and drew a large body of men into Oasaca.

But it is doubtful if even this will ease the Tycoon's sinking fortune, or restore his person to Yedo, for within a few days past the Gorogio have appealed to the French for material aid. While the Gorogio were thus striving to save their falling fortunes, let us see what was occurring contemporaneously elsewhere.

The American merchant steamer Pembroke left this port on the 21st of June for Shanghai, via the "Inland Sea." This sea is the *Suwo Nada* of the maps, lying between the islands of Nipon and Sikok. The usual passage is to enter the Kino Channel, at the eastern extremity, and to pass out through the Straits of Simonoseki, a narrow strait between the islands of Nipon and Kiusiu, varying from half a mile to a mile in width.

The Pembroke reached the entrance of Simonoseki Strait on the 25th and anchored for the night. A Japanese bark, armed and full of men, passed her at her anchorage, and anchored between the Pembroke and the entrance of the strait, a quarter of a mile distant. As there was nothing in this proceeding especially out of the way, the officers of the Pembroke took no alarm. But about 1 A.M. the following morning, the night being so dark that the position of the vessels could only be distinctly seen by the lightning flashes of an approaching storm, the Japanese bark opened fire on the Pembroke, and had fired but a few shots when a Japanese armed brig (lately purchased of an English house at Yokohama) bore down on the Pembroke and then passing within forty yards of the little steamer, its crew raising hideous yells as they passed, came also to anchor near the bark, and likewise opened fire. The firing was now rapid and continuous from both vessels. The Pembroke had a small armament, but her small crew were wholly occupied with getting up steam and getting the vessel under way, which they fortunately did before receiving any injury, and made their escape through the darkness out of the Bungo channel, an unfrequented passage between the islands of Sikok and Kiusiu.

The news of this wanton attack did not reach Kanagawa till the 10th of July, when it was communicated to the American Minister by the Japanese authorities. The following day full particulars were received from Shanghai. The Yedo Government at once disavowed the act, and said that the perpetrators had neither its sanction or protection; the attacking vessels belonging to Mowori, Prince of Chosiu, or Nagato, whose principality lies on the north side of Simonoseki Strait, a powerful chief, linked to the Miaco party, and so hostile to the Tycoon and foreigners alike. It was therefore determined that the United States corvette Wyoming, Capt. McDougal, then fortunately in port, should proceed at once to the scene of this attack in quest of the assailing vessels. The Wyoming, having to take in coals, was not ready for sea till the morning of the 13th, when she departed.

The Wyoming had hardly left port when the news arrived that the French Government dispatch steamer Kienchang, which had left this port on the 2d of July for Nagasaki, while attempting to pass through the same Strait of Simonoseki, had been fired into not only by the named vessels but by shore batteries on the north side, in the principality of the same Mowori, or Daipen no Dajboo, as he is very commonly called. The Kienchang, having run the gauntlet of a heavy fire, also escaped without serious injury.

This news came on the 15th inst., and the French Admiral Juarez at 3 o'clock the next morning was on his way to pay his respects to the fire-eating Mowori, in his flagship, the steam frigate Semiramis, with 35 guns and the steamer Tancrede, 42 guns together carrying six or seven hundred men, and, with true French spirit, ready for the fray.

Events thickened rapidly; the Semiramis was only out of sight when the Dutch steam corvette Medusa, 18 guns, came in on the 17th, and had a yet more serious story to tell. The Medusa left Nagasaki for Kanagawa on the 9th inst., via the inland sea, and when just out of the harbor, met the Kienchang coming in, and, so learned of the perils by the way. Thus the Medusa was fortunately forewarned, and, being a fine vessel, well armed with a full complement of men, did not shrink from the trial. On the 11th inst. she entered the narrow strait from the west. Her decks were cleared for action, and none too soon. At 7 A.M. two signal guns from the shore announced her approach to the batteries of Simonoseki, which as she came up within range, opened fire simultaneously with the brig and bark. The Medusa stood on her course, slowly steaming, and exchanging broadsides with the enemy. After an hour and a half she came out from the shower of shot and shell that had rained upon her from the vessels and batteries, with twenty shots in her hull, several of them as close to the water line as to require instant repair. One shell had exploded in her engine room, and a twelve pound hot shot had at one time ignited her wooden walls. Four men were killed and four were severely wounded.

The Medusa had passed in all nine batteries of six, 12, 24 and 32-pounders. One battery was an eight-gun battery of 32s. Owing to the short range—the batteries less than half a mile distant, and the vessels not more than three cables' length—the firing was necessarily effective.

The existence of such powerful batteries was not known when the Wyoming left this port, and as she did not chance to meet the Medusa, some apprehension was felt for her fate if she got entangled in that narrow pass. But we were all gratified on the 20th inst. by seeing our noble vessel coming back into port apparently unharmed, though two shots through her smokestack were plainly visible. The news was soon known.

On the morning of the 16th inst. the Wyoming, unconscious of the warm reception that awaited her, had steamed cautiously into the narrow straits, and soon caught sight of the frowning batteries, and lying under their protection, the vessels she had come in search of, and in addition to these, the fine British steamer Lancefield, sold to Mowori a few months ago. Signal guns from the shore gave the alarm, then came the first fire from a battery of three guns. Up went the old bunting, and as it went up, a second battery joined in; then the Wyoming replied with her broadside of four guns, and now all the batteries commenced firing as she came within the same easy range that the Medusa had. Here the Captain of the Wyoming took a bold course, which no doubt saved many lives of his men and much damage to the ship. Leaving the usual channel, he took his vessel so close into the northern shore that the batteries lost their range and fired over: at the same time, this brought him between the Japanese steamer and the shore, and rendered useless the most of her guns, which had been trained to the side toward the open channel.

The bark gave the Wyoming its broadside of six-pounders as she closely passed, the brig followed suit at less than 50 yards range, and the Wyoming returned her heavy compliments to both. The Wyoming next passed the Lancefield within 50 yards and gave the latter her 32-pounders, to which the Lancefield made feeble reply with the only two small guns she had left on that side. The Wyoming having now passed the batteries on the Lancefield, which brought her 10-inch guns to bear on the Lancefield, which was now steaming out of action. One well-directed 10-inch shell struck the Lancefield amidships, and the explosion that followed accompanied with volumes of steam and smoke, told that the work was done for her. The Wyoming again ran the gauntlet of this terrible fire, to which she replied as rapidly as her guns would permit, but those 10-inch shells made their mark, now bursting in the batteries, now exploding among the houses of the town, until one more turn in the shore separated the combatants in this unequal strike. The Lancefield was destroyed, the brig was left sinking, and what damage more had been done to town and batteries

was best known to the Japanese. The Wyoming's casualties were four killed and seven wounded—one has since died. She received 11 shots of shells in her hull which did trifling damage. A fragment of a shell had crushed Lieut. Barton's sword hilt doing him no personal injury. Capt. McDougal speaks in the warmest terms of the conduct of his men and officers.

Nor can we fail to admire the determination and courage of this Daimio who single-handed, defies the ships of every nation. We now await the return of the French Admiral who with his landing corps has doubtless finished what the Medusa and Wyoming so gallantly began.

The great question of interest is will the other Daimios come to Mowori's aid, or leave him to perish alone? He is but carrying out the resolution to which they had all come at Miaco for the expulsion of foreigners, and which decree was issued by the Mikado more under the instigation of this man than any other. Thus, the Yedo Government disavows him, and why?—because its own stability depends on crushing out the power of the great Daimios, not one of whom is today a friend of foreign intercourse, if we judge opinions and events impartially.

Saturday, July 25, 1863

We have today a report of the *Semiramis'* doings. This vessel and the *Tancrede* arrived at the entrance to the straits on the 20th. As usual the signal battery announced their approach, when abreast the second battery the *Semiramis* anchored, the *Tancrede* steamed a little further in and received the fire of one or more batteries. The *Semiramis* received no fire from the battery near her, although at one time she was exposed to a raking fire for half an hour. She was out of the range of the other batteries. Admiral Juarez not deeming it prudent to take his vessel into the narrow strait where she might become unmanageable. The *Semiramis* bombarded this battery for a length of time and afterwards landing a force of 150 men advanced to the assault, but no opposition was made, the few armed men seen fled, and but few shots were fired on the attacking party. The battery was empty when they reached it, two guns had been disabled by the frigate's fire and there were pools of blood showing that some must have been killed or wounded, though none were seen. At the fort and a house nearby a large quantity of powder was found which was thrown into the sea. An adjoining village, which had evidently been the headquarters of soldiers, was destroyed by fire. The party then returned to the ship and this action closed. The *Tancrede* had not been much under fire being also out of range of the main batteries. Both the *Semiramis* and *Tancrede* were not near enough to the town of Shimonoseki or the batteries behind the town to draw their fire. The casualties were trifling: three of the *Semiramis* men were wounded, the *Tancrede* had her fore topmast shot away, receiving two other shots beside. Indeed this French expedition which was "to sweep away" all these batteries, and the town of Shimonoseki, has performed feebly to its vainglorious threats, having done far less than the *Wyoming*. It is amusing to hear the talk among the Japanese of the exploits of the *Wyoming* which is the theme at "bath houses" (where all public affairs are discussed), "terrible fellows," those Americans, they say. Another of the *Wyoming*'s wounded has died.

[On July 25, 1863, Hall sent the second letter to the *New York Tribune* that was published by the *Tribune* on its front page of October 2, 1863, under the headline "THE NAVAL FIGHT WITH THE JAPANESE."]

The Semiramis, with the French Admiral Juarez on board, returned to this port yesterday—her performance having been hardly up to the promise given out. The Semiramis and Tancrede reached the eastern entrance of Simonoseki Strait on the 20th inst. The Semiramis, being a large, unwieldy vessel for so narrow a passage, lay outside of the strait and engaged the small outer batteries at long range—so long a range that the Japanese fire could not

reach in reply. The Tancrede ventured a little further in, but not far enough to come under the fire of the main batteries of Simonoseki where the Medusa and Wyoming were so hotly engaged. No vessels were to be seen, but the mainmast of one, supposed to be that of the brig sunk by the Wyoming, was seen sticking in the water. The Semiramis landed 150 men, who took the outer battery without resistance, and burned an inoffensive village on the coast. The native soldiers stationed there ingloriously fled at the first approach, though a few crossed their long swords against French bayonets, and fell. It is said of some of these men thus cut down, that they seized the legs of the French soldiers, biting them in their dying hate.

From all accounts that we can gather from both French and Japanese sources it appears that little real injury was done by this expedition, which left with a great flourish of trumpets, the town and forts of Simonoseki being left unharmed and doubtful, even if seen by it. The Japanese account says that it destroyed "one small signal battery and burned up a village of poor laborers and fishermen who had done no one any harm." At all events the injury inflicted was much less than that done by the Wyoming, which, according to native accounts, was more severe than at first supposed. These accounts acknowledge a loss of forty killed or scalded to death by the explosion of the Lancefield's boilers, of many more killed on the other vessels and in the town and batteries by the close and murderous fire of her pivot guns. Those 10-inch shells astonished the natives as they plowed through the town of Simonoseki, spreading destruction wherever they went. Everywhere in our streets, one understanding the language will overhear the knots of people talking about "those great guns" and the "terrible Americans." Capt. McDougal deserves great credit for his coolness and intrepidity, particularly for the skillful manner in which he cut off the Japanese steamer, avoiding at the same time the full force of that storm of shot, shell and shrapnell from thirty-five or forty guns on shore, beside the broadsides of the brig and bark of six and ten guns respectively.

With this I send you a map of the scene of these affairs, with the course of the Wyoming laid down, and a fuller account of her engagement by an eye-witness on board.

As the French expedition failed to destroy the principal batteries as was expected, it is probable that a second joint expedition may be sent to complete the work. The Japanese certainly deserve credit for the gallant beginning they have made in the art of war, an art disused by them for two centuries. In the battery taken by the French several books of instruction in the art of war were found, one of them open at a marked page giving instructions how batteries should act against a vessel assailing them during a difficult tideway.

It must be remembered that these are the acts of a single chief, and he not the most powerful of those hostile to foreign intercourse. Should they all band together in armed opposition to the foreign Powers, their resistance will not be despicable. It must now be speedily determined whether the other Daimios will come to Mowori's rescue, or leave him to perish alone, fighting gallantly and single-handed for his country. On the part of the foreign Powers, the matter cannot rest here for Mowori, although injured is not vanquished, and yet today with his batteries, holds the passage to the inland sea against all comers.

On the south side of the same strait are also heavy batteries belonging to another chief, which have not yet opened their fire upon foreign vessels. When they do, the strait will become impassable.

The Jamestown is now daily expected from the China coast where she was last heard from.

Yedo has again been visited by the most destructive fire known for years, which occurred in the court quarter of the city. A great number of Daimios' palaces, it is said 30 in all, were destroyed, and the flames impelled by a violent wind leaped the citadel walls, and a second time since this port

was opened, destroyed the Tycoon's palace.

But fortunately a Japanese palace is not a gold-pillared, diamond-windowed abode of kings, but an affair of clean fir-wood, nice straw mats, and paper windows, neither very sumptuous or extravagant.

[Hall's letter was accompanied by the account of the battle written by his friend E. S. Benson.]

The following account of the trip of the United States steamer Wyoming is by E. S. Benson, esq., who was passenger on board:

"Information having reached Yokohama on the 11th instant that the American steamer Pembroke had been fired into by two Japanese armed vessels, Capt. McDougal immediately issued the necessary orders to prepare for sea. Coal and stores having been taken on board, we got under way at 5 o'clock on the morning of the 13th instant; entered the Bungo Channel on the 15th and anchored at the Island of Hime Sima. The next morning (16th inst.) we proceeded toward the Straits of Simonoseki, the western entrance of the Inland Sea. On the northern shore of the narrow passage is the Province of Nagato, governed by the Prince of Tcho-shu.

Within the past year he purchased the steamer Lancefield and the brig Lanrick, the former for $125,000, and the latter for about $25,000.

On nearing the Straits a signal gun was fired from a masked battery on the northern shore, which was repeated by two others to the westward toward Simonoseki.

Rounding the point on the southern side of the entrance, a bark, brig, and steamer were discovered lying at anchor close to the north shore; the steamer and the brig were immediately made out to be the Lancefield and Lanrick; the bark's name we did not know. All the vessels were flying the Japanese flag at the peak, and the private colors of the Prince of Nagato at the main. We now steered directly for the vessels, when a battery of three guns on the northern shore, about 50 feet above the level of the sea, opened fire on us, cutting up the rigging between the main and mizzen masts. We then ran up the American flag, and, still steaming on, were fired on by a battery of four guns; to this we replied with a broadside.

We were now rapidly approaching the vessels; the bark was close in shore; about fifty yards outside of her, and one length ahead, lay the brig another length ahead; and fifty yards outside the brig was the steamer.

The main channel was outside of all these vessels. Captain McDougal gave orders to run the "Wyoming" between the steamer and the brig. As we got abreast of the bark she opened a broadside fire from three guns; in less than two minutes we were abreast of the brig and received her fire from four brass 32-pounders. We now had the steamers on our port side, her guns, like the others, being trained on the channel, she fired a few swivels and small arms only. In passing we gave them all our guns on both sides, hulling both the brig and steamer. Keeping close round the bows of the steamer we stood over toward the southern shore, receiving a constant fire from six batteries, the steamer, brig, and bark. We here got aground, but backed off without much difficulty. The steamer Lancefield having steam up, slipped her cable, keeping close along the northern shore, with the intention of escaping, or of running on shore to examine the damage caused by our first shots. The Wyoming was now maneuvered into position, and an eleven inch shell was planted in the steamer directly at midships, about one foot above the water line. In an instant volumes of steam and smoke issued out of her fore and aft—her boiler was exploded. After dropping two more shells into her hull, the order was given to cease firing on the steamer, and to direct the shots upon the different batteries, the bark, and the brig, all of which were loading and firing as rapidly as possible. Quite a number of shell exploded in the batteries, and considerable damage was done to the town.

In passing out of the Straits, we delivered a few very effective shots into the brig, and the last seen of her she was fast settling by the stern. The fire from the batteries was kept up throughout, but somewhat slackened on our return.

By that time we had four men killed outright and seven wounded (one since died). The armament of the Wyoming being only four 32-pounders and two pivot guns, opposed to six shore batteries of an average of three guns each, the bark six, the brig eight, and the steamer two, making in all thirty-four guns, mostly 32-pounders; Capt. McDougal very wisely concluded to withdraw from so unequal a contest and proceeded to Yokohama for more force. The captain, all his officers and crew behaved with the utmost coolness and enemy's vessels, receiving and returning broadsides at pistol range, at the same time sustaining a hot and continuous fire from shore batteries. When the successful shot struck the steamer our crew gave three hearty cheers. The action lasted one hour and ten minutes; thirty shots in the masts, rigging and smokestack.

One 32-pound shell came through, immediately below the tackles of the forward broadside gun, and exploding, killed one man and wounded five others."

Sunday, July 26, 1863

Wilhemina Elize left for San Francisco this morning.

There was a meeting of foreign ministers yesterday and it was agreed that it should be left with the commanders of the fleet to say what further actions should be taken to punish the Prince of Nagato.

Wednesday, July 29, 1863

The English and French Admirals and the American and Dutch Captains had a conference this morning to act on the discretion placed in their hands by the foreign ministers. The result has not transpired.

For two or three days past there have been serious riots in the courtesan's quarter arising out of the arrest of some bettos by the police. The bettos of the place in a body rescued their comrades and chastised those who had put them in durance. The following day the police again made arrests of the rioters and the same night the bettos again attacked the police and two were severely wounded or killed. The following day the emuete continued and the bettos were resolved on further riotous acts when some arrangement was come to. But this whole incident is instructive as to the character of this government, which seems not to have vigorously interfered at all but to have left the quarrel to go on between the bettos and local police.

Memo: From scenes of a wrestling match. The spectators signify their approbation of their favorites' skill not by throwing bouquets and jewels, but throwing their clothes into the arena, and afterwards redeeming them with money. Men thus often strip themselves in a public assembly, and a friend of mine saw at one of these entertainments a woman denude herself to the last skirt which covered her loins, all the rest was thrown into the ring—literally a ring made of straw.

The policeman carries a rattling staff and an iron baton suspended to the wrist by a cord.

Saturday, August 1, 1863

Three or four Japanese steamers were seen to pass up to Yedo this morning, and it is currently reported that the Tycoon has returned. The *Coquette* also came back this morning from the inland sea. This vessel did not enter the strait of Shimonoseki, but communicated with the shore this side; a boat came off and offered them every civility, said that they should not fire into the vessel, and hoped the vessel would not fire into them. This is supposed to be where the *Semiramis* had her encounter with the outer battery belonging, as the Japanese say, to a small daimio who has taken no part in the previous hostilities. The Prince of Chosiu's people were not communicated with.

Sunday, August 2, 1863

A delightful cool day which I have enjoyed exceedingly sitting at this window on my verandah looking out in the trees and to the bay beyond reading and conversing. The cool has been blowing in over the water, a delightful change from our recent hot weather.

It is officially announced today that the Tycoon has returned to Yedo and again do the affairs of Japan wear a new aspect. More unfathomable than ever is this political riddle. What has been the situation of the Tycoon at Miako—who knows?

Monday, August 3, 1863

Ogoshowara [Ogasawara Nagamichi], who had the management of affairs at Yedo part of the time during the Tycoons absence, and who made the payment of the English demand is a state prisoner at Miako, confined to his own house. This man is put forward to settle affairs and then punished for the settlement, thus to maintain imperial dignity. The Tycoon issues an order that the demands shall not be paid, but that the foreigner shall be expelled, the order is for the public ear—Ogoshowara is privately ordered to comply with the demands, and again is publicly punished for his disobedience to the public command. We should expect just such a course among the barbarous tribes of Africa.

Tuesday, August 4, 1863

Copies of a circular have been obtained purporting to be a circular from the Tycoon to all the chief daimios of the empire calling them to a council at Yedo to derive measures for the carrying into execution of the commands of the Mikado for the removal of foreigners from Japan. I no longer attribute any importance to any such papers, 1st we can have no reliance in their genuineness, and 2nd no reliance, if genuine, that they are promulgated except for effect.

Thursday, August 6, 1863

Seven vessels of the English squadron left this morning for Kagoshima. The Yedo Government have been desirous to prevent the squadron's going there, and have offered to pay the money demand £25,000 here; but as they could not produce the murderers of Richardson also, the offer was not accepted. Contrary to the English Minister's express wishes the *Jinkee*, government steamer, left about six hours before the squadron, as is supposed, to convey information to Satsuma. The general impression is that this mission will have a peaceful result, and so residents of Nagasaki strongly assert.

Saturday, August 15, 1863

Takamoto Hiato-no-kami[16] has not been seen since Ogoshowara's disgrace; it is suspected that he, too, has fallen into displeasure on account of the indemnity payment. A new man has been called to the prime ministry, a daimio of 150,000 koku revenue, as this place has heretofore been filled by small daimio this change of old custom has some reason—what we know not—indeed we were never more at a loss to fathom the policy of this country. The ministers have few and very unsatisfactory interviews with the Governors for Foreign Affairs. The Goroju are very seldom seen. We hope that the English expedition to Satsuma will throw some light upon affairs.

Sunday, August 16, 1863

Now we hear that Stotsbashi [Hitotsubashi] of the family of Mito, who was sent up to Yedo from Miako to prevent the settlement with the English, but afterwards did allow the settlement, has committed hara kiri. The report wants authenticity yet.

[16] Takemoto Masaaki. See note 10.

Tuesday, August 18, 1863

With usual Japanese contradictoriness the reports of today assume another phase, viz., that the Princes of Echizen (he who espoused the foreigners' side at the Miako council), Kaga, and Sendai, have sent envoys to Satsuma to say that if he proposes to inaugurate a more favorable foreign policy, one looking to open intercourse, they wish to join with him and propose to put down Choshiu and all his agents. While from Nagasaki we hear that Choshiu, yet undaunted, is prepared to renew his attacks upon all vessels that seek to pass the strait of Shimonoseki, and that the Prince of Hizen has consented to join him.

Wednesday, August 19, 1863

The Governor informed the American Consul today that numbers of ronins were arriving in Yokohama disguised as servants, laborers, etc., and that arms had also been brought in secreted in boxes of tea and other merchandise, and he feared a plot was afoot to murder the foreigners. We hear such things now apathetically. Our whole situation here is a mystery, why we are permitted to stay, or why we are not made more welcome, are alike mysteries, who rules Japan is a mystery, what the policy of the government is is a mystery, it's all mystery. That anybody is killed is a mystery, that any of us are left alive is a mystery, the solving of the riddle seems more hopeless and distant than ever, unless the English expedition to Kagoshima throws some light on the matter.

Friday, August 21, 1863

Startling tidings again today. The *Cormorant* is in from Shanghai and has spoken [to] the Satsuma expeditionary fleet in Van Diemen strait which is on its return to our port. The brief story we have is that after several days negotiation at Kagoshima, Satsuma appealed to the *ultima ratio regum* [the final resort of kings—force], and opened his batteries on the

English fleet while quietly riding at anchor. A fresh breeze betokening a gale was blowing on shore at the time. 70 guns opened fire, and the fleet responded. After an engagement of three hours the fleet drew out of fire, having lost sixty killed and wounded including among the former the Captain and Lieutenant Commander of the *Euryalus*, flagship of Rear Admiral Kuper. The fleet destroyed three steamers, a great number of junks, fired the city of Kagoshima, and probably did much other execution with its heavy fire from 91 guns. So "what Satsuma will do" is settled. Choshiu no longer stands alone. The strife between Japanese exclusiveness and Western liberalism is fairly grim. The fleet, hourly expected, [can] give us the needed particulars of this important affair.*

For particulars of the affair at Kagoshima see printed account preserved with this.[17]

[On August 27, 1863, Hall sent the following letter and account from the *Japan Herald* to the *New York Tribune*, which was published November 17, 1863.]

When, after long and vacillating negotiations, the Tycoon's Government consented to the payment of the English demand, there remained one question to be unsettled [*sic*]. In addition to the demand on the Tycoon for £110,000, there was a further demand on the Prince of Satsuma for £25,000, and the surrender for capital punishment those of his followers who committed the assault in the *Tokaido* when Mr. Richardson was slain and others wounded, now nearly a year since. This additional sum the Tycoon's Government offered to pay but the rendition of the murderers was impossible; and when on this state of affairs Col. Neale declared his intention of renewing this demand in Satsuma's capital city of Kagosima, the Yedo Government became urgent that the £25,000 should be received here, and the question about the murderers left open for further negotiation.

The English Charge d'Affaires turned a deaf ear to this request, and persisted in his intention of going to Satsuma's principality. On the 6th inst. the expeditionary squadron left the port. It consisted of seven steam vessels meaning ninety guns, led by the Euryalus, the flagship of Rear-Admiral Kuper, and having on board Col. Neale and his suite. From all that could be gathered beforehand, the expectation had daily grown stronger and stronger that the expedition would accomplish its object in peace. Two vessels of this squadron returned on the 22d, followed by the remainder on the 24th inst. Of what happened in the interim, the arrival at Kagosima, the demand, the evasive negotiations, the seizure of the prizes, the attack on the fleet, and the fierce battle and destruction that followed, I refer you to the published accounts of eye-witness sent herewith.

Satsuma was punished but not humiliated. His city was burned, his steamers destroyed, and many lives were doubtless lost, but his power to strike back fearfully avenging blows has been but little impaired. He is rather a more dangerous enemy today for he is exasperated by the loss of property, the fears of loosing which will no longer deter him. His foundries filled with machinery of European make are his heaviest loss.

What is to follow these affairs of the Strait of Simonoseki and the Bay of Kagosima is to the foreign resident on these shores a matter of the greatest solicitude. The Princes of Nagato and Satsuma have been punished we fear to the point of exasperation rather than that of submission, nor are they likely to be deserted of their brother chiefs in this hour of their calamity. We may be sure that the bloody baptism of Japan into the communion of nations has begun. England is little likely to leave Satsuma's affront unavenged and Nagato

[17] There is no printed acount with the manuscript of the journal, but the letter Hall sent to the *New York* *Tribune* on August 27 included such an account from *The Japan Herald*.

has thrown down the glove to all comers. So far as the Japanese are concerned nationalities are lost sight of; Americans, English, French, or Dutch, we are all of the hated blood and they will little reek on whom their avenging blows fall.

The Japanese accounts of the affair of the Wyoming increase the credit due to Capt. McDougal for his gallant conduct. They praise highly his skillful maneuvering to escape their heavy fire, and the accuracy of his own gunnery. Of the three vessels which attacked him the steamer and bark were sunk and the brig knocked to pieces. Great damage was done also to the batteries and town.

When a ten-inch shell had exploded the steamer's boilers, by which many were scalded to death, the Japanese viewing the peeled bodies of these afterwards, greatly wondered what medicine was in the foreigners' powder to turn red the bodies it killed.

P.S.—The Jamestown and Wyoming are both in port; the latter expecting to leave shortly.

THE OPERATIONS OF THE BRITISH FLEET

From the Yokohama (Japan) Herald, August 22.

The fleet, consisting of the Euralyis (25) Admiral Kuper's flagship, Pearl (21), Argus (6), Perseus (17), Coquette (4), Racehorse (4), Havoc (2) left here on the 6th, hence for Kagosima Bay on the afternoon of Tuesday the 11th. The Bay is described as forming a very splendid harbor, and is surrounded by that lofty and picturesque scenery so graphically described by Osborne and others, and by some its defenses would be considered next to impregnable.

The fleet was anchored some distance from Kagosima, a city of vast extent, said to contain 180,000 inhabitants, and having its factories, warehouses, etc., on a most extensive scale.

On the 12th the fleet moved up, and anchored opposite the town in 20 fathoms water, about 1200 yards from the batteries, which extend along the whole of the town front—say about two miles from the extreme south to the extreme north.

At 6 a.m. several of Satsuma's high officers went on board the flagship. It was observed by many, that their demeanor was far from that courteous and conciliatory kind we are accustomed to, indeed that there was an amount of swaggering and bullying about their manner, reminding one of the looks of a caged tiger when his human tutor enters at the door whip in hand. Colonel Neale had, it was clear, needs before him for the exercise of all his patience and watchfulness, and some then began to foresee the necessity for the firm application of the iron lash. They said that Satsuma was not now at Kagosima but at Kiusimi, a city 20 km. off. They received the letter of demands, and having been told that the reply was expected in 24 hours, they took their departure.

On the following day all was quiet on board the fleet. Col. Neale being busily engaged in diplomatic negotiations, his recently tested and proved forbearance had to endure another trial: The Yankonins were constantly running backward and forward, always bringing with them some evasive reply, and leaving without any definite conclusion.

On the afternoon of the 13th, the allotted time having long expired, an officer arrived who said he had brought a letter of reply, but since he had left the shore a messenger had been sent after him to recall it, "as there was a mistake in it." It could not be extracted from him, and he left, saying another should be sent immediately. None arrived until at 9 o'clock that night, when one of a most impertinent character was sent. This document we hope to place before our readers before long.

Still Col. Neale was patient. On the 14th, about 9 o'clock, two officials went on board, saying they had been sent for a receipt for the reply. They then stated that when at Kioto, Stotsbashi (the Vice-Tycoon) and two members of the Gorogio had most distinctly ordered Shimadzo Saburo that Satsuma was not to take any steps in respect to the murder of the foreigner by his retainer, and that the Tycoon's Government would settle all the matter themselves. They pretended that it was believed that the whole matter was settled at Yedo; that they had heard nothing from Yedo on the subject, and could not at first imagine what could have brought the fleet to Satsuma; and asserted that, according to Japanese law and custom, Satsuma had no power to settle the affair himself, either by acceding to or refusing the demands of the British.

All hope of settlement being crushed, deceit and subterfuge appearing to be the only aim, Col. Neale now stepped aside and the Admiral took the matter in hand. On the afternoon of the 14th there was a general shifting of the disposition of the fleet, the greater part of which were placed under the island, out of range of the guns of the fort, in the middle of the channel, say 1700 yards on either side.

The Euryalus, although shifting, still remained within range, as did also the Perseus. On the morning of the 15th the Pearl, Coquette, Argus, Havoc, and Racehorse proceeded up the bay, and took as hostages three steamers there at anchor, said to be the England, purchased by Satsuma in 1861 for $120,000, the Sir George Grey for $40,000, and the Contest, which cost him $80,000 in May last. The locality of the anchorage of these vessels was snugly behind Point Wilmot.

The weather, which had been stormy during the whole morning, now became worse; it was raining in torrents, and the wind blowing a hurricane round the bay. At 10 o'clock the above named vessels, English and Japanese, had returned and at 12 the bunch were just piped to dinner, and nothing immediate expected, when suddenly the battery on the main, covering the Euryalus, and that on the island, covering the Perseus, opened fire. The three hostage steamers were forthwith fired (the crews having been previously sent ashore, and one of the head officers on board recognized as having belonged to the staff of the late Ambassadors to Europe, and an-

other officer, at their own request, having been taken on board the flagship, where they now remain). All the ships weighed and formed line of battle.

The Perseus then engaged the battery that had been firing at her, in beautiful style, as we are informed, knocking her antagonist's guns over, one after the other, and when she had completed that, as though she had been only getting her hand in, she passed over to the other side and engaged the battery on the opposite shore. All the batteries were then engaged by the ships at point-blank range, at from 400 to 800 yards respectively (the Euryalus being within 200 yards), commanding with the northernmost and passing down the entire line to the Spit battery, at slow speed. During this time it was blowing tremendously. About dusk the town was fired in several places by our shells, and three of the forts silenced. All the ships then returned to their anchorage, save the Racehorse, which had got ashore within 200 yards of the nearest battery, of which accident she availed herself in true British style to pour her metal into it until it was effectually silenced. The Argus was sent to get her off, which she accomplished after about an hour's delay, during the whole of which time she was under fire from one of the other batteries.

This was Saturday, the 15th, during the whole of which day it had been raining and blowing fiercely. The loss on this day to us was 11 killed and 39 wounded; among the former there will be general regret that we have to name Capt. Joslin of the flagship, an officer esteemed and respected by all who knew him in ordinary times as mild and gentle, as, when the lion was aroused within him, he was bold and daring—a true type of a British officer. Commander Edward Wilmott (late of the Agamemnon), of whose character all speak in the like glowing terms, met a glorious death by the same shot. Both were standing on the bridge of the flagship, about the middle of the engagement (3:30), when a shot passed through the boat and struck them both instantaneously into eternity. The Admiral escaped death by the same shot in a wonderful manner, both he and the Master standing on the narrow bridge when the Captain fell.

About 9 o'clock the whole of one side of the town was blazing.

The following day (Sunday) the weather cleared up, the dead (2 officers and 7 men) were consigned to their sailor's grave in Euryalus Bay at 11 o'clock, and the fleet stood out, passing close to the batteries on the island, which it engaged the whole way.

The destruction accomplished by the fleet appears to have been enormous.

There can be no doubt that the whole city is now one mass of ruins, including the Palace, the factories, and the arsenals and warehouses; the batteries also have been seriously damaged; not one of them which had been engaged during the first day fired a shot on the second day as the fleet passed out.

The three destroyed ships alone have cost Satsuma $245,000, upward of half of which he has paid very recently. Several large junks also were destroyed. The Japanese are said to have stood well to their guns so long as the play was at long range, but seemed somewhat taken aback when our ships came to such close quarters.

Their metal appears to have consisted of 13-inch and 8-inch shells; four 150-pounders, ten 80-pounders, and the remainder 32-pounders, etc.

It will take some time to bring out all the little interesting episodes of the affair, but we have already heard of some surprising instances of pluck, and many more of the good practice of our guns.

Considering the close firing, as we have said in some cases only 200 yards, the amount of damage done to our ships is wonderfully small. The "Euryalus," of course, suffered most, and her damage appears to have been principally in her boats and rigging.

Euryalus, 10 killed, 21 wounded; Pearl, 7 wounded; Argus, 6 wounded; Coquette, 2 killed, 4 wounded; Racehorse, 3 wounded; Perseus 1 killed, 9 wounded.

We had nearly omitted to mention that several most pressing requests were sent to Colonel Neale to attend with as many of his suit as he chose on shore, at a conference, in a place prepared to receive them, a courtesy declined with thanks.

It is useless to attempt to speculate at present, what will be the next step taken to bring this haughty Prince to reason.

The description of ammunition used by Satsuma's forts must have been of a superior description. The quantity expended by us was considerable, and as matters have evidently not come to a conclusion, we may congratulate ourselves that a large further supply has arrived in the Cormorant and Barossa.

We need scarcely inform our readers that, as to the long story published elsewhere as to Matzdaira Etzizen no Kami having received secret information that Satsuma intended to receive the British Admiral in peace and good feeling, and that the Great Daimios Hosokawa, Kanga, and Sendai had decided to send their envoys to the Prince of Satsuma to congratulate him on his decision, and to offer him their moral and material support in sustaining his course before the Mikado, etc., was just so much word writing, or another instance of blind Tom leading blind Jack, some cunning son of Nipon performing the role of Dog Tray and sousing them both the one to his ears and the other to the gold band on his cap, in that very disagreeable quagmire, Public Ridicule.

Friday, August 28, 1863

There is a mail from Nagasaki today. News of the fight at Kagoshima had come to Nagasaki by native sources. The reports charge the British envoy and Admiral with perfidy in the seizure of the steamers; that in consequence of this act the fleet was fired into. They say the battle lasted two days during which the steamers and 1/2 the town were burned, when the fleet withdrew, having received, as they thought, more injury than they had inflicted.

Saturday, August 29, 1863

Deputy American Consul Mann died this P.M. of cholera; there are many cases among the natives.[18]

Friday, September 4, 1863

This week the Ministers have been officially informed that the Prince of Nagato has seized the shores of Shimonoseki strait opposite to his principality and that the Government at Yedo will take measures to put down this rebellious chief. Three daimios are charged with the execution of this work. The territory invaded belongs to Ogoshowara [Ogasawara], late Prime Minister.

Thursday, September 10, 1863

Walking along the street last evening I noticed a fruit seller. The man was squatted on a mat by the street side and such portion of the mat as he did not occupy was loaded with fruit, principally pears. His leisure intervals were employed in the care of a very young infant which he was folding to his bosom as carefully as any young mother might. Here, thought I, was a practical illustration of the good time coming when such light occupations as selling fruits and taking care of babies shall fall to the lot the men, while their spouses enjoyed their knitting work at home or gossiped in the streets. Japan is not without many illustrations of the saw that the "Gray mare is the better horse." The women are very diligent shopkeepers and one was a long time known as a produce broker. In the fields they are often seen working side by side with their husbands and children.

Saturday, September 12, 1863

News of Vicksburgh's capture and Lee's defeat at Gettysburg.

Wednesday, September 16, 1863

We learn from the Japanese today that two Oasaca merchants who have branch houses here have been assassinated at Oasaca because they sold too many goods to foreigners. Two others have fled. This report, which seems not without foundation, has caused some fluttering among the native merchants at this port. This process of intimidation is just what we have to fear most and it is only strange that it has not been begun before. Hitherto the blows of the discontented party have fallen on the foreigners who came to buy, let them once change their policy and strike at those who sell to foreigners and our trade is broken up.

Connected with this, it is a noticeable fact that very little silk arrives now to our market, although several thousands of bales are said to be accumulated in Yedo.

Friday, September 18, 1863

Sadajirō, who has come down from Yedo today, confirms the accounts of the murder of Oasaca merchants. One silk, and one lacker, merchant, have been killed, and Heco reports today that the chief inspector of silk at Yedo has also been killed.[19] S[adajirō] says also that the reason no more silk arrives is because the dealers are intimidated by threats of assassination from bringing it forward. He also says that the report of an expedition to punish Chosiu is groundless; that only envoys have been sent as yet. The story of the Tycoon having seized his [Choshu's] houses at Yedo he accounts for on this wise, that all the locations of the Princes in Yedo are gifts of the government and when a daimio wishes to repair or

---

[18] This was George Mann.

[19] Heco wrote in his own diary under the same date: "Still more disquieting intelligence. At Yedo, some five days ago, one of the leading raw-silk dealers was killed

by *Rōnin*, who lay the rise in price of that commodity to his charge" (Joseph Heco, *Narrative of a Japanese* (San Francisco: American-Japanese Publishing Association, n.d.), vol. 2, p. 13).

rebuild he does not himself undertake it as it would be a breach of etiquette towards the giver. So in Chosiu's case he wished to repair two of his yashikis and the emperor gives him two others in their place and even receives exchange money from Chosiu. Thus conflicting are all, or nearly all, the accounts we have.

Sunday, September 20, 1863

Took a walk to Bookengi [Bukenji] in Kanagawa. On the Kanagawa side of the bay a *staban* from the guard house followed us as an escort. It was an absurd idea for one man to protect three who were duly armed with revolvers; but he would follow, so we hastened our steps and the guardsman found it difficult to keep up. A halt at the inn of Simodaya to get a cup of tea enabled him to catch up with us. On leaving the inn we struck off the Tokaido up the steep hillside, our guard who had caught his breath again following. The path was zigzag as well as steep, and now we laid a brisk step, then a trot, then a run, up the steep face of the hill. Alas for our poor guardsman encumbered with long tunic and heavy swords and shod with straw sandals. His will was good but his flesh was weak. We turned our heads and laughed at him, the housewives at the windows below enjoyed his discomfiture and laughed too, and he tried to grin over his own misfortune when a turn in the road shut him from our sight and he was no more seen.

It is a lovely day, the skies are clear and the sun not overpowering, the vegetation still wears all its summer beauty. One of our party who is an invalid catches new life from the wholesome atmosphere. An hour's walk brings us to the temple, or rather the monastery of Bookengi, for the temples are only central to numerous sunny cottages where the indolent priests reside. The indolent priests who have no heavier labor than to sweep the broad avenues, trim the green turf banks and thrifty hedgerows that surround the thatched cottages, or in the temples up the grassy slope chant their monotonous morning, midday, and evening prayers. We sat down at the top of a flight of stone steps where on a shelf against the green sward bank of the neighboring hill-

side the upper temple stands embowered in shade. There is not a stone or fallen leaf or any one of the marauding weeds and grasses that can intrude for a moment on the clean sanctity of the paths that stretch before us. The air is full of repose under the tall cedars over our heads, only now and then the faint trills of a sparrow is heard. The lazy acolyte, a thin visaged boy of spare frame, was swinging his hands on a pole in the open verandah of one cottage, while within a priest was airing his library and spreading it to dry on the mats, for I know, by sad experience, how the mold of this moist climate destroys fine bindings and mars the fairest paper. A thousand volumes of old lore, fabulous history of fabulous divinities, the old priest says his library can boast.

Down the avenue we go counting in fifty yards eight different hedges, cryptomeria, cedar, pine, thuya, evergreen oak, box, and retinospora. In front of the main temple stand a noble salisburia, and a sciadopitys, most beautiful of evergreen conifers. At the left is a spacious kitchen whose polished floors of elm forbid the unhallowed tread of our soiled feet. In the refectory stood some trays of fruit and cakes which the lank boys of lack luster visage who are growing up into more lazy priests do not think of offering to us. I do not know any class of people in Japan more repulsive than these stupid looking young priests with their joyless eyes and blank unmeaning faces.

We left the monastery of Bookengi and its clustering cottages and scenes of aimless lives to its vacuum quiet and again through the farm roads enjoyed the pleasant wayside industry that had some hopes and material comforts at least. We were struck at the temple by the marked contrast in the face of a fat ruddy farmer's boy who was at play with the lean kind of the priesthood—greatly to the farmer boy's advantage was the contrast.

We came back to the boat landing and inquired for our attendant guard. He had not returned his fellow *stabans* said, and we had a joke at his expense in which they joined, all but one man, who was flushed with sake, and admonished us that we might have our heads cut off next time if we neglected to receive their protection. But we laughed only the more and told him the next time "not to send one whose legs were too short." But he only intimated by significant gestures that we might find our heads shorter than his legs.

Thursday, September 24, 1863

There is now no doubt that two or three shops of native traders have been closed by intimidation from some source. The largest tea house, one of the largest lacker-ware shops, and another tea shop is said to be closed. Of the first two there is no doubt. The intimidation is attributed to ronins as usual.[20]

The good news from the States to July 15th has electrified us all today with the announcement of the fall of Vicksburg and Port Hudson and the victory of Gettysburg.

Monday, October 5–Tuesday, October 6, 1863

Regatta.

Saturday, October 10, 1863

The week has gone by with its usual rumors of disturbances at Oasaca and Kioto, or Miako, fights between Chosiu men and the Mikado's men;[21] threats against merchants engaged in foreign trade, and even their murders, but what is true and what is false we have no means of determining. We hear that two Oasaca merchants interested in foreign trade were beheaded, their heads exposed in a public place with the warning that the like fate awaited others.[22] Several shops have closed, or made a show of closing. Still business is not interrupted, tea, silk, and cotton come to market as before.

From Nagasaki we hear of fresh disturbances. Some bands of Chosiu's men are said to have entered the city and given great alarm to natives and foreigners by their threats. The Governor when appealed to for aid told the Consuls that his own life was in enough danger from them, and they [should] take care of themselves. Consequently marines were landed from the men-of-war to protect the foreign population. We wait further tidings.

[20] Joseph Heco recorded on September 20 news from Kyoto that underscored the widespread intimidation of merchants by *rōnin*. He writes: "At the dawn of the 25th day of the 7th moon a head, apparently just cut off, was found stuck on a wooden pole at the Western end of the Sanjo-bridge in that city. As daylight came on the grisly object was recognized as the head of Yamatoya Wohe, one of the leading merchants of Kiōtō. Below the head the following notice was affixed to the pole: 'Genjiro, Hikotaro, Ichi-jiro and Shobe, these four persons were not at home when this occurence took place, but the Mikado's punishment which they have merited shall be meted out to them hereafter. A few years ago, the Shōgun made treaties with outside nations without the consent of the Sovereign (the Mikado). And these people, taking advantage of these treaties, have been dealing largely with foreigners and made much profit, without considering or caring how much others suffered by reason of their conduct. They have trafficked in copper cash, silk, wax, oil, salt, tea,— in fact in all the staples of the land, in articles necessary for the use of the people of the country. They have bought them up and sent them to Nagasaki, and Kana-

gawa or Yokohama, and there sold them to foreigners for their own gain. By so doing they have enhanced the price of all articles and all but themselves suffer. . . . On account of all this, we can no longer remain blind to the suffering of the people. . . . Take note all those who may disregard the above warning . . . we the *Rōnin* shall watch and investigate the conduct of all merchants, and shall exterminate all those who deal with foreigners' " (Heco, *Narrative of a Japanese*, vol. 2, pp. 13–15).

[21] The incident referred to here took place on September 30 in Kyoto. In a quick coup Aizu and Satsuma units seized the gates of the Imperial Palace and barred Chōshū troops from entering. Chōshū loyalist forces were driven from Kyoto in disarray, taking with them a number of the leading loyalist court nobles including Sanjo Sanetomi. See W. G. Beaseley, *The Meiji Restoration* (Stanford, Calif.: Stanford University Press, 1972), p. 217.

[22] Although Hall states that these are Osaka merchants he may have confused Kyoto with Osaka. What he seems to be referring to here is the same incident recorded by Joseph Heco and quoted in footnote 20.

Wednesday, October 14, 1863

A year and eleven days have passed since the murder of Richardson on the Tokaido when our community is again shocked by the news of a fresh assassination. Word came to the foreign consuls that a man had been killed on a country road much frequented by us all for walking or riding, and distant a mile and a half from the settlement. Parties of citizens, officials, and guards hastened to the spot and there found the body of a Frenchman, a sub lieutenant of the Chasseurs d'Afrique, literally hewn to pieces. The deceased was a young man of 20 years old, well educated, and of a marked mild and winning disposition and was the favorite of the French forces and an intimate friend of Admiral Juarez. He had gone out for a ride according to his usual custom, was alone and unarmed, when he must have been set upon by more than one man and murdered in a spot that we had all considered safe. His bridle arm with the reins still wound about it was severed from his body, his face cut open in several hideous wounds, the jugular vein severed, his vitals protruding from two deep gashes in either side, his shoulder cleft down to the ribs—in all more than twenty cuts. Though this happened in a much frequented road, near to the village, and among cultivated fields where more or less farmers are always busy, all denied knowledge of the occurrence, except one boy, who said that while at work in the fields he saw three men attack the stranger on horseback. No other information was elicited. The horse, also slightly wounded by a sword cut, was tied to a tree nearby. Lieut. Camus left home about 12 and the murder was committed between that and 2 P.M. Tidings reached Yokohama at 3. The body was placed on a stretcher and accompanied by a large force of marines, chasseurs, and civilians was brought home to the French Minister's and will be buried tomorrow. The streets were crowded with native spectators as the cortege passed through who looked on indulging the same levity they do when they bury their own dead from their own households.

It is noticeable that a few days since the deceased was advised to go armed in his rides. "No," he said, "the Japanese are an inoffensive people whom I like and do not fear."[23]

Thursday, October 15, 1863

The remains of Lieut. Camus were followed to their grave on the hillside today by a large concourse of military and citizens. Ministers and attaches of Legations, officers of the fleet and land forces were in full dress and all was done that was possible to make the ceremonies imposing. Thus in a little more than twenty four hours a life was stung in death and its tenement buried out of our sight.

A few days previously at the Catholic Chapel where the funeral services were performed a new bell had been consecrated and Lieut. Camus was present: today the bell gave forth its first speech in a farewell toll over his remains. The English *charge* significantly said as he listened "that bell tolls for the fate that hangs over Japan."

Friday, October 16, 1863

According to the story prevalent among the Japanese common people today the French Lieutenant was killed by three samurai, evidently without provocation as they themselves believe.

The Japanese Government as usual profess the deepest regret and promise to make every exertion to secure the offenders. The French Minister Bellecourt and Admiral Juarez demand nothing less than the seizure of the assassins, and intimate to the Governor that a

---

[23] The death of Camus is also commented on by Dr. William Willis of the British consulate, who echoed some of the frustration that Westerners felt with regards to such incidents. Willis wrote home on the same day: "The Japanese are a hopeless set of people to deal with in such matters. . . . We must burn and destroy some of these Daimyo palaces and I imagine it would produce good results. We must make some terrible examples if we are to live in this country with any ordinary degree of security." Hugh Cortazzi, *Dr. Willis in Japan, 1862–1867: British Medical Pioneer* (London: Athlone Press, 1985), p. 42.

system of exclusion of all two sworded men except those wearing a government badge within certain limits may be necessary.

Saturday, October 17, 1863

There is a good deal of uneasiness in the Japanese mind growing out of the recent event. Knowing what the English demanded, they foresee the French can demand no less. There is also increased inquiry for arms. Other shops are reported closed.

Sunday, October 18, 1863

Went with two friends to visit the scene of the late murder and found it in a much frequented road, in a broad open path, near a mia or small temple. The aspect of the place abundantly proved two things, that there was no difficulty about passing on the road, and that the affair could not have lacked sufficient spectators. Often and often I have passed alone or in company on foot or horseback this spot regarding it as one of the safest places hereabouts. There can be no doubt that the murder was wholly without cause and wanton.

Monday, October 19, 1863

Field sports and games. There was a meeting today of the foreign Ministers and Consuls to take into consideration the present position of affairs. The deliberation of this nice council ended in the agreement that a patrol of thirty men should daily do duty on shore within a radius of three miles, each nationality furnishing this patrol by turn. It is almost farcical, this inconsequential performance, having no punishment in it for the past or terror for the future, and all growing out of the fear of taking a just responsibility. There will be no protection to citizens because the daily patrol will only be known to the guard themselves, and while the murdering assassins know the guard is three miles from town in one direction they may commit their foul deeds with impunity three miles in the opposite direction.

Monday, October 26, 1863

The American Minister went to Yedo today to meet the Goroju "on important business." This proved to be nothing more or less than a proposition to close the port of Yokohama-Kanagawa.

Their argument was that it was necessary to do something to conciliate the people who were so hostile to foreign intercourse. The reply to them was, what it must needs be, that such a proposition could not for a moment be entertained. If this is the temper of the Yedo Government I suspect we may see our trade further abridged in the hope of accomplishing indirectly what they cannot gain otherwise.

Tuesday, October 27, 1863

Today is another birthday anniversary. Earth, sea, air, and sky are all charming today as possible, nature in one of her most attractive guises. Fusi rears his lofty head in the distance on which the first snows of a coming winter have fallen and the neighboring Hakone mountains peer out of the morning mists like distant islands at sea. So too the snows of coming age have begun to gather on my head and the isles of futurity loom up out of the mists of advancing years. The day is beautiful but life is sorrowful here. To a pagan it would be a day of happy omen, being thoughtful, it is a day of unhappy contrast. Why do I linger a weary lonesome life on foreign shores? What happiness remains if I return? I am a suicide in that I have lifted my hand against my own happiness.

God alone is good. How fair He has made the days, what glorious skies and soft air cover us and spread about us, and trustful in His providence why should we mourn. Away then with care and grief on such a day as this, and hopeful in His all beneficent goodness and kindness, regretful for the errors of the past, may I be watchful for the future, nor refuse the good He herewith accords my pathway.

[On October 31, 1863, Hall wrote a letter to the *New York Tribune*, which was published on January 19, 1864.]

After the affairs of Simonoseki and Kagosima, a quiet, ominous rather of new disturbances than of continued peace, settled down upon Japan. It was naturally supposed that Satsuma and Mowori, the Prince of Nagato, irritated by their conflicts and losses, would seek revenge somewhere, especially at Nagasaki, which is so near to their principalities. But it was some time before even any rumor of fresh disturbances reached us, and in these only Mowori has had a part, Satsuma to this hour giving no indication of his purposes.

Mowori, more active, not only repaired his batteries shattered by the Wyoming's excellent gunnery, but, having crossed the Strait of Simonoseki, seized upon the batteries on the south shore, in the principality of the Peaceful Prince of Boozen, and, thus gaining absolute command of this narrow passage, threw down the gauntlet against all comers.

The foreign representatives urged upon the Tycoon's Government the necessity of putting down this rebellious chieftain, and the Government, with its usual cajolery and deception, gravely informed them that an expedition had already been sent on foot for this purpose, and the proud Mowori would soon be humbled. The inner sea is still a *mare clausum*, and Mowori having deterred all foreign vessels from the passage under his batteries, turns next his attention to the Tycoon and fires into and seizes one of the Imperial steamers.

Next in order, a battery or fort of the Prince of Awa, in the island of Awadji, at the eastern entrance to this same island sea, fires on another imperial vessel and Princely Awa apologized for it, that it was the work of "wild men" who had acted contrary to his wishes, but at the same time sends a special messenger to this port to admonish all foreign vessels not to go very near the fort lest these wild men might fire on them also.

Following these events came frequent accounts of disturbances at Oasaca, of brawls between retainers of different Daimios who disagreed on the important question, not whether the foreigner should be expelled from Japan, for on that they seem pretty unanimous, but when shall the work of expulsion begin. Nay in a high council of Daimios at the Mikado's palace, two Princes are said to have come to blows, as to whether now or a few years hence was the better time to begin this work of expulsion; and so the Mikado's clean gravel walks and trim parterres were moistened with the blood of some thirty distinguished followers of each Prince, who, alas! not seeing eye to eye how to fight the hated tojin, had a free fight then and there among themselves.

From Nagasaki come tidings still more significant—the city is filled with ronins (outlaw soldiery), from Mowori's country, men of desperate adventure, and so pervading is the terrorization established, that business is universally suspended, and the native merchants fly the place. The Governor, when appealed to for protection, declares that his own life is in equal danger from these lawless men, and the foreigners must protect themselves as best they can.

Following upon all this, comes another of those horrid assassinations, which have so often shocked not only us, the dwellers in this unsafe land, but the civilized world at large.

On the 14th inst. toward evening, the foreign consuls were informed from the Custom House that a foreigner had been murdered a short distance from the settlement. A large force of soldiers and civilians immediately started for the place indicated, where, about one mile and a half from the foreign settlement, they found the body of Lieut. Camus of the Chasseurs d'Afrique, literally cut to pieces. Lieut. Camus had, at mid-day, gone out to ride horseback, as was his custom, unarmed and unattended, and here, in front of a small temple, under the shade of its sacred grove, had met his fate. This road is one daily used by foreigners for both foot and horseback exercise, constantly traveled over by the natives, and at this spot is wide enough for two carriages to pass each other. Lieut. Camus's well known amiability of character and even predilection for the Japanese, forbade the idea on his part of any intentional, as did the appearance of the place, of any accidental collision with his murderers. There are several houses in near proximity, swarming with inhabitants, yet none would confess that they had seen how or by whom the murder had been committed. Only a little boy was found, who said, that while at work in the fields at some distance he had seen the deceased assailed by three men with swords, who after finishing their bloody work, fled up the neighboring hill and out of sight. No one could be found to expose the assassins, they knew too well the fate that awaited them if they did so.

The Government as usual professed its great grief at this occurrence, in the old set phrase so often employed by them on previous similar occasions, and promised the utmost vigilance to secure the perpetrators. Two weeks have passed without bringing the faintest clue to the evil doers. No redress had been sought by the French Minister, who has referred the case to his home Government. That the French will take some decided steps, no one doubts.

It has been agreed by the foreign representatives that each nation having a force here shall furnish in turn a daily patrol of thirty men to do duty within a three mile radius from the settlement—an act of neither pith nor consequence in such an emergency, having in it no punishment for the past and small security for the future, so long as two-sworded men in daily considerable numbers are permitted to dwell in and hover about this settlement unchallenged and unknown. A dread of responsibility, and the swathing of red tape about manly thews and sinews, prevent good intentions from ripening into energetic action.

The remains of Lieut. Camus had imposing internment on the 15th. Thus in one brief twenty-four hours the drama of a human life was closed. It was not inappropriately said by one of the diplomatic corps, as he listened to the solemn tolling of the chapel bell, "That bell tolls the knell of Japan."

At the time poor Richardson's blood-money was paid to the English last Summer, it will be remembered that the Japanese coupled this payment with a demand that all foreigners should leave Japan. In a recent interview with the representatives of the United States and Holland, that demand was withdrawn, and a new one made—to wit, that the port of Kanagawa should be closed to foreign trade, and all the foreigners withdrawn to Nagasaki or Hakodadi. Nor is this new demand an idle one; on the contrary, we have reason to fear that, refused as it must be, it is but the prelude to greater embarrassments of our trade and further acts of violence.

Monday, November 2, 1863

The week past has been full of rumors about difficulties at Miako, difficulties at Oasaca, all of which are as vague as ever and as unreliable. The native merchants profess apprehension that they must leave the place. Others declare that all will be pacificated within a few days. And as usual we end by believing nothing. The foreign Ministers were requested to meet the Goroju in consultation at Yedo concerning negotiations for the departure of all foreigners from Kanagawa. The Ministers refused to have a conference discussing even such a question. The *Racehorse* from Nagasaki today reports that place as quiet as possible.

Tuesday, November 10, 1863

Yesterday, according to appointment, envoys from the Prince of Satsuma waited on Col. Neale. The interview was consumed in explanation by Col. Neale of the visit of the British fleet to Kagoshima and the events that followed. Satsuma's envoys stated that the reason the fleet was fired into was because of the seizure of the ships, or steamers, and which they supposed were to be at once carried off. The interview closed without any understanding

Satsuma Samurai in Yo-kohama. Photograph by Felice Beato.

being reached as to the settlement of affairs, and another interview appointed for the 13th.

Wednesday, November 11, 1863

Commenced alterations in the house.

Monday, November 16, 1863

The conferences between Col. Neale and the envoys from the Prince of Satsuma were concluded yesterday by the promise of the latter to pay the £25,000 originally demanded. The payment to be made in four days. The envoys proposed that there should be *mutual* apologies, which Col. Neale declined on his part.

They confessed to a great amount of damage done by the bombardment of Kagoshima and to the loss of many lives. The question regarding the giving up of the murderers was reserved, and there can be little doubt that England will forbear to press this point.

The settlement seems to argue continued peace to Japan. If Satsuma, haughtiest and most powerful of her nobles, refuses to accept the gage of war, we may be sure the others will not try it. The Japanese with all their pretensions are not bold enough for anything beyond treacherous and cowardly assassinations. Perhaps they are too wise to try strength with the western powers, and that they yield less from cowardice than a wholesome and sensible fear.

We have yet Chosiu to settle with, and the French have their affronts for which to seek reparation; but out of all war is hardly any longer to be apprehended.

Tuesday, November 24, 1863

The Japanese Government have promised today to pay the $10,000 asked for the firing into the steamer *Pembroke* by Chosiu batteries last June.

Thursday, November 26, 1863

Today is "thanksgiving day," almost forgotten, too, by our Yankee people. I shall try to keep it as best one may in a foreign shore. Tonight will dine with me Mr. Mugford, Dr. Simmons, Mr. Allen, Mr. Van Reed, Mr. Hill, Mr. Heco, besides our own family.[24]

Friday, November 27, 1863

We had a pleasant party last evening, home friends were well remembered. A Japan capon did duty for the thanksgiving turkey and none were the wiser.

Sunday, November 29, 1863

Very ill today from the effects of a cold taken a few days since and opiates taken last night. I was unable to lift my head off the bed till evening.

Monday, November 30, 1863

I am able to drag myself to the office this morning to begin the heavy mail work in hand for the States, Europe, China, and Nagasaki. My head and limbs refuse at first but afterwards are gradually drawn to their duty.

[On November 30, 1863, Hall wrote the following letter to the *New York Tribune*, which was published on February 13, 1864.]

Our affairs in Japan again look brighter. We have not felt so assured of continuing peace for a long time. It all grows out of the fact that Prince Satsuma, he with whom the English had the brush at Kagosima, has sent envoys to this place seeking an arrangement of all difficulties with the English Charge d'Affaires. He is the most powerful of all the Japanese princes, and if he is desirous of peace we feel quite sure none of the rest will seek war. As an indication of the value of our opinions, and our real estate, a lot adjoining us, with few improvements on it, size two hundred feet square, was sold yesterday for $21,000; eighteen months ago it was bought by the seller for $6500.

Yokohama, which is the local appellation, though the port is known generally as Kanagawa, is growing rapidly. Opened to commerce four years ago, it has changed from a "side beach," which its name signifies, to an opulent commercial mart. Mr. Harris, the treaty-king, first came into this bay in March, 1859, and on the present site of the town were to be seen only the cultivated fields of rice, wheat, beans, bringalls and millet, with a few cottages of the contented peasantry among the elms and evergreen oaks. He returned to Simoda, came back three months later, on the 1st of July, when the port was to be opened under the treaty, and as if some new Aladdin had again rubbed his wonderful lamp, in place of gardens and fields stood the spacious Japanese custom-houses, blocks upon blocks of official residences, three long streets built up with shops and filled with curious wares, and besides these a large number of houses built for rental to the expected com-

---

[24] C. D. Mugford and Eugene Van Reed were both members of Augustine Heard & Co., Joseph Heco and Dr. Simmons were old friends, Mr. Hill and Mr. Allen are not easily identifiable, although Mr. Hill may have

been Norman Hill who is listed as a British resident of Yokohama in M. Paske-Smith, *Western Barbarians in Japan and Formosa in Tokugawa Days, 1603–1868* (Kobe: J. L. Thomson & Co., 1930), p. 356.

ers, to say nothing of a multitude of native cottages. Our own rapidly growing country never exhibited a transformation so sudden and complete. And now today the building and extension is as rapid as ever.

The fishermen's huts, the farmers' cottages, the broad acres of grain, have all given way to structures more or less substantial and elegant of wood, mud and stone. Yet all partake of the characteristics of the country, bungalow houses; warehouses, i.e. "go—downs," of mud and stone, tile roofs, neat floors, unpainted fir ceilings, are grafted with curtains of damask, carpets of Brussels, furniture of rosewood and mahogany from beyond the seas. Brown-cheeked boys are servitors in place of handy Biddy, who I dare say, is more missed than all other home comforts whatever.

A township block, which, were it regular and compact, would represent an area three-quarters of a mile square, is crowded with foreign houses and foreign industry. A hundred lot-owners are now lords of the soil in place of the old swarthy Niponese farmers deposed. Long warehouses and two-story bungalows usurp the place of the brown chalets of the former peasantry.

We are, all told, English, Americans, Dutch, French, Prussians, Swiss, Portuguese, and nondescript, four hundred souls, already stifling for room—I have named them in the order of their numbers. Americans were once large lotholders, but Elderborn (to Japan) Esaus that they were, they have mostly sold, for the pottage mess, to later comers of all kindred and tongues. The rental of the whole area, once not over a hundred dollars of yearly value, must now multiply that sum by a thousand, and double yet the product. A lot 92 feet front by 175 deep has its standard market value of eight and ten thousand dollars, according to location, cost $265 two years ago. Here, where the farmer four years since was fain to be content with his Summer rice, and Winter harvest of turnips, commerce reaps ten millions annually of silver dollars. That is the gross of the harvest; the net profit is also a sum of fat cyphers marshaled by a not overlean digit.

Silk is the great staple of Japan trade. Then comes tea (this year raw cotton) and after this a variety of products, copper, camphor, coal, new tobacco, pulse and a variety of edibles for China consumption. For the hard dollars we pay for all these, they give us back a fifth, perhaps, for metals, cotton goods and woolens, camlets chiefly.

Thus, this spot in the remotest part of the globe, only so recently terra terribilis, if not terra incognita, is now a dear foster child of commerce. And commerce comes here full panoplied, as when, centuries ago, she conquered the Mare Mediterraneum, and so passed by to Britain, who now returns to the East. She comes with her sword and cannon, and her resonant fife and drum fill the quiet air of these isles; for today, as I write, twelve hundred British soldiers and marines are parading our streets, to give the Japanese an impress of their strength. She comes with her virtues and vices, and it will take the Eternal Accountant at last to decide whether, "the opening of Japan" brings civilization to a fearful debit or a glorious credit in the books of the Ages.

If I have been prolix and tedious excuse me, for curious thoughts are sometimes suggested, as I witness this contrast of the civilization of the Nineteenth Century with the semi-barbarism of the Fifteenth. I feel as if I were living somewhere out of my time—as if I had left the railway of your active life and gone back to something more ancient than even the old stagecoach of existence. I should not be surprised any day if some one were to ask me to go and see Cleopatra in her barge, or Titus before Jerusalem. If we are in your world, we are certainly not of it, and I am afraid to go to bed, lest I awake in the morning and find that telegraphs, steamers, and railway cars are only dreams.

Tuesday, December 1, 1863

Busy all day with the mails. The *Onward* leaves tomorrow for San Francisco; Robt. Pruyn[25] leaves us for home via Europe in the *Granache* tomorrow.

[On December 1, 1863, Hall wrote the following letter to the *New York Tribune*, which was published on January 29, 1864.]

Since my letter under date of Oct. 31, our affairs in Japan have had a sudden and unexpected change for the better.

It was reasonable to expect that the affair of the English with Satsuma at Kagosima, having sufficient of indecisiveness in it not to warrant the merit of a great achievement, would serve more to irritate than overawe that Prince. Such, indeed, was the general expectation, and English colonial journals had already begun to explore the result of that affair as unimpressive, when suddenly, some three weeks since, envoys from Satsuma made their appearance here, requesting an interview of the English Charge d'Affaires, with a view to a settlement of all past difficulties.

Several interviews were had, and at the opening one of the envoys complained that the fleet had initiated hostilities by the seizure of Satsuma's steamers, pending negotiations. This matter was set before them in its own light until the envoys were satisfied, or professed to be, that if Satsuma had suffered any wrong it was quite in the interest of law, and order, and international justice.

The envoys deprecated the least desire to come to hostilities with any of the treaty powers, or to borrow the phrase of the ring, they were ready to throw up the sponge and cry "enough." Nay, they even intimated that their Princely master, so far from being a belligerent, conservative old fogy, was the most progressive of the progressives; and had not the Tycoon been self-ish the foreigner might today have traded anywhere in dai-Nipon. For he, Satsuma, would only be too happy—to take the Customs duties, or at least his share of them, which are now flowing in one unbroken stream into the Imperial Treasury. Of course these careful envoys did not, in so many set words, confess to such an avaricious view of affairs, but it was clear enough as to "what ailed" Satsuma.

Their Prince and master would be delighted to pay the demand of £25,000 sterling; it was a mere bagatelle to such a Prince; but as for giving up the murderers, they could not. The murderers had escaped; they had been everywhere hunted for and inquired for, but had disappeared, leaving not a trace behind. They would, to be sure, keep on searching, and report progress at any time hereafter, but meantime they would like to discharge their little money obligation, and so settle affairs that no more fleets should come Kagosima-ward to topple their towns down, burn their houses and murder their people.

In a country like Japan where everybody knows what everybody is doing, has done, and may from "old custom" pretty surely tell what they will do; where every street has its local magistrate, and every five houses its responsible head—responsible to know when inquired upon all about their subjects, it hardly appears probable that murderers in so public a manner would not be known or could escape. But mind me, these murderers were privileged characters; they belong to the cast[e] of the "two sword wearers" to execute one of whom for the murder of a despicable merchant, and that merchant a barbarian foreigner, would have made every two-sworder in Japan howl and gnash its teeth in wrath unappeasable. No, a two-sworder could not be given up—a two-sworder has never been given up to justice though often culpable—and never will be given up for offense against a foreigner till stern force seizes them. He will always escape, and like these murderers of poor Richardson, "cannot be found," no matter for what foul deeds perpetrated.

---

[25] This was Robert C. Pruyn, the son of the American minister, Robert H. Pruyn.

Col. Neale, the English Charge, knows all this better than I can tell him; but Col. Neale is a bit of a philosopher as well as a diplomat. He knows that half a loaf is better than no bread; he knows that her august Sovereign, the Queen, would a little rather not spend three or five, or ten millions of pounds sterling on a Japanese war if, by any means, to be avoided. Besides, Satsuma says his murdering lieges are non-comcatibus in swamps, and who is to deny it and say he is the liar! Would the world, moreover, justify England going to war on her behalf, for an idea, and that idea, the suspicion only of a falsehood! Not a bit of it, says the gallant Colonel. So he and Satsuma's enemies come to terms.

In short, the prudent Charge says, Gentlemen Envoys, we take your money, but say to your royal master we expect him to find the murderers also if he can. On those terms we take an amicable cup of tea, Satsuma's honor and the Queen's treasure are sacred. You will get a no-kami to your name, and I a K.C.B. and vive la diplomacie. Such may not have been the words of the arrangement, but such the spirit and result, and probably, all things considered, was the best practicable. The £25,000 was to have been paid in four days; but four days, and yet other four days several times over, have passed, but Satsuma gives no sign of paying. What, or why, the delay, we know not; yet I think the money will be paid as agreed if not when agreed.

This arrangement of Satsuma's produced the greatest effect on the public mind, both Japanese and foreign. It was at once held that if Satsuma, the most puissant of Nipon's chiefs, the one most capable of conducting war, offensive or defensive, was so anxious to come to terms no fear need to be had for the rest. Confidence was mustered, and trade so revived that our markets were at once swept bare of imported merchandise, and produce to export was freely offered again. The talk about war has begun already to die out, and native shops closed through fear of the violence of this ronin or revolutionary party are opening again.

When this money is paid, few doubt that the Tycoon will be the party in reality making the payment. It will be an act of friendship toward powerful Satsuma, for the best of reasons. Nay, for my own part, I doubt not that the Imperial Treasury will disburse to Satsuma, part of the gains derived from foreign trade, something done to retrieve the losses of the bombardment of Kagosima—it will be an act of policy to do so.

But of one thing we may be sure, that this ready coming to terms of Satsuma clearly indicates that Japan will have no war with the Treaty Powers unless forced into it. The Treaty Powers may be compelled to a large forbearance, certainly to employ a careful skill to avoid war, but Japan does not wish to fight. Three centuries of peace have enervated her sword-arm. Or we may assign, perhaps, a more creditable reason that she alone of all the Oriental nations has had the sagacity to avoid conflict with the Western Powers, knowing its futility.

In this connection it is to be mentioned that a few days since the Yedo Government promised the American Minister that they would pay the $10,000 damages claimed by the owners of the steamer Pembroke for the firing into that steamer last Spring by the Prince of Nagato. This will probably be regarded by the U.S. Government as a settlement in full for all claims for that act.

In the firing upon the Wyoming, Capt. McDougal had his revenge on the spot.

Amid all these acts for compromise and settlement it is to be noted however that the Yedo Government still talks about foreigners leaving the shores of Yedo Bay. They wish to negotiate to this end, and now even talk of sending new embassies to America and Europe charged with affecting this object.

In Nagasaki quiet has again been restored. At Hakodadi there has been at no time any disturbance. Nor do we of late hear of so much of internal commotions among the great princes of the Empire. The Peace Society has eminent reason to be hopeful of this part of the world.

[Under the same date Hall added the following section on "game," which was published with his letter of November 30 in the February 13, 1864, issue of the *New York Tribune*.][26]

We have a liberal supply of game, which abounds in our markets. In the Wintertime wild geese cover the harvested rice-fields in numerous bevies; every day large flocks of them are seen in the air, and at night their peculiar scream fills the silence, as they wing on their way. I have often walked in easy pistol-shot distance of them, in my country rambles; and even in Yedo they may be seen by hundreds and thousands resting in the moat that sweeps the imperial palaces; or, more familiar still, will come down into private or temple gardens, where the fish-ponds attract their eye.

Scattered all through the farming country by which we are surrounded are numerous ponds, formed by damming the little streams at the head of every valley, for the purpose of irrigating the rice-fields. If one could hover over the landscape, he would see these gems of water as thick as the eyes in a peacock's tail, for the whole country hereabout is a succession of billowy ridges, and each interval has its own rivulet, whose waters are husbanded against the possible drought of Summer. Very many of these lakes, as you may imagine, are in quiet sequestered spots, fringed with the tall cedars or other tree growths, and so are favorite haunts of the wild duck, muscovy and mandarin, black and teal, and canvass-back for aught I know. I often come across them in my walks. One spot in particular, the "Seven Lakes," so called because seven of these irrigating ponds in proximity, is their chosen resort.

Then on the undulating hills there is a great deal of undergrowth, pollard oaks,

and chestnuts, and alders, and other trees indigenous to Japan, which form capital cover for the pheasants, green, golden, and copper, with more rarely a woodcock or quail. In the open grain fields adjoining the woods, are the wild pigeons, much like ours, but I never see them in flocks; three or four together are the most that I have seen. As the Japanese never go "for a day's shooting in the country," and seldom take life of beast or bird unnecessarily (they are not so scrupulous about a "tojin's" life), until the foreigner came, the birds had a good time of it; and the geese flew down upon the rice-fields, the ducks swam in the quiet pools, and the pigeons picked up a fat living, gleaners in the grain-fields, all unmolested.

But the "tojin" came to Japan, and human society, and old custom, and ancient law of man, not only were broken in upon, but the very birds of the air have had their peace and security invaded. The tojin has a tooth for game, the Japanese has a love for money greater than his love for beast and bird, and so woodcock and teal, wild goose and pheasant, must be caught and slain to gratify the depraved tastes of us both.

But the Japanese do not go about banging away with a blunderbuss and beating the woods with trained dogs, thus killing some and frightening for ever away more, but, more craftily going to work, he sacrifices "sport" to cunning, and snares the unwilling birds, or fastens them with bird lime. So dozens and scores and hundreds fall victims, in such a noiseless way that the rest do not take flight, and Mrs. Duck, who retires to her sedge coverlid at night, missing her lordly drake, has no idea what has happened to the dear fellow, and only suspects him of faithlessness, little thinking he is at that moment garnishing a lineal Plymouth-Rocker's Thanksgiving Day table in Nipon.

[26] It seems that the November 30 and December 1, 1863, letters were sent to the *Tribune* at the same time. Having been ill just prior to his November 30 letter, Hall apparently put off writing a more official report until December 1. The Editor at the *Tribune* seems to have reversed the publication sequence because of the news content of the December 1 letter, publishing it on January 29, 1864, and the November 30 letter on February 13, 1864. The section on "game" seems to have been part of the December 1 letter.

We regard ourselves as safe in the town limits, and, with due precaution, a little beyond them. I frequently go out for a long walk from six, eight, ten, or twelve miles, measuring both ways, but not alone. Sometimes with one friend, sometimes with two, and in my longer walks we make up a company of four, five, or six, as we can find them. In theses long walks, we go each with his trusty revolver; in the shorter ones, we sometimes go armed, and sometimes do not, as convenience serves. But there are many who do not venture outside of the smoke of our chimneys, and more still who limit themselves to "the walk on the bluffs" of two or three miles circuit. "Our walking party" ventures the furthest, owing perhaps more to our excess of leg strength and vitality than to a preponderance of courage. Having been here now a long time, and always fond of rambling and being full of "woodcraft" as to the innumerable little paths that thread the country everywhere, it falls often to my lot to be leader and guide.

We, that is, our walking club, are waiting for a day of sun which shall also be a day of leisure to make a yet longer foot excursion, boating down the shores of Yedo bay ten or twelve miles, for the pleasure of walking back. This will take us to the scene of a recent rencounter, in which three Englishmen were somewhat astonished as well as frightened, and a Japanese samowrai, or "two-sworder," as we call them, had a shoulder perforated by a pistol ball. Two weeks ago, a couple of Yankee friends recreating at an inn twelve miles in another direction, took alarm at some movements real or fancied, and without waiting for their horses to be resaddled did some tall walking on the back track. These folks were horseback, but our walking club feel more safe on foot—we know then what legs we trust, and for fight, flight, or the fence, in a broken country, there are no legs like one's own. Besides, we rely greatly upon our diplomacy to keep out of any quarrels, and if neither legs nor our diplomacy savvy, we still have in reserve something better than a horse—our little "Colts,"

frisky enough, I dare say, if properly put on their metal. Then we are actuated by principle—we have a right by treaty to go into the country ("shear the wolf"), and we will go into the country, will shear the wolf.

Yesterday I was walking in the streets of the town, when, at the turn of a corner, I came upon a mob of 200 or 300 low Japanese armed with clubs, matchlocks, firehooks and other weapons from the mob's arsenal, the street. With faces white and livid with rage, they swayed by me, not over me, fortunately, in pursuit of several Prussian sailors, who, like all Jacks ashore, had first got drunk, gone to a disreputable quarter, got into a row with the natives, nearly killed one, and now were flying for their lives; for, assuredly, if this mad mob had caught them there would have been lives lost. Luckily for the Jacks, the English barracks were not far, into which they fled, and the crossed bayonets before the gate held back the surging crowd, which had now increased to many hundreds. Thus you see we have our little excitements and variations on life—variations in the animal, not variations in the aesthetical, like opera, lecture-room and that ilk with you. This applies to north of Chambersburgh only, for south there are some pretty extensive variations in the animal.

Friday, December 4, 1863

Anytime today and yesterday the passer by in the streets has seen at the square near Benten Dori a man bound and kneeling on a mat surrounded by a crowd of spectators. Two government officials and several policemen are in attendance with the insignia of their office. The story of his arrest and punishment is told by a board nailed to a post on which it is written that all the spectators may read. It is interpreted to me thus. This man is a priest 65 years old, and united to his priestly calling that of man midwife and privately that of abortionist. In this capacity he had been called upon by two girls at different times, and the written board gives their names and residence, girls who had loved not wisely but too well.

Their story is that before operating upon them he compelled them to submit to his embraces. One of them only he appears to have operated upon. The custom of the wretched Japanese abortionist is to rupture the membranes with a pointed flexile reed, but this bungler used the rough splinter of a Japanese broom and only succeeded in giving his victim a great amount of suffering, which led to her confession to her friends of the cause, and so to the man's arrest. The other story is that this girl endeavored to extort money from him and failing in it exposed him.

After this public exposure of two days to the crowd which was always very large and contained a large proportion of women and girls, this man is to be banished to ten ri outside of imperial territory, or, as others say, he is to be banished altogether to one of the small penal islands lying off the coast. The latter seems likely, for it is at this season that a convict ship annually leaves Yedo with its freight of malefactors. Beyond banishment the hardships of these penal colonies are said to be slight, but on the contrary, that though all must labor at some business or trade, life is thus often rendered more comfortable than in their former estate.

This case is interesting as showing that the Japanese with all their social depravity punish also social crimes. This old man, though exposed to public gaze for an infamous crime, and somewhat haggard with confinement in jail, was not much cast down and bore his pillory and the gibes of the multitude with the indifference of carelessness rather than of despondency. Some foreign sailors with the usual sympathetic spirit of Jack ashore had bestowed on the old man a good supply of oranges, which he munched at his leisure and shared with his custodians, who looked upon it as a good joke, and seemed no wise inclined to make the man feel more uncomfortable than was natural from his exposed position. And when one sailor gave him a cigar, the old man bowed in acknowledgment, lighted it, nor did the young official at his side disdain to light his own pipe from the criminal's cigar. No Jack Retch at home would have treated a bound victim so familiarly or liberally.

Monday, December 7, 1863

Some of the Governors of Foreign Affairs were down again from Yedo yesterday to renew their proposition for the removal of foreigners from Kanagawa. Col. Neale refused to see them on account of his unfinished business with Satsuma. So they called upon the French Minister. It is understood that the Japanese propose to send new embassies to Europe and America to treat of this question.

We hear that several murders were committed in Yedo on Saturday night, the victims being men engaged in trade with foreigners. In one lackerman's shop three are said to have been killed. This of course produces again some consternation among the Yokohama merchants.

Monday, December 14, 1863

On Friday last Satsuma's envoys paid to Col. Neale the £25,000 ($100,000) indemnity, and coupled the payment with the promise to use every exertion to secure Richardson's murderers. No one believes that this promise will ever be fulfilled and so the case of England against Satsuma is closed.

On the other hand the Minister of the United States has received instructions to demand indemnity of the Japanese Government for the losses at the burning of the Legation in Yedo, the firing upon the *Pembroke*, and the attack upon American citizens in May last.

Envoys from Yedo have again been down to confer about the closing of this port, they had audience only of the French; and their proposal to send envoys to Europe and America to negotiate for this assumes the probability of early accomplishment. They prepare also to arrange by the same envoys the difficulties likely to spring out of the murder of Lieut. Camus.

The rumors of recent assassinations at Yedo appear to have had foundation in fact. A number of native shops have again closed under this system of terrorism. It seems astonishing that the Imperial Government should allow such a state of things to go on without any apparent check.

Among other restrictions on traffic must be

mentioned an order, whether emanating from the ronins or the government is not clear, that the supply of moosmes to the foreigners shall be restricted to the supply now on hand at Yokohama. As Macaulay says about the Pilgrims and bear baiting, the law to suppress this sport was not in mercy to the bears, but to cut off the people from their sport.

The weather has been very mild and delightful. We had no hard frost till yesterday morning. I have been picking tomatoes of late and occasionally green corn. Yesterday's frost will finish.

In a walk yesterday, a charming sunny ramble, I saw the dandelions and pyrus japonica in bloom and another yellow flower resembling the dandelion. Some American strawberries, in growth prolific, are beginning to bloom in the garden.

A horrid murder was committed Saturday night in the foreign quarter. An Englishman killed the Portuguese with whom he was boarding. The murderer was in indigent circumstances, of an excitable temperament bordering nearly on insanity, and the quarrel began out of the threat by the Portuguese to expel him from the house because he had not paid his board.[27]

Saturday, December 19, 1863

The week has had its usual rumors of ronins. From Yedo scarcely any cargo has arrived by boat, the boatmen having been threatened with vengeance if they transported goods to the foreigners. The main street shows a great many closed shops. All the porcelain stores are closed and the only silk shop, beside a number of lacker shops.

Sunday, December 20, 1863

There has been a large arrest this morning of gamblers by the officials. The reason is that gambling has become so rife that the want of money has led to repeated crimes; it is even

said that many of the so-called ronins are unfortunate gamblers seeking to recruit their purses. Some have been feigning blindness and in the guise of wandering *Amas* or (Shampooers) have gained access to houses and made their plans for robbery. We hear of fourteen removed out of town, and the whole number of arrests will reach fifty it is said.

Monday, December 21, 1863

Four of us took a boat for Kanasawa yesterday forenoon to gain our exercise by a walk back. We landed on the beach near the town and took a path across the fields into the main street. As we turned into the street we came face to a party of three roystering young blades, not more than four rods distant, who were flushed with sake and were approaching us with swaggering bravado air that was ominous of mischief. We were well armed with revolvers, and though an encounter was, however successful, to be shunned, we approached them till we came to a teahouse whose open doorway gave us a vantage ground as making their long swords less effectual and our pistols none the less. The men halted in front of the door, saluted us boisterously, but our numbers and position made us secure, though it was by no means sure what their disposition was. They proceeded on the road in precisely the direction that we wished to take.

The result of a conflict with this class of men in Japan, no matter if every assailant was slain would be to make every hour of a stay in this country an hour of danger. The assassin's sword would ever after be in waiting. So we concluded as matter of prudence that we had better take a by road which I knew, and endeavor to reach the main road in advance. So we at once started on our way and when we came into the open again saw that our drunken friends were still ahead of us. Three other sworded men were now seen coming from the opposite direction, and the three drunken young blades, when they espied us, waited in the road at the foot of the hill for us

[27] John R. Black, in *Young Japan: Yokohama and Yedo, 1858–79* (Tokyo: Oxford University Press, 1968), vol. 1, p. 280, tells us that the Portuguese was one Frank Jose and the perpetrator of the crime an Englishman named A. H. Browning.

to come up. Our excursion included the purpose to cross the hills that skirt Mississippi bay and it was a moment's consultation whether we should strike at once into the hills by the footpaths and regain the highway if we desired beyond, or whether we should take the road now and encounter these men. The men being drunk, the risk of having a shindy with them was pretty large, and we finally determined to do all that was prudent to avoid it, and so took the footpaths with the intent to regain the highway at the top of the high hill at the foot of which we both were. Once among the hills we could engage them on our own terms, if necessary, where their broadswords would have small play. We missed our road in this rough rolling land and did not regain the main path till we must have left them some distance behind and saw no more of them. Doubtless the convenient halting spots on the road, with their cups of tea and drams of sake gave them delays. Though the temptation was something to encounter these men, to show them the road was ours, we were afterwards glad that we took the more prudent course and left our minds free of the fear of assassination which would have ever been present if we had had a successful quarrel.

Thursday, December 24, 1863

If we may trust the reports of the natives, the city of Yedo is under a thorough system of terrorism from the supremacy of the ronins over the laws. Murders and outrages continue to be committed on merchants and others concerned in foreign business or trade. There can be little doubt, however, that to a great extent this cry against foreigners is only a cover for bad men to pillage and murder for money, or to gratify their depraved passions. Forty people are thus said to have recently lost their lives. Yedo is full of cargo which would gladly be forwarded to Yokohama to reap the large prices here paid; as for instance cotton which is now worth treble the customary price, but the boatmen are intimidated and scarcely a boat leaves that city for this any more. Some business is done clandestinely under the cover of the night, but that only to a small extent.

"Why," said I to one who was narrating this state of affairs to me, "why do not the people protect themselves; they are numerous and able to do so." "It was tried," he said, "a few days ago in the province of Shimosa, near Yedo, where the farmers of a small village rose up against three ronins and killed them. The weapons they used were bamboos sharpened for spears and ladders to entangle the robbers. The result was that a few days later three hundred armed men came to avenge their comrades' death. They seized the people of the village until the three or four who were chiefs in the previous affair were pointed out, and these they put to death with savage barbarity, first cutting off one finger after another, then the toes in like manner, then the lips, ears, and nose in all the suggestiveness of inhuman mutilation. "Then why do not the people all arise and exterminate their oppressors?" "They are too faint hearted" ("their liver is too weak"), was the reply. Yet he says the people, though they dare not say it, would rejoice to see the whole race of two sworders severely punished in a foreign war.

Friday, December 25, 1863

Christmas Day and general jollity among our English friends. The men-of-war are decked with green branches, and last evening the harbor resounded with the noise of mirth and gladness.

Wednesday, December 30, 1863

A cotton merchant is reported killed by ronins at Uraga and others have been threatened and to save their lives have thrown their cotton into the sea. It is however difficult to reconcile these reports with the large arrivals of stock in the market. No silk has come down from Yedo for a week, but that also may be because there is a fair stock here.

Year prepared for anything. We shall not be surprised if peace and quiet remain, we shall not be astonished if there is fresh trouble and bloodshed. We are uncertain of either our friends or enemies among the natives. If the close of the year finds us well and prosperous, or with broken business and more personal disasters, we shall be alike unsurprised.

Saturday, January 2, 1864

There is a great fire towards, or in, Yedo; it is reported to be among the joroyas of Sinagawa.

1864

Sunday, January 3, 1864

The fire at Yedo was in the mercantile quarter consuming among other large establishments the *Mitsui*, a great silk house, whose proprietors are also government bankers. The fire originated in this building and was undoubtedly an incendiary one. The popular talk is that notices were posted in Yedo ten days beforehand that in ten days this house would be burned. Again in two days a similar notice, and even on the morning of the fire, public notices were said to have been posted that this building would that day be destroyed. Strange as this may seem, it is not wholly improbable for it is quite the Japanese custom to threaten persons and places in this public manner, though these threats are not always executed.[1]

Friday, January 1, 1864

What an unlucky year this must be to all the world for beginning on a Friday!

Consul Fisher gave a grand New Year's Eve party last night and house warming. The assembly, though it could boast only a half score of ladies, was still brilliant with diplomatic, army, and navy uniforms, and passed off pleasantly. During today there has been many congratulatory calls, more than heretofore. The whole holiday week has been perfection in weather, clear, sunshining and just cold enough to exhilarate. This is a paradise land of winters.

A year ago opened auspiciously, but what a troubled year it has been of alternate hopes and fears. Our business has been threatened with destruction and our very lives in peril. One fellow citizen has fallen under assassins' swords. The year closed out in obscurity as it had begun in hope, and we enter on the New

[On January 4, 1864, Hall sent the following letter to the *New York Tribune*, which was published on March 18, 1864.]

Of all the countries in which to win the reputation of a prophet, I would pronounce Japan the most difficult. Better a "rain maker" in South Africa than a seer in Nipon, old and well settled as ancient cus-

---

[1] Conrad Totman adds that "when the Mitsui store burned, a thousand people reportedly went there in hopes of receiving distributed largesse, which suggests that the pamphleteers' message was reaching a consid- erable audience." See Conrad Totman, *The Collapse of the Tokugawa Bakufu, 1862–1868* (Honolulu: University Press of Hawaii, 1980), p. 96.

tom appears to be. So it is that if my letters at one time speak encouragingly of remaining peace and prosperity for Japan and the foreigners on her shores, and at another of wars and rumors of wars, it is because my correspondence must be a reflex of the prevailing feeling at the time now tending in one direction, and now in another.

I closed my letter of just a month since with saying that "the Peace Society has eminent reason to be hopeful of this part of the world;" but today these hopes are less fair. What with renewed intestine difficulties, multiplied assassinations, burning palaces and a score of minor difficulties here, and from abroad England's gathering wrath for the wreck of Kagosima and Holland's warlike fleet on its way, the sky of peace is obscured with ominous clouds.

True Satsuma has at last paid up his indemnity money. On the 11th ult. $100,000 were counted into the English Legation, and Satsuma fondly believes he has made his peace. Here we yet doubt if England so settles the affair of Kagosima. Meantime, the Yedo Government has not abandoned its negotiations for the permanent closing of Yedo and Kanagawa. On the contrary, they seem wholly in earnest in this matter and finding that the representatives of the Treaty Powers resident in Japan give them no encouragement they are preparing to send an embassy to Europe charged with this important business. The French Charge d'Affaires, M. Belcourt, is about to return and the present intention is that this new embassy shall either go with him or simultaneously. Another embassy will probably be sent to America on the like errand.

There is, again, a convention at Miaco, of the great Daimios of the realm, to take into consideration the affairs of the country, and to determine upon some definite public policy. The Tycoon and the Regent are shortly to leave Yedo, to be present at this council. The opinion appears strong, among the Japanese, that the result of these deliberations will be favorable to an enlightened foreign policy.

But it is high time some conclusion, that shall be felt as binding by all the Daimios and their followers, is reached. Even a determination to undertake the expulsion of the foreign element would be better than this incertitude, which is leading more and more to a petty anarchy. The *ronins*, who now seem to represent the reactionary party, are growing daily more formidable. If we may believe the continual reports from Yedo, that city is under a terrorism of outlawry, which the Government is either impotent to subdue or, for its purposes, connives at.

There have been repeated assassinations of merchants engaged in trade with foreigners, even to the petty huckster who has supplied our market with eggs and poultry. These assassinations have been perpetrated by gangs of three or four or more men entering shops and houses at dusk or in the evening. Placards threatening all who have to do with foreigners are frequently posted in the streets and on the gateposts of official quarters. The merchants openly complain that the Government takes no official steps towards their protection, and say that well-known gangs of *ronins* are recognizable in the streets in the open day, going in or coming out of Daimio palaces, and some even wearing imperial livery. For days together boats have been intimidated from leaving Yedo for this port though the distance is but fifteen miles.

The avenues of commerce by the sea have been more safe, until within a few days the slaughter of a cotton merchant at Uraga (the great entrepot of Yedo bay) shows that the foreigner is struck at on all sides through the unfortunate native who chooses to deal with him. Already a large number of the native shops at this port are closed, and unless some means be found to check this insidious warfare against foreign trade, we have reason to apprehend a general break up of business.

If the Government is conniving at all this, as some think to furnish additional reasons why foreigners should leave Yedo bay, they appear to have raised a greater storm than they can control, for a fortnight since the Imperial palace was burned to the ground leaving not a timber standing.* No one doubts that it was the work of incendiaries. The Court itself is filled with cabals, and the life of the unfortunate young Tycoon has as little security of permanency as that of an old Assyrian King, or the most ill-fated sovereign of medieval days.

Tycoon and Daimios alike cannot be blind to the dangers of a growing anarchy, and it is to be hoped, therefore, that this renewed council at Miaco may see that their common safety lies in a restoration of public order.

At this writing a Dutch fleet of nearly 300 guns is approaching these shores to demand satisfaction for the wanton attack upon the corvette Medusa in the Straits of Simonoseki, in July last. So powerful an armament sent to so distant an expedition shows that Holland means to hold her place worthily among the Powers of the world, and that she is as ready to resent a national insult as the strongest. There is something gratifying in the fact that Holland, least of all the treaty Powers, Portugal excepted, is the first to demand redress for the insults put on so many national flags last Summer in the inland sea. The lesson will be all the better for the Japanese that it is first read to them by the Power they could have feared the least and there is a further significance in it when we remember the doubtful and humiliating position Holland has held with Japan for two centuries at Desima. It is a man familiar with Desima who holds in Holland the position of Minister of the Marine. He is the avenging Nemesis.

We all hope, therefore, that this fleet will speedily arrive and that it may alone have the honor of chastizing the belligerent Prince of Nagato and of opening again the

* I think I reported this palace as burned last July; it afterward proved to be only a small portion that was thus destroyed. This time the destruction is total, and the flames of the conflagration were distinctly visible at this place.

passage of the Inland Sea and the straits of Simonoseki, now for more than six months closed.

Long before this reaches you, you will have heard of the appearance of the Alabama in the China seas, and her further depredations on American commerce, her last exploit having been the destruction of the ship Contest in Gaspar Strait, from this to New York loaded principally with rags. Capt. Semmes seldom catches so unsavory and profitless a cargo. So far as American shipping is affected we might as well be at war with all Europe, for the dread of the Alabama effectually cuts off all American bottoms from employment. In all these last Asiatic ports our ships and seamen are idly waiting a turn of affairs that will again loose their sails to the wind and give employment to willing hands.

The last heard of the Alabama was the destruction of the Contest in Gaspar Strait, at which time the Wyoming was cruising off Singapore, having intercepted letters for Capt. Semmes, which indicated his touching at that port. If they chance to meet Capt. McDougal, the hero of Simonoseki, will give a good account of himself and the Wyoming. The sloop Jamestown, Captain Price, left this harbor on the 26th ultimate bound for the China coast, at one of whose ports there was good reason to expect the Alabama.

Raw cotton is now forming an important article of export from Japan. The shipments since July 1 have been about ten millions of pounds. The staple though short is better than that of China and equal to much of that of India. Of course, not equal to the best grade of India, but bearing a fair comparative price in the London market.

The holidays just passed were ushered in and went out with all the festivities, on a reduced scale, that mark the holiday ties of more civilized lands. If we have not all your social joys how shall you match our peerless weather. Six weeks now since a drop of rain has fallen or clouds have obscured the sun, the thermometer at night falling to near the freezing point or barely a few degrees below, the midday air clear, cool, and bracing.

Monday, January 11, 1864

It is rumored that Stotsbashi [Hitotsubashi], who went a little time since to assist at the Council of Daimios in Oasaca, has been assassinated by the followers of the late Gotairo, or Regent, who was slain at the entrance of the citadel in Yedo in 1860. This strikingly illustrates the blood feud as it yet prevails in Japan. The late Emperor was assassinated by Mito's instigation, who hoped to place his son, this same Stotsbashi, on the throne. The Regent, during the minority of the present monarch, who was selected by the Council of Daimios instead of Stotsbashi, was very active in the punishment of Mito. The consequence was that he in turn was assassinated as above related, and now in turn Stotsbashi has fallen.

We hear also that two nights ago twenty-eight ronins were arrested in Yedo at one sweep, and that these ronins turned out to be "false ronin," or common vagabonds, who had assumed the somewhat honored name of ronin under which to commit their atrocities. This seems to have restored some confidence to the native merchants who have stood much in awe of these outlaws.

Tuesday, January 12, 1864

Already some of the shops which have been closed are reopening, owing to the late arrest of ronins.

Wednesday, January 13, 1864

The deed of harakiri is not yet a fable. Yesterday three officials in government employ, and living at Benten, committed suicide for fear of detection in being implicated with some merchants in smuggling silk into Yokohama without passing it through the Tongya [Toiya], or Yedo internal customs. The merchants having already been arrested, the officials feared exposure and committed suicide.

[On January 14, 1864 Hall sent the following letter to the *New York Tribune*, which was published on March 22, 1864.]

Affairs in Japan continue the same halting steps toward progress, as often recalcitrant to the old desire for seclusion—groping, stumbling, with the indecision of a blind man, inimical and dangerous to the foreign element in the Empire, puzzling to the diplomats, and wholly inexplicable, I trow, to the *Tribune*'s fireside readers.

The last mail brought us intelligence of the effect of the Kagosima affair in Europe, and there, too, it seems that naval action was regarded, as your correspondent termed it, neither decisive nor glorious. It was only unfortunate for the humane reputation of the English Admiral that he boasted as an achievement of his own what was really unavoidable, namely, the shelling of the City of Kagosima, and the consequent conflagration. The batteries could not be attacked without subjecting the town to all the horrors of a bombardment; but this is not for Admiral Kuper to plead, since he has chosen to regard it as his own heroic act. One effect of the news of this naval engagement has been to send back to Japan Sir Rutherford Alcock, the late Envoy hither, but who has now been a long time absent on leave, charged with extraordinary powers. We await his coming now daily, looked for as having an important bearing on events. But really, Col. Neale the Charge *ad interim*, seems to have so far settled the quarrel with Satsuma, that no occasion is left to reopen it.

France alone has an important business unarranged, which is the late assassination of Lieut. Camus. French officials here declare that the real business of the Japanese Embassy to Europe has for its chief object the settlement at Paris of this unfortunate murder. The Japanese declare they go hoping to secure the withdrawal of the treaty powers from Yedo and Kanagawa and the limitation of foreign trade and intercourse to the ports of Nagasaki and Hakodadi. The arrangements for the departure of the Embassy are now nearly complete. They will leave here early in February, by a French war steamer to Shanghae where they will be transferred to the French mercantile line of steamers for Marseilles via Suez. It is at their own special request that this Embassy goes in an unostentatious manner, and they asked to be received in Europe with the simplest honors due to their rank. A similar Embassy to America is talked of, but the proposition assumes, as yet, no definite shape.

The Dutch armament designed to operate on the still obdurate Prince of Nagato has not reached our shores.

In my last [letter] I alluded to the Council of Daimios at Oasaca. The Tycoon is still at Yedo, where a fleet of purchased steamers is gathering to escort him soon after the Japanese New Year, which begins with the 8th of February. Stotsbashi, son of Mito, aspirant to the throne and now or lately a quasi Regent, went down to Oasaca some time since, where, it is whispered about, he has been assassinated by the followers of the Gotairo, who was slain at the palace gates in Yedo at the instigation of old Prince Mito, his father. This act well illustrates the "blood feud" as it obtains in Japan to this day. The Tycoon with whom Mr. Harris effected his treaty died suddenly—made way with, as is generally believed, by Prince Mito, who then hoped to secure the succession in the person of his son, this same Stotsbashi. But the Council of Daimios, choosing otherwise, selected the present Emperor [Shogun], a young scion of the house of Kishiu. The Gotairo was elected Regent during the young Prince's minority. Mito, on account of the suspicion of complicity with the late Emperor's death, was, by the active influence of the Gotairo or Regent, confined a prisoner of State to his own house, and the family disgraced. Mito's followers took fearful revenge, in the summer of 1860, by the assassination of the Gotairo under the citadel walls as he was returning from Court, surrounded by his followers. The murder while decreasing the influence of the Gotairo's family, again elevated that of Mito, who belonged to the Conservative or anti-foreign party, as the Gotairo did to the progressive party. Owing to the reaction against the progressive party, the family of Mito has gradually gained position and influence until during the grave troubles of this year in early Summer, Stotsbashi was made actual regent, though not taking that title, which has continued vacant since the Gotairo's death. With the feuds of these rival families and parties the foreigners have unfortunately been involved, and Stotsbashi was expressly sent from Miaco in July to hold plenary powers at Yedo, and to inaugurate active measures against foreign foothold in Japan. On arriving at Yedo, even he was overawed by the magnitude of the danger to his country from the hostile fleets at anchor in Yedo bay, and his first act was instead of forcible opposition, the payment of $440,000 demanded by the English. The necessity of this act, the operations at Shimonoseki and Kagosima, opened the eyes of the Japanese, so far that they paused in further acts of open hostility, and the opposition to foreigners assumed the shape of intimidation by *ronins*, or outlaws, against their own traitors, who had foreign connections. Thus Stotsbashi goes down again to the Council at Oasaca somewhat shorn in his pretensions. The progressive party struggles upward again, and finally the faithful retainers of the murdered Gotairo, having nursed their hatred for three years, secure their revenge. There is hope in this blood-feud for civilization and progress.

The Government at Yedo have at last moved to some purpose against the ronins, who have been lopping off heads of those who sold silk, lackerware, or chickens to foreigners, at their own savage will. Numerous arrests have been effected at Yedo; twenty-eight having been seized in a single night. It is interesting to know that these arrests were made by a temporary police under the stimulus of high rewards offered. These arrests have given a little more confidence to the greatly intimidated native traders who had begun to arm themselves with foreign revolvers for self defense. Still the country is in a deplorably unsettled state, and trade languishes therefore.

Hara kiri, yet retains its attractions for in-

tending suicides. A sub-officer in the Yokohama Custom House, a few days since,
being implicated with some merchants in
defrauding the Government of certain imposts on raw silk, saved his honor by the
time-honored disembowelment.

The Prussian envoys, after months of
procrastination two days ago succeeded in
getting their long-time-made treaty ratified.

Oasaca has just experienced one of the
most destructive fires history records. The
burnt district is three miles in length by
one-third of a mile wide; 30,000 houses
and 250 warehouses were consumed, with
a loss of life of 500 to 1,000 souls. The fire
lasted for three days.

The Alabama, as you have already
heard, was not so snugly entrapped at
Amoy as was believed. Our news from the
southward is to the 1st of this month when
the Alabama was reported at or off Singapore, and the Wyoming at Manilla, when
last heard from.

[On January 15, 1864, Hall wrote in
addition to the *New York Tribune* a note
that was published March 22, 1864.]

I sent you tidings, a few days since, of the
detention of the Alabama at Amoy. I regret
to say this news proved false, but was regarded so trustworthy when the Rogers
left, a week since, that it was so officially
communicated to our Home Government
by the Minister Resident, General Pruyn.

Two weeks later news from the China
Seas gives no later intelligence of either the
Alabama or Wyoming since the destruction
of the Contest, except, a bare rumor that
the Alabama was seen coaling at the mouth
of the Saigon River.

Monday, January 18, 1864

Although the weather is yet cold and the
thermometer falls nightly below freezing point,
the first signs of coming spring are manifest in
the apricot blossoms opening in protected
nooks, and the swelling buds of the camellias
and daphnes. The hidden pulse of nature
throbs in the tree veins though there is no external warmth to call forth bud or blossom.

Wednesday, January 27, 1864

Foh Kien arrived.

Tuesday, February 2, 1864

Went with an excursion party to Yedo today,
going up on the steamer *Foh Kien*. The American Minister and American Consul and his
family and Mr. Forbes[2] were of the party. The
day was delightful and as we went up the bay
we had a charming view of Fusi and the neighboring mountains, their outlines all sharply defined by the light snow which had fallen a few
days previously. We dropped anchor two miles
from the landing at Yedo about eleven o'clock

[2] This was apparently Murray Forbes, the son of Robert B. Forbes who had served as a leading partner in
the American firm Russell & Co. in China at the time of
the Opium War. After making several fortunes in the
China trade, Robert B. Forbes became a major force in
the American effort to sell steamers in the Far East.
Forbes shipped out several "steamers" on the deck of
vessels such as the *Jeannie*, which was regularly consigned to Walsh, Hall and Co. It was the elder Forbes
who built and dispatched the *Pembroke* to China in
1861. This was the vessel consigned to Walsh, Hall &
Co. that was fired on in the Straights of Shimonoseki by
Chōshū. Murray Forbes was sent to China in 1863 to
work as a clerk in Russell & Co.; in 1869 he became a

full partner in this firm. See Robert B. Forbes, *Personal
Reminiscences* (Boston: Privately Printed, 1876), pp.
301ff. C. D. Mugford in a letter to Augustine F. Heard
dated January 30, 1864, writes about the arrival of the
Foh Kien: "Mr. Forbes came up in her, Walsh did not
come. She is a fine boat & the Japanese fancy her being
a wooden vessel which they seem to prefer to iron. Mr.
Forbes will go up to Jeddo in her next week and the
chances are she will be sold. I hear they want $280,000
for her." It seems that Walsh, Hall & Co. were serving
as agents in this sale. Heard Papers, Baker Library,
Harvard Business School, Heard I v. HM-57 folder II,
Letters of C. D. Mugford.

and at once went ashore. Our horses awaited us at the landing place and no time was lost getting into the saddle. Nearly fifty mounted yakunins escorted us. We went first to the American Legation and made a short halt, from there to Atago Yama, to the Castle view, so down the hill along the moat, within the citadel walls, a route familiar to me and already described in this journal.

Everything was quiet; we met nowhere any insult of word or gesture and we could not feel that Yedo was so unsafe a place to live in after all.

Notwithstanding we were riding several hours continuously, we nowhere fell upon the traces of any of those great fires which have again and again devastated the city, this alone showing how great in extent must be the entire city. Over the citadel walls we did indeed see the dismantled roofs of one of the palace towers where the late fire had raged for several hours.

In the court quarter the streets were remarkably quiet and we did not meet the usual number of trains. The moat of the citadel was lively with countless ducks that were swimming on its waters or pluming themselves on the sunny slopes of the turf banks that slope down from the grey walls above.

In the mercantile quarters the shops were busy with customers chaffering over New Year dresses, the sandal stores were crowded with new merchandise, but the street of Owari was the most pleasing, every shop nearly glittering with showy toys for children—kites, battledore, balls, miniature arms, bows, and arrows, dolls and images of every description, and all those toys that young Nippon, like the rest of the world, considers its peculiar property during the holidays.

We accomplished our jaunt successfully and were back on board our steamer with yet an hour of daylight to spare for the trip back to Yokohama.

Sunday, February 7, 1864

Today and yesterday everybody has been busy with preparations for the New Year which opens on the 8th. It is pleasant to see the clothing shops, the shoe shops, the toy shops all thronged with customers and multitudes of children looking in with eager eyes at the new things purchasing for them. The house and shop fronts are ornamented with holiday decorations. Tonight everybody will be busy closing the accounts of the year.

Monday, February 8, 1864

Japan New Year's Day. Everybody is in the streets in their new holiday clothes, and the groups of children one meets at every step look prettily in their gay robes and fresh faces. Kite flying, battledore, and ball are everywhere going on. Old heads and young are equally busy with kite flying, and some monster affairs are sent up shrilly hissing as they go held by a cord as large as my little finger. Officials in their new and stiff official suits are busy going from house to house leaving their cards at the doors of their friends. Here and there is heard the sound of noisy revelry. The toy shops are still thronged by parents and uncles and aunts as they would be in more Christian lands.

The merchants keep at home today for they have probably made a night of it last night. Tomorrow they, too, will give and receive visits and make more substantial tokens of their mutual friendships.

Wednesday, February 10, 1864

Yesterday and today the Japanese have been busy making calls on their friends and giving small presents. I have come in for my share of the latter in the shape of several neat fir boxes filled generally with cakes and sweetmeats, sometimes eggs and sugar.

Kite flying and battledore have been great pastimes. On Tuesday two large kites sent up from the main street and became entangled, there were warm words over the mishap, then blows, until the whole neighborhood became partisans—club, cotton hooks, fire poles, were freely brandished, and the actors put on all the tragic airs of the Japanese stage, but I observed that they were very careful not to hit each other. The police finally appeared on the scene and after more talking than blows the partisans of the respective kites withdrew.

Monday, February 22, 1864

Anniversary of Washington's birthday celebrated by a dinner at Consul Fisher's to which all Americans were invited.

Tuesday, February 23, 1864

Yesterday was the 16th day of the first month of the Japanese year and is strictly kept by the Japanese as a holiday by entire cessation from labor as well as the 16th day of the 7th month. Even the prisoners of the jails are allowed some freedom on these days and are provided with an extra allowance of food of better kind.

Wednesday, March 2, 1864

Alcock returned.

Friday, March 4, 1864

Rumors have reached us that one of Satsuma's steamers has been fired into and sunk by Chosiu.[3] The story goes that this steamer passed through the straits of Shimonoseki safely on her way to Oasaca, returning again with a cargo of cotton and tea, she was fired into in the straits and sunk.

Sunday, March 6, 1864

The fields begin to brighten considerably with their changing greens, but the nights are still frosty.

Friday, March 11, 1864

The Japanese with their usual readiness for invention give among themselves the following reason why the device of the Mexican Dollar is an eagle with a serpent in its mouth.

Many years ago when silver was discovered in the mountains of Mexico by the Spaniards it was impossible to mine out because the mountains were infested by dangerous serpents which prevented any approach to the treasures. The Spaniard called to his deity for aid, who sent the eagles which speedily destroyed the serpents, and in gratitude the Spaniards placed the serpent bearing eagle as the insignium of their coin. Whether this story is of Japanese invention or is an old Mexican or Spanish legend of the coin stamp I am not sure.

Wednesday, March 16, 1864

Still freezing nearly every night, but vegetation pushes itself forward. The daphnes have been slowly coming into bloom for a fortnight or more.

Friday, March 18, 1864

I saw today the official report of Satsuma to the Tycoon announcing the destruction of the steamer, *Sir Char[les] Forbes*, owned by the Tycoon and manned by Satsuma men, by the batteries of Chosiu.[4] Nine officers and thirty men lost their lives. The steamer was attacked while at anchor in the strait for the night, and although displaying the signals of the Japanese, the firing was continued till the steamer was set on fire and destroyed.

---

[3] This was the Chōshū attack on the *Nagasaki-maru* [*Sir Charles Forbes*] a shogunal steamer on loan to Satsuma on January 26. In this attack the ship was set on fire and some thirty Satsuma men lost their lives. Although the ship was clearly marked with the Japanese flag, Chōshū later claimed that it had taken the steamer to be a foreign vessel and had consequently attacked it.

This incident greatly increased Satsuma-Chōshū tensions. For more details see Albert Craig, *Chōshū in the Meiji Restoration* (Cambridge, Mass.: Harvard University Press, 1961), p. 219. See also John R. Black, *Young Japan: Yokohama and Yedo, 1858–59*, vol. 1, pp. 274–75.

[4] The "official report" mentioned here seems to be the same report presented by Satsuma officials to the

Wednesday, March 23, 1864

Received news that an Englishman had been attacked and severely wounded by a Japanese at Nagasaki.[5]

Thursday, March 24, 1864

Fine spring weather, delightful walks in the country, busy gardening, our grounds are perfumed with the blooming daphnes.

[On April 5, 1864, Hall sent the following letter to the *New York Tribune*, which was published on June 11, 1864.]

The two months that have elapsed since my last date have been two months of uneventful quiet. We have had no pillaging by outlaws, suicides *a la harakiri* of disgraceful officials, dire conflagrations, bombardments and burning of cities, or wayside assassinations of foreigners, to enliven the dull routine of our lives, or to spice up our usual correspondence, and delectate your readers withal—but hold I am writing beyond the record; such affairs are becoming to us trivial commonplaces, or I should not forget that a few days ago the mail came in from Nagasaki with its story of an attempt to assassinate a foreign resident. The victim this time was an Englishman, who was attacked in the streets by an armed Japanese, and who after losing his hand in the encounter by a sword blow at the wrist, and receiving other injuries, effected his escape, though his life, at last advices, was despaired of. The assailant was declared to be one of Nagato's men—Nagato, the fire-eating prince of Shimonoseki. And now that I have mentioned this worthy, I am reminded that he has not contributed to the quiet which I rashly asserted above as brooding over us with folded and downy wings.

On the contrary, no longer finding any foreign ships venturesome enough to come within range of his batteries, he has attacked an Imperial steamer which had anchored in the strait of Shimonoseki for the night, on its way from Oasaca to Nagasaki for repairs, in charge of Satsuma's men. This was on the 24th of January. The shore batteries, the same that fired on the Wyoming, opened on the steamer with shot and shell not-withstanding she displayed the signs agreed upon among the Japanese Daimios for Japanese vessels passing through the straits.

The steamer, finding her berth a warm one, and that her Imperial insignia afforded no protection, got up steam to move out of such dangerous proximity, but while moving caught fire and was consumed. Nine officers and thirty men lost their lives. These facts are derived from the official report of the Prince of Satsuma to the Tycoon.

A few weeks later a junk belonging to Satsuma, while anchored for the night near the same place, was boarded by Nagato men, who, finding her laden with cotton for the foreign trade at Nagasaki, summarily burned her, Semmes fashion.

These acts re-assure us of Chosiu's hostility to foreigners and to all who befriend foreigners, thus contradicting reports of recent date that he had grown weary of his hostile position, and was disposed to be friendly. His acts of hostility toward Satsuma will be understood when it is known that under the original programme of the Daimios hostile to foreign intercourse Satsuma and Chosiu of Nagato stood side by side as declared leaders of the anti-foreign movement—nay, Chosiu was led into his present position, so it is declared, more by Satsuma's persuasions than his own will. Whether Chosiu has gone beyond the bond, or Satsuma has failed to come up to it, we may never know. Perhaps Satsuma's

---

Rōju that is included in John R. Black, *Young Japan: Yokohama and Yedo, 1858–79* (Tokyo: Oxford University Press, 1968), vol. 1, p. 275.

[5] This reference is to the unprovoked attack on C. Sutton by a samurai. Sutton was badly injured and

lost his right arm. Although his life was for sometime in danger he recovered and later served as proprietor of the *Rising Sun* and *Nagasaki Express* (Black, *Young Japan: Yokohama and Yedo, 1858–79*, vol. 1, p. 297).

courage oozed out in the ashes of Kago-shima.

What bloodshed and difficulty might have been averted, had prompter measures been taken, the sequel of events in Japan will not doubtless reveal. Had the plan approved by all the naval commanders here except the English Admiral Kuper, viz.: the immediate punishment of Chosiu, after the attack on the steamers in July inst. been carried into effect we should have had none of these subsequent acts of hostility, nay, not even the bombardment of Kago-sima and its heavy losses to both sides.

To go even further back: when Shi-madzu Saburoo coolly halted for the night within four miles of the sight where Richardson had fallen a few hours previously by the swords and spears of his followers, within easy reach as he was of prompt punishment which would have had a most salutary effect in repressing for the future such fierce outbursts of savages, this same Admiral and his coadjutor the British Charge d'Affaires lamentably failed in that promptness of retaliation which so much gives to all punishment its effect and insures terror among evil doers. He afterward had full reason to believe that justice, promptly executed then, as was urged by the French authorities and the public, would have had the best possible effect. By so much as these English officials were too timid or hesitating in this instance they were too precipitate afterward at Kago-sima. Let us deal with the Tycoon and his Government with all the forbearance and consideration due to their difficulties of position, we must deal with the malcontent Princes of his empire in other measure.

A few days previous to the Japanese New Year, which came in on the 8th of February, the Tycoon again went to Oasaca and Miaco, where he still remains. The particular import of this second visit to the Spiritual Emperor within a year it is difficult to know out of many conflicting views. If we may believe the native reports it was to render homage to the Mikado and to meet the principal Daimios of the realm again assembled in council on the state of the Em-pire. It is already declared as one result that the relations of the Mikado and Tycoon have been more clearly defined and a settlement of their respective claims to authority has been had by the Tycoon's agreement to pay the Mikado an annual stipend from the foreign revenue, who, in turn, is to interfere no more in the executive affairs of the Government. A joint commission has also been agreed upon of Daimios both friendly and hostile to foreign intercourse, who are to report on a foreign policy which shall hereafter be steadily adhered to, whether its burden is one of peace or of systematic hostility toward the foreign element in Japan.

Among the names on this commission we recognize that of Shimadzu Saburo himself, brother of the late and father of the present Prince of Satsuma, whose train of followers it was that slew Richardson; also the Prince of Tosa, who is a reputed ally and friend of Chosiu of Nagato; Stotsbashi, who has sometimes been reckoned the friend, but oftener the enemy of foreigners; the venerable Prince of Echizen, who has long been known as the friend of foreign trade, and with whom on this question is associated the Prince of Aizoo; of the 6th and last name, the Prince of Oowajima we are not informed as to his antecedents. So that of the six Princes named, two are known enemies and two are known friends of the foreigner, the fifth has pursued a vacillating policy, while the sixth is unknown. The Japanese about us are sanguine that only good is to be the result, and they even hope for the general opening of the Empire to foreign intercourse, but here, doubtless, their hopes outrun any possible expectations.

While reckoning on these things, we must not forget that there is one man whose opinions are decided, and who, whatever councils at Oasaca may decree will be likely to act independently; that is Mowori, Prince of Nagato or Chosiu-Daisen-no-Daiboo [Daizen-no-tayū], as he is as frequently called.

He has thrown down the glove, and cannot fail to be looked upon by the Japanese soldiers caste as one of the heroes after that old stamp of Yoritomo and Taiko-Sama. He surely has resisted and not unsuccessfully, Dutch, and American, and French war steamers. He has kept the inland sea tight locked for now nearly a year, opening or closing the sea-gates of Shimonoseki at his pleasure. And now he undertakes to punish the enemies of his country, as he views them, at home as well as abroad, and it is much to be feared that he will create a party in Japan, who may prove to the last degree dangerous to the Yedo Government and foreign intercourse. Thus, at the opening of the year the prospect is at least doubtful and our brightest hopes are clouded or no better certainly than Japanese duplicity.

Sir Rutherford Alcock returned to his post as English Minister to the Court of Yedo a month since, and has been remarkably reticent since his return. Doubtless he is testing his position as becomes a true diplomat, and with the disturbed state of Europe operating as a check, he is little likely to try any but pacific measures with the Japanese. The French are even more anxious to keep the peace, and rebuke their Resident here for any and every warlike act or threat.

Meantime the Japanese embassy is on its way to Europe to try their arts of Eastern diplomacy at Occidental courts. Successful with Europe, they will sway the court at Washington. The last heard of them they were at Shanghae, dining and wining, and wild gossip even says, roaring drunk in their convivialities; a little practice, perhaps, against the wiles and arts of Western diplomacy.

The Swiss have, after months of patient waiting, secured their treaty with Japan. The U.S. Minister, Gen. Pruyn, has been successful in securing modifications of Mr. Harris's treaty, by which nearly all articles of import pay a duty of only 5 per cent instead of 20 per cent, as many of them formerly did. This includes liquors, which were formerly subject to a duty of 35 per cent, and consequently paid very little revenues, the temptations being irresistibly to evade the duty by undervaluation or downright smuggling. The General's temperance friends at the capital or in the Classis need not be shocked at this catholicism of views, since foreign liquors have no consumption among the natives, even the munificent gift of a dozen of Hostetter's bitters by the compounder to the Tycoon having failed to allure them from their rice whisky!

The Alabama was last heard of in the Indian Ocean, where she had burned the Emma Jane. Your news of her will be later, probably. The Wyoming is soon expected from the China coast. The Jamestown will come up also when the South monsoon blows steadily.

The Alabama-phobia has effectually squelched American freighters in this part of the world, which are seeking sales under safer flags. Here the bark Maryland has just been sold to British owners for $5,000 and under the name Yokohama loads with cotton for England. The brig Mary Capen has also been sold under the same flag for $4,500.

Your correspondent was at Yedo a short time since by courtesy of Gen. Pruyn, and rode an afternoon about that famous city. Nothing will show the magnitude of this city more than to say that, though there have lately been several destructive fires, burning over large areas, our protracted and circuitous ride revealed to our eyes none of their desolations, except that when riding under the citadel walls we could see in broken roofs traces of the late fire among the Emperor's palaces.

The universal quiet of all Yedo was noteworthy. There were very few trains of official attendants to be met in the streets, and nowhere did we encounter ill words, or harsh looks, except from one dirty soldier, who stood by the wayside looking fierce enough to swallow our entire cavalcade—but he concluded not to.

In the streets of retail shops there was more bustle consequent upon the approaching New Year holidays and it had a charmingly familiar look to see these shops thronged with buyers of New Year gifts.

The silk shops were crowded, the stocking and sandal stores were full of benevolent-looking mothers buying wooden boots and straw shoes for young Nipon, who was sometimes present to try the fit. The book and toy shops were gay with their wares, and enjoyed the most ample patronage. Balls glittering with gold and silver threads, battledore with painted and embroidered pictures; colored games, story books, and thousands of glittering toys; bows and arrows, swords, drums, war-horses, tops, dolls, big and little, houses in miniature, images of men and animals and veritable "Noah's arks" for aught I know, giving every shop of "Owari street" famous among the juveniles, a bright holiday look. There was an over-abundance of other toys that I venture to say could not be found outside of ever-indecent Japan. But the kite-shops took the lead; everybody flies a kite on New Year's Day, and purchasers and shopmen were equally busy among the gaudy kites that Nipon especially delights in.

The world, after all, is much the same everywhere when you get to the bone. The young of all animals are playful and pretty, cat or polecat; and young untrowsered Nipon with his bats and balls and warhorses on wheels, has about the same sports, boyish joys and sorrows, that better breeched young America has.

Saturday, April 16, 1864

This has been a week of charming spring weather. The hills and vallies are exceedingly beautiful with the fields of grain and rape which is now in full bloom. The branches of the deciduous trees are beginning to display the soft colors of the starting leaves. Flowering peach and cherry trees adorn the temple grounds. The first azaleas are in bloom and also the magnolias. I can hardly imagine any land more beautiful than this in the spring and early summer months.

Sunday, April 17, 1864

With Mr. Hogg and Mr. Baker[6] to "Azalea Hill" in Kanagawa; we were too early for the flowers as they are a later (the Chinese) variety. Saw two fine *Koya Maki*, one measuring 7 feet 5 inches in circumference two feet from the ground.

Monday, April 18, 1864

Fair and very warm. Mr. W.[7] gives an amusing account of his visit to Kanasawa. While at the inn an official happened to come along attended by his family and a small retinue. The landlord gave him, the official, a room adjoining W., where soon his curiosity to see foreigners overcame his reticence as a grave Japanese. Slight courtesies were exchanged and the officer was invited to partake of his champagne, which he did with infinite gusto. The fumes of the sparkling wine were soon in his head, and he so far forgot the gravity and dignity of his rank that he proffered a song and dance for his entertainment. His worthy wife and daughter were astonished to see their grave husband and papa singing a hilarious song and dancing the "Chonkina" before the strangers, but their

---

[6] As indicated earlier, Thomas Hogg was U.S. marshal in the Kanagawa consulate, Mr. Baker seems to have been O. H. Baker of Baker & Eisler, one of the American firms in Yokohama. Later in 1864 this became Eisler & Co. See Yokohama Shiyakusho, eds., *Yokohama shishikō-Sangyō hen* (Kyoto: Rinsen Shoten, 1986), p. 52.

[7] It is not clear who Mr. W. was. But given the sense of humor, he could have been Charles Wirgman, the artist and cartoonist who represented the *Illustrated London News*. Wirgman arrived in Yokohama in 1861, and launched his humorous *Japan Punch* in 1862 with a $50 loan from Rudolph Lindau. Like Hall, Wirgman was a good friend of Lindau's, and enjoyed outings in the countryside. In later years Hall referred to Wirgman as a "painter friend" from Yokohama. Hall owned two of Wirgman's oil paintings (dated 1873)—one a portrait of a Japanese official, the other a portrait of a Japanese woman—which currently hang in the Hall Memorial Library, Ellington, Connecticut. The best description of Wirgman during these early Yokohama years can be found in Rudolph Lindau, *Aus China und Japan* (Berlin: F. Fontane & Co., 1896), pp. 278–87. See also John Clark, comp., *Japanese-British Exchanges in Art 1850s–1930s* (Canberra: Privately Printed, 1989), pp. 4–95.

astonishment was swallowed up in a greater when the dancing official advanced to W. and throwing his arms about him rubbed his cheek against W.'s—token in Japan of strong attachment. The worthy gentleman's retainers were gazing from below stairs in wonder at this reciprocity of sudden friendship. We draw the curtain over the scene only imagining at evening the daughters and wife surrounding the sobered old man and beginning, the first, "Dear papa how could you," and the wife, "You made a fool of yourself, my love, today."

The services of the Reformed Dutch Church are held at the American Consulate court room where a gold "spread eagle," got up in the best gridiron and thunderbolt style, adorns the back of the platform which serves on a Sunday for a pulpit. When the doors are open to a person looking in from outside, the "spread eagle" over the preacher's head is the most conspicuous object, and any Sunday of late a group of Japanese could be seen peering through the open door at what was going on within. Such curiosity is not strange, but it appears that the Japanese have the report among themselves that the Americans get together every Sunday "to worship the eagle." They are satisfied now that they have found out the American divinity, and as the eagle is a greatly respected bird in this land also, I have no doubt we have risen highly in their estimation, since their discovery of our divinity and devotion to this "bird of the sweeping wings." Considering the American partiality for this "proud bird," the fit is not a bad one.

P. is Secretary to the American Legation.[8] He says that a short time since he was waited upon by a Japanese with a great air of mystery who had a document he wished to sell him under the ruse—this document was nothing less than a recent missive from the Mikado to the Tycoon which he had obtained in some extraordinary way and it would be worth his life to be discovered as having divulged it. The substance of the letter was this: that the Mikado had heard with deep regret that his subjects at Yedo were inclined to copy foreign fashions, particularly of dress, and he earnestly counselled the Tycoon to set his face against all

such innovations. Particularly was he to oppose the introduction of the absurd female dress among his fair subjects. So we have here a royal counterattack against crinoline.

[On April 25, 1864, Hall wrote the following article titled "Farm Life in Japan I" to the *New York Tribune*, which was published on December 1, 1864.]

The full burst of Spring is upon us, I might rather say the opening Summer, for here April is the fairy-footed May. March laughs and weeps by turns with April showers, while February trumpets with all the winds of March. The gently swelling uplands are aglow with the radiant vegetation of the new year. The crimson Camelias have faded out along the hill-sides; the daphnes have lost their odorous blossoms; apricot, plum, peach, and cherry have dropped their tinted petals. In their stead wheat and barley sway their bearded grasses to the warm south winds, interrupted by blooming patches of the Windsor bean and the golden tapestries of the rape fields. The earlier rape is passing out of flower, while the later is still in full bloom.

The surface of the country hereabout is rolling, broken into wave-like ridges of small eminence, between which the valleys run out to the sea. It is diversified with numerous clumps of timber, groves of bamboo, pine and fir woods from a few rods square to several acres in extent; no fences mar its face, but with its cleanlily cultivated fields, well trimmed banks, and luxuriant vegetation, it has a picturesqueness unsurpassed, I fancy, by few lands. With the sea and the lake-like waters of Yedo bay for its foreground, the lofty hazy ridges of the Hakone mountains for its background, and this rich middle ground of warm ridges, evergreen woods and teeming crops, what more effective grouping could the great Architect of the world have given.

The deciduous trees are now breaking into leaf. The tender green of the new foliage has for a few days only been seen on the elms, and the chestnuts and oaks have

---

[8] A.L.C. Portman was secretary and interpreter in the American legation in Edo.

yet scarcely awoke to the new life of the year. Here we see the forests putting forth their new leaves contemporaneously with the heading out of the wheat and barley. These, the wheat and barley, are both winter crops, besides which, as fall sown crops, are the two kinds of rape already mentioned (*brossica rapa and brossica orientalis*), the Windsor bean (*vicia faba*), a field pea (*pisum sativum*), and the winter radishes. I find by my own experience that our cultivated garden peas endure the winter with slight protection, and come on to blossoming early in April. Cabbages and cauliflowers fill out their succulent heads throughout the winter months.

The Japanese Spring begins according to calendar with the first day of their year, which comes in, in our February this year, corresponding with our February 8th. This is the true opening of their Spring, for although the deciduous woods and grasses remain for weeks later as bleak and bare as the Winter's cold may have left them, the alder and willow catkins are rapidly swelling, the camelias are struggling into blossom, and the apricots are also putting forth in many sheltered places under the cottage thatch.

The Japanese year is divided into lunar months, the first day of each month being that of the new moon. Every fourth year an intercalary month comes in to preserve the balance of the seasons.

A short season before the New Year and the New Year holidays, are the farmers' holidays of the year—the time when he is least crowded with out-door or in-door work. The crops of the year last to be gathered are the rice and turnip-radish crop, for the months of November and December are usually so clear and dry that this harvest is left to linger along at the farmer's convenience. The farmer has no barns for his crops—the grains are threshed on the field, and lucky is he if he has even storerooms for the threshed-out grains.

The weather favors him as to his most important crops of rice, turnip-radishes and sweet potatoes, and he harvests them as he sells them. The straw and refuse is stacked in the fields, waiting any chance purchaser, if he comes not, fire soon reduces them to ashes and manure.

The leisure the farmer has at this season is much employed in traveling near home, visiting Yedo or other market towns, and making pilgrimages to favorite temples. At this season Kanagawa is full of strangers from the country, who come from far to see the strange sight of a foreign settlement.

But for the farmer whom thrift or necessity stimulates to unceasing labor, there is plenty of work for the quiet months of midwinter also. It is the time to gather and prepare manures for the coming season. There is timber to be got out of the woods, fire wood to be cut and charcoal made. So wherever you go on a country path in Winter, in early morning you will meet strings of pack horses laden with wood, lumber, grain, charcoal, rice, fruits (oranges, pears, and persimmons), and chestnuts, large and small, black or brown, monstrous strings of radishes and other sorts of country produce, and with the load are two long empty buckets which are to be filled with such manures as the farmer can find—principally night soil which is collected in unsightly, unsavory reservoirs, at some convenient place. Many of these farmers come regularly to town, and go as regularly from house to house, each taking what he carries away as his perquisite. He would be an unthrifty farmer who would ride or lead his horse unladen back from market town to country. One learns to take the windward of these pack carriers in his country walks. These manures, thus carried into the country, are placed to ferment in large vats, under cover, by the house or wayside, giving forth the most villainous odors, as a matter of course. Where this process of fermentation is to proceed long enough, other matter is added, such as half decayed vegetable tops, to increase the mass, to which water is added and a stirring given so often as may be necessary. I have seen many a clayey hill side which had been scooped out into cave like receptacles for these manures.

There is work also for the women and

children in the latter winter and early Spring months, when every fine day—and nearly every day is fine—parties of them are to be met anywhere, in the woods among the brush or along the hill slopes and water courses gathering fuel or dead wood, decaying branches, fallen twigs, bamboo grass, reeds and leaves, which are stored in large wicker baskets, or disposed in bundles and carried home. This fuel is the general fire-wood of the farmers and countrymen, with the exception of a little charcoal for the *hibachi* or brazier around which the family gather in-doors as we around our fire places and grates. Fuel is mainly needed for cooking. The Winters in this part of Japan are not severe, and the farmers' cottages are always built with a careful regard for a sunny exposure and a situation sheltered from the northerly winds. Hence their hamlets are found along the sheltered valleys or under the lee of protecting hills. The natural defenses of the position are further improved by screens of close hedges, so that many of these hamlets, with their well-kept hedges inclosing the thatched cottages have at a little distance a charming air of comfort which the nearer approach is wont to belie.

The woods, which are all planted timber, are frequently cut over to furnish fuel for the towns, timber for building, and material for charcoal. None of the native wood, self grown, is to be seen hereabout; all is planted. We must go back to the hill ranges, forty to seventy miles distant, for any primeval woods, and even there the planting hand has been for centuries busy. The favorite trees for the planted groves are the Japan cedar (*cryptomeria japonica*), the pine (*p. deusiflora*), and the retinospora (*r. obtusa*); under their cover spring up a great variety of indigenous trees. These planted groves are supposed to attain no great age, except where they are left to adorn the surroundings of a favorite temple.

The New Year holidays well over, the Spring work fairly begins. This is first, the stirring of the earth among the fall grown crops, which is done with a mattock of long narrow blade, and which tool is to the Japanese hoe, spade and rake combined. Frequently in early Spring it is necessary to tread the wheat to set its roots, which have been disturbed either by the upheaving frosts or the winds blowing away the light soil in the dry Winter. The crops are all sown in drills; there is no exception—a broadcast sowing I have never seen. The hoeing and weeding is therefore easily performed, and in the first hoeing the earth is always drawn up freshly about the roots, no matter what the crop may be. Simultaneously with this cultivation is the application of manures, which, with very slight exceptions, are applied in a liquid state to the growing crop. This is universal on all the dry upland crops; the wet rice fields are treated differently, as I shall mention hereafter. The farmer is very busy with this work in the months of February, March, and the early part of April, going between his drills with bucket in one hand and wooden dipper in the other. Ashes, which are largely employed, are mixed with other manures, such as night soil, the drainage of cesspools, and applied in the same manner. Where other manures are difficult to be obtained, sea weed is employed, having been thrown up in large heaps to decay till even this can be put into a semi-liquid portable form.

The warm suns and frequent rains of Spring bring on the crops apace, and the first cultivation and manuring is not over before weeding follows. In this light work the whole household assists, wife and children, and most thoroughly is it done. Owing to the general use of night soil and the comparatively small use of animal manures, the weeding is not laborious, and it is a pleasure to see how clean of weeds or strange grasses every cultivated field is kept. The whole cultivated surface is laid off into patches of irregular size and shape, according to the conformation of the ground, and between these patches and dividing them are narrow edgings of turf, while threading and interlacing the fields in every direction are turf bordered paths wide enough for men and horses to freely pass. The turf in all these borders and edgings is kept closely pared to check the growth and spread of noxious weeds. Were our own farmers as persistent in this work, we should soon have done with Canada thistles; perhaps they will be when America becomes as thickly populated as Japan, labor becomes as cheap, and our agriculture becomes, as tis here, a general system of horticulture!

The manner in which these fields are laid out give to the landscape one of its chief charms. Here laid out in small and regular squares there in a semi-circular sweep along the bend of a hill or stream, again in ovals, triangles, or gourd-shaped patches, as the natural inequalities of the surface indicate, rising one above the other, or inclining with easy slope toward each other, and everywhere a uniform level surface is offered, the drills are presented to the eye at varying angles to each other so as to break up the uniformity, and thus, with the farmer's plodding work a love of order and presence of taste is ever manifest, and the ordinary laborer becomes an ornamental landscape gardener.

The effect of such training is everywhere seen in the universal "handiness" of the Japanese laborer—in his skillful management of a few simple materials where with to adorn his house or his cottage yard. Slovenly and poor enough as so many of their farm-houses seem to the passer by, yet there will nearly always be found on a closer inspection some indications of a love of the beautiful and ornamental.

In some one nook or corner, more commonly in the rear of the house, may be found a border of flowering shrubs and plants—at least thus much—and from this it may be extended to a complete garden and landscape in miniature, where are edgings of turf, box or dwarf shrubs, a mountain, lake, and lawn in miniature, or, situated as many of these cottages are, under the hill-side, there will be the cool dripping spring trickling over a mossy bank, the artificial grot, the pile of rockwork curtained with ferns, or overrun with creepers from whose interstices spring the dwarf

azaleas and ornamental grasses; there are tasty lattices of bamboo, screens of reeds, and ceilings of braided bark or wood shavings that inclose a Summer apartment, before whose entrance the wisteria swings its purple clusters, and into whose recesses creep the odors of lilies which fringe the pool without.

These effects all lie within the compass of the ready taste and practical hand of nearly every peasant you meet; they are not rarities, but common every day belongings to many a cottage whose smoky timbers, blackened thatch and untidy inmates, as seen from the wayside, give no tokens of the love of order and appreciation of the simple beauties of nature which are fostered under its roof.

[On May 10, 1864, Hall wrote the second of his series of articles on "Farm Life in Japan II" for the *New York Tribune*, which was published on December 28, 1864.]

On the 5th day of the 2d moon, corresponding this year to our March 12, is the festival of Inari, the patron deity of the farmer, who, according to Japanese mythology, descending from heaven in prehistoric ages, came to earth and taught the people the use and cultivation of rice. The white fox is his chief servant and minister, sharing propitiatory honors with his master. The fox is one of the sacred emblems of the Japanese, disputing precedence with the tortoise, stork, and the lotus flower. There are good and bad foxes; the white fox is good, the others are of doubtful reputation. In their legends of the foxes we find repeated in more romantic form the old superstition of the Will o'the Wisp. The benighted traveler sees a light which, as he follows, recedes till he is led into a hopeless wilderness—it is only the wicked fox whose breath is illuminated like a flame, and lures him on to destruction.

A youth wandering a-field encounters a beautiful and fascinating maiden with whose charms his heart is taken captive—he follows after her, she coyly retreating, and growing each moment more fascinating and beautiful, till the youth, like the benighted traveler, finds that he is lost in wood or fen, while his lovely enchantress resuming her true fox shape, disappears; or the fox spirit living in the maiden, and, like Undine, trying to recover its lost soul, allows the youth to win the charms that have enchanted him, and, overflowing with joy, he bears the beautiful bride home, lives happily with her in peace, his children growing around the door, till some day he is disenchanted of his spell by beholding beautiful wife and playful children converted into foxes before his eyes and running away—happy youth if the wicked enchantress has not first rent him in pieces. So, to say of a Japanese girl that she is as fascinating as the fox maiden is to pay the highest tribute to the power and danger of her charms.

The traveler in Japan, wherever he may go, will behold by the wayside and in the fields little chapels like exaggerated dog kennels, most of them dusty and dilapidated, open to wind and weather. Not only here, but more especially in the covert of every grove and on every leafy eminence, literally "on every high hill and under every green tree," are they found. A white paper tied to a reed stalk, a straw sandal suspended from the roof, a little rice, grain, or salt sprinkled about, or other similar emblem shows, however, that these are not wholly neglected. These chapels, of which a dozen or more may be seen during a brief walk, are sacred to Inari and his white foxes. Some of these chapels are built over fox holes on the hill-side, a door is left for ingress and egress, and within are placed trays of food and gifts for the fox. On this 5th day of the 2d moon there is no chapel, shrine or kennel, however humble, broken down, or begrimed with the dust of a twelve month, but is decked with ornaments, and with the simple offerings of the neighboring peasantry. There are flags inscribed with words and symbols of propitiation, streamers of white paper, flowers, green twigs, libations of rice wine, offerings of rice, and sandals of horses and men.

They and the paths approaching them are also hung with paper lanterns, which, at night being lighted, are as so many foxes themselves amid the woods and fields breathing flames from their nostrils as in the fable.

On this day the rural population give themselves up to the occasion, bedecking themselves in all their holiday finery, passing the day in offering, visiting, feasting, games, maskings, and dancing to the beating of drums, playing of fifes, and the evening in feasting, plays, and illuminations. In every village of importance groups of maskers go through the streets wheeled on a platform hung with all the appropriate devices for the day, or stationing themselves near a favorite temple, amuse the idle lookers on with the most grotesque of pantomimes. The chief performer is always a man wearing as a mask a fox's head and face, who goes through his absurd grimaces to the music of drum and fife, and to the apparent delight of a great crowd of admiring spectators.

This is the farmer's holiday par excellence, and fairly ushers in the long Summer season of labor, during which the whole farming population is busy. But the season is long in Japan, the climate friendly, liable to neither parching droughts or excessive moisture (I speak of the seaboard, for we know little of the interior), and except at the harvesting season the Japanese farmer is seldom driven. He goes to his work early in the morning, takes a long nooning in the mid-summer, halts occasionally to enjoy his pipe and tobacco, returns to his house at early dusk, burns few candles, lights a smudge to expel the musketoes, eats his simple fare and with wife and babies crawls under his musketo netting to his mattress of cotton quilt spread on the mat floor, and goes to his well-earned repose caring little whether it is the Tycoon in Yedo, or the Mikado in Miako, who is lord paramount of these isles, though the faith of every peasant and common man is in the demi-god ship of the latter, wakes with the new morning to the old toil, and might, if he would, truly thank

God that he was one of the happiest peasants of the world in the bliss of supreme content.

The prevailing winds from October to May are northerly; from May till October again they are southerly, blowing with nearly the regularity of the north-east and south-west monsoons on the China coast. There is no rainy season, so far as the experience of five years indicates—there are "rainy spells" lasting from a week to a month, liable to occur at any season of the year except mid-winter and mid-summer, which are always clear. That is to say, Japan is more liable to protracted rains at the change of the monsoons than during their continuance. Thunder storms are very infrequent, most common at the changes in early Spring and Fall. But Japan thunderstorms are very tame to one who remembers the thundering echoes that reverberate among the Catskills of New York, the Green and White Hills of New England, or the tornado bursts of the prairies. Earthquakes take their place in frequency, though no very alarming phenomena of this kind have occurred since foreign occupation. We have the pleasant assurance, however, that once in every seven or ten years we may confidently expect one that will crack our roofs and tumble our chimneys, if no worse. Typhoons are common on the coasts, and are at times terribly destructive, as are their congerers, the hurricanes of the West Indies. I have seen little damage done to standing crops by storm or tempest, though the millet and rice do occasionally suffer in this way.

The greatest degree of cold I have experienced at this port has been 14° of Fahrenheit, though the thermometer in Winter rarely sinks to 20°, nor in Summer rises above 90°. With this moderate temperature, and an uninterrupted succession of sunny Winter days, the frost gets no penetration into the soil, or only just sufficient to assist in a great process of pulverization which goes on all Winter between the upper and nether mill-stones of freezing nights and thawing days.

The Japanese peasant is too far advanced to be greatly terrified or impressed by meteorological or celestial phenomena. He believes that "great hairy star," the comet, is presager of evil, but acts upon that belief as little as the thousands of peasantry do who believe the same in our civilized lands. When the sun is eclipsed, he says there is poison in the air; he believes in the pot of gold at the foot of the rainbow's arch as sincerely as most boys do, and no more—he never goes to dig for it; he has his lucky and unlucky days for birth, labor, and marriage, and we have good ships that never sail to sea on Fridays, and good farmers who cure no pork at the wane of the moon. And if a three colored tomcat will preserve a ship from foundering on Japan coasts if luckily aboard, it is no more wonderful than that infant's caul which brings all manner of prosperities to its fortunate owner.

The tools of the Japanese farmer are few and simple. He listens with incredulous amazement to stories of steam plows, mowing machines and horse rakes. For hoe and spade he has the mattock; the rake or harrow he seldom uses, the soil is so light and friable that it falls to dust beneath his mattock. In the wet rice-fields plows and harrows drawn by horses or oxen are employed, both of the rudest construction, and much the same as we see pictured as in use among Chinese, Indians, or natives of Asia Minor. A knife a foot long slightly curved, and set into a handle at a right angle serves to cut his grain and to cut reeds, grasses and twigs. The gathered grain is beaten out on the field with a flail, or hatcheled. A winnowing mill, counterpart of those in every old New-England farm yard, and which has, like the old well-sweep and the two buckets over a wheel, been an institution in Japan for unknown centuries, completes the farmer's tool chest. Stout arms and a patient will supply all the rest.

The soil looks rich, but is very poor. You walk anywhere among the cultivated fields, you plunge your walking stick with ease three feet into the yielding earth, and while admiring its rich black color are reminded of fertile prairie soils at home, but the resemblance is only in appearance. The moment you leave the neighborhood of towns and villages, or the line of the coast, where manure can be had, the crops show from what a lean breast, though dark as Afric's ebony, they draw their sustenance. I have seen the soil about Nagasaki, Hakodade, Yedo and Kanagawa, and it is all the same; yielding bounteous returns only to painstaking labor. And this labor the Japanese peasant faithfully bestows till all the country laughs with fatness. For him there are no ambitions beyond honest toil, the conditions of his life are fixed irrevocably, he is haunted by no dreams of power, pursued by no restless avarice, and so his human machine runs on gently without many frets or breaks. His wife is industrious like himself, her spinning wheel sings by the door, and the shuttle of his daughter's loom flies by the window. In the rice culture and the cotton picking they labor by his side. His children, who are as numerous about his door as the sheaves in the field, have full run of the streets for their earlier years— dirty and wholesome as free grown humans are wont to be—the girl plays with dolls and dresses, the boy snares birds, robs birds nests, damns up the little rills, sails his tiny boat, bakes his mud pies in the sun, and tears his trowsers, if he has any, as all good farmers' boys have an indefeasible right to do—till such time as he is able to go to the woods for fuel, or to the fields to hoe and weed. But one thing is to be remembered, to school he must go, and the sun is hardly up before he is off to school with shining brown face and the roll of paper which makes his copy-book in hand, where he learns to read and write and make faces at his master (a regular Ichabod Crane in horn spectacles), and his task is over and he on his way home, with ink besmirched face, at an hour when our boys at home have scarcely begun their lessons for the day. It was a group of such boys full of a school boy's love for fun whom I once addressed at the door of their school room around which they had gathered at sight of a strange face: "Tell me, my fine fellow," said I to one in the best Japanese I could

muster, "tell me how old you are?" There was a pause in their roguish faces, when one whispers over the others shoulder, "tell him you are a hundred."

Friday, May 13, 1864

Today is the annual festival at Bookengi [Bukenji] temple in honor of Buddha. I went thither with a few friends to see the gathering of the people. The day was a propitious one, the sky half clouded and the air sweet with portending rain. We were early on the ground, at 1/2 past ten, and the people were just beginning to assemble. At eleven the bell was tolled and the devotees, who were now arriving in large numbers, visited the lower temple where in the open doorway under a canopy covered with evergreen twigs and flowers of the azalea, rose, and camellia, stood a bronze image of Buddha about 6 inches high. The image was in a brazier of water where was also a little dipper of wood. One after another the people, particularly the women, came up and pouring water from the dipper over the head of the image to which thereby was imparted, in their belief, healing properties, drank the water as a preventive against disease. But this consecrated water is regarded as especially effective as the cure of eye disease, and so among the devotees were many with these organs diseased, who, pouring the water into the palm of one hand, with the finger tips of the other hand bathed their eyes. Mothers were especially earnest in laving the eyes of little children and giving them of it to drink as a prophylactic against coming evil.

At midday high of the sun the services of the day began in the large upper temple, whose dark recesses under the lofty roof supported by immense columns of Japanese elm were delightfully shady and cool. Thither rapidly gathered the people from the surrounding country, all in holiday dresses. The young maidens and children looked very bright and happy in their gay robes and cunning headdresses. The central part of the temple in front of the shrine and its ornaments of images, brass candelabra, and metallic flowers, was reserved for the priests. Outside of this the people knelt in front; standing in the rear. Lighted candles of wax and incense burnt on the altar, and reading desks arranged within the reserved square awaited the ghostly officiants. These soon came from either door behind the shrine, adult priests of all ages clad in black outer tunics falling over a white robe beneath and bearing their missals in hand. Then following came a train of boy priests who took their places behind the others. Then came the priests in more gorgeous robes of silk and brocades and others of yet more exalted rank each devoutly kneeling and prostrating himself, and then began a low dolorous tone of prayer, and following this came the music of drums, fife, and reed instruments, resembling a bagpipe in tone. Then came in the high priest himself, less elegantly robed than the others, but bearing on his robes the moong of the Mikado. All prostrated themselves as he entered. He was a grave looking old man with no affectation of manner. Kneeling before the shrine with his back to the priests and people he remained bowing and silent for a few moments and then giving a signal with a bell all the priests young and old, sixty or more of them, opened their litany books and began a recitation in concert with a loud voice. At repeated signals of the bell the modulations of the voices were changed to a higher or lower key, faster, slower, now in a chanting or sing song tone, now in a rapid recitation. I observed the boy priests were the most zealous, and after half an hours practice some of them began to get winded. Meantime within, parties of well dressed people continued to arrive and took their places as at some great show. In front a shower of cash was flying over the heads of the spectators into the large altar box before the door. Out of doors other groups of people, who had come from afar, were disposing themselves at ease on the green slopes of the close cut turf beneath the shade of cedars and pines preparing to lunch, and before we left, which was yet in the middle of the day and the service, there were already many of picnicking families and neighbors picturesquely encamped for their alfresco repast. One family that we passed was a stout matronly mother with her three daughters of fifteen to eighteen years of age, a little boy, and a male servant.

Some notice of the boy opened the mother's heart and with the true hospitality of the well to do common people we were at once invited to have their lunch. The matron passed out cups of hot tea in brass saucers. The maids handed us cakes of rice and fish and pressed us to partake. We accepted their civilities and chatted with them for a few moments, they entertaining us the whole while with as much care as if we had been old friends. They had walked several miles to attend this festival and were bright and fresh with the morning exercise.

And now by the hedge at the main entrance had gathered hucksters and toy sellers of all sorts, the bulk of whose merchandise was eatables and toys for the children. Indeed the hilarity of the day had only partly opened when we left, and on our way back to our boat we met scores of people hastening to the scene, every group carrying their box of lunch tied up in a handkerchief and very many the additional little tub of sake. My friend S.,[9] who did not leave until four in the afternoon, says that at that hour the sward was covered with the picnicking groups, who had become overhospitable and hilarious in their festivities. The praying lasted till nearly three o'clock when the preaching began and had not finished when S. left. After a discourse from one of the old wheel horses of Buddhist divinity, a neophyte of twelve or thirteen years delivered his maiden discourse.

On the hill above the temple is a mia at the end of a flight of steps, the Toori gate of which was erected in stone by a courtesan of Sinagawa, a votive offering to the gods.

Monday, May 16, 1864

Mr. Alcock goes to Yedo today for the first time since his return.

---

[9] We do not know who S. was on this occasion. Although this could be Duane B. Simmons, Hall usually refers to him as Dr. S.

Monday, May 23, 1864

Returning from a walk in the hills a little time since I saw on the hill side the cremation of a dead body. A small assemblage was gathered about the fire, including several samurai from the neighboring guard house. As I came to the spot I saw the *quan*, or square box coffin, standing on two stones between which and in a little pit scooped out beneath a pit fire of pine wood was burning. The people about, not at all dispirited by the occasion, gave me lively welcome and at once made various comments on the scene before me, lead off by a stout naked fellow who was acting as fireman and who remarked "that was a very hot girl there" ("ta'san atsi moosme"). I walked round the fire to where the family of the deceased, a little girl of seven years, were standing and who were enjoying the hilarity of the occasion and the jests nearly as much as any of the indifferent lookers on, all but a little girl, a sister of the deceased and doubtless her playmate, who held her handkerchief to her nose with undisturbed gravity. Accosting a well dressed middle aged man in the mourning group, [I asked] if that was his child, he smilingly replied, yes, "and he feels very bad about it," chimed in the crowd. Just at this moment the stout heat had overcome the box which burst open until a shrunken and charred leg protruded and directly someone said, and "there is the head," and sure enough it was the head bursting open itself till the brains oozed out of the fissure. All of which was the occasion for renewed merriment and jesting, whence the naked fireman distinguished himself slapping his brawny back as he turned it to the grateful heat. But the climax of disgust was to come when the fireman thrusting his bamboo stick into the fire raked out of the embers one of the rice balls, which are placed in a funeral procession on the top or outside of the coffin, and breaking it open, offered it to the assembled people to eat. Eager they were to possess themselves of it for it seems that a rice cake roasted with a dead body is a sure prophylactic against all odors

and is a noted aphrodisiac. My sight revolted at this, and it only needed to see one breaking the cake where a deep yellow stain had disfigured it, and which a neighbor chided him not to eat, to cause me and my companion to take a sudden leave of this revolting spectacle. Surely the innate barbarism of this race was manifest.

Friday, May 27, 1864

The week past has been full of speculations on Japanese affairs, and in many foreign minds there has been a growing uneasiness in regard to the position of public affairs. It appears mostly to be one of those periodic apprehensions which have so often prevailed here, and which is fed and stimulated by mutual gossiping, rather than any real outwards dangers. What has given currency to this has been mainly the expressed opinion of our foreign officials that our relations with the Japanese were unsatisfactory and indicated a latent hostility. And they seem to derive their beliefs not so much from any particular act or declaration of the Government officials, as from the fact that our affairs do not move smoothly, and the Government showing no disposition to make them so.

On various occasions the Governors for Foreign Affairs have reiterated their desire that the foreigners should abandon the shores of Yedo Bay and have reiterated in such a way as if it was their firm purpose that we should comply. The French Minister, Mons. Roches,[10] had an interview with the Goroju a few days since, and although the visit was one of introduction and not of business, they took occasion to say that they expected Kanagawa to be abandoned, and even intimated that the abandonment of Kanagawa was the condition of peace. Such is the statement; my own idea is that the Government could hardly have come so near a threat, and that in a double interpretation or rather a treble one, the exact purport of words was not reached. Of the same tenor

[10] Leon Roches was the new French minister to Japan. He arrived in Yokohama on April 27, 1864, on the warship *Tancrede*. See Meron Medzini, *French Policy in Japan During the Closing Years of the Tokugawa Regime* (Cambridge, Mass.: Harvard University Press, 1971), p. 73.

has been the conversations with the English and American Ministers. To the former they have declared their inability to secure the protection of Yokohama, and Mr. Alcock has promptly called hither an additional force from China.

By the terms of the Treaties they are subject to a mutual revision on the first of July next[11] and some anxiety is felt to know in what way this liberty of revision is to be regarded. The Japanese have distinctly said, however, that they have always understood that they were to have the right to abrogate the treaties, if they choose, at this time. When pointed to the text of the treaties and the language employed, they reply that whatever words may have been employed in their written treaty, all their understanding in every conversation with Mr. Harris was that the treaty for five years was an experiment only, and that after that time they would be free to make such amendments as were necessary, or to do away with them altogether. That merely a mutual revision was meant, they wholly deny.

For my own part, I cannot yet believe that the Japanese mean to have an outbreak with us, if they can carry their cards by diplomacy and an appearance of a more forcible means, well and good; if they fail in this, I do not think they are ripe for bolder schemes.

It cannot be denied that the Japanese are active in learning the arts of war. They buy arms large and small freely, they are endeavoring to perfect themselves in drill, and are eager for all information on the art of war.

Thursday, June 2, 1864

A boy stopped at my gate this morning offering a great variety of chrysanthemums (cut flowers) for sale. These hawkers of flowers are now numerous on the street, and for a few cash every housewife could have her vase filled with flowers and the family altar decorated. This boy carried his flowers in two baskets at either end of a pole swung over his shoulder, and as one basket was empty he had put stones

[11] Hall corrected this in the margin writing "error not till 1870."

in it to balance the flowers. This system of compensating balance is very common. I have often met a countryman returning from his town marketing with his purchased package fastened to a bamboo laid across his shoulder one end of which was balanced by a stone.

The art of skillfully arranging flowers is one of the few elements of a lady's education in Japan. I have seen a girl arranging flowers in a flat wall vase which hung up in her apartment with as much care as if she were doing a piece of embroidery. First one position was studied then another, the relative lengths of the stems had all to be considered, what flowers produced the best effect as a center and what as a side piece, and a twig or two of suitable green leaves, or as commonly a branch of juniper or cedar, always had important places. Certainly I have seen some very tasty disposition of a few simple flowers which was the result of a studied skill in effects. I remember seeing an acquaintance (Miss Tokoo) standing before a flower vase one day which she had arranged and rearranged several times ineffectually to her liking and then lamenting that she had lost the art which she had learned as the *hokoning* [hōkōnin] or *Juchin* [jochū?] of a daimio's lady.

Saturday, June 4, 1864

Today is the fourth day of continued rain and looks like a rainy season indeed.

My Japanese friend S[adajirō] wishes to go to Yedo, but he expects the Rokugo river will be too high for ferriage. By the bye, "Rokugo" is not the name of the river but of the hamlet on the Yedo side of the river on its banks, rather still, it is a generic name for 6 hamlets as its name implies, roku (six) go (villages). The name of the river is Tamagawa, the stream takes its rise in the mountains we see in the distance to the N.W., sixty or seventy miles away. The headwaters of the stream have a sweep not far from Yedo and the water of the Yedo aqueduct is taken from this river about 8 ri from Nippon Bas. It is led by a canal to the suburbs, and then becomes a closed aqueduct of stone till it reaches the citadel whose royal inmate has the first use of the water, after which it is distributed throughout the city. Access is had to the water by well-like openings into the aqueduct. Outside the city towards the head is a reservoir.

I hear frequent confirmation of the statement that the population of the empire is much confined to large cities and populous villages, or rather to large cities and their vicinities. Even near Yedo, within 5 ri, is a wasteland (hara) in one body of 7 ri by a breadth of one to two ri, which is covered with trees, rushes, or grass. The soil is fertile enough, but there are none to cultivate it. It is a favorite breeding ground for horses. So, I am told, it is near any of the large centers. That even near Miako similar waste lands are to be found. It seems almost safe to conclude that the population of this empire is to be found on the coasts and near the great cities, the interior is sparsely settled. The lack of population is attributable to wasting diseases, such as smallpox and measles, to fatality among children, and, may we not add, to the abuse of the people in venery.

Sunday, June 5, 1864

Fair. Our five days' storm has at last cleared up, yet the whole amount of water fallen is barely four inches.

Monday, June 6, 1864

At 5 A.M. this morning we experienced one of the heaviest, if not the heaviest, earthquake shock we have ever felt. Among the natives and the oldest of the foreign residents there was a general rush to get out of doors, which was hardly effected before the shock was over. The motion seemed to be vertical, rather than horizontal, though with perhaps a general direction from south to north or vice versa. The agitation was sufficient to wash water out of tubs that were not filled by four or five inches, also to cause pools of water to foam. My friend B.,[12] in the hurry of the moment, leaped undressed from his bedroom window and landed

---

[12] The context does not allow us to determine who B. was. It is possible that this was D. C. Brower, whose marriage Hall records on June 9.

in a water tank, which was conveniently near under his dormitory.

The harvesting goes on, the first rape is gathered and the barley harvest begun.

Tuesday, June 7, 1864

The marines from the *Conqueror* were landed today and encamped in tents on the bluffs. They make a fine soldiery appearance and attract much attention from the Japanese who eagerly inquire, "what do all these soldiers wish to do here?" The contrast between their own feeble guards hutted on the hill and this fine battalion of men, one would think, would impress them with their own insignificance and clumsiness as soldiers, but oriental conceit stretches quite as wide as a western conscience in an emergency.

Wednesday, June 8, 1864

Nobori Gosekoo. This one of the Go-Sekoo [Go-sekku], or "five great holidays" of the year. It is the "flag" feast as its name implies. Its origin seems lost in obscurity. Some only dating it back to the days of the Portuguese. It is a man's holiday, as that of the 3rd moon is a woman's holiday, and is very generally observed. The flags flying in front of the houses I described last year, also the fish suspended from poles and filled out with the breeze, some of which are ten to fifteen feet long. These emblems are more particularly common where there is a young male babe in the house, especially if it be the first born son. Many families beginning with the birth year of this son keep up the observance annually, till the boy has attained his fifteenth year. The fish is regarded as an appropriate emblem, this being a fresh water fish similar to our salmon which makes its way up the stream over the falls and other obstacles, and is thus regarded as typical of the youth's progress to success in life.

Within the houses near the street door are arranged shelves on which are placed toys in abundance and elegance according as the family finances may afford. Even many humble looking cottages seem to have been prodigal for the young hope of their house. These shelves, which in the 3rd month are filled with dolls and such toys as a girl would delight in, are now all for the harder sex of youth and almost wholly emblems of war, of rank, and power. There are flags with images of great Tyco and other ancient heroes, wooden images of the same, toy swords, and suits of armor, spears, bows, plumes of horse hair and cock feathers, and such insignia as precede the norimons of men of rank when travelling. Of late years the toy musket and cannon finds a conspicuous place. These toys of the cottager's boy are carefully preserved, and though someday he may seldom hope to don the plated armor or brandish the spear of the soldier, yet he remembers that great Tyco was a groom, and in the new taxation of resources to which Nippon must inevitably be put, if she grows into civilization, the good old times of rise in rank are likely to return, too, again. But these dreams do not yet flit through the brains of the fat gaily dressed urchins rolling on the mats before their toys whose glitter keeps them attracted to the holiday shelves.

Toys for the children and drinking and feasting for the elders today. I saw some noble fish (the tai) hauled out of the water last evening for today's feast. Some doors and gateways were decorated with the stalk of the chrysanthemum and a long grass like a flag leaf. The same grass was seen often bound round the hands of the boys as an amulet.

Until the time of Gongen Sama the month had two regular holidays, the 1st, the day of the Sun, the 15th, the day of the moon. Gongen Sama instituted the 3rd on the 28th and called it after himself.

I was shown a curious mineral today called the "bech stone," this when placed on the canker would expand, curl, and writhe, like a worm and did resemble the leech. The legend says that in Kushiu where this mineral is found leeches were formerly very troublesome, but at the intercession of a pious bonze, they were converted into these stones which yet retain vi-

tality enough to writhe in their fiery tortures.

Passing a coopers shop today, Heco told me that the coopers have special privileges among the mechanics, for the shelter and safety one of the trade gave Tyco in his wars. Tyco was worsted, and fleeing for safety, entered a cooper's shop. The cooper was at work on a tub, and hastily putting the fleeing monarch underneath, went on with his cooping making a great din over the fugitive's head. The pursuers looked in on the industrious cooper, who pounded away more lustily than ever, and saved his monarch, who in gratitude bestowed upon coopers forever special privileges.

Talking with a doctor today about the 7th moon feast, the "tanabata," he told me it was derived from China and was comparatively modern. Each side of the milky-way are the stars of (what constellation?) three on one side, and two on the other, and sometimes a third appears. Whoever can thread a needle by holding the same between the eye and one of the stars becomes forever after, not only skillful with the needle, but with the pen and pencil, in music, and all accomplishments or labor requiring skill.

Thursday, June 9, 1864

Mr. Brower's wedding at the Legation in Yedo.[13]

Friday, June 10, 1864

Chowder party and target shooting at "Chowder Cove," Mississippi Bay. Caught in the rain as we were cooking our chowder. Returned at 5 P.M.

Saturday, June 11, 1864

Boy of Mr. Jaquemot died of hydrophobia.[14]

---

[13] DeWitt Clinton Brower married Jennie W. Mann on June 1, 1864, according to the consular records. This may well have been the formal civil ceremony at the legation, or a reception held by General Pruyn for

the newly married couple.

[14] This was the son of J. C. Jaquemot who was bitten by a rabid dog. As John R. Black noted, Hall had become quite concerned with the health and sanitary con-

Monday, June 13, 1864

Rumor of ronins at Kanagawa. The Governors send over some officers. The ronins are said to be some of Mito's men on their way to Oasaca to join Stotsbashi, who is said to be regularly installed in the Tycoons palace at Oasaca. Are we to have two Tycoons?

Tuesday, June 14, 1864

The Tycoon is reported to have returned to Yedo by steamer today.

Thursday, June 16, 1864

Wedding party at Consul Fisher's.

Saturday, June 18, 1864

Chowder party.

Friday, June 24, 1864

The Tycoon is reported to have returned to Yedo yesterday.

[On June 28, 1864, Hall sent the following letter to the *New York Tribune*, which was published on August 30, 1864.]

The New Japanese year opened, as my last letter stated, with doubtful auguries for the future, but on the whole with hopeful indications for peace and quietude. The only burning spot was that represented by the Prince of Nagato's obstinate hate and which was the intensified focus of all the anti-foreign feeling of Japan.

This bit of fire and fury had expanded till now it is a cloud shadow of something more than a hand's breadth in our horizon. The Council of State, or Committee on the general welfare at Oasaca, to which I before alluded, and from which something good was hoped for, if it ever has acted at all, has brought no relief to the vexed question of the foreign relations of [t]his empire. On the contrary, we hear that the good old Prince of Echizen is in a *quasi* disgrace for his avowed friendliness to progressive views, which has been signified by a Pickwickian permission to retire to his province, and not to feel himself called upon to express any further opinions or take any further action in Government affairs. Stotbashi, of the lineage of Mito, has been in some sense made generalissimo of the army, and keeps his headquarters at Miaco. How far this position conflicts with that of the Tycoon at Yedo, whose very title that he is the generalissimo and the executive power of the empire, is one of the webs that we have not yet unraveled. It is clear that it portends faction in the governing class, and looks exceedingly as if the anti-foreign party were gathering ferm and front.

This is the same Stotsbashi who was sent in hot haste hither, just a year since, to begin the work of our forcible expulsion, and who, when he arrived on the shores of our bay, and saw what manner of thing expulsion was likely to be against the powerful fleet sleeping so quietly on our waters, became a wiser if not a sadder man, and concluded instead to pay the indemnity. He has the reputation of having, since that time, sought to retrieve the dishonor of having failed to execute the orders entrusted to him by an active zeal in preparations for a like future contingency, and so has been lavish of his revenue in providing arms for his own retainers and such of his small Daimio friends as were unable to

---

ditions of the settlement. He records that in the "spring" of 1864 a public meeting was held at the residence of Mr. S. J. Gower, which was chaired by Frank Hall. "The result was the establishment of a Scavenger corps that would daily clear the streets, drains, and Bund, of any offensive rubbish, and remove it to a suitable distance from the settlement" (Black, *Young Japan: Yokohama and Yedo, 1858–79*, vol. 1, p. 295).

obtain them for themselves. In connection with his movements is the report of a fresh revolt against the Yedo Government in his father's, the Prince of Mito's, provinces.

The Tycoon has just returned from his long and second visit to the Mikado. He passed up the bay five days since with an escort of five steamers. As the Council of State have attributed any official remissness of their own, any inattention to the demands of foreign diplomats, to "the absence of the Tycoon," it is to be hoped, now that he sits in his castle over the river, we shall go on famously again. The native *on dit* is that he returns, having for his guidance eighteen regulations from the Court at Miaco touching his official rule. We hope that in due time we shall discover what these eighteen regulations concocted by the united wisdom of the Mikado and his advisers are. It would not be venturesome to suggest that one of them will be the expulsion of the hated *tojins* at the earliest practicable moment.

My last mentioned Sir Rutherford Alcock's return to the English mission in Japan. Though he has remained thus far very quiet and discreetly reticent of his opinions, so much may be said, that he regards the position of foreigners on these shores as more precarious than at any former period.

After a divided opinion among the representatives of the treaty powers, they seem now to have come to the conclusion that the Yedo Government under a seeming guise of friendship, aim at the expulsion of foreigners. That the pressure of the hostile chiefs behind the throne, (and now nearly all are known to be hostile), is such that the Government is in danger of being wholly subverted, and they are, therefore, to escape this contingency, secretly conniving at the labors of the malcontents against our longer continuance. Not that the Tycoon and his council of state for themselves would prefer this, for the condiments of foreign trade have proved exceedingly sweet to them, but that they are forced to succumb. The foreign powers would gladly give aid to the Tycoon to maintain him in

his position, but he declines that, knowing that it would be the signal for the open revolt of the Daimio. He and his advisers, for the present at least, appear to have chosen to play craftily into the hands of our enemies. It is perhaps not too much to say that the foreign representatives have, to no inconsiderable extent, been deceived by the statecraft of the Japanese, and their eyes blinded to the real danger, by the apparent importance of certain concessions, such as reduction of imposts and other minor privileges, which had a seeming of friendship in them, and of a desire for continued friendly relations. The great misfortune of all intercourse with the Japanese Government lies in its total want of truth and honesty. To lie for a desirable end is always justifiable, as in common life, so in State affairs. This duplicity and deception they practice among themselves as well as upon us intruders. Would they but honestly set forth the true position of public affairs, means might be found to allay the irritation of public feeling, the jealousy of chiefs who dread foreign encroachments, and see in open trade and intercourse the ultimate downfall of their exclusive privileges. But alas! the Yedo Government takes as much pains to conceal the secret design of their enemies and ours as if their own safety hung thereby.

Meantime the demand of the Yedo Government that Yedo and Kanagawa should be abandoned by foreigners, which it has been hoped was a mere sop thrown to the Malcontents to keep them quiet by a seeming show of acquiescence in their policy, is pressed with a tenacity that anywhere but in Japan would imply an earnestness of purpose not to be defeated. The Governor of foreign affairs have in repeated interviews with the representatives of the foreign powers, re-asserted this demand, made now nearly a year since. They have even gone so far as to intimate that our leaving the shores of Yedo bay was the question of peace and war. They have in furtherance of this declared their inability to secure the settlement of Yokohama from attacks of the hostile party, should they choose to make them. Sir Rutherford Alcock is fortunately possessed of full powers and takes the Japanese Government at their word "If you cannot protect us we will protect ourselves," is his decided reply. A more powerful English naval and land force is gathering here than was known in our troubles last year. A few days since, the "Conqueror," screw line-of-battle ship, arrived direct from England, bringing a battalion of 550 marines. The Conqueror is the old liner "Waterloo" converted; she is pierced for ninety guns, but now carries not more than half that number. The 20th regiment is daily expected from Hong Kong, when the English will have an effective land force of 1500 men, besides the ordinary marines of the fleet. The English fleet is now fifteen vessels, carrying an aggregate of about 200 guns. There are two Dutch corvettes in harbor, a third arrived this morning, and two others are daily expected, which are called hither by the aggression of Shimonoseki last summer. The French have two small steamers, one the double-decker Semiramis, Rear-Admiral Jaurez. Our American force will be represented by the Jamestown, which arrived yesterday, in good season to burn our Fourth of July powder.

There can be but little doubt that an expedition either of the English or a combined one of the treaty powers will be made against the Prince of Nagato. He is the representative man of the hostile faction, and has yet not only made no amends for his attack last summer, but has defied both the Japanese Government and the treaty powers. All that can save him will be the lying promises of the Yedo Government, in which they have already begun to move. It is to be hoped that his signal and prompt punishment may save the remainder of the Empire from a conflict with western nations, and secure a lasting peace by an exhibition to the Japanese of the danger of such a conflict.

One thing is plainly manifest—the English Government cannot afford to keep so large a force on these coasts to do guard duty, and know so well that it would be im-

minently dangerous to withdraw it. Thus arises the temptation which may pass into a necessity of bringing affairs to an issue with the Japanese, or, to borrow a medical simile, the necessity of poulticing this boil to a head, that so powerful a squadron may not, for an uncertain future, be locked up in Yedo bay.

Two hundred and fifty men of the Chasseurs d'Afrique left this place a few days since *en route* for Mexico, where they are to form a part of Maximillian's legion. Truly, from the rising to the setting sun is their road.

Monday, July 4, 1864

National anniversary, *Jamestown* salute responded to by 13 vessels of war, English, French, and Dutch. Americans kept open house to all callers. In the evening Consul Fisher gave a large party.

[On July 7, 1864, Hall sent the following letter to the *New York Tribune*, which was published on September 30, 1864.]

The brief interval since my last date, though distinguished by no particular events, has served to deepen the impression that foreign relations with Japan were never in a more satisfactory state.

That the Empire is full of discussion and debate as to what policy shall be pursued toward the hated foreigner, there can be no question, or rather it appears if there was no longer any dissension, but almost a unanimity of opposition to us, which only questions how it shall best be actively exerted.

The head of this Anti-Foreign Party, as I have said before, is at Miaco, and claims the special patronage of the Mikado. From thence we have fresh confirmation of the report that Stotsbashi, of the house of Mito, assumes executive functions there equal with the Tycoon's at Yedo. The Tycoon's ministers confess the disturbed state of public feeling, but as ever talk vaguely of what the true condition is, or what should or will be done. They appear desirous to confess and employ the fact only so far as it may serve to check any extension of our present intercourse, or even to limit the privileges we already enjoy.

In truth, for now some two years past, the Japanese Ministers have ever held up this disturbed public feeling as a sort of menace over the heads of the foreign diplomatic representatives whenever they have asked for any new favor, or a wider toleration than those already guaranteed by the treaties. To all demands the invariable answer is—"we would like to do this or that, but there are very many people already discontented with your presence in Japan, and to grant new favors, or to continue old ones even, may lead to the worse consequences." By such implied menaces as these, they have won the abandonment of Yedo as a port of trade, and, I might add as a ministerial residence; the surrender of the ports of Neegata, Hiogo, and Oasaca, the virtual concession of our right to move about within the radius prescribed by the treaties, and have further demanded the abandonment of Yokohama and Kanagawa. For two years foreign representatives have been swayed by such language and threats, but repeated disclosures of the utter mendacity of the Yedo Government, their acts in opposition to treaty rights and their large complicity in the purposes of the anti-foreign party have opened all eyes to the danger of the position.

In all this time both Government and Daimios have been steadily accumulating the munitions of war and increasing their means of resistance or aggression. The export of copper and saltpeter long since ceased, immense quantities of tin spoiter and lead have been imported; forts and batteries have sprung up along their coasts; large and small arms have been extensively manufactured and purchased; troops have been regularly drilled; new highways of communication have been cut in the interior to unite the several provinces independent of the assailable sea-way. Daimios, who, like Chosiu, Prince of Nagato, have

already been aggressive, are allowed to go unpunished, if not secretly encouraged.

But the present gathering of so large a land and naval force at this port causes even the Yedo ministers some alarm, and they are already busy with their old game of lying promises, to forestall, if possible, its action. "Let the Prince of Nagato alone," they say, "we will punish him ourselves." So they said and promised a year ago and Chosiu is today stronger than ever. He is far more powerful for an effective opposition than ever before, and our delay to punish him has rendered him defiant not only of the Tycoon, but of us. Our forbearance, like every other act of forbearance since Japan was opened, has been construed as the weakness of timidity. Thus the danger grows daily greater with the delay, that if any hereafter attempt to chastise Chosiu for the outrages of a year since, he will have the active sympathy and support of more than one of the great chiefs of the south-west portion of the Empire. We hear from Nagasaki that such will doubtless be the case, and that the Prince of Chikuzen has already sent a contingent to Chosiu's aid. There is no longer but the one opinion—that if ever there was any considerable party in Japan favorable to foreign intercourse, it has diminished now to a feeble minority. We remain by courtesy of fear and not of regard.

Our Minister, Gen. Pruyn, notified the Yedo Government a few days since of his intention to visit that city, in order to press his claims against the Government more effectually than he has been able to do here so far from Court. Since this announcement, earnest have been the remonstrances against his so doing. The old menace of danger has been held over his head. Two years ago residence in Yedo was not different; but through like menaces foreigners having once virtually abandoned their right of residence in that city, the move now is to prevent even a temporary visit for official purposes. Our Minister is thus far firm in his purpose to go to Yedo. He has the "Jamestown" to support him. To yield would be to surrender the last hold in

Yedo, viz.: the right of personal representation at the Imperial Court.

Such squadron as the Dutch could gather for a demonstration against Chosiu is now in port, and consists of four corvettes, carrying about 60 guns. They are seeking additional aid from Admiral Kuper of the English fleet, to enable them to operate effectively, for without such aid, they will make as abortive an effort as did the French last year. The English minister keeps his own counsels quiet; we only know that the Japanese are pleading lustily for more delay.

As the mail closes the latest *on dit* is, and appears worthy of some credence, that the Japanese Ministers have renewed their demand for at least a temporary suspension of trade at Yokohama; *per course* that they have been notified in turn that unless within the current month they give some guarantee for the repression of Chosiu and the reopening of the Inland Sea, a combined expedition of the treaty powers will move against the Prince of Nagato without further delay.

The 4th of July just passed received due honor from the shipping in harbor and the residents on shore. The various ships were gaily decorated, and the Jamestown's national salute was responded to by thirteen men-of-war of different flags—English, French and Dutch. The old colors seldom receive such a greeting from our European brethren. In the evening Consul Fisher and lady, ever hospitable, gave one of their handsome entertainments to a large party, where nearly every civilized land had its representatives—scarcely any part of the world but what there was some one to say, "I was once there." The band of the English flagship lent inspiring music to willing feet.

Wednesday, July 13, 1864

The U.S. Minister went to Yedo today in the *Jamestown* hoping to secure by his residence the settlement of the various claims upon the Japanese Government. The Japanese Governors made strong objection to his going there, the old plea of "danger" being the principal argument brought to bear.

Thursday, July 14, 1864

The 20th Regiment recently arrived from Hong Kong lands today.

Saturday, July 16, 1864

My Japanese friend S[adajirō] came back from Yedo last evening and reports a very bad state of affairs at the capital. The ronins have been gradually gaining strength and have recently had a conflict near Yedo with the forces of daimios sent to suppress them in which they were victorious. S[adajirō] says the wounded were known to have been brought back to Yedo. The ronins were reported 300 strong and acknowledge Mito for their leader, or chief. Much dissatisfaction exists with the government who were repeatedly enjoined by the friendly daimios to suppress these ronins but failing to do so, it is now feared that the ronins are too powerful to be suppressed. The Goroju feign illness and keep to their houses. The Tycoon is said to have been again imperatively summoned to Miako and it is rumored that he is to be deposed and Stotsbashi is to take his place. Such is the budget of news S[adajirō] brings, all of which is to be taken *cum grano salis*.

Thursday, July 21, 1864

General Pruyn came down from Yedo two days ago and reports all as very quiet in that city.

Last evening the *Barossa* and *Cormorant* steamed out of the harbor under sealed orders. There are various rumors as to their destination and objects, but the most probable is that they have gone on a reconnoitering expedition to the inland sea.

Saturday, July 30, 1864

Until yesterday we have had a succession of days remarkably cool for the season, without being too cool for health. The winds have been easterly, the sky a large part of the day slightly overcast, the thermometer barely rising to 80 degrees in the hottest part of the day. I can imagine no weather more delightful for the summer. There has been a positive luxury in the passive enjoyment of air, sky, and the rich foliage of the hills and vallies.

From Yedo and Oasaca still come many rumors, the most important of which is a reported attempt to take the Tycoon's life by poison and the arrest of three physicians charged with complicity.

The story goes that the royal taster, for Japan still has such a personage attached to the Emperor's service whose duty it is to taste all the food offered to the imperial lips, suspected some dish of which he had partaken and rejected it. The taster was made very ill, the emperor escapes, the cook declares his innocence, and suspicion fastens on the three unfortunate doctors, why or wherefore we do not hear.

This case is not the first attempt on the young emperor's life, according to general belief. At Oasaca a like attempt was made, but the emperor was warned by a white fox who appeared to him and saved his life. The fox came again the following night and said had he eaten that dish he would have perished, that he was a Yedo fox, and belonged to a temple near great Asakusa in Yedo and had come to save his royal master's life. The emperor in gratitude has since erected a handsome chapel to the fox at the place indicated as his residence, and if you don't see the fox there you may see the temple any day, so they tell us. *Quien sabe.*

The Goroju have resigned, some say on account of the poisoning affair as official etiquette required. Stotsbashi is the bête noir of all this trouble and is reported as stronger and more dangerous than ever.

Tuesday, August 2, 1864

From Dr. S[immons] I gathered some additional facts today about the official ichibu exchange. It seems that Mr. Von Brandt, the Prussian Consul, has compiled from the Custom House documents full returns of the amount of dollars changed by the Government for different individuals, and for what account the Japanese understood they were allowing this exchange. The documents are all authentic from the Custom House and show an amount of official rapacity that is lamentable to behold. The whole report will be published in Prussia in due time. Some of the items are as follows. The English fleet alone is receiving $180,000 worth of exchange per month. The *Semiramis* draws for over 1000 men and 65 officers! which is nearly if not quite double of the number she carries. A Dutch vessel with 260 men on board draws for 35 officers. The American Minister is down for over $70,000 worth of exchange for a single year, some of which is put down by the Japanese "as compensation for leaving Yedo"!! The American Consul figures for large sums given also as compensation. The late French Minister, M. Bellecourt, appears as having received on the eve of his departure a present, in the shape of a privilege to exchange $5000! To know what profit this represents, it is only to be added that those receiving exchange get for each $100, 311 ichibus less 4% (percent) for seignorage. These ichibus they have sold in the markets again the past year at 240 ichibus per $100 on an average! The average would be less than this for at times they have been able to turn back their dollars on the street at 230 ichibus per $100. The American Minister seems to have the sharpest dodge, for instead of allowing the Japanese to take 4 percent discount out of his money he exchanges for his full monthly sum of $3000 and pays them the $120 additional, thus securing exchange for $120 more than he would if the discount was deducted. Sharp work for a high official. The total amount now exchanged for officials, the fleet, and military, amounts to an annual take of over $4,000,000!! What a revelation is this of foreign rapacity in high quarters. Knowing that the Japanese pay this as a favor, or more also as a bribe, no matter with what spirit the recipients flatter themselves they receive it, what a picture it presents of our boasted civilization and our honor. Of its entire truthfulness there is no doubt. I myself am knowing personally to the U.S. Minister's monthly receipt of $3000 exchange, of his receiving 20,000 dollars exchange at a single time last year as a "special" favor; of the American Consul's receipt of nearly, or quite, half that sum. It is within bounds to say that the U.S. Minister's place was thus made worth for a single year with salary and exchange privileges alone $25,000. The U.S. Consul's at Kanagawa, eight to ten thousand. These affairs will one day be exposed to public excoriation.[15]

Wednesday, August 10, 1864

The steamers *Barossa* and *Cormorant* returned today. It appears that the object of their expedition was two fold. Quite recently two native Japanese,[16] who have been some time in Europe, returned to this port. They were anxious to return to their native province (Nagato), but were afraid to undertake the journey by the usual road. Moreover they were, or professed to be, convinced that if they could see their master, the Prince of Chosiu, they could give him such knowledge of the power and resources of the western world that he might be induced to cease his hostility towards foreigners. The English Minister therefore resolved to send these men back to Nagato hoping that they might be the means of doing a great good. It was besides important that a survey should be had of the approaches to Chosiu's principality with a view to necessary ulterior action, which survey could conveniently be made under cover of this mission, so that if it failed in one object it would accomplish the other.

According to this plan, which was indeed well conceived, the *Barossa* and *Cormorant* went down to Shimonoseki Strait. On approaching its eastern entrance they were warned by shots thrown across the straits in their advance to proceed no further. Guns from signal batteries had before given warning of their approach. The two natives were sent ashore on their errand and waiting their reply the steamers took every possible survey of the position, of all the approaches by sea and land way, and particularly of the batteries which were very numerous on shore, and some of which were so well marked that they would not have been detected but for their firing. The people on shore refused to hold intercourse with them. After a week passed in this manner the two envoys returned, having exchanged their plain robes with which they went ashore for the full dress of the yakunin. They delivered their message verbally and returned to their sovereign, and the steamers returned to this port. Their answer on behalf of their master was this: "that he, the Prince of Nagato, had no hostile feelings towards foreigners, but that in doing all he had done he was obeying the orders of his superior the Mikado and the Tycoon. If the English wished a suspension of his hostilities they should apply to the Mikado, who would doubtless give the necessary orders on being persuaded of their friendliness, and whose efforts he would aid, all of which would require some time, three months probably."

This was the unsatisfactory reply given verbally with no proofs or credentials of its veracity, and very possibly much softened down in its tone by the messengers. It was a clever evasions of the whole question, leaving the English in just the position they were before its receipt. There seem, indeed, but two courses left to the English, either assail Chosiu and demolish his batteries and weaken him for further hostile proceedings, or to go to Miako and

---

[15] John T. Comerford, who was a surgeon with the British fleet, commented on this arrangement: "Although Japan was very enjoyable, both as regards country, climate & people, I doubt if we would have liked it so much, without the itzibu exchange; this was a charming system, then recognized by the Japanese Government, by which we added considerably to our pay (in my case 4/-or 6/-per diem)." See John T. Comerford,

"An English Surgeon in Japan in 1864–65 (an extract from the *Private Journal* of John T. Comerford," in Frank Hawley, *Miscellanea Japonica*, vol. 1 (Kyoto: Privately Printed, 1954), p. 27.

[16] The two were Ito Hirobumi and Inoue Kaoru. Ernest Satow, who accompanied this expedition, describes the journey and its results in his *A Diplomat in Japan* (London: Oxford University Press, 1968), pp. 96ff.

demand audience of the Mikado and put to rest this vexed question of a divided sovereignty.

Thursday, August 11, 1864

I have neglected to record in my journal an account of the *Monitor's* experience at the Japan Sea. The *Monitor* is the property of an American Co. in Shanghai and has been fitted up with a view to a sale to the Japanese. She carries on deck a considerable armament. This steamer has recently been to Hakodade, where, failing of business, it left to return to Shanghai on the 2nd July. According to [the] owner's account, the weather coming down the Japan Sea was adverse and the ship got short of coal, and so came to anchor one evening off the coast of the Prince of Nagato's dominions at the port of Fukigawa. The steamer was boarded by officials from the shore who inquired her business. The steamer explained that she was short of coals and asked a supply. The officials replied that they would give an answer in the morning. During the night considerable noise was heard on shore, but not of a nature to excite suspicion, but at early dawn fire was opened on the steamer from cannon and muskets. The steamer, although surprised, soon had steam up and escaped, having received no injury and only been hit by the musket balls. After getting a long range out of reach of the batteries, the steamer, in turn, opened fire with a 20 pound Parrot gun and threw a score or so of shell into the town, without however apparently inflicting much damage. She then steamed away.

I learn from General Pruyn that during his recent visit to Yedo a thorough revolution was effected in government offices, and what is a little singular, without his knowledge until after his return to Yokohama. Over seventy officers were summarily dismissed for disaffection, or want of hearty cooperation with the Tycoon's government. This sweep included two members of the supreme council and a host of minor officials. The danger from the ronins who are gathering in force near Yedo seems to have determined this action. It was the only way to secure even the existence any longer of

the present dynasty. It is to be hoped that this act will be the means of committing the government completely to the foreign interests, from which power alone they can hope for aid. The regent was one of those dismissed. He had been ordered to march troops against the ronins, but had refused, because "the ronins were executing the will both of the Mikado and the people." Here at last seems to be a possible opening for successful foreign intervention.

[On August 11, 1864, Hall also sent the following letter to the *New York Tribune*, which was published on November 10, 1864.]

Another month has passed by, and still the English fleet swings idly at its anchors, while those who rule over it falter in ever-halting doubt how they shall treat the complex situation of Japanese affairs. A year of such fruitless doubting has gone by since their first essay at Kagosima, a year filled with hopeless contradictions and weary surmises, which has brought us no nearer a satisfactory conclusion than we were when the English fleet steamed out of Kagosima bay, followed by the farewell shots of the unsubdued batteries of Satsuma.

At the Court of Yedo the Tycoon has been the puppet of his ministers; flying between Yedo and Miaco the shuttle-cock of adverse parties. Deposed ministries have followed deposed ministries in rapid succession. Tycoons, Mikados, supreme councilors, regents, governors, no-kamis, daimios friendly, and daimios hostile have flitted before our eyes with all the changefulness of the magic lantern's phantasmagorfs. The same irresolution, born of hopeless doubt and ignorance, still hangs like lead on the conduct of ministers and admirals which weighed them down when first the fleet came into our waters. Sir Rutherford Alcock, accomplished and skilled in Oriental diplomacy, is no nearer the solution of his difficulties than was his baffled predecessor when he left us six months ago. For where every one, even the most experienced, are ignorant of the true position of affairs with the Japanese, where each government official is more skillful than his fellow in the art of lying so as to simulate the truth, who shall tell whether it were better to strike or forbear. So we are drifting on the surface of the flowing time, steering neither to this side or that, hoping only that some propitious wind, tide, or current will float us into our haven of ease.

The irksomeness of this delay is magnanimously borne by the fleet, whose profit, arising out of their ichibu exchange, now reaches the enormous sum of $50,000 per month! This is safer and surer than prize money. You and your readers have doubtless some remembrance of the epithets heaped on foreign merchants in Japan by Minister Alcock,[17] and echoed by every blatant orator of the House of Commons, for their (the merchants') disgusting avariciousness in wanting to change fabulous amounts of dollars into ichibus. Let it be known, then, that, by the grace of this same Minister, so sensitive for mercantile honor, a system of ichibu jobbing is going on here by officers wearing her Majesty's livery to which the offenses of the so-much-abused merchants were harmless peccadilloes. The story of this business—so discreditable to her Majesty's high officials, and not to hers only—must some day be made known, when home governments and home people will be equally astonished and ashamed for such weakness—to use no rougher term—in high quarters. This enormous subsidy from the Japanese Government is dangerous to public morals and official integrity, and should be swept away before it accomplishes its legitimate, I had almost said its inevitable, work.

If there is doubt on our side, there is more on the Japanese, who grow stronger of a resistance and more encouraged thereto by our irresolution. The Prince of Chosiu or Nagato becomes no more amiable in delay, but pushes with commendable

vigor his preparation for the trial by combat.

Recent incidents have given us proof of his unchanged temper. The armed steamer Monitor, flying the U.S. flag, and enjoying a semi-filibustering reputation, has been knocking her bones around these coasts for a year past, waiting, like Micawber, for something to turn up to her advantage by way of a sale, or possibly elsewise. At all events, last year, in a voyage from this to Nagasaki, and subsequent to the battle of Kagosima, Commodore Drake, as the Monitor's owner is familiarly known, found himself short of coals, and put into the bay of Kagosima. It was fair to suppose that Satsuma recently bereft of several steamers, might wish to avail himself of any reasonable opportunity to purchase a tight little steamer that could skim the dew, and was well armed beside. Satsuma did not see it at the time, but politely furnished the steamer with fuel to steam away again. But the Monitor, like the inevitable Monsieur Tonson, turns up again this Summer. We hear of her at Hakodadi, which port she left on July 9 for Shanghai. As ill-luck would have it, the Monitor gets short of coal again and this, too, right abreast the territory of another fighting potentate—no less a one than the Prince of Nagato.

Commodore Drake, nothing daunted, stops at the port of Fukigawa, and applies for fuel. The harbor officials politely inform him that they will send an answer in the morning, which they do in shape of shot and shell at early morning dawn. Commodore Drake, not liking this style of fuel, got up his steam in all convenient haste, and after an hour's exposure to the fire of the inefficient batteries and musketry which do him no harm, makes a convenient offing out of harm's way. And now our gallant American, whose pluck is very commendable, proceeds to return his compliments to the worthy burghers of Fukigawa with a twenty-pound Parrot, which forms a part of his armament. According to his report, he planted a score or more of shells in the town, set fire to several buildings, and then steamed away. Of course,

[17] Alcock had called the foreign merchant community in Yokohama "the scum of Europe." See Ernest Satow, *A Diplomat in Japan*, p. 25.

the next step is a liberal claim for damages. However, whatever may have been Commodore Drake's intentions or his hopes, his Majesty of Nagato was none the less unwarranted in committing a hostile act on a friendly vessel, and for which we must have proper redress. Unfortunately, we have no steamer here to repeat the Wyoming's gallant exploit, the old Jamestown being our only defense and offense in these waters.

Three weeks since the armed steamers Barossa and Cormorant were dispatched from the English fleet for the "inland sea," under sealed orders. They returned two days ago and it appears that they left here with the double purpose of having communication with the Prince of Nagato and of surveying the waters adjacent to his principality.

On approaching the eastern entrance of Shimonoseki Strait, signal guns were fired from battery to battery on shore to give notice of their approach. Afterward shots and shell were fired across the Cormorant's bows, which led the way, when the steamers stopped their progress, as they were under express orders to provoke no hostilities. Two envoys, native subjects of the Prince of Nagato, who recently returned from Europe to Kanagawa, and who were taken down in the steamers for the purpose, were sent on shore with a communication from the English Minister to the Prince of Nagato. After landing them, the steamers waited a week for their return, cruising in the vicinity and surveying the approaches to the Strait and the Strait itself, which latter duty was performed under the cover of the night. The people on shore were forbid by their rulers to visit the vessels or to furnish them supplies. Additional batteries were found to have been thrown up since last Summer, though none of them appeared of a formidable character.

After a week's delay the envoys came again on board when the steamers returned to this port. Neither the purport of the message to the Prince nor its reply have been allowed to transpire. The message could well be none other than an inquiry into Nagato's position toward foreigners, and a peremptory demand for unmolested passage past his dominions by the sea-way of Shimonoseki Strait. The returning envoys have brought only a verbal message, with no credentials for their authority to give even that. We are probably right in conjecturing, therefore, that the answer to the Minister's formal message is as unsatisfactory in matter as it has been in manner. Even a favorable reply sent in such a way would not be one on which any reliable hopes of future peace with Nagato could be built.

To diversify the monotony of our political affairs, and feed our dull ears with novelty, we have had a grand story of an attempt to poison the Tycoon, which is told in a way more horrific if not so romantic as that of the royal Alexander and his doctor Philip. It seems that in the imperial household at Yedo the function of taster of dishes offered to the royal appetite is not obsolete. On a recent occasion, this royal taster, in the discharge of his duty, had occasion to suspect a tempting dish, but why or wherefore is not said. The cook was called and forced to eat the dish his own skill had provided, and straightway died horribly before his astonished master's eyes. Whether the faithful taster was rewarded with robes of purple and fine linen, gold chains about his neck, and "the hand of the sultan's favorite daughter," the story is silent. That is the popular version, but the truth of the affair is said to be that the cook was exonerated and suspicion fastened on three of the court physicians, who were ordered under arrest, and are like enough to be condemned to eat arsenic and drink prussic acid the rest of their mortal lives!

This is not the first attempt, according to general belief, to take the Tycoon's life. Recently, while at Oasaca a similar attempt was made, and prevented of its fatal consummation by a *white fox* that came up all the way from Yedo, 400 miles, to warn his sovereign against eating a certain dish that was to be offered him the next day! The monarch abstained, and so lived to express his gratitude to the white fox by erecting a chapel to him near his favorite haunt in Yedo. Japan foxes have surely, more than their share of the cunning attributed to their race.

Considering that his two immediate predecessors suffered violent deaths, as now generally held to be true, and that the regent of his own minority was assassinated under his palace wall, the young Tycoon has some occasion to reflect on the vanity of earthly expectations and the exceeding wisdom of white foxes.

We daily hear of continued disturbances near Yedo, fomented by the party hostile to the present Government. Serious conflicts have taken place between these insurgents and the imperial troops, and though the latter are reported triumphant, the insubordination is evidently on the increase.

Our minister, Gen. Pruyn, has returned from a three week's residence in Yedo, greatly to the relief of the Japanese Government. The price of his leaving again was the settlement by the Japanese of a few outstanding claims, amounting to about $25,000. It is somewhat unfortunate for our national dignity, when our minister must trade in this manner, but if our common Uncle furnishes him no better means of enforcing just claims we must expect to descend to such paltry methods. I have taken previous occasion to deplore the abandonment of Yedo as a ministerial residence—a step which, more than any other single act has embarrassed diplomatic intercourse with the native authorities. The recent visit of our minister to Yedo serves to corroborate the conviction. Though the Japanese Government saw fit to surround the legation with several hundred swordsmen, and our minister landed a party of sixty marines and sailors from the Jamestown, there is nothing to show that Yedo is one whit more insecure for a residence than when Mr. Harris, to his great credit, so persistently remained there. Wherever Gen. Pruyn or his guest rode in the city they met nought but civility. The sooner the treaty powers insist upon their representatives residing again at the Court to

which they are accredited, the better will it be for the public welfare. At least, do not let us place our minister in a position where he must surrender not his right only but his duty to reside there, for the paltry consideration of a petty pecuniary claim. Better let our claim go down if we cannot secure it as becomes the dignity of a great nation.

Sunday, August 14, 1864

I attended last evening the funeral of Mr. Hamilton, Chaplain of the forces. He was buried just before sunset in our cemetery under the hill. A large concourse of people including officers from the fleet and land forces and the escort of the 20th regiment followed his remains to the grave. The band of the 20th playing the "Dead March in Gaul." As we stood around his open grave listening to the last services for the dead, vollies on the hill above us told that some other soldier was being interred at the same hour. Three vollies of 100 guns each were fired over the Chaplain's grave and the ceremony was over. The ground is thickly marked with fresh hillocks that mark the deposit of many a fine soldier who has succumbed to disease and not to wounds.

Monday, August 15, 1864

We had a charming day for an excursion on the steamer *Takiang*. I am busy all the morning helping poor Robertson[18] aboard of the *Houqua* bound for New York. I saw the invalid safe aboard in charge of his Indian nurse and his eyes brightened and his spirits rallied with the prospect of a return home. I hope he may safely reach his expectant friends. The *Houqua* was lashed alongside the *Takiang* that we might give her a tow down the bay. The excursionists were thirty or so in number and were guests of Mr. Gordon and Captain Andrews of the *Takiang*. We steamed down the bay till we were outside of Cape Sagami where we cast off the

[18] This was Mr. Samuel Robertson. See *Japan Herald*, August 20, 1864.

Houqua with parting cheers and saw her spread her sails "homeward bound." More than one of us longed to go. The water was smooth as a lake, the wind blowing gently and the shores were beautifully fresh and green. After casting off the *Houqua* we turned back towards Yokohama and had a beautiful dinner with plenteous libations. We steamed into the harbor long enough to drop a few guests and then went past the anchorage towards Yedo. We steamed into Yedo harbor within a mile or so of the forts and near to the shipping, had a distant view of the city and its temples, palaces, and green groves, then turned back again to Yokohama, which place we reached at 8 in the evening having had a day of unalloyed pleasure.

Tuesday, August 16, 1864

The report of the *Barossa* and *Cormorant* has stirred up action on the part of the foreign representatives. On Friday and Saturday last, conferences were held by them in conjunction with the admirals of the fleet and the conclusion arrived was to send a joint expedition against Chosiu. Preparations to this end are now rapidly pressing forward and it is thought that the expedition will sail the last of this week. The English, French, Dutch, and Americans all join in this, though the share of the latter will necessarily be insignificant. The three French vessels, the four Dutch, all go and all of the English, except two gunboats and a corvette which with the *Jamestown* are to remain for the protection of the settlement. The battalion of marines which came on the *Conqueror* are to accompany the expedition, leaving the 20th Regiment and the portion of the 67th to guard duty here. It is understood that orders were sent by the steamer on Saturday to Shanghai for the balance of the 67th and other additional forces.

Today is the second greatest holiday of the year called Bong [Bon]. It is generally observed by all classes. At Yedo ceremonious visits are made to the Tycoon. It is also the great occasion for paying rites of umbrage to dead ancestry. The graves are visited, and before them are placed offerings of rice, sake, or fruits, incense sticks are burned and fresh flowers and green twigs are placed at the graves. The stones are ornamented with symbols of paper, either plain white or stamped by the priests with sacred characters. Lanterns are suspended, which at night are lighted. On the sea, or near water, curious toy boats are launched on the water laden with food for the departed spirits that are wandering about and lighted with candles or paper lanterns. Whole fleets of these boats may be seen pulling to sea, or floating in the rivers and canals.

Today even the prisoners have a jubilee, their chains are loosed for the day and they are provided with extra food.

Wednesday, August 17, 1864

Our spell of hot dry weather is broken at last by clouds and rain. The combined expedition of the treaty powers against Chosiu is now fully determined on. All the Dutch ships are to go, all the French, all the English, but two gunboats and a corvette. The *Jamestown* also remains for the protection of the harbor, but the *Takiang* is to be chartered to accompany the expedition that the American flag may be seen with it. Of the troops the marines go, but the 20th regiment and 67th remain here. Saturday or Sunday will be the starting day.

Thursday, August 18, 1864

The rain retards the preparations of the fleet and now Sunday is mentioned as the day of departure.

Friday, August 19, 1864

We are all surprised this morning by the arrival of the P.O. Steamer [*Ganges*] with the Japanese Embassy to Europe on board. The tidings they bring has at a blow suspended all operations of the combined fleet, for they bring news of a convention with the French Government whereby the attack on the *Kien Chan*, and the murder of Camus, are settled with money and an agreement that the Tycoon shall within three months after their arrival himself open the inland sea and bring Chosiu to terms. This news was a thorough damper to the English Minister, and it is indeed unfortunate that this interruption has taken place. There are but three courses left to the foreign powers, either to abandon Japan, or to live here under humiliating conditions, or to *pacificate* this empire with the sword, now fast verging into anarchy. Concessions to the Japanese only increase the anarchy and strengthen the hands of the conservative party, and if force ever must be used, the earlier the better in the interest of humanity, before the hostile faction are strong enough to overthrow the Government at Yedo and to protract a useless resistance. The Tycoon has no power to fulfill the promises of his envoys. His first attempt thereto will bring ruin upon him and his dynasty. Chosiu is far more likely to unseat him on his throne in Yedo, than he to unseat Chosiu in Shimonoseki.

Saturday, August 20, 1864

Everyone is deeply disappointed with the failure of the contemplated expedition, for it seems as if we had to linger on here for still an indefinite period with our trade broken up and all our relations with this people of the most unsatisfactory nature.

Monday, August 22, 1864

My old friend Sadajirō has fallen into some trouble with the government and is under arrest.[19] I am anxious for his condition.

[On August 24, 1864, Hall sent the following letter to the *New York Tribune*, which was published on November 10, 1864.]

The doubtful counsels which for so long a period have embarrassed the action of

the Treaty Powers in Japan, and of which my last letter had something to say, gave way at last to vigorous resolution, but this vigorous resolution no sooner saw the light than it in turn was strangled like an untimely birth, and we are left once more drifting, still drifting in a current of events which we have forborne to guide. The happening has been in this wise:

I gave you in May last some account of the visit of Her Majesty's steamers Barossa and Cormorant to the Inland Sea of Japan, bearing a message from British Minister to the Prince of Nagato. I was mistaken in saying that the native envoys who accompanied this expedition returned to Kanagawa. This was not so; they were landed near Shimonoseki, and after a week's absence returned to the steamers bringing a brief verbal answer to the written dispatch of the Minister, and then went back again to resume their residence in their master's dominions.

This verbal message, softened in tone as it doubtless was by the friendly envoys, was briefly this: That their Chief, the Daimio of Chosiu, "in all his acts of hostility toward the foreigners, had acted under the direct orders of his sovereign, the Mikado, (not the Tycoon's it is to be observed) and that if there was any complaint of his course, it must be made to the Mikado.

The steamers returned to Kanagawa with this message and after consultation among the foreign diplomatic representatives, the conclusion was unanimously attained that every argument for peace, every motive for delay, had been exhausted, and that new measures of a more vigorous character should be instituted to bring the Japanese, or the malcontent faction of them, to respect the rights guaranteed by the treaties. It was resolved, accordingly, to send an expedition against Chosiu to reduce his fortifications in the Strait of Shimonoseki, and to take such other measures as would secure his future quiet. Further, if it were necessary, addi-

[19] Hall makes no mention of what Sadajirō's problem with the authorities was, but as he noted earlier this was a period when all Japanese with close contacts to Westerners were treated with suspicion.

tional guarantees should be required of the Mikado and his Court that they would cease their interference with the execution of the treaties by the Tycoon, even if it necessitated the sending of a force to Oasaca, and Miaco, the seat of the Mikado's government. I presume your readers do not forget that all the opposition to the treaties has been made in the name and with the real or pretended sanction of the Spiritual Emperor.

Active preparations for the expedition were at once begun, and the 20th to the 22nd instant was fixed upon for its departure from Kanagawa. It was to be a combined expedition of all the maritime Treaty Powers and though the English, from their superior force in these waters, took the leading part, the French, Dutch and Americans were to be represented to the extent of their ability. The American contingent was a steamer chartered for the purpose, which would serve the purpose of bearing our flag and showing to the Japanese our unity of purpose with the other Treaty Powers, while it could also be of no small service in various ways. The Jamestown, the only government vessel in the China station, was unfit for service in those tortuous, island-studded waters, flowing with strong current between Sikok and Nipon, while she could render efficient service by remaining behind with two gunboats and a corvette from the English squadron for the protection of Kanagawa. The Dutch contingent was four corvettes bearing 60 guns; the French, a gunboat, corvette and the Semiramis, flag-ship of Rear-Admiral Juarez, in all 80 guns, while the English contributed fifteen steamers of various armaments, mounting in all some 225 guns, under Admiral Kuper. Including a battalion of Royal Marines from the shore, the combined squadron could land in case of necessity nearly 3,000 men.

The work of preparation was nearly complete, shore messes were broken up, bills were called in, coals were put aboard, officers had taken leave of their friends, the last dollar had been converted into ichibus at the usual profit, and only the subsi-

dence of a long storm was waited for that the finishing work of preparation might be done, and the fleet steam away on its hostile errand; when lo! on the morning of the 19th, the mail steamer came from China, bringing, most unexpectedly, the Japanese Envoys returning from their visit to Europe, and with them the news of their Convention with the French Government, whereby not only had all the difficulties with the French been arranged, inclusive of the murder of Lieut. Camus, whose blood was compounded for a £7,500; but a part of that Convention was that the Envoys had pledged the Tycoon to the opening of the Inland Sea, and the repression of Chosiu within three months after their return to Japan. This was a bombshell thrown into the expeditionary fleet of the largest diameter.

Of course, the French were at once counted out of the proposed expedition, while the English by this one silent act of their beloved allies, seemed equally restricted from aggressive measures till the three months had passed by. The expedition for the present was at an end; officers took up again their pleasant shore life, the Royal Marines remained in their tents on the hill, and the pretty little game of changing dollars into ichibus, and ichibus into dollars again at 30 per cent profit, was entered into with fresh zest by admirals, captains, commanders, and such minor officers as had this privilege peculiar to gold bands and shoulder-straps.

And Chosiu, whose friends had, with cunning diplomacy, kept off the avenging blow for near a year, saw, at the hour when diplomatic intrigue could avail him no longer, help descend to him as from his gods above.

What, now, shall come of this? There is not a man in Japan, native or foreigner, but knows that those Envoys pledged the Tycoon to do something which he can no more do than he can snatch Denmark from the greedy clutch of the German. This interval of three month[s] will only serve to add to the strength of Chosiu, who is now forewarned of what he must expect, while it will add more and more to the growing anarchy of the country, which already threatens to overthrow the existing government and entail on this land the horrors of civil war, from which it has been exempt for now more than two centuries.

Had Chosiu been punished a year ago, when he was no formidable foe, it would have been for the peace of this nation and in the interest of humanity. Every month of delay adds to the distress that will yet ensue. Nothing could have been more ill-timed than this separate action of the French Government; and I doubt if after a little consideration the English will be restrained by it. The welfare of this empire, fast falling into political disorganization, demands outside compression. On the other hand, the Tycoon will be as little satisfied with the rash pledges of his Envoys that he would do what he has again and again assured the foreign ministers he could not do. It is still an even chance if the Tycoon does not repudiate the pledges of his Envoys, and they sink into disgrace, or seek that consolation of all unlucky politicians in Nipon—self immolation by hara-kiri.

It is manifest that nothing will save the present Government but the absolute putting down of the Prince of Nagato, and all his faction. We, as the foreign element, have but two alternatives, either to leave a land fast becoming a prey to internal discord, and with which we can no longer have peaceful or profitable intercourse, or to assist the Tycoon to maintain his throne, imperilled by a faction which strikes at us through him. Which is the course of humanity and civilization, which will cause the least flow of blood, there cannot be a moment's doubt. If our coming to Japan at all were an evil, our going away will now less contribute to the restoration of the ancient peace than our remaining in the discharge of the duty our position forces upon us.

[On August 25, 1864, Hall updated the above letter with the following note, which was also published in the *Tribune* on November 10, 1864.]

Since closing my letter of yesterday, it is reported, on apparent good authority, that the Tycoon has formally repudiated the action of his Envoys to Europe so far as their pledges to the French Government for the punishment of the Prince of Nagato are concerned. It is believed, therefore, that the combined expedition of the Treaty Powers against that Prince will be at once resumed.

Friday, August 26, 1864

The Japanese Governors of Foreign Affairs, after two or three days consultation with the Foreign Ministers, have formally repudiated the pledge of the European Envoys for the opening of the "Inland Sea." Having before this repeatedly assured the Ministers that it was impossible to do this, this act is a necessary consequence of those assurances. They preferred to convict their envoys of false promises than themselves of falsehoods. Besides, to have assented to this would have been to have committed themselves to acts of hostility against one of the empire's daimios, a step which they have been from the first cautious to avoid. However much they would secretly rejoice to see Chosiu punished they dare not themselves undertake it.

This repudiation again leaves the Ministers free to act, and again preparations are renewed for the combined expedition against Chosiu. The Japanese government professes to approve, and promises to pay towards its expense, but is, for all that, not to be trusted beyond the reach of controlling force. It means to take no overt act against Chosiu so that in case of disaster to the allied expedition it can wash its hands of all implication.

The Governors of Foreign Affairs have announced to the foreign authorities that Chosiu has attacked Miako and burned half of the city. Also there is report of more fighting near Yedo.

Saturday, August 27, 1864

We have confirmation of the attack on Miako from the Japanese people generally. They seem little disturbed by the preparations for the expedition against Chosiu, and many of them predict the latter's success in repelling all attacks.

Sunday, August 28, 1864

Part of the expedition, viz., the four Dutch steamers and two French, sailed this morning. The rest will follow tomorrow.

Monday, August 29, 1864

The remainder of the squadron sailed this morning at an early hour. The effective force of the fleet is 325 to 350 guns and with the ability to land nearly 3000 sailors and marines.

The *Jamestown* has come closer in shore, the other vessels left for our protection have taken up convenient positions for the defence of the settlement if need be. No one has any apprehensions, though the American Consul as a precaution has issued a circular warning his countrymen against exposure.

Tuesday, August 30, 1864

Went with the "Chowder Club" to Mississippi Bay. Dr. Hay was our guest. The water was rough going down, and I was slightly seasick. Passed a pleasant day on the beach and had a famous chowder.

[On September 1, 1864, Hall wrote the following letter to the *New York Tribune*, which was published on November 10, 1864.]

The succession of events justifies all that I ventured to predict would be the issue of affairs. After the return of the Envoys from France, the Ministers of the Tycoon were at once pressed by the representatives of the Treaty Powers with the question whether they would undertake to fulfill the pledges given by these Envoys to the Emperor, that Chosiu should be humilified and the Inland Sea opened to the passage of foreign vessels. Their reply was promptly to the effect that not only in this had the Envoys exceeded their powers, but in all they had done at the French Court. They had given dissatisfaction to the Tycoon, and their acts could not and would not be ratified. On the contrary, another embassy would leave at once for Europe to undo the mischief this one had done. They distinctly denied both their ability or wish to punish Chosiu by the force of arms, and so once more the Treaty Powers were left free to act.

The postponed expedition was at once resumed, and in a few days was ready for sea. On the mornings of the 28th and 29th ultimo, it took its departure for the Inland Sea, which it will enter by the Bungo channel. Its effective force is fifteen steamers, carrying a total of 325 guns and able to put on shore, in case of necessity, a landing party of 3,000 men. The Prince of Nagato has had ample notice to perfect his preparations to receive this powerful expedition, and we hear from native sources extravagant accounts of the opposition the fleet will have to overcome, and of the number of forces ready to resist any attempt to land. But it may safely be assumed, that the Japanese, in their long disuse of war, have feeble conceptions of the range and power of modern artillery, or the compact force of three thousand well-drilled bayonets. The first collision with Nagato men can hardly fail to result in easy victory to the allies.

The interest of the United States in this combined expedition is represented by the hired steamer Takiang, on which a party is placed from the Jamestown, and which will serve to show our flag united with those of the other treaty powers. If we had held aloof, our reasons would have been misinterpreted, and it is better that the Japanese should at once know that all the treaty powers are together on this question, and that resistance to their just demands is hopeless. The action of Gen. Pruyn in this matter should win the approval of the Government he represents, and may save us at some future day a more costly expedition.

It is proposed after the reduction of batteries at Shimonoseki, to hold the place as a guarantee of future peace and it is not improbable that this valuable port will be thrown open to *free* commerce.

Should this expedition be unsuccessful in putting down the reactionary party, we may look for further active operations on the Inland Sea which will affect Oasaka, the great commercial metropolis of the empire, and may even necessitate a march upon Miaco, where the Spiritual Emperor resides. The expedition is not expected to return to this port for a month or so, and you will hear of its exploits first from other sources than mine.

Meanwhile the malcontents are active and give the Tycoon no small trouble. To the north of Yedo they are in force, and have successfully resisted the Imperial troops sent against them, driving them back and destroying their depots of supply. Miaco has been attacked by the Chosiu men, in an attempt to seize the person of the Mikado, as in olden feudal days king or emperor was seized to win possession of the Court. The Mikado escaped, but half of the large and populous city of Miaco was laid in ashes. These events show the condition of anarchy and civil war into which these islands are fast driving, and from which nothing can save them but the sustaining hands of the foreigners toward the Tycoon.

During the absence of the fleet Kanagawa is protected by the Jamestown, 22 guns, H.B.M. Pelorous, 21 guns, and two gunboats, covering the sea approach, and the 20th regiment, part of the 67th, and part of an Indian regiment on shore. The town is under the guns of a large Japanese fort across the neck of the bay, and the battery of the Governor's hill, which overlooks

the settlement on the west. These are in the hands of the Tycoon's officers, and no danger is to be apprehended from them unless they should be surprised and held by the malcontents, the mischance of which is very slight. The ministers and consuls, however, have though it prudent to issue to their representative subjects timely cautions. I append to this the letter of Gen. Pruyn to Consul Fisher and the Consul's notification to American citizens.

This move of the foreign powers which is virtually an armed support of the Tycoon's Government is pregnant of important changes in Japan. It brings on directly the struggle between parties friendly and hostile to foreign intercourse. If the latter have the ability and disposition to enter into the contest, it will be a long time before Japan is restored to peace; but our reasonable hope is that this first demonstration against Chosiu, Prince of Nagato, will show them the futility of such a struggle. No doubt many of the great feudal chiefs of these isles have the prescience to know what the effect of extended commerce and a wide intercourse with foreign nations will be on their exclusive privileges, and some of them may, like the old Prince of Kaga when the foreign treaties were first under discussion, put their hands to their sword hilts in the council room and say, "It is better to die first."

[copy] No. 1. UNITED STATES LEGATION IN JAPAN, August 29, 1864.

Sir: The representatives of the Treaty Powers, in view of the serious interruption of trade seeking an outlet at the Straits of Shimonoseki, and of the political situation in this country, have come to the decision that the obstacles at these Straits should be removed by the combined forces of those Powers.

The safety and interests of the citizens and subjects of the Powers at the open ports have not been overlooked and while we are convinced that ample means have been provided against any attack which may be apprehended, I deem it my duty to say to you that at the present crisis great caution should be observed and no unnecessary exposure made. I desire that the citizens of the United States shall be enjoined by you to abstain from going on the Tokaido in any locality where they may be exposed to danger, not only through regard to their own lives, but also for the purpose of avoiding the complications of the political situation which might be occasioned thereby; and, for a season, I would also advise that in their customary rides they should as much as possible avoid going out alone.

ROBERT H. PRUYN
U.S. Minister Resident in Japan
To GEO. S. FISHER esq., U.S. Consul, Kanagawa

[Copy] No. 2. UNITED STATES CONSULATE, Kanagawa, Japan, Aug. 29, 1864.

OFFICIAL NOTIFICATION. In accordance with the suggestions of his Excellency the Minister Resident of the United States in Japan as per the accompanying letter, and to avoid every unnecessary complication and pretext for collision, it is earnestly requested that all citizens and persons registered at the United States Consulate and under the protection of its flag, shall, for a temporary season, refrain riding on pedestrian excursions in the Tokaido or into the country, unless in parties of not less than six persons. It is also expected and enjoined upon citizens of the United States and persons registered under our flag, unless compelled by necessity, not to hazard or expose themselves, in town or country, to any difficulty or altercation with the Japanese officials or other people. And it will be noted the purpose of this notification being only for the public good, the undersigned feels sure private pleasure will give place to wise precautions, the general welfare of the settlement and the combined interests of all the treaty powers for a season at least.

GEO. S. FISHER, U.S. Consul Kanagawa

Saturday, September 3, 1864

Dr. Simmons sailed.[20]

Friday, September 9, 1864

A typhoon not very severe passed over the place this morning. Very little damage was done owing to its short continuance.

Sunday, September 11, 1864

Letters received from Nagasaki today report a quiet condition at that port. There have been many threats made, in case Chosiu was attacked, of vengeance on the foreigners. The articles confirm the news of Chosiu's recent attempt in Miako and his signal repulse. The attacking forces entered the city in two columns and were assisted by Chosiu men within, but were defeated with the loss of nearly their entire force, but not until the shells of the assailants and defenders had set fire to the city, causing immense destruction owing to the high wind prevailing at that time. According to native accounts the fire raged two whole days destroying 78,000 houses and temples and 3700 warehouses, and laying waste nearly 1000 squares, or blocks, including Higashi Honquan-gee [Higashi Honganji], the largest temple in the empire. Three days subsequent to this affair Chosiu's son arrived at Hiogo with reinforcements of 15,000 men. Subsequently his return to Shimonoseki with his forces is announced.

Chosiu's now open revolt against the constituted government is manifest, and it is hardly to be supposed that he has undertaken this movement single handed, but as yet we do not hear of the active cooperation of any other daimios.

The wreck of the British bark *Toledo* in the recent typhoon is reported on the coast. Lives all saved.

[20] Dr. Simmons sailed on the *Delaware* for San Francisco. See *The Japan Herald*, September 3, 1864.

Monday, September 12, 1864

Since the typhoon the weather begins to put on its Septemberish character, evenings are cooler and the morns more bracing. The steamer *City of Nantes*, hence to Hakodade, but back today, having suffered some injury in the late gale whereby one boiler was shifted.

Tuesday, September 13, 1864

Dined with Sir Rutherford and Lady Alcock.

Sunday, September 18, 1864

Late last evening the *Perseus* returned from Shimonoseki bringing the first news of the Allied Fleet's success against Chosiu. The forts were easily silenced, and a subsequent landing party completed the work. The casualties were few, 12 killed and 54 wounded. The printed report of this affair preserved with this journal will give full particulars.[21]

[Although the date is not clear, it seems that Hall forwarded to the *New York Tribune* three letters from Eugene Van Reed, who was aboard the *Takiang*. Hall was working with Van Reed to sell the *Takiang* at the time. These letters were published in the *Tribune* on November 26, 1864.]

On Board the Takiang, off Straits of Simonoseki, Sept. 11, 1864.

Tshosiu has been attacked by the combined fleet which left Yokohama eighteen vessels strong, and has come to terms after removing his guns and destroying some six forts. He asserted that the Mikado and Tycoon had given him positive orders to fire upon foreigners, and that he was merely carrying out his orders. The Straits are now freely opened to any nation, and he

desires to open a port for trade: hopes that no ill feeling may exist, and supplicates for pardon. Wednesday next the troops land as an escort to the English admiral, when Tshosiu will be there to receive him. Not withstanding the heavy firing from the fleet and Takiang, they report a loss of some three hundred only. Takiang made honorable use of a 30-lb. Parot gun which was highly spoken of by Admiral Kuper. Japanese had 11-inch shells, one of which I possess. The guns, some six and a half tons weight, and sixteen feet in length were all of Russian manufacture.

Part of the fleet will winter here. We may leave for Yokohama at any moment, having some thirty wounded English on board.

Off Simonoseki, Steamer Takiang, Sept. 11, 1864.

The Tancrede leaves for Nagasaki and Shanghai at 12m., so I avail myself of the opportunity of writing a line. The tale of Tshosiu is soon told. We arrived here in naval order on the 4th, eighteen vessels in all. Monday, 2 p.m. as the tide was flowing inward, Tartar, Dupleix and Metalls Krius led the way, one after another, right past the forts, steering for the shore opposite. The Forts would not fire upon either nationality. There was a pause for about a quarter of an hour; French Admiral left his vessel and went on board the Euryalus to confer. The result was that the English Admiral threw a shell toward the strongest fort; the reply was instantaneous, and before we recognized our position, we were in the center of the fire, lying just between French and English Admirals, I can assure you that Tshosiu's fire was an energetic one with shot and shell. The Takiang threw her 30-lb. shell into a fort and set fire to it, French and English Admirals were watching us closely.

Although but a chartered steamer, we could not stand idly by and be shot at without upholding the Flag. A brisk fire was

---

[21] The report mentioned is not with the manuscript, but Joseph Heco in his diary under the same date gives the local newspaper account. See *Narative of a Japanese*

(San Francisco: American-Japanese Publishing Association, n.d.), vol. 2, pp. 64–68.

kept up until 5½ p.m., when the Japanese fire slackened. Tuesday morning Takiang, Perseus and Tancrede aided in disembarking the troops, and we anchored right opposite the forts and were in the worst position as soon as the Japanese rallied. After the forts were taken, the enemy secreted in paddy fields and (not visible) fought bravely with musketry and drove French and English soldiers near the waters edge twice. A rally was made by the English to drive the enemy from the woods and fields by 6 p.m., when the enemy ran and got behind a stockade, where they fought desperately and killed some ten men and wounded 22, Captain Alexander was wounded and will probably lose his leg. Thursday flag of truce on board Euryalus 2 p.m., French tried to burn the town with shells even to half an hour after flag went up. Two Japanese came off to say that Tshosiu was willing to come to any terms, and would send his Prime Minister to see the Admiral Saturday, 12 m. Admiral ordered us (with twenty-five English wounded on board) to go to Himesima and bring up any vessels there might be with coals for the fleet. We returned yesterday 2 p.m., when we heard that Japanese were punctual, arriving 20 minutes before 12 o'clock. In the Japanese letter to Americans he says that all was a mistake, that we might have passed this without trouble. That Mikado and Tycoon last year ordered him to fire upon all foreigners, that we think him unfriendly, that he has no ill-will, and supplicates for peace and pardon.

Wednesday admirals go ashore with troops to meet Tshosiu, and sign a Treaty. It is rumored that he will give up all the forts and cannon, and allow free passage to any nation through the Straits; is desirous of opening a port.

I have visited the forts, and find but little execution was effected by our guns. Sand Batteries, guns 11-inch shell, cannon 20 feet long, weighting 6½ tons, all made by the Russians. Tshosiu says the Tycoon is to blame.

The lower orders of people were very friendly; silk, tea, cotton, and all produce passes here, and the place looks flourishing.

We may be ordered to Yokohama with the wounded, day after tomorrow.

Part of the fleet will winter here and see that Tshosiu carries out his promises.

The Japanese say they lose 200 to 300 men; we have lost about 30, and some 40 wounded. Medusa fought well; iron chains around her sides. Perseus was ashore on a rock for 48 hours; no damage.

On Board U.S.S. Takiang, Simonoseki, Sept. 15, 1864.

Our movements here have been very successful, as far as punishing the Prince of Tshosiu for his continued attacks upon all foreigners endeavoring to pass through these Straits.

The forts belonging to Tshosiu as well as guns have been removed, and there is no obstacle to our passing through the Straits. I have just learned the result of negotiations with Tshosiu. It is stated that Tshosiu is forced to pay an indemnity, (don't know what amount) that the Straits are to be free and unrestricted for all nations, that no more forts are to be erected in his dominions, that the town of Simonoseki is to be opened to foreign trade; that perfect safety is to be guaranteed all foreigners coming here. This embraces about all the principal stipulations that have transpired thus far. We are anchored in 6 fathoms, tide runs 7 knots per hour, and in tide way 15 fathom chain is of no service, no holding ground. The town stretches for nearly two miles; the banks of the Straits are crowded with large junks (I have counted 94 to-day) laden with rice, copper cash, cotton and sugar. Seaweed appears to be the principal article of trade with dried fish. Oil, copper and cotton are also visible.

Of course the town appears to be a poor one, the Japanese living without much ostentation. Were foreigners to trade here, I believe that much of the produce which now passes by would be centered here next to Hiyogno [Hyogo]. Now that a basis for a Treaty has been established, the Ministers will have to be present to see it ratified, and as a consequence, I think that Hiyogno will shortly be opened to us. However, one thing has been discovered to our satisfaction, and that is that the Tycoon has been playing us false, while the Daimios are desirous of our friendship. What course will be pursued with the Tycoon, now that his treachery is exposed, remains to be seen.[22]

Monday, September 19, 1864

All the mercantile community are rejoiced to learn that the mail of Saturday brought orders to the English Minister that no more exchange should be received at the Custom House by foreign officials in the English service. It is expected that the other Treaty Powers will soon be under like instructions. We hope that our officials will now set earnestly to work to rearrange our disturbed currency.

Wednesday, September 21, 1864

The *Takiang* returned this evening from Shimonoseki bringing little news. The squadron were expected to leave in a day or two later for Oasaca and Kanagawa. Some details of the recent affair are brought showing that the Japanese could have had only a small force to resist the Allies, probably not more than man for man. Nor were they deficient in courage. One instance is related when a single Japanese was seen walking along the hill side, instantly hundreds of muskets were fired and shell from two cannon, but our hero walked on unmoved till within a few rods of the native fort when he broke into a run for cover. Another incident is of a native, who concealed partly by the bush, fired and brought down a soldier, a volley was returned in reply and a rush made for him, but before he was reached he had brought down his second man and then strove to kill himself, but was killed by his assailants.

Friday, September 23, 1864

Several Japanese merchants have been detected in smuggling silk into the settlement concealed in bales of cotton, hay, and other produce. That the Japanese merchant is willing to undergo all this risk to sell his goods at a less price than he could get if brought in with the sanction of his government is conclusive that it is the government who restricts our trade.

Wednesday, September 28, 1864

We hear that the recent rains produced no little mischief in the provinces of Fitatsi [Hitachi] and Simosa [Shimosa] to the north and east of Yedo. Rivers overflowed their banks and swept away houses, cattle, grain, and some lives also are reported lost. On the sea coast of Fitatsi the sea carried away some houses along the shore.

[We do not know the precise date on which Hall sent to the *New York Tribune* the third of his articles "Farm Life in Japan III"; it is simply dated Kanagawa, September 1864. This article was published on March 24, 1865.]

In the latter part of April, whichever way the eye turns, it beholds a boundless sea of verdure. The forests are heavy with leaf, and the hill-sides are dense with waving grain and the luxuriant rape. The early bare and brown spots are the intervals let for rice planting. Rice is the staple crop of the country, as well as its most valuable. The coming of the foreigner with his wants for export trade, has, however enhanced the value of other crops, and made many an unremunerative acre valuable. Wheat that hitherto indifferently repaid the farmer for his toil, by his coming threatened to rise in value about the open ports

---

[22] The first and third of these letters were clearly written by Eugene Van Reed, although the middle letter may have been by another author. For the Van Reed letters see the Augustine Heard & Co. Papers, Heard I, HM-58-I, in the Baker Library, Harvard Business School.

to such an extent that the Government threw every obstacle in the way of its export, ending with a positive prohibition. So with rape seed oil, essential alike for light and cookery; while the product of silkworms and mulberry trees has doubled and trebled in price, and raw cotton quadrupled. As all farming lands susceptible of rice culture pay their rents in tithes of rice, it became at once the interest of the proprietors not to allow the substitution of other crops, which paid no rates.

The increased demand for vegetables, fire-wood, charcoal, lumber and other daily supplies, has penetrated many a league into the country round about each open port with enhanced prices. Farm labor and its rewards have thus been to some extent equalized so that our best, almost our only friends in this land to-day are among the farmers and merchants, while the classman yet looks at us with eye askant, and even an itching palm for his sword-hilt.

True, the farmer pays more to-day for the coarse cotton robes that he, his wife and children wear; more for his daughter's silken skirts which she must wear on New Year and other holidays, and clad in which she goes to the temple festivals, whither her piety or her superstition, as we may choose to regard it, calls her, but his boys' dress and his own, too, for that matter, for a good share of the year are their own stout sun-tanned envelopes, which have grown no dearer from our coming, but possibly more sleek from better feeding.

As a rule, all land capable of growing a fair crop of rice is set apart for that purpose. This includes all the valleys, or wherever irrigation can be had. In Japan, fortunately, living streams are numerous, and at the head of the hill ravines, or of such open valleys as are girt with sufficient water shed, it is common to see the waters collected in a reservoir as a precaution against the chance of a protracted dry season. These ponds of water are quite commonly surrounded with planted growths of timber or indigenous shrubbery, where, hid away in unfrequented spots, they become the resort of wild fowls, the gay plumaged ducks and the screaming her-

ons. Pond-lilies, the delicate leaves of the water chestnut, and often times the broad disks and flame-tipped blossoms of the lotus add their attractions to these miniature lakes.

Though in midsummer there are several weeks usually with a small fall of rain, the ground does not parch rapidly; there are copious night-dews and always some moisture in our island atmosphere. The Fall-sown crops are harvested before the extreme heats of Summer begin, and one or two copious midsummer rains will carry the later crops on to the falling days of Autumn. So it happens it is only in occasional years that those pent up lakes are let away for even a crop requiring so much water as rice. If the experience of five years is a criterion, we can say that the Japanese farmer labors in the golden clime of toil. Neither floods or droughts, burning suns or pinching cold enter largely into his calculations for the year's product—to him, indeed, seedtime and harvest never fail.

But it is not the valleys alone that yield a crop of rice. Porous as the upper soil is, and underlaid as the hills are, with a soft clayey grit rock or beds of gravel, the rains of Spring and Fall are readily drunk up and held and thus little streams are gushing out way up on the hill-sides, which live long enough to accomplish the good end of a short but busy life. These waters, too, are gathered on the highest point, and step by step are led down the terraced hill-sides, to the joy of the horny-handed laborer who watches and controls them, giving moisture to many a field leveled out against the hill-side centuries ago, and finish their life of usefulness scattered by many a silver thread among the broad rice plains below.

Japan produces also one or more varieties of upland rice, not common about the open ports, seed of which has been obtained by our Minister Resident, Gen. Pruyn, and forwarded to the Patent Office. The fields designed for a rice crop are continually covered with a slight depth of water, so that the soil is in a semi-liquid state the year round. In early May the farmers break up small patches for nursery beds, from which they will afterward transplant to the larger fields. The spot for this nursery is duly chosen, regard being had to a warm locality where there is a good supply of living water abundant without danger of overflow. This much done for the rice, other crops for a month will require the farmer's attention, for the rape plant, wheat, and barley are coming in apace and need a last hoeing and weeding.

We shall also see in early May in every farm-yard the sweet potato hot-bed. This is simply made—a bed a foot and a half deep, with chopped straw and leaves is wet down with water, or, better still, with slops from the farm-house where, exposed in a sheltered place to the hot sun, aided by some fermentation, it gains warmth sufficient to start the tubers for an after transplanting. The sweet potato is a greater staple of the country than rice even. Wherever it can be grown it is a universal article of food. No wayside cookshop is more common than the sweet potato bakery, and many a dame, wrinkled, toothless and old, supports herself by her baking kettle stationed at a street corner or by the side of a much traveled thoroughfare, where she is as well patronized by the boys and girls as the apple or peanut women at home, and is, I fear, the victim of as many childish pranks. I remember such a one whom I have known since my first residence in Japan and not one whit older has she grown, and the boys and girls who are her patrons are of just the same assorted sexes and sizes, fresh relays of never-ending youth. Her establishment is where the Tokaido to Yedo crossing a bridge intersects also a main road to the country, and consists of a bake-kettle two feet in diameter, supported by a wood furnace, and provided with a wooden-cover. Into this all day go incessant supplies of sliced potatoes; and by some marvelous instinct of smell, which I never fathomed, the whole neighborhood knows when the last bake is ready, perhaps long habit has taught them every gradation of the savory odor, till the potatoes are done to a turn. Eleven in the forenoon, is the busy hour. Then the travelers halt for the noonday meal, and the teamsters bait their horses out of nose-bags, while daily is the old lady ready for the pressing emergency, with smoking tubers in never failing supply. Boys in every degree of nudity, girls with babies on their backs almost as big as themselves, are clamorous customers, vying with each other for the large slices, then scampering away with blistering tongues or tingling fingers.

On the island of Yesso to the northward the sweet potato is little cultivated, but its place is being rapidly supplied by our own American root. I was on this island in 1860 and wherever I went in the country I found the American potato in cultivation. Although this potato has undoubtedly been known to Japan for a long time and bears the name that indicates its introduction from Java, by the Dutch probably, it was a little singular that at Hakodadi its introduction was attributed to Commodore Perry's expedition. The supply of fresh seed by this expedition may, perhaps, have given a new stimulus to its culture. So too, I have found wheat spoken of as an introduction from our land, but whether this alludes to some particular variety that may have been brought hither by American vessels, or whether the meaning was that wheat was introduced from the West, I have never been able satisfactorily to determine, probably the latter.

By the middle of May the rape, wheat, and barley fields begin to turn, and under the warm suns this ripening is rapidly perfected. Harvesting begins from the 25th of May to the 1st of June. These dates are particularly for the country about Yedo Bay. And now in whatever direction we may look, is seen smoke rising from every hill-side and valley. The farmers are pulling the rape, the dry stalks are gathered in heaps, the seed is trodden out, the refuse is burned, and the ashes carefully saved for manure. The few days that are required for the rape harvest bring forward the barley to its ripening. The barley harvest is still going on when the wheat and later rape come in, making the month of June a busy harvest month.

The wheat and barley are cut with the grass knives, the rude kind of sickle which I have before mentioned. The morning's work is laid in the sun to dry, and in the afternoon the heads are whipped or cut off by a hatchel of bamboo, or sometimes of iron, resembling a rake with closely set short pointed teeth. Mats are spread on the ground to catch the falling heads, and then the grain is beaten out with a clumsy flail. The threshed grain is winnowed or gathered in baskets and taken to the farm yard, where stand a fan-mill, exact counterpart of those found in every New England farm yard a quarter of a century ago. Each day's work is cleared up as it goes along.

But oftentimes the harvest season is interrupted by frequent rains, when the Japanese employ a process peculiar to themselves. The grain is gathered in the sheaf, carried to some convenient spot where a fire is lighted. The farmer holds a handful of the sheaf in one hand and with a lighted wisp of straw in the other singes the bearded heads till they fall from the stalks in a heap at his feet. This process is repeated till all the grain has been treated in like manner, and the fire, though sufficient to singe the awns and burn off the straw, appears to do no injury to the berry. The still warm heap is gathered up and taken to the farm house, where the grain is beaten out on the granary floor of hard earth or oyster shell lime, and after this scorching separates readily from the remaining chaff. In a wet June month the continual smoke of their fires is everywhere seen ascending.

In all this harvest labor, but especially in a wet season, the farmer's wife and daughter come into the field again. When the winnowing is done in the open fields, as it more commonly is, this generally falls to the woman's share. If there is a fine breeze blowing the winnowing is done by the simple process nature indicates. If the breeze is wanting, a fan made of the outspread fibers of the palm leaf, covered with paper, supplies it. "Whose fan is in his hand," says the ancient record, and the old custom still holds from Judea's hills across the steppes of Asia to these isles of the sea.

Friday, September 30, 1864

Sold and delivered the *Takiang*.[23]

Sunday, October 2, 1864

Fleet returned from Shimonoseki.

[On October 12, 1864, Hall sent the following letter to the *New York Tribune*, which was published on December 15, 1864.]

The victory of the allied fleet at Shimonoseki was as decisive as it was easy. Indeed the resistance was almost too feeble to be dignified with the name. Chosiu was no less overpowered by the weight of metal brought to bear against him than he was outnumbered by his assailants. The battle of Shimonoseki will not be counted in history as one of the remarkable instances of the resistance of forts and earthworks to an

---

[23] Hall acted as commission agent in the sale of the *Takiang*. The ship was put up for sale by Augustine Heard & Co., whose agent in Yokohama was Hall's acquaintance, Eugene Van Reed. Van Reed, writing to Albert F. Heard from Kanagawa on August 20, 1864, noted, "the *Takiang* was chartered by General Pruyn to accompany the vessels south for $9500 per mo.; if lost, to pay 120 thousand." On October 1, 1864, Van Reed wrote to Heard, "I have to report the sale of the steamer *Takiang* to the Japanese government, which was accomplished yesterday afternoon, the sum paid was $72,000; the owners will probably realize after charges etc. $60,000. Walsh [Hall] & Co. asked

$100,000 but upon the return from Simonoseki, were willing to accept a less amount. The contract with the English government to bring troops over, and finally the move of the American Minister in chartering her for the southern expedition were the great inducements to her sale." These letters are contained in the Heard Collection, Box HM-58, Albert F. Heard Letters received from E. M. Van Reed, 1836–66, Baker Library, Harvard Business School. See also Fukunaga Ikuo, "Vuan Riido hyōron," *Eigakushi kenkyū* (Nihon Eigakushi Gakkai), no. 18 (11/1/1985), p. 69. I am indebted to Mr. Fukunaga for alerting me to the existence of these letters.

assailing fleet! A half hour's practice—three quarter at most—and all was over.

The Japanese abandoned their guns, not one of which was so much as scratched nor a single carriage broken. There was a little skirmishing the following day, to carry a stockade, when the campaign of Shimonoseki was finished.

The printed accounts which I send you will give the details of the affair. The number of casualties to the allies are summed up in 12 killed and 56 wounded. How much loss was inflicted on the Japanese no one knows, for when the forts were seized by the landing party there were neither dead or wounded to be seen—some blood stains proved that there had been wounded. So at the stockade, which was carried just at nightfall, neither dead or wounded were to be seen the following morning. We conclude that the casualties to the Japanese were few, nor is it generally supposed, that in this inglorious engagement they more than, if they so much as equaled the number of their foes, man for man. We can only account for Chosiu's bringing so small a force in the field on the ground either that his troops were still absent in his raid against Miaco, or, as is more probable, that he already had as many and more men than he could properly arm, for bows and arrows were used in this engagement, one soldier, at least, having been slain by them.

The Japanese were as successful in keeping their arms as they were in removing and concealing their dead and wounded. True they lost all their heavy guns in position, which, to the number of seventy or eighty, were carried off by the victors, but of small arms not so much as a sword or musket was carried off as a trophy. Trophies are not wanting among the returned heroes, but rumor says that after the truce the clever shop-keepers of Shimonoseki turned a handsome penny selling their old and battered stock of swords and armor as battlefield relics.

Compared with this exploit, the gallant feat of our "Wyoming" last year, when single-handed she engaged for two hours those shore batteries and an armed steamer and two armed brigs besides, is a better one of which a nation may proudly boast. To this day the Japanese do not cease to speak of and admire her bold adventures.

This time our navy was represented by the chartered American steamer Takiang, the property of Mssrs. Olyphant & Co. of China and New York, which rendered efficient service, as the reports herewith show. Her employment was the fortunate suggestion of our minister, Gen. Pruyn, in order that our flag might appear in concert with the other treaty powers. A thirty-two-pounder Parrott from the United States sloop Jamestown was put on board the Takiang, whose long range and precision of fire attracted much attention from both the English and French naval commanders. Capt. Price was unfortunate in being debarred from going thither in the Jamestown, the heavy tide-way of the Straits rendering the employment of sailing vessels wholly impracticable; but he lent hearty cooperation by fitting out the Takiang with his Parrott rifled gun and lending Lieut. Pearson and a squad of men to serve it. Lieut. Pearson and his little band are handsomely mentioned by Admiral Kuper in the events of the day.

It proves in Japan, as elsewhere, that when a man is down there is a general desire to trample on him, for no sooner is the victory over Chosiu achieved by foreign arms than His Majesty the Tycoon, in a very flourishing and theatrical way, issues orders to twenty-three Daimios to furnish consignments to a force which shall uproot and destroy that belligerent chief. A great show of preparation is going on for this "hitting when he's down" business. But I fancy, first that a goodly proportion of the Daimios ordered will not comply, and second, that those who do will not find so cheap a victory as did the allies who have gone before them.

To the foreigners Chosiu promises any conditions of peace required, and negotiations are now in progress between the foreign representatives and the Japanese Ministers of State, which are likely to secure a substantial indemnity for the trouble Chosiu has put them to.

We have now fuller accounts of Chosiu's attack (prior to the Shimonoseki engagement) upon Miaco, the capital city of his spiritual highness the Mikado, and the attempt to seize his person. This was in August. Chosiu's forces, indifferently armed, were encamped outside the city, and suddenly one morning moved in two columns to its attack, while at the same time his followers within the city rose to their aid.

The attacking columns, which were less than five thousand together, were vigorously opposed by the retainers of the Daimios whose duty it was to guard the city and the Mikado's person, conspicuous among whom were the Daimios of Satsuma, Aidzu, Echizen, and the son of the Regent assassinated at Yedo in 1860. Some of the Tycoon's household troops were also assisting, for the Tycoon has a palace at Miaco as well as at Yedo. The attacks of the assailants were chiefly directed against the respective citadels of the Tycoon and Mikado, from both of which they were finally repulsed, but not until the Mikado's outermost buildings had been sacked and destroyed. The assailants were overpowered, driven back, and cut to pieces, few of them escaping.

The consequences of this hand-to-hand fighting in the heart of one of the most populous cities of the world produced a destruction of property unparalleled in modern warfare. The shells of both assailants and defenders exploding amid the crowded buildings set fires in many places, which caught up by a high wind then blowing, raged unchecked until the populous city was reduced to ashes.

According to the native accounts, the fire raged two entire days, laying in waste nearly one thousand blocks or squares, destroying seventy-eight thousand houses and temples, and three thousand seven hundred ware-houses. About five-sixths of the city was in ashes and we may imagine, though words cannot describe, the scene of devastation which made half a million people homeless. Japanese houses are not al-

together such paste and paper affairs as the burners of Kagosima would have us believe. A very large portion of the European peasantry are sheltered by no better. The great temple of Hun-quan-gee, the most famous in the empire, was burned.

The young Prince of Nagato was about to renew the attack with increased force, when the affairs at Shimonoseki intervened, and we shall probably hear no more of it.

Now that Chosiu has been thoroughly humbled by foreign arms, we wait to see what good shall come of it. If it will lead the Japanese generally to see that trade and intercourse with foreign nations, however disagreeable, is a fixed necessity, and how futile any resistance will be, we may rejoice that the lesson has been taught them with so little bloodshed.

Sunday, October 16, 1864

Ida D. Rogers arrived.

Wednesday, October 19, 1864

Today there was a review of Japanese soldiers near the Governor's residence. I was not present, but the scene is described as having been very unique. It was a drill with native arms.

Thursday, October 20, 1864

This morning there was a drill of the English forces stationed here, which was got up more particularly in return to the Japanese for their display of yesterday. A council is now holding here between the native and foreign officials, and some high dignitaries of the government are present, among them the commander of the forces. These were on the parade ground today first as spectators and afterwards going through their own drill. There were less than 200 of them, most of whom were clad in the suits of chain and plate armor and gorgeously appareled in silk robes. There were men on horseback in complete armor with their attendant esquires. Burnished helmets and gilded casques shone in the sun, the spearsmen and swordsmen and bannerets were picturesquely grouped about the knights on horseback. On the balcony of a foreign house overlooking the field were several foreign ladies, and every one could not help feeling the resemblance to the olden days so quaintly discussed by Froissart and other chroniclers. Here was a squire holding his master's helmet, another "iron clad" warrior was leaning on his spear, there were bareheaded youths with a scarf of white cotton knotted about their heads. The scene was theatrical in the extreme, and their exhibitions not less so. The word of command was indicated by a wand of paper cut into strips which as it was shaken in the air, or thrown to one side or the other, indicated in some mysterious manner the order to be obeyed. The theatrical effect was heightened by seeing such small forms clad in such heavy suits as though children were playing with their father's garments. There was no conformity in their dress, each one wore such armor or no armor at all, as best suited his fancy. Some wore quilted cotton robes which alone would give no little resistance to spear, arrow, or sword, and I observed that nearly all who wore chain armor wore underneath quilted garments that added greatly to its efficiency of protection. It was the 14th and 19th century suddenly brought together, in one part of the field were battalions of modern troops armed with terrible efficiency for modern warfare, in another part, far gayer and more strikingly costumed were represented the long disused modes of ancient warfare. For a holiday purpose their's was the showier, for actual service who could doubt. One knight in a suit of burnished black armor and black bossed helmet from which two gilt horns ascended in a crescent might have stood for the Black Prince of Poitiers. Another knight had on a sumptuous armor of massive gilded plates which nearly crushed him to his saddle. Stuck in his belt at his back was a staff supporting over his head a small banner. The political significance of the affair was perhaps the most important, after all, that English and Japanese soldiers should be drilling in the same field in great friendliness. When the native drill was over the English soldiers, to the number of 1500 or more, gave three rousing English cheers and the camp broke up.

Friday, October 21, 1864

The moonlight nights of October have been very brilliant. On the 13th of this moon (9th Japanese) is the evening festival of (Tsooki miroo [tsuki miru]) or "Moon Sight." It is the day of the full moon, and the evening is given to social festivity, parties sit on the balconies overlooking gardens, or the water, where the moon falls brightly, and with dancing women, feasting, and drinking, pass the night away.

Saturday, October 22, 1864

Boat excursion to Mississippi Bay. Capt. Tilden of the 20th Mass. is our guest. A lovely Indian summer day.

Thursday, October 27, 1864

My birthday anniversary. A charming beautiful day it is. I might be disposed to moralize over advancing years, did not a cold in the head render me too stupid for any reflections. My sister E[liza] at home, who never forgets these anniversaries, thinks of her brother away today. One more in Japan, the next, with God's blessing, in America. Reception at Lady Alcock's this evening.

Friday, October 28, 1864

At Lady Alcock's reception last evening. A large assembly, scarlet with uniforms, glittering with decorations, a few ladies, more punch and chocolate ice, music by the *Euryalus* band, and "God Save the Queen" at 11 bids us depart. On the whole pleasant, our lady and lord receiving very pleasantly and with no restraint.

Teahouses in Yokohama.
Photograph by Felice
Beato.

Tuesday, November 1, 1864

The *Nepaul* which left this morning with
1850 bales of silk, value $1,000,000, struck a
rock in Uraga channel and returned leaking
badly. A good deal of silk injured.

Monday, November 14, 1864

General Pruyn gave an exhibition of top
spinning today to invited guests. The adroit-
ness of the spinners was very fine. Perhaps the
most curious feat was spinning the top on a
closed fan which the performer opened and
fanned himself with while the top was in rapid
motion. The fan proved to be quite an ordinary fan, possibly a little stiffer than usual,
with the edge bound with gilt paper in the
usual manner. The most pleasing feat was
spinning a top in a cup of water which threw a
handsome jet through the top of the spindle.
He also spun a top on the edge of a sharp
sword handed him by one of the spectators,
though he had several failures before he succeeded. The top spun and traveled from hilt to
point and back again. He also spun a top on a
small card, but what was more curious, he
would throw the top up, catch it in the angle
where spindle and wood meet, where nicely

balanced the top seemed to lose none of its ve-
locity, but was repeatedly tossed up and caught
in like manner. Again the top was nicely spun
on the tip of a small hen's egg, and more difficult still, was taken off the egg by a small
spoon-like instrument without impairing its
balance.

The two feats which were most pretentious
were these, first an inclined plain made by two
parallel bars led up to a small temple placed
against the wall. The temple being four feet or
so higher than the base of the plain and eight
or ten feet distant. The parallel bars were interrupted at one point by a fall of a foot, and
again at a little interval by a rise of a foot. The
top was set in motion and turned on its side so
that the spindle rested on the bars and the
wood between. The spinner let go his hold and
the top sprang up the stairway, or plain,
leaped down one declivity and up the ascent,
passed through a gate, and knocking open the
doors of the miniature temple, entered. While
within, out of sight, it turns to a right angle
from its entrance, makes its exit into a miniature garden, comes out of the garden gate,
travels three feet and leaps down upon a drawbridge which no sooner feels the tread than it
springs up and throws the top into a little
tower passing in by a curtained window. This
tower is a foot or so above the temple level.

While within, the performer turns the tower with a bamboo rod in his hand by a sudden tap, when out pops the top at a right angle from its entrance, descends an inclined plain of a few feet, enters a summer house, makes another turn, comes out, proceeds a little way on to another drawbridge which rises, tosses the top into another miniature temple on a level with the tower and also against the wall, emerges at a right angle, enters another temple from which it again emerges at a right angle and descends a long walk which is interrupted by two arched bridges over which it crosses and finally drops off its walk into the performer's hands having made a circuitous travel of thirty or forty feet.

Again the top is set in motion, climbs a like parallel plain and enters the top of a castle surmounted with a belfry and clock face. This castle belfry stands three feet high and the industrious top is heard within leaping down one stair case after another, while at each fall the bell strikes one, then two, then three, on up to eight, when lo! the spinning traveller emerges from a corner opposite to that which it went in, through the arched doorway of the castle and runs across the walk to his master's hands again.

There were other feats such as spinning some huge tops, one of which would weigh forty or fifty pounds, spun by a loose cotton cable as large as my arm.

The butterfly trick was given, and a clever trick with a cup of water and some white sheets of paper transmuted into pictures after the cup had been inverted on the paper.

The performer was attended by a little girl whose quaint ways and music on the shamisen added to the interest of the entertainment.

[On November 15, 1864, Hall sent the following letter to the *New York Tribune*, which was published on February 15, 1865.]

The affair of Shimonoseki was not without its effect on the minds of the Japanese rulers.

The smoke of the battle had hardly cleared away before the combined fleet was followed back to Kanagawa by envoys from Prince Chosiu, bearing handsome gifts to the ministers of the treaty powers, with assurances of his desire for future peace. Here at the same time the Japanese Governors of Foreign Affairs were daily closeted with our representatives in putting into set terms the concessions they were prepared to make through virtue of Enfield and Armstrong persuasion.

The first benefit derived was that the passage of the Suwo Nada or "Inland Sea" was declared free, and its passage has since been repeatedly made without further molestation.

The next was that foreign export trade was at once relieved of all those government impediments and restrictions which for now some months past had palsied the commerce of Yokohama and threatened to break up every mercantile establishment.

Raw silk, which had become nearly as *rara avis* as a silver dollar in the United States, came down again from Yedo, in such quantities, that not only did a single vessel bear away a million dollars worth at a trip, but it was followed at short intervals by other cargoes nearly as valuable.

Thus the Japanese Governors who had been so industriously lying for the year past, that the suspension of trade was no fault of theirs, now, with an effrontery equally unblushing admitted the falsehood, acknowledging that they had forbidden the sale of raw silk to foreigners, "because it gave displeasure to the anti-foreign party in Japan." The guns of Shimonoseki aroused them to the conviction that there were others to be considered besides the treaty-breaking Princes of the Empire.

After all is said, some allowance must be made for the peculiar position of the Tycoon, threatened by foreign arms from without and by anarchy and civil war within. It would have been better for him to have ventured the honest game, but oppressed by his difficult situation, which threatened destruction on either hand it is not so much to be wondered at that a semi-barbarous court should have temporized with its difficulties, hoping to see them removed by some chance stroke of good fortune. For these and other reasons which will appear, the final settlement of the foreign representatives with the Tycoon's Ministers is open to a degree of censure, as one which, while securing no additional safeguards to our personal safety in the empire, was not as respected other matters worthy our forbearance and generous clemency. What we need most of all is security for our personal property, and unrestricted freedom of trade as guaranteed by the treaties. Whereas the terms prescribed were simply and severely punitive.

The terms on which the Tycoon purchased peace were, beside some minor matters, such as wordy promises to keep the treaties and additional grants of building sites at Yokohama, these, the payment of an indemnity of three million of dollars, to be divided *spolia optima* among his victors, or the opening of a new port—the Tycoon to have his choice of the alternatives. These conditions are, moreover, subject to the approval of the Home Government, who, I hope, will reject the one alternative as a needless and the other as an exorbitant demand.

As to ports, we have three already unopened which were by treaty to be opened, and because our difficulties were already sufficiently great with securing ourselves at those we have opened, to both the Japanese and us the opening of a new port would bring only increased complications; and whatever might have once been deemed best, few now would advocate the opening of a new port until affairs are arranged on a more solid basis with this Government. But our wise diplomats have no expectation of a new port. Severe as the payment of three millions would be to the Japanese, they know they will strive to meet it rather than to further embarrass themselves by the opening of a great port like that of Oasaca. Thus the alternative presented to the Japanese is like that of the highwayman's—"Your purse or your life." He has no more doubt as to which will be

chosen than had the foreign representatives when they put their hands at the throat of the unfortunate Tycoon. If the indemnity was more needed, let it have been an indemnity—one reasonable in amount, considering that it was a rebel against the Tycoon as well as against us whose aggressions were the pretext for demanding any indemnity. But there is a secret history of those negotiations which renders this demand even more shameful to the negotiators. It is this:

The foreign representatives came into Council, a ruling majority of them prepared to demand two millions as a first equivalent; a moiety of which was to go to the English, and justly so, for England had borne the brunt of the affair, and the balance was to be divided among the Dutch, Americans, and French, the latter taking the lion's share. But alas! for this well digested plan. French jealousy was aroused, and not a dollar less would France receive than fell to England's share. "It was a question of recompense to outraged national dignity, not wages for service rendered." If so, will money heal a torn and bleeding dignity, or is the healing in proportion to the size of the medicating plaster? If so, were the United States most of all entitled to the larger heap of shining dollars, and Holland next? These two could, without offense, be kept out in the cold that the pair of loving allies might be kept warm.

How was this hitch avoided; by a redivision of the demand which had been agreed as the first thing! By no means, to the shame of all such diplomacy be it said poor Japan was made the victim of this disagreement, and a fresh million was demanded and wrung out of their victim. It is for this, especially, that those who have suffered most and longest from Japanese ill-kept faith still earnestly hope that the Home Governments will repudiate the arrangement for one which shall better show that we know how to temper justice with mercy.[24]

But there is a consideration beside that

[24] Unfortunately the $3,000,000 indemnity was not repudiated by the home governments as Hall hoped

and became an overwhelming financial burden not only for the Tokugawa regime, to whose downfall it contrib-

of fair play. The fine was an impolitic one. For the imposition of a three million indemnity on Japan is an imposition of a three millions tax on the foreign trade! No one at all conversant with Japanese affairs will deny this. The tax is at last to be paid by England, France, Europe generally, and the United States. It comes in the end out of our own pockets, first, by the depreciation of the dollars we bring hither, so that the Yedo mint can coin them into the local currency at a seigniorage of 25 to 33 per cent. Since this agreement was entered into, the dollar has fallen an additional seven per cent, so that we see it depreciated from its standard value of 311 Ichibus, as per treaty, to 215 Ichibus. Count for yourselves what this difference will yield on a yearly importation of ten millions of silver dollars. A gain of, in round numbers, $30 in every hundred brought hither. How long will it take Japan to pay an indemnity the treaty powers may see fit to demand?

Again, this three million indemnity is a mortgage on the productive industry of the country, to be paid out of our pockets in enhanced prices for every article we buy for export or consumption. Already the peasant complains of new imposts on his coal, his firewood, his rice, his wheat, and his cotton, to secure the growing expenses of the Imperial Government through foreign intercourse.

Meantime, what are the foreign Ministers themselves doing while thus imposing a heavy burden on the foreign trade with this country. These ministers, consuls, admirals and officials of every grade are receiving a yearly subsidy from the Japanese Government doubling or trebling the salaries they receive from their own Government. And how is this subsidy to be paid. I have already said that the dollar is depreciated as toward the local currency 25 to 30 per cent from its standard value, but the foreign officials are allowed by the Japanese the privilege of exchanging monthly a certain sum of dollars with the Government broker at the standard value. The Minister, consul, admiral, or whoever he may be, resells this native coin to the foreign merchant who must have it for trade purposes, and who is blessed with no such diplomatic privilege of exchange, at the round profit aforesaid of thirty dollars in the hundred. The amount thus exchanged by foreign officials doubles and trebles their salaries as I have before said. Do the astute Japanese suppose they get no return for this favor? Is it wholesome for the purity of official intercourse that a diplomatic representative should receive from the sovereign to whom he is accredited *twice the salary* that he gets from the country that sent him thither? Yet these be the stern facts.

But as ill fate would have it, an avenging Nemesis already threatens the exacting convention of our representatives. The Tycoon's Ministers glibly promised the sanction of the Mikado, or Spiritual Emperor, to this arrangement for the settlement of our troubles, past, present and prospective; but within the past day or two it creeps out that the Mikado has refused to ratify this arrangement, as he might have done one more liberal. Nay, the very forces ordered with so much flourish to proceed against Chosiu have been found so unwilling for the work that the Tycoon fears lest their swords should be turned against himself. Thus at this very hour all the gain we made by the shedding of some blood and the burning of much powder at Shimonoseki threatens to be lost for want of a greater magnanimity in our subsequent councils. We

---

uted, but also for the new Meiji administration. After numerous delays in completing the payment schedule the indemnity was finally paid off by the Japanese in 1874. The United States received in total $785,000 as its portion of the settlement. Never fully comfortable with this indemnity, which far exceeded American damage claims, Congress decided in 1884 to return the $785,000 to Japan. It should be added, however, that interest on the fund had increased it to $1,839,533 by that year and the remaining sums went into the U.S. treasury. The Japanese used the returned funds to construct the breakwater in Yokohama harbor. See Payson J. Treat, *The Early Diplomatic Relations between the United States and Japan, 1853–1865* (Baltimore, Md.: Johns Hopkins University Press, 1917), pp. 412ff.

are not to-day one whit better assured of our continued trade or our personal safety than before this unfortunate convention.

Tuesday, November 22, 1864

We have tidings this morning of the murder of two officers of the 20th Regiment near Kamakura. So far as we can learn the men were attacked on the highway from Kamakura to Yenosima and cruelly hacked to pieces with the usual marks of Japanese atrocity. From the peaceful character of the men, the attack is supposed to have been wholly unprovoked. One of them still grasped a pistol in his hand, the barrel of which (one cylinder) had been discharged.

The affair creates less than the usual excitement, perhaps because these assassinations have become so frequent.

The heavy payments of money before exacted, the terror of Shimonoseki, have not made life one whit more secure. It is doubtful if any security can be effected except by such measures in terrorism as would shock quiet peoples living in English homes, who would say, "how cruel." Yet is it not as well that some innocent, even of the Japanese, should suffer as that innocent foreigners should continue to be butchered.

Thursday, November 24, 1864

Thanksgiving day. Dr. H[epburn], Dr. V[isscher],[25] Lieut. R., I. S. B[lydenburgh], Esq.,[26] Mr. J[oseph] H[eco], and H. A., Jr.,[27] dined with me.

The remains of Major Baldwin and Lieut. Bird were buried today with imposing military ceremonies. The 20th Regiment escorted, Minister, Admirals, Consuls, Captains, etc., were present in full dress. The procession presented a striking appearance as it wound down the hill and among the green woods of the cemetery. Drawn up in a semicircle on the slope of

the hill three vollies were fired by the 20th over the grave of their late officers and the pageant was over. These men make the ninth victims of native atrocity buried in our midst, two more are buried at Yedo.

The inquest now going on throws some light on the affair of the murder. The men are now supposed to have been down the avenue from the temple of Hachiman near the sea sketching, and were surprised by their assailants as they were remounting their horses to ride away. It is supposed the assailants were only two. A hat has been found near the spot with a letter in it, which, it is hoped, may give some clue to the assassins. It came out also that one of the victims, declared to be Lieut. Bird, lived until 2 A.M. of the following morning and spoke, calling for water, and other words which the natives did not understand, offering them also money. As his body was found with a sword cut deeply severing his neck and cutting in two the spinal column, the inevitable suspicion arises that the poor fellow survived his first wounds and in the dead of night received the additional blow. But from whom? He should have been under the guardianship of imperial officers. The Governor of Yokohama was apprised of the fact, as he himself says, at 9 P.M., and, now it is said, to [have] known that had the foreigners been promptly apprised of the affair one of the victims might have been seen yet alive.

Wednesday, November 30, 1864

The hard work of the mails has brought me down with an attack of neuralgia so that I am scarcely fit to be about.

[On November 30, 1864, Hall dispatched the following letter to the *New York Tribune*, which was published on February 15, 1865.]

I laid down my pen a few days ago, not

---

[25] Dr. C.H.D. Visscher is listed in *The Chronicle and Directory for China, Japan and the Philippines for 1865* (Hong Kong: Daily Press, 1865), p. 239.

[26] I. S. Blydenburgh is listed as a member of Smith, Archer & Co., ibid.

[27] H. A., Jr., was Henry Allmand, Jr.

View near Kamakura where Major Baldwin and Lieutenant Bird were murdered. Photograph by Felice Beato.

thinking that I should have occasion to take it up again before the mail's departure, or that I would have the sorrowful record, I am now called upon to write, read in the light of that just written.

Too soon have we been taught how vain are all arrangements with this treacherous race which compound blood for dollars, and hush up felony with a bribe. After a series of the most cowardly and atrocious assassinations ever known, and for which we have hitherto found no punishment except the taking of blood-money in full satisfaction, we have to record one more brutal, if possible, than any of its antecedents.

On the 22d inst. two officers, a Major and Lieutenant of H.B.M's 20th Regiment stationed at this port, while out on a short excursion in the country, were waylaid and murdered by unknown hands.

The blameless and quiet character of the victims, the circumstances so far as known or surmised, preclude any other idea than this, that they were without offense treacherously waylaid while momentarily off their horses, sketching in an avenue of trees, leading from the great temple of Kamakura to the sea side, an open highway, and maimed, wounded, and cut to pieces in the most frightful manner, were left for dead or to die. The scene of the murder was one with which we are all familiar, it being one of our favorite places of recreation.

Word came to town late in the evening of the 22d that two foreigners had been attacked at Kamakura, one of whom was dead and the other still living. Assistance was at once sent forward, but ere it arrived both were dead.

One was pointed out as having survived the assault from the middle of the afternoon until 2 o'clock on the next morning. As this one's body was found with a deep sword cut at the base of the neck completely severing the spinal column, a wound that must have been followed by instant death, the suspicion becomes a certainty that after living several hours from the first attack, some hand was found brutal enough to give him the last and mortal blow. The other had long been dead.

Their remains were brought to Yokohama and interred on the 24th instant with military ceremony, the Japanese Governor of Kanagawa and suite following the procession.

The British authorities are prosecuting with the best means in their power the search for the perpetrators. The Japanese authorities profess the greatest anxiety to discover them also—so they have done before, and if their endeavors are any less futile and a mockery than they have been found in every similar case hitherto, we shall all greatly rejoice. How much hope of success there is your readers can imagine, when out of a village of more than a thousand souls, within whose precincts this deed was done in the full blaze of day, where no foreigner could wander without being followed and watched by curious eyes, nobody knows anything of it! The men were found wounded to death, one calling for water, the only word he knew in Japanese, mutely offering them money for some assistance that was never given—this was all the villagers knew.

Thus we continue to pay our annual or semi-annual toll of human sacrifice to Japanese ferocity and hate, and yet no one is yet found wise enough or courageous enough to apply a remedy more befitting than compounding for a price in dollars, blood against gold.

In this connection it is well to mention that Sir Rutherford Alcock, the English Minister, is under orders for recall because of his furtherance of other measures of reparation against Japanese offenses than the taking of money. His departure will be universally regretted, as his long acquaintance with colonial life peculiarly qualifies him for the place he has, as a whole, so honorably filled. We shall have the consolation of knowing that he may be able to assist us more by his counsels to the Government at home than he could by his administration here.

Wednesday, December 1, 1864

The [Ida D.] Rogers left for California this morning and I feel relieved. I am an idle man today seeking only to recover from my fatigue.

Sunday, December 5, 1864

J.G.W. arrived.[28]

Thursday, December 16, 1864

It was announced yesterday to the foreign Ministers that two men who had been arrested as associates of the murderers of the English officers at Kamakura were to be executed this afternoon. According to the account of the Japanese Government officials these two men, who are *samurai*, were arrested within a few miles of Yokohama in an attempt to rob some farmers. They were ronins vagabondizing and demanded food and money of the farmers. On being refused they threatened the farmers that if they did not comply that they would "serve them as the two Englishmen were served at Kamakura." After their arrest, which the farmers and village people effected, they were examined by the Government officers here and confessed under torture that they belonged to a band of desperadoes who had for their object the assassination of foreigners and that although they had nothing to do with the Kamakura murders they belonged to the same association. This confession seems to have been sufficient to justify the Government in their execution as a show of their desire to punish all who lifted their murderous hands against foreigners, for Sir Rutherford Alcock had demanded of the authorities the arrest and punishment of the Kamakura murderers before his departure for England which was now near at hand. How much effect this demand had upon the minds of the Government officials in making this show of stern justice they best know, but knowing, as we also do, what these murderers have cost the Government hitherto in after fines and indemnities, bombardments, and burnings of cities, the opinion is common—universal—that the authorities might have strained a point to placate Sir Rutherford before his departure.

At all events, the men were publicly beheaded today in presence of a large body of

[28] John Greer Walsh, U.S. consul in Nagasaki and Hall's partner in Walsh, Hall & Co.

foreign spectators and three special witnesses sent thither by the British Minister. They were led out from the jail blindfolded and with their arms pinioned. The executioner had been for some time awaiting them and hurrying the preparations with a self-satisfied knowing look. These preparations were simple enough. Two holes were dug in the earth a little ways apart, and over the earth thrown out a mat was spread. By the side of the executioner was an attendant with a bucket of water. The executioner was a man of middle age who seemed to take pride in his office as he walked looking into the holes, adjusting the mats, feeling the keen edge of his sword, a long heavy two handed weapon with a rough bamboo handle, to secure a firm grip.

The first victim came forward and kneeled upon the mat facing one of the holes. He was a man apparently 28 years of age of robust habit and showing no signs of trepidation. The executioner bid him kneel with his head thrown forward and then, having with his own hand removed his clothing from the back of his neck, the attendant poured water over the sword blade which the executioner lifted aloft, poised it in the air for a second, when the glittering blade again fell with no visible impulse from the executioner's hand the head rolled into the pit prepared for it. The cut was a clean smooth cut, not staining the sword blade which passed through the neck so quickly that for an instant before the head dropped it was seen beneath the neck and withdrawn.

The second victim was a younger man by a few years with haggard face and evidently overcome with terror. He was carried out from the jail doorway and placed in position by the pit, and in another instant his head fell into its pit also, and the scene was over. So quietly was the work done and with adjuncts so little cruel or revolting that it seemed to have left small impression on the spectators of any brutality connected with the act or the witnessing of it. Few executions in any land could have been more decorous, certainly no public ones so much so.

Now that it is all over, few more beside the foreign Ministers themselves, express any satisfaction with the affair. They accept the facts, without questioning given them by the Japanese Government. But among natives and foreigners alike no one believes that these men had the slightest complicity with the murders of the English officers. They are declared to be old offenders who have justly suffered for other crimes, and who possibly in a mistaken moment made the threat as related, but were only "fools" not criminals "for doing so."

The Japanese authorities have posted in the public place announcements of the execution of these men, giving, as they say, the cause that they were implicated in the murders. If so, to the public the point has been gained that the Japanese Government show to their own people that they will execute their citizens for the murder of foreigners. If they execute men innocent of the crimes, the shame is ever the deeper to them.

Friday, December 24, 1864

Last evening it was officially announced to the British Minister that one of the murderers of the officers at Kamakura had been arrested and was now in jail. Sir Rutherford in his joy at the intelligence took off his watch and presented it to the head of the police who brought the news.

The man confessed the crime; says he had two accomplices, one assisted in the murder and the other kept a look out. They surprised their victims as they came long the road. Against those in particular they had no enmity. They had never seen them before. They believed it a proper thing to kill foreigners, and had selected that place knowing that foreigners made Kamakura a resort. It is hoped that the arrest of this man will lead to other discoveries.

Sir Rutherford Alcock left this morning by steamer en route for home.

Saturday, December 25, 1864

Many English residences are decked with Christmas greens and berries and the mast heads of the fleet bear evergreen branches. This is the land of Christmas greens and scarlet berries, of the latter there are many varieties and profusion of glossy green leaves.

Sunday, December 26, 1864

The brig *Jeannie* arrived today and Mr. Forbes is my guest.[29] General Pruyn, Capt. P[rice] of the *Jamestown* and Consul Fisher helped me eat a Christmas turkey.

Monday, December 27, 1864

Shimidzu Seji [Shimizu Seiji], the man arrested for the murder of the English officers was brought down from Yedo today for execution. At Yedo he has been examined under torture and confessed to the fact. He refused to give the name of his country, but it is generally believed that he is a Mito ronin. By his own confession he committed the murder with the aid of two accomplices, one of whom kept watch, while the others used their swords. His victims were men whom he had never seen before, and whom he killed because he believed it was a good thing to kill the detested foreigner. His accomplices and himself fled immediately after the murder, taking separate directions to avoid detection. Since that day, he has heard nothing of them. He was arrested at a small village near Yedo in a joroya.

The two men who were executed the other day had nothing to do with the murder, he said, but were "green" accomplices, whom he had picked up a few months ago, "craven fellows."

On his arrival at Yokohama he was confronted with witnesses from Kamakura who recognized him as one of the men who committed the murders. To the English officials who asked him if "he was truly the man who murdered the Englishmen," he said, "you may be sure there is no lie about that." His identification seems complete enough, indeed, the whole bearing of the bold man was evidence that he would not have condemned himself unjustly. Yet it is to be regretted that time was not taken to examine him fully, with the hope of obtaining some information of the much

talked of ronins of whom he was clearly an important fellow. The Japanese were anxious to hurry the execution because they said the man was so exhausted by torture that he was not likely to live another day, a great falsehood as the man's after appearance fully showed.

It was the desire of Col. Brown of the Regiment to which the murdered officers belonged and senior military officer of the court that his execution should be before the regiment, and a postponement of Seji's execution was demanded until the following day. This the Japanese declared impossible, as the next day was a great official holiday and proceeded with the arrangements for his execution.

The criminal was brought forth, seated on a pack horse, his arms piniered behind him, and was conducted through the principal street of Yokohama. He was escorted by a small force of Japanese infantry, a body of police, and a few Custom House officials. Before him was carried a banner made of a large sheet of paper on which was inscribed the offence for which he was to suffer, his name, age, and other personal particulars. This was repeated again on a board which was afterwards to serve as a monument where his head was to be exhibited. Crowds of people thronged the streets to gaze on the man's face who had become notorious by his foul crime. He had an indifferent air, gazing upon the crowd that followed him and laughing as if in scorn of their curiosity. As the procession proceeded he broke into song, reciting the improvised verses with a full clear voice. His quiet resolute eye, as well as his firm mouth and chin, showed his spirit. There was nothing of the craven about him. After making the circuit of the town he was led towards the execution hill near the Governor's residence. On the way refreshment was provided for him at a tea house, which he partook sitting on his horse and eating voraciously. He continued to talk at intervals giving snatches of what he had done, remarks upon the people and place, and showed the utmost courage in face of his approaching doom.

It was dark before the procession reached the place of execution and lanterns were lighted. I could not refrain from following the crowd to the spot. On arriving there we found

[29] Murray Forbes, the son of Robert B. Forbes who had built the *Jeannie* and who had been a leading partner in Russell & Co. in China.

on a small elevation girt with trees and facing a broad plateau the preparations for the execution; fires were blazing and lanterns were suspended from poles and crowds of people were standing about a shallow pit which was to receive the decapitated head of the malefactor. A mat was placed for the criminal to kneel upon while the executioner did his work, who stood nearby sword in hand ready to do his work.

For a long time we waited in the dark but the execution did not take place. It was a striking group, the prisoner bound, seated on his horse in the midst, the guard, the spectators. The blazing bonfires, the many colored lanterns, and the thick darkness beyond the circle. After a long delay it was understood that the execution would be postponed till morning at the urgent request of Col. Brown, and the crowd in little squads one by one began to go away, leaving others to await every possible chance of an execution.

A party of a half dozen of us started to come away together and we had a merry time plunging through mud and darkness, buying out a lantern shop, and having a race home. There was no execution this night.

Tuesday, December 28, 1864

This morning it was known the criminal was to be executed at ten o'clock and curiosity to see how this bold fellow would bear himself when at last face to face with death again attracted me in common with many others to the execution ground.

The arrangements were the same as the night before, the pit, the mat, the smiling executioner, the crowd of people. This morning was added a large body of the forces in garrison here, especially the 20th Regiment to which the murdered men had belonged. These men were drawn up on three sides of a square facing and flanking the execution ground. After considerable delay the prisoner was again escorted to the fatal spot, this time brought in a norimon. He seemed to be talking incessantly. As he stepped out of the norimon (one with bars and for criminals) refreshment was again offered him. It seemed an outrageous

mocking to offer to feed a man within a moment of his death. Perhaps the old truth was recognized that food and wine give courage. The prisoner drank a little sake, but seemed to care little for the food. This over he walked with a firm step and unchanging face to one side of the pit and kneeling down on the mat placed himself with an easy smile in the hands of the executioner and his assistants. A bandage for his eyes was brought. "No he said, spare me that, if I am to die before these foreigners, let them see that a Japanese knows how to die bravely for his country." Then lifting his head he exclaimed with slow loud tones and great force of manner, every look and motion of his face breathing defiance, "It is a disgrace and shame to Japan that she sees one of her own people dying for a foreigner." Then turning to the executioner he said in quiet tones. "Please do your work skillfully and quickly," and leaned his head forward over the pit stretching out his neck to the expected blow. It was a shuddering sight to see these men deliberately smoothing his hair up over his head and preparing his clothing away from his neck and shoulders to give the headsman a clear way. Once when all seemed to be ready, the man said, "wait," to adjust his position evidently, again all was ready and as the glittering sword descended there came one wild cry and all was over, though so unskillful was the executioner that two more blows were needed to complete the severance.

By the time the procession returned, at the gate of the Yoshida bridge leading into town the criminal's head was already exposed on a bench prepared for the purpose, there to remain for the public gaze for three days.

There were many white faces among the spectators as they rose up to depart.

Thus ended the career of a man of whose antecedents little was known. It was manifested that he was a man of education as education goes in Japan and no one could doubt that they had at last seen a real ronin, and all felt if there were many like him, active, bold, and unsparing, foreigners held their lives here in no small danger.

Many things were said by the prisoner worthy of record, and the officials have furnished his written confession which is to be published, and which I shall preserve for anyone who is curious to know more of this man.[30]

[30] Hall does not include Shimizu Seiji's "confession," but his friend Rudolph Lindau, who wrote a lengthy account of Shimizu's execution in his article, "Account of the Murder of Major Baldwin and Lieutenant Bird," does include it. For Lindau's account see M. Paske-Smith, *Western Barbarians in Japan and Formosa in Tokugawa Days, 1603–1868* (Kobe: J. L. Thompson & Co., 1930), pp. 365–85. Paske-Smith lists Lindau as Robert rather than Rudolph. The translator of the article was a Miss Hall.

1865

Sunday, January 1, 1865

A wet disagreeable day for New Year's. Our English friends are making calls, also the Germans and French. The Americans are waiting for tomorrow.

Monday, January 2, 1865

Rained heavily all the morning but by noon the sun came out and the roads dried sufficiently for New Year's callers to get around. Made many calls with J.G.W.[1]

In the evening Consul Fisher gave his annual New Year's party which was very brilliant.

Friday, January 6, 1865

I see it related in the papers that the Empress of China has issued an edict that "Since thanks are due to the gods for their aid in putting down the rebellion in China it is or-

[1] John Greer Walsh, Hall's partner in Walsh, Hall & Co.

dered that the Board of Rites be directed to inquire into the relative merits due to the different divinities."

Thursday, January 12, 1865

The sunsets are now extremely beautiful. Fusi and the chain of peaks that bound our south-western horizon are covered with snow, and after the sun has gone down their glistening outlines stand out in clear relief against the golden sky with all the sharpness of a silhouette profile. It seems as if a lambent flame played behind the mountain tops and sent its glow along the sky. It is wonderful, too, what a beautiful light is shed over the landscape and the waters of the bay in which every object stands out with a clearness not apparent in the broad glitter of day. The hulls and spars of the shipping show every line with minute distinctiveness. The twilight fades away, and an ashen gray steals over the white houses, a cloud of night comes up out of the eastern horizon and folds all in its mantle. But again the moon, now at its full, rises over the waters of the bay. The western mountains are lost, and we have now the wooded shores of Kanagawa and the restless waters of the sea in our horizon, bathed in no longer a golden light, but the silvery gleam of the moon.

Thursday, January 19, 1865

An old grey-beard physician who was in the compound today told me that when he reaches a century of years, as he expected to, he would be supported by the Tycoon according to custom. The old man, now over seventy and very hale and hearty, seemed to think it would be a great honor to be thus fed at the Emperor's hand. His father had lived till ninety, and his grandmother died at 103 years of age, thus being of long lived stock, he counted on his century very strongly.

I learned sometime since that it was the custom that a mother who had given birth to three children at once should be cared for by the state and supported by the imperial family.

Friday, January 20, 1865

In Japanese suits for collection of debts which are held before the local *nanushi* or the Yedo Governors, *machi bunios* [machi bugyos], the complainant is debarred interest from the commencement of the suit.

[On January 21, 1865, Hall sent the following letter to the *New York Tribune*, which was published on May 13, 1865.]

My last letter gave your readers some account of the murder at Kamakura of the English officers attached to the 20th Regiment in garrison at this port. It appeared when I wrote as if this affair was to take the course of the many that had preceded it. There were the customary protestations of regret on the part of the native officials, the old promises to be diligent in search of the offenders were renewed, but so often baffled as we had been before, they were no longer trusted.

It is indeed, gratifying for once to say something commendatory of an honest purpose in our Japanese rulers; an honesty begotten of policy if you will, but in the work it has wrought none the less gratifying. Briefly, then, after fourteen foreigners have been killed and several more been wounded out of our little community, at the hands of Japanese assassins, during the brief six treaty years of our intercourse with this people, we have at last a murderer brought to justice.

Fortunately, without doubt, for the good issue of this affair, Sir Rutherford Alcock, the British Minister, was on the eve of departure for England, and he duly represented to the Japanese Government their embarrassed position if he returned to his country bearing news of this fresh outrage, and their inefficiency to prevent or punish the oft recurring wrongs of this kind. The Japanese beside had freshly in their minds the cost to them of their former supineness and with all these influences bearing on them seem for once to have abandoned their traditional policy of procrastination and a barren display of zeal that brings no fruit. They promised unsparing efforts to ferret out the assassins, and set at once to work about it. And now the sequence of events unraveling the whole story of this double murder, thread by thread, proves the truth of all we have heard of the thoroughness of Japanese espionage, proving also that the same exertion on the part of the Government before would have produced a like result. It convinced us, moreover, if we needed convincing, that it was no idle boast of the Japanese people that the murderers of Heusken, of Camus, of Richardson, and others, were well known to the Yedo Government, and that it could at any moment have laid its hand upon them had they seen fit to do so. In Heusken's case especially (the late Secretary of the United States Legation) the midnight murder was a matter of open jest and boast.

An examination into the Kamakura assassinations was promptly begun by the native authorities and the British Consul, Dr. Winchester, who is deserving great credit for the zeal and intelligence that accompanied his labor.

On inquiry witnesses were found who saw the murdered officers before life was extinct; others who saw their murderers in wait by the roadside prepared for the fray. The priests of the great temple of Hachiman in whose avenue of century-old pines the bodies were found, remembered two men armed with swords who worshipped at their temple a brief interval before the assault. A boy and girl who came upon the assassins as they lay in wait for their victims were warned off as "something horrid was [a]bout to happen." A peasant in the field heard the noise of the attack and looking up from his work saw a man with a drawn sword running by the side of a mounted foreigner dealing blows as he ran, till the foreigner fell from his saddle. The deed itself was clear enough; the unsuspecting officers were riding home from a pleasure trip in the country, when, without having given any provocation, they were surprised by men in ambush and slain. Their assailants had escaped, leaving no clue behind except a lost shoe or wooden clog, and a hat with a letter in it which have no individual information.

Fortunately the native officials were faithful in their work and traced the fleeing men, or one of them, to a neighboring village where he had supped; they discovered where he had crossed the River Rokingo, on the road to Yedo, at an obscure ferry. The sellers of the shoe and the hat were found in a quarter of the city of Yedo frequented by the north country ronins, or outlaws. Here the trail was for a time lost, and if the murderers had used ordinary discretion they would probably have escaped.

A few days subsequently at a village thirty or forty miles from Yedo on the road to Oasaca, three armed Japanese entered the house of a wealthy farmer, and with threats of violence robbed him of a large sum of money. The robbers were followed and two of them were arrested; the third, after a severe struggle, escaped. On examination of these two under torture they denounced their escaped associate as their leader, and as one of the men who committed the Kamakura murders. The native police were thus put on the murderer's track again, and did not relinquish it until, by one step and another, they tracked him to his hiding place in a village a little way out of Yedo. Thither he frequently came to meet his mistress. With her the authorities soon came to an understanding for his betrayal. On a given night he was applied with sake until suspicion was blinded, when he was seized by the native police, though not without a desperate struggle, and handed over to the officers of justice. Meantime his two accomplices in the robbery had been tried, condemned to death, and publicly beheaded at Yokohama.

This man, Seiji, boldly confessed his crime. He said that he had been long inspired with the desire of killing foreigners as a meritorious act toward his country. Twice before he had made the attempt to carry this idea into execution. Once he had been betrayed by an associate, but made his escape. At another time he drew his sword upon a party of foreigners at the entrance of Yokohama from the *Tokaido*, but was foiled by their drawing their pistols in defense. After these unsuccessful efforts, fearing detection if he lingered about Yokohama, he went to Kamakura, where he heard foreigners frequently came.

On arriving at Kamakura he met another *ronin*, whom "he found to be of the right stamp," and unfolded to him his designs. His new found friend heartily acquiesced. They visited the temple at Kamakura, and on coming out walked down the long avenue of pines toward the sea. As they walked they saw two foreigners approaching on horseback, and at once resolved on their destruction. They prepared themselves for the attack, and how successfully they accomplished their object we know. Immediately after the murder they fled in different directions, and he, Seiji, had not seen or heard of his accomplice from that day to this.

Short shrift was allowed the criminal. His arrest was heard of one day at Yokohama and on the next he was brought down from Yedo to be executed. He admitted to the English officers sent to examine him what he had already done to his own country officials, that he was indeed the murderer of Kamakura. He was then paraded through the streets pinioned and on horseback, after the manner of condemned criminals, and was followed by a large crowd of natives and foreigners to the hill of execution. It was already night when the procession reached the spot where he was reprieved till the following morning, in order that his execution might be before the 20th Regiment whose officers he had murdered. On the following morning he was again led forth to the execution ground still preserv-

ing the same bold, undaunted manner which had characterized his actions from the first. With clear, unbroken voice he sang songs as he rode through the crowds and before the pit which was to receive his head as it should fall beneath the executioner's blow. His last words were as he kneeled to the headsman's hand, saying to his countrymen in loud accents, "It is a shame and reproach that a Japanese should die for a foreigner." In another moment his head rolled into the pit and the fate of the outlaw was completed.

To all who saw the bold, resolute air of the man, and who heard his confession was present the thought that if our footsteps continue to be watched as we go out or come in by such fanatical assassins no one in Japan can count his life secure if he strays from the protection of the foreign settlement. This event has given the key to the many tragical affairs which have preceded it. Nor can we believe that with the death of Seiji have died out all the fierce outlaws who would compass our destruction if they could.

Sunday, January 22, 1865

The rumor is current that Chosiu has made terms with the Government by ordering three of his ministers, who have been most active in prosecuting the rebellion, to commit harakiri and afterwards sending their heads to the Mikado at Miako suing for terms.[2] It is alleged that from the first Prince Chosiu has been hostile to the revolutionary movement, but that it was fomented and directed by his son the Prince of Nagato.

[2] The three Chōshū elders, Masuda, Kunishi, and Fukuhara, were ordered to commit suicide on November 11, 1864, and their heads were delivered to Tokugawa Keisho, the commander of the 150,000 troops sent against them, at Hiroshima. The final settlement of the First Chōshū Expedition took place on January 24, 1865, with Chōshū's acceptance of the peace terms offered by the Tokugawa forces. As this entry indicates, Hall appears to have received word of this imminent settlement. For details of the Chōshū side of the story see Albert Craig, *Chōshū in the Meiji Restoration* (Cambridge, Mass.: Harvard University Press, 1961), pp. 247ff.

Wednesday, January 25, 1865

The Japanese are busy with their preparations for their New Year's holidays which commences tomorrow. The houses are being decorated in the usual manner, the shops are full of purchasers of New Year's gifts, and the shopmen make a great display of their wares, evidently more for the purpose of ornament than to attract customers—for even the lumber dealers and the wood and coal merchants have their commodities brought to the street front and there symmetrically displayed in piles neatly laid up.

Last night at Benten there was a candlelight fair for the sale of all small commodities, domestic wares, household furniture, clothing, provisions, toys, confectionery, for I notice that Japanese New Year gifts really take the useful form. The cake and confectionery shops and the sugar stores have been very busy all day selling their wares neatly put up in small paper packets or ornamented boxes tied with the customary colored strings.

The kite shops, battledore shops, and ball shops, have the largest share of attraction for the juveniles.

Thursday, January 26, 1865

Dr. Lindau returned today from a week's visit at Yedo.[3] He reports the city is very quiet, though busy with holiday preparations.

As he was going into the city on his way up, he met a train of policemen and officers escorting a woman to execution. She was mounted on a pack horse, with pinioned arms, and with the customary board placard and paper banner detailing her name, birth place, age and crime, was going to her doom as we at Yokohama saw Seigi carried a few days ago.

Her crime was the murder of her husband in a fit of jealous passion. L[indau] describes her as being very coarsely clad with dirty disheveled hair and coarse hard features, a woman of less than thirty years old. She paid no attention to surrounding objects but was going doggedly and abjectly to her horrid fate, which was to be suspended on a crucifix by rope lashings and to have spears passed obliquely through her body from the lower ribs to the shoulders. Death follows the impalement speedily. What struck L[indau]'s attention particularly was that the sight of this woman going to such a fate attracted the merest passing attention from the numerous dwellers by the wayside, revealing that the spectacle was no strange one there, whereas a few days previous at Yokohama thousands had gathered to see the less melodramatic spectacle of beheading.

Friday, January 27, 1865

Japanese New Year's. Charming weather ushers in the New Year and our native friends are disposed to make the most of it. Today the callers are the official and two-sworded class and the street is alive with them decked out in their *kamishimos*, attended by servants, calling at friends' houses and paying visits in person or leaving their cards at the door, the latter more frequently the two-sworded class callers.

The streets were full of children in new and gay dresses wandering about from shop to shop making their little purchases of toys, cakes, sweetmeats. At nearly every corner is a pastry man who disposes of his sugary stock in trade by the lottery of wheel, or dice, or teetotum, and boys and girls surround them in groups laying down their own cash for a venture. Ruder groups are gambling in the less frequented thoroughfares at a sort of penny

---

[3] This was Rudolph Lindau who had just published his book, *Un Voyage Autour du Japon* (Paris: Librairie de L. Hachette et Cie, 1864), and who later published *Aus China und Japan* (Berlin: F. Fontane & Co., 1896). Lindau had been a good friend of the Walsh brothers in China and Nagasaki, had spent nearly a year in Japan in 1859–1860, and accompanied them on a trip to Hakodate, Yokohama, and Edo in 1861. Lindau later became a good friend of Hall's in Yokohama and subsequently went on to become a writer of some reputation in Europe. While in Yokohama Lindau was engaged in the publication of an "English and also a Japanese newspaper" (*Aus China und Japan*, p. 284) and for a time served as Swiss consul (*The Chronicle and Directory for China, Japan and the Phillipines for 1865*, p. 235).

pitch and toss game, while their elders are playing at hazard in larger sums at the street corners. In this street groups of tidily dressed girls with their mothers, aunts, or nurses are playing at battledore; the next is given up to the kite flyers, from the little toddler who is assisted to set his toy afloat in the air by his comrades, to the old grey-beard who renews his youth in juvenile sport. There are kites of all shapes, from one peers out the prim head of some old hero, divinity, or minister of fable, from another looks out more sweetly the almond eyes of a Nippon belle, bugs in paper, flying fans, birds and serpents flap in the faces of passing pedestrians, kite strings trip your feet, but it is Nippon carnival time and the boys and girls have the license of the road.

Nor are pious sites forgotten, favorite temples are visited especially by women and children, the bell is struck to draw the attention of a benignant divinity, the head is bowed, hands struck together, and a few words uttered, then the supplicant wraps a few cash in paper which is thrown into the offering box and the New Year is bravely begun.

The day passes by in spirit and ceremony, nor is feasting forgotten. The cook shops displaying their choicest viands, large and rare fish hang temptingly in the doorways. The sake shops display their fat tubs of rice-distilled liquor covered with ornamental devices, and there is a profusion of little covered tubs holding a quart or so each floating about in a reservoir of clean water ready to be filled at any customer's service.

Saturday, January 28, 1865

The New Year festivities go on with unabated vigor. Yesterday was the two-sworders' day, today the merchants and common gentry give and receive calls, while among the young folks kite flying, battledore playing, and toy purchasing is vigorous as ever.

Today the business year is opened, but only a show of business is made. The merchant makes some formal purchases and sales, and every trade in like manner makes a display of opening the New Year's business. None are more demonstrative in this than the public

porters and carters, and many a new cart is inaugurated on this day. These carts are drawn by men, several of whom usually club together in the ownership and use. These fellows were very busy today decked out in their holiday attire going to their merchant patrons to get a loading, which sometimes or generally would be of empty bales or boxes only. Other groups were carrying huge sticks of timber from the lumber yards, but the jolliest group was one drawing a cart on which was a plethoric sake tub bestrode by one of their companions. The tub was ornamented with the usual New Year insignia of rice cake, evergreens, and paper ornaments. The boatmen likewise went out on the bay rowing, shouting, and flinging iron cash into the water for good luck. Other boatmen were carrying their boats through the streets with loud demonstrations of joy. Towards night, reeling individuals in good natured inebriation were corkscrewing their way home. The farmers also made a beginning of the year's work by sewing seed in little patches. Others saddle their pack horses and ride them up and down the country roads as if going to market.

In the courtesan's quarter, a populous portion of our city, the holidays are none the less observed. The girls are presented with new dresses, sumptuously feasted, and for three days can, if they choose, cease their customary avocations.

The second day is rather more riotous than its predecessor. There is something after all cheerful in seeing a whole population so given up to their annual holidays. Whatever want or squalor there may be, it is all disguised today by new dresses and happy faces. Whatever their circumstances of life may be, few families fail to provide their children with an entire new outfit of dress from head to the new wooden shoes and socks on their feet. There is indeed poverty where this custom cannot be observed.

My friend Dr. L[indau], who has just returned from Paris says that a modest man who goes home from Japan desirous only to tell the truth, is listened to with no interest after the sensation stories of less scrupulous travellers. Says one gentleman to him, "how remarkably enlightened and intelligent those Japanese are.

I saw a returned visitor the other day who narrates that a Japanese came to one of the resident missionaries and said he 'wished to be converted.' Very well says the missionary, that I can do for you very easily, but I must first question you on the groundwork of your faith. Very well say the Japanese, I am ready. Whereupon the missionary propounds a great variety of questions taking in nearly the whole scope of theology all of which the catechumen answers satisfactory and the missionary says 'very well my friend you are now converted, but tell me where did you learn so much?' Oh, said the Japanese I have been reading so and so's works on theology naming the ancient and rare works of a father in the church and there I learned all." Dr. L. gives this story as an illustration of the intelligence with which people he met talked about Japan.

Sunday, January 29, 1865

The 3rd and last day of the New Year festivities, strictly speaking. Tomorrow the laborers begin to return to their work, the shops are re-opened, and business begins to flow in its wonted channels. On the 7th day there will be a general holiday again, but not so strictly observed by the laboring classes. And so there are occasionally days of observance of certain ceremonies until the 15th day of the 1st moon makes a final closing up of the New Year holidays.

[In January 1865 Hall sent to the *New York Tribune* the last two articles of his series "Farm Life in Japan." The first bears no date of composition, but the second is datelined simply "January, 1865"; they were published on February 3, 1866, and February 17, 1866, respectively.]

Besides the regular labors of the farm, in the production of staple crops, our Japanese farmer, like his congener in other lands, directs his eye to those adjuncts of farm labor which help "to eke out a comfortable living." Here is a sandy tract devoted to the growth of melons, the various kinds of which find an enormous consumption during the Summer months. In yonder sheltered valley bloom orchards of the apricot, plum and peach, around the farm houses stand the persimmon, orange, fig, and loquat trees. The fruits of the first three, with true oriental reversion of taste are prized green rather than ripe, and a sour plum steeped in a sourer pickle, is the morning phlegm-cutter. The persimmon is not our small and puckery globe of verjuice, but a large, luscious fruit, extra specimens of which will weigh a pound. A narrow tongue of land running into Yedo bay, a few miles from Kanagawa is famous for its pear orchards, where are orchards of many acres in extent, in which the pear-tree is grown as a standard to the height of four and a half to five feet, and then the branches are spread and trained horizontally, so thoroughly done, so evenly cut and trimmed that throughout the whole extent of these orchards a flat surface of foliage is presented to the eye, a natural trellis of posts, rafters, and leaves under whose shade an army might camp and sleep. The product of these orchards are russet pears, apple-shaped, of immense size, whose insipidity is in inverse ration to their bigness. About forty miles west of Kanagawa and equal-distant from Yedo, are the vineyards of Koshiu, where the native sweet-water grape is largely cultivated, being trained altogether on trellises. The supply of Yedo with these grapes, which is one of the few good fruits this country can boast, and of the still fewer which are ripened and prized as we prize fruits, brings to the grower an annual good result. It may be of consolation to our cultivators to know that in Japan, remote and tucked away in the furthermost corner of the globe, seagirt and isolated as she is, the May bug comes down in annual swarms on the vine-leaves, and the "stripedbug" devours the melon patches. The Japanese has an ally which he is too wise not to employ in his war against the predatory insect rovers. A little bird which breeds in countless numbers about his door finds no obstacle to an offensive and defensive alliance save in the housewife's pet grimalkin. The manufacture of wine from those grapes is an art wholly unknown. Grapes coated with sugar, as our confectioners do almonds, are in the Winter season an article of luxury, and considered worthy of being passed as gifts among the highest in the land.

There are other farmers who unite to their ordinary labors such manufactures as they or their households can pursue in the intervals of field labor. By far the finest farm buildings I have seen hereabout were those of a whisky-distiller, whose large and well-built house, numerous outbuildings, ample grounds girt with hedge rows planted with shade and ornamented with the gardener's best care, attracted by attention as I was riding by into the back country. I pulled my horse up at the gate for a minute's chat with the proprietor, who came forward to meet me and warmly pressed me to dismount and partake of his hospitalities. He seemed to take great pride in his snug establishment, told me that he was a distiller of rice whisky, for which purpose he bought up the surplus crop of the neighboring farmers, and though he did not tell me so, no doubt before the year rolled round resells their rice to them in the new form at a paying profit.

It was on the same excursion that another noon-day halt brought me to a little inn on the banks of the Suruga river, and to as clean and quiet a country inn as one would care to find. At one end of a range of cottage rooms I was provided with a neatly matted apartment overlooking the garden and the brawling river beyond; at the remove of a partition or two was what we so well know in the States as a "country store," where everything was to be had, from a horse's straw shoe to a silk robe; at one remove further was a farm kitchen and its appendages of servants, rooms, stables, granaries, and out-houses, showing that my thrifty host, on the banks of this mountain torrent, was successfully carrying out his tripartite profession of innkeeper, merchant, and farmer.

At the religious festival, held at a noted temple in a farming region, where it was my pleasure to be a witness of the crowd gathering from the adjacent country, all in their bright holiday dresses, and clearly caring more for the pic-nicing and drinking on the uncovered green sward than for the wearisome ceremonies that were dragging on in the temple, decidedly the belle of the occasion was a whisky-distiller's daughter from a neighboring village.

The farmers about the open ports are, as a class very small landholders, but in the interior, more especially near Miaco, the seat of the spiritual Emperor, we hear of large estates in the possession of a single family, whose Chief keeps up the state of a hereditary noble of smaller class, and appears in public wearing two swords, the badges of the privileged classes, and is followed by a train of armed attendants, a country squire with a country squire's importance in other and older days. These large estates and the privileges of rank accorded with them, were, we are told, the grants of former Emperors, in long ago days, and recompense for personal or public service. Here the old feudal customs of Europe are extant in many ways, and to-day the reward of merit in civil life or military service is the grant of certain lands, with the right to their incomes and the direction of its descent. A hereditary bestowal to be forfeited in like manner as it was gained, by disservice to the Imperial will. I have known one such family so decayed, however, that what was left of the ancestral acres barely sufficed to keep up the shabby old farm house and maintain the few servants who were attached to it, while its lord found the air of Yedo and its coast more congenial than that of his patronymic estate. Still the ancient spear and bow of the family hung conspicuous on the walls in the vestibule, as they had done for centuries perhaps.

The farmers as a class hold an intermediate rank in the social scale. Of all whose position is not hereditary, they hold the best place. It is from their ranks that the Government infuses new strength into the soldier caste and the grades of civil service are possible to conspicuous and well sustained merit. And in a land like this, where family alliances are the touchstone of caste, it is no misalliance for a noble to wed the daughter of the great landholder, and the proudest Chief in the land lifts to his side as concubine the farmer's daughter, by whose charms of person he has been captivated, and whose offspring may inherit all his rank and privileges. She may not be his wife, but she may be his "side-wife," as her title indicates, and may, as in patriarchal days, be his best beloved and the mother of his heirs. For, though other things being equal, the son of the real wife has precedence by custom, there is nothing to prevent the course of descent being directed, when interest or love, or pride, or natural incapacity or unfitness in the wife's children intervenes, to the children of the side-wife or even to an adopted son.

Among the humbler population of Japan the birth of female children is not regarded a misfortune as in China—a misfortune to be averted by infanticide. Here sufficient avenues for employment are not wanting. Beside the light labors of the farm and loom, the picking of tea, the culture of silk-worms, there is employment in many light manufactures, in the shops as assistants, saleswomen, keepers of the accounts, keepers of the purse, for more indolent, or unoccupied, or possibly more submissive husbands. Let our "social reformers" take heart that this is in conservative Japan—a place shut up and sealed up three centuries ago from the benign influences of occidental civilization!

The great towns make their continual draughts on the country also. The Yedo Yashkis, or palaces of the hereditary nobles, employ a large number of female servants and each mistress of such Yashki is surrounded by a bevy of maids whose idle and luxurious life is the coveted position to which many a simple country maid aspires, knowing in what arts and accomplishments she will there be educated, to the better adornment of her position. The tea-gar-

dens, the eating houses and inns, everywhere numerous, have their large demands also, to say nothing of that special class whose numbers are certainly not less in the general ratio than those of other countries. Thus it is that the foreign resident never hears any complaint of an excess of female population as he would in China, nor hears of a single instance of that unnatural crime which is there the remedy.[4]

The Japanese farmer holds his estate by a sort of copyhold tenure. The same glebe descends from father to son uninterruptedly so long as the rental is paid, and here, where adoption gives all, or nearly all, the rights of birth, the farmer need never be without a legitimate heir. The whole empire is divided into a few landholdings. First and largest of all are the imperial [shogunal] domains, then those of the greater or lesser daimios, then those of the *hatamoto* or official class whose service is always due to the reigning Emperor [shogun], and whose titles and estates are not hereditary, but dependent on the pleasure or caprice of the reigning monarch. These men fill all the places on the civil list owing military service as well, and are said to number sixty to eighty thousand souls.

Then there are the temple glebes, inalienable grants to temple-foundations by successive monarchs; the large estates granted to faithful followers, and those of the great farmers or landholding squires already named.

To all landlords, whoever he may be, the farmer pays in kind and the rates vary with the master as well as with the product of the soil. The tenants on the Imperial estates are generally regarded as the most favored, although their payment in kind on the rice crop is said to amount to 40 per cent of the annual yield. On the other hand, there are daimios like him of Matsmai on the island of Yeso, who stimu-

---

[4] It seems curious that Hall, who notes the existence of abortionists while living in Yokohama, remains unaware of the practice of infanticide, which served as a major form of population control in the latter half of the Tokugawa period.

late emigration from Nipon by offering "land to the landless"—or, at most charging them with moderate exactions. Thus it was that on this island in 1860 I saw what I have never seen elsewhere in Japan, a new village built upon a before uninhabited site.

Payment in kind has chiefly, often only, reference to the rice crop. This crop is to Japan what corn, wheat, and other grains are to other countries. Where there are rice lands the payment of this, at a fixed rate, usually remits taxes on all of the crops, though in some districts there is a small pecuniary compensation for this remission. In some principalities where rice is sparsely produced, the lord of the soil claims the whole of the rice. As a rule notwithstanding the heavy exaction of the landlord, it is better for the farmer to grow what rice he may, for rice is the one exchangeable product for anything else that Japan makes or produces. Where it is not interest, the terms of the lease make it duty, and no rice lands are neglected. Though the great burden of the rent thus appears to fall on the rice crop, other commodities do not escape. Tea, cotton, and silk, whether raw or manufactured, do not pass from the estate where they are grown or manipulated without paying a moderate tax to the lord of the soil, collected at established toll houses. So with the manufacture of salt and other articles.

While the planted groves of trees belong to the farm and the farmers who have nurtured them, the original forests of valuable timber belong to the proprietor, and are sold as wanted by his own especial forest guardians. Likewise the mines belong, on the imperial lands, to the Emperor, and in the principalities, to each petty chief exercising jurisdiction.

It is the duty of the lord of the soil to establish and maintain the public roads through his estate, to build and repair bridges, to protect the lands from encroachments of running waters, and to repair the ravages made thereby. The traveler about the country will occasionally pass a farm-house and outbuildings of a more pretentious character, whose entrance through the thick-set living hedge is by an imposing gateway. These may be the residences of large and thriving farmers, or, as is more probable, of the factor of the emperor, prince, or lord, to whom the particular estate may belong, and whose duty it is to oversee the lands and to gather in the rents. Large discretion is given to this factor, who is usually also the *nanooshi* or head man of the village, the local magistrate who sits upon and decides all neighborhood quarrels, and who may summarily arrest for offenses against the established order and deliver his victim to the district governor, or himself punish him for petty offenses. When seasons are unpropitious and crops fail, or misfortune befalls any household, it is for him to say what deduction and allowance shall be made in the annual rents. So long as he rules with fairness and justice there is no appeal from his magistracy. He was, when chosen, rather the chosen man of his neighborhood than that of his lord, for their expressed wish is usually followed. If he is a hard and exacting man, there is an appeal to the power above him, and cases are not wanting where justice being slow, the entangled peasantry have risen against their petty oppressor and with mild force expelled him from their midst. The lord of the soil listens patiently to his aggrieved tenantry, and is seldom found unwilling to do them substantial justice. On the other hand, the factor may be simply corrupt, one whose open palm is ever ready for that metallic anointing which infects him with a marvelous liberality toward the tenantry, and rents go down as his profits of place come up, so long as farmers and factors keep their mutual secret safe enough.

A residence of several years in Japan has more and more impressed me with the conviction that although the farming class in Japan submits like the patient ox to the laws, regulations, and customs imposed by the titled class above him, that same ruling class have a wholesome respect for his really independent position, and while they may inflict upon him ceremonious observances, seldom deny him substantial justice or trample upon his equally well established privileges. The Government to-day is as much of the patriarchal as the despotic character, whose laws, while severe, are protective, seeking to guard the interests of its subjects by the preservation of order and such public morality as their feeble moral sense recognizes and the quiet comfort of the mass of the people. Again and again have I stood in their valley hamlets where there were no signs but those of peaceful industry and content, each hamlet to all intents a little republic by itself, knowing little and caring less for the outside world; to whom a change of rulers or revolution in the State would have no significance as great as the death of their own *nanooshi* or head man—people who know no oppression because they feel none, whose lives have fewer disturbing elements, perhaps, than any other people on whom the sun in its daily revolutions falls.

The Japanese farmer is not unlike his kindred laborer in other lands, in certain characteristics peculiar to themselves. To the stranger who wanders among their quiet hamlets, seeing so much of worldly peace and apparent content, and certainly so little of poverty or distress, there seems to be nothing wanting to their rustic happiness. Yet our Japanese farmer also likes to grumble amid all his thrift. If you stop him at his labor to inquire after his crops and his prosperity, he leans on his mattock handle and tells you in language whose words but not their import is unfamiliar, how "hard it is for the poor farmer to get along in these times." The skies are unfriendly, although he has placed no end of straw ropes and paper streamers and other lucky devices about his patronymic acres; it is either too dry for his rice fields or too wet for his uplands, or the wind is mischievous, or later or early frosts do him harm, or the markets are dull; in fact he says "times are not as they used to be," and, "if they keep on he don't know how he's going to get on with an ailing wife and house full of babies," while, as for the taxes, they "quite eat him up!" The farmer's life, he is sure, is the hardest of all and having thus freed his mind, he goes on industriously at his work again, not wholly a long suffering and much abused man.

As a class the farmers have in Japan the same comparative good repute for a quiet and order-loving people; here, too public virtue is supposed to reside in rustic bosoms. In Japan, also, it is the town that is corrupt. Nor is this good character to the wholesomeness of rural life without some foundation. When Kanagawa was opened to foreign access, it was, as it is now, a large straggling town deriving its support from its situation on the great traveled road from Miaco to Yedo, gathering its gains out of the daily passing crowds. It had its large inns and tea houses, and other large establishments of less reputable character which so naturally spring up on the banks of such a stream of life. But these latter, by order of Government, were closed on the foreigner's advent, and with them ceased much of the patronage of the inns and tea houses also. The petty tradesmen, the fishermen themselves who daily vexed the sea with their nets lost their best customers, while the town itself, having been shorn of its former attractions to travelers, was threatened with decay. The inhabitants then resolutely petitioned the Government for the renewal of their former privileges and continuing to do so with the pertinacity of their prototypes of Ephesus who saw their craft endangered, their prayer was listened to so soon as the foreign population removed across the bay to Yokohama and Kanagawa was restored to its ancient uncleanly thrift. But this success was not effected without a struggle between the townspeople and the adjacent farmers. The latter counter-petitioned that Kanagawa might not be reinstated in its former privileges, urging their reasons that it was thence sprang disorder and corruption among their own children, and they begged that the temptation to wrong might be done away with forever, as it now had been done for a period of three or four years. Unfortunately the farmers, though aided by the discreeter portion of the villagers, fought their battle of good order in vain, and through old custom, solicitation, and no doubt bribery, carried the day against them. It is pleasant to make this good record of their efforts.

Such is our sketch of the farmer's life and labor for the year; we took him up with the opening Spring and we leave him with his twelve months' labor finished, still in that humble cottage and in those inherited fields whose little area is his whole world. He has vague ideas how the same sun which warms his planted seed into flower and fruit, and ripens his serried ranks of grain, carries also lite and blessing to a great world of which he is such a little atom, or that of the stars which shine at night into his secluded valley home have a much wider range than the hilly horizon he has known from boyhood. It was my father's cot for long generations before, here will I live and die, and here will my sons live in the long generations that shall follow and there shall, as there has been, be seed time and harvest, the rain and dew, and light, warmth, food—blessing: this is the sum of his existence, the simple thread on which all his being hangs.

Friday, February 3, 1865

The eighth day of the first moon. Age day, from which the age is counted—its annual increase. Also Bean day, from the superstition of throwing beans for good luck. (See under the 10th.)

Sunday, February 5, 1865

Walked to Mississippi Bay; found the plum trees in that vicinity in full bloom. The plum orchards at Soongita [Sugita] are now the resort of pleasure parties of natives, picnic parties.

Monday, February 6, 1865

Koorabiraki. See next page.

Friday, February 10, 1865

I have not heretofore rightly apprehended the custom of bean day. This day is the last day of winter and may fall before or after the New Year. Its place in the calendar is forced by the native almanac. The customs connected with [it] are among the oldest known to Japan. It is from this day, and not from New Year, that all date their ages, old and young, male and female. Just after sunset the youngest male member of each household, that is the last one who has reached his majority, *tosi otoko*, or, "year man," as he is called, goes outside and throws white beans against the house. This operation is supposed to drive away the demons of sickness and poverty for the year about to be entered on, and to keep the devil out (ongee) [oni]. To secure the house against the devil's reentrance the head of a sardine and sharp pointed leaf are placed over the lintels of the main entrance, or over the door. The dead eye of the sardine is supposed to own mysterious watchfulness and power. If the *ongee* escapes that, and tries to enter, the sharp point of the leaf pierces his eye and repulses him.

We have the custom of giving one as many strokes on his birthday as he has attained years. The Japanese on this day eats as many beans as he has completed years. Thus if a boy finishes his fifteenth year on bean day, he has fifteen beans to eat for good luck to his sixteenth. If the *tosi otoko*, the "year man," attains his majority (in Japan 18 years) on bean day it is a day of feasting and presents.

This custom is universal and is observed by the Tycoon as well as his commonest subjects. In the Tycoon's household one of his councilors of state has the duty of throwing beans against the imperial palace. And in every princely residence the office is performed by some official member of his staff.

The 11th day is Koorabiraki (Koora hiraku) [kurabiraki], which means, "warehouse opening." For this is the day that the great merchants and the princes who sell their surplus rice formally open their *kooras*, or warehouses, for the business of the new year. So this is a day of feasting among the tradesmen again, and is kept as a holiday.

The 20th is called (_____) [blank in original] and is also regarded as the closing holiday of all the New Year's holidays. Play and feasting are over and the sober business of the year goes on in fill stride. Even the battledores and shuttlecocks of the little girls are laid aside for the New Year, and kite flying is given up by the men and grey-beards to the boys whose season of kite flying lasts them till the genial airs of full spring, a month or so later, call them to other occupations.

Friday, February 17, 1865

On Thursday morning the atmosphere being very clear, Mr. Hogg[5] and myself went out upon the bluffs two miles distant overlooking the valley to get a view of the distant mountains. We were well rewarded for our pains. Fusi seen through a glass appeared in the transparent atmosphere to have come so near that the smallest moving object would be visible on its glistening snows. True, it was a delusion, but it was difficult not to believe that we could have seen a snowball rolling down its smooth surface. Mount Hiacone was even more grand with its rugged faces sprinkled with white. The old volcanic chasms were plainly perceptible, and one face was what, if it was not indeed an extinct crater, something much resembling it. The mountains to the right of Fusi were very plain in all their rugged broken heaped up cavernous outline. I doubt if a nearer view could have given so complete satisfaction as this distant one which gave us command of the whole at a glance.

Sunday, February 19, 1865

Today is a fete day at the old temple in the swamp near Yoshida bashi. Visited the temple in the afternoon and found crowds of natives going thither and all in their holiday clothes, and as usual women, girls, and children having the preponderance. The approach to one of the shrines within which priests were loudly vociferating their prayers was lined on either

[5] As stated earlier, Thomas Hogg was the U.S. marshal in Kanagawa.

side with beggars who were beating bells and drums and joining their voices in the chorus. One little shock headed dirty boy was the noisiest party. In the rear of the temple was a small stone image of Buddha which the devotees laved with water to propitiate good fortune. Some scrubbed the image with little brushes of straw provided for the purpose, touching that part of the body in which themselves were afflicted. One dame, who had rheumatism in her shoulders, scrubbed the stone god's arm to bring healing to her own.

Wednesday, February 22, 1865

Salutes fired in honor of the day. [Washington's Birthday]

Tuesday, February 28, 1865

Sharp earthquake in the evening while at Consul Fisher's. The peculiarity and frequency of earthquakes of late was the subject of conversation and the question was mooted if they were not ominous of something more serious. The shocks have had at times a suddenness of jar and been accompanied with an unusual roaring.

[On March 10, 1865, Hall sent the following letter to the *New York Tribune*, which was published on June 9, 1865.]

Not for a long time has there been such a period of quiet in Japan as at present, certainly not for the past two years. I allude particularly to the foreign relations of this country, and to foreign life in it. But I might almost extend the remark to the internal affairs of Japan as well. The clouds so long threatening, and which burst in a storm of fire first at Kagosima and more recently at Shimonoseki, have cleared away. The Japanese seem at last to have accepted our continued presence within their borders as a fixed fact, possibly as an inevitable evil, though we hope in the end they will discover the eventual good of our coming.

Their annual New-Year holidays have

just passed by, coming in our February. This is the grand settling-time of their year, when woe to the credit of the unfortunate tradesman who has not squared his books by prompt payments before the dawn of New Year's morning. During the last night of the expiring year, shops and stores are kept open till the light of the old year's lamp pales before the morning dawn of the new. One might readily call up at the sight Dr. Watts's well-known couplet,

"And while the lamp holds out to burn," etc., [The vilest sinner may return]

substituting the poor, hard-up debtor for the vile sinner in the application.

At no recent New-Year's time have our native friends appeared to close old accounts so readily or to show a better spirit of renewed enterprises. The disturbed state of affairs last year throughout the empire kept down the zeal of speculation, and consequently, while a business of less extent was done, it was remuneratively done. Few were ready to take uncertain engagements. Again, the wide-reaching demand for raw cotton at prices on an average quadruple of its customary value, put large profits into the hands of a far more numerous class of producers than the tea cultivators and silk-spinners.

So, as I have said, the Japanese settled up last year's accounts easily, with a balance to the right side, celebrated their round of New-Year festivities with unusual jollity, and looked forward into the open year with assured courage.

Two things embarrass the New-Year's opening trade—one is the always fluctuating value of the foreigners' imported silver dollar to the local currency, which fluctuation is chiefly owing to the immense currency exchange business, a monopoly of foreign resident officials, to their shame and the general injury of foreign trade. As I have before had occasion to say, this exchange monopoly is a favor allowed foreign officials by the Japanese, by which their salaries and places are doubled, trebled or quadrupled in value—a corrupt state of affairs which if understood in all its

influences for evil by the Western Powers would be at once and forever forbidden to the officials they send hither.

In the second place, the Japanese are not yet educated to the course of foreign trade. With them to have once received a great price for any article of export is reason sufficient why they should always demand it. Understanding well enough the law of demand and supply in their own internal trade, they are too ignorant of foreign affairs to see how the same law operates with their foreign customers. They look upon foreigners as men possessed of fabulous wealth which they are only too anxious to convert.

Thus it is that they have withheld, virtually, the entire cotton crop of last Summer's production, because they do not now get the price they once got and still expect; though more than treble old values have been at any time available to them.

Time will remedy all this. Grant only a continuance of the present quiet and the "hands off" of the native government, and commerce and its needs will give to Japan trade its normal development.

Not only could the common people on New Year's day rejoice in the happy turn of affairs, but their rulers had occasion for self congratulation. The expedition which the Tycoon launched against the Prince of Chosiu, of such formidable dimensions, has accomplished its purpose. It is many long years since Japan has witnessed such a warlike demonstration. The Prince of Owari, of the royal lineage, was the leader of the expedition, and around his standard were gathered the chief princes of the empire, each with his contingent of bowmen, spearmen, or musketeers, as they chanced to be armed. Oasaca was made the place of rendezvous, distant a few day's marches by land, and scarcely more than a day by the sea from Chosiu's principality.

While the clans were gathering at Oasaca, Chosiu became alarmed, and, dreading the outbreak of the storm, sent in proposals for terms, accompanying them as tangible evidence of his desire for peace with the heads of his three ministers, who were charged with the fault of having instigated his (Chosiu's) revolt. Other accounts place the affair in a less revolting shape, which say that the ministers, disgraced by the failure of their position, committed, according to time-honored national precedent, the self-immolation of *hara-kiri*, after which their heads were severed and forwarded to the court of the spiritual Emperor as tokens of submission. Perhaps our great arch-Rebel who leads the Secession revolt may take a timely hint when furnishing his peace-suing ambassadors with their credentials.

But Chosiu's apologies with even such remarkable backing were unavailing to hinder the departure of the expedition from Oasaca and its gathering in force on the confines of his territory. To the assembled chiefs now ready to commence offensive operations, Chosiu again sent messengers abjectly suing for peace on any terms. These messengers announced his abdication of his throne in favor of his son, the young Prince of Nagato, and his refuge in a monastery, where he awaited such conditions as their clemency might impose. Since there was no one to fight, the expedition necessarily came to an end, and the large force was disbanded. And now we hear that a grand council of nobles of the empire, with the Tycoon at their head, is to be convened at Miaco to determine what shall be done with the unfortunate Chosiu.

While referring to the misfortunes of this chief, whose name is foremost among Niphon's aristocracy, let me correct a paragraph which has had a wide circulation in Western journals and seems to have been generally credited respecting the revenge taken upon the prince's family and followers at Yedo. The purport of it is this: that the Yedo Government took a base and cowardly revenge in destroying the city palaces of this chief, and putting to death several hundred inoffensive men, women and children who resided in them. I am glad to brand this story as an atrocious falsehood. Such a cold-blooded atrocity would have sent a thrill of horror throughout Japan and reacted on the perpetrators. I am glad to say that the Japanese Government, with all its faults, has yet too much humanity to commit so dark a deed. True, Chosiu's Yedo residences were razed to the ground—"confiscated" is the milder war term—and the inmates, who were unarmed servants, women and children were removed, but instead of being slaughtered at the palace gates, as this story runs, they were handed over to the charge of their friends in the city—scarcely so much as placed under Government surveillance. Not a life was lost.

Your readers may remember that our flag two years ago was gallantly carried into action with the batteries of this same Chosiu at Shimonoseki by Capt. McDougall, of the Wyoming, unsupported by any other vessel. In acknowledgement of his brave conduct on that occasion, the American residents at Kanagawa have presented to Capt. McDougall a tea and breakfast service of solid silver, the principal pieces of which were engraved with a representation of the Wyoming in action after a drawing on the spot by C. Wirgman, esq., artist of *The London Illustrated News*. Capt. McDougall has since returned home, and, at last dates was commandant at Mare Island, Cal.

The Jamestown, Capt. Price, is still "piling up beef bones" in our harbor, and may yet demand the attention of the port police if she don't "move on." Her departure on the 1st prox. is talked of.

Gen. Pruyn, the United States Minister Resident contemplates availing himself at an early day of the leave of absence long since granted him, by a visit to the States.

Japan was opened to foreign trade not quite six years ago, at which time, and since, allotments of land have been granted for foreign occupation of limited extent. A recent sale of a compound containing two acres situated on the sea front, for 90,000 Mexican dollars, or over $200,000 greenbacks at current exchange, will illustrate the present value of what was so few years ago only worth its productiveness in turnips. It illustrates as well the march of commerce in these hitherto secluded isles. Real estate can hardly be regarded as fixed property in this land of earthquakes. These ague chills have been frequent of late as well as peculiar in their symptoms—having much the feeling of a sudden sharp blow at first, succeeded by the usual wave-like motion. Such a one we experienced a few nights since, which shook our houses out of perpendicular and ourselves out of serene propriety, opening our doors, spilling our pitchers, stopping our clock pendulums, and such minor freaks. Still old Fusi looks calm, placid and venerable under his increasing weight of winter snows, quite too respectable for any such juvenile pranks. I suspect, however, he has less to do with it than his younger brother of Oho-Sima, whose meerschaum is always alight.

But why is it that earthquakes most abound in falling weather? Such is the observed coincidence, if that only we are to call it, in Japan.

Sunday, March 12, 1865

Walking in the outskirts this P.M., my attention was attracted by a review of Japanese infantry at the barracks beyond Yoshida-bashi. There were four or five hundred soldiers at drill. Their proficiency in firing was particularly noticeable.

Thursday, March 23, 1865

Ida D. Rogers arrived.

Friday, March 24, 1865

Yesterday and today busy gardening. Planted seeds, onions, beets, cabbages, celery, radish, etc., in open ground. Strawberries begin to bloom more freely. Japan green peas in pod in market.

Wednesday, March 29, 1865

Festival of the 3rd day of 3rd moon.

Thursday, March 30, 1865

S[adajirō] is down from Yedo and reports that the Chosiu difficulty is by no means settled. It had been arranged that Chosiu should interchange with the Tycoon expressions of regret for the late affairs and so the difficulty be settled. This course is said to give great displeasure to the Mikado. When the peace offering of Chosiu's ministers, three heads, were presented to him he refused to see them, saying he "wanted men not heads." Owari, the chief of the late expedition, is greatly indignant. Preparations for a further expedition are said to be in foot.

Tuesday, April 4, 1865

A fine day again after much dull disagreeable weather which I improved in a long walk over the bluffs and back through the valley in company with I.S.B., C. B., E. B. and A.L.C.P.[6] On our return we stopped at a fine looking farmhouse which we found to combine with farming the profit to be derived from sake selling, and sale of refreshments. The house itself was remarkably well built. Overhead were huge beams of the beautiful Japanese elm smoothly planed and polished, the uprights were of the same, and the wood work of the doors and windows was of clear pine handsomely dressed and polished. We entered the kitchen part of the house with its flooring of hard trodden earth. Here was the cooking range, steaming away with its ever ready hot water. Sacks of rice were piled up to the ceiling in one corner, and ranged against the wall were tubs and jars of white sake. This sake is so called because the liquid is not drawn clear

[6] I.S.B. appears to have been I. S. Blydenburgh of Smith, Archer & Co; E. B. may have been Edward Banks, who also served as U.S. marshal; and A.L.C.P. was A.L.C. Portman, the secretary and interpreter of the U.S. legation. It is not clear who C. B. was, unless he was Colgate Baker, who worked with Blydenburgh at Smith, Archer & Co. See *The Chronicle and Directory for China, Japan and the Philippines for 1865* (Hong Kong: Daily Press, 1865), p. 239.

from the broken rice of which it is made but they are left together making a thick pungent drink highly intoxicating.

On the mats raised above the earth floor, in a clean cheerful compartment facing the pleasant south sun of winter, two old women and two girls were busy ginning cotton. One, a stout red faced old lady evidently the mistress of the house, bade us welcome. A young man was kneading a paste of buckwheat flour preparatory to making macaroni thereof. An old traveller was sitting on a bench drinking his rice whiskey and eating fried cakes. A young woman about twenty was serving him.

We went through the house into a back kitchen where were all the implements of the scullery stood in order or hung up in a cleanliness worthy of such a fine farmhouse. Still outside of this was a pond for the breeding of gold fish, another adjunct of wealth, and fringing the little homestead were a few fruit and ornamental trees the favorite of which in their eyes was a flowering peach just now in its full blossom.

Under the kitchen shed the wash board, basins of copper, the tooth brushes sticking in the cracks of the clapboards, and the bath tub, denoted that personal ablution was duly cared for. As we came back into the house, the rice wine was offered us, the old lady with her own hands carefully prepared her tea and offered it to us in tiny porcelain cups with a spread of sweet cakes and confectionery. As we sipped our tea, the stout wife of some neighboring farm house came in with two glass bottles (acquisitions from our foreign life) to be filled with whiskey, and soon after a group of farmers and laborers returning from their day's works. Seeing that the evening tide of customers was set in, we left our hospitable dame with many kindly expressions on both sides.

As we passed near another house we saw at the door a pail full of snails just taken from the shells which lay in a heap about the door. A boy with eyes of the blackest and sharpest, and face besmirched with ink, explained to us the "delicious taste" of these shell fish and answered our inquiries with a quickness that pleased us greatly. We liked him better still when at one corner of the yard we saw his copy books hung up to dry on a pole resting in two crotched sticks which he had neatly put up for the purpose.

Thursday, April 6, 1865

Garrison races came off today. The most striking feature was a race ridden by several Japanese, all samurai, some of them boys, sons of high local officials. Their general good riding was greatly admired and the victors were handsomely rewarded by the spectators.

Friday, April 28, 1865

American Minister left for home.

Sunday, April 30, 1865

Had a pleasant walk on the Kanagawa side.
This day completes my three years of partnership with Walsh, Hall, & Co. I have agreed to extend the time until the end of December. Half regretting that I have done so after all. Now I must bend all my energies to make these eight months prosperous so that I may have my reward of once again revisiting home and may Providence bless my efforts.

Wednesday, May 3, 1865

Annual festival at Bookengi [Bukenji]. On account of the rain its pleasure is broken up.

Sunday, May 14, 1865

Walk over the Governor's hill.

Saturday, May 27, 1865

During this week the Japanese have again been buying arms in considerable quantities anticipatory of the Tycoon's proposed departure to Miako and an expedition against Chosiu. It appears that the relations of the Yedo Government with this chief are by no means settled. The general rumor is that Chosiu himself would be content to ratify the terms of the amnesty he had last summer but that a large body of his followers openly resist any settlement which will deprive them of their revenues and position and prefer all the chances of strife to what they consider a dishonorable peace.

The *Tee-pang*, formerly the *Monitor*, an American armed steamer, has been repeatedly to Shimonoseki and is said to have supplied Chosiu with considerable quantities of arms and ammunition. The Tycoon's vessels have not been permitted to pass the straits of Shimonoseki since the affair of last summer. The Japanese openly talk of the new expedition to reduce Chosiu.

Sunday, June 4, 1865

The mail arrived at a late hour last evening bringing news of Lee's defeat and the evacuation of Richmond. And a final telegram announces the murder of Lincoln and Seward! Although we cannot trust the correctness of this last telegram, yet we are all saddened by the belief that it may be true. Men of all nationalities seem equally shocked with the tidings.

Saturday, June 10, 1865

Today was the day appointed for the Tycoon to pass along the Tokaido on his way to Miako. By an arrangement with the foreign consuls, foreigners, contrary to the usual custom, were to be allowed to witness the grand cortege, and a place was designated for them where to assemble. The foreign population began streaming out on the Kanagawa road at an early hour in the morning, as the precise hour of the procession was not known. The Tycoon left Yedo yesterday and passed last night at Kawasaki. This morning he was to leave Kawasaki, halt at Kanagawa, and rest at Hodoriya [Hodogaya]. The place selected for the foreign spectators was by the roadside near the latter place. I did not go out until noon, and when I arrived after an hour's walk found a large

crowd awaiting the cortege some of whom had been on the ground since morning. Our Japanese friends had had some consideration for our comfort in choosing a spot where we could have the shelter of a fine grove within a few rods of the highway from which we were debarred by a cordon of ropes stretched from post to post. All Yokohama appeared to have turned out, saddle horses were picketed about more numerous than at a Kentucky camp meeting, and some thoughtful ones had brought hampers of provisions and made a picnic of the occasion. Late as I had arrived, I still had to wait until the middle of the afternoon before the preliminary stragglers which announce a chief's train made their appearance. Baggage bearers began to pass, single soldiers, then couples and triplets, and more baggage, the Tycoon's camp chests, bedding, clothing, armor, the imperial lanterns. The stream began to thicken, policemen went about cleaning the road and driving back the crowds of natives who had gathered as much to see the foreign spectators as their own emperor. Officers of the government got into a bustle, about nothing, hastened some unlucky straggler off the road. The people fell down on their knees, the passing stream of baggage bearers and guards grew yet thicker, one youth who carried a red carpet bag of foreign make as his share of the burden, attracted especial attention; some one suggested he carried the emperor's night gown and hair brush and a clean shirt. Then there was a pause in the crowd, then a roll of drum was heard, and a battalion of native infantry made its appearance, uniformed in imitation of foreign style and in heavy marching order. The officers were dressed after their own fancy and generally managed to unite the uniforms of infantry, artillery men, and hussars all in one single. Then trains of native soldiers in the old style of country swordsmen and spearsmen and bowmen, escorting dignitaries on horseback, who were dressed in gorgeous style, brocade dresses, stiff with embroidery and gold, armor and helmets, like knights of the olden times. Then came more troops fantastically dressed, then a long roll of drums and a dozen drummer boys marched by leading another battalion of infantry, rather stout good looking

fellows; then came a gay cavalcade of horsemen with banners and plume, and casque and
helm, and gay robes glittering in the sun, moving with slow walk, all mounted, their horses as
gaily decked as themselves. Were we really in
the 19th century, or had I been reading a saga
of Froissart and fallen asleep dreaming? I
blinked my eyes, no, here was the bay of Kanagawa and the familiar woods and hills and the
daily faces I knew. At all events it was a procession of the middle ages passing through our
material century. In the midst of this cavalcade
rode nine horsemen three abreast at once recognizable as the men of mark. They were su-
perbly mounted, and language fails to give any
description of their singular dress. It was very
brilliant and striking and ornamented. Each
wore the broad circular hat of steel lacker and
highly ornamented with insignia of rank
stamped thereon. These were officers of the
court and one of them was the Tycoon himself, but just which one we did not know. So we
took a good stare at them all, and so saw the
Tycoon if there was any Tycoon there whatever. I picked out the middle man of the middle row, but he was a fine looking fellow, one
that looked the monarch, while the real Tycoon is rather inferior in personal appearance,
I am told. These were followed by other
mounted men, then more infantry, and high
officers of the empire, each with his escort,
and then a cluster of stragglers and the procession was past.

Tuesday, July 4, 1865

The usual calls and festivities with which we
have heretofore observed this anniversary
were omitted this year as we had recently received the sad news of President Lincoln's assassination. Even the joy we felt in our victories
at home was lost in the deeper grief over this
event. The Americans assembled at the Consulate where appropriate exercises were had consisting of a discourse by the Rev. Mr. Ballagh,
singing of appropriate hymns, reading of resolutions, the whole closing with the John Brown
song. During the ceremonies, which were attended by members of the various legations
and consulates, flags on these and on the ship-

ping were dropped [to] half mast. We had no
national vessel to fire the usual salute, but a
merchant ship did the honor to the best of its
ability with a pair of guns.

The news of Lincoln's death was announced
by telegram nearly three weeks ago, but it was
not until a week ago that the report was believed on confirmation of a later mail. All nationalities unite in the reprobation of the foul
deed.

Thursday, July 13, 1865

A native friend from Yedo reports that the
recent forced loan tax levied by the Government has excited much opposition on the part
of the smaller tax payers. Placards have been
posted and circulated in the city threatening
death to the leading officers of the government if they persisted in its exaction. The consequence has been that the loan has been
remitted on all who were required a contribution of hundred rios or under. By this new arrangement 1300 men pay an aggregate of
630,000 rios. In Oasaca the great merchants
themselves opposed the general distribution of
this loan, saying that it would produce trouble
and embarrass trade and they would prefer
themselves to make the necessary advances to
the Government. Accordingly sixteen (16) Oasaca merchants step forward and proffer to
advance unitedly 850,000 rios. Enormous as
this sum is for sixteen men to pay, it is said
that the two heaviest merchants are not con-
tributors being under the Government ban,
one of them for his large loans to the rebellious Prince of Nagato and who is confined to
his house under official surveillance.

Sunday, July 23, 1865

Illustrative of the clanship of trades in Japan
a friend tells me of a feud between the tailors
and bathmen and barbers in Yokohama. It
grew out of some insignificant [cause] between
individuals of their respective trades, and soon
involved the whole fraternity on either side in
both Yokohama and the neighboring village of
Honmura. The bathmen assembled in force to

demolish the house or shop of the chief of-fending tailor, but the tailors were prepared for them and from the roofs of the adjoining houses plied defensive missiles so vigorously that the barbers and bathers were defeated. Several were severely injured, and two or three likely to die. The authorities now stepped in and arrested several of the ringleaders and the feud was quieted.

Tuesday, August 1, 1865

The summer this far has been remarkably wet and cool, beyond the memory of the ubiq-uitous personage "the oldest inhabitant." Much apprehension is expressed for the rice crop. The price has nearly trebled its customary value and is now twelve ichibus per picul. The cotton crop is equally endangered and the price in the native town has advanced to $28.

Thursday, August 17, 1865

Races.

Friday, August 18–Saturday, August 19, 1865

Regatta.

Friday, September 15, 1865

Took the little steamer and went down with a party of friends to Coquimbo (Jap. Yokoska) Bay. We found a charming bay with deep wa-ters and bold, picturesque shores. Selecting a shady spot on the terrace of a hillside we landed our camp materials and soon had our pot boiling with a fish chowder. The fish we bought of the fishing boats as we came down and all the necessary ingredients and appara-tus were in one camp chest. We amused our-selves with pistol and rifle shooting till the chowder was pronounced ready and then sat

to with the good appetites our jaunt had given us. Chowder disposed of we amused ourselves as picnickers are wont to do until it came time to return. Just at sunset we steamed out of the beautiful little bay whose shores were all green and gold in the departing sunlight.

Wednesday, September 20, 1865

Returned today from a pleasant trip to Yedo. I left Yokohama at 7 o'clock Monday morning having as guests Mr. Mangum, the new Consul to Nagasaki, Mr. Capes of N.Y. the planner of the *Dictator*, Mr. Church of our Na-gasaki house, and Capt. Johnson and Engineer Seil of the Steamer *Pembroke*, who took charge of our little boat.[7] We took saddle and bridles with us relying on Yedo stables for our horses.

As we got out of the anchorage we encoun-tered a heavy sea and head wind, but we were delighted to see how our little craft fifty feet by twelve put herself through. The spray flew over us some but few seas boarded us and those barely wet our decks. On my own part I stood the rough seas finely, not being in the least seasick as is my wont. We had a lunch on board, and after two-and-three-quarter hour's steaming reached the forts at Yedo. Tide was out and we found it difficult to to make our landing a good mile distant across the mud flats. Mr. Portman saw us from the shore and sent a light boat off to bring us in. We landed at the familiar hatoba and were soon on the way to the U.S. Legation escorted by the usual crowd of officers. Mr. Portman received us very hospitably in his new house built by the Japanese and yet unfinished. We had a break-fast at twelve and then started off on a ride to Atago Yama and Asakusa. We had brought our saddles with us and procured our horses from the Japanese stables. We rode out accom-panied as on former occasions by a mounted guard strong in numbers if not in power. From the top of Atago Yama we had again the charming view of Yedo which is always fresh to me, and after a cup of tea rode on to Asakusa. The temple of Asakusa Quanon was less

[7] Willie P. Mangum replaced John G. Walsh, Hall's partner, as U.S. consul in Nagasaki in 1865; S. Howard Church was a member of Walsh & Co. in Nagasaki.

crowded than on my previous visits, we entered it, stood a few minutes before its great treasure box for offerings, and passing out at a side door went into the shady gardens at the side where we had our refreshing tea again. After this a stroll among the curiosities which surround the temple, a remount and return home to the Legation. I was greatly struck with the quiet look of Yedo. Its streets were less crowded and there was a marked absence of sworded men. All this is accounted for by the absence of the Tycoon and princes with their retainers and followers on the Chosiu expedition. Yedo complains in its shopkeepers of the desertion and there is said to be even real distress. Rice is dearer than known in long years before.

We made a twelve or fourteen mile ride without molestation. However, while walking about Asakusa we met a group of drunken young officers, one of whom made some gestures of defiance at us, and shortly after a stone was thrown into our midst which passing my head struck Mr. Portman without injury.

Mr. Portman gave us a refreshing dinner after our exercise and we passed a long delightful evening around the table talking of adventures and incidents in all parts of the world.

We preferred to return to Yokohama the following day, and some of our party being over fatigued by yesterday's jaunt, we kept quietly in the house until the time came to take our leave of our hospitable host. Bag and baggage we went down to the sea and found a south wind blowing up the bay with such force, and the sea so rough, that we gave up the attempt to fight it out with our tiny steamer and returned to the Legation to pass the night. Our host's good cheer, and our pleasant surroundings, caused the time to pass without weariness.

The following morning we took an early start and were soon steaming away down the bay touching a shoal once, backing off, and reaching Yokohama anchorage in two hours and a quarter steaming.

Friday, October 27, 1865

Today is the anniversary of my birth; it is also Dr. and Mrs. Hepburn's 25th anniversary of their marriage, their Silver Wedding. I took dinner with them and met as guests Mr. and Mrs. L. of Hong Kong, Col. and Mrs. C. of the 20th and two merchants.[8] The weather was dreary out but we had sunshine and merriment within, passing a most agreeable afternoon, and Dr. and Mrs. H.'s lively feelings quite belie their years. For me another mile stone checked off in the journey road of life. The traveller in an unknown land, tho' he remembers the inn which he left in the morning knows not where he shall tarry for the night, or how far he may be from his rest.

Wednesday, November 1, 1865

A combined fleet, English, French and Dutch, sailed this morning for the Inland Sea and Oasaca, taking with it the diplomatic representatives of England, France, The United States, and Holland. The object of its visit is not made public, but it is understood to be to make a demonstration in favor of our treaties with the Tycoon; perhaps to demand of the Mikado a formal ratification of the treaties, at all events, to give the Mikado and his court and all factious daimios to understand that we expect the treaties to be respected, and that, so long as the Tycoon honestly endeavors to carry them out, he will be sustained by all the Treaty Powers to every necessary extent, and that there must be an end to all factions that originate in their policy towards foreigners. The Tycoon is still at Miako or Oasaca and the foreign powers feel the necessity of understanding what is going on at these courts, for at Yedo there is barely the form of a government.

Mr. Portman our *charge* is a guest on the *Pelorus*.

[8] The L.'s are not identifiable, but Col. and Mrs. C. were Col. A. H. Cobbe and his wife.

Thursday, November 30, 1865

Thanksgiving Day. As usual kept by few. Having a sick guest in my home I had made no preparations for the day, and well, for poor Melliss quietly died this afternoon at 4 o'clock.[9] He arrived here two months ago in a moribund condition from dysentery and has slowly died out under my care. I have had five men whose sole business was to attend him and the care was great.

In the evening dined with Consul Fisher and wife and a small party of friends.

Friday, December 1, 1865

Buried poor Melliss. The allied squadron returned on the 26th and 27th ult from Hiogo having accomplished their mission peacefully. The results obtained were the ratification of the treaties by the Mikado, the payment (in installments) of $3,000,000 indemnity for the aggressions at Shimonoseki, and a revision of the tariff on imports and exports. On the other hand, Hiogo is to remain closed until the stipulated time, January 1868, unless events should force its earlier opening.

The ratification by the Mikado, which consists of an order to the Tycoon to execute the treaties, was not obtained without some delay and difficulty. The foreign representatives conducted their negotiations with the Tycoon's ministers, and not directly with any representatives of the Mikado. The ratification is desirable, and if it carries any weight ought to do much to settle the perturbed state of this empire. It remains to be seen, however, whether this ratification will quiet down the malcontent princes who have been represented by the Mikado as their head. I am still of the opinion that the Mikado's power is nominal, rather than real, and that we have the body of the daimios to deal with now as much as before the ratification.

[9] Melliss is not identified further and we do not know from where he arrived or why Hall was nursing him.

Monday, December 25, 1865

Merry Christmas. Business suspended and the day given to festivity. Some are out riding, some hunting, some walking, and dinner parties are numerous. The Japanese call it the "tojin's *big sunday*". We are very quiet. I have again an invalid guest and have omitted my usual dinner party, but kept the day quietly, hoping that my next Christmas may be at home.

Thursday, December 28, 1865

Last evening the Belgian Minister, M. de Roodenbeck, the Dutch Consul General,[10] Swiss ditto,[11] and Prussian ditto,[12] dined with me. The Mexican Empires and Ott's murder were among the subjects discussed.

[10] D. de Graeff van Polsbroek.
[11] Rudoph Lindau.
[12] Max von Brandt.

family were represented in letters from Ellington, Centre Brook, Newton, Syracuse, and Elmira. No New Year gifts could have been more appropriate or acceptable.

Sunday, January 7, 1866

Bookengee with guests from R. & Co.[1]

Wednesday, January 10, 1866

Oriflamme and *Jeanie* got to sea.

Tuesday, January 23, 1866

Farci Gama arrived.

Sunday, February 11, 1866

A charming sunny day; walked with B.[2] through the native town out by the Governor's residence and so into the open country. Everywhere there are proclamations of the New Year. The shops are displaying their wares in the most attractive manner and the decoration of the streets and shop fronts has begun. In the country we stopped at a farm house where the neighbors were making the annual rice cakes. We took our turn at the pounding or kneading mallets to the great delight of the rustics, among whom was a girl of sixteen or seventeen of particularly comely face and attractive hazel eyes. The year has been a prosperous one with our native friends and they seem fully intent on their festivities. The New Year is now only four days off.

Wednesday, February 14, 1866

This is the closing day of the Japanese year. The streets are ornamented as usual and every preparation made for the holidays. At 1/2 past 10 in the evening I went through the principal

1866

Monday, January 1, 1866

Yesterday closed my partnership arrangement with Walsh, Hall, & Co., but as my successor has not arrived I continue on until relieved. It is a pleasant thought this New Year's Day that I may so soon revisit home and friends. To that my longing expectations reach. The day is calm soft and beautiful, the very sunshine of peace broods over us, may it be typical of the New Year upon which we have entered.

The *Lubra* arrived this morning from San Francisco and interrupted the morning's leisure, but in the afternoon I called on all my friends and coming home found my table bestowed with cards.

Thursday, January 4, 1866

The English mail arrived this morning and brought me a gracious New Year's offering in a fine parcel of letters from home. The whole

[1] Russell & Co.
[2] It is not clear whether this is S. R. Brown or Edward Banks. Banks is usually referred to as E. B. in the Journal, so it may have been the former.

street finding the retail shops open and busy with traffic. Some of the streets presented a very gay and animated spectacle. As I returned I encountered a mob in the street gathered about two men who were quarreling, but the police were quickly on hand and one offender was summarily taken to the station house.

Thursday, February 15, 1866

Japanese New Year. A beautiful sunny quiet day. All the natives old and young are out in their holiday dresses. Children by hundreds, thousands I might say, in the streets flying kites, playing battledore etc. All gaily decked out in new attire and bright shining or painted faces. Everyone seemed happy as possible. Called with Heco on Kaiya's wife who hospitably entertained us with sweetmeats, egg and celery soup, toso, hot sake and tea.[3] She expressed many polite regrets that I was so soon to leave Japan.

Friday, February 16, 1866

Today business is supposed to re-open and the custom is for the merchants to commence by some business to inaugurate the New Year's trade.

While I was sitting in my office I heard a great noise without and going to the door saw several cart loads of tea coming into the compound, each cart drawn by several Japanese laborers attired in holiday suits, pulling with new straw ropes. On the top of the last cart sat a boy with a mask who was amusing the following crowd by his grotesqueries. Thus was my New Year trade in good omen inaugurated.

Monday, February 19, 1866

The Japanese keep up their holiday festivities with unwonted spirit. Saturday was a rainy

day and a damper on their festivities but I was pleased to see as I passed a well known merchant's shop on a street corner that he had given up his shop to the children, who to the number of fifteen or twenty boys and girls, were playing battledore and romping merrily on his new mats. Think of a well-to-do merchant on a rainy New Year day at home letting the neighborhood children have his carpeted parlor to play in!

Since the 2nd of the New Year the strings of carts have been numerous laden with boxes and bales of merchandise going to and from the foreign settlement, much in the manner described above, tho' the maskers were not always quite so decent. The procession of the sake tub seemed generally to have the most admirers and followers. It was really a little comical to see even the stone merchants and lumber merchants inaugurating the New Year's business with carts laden with stone or heavy pieces of timber which it was no joke to haul. Everybody who wishes to be successful for the New Year must begin with some trade, and arrangements are often made just before New Year to do a certain business on the 2nd day of the New Year. In this way I sold some imported merchandise, delivery of which was taken with due ceremony as above named.

Saturday, March 10, 1866

Lubra left.

Sunday, March 25, 1866

Ida D. Rogers sailed.

Sunday, April 1, 1866

Gave up management of Walsh, Hall, & Co.'s business to my successor [John A. Cunningham]

---

[3] Kaiya Kyūjirō was one of the leading Yokohama merchants who traded in a wide variety of goods that ranged from silk and tea to ceramics, paper, and tobacco. See Yokohama Shi, eds., *Yokohama shishi* (Tokyo: Tosho Insatsu Kabushiki Kaisha, 1959), vol. 2, p. 7. Heco was, of course, Joseph Heco with whom Hall maintained a close friendship throughout his stay in Japan.

Thursday, April 26, 1866

Went to Kanazawa, Kamakura and Daibuts with a party of friends. Our guests were Mr. Middleton, Nichols, and Mr. Andrews.[4] We had the usual charming ride over the hills and along the familiar road described before. At Kamakura the only sight this time novel was the multitude of wild fowl (teal) covering the ponds on either side of the walk up to the temple of Hachiman. The water was covered with them swimming about among the lotus, and so tame were they that we came up to the water's edge without disturbing them. We dined at Kanazawa and most of our party returned by boat, Mr. M. and myself keeping to our horses.

Sunday, May 13, 1866

Went over to Kanagawa for a walk with I.S.B.[5] The country was looking beautifully. We wandered through the narrow paths out into the "great valley" where the rain overtook us and we had a wet walk home.

Wednesday, May 16, 1866

Took a kango [kago] excursion into the country with Heco to visit a silk district. We went to Kanagawa by boat to meet Heco's native friend Bohe, who was to furnish us with chairs or "baskets."[6] Bohe had been waiting for us all the morning and had just gone out as we came to his house. An hour's delay followed in hunting him and the chair bearers up. We got off at 1/2 past nine, taking the Tokaido to Hodoriya [Hodogaya], where we struck off through a wide long valley, following it up till we ascended higher ground and finally came into the Hachioji road. We followed this road several miles halting once for lunch at a wayside house. From this road we branched into the Atsoogi [Atsugi] road and from this again we struck off by country paths towards the village of Seya, which place we reached at 12 1/2

o'clock. The country everywhere looked fresh and beautiful. The wheat and barley were in full head. A recent frost had cut off most of the young mulberry leaves and the paths of the cold were plainly seen where leaves were nipped and on either side left unharmed. At Seya some of the farmers had thrown away the young worms for want of food.

Bohe had commended us to the care of the principal farmer of the town, the nanooshi Taksho, and we were hospitably received at his well kept farm house. The house was large, forming as usual the rear of an enclosed quadrangle with the customary outhouses, gates, and gardens in front and on either side. We were shown into quiet apartments at one end of the house, as usual, scrupulously neat, the walls hung with scrolls of writing and pictures. A single vase stood on a shelf and two folding screens completed the furniture of the apartment. The house had been built a century [earlier] and was in [such] thorough repair that I did not suspect more than a quarter of that age. Our host was a plain and quiet man, but his good looking wife was more bustling. Apologies were made for want of suitable entertainment as tea and sweet meats were presented us.

We inquired for the silkworms and were taken up a ladder into the peaked loft of the house where a colony of worms were feeding on mats which had been first strewn with millet husks. The worms were yet quite young. The floors of this loft was of loose boards directly above the kitchen and so the room was at an agreeable temperature. We were told that quite in the same way worms were reared in the cottages scattered about the plain where the village of Seya stands. Our host sent a guide with us to show us the same process repeated at another large farmer's a mile distant. While making this visit we were the center of curiosity to all the children of the neighborhood and many grown people besides.

On our return to the house of our host we were offered a Japanese dinner neatly served if not luxurious. Boiled rice, broiled salt

---

[4] It is not clear who these men were.

[5] I.S.B. was I. S. Blydenburgh of Smith, Archer & Co.

[6] This appears to have been the Kanagawa merchant, Saigaya Buhee, with whom Hall also did business. See footnote 3 for the year 1860 for reference to this merchant.

salmon rather ancient in flavor, boiled lotus roots, young bamboo sprouts, seasoned with pickled slices of cucumber formed our repast. It made bulk if not nutriment and, as we were sharp-set, was on the whole quite palatable. We had our own stores but our hosts were so attentive that we feared to offend them by refusing their food for ours. A bottle of wine, however, helped our meal and was a curiosity to our newly made friends.

Beyond the silkworms there was nothing to see in Seya and at three o'clock we said saionara to our hosts and took our baskets again for the return. Rain began to fall at intervals and we were therefore glad to reach Yokohama at 6 1/2 P.M. having had an enjoyable day of walking and basket riding.

Thursday, May 17, 1866

My friends the Cobbes left today with the 20th Regiment for Hong Kong. I was sorry to part with them.[7]

Tuesday, May 22, 1866

Went to Kanagawa today to attend the annual fete at Bookengee [Bukenji] temple. There was the usual crowd of people, services in the temple, washing of Buddha, and other ceremonies before described in these pages. There did not appear to be so many present as formerly, nor, of these, so many of the respectable Japanese. Picnic parties were scattered all over the green ground under the trees, and many were the invitations to partake of their food and drink. As the day wore away many were overpowered by their potations and became noisy and rude. One female whose earlier potations made her extremely jolly grew sullen and then pugnacious under deeper cups till after having had a scuffle with one of her

own sex she came with the flashing eyes and inflamed face of a fury at our party. We laughed at her, dodged her, and finally beat a retreat to get out of her way. In another family party were two girls and a boy, the latter and one of his sisters had drunk a little too freely and amused us by their antics. But the drinking was prolonged and the men also were getting high, including some young officers wearing swords. We concluded it prudent to say our saionaras and depart.

Monday, June 11, 1866

Trip to the mountains see under June 16th.

Saturday, June 16, 1866

Returned last evening from a trip to the mountains west of Yokohama in company with Mr. J. H.,[8] Dr. J.C.H.[9] and Mr. E.S.B.[10] We left Yokohama on Monday morning June 11th at 6 o'clock. Our object was to penetrate into the mountains to the westward towards Fusi Yama and to reach at or near the base of that mountain if practicable. Our first destination was Miangaze [Miyagase] 32 miles west of Yokohama.[11] To this point we had dispatched, on the previous day, a pack horse laden with supplies of food and wine, and Mr. B[enson]'s servant as chief of the commissariat to procure us such lodgings as could be had in advance of our own arrival. B[enson] was an old campaigner in California's early days and was skillful in arranging our outfit of smoked, salt, and preserved meats, tin plates, frying pan, and such other necessaries and conveniences as one stout beast might carry.

The morning of our start was cloudy, and this being a season when abundant rain was liable to fall, we were not without some misgivings as to the result. We took an easy gait on

---

[7] This was Col. and Mrs. A. H. Cobbe of the 20th Regiment.

[8] J. H. was Joseph Heco.

[9] Dr. J.C.H. was J. C. Hepburn.

[10] E.S.B. was E. S. Benson, one of the Yokohama merchants with whom Hall was friendly.

[11] For contemporary photographs of the village of Miyagase by Felix Beato see *F. Beato bakumatsu nihon shashin shū* (Yokohama: Yokohama Kaikō Shiryō Kan, 1987), pp. 38–39. The Nakatsu valley is still known for its beautiful scenery, particularly its fantastic rocks and hanging cliffs.

our horses closely followed by our bettos out of Yokohama to the Miako road, which we again left about 2 miles from Yokohama for the high plains rolling country and bridle roads that diverged on our right towards Atsoogi [Atsugi] on the Sagami River, being for several miles the same track passed over by Heco and myself a few days previously (May 16th). We were all well mounted and carried our rain coats at our saddles' peak in case of need.

The ride across the rolling country towards Atsoogi was extremely pleasant and we sauntered along leisurely enjoying the prospect spread around us. We reached Kokooboo [Kokubu] near the left bank of the Sagami River at 11 A.M. after a ride of eighteen miles, and finding a quiet pleasant inn on the edge of the river terrace we halted for rest and refreshments. We were kindly received by our host, who had never entertained foreigners before, and opening our knapsacks made a substantial lunch. We rested until one o'clock and remounted after paying our inn charges for 4 foreigners and four native servants and 4 horses, all told 3 ichibus or $1.

We rode down the river terrace and from its brink had a fine view of the wide valley which flanks the Sagami for a mile on either side and the mountains across the river to which we were bound. These truly magnificent plains were everywhere devoted to rice culture. We crossed the Sagami at 1 P.M. by a ferry boat propelled by setting poles, the river being neither wide nor deep, though its extended banks and gravel beach showed that in other times it might become a powerful stream. On the right bank we passed through the important village of Atsoogi without a halt, and crossing the same river plain on the right bank that we had crossed on the left, struck into the mountains from whose gorges issued the head waters of the Sagami. For the last three hours of our ride we had been passing through a succession of mulberry groves and as we began the mountainous ascent, silk culture seemed to be the absorbing pursuit of all the farmers.

The mountains which extend from the Sagami River to Fusi Yama, 40 or 50 miles distant, are a succession of broken ridges thrown up by volcanic agency in the utmost irregularity and tho' the mountains were bold and

rough the road was nevertheless not difficult to make by crossing the spurs of the least precipitous and tracking around among the vallies. The distance from the foot of the hills to Miangaze, our halting place 2500 feet above the river, was a good mountain road, well laid out along the slopes and in general good repair. Throughout this distance we were surprised to find a numerous population living with all the evidences of thrift as indicated in their neat substantial farm houses and good order of their farms. The original growth of timber must have disappeared from these hills centuries ago, all the timber with few exceptions here and there being planted by the present generation. The farmers preferred the small wood for charcoal burning. Mountain streams were everywhere running down to the valley with swift current over their rocky beds; there were living waters everywhere. Very many of the farm houses were picturesquely planted at road-side angles, on terraces supported by stone walls, and garnished with magnificent shade trees. Water brought to the door in bamboo pipes was the common adjunct of a large portion of the farm yards. Overhanging these houses, or standing in thick groves around their temples, we saw splendid specimens of the Japan cedar (C. Japonica), firs (Abies bifida), magnificent torreas [torreya—or stinking cedar], elms, retinosporas [a variety of cypress], and thujas. Between the hills were occasional valleys of good breadth and length, some of which appeared to us as the most covetable farms we had ever seen in Japan or almost any land. The mountains which range in altitude from a few hundred to five thousand feet were cultivated and foraged to their summits. Wheat and millet were common crops against their steep sides. Much clearing up of brush was going on for new soils and new thatches and other repairs to houses and otherwise betokened the profitable activity of the inhabitants. The hillsides were covered with long grasses and succulent shrubs, and the pack bullocks, which we frequently met, were, despite their labor, sleek and fat as such pasture could make them.

We had frequently to cross the mountain streams over wide bridges of natural trunks supported on uprights and laid over with

Road to "Miangaze" near
Eiyama. Photograph by
Felice Beato.

young round wood and turf. These bridges
are frequently carried away by the mountain
freshets and as often renewed.

A storm overtook us in the mountains and
the last two hours of our journey was in the
rain. We rejoiced therefore at 5 P.M. to reach
our journey's end for the day at a farm house
turned into an inn. Our commissariat train
had arrived several hours before and we were
soon off our horses and stretched to rest on
the inviting mats. Our horses were stabled under sheds, our hampers unpacked, and we began to make preparations for the dinner and
rest we so much needed.

Miangaze [Miyagase] is a low straggling village lying along the sunny slope of one of the
mountains, our inn being at its western extremity. Above us was the mountain top, on
every side peaks and ridges, in a ravine below
the house brawled a delightful mountain
stream, afterwards to become very dear to us
for its treasures of spreckled trout and its cool
morning baths in its sandy bottomed pools. We
were all from mountain regions at home and it
was a pleasant association to be embowered
amidst such green hills, to hear the prattle and
roar of mountain streams, and to breath the
invigorating atmosphere of these heights.

We made ourselves merry over our meal
preparing, and, delighted and weary, dropped
off to sleep at an early hour. We had brought
blankets with us but the indefatigable fleas
penetrated through every envelope and often
awoke us to listen to the roar of the mountain
torrent or the sweeping of the wind across the
breezy height above us.

We awoke at an early hour and were off
down the mountain side for a cool plunge
which sharp-set us for breakfast. We had engaged the night before guides to conduct us on
our farther way through the mountains. These
were with us betimes, one of them proving
throughout our stay a good assistant, helping
to cook our meals and arranging for our comfort. It was our hope that today we might well
get on our way towards Fusi, but inquiries
among the natives developed the possibility of
interruption. We set forth however, taking all
our baggage with us, determined to go as far
through the mountains as possible. After a
mile of rough road we struck into better paths,
and though we ascended and descended one
hill after another we gradually ascended until
we could see about us a vast outspread panorama of mountain peaks. As we rode through
the woods we had the melody of two kinds of
singing birds whose notes scarcely parted us a
moment. We passed the village of Oochiai, or
the "Meeting of the Waters," where two mountain streams united, and again the more im-

portant village of Toya, then crossing a mountain plain of some breadth we struck again into the hills. As on the day before we found a well-watered country and numerous cascades enlivened our way with their song of rushing waters. We emerged from the hills again into the valley of the head waters of the Sagami near the large village of Owenohara [Uenohara]. An affluent of this river crossed our road and plunged down an abyss of 150 feet or more in three or four successive plunges. On this, as in other of these mountain streams, we found rice stamps and stones for flour grinding busily at work.

Our fears as to the difficulty of passing in the road assumed at this village tangible shape, for a guard house was reported by our guide as barring our further progress. This guard house was well situated where the road which enters Owenohara [Uenohara] is compressed in a bend of the river between the hills on one side and the abyss of the fall on the other. We halted at the mill house at the foot of the declivity on which the road wound up to the gate, under the shade of a grove of elms and conifers and sent our guides to parley with the gate keepers for our passage. We waited a long time for an answer, and none coming, we concluded to move ourselves. As we ascended the winding road a turn brought us suddenly before the open gateway. There were but few persons standing who shouted "close the gates," and an attempt was made to bar the passage in our faces, but we were too quick and pushed ourselves through the half folded door. The gate keeper, an old man of fifty years or more, came running down the hill from the opposite side and jumping into his accustomed seat within the guard house faced us with irate countenance demanding that we should instantly depart through the gateway by which we had entered, at the same time the villagers began to flock about us, men, women, and children, all in a state of surprise and excitement at this unexpected appearance of foreigners in their midst. We proposed to parley with the old gatekeeper, but he said he would

not have a word with us until we rose up from sitting on the floor of his guard house and went outside the gate again. We replied that we would get off his floor, but would not go outside the gate without some reason why we should do so. The old man's eyes flashed fire and his voice was trembling in his wrath, or perhaps in fear of what the personal consequences might be to him who had thus permitted foreigners to pass this gateway. Finding that we could converse with him in his own tongue, he explained to us that he was placed in charge of this gate, which was outside of the limit in which foreigners were permitted to travel and his instructions were on no account to allow foreigners to pass, and that we must at once leave. He had no discretion in the matter, his orders were imperative. At this juncture one of the villagers inquired if "he should put us out." This amused us, but the proposition did not have the gate keeper's assent, who hoped doubtless to persuade us to yield. B[enson] now produced his pocket flask and asked the old gentleman if he drank sake. The instantaneous change in the old man's face produced a roar of laughter as he replied "of course I do," and extended a cup that would hold a pint to receive the proffered dram, begging B[enson] to increase the quantity, as after a liberal outpouring he was about to withhold the flask. A draft of old "Bourbon" mollified the old gentleman so much that we argued with him the propriety of allowing us to pass, who were only peaceful travellers that wished to visit the summit of Yakeyama, or Burnt Mountain, whose head we could see four or five miles distant.[12] Despite all the reductive influences of Bourbon our old gatekeeper was inflexible, and when we hinted that we could pass on in spite of him were we disposed, he replied that it was as much his duty to resist us as tho' he had the effective force to do it. All this colloquy went on with a crowd of the villagers at our backs who cared far less [than] the officious gatekeeper whether we passed or not.

As we knew this gateway stood on daimio's

---

[12] The mountain Hall appears to be referring to here is Gongen-Yama which lies northwest of Uenohara and overlooks the valley of the Nakatsu-gawa, along which the Koshū Kaidō makes its way towards the Kanto plain. Yake-Yama (or "Burnt Mountain") may well have been the nickname given to this mountain by local villagers. Later Hall tells us the mountain was dedicated to Gongen, from which stemmed its other name.

domain, whereas the gatekeeper was a Tycoon's officer, we called for the daimio's local magistrate, who might give us the desired pass if he would. A messenger was dispatched for him, but as he lived two miles distant we had little hope of seeing him, we waited an hour for him, but hearing no tidings of him, except that he was "eating his dinner and would come by and by," we concluded it useless to expect a peaceable passage of the gate, a forcible one we did not wish to make. We were clearly beyond the limits allowed by treaty and to have forced our way would have been to have given just cause of complaint to the government officers and would have rendered them less liberal in conceding privileges to foreigners hereafter. There was a more potent motive, if one were needed, in the fact that however well we might get through, our servants and baggage could not pass, for they at least must obey the commands of their superiors. So we refreshed the old gatekeeper's thirsty soul with more Bourbon and told him we would withdraw to the mill below and await an answer from the nanooshi or local magistrate. As we yielded the old gentleman became momently more bland regretting that he could not do more according to our wishes and hoped we should have a good time with the nanooshi.

We sat down in the old mill house under the shadow of the elms, listening to the plash of the mill and the sound of the waterfall, laughing over our mishaps, finishing what little Bourbon the old Bansha had left while our bettos picketed our horses about on the young twigs and grasses that grew on the river's bank, and our commissariat beast and his driver were the picture of disappointed hopes as he smoked and the beast whisked off the flies with disconsolate air.

The villagers, especially the younger portion, came out and fringed the steep bank above us as they stood gazing. A bevy of maidens sat down on the grassy slope watching us and commenting on us. We tried to be on friendly terms with them, but they fled whenever we approached, and would only allow our glances of admiration from a distance. I undertook to propitiate the fairest of them all by the gift of a mirror, but in vain did I attempt to bear my own gift, and was compelled to employ a native to carry to Miss. Ohatsan, the

prize. The mirror made a decided sensation, and all the girls took turn in gazing at their features as seen in this new light.

Another hour rolled by, but still the nanooshi had not finished his dinner, and impatient of longer delay we concluded to retrace our steps and make a fresh attempt to outflank the bansha of Owenohara some other day. So we rode back by the way we came having been deflected for this day at least in our attempt to reach Fusi Yama.

Our host at Miangaze [Miyagase] was not surprised to see us return, indeed, he expected no other result, and consoled us by a couple of baskets of trout just taken from the stream below, which gave an agreeable change to our ham and bacon diet. In the evening we counseled for a fresh attempt to penetrate into the hills, and learning from our guides that we could reach the Burnt Mountain by a flank movement around the Bansho of Owenohara [Uenohara], through mountain paths we made our arrangements to that end and went to bed hopefully.

June 13th. Weather still fine and our morning bath in the trout steam gave us fresh strength for our day's journey which must be on foot over the mountains. We started at an early hour taking our two guides and a coolie, each of whom carried something to assist the day's adventure. We struck directly up the hill which lay before our inn's door and were soon treading our way through the intricate wood paths. The dew was heavy on the bushes, and we were soon wet to the skin, especially myself, who had the lead and took the first brushing. Up and down steep ridges, winding through narrow ravines and more open vallies, with sometimes a good "mountain path," and then scarcely a trail to be found, we kept on for several miles leaving our yesterday's road far to the right. We skirted the village of Toya on its extreme right edge, having yesterday left it on our left. From Toya we began at once the ascent of the mountains which were our destination. Through the lower part of the hills was a good path, passable by beasts of burden, and on either side were thick growing woods. Rising higher we emerged from the woods upon a long grassy elevation which was the immediate approach to Yakeyama. No young wood covered these hills. Here and there stood a solitary pine. Before and above us was the mountain peak we aspired to, its head half held in the clouds which were sweeping over its summit and three of the taller hills. We began our ascent by a thin trail which wound along the sides or across the summits of lesser peaks. We occasionally came to a path beaten by horses' feet who were led up these steep hill sides to bring back a burden of grass or young brush. There were no difficulties on our way of any importance; our path lay along the steep hill sides where a false step might have given us a disagreeable downward impulse. There were a few ledges of rock to be overcome. As we neared the top, after a long pull, the road became exceedingly steep, and our progress was by slow clambering and with frequent halts which fatigued us much. H[eco] was at last compelled to give up the struggle and lay down by the pathside to await our descent.

After a short clamber over broken rock, old sedimentary rock, with perpendicular strata crumbling with dirt, we reached the last 200 feet of our way over an easy upward slope. All the mountain side had been thickly bestrewn with the day lily (Hemerocallis), and near the summit the surface was liberally carpeted with them not yet in bloom. One more push and we were at the top amid the drifting clouds. To the right of us, left of us, before and behind us, were kindred peaks each and all enveloped in their misty veils. Though our view was limited by the clouds, we nevertheless had a grand view of the tumbled precipitous masses of hills which fill up all this country. Below us ran the Doshigawa [Nakatsu-gawa?],[13] chief affluent of the Sagami River, through a valley clustered with villages. Along its banks ran the road to Fusi, the road which we had tried to travel the day before. Owenohara and its bansha were outflanked, we had reached several miles beyond the position. To the west of us were the higher hills of Koshiu and Sinshiu, and further west, hidden by the clouds but not more than 20 miles distant, lay Fusi Yama. On a clear day the prospect from this summit must be truly magnificent. We could dimly discern the great

valley of the Sagami and the country rolling beyond to the bay near Yokohama. More to the southward was a wide reach of flat country, bounded by the high promontory of Idzu and the waters of the Pacific rolling into the great bay of Odawara. To the north the valley of the Sagami, and at intervals, stretching towards Hachioji and Yedo, lovely mountains, valleys, and farms, whose beauty and seclusion were enticing to come and dwell in their hills. Had we been permitted yesterday to pass Owenohara [Uenohara] we should have at once debouched from the mountainous path upon the nearly level road which winds along the headwaters of the Sagami. We could see strategically how well the gate was placed to guard this last pass into the Sagami valley. We had already learned that this was an old gate, placed to guard the back road toward Hiacone [Hakone], as well as the mountain approach to Fusi. Had we been able to pass we should have encountered yet two other guard houses on our way.

The summit of Yakeyama is devoted to the worship of Gongen Sama and we found small mias of dog kennel proportions erected to his honor. One elevated position gave us a more distinct impression of the mountain ranges, which with all their irregularities had yet some regularity of course. The whole country as far as the eye could reach was broken up into isolated hills or sharp short ridges whose general direction was N. by S. or N.E. by S.W. All were clothed with vegetation, some were covered with a young growth of timber, while others had only small bushes and long reed like grasses, like the hill on which we had stood. Yet everywhere it was evident that man's hand had been for centuries at work in planting, denuding, and replanting these hills. So testified the numerous villages also, and after passing the sparsely inhabited plains which are to be found below, we were the more astonished to see the active and prosperous population in the mountains.

The only animals found on these hills are the wild boar, quite numerous, bears (cave bears), deer—traces of all of which we saw—

[13] The river that Hall refers to here may have been a stream that flowed into the Nakatsu-gawa which, as Hall correctly notes is the chief affluent of the Sagami River.

and wild monkeys, which, although plentiful, we saw none of. We were surprised to find the monkey an inhabitant of these hills where snow falls sometimes to a foot or more depth continuing on the ground for several days.

After a few minutes rest on the summit I returned to Mr. H[eco], whom I found quietly resting, and as he was overcoming his fatigue I returned to my companions on the summit. The clouds still shut us in, so that after waiting in the vain hope to see them break away, we all rejoined Mr. H[eco] and took the lunch we had brought with us. No champagne ever tasted better than ours on Yakeyama.

We saw that there was a good path practicable even for horses ascending the hill from the north side from the village of Nishinowo two and a half miles west of Owenohara. To reach it from below one must needs pass through the latter village and its guard house. We reached the summit of Yakeyama at 1 P.M. and commenced our descent at 2 o'clock. Returning we made a better path by passing through the village of Toya, and joining the road we had passed over yesterday. Late in the afternoon we reached our inn at Miangaze. All were thoroughly jaded by our day's work.

We proposed to return the following day, as any further attempt to reach Fusi would be in vain. To go with our horses was impractical and to reach it by bye roads across the mountains would require some preparations which we could not make on the mountains. During our stay Dr. H[epburn] was often visited by the mountaineers in quest of remedies for their diseases, so that every night and morning we were like a travelling dispensary. I can imagine no life of apparently fewer cares and exactions than that of these mountaineers, well housed and clad, with good soil, air, and water, they should be, as I have no doubt they are, as happy as any peasantry in the world. In every house at the time of our visit silk worms were rearing. The mulberry trees lined the hills everywhere, and all day long men, women, and children were bringing in the gathered branches to feed the worms. The large share of this work falls on the women and girls, stout, buxom, and somewhat untidy lasses. When not engaged in this, they were busy gathering leaves, twigs, reeds, and grasses, for

manure. These are brought to the farm yards, there chopped up, and thrown into a heap which receives the slop of the house and is fermented until it is fit for the wheat and millet fields. It seemed to be the chief avocation of the village to bring food for the worms and grasses for the manure.

Thursday, June 14th. Our horses were saddled for the road when the clouds which had hung over us threatening began to pour down the contents and we abandoned our intentions for another day's halt among the hills. All day long the rain poured, keeping us within doors. We were not wholly sorry to have the rest we needed so much. Choojiro [Chujirō], our guide, was very attentive looking up trout if any of the villagers had caught any, helping to cook our meals, and doing many odd jobs which gave him great favor with us.

The rain fell all day and all night, and when we arose, Friday, June 15th, it was still falling. We were apprehensive lest the Sagami might become swollen to an extent that crossing at Atsoogi [Atsugi] would be impossible and despite the rain resolved to start. Our horses were saddled, our commissariat beast reladen with a lighter load than that he had come up with, we discharged all dues to our host, and enveloping ourselves in waterproof garments bade adieu to Miangaze [Miyagase].

The mountain streams were full in volume, cascades were leaping over the rocks on every side, the mountain clouds wrapped us in their packing sheets and the rain driving in thick scud we wound our way down the mountain roads. It was a glorious sight to see the play of the waters among the hills. As we descended it became clearer at every step, and before we had reached the plain the rain ceased, the clouds were left above us, and under our overcast sky we enjoyed the freshness and perfume the storm had imparted to the woods, vegetation, and atmosphere. We reached the Sagami River at 10 A.M. and were delighted that the crossing was practicable, although the river had nearly doubled its width and volume. We halted at Kokooboo [Kokubu] for our lunch, and then rode across the immense plains which spread from Atsoogi toward Hachioji of many miles in extent, quite prairie-like in extent, but dotted everywhere with copses and

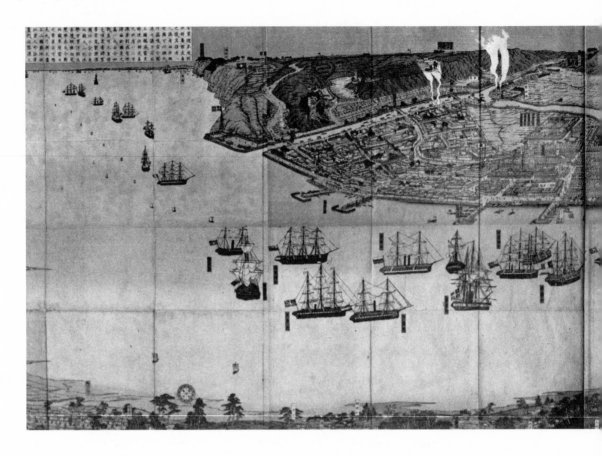

belts of planted timber watered with streams and teeming with crops. Some portions of these plains are very sparsely inhabited and left almost uncultivated, probably owing to the thinness of the soil and the inability under their mode of culture to receive sufficient manure to put the soil in condition.

We reached Yokohama at 5 P.M. rejoicing in the prospect of more beds and less fleas and a relapse to old ways [in] spite of all the benefits of mountain air and appetites.

Thursday, July 5, 1866

Left Japan. Brig *Jeanie*, Pacific Ocean. The last few entries of this page bring my journal of a residence in Japan to a close. My business engagements with Walsh, Hall, & Co. ended by limitation of partnership the 30th of April 1865, but by agreement the partnership was prolonged to Dec. 31st, 1865, when Walsh & Co., not yet being able to relieve me, I consented to remain until such time as they could relieve me without embarrassment to themselves. On the 30th of March 1866 I was relieved by Mr. Walsh's arrival, and soon after my immediate successor, Mr. Cunningham, arrived.[14] I was still not able to leave Japan for want of an opportunity to San Francisco, wither I wished to go at first. It was not till the *Jeanie's* departure on the 5th of July that I was able to get away. This long delay, though in itself tedious and annoying on my impatience to go home, was of valuable service in enabling me to settle definitively all my Japan business

---

[14] On May 18, 1866, the *Japan Times' Daily Advertiser* ran the following notice: "The interest and responsibility of Mr. FRANCIS HALL in our firm ceased on the 31st March last, and Mr. JOHN A. CUNNINGHAM was admitted as partner on the 1st instant. Walsh, Hall & Co., May 14, 1866." See Utsumi Takashi, "Uorushiyu-Hōru shōkai," *Kaikō no hiroba* (Yokohama kaikō shiryōkan kanhō), no. 16 (1886), p. 6.

Sadahide's 1866 pictorial map depicting Yokohama at the time of Francis Hall's departure. Much of the city shown here was destroyed in the great fire of October 1866.

affairs. My settlements with Walsh, Hall, & Co. were made on a liberal and satisfactory basis and I could not but be pleased with the out-turn of my years of travel. One thing only remained, to go home and find my friends alive and well, as the crown of my joy.

My last days in Japan were memorable ones for the many expressions of kindness and regret at my departure from Yokohama friends. I cannot fail to carry the memory of it all to the end of life. On the Friday before I left I met the American residents of Yokohama by their invitation at a pleasant reunion at the French Hotel. Nothing could be more flattering than the abundant overflow of their sentiments on this occasion. Again on Monday evening we all met again at Walsh, Hall, & Co.'s table and took another good-bye. The *Jeanie* had intended to sail on Saturday, but sailing day was postponed until Tuesday, and again until Wednesday morning. So I had my many good-byes said long in advance of my actual departure.

On Tuesday evening at a late hour I went on board. It had rained all day, but about 10 P.M. there was a lull in the storm. All our servants headed by our compradore, Assing, had planned to honor my departure after their own fashion. They gathered round the door of our house, each bearing a lantern made for the occasion and inscribed with the U.S. flag. In the number of twenty or more they escorted me to the pier, and as I took leave of them at the boat the manifestations of their regret at my departure were equally touching and gratifying; as the boat pushed off from the shore they made the quay alive with the bursting of fire crackers, and shouts, keeping it up until the boat was well off the shore. This was in accordance with the Chinese custom to propitiate success to my homeward voyage. On arriving on board the *Jeanie* I found that owing to the heavy looking weather the *Jeanie* would not make an early start, and that all the passengers would sleep ashore, and after all this demonstrative leave taking I had to go back again. I am afraid my China servants regarded this as a bad omen.

Wednesday remained calm all day. I went off on board in the morning and waiting in turn till noon for a breeze returned once more on shore. I watched late at night for a breeze, and surely enough in the evening a stout norther came down the bay, but as the captain fired no signal to call us on board, I slept that night on shore.

I was up betimes on Thursday morning hoping to greet the usual morning land breeze, but still a calm weighed down the waters. My good-byes had been said, and said over again, and I kept quietly at home watching the wind, water, and our brig riding at anchor in the offing she had taken. At 3 P.M. a light breeze began to spring up and I saw the *Jeanie* filling her sails in an attempt to tack out. Once more I left the shore, this time very quietly. Mr. Walsh and Mr. Morse[15] accompanying me. At 4 P.M. I was on board, and it was evident that the brig would be able to beat several miles at least down the bay before dark. Accordingly Walsh and Morse gave me a last good-bye; my eyes filled to say the final words, and we at last stood out *"homeward bound!"* We anchored at night near Perry's Island about twelve miles from Yokohama.

[15] This was W. H. Morse who worked with Hall at Walsh, Hall & Co.

Friday morning was again calm, but about 8 A.M. a light breeze came up the bay and we shook out our sails to beat out. Here Consul Fisher, who had accompanied us thus far with his wife and child who were of our passengers took leave of us, and our last shore tie was cut. We beat slowly down the bay, having charming views of the beautiful shores of Yedo bay in our slow progress. It was a delightful summer day, such a day as I would have had to say adieu to dear old Nippon, which I was leaving with so much regret. Those were after all, I saw, golden years of my life that I had passed on these shores. Nightfall found us scarcely outside of Cape Sagami with a light head wind.

Saturday morning we were off Ohosima, having made little progress during the night, but now there was a southeast wind and considerable sea running and we fairly pulled away on our course. I had hoped to see old Fusi's sunny head yet once more but the clouds forbade me. The rough sea made me sea sick and I kept my berth all day. In the afternoon Capt. Morehouse called to me to take my last look at Japan. I opened my window and saw in the receding distance the hilly coast of Nippon between Cape King and Cape Blunce and this was indeed my last sight of dear old Nippon.

INDEX

275, 400–401; misinformation about Japan in, 51

Westerners in Hakodate, 231

Westerners in Japan: acceptance of, 596; and accidental injury of Japanese, 402; believed to kill Japanese for their livers, 365; carrying of firearms by, 83–84, 121, 137, 144, 147, 152, 161, 163, 165, 219, 220, 243–44, 268, 280, 282, 283, 447, 455, 507, 519, 521, 587, 603 (*see also* Moss Case); controls over, 52, 197, 225n.85; displays of friendship toward, 225, 236, 246, 247, 293–94, 301–3, 314, 315, 337, 338, 380, 396, 542, 609; in Edo, 192; fear of, 103–4, 114, 222, 317, 380, 613; and fears of attacks by Japanese, 130, 132, 137–38, 144, 161, 291, 296, 352, 356, 462, 472, 476, 479, 519, 578; government reportedly plans to deport, 87, 441, 466–67, 548; hostility toward, 84, 218, 295, 297, 372, 374–75, 377, 604; limits on travel by, 253, 418–21, 550, 612–13; as objects of curiosity, 66, 72, 73, 76, 77, 90, 103–4, 107, 122, 132, 152, 156, 164, 195, 228, 251–52, 260, 315, 316–17, 327, 330, 377, 398, 409, 410, 415, 601, 608; opinions of them by Japanese, 93; restricted in aiding Japanese emigration, 165; surveillance over, 82, 140, 206, 222, 228, 247, 250, 313, 329, 333, 372, 409, 417, 418–19. *See also* Assassinations; Currency exchange; Merchants, American; Merchants, foreign; Murders; Treaty Powers; Xenophobia

Westerners in Yokohama, 54–55; and armed defense groups, 144, 147, 161, 163, 280, 456, 457, 458, 473, 510, 512 (*see also* Moss Case); foreign troops provide guards for, 130, 132, 137, 280, 356, 455–56, 494, 558; and Hall's "walking party," 519; hunting by, 279–81, 283, 605; meetings of, to discuss British reparations demands, 469, 470, 476–77; numbers of, 515; and purchase of land, 33, 35, 36, 84, 103n.6, 122, 168, 172, 178, 204, 204n, 303, 305, 306, 320, 337, 361n, 390–91n.3, 466; reported plot to burn houses of, 455–56; and Scavenger corps,

547n; women take refuge on British ships, 472, 473

Whaling, 251

Whampoa, 17

What Cheer (ship), 36, 390

Whipple, Edwin Percy, 10

White, Mr., 180

Wigs, 200

Wilhemina Elize (ship), 499

Williams, Channing Moore, 87, 192

Williams, S. Wells, 14n.65

Willis, William, 509n

Wilmott, Comdr. Edward, 504

Winchester, Charles A., 489, 490; and investigation of Baldwin and Bird murders, 586; and letter on reparation demands, 471

Windows, paper, 414–15

Winds: prevailing patterns of, 540

Wine, 154, 405, 591

Wirgman, Charles, 345n.42, 367n, 534n.7; and drawing of *Wyoming* battle with Chōshū, 598; paintings by, 61n.192, 367n, 534n.7

Women, 112, 117–18; accomplishments expected of, 224; arrested for having relations with foreigners, 362; attitudes toward by men, 178, 592; barred from religious sites, 421; as beggars, 425–26; and class distinctions in appearance of, 407–8; crimes committed by, 334–35, 588; and customary deference to husbands, 101; dressed as men, 199; and festival of Hinari (the Dolls), 326, 405–6; foreign, Japanese attitude toward, 42; improvement in position of, 400; legal rights of, 221, 592; men dressing as, 198, 202, 204; as Mikados, 394; occupations of, 506; prohibited on Edo Bay, 379; and religion, 207, 366–67; seclusion of, 263–64, 366, 400, 458; social status of, 592; as travelers, 76; and trust in strangers, 151, 152; work done by, 171, 176, 182, 274, 282–83, 310, 322, 330, 343, 378–79, 388, 409, 431, 536–37, 541, 569, 570, 592, 600, 615; at wrestling matches, 127; as writers, 215–16. *See also* Clothing: of women; Courtesans; Jorōya houses; Jorōyas; Marriage; Mistresses; Prostitution

Wong, Dr. (surgeon in Canton), 18n.83

Wood, Henry, 14n.65

Woodlawn Cemetery (Elmira, N.Y.), 12

Work: intensity of, 213–14

Workers: and clashes with employers, 391; effect of daimyō withdrawal from Edo on, 453, 463; feuds among, 602–3; guildlike organization among, 46, 602–3; and holidays, 590; representation of, in festivals, 199

—and specific occupations: agriculture, 115; attendants at travelers' halts, 91, 318; bakery workers, 100; barbers, 602–3; bath attendants, 602–3; boatmen, 116–17, 160, 174, 205–6, 215, 219, 222, 263, 364, 372–73, 397, 589; carpenters, 105, 391 (*see also* Takaradaya; Tarakagi); carters, 589; cooks, 265; coolies, 146, 183, 272, 287, 387, 425, 475, 613; crematorium workers, 247–48; dockworkers, 73–74; fishermen, 77, 148, 154, 444 (*see also* Fishing); grooms (bettos), 90, 429, 500 (riots by), 610; guides, 611, 613, 615; gymnasts, 85; at inns, 318, 376; ironworkers, 76; laborers, 91, 95–96, 153, 383, 590; leather dressers, 46, 148, 154–55; norimon bearers, 94, 141, 272, 463; pearl divers, 329; porcelain makers, 248; porters, 589; postal workers, 161, 272; rice pounders, 73; sedan chair bearers, 50, 159–60, 446; street peddlers, 76, 77, 91, 101, 117, 169, 177, 195, 201, 245, 246, 405, 445, 506, 542, 544; at tea houses, 75, 88. *See also* Crafts; Farmers; Inns; Professions; Servants; Tea houses; Wages

Wrestling, 124–28, 195, 262, 285, 286–87, 500; by children, 422

Writers: women as, 215–16

Wycoff, Rev. Isaac N., 11

Wyoming (ship), 472, 476, 490, 533; aids *Viking* after wreck, 480, 484; and expedition against Chōshū, 26, 50, 491–92, 493, 495–96, 497–99, 503, 517, 556, 571, 598; Hall's report on, 50; searches for the *Alabama*, 525, 528; women take refuge on, 479

Xavier, Francis, 19

Xenophobia: in China, 18; in Japan, 24, 27, 28, 130, 218; in Yokohama, 54–55